3rd Edition

토익 문법·독해·어휘 입문서

기본
RC 완성

초 판 1쇄 발행 2016년 4월 29일
개 정 판 1쇄 발행 2016년 12월 26일
개정2판 10쇄 발행 2021년 12월 1일

지 은 이 | 파고다교육그룹 언어교육연구소, 홍수림
펴 낸 이 | 고루다
펴 낸 곳 | Wit&Wisdom 도서출판 위트앤위즈덤
임프린트 | **PAGODA Books**
출판등록 | 2005년 5월 27일 제 300-2005-90호
주　　소 | 06614 서울특별시 서초구 강남대로 419, 19층(서초동, 파고다타워)
전　　화 | (02) 6940-4070
팩　　스 | (02) 536-0660
홈페이지 | www.pagodabook.com

저작권자 | ⓒ 2019 파고다아카데미, 위트앤위즈덤

ISBN 978-89-6281-819-2 (13740)

도서출판 위트앤위즈덤　　www.pagodabook.com
파고다 어학원　　　　　　www.pagoda21.com
파고다 인강　　　　　　　www.pagodastar.com
테스트 클리닉　　　　　　www.testclinic.com

|PAGODA Books는 도서출판 Wit&Wisdom의 성인 어학 전문 임프린트입니다.
낙장 및 파본은 구매처에서 교환해 드립니다.

3rd Edition

토익 문법·독해·어휘 입문서

기본 완성

RC

목차

PART 5 GRAMMAR

PART 5 VOCA

파고다토익 기본 완성 RC

PART 6

PART 7

이 책의 구성과 특징

>> **PART 5** GRAMMAR 토익 입문자들에게 꼭 필요한 기초 토익 문법과 핵심 기본 문제 유형을 학습한다.
　　문장의 구조와 틀을 이해하고 해석하는 능력을 길러 각 문제를 푸는 방법을 익힌다.

>> **PART 5** VOCA Part 5, 6, 필수 동사, 명사, 형용사, 부사 어휘를 핵심 어휘 문제로 풀어본다.

>> **PART 6** Part 5에서 학습한 어법 적용 문제, 어휘 문제, 글의 흐름상 빈칸에 알맞은 문장을 삽입하는 문제에도
　　충분히 대비한다.

>> **PART 7** 문제 유형별 해결 전략과 지문의 종류 및 주제별 해결 전략을 학습한다.

OVERVIEW

본격적인 학습의 준비 단계로, 각 Part별 출제 경향 및 문제 유형,
바뀐 신토익 소개 및 그에 따른 접근 전략을 정리하였다.

기본 개념 이해하기

Part별 문제 풀이에 앞서, 해당 Part의 기본 개념을 예문과 함께 익히고, 정답에 쉽게 접근할 수 있는 문제 풀이 전략을 제시하였다.

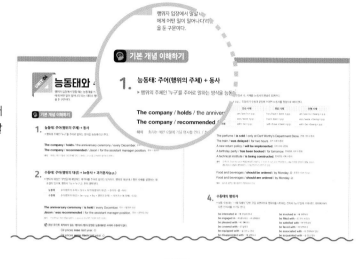

질문·지문 유형 확인하기

본격적인 학습에 앞서, UNIT별 기본 개념과 최신 토익 경향 Tip을 제시하여 보다 효율적으로 학습 전략을 세울 수 있도록 구성하였다.

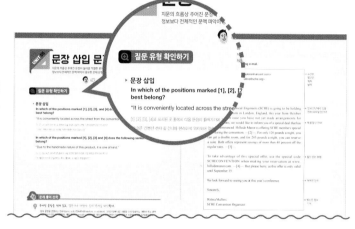

핵심 문제 유형

앞서 학습한 내용을 실제 문제에 적용해 볼 수 있도록 해당 유형의 대표 문제들을 제시하였다.

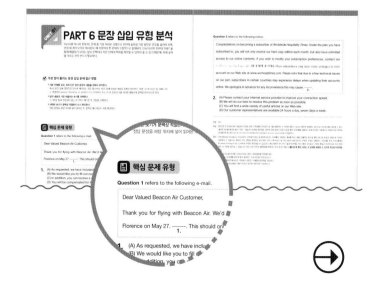

이 책의 구성과 특징

Practice

다양한 토익 실전 문제를 접할 수 있도록
핵심 빈출 유형과 신유형 및 고난도 문제를
각 Part별로 골고루 구성하였다.

PART 5 GRAMMAR : 20문항
　　　　　 VOCA : 10문항
PART 6 : 16문항
PART 7 질문 유형 : 4지문
　　　　　 지문 유형 : 2~4지문

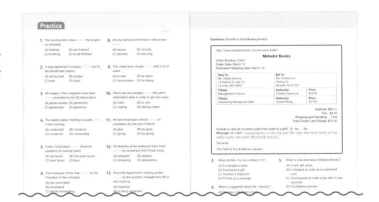

REVIEW TEST

각 Part별 학습한 내용을 마지막으로 체크
할 수 있도록 정기 토익 시험과 동일한 유
형과 난이도로 구성하였다.

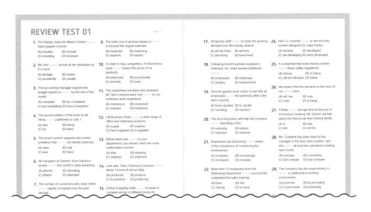

MINI TEST

5회분의 풍부한 연습 문제를 통해 전반적인 실력을 파악할 수 있도록 구성하였다.

PART 5: 10문항
PART 6: 4문항
PART 7: 5~6지문 / 16문항

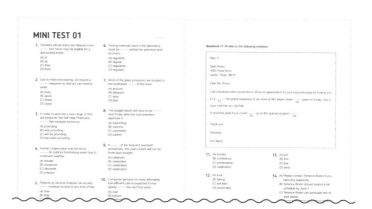

ACTUAL TEST

토익 시험 전 학습한 내용을 최종 점검할 수 있도록 실제 정기 토익 시험과 가장 유사한 형태의 모의고사 1회분을 제공하였다.

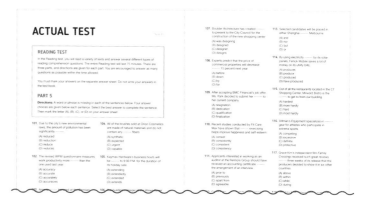

해설서

기본 완성을 위한 철저한 정·오답 분석과 상세한 해설로 혼자서도 학습이 가능하도록 상세하게 구성하였다.

토익이란?

TOEIC(Test Of English for International Communication)
은 영어가 모국어가 아닌 사람들을 대상으로 일상생활 또는 국제
업무 등에 필요한 실용 영어 능력을 평가하는 시험입니다.

상대방과 '의사 소통할 수 있는 능력(Communication ability)'을
평가하는 데 중점을 두고 있으므로 영어에 대한 '지식'이 아니라 영
어의 실용적이고 기능적인 '사용법'을 묻는 문항들이 출제됩니다.

TOEIC은 1979년 미국 ETS(Educational Testing Service)에 의
해 개발된 이래 전 세계 150개 국가 14,000여 개의 기관에서 승
진 또는 해외 파견 인원 선발 등의 목적으로 널리 활용하고 있으며
우리나라에는 1982년 도입되었습니다. 해마다 전 세계적으로 약
700만 명 이상이 응시하고 있습니다.

>> 토익 시험의 구성

	파트	시험 형태		문항 수	시간	배점
듣기 (LC)	1	사진 문제		6	45분	495점
	2	질의응답		25		
	3	짧은 대화		39		
	4	짧은 담화		30		
읽기 (RC)	5	단문 빈칸 채우기		30	75분	495점
	6	장문 빈칸 채우기		16		
	7	독해	단일 지문	29		
			이중 지문	10		
			삼중 지문	15		
계				200	120분	990점

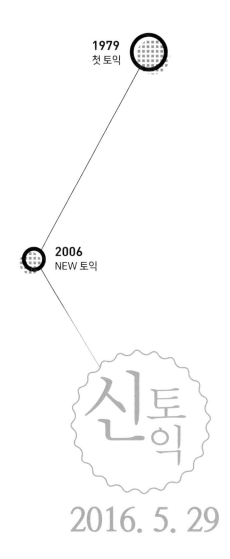

1979
첫 토익

2006
NEW 토익

2016. 5. 29

토익 시험 접수와 성적 확인

토익 시험은 TOEIC 위원회 웹사이트(www.toeic.co.kr)에서 접수할 수 있습니다. 본인이 원하는 날짜와 장소를 지정하고 필수 기재 항목을 기재한 후 본인 사진을 업로드하면 간단하게 끝납니다.

보통은 두 달 후에 있는 시험일까지 접수 가능합니다. 각 시험일의 정기 접수는 시험일로부터 2주 전까지 마감되지만, 시험일의 3일 전까지 추가 접수할 수 있는 특별 접수 기간이 있습니다. 그러나 특별 추가 접수 기간에는 응시료가 4,000원 더 비싸며, 희망하는 시험장을 선택할 수 없는 경우도 발생할 수 있습니다.

성적은 시험일로부터 16~18일 후에 인터넷이나 ARS(060-800-0515)를 통해 확인할 수 있습니다.

성적표는 우편이나 온라인으로 발급 받을 수 있습니다. 우편으로 발급받을 경우는 성적 발표 후 대략 일주일이 소요되며, 온라인 발급을 선택하면 유효 기간 내에 홈페이지에서 본인이 직접 1회에 한해 무료 출력할 수 있습니다. 토익 성적은 시험일로부터 2년간 유효합니다.

시험 당일 준비물

시험 당일 준비물은 규정 신분증, 연필, 지우개입니다. 허용되는 규정 신분증은 토익 공식 웹사이트에서 확인하기 바랍니다. 필기구는 연필이나 샤프펜만 가능하고 볼펜이나 컴퓨터용 사인펜은 사용할 수 없습니다. 수험표는 출력해 가지 않아도 됩니다.

시험 진행 안내

시험 진행 일정은 시험 당일 고사장 사정에 따라 약간씩 다를 수 있지만 대부분 아래와 같이 진행됩니다.

≫ 시험 시간이 오전일 경우

AM 9:30 ~ 9:45	AM 9:45 ~ 9:50	AM 9:50 ~ 10:05	AM 10:05 ~ 10:10	AM 10:10 ~ 10:55	AM 10:55 ~ 12:10
15분	5분	15분	5분	45분	75분
답안지 직싱에 관한 Orientation	수험자 휴식 시간	신분증 확인 (감독교사)	문제지 배부, 파본 확인	듣기 평가(LC)	읽기 평가(RC) 2차 신분증 확인

* 주의: 오전 9시 50분 입실통제

≫ 시험 시간이 오후일 경우

PM 2:30 ~ 2:45	PM 2:45 ~ 2:50	PM 2:50 ~ 3:05	PM 3:05 ~ 3:10	PM 3:10 ~ 3:55	PM 3:55 ~ 5:10
15분	5분	15분	5분	45분	75분
답안지 작성에 관한 Orientation	수험자 휴식 시간	신분증 확인 (감독교사)	문제지 배부, 파본 확인	듣기 평가(LC)	읽기 평가(RC) 2차 신분증 확인

* 주의: 오후 2시 50분 입실 통제

파트별 토익 소개

PART 5
INCOMPLETE SENTENCE
단문 빈칸 채우기

Part 5는 빈칸이 있는 문장이 하나 나오고, 4개의 선택지 중 빈칸에 가장 적합한 단어나 구를 고르는 문제로써 총 30문항이 출제된다.

문항 수	30문항 (101번 ~ 130번)
문제 유형	**[어형 문제]** 문제의 빈칸이 어떤 자리인지를 파악하여 네 개의 선택지 중에 들어갈 적절한 품사 및 형태를 묻는 문제이다. 보통 10문항 정도가 출제되는데 어형 문제는 품사에 관한 기초만 탄탄히 하면 쉽게 풀 수 있는 비교적 난이도가 낮은 문제이다.

[어휘 문제] 어휘의 정확한 용례를 알고 있는지 묻는 문제로 같은 품사의 서로 다른 어휘가 선택지로 나온다. 어휘 문제는 다른 Part 5 문제들보다 어려운 편인 데다가 전체 30문항 중 절반가량이 어휘 문제일 정도로 출제 비중이 점점 높아지고 있다.

[문법 문제] 문장의 구조 파악과 구와 절을 구분하여 전치사와 접속사 또는 부사 자리를 구분하고, 접속사가 답인 경우는 접속사 중에서도 명사절, 형용사절, 부사절을 구분하는 문제가 출제된다. 보통 6~7문항이 출제되는데 쉬운 문제부터 상당히 어려운 문제까지 난이도는 다양하다.

어형 문제
»

101. If our request for new computer equipment receives -------, we are going to purchase 10 extra monitors.

    (A) approval   (B) approved
    (C) approve   (D) approves

어휘 문제
»

102. After being employed at a Tokyo-based technology firm for two decades, Ms. Mayne ------- to Vancouver to start her own IT company.

    (A) visited   (B) returned
    (C) happened   (D) compared

문법 문제
»

103. ------- the demand for the PFS-2x smartphone, production will be tripled next quarter.

    (A) Even if   (B) Just as
    (C) As a result of   (D) Moreover

정답 101. (A) 102. (B) 103. (C)

PART 6

TEXT COMPLETION
장문 빈칸 채우기

Part 6은 4문항의 문제가 있는 4개의 지문이 나와 총 16문항이 출제된다. 각각의 빈칸에 가장 적절한 단어나 구, 문장을 삽입하는 문제로 Part 5와 Part 7을 접목한 형태로 볼 수 있다.

문항 수	4개 지문, 16문항 (131번 ~ 146번)
지문 유형	설명서, 편지, 이메일, 기사, 공지, 지시문, 광고, 회람, 발표문, 정보문 등
문제 유형	**[어형 문제]** 빈칸의 자리를 파악하여 네 개의 선택지 중에 들어갈 적절한 품사 및 형태를 묻는 문제로 Part 5와 같은 유형의 문제들이다. 전체 16문항 중 3~4문항 정도가 출제된다.
	[어휘 문제] 네 개의 선택지 중 의미상 가장 적절한 어휘를 고르는 문제로, 전후 문맥을 파악하여 풀어야 하므로 Part 5의 어휘 문제들보다 어려운 편이다. 보통 5~6문항이 출제된다.
	[문법 문제] 구와 절, 즉 문장 구조를 파악하는 문제로 Part 6에서는 출제 빈도가 낮은 편이지만 Part 5보다 상당히 어려운 문제들로 출제된다. 전체 16문항 중 1~2문항 정도가 출제된다.
	[문장 삽입 문제] Part 7처럼 전반적인 지문의 흐름을 파악하여 4개의 선택지 중에 가장 적절한 한 문장을 선택하는 가장 난이도가 높은 문제이며, 지문마다 한 문제씩 총 4문항이 출제된다.

Questions 131-134 refer to the following e-mail.

To: sford@etnnet.com
From: customersupprt@interhostptimes.ca
Date: July 1
Re: Your Subscription

Congratulations on becoming a reader of *International Hospitality Times*. --131.-- the plan you have subscribed to, you will not only have unlimited access to our online content, but you will also receive our hard copy edition each month. If you wish to --132.-- your subscription preferences, contact our Customer Support Center at +28 07896 325422. Most --133.-- may also make updates to their accounts on our Web site at www.interhosptimes.ca. Please note that due to compatibility issues, it may not be possible for customers in certain countries to access their accounts online. --134.--. Your business is greatly appreciated.

International Hospitality Times

문법 문제
>>
131. (A) Besides
(B) As if
(C) Under
(D) Prior to

어휘 문제
>>
132. (A) purchase
(B) modify
(C) collect
(D) inform

어형 문제
>>
133. (A) subscribe
(B) subscriptions
(C) subscribers
(D) subscribing

**문장 삽입
문제**
>>
134. (A) We have branches in over 30 countries around the globe.
(B) We provide online content that includes Web extras and archives.
(C) We are working to make this service available to all readers soon.
(D) We would like to remind you that your contract expires this month.

정답 131. (C) 132. (B) 133. (C) 134. (C)

PART 7

READING COMPREHENSION
독해

Part 7은 지문을 읽고 그에 해당하는 각각의 질문(2~5개)에 알맞은 답을 고르는 문제이다. 지문의 종류가 다양하며 그 형태도 1개의 지문으로 된 것과 2개, 3개의 지문으로 된 것이 있다.

문항 수	54문항 (147번 ~ 200번) → 단일 지문: 10개 지문, 19문항
	이중 지문: 2개 지문, 10문항
	삼중 지문: 3개 지문, 15문항
지문 유형	편지, 이메일, 광고, 공지, 회람, 기사, 안내문, 웹페이지(회사나 제품소개, 행사 소개, 고객 사용 후기), 청구서 또는 영수증, 문자, 온라인 채팅 대화문 등
문제 유형	- 주제 · 목적 문제
	- 세부사항 문제
	- 암시 · 추론 문제
	- 사실확인 문제
	- 동의어 문제
	- 화자 의도 파악 문제
	- 문장 삽입 문제

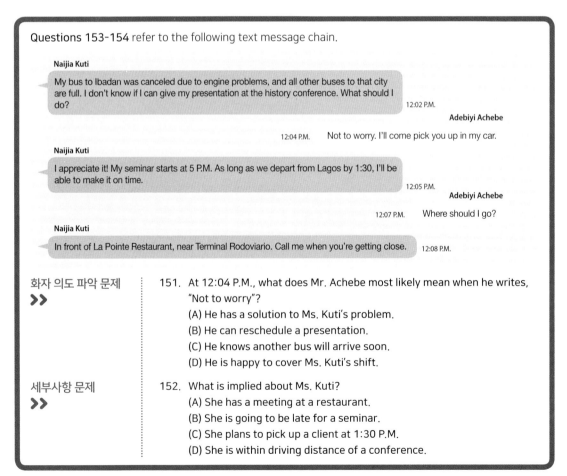

Questions 153-154 refer to the following text message chain.

Naijia Kuti
My bus to Ibadan was canceled due to engine problems, and all other buses to that city are full. I don't know if I can give my presentation at the history conference. What should I do?　　12:02 P.M.

Adebiyi Achebe
12:04 P.M.　　Not to worry. I'll come pick you up in my car.

Naijia Kuti
I appreciate it! My seminar starts at 5 P.M. As long as we depart from Lagos by 1:30, I'll be able to make it on time.　　12:05 P.M.

Adebiyi Achebe
12:07 P.M.　　Where should I go?

Naijia Kuti
In front of La Pointe Restaurant, near Terminal Rodoviario. Call me when you're getting close.　　12:08 P.M.

화자 의도 파악 문제
≫

151. At 12:04 P.M., what does Mr. Achebe most likely mean when he writes, "Not to worry"?
(A) He has a solution to Ms. Kuti's problem.
(B) He can reschedule a presentation.
(C) He knows another bus will arrive soon.
(D) He is happy to cover Ms. Kuti's shift.

세부사항 문제
≫

152. What is implied about Ms. Kuti?
(A) She has a meeting at a restaurant.
(B) She is going to be late for a seminar.
(C) She plans to pick up a client at 1:30 P.M.
(D) She is within driving distance of a conference.

정답 151. (A) 152. (D)

Questions 158-160 refer to the following Web page.

http://www.sdayrealestate.com/listing18293

Looking for a new home for your family? This house, located on 18293 Winding Grove, was remodeled last month. It features 2,500 square feet of floor space, with 5,000 square feet devoted to a gorgeous backyard. Also included is a 625 square feet garage that can comfortably fit two mid-sized vehicles —[1]—. Located just a five-minute drive from the Fairweather Metro Station, this property allows for easy access to the downtown area, while providing plenty of room for you and your family. —[2]—. A serene lake is just 100–feet walk away from the house. —[3]—. A 15 percent down payment is required to secure the property. —[4]—. For more detailed information or to arrange a showing, please email Jerry@sdayrealestate.com.

세부사항 문제
➤➤

158. How large is the parking space?
(A) 100 square feet
(B) 625 square feet
(C) 2,500 square feet
(D) 5,000 square feet

사실확인 문제
➤➤

159. What is NOT stated as an advantage of the property?
(A) It has a spacious design.
(B) It has been recently renovated.
(C) It is in a quiet neighborhood.
(D) It is near public transportation.

문장 삽입 문제
➤➤

160. In which of the positions marked [1], [2], [3], and [4] does the following sentence best belong?

"A smaller amount may be accepted, depending on the buyer's financial situation."

(A) [1]
(B) [2]
(C) [3]
(D) [4]

정답 158. (B) 159. (C) 160. (D)

학습 플랜

4주 플랜

DAY 1	DAY 2	DAY 3	DAY 4	DAY 5
[PART 5 GRAMMAR] Unit 01. 문장의 구조와 동사 Unit 02. 수 일치 Unit 03. 시제 Unit 04. 능동태와 수동태	REVIEW TEST 01 REVIEW TEST 01 다시보기	Unit 05. 명사 Unit 06. 대명사	Unit 07. 형용사 Unit 08. 부사 Unit 09. 전치사	REVIEW TEST 02 REVIEW TEST 02 다시보기

DAY 6	DAY 7	DAY 8	DAY 9	DAY 10
Unit 10. 접속사 Unit 11. 명사절 접속사 Unit 12. 형용사절 접속사	REVIEW TEST 03 REVIEW TEST 03 다시보기	Unit 13. to부정사 Unit 14. 동명사 Unit 15. 분사 Unit 16. 비교	REVIEW TEST 04 REVIEW TEST 04 다시보기	[PART 5 VOCA] Unit 01. 동사 Unit 02. 명사 Unit 03. 형용사 Unit 04. 부사

DAY 11	DAY 12	DAY 13	DAY 14	DAY 15
Part 5 VOCA REVIEW TEST Part 5 VOCA REVIEW TEST 다시보기	[PART 6] Unit 01. PART 6 문장 삽입 유형 분석 Unit 02. 실전 연습 01 Unit 03. 실전 연습 02 Unit 04. 실전 연습 03 Unit 05. 실전 연습 04	Part 6 REVIEW TEST Part 6 REVIEW TEST 다시보기	[PART 7] Unit 01. 주제·목적 문제 Unit 02. 세부사항 문제 Unit 03. 사실확인 문제	Unit 04. 암시·추론 문제 Unit 05. 문장 삽입 문제 Unit 06. 동의어 문제

DAY 16	DAY 17	DAY 18	DAY 19	DAY 20
Unit 07. 문자 대화문과 화자 의도 Unit 08. 편지·이메일 Unit 09. 광고 Unit 10. 공지·회람	Unit 11. 기사 Unit 12. 양식 Unit 13. 이중 지문 Unit 14. 삼중 지문	Part 7 REVIEW TEST Part 7 REVIEW TEST 다시보기	MINI TEST 01 MINI TEST 02 MINI TEST 03 MINI TEST 04 MINI TEST 05	ACTUAL TEST

8주 플랜

DAY 1	DAY 2	DAY 3	DAY 4	DAY 5
[PART 5 GRAMMAR] Unit 01. 문장의 구조와 동사 Unit 02. 수 일치	Unit 03. 시제 Unit 04. 능동태와 수동태	REVIEW TEST 01 REVIEW TEST 01 다시보기 - 틀린 문제 다시 풀어보기 - 모르는 단어 체크해서 암기	Unit 05. 명사 Unit 06. 대명사	Unit 07. 형용사 Unit 08. 부사 Unit 09. 전치사

DAY 6	DAY 7	DAY 8	DAY 9	DAY 10
REVIEW TEST 02 REVIEW TEST 02 다시보기 - 틀린 문제 다시 풀어보기 - 모르는 단어 체크해서 암기	Unit 10. 접속사	Unit 11. 명사절 접속사 Unit 12. 형용사절 접속사	REVIEW TEST 03 REVIEW TEST 03 다시보기 - 틀린 문제 다시 풀어보기 - 모르는 단어 체크해서 암기	Unit 13. to부정사 Unit 14. 동명사

DAY 11	DAY 12	DAY 13	DAY 14	DAY 15
Unit 15. 분사 Unit 16. 비교	REVIEW TEST 04 REVIEW TEST 04 다시보기 - 틀린 문제 다시 풀어보기 - 모르는 단어 체크해서 암기	[PART 5 VOCA] Unit 01. 동사 Unit 02. 명사	Unit 03. 형용사 Unit 04. 부사	Part 5 VOCA REVIEW TEST Part 5 VOCA REVIEW TEST 다시보기 - 틀린 문제 다시 풀어보기 - 모르는 단어 체크해서 암기

DAY 16	DAY 17	DAY 18	DAY 19	DAY 20
[PART 6] Unit 01. PART 6 문장 삽입 유형 분석 Unit 02. 실전 연습 01 Unit 03. 실전 연습 02	Unit 04. 실전 연습 03 Unit 05. 실전 연습 04	Part 6 REVIEW TEST Part 6 REVIEW TEST 다시보기 - 틀린 문제 다시 풀어보기 - 모르는 단어 체크해서 암기	[PART 7] Unit 01. 주제·목적 문제 Unit 02. 세부사항 문제	Unit 03. 사실확인 문제 Unit 04. 암시·추론 문제

DAY 21	DAY 22	DAY 23	DAY 24	DAY 25
Unit 05. 문장 삽입 문제 Unit 06. 동의어 문제	Unit 07. 문자 대화문과 화자 의도 Unit 08. 편지·이메일	Unit 09. 광고 Unit 10. 공지·회람	Unit 11. 기사 Unit 12. 양식	Unit 13. 이중 지문

DAY 26	DAY 27	DAY 28	DAY 29	DAY 30
Unit 14. 삼중 지문	Part 7 REVIEW TEST Part 7 REVIEW TEST 다시보기	PART 5 GRAMMAR 단원 복습	PART 5 VOCA 단원 복습	PART 6 단원 복습

DAY 31	DAY 32	DAY 33	DAY 34	DAY 35
PART 7 단원 복습	MINI TEST 01	MINI TEST 02	MINI TEST 03	MINI TEST 01-03 다시보기 - 틀린 문제 다시 풀어보기 - 모르는 단어 체크해서 암기

DAY 36	DAY 37	DAY 38	DAY 39	DAY 40
MINI TEST 04	MINI TEST 05	MINI TEST 04-05 다시보기 - 틀린 문제 다시 풀어보기 - 모르는 단어 체크해서 암기	ACTUAL TEST	ACTUAL TEST 다시보기 - 틀린 문제 다시 풀어보기 - 모르는 단어 체크해서 암기

PAR

KEY
WORDS

GRAMMAR

RT5

단문 빈칸
채우기

OVERVIEW

PART 5는 빈칸이 있는 문장이 하나 나오고, 4개의 선택지 중 빈칸에 가장 적합한 단어나 구를 고르는 문제로써 총 30문항이 출제된다.

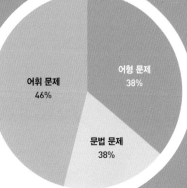

어휘 문제
46%

어형 문제
38%

문법 문제
38%

문제 유형

문장 구조 문제 | 빈칸의 자리를 파악하여 선택지 중 알맞은 품사나 형태를 고르는 문제
문법 문제 | 같은 품사의 네 개 어휘 중 정확한 용례를 파악하여 알맞은 단어를 고르는 문제
어휘 문제 | 문장의 구조 파악과 구와 절을 구분하여 접속사나 전치사, 부사를 고르는 문제

출제 포인트

• 문법적 지식과 어휘력을 동시에 묻는 문제들이 증가하고 있다.
  ⋯ 명사 자리인데 선택지에 비슷하게 생긴 명사가 두 개 이상 나오는 문제가 출제된다.

• 두 가지 이상의 문법 포인트를 묻는 문제들이 출제되고 있다.
  ⋯ 동사의 문장 형식을 이해하고 태를 결정하는 문제가 출제된다.

• 다양한 품사의 선택지로 구성된 문제들이 출제되고 있다.
  ⋯ 부사 문제이지만 전치사, 접속사, 관용 표현 등으로 선택지가 구성된다.

PART 5 이렇게 대비하자!

• 무조건 해석부터 하지 말고 선택지를 보고 [어형문제 / 어휘문제 / 문법문제] 중 어떤 문제인지부터 파악한다. 어형 문제는 해석 없이도 답이 나오는 문제가 대부분이므로 최대한 시간을 절약할 수 있는 방법으로 풀어나가야 한다.

• 고득점을 얻기 위해서는 한 단어를 외우더라도 품사, 파생어, 용법을 함께 암기해야 한다. 예를 들어, announce와 notify를 똑같이 '알리다'라고 외워두면 두 단어가 같이 선택지로 나오는 어휘 문제는 풀 수 없다. notify 뒤에는 사람만이 목적어로 나온다는 사실을 꼭 알아 두어야 한다.

단계별 문법 학습 전략

(1) 문장의 구조를 결정하는 5형식 동사와 품사별 문장 성분 역할과 문법을 학습한다.
(2) 구와 절을 연결하여 문장을 확장시켜주는 전치사와 접속사의 역할을 학습한다.
(3) 동사의 시제와 태, 가정법, 분사 구문 등의 다소 까다로운 문법 지식을 습득한다.

PART 5 문제 유형별 문제 풀이 접근법

1. 어형 문제

아래 문제처럼 한 단어의 네 가지 형태가 선택지로 나오는 문제를 어형 문제 또는 자리 찾기 문제라고 한다. 어형 문제는 빈칸이 [주어, 동사, 목적어, 보어, 수식어] 중에 어떤 자리인지를 파악해서 선택지 중 알맞은 품사나 형태를 고르는 문제이다.

Billy's Auto Repair has ------- with 15 different parts suppliers.

(A) contracting   (B) contracts
(C) contractor   (D) contract

빈칸은 이 문장의 목적어 자리로 명사가 들어갈 자리인데 명사가 보기에 (B), (C), (D) 이렇게 세개나 나와 있다. 이런 문제들은 자리만 찾는 것으로 끝나지 않고 한 단계 더 나아가 명사의 특성을 알고 있어야 풀 수 있는 문제이다. 한정사 없이 가산 단수 명사는 쓸 수 없으므로 복수명사 (B)가 답이 되는 문제이다.

2. 어휘 문제

아래 문제처럼 같은 품사의 네 가지 다른 단어가 선택지로 나오는 문제를 어휘 문제라고 한다. 한 어휘 문제는 최소한 빈칸 주변을 해석해야만 풀 수 있고, 어려운 문제의 경우에는 가산/불가산 명사의 구분, 자/타동사의 구분과 같은 문법 사항까지 같이 포함되어 출제되기도 한다.

I have enclosed a copy of my résumé for your ------- and look forward to hearing from you soon.

(A) explanation   (B) participation
(C) reference   (D) consideration

빈칸은 전치사 for의 목적어 자리에 어떤 명사 어휘를 넣으면 가장 자연스러운지를 고르는 문제인데 '당신의 고려를 위해 제 이력서를 첨부합니다' 정도는 해석해야만 정답 (D)를 고를 수 있는 문제로 어형 문제보다는 훨씬 난이도가 높다.

3. 문법 문제

아래 문제처럼 종속접속사, 등위접속사, 전치사, 부사 등이 선택지에 같이 나오는 문제를 문법 문제라고 한다. 문법 문제는 그 문장의 구조를 파악하여 구와 절을 구분하고 절이라면 여러 가지 절 중 어떤 절인지를 파악해야 하는 어려운 문제들로 대부분 해석까지도 필요하다.

We need more employees on the production line ------- production has increased by 60 percent.

(A) although   (B) since
(C) because of   (D) so

빈칸은 전치사 두 개의 절을 연결하는 종속 접속사자리이다. 전치사인 (C)와 등위접속사인 (D)는 답이 될 수 없고, 접속사 (A)와 (B) 중에서 '생산이 증가했기 때문에 추가직원을 고용해야 한다' 는 의미에 맞는 (B)를 답으로 고르는 문제이다.

문장의 구조와 동사

영어 문장은 주어, 서술어, 목적어, 보어, 수식어로 이루어지며, 동사 뒤에 오는 목적어나 보어의 유무에 따라 크게 5가지로 구분된다.

Tip! 문장 구조를 파악할 때는 반드시 주어, 동사, 목적어, 보어를 먼저 확인하고, 나머지는 수식어구로 간주하면 된다!

 기본 개념 이해하기

1. 문장 성분

▶ 영어 문장은 최소 주어와 동사로 이루어진다. 주어는 '~은/는/이/가'에 해당하는 말이고, 동사는 '~하다/~이다'라는 의미로 해석되며 주어의 동작이나 상태를 나타낸다.

▶ 동사는 혼자서 주어를 설명할 수도 있지만, 전달하려는 의미에 따라 보어나 목적어가 필요하다. 보어는 불완전한 동사를 보충하는 말로 주어나 목적어의 상태나 성질을 설명하는 말이고, 목적어는 '~을/를'에 해당하는 말로 동사 동작의 대상이 되는 말이다.

Sales / **increased** / last month. 주어 + 동사 + (수식어)

The personal information / **is** / strictly **confidential**. 주어 + 동사 + 보어

The company's first minivan model / **received** / positive **reviews**. 주어 + 동사 + 목적어

해석 매출이 지난달에 증가했다. / 개인 정보는 엄격히 기밀이다. / 그 회사의 첫 번째 미니밴 모델은 긍정적인 평가를 받았다.

2. 주어, 목적어, 보어의 자리

▶ 주어, 목적어, 보어의 문장 성분은 동사를 기준으로 한 어순과 품사로 파악한다.

주어		동사의 앞에 오며 동작의 주체를 나타내는 (대)명사
목적어		동사의 뒤에 오며 동작의 대상을 나타내는 (대)명사
보어	주격 보어	동사의 뒤에 오는 명사 또는 형용사 * 명사 보어는 주어와 동격을 나타내고, 형용사 보어는 주어의 상태를 나타낸다.
	목적격 보어	목적어 뒤에 오는 명사 또는 형용사 * 명사 보어는 목적어와 동격을 나타내고, 형용사 보어는 목적어의 상태를 나타낸다.

The **manager** / is going to make / a **presentation**. 주어(명사) + 동사 + 목적어(명사)

The **historic district** / is / easily **accessible**. 주어(명사) + 동사 + 보어(형용사)

A new **Web site** / will make / your **business** / more **attractive**.
주어(명사) + 동사 + 목적어(명사) + 보어(형용사)

해석 부서장이 발표를 할 것이다. / 유적지는 쉽게 갈 수 있다. / 새 웹사이트는 당신 회사를 더 매력적이게 해줄 것이다.

3. 1형식 문장: 「주어 + 동사」

▶ 「주어 + 동사」 형태로 동사만으로 주어의 동작이나 상태를 설명하는 문장 형식이다. 보통 동사 뒤에 '어떻게, 어디서, 언제' 등을 나타내는 부사나 전치사구 등의 수식어가 붙는다.

꼭 외워야 할 1형식 동사		
go 가다	come 오다	work 일하다
travel 여행하다	live 살다	reside 거주하다
rise 증가하다	fall 떨어지다	arise 발생하다
occur 발생하다	take place 발생하다	happen 발생하다
land 착륙하다	arrive 도착하다	exist 존재하다
participate 참가하다	emerge 나타나다	appear 나타나다
depart 출발하다	compete 경쟁하다	cooperate 협력하다
collaborate 협력하다	speak 이야기하다	talk 이야기하다
last 지속하다	grow 성장하다	persist 집요하게 계속하다(계속되다)
proceed 진행하다	vary 다르다, 달라지다	differ 다르다

Unemployment / **fell**. 동사

Unemployment / **fell** sharply. 동사 + 수식어(부사)

Unemployment / **fell** in December. 동사 + 수식어(전치사구)

해석 실업률이 하락했다. / 실업률이 급격하게 하락했다. / 실업률이 12월에 하락했다.

✅ **문법 포인트** 1형식 동사는 뒤에 부사나 전치사구를 보고 선택지 중에 1형식 동사를 고르는 문제와 앞에 1형식 동사를 보고 뒤에 부사를 고르는 문제가 주로 출제된다.

4. 2형식 문장: 「주어 + 동사 + 보어」

▶ 「주어 + 동사 + 보어」 형태로 be, become, remain 등의 동사 뒤에는 주어의 상태나 성질을 설명하는 형용사나 보어나 주어가 무엇인지를 설명하는 명사 보어가 온다.

꼭 외워야 할 2형식 동사		
be ~이다	become ~되다	remain 여전히 ~이다
appear ~하게 보이다	seem ~하게 보이나	prove ~임이 판명되다
stay 계속 ~인 상태이다	look ~하게 보이다	feel ~한 느낌이 들다
sound ~인 것 같다, ~처럼 들리다	smell ~한 냄새가 나다	taste ~한 맛이 나다

The prices / **are** / **reasonable**. 동사 + 보어(형용사)

My supervisor / **became** / **a general manager**. 동사 + 보어(명사)

해석 가격들이 합리적이다. / 나의 상사는 총지배인이 되었다.

✅ **문법 포인트** 2형식 동사 뒤에 오는 보어는 주어를 설명해 주는 보어라는 의미로 주격 보어라고 부른다.
주격 보어 자리에는 명사와 형용사가 올 수 있는데, 명사 보어는 주어와 동격(동일한 대상)일 때에만 쓴다. 토익 시험에서는 명사 보어는 거의 출제되지 않고 형용사 보어를 고르는 문제가 주로 출제된다.

5. 3형식 문장: 「주어 + 동사 + 목적어」

▶ 「주어 + 동사 + 목적어」 형태로 동사 뒤에 '무엇을, 누구를'에 해당하는 목적어가 따라오는 문장 형식이다.

They will / **inspect** / the **factory** / in June. 동사 + 명사(목적어) + 전치사구(수식어)

The company / **expanded** / its **services**. 동사 + 명사(목적어)

해석 그들은 6월에 공장을 점검할 것이다. / 그 회사는 서비스를 확장했다.

6. 4형식 문장: 「주어 + 동사 + 목적어 + 목적어」

▶ 「주어 + 동사 + 간접 목적어(~에게) + 직접 목적어(~를)」 형태로 목적어가 두 개이다. 간접 목적어는 '~에게'에 해당되는 목적어로 주로 사람이 오고, 직접 목적어는 '~을/를'에 해당하는 목적어로 주로 사물이 온다.

▶ '(~에게) …을 주다'라는 기본 의미를 가진 동사인 give, offer 등이 4형식으로 쓰인다. 모든 4형식 동사들은 사람에 해당하는 간접 목적어 없이 직접 목적어만 나와서 3형식으로도 쓰인다.

꼭 외워야 할 4형식 동사 (수여동사)		
give 주다	offer 제공하다	send 보내다
grant 수여하다, 승인해 주다	award 수여하다	assign 할당해 주다
show 보여주다	bring 가져다 주다	teach 가르치다
lend 빌려주다		

The store / will **offer** / **customers** / a **discount**. 동사 + 명사(간접 목적어) + 명사(직접 목적어)

The company / **grants** / **employees** / **bonuses**. 동사 + 명사(간접 목적어) + 명사(직접 목적어)

해석 그 가게는 고객들에게 할인을 제공할 것이다. / 그 회사는 직원들에게 보너스를 수여한다.

7. 4형식 문장: 「주어 + 동사 + 사람 목적어 + that절」

▶ 다음의 동사들은 4형식으로 쓰일 때, 사람 또는 통지 대상이 간접 목적어 자리에 오고 that절이 직접 목적어로 온다. 이 동사들은 3형식으로 바뀌어도 뒤에 사람 또는 통지 대상이 오는 것은 바뀌지 않는다.

꼭 외워야 할 4형식 동사 (notify류 동사)		
notify ~에게 알리다	inform ~에게 알리다	+ 사람(통지 대상) + that절 → 4형식
remind ~에게 상기시키다	assure ~에게 확언해 주다	
advise ~에게 알리다	convince ~에게 납득시키다	+ 사람(통지 대상) + of 명사 → 3형식
warn ~에게 경고하다		

* 이 중 remind, convince, warn 동사는 「remind, convince, warn + 사람(통지대상) + to 부정사」 형태로 사람 목적어 뒤에 to 부정사가 오는 형태로 출제되기도 한다.

Ms. Han / **reminded** / **employees** of the policy changes. 3형식

Ms. Han / **reminded** / **employees** / **that** the policy changes are necessary. 4형식

Ms. Han / **reminded** / **employees** / **to implement** the policy changes. 5형식

해석 Ms. Han은 직원들에게 정책 변경에 대해 상기시켰다. / Ms. Han은 직원들에게 정책 변경이 필요하다는 것을 상기시켰다. / Ms. Han은 직원들에게 정책 변경을 시행할 것을 상기시켰다.

✅ **문법 포인트** '알리다'라는 의미의 inform이나 notify는 뒤에 사람(통지 대상) 목적어가 오지만 같은 의미의 announce는 뒤에 사람이 올 수 없고 알리는 내용이 온다는 점을 꼭 기억해야 한다.

Mr. Keith has [~~announced~~ / **informed**] us that the samples should arrive by this Wednesday.

Mr. Keith has [**announced** / ~~informed~~] (to us) that the samples should arrive by this Wednesday.

해석 Mr. Keith가 우리에게 샘플이 수요일까지 도착할 것이라는 것을 알려 주었다.

8. 5형식 문장: 「주어 + 동사 + 목적어 + 형용사 / 명사」

▶ 「주어 + 동사 + 목적어 + 목적격 보어」로 이루어진 문장을 5형식 문장이라고 한다.

▶ 목적격 보어로 목적어의 상태를 설명해 주는 형용사가 오는데, 형용사 보어는 '~하게'로 해석되므로 부사를 쓰지 않도록 주의한다.

▶ 목적격 보어로 목적어가 무엇인지를 설명해 주는 명사가 온다. 이때 목적어와 명사는 서로 동일한 대상이다.

꼭 외워야 할 5형식 동사 (형용사 / 명사 목적격 보어)		
make ~을 ~하게 하다 consider ~라고 여기다 leave 계속 ~하게 하다	find ~라고 여기다, ~라고 생각하다 keep 계속 ~하게 하다	+ 목적어 + 형용사
name 지명하다, 임명하다 call ~라고 부르다	appoint 임명하다 elect 선출하다	+ 목적어 + 명사

The training program / **keeps** / employees / **safe**. 동사 + 명사(목적어) + 형용사(목적격 보어)

They / **elected** / her / **mayor**. 동사 + 명사(목적어) + 명사(목적격 보어)

해석 그 훈련 프로그램은 직원들을 안전하게 해준다. / 그들은 그녀를 시장으로 선출했다.

9. 5형식 문장: 「주어 + 동사 + 목적어 + to부정사」

▶ want, ask, tell 등은 '(누가) ~하기를 …하다'라는 의미를 가지고 있으므로, **'누가** 하는지'를 나타내는 목적어와 **'무엇을** 하는지'를 나타내는 to 부정사 목적격 보어가 필요하다.

▶ help는 목적격 보어로 원형부정사와 to부정사가 올 수 있다.

꼭 외워야 할 5형식 동사 (to부정사 목적격 보어)			
advise 조언(충고)하다 ask 요청하다 enable 가능하게 하다 help 돕다 invite 초대하다	allow 허락하다 cause 야기시키다, 일으키다 expect 예상하다 require 요구하다 force 강요하다	permit 허가하다 persuade 설득하다 want 원하다 encourage 장려하다 urge 권고하다, 재촉하다	+ 목적어 + to부정사

The manager / **asked** / the applicants / **to submit their** résumés by mail.
동사 + 명사(목적어) + to부정사(목적격 보어)

Regular exercise / will **help** / **you** / **(to) relieve** stress. 동사 + 명사(목적어) + to부정사(목적격 보어)

해석 그 관리자는 지원자들에게 그들의 이력서를 우편으로 제출하라고 요구했다. / 규칙적인 운동은 스트레스를 해소하는 데 도움이 될 것이다.

Q1 [주어 자리] + 동사

------- for the musical audition will receive responses by April 7.

(A) Applied   (B) Applications   (C) Applicants   (D) Applies

>> **출제 포인트 동사 앞에는 주어 역할을 하는 명사가 나온다.**

1 선택지 확인 | 빈칸에 들어갈 알맞은 품사를 고른다.

2 빈칸 확인 | 주어 자리 → for the musical audition은 주어를 뒤에서 꾸며주는 전치사구이며, 주어 자리에는 명사가 들어가야 한다. → 동사 (A) Applied ❌ (D) Applies ❌

3 정답 확인 | 뮤지컬 오디션의 지원서가 4월 7일까지 응답을 받을 것이다. (B) Applications ❌
뮤지컬 오디션의 지원자가 4월 7일까지 응답을 받을 것이다. → (C) Applicants ⭕

정답 (C) Applicants / for the musical audition / will receive / responses / by April 7.
해석 지원자들은 / 뮤지컬 오디션의 / 받을 것이다 / 응답을 / 4월 7일까지

출제 포인트 ❶ 명사나 대명사는 주어 역할을 한다.

Construction on Main Street / will continue / until the end of the year. 명사 주어
He / forwarded / the evaluation / to my supervisor. 대명사 주어
Recovering lost files / is not an easy job. 동명사 주어
The department [manager / ~~manage~~] will be away on business this week. 명사 주어

주의! 동사나 형용사는 주어가 될 수 없다.

해석 Main가의 공사는 올해 말까지 계속될 것이다. / 그는 내 상사에게 평가서를 전달했다. / 잃어버린 파일들을 복구하는 것은 쉬운 일이 아니다. / 부서장은 이번 주에 출장을 갈 것이다.

해설서 p.2

➕ check

1. All of the laboratory ------- must attend the safety training session this afternoon.

(A) assistance   (B) assistants   (C) assisting   (D) assists

Q2 주어 + [동사 자리]

The concert ------- with a performance by a famous singer.

(A) concluding   (B) to conclude   (C) concluded   (D) conclusion

>> 출제 포인트 동사 자리에는 준동사가 올 수 없다.

1 **선택지 확인** | 빈칸에 들어갈 알맞은 품사를 고르고, 올바른 형태를 선택한다.

2 **빈칸 확인** | 동사 자리 → 준동사나 명사는 동사 자리에 올 수 없다. → (A) 동사-ing ❌ (B) to부정사 ❌ (D) 명사 ❌

3 **정답 확인** | (C) 「conclude + with: ~로 끝맺다」 → 동사는 (C) concluded ⭕

정답 The concert / **(C) concluded** / with a performance / by a famous singer.
해석 콘서트는 / 끝이 났다 / 공연으로 / 유명 가수의

출제 포인트 ② 모든 문장에는 주어와 동사가 있지만, 명령문은 주어를 생략하고 동사원형으로 시작한다.

(Please) **direct** / all inquiries and applications / to Human Resources Director / Maria Ramirez.

해석 모든 문의사항과 지원서들은 인사과 책임자인 Maria Ramirez에게 보내주세요.

출제 포인트 ③ 수식어(구)는 문장의 형식에 포함되지 않으며 명사, 동사, 형용사, 부사를 수식한다.

형용사	명사를 수식한다.
부사	형용사, 동사, 다른 부사를 수식한다.
전치사구	형용사나 부사 역할을 하여 명사나 동사를 수식한다.

The **local** economy / improved. 형용사: 명사 수식

The local economy / (**in the Caribbean**) / improved. 전치사구: 명사 수식

The local economy / (in the Caribbean) / improved (**quickly**). 부사: 동사 수식

The local economy / (in the Caribbean) / improved quickly (**in the second quarter**). 전치사구: 동사 수식

해석 지역 경제가 호전되었다. / 카리브해의 지역 경제가 호전되었다. / 카리브해의 지역 경제가 빠르게 호전되었다. /
카리브해의 지역 경제는 2분기에 빠르게 호전되었다.

출제 포인트 ④ 조동사 뒤에는 동사원형이 나오며, 동사의 의미를 더해준다.

조동사 + 동사원형

can(~할 수 있다), may(~해도 좋다), must(~해야한다), will(~할 것이다), should(~해야한다), do not / does not / did not(부정문)

Normal service **will resume** on July 21.

해석 정상적인 서비스는 7월 21일에 재개될 것이다.

⭐check

2. All on-site factory supervisors must ------- their timesheets by Monday.

(A) submitted   (B) submit   (C) submission   (D) to submit

Q3 주어 + 동사 + [목적어 자리]

We offer free ------- if your order is more than $50.

(A) deliver (B) delivery (C) deliverable (D) delivers

>> 출제 포인트 3형식 동사 뒤에는 목적어 역할을 하는 명사가 온다.

1 선택지 확인 | 빈칸에 들어갈 알맞은 품사를 고른다.

2 빈칸 확인 | 동사 뒤의 목적어 자리 → 목적어 자리에는 명사가 온다. → (A) 동사 ❌ (C) 형용사 ❌ (D) 동사원형-(e)s ❌

3 정답 확인 | 「offer + 목적어: ~을 제공하다」 → 동사의 목적어는 명사 (B) delivery ⭕

정답 We / offer / free **(B) delivery** / if your order is more than $50.
해석 우리는 / 제공합니다 / 무료 배송을 / 귀하의 주문이 50달러 이상이면

출제 포인트 ❹ 명사나 대명사는 목적어 역할을 한다.

Samfen Architecture, Inc. **completed** / **construction** of the bridge as scheduled. 명사 목적어

We can **send** / **you** / the product within a week. 대명사 목적어

They **planned** / **to open** a new branch in June. to부정사 목적어

They **postponed** / **opening** a new branch in June. 동명사 목적어

A recent survey **indicates** / **that** 60 percent of the population owns an automobile. 명사절 목적어

해석 Samfen 건축회사는 다리 공사를 예정대로 끝냈다. / 일주일 내에 당신에게 물건을 보내줄 수 있다. / 그들은 6월에 새로운 지점을 열기로 계획했다. / 그들은 6월에 새로운 지점을 여는 것을 연기했다. / 최근의 조사는 인구의 60퍼센트가 자가용을 소유하고 있다는 것을 보여 준다.

+ check

3. Bitec Gaming Ltd. has made ------- to renovate the company's Hillstown manufacturing facility.

(A) plans (B) will plan (C) to plan (D) planner

Q4 주어 + 동사 + 목적어 + [보어 자리]

The seminar attendees found the president's speech -------.

(A) impressive　　　(B) impressively　　　(C) impress　　　(D) impression

---

>> **출제 포인트 5형식 동사의 목적어 뒤에는 보어 역할을 하는 명사나 형용사가 온다.**

1 선택지 확인 | 빈칸에 들어갈 알맞은 품사를 고른다.

2 빈칸 확인 | 목적어 뒤의 보어 자리 → 목적격 보어 자리에는 명사/형용사가 온다.
　　　　　　　→ 부사 (B) impressively ❌ 동사 (C) impress ❌

3 정답 확인 | 「find + 목적어 + 목적격 보어: ~를 …하다고 생각하다」 → 목적격 보어자리에 목적어의 상태를 설명하면
　　　　　　　형용사, 동격(동일한 대상)이면 명사 자리이다. → (A) impressive ⊚

정답 The seminar attendees / found / the president's speech / **(A) impressive**.
해석 세미나 참석자들은 / 생각했다 / 그 회장의 연설이 / 인상적이라고

출제 포인트 ⑤ 형용사는 목적어 뒤에서 목적어를 설명해 주는 보어 역할을 한다.

동사 find, consider, make는 목적어 자리에 가목적어 it이 오는 구조로도 쓰인다.

Mr. Lee **found** / the company's benefits package / **attractive**. find + 목적어 + 목적격 보어(형용사)

The interviewers **considered** / Ms. Hue / **qualified** for the position. consider + 목적어 + 목적격 보어(형용사)

Businesses can **make** / customers / **satisfied** / by solving problems quickly.
make + 목적어 + 목적격 보어(형용사)

해석 　Mr. Lee는 그 회사의 복리 후생 제도가 매력적이라고 생각했다. / 면접관들은 Ms. Hue가 그 자리에 적격이라고 생각했다.
　　　　회사는 문제점을 빠르게 해결해 줌으로써 고객들을 만족시킬 수 있다.

⊕check

4. Skymet Electronics will keep its customers ------- by offering products at the most affordable prices.

(A) to satisfy　　　(B) satisfies　　　(C) satisfaction　　　(D) satisfied

Practice

해설서 p.2

1. The Finance Department is very ------- this month with their budget report.

   (A) busyness   (B) busier
   (C) busily   (D) busy

2. Jaygen Holdings ------- its workforce by 20 percent this year.

   (A) will increase   (B) increasing
   (C) to increase   (D) being increased

3. Responses from our monthly customer survey are ------- positive.

   (A) consistency   (B) consistencies
   (C) consistently   (D) consistent

4. The President of S&B Communications ------- to offer internships to students.

   (A) deciding   (B) decided
   (C) decision   (D) to decide

5. The varying quality of products can make purchase decisions quite -------.

   (A) difficulties   (B) difficulty
   (C) difficultly   (D) difficult

6. You can renew ------- to *Beauty Updates Magazine* online or by telephone.

   (A) subscribers   (B) subscribes
   (C) subscriptions   (D) subscribe

7. This Saturday, the department store will be offering all ------- a 15 percent discount.

   (A) shoppers   (B) shopping
   (C) shop   (D) shops

8. The ------- of the company's headquarters to Miami will occur in April.

   (A) relocate   (B) relocated
   (C) relocation   (D) relocates

9. The government's new employment policy will enable businesses ------- many jobs.

   (A) to create   (B) creating
   (C) created   (D) create

10. Plaxco Accounting grew ------- from a small company to a large firm with over 500 staff members.

    (A) quicker   (B) quickly
    (C) quickest   (D) quick

11. ------- at the Johnsonville Factory receive their salary at the end of each month.

    (A) Work   (B) Workers
    (C) Working   (D) Works

12. The President informed employees of the ------- in the payroll system.

    (A) to change   (B) changing
    (C) changed   (D) change

13. Some customers complained that the chef's new dessert was too --------.

    (A) sweetness   (B) sweet
    (C) sweeten   (D) sweetly

14. The first train to Frankston will depart ------- at 10 A.M. today.

    (A) precisely   (B) precise
    (C) precision   (D) preciseness

15. The upgraded computer system is now fully ------- and ready for use.

(A) operation   (B) operational
(C) operates   (D) operate

16. The Marketing Department encouraged employees ------- their feedback reports as soon as possible.

(A) to submit   (B) submitting
(C) submitted   (D) submit

17. Mr. Song ------- positions in many areas of the company prior to becoming the CEO.

(A) occupational   (B) occupation
(C) occupying   (D) occupied

18. The Nahaju Group ------- a bigger office complex in the suburbs next year.

(A) will build   (B) building
(C) to build   (D) builder

19. Moonfield Shopping Center reminded customers ------- their business hours will change from March 1.

(A) to   (B) that
(C) of   (D) for

20. ------- of this task is not expected until early April.

(A) Completed   (B) Completely
(C) Completion   (D) Completes

기본 완성 훈련 ▷ 다음은 앞서 풀어 본 연습문제의 문장들입니다. 주어(S), 동사(V), 목적어(O), 보어(C)를 찾아 밑줄을 긋고 품사를 표시하세요.

1. The Finance Department is very busy this month with their budget report.

2. The President of S&B Communications decided to offer internships to students.

3. The varying quality of products can make purchase decisions quite difficult.

4. You can renew subscriptions to *Beauty Updates Magazine* online or by telephone.

5. The government's new employment policy will enable businesses to create many jobs.

6. The President informed employees of the change in the payroll system.

7. The upgraded computer system is fully operational now and ready for use.

8. The Marketing Department encouraged employees to submit their feedback reports as soon as possible.

9. Moonfield Shopping Center reminded customers that their business hours will change from March 1.

10. Completion of this task is not expected until early April.

수 일치

모든 주어와 동사는 반드시 수 일치가 되어야 한다!

문장의 주어 역할을 하는 명사는 단수와 복수가 있으며, 동사는 주어의 수에 따라 단수형과 복수형을 구분해서 쓴다.

 기본 개념 이해하기

1. 주어와 동사의 수 일치

▶ 명사는 하나를 의미하는 단수형과 둘 이상을 의미하는 복수형이 있으며, 복수형은 대부분 -(e)s가 붙는다.
주어가 단수 명사이면 단수 동사를, 복수 명사이면 복수 동사를 쓴다. 명사는 복수형일때 -(e)s가 붙지만, 동사는
단수형 동사에 -(e)s가 붙는다.

| 단수 명사 | 하나 | A / An + 명사 + 단수 동사 | **An** employee / **works** in the office. |
| 복수 명사 | 둘 이상 | 명사 + -(e)s + 복수 동사 | Employee**s** / **work** in the office. |

해석 한 직원이 사무실에서 근무한다. / 직원들이 사무실에서 근무한다.
풀이 단수 주어(An employee) 뒤에는 단수 동사 works를 쓰고, 복수 주어 Employees 뒤에는 복수 동사 work를 쓴다.

2. 일반 동사의 단수형과 복수형

▶ 일반 동사의 단수형은 「동사원형 + -(e)s」를 쓰고, 복수형은 동사원형을 그대로 쓴다. 단, 과거 시제일 때는
주어의 수와 상관없이 동일한 형태로 쓴다.

		현재	과거
단수 주어	단수 동사	works, does, has	worked, did, had
복수 주어	복수 동사	work, do, have	

The company / **provides[provided]** / free e-mail service. 단수 동사[과거형]
Many companies / **provide[provided]** / free e-mail service. 복수 동사[과거형]

The price / **does not[did not]** include / any delivery charges. 단수 동사[과거형]
The prices / **do not[did not]** include / any delivery charges. 복수 동사[과거형]

The manager / **has[had]** / new applications / to review. 단수 동사[과거형]
The managers / **have[had]** / new applications / to review. 복수 동사[과거형]

해석 그 기업은 무료 이메일 서비스를 제공한다[제공했다]. / 많은 기업들이 무료 이메일 서비스를 제공한다[제공했다].
그 가격은 배달 요금을 포함하지 않는다[않았다]. / 그 가격들은 배달 요금을 포함하지 않는다[않았다].
그 매니저는 검토해야 할 새로운 지원서들이 있다[있었다]. / 매니저들은 검토해야 할 새로운 지원서들이 있다[있었다].

3. be동사의 단수형과 복수형

▶ be동사는 일반동사와 달리 현재 시제와 과거 시제 모두 수 일치가 필요하다. 단수형은 is/was를 쓰고, 복수형은 are/were를 쓴다.

		현재	과거
단수 주어	단수 동사	is	was
복수 주어	복수 동사	are	were

The product / **is** popular / in overseas markets.

The products / **are** popular / in overseas markets.

The conference / **was** informative.

The workshops / at the conference / **were** informative.

해석 　그 제품은 해외 시장에서 인기가 있다. / 그 제품들은 해외 시장에서 인기가 많다.
　　　그 학회는 유익했다. / 그 학회에서의 워크숍들은 유익했다.

4. 인칭대명사 주어와 동사의 수 일치

▶ 인칭대명사는 3인칭 단수일 때는 단수 동사를 쓰지만, 3인칭 복수와 1, 2인칭에서는 복수 동사(동사원형)를 쓴다.

		일반 동사		be 동사	
		현재	과거	현재	과거
3인칭 단수 주어 He/She/It	단수 동사	works, does, has		is	was
3인칭 복수와 1, 2인칭 주어 We/You/They/I	복수 동사	work, do, have	worked, did, had	are (I am)	were (I was)

She / **attends** / the seminar / every year. 3인칭 단수 + 단수 동사

They / **attend** / the seminar / every year. 3인칭 복수 + 복수 동사(동사원형)

I / **attend** / the seminar / every year. 1인칭 단수 + 복수 동사(동사원형)

He **is[was]** responsible / for marketing the product. 3인칭 단수 + is[was]

They **are[were]** responsible / for marketing the product. 3인칭 복수 + are[were]

I **am[was]** responsible / for marketing the product. 1인칭 단수 + am[was]

해석 　그녀는 매년 그 세미나에 참석한다. / 그들은 매년 그 세미나에 참석한다. / 나는 매년 그 세미나에 참석한다.
　　　그는 그 제품 마케팅을 책임지고 있다[있었다]. / 그들은 그 제품 마케팅을 책임지고 있다[있었다]. / 나는 그 제품 마케팅을 책임지고 있다[있었다].

Q1 고유 명사 주어 + [단수 동사 vs. 복수 동사]

XTM Labs ------- qualified candidates to fill the two vacant technician positions.

(A) seeking   (B) is seeking   (C) are seeking   (D) to seek

>> **출제 포인트 주어의 수에 동사의 수를 일치시킨다.**

① 선택지 확인 | 빈칸에 들어갈 동사의 알맞은 형태를 묻는 동사 어형 문제이다.

② 빈칸 확인 | 동사의 자리 → 동사 자리에 올 수 없는 (A) 동사-ing ❌ (D) to부정사 ❌

③ 정답 확인 | 주어 XTM Labs는 -s로 끝나고 있어 복수명사로 보기 쉽지만 회사 이름은 고유명사로 단수 취급을 해야 하
므로 (C) are seeking ❌ 정답은 (B) is seeking ⭕

정답 XTM Labs / **(B) is seeking** / qualified candidates / to fill the two vacant technician positions.

해석 XTM Labs는 / 찾고 있다 / 자격을 갖춘 지원자들을 / 두 개의 기술직 공석을 채우기 위해

출제 포인트 ❶ 불가산 명사(물질명사, 추상명사), 고유명사, 학문명은 끝에 -s가 붙어 있든 붙어 있지 않든 항상 단
수 취급한다.

물질명사	furniture 가구 equipment 기구 money 돈 cash 현금 change 잔돈 baggage 수하물 luggage 수하물
추상명사	access 접근 advice 조언 information 정보
고유명사	Brooks Brothers 브룩스 형제(업체명) the United States 미국 Mr. Louis Louis 씨
학문명	economics 경제학 statistics 통계학 mathematics 수학

Network **access** / **is** denied. 불가산 명사 + 단수 동사

Economics / **is** a challenging subject for Sally. 학문명 + 단수 동사

해석 네트워크 접근이 거부되었다. / 경제학은 Sally에게 힘겨운 과목이다.

출제 포인트 ❷ one, each, every, everything은 단수 취급한다.

one과 each는 「of the + 복수 명사」가 뒤따라 올 수 있으며, every와 each는 「every / each + 단수 명사」 형태로 사용하고,
everything, everybody, everyone은 의미상 복수이지만 단수 취급한다.

One of the products[**One** product] / **is** defective. 주어 (수식어구) + 동사

Each of the products[**Each** product] / **is** individually wrapped. 주어 (수식어구) + 동사

Everything / **depends** on you.

해석 그 제품들 중의 하나는 결함이 있다. / 각각의 제품들은 개별 포장된다. / 모든 것은 당신에게 달려 있습니다.

➕ check .... 해설서 p.4

1. The Arts Marketing Association ------- its annual conference at the Zenco Hotel tonight.

    (A) hold   (B) is holding   (C) holding   (D) have held

Q2 「수량 표현 of + 복수 명사」+ [단수 동사 vs. 복수 동사]

Most of the candidates ------- well-qualified for the position.

(A) is   (B) was   (C) being   (D) were

≫ 출제 포인트 「수량 표현 of + 명사」는 명사의 수에 동사의 수를 일치시킨다.

① **선택지 확인** | 빈칸에 들어갈 동사의 알맞은 형태를 묻는 동사 어형 문제이다.

② **빈칸 확인** | 동사의 자리 → 준동사는 동사 자리에 올 수 없다. → (C) 동사-ing ✕

③ **정답 확인** | Most of the + 복수 명사(candidates) 뒤에는 candidates에 수를 일치시켜 복수 동사가 와야 한다.
→ 3인칭 단수형인 (A) is ✕ (B) was ✕ be동사의 과거 시제 복수형 (D) were ◎

정답 Most of the candidates / **(D) were** well-qualified / for the position.
해석 지원 후보자의 대부분은 / 자격을 잘 갖추고 있다 / 그 직책에 대해

출제 포인트 ❸ most, all, some, half 등은 전치사 of 뒤에 오는 명사의 수에 동사의 수를 일치시킨다.

most, all, some, half, percent, the rest	of the + 단수 명사 + 단수 동사
	of the + 복수 명사 + 복수 동사

Most of the information / **is** available free of charge. most of + 단수 명사(불가산 명사) + 단수 동사
Half of the employees / **want** to participate in the workshop. half of + 복수 명사 + 복수 동사

해석 그 정보의 대부분은 요금 없이 무료로 이용 가능하다. / 직원들 중 절반이 워크숍에 참여하고 싶어 한다.

출제 포인트 ❹ 「both / a couple of / a number of + 복수 명사 + 복수 동사」

Both of her parents / **are** from Germany. both of + 복수 명사 + 복수 동사
A couple of ideas / **were** approved by the board of directors. a couple of + 복수 명사 + 복수 동사
A number of students / **are** studying. a number of(=a lot of) + 복수 명사 + 복수 동사
The number (of students) / **is** going to increase. the number of + 복수 명사 + 단수 동사

해석 그녀의 부모님은 두 분 다 독일 출신이다. / 두어 가지 아이디어들이 이사회의 승인을 받았다. / 많은 학생들이 공부하고 있다. / 학생 수가 증가할 것이다.

✓ 문법 포인트 「A number of + 복수명사 + 복수동사」 vs. 「The number of + 복수명사 + 단수동사」

- 「A number of + 복수명사」가 주어로 나올 때에는 a number of는 '많은'이라는 의미로 수식어에 불과하고 뒤에 있는 복수명사가 주어이므로 동사도 복수동사로 일치시킨다.
- 「The number of + 복수명사」가 주어로 나올 때에는 of 이하의 전치사구가 앞에 있는 명사 number를 수식해주는 형태로 '~의 숫자'라는 의미로 단수명사인 number가 주어이므로 동사는 단수동사로 일치시킨다.

⊕ check

2. Each of the tourists ------- given some brochures before leaving for the next destination.

(A) is   (B) were   (C) to be   (D) being

Q3 주어 + 수식어 + [단수 동사 vs. 복수 동사]

A master's degree, one of our requirements, ------- essential.

(A) being   (B) are   (C) is   (D) be

>> **출제 포인트** 주어와 동사 사이의 수식어는 수 일치에 영향을 주지 않는다.

① 선택지 확인 | 빈칸에 들어갈 동사의 알맞은 형태를 묻는 문제이다.

② 빈칸 확인 | 동사의 자리 → 동사 자리에 올 수 없는 (A) 동사-ing ❌

③ 정답 확인 | 단수 주어(A master's degree) + 동격어구(one of our requirements) → 동격어구는 주어, 동사 사이에 들어간 수식어구일 뿐이므로 수 일치에 영향을 주지 않는다 → 주어 degree에 수를 일치시켜 be동사의 3인칭 단수형이 와야 하므로 (B) are ❌ 동사원형 (D) be ❌ 정답은 (C) is ⭕

정답 A master's degree, / one of our requirements, / **(C) is** / essential.
해석 석사 학위는 / 요구 조건 중의 하나인 / 필수적이다.

출제 포인트 ⑤ 주어와 동사 사이에 앞에 있는 주어를 수식하는 전치사구, 형용사구, 분사구, to부정사, 형용사절, 동격어구 등의 수식어가 올 수 있지만, 수 일치에는 영향을 주지 않는다. 동사 바로 앞의 명사를 주어로 착각하면 안된다.

The **products** (of the company) / **are** popular. 복수 주어 (전치사구) + 복수 동사

Mr. Hong, (one of the instructors), / **works** / hard. 단수 주어 (동격어구) + 단수 동사

The **company**, (founded by several architects), / **has** / a good reputation. 단수 주어 (분사구) + 단수 동사

The **customers** (who used our rental service) / **were** satisfied. 복수 주어 (형용사절) + 복수 동사

The **departments** (responsible for marketing data) / **are** listed below. 복수 주어 (형용사구) + 복수 동사

Ms. Chen's **ability** (to attract customers) / **was** impressive. 단수 주어 (to부정사) + 단수 동사

해석 그 회사의 제품들은 인기가 좋다. / 강사들 중 한 명인, Mr. Hong은 열심히 일한다. / 몇몇 건축가들에 의해 설립된 그 회사는 좋은 평판을 가지고 있다. 우리의 대여 서비스를 이용했던 고객들은 만족스러워 했다. / 마케팅 데이터를 관리하는 부서가 아래에 열거되어 있다. 고객들을 끌어들이는 Ms. Chen의 능력은 인상적이었다.

+check

3. Over the last several years, the costs related to owning a car ------- many commuters from driving to work.

(A) have prevented   (B) preventive   (C) has prevented   (D) prevention

Q4 단수 주어 + [과거 동사 vs. 복수 동사]

The developer ------- the new software program to us.

(A) introduced　　　(B) introduce　　　(C) introducing　　　(D) to introduce

>> **출제 포인트 일반동사의 과거형은 단수와 복수를 구분하지 않는다.**

➊ 선택지 확인 | 빈칸에 들어갈 동사의 알맞은 형태를 묻는 문제이다.

➋ 빈칸 확인 | 동사의 자리 → 동사 자리에 올 수 없는 (C) 동사-ing ✖ (D) to부정사 ✖

➌ 정답 확인 | 단수 주어(The developer) → 일반동사의 현재 시제는 단수형을 써야 하므로 (B) introduce ✖
　　　　　　　과거 시제는 단수와 복수 구분이 없으므로 정답은 (A) introduced ◉

정답 The developer / **(A) introduced** / the new software program / to us.
해석 개발자가 / 소개했다 / 새로운 소프트웨어 프로그램을 / 우리에게

출제 포인트 ➎ 「**There + 동사(be) + 주어**」 구문에서 동사는 뒤따라 오는 주어와 수를 일치시킨다.

There / **is a change** / to the terms and conditions of the contract. There + 단수 동사 + 단수 명사

There / **are** some **changes** / to the terms and conditions of the contract. There + 복수 동사 + 복수 명사

해석　계약 조항 및 조건에 한 가지 변경 사항이 있다. / 계약 조항 및 조건에 몇 가지 변경 사항들이 있다.

출제 포인트 ➐ 조동사 뒤에는 주어의 수와 상관없이 동사원형이 온다.

Each application / **must be received** / before March 1. 단수 주어 + 조동사 (must) + 동사원형

Visitors / **can** easily **find** / tour brochures / at the front desk. 복수 주어 + 조동사 (can) + 동사원형

해석　각 지원서는 3월 1일 전에 수령되어야 한다. / 방문객들은 안내 데스크에서 여행 책자를 쉽게 찾을 수 있다.

check

4. Kelly Brady in Marketing ------- her ideas on promoting new products at last week's meeting.

(A) present　　　(B) presenting　　　(C) to present　　　(D) presented

Practice

해설서 p.4

1. Mr. Lee, the restaurant manager, regularly ------- new menus.

(A) develops (B) develop
(C) to develop (D) development

2. The new LX555 camera, designed for beginner photographers, ------- popular among young people.

(A) is (B) are
(C) be (D) being

3. The sales director closely ------- the new interns' training.

(A) monitor (B) to monitor
(C) monitors (D) monitoring

4. Our solid wood furniture ------- with an extensive five-year warranty.

(A) come (B) coming
(C) to come (D) comes

5. It is expected that ------- at the Thorndon Factory is going to increase this quarter.

(A) productivity (B) productive
(C) products (D) produce

6. Ms. Felix ------- a considerable donation to the local community.

(A) have made (B) has made
(C) having made (D) making

7. The customer service ------- is trained to deal with various complaints from customers.

(A) departed (B) department
(C) to depart (D) departments

8. Comfy Dress, Inc. ------- retailers with affordable and trendy clothes for over 10 years.

(A) having supplied (B) has supplied
(C) to supply (D) have supplied

9. Orders placed on the Cheap Buy Web site typically ------- four days to process.

(A) takes (B) taking
(C) take (D) to take

10. Please ------- the manual carefully before installing your new word processing software.

(A) reading (B) read
(C) to read (D) reads

11. All construction workers must ------- the health and safety training by October 11.

(A) completes (B) completing
(C) complete (D) completed

12. Some of the defective products ------- going to be shipped to the Newlands warehouse.

(A) was (B) to be
(C) be (D) are

13. More than 2,000 people ------- to *Jay's Fashion Magazine*.

(A) subscribes (B) subscribing
(C) to subscribe (D) subscribe

14. There ------- many suitcases at the hotel lobby this morning.

(A) were (B) be
(C) was (D) is

15. One of the candidates ------- some inaccurate information in his résumé.

(A) including   (B) included
(C) include   (D) to be included

16. If you ------- questions about the product, please contact our help desk at 555-2349.

(A) has   (B) having
(C) have   (D) to have

17. The number of participants in this year's Technology Conference ------- expected to decrease.

(A) is   (B) are
(C) been (D) were

18. Ms. Rares ------- more information about the workshop before she can decide whether to attend.

(A) needs   (B) needing
(C) need   (D) to need

19. Tom's Bistro ------- customers friendly service as well as a variety of healthy foods.

(A) have offered   (B) are offered
(C) offer   (D) offers

20. Commuters can easily ------- the central business district by taking the Yellow Rail Line.

(A) reaches   (B) reach
(C) to reach (D) reaching

기본 완성 훈련 다음은 앞서 풀어 본 연습문제의 문장들입니다. 주어, 동사를 찾아 밑줄을 긋고, 주어가 단수인 경우 문제 번호에 ○를 치세요.

1. The new LX555 camera, designed for beginner photographers, is popular among young people.

2. Our solid wood furniture comes with an extensive five-year warranty.

3. It is expected that productivity at the Thorndon Factory is going to increase this quarter.

4. Ms. Felix has made a considerable donation to the local community.

5. The customer service department is trained to deal with various complaints from customers.

6. Orders placed on the Cheap Buy Web site typically take four days to process.

7. Please read the manual carefully before installing your new word processing software.

8. Ms. Rares needs more information about the workshop before she can decide whether to attend.

9. Tom's Bistro offers customers friendly service as well as a variety of healthy foods.

10. Commuters can easily reach the central business district by taking the Yellow Rail Line.

시제

동사의 때를 표현하는 시제에는 현재, 과거, 미래 시제가 있다. 세부적인 의미에 따라 단순 시제, 진행 시제, 완료 시제로 나뉜다.

 기본 개념 이해하기

1. 시제의 형태

	단순 시제	완료 시제	진행 시제	완료 진행 시제
현재	attend / attends	has / have attended	is / are attending	has / have been attending
과거	attended	had attended	was / were attending	had been attending
미래	will attend	will have attended	will be attending	will have been attending

2. 단순 시제

현재 시제	동사원형 / 동사원형-(e)s	늘상 일어나는 반복적인 일(repeated events)이나 현재의 일반적인 사실(general facts)을 말할 때
과거 시제	동사원형-(e)d / 불규칙 변화	이미 끝난 일(finished events) 또는 과거의 사실이나 습관을 말할 때
미래 시제	will + 동사원형	앞으로의 일(predicted events)을 예상하거나 앞으로 할 일을 말할 때

Canota, Inc. / **conducts** / a customer satisfaction survey / every year. 현재 시제

Ms. Leroy / **works** / here / as a nurse. 현재 시제

Canota, Inc. / **conducted** / a customer satisfaction survey / last month. 과거 시제

Ms. Leroy / **worked** / here / as a nurse. 과거 시제

Canota, Inc. / **will conduct** / a customer satisfaction survey / next week. 미래 시제

Ms. Leroy / **will work** / here / as a nurse. 미래 시제

해석　Canota 사는 고객 만족도 조사를 매년 수행한다. / Ms. Leroy는 여기서 간호사로 일한다.
　　　Canota 사는 지난달에 고객 만족도 조사를 수행했다. / Ms. Leroy는 여기서 간호사로 일했다.
　　　Canota 사는 다음 주에 고객 만족도 조사를 수행할 것이다. / Ms. Leroy는 여기서 간호사로 일할 것이다.

3. 완료 시제

▶ 현재, 과거, 미래의 기준 시점까지 그 이전에 일어난 어떤 사건이나 상태가 영향을 미치고 있음을 나타낸다.

현재완료 시제	have / has + p.p.	'과거부터 지금까지 계속되고 있는 일' 또는 '과거에 일어난 일'을 현재와 연결시켜 '현재까지 남아 있는 결과, 경험한 일, 완료한 일'로 묘사한다.
과거완료 시제	had + p.p.	'과거의 기준 시점보다 먼저 일어난 일'을 의미한다. 주로 과거에 일어난 일들의 순서를 명확하게 나타낼 필요가 있을 때 쓴다.
미래완료 시제	will have + p.p.	'미래의 기준 시점보다 먼저 일어난 일' 또는 '과거에 시작된 일이 미래시점에 완료될 일'을 의미한다.

Ms. Hagen / **has worked** / here / for four years. 현재완료 시제: 과거부터 지금까지 계속되고 있는 일

Mr. Tran / **has injured** / his leg, / and (he) / cannot move.
현재완료 시제: 현재까지 남아 있는 결과(~한 상태로 남아 있다)

Before Mr. Lee arrived at the office, / the meeting / **had started**. 과거완료 시제

= After the meeting **had started**, / Mr. Lee / arrived / at the office. 과거완료 시제

Ms. Perez / **will have worked** / here for four years by next October. 미래완료 시제

해석 Ms. Hagen은 여기서 4년간 일하고 있다. / Mr. Tran은 다리를 다쳐서 움직이지 못한다. / Mr. Lee가 사무실에 도착하기 전에 회의가 시작됐다. / 회의가 시작한 후에 Mr. Lee는 사무실에 도착했다. / Ms. Perez는 돌아오는 10월이면 여기서 일한 지 4년이 된다.

4. 진행 시제

▶ 현재, 과거, 미래의 한 시점에서 진행 중인 동작이나 그 시점에서의 상태를 나타낸다.

현재진행 시제	is / are + V-ing	현재 시점에서의 진행 중인 동작이나 상태, 가까운 또는 확정된 미래를 나타내기도 한다.
과거진행 시제	was / were + V-ing	과거 시점에서의 진행 중인 동작이나 상태
미래진행 시제	will be + V-ing	미래 시점에서 진행 중인 동작이나 상태의 예상

Ms. Lund / **is attending** / the staff meeting / now. 현재진행 시제

Ms. Lund / **is attending** / the staff meeting / tomorrow. 현재진행 시제(가까운 미래)

Ms. Lund / **was attending** / the staff meeting / when we arrived here. 과거진행 시제

Ms. Lund / **will be attending** / the staff meeting / after lunch. 미래진행 시제

해석 Ms. Lund는 지금 직원 회의에 참석 중이다. / Ms. Lund는 내일 직원 회의에 참석할 것이다. / 우리가 여기 도착했을 때 Ms. Lund는 직원 회의에 참석 중이었다. / 점심 이후에 Ms. Lund는 직원 회의에 참석 중일 것이다.

Q1 단순 시제

Some of the managers ------- a guided tour of the factory next Monday.

(A) will take   (B) take   (C) took   (D) were taking

>> 출제 포인트 현재 / 과거 / 미래를 나타내는 단서 표현을 찾아 동사의 시제를 정한다.

➊ 선택지 확인 | 빈칸에 들어갈 알맞은 동사의 형태를 고른다.

➋ 빈칸 확인 | 동사의 자리 → (A) 미래 시제, (B) 현재 시제, (C) 과거 시제, (D) 과거진행형 모두 동사 자리에 올 수 있다.

➌ 정답 확인 | next Monday(다음 주 월요일)는 미래의 시점을 나타낸다. → 미래 시제 (A) will take ◎

정답 Some of the managers / **(A) will take** / a guided tour of the factory / next Monday.
해석 일부 매니저들이 / 할 것이다 / 공장 견학을 / 다음 주 월요일에

출제 포인트 ❶ 단순 시제와 함께 쓰이는 시간 부사(구)가 시제 문제의 결정적 단서가 된다.

현재 시간 부사(구)	currently 현재 regularly 정기적으로 each year 매년 frequently 빈번하게 occasionally 가끔	typically 보통 periodically 주기적으로 always 항상 usually 보통	normally 보통 every week 매주 often 자주 sometimes 가끔
과거 시간 부사(구)	last month 지난달에 yesterday 어제	recently 최근에 in 2000 2000년도에	two years ago 2년 전에
미래 시간 부사(구)	next year 내년에 tomorrow 내일	soon 곧, 머지않아 as of tomorrow 내일부터	shortly 곧, 머지않아

Jacky's Café / offers / free beverages / to its customers **every month**. 현재 시간 부사(구)
Jacky's Café / offered / free beverages / to its customers **last month**. 과거 시간 부사(구)
Jacky's Café / will offer / free beverages / to its customers **soon**. 미래 시간 부사(구)

해석   Jackey's Café는 매달 고객들에게 무료 음료를 제공한다. / Jacky's 카페는 지난달에 고객들에게 무료 음료를 제공했다.
       Jacky's Café는 고객들에게 곧 무료 음료를 제공할 것이다.

➕check .... 해설서 p.6

1. Lake Yohanas last ------- completely a decade ago.

(A) froze   (B) freeze   (C) frozen   (D) freezing

Q2 완료 시제

Saritex Group ------- its business in developing countries in the last three years.

(A) expansion   (B) expands   (C) expanding   (D) has expanded

>> 출제 포인트 완료 시제와 함께 쓰이는 단서 표현을 찾아 동사의 시제를 정한다.

❶ **선택지 확인** | 빈칸에 들어갈 알맞은 동사의 형태를 고른다.

❷ **빈칸 확인** | 동사 자리 → 명사와 준동사는 동사 자리에 올 수 없다. → (A) 명사 ✖ (C) 동사원형-ing ✖
        (B) 현재 시제와 (D) 현재완료시제는 동사 자리에 올 수 있다.

❸ **정답 확인** | in the last three years(지난 3년 동안)은 '과거부터 지금까지의 기간'을 의미한다.
        → 현재완료 (D) has expanded ⓞ

정답 Saritex Group / **(D) has expanded** / its business / in developing countries / in the last three years.
해석 Saritex 그룹은 / 확장해 왔다 / 사업을 / 개발도상국가들에서 / 지난 3년 동안

출제 포인트 ② 완료 시제와 함께 쓰이는 시간 부사(구)가 시제 문제의 결정적 단서가 된다.

현재완료 시간 부사(구)	over[during / for / in] the last[past] three years 지난 3년 동안 「since + 과거 시점」(과거 시점) 이후로 (지금까지) 「since + S + 과거 시제」(과거 시점에 ~한) 이후로 (지금까지) recently / lately 최근에 so far / until now 지금까지 for two months 두 달 동안 during the summer 여름 동안
과거완료 시간 부사(구)	「Before S + 과거 시제, S + 과거완료 시제」~하기 전에 이미 ~했었다 「After S + 과거완료 시제, S + 과거 시제」이미 ~한 후에 ~했다 「By the time S + 과거 시제, S + 과거완료 시제」~했을 때(쯤) 이미 ~했었다
미래완료 시간 부사(구)	「By the time S + 현재 시제, S + 미래완료 시제」~할 때까지면 ~했을 것이다

Vitpro Co. / has enforced / the new policies / **for three months**.
Vitpro Co. / has been enforcing / the new policies / **over the last three months**.
Vitpro Co. / has enforced / the new policies / **since last April**.
Vitpro Co. / has enforced / the new policies / **since the new manager took office**.
By the time Ms. Feng **became** the manager, she / **had worked** / here / for five years.
By the time our R&D team **finishes** developing the new product, our marketing team / **will have set** / the marketing strategies.

해석 Vitpro 사는 3달 동안 새로운 정책들을 시행해왔다. / Vitpro 사는 지난 3달 동안 새로운 정책들을 시행해오고 있다.
     Vitpro 사는 지난 4월 이후로 새로운 정책들을 시행해왔다. / Vitpro 사는 새로운 매니저가 일을 시작한 이후로 새로운 정책들을 시행해왔다.
     Ms. Feng이 매니저가 되었을 때 쯤 그녀는 여기서 5년간 일했었다. / R&D 팀에서 신제품 개발을 끝낼 때까지 마케팅 팀은 마케팅 전략을 수립해 놓을 것이다.

✚ check

2. The exports of our mobile phones ------- over the past three years.

     (A) have increased   (B) increasing   (C) will increase   (D) increase

핵심 문제 유형

Q3 시간·조건절의 시제

If you get this position, you ------- overseas for the next three years.

(A) has worked   (B) will work   (C) work   (D) working

>> **출제 포인트** 시간·조건절의 미래 시제는 현재 시제로 대신한다.

① **선택지 확인** | 빈칸에 들어갈 알맞은 동사의 형태를 고른다.

② **빈칸 확인** | 동사의 자리 → 준동사는 동사 자리에 올 수 없다. → (D) 동사원형-ing ❌

③ **정답 확인** | if절에는 현재 시제가 쓰였지만, 주절은 문맥상 for next three years(앞으로 3년 동안)와 일치하는
(B) will work ⭕

정답 If you get this position, you / **(B) will work** / overseas / for the next three years.
해석 당신이 이 자리를 얻게 된다면, 당신은 / 일하게 될 것이다 / 해외에서 / 앞으로 3년 동안

출제 포인트 ③ 시간·조건을 나타내는 부사절에서 미래 시제는 현재 시제로 대신한다.

시간 부사절 접속사	when ~할 때, ~하면 after ~한 후에 while ~하는 동안	as ~할 때 as soon as ~하자마자	before ~하기 전에 until ~할 때까지
조건 부사절 접속사	if ~라면	unless ~가 아니라면	once 일단 ~하면

When the manager **arrives**, the meeting / **will** begin.
When Ms. Malik **returns** from her trip next month, she / **will** visit / the new plant.

해석 매니저가 도착하면, 회의가 시작될 것이다. / Ms. Malik이 다음 달에 여행에서 돌아오면, 그녀는 새 공장을 방문할 것이다.

If the company **builds** another factory, production capacity / **will** improve.
If there **is** heavy rain, some flights / **will** be suspended.

해석 회사가 또 다른 공장을 설립한다면 생산 능력이 개선될 것이다. / 폭우가 내리면, 일부 비행편이 중단될 것이다.

+ check

3. After employees ------- the satisfaction survey, they will send the form to the Human Resources Manager.

(A) completed   (B) will be completing   (C) are completing   (D) complete

Q4 당위성을 나타내는 that절의 동사

The manager recommended that Mr. Park ------- the report by Friday.

(A) submit   (B) submits   (C) submitted   (D) will submit

>> **출제 포인트** 주장·제안·명령·요청을 나타내는 동사 뒤의 목적어 that절에는 should가 생략된 동사원형을 쓴다.

① 선택지 확인 | 빈칸에 들어갈 알맞은 동사의 형태를 고른다.

② 빈칸 확인 | 동사의 자리 → (A), (B) 현재 시제, (C) 과거 시제, (D) 미래 시제 모두 동사 자리에 올 수 있다.

③ 정답 확인 | 「recommend는 '~할 것을 권고하다」의 의미이므로 that절에는 should가 생략된 동사원형
     (A) submit ⊙

정답 The manager / recommended / that Mr. Park **(A) submit** the report by Friday.

해석 매니저는 / 권고했다 / Mr. Park가 리포트를 다음 주 금요일까지 제출하라고

출제 포인트 ④ 주장·명령·제안·요청을 나타내는 동사 또는 중요·필수를 나타내는 형용사 뒤에 오는 that절은 문맥상 당위성(~해야 한다)을 나타내는 데, 동사 앞에 보통 should가 생략된 동사원형이 온다.

주장·명령·제안·요청을 나타내는 동사	주어 +	ask 요청하다 require 요구하다 advise 권고하다 suggest 제안하다 insist 주장하다	request 요청하다 demand 요구하다 recommend 권고하다 propose 제안하다 order 명령하다	+ that 주어 + (should) + 동사원형
중요·필수·의무를 나타내는 형용사	It is +	necessary 필요한 important 중요한 vital 필수적인	imperative 필수의 essential 필수의 crucial 중대한	+ that 주어 + (should) + 동사원형

Mr. Kumar suggests / that the company / **(should) hire** / more employees. ⊙ (should) + 동사원형

Mr. Kumar suggests / that the company / **hires** / more employees. ⊗

해석 Mr. Kumar는 회사가 더 많은 직원들을 고용해야 한다고 제안한다.

It is essential / that every employee / **(should) wear** / protective clothing. ⊙ (should) + 동사원형

It is essential / that every employee / **wears** / protective clothing. ⊗

해석 모든 직원들은 방호복을 입는 것이 필수적이다.

● check

4. Flight attendants may ask that your carry-on luggage ------- in a designated compartment.

(A) kept   (B) be kept   (C) keeps   (D) is keeping

해설서 p.6

1. Mr. Rockwell has been supervising the production schedule since he ------- appointed factory manager.

(A) was   (B) to be
(C) is   (D) been

2. Mr. Garcia ------- the marketing project last Monday.

(A) completes   (B) completed
(C) is completing (D) will complete

3. Dr. Cruz recommends that every patient ------- his hospital for a routine checkup at least once a year.

(A) visited   (B) visits
(C) is visiting   (D) visit

4. Mr. Nakamoto, an expert in the field of science, ------- recently elected city mayor.

(A) were   (B) was
(C) will be   (D) have been

5. We always ------- your efforts to improve product quality.

(A) appreciate   (B) are appreciating
(C) will appreciate (D) appreciated

6. An increasing number of restaurants ------- customers discount coupons in the last few years.

(A) will offer
(B) have offered
(C) have been offered
(D) to offer

7. The city's plan to build the factory ------- next week.

(A) was finalized
(B) will be finalized
(C) has been finalized
(D) had been finalized

8. Customers usually ------- to Sador's Diner due to its excellent service and delicious food.

(A) return   (B) has returned
(C) returns   (D) have been returned

9. Since Ms. Pham joined the company, sales ------- almost by 30 percent.

(A) increased
(B) had increased
(C) have increased
(D) will have increased

10. Until Ms. Kim ------- to the Beijing branch, she will be handling the Drefus account.

(A) relocated   (B) relocate
(C) had relocated (D) relocates

11. Kirks Department Store ------- open for over 20 years.

(A) have been   (B) has been
(C) is   (D) to be

12. ------- the past two months, attendance at Professor Hu's lectures has increased dramatically.

(A) Behind   (B) Above
(C) Into   (D) During

13. Mr. Johnson was able to get a seat at the arts festival only because he ------- in advance.

(A) will book   (B) had booked
(C) booking   (D) to book

14. Mr. Randall ------- a new database over the past two months.

(A) is developing
(B) has been developing
(C) will be developing
(D) would have been developing

15. Ms. Reddy ------- operations of the new factory when it opens next April.

(A) had overseen   (B) oversaw
(C) will oversee   (D) overseeing

16. The IT Department ------- suggestions for the new security program until the end of this week.

(A) have accepted   (B) will be accepting
(C) to accept   (D) accepting

17. Starting next Wednesday, the Vianox Shopping Center ------- its business hours until 10 P.M.

(A) was extending   (B) had extended
(C) are extending   (D) will be extending

18. Both Ms. Li and Ms. Chau ------- at Wantari group for over seven years.

(A) work   (B) will be working
(C) works   (D) have worked

19. Phone calls received after 8 P.M. at the office ------- the following morning.

(A) will be returned
(B) had returned
(C) was returned
(D) is return

20. Baprix Industries will ------- expand its manufacturing facilities in Detroit.

(A) usually   (B) recently
(C) soon   (D) formerly

기본 완성 훈련 다음은 앞서 풀어 본 연습문제의 문장들입니다. 주어(S), 동사(V), 목적어(O), 보어(C)를 찾아 표시하고, 시간 부사(구) 또는 시간 부사절에 ○를 치세요.

1. Mr. Rockwell has been supervising the production schedule since he was appointed factory manager.

2. Dr. Cruz recommends that every patient visit his hospital for a routine checkup at least once a year.

3. Mr. Nakamoto, an expert in the field of science, was recently elected city mayor.

4. An increasing number of restaurants have offered customers discount coupons in the last few years.

5. Since Ms. Pham joined the company, sales have increased by almost 30 percent.

6. Until Ms. Kim relocates to the Beijing branch, she will be handling the Drefus account.

7. Kirks Department Store has been open for over 20 years.

8. Mr. Randall has been developing a new database over the past two months.

9. The IT Department will be accepting suggestions for the new security program until the end of this week.

10. Starting next Wednesday, the Vianox Shopping Center will be extending its business hours until 10 P.M.

UNIT 04 능동태와 수동태

행위자 입장에서 말할 때는 능동태를 쓰고 행위의 대상 입장에서 말할 때는 수동태를 쓴다. 수동태는 '주어에게 어떤 일이 일어나다'라는 의미로 행위의 주체보다는 행위의 영향을 받는 대상이나 행위 자체에 초점을 둔 구문이다.

기본 개념 이해하기

1. 능동태: 주어(행위의 주체) + 동사

▶ 행위의 주체인 '누구'를 주어로 말하는 방식을 능동태라고 한다.

The company / **holds** / the anniversary ceremony / every December. 주어 = 행위자
The company / **recommended** / Jason / for the assistant manager position. 주어 = 행위자

해석 회사는 매년 12월에 기념 행사를 연다. / 회사는 Jason을 부지배인 자리에 추천했다.

2. 수동태: 주어(행위의 대상) + be동사 + 과거분사(p.p.)

▶ 행위의 대상인 '무엇을'에 해당하는 목적어를 주어로 말하는 방식이다. 행위의 대상이나 행위 자체를 설명하는 데 초점이 있으며, 행위자 「by + 누구」는 흔히 생략된다.

능동태	주어(행위의 주체) + 동사 + 목적어(행위의 대상) → 주어가 ~를 ~하다
수동태	주어(행위의 대상) + be + p.p. + (by + 행위의 주체) → 주어가 (~에 의해) ~되다

The anniversary ceremony / **is held** / every December. 주어 = 행위의 대상
Jason / **was recommended** / for the assistant manager position. 주어 = 행위의 대상

해석 기념 행사는 매년 12월에 열린다. / Jason은 부지배인 자리에 추천 되었다.

✓ **문법 포인트** 목적어가 없는 1형식과 2형식 문장은 능동태로만 쓰이며 수동태가 없다.
Oil prices **rose** last year. ◉
Oil prices **were risen** last year. ✕

해석 작년에 기름 가격이 올랐다.

3. 수동태의 형태

▶ 수동태는 주어의 인칭과 수, 시제를 be동사의 변화로 표현한다.

▶ 「조동사 + be + p.p.」: 조동사가 수동태 문장에 쓰이면 be동사를 원형으로 써야 한다.

	단순 시제	완료 시제	진행 시제
현재	am / are / is + p.p.	has / have + been + p.p.	am / are / is + being + p.p.
과거	was / were + p.p.	had + been + p.p.	was / were + being + p.p.
미래	will + be + p.p.	will + have + been + p.p.	will + be + being + p.p.

The perfume / **is sold** / only at Dart Worthy's Department Store. 현재 시제 수동태

The train / **was delayed** / for two hours. 과거 시제 수동태

A new return policy / **will be implemented**. 미래 시제 수동태

A birthday party / **has been booked** / for tomorrow. 현재완료 시제 수동태

A technical institute / **is being constructed**. 현재진행 시제 수동태

해석 그 향수는 Dart Worthy's 백화점에서만 판매된다. / 기차가 두 시간 동안 연착되었다. / 새로운 반품 정책이 시행될 것이다. 생일 파티가 내일로 예약되었다. / 기술 연구소가 지어지고 있다.

Food and beverages / **should be ordered** / by Monday. ◎ 조동사 + be + p.p.

Food and beverages / **should are ordered** / by Monday. ✗

해석 음식과 음료는 월요일까지 주문되어야 한다.

4. 수동태의 행위자

▶ 보통 수동태는 '~에 의해서' 당한 것을 표현하므로 행위자를 나타내는 전치사 by가 많이 쓰이지만, 의미에 따라 다른 전치사를 쓰기도 한다.

be interested in ~에 관심이 있다	**be involved in** ~에 관련되다
be engaged in ~에 종사하다, ~에 관여하다	**be filled with** ~로 가득 차 있다
be pleased with ~에 기뻐하다	**be satisfied with** ~에 만족하다
be covered with ~로 덮이다	**be faced with** ~에 직면하다
be equipped with ~을 갖추고 있다	**be associated with** ~와 연관되어 있다
be disappointed with ~에 실망하다	**be acquainted with** ~을 알고 있다
be committed to ~에 전념하다	**be dedicated to** ~에 전념하다
be devoted to ~에 전념하다	**be related to** ~과 관련이 있다
be exposed to ~에 노출되어 있다, ~에 드러나다	**be worried about** ~을 걱정하다
be concerned about ~을 걱정하다	**be concerned with** ~에 관심이 있다
be surprised at ~에 놀라다	**be amazed at** ~에 놀라다
be shocked at ~에 충격 받다	**be based on(upon)** ~에 기초하다
be known for ~로 알려져 있다, ~로 유명하다	**be known to** ~에게 알려져 있다
be known as ~로(써) 알려져 있다	**be divided into** ~로 나뉘어지다

핵심 문제 유형

Q1 자동사와 수동태

The company's total revenue ------- unchanged.

(A) remaining   (B) remains   (C) is remained   (D) to remain

>> **출제 포인트 목적어가 없는 자동사는 수동태가 불가능하다.**

1 선택지 확인 | 빈칸에 들어갈 알맞은 동사의 형태를 고른다.

2 빈칸 확인 | 동사 자리 → 동사 자리에 올 수 없는 준동사 (A) 동사원형-ing ❌ (D) to부정사 ❌

3 정답 확인 | 「remain + 형용사: 계속 ~인 채로 남아 있다」 → 목적어가 오지 않는 2형식 동사로, 수동태가 불가능하다.
→ (C) is remained ❌   (B) remains ⭕

정답   The company's total revenue / **(B) remains** / unchanged.
해석   회사의 총수입은 / 남아 있다 / 변하지 않은 채로

출제 포인트 ❶ 2형식 동사 뒤에 오는 명사는 목적어가 아니라 보어이기 때문에 수동태가 불가능하다.

Mr. Stallard / **became** / a successful businessperson. ⭕
A successful businessperson / ~~was become~~. ❌

해석   Mr. Stallard는 성공적인 사업가가 되었다.

출제 포인트 ❷ look, seem 등은 '~하게 보이다'로 해석되어 수동태로 착각하기 쉽지만, 행위의 대상이 없는 자동사이므로 수동태 표현도 없다.

수동태로 착각하기 쉬운 자동사
look / appear / seem / sound ~인 것 같다   happen 발생하다   occur 일어나다   consist of ~로 구성되다

The intern's suggestion / **sounds** / useful. ⭕
The intern's suggestion / ~~is sounded~~ / useful. ❌

해석   인턴의 제안은 유용한 것 같다.

출제 포인트 ❸ 동사구의 수동태: 「자동사 + 전치사」는 하나의 동사처럼 취급하여 수동태를 만든다.

This issue / should be **taken care of** / as soon as possible.
The concert / **was called off** / by the band.

해석   이 문제는 가급적 빨리 처리되어야 한다. / 콘서트가 그 밴드에 의해 취소되었다.

+ check .... 해설서 p.8

1. A recent report shows that tourism has remained ------- strong even in the current economic recession.

(A) surprising   (B) surprisingly   (C) surprised   (D) surprise

Q2 **3형식 동사의 수동태**

The office complex ------- on the outskirts of Seoul next year.

(A) will be built   (B) built   (C) was built   (D) building

>> **출제 포인트** **3형식 동사 뒤에 목적어가 없으면 수동태이다.**

① **선택지 확인** | 동사와 명사 중 빈칸에 들어갈 알맞은 품사를 고르고 올바른 형태를 선택한다.

② **빈칸 확인** | 동사 자리 → 동사 자리에 올 수 없는 준동사 (D) 동사-ing / 명사 ✘

③ **정답 확인** |「build + 목적어: ~을 짓다」→ 동사 뒤에 목적어가 있어야 하는 3형식 동사인데, 빈칸 뒤에 목적어 없이 전치사구가 연결되어 있다. → 능동태의 과거형 (B) built ✘ → 수동태 (A), (C) 중 문장 맨끝에 미래 시간 부사구 next year가 있다. → (D) was built ✘ (A) will be built ◎

정답 The office complex / **(A) will be built** / on the outskirts of Seoul next year.

해석 복합 사무동이 / 지어질 것이다 / 서울 근교에 / 내년에

출제 포인트 ④ **3형식 동사의 수동태 뒤에는 아무것도 오지 않거나 부사나 전치사구가 온다.**

The manufacturer / **provides** / warranty information / online. 동사 + 목적어 ⋯ 능동태
Warranty information / **is provided** / online. 동사 ⋯ 수동태

해석   그 제조업체는 품질 보증 정보를 온라인으로 제공한다. / 품질 보증 정보가 온라인으로 제공된다.
풀이   3형식 동사 provide 뒤에 목적어가 없으면 수동태 문장이다.

✓ 문법 포인트 3형식 동사 provide 뒤에 목적어가 없으면 수동태 문장이다.
                    이 때 빈칸 뒤에 있는 부사 online(온라인으로)을 목적어로 착각해서 능동태를 고르면 안 된다. 다음과 같은 부사나 부사구는 목적어로 착각하기 쉬우므로 주의한다.

목적어로 착각하면 안 되는 부사/부사구

company wide 전사적으로	**worldwide** 전세계적으로	**online** 온라인으로
the following morning 다음날 아침	**this morning** 오늘 아침	**another day** 또 다른 하루

Students / **will wear** / complete uniforms. 동사 + 목적어 ⋯ 능동태
Complete uniforms / will **be worn**. 동사 ⋯ 수동태

해석   학생들이 모든 것을 갖춘 유니폼을 착용할 것이다. / 모든 것을 갖춘 유니폼이 착용될 것이다.

✓ 문법 포인트 3형식 동사 wear 뒤에 목적어가 없으면 수동태 문장이다.

⊕ check

2. Productions at Birnham Theater are ------- mainly by local sponsors.

    (A) funds   (B) funded   (C) funding   (D) fund

Q3 4형식 동사의 수동태

Verma Medical Lab ------- a research grant from the government for the last five years.

(A) has awarded   (B) has been awarded   (C) was awarded   (D) are awarding

>> **출제 포인트** **4형식 동사의 수동태 뒤에는 목적어가 한 개 온다.**

❶ 선택지 확인 | 빈칸에 들어갈 알맞은 동사의 형태를 고른다.

❷ 빈칸 확인 | 동사의 자리 → 수 일치에 어긋나는 (D) are awarding ❌ → 문장 끝에 현재 완료시제와 어울리는 시간부사구 for the last five years가 나와 있으므로 과거시제 (C) was awarded ❌

❸ 정답 확인 | 「award + 누구 + 무엇: 누구에게 무엇을 수여하다」 → '누구에게'와 '무엇을'에 해당하는 목적어가 두 개 있어야 하는 4형식 동사인데, a research grant 한 개 밖에 없다. → 능동태 (A) has awarded ❌
수동태 (B) has been awarded ⭕

정답 Verma Medical Lab / **(B) has been awarded** / a research grant / from the government for the last five years.
해석 Verma 의료 연구소는 / 지급받았다 / 연구 보조금을 / 정부로부터

출제 포인트 ❺ 사람을 나타내는 간접목적어가 수동태의 주어가 되는 경우가 많다. 직접목적어가 주어가 될 때에는 간접목적어 앞에 전치사 to, for, of 등을 쓴다.

The store / **offered** / customers / a discount coupon. 동사 + 간접목적어 + 직접목적어 → 능동태
Customers / **were offered** / a discount coupon (by the store). 동사 + 직접목적어 → 수동태
A discount coupon / **was offered** (to customers) (by the store). 동사 → 수동태

해석 그 가게는 고객들에게 할인 쿠폰을 제공했다. / 고객들은 그 가게에 의해서 할인 쿠폰을 제공 받았다. / 할인 쿠폰은 가게에 의해서 고객들에게 제공되었다.
풀이 4형식 동사 offer 뒤에는 목적어(명사)가 두 개 있어야 하는데 목적어가 하나만 나오거나 목적어가 없으면 수동태이다.

☑ **문법 포인트** 4형식 동사 offer 뒤에는 목적어가 두 개 있어야 하는데 목적어가 하나만 나오거나 목적어가 없으면 수동태이다.

주의 그러나 모든 4형식 동사들은 3형식 동사로도 쓰이므로 빈칸 뒤에 명사가 하나 있을 경우 무조건 수동태를 고르지 말고 해석을 통해서 '주다'라고 해석이 되면 능동태를, '받다'라고 해석이 되면 수동태를 고른다.

The management team at Oram International [**offers** / ~~is offered~~] incentives to increase employee productivity.

해석 Oram 인터네셔널의 경영팀에서는 직원 생산성을 향상시키기 위해 장려금을 제공한다.
풀이 offer는 4형식으로도 쓰이지만 목적어가 하나 있는 3형식으로도 많이 쓰인다. 이 문장에서는 경영팀이 직원들에게 장려금을 '제공하다'라고 능동의 의미로 해석이 되어야 하므로 뒤에 목적어가 하나만 있지만 능동태를 골라야 한다. 이 때 offer는 3형식 동사로 쓰임에 유의한다.

🔊 check

3. Winners of 59.2 FM's monthly contest ------- the opportunity to come to the studio and meet famous radio hosts.

(A) will be given   (B) gave   (C) given   (D) would have given

Q4 5형식 동사의 수동태

The travelers ------- to check their luggage by the tour guide.

(A) advised   (B) advise   (C) were advised   (D) will advise

>> **출제 포인트** 5형식 동사의 수동태 뒤에는 목적어가 아닌, 목적격 보어가 나온다.

① **선택지 확인** | 빈칸에 들어갈 알맞은 동사의 형태를 고른다.

② **빈칸 확인** | 동사의 자리 → (A) 과거 시제 능동태, (B) 현재 시제 능동태, (C) 과거 시제 수동태, (D) 미래 시제 수동태, 모두 동사 형태이다.

③ **정답 확인** | 「advise + 사람 + to부정사: ~에게 …하라고 조언하다」 → 목적어 없이, 목적격 보어에 해당하는 to부정사가 바로 이어져 있다. → 능동태 ❌ 수동태 (C) were advised ⭕

정답 The travelers / **(C) were advised** / to check their luggage / by the tour guide.
해석 그 여행자들은 / 충고를 받았다 / 짐을 살펴보라고 / 여행 가이드로부터

출제 포인트 ⑤ 5형식 동사의 수동태 뒤에는 목적어가 없고 보어가 나온다.

5형식 문장 「동사 + 목적어 + 목적격 보어」의 수동태는 목적어만 수동태의 주어가 될 수 있으며, 목적격 보어(명사, 형용사, to부정사, 분사)는 동사 뒤에 그대로 쓴다.

The board / **considered** / the policy / necessary. 동사 + 목적어 + 형용사
The policy / **was considered** / necessary (by the board). 동사 + 형용사 → 수동태

해석 이사회는 그 방침을 필요한 것으로 여겼다. (이사회는 그 방침이 필요하다고 생각한다.) / 그 방침은 이사회에 의해 필요한 것으로 여겨졌다.

☑ **문법 포인트** 5형식 동사 consider 뒤에 목적어 없이 목적격 보어(형용사)만 나오면 수동태이다.

    반대로 5형식 동사의 수동태 뒤에 부사와 형용사 중에 고르는 문제가 출제되면 부사를 고르기 쉽지만 목적격 보어인 형용사를 골라야 한다.

    Mr. Mueller's budget proposal was considered [**feasible** / **feasibly**] by the board.

      해석 Mr. Mueller의 예산 제안서는 이사회에 의해 실현 가능하다고 여겨졌다.

Management **asked** / employees / to submit the evaluation form. 동사 + 목적어 + to부정사 → 능동태
Employees / **were asked** / to submit the evaluation form / (by management). 동사 + to부정사 → 수동태

해석 경영진은 직원들에게 평가서를 제출하라고 요청했다. / 직원들은 평가서를 제출하라고 경영진에 의해 요청을 받았다.

☑ **문법 포인트** to부정사를 목적격 보어로 취하는 5형식 동사 ask 뒤에 목적어 없이 바로 목적격 보어(to부정사)가 나오면 수동태이다.

to부정사 목적격 보어	be asked to ~하라고 요청 받다 be urged to ~하라고 요구 받다 be allowed to ~하도록 허락 받다 be advised to ~하라는 충고를 듣다	be required to ~하라고 요구 받다 be told to ~하라는 말을 듣다 be invited to ~하라고 권유 받다 be encouraged to ~하라고 권고 받다	be requested to ~하라고 요청 받다 be expected to ~하리라 기대되다 be permitted to ~하도록 허락 받다

>>**check**

4. For security purposes, all personnel ------- to show their ID cards when entering the facility.

    (A) ask   (B) asking   (C) is asking   (D) are asked

Practice

해설서 p.9

1. The construction crews ------- the project on schedule.
   (A) finished
   (B) are finished
   (C) finishing
   (D) to be finished

2. A large apartment complex ------- next to the Barhill train station.
   (A) will be built
   (B) builder
   (C) built
   (D) build

3. All images in the magazine have been ------- provided by the SE Association.
   (A) generousness
   (B) generosity
   (C) generously
   (D) generous

4. The weekly sales meeting is usually ------- in the morning.
   (A) conducted
   (B) conducts
   (C) conductor
   (D) conducting

5. Furiko Corporation ------- financial problems for several years.
   (A) has faced
   (B) has been faced
   (C) have faced
   (D) face

6. The Employee of the Year ------- by the President of the company.
   (A) has nominated
   (B) nominated
   (C) will be nominating
   (D) has been nominated

7. Changes to delivery schedules ------- to the shipping manager directly.
   (A) has been reported
   (B) will be reporting
   (C) may have reported
   (D) should be reported

8. All your personal information will be kept -------.
   (A) secure
   (B) security
   (C) secures
   (D) securing

9. This medication should ------- with a lot of water.
   (A) to take
   (B) be taken
   (C) having taken
   (D) be taking

10. Hikers are encouraged ------- the park's information desk in order to get trail maps.
    (A) visits
    (B) to visit
    (C) visiting
    (D) having visited

11. All new employees should ------- an orientation by the end of March.
    (A) give
    (B) be given
    (C) giving
    (D) be giving

12. All desserts at the restaurant have been ------- by renowned chef Christy Kang.
    (A) prepared
    (B) prepare
    (C) preparing
    (D) preparation

13. Bromville Apartments' heating system ------- by the property management office this morning.
    (A) inspector
    (B) is being inspected
    (C) was inspecting
    (D) inspection

14. All team members can apply for a bonus once they ------- here for one year.
    (A) have worked
    (B) have been worked
    (C) are working
    (D) work

15. Mr. Hassan will ------- all hotel reservations while Ms. Yang is away.

(A) handling   (B) handle

(C) be handled   (D) is handling

16. Applicants interested in the position ------- to submit their résumés by November 30.

(A) require   (B) requires

(C) are required   (D) has required

17. The main cause of the flight delay was related ------- engine failure.

(A) to   (B) for

(C) at   (D) by

18. Any requests for a vacation must be ------- to the supervisor at least one week in advance.

(A) submitted   (B) submission

(C) submit   (D) submitting

19. The laboratory test results ------- that the experiment was successful.

(A) indicates   (B) indicate

(C) was indicated   (D) has been indicated

20. The conference organizers ------- transportation for the attendees.

(A) have arranged

(B) arrangement

(C) was arranged

(D) arranging

기본 완성 훈련 다음은 앞서 풀어 본 연습문제의 문장들입니다. 주어(S), 동사(V), 목적어(O), 보어(C)를 찾아 표시하고, 수동태 문장인 경우 문제 번호에 ○를 치세요.

1. A large apartment complex will be built next to the Barhill train station.

2. The Employee of the Year has been nominated by the President of the company.

3. Changes to delivery schedules should be reported to the shipping manager directly.

4. This medication should be taken with a lot of water.

5. Hikers are encouraged to visit the park's information desk in order to get trail maps.

6. All desserts at the restaurant have been prepared by renowned chef Christy Kang.

7. Bromville Apartments' heating system is being inspected by the property management office this morning.

8. All team members can apply for a bonus once they have worked here for one year.

9. Applicants interested in the position are required to submit their résumés by November 30.

10. Any requests for a vacation must be submitted to the supervisor at least one week in advance.

REVIEW TEST 01

해설서 p.11

1. The holiday menu for Mauri's Diners ------- black pepper chicken.

  (A) includes   (B) include
  (C) including   (D) inclusion

2. Ms. Kim ------- arrives at her workplace at 8 o'clock.

  (A) strongly   (B) evenly
  (C) excellently   (D) usually

3. The accounting manager expects the budget reports to ------- by the end of the month.

  (A) complete   (B) be completed
  (C) be completing (D) have completed

4. The second edition of the book by Mr. Hong ------- published on July 1.

  (A) was   (B) being
  (C) be   (D) were

5. The recent system upgrade discovered problems that ------- not initially detected.

  (A) were   (B) had
  (C) was   (D) have

6. All managers at Geimon Tech Solutions should ------- this month's sales workshop.

  (A) attends   (B) attending
  (C) attend   (D) attended

7. The number of customers who shop online ------- rapidly increased over the past decade.

  (A) have   (B) has
  (C) was   (D) were

8. The technical specifications for the computer ------- in the user manual.

  (A) were detailing (B) are detailed
  (C) to detail   (D) will detail

9. The total cost of window repairs is ------- to exceed the original estimate.

  (A) expected   (B) expecting
  (C) expects   (D) expect

10. In order to stay competitive, HI Electronics store ------- lowers the prices of its products.

  (A) previously   (B) occasionally
  (C) recently   (D) soon

11. The committee members who reviewed Mr. Tam's résumé were very ------- by his extensive work experience.

  (A) impression   (B) impressed
  (C) impress   (D) impresses

12. LM Business Store ------- a wide range of office and stationery products.

  (A) supply   (B) supplies
  (C) have supplied (D) is supplied

13. Before items are ------- to your department, you should check the order confirmation number.

  (A) ship   (B) shipping
  (C) shipped   (D) shipment

14. Last year, Tofuo Chemical Company ------- about 14 tons of silicon daily.

  (A) produced   (B) produce
  (C) to produce   (D) producing

15. Online shopping malls ------- it easier to compare prices of different products.

  (A) making   (B) make
  (C) are made   (D) to make

16. Perstrom Corporation ------- electronic goods for over 30 years.

  (A) has manufactured
  (B) is manufacturing
  (C) manufacture
  (D) has been manufactured

17. Temporary staff ------- to meet the growing demand over the holiday season.

(A) will be hired   (B) will hire
(C) are hiring   (D) have hired

18. Following recent business expansion, Chentora, Inc. hired several additional -------.

(A) employees   (B) employee
(C) employ   (D) employment

19. Security guards must check to see that all employees ------- the premises after a fire alarm sounds.

(A) have vacated   (B) to vacate
(C) vacating   (D) vacancy

20. The recycling policy will help the company ------- operating costs.

(A) reducing   (B) reduce
(C) reduced   (D) reduces

21. Businesses are becoming ------- aware of the importance of conserving the environment.

(A) increases   (B) increasingly
(C) increased   (D) increase

22. More than 15 employees from the Marketing Department ------- successfully completed the sales training.

(A) have   (B) has
(C) having   (D) to have

23. Employees who registered for the workshop will ------- monthly newsletters.

(A) receives   (B) receiving
(C) receive   (D) to receive

24. Nari Co. recently ------- a new security system designed for major banks.

(A) develop   (B) developed
(C) are developing (D) were developed

25. It is essential that every factory worker ------- these safety regulations.

(A) follows   (B) to follow
(C) will be followed (D) follow

26. We expect that the demand for the new X5 car ------- soon.

(A) will rise   (B) rose
(C) risen   (D) is rising

27. If there ------- enough time at the end of tomorrow's meeting, Mr. Garson will talk about the Vancouver Arts Festival briefly.

(A) is   (B) was
(C) are   (D) will be

28. Ms. Ouellette has been hired as the manager of the new store location, and she ------- all business operations starting next month.

(A) oversaw   (B) overseeing
(C) will oversee   (D) had overseen

29. The company has the responsibility to ------- a collaborative working environment.

(A) promote   (B) be promoted
(C) is promoted   (D) promoting

30. The results from the staff satisfaction survey were ------- positive by the management.

(A) considering   (B) consider
(C) consideration (D) considered

명사

명사(noun)는 문장에서 주어, 목적어, 보어 등의 역할을 한다. 명사에는 가산 명사와 불가산 명사가 있으며, 보통 관사나 형용사 등의 수식어와 결합된 구(phrase)로 쓰인다.

명사는 주어, 목적어, 보어 자리 및 관사나 형용사, 소유격 뒤에 올 수 있다. 명사 자리에 형용사나 동사가 올 수 없으며, 가산 명사가 단수일 때는 명사 앞에 관사(a / an)를 쓰고, 복수일 때는 명사 뒤에 -(e)s를 붙인다. 단, 불가산 명사는 앞에 관사 a / an이나, 뒤에 -(e)s를 붙이지 않도록 반드시 주의하자!

🧠 기본 개념 이해하기

1. 명사의 종류

▶ 명사(Nouns)는 같은 부류의 사람이나 장소, 사물, 개념 등을 통칭하여 '무엇'이라고 부르는 이름이다. 특정한 사람이나 장소, 사물 등에 붙여진 개별적인 이름은 고유명사(proper nouns)라고 한다.

보통명사	사람, 동식물, 사물, 장소 등의 이름	employee, office, product, computer, desk
집합명사	구성원들이 모인 집합체의 이름	family, class, audience, staff, committee, crowd
물질명사	일정한 형태가 없는 물질의 이름	furniture, money, paper, sugar, water
추상명사	추상적인 개념의 이름	friendship, hope, luck, value, happiness, honesty
고유명사	특정한 사람 등의 개별적인 이름	Ms. Clark, Central Park, Seoul

2. 가산 명사와 불가산 명사

▶ 명사는 셀 수 있는 가산 명사와 셀 수 없는 불가산 명사로 구분된다.

▶ 가산 명사는 '하나'를 의미하는 단수형과 둘 이상을 의미하는 복수형이 있다. 가산 명사 단수형 앞에는 관사 a/an과 같은 한정사가 반드시 있어야 하고, 복수형은 명사 뒤에 -(e)s를 붙이고 관사와 같은 한정사 없이 쓸 수 있다.

▶ 불가산 명사는 셀 수 없기 때문에 복수형이 없고 항상 단수형으로만 쓰고 한정사 없이 쓸 수 있다.

명사	가산 명사	단수형(하나)	**an** employee 직원(한 명)
		복수형(둘 이상)	employee**s** 직원(여러 명)
	불가산 명사		information 정보(셀 수 없음)

✅ **문법 포인트** 셀 수 있는 가산 명사 employee는 홀로 쓰이지 않고, '하나'를 의미하는 부정관사 an을 쓰거나 복수형 -(e)s으로 쓴다. 반면, 셀 수 없는 불가산 명사인 information은 '하나'를 의미하는 부정관사 an을 쓸 수 없고, 복수형 -(e)s가 붙지 않는다.

EX employee ⊗ **an** employee ⊙ employee**s** ⊙
information ⊙ ~~**an** information~~ ⊗ ~~information**s**~~ ⊗

3. 명사의 한정사

▶ 명사의 대상이나 수량을 표시하는 관사나 소유격, 지시 형용사, 수량 형용사, 부정 형용사들을 명사의 한정사라고 한다.

▶ 가산 단수 명사, 가산 복수 명사, 불가산 명사 앞에 붙을 수 있는 한정사가 정해져 있기 때문에 한정사의 종류는 반드시 외워 두어야 한다.

a(n) 하나의 │ every 모든 │ each 각각의 │ another 또 다른 하나의	+ 가산 단수명사
many / a number of / numerous 많은 │ a few / several 몇몇의 │ few 거의 없는	+ 가산 복수명사
much 많은 │ a little 적은 │ little 거의 없는	+ 불가산 명사
all 모든 │ some 약간의 │ most 대부분의 │ other 다른	+ 가산 복수 / 불가산 명사
소유격(his, Mr. Gupta's) ~의 │ no 어느 ~도 ~아니다 │ any 어느 ~든지, 모든 │ the 그	+ 가산단수 / 가산복수 / 불가산 명사

✓ **문법 포인트**　정관사 the와 소유격 등은 가산 명사 단수형과 복수형, 불가산 명사 앞에 모두 쓰인다. 이 때, 지시형용사(this, these)나 소유격(your, his, her)도 명사의 대상을 구체화시킨다.

　　　　EX　**the** employee ⊙　**the** employees ⊙
　　　　the information ⊙　**this** information ⊙　**your** information ⊙

4. 명사의 형태

▶ -tion / -sion / -ment / -ness / -ity / -ence 등으로 끝나는 단어는 대부분 명사이다.

▶ -al, -ive와 같이 형용사처럼 생긴 명사나 -ing로 끝나는 명사에 주의해야 한다.

기본적인 명사형 어미	location 장소 │ permission 허가 │ development 발달 │ happiness 행복 │ ability 능력 │ emergency 비상 │ difference 차이 │ failure 실패 │ attendee 참석자 │ worker 직원 │ creator 창조자
형용사처럼 보이는 사람 명사	critic 비평가 │ representative 대표자 │ respondent 응답자 │ individual 개인 │ professional 전문가 │ client 고객 │ attendant 종업원 │ assistant 보조원 │ participant 참가자 │ accountant 회계사 │ consultant 상담자 │ applicant 지원자 │ correspondent 기자, 특파원
형용사처럼 보이는 사물 명사	alternative 대안 │ objective 목적 │ characteristic 특징 │ potential 잠재력 │ approval 승인 │ proposal 제안(서) │ renewal 갱신 │ removal 제거 │ arrival 도착 │ terminal 터미널 │ rental 임대, 대여
-ing로 끝나는 명사	planning 계획 수립 │ accounting 회계 │ funding 자금(재정) 지원 │ dining 식사 │ opening 공석, 개막식 │ training 훈련 │ marketing 마케팅 │ spending 지출 │ understanding 이해 │ boarding 탑승 │ housing 주택 │ widening 확장 │ meeting 회의

Q1 한정사 + [명사 자리]

The ------- can be purchased online or in stores.

(A) production   (B) products   (C) productive   (D) produces

>> **출제 포인트** 관사, 소유격, 형용사의 꾸밈을 받는 말은 명사이다.

1 선택지 확인 | 빈칸에 들어갈 알맞은 품사를 고른다.

2 빈칸 확인 | 정관사 the 뒤의 명사 자리인 동사에 주어 자리 → 명사 자리에 올 수 없는 (C) 형용사 ✗ (D) 동사 ✗

3 정답 확인 | '주어가 온라인 또는 매장에서 구매될 수 있다'라는 의미이므로 정답은 문맥상 (A) production 생산 ✗
(B) products 제품들 ⭕

정답 The **(B) products** / can be purchased / online or in stores.
해석 그 제품들은 / 구매될 수 있다 / 온라인 또는 매장에서

출제 포인트 ① 한정사(관사, 소유격, 형용사)의 꾸밈을 받는 자리는 명사 자리이다.

The **products** / in question / are scheduled / to be tested. 관사 뒤
He / will talk / briefly about the corporation's **history**. 소유격 뒤
Some **items** / will not be included / in the sale. 수량형용사 뒤

해석 의심을 받고 있는 제품들은 실험될 일정이 잡혀 있다. / 그는 회사의 약력에 대해 간략하게 말할 것이다.
몇몇 제품은 할인 판매에 포함되지 않을 것이다.

출제 포인트 ② 명사는 동사의 주어, 목적어, 보어 및 전치사, 준동사의 목적어 역할을 한다.

All **employees** / must wear / uniforms. 동사 앞: 주어 자리
The manager / introduced / a new **employee**. 타동사 뒤: 목적어 자리
He / is / the hotel's head **chef**. 자동사 뒤: 보어 자리
I / got / the manual / from their **Web site**. 전치사 뒤: 목적어 자리

해석 전 직원이 유니폼을 입어야 한다. / 매니저가 한 신입직원을 소개했다.
그는 그 호텔의 수석 요리사이다. / 나는 그 매뉴얼을 웹사이트에서 구했다.

⊕ check ·· 해설서 p.13

1. In order to access the database, a completed request form and a written ------- from Ms. Wood are required.

(A) to authorize   (B) authorized   (C) authorize   (D) authorization

가산 명사 vs. 불가산 명사

A ------- in English proficiency is necessary for the position.

(A) certificate   (B) certification   (C) certifying   (D) certifies

>> **출제 포인트** 부정관사 a(an) 뒤에는 가산 단수 명사가 온다.

1 선택지 확인 | 빈칸에 들어갈 알맞은 품사를 고른다.

2 빈칸 확인 | 부정관사 a 뒤의 명사 자리인 동시에 주어 자리 → 부정관사와 함께 쓰지 않는 (C) 동사-ing ❌
(D) 동사 ❌

3 정답 확인 | 부정관사 a 뒤에 올 수 있는 가산 명사이고, '그 직책에는 영어 시험 인증서가 필요하다'는 의미가 적절하므로
(B) certification 증명 ❌ (A) certificate 증명서 ◉

정답 A **(A) certificate** / in English proficiency / is necessary / for the position.
해석 인증서는 / 영어 숙련도에서의 / 필수이다 / 그 직책에는

출제 포인트 ❸ 가산 명사 단수형은 반드시 부정관사 a(an)이나 소유격, 수량 형용사 등의 한정사와 함께 쓰이지만,
가산 명사 복수형과 불가산 명사는 한정사 없이도 단독으로 쓸 수 있다.

가산 명사		불가산 명사	
a discount 할인	an effort 노력	approval 승인	advice 충고
a decision 결정	an increase, rise 증가	access 이용(기회), 접근(권한)	production 생산
a request 요청	a delay 지연	productivity 생산성	arrival 도착
a requirement 자격요건	an opening 공석	delivery 배달	consent 동의
a visit 방문	a purchase 구매	growth 성장	equipment 장비
a change 변경사항	a task 과제, 업무	change 잔돈	work 일, 작업
a permit 허가증	a prospect 전망	interest 관심	support 지원, 지지
a work 작품	a refund 환불	information 정보	mail 우편물
a rate 가격, 요금	a load 짐	research 연구	operation 운영, 영업
an expense 비용	a contribution 기여, 기부금	planning 기획	certification 증명
a certificate 증명서(자격증)	an approach 접근법	staff 직원	money 돈
a detail 세부사항	a price 가격	cash 현금	furniture 가구
a compliment 칭찬	a complaint 불평, 불만	clothing 의류	luggage, baggage 짐
a result 결과	a mistake 실수	permission 허가	part 일부, 일원
an offer 제안	a part 부분; 부품		

check

2. Modern Office Furniture is offering ------- of up to 30 percent on select items.

(A) discount   (B) discounts   (C) discounter   (D) discounted

Q3 사람 명사 VS. 사물/추상명사

Mr. Hong will share important ------- about starting a business during the conference.

(A) advice   (B) adviser   (C) advises   (D) advised

>> **출제 포인트** 사람 명사와 사물/추상 명사를 상황에 맞게 써야 한다.

① **선택지 확인** | 빈칸에 들어갈 알맞은 품사를 고른다.

② **빈칸 확인** | 빈칸은 목적어 자리 → 명사 자리이므로 동사 (C) advises (D) advised ✖

③ **정답 확인** | 사람 명사는 셀 수 있는 가산 명사이므로, an adviser나 advisers로 써야지, adviser 단독으로 쓸 수 없으므로 추상명사로 불가산 명사인 (A) advice 조언 ⭕

정답 Mr. Hong / will share / important **(A) advice** / about starting a business / during the conference.
해석 Mr. Hong은 / 공유할 것이다 / 중요한 충고를 / 사업을 시작하는 것에 관한 / 컨퍼런스 기간 동안

출제 포인트 ④ 사람 명사는 가산 명사이므로 한정사 없이는 단수 형태로 쓸 수 없다는 점에 유의한다.

사람 명사		사물/추상 명사	
advisor 고문	analyst 분석가	advice 충고	analysis 분석
assistant 보조자	applicant 지원자	assistance 지원	application 지원(서)
professional 전문가	competitor 경쟁자	profession 직업	competition 경쟁
founder 설립자	enthusiast 애호가	foundation 설립	enthusiasm 열정
marketer 마케터	inspector 검사관	marketing 홍보	inspection 검사
instructor 강사	permitter 허가자	instruction 지시사항	permission 허락, 허가
contributor 기여자	performer 공연자	contribution 기여	performance 공연
participant 참가자	supervisor 상사	participation 참가	supervision 감독
subscriber 구독자	distributor 배급업자	subscription 구독	distribution 배급, 배포
correspondent 통신원, 기자	visitor 방문자	correspondence 서신	visit 방문

⊕ check ....

3. Please read the enclosed ------- on how to sign up for a membership at the Goldland Gym.

    (A) instructive   (B) instructor   (C) instructs   (D) instructions

Q4 명사 + 명사 = 복합 명사

Doha Consulting offers tips on improving employee -------.

(A) productively   (B) produced   (C) productivity   (D) produce

>> **출제 포인트 복합 명사는 앞의 명사가 뒤의 명사를 꾸며주는 형태이다.**

❶ 선택지 확인 | 빈칸에 알맞은 품사를 고른다.

❷ 빈칸 확인 | 이미 동사 offer가 있다. → 동사 형태인 (B) produced ❌ (D) produce ❌ → 빈칸은 동명사 improving 의 목적어 자리인데, 빈칸 앞에 목적어처럼 보이는 employee가 있어서 빈칸에 「동명사 + 목적어」를 수식하 는 부사 (A) productively를 선택할 수 있으나 가산 단수 명사인 employee 앞에 어떠한 한정사도 없기 때 문에 목적어가 될 수 없다. 따라서 employee와 함께 복합명사를 이루는 명사 (C) productivity가 정답이다.

❸ 정답 확인 | 「명사 + 명사」 복합 명사 형태로 improving의 목적어가 되어야 문맥상 자연스러우므로 (C) productivity ◉

정답 Doha Consulting / offers / tips / on improving employee **(C) productivity**.
해석 Doha 컨설팅은 / 제공한다 / 조언들을 / 직원 생산성 개선에 대한

출제 포인트 ⑤ 「명사 + 명사」의 형태를 복합 명사라 하며, 앞의 명사가 뒤의 명사를 수식하는 형태이다.

「명사 + 명사」의 형태인 복합 명사		
retail sales 소매 판매	refund policy 환불 정책	safety regulation 안전 규칙
sales representative 영업 사원	water shortage 물 부족	interest rate 이자율, 금리
safety precaution 안전 예방책	registration form 신청서	tourist attraction 관광 명소
office supplies 사무용품	baggage allowance 수하물 제한량	contingency plan 비상 계획
sales figures 매출액	media coverage 언론 보도	bank statement 입출금 내역서
production line 생산 공정	bank account 은행 계좌	
job opening 공석, (직장의) 빈자리	employee productivity 직원 생산성	

check

4. Despite efforts to boost the construction business, requests for building ------- have decreased.

  (A) permit   (B) permitted   (C) permitting   (D) permits

Practice

해설서 p.13

1. Gihans Architects received ------- for the building project from the town council.

(A) approve   (B) approval
(C) approves   (D) approved

2. Mr. Morgan's ------- to communicate with his clients is impressive.

(A) ably   (B) ability
(C) able   (D) ablest

3. MT Mart will provide ------- for all Reef Beauty Products purchased before August 12.

(A) refund   (B) refunded
(C) refunding   (D) refunds

4. The latest vehicle model is expected to be a ------- in the European market.

(A) successfully   (B) success
(C) succeed   (D) successful

5. Office supply ------- should be approved by Ms. Kang.

(A) purchase   (B) purchases
(C) purchaser   (D) purchased

6. Due to the current drought conditions, agricultural water ------- will increase.

(A) usefully   (B) usage
(C) useless   (D) useful

7. ------- by popular musicians attracted large crowds at the festival.

(A) Performances   (B) Performance
(C) Performed   (D) Perform

8. To complete the project on time, we need to hire an -------.

(A) assistance   (B) assistant
(C) assist   (D) assisted

9. The ------- about the security program was rescheduled.

(A) presenter   (B) presented
(C) presents   (D) presentation

10. The seminar will focus on how businesses can increase ------- sales through online services.

(A) they   (B) their
(C) them   (D) theirs

11. McJessop Consulting recently employed additional ------- to join their finance team.

(A) accountable   (B) accounting
(C) accountants   (D) accounts

12. Mr. Park, an ------- for the customer service position, will be meeting with the interviewers tomorrow.

(A) apply   (B) application
(C) applied   (D) applicant

13. It is recommended that ------- renew their memberships by the end of the month.

(A) subscribers   (B) subscribes
(C) subscriptions   (D) subscribing

14. Vabimo Group's recent ------- of Pexor Company helped expand its production capacities.

(A) acquired   (B) acquire
(C) acquisition   (D) acquiring

15. Please call our customer service line to arrange your furniture ------- this week.

(A) delivers (B) deliver

(C) delivered (D) delivery

16. ------- of the Klarksson project is expected to increase the company's sales.

(A) Completely (B) Completed

(C) Completion (D) Complete

17. ------- at the annual travel conference must show their tickets at the main door.

(A) Attends (B) Attendance

(C) Attendees (D) Attend

18. According to ------- collected by Terisan Communications, the BX555 laptop is popular among graphic designers.

(A) information (B) informing

(C) inform (D) informative

19. The Allwalk Shoe Store offers 10 percent discount coupons to first-time -------.

(A) buyer (B) buy

(C) bought (D) buyers

20. A digital ------- of 1,000 books and business journals will be displayed in the Hargort Library.

(A) collect (B) collections

(C) collection (D) collected

기본 완성 훈련 다음은 앞서 풀어 본 연습문제의 문장들입니다. 명사를 찾아 밑줄을 긋고, 복합 명사에는 ○를 치세요.

1. Gihans Architects received approval for the building project from the town council.

2. Mr. Morgan's ability to communicate with his clients is impressive.

3. MT Mart will provide refunds for all Reef Beauty Products purchased before August 12.

4. Due to the current drought conditions, agricultural water usage will increase.

5. Performances by popular musicians attracted large crowds at the festival.

6. The seminar will focus on how businesses can increase their sales through online services.

7. Mr. Park, an applicant for the customer service position, will be meeting with the interviewers tomorrow.

8. Vabimo Group's recent acquisition of Pexor Company helped expand its production capacities.

9. Please call our customer service line to arrange your furniture delivery this week.

10. Attendees at the annual travel conference must show their valid tickets at the main door.

UNIT 06

대명사

대명사(pronoun)는 앞에 나온 명사의 반복을 피하기 위해 대신 쓰는 말로 명사와 마찬가지로 주어, 목적어, 보어 역할을 한다. 가리키는 대상에 따라 인칭대명사, 소유대명사, 재귀대명사, 지시대명사, 부정대명사가 있다.

🧠 기본 개념 이해하기

1. 인칭대명사의 격과 수

▶ 대신하는 명사의 수나 인칭, 성별에 따라 알맞은 형태로 써야 한다. 주어로 쓰이면 주격으로, 동사나 전치사의 목적어일 때는 목적격으로 쓴다.

Mr. Smith / will start work / in Greenville next week. **He** / will be overseeing / the Sales Department. 주격(He = Mr. Smith) + 동사

To maintain relationships with our customers, / we / contact / **them** / regularly.
동사 + 목적격(them = our customers)

The manager / is not available / right now, but / you / can talk / to **her** / tomorrow afternoon. 전치사 + 목적격(her = the manager)

해석   Mr. Smith는 다음 주부터 Greenville에서 근무를 시작할 것이다. 그는 영업부를 관리할 것이다. / 고객들과의 관계를 유지하기 위해서, 우리는 그들에게 정기적으로 연락한다. / 매니저는 지금 시간이 안 되지만, 내일 오후에 그녀와 얘기 나눌 수 있다.

2. 소유격과 소유대명사

▶ 소유격은 '~의'라는 뜻으로 명사 앞에 붙어서 사용되고, 소유대명사는 '~의 것(= 소유격 + 명사)'이라는 의미이다. it은 소유대명사가 없다.

소유격	my	your	his	her	its	our	your	their
소유대명사	mine	yours	his	hers	없음	ours	yours	theirs

Mr. Anderson / is famous / for **his** innovative designs. 소유격

Mr. Mui / accepted / Stacey's proposal, / but he / asked / me / to revise **mine**.
소유대명사(mine = my proposal)

해석   Mr. Anderson은 그의 혁신적인 디자인들로 유명하다. / Mr. Mui는 Stacey의 제안서는 수락했지만, 그는 내게 내 것(내 제안서)을 수정할 것을 요청했다.

3. 재귀대명사

▶ 재귀용법: 동사나 동사구(동사 + 전치사)의 목적어가 주어와 같을 때 '~ 자신'이라는 의미로 재귀대명사를 쓴다.

▶ 강조용법: 재귀대명사는 '직접, 스스로'라는 뜻으로 주어, 목적어, 보어 등을 강조하는 용법으로도 쓰인다. 강조하는 말 바로 뒤에 오거나 문장 끝에 올 수 있다.

재귀대명사	myself	yourself	himself	herself	itself	ourselves	yourselves	themselves
목적격	me	you	him	her	it	us	you	them

Ms. Anderson / proved / **herself** / to be capable of the task. 재귀용법(Ms. Anderson = herself)

If you receive the packages, please / send / **them** / to the Sales Department. 목적격

Mr. Kim / gave / the presentation / to the prospective investors / **himself**. 강조용법

Ms. Lee / made / handouts / for the sales meeting / **by herself**. 관용 표현

해석　　Mr. Anderson은 그녀 자신이 그 일을 할 수 있는 능력이 있다는 것을 입증했다. / 그 소포들을 받으면 그것들을 영업팀으로 보내 주세요.
Mr. Kim은 유망한 투자자들에게 자신이 직접 프레젠테이션을 했다. / Mr. Lee는 영업 회의를 위해 그녀 혼자서 유인물을 만들었다.

4. 부정대명사

▶ 수량을 나타내는 형용사 one, some, any, many, much, all, each 등은 불특정한 사람이나 사물을 가리키는 부정대명사로도 쓰인다.

▶ 명사를 반복하는 대신 명사와 같은 종류인 '하나, 몇몇, 약간, 다수, 다량, 모두, 각각' 등으로 표현할 때 쓰인다.

I / lost / my wallet. I / am looking / for **the wallet**.

⋯▸ I / am looking / for **it**. 나는 그것을 찾고 있다. [it = the wallet]

I / lost / my wallet. I / want to buy / **a wallet**.

⋯▸ I / want to buy / **one**. 나는 하나 사기를 원한다. [one = a wallet]

The local market / sells / **home-grown vegetables**.

⋯▸ **They** / are fresh and safe. 그것들은 신선하고 안전하다. [They = The home-grown vegetables]

You / should eat / many **vegetables**.

⋯▸ Seasonal **ones** / are less expensive and taste better.
계절 채소는 덜 비싸고 맛이 더 좋다. [ones = vegetables]

풀이　　they vs. ones: 앞에서 언급된 바로 그 복수 명사는 they로, 불특정한 복수 명사는 ones로 대신한다.

5. 지시대명사

▶ 단수 명사를 대신하면 that, 복수 명사이면 those를 쓴다. that과 those 뒤에는 전치사구와 같은 수식어가 붙어 주로 「that of: ~의 그것」, 「those of: ~의 그것(들)」 형태로 쓰인다

The **result** / will be more positive / than **that** of last year. that + 전치사구

The **profits** of Fremont Company / are higher / than **those** of Alberta, Inc. those + 전치사구

해석　　결과가 작년의 그것보다 더 긍정적일 것이다. / Fremont 사의 수익은 Alberta 사의 그것보다 더 높다.

Q1 [소유격 vs. 목적격] + 명사

Mr. Weiser will be honored for ------- dedication to the company.

(A) he   (B) himself   (C) his   (D) him

>> **출제 포인트** **대명사는 역할에 따라 주격, 목적격, 소유격으로 쓴다.**

① **선택지 확인** | 빈칸에 들어갈 알맞은 대명사의 격을 고른다.

② **빈칸 확인** | 명사 앞의 수식어 자리 → 앞에 전치사가 있지만, 뒤에 명사가 나오므로 전치사의 목적어 자리가 아니다.
   (D) him ✗

③ **정답 확인** | 명사 dedication을 수식하는 자리이므로 정답은 소유격 (C) his ◎

정답 Mr. Weiser / will be honored / for **(C) his** dedication / to the company.

해석 Mr. Weiser는 / 표창을 받을 것이다 / 그의 헌신에 대해서 / 회사에 대한

출제 포인트 **①** 대명사의 역할과 격

Ms. Diaz / believes / that **she** is highly qualified for the position of branch manager. 주격: 주어 자리

Let / **me** / know / when the Vice President is leaving. 목적격: 목적어 자리

Ms. Simpson / will review / the final draft of the report / before the meeting.

Please / fax / it to **her** / before Friday. 목적격: 전치사의 목적어 자리

Employees / are invited / to talk / about **their** retirement plans. 소유격: 명사 앞

해석 Ms. Diaz는 그녀가 지점장 자리에 매우 적합하다고 믿고 있다. / 부사장님이 언제 떠나는지 저에게 알려 주세요.
Ms. Simpson이 회의 전에 보고서의 최종본을 검토하려고 해요. / 금요일 전까지 그녀에게 그것을 팩스로 보내 주세요.
직원들은 그들의 은퇴 계획에 대해 이야기하기 위해서 초대된다.

---

check .... 해설서 p.15

1. Ms. Yamato has been promoted to department head because of ------- excellent communication skills.

(A) she   (B) her   (C) herself   (D) hers

Q2 재귀대명사 vs. 목적격 대명사

At the training session, Ms. Schwartz proved ------- to be competitive.

(A) she   (B) herself   (C) her   (D) hers

>> **출제 포인트** 목적어가 주어와 동일할 때 재귀대명사를 쓴다.

1 선택지 확인 | 빈칸에 들어갈 알맞은 대명사를 고른다.

2 빈칸 확인 | 목적어의 자리 → 주격 (A) she ✖

3 정답 확인 | 'Ms. Schwartz는 자기 자신이 경쟁력이 있음을 증명해 보였다'라는 의미이므로 목적어가 주어와 동일한 대상이다. 정답은 재귀대명사 (B) herself ⭕

정답 At the training session, / Ms. Schwartz / proved / **(B) herself** / to be competitive.

해석 교육에서 / Ms. Schwartz는 / 증명했다 / 그녀 자신을 / 경쟁력이 있다고

출제 포인트 ❷ 재귀대명사의 재귀 용법과 강조 용법

1) 재귀대명사의 재귀 용법

목적어가 주어와 같은 대상일 때 목적어 자리에 목적격 대명사 대신에 재귀대명사를 쓴다. '주어가 자기 자신을 ~하다'라고 해석된다.

Employees / must familiarize / **themselves** / with the safety manual. (Employees = themselves)

해석 직원들은 자신들을 안전 수칙에 익숙하도록 해야 하다(스스로 안전 수칙을 숙지해야 한다).

2) 재귀대명사의 강조 용법

부사와 같이 문장 끝에 오는 경우가 대부분 출제되며, '자신이 직접'이라는 의미로 해석이 된다.

The general manager / took / the visitors / on the tour of the plant **himself**.

해석 총지배인은 자신이 직접 방문객들을 공장 견학에 데려갔다.

출제 포인트 ❸ 재귀대명사의 관용 표현

by oneself 혼자서 | for oneself 혼자 힘으로 | in itself 본질적으로 | of itself 저절로

The speakers / prepared / the presentation materials / **by themselves**.

해석 발표자들은 프레젠테이션 자료를 스스로 준비했다.

⊕ check

2. Studio production interns often find ------- working overtime.

(A) them   (B) their   (C) themselves   (D) they

Q3 [They vs. Those] + who + 복수 동사

------- who were absent from work received a written warning.

(A) They   (B) That   (C) Anyone   (D) Those

>> 출제 포인트 those는 전치사구나 형용사절의 수식을 받을 수 있다.

1 선택지 확인 | 빈칸에 들어갈 알맞은 대명사를 고른다.

2 빈칸 확인 | 형용사절의 꾸밈을 받는 자리인 동시에 주어의 자리 → 수식어의 꾸밈을 받지 못하는 인칭대명사 (A) They ✕

3 정답 확인 | '~했던 사람들은 서면 경고를 받았다'라는 의미로 '사람들'을 뜻하는 대명사가 와야 한다. who 뒤의 동사가 복수이므로 단수 (C) Anyone ✕ 복수 (D) Those ⭕

정답 **(D) Those** who were absent from work / received / a written warning.

해석 결근했던 사람들은 / 받았다 / 서면 경고를

출제 포인트 **④** those는 '사람들(people)'이라는 의미로도 쓰이며, 인칭대명사 they와 달리 who 관계대명사절, 분사, 전치사구 등의 수식어가 뒤따라올 수 있다.

Those / who **work** in the Marketing Department / received / a bonus.
= **People** / who **work** in the Marketing Department / received / a bonus.
= **Anyone** / who **works** in the Marketing Department / received / a bonus.

해석 마케팅 부서에서 일하는 사람들은 (누구든) 보너스를 받았다.

출제 포인트 **⑤** 지시대명사 that과 those는 뒤에 전치사구가 붙어서 앞에 나온 명사와 같은 대상을 나타낼 때 사용한다.

Although Angelo Meyers is new to the sales team, his skillful **presentations** seemed like **those** of an experienced salesperson.

해석 Angelo Meyers는 영업팀에 새로 왔지만, 그의 능숙한 발표는 경력 많은 영업사원의 그것(발표)과 같았다.

✔ 문법 포인트 앞에 있는 presentations과 같은 대상을 나타내고 있긴 하지만, 앞의 presentation은 Angelo Meyers의 발표이고 뒤에 나오는 those는 다른 영업사원의 발표를 가리킨다.

that of / those of	~의 그것 / 그것들
those + who + 복수 동사 those + -ing / p.p. those + with ~	~한 사람들
anyone / everyone + who + 단수 동사 anyone / everyone + -ing / p.p. anyone / everyone + with ~	~한 사람은 어느 누구나 / 모두

➕ check

3. Only ------- holding current parking permits may bring their vehicles to the company.

(A) whose   (B) they   (C) each   (D) those

Q4 부정대명사 others vs. other

A weekly rail pass is the most economical option for commuters, but ------- are available.

(A) other   (B) others   (C) the other   (D) another

>> **출제 포인트 부정대명사의 수 일치**

① **선택지 확인** | 빈칸에 들어갈 형용사 또는 대명사를 고른다.

② **빈칸 확인** | 주어 자리 → 주어 자리에 올 수 없는 형용사 (A) other ❌

③ **정답 확인** | 뒤에 동사가 are이므로 단수 (C) the other ❌ (D) another ❌ 정답은 복수인 (B) others ⭕

정답 A weekly rail pass / is the most economical option / for commuters, / but / **(B) others** / are available.
해석 열차 일주인권은 / 가장 경제적인 선택이다 / 통근자들에게 / 그러나 / 다른 것들도 / 이용 가능하다

출제 포인트 ⑤ 부정대명사 **another, one, the other(s), some, others**의 쓰임새 차이를 구분할 수 있어야 한다.
other는 형용사이기 때문에 주어나 목적어 자리에 명사 없이 단독으로 쓰이지 않는다.

	의미	품사	대명사일 때 수	형용사일 때 뒤에 오는 명사
one	하나/하나의	형용사/대명사	단수	+ 가산 단수명사
the other	나머지 하나/나머지 하나의	형용사/대명사	단수	+ 가산[단수 복수]명사
another	또 다른 하나/또 다른 하나의	형용사/대명사	단수	+ 가산 단수명사
the others	나머지 것(사람)들	대명사	복수	
others	다른 것(사람)들	대명사	복수	
other	다른	형용사		+ 가산 복수/불가산 명사
any other	다른 어떤	형용사		+ 가산 복수/불가산 명사
each other	서로	대명사		
one another	서로	대명사		

주의 each other와 one another는 주어 자리에 올 수 없다.

Because this store is crowded with people, I / will go / to **another**.
Some employees / like / the movie, / but **others(=other employees)** / don't like / it.
Among ten applicants, / **two** applicants / were impressive, / but **the others** / were not impressive.

해석 이 가게가 사람들로 붐비기 때문에 나는 다른 곳으로 갈 것이다. / 일부 직원들은 그 영화를 좋아하지만, 다른 직원들은 그 영화를 좋아하지 않는다.
열 명의 지원자 중에서 두 명은 인상적이었으나 나머지 지원자들은 인상적이지 않았다.

◆ check

4. Department managers urge their staff to communicate with -------.

(A) one another   (B) the other   (C) another   (D) other

Practice

해설서 p.16

1. Mr. Park wants all staff to communicate directly with ------- about the new marketing project.
   - (A) he
   - (B) his
   - (C) him
   - (D) his own

2. While Dr. Kim is out of the office, please call ------- administrative assistant.
   - (A) she
   - (B) her
   - (C) hers
   - (D) herself

3. All employees who have unused vacation days should use ------- by October 30.
   - (A) they
   - (B) their
   - (C) them
   - (D) themselves

4. The company policy requires that ------- computers be protected with a secure password.
   - (A) we
   - (B) ours
   - (C) us
   - (D) our

5. Anopar Industries will acquire ------- main competitor, Pukom Enterprises, in March.
   - (A) itself
   - (B) themselves
   - (C) its
   - (D) them

6. ------- of the new XV20 laptops were damaged during transit.
   - (A) Anything
   - (B) Every
   - (C) Each
   - (D) Some

7. After the proposal had been reviewed by three managers, ------- was finally accepted.
   - (A) it
   - (B) its
   - (C) its own
   - (D) itself

8. Most of the computers used by our employees are not ------- but are provided by the company.
   - (A) they
   - (B) them
   - (C) their
   - (D) theirs

9. Mr. Jang has proven ------- to be a hardworking and useful member of the R&D Department.
   - (A) he
   - (B) itself
   - (C) its
   - (D) himself

10. The secretary could not repair the copy machine because ------- parts were not available.
    - (A) his
    - (B) its
    - (C) our
    - (D) their

11. If ------- has completed their quarterly reports, please inform the team leader.
    - (A) yourself
    - (B) other
    - (C) anyone
    - (D) himself

12. Although Carlam Beauty Products and GoodNature Cosmetics were unprofitable this year, ------- expect revenues to rise next year.
    - (A) another
    - (B) both
    - (C) other
    - (D) the other

13. The brand's sales have been much better than ------- of last year.
    - (A) this
    - (B) that
    - (C) these
    - (D) those

14. Although ------- disagreed with Ms. Wilson's opinion, Mr. Taylor agreed with it.
    - (A) the other
    - (B) many
    - (C) himself
    - (D) other

15. Ms. Hong managed to move the heavy desk by -------.

(A) she   (B) hers
(C) herself   (D) her own

16. La Rouge Pictures is one of the leading film distributors in ------- of Europe.

(A) all   (B) other
(C) every   (D) the other

17. Many students at Korire University work as interns before starting ------- first professional job.

(A) they   (B) their
(C) them   (D) theirs

18. Please inform Ms. Lin that ------- visit to the Hong Kong office has been canceled.

(A) my   (B) me
(C) mine   (D) myself

19. At Giny's Store, we take pleasure in providing ------- of our customers with excellent service.

(A) each   (B) the other
(C) other   (D) every

20. ------- people attended the music festival despite the bad weather.

(A) Others   (B) The others
(C) Every   (D) Many

기본 완성 훈련 다음은 앞서 풀어 본 연습문제의 문장들입니다. 대명사를 찾아 밑줄을 긋고, 해당 대명사가 가리키는 명사가 있다면 ◯를 치세요.

1. Mr. Park wants all staff to communicate directly with him about the new marketing project.

2. All employees who have unused vacation days should use them by October 30.

3. The company policy requires that our computers be protected with a secure password.

4. After the proposal had been reviewed by three managers, it was finally accepted.

5. Mr. Jang has proven himself to be a hardworking and useful member of the R&D Department.

6. If anyone has completed their quarterly reports, please inform the team leader.

7. The brand's sales have been much better than those of last year.

8. Ms. Hong managed to move the heavy desk by herself.

9. Many students at Korire University work as interns before starting their first professional job.

10. At Giny's Store, we take pleasure in providing each of our customers with excellent service.

형용사

형용사(adjective)는 명사 앞에서 명사가 가리키는 대상이나 수, 특성 등을 한정해 주는 수식어 역할을 하거나 동사나 목적어 뒤에서 주어나 목적어의 상태를 설명해 주는 보어 역할을 한다.

 기본 개념 이해하기

1. 형용사의 형태

형용사형 어미	-ive (creative 창의적인) -y (healthy 건강한) -ic (realistic 현실적인) -al (final 마지막의) -able (refundable 환불 가능한) -ible (eligible 자격이 있는) -ous (dangerous 위험한) -ful (careful 조심하는, 주의 깊은) -less (useless 쓸모없는) -ant (important 중요한)
현재분사형	growing 증가하는 leading 선두적인 outstanding 뛰어난 challenging 도전적인
과거분사형	detailed 상세한 attached 첨부된 experienced 경험이 있는 qualified 자격이 있는
명사 + ly	hourly 매시간의 weekly 매주의 monthly 매달의 quarterly 매 분기마다의 yearly 매년의 timely 시기적절한 costly 비싼 orderly 질서 정연한 friendly 친절한 likely ~일 것 같은

A **detailed** itinerary / is included / in the attached file.
The Best Earth Shop / sells / environmentally **friendly** products.

해석 상세한 일정표가 첨부 파일에 포함되어 있다. / Best Earth Shop은 친환경 제품을 판매한다.

✅ **문법 포인트** 「형용사 + ly」는 부사이지만, 「명사 + ly」는 형용사라는 점에 유의한다.

2. 명사 앞에 오는 수식어

▶ 명사 앞에는 명사의 대상(a, an, the, this, your)이나 수량(some, any)을 나타내는 한정사와 특성·상태를 설명하는 일반 형용사가 온다.

▶ 「형용사 + 형용사 + 명사」: 명사를 수식하는 일반 형용사는 두 개 이상 올 수 있다.

The book / contains / some **useful** information. 수량 형용사 + 형용사 + 명사
Her **effective** strategy / helped / sales / to increase. 소유격 + 형용사 + 명사
It / is an extremely **successful** policy. 관사 + 부사 + 형용사 + 명사
The government / seeks / to maintain a **steady economic** growth. 관사 + 형용사 + 형용사 + 명사

해석 그 책은 유익한 정보를 담고 있다. / 그녀의 효과적인 전략은 판매가 증가되도록 도왔다.
그것은 매우 성공적인 정책이었다. / 정부는 지속적인 경제 성장을 유지하는 것을 모색한다.

3. 명사 뒤에 오는 수식어

▶ 형용사가 전치사구 등의 수식어구와 함께 쓰여 길어질 때, 명사의 뒤에 온다.

There are some new products / **available** at the store. 명사 + 형용사 + 전치사구

Please contact / the manager / **responsible** for the service. 명사 + 형용사 + 전치사구

해석   그 매장에서 구매할 수 있는 몇몇 새로운 물건들이 있다. / 그 서비스를 담당하고 있는 매니저에게 연락해 보세요.

4. 주어나 목적어를 설명하는 보어

▶ 2형식 동사 (be, become, remain, seem, appear) 등의 뒤에 와서 주격 보어 역할을 한다.

▶ 5형식 동사 (make, find, keep, leave, consider) 등의 목적어 뒤에 와서 목적격 보어 역할을 한다.

The product / is very **useful**. 동사 + 형용사

I found / the product / very **useful**. 동사 + 목적어 + 형용사

해석   그 제품은 매우 유용하다. / 그 제품이 매우 유용하다고 생각했다.

5. 수량 형용사의 종류

one 하나의 every 모든 each 각각의 another 또 다른 하나의 either 둘 중 하나의 neither 둘 중 하나도 ~아니다	+ 가산 단수 명사 EX every product
two 두 개의 both 둘 다 a few 몇몇의 several 몇몇의 many 많은 numerous 많은 a number of 많은 various 다양한 a variety of 다양한	+ 가산 복수 명사 EX many products
a little (양이) 적은 little (양이) 거의 없는 much (양이) 많은 a large amount of 많은 a great deal of 많은	+ 불가산 명사 EX much information
some 약간의 all 모든 more 더 많은 most 대부분의 plenty of 많은	+ 가산 복수 명사 EX all products + 불가산 명사 EX all information
any 어느 ~든지, 모든 no 어느 ~도 ~가 아니다	+ 가산 단수 명사 EX any product + 가산 복수 명사 EX any products + 불가산 명사 EX any information

A few students / missed / the deadline. A few + 가산 복수 명사

Every employee / must submit / the sales report. Every + 가산 단수 명사

All applicants / are eligible / for the position. All + 가산 복수 명사

All information / in this report / is important. All + 불가산 명사

해석   몇몇 학생들이 마감일을 놓쳤다. / 모든 직원들은 판매 보고서를 제출해야 한다.
       모든 지원자들은 그 자리에 대해 자격을 갖추고 있다. / 이 보고서의 모든 정보는 중요하다.

Q1 관사 + [형용사 자리] + 명사

In addition to an ------- salary, the company offers various benefits.

(A) attract   (B) attractively   (C) attractive   (D) attraction

>> **출제 포인트** **명사 앞의 수식어 자리에는 형용사가 온다.**

1 선택지 확인 | 빈칸에 들어갈 알맞은 품사를 고른다.

2 빈칸 확인 | 부정관사와 명사 사이의 수식어 자리 → 동사 (A) attract ❌ 부사 (B) attractively ❌

3 정답 확인 | attraction salary는 의미가 통하지 않으므로 (D) attraction ❌ salary를 꾸며주는 형용사가 와야 한다.
정답은 (C) attractive ⓞ

정답 In addition to an **(C) attractive** salary, / the company / offers / various benefits.

해석 높은 급여에 / 그 회사는 / 제공한다 / 다양한 복리후생을

출제 포인트 ❶ 명사 앞에는 〈관사 / 소유격 / 지시형용사 + 수량형용사 + 일반형용사〉 순으로 온다.

명사 앞에 오는 형용사의 순서

① **관사 / 소유격 / 지시형용사**: a, an, the, your, this, these 등
② **수량형용사**: some, any, many, much, a few, a little, one, two 등
③ **특성 및 상태를 나타내는 일반형용사**: informative, spacious, attractive 등

Authorized managers / have access / to this information. 형용사 + 명사
A few authorized managers / have access / to this information. 수량형용사 + 형용사 + 명사
The authorized managers / have access / to this information. 관사 + 형용사 + 명사

해석 승인 받은 매니저들은 이 정보에 접근할 수 있다. / 몇몇 승인 받은 매니저들은 이 정보에 접근할 수 있다.
그 승인 받은 매니저들은 이 정보에 접근할 수 있다.

+ check .... 해설서 p.18

1. Linear Stage's ------- theatrical performances highlight contemporary social issues.

(A) innovative   (B) innovator   (C) innovated   (D) innovation

Q2 동사 + 목적어 + [형용사 자리]

Jason's supervisor found his proposal very -------.

(A) creative   (B) create   (C) creatively   (D) creation

>> **출제 포인트** 목적어를 설명하는 보어 자리에는 형용사가 온다.

1 선택지 확인 | 빈칸에 들어갈 알맞은 품사를 고른다.

2 빈칸 확인 | 목적격 보어 자리 → 5형식 동사 find의 목적격 보어 자리에 올 수 없는 동사 (B) create ❌
부사 (C) creatively ❌

3 정답 확인 | 목적격 보어 자리에는 목적어와의 의미를 고려하여 목적어의 상태를 나타내면 형용사, 목적어와 동격이면 명사
를 고른다. → Jason의 상사는 그의 제안서가 매우 창의적이라고 생각했다'라는 의미로 목적어의 상태를 나타
내므로 빈칸에는 형용사가 들어가야 적절하다. 정답은 (A) creative ⭕

정답 Jason's supervisor / found / his proposal / very **(A) creative**.
해석 Jason의 상사는 / 생각했다 / 그의 제안서가 / 매우 창의적이라고

출제 포인트 ❷ 「2형식 동사 + 형용사 주격 보어」
형용사 주격 보어는 주어의 상태를 설명해준다.

be ~이다	become ~되다	remain 여전히 ~이다	appear ~하게 보이다	
seem ~하게 보이다	prove ~임이 판명되다	stay 계속 ~인 상태이다	look ~하게 보이다	+ 형용사 주격 보어
feel ~한 느낌이 들다	sound ~인 것 같다	smell ~한 냄새가 나다	taste ~한 맛이 나다	

The concert / is not **affordable** for most students. 동사 + 형용사
Jack's decision / to open a fitness center / is **timely**. 동사 + 형용사

해석 그 콘서트 티켓은 대부분의 학생들이 부담하기 어려운 가격이다. / 헬스 클럽을 열기로 한 Jack의 결정은 시기적절하다.

☑ **문법 포인트** 「be, become + 명사 주격 보어」: 명사 주격 보어는 주어와 동격으로 주어가 무엇인지를 설명해 준다. (주어 = 보어)
The firm has quickly become **a threat to its competitors**. (The firm = a threat ~ competitors)
해석 그 회사는 빠르게 경쟁사들에게 위협이 되었다.

출제 포인트 ❸ 「5형식 동사 + 목적어 + 목적격 보어」

make ~하게 하다	find ~라고 여기다 / 생각하다	consider ~라고 여기다	+ 목적어 + 형용사 목적격 보어
keep 계속 ~하게 하다	leave 계속 ~하게 하다		

Team members / are asked / to keep / all the information / **confidential**. 동사 + 목적어 + 형용사
The manager / made / the process / **simple**. 동사 + 목적어 + 형용사

해석 팀 구성원들은 모든 정보를 기밀로 유지하도록 요청받는다. / 그 매니저는 과정을 간소하게 만들었다.

☑ **문법 포인트** 「appoint, name, call, elect + 목적어 + 명사」: 명사 목적격 보어는 목적어가 무엇인지를 설명해 준다. (목적어 = 보어)
They elected **him the temporary captain** of their company. (him = the ~ captain)
해석 그들은 그를 회사의 임시 회장으로 선출했다.

⊕ check

2. You should make your sales presentation ------- to increase the possibility of acquiring the client.

(A) persuade   (B) to persuade   (C) persuasive   (D) persuaded

Q3 사람과 사물을 구분해서 수식하는 형용사

BNQ Motors has created an ------- client base in just two months.

(A) impressive   (B) impression   (C) impressively   (D) impressed

>> **출제 포인트** 사람 명사나 사물 명사에 주로 쓰이는 형용사를 구별해야 한다.

❶ 선택지 확인 | 빈칸에 들어갈 알맞은 품사를 고르고, 비슷한 형태의 다른 의미를 가진 형용사를 구별한다.

❷ 빈칸 확인 | 관사와 명사 사이의 수식어 자리 → 형용사가 들어갈 자리이므로 명사 (B) impression ✖
     부사 (C) impressively ✖

❸ 정답 확인 | (A) impressive는 '인상적인'이란 의미로 주로 사물을 수식하는 형용사이며, (D) impressed는 '감명 받은'
     이란 의미로 사람을 수식하는 형용사이다. 빈칸 뒤의 명사가 사물이라는 점에서 정답은 (A) impressive ◉

정답 BNQ Motors / has created / an **(A) impressive** client base / in just two months.

해석 BNQ 자동차는 / 창출했다 / 인상적인 고객층을 / 단 2달 만에

출제 포인트 ❹ 사람과 사물을 구분해서 수식하는 형용사

사람 명사와 주로 쓰이는 형용사	사물 명사와 주로 쓰이는 형용사
considerate 사려 깊은	considerable 상당한
impressed 감명 받은	impressive 인상적인
pleased 기쁜	pleasing (남에게) 기쁨을 주는
satisfied 만족하는	satisfactory 만족스러운
interested 흥미를 느끼는	interesting 흥미로운
encouraged 고무된	encouraging 고무적인
understanding 이해심 있는	understandable 이해할 수 있는
argumentative 논쟁을 좋아하는	arguable 논란의 여지가 있는

The seminar / was informative and [**encouraging** / ~~encouraged~~].

해석   그 세미나는 정보가 유익하고 고무적이었다.

⊕ check

3. Sales representatives must dress professionally and avoid becoming ------- with demanding customers.

(A) arguable   (B) argument   (C) argumentative   (D) argumentatively

Q4 비슷한 형태의 형용사

The new marketing manager implemented a ------- strategy of attracting customers.

(A) succeed   (B) successive   (C) successful   (D) successfully

>> **출제 포인트** 형태는 비슷하지만, 의미가 다른 형용사에 유의한다.

❶ 선택지 확인 | 빈칸에 들어갈 알맞은 품사를 고르고, 비슷한 형태의 다른 의미를 가진 형용사를 구별한다.

❷ 빈칸 확인 | 관사와 명사 사이의 수식어 자리 → 형용사 자리이므로 동사 (A) succeed ❌ 부사 (D) successfully ❌

❸ 정답 확인 | 고객들을 끌어들일 '성공적인 방법'이란 의미가 적절하므로, '연속적인'이란 뜻의 (B) successive ❌
정답은 (C) successful ⊙

정답 The new marketing manager / implemented / a **(C) successful** strategy / of attracting customers.
해석 새 마케팅 매니저는 / 도입했다 / 성공적인 전략을 / 고객들을 끌어들일

출제 포인트 ❺ 비슷한 형태의 형용사

additional 추가의	addictive 습관성의
complimentary 무료의, 칭찬하는	complementary 보충의
comprehensive 종합적인, 포괄적인	comprehensible 이해할 수 있는
economic 경제성이 있는	economical 절약하는
informative 유익한	informed 잘 아는
persuasive 설득력 있는	persuadable (사람이) 설득되는
reliable 신뢰할 만한	reliant 의존하는
responsible for ~에 책임이 있는	responsive to ~에 반응하는
successful 성공적인, 합격한	successive 연속적인
sensitive 민감한	sensible 분별 있는
complete (서술적 용법) 완전한, 완료된	completed 완료된, 작성된
confidential 비밀의	confident 확신하는
favorable 우호적인	favorite 가장 좋아하는
respective 각각의	respectful 공손한

Interns / will receive / specific training in their [**respective** / ~~respectful~~] departments.
해석 인턴사원들은 각자의 부서에서 구체적인 훈련을 받을 것이다.

🔵 **check**

4. With the new accounting software program in place, most bookkeeping errors are -------.
(A) preventing   (B) preventable   (C) preventive   (D) prevention

해설서 p.18

1. Elbart Bay is a popular holiday destination among young travelers due to its ------- accommodation.

(A) affordable   (B) affords
(C) affordably   (D) afford

2. Many people today are too ------- to pay attention to their diet.

(A) busyness   (B) busily
(C) more busily   (D) busy

3. Because this is an ------- teaching method, Dr. Wu wants to receive student feedback.

(A) experiment   (B) experiments
(C) experimental   (D) experimentally

4. Mr. Jones plans to conduct training with ------- members of the sales team.

(A) another   (B) each
(C) several   (D) every

5. After months of negotiations, the two companies appeared ------- to the terms of the merger.

(A) agree   (B) agreement
(C) agreeable   (D) agrees

6. Carefully reviewing comments from ------- customer will help improve our services.

(A) each   (B) a few
(C) all   (D) most

7. Once the factory is fully -------, it will need a workforce of 500.

(A) operational   (B) operation
(C) operates   (D) operationally

8. Mr. Pareto was hired by Gofirst Travels thanks to his ------- understanding of the tourism industry.

(A) deep   (B) deeply
(C) deepen   (D) depth

9. The controversial policy change was resolved in a ------- manner.

(A) time   (B) timing
(C) timely   (D) times

10. According to the survey results, most customers found Lebtro's new leather jackets very -------.

(A) attractive   (B) attraction
(C) attractively   (D) attract

11. The suitcases made by CariBags are both ------- and trendy.

(A) durable   (B) durability
(C) durableness   (D) durably

12. Bahilo Advisory Group provides a ------- variety of financial services.

(A) wide   (B) widen
(C) widely   (D) widest

13. Some of the Frankston Line trains are in need of ------- repairs.

(A) extensive   (B) extension
(C) extended   (D) extensively

14. Despite being dropped on the floor a few times, the mobile phone is still -------.

(A) function   (B) functional
(C) functionally   (D) functionality

15. Customers at Hurley's Café said that the new iced tea is ------- enough.

(A) sweet
(B) sweetly
(C) sweeten
(D) sweetest

16. Everyone at the staff meeting agreed that safety was one of the most ------- priorities.

(A) importance
(B) important
(C) import
(D) importantly

17. The advertising campaign was ------- in increasing the company's sales.

(A) success
(B) successive
(C) successful
(D) successfully

18. It is crucial that all client information is kept -------.

(A) confidential
(B) confidence
(C) confidentially
(D) confidentiality

19. Perco Industries has been ------- in organizing environmental activities for over 20 years.

(A) active
(B) activists
(C) actively
(D) activities

20. Many road accidents are ------- through careful planning and driver education.

(A) preventing
(B) preventable
(C) prevention
(D) prevents

기본 완성 훈련 다음은 앞서 풀어 본 연습문제의 문장들입니다. 형용사에 밑줄을 긋고 해당 형용사가 수식 또는 서술하는 대상에 ○를 치세요.

1. Mr. Jones plans to conduct training with several members of the sales team.

2. After months of negotiations, the two companies appeared agreeable to the terms of the merger.

3. Carefully reviewing comments from each customer will help improve our services.

4. Once the factory is fully operational, it will need a workforce of 500.

5. The controversial policy change was resolved in a timely manner.

6. According to the survey results, most customers found Lebtro's new leather jackets very attractive.

7. Bahilo Advisory Group provides a wide variety of financial services.

8. Despite being dropped on the floor a few times, the mobile phone is still functional.

9. The warm weather is likely to last throughout the month.

10. It is crucial that all client information is kept confidential.

UNIT 08 부사

부사(adverb)는 동사나 형용사, 부사 또는 문장 전체를 꾸며주는 수식어 역할을 한다. 주로 동사 뒤, 또는 형용사나 부사 앞에 위치하며, 문장 전체를 꾸며줄 때는 보통 문장의 맨 앞에 온다.

기본 개념 이해하기

1. 부사의 형태

▶ 형용사와 부사의 형태가 동일한 단어들 또는 형태는 비슷하지만 의미가 전혀 다른 부사에 주의한다.

형태는 비슷하나 의미가 다른 부사		
	hard 형 근면한 부 열심히	**hardly** 부 거의 ~않다
	near 형 가까운 부 가까이	**nearly** 부 거의 (=almost)
	high 형 높은 부 높게	**highly** 부 매우
	late 형 늦은 부 늦게	**lately** 부 최근에 (=recently)
	close 형 가까운 부 가깝게	**closely** 부 면밀하게, 밀접하게

The employees / worked **hard** to meet the deadline.
Finishing the project on time / is **hardly** possible.

해석　그 직원들은 마감 기한을 맞추기 위해 열심히 일했다. / 그 프로젝트를 제때에 끝내는 것은 거의 가능하지 않다.

2. 형용사, 부사, 전치사구를 수식하는 부사

▶ 부사는 형용사와 다른 부사 또는 전치사구 형태의 부사구 앞에서 수식어 역할을 한다.

We / are discussing / a **reasonably** important issue. 관사 + 부사 + 형용사 + 명사
This location / is **easily** accessible by public transport. be동사 + 부사 + 형용사
The manager is concerned that the project is progressing **too** slowly. 강조 부사 + 부사
Despite its high price, Koruntis' winter jacket is selling **quite** well. 강조 부사 + 부사
The weather was **very[really]** nice yesterday for the company picnic. 강조 부사 + 형용사
The chef's new menu received **pretty** good reviews from the critics. 강조 부사 + 형용사
Preview tickets / go on sale / **exclusively** / to our members. 부사 + 전치사구

해석　우리는 상당히 중요한 문제에 대해서 논의하고 있다. / 이 장소는 대중 교통으로 접근하기 쉽다. / 그 관리자는 프로젝트가 너무 느리게 진행되고 있는 점을 걱정하고 있다. / 높은 가격에도 불구하고, Koruntis'의 겨울 재킷은 꽤 잘 팔리고 있다. / 어제 회사 야유회를 하기에 날씨가 매우[정말로]좋았다. / 그 요리사의 신 메뉴는 비평가들로부터 매우 좋은 평가를 받았다. / 시사회 티켓은 우리 회원들에게만 할인 판매된다.

3. 동사를 수식하는 부사

▶ 주어와 동사 사이에 동사를 앞에서 수식하는 부사를 고르는 문제가 자주 출제된다.

▶ 부사가 동사 뒤에서 수식할 경우, 자동사를 수식하는 부사는 동사 바로 뒤에 오고 타동사를 수식하는 부사는 목적어 뒤에 온다.

▶ 조동사가 있을 때는 조동사와 동사 사이에 부사가 올 수 있다. 진행형과 수동태에서는 be동사와 현재분사/과거분사 사이에 올 수 있다.

The R&D Department / cooperates / **closely** / with the laboratory staff. 동사 + 부사

Please enter / your personal information / **accurately**. 동사 + 목적어 + 부사

Ms. Kim / will **gladly** give / you / a ride to the airport. 조동사 + 부사 + 동사원형

We / have **recently** inspected / the facility. have + 부사 + 과거분사

Our office / is **conveniently** located / near the subway station. be동사 + 부사 + 과거분사

We / are **currently** inspecting / the facility. be동사 + 부사 + 현재분사

해석　R&D 부서는 그 연구소 직원들과 긴밀하게 협력한다. / 귀하의 개인 정보를 정확하게 입력하세요. / Ms. Kim은 기꺼이 당신을 공항까지 태워다 줄 것이다. / 우리는 최근에 그 설비를 검사했다. / 우리 사무실은 편리하게 지하철역 부근에 위치해 있다. / 우리는 현재 그 설비를 검사하고 있다.

4. 숫자를 수식하는 부사

▶ 숫자 앞에는 '대략'이라는 뜻의 almost, approximately, roughly, nearly, about이 올 수 있다.

	숫자를 수식하는 부사
약, 대략, 거의	approximately, nearly, almost, about, around, roughly
이상	more than, over
미만	less than
적어도	at least
까지	up to

It / takes / **approximately** 30 minutes / to get to the station.

해석　역에 도착하는 데 대략 30분이 걸린다.

5. 문장 전체를 수식하는 부사

▶ 문장 맨 앞에서 문장 전체를 수식할 수 있다.

Fortunately, Mr. Thompson / passed / the first round of interviews.

Unfortunately, that model / is out of stock.

Perhaps, it / will rain / in the evening.

해석　다행히도, Mr. Thompson은 첫 번째 면접을 통과했다. / 애석하게도, 그 모델은 재고가 없다. / 아마도, 저녁에 비가 올 것이다.

Q1 관사 + [명사 vs. 부사] + 형용사 + 명사

Mr. Wong is a ------- renowned expert in transportation planning.

(A) nation   (B) national   (C) nationally   (D) nationalistic

>> 출제 포인트 부사는 형용사를 수식한다.

1 선택지 확인 | 빈칸에 들어갈 알맞은 품사를 고른다.

2 빈칸 확인 | 관사와 형용사(renowned) 사이의 부사 자리 또는 renowned와 함께 명사 expert를 꾸며주는 형용사 자리
→ 명사 (A) nation ❌

3 정답 확인 | '전국적으로 알려진 전문가'라는 의미가 적절하므로 형용사 renowned를 꾸며주는 부사가 와야 한다.
정답은 (C) nationally ⭕

정답 Mr. Wong / is a **(C) nationally** renowned expert / in transportation planning.
해석 Mr. Wong은 / 전국적으로 유명한 전문가이다 / 교통 계획 분야에서

출제 포인트 ❶ 부사는 형용사, 부사, 전치사구 등을 수식한다.

[부사] + 형용사	Ms. Lee is an **exceptionally** valuable client of our hotel.
[부사] + 부사	You should compare all the benefits **extremely** carefully.
[부사] + 전치사구	Some of the equipment broke down, **reportedly** due to poor maintenance.

해석 Ms. Lee는 우리 호텔의 특별하게 소중한 고객이다. / 모든 혜택을 매우 주의깊게 비교해야 한다. / 장비 일부가 고장 났는데 보도된 바로는 유지 보수가 제대로 되지 않아서이다.

출제 포인트 ❷ 부사는 동사 앞뒤에 올 수 있으나, 동사와 목적어 사이에는 오지 않는다.

자동사 + [부사]	Employee productivity improved **significantly** last year.
동사 + 목적어 + [부사]	The government changed the system **successfully**.
[부사] + 동사 + 목적어	The government **successfully** changed the system.
2형식 동사 + [부사] + 형용사	Mr. Choi was **largely** responsible for the increase in expenses.

해석 직원 생산성이 지난해 크게 향상되었다. / 정부는 성공적으로 시스템을 변경했다. / 정부는 성공적으로 시스템을 변경했다. /
Mr. Choi는 비용 증가에 큰 책임이 있다.

해설서 p.20

✚ check

1. Analysts expect Halcyon Tech to gain ------- more revenue this year.

(A) substantial   (B) substantially   (C) substantiate   (D) substance

Q2 주어 + 동사 + [형용사 vs. 부사]

Employees should work ------- to meet the project deadline.

(A) cooperation   (B) cooperate   (C) cooperative   (D) cooperatively

>> **출제 포인트 1형식 동사 뒤에는 부사가 온다.**

1 선택지 확인 | 빈칸에 들어갈 알맞은 품사를 고른다.

2 빈칸 확인 | 1형식 동사 뒤는 부사 자리 → 명사 (A) cooperation ✕ 동사 (B) cooperate ✕
형용사 (C) cooperative ✕

3 정답 확인 | '협력하여 일하다'라는 의미로 1형식 동사 'work' 뒤에는 부사가 와야 한다. 정답은 (D) cooperatively ◎

정답 Employees / should work / **(D) cooperatively** / to meet the project deadline.
해석 직원들은 / 일해야 한다 / 협력하여 / 마감일을 맞추기 위해

출제 포인트 ❸ 조동사와 동사 사이에 부사가 온다.

| 조동사 + [부사] + 동사 + 목적어 | You will **automatically** receive the information through your e-mail. |

해석 당신은 당신의 이메일로 그 정보를 자동으로 받게 될 것이다.

출제 포인트 ❹ 진행형과 수동태에서 부사는 be동사와 현재분사(V-ing)/과거분사(p.p.) 사이에 올 수 있다.

| be동사 + [부사] + -ing: 현재진행형 | Karen is **currently** studying business at Gemnus University.
= Karen is studying business at Gemnus University **currently**. |
| be동사 + [부사] + p.p.: 수동태 | All the résumés will be **carefully** reviewed.
= All the résumés will be reviewed **carefully**. |

해석 Karen은 요즘 Gemnus 대학에서 경영학을 배우고 있다. / 모든 이력서는 면밀하게 검토될 것이다.

☑ **문법 포인트** 일반적인 3형식 동사의 수동태 뒤에 빈칸이 있는 경우 무조건 부사를 고른다.

Our new product has generally been reviewed **favorably**.

해석 우리 신제품은 일반적으로 좋게 평가 받았다.

---

check

2. Canterra's consulting services are designed ------- to meet the requirements of medium-sized retail businesses.

(A) specifies   (B) specifics   (C) specifically   (D) specific

Q3 [형용사 vs. 부사] + 동명사

The project helps improve the environment by ------- investing in clean energy.

(A) heavy   (B) heavily   (C) heaviness   (D) heavier

>> 출제 포인트 **동명사는 부사의 수식을 받는다.**

1 선택지 확인 | 빈칸에 들어갈 알맞은 품사를 고른다.

2 빈칸 확인 | 전치사 by의 목적어인 동명사의 수식어 자리 → 형용사나 명사는 동명사의 수식어 자리에 올 수 없다.
(A), (C), (D) ✖

3 정답 확인 | 동명사는 동사와 마찬가지로 부사의 꾸밈을 받으므로 정답은 부사 (B) heavily ◉

정답 The project / helps / improve the environment / by **(B) heavily** investing in clean energy.
해석 그 프로젝트는 / 돕는다 / 환경 개선을 / 청정 에너지에 대규모로 투자함으로써

출제 포인트 ⑤ 동명사를 꾸며 주는 품사는 부사이다.

Mr. Wright / increased / productivity / by **efficiently** managing employees. 부사 + 동명사

해석 Mr. Wright는 직원들을 효율적으로 관리함으로써 생산성을 높였다.

출제 포인트 ⑥ to부정사를 꾸며 주는 품사는 부사이다.

It / is important / to **thoroughly** review all the terms of the contract. to + 부사 + 동사원형

해석 계약서의 모든 조항들을 철저하게 검토하는 것은 중요하다.

+ check

3. Kamal Electronics is hoping to increase sales by ------- interacting with customers.

(A) actively   (B) activate   (C) active   (D) activation

Q4 비슷한 형태의 부사

Homefront Furniture sells its products at ------- reasonable prices.
(A) height   (B) high   (C) highly   (D) highness

>> 출제 포인트 형용사와 형태가 비슷한 부사에 유의한다.

1 **선택지 확인** | 빈칸에 들어갈 알맞은 품사를 고른다.

2 **빈칸 확인** | 형용사 reasonable을 수식하는 부사 또는 reasonable과 함께 명사 prices를 수식하는 형용사 자리
→ 명사 (A) height, (D) highness ✖

3 **정답 확인** | '매우 합리적인 가격'이라는 의미가 적절하므로 빈칸은 형용사 reasonable을 수식하는 부사 자리이다.
→ (B) high가 부사로 쓰이면, '(위치가) 높이, 높은 곳에'라는 의미이다. ✖ 정답은 '매우'라는 뜻의 부사
(C) highly ◎

정답 Homefront Furniture / sells / its products / at **(C) highly** reasonable prices.
해석 Homefront 가구는 / 판매한다 / 그 회사 제품들을 / 매우 합리적인 가격으로

출제 포인트 ❼ 비슷한 형태의 부사

Flour prices / are / **high** this month. 형용사: 높은
I / **highly** recommend / that you hire Ms.Yang. 부사: 매우
해석 이번 달 밀가루 가격이 높다. / 나는 Ms. Yang을 채용할 것을 강력하게 추천한다.

The employees / worked **hard** to meet the deadline. 부사: 열심히
Finishing the project on time / is **hardly** possible. 부사: 거의 ~않다
해석 직원들은 마감을 맞추기 위해 열심히 일했다. / 그 프로젝트를 제시간에 끝내는 것은 거의 불가능하다.

The hotel / is located **near** the station. 전치사: ~근처에
I / have / **nearly** four years of banking experience / as a loan officer. 부사: 거의, 대략
해석 그 호텔은 역 근처에 위치해 있다. / 나는 대출 업무 담당자로 거의 4년의 은행 업무 경력이 있다.

+ check
....

4. According to the notice which will be posted -------, the main entrance will be closed for repairs.
(A) short   (B) shorter   (C) shorten   (D) shortly

해설서 p.20

1. The Goodread Bookstore on Riverside Street ------- hosts big discount events.

(A) frequent (B) frequency
(C) frequented (D) frequently

2. Almost 200 employees have ------- completed our basic courses.

(A) succeeded (B) to succeed
(C) successful (D) successfully

3. Ms. Chen has been ------- involved in the creation of Broaden's security system.

(A) depth (B) deep
(C) deeply (D) deepen

4. By hiring additional employees, productivity increased ------- at Woodtown Manufacturing.

(A) substantial
(B) most substantial
(C) more substantial
(D) substantially

5. One of the most ------- respected jazz events is held in Seoul.

(A) width (B) widely
(C) widest (D) wider

6. All production floor workers must receive training on workplace ------- prior to operating machinery.

(A) safety (B) safely
(C) safest (D) safe

7. The new surgical laser is designed to ------- shorten patients' recovery times.

(A) most significant
(B) significant
(C) significance
(D) significantly

8. Froissart Co. has purchased Metz Heavy Industries for ------- $10 million.

(A) approximation (B) approximated
(C) approximately (D) approximate

9. Customers' responses to the new product packaging have been ------- positive.

(A) consistency (B) consistent
(C) consistently (D) consistencies

10. Management was not ------- satisfied with the redesigned company logo.

(A) completing (B) completes
(C) completely (D) completion

11. Fragile items should be packaged -------.

(A) separating (B) separation
(C) separately (D) separates

12. Candidates for the office receptionist position must be able to relay messages -------.

(A) accuracy (B) accurate
(C) accurately (D) accurateness

13. A marketing campaign designed by EPPN Advertising will make your products more ------- to consumers.

(A) attracting (B) attraction
(C) attractive (D) attractively

14. Staff members are expected to work ------- to complete projects in a timely manner.

(A) collaboration (B) collaborative
(C) collaborate (D) collaboratively

15. Kamal Electronics is hoping to increase sales by ------- interacting with customers.

(A) actively
(B) activate
(C) active
(D) activation

16. ------- 1,000 customers recently subscribed to *Rover Auto Magazine*.

(A) Any
(B) Very
(C) Other
(D) Over

17. Regend University is well-known for its ------- diverse student body.

(A) remarks
(B) remarkably
(C) remark
(D) remarked

18. Attendees are asked to exit the room ------- at the end of the meeting.

(A) quiet
(B) quietly
(C) quietness
(D) quietest

19. Providing more public transportation options has proven ------- in reducing air pollution in the city.

(A) effective
(B) effected
(C) effectiveness
(D) effectively

20. -------, Mr. Ko has been working overtime in order to meet the project deadline.

(A) Late
(B) Latest
(C) Later
(D) Lately

기본 완성 훈련 다음은 앞서 풀어 본 연습문제의 문장들입니다. 부사를 찾아 괄호로 묶고, 해당 부사가 수식하는 대상에 밑줄을 그으세요.

1. The Goodread Bookstore on Riverside Street frequently hosts big discount events.

2. By hiring additional employees, productivity increased substantially at Woodtown Manufacturing.

3. One of the most widely respected jazz events is held in Seoul.

4. The new surgical laser is designed to significantly shorten patients' recovery times.

5. Customers' responses to the new product packaging have been consistently positive.

6. Fragile items should be packaged separately.

7. Over 1,000 customers recently subscribed to *Rover Auto Magazine*.

8. Regend University is well-known for its remarkably diverse student body.

9. Providing more public transportation options has proven effective in reducing air pollution in the city.

10. Lately, Mr. Ko has been working overtime in order to meet the project deadline.

전치사

전치사는 명사나 동명사, 명사절과 결합하여 명사 뒤에서 수식어 역할을 하거나, 동사나 문장 전체의 수식어 역할을 한다.

1. 전치사구 형태

▶ 전치사는 명사나 대명사, 동명사 또는 명사절을 목적어로 취하여 형용사구와 부사구를 만든다.

Due to security concerns, access to the server room is strictly limited. 전치사 + 명사 = 부사구
This document explains the process **of receiving a family discount.** 전치사 + 동명사 = 형용사구

해석　보안상의 염려 때문에, 서버실로의 접근은 엄격히 제한되어 있다. / 이 서류는 가족 할인을 받는 절차를 설명하고 있다.

2. 시간 전치사

시간	at + 시각, 구체적인 때	~에	**at** 4 P.M. 오후 4시에 ┃ **at** noon 정오에 ┃ **at** midnight 자정에 **at** the end of this fiscal year 이번 회계연도 말에
	on + 날짜, 요일, 특정한 날	~에	**on** May 10 5월 10일에 ┃ **on** Friday 금요일에 ┃ **on** Wednesday afternoon 수요일 오후에 ┃ **on** Christmas 크리스마스에
	in + 오전/오후, 월, 계절, 연도	~에	**in** the morning 아침에 ┃ **in** August 8월에 **in** summer 여름에 ┃ **in** 2015 2015년에
시점	from + 시점	~로부터	**from** May to August 5월부터 8월까지
	since + 과거 시점	~이후로	**since** last Friday 지난 금요일 이후로
	by + 완료시점	~까지	submit the report **by** Friday 보고서를 금요일까지 제출하다
	until + 계속되는 시점	~까지	be postponed **until** Friday 금요일까지 연기되다
	before / prior to + 시점	~전에	**before** his arrival 그의 도착 전에 3 hours **prior to** your arrival 당신의 도착 3시간 전에
	after / following + 시점	~후에	**after** 6 P.M. 오후 6시 후에 **following** a short test 짧은 테스트 후에
기간	during + 기간	~동안	**during** the conference 회의 동안 **during** the last three years 지난 3년 동안
	for + 숫자 기간	~동안	**for** three years 3년 동안 ┃ **for** the last three years 지난 3년 동안
	over + 기간	~동안	**over** the last three years 지난 3년 동안
	in + 기간	~동안/~후에	**in** the last three years 지난 3년 동안 **in** two weeks 2주 후에
	between A and B	A와 B사이에	**between** Monday **and** Friday 월요일과 금요일 사이에
	throughout + 기간	~내내	**throughout** the year 1년 내내
	within + 기간	~이내에	**within** 30 days 30일 이내에

3. 장소 전치사

장소	at + 구체적인 한 지점, 번지	~에	**at** the corner 모퉁이에 **at** the press conference 기자회견에서 **at** 55 Main Street Main 가 55번지에서
	on + 접촉면, 도로, 교통수단	~(위)에	**on** the table 탁자 위에 **on** Main Street Main 가에서 **on** the bus / train / plane 버스/기차/비행기에서
	in + 공간, 도시, 국가 / 대륙	~(안)에	**in** the lobby 로비에서 **in** Seoul 서울에 **in** Asia 아시아에
	within + 장소, 거리	~내에서	**within** walking distance 걸을 수 있는 거리 이내에
	across / throughout + 장소	~전체에	**across** the nation 전국적으로 throughout Europe 유럽 전역에
방향	to + 도착점	~로	be delivered **to** the front desk 프론트 데스크로 배달되다
	from + 출발점	~로부터, ~에서	relocate across the street **from** its former location 이전 위치에서 길 건너편으로 이전하다
	towards	~방향으로	trend **towards** earlier retirement 조기 퇴직을 향한 추세
	into	~(안)으로	expand **into** three more communities 세 개 지역으로 더 확장하다
	out of	~밖으로	**out of** town (출장 등으로) 도시 밖으로
	across from / opposite	~맞은 편에	opens its doors **across from** (= **opposite** the convention) center 컨벤션 센터 맞은 편에 문을 열다
	for	~를 향해, ~행	leave **for** ~를 향해 떠나다
	through	~를 통해	highway **through** town 도시를 통해 지나가는 고속도로
	along	~을 따라	**along** the street 도로를 따라
위치	above	~위쪽에	signs **above** the door 문 위쪽에 있는 표지판들
	over	~바로 위에	**over** the bridge 다리 바로 위에
	below	~아래쪽에 / 이하	**below** warehouse prices 창고 출하 가격 이하로
	under	~바로 밑에 ~중인, ~하에	**under** the desk 책상 아래에 **under** construction 공사 중인 **under** the new rules 새로운 규칙 하에서
	beside / next to / by	~옆에	**beside** the stand 연단 옆에 sit **next to** the aisle 통로 옆자리에 앉다
	near	~근처에	**near** the rear entrance 후문 근처에
	in front of	~앞에	**in front of** the building 빌딩 앞에
	behind	~뒤에	**behind** the building 빌딩 뒤에
	among + 복수 명사	~사이에 / 중에	**among** the guests 손님들 사이에
	between A and B	A와 B 사이에	**between** Maron Boulevard **and** Hoover Street Maron 가와 Hoover 가 사이

4. 기타 전치사

이유	due to / because of	~때문에	**due to** limited space 제한된 공간 때문에
양보	in spite of / despite	~에도 불구하고	**despite** the issue 그 문제에도 불구하고
주제	about / regarding / concerning	~에 관하여 / 관한	information **about** the program 프로그램에 관한 정보
추가	in addition to	~외에도	**in addition to** this benefits 이러한 혜택 외에도
	including	~를 포함하여	**including** client testimonial 고객 추천글을 포함하여
제외	except / excluding	~를 제외하고	**except** Sundays 일요일만 제외하고
조건	without	~없이, ~가 없다면	**without** permission 허가 없이는
	in case of / in the event of	~인 경우에는	**in case of** rain 비가 오는 경우에는
결과	as a result of	~의 결과로	**as a result of** the continuing training 지속적인 교육의 결과로
목적	for	~을 위해 / 위한	**for** your convenience 당신의 편의를 위해서
자격	as	~로서	**as** a lawyer 변호사로서
행위자	by	~에 의해	be presented **by** members 회원들에 의해 발표되다
방법	by	~함으로써, ~로	**by** e-mail 이메일로 **by** turning off the equipment 장비 전원을 끔으로써
	through	~을 통해	**through** the survey 설문조사를 통해서
동반 / 소지 / 수단	with	~와 함께, ~을 가지고	**with** the President 회장님과 함께
	along with	~와 함께	**along with** your application 당신의 신청서와 함께
예시	such as	~와 같은	facilities **such as** the gym 체육관과 같은 편의시설
	like / unlike	~와 같이 / ~와는 달리	respected instructors **like** Dylan Andersson Dylan Andersson과 같이 존경 받는 강사들
기타	instead of	~대신에	**instead of** participating 참가하는 대신에
	by ~ing	~함으로써(방법)	**by expanding** our operation 영업을 확장함으로써
	according to	~에 따르면	**according to** the agreement 계약서에 따르면
	in response to	~에 부응하여	**in response to** high demand 높은 수요에 부응하여
	regardless of	~와는 상관없이	**regardless of** how many guests attend 얼마나 많은 손님들이 참가하는지와는 상관없이

5. 전치사의 관용표현

자동사 + 전치사

comply with 준수하다

specialize in ~을 전문으로 하다

enroll in ~에 등록하다

rely on(upon) ~에 의존하다

contribute to ~에 기여/공헌하다

apply to ~에 해당되다

respond to ~에 응답하다

qualify for ~할 자격이 있다

register for ~에 등록하다

apply for ~에 지원/신청하다

deal with 다루다, 처리하다

participate in ~에 참가하다

result in ~의 결과를 낳다

depend on(upon) ~에 의존하다/달려있다

subscribe to ~에 가입하다, 구독하다

reply to ~에 응답하다

lead to ~로 이어지다, ~를 초래하다

account for ~을 설명하다

search for ~를 찾다, 검색하다

benefit from ~로부터 혜택을 얻다

명사 + 전치사

decrease in ~의 감소

rise in ~의 증가

access to ~의 이용(기회), 접근(권한)

subscription to ~의 구독

dedication to ~에 대한 전념

contribution to ~에 대한 공헌(기여)

questions about ~에 관한 질문

inquiry about ~에 관한 문의

problem with ~에 대한 문제

increase in ~의 증가

interest in ~에 대한 관심

objection to ~에 대한 반대

commitment to ~에 대한 전념

resolution to ~에 대한 해결책

demand for ~에 대한 수요

information about ~에 관한 정보

detail about ~에 관한 세부사항

compliance with ~의 준수

be동사 + 형용사 + 전치사

be accessible to ~에 가기 쉽다, ~을 이용하다

be familiar with ~를 잘 알다, ~에 익숙하다

be finished with ~을 끝내다

be concerned about ~에 대해 걱정하다

be responsible for ~에 책임이 있다

be aware of ~를 알다, 알고 있다

be dependent on(upon) ~에 의존하다/달려있다

be opposed to ~에 반대하다

be pleased with ~에 기뻐하다

be equipped with ~를 갖추고 있다

be interested in ~에 흥미가 있다

be eligible for ~할 자격이 있다

be based on ~에 기반하다, 근거를 두다

be reliant on(upon) ~에 의존하다

Q1 시점·기간

Please return defective products ------- seven days of the purchase date.

(A) within   (B) through   (C) after   (D) by

>> 출제 포인트 시점·기간을 나타내는 전치사를 구별해야 한다.

① 선택지 확인 | 빈칸에 들어갈 알맞은 전치사를 고른다.

② 빈칸 확인 | 기간(seven days)을 나타내는 표현 앞에 오는 전치사 자리 → 시점을 나타내는 전치사는 올 수 없다.
→ (C) after ✗ (D) by ✗

③ 정답 확인 | 결함이 있는 제품을 '주어진 기간 안에' 반품해 달라는 의미이므로 '기간 내내'를 의미하는 (B) through ✗
정답은 '기간 이내에'를 의미하는 (A) within ✓

정답 Please return / defective products / **(A) within** seven days of purchase date.
해석 반품해 주세요 / 결함 있는 제품은 / 구입한 날로부터 일주일 이내에

출제 포인트 ❶ 시점 vs. 기간을 나타내는 전치사
특정 시점과 함께 하는 전치사와 소요 기간과 함께 하는 기간 전치사를 구분한다.

Oil prices / have risen / **since** August 15. since: 시점
Oil prices / have risen / **for** eight months. for: 기간
해석   유가가 8월 15일 이후로 상승했다. / 유가가 8개월 간 상승했다.

출제 포인트 ❷ by vs. until

by	동작이 완료되는 시점	submit, finish, complete 등과 주로 출제
until	동작이 계속되는 시점	postpone, remain, stay, last, continue 등과 주로 출제

The report / should be submitted / **by** March 7. by: ~까지 완료
Ms. Kim / must finish / the project / **by** Wednesday.
해석   그 보고서는 3월 7일까지 제출되어야 한다. / Ms. Kim은 그 프로젝트를 수요일까지 끝내야만 한다.

We may need to postpone payments to some of our suppliers **until** next week. until: ~까지 계속
The ski season / will last / **until** early March.
해석   우리는 대금 지불을 다음 주까지 연기해야 할지도 모른다. / 스키 시즌은 3월 초까지 지속된다.

+ check .... 해설서 p.22

1. Please be sure to return all borrowed books to the library ------- next Monday.

(A) within   (B) onto   (C) before   (D) about

Q2 장소·방향

The tourists are scheduled to leave ------- Walvis Bay, where they will enjoy a boat trip to the bird sanctuary.

(A) into   (B) for   (C) between   (D) to

>> **출제 포인트 장소·방향을 나타내는 전치사를 문맥에 맞게 사용한다.**

❶ 선택지 확인 ┃ 빈칸에 들어갈 알맞은 전치사를 고른다.

❷ 빈칸 확인 ┃ 장소를 나타내는 표현 앞에 오는 전치사 자리이다.

❸ 정답 확인 ┃ 관광객들이 Walvis Bay를 '향해' 떠나기로 예정되어 있으므로 '어떤 장소를 향하여'라는 의미의 전치사가 필요하다. 정답은 (B) for ⊙

정답 The tourists / are scheduled / to leave **(B) for** Walvis Bay, / where they will enjoy a boat trip to the bird sanctuary.
해석 관광객들은 / 예정되어 있다 / Walvis Bay로 떠나기로 / 그곳에서 그들은 조류 보호구역으로 가는 보트 여행을 즐길 것이다.

출제 포인트 ❸ 장소를 나타내는 전치사

in은 넓은 장소와 건물 안, on은 표면 위, at은 구체적인 장소를 나타낸다.

Mr. Yang / lives / **in** Los Angeles. in: 넓은 장소
I / met / Mr. Yang / **in** the bank. in: 건물 안
Mr. Yang / lives / **at** 718 Oak Street, Los Angeles. at: 정확한 주소
Mr. Yang / placed / the folder / **on** his desk. on: 표면 위

해석   Mr. Yang은 로스앤젤레스에서 산다. / 나는 Mr. Yang을 은행 안에서 만났다.
  Mr. Yang은 로스앤젤레스, Oak 가 718번지에 산다. / Mr. Yang은 그의 책상 위에 폴더를 두었다.

출제 포인트 ❹ 방향을 나타내는 전치사

The company / sent / Ms. Sato / **to** the New York branch. to: ~로(도착점)
The train / leaves / **for** London. for: ~를 향하여
Mr. Wu / was walking / **toward** us. toward: ~ 방향으로

해석   그 회사는 Ms. Sato를 뉴욕 지사로 보냈다. / 그 열차는 런던 행이다.
  Mr. Wu가 우리 쪽으로 걸어오고 있었다.

+ check

2. This Saturday is the official opening of our bank's latest branch located ------- the town's financial district.

(A) to   (B) below   (C) in   (D) until

Q3 구전치사

The flight has been delayed ------- unexpected mechanical problems.

(A) considering   (B) because of   (C) since   (D) in addition to

>> **출제 포인트 두 단어 이상으로 이루어진 구전치사를 알아둔다.**

❶ 선택지 확인 | 빈칸에 들어갈 알맞은 전치사를 고른다.

❷ 빈칸 확인 | 명사구(unexpected mechanical problems) 앞의 전치사 자리이다.

❸ 정답 확인 | 문맥상 '비행기가 돌발적인 기계 결함 때문에 지연되고 있다'라는 의미가 되어야 하므로 이유를 나타내는 전치사가 와야 한다. 정답은 (B) because of ◉ (C) since는 접속사로 쓰일 때는 '(특정 시점) 이후로'와 '~때문에'의 두 가지 의미 모두 가능하지만, 전치사로 쓰일 때는 이유를 나타내는 '~때문에'의 의미로 쓰일 수 없다는 점에 유의한다.

정답 The flight / has been delayed / **(B) because of** unexpected mechanical problems.

해석 그 비행기는 / 지연되고 있다 / 돌발적인 기계 결함 때문에

출제 포인트 ❺ 두 단어 이상의 구전치사

in front of ~의 앞에	according to ~에 따르면
except for ~을 제외하고	instead of ~대신에
such as ~와 같은	prior to / ahead of ~보다 앞서, ~전에
as a result of ~의 결과로	regardless of ~와는 상관없이
in case of / the event of ~의 경우에는	on behalf of ~을 대신/대표해서
because of / due to ~때문에	in terms of ~의 관점에서
in response to ~에 부응하여	pertaining to ~에 관하여

Prior to her employment at Flazi Consulting, / Ms. Han / was / a TV correspondent.

해석 Flazi 컨설팅에서 근무하기 전에, Ms. Han은 TV 통신원이었다.

+ check

3. ------- your reception party, one of our caterers will call you to confirm the number of guests and menu choices.

     (A) When   (B) As long as   (C) Prior to   (D) Together with

Q4 전치사의 관용 표현

Of the eight candidates, Kathy Swanson is the most eligible person ------- the job.

(A) on　　　　　　(B) to　　　　　　(C) with　　　　　　(D) for

>> 출제 포인트 전치사의 관용 표현을 알아둔다. (91 페이지 참조)

1 선택지 확인 | 빈칸에 들어갈 알맞은 전치사를 고른다.

2 빈칸 확인 | 명사구 앞의 전치사 자리이다.

3 정답 확인 | 문맥상 'Kathy Swanson이 그 업무에 가장 적격인 사람이다'라는 의미가 되어야 하므로 「be eligible for: ~에 자격이 있다」 구문을 써야 한다. 정답은 (D) for ⊙

정답 Of the eight candidates, / Kathy Swanson / is the most eligible person / **(D) for** the job.
해석 여덟 명의 후보자들 중에서 / Kathy Swanson이 / 가장 적격인 사람이다 / 그 업무에

출제 포인트 ⑥ 「동사 + 전치사」

Although they were newly hired, / Mr. Shin and Ms. Lee / are good / at **dealing with** customer inquiries.
Our Web site / **provides** / you / **with** information / regarding global warming and its effects.

해석 비록 Mr. Shin과 Ms. Lee는 신입사원이었지만 고객 문의를 처리하는 데 능숙하다. / 우리의 웹사이트는 지구 온난화와 그 영향에 대한 정보를 제공한다.
풀이 「dealing with: ~를 처리하다」「provides A with B: A에게 B를 제공하다」

출제 포인트 ⑦ 「명사 + 전치사」

A lot of people / are without **access** / **to** safe drinking water.
There / has been a dramatic **increase** / **in** the number of new jobs created.

해석 수많은 사람들이 안전한 식수를 이용하지 못하고 있다. / 새로 생기는 일자리의 수가 급격하게 증가했다.

출제 포인트 ⑧ 「형용사 + 전치사」

The staff / are fully **aware** / **of** the needs of the industry.
Employees / are rated / **based on** their performance.

해석 그 직원들은 그 산업의 요구 사항에 대해 충분히 알고 있다. / 직원들은 그들의 성과에 기반하여 평가를 받는다.

⊕ check

4. Since small retailers can ------- from cooperating with one another, they form local business associations.

(A) benefit　　　　　　(B) serve　　　　　　(C) assist　　　　　　(D) help

1. The Spicy Leaf Restaurant will be closed on Monday, July 10, ------- a private event.

(A) from   (B) for
(C) across   (D) since

2. Applications for Panjala Business School are accepted ------- the year.

(A) throughout   (B) across
(C) when   (D) in

3. Starzie Chemicals purchased new lab equipment ------- the extra funds.

(A) over   (B) at
(C) on   (D) with

4. Commuters can help conserve energy ------- taking public transportation.

(A) to   (B) into
(C) by   (D) for

5. Because it is cold and has been snowing heavily, the ski season will last ------- the end of March.

(A) until   (B) for
(C) by   (D) in

6. Elkor Spa resort is conveniently located ------- walking distance of major tourist attractions.

(A) within   (B) furthermore
(C) finally   (D) until

7. Patrons can get help from librarians ------- the library's online help desk.

(A) through   (B) in case of
(C) among   (D) such as

8. Please read the instructions in the manual ------- assembling the couch.

(A) prior to   (B) outside of
(C) according to   (D) in front of

9. The conference room is located ------- the entrance of the building.

(A) from   (B) next
(C) near   (D) for

10. Mr. Jang has worked at Sognet Industries ------- more than eight years.

(A) for   (B) from
(C) after   (D) near

11. The estimate for your office renovation will be provided ------- two working days.

(A) when   (B) within
(C) by   (D) since

12. All tenants must follow the rules included ------- the lease agreement.

(A) near   (B) over
(C) in   (D) next

13. H&PCH Architects will not make changes to the floor plan ------- the client's prior approval.

(A) about   (B) except
(C) toward   (D) without

14. Before he came to Busan, Mr. Kang had worked ------- a bank manager.

(A) on   (B) in
(C) to   (D) as

15. The tour may differ from the description in the brochure depending ------- the weather conditions.

(A) in (B) upon
(C) there (D) with

16. Please note that e-mails received ------- 10 P.M. will be checked the following morning.

(A) such as (B) between
(C) during (D) after

17. Employees who are responsible ------- cleaning the staff lounge should check the area three times a day.

(A) of (B) on
(C) for (D) in

18. Please save all important files ------- installing the new security update.

(A) before (B) about
(C) of (D) into

19. ------- the past three months, the number of students at Pullmans Academy has increased dramatically.

(A) Near (B) Above
(C) Behind (D) During

20. Due to broken water pipes, Blues Restaurant will be closed ------- further notice.

(A) except (B) through
(C) around (D) until

기본 완성 훈련 다음은 앞서 풀어 본 연습문제의 문장들입니다. 전치사구를 찾아 괄호로 묶고, 해당 전치사에 밑줄을 그으세요.

1. Elkor Spa Resort is conveniently located within walking distance of major tourist attractions.

2. Patrons can get help from librarians through the library's online help desk.

3. Please read the instructions in the manual prior to assembling the couch.

4. The conference room is located near the entrance of the building.

5. The estimate for your office renovation will be provided within two working days.

6. H&PCH Architects will not make changes to the floor plan without the client's prior approval.

7. Before he came to Busan, Mr. Kang had worked as a bank manager.

8. The tour may differ from the description in the brochure depending upon the weather conditions.

9. Please note that e-mails received after 10 P.M. will be checked the following morning.

10. During the past three months, the number of students at Pullmans Academy has increased dramatically.

REVIEW TEST 02

해설서 p.24

1. Jorcom Advertising aims to hire salespeople with ------- skills.

(A) organizational (B) organize
(C) organizations (D) organizes

2. In most cases, you can recover ------- your files from your computer with the software.

(A) as (B) all
(C) every (D) next

3. Dreambird Furniture offers a money-back guarantee on all -------.

(A) purchase (B) purchaser
(C) purchasers (D) purchases

4. Sales at the Tokyo branch have been ------- higher than those at the Beijing branch.

(A) notice (B) noticing
(C) noticeably (D) notices

5. Mr. Oh will send the agenda ------- the staff meeting tomorrow.

(A) by (B) into
(C) over (D) for

6. El Grande Restaurant uses only ------- ingredients for all its dishes.

(A) superiors (B) superior
(C) superiority (D) superiorities

7. The environmentally-friendly features make the product -------.

(A) value (B) values
(C) valuable (D) valuably

8. Frequent mailing-list updates have ------- contributed to targeting the markets.

(A) succeeded (B) succeed
(C) successful (D) successfully

9. Jassom Ltd. welcomes your ------- concerning new products.

(A) suggests (B) suggest
(C) suggested (D) suggestions

10. As a result of the collaboration of ------- departments, the meeting went smoothly.

(A) various (B) variety
(C) variable (D) variation

11. The air conditioner may be returned ------- six months of the purchase date free of charge.

(A) by (B) until
(C) within (D) on

12. The company's new Web site will make product information more ------- accessible to consumers.

(A) ready (B) readily
(C) readied (D) readier

13. ------- the lease agreement, the tenant must pay a fine if the rent is late.

(A) Except for (B) According to
(C) Such as (D) Instead of

14. As a result of increasing -------, the company is offering its employees incentives.

(A) producer (B) produces
(C) productive (D) productivity

15. Whether the issues are about product defects, damaged items or missing merchandise, ------- are forwarded to Ms. Cherry.

(A) all (B) another
(C) each (D) one

16. Passengers on board can obtain the customs forms ------- flight attendants.
    (A) instead of   (B) following
    (C) from   (D) within

17. According to the minutes from last month's meeting, all of the members were in -------.
    (A) attendant   (B) attendance
    (C) attended   (D) attending

18. Analysts believe that fuel ------- will rise next year.
    (A) priced   (B) prices
    (C) to price   (D) price

19. Workers at the factory should wear hearing ------- devices.
    (A) protect   (B) protection
    (C) protected   (D) protects

20. Ms. Lee will interview the top candidates for the marketing position -------.
    (A) she   (B) her
    (C) hers   (D) herself

21. ------- who want to attend the seminar should contact Mr. Chang.
    (A) Those   (B) Anyone
    (C) Other   (D) Themselves

22. Ms. Smythe had to work overtime to finish the design as ------- designer was away on vacation.
    (A) the other   (B) others
    (C) the others   (D) other

23. Many colleagues stay in touch with ------- after they've left their companies.
    (A) one another   (B) another
    (C) other   (D) each

24. ------- students are expected to attend Professor Kumar's history lecture.
    (A) Another   (B) Much
    (C) Every   (D) Many

25. Several employees found the noise from the road repairs ------- to their work.
    (A) disruptive   (B) disrupt
    (C) disruptions   (D) disruptively

26. Customer service associates should ------- respond to all complaints and inquiries.
    (A) promptness   (B) prompt
    (C) promptly   (D) prompting

27. Companies are becoming ------- aware of the importance of workplace equality.
    (A) increasing   (B) increasingly
    (C) increased   (D) increase

28. All the office computers are now working ------- with the updated software.
    (A) correcting   (B) correction
    (C) corrects   (D) correctly

29. Additional details ------- the workshop will be confirmed tomorrow.
    (A) concerning   (B) across
    (C) in spite of   (D) through

30. The Garrison Law Center has served the local community for ------- two decades.
    (A) between   (B) over
    (C) from   (D) during

접속사(부사절·등위·상관접속사)

주어와 동사를 갖춘 문장을 절(clause)이라고 하며, 절이 문장에서 명사, 형용사, 부사 역할을 할 때를 종속절이라고 하고 이러한 종속절을 포함하는 절을 주절이라고 한다. 두 개 이상의 절이 and, but, or, so 등으로 대등하게 연결되는 절은 대등절이라고 한다.

 기본 개념 이해하기

1. 부사절과 부사절 접속사

▶ 부사절은 「부사절 접속사 + 주어 + 동사」 형태로 주절에 시간, 조건, 이유 등의 부가 정보를 덧붙인다. 부사절은 주절의 앞이나 뒤에 오며, 부사절이 주절 앞에 나오면 그 뒤에 콤마(,)를 찍어 주절과 구별해 준다.

시간	when / as ~할 때 before ~전에 until ~까지 as soon as / once ~하자마자	while ~하는 동안에 after ~후에 since ~이후로 by the time ~할 때(쯤)
조건	if / provided (that) / assuming (that) ~라면 as long as ~하기만 한다면 once 일단 ~하면	unless ~가 아니라면 in case (that) / in the event (that) ~인 경우에는
이유	because / as / since ~때문에	now that ~때문에
양보	though / although / even though / even if / while 비록 ~이긴 하지만	
대조	whereas / while ~인 반면에, ~지만	
목적	so (that) / in order that ~할 수 있도록 주의! 「in order to + 동사원형」 ~할 수 있도록	
결과	「so + 형용사/부사 + that」 너무 ~해서 ~하다	

Please / speak / clearly / **when** you explain a problem. 시간

If you have any questions, / feel free / to contact us. 조건

Now that the Copper Tunnels have been completed, / many commuters' driving times / have been cut / in half. 원인 [now that: ~이니까, ~인 이상]

Even though the budget was not sufficient, / the project / was successfully completed. 양보

해석　문제를 설명할 때는 분명하게 말하세요. / 질문이 있으면 주저 없이 우리에게 문의해 주세요.
　　　Copper 터널이 완공되었으므로 많은 통근자들의 운전 시간이 반으로 줄었다. / 예산이 불충하긴 했지만, 그 프로젝트는 성공적으로 수행되었다.

2. 접속부사

▶ 접속부사는 두 문장을 의미상 연결해 주지만 접속사는 아니므로, 두 문장을 연결할 때는 접속사나 세미콜론(;) 뒤에 온다.

접속부사의 위치	주어 + 동사~. **접속부사**, 주어 + 동사 ~
	주어 + 동사~; **접속부사**, 주어 + 동사 ~
	주어 + 동사 ~ 접속사 and + **접속부사**, 주어 + 동사 ~

The company / is trying / to boost sales. **As a result**, it / plans / to advertise more.
= The company / is trying / to boost sales; *as a result*, it / plans / to advertise more.

해석　그 회사는 판매량을 늘리고자 한다. 그 결과, 그 회사는 광고를 더 할 계획이다.

3. 등위접속사

▶ 등위접속사는 단어와 단어, 구와 구, 절과 절을 대등하게 연결해 준다. so는 문장만 연결한다.

등위접속사	**and** 그리고	**but(=yet)** 그러나	**or** 또는	**so** 그래서

He / reviewed / my proposal **and** agreed / to discuss it at the meeting. 동사구 and 동사구
The new model / is costly **but** energy-efficient. 형용사 but 형용사
Mr. Brown **or** Mr. Robinson / should be responsible for it. 주어 or 주어
She / worked / hard, **so** she / was selected / as the employee of the month. 절 so 절

해석　그는 내 제안서를 검토했고, 그것을 회의에서 논의하는 것에 동의했다. / 새로운 모델은 비싸지만 에너지 효율이 높다.
　　　Mr. Brown이나 Mr. Robinson이 그것을 책임져야 한다. / 그녀는 열심히 일했다. 그래서 그녀는 이달의 직원으로 선정되었다.

4. 상관접속사

▶ 상관접속사는 등위접속사 중에서 반드시 짝으로 사용되는 접속사를 말한다.

상관접속사	both A and B	A와 B 둘 다	not A but B	A가 아니라 B인
	not only A but also B	A뿐만 아니라 B도	either A or B	A 또는 B 둘 중에 하나
	A as well as B	B뿐만 아니라 A도	neither A nor B	A도 B도 둘 다 아닌

Both Jack **and** Sally / help / with the final quarterly reports. 주어 연결
Not only you **but also** David / is responsible for the presentation. 주어 연결
Neither the manager **nor** the staff / has / access to the information. 주어 연결
Successful candidates / will be based / in **either** New York **or** Boston. 부사구 연결

해석　Jack과 Sally 둘 다 마지막 분기 보고서 작성을 돕는다. / 당신뿐 아니라 David도 그 발표에 책임이 있다.
　　　관리자나 직원들 모두 그 정보를 열람할 수 없다. / 최종 합격자들은 뉴욕이나 보스턴 둘 중 한 곳으로 발령이 날 것이다.

Q1 문맥에 맞는 부사절 접속사 선택

The CEO finally approved the budget proposal ------- it had been revised several times.

(A) during   (B) then   (C) after   (D) although

>> **출제 포인트** **문맥에 어울리는 부사절 접속사를 선택한다.**

① **선택지 확인** | 빈칸에 들어갈 알맞은 접속사를 고른다.

② **빈칸 확인** | 빈칸을 기준으로 앞과 뒤에 모두 절이 연결되어 있으므로 접속사 자리 → 전치사 (A) during (동안에) ❌
부사 (B) then (그리고 나서) ❌

③ **정답 확인** | 문맥상 '제안서가 여러 번 수정된 후에 CEO가 마침내 그것을 승인했다'는 의미가 자연스러우므로 정답은 접속사 (C) after (~이후에) ⊙

정답 The CEO / finally / approved / the budget proposal / **(C) after** it had been revised several times.

해석 CEO가 / 마침내 / 승인했다 / 그 예산안을 / 그것이 여러 번 수정된 후에

출제 포인트 ❶ 부사절 접속사

Employees can take a day off / **when** they are sick. 시간
= **When** employees are sick, / they can take a day off.

해석   직원들은 아플 때 하루 쉴 수 있다.

You can ask me / **if** you cannot solve the problem. 조건
= **If** you cannot solve the problem, you can ask me.

해석   그 문제를 풀지 못한다면 제게 물어보세요.

Ms. Ha's English has not improved / **although** she has lived in Canada for several years. 양보
= **Although** she has lived in Canada for several years, Ms. Ha's English has not improved.

해석   Ms. Ha가 캐나다에서 수년간 살았지만 그녀의 영어는 나아지지 않았다.

Mr. Lee is a technical expert / **because** he majored in computer science. 이유
= **Because** he majored in computer science, / Mr. Lee is a technical expert.

해석   Mr. Lee는 컴퓨터 공학을 전공했기 때문에 기술 전문가이다.

⊕ check   해설서 p.27

1. The board of directors will not approve the merger with Skycross Airliners ------- their CEO makes the contract terms satisfactory.

(A) whereas   (B) because   (C) unless   (D) when

Q2 접속사 vs 전치사

------- Mr. Kang arrived late, he was able to participate in the meeting.
(A) Even though　　(B) Despite　　(C) Because　　(D) In case of

>> **출제 포인트** 빈칸 뒤의 구조를 보고, 접속사 자리인지 전치사 자리인지 파악한다.

1 선택지 확인 | 빈칸에 들어갈 알맞은 접속사 또는 전치사를 고른다.

2 빈칸 확인 | 빈칸을 기준으로 모두 절이 연결되어 있으므로 접속사 자리 → 전치사 (B) Despite (~에도 불구하고), (D) In case of (~인 경우에 대비하여) ✘

3 정답 확인 | 문맥상 '비록 Mr. Kang이 늦게 도착했지만, 회의에 참가할 수 있었다'는 의미가 자연스러우므로 정답은 접속사 (A) Even though (비록~이긴 하지만) ◎

정답 (A) Even though Mr. Kang arrived late, / he / was able to participate / in the meeting.

해석 비록 Mr. Kang이 늦게 도착하긴 했지만, / 그는 / 참가할 수 있었다 / 회의에

출제 포인트 ❷ 접속사 뒤에는 절이 오고, 전치사 뒤에는 명사가 온다.

다음은 뜻이 비슷하여 혼동되는 접속사, 전치사, 부사들이다. 각 품사에 따른 의미적 차이를 유의하여 암기해두도록 하자.

	접속사	전치사	부사
시간	while ~하는 동안에 before ~전에	during ~동안 before / prior to ~전에	meanwhile 그러는 동안에 in advance 미리
조건	unless ~하지 않는다면	without ~없이	otherwise 그렇지 않으면
이유	because / as / since ~때문에	due to / because of ~때문에	therefore 그러므로
양보	though / although even though ~이긴 하지만	despite / in spite of ~에도 불구하고	nevertheless 그럼에도 불구하고 however 그러나

☑ **문법 포인트** 접속사와 전치사로 둘 다 쓰이는 단어들

	접속사	전치사		접속사	전치사
until	~까지	~까지	since	~이후로, ~때문에	~이후로
after	~후에	~후에	as	~할 때, ~때문에	~로써
before	~전에	~전에			

Janet studied / **until** the library closed at 10 P.M. 접속사 + 절
Janet studied / **until** 10 P.M. 전치사 + 명사

해석 Janet은 밤 10시에 도서관이 문 닫을 때까지 공부했다. / Janet은 밤 10시까지 공부했다.

⊕ check

2. Shoppers will receive a coupon ------- they make a new purchase.
　　(A) when　　　　(B) from　　　　(C) above　　　　(D) even

Q3 접속사 vs. 접속부사

------- the new lockers have been installed, gym members can now bring bigger bags to the fitness center.

(A) Nevertheless   (B) Because   (C) Due to   (D) Therefore

>> **출제 포인트 접속부사는 접속사 자리에 들어갈 수 없다.**

① 선택지 확인 | 빈칸에 들어갈 알맞은 접속사, 전치사, 또는 접속부사를 고른다.

② 빈칸 확인 | 빈칸을 기준으로 모두 절이 연결되어 있으므로 접속사 자리 → 전치사 (C) Due to (~때문에) ❌ 접속부사 (A) Nevertheless (~에도 불구하고), (D) Therefore (그러므로) ❌

③ 정답 확인 | 해석 없이도 답이 될 수 없는 보기를 모두 소거하고 남은 (B) Because ⭕

정답 **(B) Because** the new lockers have been installed, / gym members / can now bring / bigger bags / to the fitness center.

해석 사물함이 새로 설치되었기 때문에 / 체육관 회원들은 / 이제 가져올 수 있다 / 더 큰 가방들을 / 체육관에

출제 포인트 ❸ 접속사 vs. 접속부사

Although she was sick, Ms. Wilson went to work. 접속사
= Ms. Wilson went to work **although** she was sick. 접속사
Ms. Wilson was sick, **but** she went to work. 접속사

Ms. Wilson was sick. **However,** she went to work. 접속부사
= Ms. Wilson was sick; **however,** she went to work. 세미콜론 + 접속부사
Ms. Wilson was sick, **however** she went to work. ❌ 접속부사는 접속사처럼 두 문장을 연결하지 못한다.

해석 Ms. Wilson은 아팠지만 출근했다.

✓ 문법 포인트 접속부사의 종류

양보	however 그러나 nevertheless 그럼에도 불구하고
결과	therefore / thus 그러므로 as a result 그 결과
부가	in addition / moreover / furthermore / besides 게다가
추가 설명	indeed 정말로, 확실히 in fact 사실상
대조	contrarily / in contrast 그에 반해서 on the other hand 반면에 on the contrary 그와는 반대로
순서	then 그리고 나서 thereafter / afterwards 그 후에
가정	then 그러면 otherwise 그렇지 않으면
화제 전환	meanwhile 그러는 동안에

+ check

3. Our department meeting this week will be postponed ------- some of the employees will be away for a conference.

(A) whether   (B) because   (C) therefore   (D) in addition

Q4 상관접속사

Commuters are encouraged to travel by ------- bus or train to reduce traffic congestion.

(A) neither   (B) both   (C) nor   (D) either

>> **출제 포인트 상관접속사는 항상 짝을 이룬다.**

1 선택지 확인 | 빈칸에 들어갈 알맞은 상관접속사를 고른다.

2 빈칸 확인 | 전치사 by의 목적어를 연결하는 상관접속사의 자리 → 뒤에 나오는 or와 짝을 맞춰야 한다.
→ (A) neither (A nor B) ✖ (B) both (A and B) ✖

3 정답 확인 | 문맥상 '자전거 또는 열차 둘 중의 하나'라는 의미가 되어야 한다. 정답은 (D) either (A or B) ⭕

정답 Commuters are encouraged / to travel by **(D) either** bus or train / to reduce traffic congestion.
해석 통근자들에게 권장된다 / 버스나 기차로 다니도록 / 교통 체증을 감소시키기 위해

출제 포인트 ④ 등위접속사나 상관접속사는 문법적 역할(주어, 목적어 등)이나 형태(명사, 형용사, 구, 절 등)가 같은 의미 단위를 연결한다.

Most people attended the party, / **but** I stayed at home. 등위접속사: 문장과 문장을 대등하게 연결

I was sick yesterday, / **so** I was not at work. 등위접속사: 문장과 문장을 대등하게 연결

~~And~~ Mr. Clarke became the president of the company. ✖ 등위접속사는 문두에 올 수 없다.

해석 대부분의 사람들은 파티에 참석했지만 나는 집에 머물렀다. / 나는 어제 아팠다 그래서 나는 직장에 결근을 했다.
그래서 Mr. Clarke는 그 회사의 최고 경영자가 되었다.

Both Sue **and** Kate / are my coworkers. 상관접속사: 명사와 명사 연결

James / is **not only** talented **but also** hardworking. 상관접속사: 형용사와 형용사 연결

This video / is **not only** interesting **but also** instructive. 상관접속사: 주격 보어와 주격 보어 연결

This program / can keep / people / healthy **and** happy. 상관접속사: 목적격 보어와 목적격 보어 연결

해석 Sue와 Kate 둘 다 내 동료이다. / James는 재능이 있을 뿐만 아니라 성실하다. / 그 비디오는 흥미로울 뿐 아니라 교훈적이다.
이 프로그램은 사람들을 건강하고 행복하게 유지시킬 수 있다.

∙ check

4. Mr. Watts suggests that assistant managers participate in ------- the training session in June and the workshop in July.

(A) both   (B) nor   (C) so   (D) some

Practice

해설서 p.27

1. Halmont is a popular tourist destination, ------- welcomes foreign investment.

(A) despite
(B) due to
(C) and
(D) although

2. ------- free delivery, the company offers discounts on large orders.

(A) Furthermore
(B) Due to
(C) Yet
(D) In addition to

3. ------- joining our company, Ms. Patel worked for a competing firm.

(A) As
(B) Prior to
(C) As long as
(D) When

4. The cafeteria will be closed ------- it undergoes renovations.

(A) while
(B) during
(C) against
(D) near

5. ------- employees were only required to work until 6, many often stayed later.

(A) In spite of
(B) So as to
(C) Regarding
(D) Even though

6. The internet helps companies connect with customers ------- make new business contacts.

(A) as well as
(B) both
(C) either
(D) not only

7. The recycling policy will be approved ------- it can decrease expenses.

(A) on
(B) meanwhile
(C) as if
(D) because

8. Employees may join the workshop ------- they sign up in advance.

(A) despite
(B) so as to
(C) as though
(D) as long as

9. The new store is ------- popular that it had to hire additional staff.

(A) so
(B) very
(C) truly
(D) such

10. The heating system will be upgraded ------- its poor energy efficiency.

(A) due to
(B) however
(C) since
(D) because

11. The budget was changed ------- produce two television advertisements.

(A) when
(B) in order to
(C) due to
(D) in addition

12. We will not disclose our customers' information ------- their consent.

(A) although
(B) unless
(C) when
(D) without

13. Contest winners can choose to receive ------- a store gift certificate or cash.

(A) either
(B) taken
(C) both
(D) addition

14. Staff will not be eligible for a bonus ------- they meet or exceed their sales quotas.

(A) thus
(B) unless
(C) besides
(D) despite

15. ------- RZAI, Inc. has done so well in Los Angeles, it will open a branch in Seoul.

(A) Unless   (B) Since
(C) Therefore   (D) Rather

16. ------- the success of her novel, Kylie Chung has now written a film script.

(A) Because   (B) When
(C) Following   (D) Already

17. The amount charged for the repair was inaccurate, ------- we have attached a new invoice.

(A) and   (B) nor
(C) or   (D) yet

18. This luggage brand is known for being ------- lightweight and durable.

(A) both   (B) either
(C) neither   (D) as well as

19. The client database system was updated ------- employees could find information more quickly.

(A) because of   (B) whereas
(C) so that   (D) in spite of

20. All employees are required to attend next week's safety training session ------- they participated in it last year.

(A) between   (B) despite
(C) even if   (D) during

기본 완성 훈련 다음은 앞서 풀어 본 연습문제의 문장들입니다. 부사구 또는 부사절을 찾아 밑줄을 긋고, 부사절 접속사에 ○를 치세요.

1. In addition to free delivery, the company offers discounts on large orders.

2. Prior to joining our company, Ms. Patel worked for a competing firm.

3. The internet helps companies connect with customers as well as make new business contacts.

4. Employees may join the workshop as long as they sign up in advance.

5. The new store is so popular that it had to hire additional staff.

6. The heating system will be upgraded due to its poor energy efficiency.

7. We will not disclose our customers' information without their consent.

8. Staff will not be eligible for a bonus unless they meet or exceed their sales quotas.

9. Since RZAI, Inc. has done so well in Los Angeles, it will open a branch in Seoul.

10. The client database system was updated so that employees could find information more quickly.

명사절 접속사

문장에서 주어, 목적어, 보어 역할을 하는 절을 명사절이라고 한다. 명사절은 접속사 that, what, if, whether, 의문사, 복합관계대명사가 이끈다.

기본 개념 이해하기

1. 명사절

▶ 명사절은 「명사절 접속사 + 주어 + 동사」 형태로 문장의 주어, 목적어, 보어 역할을 한다.

Whether Mr. Cho has good management skills / is not known. 주어 역할

We / do not know / **if** Ms. Kim will buy that house. 목적어 역할

The customer's complaint / is / **that** the computers are too slow. 보어 역할

해석　Mr. Cho가 훌륭한 관리 기량을 갖추고 있는지는 알려지지 않았다. / 우리는 Ms. Kim 부부가 그 집을 살 것인지 알지 못한다.
그 고객의 불만은 컴퓨터들이 너무 느리다는 것이다.

2. 명사절 접속사 that

▶ 주어, 목적어, 보어 역할을 한다. 목적어로 쓰이는 경우, that을 생략하기도 한다. 단, 전치사의 목적어로는 쓰이지 않는다.

▶ news, fact, idea 등의 명사 뒤에 와서 그 내용을 나타내는 동격절로 쓰인다.

That the CEO approved the plan / was surprising. 주어

= **It** / was surprising / **that** the CEO approved the plan. 가주어 It ~ that

Management / announced / **(that)** the CEO approved the plan. 목적어 (that 생략 가능)

The surprising news / is / **that** the CEO approved the plan. 보어

I / believe in / **the idea** / **that** 10,000 hours of practice makes an expert. the idea = that

They / talked / **about that** the CEO approved the plan. ✕ 전치사의 목적어로 불가

해석　최고경영자가 그 계획을 승인했다는 것이 놀라웠다. / 경영진은 최고경영자가 그 계획을 승인했다는 것을 공지했다.
놀라운 소식은 최고경영자가 그 계획을 승인했다는 것이다. / 나는 일만 시간 동안의 훈련이 전문가를 만든다는 생각을 믿는다.

3. 명사절 접속사 whether ~ (or not)

▶ '~인지 아닌지'라는 의미이다. whether 명사절은 주어, 목적어, 보어 역할을 하지만, 같은 의미의 if 명사절은 목적어로만 쓰인다. whether이나 if절 끝에는 or not을 쓸 수 있다. 이 때, or not은 생략 가능하다.

▶ whether 뒤의 절을 축약하여 「whether + to부정사」 형태로도 자주 출제된다.

Whether the storm will hit **(or not)** / is unclear. 주어 역할

We / do not know / **whether[if]** the plane will take off **(or not)**. 목적어 역할

The question / is / **whether** we have enough time **(or not)**. 보어 역할

Ms. Lee / has not decided / **whether to accept** the position **(or not)**. whether + to부정사

해석　폭우가 몰아칠지(안 칠지) 확실하지 않다. / 우리는 비행기가 이륙할지(안 할지) 모르겠다.
문제는 우리가 충분한 시간이 있는지의 여부다. / Ms. Lee는 그 자리를 수락할지(안 할지) 결정하지 못했다.

4. 명사절을 이끄는 의문사

▶ 의문문이 다른 문장의 주어, 목적어, 보어, 전치사의 목적어 등으로 포함되면, 「의문사 + 주어 + (조)동사」가 된다.

When does / the local job center / **open**? 의문사 + 조동사 + 주어 + 동사

⋯▶ They / have not noticed / **when** the local job center **opens**. 동사 + 목적어(의문사 + 주어 + 동사)

해석　지역 직업 센터가 언제 문을 여나요? → 그들은 지역 직업 센터가 언제 문을 여는지 알아채지 못했다.

5. 관계대명사 what과 복합관계대명사

▶ **what**: '~것'이라는 의미로 다른 관계대명사와 달리 명사절을 이끌어 문장에서 주어, 목적어, 보어로 쓰인다.

▶ **복합관계대명사**: 「관계대명사 + ever」의 형태이고, '~든지'의 의미로 명사절을 이끈다.

what(= the thing that / which) ~것	**whatever**(= anything that) ~하는 것은 무엇이든지
whoever(= anyone who) ~하는 사람은 누구든지	**whichever**(= any one of the things that) ~하는 것(사람)은 어느 것(사람)이든지

What Ms. Moore said / is / true. 주어

Whoever gives the correct answer first / will get / a free gift. 주어

You / can have / **whichever** you like. 목적어

Whatever has a beginning / also has / an end. 주어

해석　Ms. Moore이 말한 것은 사실이다. / 누구든지 처음으로 정답을 맞히는 사람은 사은품을 받을 것이다.
당신이 좋아하는 것은 어느 것이든 가지세요. / 시작이 있는 것은 무엇이든지 끝이 있다.

핵심 문제 유형

Q1 명사절 접속사 자리

Economists predict ------- the merger of the two companies will be completed in March.

(A) that　　　　(B) whether　　　　(C) because　　　　(D) it

>> **출제 포인트 명사절을 이끄는 접속사가 무엇인지를 묻는다.**

1 선택지 확인 | 빈칸에 들어갈 알맞은 접속사나 대명사를 고른다.

2 빈칸 확인 | 동사 뒤에 오는 목적어 자리이다. 빈칸 뒤에 완전한 문장이 이어지고 있다. → 명사절을 이끄는 접속사가 필요하다. 부사절 접속사 (C) because ❌ 대명사 (D) it ❌

3 정답 확인 | 「predict + 접속사 + 절: ~하는 것을 예상하다」→ 어떤 사실을 전달하는 명사절 접속사가 필요하다. → 문맥상 '~인지 아닌지'라는 의미의 접속사 (B) whether ❌ 정답은 (A) that ⭕

정답 Economists / predict / **(A) that** the merger of the two companies will be completed in March.

해석 경제학자들은 / 예상한다 / 두 회사의 합병이 3월에 마무리될 것으로

출제 포인트 ❶ 동사 + that절

announce (that) ~을 발표하다	recommend (that) ~을 추천하다
indicate (that) ~을 나타내다	suggest (that) ~을 제안하다
mention (that) ~라고 언급하다	propose (that) ~을 제안하다
explain (that) ~을 설명하다	ask (that) ~을 요청하다
note (that) ~라고 언급하다, 유념하다	ensure (that) 확실히 ~하다
determine (that) ~을 결정하다	make sure (that) 확실히 ~하다
notify 사람 that ~에게 ~라는 것을 통지하다	inform 사람 that ~에게 ~라는 것을 알리다

출제 포인트 ❷ 형용사 + that절

be aware that + 완전한 문장 ~을 알다	be [happy / glad / delighted] that + 완전한 문장 ~해서 기쁘다
be convinced that + 완전한 문장 ~을 확신하다	make sure that + 완전한 문장 ~를 확실히 하다
be confident that + 완전한 문장 ~을 확신하다	be sure that + 완전한 문장 ~를 확신하다
be afraid that + 완전한 문장 ~을 두려워하다	

I / am **aware** / **that** Ms. Clarke will arrive on Tuesday.

해석 나는 Ms. Clarke가 화요일에 도착할 것을 알고 있다.

+check .... 해설서 p.29

1. Please inform Ms. Chang ------- my trip to Taiwan has been postponed to a later date.

(A) to　　　　(B) that　　　　(C) of　　　　(D) because

명사절 접속사 what vs. that

The safety instruction manual explains ------- new employees should know while they are working in the field.

(A) what   (B) that   (C) which   (D) how

>> **출제 포인트** **불완전한 문장을 이끄는 명사절 접속사를 묻는다.**

1 **선택지 확인** | 빈칸에 들어갈 알맞은 접속사를 고른다.

2 **빈칸 확인** | 동사 뒤에 오는 목적어 자리이다. 빈칸 뒤에 목적어가 없는 불완전한 문장이 이어지고 있다. 목적어와 접속사 역할을 할 수 있는 명사절 접속사가 필요하다. → 완전한 문장을 이끄는 접속사 (B) that, (C) which, (D) how ❌

3 **정답 확인** | 문맥상 '새로운 직원들이 알아야 할 것을 설명하다'라는 뜻이 되어야 하므로 정답은 (A) what ⭕

정답 The safety instruction manual / explains / **(A) what** new employees should know / while they are working in the field.

해석 그 안전 지침 안내서는 / 설명한다 / 새로운 직원들이 알아야 할 것을 / 그들이 현장에서 일하는 동안에

출제 포인트 ③ **명사절 접속사 that vs. what**
뒤에 완전한 구조의 절이 오면 that, 불완전한 구조의 절이 오면 what이 필요하다.

that	주어, 목적어, 보어 역할	완전한 문장을 이끈다.	오로지 접속사 기능
what	주어, 목적어, 보어, 전치사의 목적어 역할	불완전한 문장을 이끈다. (주어나 목적어, 보어가 빠진 문장)	「접속사 + 주어/목적어/보어」 기능

What Mr. Khan wrote / became a bestseller. 주어
The writer / wanted to share / **what** he experienced during his travels. 목적어
What you dream / is / **what** you are. 보어

해석 Mr. Khan이 집필한 것이 베스트셀러가 되었다. / 그 작가는 여행에서 자신이 경험한 것을 나누기를 원했다. / 당신이 꿈꾸는 것이 바로 당신이다.

⊕ check

2. We need to determine ------- can be accomplished in order to provide the most accurate information.
(A) that   (B) what   (C) there   (D) whether

Q3 명사절 접속사 [whether vs. that]

Residents attended the meeting to ask ------- the historic properties will be preserved.

(A) although   (B) since   (C) whether   (D) that

>> **출제 포인트 문맥상 알맞은 명사절 접속사를 묻는다.**

1 선택지 확인 | 빈칸에 들어갈 알맞은 접속사를 고른다.

2 빈칸 확인 | to ask 뒤에 목적어(명사)가 필요하며, 빈칸 뒤에는 완전한 절이 이어지고 있다. → 명사절을 이끄는 접속사가 필요하다. 부사절 접속사 (A) although, (B) since는 뒤에 절을 연결하긴 하지만, to ask의 목적어(명사) 역할을 할 수 없으므로 답이 될 수 없다. → (A) although ✕ (B) since ✕

3 정답 확인 | 명사절 접속사 (C)와 (D) 중, 문맥상 "역사적 물건들이 보존될 것인지 아닌지를 물어보기 위해"라는 뜻이므로 정답은 (C) whether ⭕

정답 Residents / attended / the meeting / to ask / **(C) whether** the historic properties will be preserved.
해석 주민들은 / 참석했다 / 회의에 / 물어보려고 / 역사적 물건들이 보존될 것인지 아닌지를

출제 포인트 ❹ if절 / whether

if절은 ask, know, see, check, try, wonder, doubt과 같이 의문 사항이나 사실 여부를 묻는 동사의 목적어로 사용될 때만 명사절로 분류된다.

if	타동사 목적어 역할	완전한 문장을 이끈다.
whether	주어, 목적어, 보어, 전치사의 목적어 역할	완전한 문장을 이끈다.

Nobody / knows / **whether[if]** Mr. Patel lives in Seoul. 목적어
The problem / is / **whether** the company invests in the project. 보어
I / cannot answer / your question / of **whether** we will adopt the policy. 전치사의 목적어

해석 아무도 Mr. Patel가 서울에서 사는지 살지 않는지를 모른다. / 문제는 그 회사가 그 프로젝트에 투자를 하는지 하지 않는지이다.
나는 우리가 그 정책을 채택할지 하지 않을지에 관한 너의 질문에 대답할 수 없다.

✔ **문법 포인트** whether 뒤의 절을 축약하여 「whether + to부정사」 형태로도 자주 출제된다.
They / do not know / **whether to answer** the question. whether + to부정사
해석 그들은 그 질문에 대답을 할지 하지 않을지를 모른다.

➕ check
....

3. The Chief Financial Officer will decide ------- the firm will order office supplies from Faremex Co. or from Callico, Inc.

(A) although   (B) to   (C) whether   (D) that

Q4 명사절을 이끄는 의문사

We will decide ------- will recruit study circle participants and find a suitable location.

(A) what　　　　(B) who　　　　(C) she　　　　(D) which

>> **출제 포인트** 명사절을 이끄는 의문사를 묻는다.

1 선택지 확인 | 빈칸에 들어갈 알맞은 의문사를 고른다.

2 빈칸 확인 | 동사 뒤의 목적어 자리이다. 빈칸 뒤에 주어가 없는 불완전한 문장이 이어지고 있다. 주어 역할을 할 수 있는
의문사가 필요하다. → (C) she ✗

3 정답 확인 | 문맥상 주어는 동사 recruit과 find의 주체 역할을 하는 사람이어야 하므로 정답은 (B) who ✓

정답 We / will decide / **(B) who** will recruit study circle participants and find a suitable location.
해석 우리는 / 결정할 것이다 / 누가 연구 그룹 참여자들을 채용하고, 적절한 장소를 찾을지를

출제 포인트 ⑤ 의문사가 이끄는 명사절

의문대명사	who, what, which	불완전한 문장을 이끈다.	「접속사 + 주어/목적어/보어」 기능
의문형용사 + 명사	which / what / whose + 명사	불완전한 문장을 이끈다.	「접속사 + 형용사」 기능
의문부사 + 절	when, where, how, why	완전한 문장을 이끈다.	오로지 접속사 기능

Mr. Wood / is unsure / **who** is going to review this file. 의문대명사 = 의문사절의 주어
We / do not know / **what color** the client wants to paint her room. 의문형용사 + 명사 = 의문사절의 목적어
Please / tell / me / **when** the conference will be held. 의문부사 + 절

해석　Mr. Wood는 누가 이 파일을 검토할 것인지 잘 모른다. / 우리는 그 고객이 그녀의 방을 어떤 색으로 칠하기를 원하는지 모른다.
　　　컨퍼런스가 언제 열리는지 말해 주세요.

✔ **문법 포인트** 주어 자리에 있는 긴 명사절을 문장 끝으로 보내고 가주어 It를 쓰기도 한다.

Where[When / How / Why] Ms. Cho purchased the equipment / is unknown. 의문사절 = 주어
⋯ **It** / is important / **where[when / how / why]** Ms. Cho purchased the equipment. 가주어 it ~ 의문사절

해석　어디서[언제/어떻게/왜] Ms. Cho가 그 장비를 구입했는지는 알려져 있지 않다.
　　　어디서[언제/어떻게/왜] Ms. Cho가 그 장비를 구입했는지는 중요하다.

● check

4. Once Mr. Yoon has evaluated all the entries, he will determine ------- work will be chosen.

(A) who　　　　(B) whose　　　　(C) whom　　　　(D) that

해설서 p.29

1. The warranty guarantees ------- the machine will be replaced if it has defects.

(A) that   (B) and
(C) what   (D) because

2. The recent survey result indicates ------- most travelers book their flights online.

(A) which   (B) what
(C) those   (D) that

3. The President will decide ------- to merge with the company.

(A) whether   (B) either
(C) even if   (D) so that

4. Regardless of ------- a candidate is hired, we keep all applications on file for one year.

(A) even   (B) whether
(C) although   (D) even if

5. Nobody knew the fact ------- oil prices would increase last quarter.

(A) that   (B) if
(C) whether   (D) because

6. The instruction manual states ------- the blender can be used for making both cold and hot drinks.

(A) but   (B) that
(C) so   (D) while

7. The study will determine ------- our new product will appeal to younger buyers.

(A) what   (B) while
(C) either   (D) whether

8. The board ------- several changes be made to the company's insurance policy.

(A) proposed   (B) proposing
(C) will be proposed   (D) to propose

9. City officials insist ------- the new fuel tax will reduce traffic congestion.

(A) that   (B) what
(C) if   (D) whether

10. The company will end its weekly newsletter ------- the graphic designer is too busy.

(A) whether   (B) because
(C) in addition   (D) therefore

11. The poll shows ------- consumers aged 21-35 prefer our competitor's product.

(A) that   (B) what
(C) whether   (D) if

12. Please be aware ------- the HR Department will be interviewing new employees in conference room A today.

(A) that   (B) whether
(C) if   (D) because

13. Our records indicate that ------- is time for your annual eye exam.

(A) it   (B) itself
(C) its   (D) them

14. Given his excellent sales record, it is hardly surprising ------- Mr. Wang received a salary increase.

(A) that   (B) what
(C) whether   (D) when

15. Mr. Kim said ------- he would be gone for four days on a business trip.

(A) that
(B) what
(C) and
(D) while

16. The technician will determine exactly ------- caused the building's power failure.

(A) what
(B) that
(C) those
(D) whose

17. Please ensure ------- all labels are put on the boxes properly before sending them to the warehouse.

(A) such as
(B) that
(C) if
(D) whether

18. ------- Milleott Co. builds a new factory depends on long-term market trends.

(A) While
(B) Whether
(C) Although
(D) Despite

19. ------- the increased volume, 96 percent of the packages were delivered on time.

(A) That
(B) Whether
(C) If
(D) Despite

20. Tamiloy Jewelry customers can get 10 percent off their purchases ------- they spend $300 or more.

(A) than
(B) that
(C) even
(D) as long as

기본 완성 훈련 다음은 앞서 풀어 본 연습문제의 문장들입니다. 명사절을 찾아 밑줄을 긋고 문제 번호에 ○를 치세요.

1. The warranty guarantees that the machine will be replaced if it has defects.

2. The recent survey result indicates that most travelers book their flights online.

3. The President will decide whether to merge with the company.

4. Regardless of whether a candidate is hired, we keep all applications on file for one year.

5. City officials insist that the new fuel tax will reduce traffic congestion.

6. Please be aware that the HR Department will be interviewing new employees in conference room A today.

7. The technician will determine exactly what caused the building's power failure.

8. Please ensure that all labels are put on the boxes properly before sending them to the warehouse.

9. Despite the increased volume, 96 percent of the packages were delivered on time.

10. Tamiloy Jewelry customers can get 10 percent off their purchases as long as they spend $300 or more.

형용사절 접속사

관계대명사나 관계부사가 이끄는 절은 앞에 오는 명사를 꾸며 주는 형용사 역할을 한다.

기본 개념 이해하기

1. 형용사절

▶ 형용사절은 주절의 주어, 목적어, 보어 자리에 있는 명사를 뒤에서 꾸며 주거나 설명해 준다. 이때 형용사절이 수식하는 앞 명사를 선행사라고 한다.

▶ 형용사절의 구조는 「접속사 + (주어) + 동사 + (목적어)」 형태인데 접속사 자리에 관계대명사나 관계부사가 온다.

A team of doctors / developed / a system / **that** detects heart failure. 선행사 + 관계대명사
Mr. Baxter / went / to the airport / **where** he picked up the CEO. 선행사 + 관계부사

해석　의료진은 심장 질환을 감지하는 시스템을 개발했다. / Mr. Baxter는 CEO를 픽업했던 공항으로 갔다.

2. 관계대명사: 「접속사 + 대명사」

▶ 관계대명사는 꾸며 주는 주절의 명사(선행사)를 가리키는 대명사이자 형용사절 접속사 역할을 한다.

▶ 관계대명사절에서 관계대명사는 주어, 목적어, 소유격 대명사의 역할을 하며, 주격, 목적격, 소유격으로 써야 한다.

▶ 선행사가 사람이면 who(m), 사물이나 동물이면 which를 쓴다. 목적격 관계대명사 whom은 who로 대신할 수 있다. which는 주격과 목적격이 동일하다. 선행사와 상관없이 주격과 목적격은 that으로도 쓸 수도 있다.

선행사	주격	소유격	목적격
사람 명사	who/that	whose	who(m)/that
사물 명사	which/that	whose/of which	which/that

Visitors / **who** have an appointment / can park / in the underground garage. 주격
This / is a water-saving device / **which** you can use in your kitchen. 목적격
The HR Department hired / a manager / **whose** experience is suitable for the job. 소유격

해석　예약을 한 방문객들은 지하 주차장에 주차할 수 있다. / 이것은 주방에서 사용할 수 있는 절수 장치이다.
　　　인사과는 그 일에 적합한 경력이 있는 매니저를 고용했다.

3. 관계부사: 「접속사 + 부사」

▶ 관계부사절이 꾸며 주는 선행사가 장소, 시간, 이유, 방법 중 무엇이냐에 따라 where, when, why, how를 쓴다.

▶ 선행사 the way와 관계부사 how는 함께 쓰지 않고, 둘 중 하나만 쓴다. 선행사가 the time, the day, the place, the city, the reason 등일 때 선행사와 관계부사 중 하나를 생략할 수 있다.

Mr. Kline / remembers / **the time** / **when** he first saw the prototype. 선행사 + 관계부사
= Mr. Kline / remembers / **the time** he first saw the prototype. 관계부사 생략
= Mr. Kline / remembers / **when** he first saw the prototype. 선행사 생략

해석   Mr. Kline은 그가 처음 견본을 봤을 때를 기억한다.

The manual / explains / **the way** we handle personal information. 선행사 + 관계부사 생략
= The manual / explains / **how** we handle personal information. 선행사 생략 + 관계부사

해석   그것은 우리가 개인정보를 어떻게 다루는지에 대해 설명한다.

4. 관계대명사의 제한적 용법과 계속적 용법

▶ **제한적 용법:** 관계대명사절이 선행사의 의미를 한정한다.

▶ **계속적 용법:** 관계대명사절이 선행사에 대해 부가적인 설명을 덧붙인다. 관계대명사 앞에는 콤마(,)를 찍는다.
이때, that은 계속적 용법으로 쓰지 않는다.

Susan / has / a water heater / **that** runs on solar power. 제한적 용법(온수기의 의미를 한정)
Susan / has / a water heater, / **which** runs on solar power. 계속적 용법(온수기에 대한 부가설명)

해석   Susan은 태양열로 작동하는 온수기를 가지고 있다. (=일반 전기 등으로 작동하는 온수기도 가지고 있을 수 있다.)
        Susan은 온수기를 가지고 있는데, 그것은 태양열로 작동한다. (=Susan이 가진 온수기는 태양열로 작동하는 것 한 개뿐이다.)

5. 관계대명사: what vs. that

▶ **what:** '~것'을 뜻하는 관계대명사 what는 선행사를 포함하는 관계대명사로서 [the thing(s) + that/which(선행사 + 관계대명사)]를 대신해서 쓸 수 있다. 또한, 다른 관계대명사와 달리 명사절을 이끌어 문장에서 주어, 목적어, 보어로 쓰인다.

▶ **that:** 관계대명사 that는 선행사의 종류나 격에 상관없이 who, whom, which를 대신해서 쓸 수 있는 반면에, 명사절 접속사 that(~하는 것)는 뒤에 완전한 절을 이끌어 문장에서 주어, 목적어, 보어로 쓰인다.

What(=The thing which) surprised the critics / was the movie's popularity.
what + 불완전한 문장

That the movie was popular / surprised the critics. that + 완전한 문장

해석   비평가들을 놀라게 했던 것은 그 영화의 인기였다. / 그 영화가 인기 있었다는 것이 비평가들을 놀라게 했다.

핵심 문제 유형

Q1 명사 + [주격 관계대명사] + 동사

Only employees ---------- have received training may use the lab's equipment.

(A) whose   (B) whom   (C) who   (D) which

>> **출제 포인트 관계대명사는 선행사와 격의 종류에 따라 달라진다.**

❶ 선택지 확인 | 빈칸에 들어갈 알맞은 관계대명사를 고른다.

❷ 빈칸 확인 | 주어(명사)는 Only employees, 동사는 may use이며, 빈칸은 주어와 동사 사이에 주어(Only employees)를 수식할 수 있도록 관계대명사가 필요한 자리이다. 관계절의 동사 'have received' 앞에 주어가 없는 것으로 보아 주격관계대명사가 필요하다. → 소유격 (A) whose ✖ 목적격 (B) whom ✖

❸ 정답 확인 | 선행사가 employees로 사람이다. → (D) which ✖ 정답은 (C) who ⓞ

정답 Only employees / **(C) who** have received training / may use / the lab's equipment.
해석 직원들만이 / 교육을 받았던 / 이용할 수 있다 / 실험실 장비를

출제 포인트 ❶ 「주격 관계대명사 + 주어가 없는 불완전한 문장」
주격 관계대명사 자리 뒤에는 주어 없이 바로 동사가 나온다.

The police officer / **who** is standing near the entrance / will help / you. 주격 관계대명사 + 동사
해석 출입문 근처에 서 있는 경찰관이 당신을 도와줄 거예요.

출제 포인트 ❷ 주격 관계대명사와 be동사는 함께 생략될 수 있다.
The company / **(which is) producing** the most affordable merchandise / will be popular.
= The company / **producing** the most affordable merchandise / will be popular.
   주격 관계대명사 + be동사 생략

해석 가장 알맞은 가격의 상품을 생산하는 회사가 인기를 끌 것이다.

Mr. Kroloff / attended / the conference / **(which is) held** by the government.
= Mr. Kroloff / attended / the conference / **held** by the government. 주격 관계대명사 + be동사 생략

해석 Mr. Kroloff는 정부에 의해 개최되는 회의에 참석했다.

Those **(who are)** available for the workshop are listed on the Web site.
=Those / **available** for the workshop / are listed on the Web site. 주격 관계대명사 + be동사 생략

해석 워크숍에 참석 가능한 사람들이 웹사이트 상에 열거되어 있다.

+ **check** ·· 해설서 p.31

1. Shireton Manor on Kellogg Street, ------- served as Statusville's first elementary school, will be completely remodeled.

(A) who   (B) which   (C) what   (D) they

Q2 명사 + [목적격 관계대명사] + 주어 + 동사

Mr. Jansen interviewed the applicant ------- his colleague recommended.

(A) which   (B) whom   (C) what   (D) whose

>> **출제 포인트 관계대명사는 선행사의 종류에 따라 달라진다.**

1 선택지 확인 | 빈칸에 들어갈 알맞은 관계대명사를 고른다.

2 빈칸 확인 | 명사 뒤에 오는 관계대명사 자리이다. 관계대명사절의 주어(his colleague)와 동사(recommended) 뒤에
목적어가 없다. → 목적격 관계대명사가 필요하다. → (C) what ❌ (D) whose ❌

3 정답 확인 | 선행사가 사람(the applicant)이다. → 정답은 (B) whom ⭕

정답 Mr. Jansen / interviewed / the applicant / **(B) whom** his colleague recommended.
해석 Mr. Jansen은 / 면접을 봤다 / 지원자를 / 그의 동료가 추천한

출제 포인트 ❸ 「목적격 관계대명사 + 목적어가 없는 불완전한 문장」

목적격 관계대명사 자리 뒤에는 주어와 동사만 있고, 목적어가 없는 불완전한 문장이 나온다.

The product / **which** Ms. Cho ordered / has not arrived yet. 목적격 관계대명사 + 목적어가 없는 문장 (주어 + 동사)

해석   Ms. Cho가 주문한 제품이 아직 도착하지 않았다.

출제 포인트 ❹ 목적격 관계대명사의 생략

목적격 관계대명사 who(m), which, that은 생략할 수 있다.

These are / the top 10 dream jobs / (**which / that**) students want. 목적격 관계대명사 생략

해석   이들은 학생들이 원하는 열 개의 선망 직종들이다.

⊛ check

2. Please find the attached membership application ------- you requested, and fill it out completely.

(A) then   (B) what   (C) that   (D) when

Q3 명사 + [소유격 관계대명사] + 명사

The applicant ------- résumé most impressed Ms. Hong was selected for the position.

(A) who   (B) whose   (C) how   (D) which

>> **출제 포인트 관계대명사는 선행사와 격의 종류에 따라 달라진다.**

① 선택지 확인 ㅣ 빈칸에 들어갈 알맞은 관계대명사 또는 관계부사를 고른다.

② 빈칸 확인 ㅣ 주어는 the applicant이고, 동사는 was selected이므로 빈칸은 주어와 동사 사이에서 명사 the applicant 를 수식할 수 있는 관계대명사 또는 관계부사자리이다. 빈칸 뒤에 명사가 있으며, 빈칸 뒤의 문장이 완벽하다.
→ (A) who ❌ (D) which ❌

③ 정답 확인 ㅣ 선행사가 사람인 applicant가 왔으므로 관계부사가 아닌, 사람을 선행사로 취하는 소유격 관계대명사가 와야 한다. 따라서 정답은 (B) whose ⭕

정답 The applicant / **(B) whose** résumé most impressed Ms. Hong / was selected / for the position.
해석 그 지원자가 / 그의 이력서가 Ms. Hong에게 가장 깊은 인상을 준 / 선정되었다 / 그 자리에

출제 포인트 ⑤ 「소유격 관계대명사 + 완전한 문장」

소유격 관계대명사 자리 뒤에는 관사나 소유격이 없는 명사가 주어로 온다.

The orchestra / **whose** last performance was very impressive / will hold / another concert / soon.
whose + 완전한 문장

Employees / **whose** jobs involve public interaction / are required / to dress professionally.
whose + 완전한 문장

해석 지난 공연이 아주 인상적이었던 그 오케스트라가 곧 다른 콘서트를 열 것이다.
대중을 상대하는 업무를 하는 직원들은 전문가 답게 옷을 입는 것이 요구된다.

+check

3. All artists ------- work has been chosen for the gallery will be contacted by April 2.

(A) who   (B) whom   (C) whoever   (D) whose

Q4 명사 + [관계대명사 vs. 관계부사] + 완전한 문장

The CEO visited the factory ------- most of the company's products are manufactured.

(A) where   (B) when   (C) who   (D) which

>> **출제 포인트** 장소·시간·이유·방법을 수식하는 관계부사절 뒤에는 완전한 문장이 나온다.

1 선택지 확인 | 빈칸에 들어갈 알맞은 관계대명사 또는 관계부사를 고른다.

2 빈칸 확인 | 명사 뒤에 오는 관계대명사 또는 관계부사 자리인데, 빈칸 앞뒤로 완전한 문장이 연결되어 있다.
→ 주격 또는 목적격 관계대명사는 올 수 없다. (C) who ✗ (D) which ✗

3 정답 확인 | 빈칸 앞의 선행사가 장소(the factory)를 나타낸다. → 장소를 수식하는 관계부사가 와야 하므로 정답은
(A) where ⊙

정답 The CEO / visited / the factory / **(A) where** most of the company's products are manufactured.
해석 최고경영자가 / 방문했다 / 공장을 / 그 회사 제품의 대부분이 생산되는

출제 포인트 ⑥ 「관계부사 + 완전한 문장」
앞에 오는 장소, 시간, 이유, 방법 등을 나타내는 명사를 꾸며 주는 관계부사 뒤에는 완전한 문장이 온다.

This / is **the place** / **where** my friends worked. where + 완전한 문장
The manager / notified us / of **the date** / **when** the conference would be held. when + 완전한 문장
I / know / **the reason** / **why** Mr. Ruiz is learning English. why + 완전한 문장
What makes their business exceptional / is / **the way** they create the products very quickly.
the way + 완전한 문장

해석 이곳은 내 친구들이 일했던 곳이다. / 그 관리자는 우리에게 컨퍼런스가 개최될 날짜를 알려 주었다.
나는 Mr. Ruiz가 영어를 배우는 이유를 알고 있다. / 그들의 사업을 특별하게 만드는 것은 그들이 제품들을 빨리 만든다는 것이다.

출제 포인트 ⑦ 「전치사 + 관계대명사 + 완전한 문장」
관계부사는 「전치사 + 관계대명사」로도 쓸 수 있으며, 뒤에는 완전한 문장이 온다.

Ms. Lanson / found / a **place**. + RP&K Industries / can hold / the event /(in)that place.
해석 Ms. Lanson은 한 장소를 발견했다. + RP&K 산업이 그 장소에서 행사를 열 수 있다.

= Ms. Lanson / found / a **place** /(in)which RP&K Industries can hold the event.
= Ms. Lanson / found / a **place** / **where** RP&K Industries can hold the event.

해석 Ms. Lanson은 RP&K 산업이 행사를 열 수 있는 장소를 찾았다.

⟡check

4. In box five of the application, please indicate the particular date ------- you are most available for an interview.

(A) what   (B) that   (C) when   (D) where

해설서 p.32

1. Many of the applicants ------- applied for the job were well-qualified.

(A) they　　　　(B) when
(C) who　　　　(D) what

2. The proposal ------- we reviewed will be presented to the board of directors.

(A) which　　　(B) whom
(C) who　　　　(D) whose

3. Starshine Corp., ------- advertisements appear frequently on TV, is launching a new product.

(A) why　　　　(B) whose
(C) which　　　(D) that

4. The document which ------- the new marketing strategies will be on your desk by tomorrow.

(A) describe　　(B) describing
(C) describes　　(D) to describe

5. Crowde Developing announced ------- the design for the Falcon Central Complex is almost completed.

(A) what　　　　(B) that
(C) because　　　(D) while

6. ------- who do not receive their magazines by August 15 should contact the customer service center.

(A) Subscribers　(B) Subscriber
(C) Subscription　(D) Subscriptions

7. Dr. Kim requested that ------- not eat for 12 hours before the annual health check-up.

(A) we　　　　　(B) us
(C) ours　　　　(D) ourselves

8. Red Cedar Plant, ------- manufactures recycled paper products, has relocated to Midville.

(A) while　　　　(B) which
(C) where　　　　(D) that

9. One of the interns the sales team hired ------- performing exceptionally well.

(A) is　　　　　(B) are
(C) be　　　　　(D) to be

10. A training session for those ------- will use the new software is scheduled for 9 A.M.

(A) who　　　　(B) which
(C) they　　　　(D) whom

11. Some replacement parts that ------- to LNK Warehouses never arrived.

(A) ship　　　　(B) was shipped
(C) were shipped　(D) shipping

12. The list of employees ------- are promoted will be announced tomorrow.

(A) who　　　　(B) which
(C) what　　　　(D) whom

13. The study was conducted by three researchers ------- have won awards in the field of biology.

(A) because　　　(B) who
(C) whose　　　　(D) what

14. The expanded PG Sports Complex, ------- can accommodate 5,000 spectators, is going to open in October.

(A) this　　　　(B) which
(C) that　　　　(D) what

15. Mr. Kang, ------- currently manages AC Technology's plant in Seoul, will be promoted to Vice President of Operations next month.

(A) that
(B) who
(C) which
(D) when

16. Ms. Lang wants to know ------- Mr. Yoon submitted his budget report late.

(A) where
(B) while
(C) why
(D) who

17. The company recently carried out a survey ------- asked employees about their retirement plans.

(A) that
(B) whether
(C) if
(D) since

18. JAK Frequent Traveler members ------- enrollment ends this month should pay their fees by the 26th.

(A) who
(B) whom
(C) what
(D) whose

19. Fuel -------, which have increased steadily for months, are forecast to go down in September.

(A) priced
(B) prices
(C) pricing
(D) price

20. Any items left in the building which ------- not claimed within a week will be discarded.

(A) is
(B) are
(C) has
(D) have

기본 완성 훈련 | 다음은 앞서 풀어 본 연습문제의 문장들입니다. 형용사절을 찾아 괄호 표시를 하고, 선행사가 있는 경우 밑줄을 그으세요.

1. Many of the applicants who applied for the job were well-qualified.

2. Starshine Corp., whose advertisements appear frequently on TV, is launching a new product.

3. The document which describes the new marketing strategies will be on your desk by tomorrow.

4. Subscribers who do not receive their magazines by August 15 should contact the customer service center.

5. Red Cedar Plant, which manufactures recycled paper products, has relocated to Midville.

6. Some replacement parts that were shipped to LNK Warehouses never arrived.

7. The list of employees who are promoted will be announced tomorrow.

8. JAK Frequent Traveler members whose enrollment ends this month should pay their fees by the 26th.

9. Fuel prices, which have increased steadily for months, are forecast to go down in September.

10. Any items left in the building which are not claimed within a week will be discarded.

REVIEW TEST 03

해설서 p.34

1. Any employee ------- idea is adopted for the project will receive a cash award.

(A) that
(B) their
(C) whose
(D) who

2. ------- various efforts to boost sales, the company's revenue did not increase.

(A) Even
(B) Despite
(C) Although
(D) Because

3. Ms. Wilson, ------- is retiring soon, will be presented with an outstanding employee award.

(A) she
(B) who
(C) her
(D) which

4. The steak dish at Jackie's Diner comes with a side of either rice ------- sweet potatoes.

(A) neither
(B) or
(C) but
(D) and

5. Stores that ------- heavily on younger workers are struggling to find suitable candidates.

(A) relying
(B) relies
(C) reliant
(D) rely

6. The assembly machine will be fixed tomorrow, ------- the necessary parts arrive today.

(A) because of
(B) unless
(C) in spite of
(D) as long as

7. The conclusion of the tax consulting firm was ------- the company needed to improve its budgeting.

(A) whose
(B) what
(C) that
(D) which

8. The lease agreement will be official ------- the tenant and the landlord sign it.

(A) once
(B) despite
(C) but
(D) until

9. Go Aid is an organization ------- goal is to improve living conditions across Asia.

(A) who
(B) which
(C) whose
(D) what

10. ------- FG Advertising offers reasonable rates, DTO Ads has a better reputation.

(A) As soon as
(B) And
(C) However
(D) While

11. At the 10th Landscaping Conference, Ms. Petal will present the gardening plan ------- designed last month.

(A) she
(B) herself
(C) her own
(D) hers

12. The Purchasing Department will decide ------- to purchase the new photocopier from Adalet Corp.

(A) whether
(B) neither
(C) that
(D) even if

13. The law which ------- international trade has been changed.

(A) regulate
(B) regulates
(C) regulating
(D) is regulated

14. ------- we requested immediate replacement of the parts, it took several days to book a service appointment.

(A) However
(B) Although
(C) Otherwise
(D) Yet

15. We started a project ------- will increase our sales in the Asian markets.

(A) that
(B) nor
(C) unless
(D) yet

16. ------- Ms. Kang nor Ms. Lee was appointed to the planning committee.

(A) None   (B) Both
(C) Neither   (D) Not only

17. Customers will receive 24-hour technical support ------- they have outstanding payments.

(A) without   (B) otherwise
(C) unless   (D) when

18. Ms. Kang was unable to attend the shareholder meeting ------- her flight was delayed.

(A) owing to   (B) as
(C) where   (D) despite

19. ------- after receiving many customer complaints, B&C Stores changed their return policy.

(A) Provided that   (B) As soon as
(C) Shortly   (D) Despite

20. Please turn off your computer ------- leaving the building to save energy.

(A) nevertheless   (B) because
(C) before   (D) so that

21. We have a new device ------- can check the entire assembly line for problems.

(A) that   (B) what
(C) so   (D) near

22. ------- the production delay, the company released its new RVM-593 phone on schedule.

(A) Whether   (B) Either
(C) Thus   (D) In spite of

23. We require all guides to arrive by 9 A.M. ------- tours can begin promptly at 10 A.M.

(A) whether   (B) even if
(C) while   (D) so that

24. All service contracts have to be signed by ------- a manager and a sales representative.

(A) both   (B) whether
(C) not only   (D) either

25. ------- who wants to attend the seminar should contact Ms. Lee by October 24.

(A) Those   (B) Anyone
(C) They   (D) Their

26. The report has some figures that Carol ------- before the meeting.

(A) correct
(B) has been corrected
(C) to correct
(D) will correct

27. Ms. Kim is working on the report ------- is due tomorrow.

(A) that   (B) since
(C) whose   (D) whom

28. Part-time staff should check the schedule ------- was revised last night.

(A) which   (B) whose
(C) whom   (D) where

29. Please let Ms. Shim know ------- you are available to lead the project by Friday.

(A) than   (B) such
(C) whether   (D) whereas

30. The article about the new community center will be published ------- it is reviewed by the chief editor.

(A) because of   (B) as soon as
(C) in addition to   (D) moreover

to부정사

주어, 목적어, 보어 등의 자리에 명사 외에 동사가 나타내는 행위(activities)나 상태(states)를 명시할 때 to부정사나 동명사를 쓴다. to부정사와 동명사는 동사처럼 목적어, 보어, 수식어를 동반하며 시제와 태가 있다.

기본 개념 이해하기

1. to부정사의 형태와 역할

▶ to부정사는 「to + 동사원형」의 형태이며, 동사처럼 목적어, 보어, 수식어구를 동반하며 명사, 형용사, 부사 역할을 한다.

Pinoca Co. decided / **to hire** a part-time receptionist.

해석 Pinoca 사는 파트타임 접수원을 고용하기로 결정했다.
풀이 to hire는 목적어 a part-time secretary를 동반하고 있으며, 문장의 동사 decided의 목적어 역할을 한다.

2. 명사적 용법

▶ to부정사는 명사처럼 주어, 목적어, 보어 역할을 하며, 전치사의 목적어로는 쓰이지 않는다.

To finish the work / is not easy. 주어

The employees wish / **to save** time. 목적어

Mr. Chen's job is / **to review** résumés. 주격 보어

The manager asked me / **to send** the letter. 목적격 보어

I found Ms. Duvall / **to be** a reliable business partner. 목적격 보어

해석 그 일을 끝내는 것은 쉽지 않다. / 직원들은 시간을 줄이기를 바란다. / Mr. Chen의 일은 이력서를 검토하는 것이다.
그 관리자는 내게 그 편지를 보내달라고 했다. / 나는 Ms. Duvall이 믿을 만한 사업 파트너라는 걸 알았다.

3. 가주어 it

▶ to부정사 주어를 대신하여 주어 자리에 가주어 it을 쓰고, 진주어 to부정사를 문장 뒤에 위치시킨다.

To meet with the client / is important.

= **It** / is important / **to meet** with the client.

해석 고객을 만나는 것은 매우 중요하다.

4. 형용사적 용법과 부사적 용법

▶ **형용사적 용법:** '~할, ~해야 할'의 의미로 앞에 오는 명사나 대명사(something, anything 등)를 수식한다.

▶ **부사적 용법:** 동사, 형용사, 부사, 문장 전체를 수식하며 목적, 감정의 원인, 결과, 판단의 근거 등을 나타낸다.

You should make an effort / **to help** Mr. Jones. 명사 수식(목적)

We are employing staff / **to work** overseas. 명사 수식(목적)

해석 당신은 Mr. Jones을 도우려는 노력을 해야 한다. / 우리는 해외에서 근무할 직원을 채용하고 있다.

I am glad / **to hear** the good news. 형용사 수식(감정의 원인)

Ms. Pang worked hard / (in order) **to get** a promotion. 부사 수식(목적)

해석 나는 좋은 소식을 듣게 되어서 기쁘다. / Ms. Pang은 승진을 하기 위해 열심히 일했다.

☑ **문법 포인트** 목적을 나타내는 to부정사는 보통 「in order to + 동사원형: ~하기 위해서」 형태로도 자주 출제된다. to 앞의 in order는 생략 가능하다. 동사원형 앞에 같은 의미의 부사절 접속사인 so that과 in order to 중에서 in order to를 고르는 문제와 in order to 뒤에 동사원형을 고르는 문제가 출제된다.

5. to부정사의 의미상 주어

▶ to부정사의 의미상의 주어가 문장의 주어와 일치할 때나 문맥 속에서 파악 가능할 때는 따로 표시하지 않는다.

▶ to부정사의 행위자를 따로 밝혀야 할 때 대개 「for + 목적격」의 형태로 표시한다.

Jack hoped / **to get** a telescope as a birthday present. 의미상 주어 = 문장의 주어(She)

It is not easy / **for beginners to choose** their first telescope. 의미상 주어(for beginners) ≒ 문장의 주어(It)

해석 Jack은 생일 선물로 망원경을 받기를 희망했다. / 초보자들이 그들의 첫 망원경을 선택하는 것은 쉽지 않다.

6. to부정사의 부정, 시제, 태

▶ to부정사의 부정형은 「not/never + to + 동사원형」이다.

▶ 시제: to부정사의 사건이 본동사보다 먼저 일어났을 때 「to have + 과거분사」 형태를 쓴다.

▶ 태: to부정사와 의미상 주어가 수동의 관계일 때 「to be + 과거분사」 형태를 쓴다.

Remember / **not to stop** planning. 부정

I am happy / **to have completed** the project. 과거 시제

A shopping center is expected / **to be constructed** along with other facilities. 수동태

해석 계획하는 것을 멈추지 말 것을 기억하세요. / 나는 그 프로젝트를 완료해서 기쁘다.
다른 시설들과 더불어 쇼핑센터가 건축될 예정이다.

Q1 to부정사의 의미상 주어

It is important ------- every employee to respond to customer complaints as promptly as possible.

(A) so   (B) when   (C) that   (D) for

>> 출제 포인트 to부정사의 의미상 주어를 묻는다.

❶ 선택지 확인 | 빈칸에 들어갈 알맞은 전치사를 묻는 문제이다.

❷ 빈칸 확인 | 가주어 it과 진주어 to부정사로 이루어진 문장이고, to부정사 앞에는 행위자를 표시하는 전치사가 와야 한다.
→ (A) so, (B) when, (C) that ❌

❸ 정답 확인 | to부정사의 행위자는 「for + 목적격」의 형태로 표시한다. → (D) for ⭕

정답 It is important / **(D) for** every employee / to respond to customer complaints as promptly as possible.
해석 중요하다 / 모든 직원이 / 가능한 한 즉각적으로 고객 불만에 응답하는 것이

출제 포인트 ❶ to부정사의 의미상의 주어

I would love / **to visit** our branch in Paris next time. 문장의 주어=의미상의 주어

I would love / **you to visit** our branch in Paris next time. 목적격=의미상의 주어

It is necessary / **(for us) to exercise** regularly. 일반인 주어=의미상의 주어

It is necessary / **for her to exercise** regularly. for + 목적격=의미상의 주어

해석 나는 다음에 우리 파리 지사를 방문하고 싶다. / 나는 당신이 다음에 우리 파리 지사를 방문했으면 좋겠다.
(우리가) 규칙적으로 운동하는 것은 필수적이다. / 그녀가 규칙적으로 운동하는 것은 필수적이다.

➕ check   해설서 p.36

1. Dytex, Inc. makes it a requirement ------- all managers to attend a quarterly workshop.

(A) for   (B) off   (C) with   (D) by

Q2 to부정사의 수식을 받는 명사

The staff made every ------- to resolve the claim in a timely manner.

(A) talent   (B) effort   (C) explanation   (D) response

>> **출제 포인트 to부정사의 수식을 받는 명사를 묻는다.**

❶ 선택지 확인 | 빈칸에 들어갈 알맞은 의미의 명사를 고른다.

❷ 빈칸 확인 | 빈칸 뒤에 to부정사(to resolve)가 연결되어 있으므로 to부정사의 수식을 받을 수 있는 명사를 고른다. 전치사 to를 동반하는 (D) response ✖

❸ 정답 확인 | to부정사를 동반하면서, '해결하기 위해 모든 노력을 했다'라는 의미가 적절하므로 정답은 (B) effort ◎

정답 The staff / made every **(B) effort** / to resolve the claim in a timely manner.
해석 직원들은 / 모든 노력을 했다 / 그 클레임을 시기적절하게 해결하기 위해

출제 포인트 ❷ to부정사의 수식을 받는 명사들

plan to ~할 계획	time to ~하기 위한 시간
way to ~하기 위한 방법	effort to ~하기 위한 노력
chance / opportunity to ~할 기회	decision to ~하기 위한 결정
need to ~하기 위한 필요성	ability to ~할 수 있는 능력
right to ~할 권리	claim to ~하고자 하는 주장

They don't have enough **time** / **to solve** the problem.

해석 그들은 그 문제를 해결할 충분한 시간이 없다.

출제 포인트 ❸ to부정사를 취하는 형용사

be [able / unable] to ~할 수 [있다/없다]	be about to 막 ~하려고 하는 참이다
be ready to ~할 준비가 되다	be likely to ~할 것 같다
be willing to 할 의향이 있다	be pleased to 기꺼이 ~하다
be eager to 열성적으로 ~하다	be [easy / difficult] to ~하기 [쉽다/어렵다]
be good to ~하는 것이 좋다	be used to ~하는 데 사용되다

The local farmers / **are willing to** plant / a new variety of crops.

해석 지역 농민들은 새로운 품종의 다양한 작물을 심을 의향이 있다.

+check

2. One of the most popular ways ------- a company's anniversary is having a picnic.

(A) celebration   (B) celebrates   (C) to celebrate   (D) in celebration

Q3 목적어로 to부정사를 취하는 동사

Local environmentalists hope ------- awareness of air pollution through weekly seminars.

(A) raising   (B) to raise   (C) having raised   (D) to be raised

>> 출제 포인트 to부정사만을 목적어로 취하는 동사를 알아야 한다.

1 **선택지 확인** | 빈칸에 들어갈 알맞은 형태를 고른다.

2 **빈칸 확인** | 'hope'라는 동사는 목적어로 to부정사를 취한다. → (A) raising ❌ (C) having raised ❌

3 **정답 확인** | to raise 의 목적어 awareness가 있으므로 to부정사의 능동 형태를 고른다. (D) to be raised ❌
정답은 (B) to raise ⭕

정답 Local environmentalists / hope / **(B) to raise** awareness / of air pollution / through weekly seminars.
해석 지역 환경운동가들은 / 희망한다 / 인식을 높이기를 / 공기 오염에 대한 / 주간 세미나를 통해서

출제 포인트 ❹ 목적어로 to부정사를 취하는 3형식 동사

기대, 희망, 필요	hope to ~하기를 희망하다 need to ~하는 것을 필요로 하다	wish to ~하기를 바라다 want to ~하기를 원하다	expect to ~하기를 기대하다
계획, 약속	plan to ~할 것을 계획하다 refuse to ~하기를 거부하다	decide to ~할 것을 결정하다 promise to ~할 것을 약속하다	agree to ~하는 데 동의하다
제시, 제안	ask to ~할 것을 요청하다	offer to ~할 것을 제시하다	propose to ~할 것을 제안하다
성패 여부, 수완	manage to ~해 내다	afford to ~을 할 수 있는 여건이 되다	fail to ~하는 데 실패하다

The part-time worker / **managed to earn** / a reasonable wage.
해석 그 시간제 근로자는 적절한 임금을 벌어들였다.

⊕ check

3. We sincerely hope ------- from you in the near future.

(A) to hear   (B) hear   (C) hearing   (D) heard

Q4 목적어 + [to부정사 vs. 동사원형]

Although the employees strongly objected, the company will no longer allow them ------- casual attire in the workplace.

(A) wears   (B) wearing   (C) wear   (D) to wear

>> **출제 포인트 목적어 뒤에 오는 to부정사를 묻는다.**

1 선택지 확인 | 빈칸에 들어갈 알맞은 형태를 고른다.

2 빈칸 확인 | allow가 5형식 동사이므로, 빈칸은 목적어(them) 뒤 목적격 보어자리이다. → 목적격 보어 자리에 올 수 없는 동사 (A) wears ❌ (C) wear ❌

3 정답 확인 | 문맥상 '그들이 직장에서 평상복을 입는 것을 허락하지 않는다'라는 의미가 되어야 한다. 5형식 동사 allow는 「allow A to B: A가 B하는 것을 허락하다」 용법으로 쓰여 목적격 보어로 to부정사를 취하므로 정답은 (D) to wear ⭕

정답 Although the employees strongly objected, the company / will no longer allow / them **(D) to wear** casual attire in the workplace.

해석 비록 직원들이 강력하게 항의했지만, 회사는 / 더 이상 허락하지 않을 것이다 / 그들이 직장에서 평상복을 입는 것을

출제 포인트 ⑤ 목적격 보어로 to부정사를 취하는 5형식 동사

다음 타동사들은 「타동사 + 목적어 + 목적격 보어」에서 목적격 보어로 to부정사를 동반한다.

ask A to A에게 ~하도록 요청하다	request A to A에게 ~하도록 요청하다
want A to A가 ~하기를 원하다	tell A to A에게 ~하라고 말하다
get A to A에게 ~하라고 시키다	instruct A to A가 ~하도록 지시하다
advise A to A에게 ~하도록 충고하다	cause A to A가 ~하도록 원인을 제공하다
expect A to A가 ~할 것을 기대하다	encourage A to A가 ~하도록 격려하다
allow A to A가 ~하는 것을 허락하다	persuade A to A가 ~하도록 설득하다

The dentist / **advised** the patient **to visit** / his office next month.

해석 그 치과 의사는 환자에게 다음 달에 병원을 방문하라고 권했다.

✔ **문법 포인트** [be committed to/be dedicated to:~에 헌신하다, 전념하다]와 같은 표현의 to는 to부정사가 아닌 전치사로 뒤에 동사원형이 아니라 명사나 동명사가 나오는 것에 유의한다.

check

4. Emerson expects all of its employees ------- their business dealings with honesty and fairness.

(A) to conduct   (B) conductor   (C) conduct   (D) be conducting

Practice

1. Because the weather is unusually cold, Matton Hotels are currently offering discount coupons ------- customers.

   (A) to attract
   (B) attracts
   (C) attracted
   (D) to attracting

2. Due to the low sales figures, we made a decision ------- the Bluestone Bicycle line.

   (A) will discontinue
   (B) was discontinuing
   (C) discontinued
   (D) to discontinue

3. The Human Resources Department asked employees ------- ideas to improve workplace performance.

   (A) to submit
   (B) submitting
   (C) submitted
   (D) submits

4. The President of JBK Company ------- to offer university students internships this summer.

   (A) decision
   (B) has decided
   (C) to decide
   (D) being decided

5. The employees are happy ------- ways to improve customer services.

   (A) discussion
   (B) to discuss
   (C) discussed
   (D) discusses

6. The company is committed to ------- its domestic sales.

   (A) increasing
   (B) increase
   (C) increased
   (D) increases

7. ------- for the editor position include a journalism degree.

   (A) Requiring
   (B) To require
   (C) Requirements
   (D) Required

8. Okoms Global Bank wants to hire employees with a strong interest in ------- foreign languages.

   (A) to learn
   (B) will learn
   (C) learns
   (D) learning

9. The heat wave is likely ------- through the end of the month.

   (A) last
   (B) lasted
   (C) to last
   (D) lasting

10. ------- for this job, visit the company Web site.

    (A) Applicants
    (B) Apply
    (C) To apply
    (D) Applicable

11. All items ------- at the auction must be inspected beforehand.

    (A) to be sold
    (B) is selling
    (C) has been sold
    (D) to sell

12. The owners plan ------- the restaurant to attract more customers.

    (A) remodeling
    (B) remodeled
    (C) to be remodeled
    (D) to remodel

13. In order to ------- your subscription, you have to fill out an online survey first.

    (A) renew
    (B) renewal
    (C) renews
    (D) renewing

14. Human Resources hopes ------- more employees with IT experience.

    (A) to hire
    (B) hiring
    (C) hire
    (D) hired

15. The restaurant is planning a special menu ------- its fifth anniversary.

(A) to celebrate   (B) celebrates
(C) celebrated   (D) in celebration

16. To get to the Roseblossom Café, ------- the elevator on the south side of the lobby.

(A) use   (B) used
(C) using   (D) to use

17. It is essential ------- us to analyze customer feedback carefully.

(A) for   (B) of
(C) so   (D) that

18. Mr. Park, the President of Drytech, Inc., announced his ------- to retire in March.

(A) intended   (B) intentional
(C) intends   (D) intention

19. Workers need to become more ------- with the new safety standards.

(A) familiar   (B) familiarity
(C) familiarly   (D) to familiarize

20. The city council organized the town hall meeting to be ------- on May 20.

(A) holding   (B) held
(C) hold   (D) holds

기본 완성 훈련 다음은 앞서 풀어 본 연습문제의 문장들입니다. to부정사를 찾아 밑줄을 긋고, 부사적 용법으로 쓰인 경우 문제 번호에 ○를 치세요.

1. Because the weather is unusually cold, Matton Hotels are currently offering discount coupons to attract customers.

2. Due to the low sales figures, we made a decision to discontinue the Bluestone Bicycle line.

3. The Human Resources Department asked employees to submit ideas to improve workplace performance.

4. The President of JBK Company has decided to offer university students internships this summer.

5. The employees are happy to discuss ways to improve customer services.

6. The company is committed to increasing its domestic sales.

7. Requirements for the editor position include a journalism degree.

8. The restaurant is planning a special menu to celebrate its fifth anniversary.

9. To get to the Roseblossom Café, use the elevator on the south side of the lobby.

10. The city council organized the town hall meeting to be held on May 20.

동명사

동명사는 주어, 목적어, 보어, 전치사의 목적어 역할을 한다. 명사와 달리 동사처럼 목적어, 보어, 수식어를 동반하며 시제와 태가 있다.

기본 개념 이해하기

1. 동명사의 형태와 역할

▶ 동명사는 「동사원형-ing」의 형태로, '~하는 것'으로 해석한다.

▶ 동명사는 주어, 목적어, 보어, 전치사의 목적어 자리에 쓸 수 있다.

▶ 동명사 주어는 단수로 취급하므로 3인칭 단수형 동사를 쓴다.

▶ 동명사는 동사의 목적어로도 쓰이며, mind, consider, postpone 등은 목적어로 to부정사는 못 나오며 동명사를 취한다.

Assisting customers promptly / is our top priority.

⋯▸ **Assistance** ⊗ **Assist** ⊗ **Assisted** ⊗

The company considered **hiring** Mr. Shin / based on his strong communication skills.
⋯▸ **to hire** ⊗

해석 고객들을 신속하게 돕는 것이 우리가 최우선으로 하는 것이다. / 그 회사는 Mr. Shin의 뛰어난 의사소통 기술을 근거로 그를 채용하는 것을 고려했다.

2. 전치사의 목적어 역할

▶ 동명사는 시험에 전치사의 목적어 자리로 가장 많이 출제된다. 전치사 바로 뒤에 명사, 동명사, 형용사를 고르는 문제가 출제되므로 주의해야 한다. 특히 전치사와 관사나 소유격과 같은 한정사가 붙어 있는 명사 사이에는 무조건 동명사를 고른다.

전치사 + [명사] (+ 전치사구 등 수식어)   전치사 + [동명사] (+ 한정사) + 명사

As a coordinator, he will be responsible for **arranging** employee shifts. 전치사 + 동명사 + 명사

⋯▸ **arranged** ⊗ **arrangement** ⊗ **to arrange** ⊗

Hamoor Bistro succeeded in **opening** several restaurants in the neighborhood.
전치사 + 동명사 + 한정사 + 명사

⋯▸ **opened** ⊗ **to open** ⊗

해석 진행자로서, 그는 직원 교대를 조정하는 것을 담당하게 될 것이다. / Hamoor 식당은 인근에서 다수의 레스토랑을 개업하는 데 성공했다.

3. 명사와 동명사의 차이

▶ 동명사는 목적어, 보어, 수식어를 동반할 수 있으며, 부사의 수식을 받는다.

▶ 동명사 앞에는 관사나 형용사가 올 수 없다.

▶ 명사는 관사나 형용사가 앞에 올 수 있지만, 목적어나 보어를 동반할 수 없다.

	관사	수	수식어	목적어
명사	O	단/복수 구분	형용사	X
동명사	X	단수 취급	부사	O

Mr. Park will begin **creating** invitations. ◉

Mr. Park will begin / **creation** invitations. ✖

The security guards kept the crowd / from **approaching closely**. ◉

The security guards kept the crowd / from **approaching close**. ✖

The ship has made / a **close approach** to the harbor.

해석　Mr. Park는 초대장을 만들기 시작할 것이다. / 보안 요원들은 군중들이 가까이 접근하는 것을 막았다. / 배가 항구에 근접했다.
풀이　원래 목적어가 없는 자동사는 동명사가 되더라도 뒤에 목적어가 없다.

4. 동명사의 의미상 주어, 부정, 시제, 태

▶ 동명사의 의미상 주어는 동명사 앞에 소유격으로 표시한다.

▶ 동명사의 부정형은 「not / never + 동사원형-ing」이다.

▶ 시제: 동명사의 사건이 본동사의 시점보다 먼저 일어났을 때 「having + 과거분사」 형태의 완료 동명사를 쓴다.

▶ 태: 동명사가 의미상의 주어와 수동의 관계일 때 「being + 과거분사」 형태를 쓴다.

We are so proud of **her** / **winning** the recent contest. 소유격: 동명사의 의미상 주어

The business got fined / for **not paying** its taxes. not + 동사원형 -ing: 부정

Everyone was surprised / at her **having won** the prize. having + 과거분사: 완료형

To avoid **being charged** for services he never received, Gary asked for an itemized bill. being + 과거분사: 수동형

해석　우리는 그녀가 최근 경연 대회에서 우승한 것을 매우 자랑스럽게 생각한다.
그녀가 그 상을 수상했었다는 것에 다들 놀랐다. / 그 사업장은 세금을 내지 않아서 벌금을 물었다.
Gary는 받지 않은 서비스에 대해 비용이 청구되는 것을 피하기 위해 요금 상세 내역서를 요청했다.

Q1 동명사의 자리

------- a conference for over 1,000 people is one of the most demanding projects that our team has undertaken.

(A) Being planned   (B) Plans   (C) Planning   (D) Will have planned

>> 출제 포인트 동명사는 명사 자리에 온다.

1 선택지 확인 | 빈칸에 들어갈 알맞은 형태와 품사를 고른다.

2 빈칸 확인 | 주어 자리 → 주어의 역할을 하는 명사나 동명사가 와야 하므로 동사 (D) Will have planned ❌

3 정답 확인 | a conference를 목적어로 받고 동사 is의 주어 역할을 하는 동명사가 와야 하므로 (A) Being planned, (B) Plans ❌ (C) Planning ⭕

정답 **(C) Planning** a conference for over 1,000 people / is one of the most demanding projects / that our team has undertaken.

해석 1,000명 이상의 사람들을 위한 컨퍼런스를 계획하는 것이 / 가장 힘든 일 중 하나이다 / 우리 팀이 겪어온

출제 포인트 **❶ 동명사는 명사 역할을 한다.**

Reducing operating costs / is not easy.   주어

Ms. Ross considered / **helping** me.   목적어

Mr. O'Neill talked about / **moving** to another apartment.   전치사의 목적어

Our goal is / **making** clients happy.   동명사 보어

해석   운영비를 줄이는 것은 쉽지 않다. / Ms. Ross는 나를 돕는 것을 고려했다.
Mr. O'Neill은 다른 아파트로 이사하는 것에 대해 이야기를 했다. / 우리의 목표는 고객을 행복하게 하는 것이다.

해설서 p.38

check

1. Please inform your event organizer of any special meal requests before ------- a catering service.

(A) book   (B) books   (C) booking   (D) booked

Q2 명사 vs. 동명사

Offering frequent discounts is a good way of ------- more customers to a business.

(A) attracts   (B) attraction   (C) attractive   (D) attracting

>> **출제 포인트 동명사는 명사와 달리 동사의 성질에 따라 목적어나 보어를 동반한다.**

1 선택지 확인 | 빈칸에 들어갈 알맞은 품사를 고른다.

2 빈칸 확인 | 전치사 뒤 → 동사인 (A) attracts ✗ → 명사 (B) attraction은 전치사 뒤에 들어갈 수 있으나, 빈칸 뒤의 명사구(more customers)와 연결될 수 없다. (B) attraction ✗

3 정답 확인 | 명사구(more customers)를 목적어로 취하면서 전치사(of)의 목적어 자리에 들어갈 수 있는 품사는 동명사이므로 정답은 (D) attracting ◉ 형용사 (C)도 가능하지만 문맥상 '매력적인 고객들의 방법'은 어색하므로 답이 될 수 없다.

정답 Offering frequent discounts / is a good way / of **(D) attracting** more customers / to a business.
해석 할인을 자주 제공하는 것이 / 좋은 방법이다 / 더 많은 고객들을 유치하는 / 사업에서

출제 포인트 ❷ 명사와 동명사의 차이

명사	관사가 앞에 올 수 있다.	형용사의 수식을 받는다.	목적어나 보어가 없다.
동명사	관사가 앞에 올 수 없다.	부사의 수식을 받는다.	목적어나 보어가 따라올 수 있다.

출제 포인트 ❸ -ing로 끝나는 명사

-ing로 끝나지만 동명사가 명사로 굳어진 단어들에 유의해야 한다.

findings 발견	covering 덮개	processing 처리
shopping 쇼핑	ticketing 발권	earnings 소득, 이득
advertising 광고업	meaning 의미	sightseeing 관광
recording 녹화, 녹음	setting 설정, 설치	opening 공석, 시작 부분, 개막식
parking 주차	warning 경고	housing 숙소, 주거
learning 학습	spending 지출	marketing 마케팅
belongings 소유물	seating 좌석 배치	surroundings 환경, 상황
cleaning 청소	packaging 상품 포장	gathering 모임
funding 자금 지원	training 훈련	accounting 회계
understanding 이해	savings 저축, 저금	beginning 시작

⊕ check

2. The security team is responsible for ------- safety regulations and guidelines for the guests and employees of Westland Hotel.

    (A) established   (B) establish   (C) establishment   (D) establishing

Q3 동사 + [동명사 vs. to부정사]

Mr. Tenor should reconsider ------- another store in San Francisco because of the city's high property prices.

(A) open   (B) opening   (C) to open   (D) opens

>> **출제 포인트** 동사에 따라 목적어로서 동명사 또는 to부정사를 구별해서 사용해야 한다.

1 선택지 확인 | 빈칸에 들어갈 알맞은 형태와 품사를 고른다.

2 빈칸 확인 | 동사의 목적어이자 빈칸 뒤에서 목적어를 동반하는 준동사 자리 → 동사/형용사 (A) open ❌
동사 (D) opens ❌

3 정답 확인 | 동사 reconsider은 동명사를 목적어로 취하는 동사이다. → to부정사 (C) to open ❌
동명사 (B) opening ⭕

정답   Mr. Tenor / should reconsider / **(B) opening** another store / in San Francisco / because of the city's high property prices.
해석   Mr. Tenor는 / 재고해야 한다 / 또 다른 상점을 여는 것을 / 샌프란시스코에서 / 그 도시의 높은 부동산 가격 때문에

출제 포인트 ❹ 동명사만을 목적어로 취하는 타동사

즐김, 상상	enjoy -ing 즐기다	miss -ing 그리워하다	imagine -ing 상상하다
제안, 인정	suggest -ing 제안하다 admit -ing 인정하다	recommend -ing 권유하다	consider -ing 고려하다
지속, 중단	keep -ing 계속하다 give up -ing 포기하다 delay -ing 미루다	finish -ing 끝마치다 discontinue -ing 중단하다 postpone -ing 연기하다	quit -ing 그만두다 prevent -ing 막다 resume -ing 재개하다
싫음, 거부	avoid -ing 피하다 deny -ing 거부하다	dislike -ing 싫어하다 resist -ing 저항하다	mind -ing 싫어하다

Ms. Stacey **enjoys** / **listening** to various genres of music.

해석   Ms. Stacey는 다양한 장르의 음악을 듣는 것을 즐긴다.

+ check

3. To find your desired book, we strongly recommend ------- the library's newly updated electronic database.

(A) utilization   (B) to utilize   (C) utilizing   (D) utilized

Q4 형용사 + [전치사 to vs. to부정사]

The instruction manual is dedicated ------- how to properly assemble the Cool Jet Spa.

(A) explaining　　　(B) to explain　　　(C) to explaining　　　(D) explained

>> **출제 포인트** 「전치사 to + 동명사」 관용 표현을 묻는다.

1 선택지 확인 | 빈칸에 들어갈 알맞은 형태와 품사를 고른다.

2 빈칸 확인 | 「be dedicated to: ~하는 데 전념하다」 관용 표현을 알고 있어야 한다.

3 정답 확인 | be dedicated to의 to는 전치사이므로 to부정사로 착각해서 동사원형을 쓰면 안 된다. 전치사 뒤에는 동명사가 나오므로 정답은 (C) to explaining ⊙

정답　The instruction manual / is dedicated / **(C) to explaining** how to properly assemble the Cool Jet Spa.
해석　그 설명서는 / 전념한다 / Cool Jet Spa를 제대로 조립하는 방법을 설명하는 데

출제 포인트 ⑤ 전치사 to와 to부정사를 혼동하지 않도록 한다.

be committed to -ing ~에 헌신하다
look forward to -ing ~하는 것을 고대하다
object to -ing ~에 반대하다
be devoted to -ing ~하는 데 전념하다

contribute to -ing ~하는 데 공헌하다
be used to -ing ~하는 데 익숙하다
be opposed to -ing ~하는 데 반대하다
be subject to -ing ~하기 쉽다

We are **looking forward / to having** a mutually beneficial partnership.

해석　우리는 상호간에 수혜적인 협력 관계를 맺기를 고대한다.

출제 포인트 ⑥ 동명사 관용 표현

have difficulty (in) -ing ~하는 데 어려움을 겪다
be busy -ing ~하느라 바쁘다
keep (on) -ing 계속해서 ~하다
cannot help -ing ~할 수밖에 없다
insist on -ing ~하기를 고수하다

on -ing ~하자마자
be worth -ing ~할 가치가 있다
feel like -ing ~하고 싶다
It's no use -ing ~해봐야 소용없다
when it comes to -ing ~에 관하여 말하자면

I had **difficulty / performing** the software update.

해석　나는 그 소프트웨어 업데이트를 실행하는 데 어려움을 겪었다.

▶check

4. PS Consultants is committed to ------- the skills that allow workers to perform more efficiently on the job.

(A) provides　　　(B) providing　　　(C) provider　　　(D) provided

해설서 p.39

1. ------- to the construction site must wear a protective helmet and glasses.

(A) Visit (B) Visitors
(C) Visiting (D) Visits

2. ------- additional engineers for the project will be our first priority.

(A) Hiring (B) Hire
(C) Hires (D) Hired

3. This notice is intended to inform drivers of ------- on oversized vehicles in the parking garage.

(A) restricting (B) restricts
(C) restrictive (D) restrictions

4. Lulpite Corporation discontinued ------- home appliances.

(A) to produce (B) producing
(C) production (D) produced

5. All the information about interviewing ------- is kept in the HR office.

(A) applicants (B) applications
(C) applied (D) apply

6. The trays of the Kitchen-Pro stove can be removed for easy -------.

(A) clean (B) cleaners
(C) cleaning (D) cleaned

7. The theater owner prevented the audience from ------- the performance.

(A) recording (B) record
(C) to record (D) recorded

8. By ------- the assembly line process, production numbers can be increased.

(A) updates (B) updating
(C) updated (D) update

9. Bostex, Inc., a global consumer appliance -------, works to meet the demand for steam irons.

(A) supplier (B) supplying
(C) supplied (D) supplies

10. After ------- reviewing the seating chart, let me know what changes should be made.

(A) carefully (B) to care
(C) careful (D) care

11. After ------- a promotion, Mr. Jang began looking for an assistant.

(A) acceptable (B) accepts
(C) accepting (D) accepted

12. Next Wednesday marks the third anniversary of KJ Bank's -------.

(A) opened (B) openness
(C) open (D) opening

13. Purchasing a movie ticket through the Web site ------- only a few minutes.

(A) taken (B) take
(C) takes (D) taking

14. A good way of ------- customers is to give them a money-back guarantee.

(A) attracts (B) attraction
(C) attracting (D) attracted

15. Please make sure to confirm ------- of order #9734, which will be arriving later today.

(A) receipt   (B) received
(C) receive   (D) receiving

16. Students are assigned a recommended reading list as a ------- to the material in the textbook.

(A) supplemented
(B) supplement
(C) supplementing
(D) supplementary

17. The BRT sports watch can be worn in the water without losing -------.

(A) functioned   (B) functional
(C) functionality   (D) functionally

18. Customers will receive free movie tickets, for ------- in the survey.

(A) participates   (B) participate
(C) participating   (D) participated

19. Festival ------- can try authentic dishes from around the world.

(A) attending   (B) attends
(C) attendees   (D) attendance

20. The person in charge of dealing with urgent ------- is Mr. Morales.

(A) request   (B) requesting
(C) requested   (D) requests

기본 완성 훈련 다음은 앞서 풀어 본 연습문제의 문장들입니다. 동명사를 찾아 밑줄을 긋고, 동명사를 포함한 명사구에 괄호 표시를 하세요.

1. Hiring additional engineers for the project will be our first priority.

2. Lulpite Corporation discontinued producing home appliances.

3. All the information about interviewing applicants is kept in the HR office.

4. The theater owner prevented the audience from recording the performance.

5. By updating the assembly line process, production numbers can be increased.

6. Bostcx, Inc., a global consumer appliance supplier, works to meet the demand for steam irons.

7. After carefully reviewing the seating chart, let me know what changes should be made.

8. A good way of attracting customers is to give them a money-back guarantee.

9. Customers will receive free movie tickets for participating in the survey.

10. The person in charge of dealing with urgent requests is Mr. Morales.

UNIT 15

분사

분사는 동사처럼 목적어, 보어, 수식어를 동반하며 시제와 태가 있다. 현재분사와 과거분사는 동사의 진행형이나 완료형 또는 수동태의 일부로 쓰이거나 형용사처럼 명사 앞의 수식어 또는 주어나 목적어를 보충 설명하는 보어 역할을 한다.

기본 개념 이해하기

1. 분사의 형태와 의미

▶ 현재분사는 「동사원형-ing」 형태이며, '능동(~하는)'이나 '진행(~하고 있는)'의 의미가 있다.

▶ 과거분사는 「동사원형-ed」 형태이며, '수동(~된)'이나 '완료(~한)'의 의미가 있다.

현재분사	능동, 진행의 의미	a **leading** company	선두 기업
과거분사	수동, 완료의 의미	an **attached** file	첨부된 파일

▶ 수식 받는 명사 또는 주어와의 능동·수동 관계에 따라 현재분사나 과거분사를 쓴다.
  타동사의 과거분사는 '수동(완료)'을 의미하며, '수동'의 개념이 없는 자동사의 과거분사는 '완료'의 의미만 있다.

2. 분사의 역할

▶ 형용사와 같이 명사의 수식어 역할과 주어와 목적어를 보충 설명하는 보어 역할을 한다.

Learn more / about the recently **announced** changes to the program.
분사(수식어) + 명사(changes)

The new technology / is very **promising**. be동사 + 분사(보어)

해석 최근에 발표된 그 프로그램에 생긴 변동 사항에 대해 좀 더 알아 보세요. / 그 새로운 기술은 전망이 매우 좋다.

3. 명사를 뒤에서 꾸며 주는 분사

▶ 분사 뒤에 목적어나 보어, 수식어구 등이 따라와서 길어질 때는 명사를 뒤에서 꾸며 준다.

The Web site is a great resource for people / **seeking** travel information.
명사(people) + [분사(seeking) + 목적어(travel information)]

We have some problems / **related** to the system.
명사(problems) + [분사(related) + 전치사구(to the system)]

해석   그 웹사이트는 여행 정보를 찾는 사람들에게 훌륭한 자료가 된다. / 우리는 그 시스템과 관련하여 약간의 문제가 있다.

✓ 문법 포인트   준동사란?

to부정사, 동명사, 현재분사나 과거분사처럼 동사의 모양이 바뀌어 서술어가 아닌 다른 여러 가지 문장 성분으로 사용되는 형태를 준동사라고 한다. 준동사는 단독으로도 쓰이지만, 동사와 마찬가지로 뒤에 목적어나 보어가 올 수 있으며, 부사어구의 꾸밈을 받을 수 있다. 또한 시제나 수동태를 나타낼 수 있고, 부정형도 있다.

4. 분사 구문

▶ 「접속사 + 주어 + 동사」 형태의 부사절을 분사를 이용해서 간결하게 나타낼 수 있다. 부사절의 주어가 주절과 같은 경우 부사절의 접속사와 주어를 지우고 동사를 분사로 바꾼다.

▶ 시간, 조건, 이유, 동시 동작, 양보 등을 나타내며, 접속사를 생략하지 않는 경우도 있다.

| 능동 분사 구문 | (While) **Walking** outside, Martha saw the mailman arrive. |
| 수동 분사 구문 | (If) **Handled** carelessly, this product can be damaged. |

Not **having** any cash, / Mr. Amoto paid for the item with his credit card.

= As he didn't have any cash,

해석   현금이 없어서 Mr. Amoto는 그 상품을 신용카드로 결제했다.
풀이   접속사 As와 주어 he를 생략하고 동사 have를 분사 having으로 바꾼다. 부정어 not은 having 앞에 써 준다.

As **discussed** in the meeting, / the new policies will bring significant benefits in cost savings.

= As they were discussed in the meeting,

해석   회의에서 논의된 바와 같이, 새로운 정책들은 비용 절감에 상당한 이익을 가져다줄 것이다.
풀이   접속사 As(~대로)를 생략해 버리면 '논의한 바와 마찬가지로'라는 의미가 정확하게 전달되지 않으므로 그대로 남겨둔다.

The system **being** too complicated, / the programmer attempted to automate the process.

= Because the system was too complicated,

해석   그 시스템은 너무 복잡했기 때문에 그 프로그래머는 그 절차를 자동화하려고 애썼다.
풀이   complicated와 attempted의 주어가 다르므로 이를 밝혀 주어야 한다. '그 프로그래머'가 아닌 '그 시스템'이 복잡한 것이다.

Q1 명사를 앞에서 수식하는 분사

The university dean will review the ------- changes to the undergraduate admissions process.

(A) proposed   (B) proposal   (C) proposing   (D) propose

>> **출제 포인트** 수식을 받는 명사와 분사의 능동·수동 관계를 확인해야 한다.

1 선택지 확인 | 빈칸에 들어갈 알맞은 품사를 고른다.

2 빈칸 확인 | 관사와 명사 사이의 형용사 자리 → (D) propose ✕ (B)는 생김새가 형용사같지만 명사이므로 주의가 필요하다.

3 정답 확인 | 문맥상 '제안하는 변경 사항들'이 아닌, '제안된 변경 사항들'이므로 명사와 '수동' 관계인 과거분사가 와야 한다. 정답은 (A) proposed ◎

정답 The university dean / will review / the **(A) proposed** changes / to the undergraduate admissions process.

해석 그 대학 학과장이 / 검토할 것이다 / 제안된 변경 사항들을 / 학부생 입학 절차에 대한

출제 포인트 ❶ 명사 앞에 자주 나오는 분사

현재분사 (V-ing) 표현		과거분사 (p.p.) 표현	
lasting impression	오래 남는 인상	damaged items	손상된 제품
rising price	오르는 가격	detailed information	세부적인 정보
growing demand	증가하는 수요	limited time	한정된 기간
existing product line	기존의 제품 라인	enclosed brochure	동봉된 안내책자
remaining paperwork	남아있는 서류 작업	attached document	첨부된 서류
surrounding community	인근 지역	updated manual	최신의 설명서
leading company	선두적인 기업	complicated order	복잡한 주문
demanding work	힘든 작업	qualified applicant	자격을 갖춘 지원자
promising new musicians	유망한 신인 음악가	written notice	서면의 공지
rewarding effort	보람 있는 노력	designated parking area	지정된 주차구역
winning entry	우승한 출품작	revised budget	개정된[수정된] 예산
challenging tasks	어려운 업무	experienced / skilled programmer	숙련된 프로그래머
emerging company	떠오르는 회사	specialized hiking boots	전문화된 등산화

➕check   해설서 p.41

1. Passengers must be in their ------- seats by 9 A.M. in order for the flight to take off on time.

(A) assigned   (B) assign   (C) assigns   (D) assigning

Q2 명사를 뒤에서 수식하는 분사

All trains ------- from New York have been delayed, but service is expected to resume this afternoon.

(A) origin   (B) will originate   (C) originating   (D) originate

>> 출제 포인트 동사처럼 목적어나 전치사구를 동반하는 분사는 명사 뒤에 온다.

1 선택지 확인 | 빈칸에 들어갈 알맞은 품사를 고른다.

2 빈칸 확인 | 주어는 All trains, 동사는 have been delayed이며, 「------- + 전치사구」는 All trains를 꾸며 주는 수식어구이다. → 전치사구를 동반할 수 없는 명사는 빈칸에 올 수 없다. (A) origin(기원) ✘ → 동사 자리가 아니므로 (B) will originate(기원할 것이다), (D) originate(기원하다) ✘

3 정답 확인 | 문맥상 '~에서 출발하는'이라는 의미가 되어야 하므로 꾸밈을 받는 명사와 '능동' 관계의 현재분사가 와야 한다. 정답은 (C) originating(기원하는, 출발하는) ◎

정답 All trains / **(C) originating** from New York / have been delayed, but service is expected / to resume this afternoon.
해석 모든 기차들은 / 뉴욕에서 출발하는 / 연기되었다, 그렇지만 서비스는 기대된다 / 오늘 오후에 재개될 것으로

출제 포인트 ❷ 명사 뒤에 오는 분사
목적어나 수식어구를 동반한 현재분사나 과거분사는 명사를 뒤에서 수식한다.

Workers / **renovating** the building / removed the old tile flooring. 명사 뒤에서 수식
A traffic jam / **caused** by the car accident / made the clients late. 명사 뒤에서 수식
해석 그 빌딩을 개조하는 일꾼들은 낡은 타일 바닥을 제거했다. / 차 사고로 인한 교통 정체는 고객들이 늦어지게 했다.

- -

⊕check

2. Tungston Manufacturing intends to offer employees various training programs ------- on workplace safety.

(A) focus   (B) focusing   (C) will focus   (D) have focused

Q3 보어 자리의 분사

Although Mr. Yisida was ------- with this quarter's sales figures, he is still planning to expand his business.

(A) disappointing   (B) disappointment   (C) disappoint   (D) disappointed

>> **출제 포인트** 분사는 주어나 목적어를 설명하는 보어 역할을 할 수 있다.

① **선택지 확인** | 빈칸에 들어갈 알맞은 품사를 고른다.

② **빈칸 확인** | be동사 뒤 주격 보어자리이므로 명사나 형용사가 필요하다. → 빈칸에 올 수 없는 동사원형 (C) disappoint ❌

③ **정답 확인** | 문맥상 '~에 실망하다'라는 뜻이 되어야 한다. 주어인 Mr.Yisidark가 외부의 자극으로 실망한 감정을 나타내야 하며, 감정 동사(disappoint)는 사람을 수식/서술할 때 과거분사를 취하므로 정답은 (D) disappointed ⭕

정답 Although Mr. Yisida was **(D) disappointed** / with this quarter's sales figures, he is still planning / to expand his business.

해석 Mr. Yisida가 실망했어도 / 이번 분기의 매출액에, 그는 여전히 계획하고 있다 / 그의 사업을 확장할 것을

출제 포인트 ❸ 감정을 나타내는 분사

현재분사형 형용사는 주로 사물을 수식/서술하고, 과거분사형 형용사는 사람을 수식/서술한다.

감정 동사		현재분사(V-ing)		과거분사(p.p.)	
excite	신나게 하다	exciting	신나는, 들뜨게 하는	excited	신이 난, 들뜬
please	기쁘게 하다	pleasing	기쁘게 하는	pleased	기뻐하는, 만족스러운
surprise	놀라게 하다	surprising	놀라운	surprised	놀란
disappoint	실망시키다	disappointing	실망시키는	disappointed	실망한
satisfy	만족시키다	satisfying	만족을 주는	satisfied	만족한
interest	흥미를 일으키다	interesting	흥미 있는	interested	흥미를 가진
confuse	혼동을 일으키다	confusing	혼동을 일으키는	confused	혼란스러워 하는
amuse	즐겁게 하다	amusing	재미있는	amused	재미있어 하는
tire	지치게 하다	tiring	피곤하게 하는	tired	피곤한, 지친
disturb	방해하다	disturbing	방해가 되는	disturbed	방해 받은, 산란한
embarrass	당황하게 하다	embarrassing	당황스럽게 하는	embarrassed	당황한, 난처한
worry	걱정시키다	worrying	걱정을 끼치는	worried	근심에 싸인

➕ check

3. It is quite ------- that Tory Motors has become the leader in the electric car industry in just five years.

(A) amaze   (B) amazing   (C) amazed   (D) amazes

Q4 분사 구문

The book inspires you to try different approaches to resolving a problem when
------- with obstacles.

(A) face   (B) faced   (C) facing   (D) to face

▶▶ 출제 포인트 분사 구문은 부사절을 대신할 수 있다.

❶ 선택지 확인 | 빈칸에 들어갈 알맞은 동사의 형태를 고른다.

❷ 빈칸 확인 | 「접속사 + 빈칸 + 전치사구」는 부사어구이다. → 접속사와 전치사구를 동반하여 부사어 역할을 할 수 있는 동사의 형태는 현재분사와 과거분사이다. → 동사 (A) face ✗ to부정사 (D) to face ✗

❸ 정답 확인 | 문맥상 '당신이 장애에 직면했을 때'라는 의미가 되어야 한다. → 정답은 when you are faced with obstacles에서 you are가 생략된 형태인 (B) faced ◎

정답 The book inspires you / to try different approaches to resolving a problem / when **(B) faced** with obstacles.
해석 그 책은 당신을 고무시킨다 / 어떤 문제를 해결하기 위해 다른 방식들을 시도해 보도록 / 장애에 직면했을 때

출제 포인트 ❹ 분사 구문

Turning to the right, you'll see the magazine section.
= If you turn to the right,

해석 오른쪽으로 돌면, 잡지 섹션이 보일 것이다.

When sending the payment, / be sure to include the list of items you purchased.
= When you send the payment,

해석 지불 금액을 보낼 때, 당신이 구입한 물품 목록을 첨부하는 것을 잊지 마세요.

Compared with bids from other firms, / your prices are steep.
= When your prices are compared with the bids from other firms,

해석 타사들의 입찰과 비교할 때, 귀하의 가격은 비쌉니다.

⊕check

4. Mr. Doan will give staff members a one week notice when ------- annual performance reviews.
   (A) scheduled   (B) schedules   (C) scheduling   (D) will schedule

1. WBC Health manufactures ------- medical equipment for use in hospitals and clinics.
   (A) disposable   (B) disposed
   (C) disposing   (D) disposal

2. New workers must attend the ------- training sessions taking place this week.
   (A) assigned   (B) assigns
   (C) assign   (D) assigning

3. *Jenny's Adventures* is one of the most ------- movies of this coming holiday season.
   (A) anticipation   (B) anticipated
   (C) anticipating   (D) anticipate

4. Because of the ------- population, home builders are in high demand.
   (A) growing   (B) growth
   (C) grown   (D) to grow

5. The ------- logo for *Beauty Tips Magazine* has won several awards.
   (A) redesign   (B) redesigns
   (C) redesigning   (D) redesigned

6. Candidates ------- in applying for the position should contact the Personnel Department.
   (A) interests   (B) interest
   (C) interesting   (D) interested

7. The recently ------- report shows that fourth quarter sales increased.
   (A) released   (B) releasing
   (C) to release   (D) was released

8. Customers ------- items in bulk may be eligible for volume discounts.
   (A) purchase   (B) purchasing
   (C) purchased   (D) purchases

9. ------- repairs are needed before the bridge over Sunflower Creek can reopen.
   (A) Extensive   (B) Extend
   (C) Extending   (D) Extends

10. Newly hired employees are required to attend a very ------- three-week training course.
    (A) demand   (B) demanded
    (C) demanding   (D) demands

11. The Web site ------- by J&J Tech won an industry award in April.
    (A) created   (B) creating
    (C) creatively   (D) creation

12. The organizers hope that the company picnic is ------- and enjoyable.
    (A) excitement   (B) exciting
    (C) excitably   (D) excited

13. Upper management worries that the user manual is ------- and may need to be rewritten.
    (A) confusing   (B) confusion
    (C) confuses   (D) confused

14. The hotel's ------- Web site will allow customers to book reservations online.
    (A) updating   (B) updated
    (C) update   (D) to update

15. CSG, also ------- as the Camera Servicing Group, hosts monthly classes for professionals.

(A) knowing   (B) was known
(C) known   (D) knew

16. Many customers were ------- because the product did not work as advertised.

(A) disappointing   (B) disappointed
(C) disappoint   (D) disappoints

17. Despite the convenience of online shopping malls, consumers are still ------- to buy clothes they cannot try on first.

(A) hesitated   (B) hesitantly
(C) hesitance   (D) hesitant

18. To keep employees ------- of the most recent project developments, we update the company Web site daily.

(A) inform   (B) informed
(C) informing   (D) informs

19. All boxes ------- behind the loading dock will be discarded this weekend.

(A) left   (B) leaves
(C) leaving   (D) leave

20. Our company will hold interviews for ------- programmers next month.

(A) to experience   (B) experience
(C) experiences   (D) experienced

기본 완성 훈련 다음은 앞서 풀어 본 연습문제의 문장들입니다. 분사를 찾아 밑줄을 긋고, 분사가 수식하는 대상에 ○를 치세요.

1. WBC Health manufactures disposable medical equipment for use in hospitals and clinics.

2. New workers must attend the assigned training sessions taking place this week.

3. The redesigned logo for *Beauty Tips Magazine* has won several awards.

4. The recently released report shows that fourth quarter sales increased.

5. Customers purchasing items in bulk may be eligible for volume discounts.

6. Extensive repairs are needed before the bridge over Sunflower Creek can reopen.

7. Newly hired employees are required to attend a very demanding three-week training course.

8. Despite the convenience of online shopping malls, consumers are still hesitant to buy clothes they cannot try on first.

9. All boxes left behind the loading dock will be discarded this weekend.

10. Our company will hold interviews for experienced programmers next month.

비교

둘 이상의 대상을 하나의 기준에 빗대어 그 수량이나 성질의 상대적 관계를 표현하는 비교 구문에는 원급, 비교급, 최상급 비교가 있다.

1. 형용사·부사의 급

▶ be동사 등의 보어 역할을 하거나 명사를 꾸며 주는 형용사, 또는 동사, 형용사 등을 꾸며 주는 부사는 원급, 비교급, 최상급으로 그 급이 변화한다.

원급	기본형	small	big	beautiful	두 비교 대상의 위상이 서로 동등함을 나타냄
비교급	원급 + -er more + 원급	smaller	bigger	**more** beautiful	두 비교 대상 중 하나의 위상이 상대적으로 더 높음을 나타냄
최상급	원급 + -est most + 원급	smallest	biggest	**most** beautiful	셋 이상의 비교 대상 중 하나의 위상이 가장 높음을 나타냄

2. 원급

▶ 「as + 형용사/부사의 원급 + as」 형태로 비교하는 두 대상이 서로 비슷할 때 사용한다. '~만큼 …한/하게'의 뜻이다.

▶ 부정문에 쓰이면 '~만큼 …하지 않은/않게'를 의미한다.

The food was good.

⋯▶ The food / was **as good as** the customer expected. 형용사 자리의 원급 비교

해석   그 음식이 훌륭했다. / 그 음식은 고객이 기대했던 만큼 훌륭했다.

The new employee works efficiently.

⋯▶ The new employee works / **as efficiently as** Steve does. 부사 자리의 원급 비교

해석   새로 온 직원은 효율적으로 일한다. / 새로 온 직원은 Steve만큼 효율적으로 일한다.

This product / is **not as popular as** that one. 부정문에 쓰인 원급 비교

⋯▶ This product / is **less popular** than that one.

해석   이 제품은 저것(=제품)만큼 호응이 좋지 않다.

3. 비교급

▶ 「원급 + -er than / more + 원급 than」 형태로 한쪽이 우월할 때 사용한다. '더 ~한/하게'의 뜻이다.

▶ 반대로 '덜 …한/하게'는 「less ~ than」으로 표현한다.

The test / was **easier than** expected. 형용사 자리의 비교급 비교

The instructions / were **more complex than** expected.

해석 그 시험은 예상보다 쉬웠다. / 그 설명서는 기대한 것보다 복잡했다.

Ms. Rose works **harder** / **than** Mr. Davis does. 부사 자리의 비교급 비교

Ms. Rose works **more efficiently** / **than** Mr. Davis does.

해석 Ms. Rose는 Mr. Davis보다 열심히 일한다. / Ms. Rose는 Mr. Davis보다 더 효율적으로 일한다.

Most of the applicants / were **less qualified** / than we expected. 형용사 자리의 비교급 비교

해석 지원자들 대부분이 우리가 기대했던 것보다 자격을 덜 갖추고 있었다.

4. 최상급

▶ 최상급은 세 개 이상의 대상을 놓고 비교할 때 사용한다. '~중에서 / ~에서 가장 …한/하게'를 의미한다.

| the / 소유격 + [부사 / 형용사-est] + of 대상 / in 장소 |
| the / 소유격 + [most 부사 / 형용사] + of 대상 / in 장소 |

~중에서 / ~에서 가장 …한/하게

The advertisement for Vocalola / was voted **the most influential** / of all the advertisements.

= Of all the advertisements, the advertisement for Vocalola / was voted **the most influential**.

해석 Vocalola의 광고가 모든 광고들에서 가장 영향력 있는 것으로 선정되었다.
모든 광고들 중에서 Vocalola의 광고가 가장 영향력 있는 것으로 선정되었다.

5. 강조 표현

▶ 비교급을 강조하는 부사: much / even / far / still / by far / a lot + 비교급(훨씬)

▶ 최상급을 강조하는 부사: even(심지어) / by far(단연코) + 최상급

The new assembly line process contained / **even more cost-effective** measures. 비교급 강조

Our technician answers / **even the most difficult** questions / about our products. 최상급 강조

해석 새로운 조립 라인 공정은 훨씬 더 비용 효율이 높은 방법들을 포함했다. / 저희 기술자가 저희 제품에 관한 가장 어려운 질문들조차도 답변해 드립니다.

Q1 ~만큼 ~한/하게

Stax Electronics' tablet PCs are as popular ------- its main line of smartphones.

(A) as   (B) of   (C) either   (D) like

>> **출제 포인트 원급 비교 표현을 묻는다.**

① **선택지 확인** | 빈칸에 들어갈 알맞은 단어를 고른다.

② **빈칸 확인** | 빈칸 앞 'as + 원급 형용사(popular)'를 보고 원급 비교 표현 「as + 원급 형용사/부사 + as」을 떠올릴 수 있어야 한다.

③ **정답 확인** | 「as + 원급 형용사 + as」는 '~만큼 …하다' 라는 의미이므로 정답은 (A) as ⓞ

정답 Stax Electronics's tablet PCs / are / as popular **(A) as** its main line of smartphones.

해석 Stax 전자의 태블릿 PC가 / 그 회사 스마트폰의 주력 라인만큼 인기가 좋다.

출제 포인트 ❶ 여러 가지 원급 비교 표현

as 수량 형용사 + 명사 as	~만큼 많은(적은) …	the same ~ as	~와 같은 …
as 원급 as possible	가능한 한 ~하게	not as 원급 as	~만큼 …하지 않은

Please take / **as many** brochures **as** you need.
Mr. Mendez needs the sales information / **as soon as possible**.
I would like / to set up franchise stores in / **as many** places **as possible**.
The digital camera has many of / **the same** features / **as** film models.
Selecting a good financial investment is **not** / **as** easy **as** it may seem.

해석 필요한 만큼 책자를 가져가세요. / Mr. Mendez는 가능한 빨리 매출액 정보가 필요하다.
나는 가능한 많은 곳에 가맹점들을 차리고 싶다. / 그 디지털 카메라는 필름 카메라와 같은 기능들을 많이 가지고 있다.
좋은 금융 투자처를 고르는 일은 보이는 것처럼 쉬운 일이 아니다.

해설서 p.43

✚ check

1. If you need to reschedule your appointment, please contact us as ------- as possible.

(A) early   (B) earliness   (C) earlier   (D) earliest

Q2 더 ~한/하게

Calton Exports' warehouse manager concluded that replacing the broken equipment would be ------- than fixing it.

(A) cheaper   (B) cheapest   (C) more cheaply   (D) most cheaply

>> **출제 포인트 여러 가지 비교급 표현을 묻는다.**

1 선택지 확인 | 빈칸에 들어갈 알맞은 어형을 고른다.

2 빈칸 확인 | 형용사의 자리 → 형용사의 자리에 올 수 없는 부사 (C) more cheaply, (D) most cheaply ❌

3 정답 확인 | 「형용사 비교급 + than」의 표현으로 '~보다 더 …하다'를 의미하므로 정답은 (A) cheaper ⭕

정답 Calton Exports' warehouse manager concluded / that replacing the broken equipment would be **(A) cheaper** than fixing it.

해석 Calton Exports'의 물류 담당자는 결론지었다 / 고장 난 장비를 교체하는 것이 수리하는 것보다 더 저렴할 것이라고

출제 포인트 ② 여러 가지 비교급 표현

수량 형용사 + 명사 than	~보다 많은(적은) ~	the 비교급 of the two	둘 중에 더 ~한
the 비교급 ~ the 비교급	~할수록 더 ~한		

We sold / **more** devices this month than ever before.
The faster the Web site loads, / **the more** visitors we can get.
Royal Doctors is / **the more** famous **of the two charities**.

해석 우리는 이번 달에 그 어느 때보다 더 많은 기기들을 팔았다. / 웹사이트의 로딩 속도가 더 빠를수록 더 많은 방문객들을 얻을 수 있다.
그 두 자선 기관 중에서 Royal Doctors가 더 유명하다.

⬢ check

2. Liv Diner's success is attributed to the fact that it serves customers ------- than the other restaurants do.

(A) more quickly   (B) quick   (C) quickest   (D) most quickly

Q3 가장 ~한/하게

The Tito Carrier is known to have transported some of the ------- cargo in the company's history.

(A) heavy   (B) heavily   (C) heavier   (D) heaviest

>> 출제 포인트 형용사나 부사의 최상급 표현을 쓸 때는 비교할 범위를 한정해준다.

1 선택지 확인 | 빈칸에 들어갈 알맞은 어형을 고른다.

2 빈칸 확인 | 관사와 명사 사이의 형용사 자리 → 형용사 자리에 올 수 없는 부사 (B) heavily ✗

3 정답 확인 | 비교 범위 대상인 'in the company's history' 가 제시되었고, '문맥상 회사 역사상 가장 무거운'이라는 의미이므로 정답은 최상급 (D) heaviest ◎

정답 The Tito Carrier / is known to have transported / some of the **(D) heaviest** cargo / in the company's history.
해석 Tilto Carrier는 / 수송해왔던 것으로 잘 알려져 있다 / 가장 무거운 화물 중 일부를 / 회사 역사상

출제 포인트 ❸ 여러 가지 최상급 표현과 최상급 의미를 나타내는 표현들

One of the 최상급 + 복수 명사	가장 ~한 …중의 하나
비교급 than any other 단수 명사	다른 어떤 ~보다 더 …한
no other 명사/nothing is as 원급 as	어떤 ~도 …만큼 ~하지 않다
no other 명사/nothing is 비교급 than	어떤 ~도 …보다 더 ~하지 않다
have never been 비교급	더 ~해본 적이 없다

The TX 3000 / is **one of the most** advanced mobile phones / on the market.
China has / **more** natural resources **than any other** country / on the planet.
No other product on the market / is **as** useful **as** this one.
Nothing is more valuable **than** time.
The company has **never** been **more** profitable / **than** it is now.

해석 TX 3000은 시중에 나와 있는 가장 진보한 휴대폰 중 하나이다. / 중국은 지구상의 다른 어떤 나라보다도 많은 천연자원을 가지고 있다. 시장에 나와 있는 다른 어떤 제품도 이것만큼 유용하지 않다. / 시간보다 더 귀중한 것은 없다. / 그 회사는 지금처럼 수익이 높은 적이 없었다.

⊕ check

3. Of the sales clerks at Office Network, Mr. Bryson is the ------- about the products displayed in the store.
　(A) knowledgeable   (B) knowledge   (C) more knowledgeable   (D) most knowledgeable

관용 표현

Due to its many successful products, AceSoft has become the single ------- software company in the state.

(A) large   (B) larger   (C) largest   (D) largely

>> **출제 포인트** 비교급과 최상급의 관용 표현을 묻는다.

1 선택지 확인 | 빈칸에 들어갈 알맞은 어형을 고른다.

2 빈칸 확인 | 관사와 명사 사이의 형용사 자리 → 형용사 자리에 올 수 없는 부사 (D) largely ✖

3 정답 확인 | 「the single + 형용사 최상급」으로 '단 하나'만을 강조하는 표현이므로 정답은 최상급 (C) largest ✔

정답 Due to its many successful products, / AceSoft has become / the single **(C) largest** software company in the state.

해석 많은 제품의 성공으로 인해 / AceSoft 사는 되었다 / 그 주에서 가장 큰 단일 소프트웨어 회사가

출제 포인트 ❹ 관용 표현

more than / less than	~이상 / ~이하	no later than	늦어도 ~까지는
would rather ~ than	~하느니 차라리 …하다	no sooner ~ than	~하자마자 …하다
no longer	더이상 ~않다	more than	~이상

The factory has been running / for **more than** a week.
The next annual meeting / will be held **no later than** next July.
Research suggests that passengers **would rather** pay less / **than** have comfortable seating.
No sooner did the presentation begin / **than** the projector broke.

해석 그 공장이 일주일 넘게 가동되고 있다. / 다음 연례 회의는 늦어도 내년 7월에는 열릴 것이다.
연구 자료는 승객들이 좌석이 편한 것보다 돈을 덜 지불하는 것을 선호한다는 것을 보여 준다. / 발표가 시작하자마자 프로젝터가 고장 났다.

+ check

4. Once the new software is installed, the XM120 smartphone will ------- longer support the old video application.

(A) none   (B) not   (C) no   (D) nowhere

Practice

1. Geartech's flagship product is more expensive ------- that of Noble Connect's.

(A) than
(B) instead
(C) from
(D) around

2. The industry association is looking for a conference venue that is ------- larger than MC Convention Center.

(A) such
(B) very
(C) too
(D) even

3. It is important to use the ------- packing materials possible to avoid accidental damage.

(A) strengthens
(B) strengthen
(C) strongest
(D) strongly

4. Clover Suites is the ------- among the area's many resorts.

(A) most beautiful
(B) beautifully
(C) more beautifully
(D) more beautiful

5. DRM Tech yesterday released the ------- tablet PC on the market.

(A) small
(B) smaller
(C) most small
(D) smallest

6. Mr. Lee would like a suitcase as ------- as the one he bought last year.

(A) durable
(B) more durable
(C) durably
(D) durableness

7. Cedar Taxi Co.'s airport pick-up service is more ------- than any of its competitors'.

(A) convenient
(B) conveniently
(C) convenience
(D) conveniences

8. Islet Travel is famous for offering the ------- flights available from Chicago to New York.

(A) cheapness
(B) cheaply
(C) cheapen
(D) cheapest

9. The city planners were convinced more ------- once they had seen the building's plans.

(A) easiest
(B) easy
(C) easier
(D) easily

10. Martin Co. plans to have the ------- network of bus routes in the country by next year.

(A) extends
(B) more extensive
(C) most extensive
(D) extensively

11. With the new software, employees can analyze customer feedback ------- than before.

(A) accuracy
(B) more accurate
(C) more accurately
(D) accuracies

12. JH Company's new computer monitor is much ------- than its model from the year before.

(A) slim
(B) slimmer
(C) sliming
(D) slimness

13. Marrich, Inc. believes its product is superior ------- those made by its competitors.

(A) to
(B) than
(C) such
(D) very

14. Print advertising is usually ------- than online advertising due to additional overhead costs.

(A) expensive
(B) expensively
(C) more expensive
(D) expense

15. No one at the Anderson Corporation has worked ------- for the launch of the new smartphone than Justine Kim.

(A) more energetic   (B) energetic
(C) energetically   (D) more energetically

16. Of all the applicants, Mr. Hong seems to be the most -------.

(A) qualify   (B) qualifies
(C) qualified   (D) qualifier

17. Our client meeting was postponed because their flight was delayed by more ------- five hours.

(A) from   (B) of
(C) as   (D) than

18. Most customer complaints nowadays are resolved ------- easily than before.

(A) right   (B) very
(C) later   (D) more

19. Mr. Kim's ------- article about Lapan Tech is encouraging to investors.

(A) recently   (B) most recent
(C) more recently (D) most recently

20. Falanx Corp. has been more ------- focused on manufacturing computer components in recent years.

(A) narrows   (B) narrowing
(C) narrower   (D) narrowly

기본 완성 훈련 ▶ 다음은 앞서 풀어 본 연습문제의 문장들입니다. 비교급 또는 최상급 표현에 밑줄을 긋고, 비교 대상에 괄호 표시를 하세요.

1. Geartech's flagship product is more expensive than that of Noble Connect's.

2. The industry association is looking for a conference venue that is even larger than MC Convention Center.

3. Islet Travel is famous for offering the cheapest flights available from Chicago to New York.

4. Martin Co. plans to have the most extensive network of bus routes in the country by next year.

5. JH Company's new computer monitor is much slimmer than its model from the year before.

6. Marrich, Inc. believes its product is superior to those made by its competitors.

7. Print advertising is usually more expensive than online advertising due to additional overhead costs.

8. No one at the Anderson Corporation has worked more energetically for the launch of the new smartphone than Justine Kim.

9. Of all the applicants, Mr. Hong seems to be the most qualified.

10. Falanx Corp. has been more narrowly focused on manufacturing computer components in recent years.

REVIEW TEST 04

1. The final ------- should submit the proposal to the board of directors tomorrow morning.
   - (A) reviews
   - (B) reviewing
   - (C) reviewer
   - (D) reviewed

2. The new factory equipment can be set to the ------- height with the lever.
   - (A) desires
   - (B) desire
   - (C) desired
   - (D) desiring

3. Customers wishing ------- the botanical gardens may purchase tickets online or at the front gate.
   - (A) will explore
   - (B) explore
   - (C) exploring
   - (D) to explore

4. The new software enables people to organize complex projects with -------.
   - (A) easy
   - (B) ease
   - (C) easing
   - (D) easily

5. Before ------- the new product, Xpando Corp did extensive research.
   - (A) develop
   - (B) developing
   - (C) developed
   - (D) to develop

6. The Rousse Bistro's ------- new menu has increased the monthly revenue by 20 percent.
   - (A) impress
   - (B) impresses
   - (C) impressed
   - (D) impressive

7. The company's main plant is planning ------- production next month.
   - (A) to increase
   - (B) increasing
   - (C) increase
   - (D) increases

8. ------- to reserve the meeting room should be submitted to the receptionist.
   - (A) Request
   - (B) Requesting
   - (C) Requested
   - (D) Requests

9. The report about the ------- merger will be released tomorrow.
   - (A) proposed
   - (B) proposing
   - (C) propose
   - (D) proposal

10. LPS Machinery hopes its new product will be a ------- in the retail marketplace.
    - (A) succeed
    - (B) success
    - (C) successfully
    - (D) succeeding

11. All current employees are eligible to apply for the newly ------- administrative assistant position.
    - (A) creates
    - (B) created
    - (C) creator
    - (D) creation

12. In order to boost skills in the workforce, devoting a ------- amount of money for training is unavoidable.
    - (A) reasonably
    - (B) reasons
    - (C) reasonable
    - (D) reasoning

13. Please submit the ------- quarterly report tomorrow for the store manager's review.
    - (A) revise
    - (B) revised
    - (C) revising
    - (D) revision

14. The oversupply of steel has made supplier prices very -------.
    - (A) attractive
    - (B) attraction
    - (C) attracted
    - (D) attracts

15. Proper safety precautions should make all workplace accidents -------.
    - (A) preventing
    - (B) preventable
    - (C) prevent
    - (D) prevention

16. All passengers are asked to ------- their airline ticket and passport to the boarding agent.
    - (A) presented
    - (B) presenting
    - (C) present
    - (D) presents

17. B.N. Enterprises is seeking ------- and motivated employees.

(A) to experience   (B) experienced
(C) experiences   (D) experience

18. All properties on Mulberry Lane have driveways that are capable of ------- two vehicles.

(A) parking   (B) parker
(C) parks   (D) park

19. The Vice President of the company was completely ------- with our presentation.

(A) satisfy   (B) satisfies
(C) satisfying   (D) satisfied

20. Genhardt Motors is currently considering ------- their supply tracking software.

(A) to change   (B) changing
(C) being changed   (D) changed

21. One of the ------- made by the committee will be implemented immediately.

(A) recommendations
(B) recommending
(C) recommenders
(D) recommendation

22. An initial budget ------- should be submitted to Accounting by Friday.

(A) estimates   (B) estimate
(C) estimating   (D) estimations

23. Those interested in ------- professional development skills at the conference should sign up by October 10.

(A) to teach   (B) will teach
(C) teaching   (D) teaches

24. Before ------- the next tour stop, make sure that all of the participants are seated in the bus.

(A) announced   (B) announcer
(C) announcement   (D) announcing

25. The ------- issues that users experience with Goldway Bank's mobile application will be resolved in the new version.

(A) occasioned   (B) occasion
(C) occasional   (D) occasionally

26. Mr. Jones will be giving a speech to an ------- audience at the conference tomorrow.

(A) invite   (B) invitation
(C) inviting   (D) invited

27. The ------- corporate sponsors for the event are Indulsion, Inc. and M&K Enterprises.

(A) prominently
(B) more prominently
(C) most prominent
(D) prominence

28. Consumers ------- await the day the next generation of Mango laptops go on sale.

(A) more eager   (B) eagerly
(C) eager   (D) eagerness

29. The decline in profits made it ------- than ever to hire extra sales associates.

(A) harden   (B) hard
(C) harder   (D) hardly

30. The apple salad is ------- than the kiwi salad she made yesterday.

(A) sweet   (B) sweeter
(C) sweetly   (D) sweetest

VOCA

RT5

단문 빈칸
채우기

동사

1 **acquire** [əkwáiər] 획득하다, 인수하다, 습득하다

2 **advertise** [ǽdvərtàiz] 광고하다

3 **anticipate** [æntísəpèit] 예상하다, 예측하다, 고대하다

4 **apologize** 미국 [əpálədʒàiz] 영국 [əpɔ́lədʒàiz]
사과하다

5 **appeal** [əpí:l] 매력적이다, 호소하다, 간청하다

6 **appoint** [əpɔ́int] 임명하다, 지명하다, 정하다

7 **appreciate** [əprí:ʃièit] 고마워하다

8 **approve** [əprú:v] 승인하다

9 **arrange** [əréindʒ] 마련하다, 준비하다, 처리하다, 정리하다,
배열하다

10 **ask** [æ:sk] 요청하다, 묻다

11 **attach** [ətǽtʃ] 첨부하다, 붙이다

12 **attend** [əténd] 참가[참석]하다

13 **award** [əwɔ́:rd] 수여하다

14 **begin** [bigín] 시작하다

15 **believe** [bilí:v, bə-] 믿다

16 **boost** [bu:st] 신장시키다, 북돋우다

17 **charge** [tʃɑ:rdʒ] 청구하다 (n. 요금)

18 **claim** [kleim] 주장하다, 요구하다, 청구하다

19 **complete** [kəmplí:t] 완료하다, 끝마치다
(adj. 완벽한, 완전한, 모든)

20 **confuse** [kənfjú:z] 혼란시키다, 혼란스럽게 만들다

21 **contact** 미국 [kántækt] 영국 [kɔ́ntækt]
연락하다, 접촉하다 (n. 연락, 접촉)

22 **cooperate** 미국 [kouá:pərèit] 영국 [kouɔ́pərèit]
협력하다, 협조하다

23 **create** [kriéit] 만들다, 창조하다

24 **decrease** [dikrí:s] 줄다, 감소하다 (n. 감소, 하락)

25 **delay** [diléi] 미루다, 연기하다 (n. 지연, 지체)

26 **deliver** [dilívər] 배달하다, (연설 등을) 하다

27 **depend** [dipénd] ~에 달려 있다, 의존하다

28 **designate** [dézignèit] 지정하다, 지명하다

29 **discard** [diská:rd] 버리다, 폐기하다

30 **discontinue** [dìskəntínju:] 중단하다

31 **divide** [diváid] 나누다

32 **elect** [ilékt] 선출하다

33 **enclose** [inklóuz] 에워싸다, 동봉하다, 두르다

34 **enjoy** [indʒɔ́i] 즐기다

35 **enlarge** [inlá:rdʒ] 확대/확장하다

36 **enter** [éntər] 출품하다, 출전하다, 들어가다

37 **exchange** [ikstʃéindʒ] 교환하다 (n. 교환)

38 **exit** [égzit, éksit] 나가다 (n. 출구)

39 **expand** [ikspǽnd] 확대되다, 팽창시키다

40 **expect** [ikspékt] 기대하다, 예상하다, 고대하다

41 **feature** [fí:tʃər] 특별히 포함시키다, 특징으로 삼다 (n. 특징)

42 **finalize** [fáinəlàiz] 마무리 짓다, 완결하다

43 **focus** [fóukəs] 집중하다, 초점을 맞추다 (n. 초점, 주목)

44 **gain** [gein] 얻다 (n. 이득)

45 **handle** [hǽndl] 다루다

46 **hire** [haiər] 고용하다

47 **honor** 미국 [ánər] 영국 [ɔ́nər]
존경하다, 공경하다 (n. 명예, 영예)

48 improve [imprúːv] 개선하다, 향상시키다

49 include [inklúːd] 포함하다

50 increase [inkríːs] 증가하다 (*n.* 증가)

51 indicate [índikèit] 나타내다

52 interrupt [intərʌ́pt] 방해하다, 가로막다, 중단시키다

53 issue [íʃuː] 발행하다, 발표하다 (*n.* 쟁점, (잡지의) 호, 발행)

54 join [dʒɔin] 가입하다, 입사하다, 합류하다

55 keep [kiːp] 유지하다

56 leave [liːv] 떠나다, 남기다

57 load [loud] (짐을) 싣다 (*n.* 짐)

58 maintain [meintéin] 유지하다

59 modify 미국 [mádəfài] 영국 [mɔ́dəfài] 수정하다, 변경하다

60 name [neim] 지명하다, 임명하다, 명명하다 (*n.* 이름)

61 need [niːd] 필요로 하다 (*n.* 필요성)

62 notify [nóutəfài] 알리다, 통보하다

63 occur [əkə́ːr] 발생하다

64 offer 미국 [ɔ́ːfər] 영국 [ɔ́fər] 제공하다, 제안하다 (*n.* 제의, 제안)

65 organize [ɔ́ːrgənàiz] 준비하다, 정리하다, 체계화하다

66 oversee 미국 [òuvərsíː] 영국 [əuvəsíː] 감독하다

67 perform [pərfɔ́ːrm] 수행하다, 공연하다

68 permit [pərmít] 허가하다 (*n.* 허가증)

69 postpone [poustpóun] 연기하다, 미루다

70 prepare [pripéər] 준비하다

71 preregister [príːredʒistə(r)] 사전 등록하다

72 provide [prəváid] 제공하다

73 purchase [pɔ́ːrtʃəs] 구매하다 (*n.* 구매, 구매품)

74 receive [risíːv] 받다, 수령하다

75 recognize [rékəgnàiz] 인정하다, 알아보다, 인식하다

76 recommend [rèkəménd] 추천하다

77 reduce [ridjúːs] 감소하다, 낮추다

78 relate [riléit] 관련시키다

79 relieve [rilíːv] 완화하다, 안심시키다

80 relocate [riːloukeit] 이전하다, 이전시키다

81 remember [rimémbər] 기억하다

82 remind [rimáind] (잊지 않도록) 다시 알리다, 상기시키다

83 renew 미국 [rinúː] 영국 [rinjúː] 갱신하다

84 renovate [rénəvèit] 개조하다

85 repair [ripéər] 수리하다 (*n.* 수리)

86 reserve [rizə́ːrv] 예약하다, (권한 등을) 보유하다

87 return [ritə́ːrn] 돌아오다, 돌려주다

88 review [rivjúː] 평가하다, 재검토하다 (*n.* 평가, 재검토)

89 rise [raiz] 오르다 (*n.* 증가)

90 select [silékt] 선택하다, 선발하다

91 serve [səːrv] (음식을) 제공하다

92 share [ʃɛər] 공유하다

93 show [ʃou] 보여주다 (*n.* 쇼, 공연물)

94 sort [sɔːrt] 분류하다, 구분하다 (*n.* 종류, 유형)

95 spend [spend] (시간, 돈을) 쓰다, 소비하다

96 submit [səbmít] 제출하다

97 suggest [sədʒést] 제안하다, 암시하다

98 support [səpɔ́ːrt] 지지하다, 후원하다 (*n.* 지지, 후원)

99 vote [vout] 투표하다 (*n.* 투표, 표결, 표)

100 work [wəːrk] 일하다, 작동하다 (*n.* 일)

≫ 출제 포인트

Q1
Editors' responsibilities are to ------- the text thoroughly.

(A) review (B) purchase
(C) receive (D) advertise

 주어진 목적어와 어울려 쓸 수 있는 동사를 찾는다.

정답 (A)
해석 편집자들의 책무는 철저하게 본문 글을 검토하는 것이다.
해설 빈칸 주변에 힌트가 있는데 빈칸 뒤에 text라는 단어가 있다. text는 빈칸에 들어갈 동사 어휘의 목적어이므로 목적어와 제일 어울려 쓸 수 있는 동사 어휘를 찾아야 한다. text(본문, 글)를 목적어로 가장 자연스럽게 연결할 수 있는 동사를 찾자. text를 (B) 구매하는 것도, (C) 받는 것도, (D) 광고하는 것도 아니다. 본문 글을 (A) 검토하는 (review) 것이다. 정답은 (A) review이다.

Q2
The car maker ------- the plan to invest in non-polluting cars.

(A) appeals (B) relates
(C) focuses (D) supports

 선택지 동사 뒤에 연결되는 전치사를 힌트로 삼는다.

정답 (D)
해석 자동차 제조업체는 무공해 차량에 투자하기 위한 계획을 지지한다.
해설 모두 해석할 필요 없이 전치사를 힌트로 삼자!
support는 3형식 동사로 전치사 대신 목적어를 취한다. 전치사 없이 목적어 the plan이 나오므로 정답은 (D) supports이다.
• appeal to + 명사 ~에 호소하다
• relate + 목적어 + to + 명사 ~에 관련시키다
• focus on + 명사 ~에 집중하다

Q3
The Marketing Department ------- its employees to use the company's products in public.

(A) keeps (B) maintains
(C) responds (D) encourages

 필수 5형식 동사만 알고 있으면 쉽게 풀 수 있는 문제가 나온다.

정답 (D)
해석 마케팅 부서는 직원들에게 제품을 공개적으로 사용해 볼 것을 장려한다.
해설 모두 해석해 보지 않아도 문장 형태가 「동사 + 목적어 + to 부정사」 구조이므로 목적격 보어에 to부정사를 취하는 5형식 동사 encourage가 적절하다. 따라서 정답은 (D) encourages이다.

Q4
His proposal to attract new customers has been ------- by the President of the company.

(A) confused (B) increased
(C) accepted (D) reminded

Point 주어와 동사의 관계를 확인한다.

정답 (C)
해석 새로운 고객을 유치하기 위한 그의 제안서는 회사 대표에 의해서 받아들여졌다.
해설 동사 어휘를 물어본다면 먼저 주어와 동사의 관계를 확인해 보자. 문장 구조 중간에 수식어구는 보지 않아도 된다. 주어가 '제안서'이므로 제안서와 어울려 쓸 수 있는 동사 어휘는 '받아들이다'라는 뜻을 가진 accept이다. 현재완료 수동태 문장이므로 과거분사 형태를 취하고 있다.

Q5
The restaurant was ------- a Top Restaurant by the CS Association.

(A) named (B) committed
(C) attracted (D) related

Point 수동태를 힌트로 삼는다.

정답 (A)
해석 그 레스토랑은 CS 협회에 의해서 '최고의 레스토랑'으로 명명되었다.
해설 선택지에서 어떤 정답을 찍어도, 모두 수동태인 것을 확인할 수 있다. 수동태는 목적어가 빠져 있어야 하는데 빈칸 뒤에 명사(a Top Restaurant)가 또 나와 있다. 4형식 동사는 목적어가 2개이므로 하나가 빠져도 하나가 남는다. 5형식 동사는 목적어가 빠지면 목적격 보어인 명사나 형용사가 뒤에 남는다. 따라서 해석하지 않고도 4, 5형식 동사를 찾으라는 것임을 알 수가 있다. name은 이름이라는 명사도 있지만, '목적어를 ~라고 명명하다'라는 뜻의 5형식 동사이기도 하다. 따라서 정답은 (A) named이다. (B)와 (D)는 전치사 to를 동반해야 하고, (C)는 3형식 동사이다.

Practice

1. To ------- customers, Blue Stone Hotels are currently offering discounts.

(A) await
(B) contact
(C) attract
(D) reimburse

2. The new color printer ------- up to 10,000 pages of documents from one toner cartridge.

(A) categorizes
(B) limits
(C) produces
(D) spends

3. All customers were ------- discount coupons for purchases over $10.

(A) offered
(B) received
(C) created
(D) advertised

4. We ------- employees to wear their identification badges at all times while inside the office.

(A) check
(B) ask
(C) prove
(D) contain

5. All employees must ------- with company policies.

(A) give
(B) comply
(C) update
(D) assign

6. Hidden Studios and Cliff Productions have ------- an agreement to work collaboratively on the movie.

(A) resulted
(B) earned
(C) informed
(D) reached

7. You can ------- from joining local business associations.

(A) benefit
(B) assist
(C) serve
(D) help

8. Hill Company's flooring ------- in a variety of shapes, sizes, and colors.

(A) provides
(B) purchases
(C) comes
(D) gets

9. Request forms for sick leave must be ------- by e-mail to the department manager.

(A) selected
(B) needed
(C) solved
(D) submitted

10. All employees are ------- to clean their desks.

(A) created
(B) invited
(C) required
(D) worked

명사

1 **account** [əkáunt] 계좌, (정보·서비스의) 이용 계정

2 **acquisition** [ækwizíʃən] 인수, 획득, 습득

3 **advice** [ədváis] 충고

4 **agreement** [əgríːmənt] 협정, 합의, 동의

5 **amount** [əmáunt] 총액, 총계, 양, 액수

6 **area** [ɛ́əriə] 지역, 구역

7 **article** [áːrtikl] 글, 기사

8 **attendee** [ətèndíː] 참석자

9 **audience** [ɔ́ːdiəns] 청중, 관중

10 **benefit** [bénəfit] 혜택, 이득 (v. ~에서 혜택을 보다)

11 **brochure** 미국 [brouʃúər] 영국 [bróuʃə] (안내) 책자

12 **change** [ʧeindʒ] 변화 (v. 변화하다, 변화시키다)

13 **chemistry** [kéməstri] 화학

14 **clerk** 미국 [kləːrk] 영국 [klaːk] 점원, 판매원

15 **client** [kláiənt] 고객, 의뢰인

16 **company** [kʌ́mpəni] 회사

17 **consumer** 미국 [kənsúːmər] 영국 [kənsjúːmər] 소비자

18 **content** [kántent] 내용물, 내용, 목차

19 **contract** [kántrækt, kɔ́n-] 계약(서) (v. 계약하다)

20 **copy machine** 복사기

21 **customer service** 고객 서비스

22 **customer** [kʌstámər] 고객

23 **decision** [disíʒən] 결정, 판단

24 **delivery** [dilívəri] 배달

25 **demand** 미국 [diménd] 영국 [dimáːnd] 수요, 요구 (v. 요구하다)

26 **demonstration** [dèmənstréiʃən] 입증, (시범) 설명

27 **department** [dipáːrtmənt] 부서

28 **development** [divéləpmənt] 개발, 발달, 성장

29 **director** [diréktər] 임원, 감독, 책임자

30 **duration** 미국 [djuréiʃən] 영국 [djúəréiʃən] 지속, 기간

31 **economy** 미국 [ikánəmi] 영국 [ikɔ́nəmi] 경제

32 **editor** [édətər] 편집자

33 **effort** [éfərt] 노력

34 **electronics** 미국 [ilektrániks] 영국 [ilektrɔ́niks] 전자 공학, 전자 기술

35 **employee** [implɔ́iiː, èmplɔ́iː] 직원

36 **equipment** [ikwípmənt] 장비

37 **executive** [igzékjutiv] 경영(운영) 간부, 경영진, 운영진

38 **expert** [ékspəːrt] 전문가

39 **exposure** [ikspóuʒər] 노출

40 **fee** [fiː] 수수료, 요금

41 **field** [fiːld] 분야

42 **firm** [fəːrm] 회사 (adj. 단단한, 확고한)

43 **fuel** [fjúːəl] 연료

44 **furniture** [fə́ːrniʧər] 가구

45 **heating system** 난방 시스템

46 **human resources director** 인사 부장

47 **identification** [aidèntifəkéiʃən] 신분증, 신원 확인

48 **innovation** [ìnəvéiʃən] 혁신, (사상, 방법 등) 획기적인 것

49 **instance** [ínstəns] 사례, 경우 (v. ~을 예로 들다)

50 **interest** [íntərəst] 관심, 흥미 (v. ~의 흥미를 끌다)

51 **internship** [íntəːrnʃip] 인턴 직, 인턴사원 근무

52 **invoice** [ínvɔis] 청구서, 송장

53 **journey** [dʒə́ːrni] 여행, 여정

54 **laboratory** 미국 [lǽbərətòːri] 영국 [ləbɔ́rətəri] 실험실

55 **maintenance** [méintənəns] 유지, 지속

56 **market** [máːrkit] 시장 (v. 상품을 내놓다, 광고하다)

57 **material** [mətíəriəl] 재료, 소재, 직물, 천, 내용

58 **notification** [nòutəfikéiʃən] 알림, 통지

59 **opening** [óupəniŋ] 개막식, 공석, 결원

60 **operating expense** 운영비, 경영비

61 **order** [ɔ́ːrdər] 주문(품), 순서, 질서, 명령 (v. 명령/주문하다)

62 **organization** 미국 [ɔ̀rgənizéiʃən] 영국 [ɔ̀rgənaizéiʃən] 조직, 단체

63 **package** [pǽkidʒ] (포장용) 상자, 포장물, 패키지

64 **parts** [paːrts] 부품

65 **patient** [péiʃənt] 환자

66 **personnel** [pə̀ːrsənél] 인사과, 직원들

67 **policy** 미국 [pάləsi] 영국 [pɔ́ləsi] 정책, (보험) 증권

68 **preference** [préfərəns] 선호(도)

69 **president** [prézədənt] 사장, 회장, 대통령

70 **price** [prais] 가격, 값, 물가

71 **process** [práses] 과정, 절차, 가공 (v. 처리하다)

72 **product** 미국 [prάdʌkt] 영국 [prɔ́dʌkt] 제품

73 **production capacity** 생산 능력

74 **project** [práːdʒekt] 프로젝트, 계획된 일

75 **proposal** [prəpóuzəl] 제안, 제안서

76 **publication** [pʌ̀bləkéiʃən] 출판(물), 발행

77 **quality** 미국 [kwάləti] 영국 [kwɔ́ləti] 품질

78 **reason** [ríːzn] 이유, 근거, 이성, 사고력

79 **renovation** [renəvéiʃən] 수리, 개조

80 **representative** [rèprizéntətiv] 대표(자), 대리인

81 **researcher** [risə́ːrtʃər] 연구원

82 **resident** [rézədnt] 거주자, 주민

83 **responsibility** 미국 [rispάnsəbíləti] 영국 [rispɔ́nsəbíləti] 책임(감), 책무

84 **route** [ruːt] 길, 경로, 노선

85 **salespeople** 영업사원, 판매원들

86 **setting** [sétiŋ] 환경, 무대, 설정, 세팅(차려놓은 것)

87 **shipment** [ʃípmənt] 수송, 수송품

88 **shipping company** 운송 회사, 택배 회사

89 **space** [speis] 공간

90 **subscriber** [səbskráibər] 구독자

91 **subscription** [səbskrípʃən] 구독

92 **supervisor** 미국 [súːpərvàizər] 영국 [sjúː-] 감독관, 관리자

93 **survey response** 설문 조사 반응

94 **task** 미국 [tæsk] 영국 [taːsk] 임무, 과제

95 **technician** [teknéʃən] 기술자

96 **transportation** 미국 [træspərtéiʃən] 영국 [trænspɔːtéiʃən] 수송, 교통

97 **travel cost** 여행 비용

98 **value** [vǽljuː] 가치 (v. 가치 있게 여기다)

99 **visitor** [vízitər] 방문자

100 **weather** [wéðər] 날씨

>> 출제 포인트

 Q1 Please follow the safety ------- when using machines in the factory.

(A) precautions   (B) prescriptions
(C) descriptions   (D) subscriptions

Point 덩어리 표현과 복합 명사를 힌트로 삼는다.

정답 (A)
해석 공장에서 기계를 이용할 때 안전 예방책을 따르시기 바랍니다.
해설 safety가 나오면 바로 safety precautions가 정답이다. 이 복합 명사는 '안전 예방책'이라는 뜻이다. 같이 다니는 덩어리 표현 또는 복합 명사를 찾으면 쉽게 답을 찾을 수 있다. 정답은 (A) precautions이다.

 Q2 Ms. Park is a ------- of the company at all trade shows and conferences.

(A) client   (B) resident
(C) proposal   (D) representative

Point 각 보기의 의미를 대입하여 정답을 찾는 어휘 문제가 나온다.

정답 (D)
해석 Ms. Park는 모든 무역 박람회와 학회에서 회사의 대표자이다.
해설 representative는 생김새는 형용사 같지만 '대표자'라는 뜻의 명사이다. 시험에 자주 출제되는 어휘이므로 꼭 알아두자. 보통 이럴 땐 형태(생김새)와 실제 품사가 다른 어휘가 다른 명사들보다 정답이 될 확률이 높다. 빈칸에는 사람 명사가 와야 하므로 정답은 (D) representative 이다.

 Q3 In an ------- to boost sales, the company hired a PR expert.

(A) advice   (B) item
(C) issue   (D) effort

Point to부정사의 수식을 받는 명사를 찾는다.

정답 (D)
해석 매출을 증대시키려는 노력의 일환으로, 회사는 홍보 전문가를 고용했다.
해설 빈칸 뒤에 to부정사가 나왔으므로 to부정사의 수식을 받아 자연스러운 의미가 되는 어휘를 찾아야 한다. '매출을 증대시키려는 (A) 조언으로, (B) 물품으로, (C) 이슈로'는 의미가 모두 어색하다. 따라서 정답은 (D) effort이다.

 Q4 Ms. Brown will deliver a speech about the ------- traffic jams have on air pollution.

(A) transfer   (B) development
(C) impact   (D) requirement

Point 명사 뒤에 나오는 전치사를 힌트로 삼는다.

정답 (C)
해석 Ms. Brown은 교통 체증이 대기 오염에 끼치는 영향에 대하여 연설할 것이다.
해설 빈칸 뒤에 나온 전치사가 정답의 단서를 제공한다. 보기에 나온 명사 어휘 중 전치사 on을 취하는 것은 impact 뿐이다. 정답은 (C) impact이다.
　• have an impact on ~에 영향을 끼치다

 Q5 The ------- for applying for membership to the association is not simple.

(A) ability   (B) procedure
(C) capacity   (D) creation

Point 수식어구를 모두 제외하고 문장의 뼈대만 보고 정답을 찾는다.

정답 (B)
해석 그 협회의 회원 신청 절차는 간단하지 않다.
해설 필요 없는 수식어구 (for applying for membership to the association)를 빼고 주어와 그 뒤에 나온 어휘와 일치시켜 보자. (A) 능력, (C) 수용력, (D) 창조가 간단하지 않다는 것은 말이 안 된다. '절차가 간단하지 않다'고 하는 것이 가장 자연스러우므로 정답은 (B) procedure이다.

Practice

해설서 p.49

1. The new restaurant offers a wide ------- of healthy dishes.

   (A) sense
   (B) situation
   (C) variety
   (D) condition

2. The labor costs indicated in the invoice are a rough -------.

   (A) development
   (B) estimate
   (C) attempt
   (D) requirement

3. The ------- of the Platinum Award will be featured in next month's *Technological Spotlight Magazine*.

   (A) customer
   (B) partner
   (C) recipient
   (D) member

4. Hanscro Supermarket sells a full ------- of organic products to attract health-conscious shoppers.

   (A) range
   (B) degree
   (C) focus
   (D) growth

5. QVPE Company announced its ------- to buy Kavabean Ltd. this quarter.

   (A) ideal
   (B) intention
   (C) creation
   (D) explanation

6. In ------- of your continued business, we would like to offer you a membership card.

   (A) response
   (B) mention
   (C) appreciation
   (D) comment

7. To improve customer -------, we are committed to increasing product quality.

   (A) satisfaction
   (B) design
   (C) consideration
   (D) hospitality

8. We discussed the most effective ------- to save on operating costs.

   (A) ways
   (B) specifications
   (C) qualifications
   (D) accommodations

9. ------- for Employee of the Month should be submitted by 4 P.M. today.

   (A) Performances
   (B) Nominations
   (C) Incidents
   (D) Authorities

10. Sales representatives must take the ------- and make contact with potential customers.

    (A) initiative
    (B) outcome
    (C) advice
    (D) prediction

형용사

1 **available** [əvéiləbl] (서비스·사물 등이) 이용 가능한, (사람이 시간적) 여유가 있는

2 **accidental** [æksədéntl] 우연한, 돌발적인

3 **additional** [ədíʃənl] 추가적인

4 **affordable** [əfɔ́ːrdəbl] (가격이) 알맞은, 감당할 수 있는

5 **anxious** [ǽŋkʃəs] 염려하는, 불안해 하는, 열망하는

6 **appointed** [əpɔ́intid] 정해진, 지정된, 약속된, 임명된

7 **appropriate** [əpróupriət] 적절한

8 **aware** [əwéər] 알고 있는, 인식하고 있는

9 **beneficial** [bènəfíʃəl] 유익한, 이로운

10 **bright** [brait] 밝은

11 **careful** [kéərfəl] 조심스러운, 신중한

12 **cautious** [kɔ́ːʃəs] 조심스러운, 신중한

13 **certain** [sə́ːrtn] 틀림없는, 확신하는, 어떤

14 **colored** [kʌ́lərd] ~한 색깔의, 색깔이 있는

15 **compatible** [kəmpǽtəbl] 호환이 되는, (생각, 방법이) 양립될 수 있는

16 **competent** 미국 [kámpətənt] 영국 [kɔ́mpətənt] 능숙한

17 **conditional** [kəndíʃənl] 조건부의

18 **confident** 미국 [kánfədənt] 영국 [kɔ́nfədənt] 자신감 있는, 확신하는

19 **considerable** [kənsídərəbl] 상당한

20 **controversial** 미국 [kàntrəvə́ːrʃəl] 영국 [kɔ̀ntrəvə́ːrʃəl] 논란이 많은

21 **deep** [diːp] 깊은

22 **dependent** [dipéndənt] 의존적인, ~에 좌우되는

23 **desirable** [dizáiərəbl] 바람직한, 호감 가는, 가치 있는

24 **different** [dífərənt] 다른

25 **difficult** 미국 [dífikʌlt] 영국 [dífikəlt] 어려운

26 **distinctive** [distíŋktiv] 독특한

27 **eager** [íːgər] 열렬한, 간절히 바라는, 열심인

28 **educational** [èdʒukéiʃənl] 교육적인

29 **efficient** [ifíʃənt] 능률적인, 효율적인

30 **enough** [inʌ́f] 충분한

31 **entire** [intáiər] 전체의

32 **every** [évri] 모든, 매, ~마다

33 **excellent** [éksələnt] 훌륭한

34 **exclusive** [iksklúːsiv] 독점적인, 전용의

35 **expensive** [ikspénsiv] 비싼

36 **experienced** [ikspíəriənst] 경험 있는, 경력이 있는

37 **favorite** [féivərit] 가장 마음에 드는, 매우 좋아하는

38 **following** 미국 [fálouiŋ] 영국 [fɔ́louiŋ] 그 다음의, 다음에 나오는

39 **free** [friː] 무료의, 자유로운

40 **frequent** [fríːkwənt] 빈번한

41 **furnished** 미국 [fə́ːrnɪʃt] (집·방 등이) 가구가 비치된

42 **heavy** [hévi] 무거운

43 **historical** 미국 [histɔ́ːrikəl, histárikəl] 역사적인, 역사상의

44 **ideal** 미국 [aidíːəl] 영국 [aidíəl] 이상적인, 가장 알맞은

45 **important** [impɔ́ːrtənt] 중요한

46 **impressive** [imprésiv] 인상적인

47 **indefinite** [indéfənit] 무기한의

48 **initial** [iníʃəl] 처음의, 초기의

49 **interested** [íntərəstid, -tərèst-] 흥미가 있는, 관심 있는

50 **international** [intərnǽʃənəl] 국제적인

51 **leading** [líːdiŋ] 이끄는, 선두적인

52 **leisurely** 미국 [líːʒərli] 영국 [léʒ-] 한가한, 여유로운

53 **likely** [láikli] ~할 것 같은, ~할 가능성이 높은

54 **local** [lóukəl] 지역의, 현지의

55 **low** [lou] 낮은

56 **loyal** [lɔ́iəl] 충실한, 충성스러운

57 **magnificent** [mægnífəsnt] 훌륭한, 감명 깊은

58 **major** [méidʒər] 주요한, 중대한, 주된

59 **natural** [nǽʧərəl] 자연의, 당연한, 정상적인, 자연스러운

60 **necessary** 미국 [nésəsèri] 영국 [nésəsəri]
필요한, 필수적인, 필연적인, 불가피한

61 **notable** [nóutəbl] 주목할 만한, 눈에 띄는, 중요한, 유명한

62 **ongoing** 미국 [ɑːngoʊiŋ;ɔːn-] 영국 [ɒngəʊiŋ]
계속 진행 중인

63 **operational** 미국 [àpəréiʃnel] 영국 [ɔp-]
운영의, 사용할 준비가 갖춰진

64 **opposed** [əpóuzd] (~에) 반대하는

65 **original** [ərídʒənl] 원래의, 원본의, 독창적인

66 **personal** [pɑ́rsənl] 개인적인, 개인의

67 **plenty of** 많은

68 **prevalent** [prévələnt] 일반적인, 널리 퍼져 있는

69 **probable** 미국 [prábəbl] 영국 [prɔ́bəbl] 사실일 것 같은

70 **productive** [prədʌ́ktiv] 생산하는, 생산적인

71 **professional** [prəféʃənl] 전문적인, 전문가의, 능숙한 (n. 전문가)

72 **profitable** 미국 [práfitəbl] 영국 [prɔ́fitəbl]
수익성이 있는, 이득이 되는, 유익한

73 **promotional** [prəmóuʃənl] 홍보의

74 **proposed** [prəpóuzd] 제안된

75 **quick** [kwik] 빠른

76 **reasonable** [ríːzənəbl] 합리적인, 타당한

77 **recent** [ríːsnt] 최근의

78 **redesigned** [riːdizáind] 다시 디자인된

79 **regional** [ríːdʒənl] 지방의, 지역의

80 **related** [riléitid] 관련된

81 **relevant** [réləvənt] 관련 있는, 적절한

82 **remote** [rimóut] 외딴, 먼, 원격의

83 **renowned** [rináund] 유명한, 명성 있는

84 **routine** [ruːtíːn] 일상적인, 판에 박힌, 지루한

85 **satisfied** [sǽtisfàid] 만족하는, 만족스러워하는

86 **seasonal** [síːzənl] 계절적인, 계절에 따라 다른

87 **secure** [sikjúər] 안심하는, 안전한, 확실한

88 **several** [sévərəl] 몇몇의

89 **significant** [signífikənt] 상당한, 중요한, 의미심장한

90 **steady** [stédi] 꾸준한

91 **surrounding** [səráundiŋ] 인근의, 주위의

92 **technical** [téknikəl] 기술적인, 기술의

93 **tolerant** 미국 [tálərənt] 영국 [tɔ́lərənt] 관대한, 잘 견디는

94 **unexpected** [ʌnikspéktid] 예기치 않은, 뜻밖의

95 **unique** [juːníːk] 독특한

96 **upcoming** [ʌpkʌmiŋ] 다가오는, 곧 있을

97 **updated** [ʌpdeitid] 최신의, 갱신된

98 **valid** [vǽlid] (법적·공식적으로) 유효한

99 **warm** [wɔːrm] 따뜻한

100 **weekly** [wíːkli] 매주의, 주 1회의, 주간의

>> 출제 포인트

Q1

Many employees in the company remain ------- to the new vacation policy.

(A) opposed   (B) eager
(C) interfered   (D) anxious

 Point 전치사를 보고 형용사를 결정한다.

정답 (A)
해석 그 회사의 많은 직원들은 새 휴가 정책에 계속 반대하는 상태이다.
해설 빈칸 뒤에 명사구 the new vacation policy를 이끄는 전치사 to가 나와 있다. 「be eager[anxious] to + 동사원형」은 '~하길 열망하다'라는 뜻으로 to부정사를 취한다. 「interfere with」는 '~을 간섭[방해]하다', 「be opposed to + 명사」는 '~에 반대하다'란 뜻으로 전치사 to를 취한다. 따라서 정답은 (A) opposed이다.

Q2

Cold weather is ------- to last throughout the month.

(A) considerable   (B) seasonal
(C) frequent   (D) likely

 Point to부정사와 어울려 쓸 수 있는 형용사를 찾는다.

정답 (D)
해석 추운 날씨가 한 달 내내 지속될 확률이 높다.
해설 어휘 문제라고 해서 모두 다 읽을 필요는 없다. 빈칸 뒤에 to부정사가 나왔으므로 to부정사와 어울려 쓸 수 있는 형용사를 찾는다. 「be likely to + 동사원형」은 '~할 가능성이 높다'라는 뜻으로 정답은 (D) likely이다. 잘 기억이 나지 않는다면, to부정사와 어울려 쓸 수 있는 형용사 어휘가 정리되어 있는 to부정사의 Grammar 파트를 다시 한번 펼쳐 보자.

Q3

Employees were pleased to receive an ------- $500 bonus for their sales in April.

(A) indefinite   (B) equipped
(C) inexperienced   (D) unexpected

Point 각 보기의 의미를 대입하여 정답을 찾는 어휘 문제가 나온다.

정답 (D)
해석 직원들은 4월 판매에 대해 기대하지 않은 500달러 보너스를 받게 되어 기쁘다.
해설 분사 형용사를 물어보는 문제이다. unexpected는 '기대하지 않은'이란 뜻으로 자주 나오므로 꼭 알아두자. 정답은 (D) unexpected이다.

Q4

According to the article, the interest rate will fall in the ------- future.

(A) prevalent   (B) appreciable
(C) foreseeable   (D) ongoing

Point 명사와 의미상 어울리는 형용사를 찾는다.

정답 (C)
해석 기사에 따르면, 이자율이 가까운 미래에 떨어질 것이다.
해설 어휘 문제라고 해서 모두 다 읽을 필요 없이 빈칸에 올 형용사가 future라는 명사를 꾸밀 수 있는지 확인한다. 따라서 빈칸에 들어갈 말은 '미래'라는 말과 제일 잘 어울리는 단어이어야 한다. foreseeable이 '미리 볼 수 있는, 예측 가능한'이라는 뜻인데, '예측이 가능한 미래'란 '가까운 미래'를 의미한다. 정답은 (C) foreseeable이다.

Q5

You can enjoy a ------- stroll through McFinley Park.

(A) conclusive   (B) tolerant
(C) leisurely   (D) difficult

 Point 예사롭지 않은 모양의 형용사를 찾는다.

정답 (C)
해석 당신은 McFinley 공원에서 여유로운 산책을 즐길 수 있다.
해설 「형용사 + ly」는 부사이고 「명사 + ly」는 형용사이다. leisurely는 부사처럼 보이지만 실제 품사는 형용사이다. 이럴 때, 생긴 것과 실제 품사가 다른 것이 간혹 답이 될 수도 있다는 점에 유의하자. 정답은 (C) leisurely이다.

Practice

해설서 p.50

1. ------- technicians take just 10 minutes to identify most computer problems.

(A) Relative
(B) Experienced
(C) Conclusive
(D) Advantageous

2. You should check if the new software is ------- with your operating system.

(A) reflective
(B) reportable
(C) compatible
(D) irregular

3. Golden Organic Farm considers environmentally ------- practices important.

(A) general
(B) exposed
(C) friendly
(D) considerate

4. Participants must show a ------- photo ID to enter the convention.

(A) valid
(B) steady
(C) mixed
(D) fast

5. Please contact Mr. Hong for ------- assistance with the application.

(A) technical
(B) interested
(C) dependent
(D) historical

6. Employees have to do their work in a ------- manner.

(A) favorite
(B) timely
(C) renewed
(D) recent

7. Please be ------- of the contract's terms and conditions.

(A) noted
(B) proposed
(C) aware
(D) known

8. The company welcomes all applicants ------- to work in the field of chemistry.

(A) eager
(B) capable
(C) probable
(D) possible

9. Due to the ------- power outage, several employees were unable to save some important files.

(A) convenient
(B) sudden
(C) inadequate
(D) upcoming

10. During Mr. Nguyen's ------- absence, one of his colleagues will be covering his duties at the workplace.

(A) strong
(B) productive
(C) important
(D) brief

부사

1 **accordingly** [əkɔ́ːrdiŋli] 그에 부응해서, 그에 맞춰, 그런 이유로

2 **accurately** [ǽkjurətli] 정확하게, 정밀하게

3 **actually** [ǽktʃuəli] 실제로, 정말로

4 **additionally** [ədíʃənli] 추가적으로

5 **ahead** [əhéd] 앞으로, 미리, 앞서

6 **almost** [ɔ́ːlmoust] 거의, 대체로

7 **already** [ɔːlrédi] 이미

8 **always** [ɔ́ːlweiz, -wiːz] 항상

9 **annually** [ǽnjuəli] 일 년에 한 번

10 **approximately** 미국 [əpráksəmətli] 영국 [əprɔ́ksəmətli] 거의, ~가까이, 대략

11 **at least** 적어도, 최소한

12 **attractively** [ətrǽktivli] 보기 좋게

13 **automatically** [ɔ̀ːtəmǽtikəli] 자동적으로

14 **briefly** [bríːfli] 잠시, 간단히

15 **brightly** [bráitli] 밝게, 빛나게, 환히

16 **collaboratively** [kərábərèitivli] 협력적으로, 합작으로

17 **completely** [kəmplíːtli] 완전히

18 **considerably** [kənsídərəbli] 상당히

19 **constantly** 미국 [kánstəntli] 영국 [kɔ́nstəntli] 끊임없이, 거듭

20 **correctly** [kəréktli] 바르게, 정확하게

21 **decidedly** [disáididli] 확실히, 분명히, 단호히

22 **directly** [diréktli, dai-] 곧장, 똑바로, 즉시, 곧

23 **dramatically** [drəmǽtikəli] 극적으로

24 **eagerly** [íːgərli] 열망하여, 열심히, 간절히

25 **easily** [íːzili] 쉽게

26 **electronically** 미국 [ilektránikəli] 영국 [-trɔ́n-] 온라인으로, 전자적으로

27 **equally** [íːkwəli] 동일하게, 똑같이

28 **even** [íːvən] ~도[조차], 심지어, (비교급 강조) 훨씬

29 **eventually** [ivéntʃuəli] 결국에

30 **exactly** [igzǽktli] 정확히, 꼭, 틀림없이

31 **exceptionally** [iksépʃənli] 특별히, 유난히, 예외적으로

32 **expertly** [èkspəːrtli] 훌륭하게, 전문적으로

33 **extremely** [ikstríːmli] 대단히, 몹시, 극도로

34 **fairly** [féərli] 상당히, 꽤, 공정하게

35 **favorably** [féivərəbli] 호의적으로, 유리하게

36 **finally** [fáinəli] 마지막에, 결국에

37 **frankly** [frǽŋkli] 솔직히, 솔직히 말하면

38 **free of charge** 무료로

39 **frequently** [fríːkwəntli] 자주, 빈번하게

40 **fully** [fúli] 완전히, 충분히

41 **gradually** [grǽdʒuəli] 점차적으로, 서서히

42 **greatly** [gréitli] 대단히, 크게

43 **hardly** [háːrdli] 거의 ~ 아니다/없다

44 **highly** [háili] 매우

45 **ideally** 미국 [aidíːəli] 영국 [aidíəli] 이상적으로, 원칙적으로

46 **immediately** [imíːdiətli] 즉시

47 **in advance** 미리

48 **just** [dʒʌst] 막[방금], 단지[오로지], 정확히

49 late [leit] 늦게 (adj. 늦은)

50 lately [léitli] 최근에

51 loosely [lúːsli] 느슨하게, 헐겁게, 막연히, 엄밀하지 않게

52 mainly [méinli] 주로

53 moderately 미국 [mádərətli] 영국 [módərətli] 중간 정도로, 적당히

54 mutually [mjúːtʃuəli] 서로 상호간에, 공통으로

55 near [niər] 가까이 (adj. 가까운 prep. ~근처에)

56 nearly [níərli] 거의, 대체로

57 never [névər] 결코 ~하지 않다

58 newly [njúːli] 새롭게

59 noticeably [nóutisəbli] 두드러지게, 현저히

60 once [wʌns] 한 번, (과거) 언젠가, 한때

61 only [óunli] 오로지, 단지, ~만 (adj. 유일한, 오직 ~만의)

62 overseas 미국 [ouvərsíːz] 영국 [əuvəsíːz] 해외로

63 partially [páːrʃəli] 부분적으로

64 particularly [pərtíkjulərli] 특히, 특별히

65 positively [pázətivli, óz-] 긍정적으로

66 potentially [pəténʃəli] 잠재적으로, 가능성 있게

67 precisely [prisáisli] 정확히, 바로, 꼭

68 previously [príːviəsli] 이전에, 미리, 사전에

69 probably 미국 [prábəbli] 영국 [próbəbli] 이미

70 promptly 미국 [prámptli] 영국 [prómptli] 지체 없이, 제시간에, 즉시

71 quietly [kwáiətli] 조용하게

72 quite [kwait] 꽤, 상당히

73 radically [rǽdikəli] 근본적으로; 급진적으로

74 rarely [réərli] 드물게, 좀처럼 ~하지 않는

75 rather 미국 [rǽðər] 영국 [ráːðər] 꽤, 약간, 상당히, 오히려, 차라리

76 recently [ríːsntli] 최근에

77 relatively [rélətivli] 비교적으로, 상대적으로

78 seldom [séldəm] 좀처럼 (거의) ~않는

79 severely [sivíərli] 심하게, 엄하게, 엄격하게

80 shortly [ʃɔːrtli] (시간상으로) 머지 않아, 곧

81 significantly [signífikəntli] 상당히, 중요하게

82 simply [símpli] 단지, 간단히, 요약하면

83 simultaneously 미국 [sàiməltéiniəsli] 영국 [sìm-] 동시에

84 slightly [sláitli] 약간, 조금

85 soon [suːn] 머지않아, 곧

86 specially [spéʃəli] 특별히

87 specifically [spisífikəli] 구체적으로 말하면

88 steadily [stédili] 꾸준히, 착실하게, 지속적으로

89 still [stil] 아직도, 그런데도 (비교급 강조) 훨씬

90 strongly [strɔ́ːŋli] 강하게, 강경히

91 successfully [səksésfəli] 성공적으로

92 temporarily 미국 [tèmpərérəli] 영국 [témpərərəli] 일시적으로, 임시로

93 thoroughly 미국 [θɔ́ːrouli] 영국 [θʌrəuli] 대단히, 완전히, 철저히

94 totally [tóutəli] 완전히, 전적으로

95 traditionally [trədíʃənəli] 전통적으로

96 truly [trúːli] 정말로, 진심으로

97 ultimately [ʌltəmətli] 궁극적으로, 결국

98 unanimously [juːnǽnəməsli] 만장일치로

99 unfortunately 미국 [ʌnfɔ́ːrtʃənətli] 영국 [ʌnfɔ́ːtʃənətli] 불행하게도, 유감스럽게도

100 very [véri] 매우

>> 출제 포인트

Q1
Review the manual ------- before contacting the Customer Service Department with any questions.

(A) thoroughly   (B) greatly
(C) previously   (D) relatively

 Point 동사를 수식하기에 알맞은 부사를 찾는다.

정답 (A)
해석 어떤 질문들을 가지고 고객서비스 부서에 연락하기 전에 매뉴얼을 꼼꼼하게 검토하시오.
해설 부사가 무엇을 꾸미는지를 보아야 한다. 빈칸에 들어가는 부사는 명사를 꾸밀 순 없으므로 동사 review를 꾸미게 된다. 그럼 전부 읽을 필요 없이, 동사 review와 어울리는 부사 어휘를 찾는 것이 이 문제의 출제 포인트다. '꼼꼼하게[철저하게] 재검토하라'가 어울리므로 정답은 (A) thoroughly이다.

Q2
Safety inspectors will visit the factory to check on the ------- installed fire alarms.

(A) immediately   (B) recently
(C) afterward   (D) briefly

 Point 형용사 및 부사 또는 문장 전체를 수식하기에 알맞은 부사를 찾는다.

정답 (B)
해석 안전 검사관들이 최근에 설치된 화재 경보기들을 살펴보기 위해 공장을 방문할 것이다
해설 빈칸을 과거 분사 형용사 installed (설치된)를 수식하기에 적절한 부사 자리로 '최근에 설치된 화재 경보기'라는 의미가 적절하므로 (B) recently가 정답이다.

Q3
With only two months before Granville's annual music festival, the organizers have ------- to determine the performance locations.

(A) yet   (B) finally
(C) not   (D) already

Point 관용 표현을 완성하는 부사를 찾는다.

정답 (A)
해석 Granville의 연례 음악 축제를 단 두 달 앞두고, 조직위원들은 아직 공연 장소도 결정하지 못했다.
해설 관용 표현 「have yet to + V」는 '아직 ~하지 못하다」라는 의미의 관용 표현이다. 따라서 빈칸 앞뒤의 단어와 항상 같이 쓰이는 부사를 고를 수 있어야 한다. 정답은 (A) yet이다.

Q4
Although ------- two weeks have passed, I haven't received my TV yet.

(A) incompletely   (B) thoroughly
(C) nearly   (D) quickly

Point 숫자 앞에 들어갈 부사를 찾는다.

정답 (C)
해석 거의 2주가 흘렀음에도 불구하고, 나는 내 TV를 아직 받지 못했다.
해설 '2주'라는 숫자가 나왔다. 숫자가 나왔을 경우 '대략'이라는 부사를 찾아야 한다. '거의, 대략'이라는 뜻의 (C) nearly가 정답이다.

Q5
According to the sales report, the company will ------- turn a profit.

(A) lately   (B) newly
(C) soon   (D) once

 Point 특정 시제에 어울리는 부사를 찾는다.

정답 (C)
해석 판매 보고서에 따르면, 그 회사는 곧 수익을 낼 것이다.
해설 부사 문제처럼 보이지만 사실 시제를 물어보는 문제이다. 미래 시제가 나왔으므로 미래 시제와 가장 잘 어울리는 부사 (C) soon이 정답이다. '최근에, 새로'를 뜻하는 newly는 과거분사나 형용사 앞에 쓰인다. 또한 lately는 현재완료와 쓰이고, once는 과거 시제와 주로 쓰인다.

해설서 p.51

1. Please ------- fill out the baggage claim form before submitting it to the guest services center.

(A) comparatively
(B) sometimes
(C) completely
(D) massively

2. You should write ------- three pages for the article.

(A) more
(B) rather
(C) about
(D) quite

3. Because of low salaries, the company's employees ------- requested a pay raise.

(A) repeatedly
(B) incredibly
(C) shortly
(D) exactly

4. According to a recent study, the unemployment rate among college graduates is ------- higher this year.

(A) deeply
(B) considerably
(C) densely
(D) nearly

5. The new GX890 printer is ------- recommended by industrial designers.

(A) loosely
(B) readily
(C) highly
(D) gradually

6. Although she was late today, Ms. Kim ------- arrives at work at 8 o'clock.

(A) hardly
(B) evenly
(C) weakly
(D) usually

7. Many of the intensive training programs for employees are ------- successful.

(A) courteously
(B) optionally
(C) experimentally
(D) extremely

8. Ober Apparel sells ------- priced business attire to attract more customers.

(A) specifically
(B) totally
(C) reasonably
(D) slightly

9. The bus takes ------- 40 minutes to get from the Maxerit Hotel to the city center.

(A) neatly
(B) finally
(C) approximately
(D) closely

10. The surveys that we are ------- conducting for your company will be compiled by next Tuesday.

(A) previously
(B) lately
(C) ordinarily
(D) currently

REVIEW TEST

해설서 p.52

1. The physical therapy department is located far from the hospital's -------.

(A) distance
(B) entrance
(C) format
(D) dimension

2. PT Beverages' marketing director ------- Ms. Kanakuro for the position.

(A) recommended
(B) concluded
(C) deserved
(D) recorded

3. When attending an interview, it is helpful to have ------- knowledge about the company.

(A) basic
(B) anxious
(C) hard
(D) reckless

4. It is crucial to read the information included on the shipping ------- before opening a package.

(A) driver
(B) label
(C) signal
(D) type

5. Ms. Johnson was ------- first prize for her painting in the national art contest.

(A) gotten
(B) won
(C) obtained
(D) awarded

6. Stern Bistro's executive chef orders -------, organic produce from local farms.

(A) fresh
(B) gentle
(C) durable
(D) effective

7. Riverton's Transportation Department ------- the city's bus and subway services.

(A) predicts
(B) oversees
(C) views
(D) commutes

8. The ------- for Ms. Nguyen's startup company was formed during her vacation in New Zealand.

(A) content
(B) fact
(C) value
(D) idea

9. The special discount from Heilen Groceries is available ------- until September 15.

(A) hardly
(B) only
(C) barely
(D) carefully

10. *Essential Knife Techniques* will make a ------- addition to any aspiring chef's video library.

(A) like
(B) great
(C) high
(D) constant

11. In Mr. Ido's -------, the assistant manager will run the store.

(A) situation
(B) example
(C) absence
(D) duty

12. Dyno, Inc. surpassed its projected -------, so staff members will receive bonuses at the end of the year.

(A) employees
(B) combinations
(C) earnings
(D) trips

13. Please confirm the data in the budget proposal and call Mr. Patel if you have any -------.

(A) operations
(B) policies
(C) comments
(D) prices

14. Lamar Wireless internet sincerely apologizes for the ------- reception in the Heather Hill district this morning.

(A) pale
(B) mild
(C) poor
(D) less

15. All lab technicians must adhere to official safety ------- when handling dangerous chemicals.

(A) matters
(B) buildings
(C) procedures
(D) installations

16. To get early notifications about ------- events, please provide your contact information.

(A) latest   (B) upcoming
(C) prepared   (D) advanced

17. The garden at Lascaux Plaza was ------- by popular outdoor artist Jean Dernier.

(A) concerned   (B) assumed
(C) planned   (D) affected

18. For the past few months, it was unusually warm, but -------, it has snowed heavily, benefitting local ski resorts.

(A) soon   (B) next
(C) recently   (D) evenly

19. The manufacturer's decision on which model to produce is ------- on the study results.

(A) responsive   (B) dependent
(C) reliable   (D) subsequent

20. All library ------- must thoroughly organize the bookshelves at the end of the day.

(A) research   (B) personnel
(C) system   (D) information

21. Designed last November, Fleet Footwear's new training shoes will ------- begin production next week.

(A) extremely   (B) precisely
(C) finally   (D) lately

22. A retirement reception for the Vice President will be ------ on Saturday, November 24, at the Morely Auditorium in Webster Center.

(A) opened   (B) secured
(C) invited   (D) held

23. Dr. Nasseri was ------- the department manager due to his impressive credentials.

(A) situated   (B) appointed
(C) provided   (D) decided

24. Starker Restaurant offers an ------- of menu items to appeal to diners of all ages.

(A) ingredient   (B) object
(C) array   (D) entity

25. ------- a month, Gatlin Construction Materials inspects the stock in all of its warehouses.

(A) Instantly   (B) Once
(C) Already   (D) every

26. The Wraith 1200 tablet PC ------- an improved, shatter-resistant screen.

(A) samples   (B) endures
(C) adjusts   (D) features

27. Due to mechanical problems that are ------- unspecified, the flight has been canceled.

(A) early   (B) still
(C) well   (D) much

28. Although she studied chemical engineering, Ms. Phan ------- works in Marketing and Sales.

(A) now   (B) therefore
(C) fairly   (D) quite

29. ------- machinery has enabled the factory to produce more units in a shorter amount of time.

(A) Upgraded   (B) Anticipated
(C) Imposed   (D) Permitted

30. Dr. Berringer's ------- for helping patients at Smith Hospital remains high after 20 years.

(A) likeness   (B) enthusiasm
(C) addition   (D) collection

PAR

RT 6

▼

장문 빈칸
채우기

OVERVIEW

PART 6은 4문항의 문제가 있는 4개의 지문이 나와 총 16문항이 출제된다.
각각의 빈칸에 가장 적합한 단어나 구, 그리고 문장을 고르는 문제로
PART 5와 PART 7을 접목한 형태로 볼 수 있다.

문법 문제
12%

어형 문제
19%

어휘 문제
45%

문장 삽입
25%

문제 유형

어형 문제 | 빈칸의 자리를 파악하여 선택지 중 알맞은 품사나 형태를 고르는 문제
어휘 문제 | 같은 품사의 네 개 어휘 중 정확한 용례를 파악하여 알맞은 단어를 고르는 문제
문법 문제 | 문장의 구조를 파악하여 구와 절을 구분하여 접속사나 전치사, 부사를 고르는 문제
문장 고르기 | 앞뒤 문맥을 파악하여 네 개의 문장 중에 알맞은 문장을 고르는 문제

지문 유형

편지·이메일/기사/공지/지시문/광고/회람/설명서/발표문/정보문 등

출제 포인트

• 앞뒤 문맥을 통해 시제를 결정하는 문제의 출제 비중이 높다. 시제를 묻는 문제는 Part 5에서는
  시간 부사구로 결정하지만, Part 6에서는 맥락으로 파악해야 한다.
• 두 문장을 자연스럽게 이어주는 접속부사를 선택하는 문제가 많이 출제된다.
• 맥락상으로 파악해야 하는 대명사의 인칭 일치 문제, 수 일치 문제가 출제된다.
• 어휘는 그 문장만 보고는 문제를 풀 수 없고 앞뒤 문맥을 파악하여 고르는 문제가 출제된다.

PART 6 이렇게 대비하자!

• Part 5처럼 단순히 문장 구조나 문법을 묻는 문제도 출제되지만, 전체적인 내용이나 앞뒤 문장
  내용과 연결되는 어휘나 시제, 접속부사를 묻는 문제들이 주로 출제된다는 것에 유의한다.
• 문맥상 적절한 문장 고르기는 문제는 빈칸 앞뒤 문장의 대명사나 연결어 등을 확인하고 상관
  관계를 파악한다.
• 지문의 길이가 짧기 때문에 전체 내용을 파악하는 데 많은 시간이 걸리지 않으므로 정독해서
  읽으면 오히려 더 쉽게 해결할 수 있다.

PART 6 문제 유형별 문제 풀이 접근법

Questions 143-146 refer to the following article.

Jakarta, INDONESIA (5 June) - An Indonesian steelmaker, Irwan Steel Company, announced that it had named Maghfirah Baldraf its new Chief Operating Officer of the Java Division effective 1 September. His 30 years of experience in the ------- made him the obvious choice for the position.
143.
Baldraf majored in metal engineering at the National University of Indonesia. After graduation, he then ------- his career in the quality control department at Putirai Metal. 15 years ago, he joined
144.
Irwan Steel Company. -------. Baldraf will go to Java to oversee the daily operations of Irwan Steel
145.
Company ------- its inauguration on September 1.
146.

1. 어휘 문제

Part 5 어휘 문제와는 달리 그 한 문장만 봐서는 여러 개가 답이 될 수 있을 것 같은 선택지들이 나온다. 따라서 Part 6의 어휘 문제는 앞뒤 문맥을 정확히 파악하여 답을 골라야 한다.

143.	(A) license	(B) industry	(C) outset	(D) program

이 문제에서는 '그 산업 분야에서의 30년 경력 때문에 그가 그 자리에 확실한 선택이었다'라는 의미를 파악해서 (B)를 골라야 한다

2. 어형 문제

한 단어의 네 가지 형태가 나오는 문제를 어형 문제 또는 자리 찾기 문제라고 한다. Part 5와 마찬가지 방법으로 풀면 되지만, 동사 시제 문제는 문맥을 파악하는 까다로운 문제로 출제된다.

144.	(A) started	(B) had started	(C) was starting	(D) will start

이 문제는 동사의 시제를 고르는 문제로 문맥상 이 사람이 처음으로 직장 생활을 시작한 것을 이야기하고 있으므로 과거 시제인 (A)가 답이 되며, then도 힌트가 될 수 있다.

3. 문장 고르기 문제

Part 6에서 가장 어려운 문제로 전체적인 문맥을 파악하고, 접속부사나, 시제 등을 종합적으로 봐야 답을 고를 수 있다.

145.	(A) The company also has a division in Singapore.
	(B) He has been interested in engineering since he was young.
	(C) Most recently, he has served as Vice President of Development of Irwan Steel Company.
	(D) As soon as Baldraf is appointed, the company will go through a major restructuring.

이 문제에서는 대학교 졸업 후부터 이 사람의 경력을 나열하고 있으므로 (C)가 답이 된다.

4. 문법 문제

문법 문제는 보통 문장의 구조를 파악하여 구와 절을 구분하는 문제이다.

143.	(A) by the time	(B) as soon as	(C) when	(D) after

이 문제에서는 빈칸 뒤에 명사구가 있으므로 명사를 목적어로 취하는 전치사가 답이 되어야 하는데 보기 중에 전치사로 쓰일 수 있는 것이 (D)뿐이다.

PART 6 문장 삽입 유형 분석

Part 6뿐 아니라 전체 RC 문제 중 가장 어려운 유형으로 빈칸에 들어갈 가장 알맞은 문장을 골라야 하며, 문장 네 개가 보기로 제시된다. 매 지문마다 한 문제씩 고정적으로 출제된다. 단순히 빈칸 주변의 키워드를 통해 해결되기 보다는 앞뒤 문맥이나 지문 전체의 맥락을 파악할 수 있어야 풀 수 있기 때문에, 독해 실력을 기르는 것이 반드시 필요하다.

✔ 가장 많이 틀리는 문장 삽입 문제 접근 방법

▶ **지문 전체를 읽되, 특히 빈칸 앞뒤 문장의 내용을 정확히 파악한다.**
특히, 빈칸 앞에 결정적인 단서가 제시되는 경우 많으므로, 빈칸 앞에 언급된 내용을 정확히 파악한다. 또한, 보기나 빈칸 앞 뒤에 나오는 연결어(however, therefore, in addition to), 지시어(it, this, that) 등을 단서를 최대한 활용하여 문맥을 파악하도록 한다.

▶ **앞뒤 내용과 가장 어울리는 보기를 선택한다.**
소거법을 통해 연관성이 없는 보기부터 제거한 후, 정답을 선택한다.

▶ **선택한 보기가 문맥상 적절한지 다시 확인한다.**
정답 문장을 해당 위치에 넣어 읽어본 후, 문맥상 매끄러운지 최종 확인한다.

📋 핵심 문제 유형

Question 1 refers to the following e-mail.

Dear Valued Beacon Air Customer,

Thank you for flying with Beacon Air. We'd like to know about your recent flight from St. Louis to Florence on May 27. -------. This should only take a few minutes of your time.
      1.

1. (A) As requested, we have included a list of recommended hotels.
(B) We would like you to fill out our satisfaction survey.
(C) In addition, you can receive a discount on your next flight.
(D) You will be compensated for the delayed flight.

정답 (B)

해설 앞 문장에서는 최근 비행 경험에 대해 알고 싶다고 했으며, 뒷문장은 이것을 하는 데 몇 분밖에 걸리지 않을 거라고 했으므로 보기 중 '만족도 설문을 작성해주기를 원한다'는 문장이 들어가야 문맥상 적절하다. 따라서 (B) We would like you to fill out our satisfaction survey.가 정답이다.

해석 소중한 Beacon 항공 고객님께.
Beacon 항공을 이용해 주셔서 감사합니다. 저희는 고객님의 5월 27일 St. Louis 발 Florence행 최근 비행에 관하여 알고 싶습니다. **1** 저희는 귀하께서 만족도 설문을 작성해 주셨으면 합니다. 이것은 몇 분밖에 걸리지 않을 것입니다.
(A) 요청하신 대로, 추천 호텔 목록을 포함해드렸습니다.
(B) 저희는 귀하께서 만족도 설문을 작성해 주셨으면 합니다.
(C) 게다가, 다음 비행 시 할인을 받으실 수 있습니다.
(D) 비행기 지연에 대해 보상을 받게 될 것입니다.

Question 2 refers to the following notice.

Congratulations on becoming a subscriber of *Worldwide Hospitality Times*. Under the plan you have

subscribed to, you will not only receive our hard copy edition each month, but also have unlimited

access to our online contents. If you wish to modify your subscription preferences, contact our

customer service team at +65-04975-614733. Most subscribers may also make changes to their

account on our Web site at www.worhosptimes.com. Please note that due to a few technical issues

on our part, subscribers in certain countries may experience delays when updating their accounts

online. We apologize in advance for any inconvenience this may cause. -------.
2.

2. (A) Please contact your internet service provider to improve your connection speed.
(B) We will do our best to resolve this problem as soon as possible.
(C) You will find a wide variety of useful articles on our Web site.
(D) Our customer representatives are available 24 hours a day, seven days a week.

정답 (B)

해설 빈칸 앞 두 문장에 걸쳐 기술상의 문제로 일부 구독자들이 온라인으로 계정 업데이트 시 지연을 겪을 수 있다고 하면서 사과하고 있으므로 문제점 뒤에 이어질 수 있는 해결책 제시를 예상해 볼 수 있다. '기술상의 문제로 업데이트 지연이 되어 사과 드리며, 되도록 빨리 이 문제를 해결하기 위해 최선을 다하겠다'는 자연스러운 문맥을 완성하므로 (B) We will do our best to resolve this problem as soon as possible.이 정답이다.

해석 〈Worldwide Hospitality Times〉의 구독자가 되신 걸 축하드립니다. 귀하께서 구독하신 계획에 따라, 매월 인쇄판을 받으실 뿐만 아니라 온라인 콘텐츠도 무제한 이용하실 수 있습니다. 귀하의 구독 선택을 변경하고 싶으시면, 저희 고객 서비스 팀 +65–04975–614733으로 연락해 주세요. 대부분의 구독자들 또한 저희 웹사이트 www.worhosptimes.com에서 계정을 변경하실 수 있습니다. 저희 파트의 몇 가지 기술상의 문제로 인해. 특정 국가들의 구독자 분들은 온라인으로 계정 업데이트 시 지연을 겪으실 수 있습니다. 이로 인한 어떠한 불편함에 대해서든 미리 사과 드립니다. **2 되도록 빨리 저희는 이 문제를 해결할 수 있도록 최선을 다하겠습니다.**
(A) 연결 속도를 개선하기 위해 인터넷 서비스 제공업체에 연락해주세요.
(B) 저희는 이 문제를 되도록 빨리 해결하기 위해 최선을 다하겠습니다.
(C) 저희 웹사이트에서 아주 다양하고 유용한 기사들을 발견하실 것입니다.
(D) 저희 고객 담당자들은 하루 24시간, 일주일 내내 이용 가능합니다.

실전 연습 01

Questions 1-4 refer to the following instructions.

해설서 p.55

Maintenance Instructions

-------. Please ------- the table with a dry cloth. Any remaining stain can be removed with a
　　1.　　　　　2.

damp cloth. When the surface is clean, it's good to apply wax. This will make the table -------.
　　3.

You should ------- the process three to four times.
　　　　　　4.

---

1. (A) You will never have to use this method more than once.
(B) Follow these instructions for maximum performance.
(C) This method is not effective for getting rid of stains.
(D) Make sure that the cloth you are using is damp.

2. (A) wipe
(B) to wipe
(C) wiped
(D) wiping

3. (A) shined
(B) shiny
(C) shines
(D) to shine

4. (A) enter
(B) repeat
(C) check
(D) study

해결 TIP

1. **문장 삽입:** 문맥에 맞는 문장 삽입
2. **동사 자리:** Please + 동사원형
3. **형용사 자리:** make의 목적격 보어 자리
4. **동사 어휘:** 능동태의 동사 어휘는 목적어를 확인

VOCA ···

maintenance *n.* 유지, 보수, 정비 I **instruction** *n.* 지시, 설명, 지침서 I **dry** *adj.* 마른, 건조한 I **remaining** *adj.* 남아있는 I **remove** *v.* 제거하다 I **cloth** *n.* 천 I **surface** *n.* 표면 I **apply** *v.* (크림 등을) 바르다, 신청하다, 적용하다 I **process** *n.* 과정 I **method** *n.* 방법 I **once** *adv.* 한 번 I **maximum performance** 최대의 효과 I **effective** *adj.* 효과적인 I **get rid of** ~를 없애다 I **stain** *n.* 얼룩 I **damp** *adj.* 축축한 I **shiny** *adj.* 빛나는

Questions 5-8 refer to the following e-mail.

To: Sue77@mymail.net
From: JayJang@pinkinc.com
Date: April 8

Dear Ms. Song,

We recently reviewed your résumé for the opening in the Marketing Department.

Although you do not ------- work experience, your strong academic performance and letter of
5.

self-introduction ------- very impressive. For these reasons, our manager, David Kim, and I would
6.

like to speak with you by phone. -------. Please ------- when a convenient time to call is.
7.   8.

I look forward to your response.

Best regards,

Jay Jang
Hiring Director, PINK, Inc.

5.
(A) have
(B) has
(C) having
(D) to have

6.
(A) are
(B) is
(C) to be
(D) been

해결 TIP

5. **동사 자리**: 조동사(do) + 동사원형
6. **동사 자리**: 동사의 수 일치
7. **문장 삽입**: 문맥에 맞는 문장 삽입
8. **동사 자리**: Please + 동사원형

7.
(A) We think this will be most convenient for all of us.
(B) It was very nice to speak with you on the telephone last week.
(C) That way, we can have your job interview in person.
(D) Mr. Kim is looking forward to having lunch with you soon.

8.
(A) confirming
(B) to confirm
(C) confirmed
(D) confirm

VOCA ···

résumé n. 이력서 | **opening** n. 공석, 빈자리 | **academic** adj. 학업의, 학교의 | **self-introduction** n. 자기소개서 | **impressive** adj. 인상 깊은 |
convenient adj. 편리한 | **look forward to -ing** ~를 고대하다 | **response** n. 응답, 반응, 답변 | **confirm** v. 확인하다

Questions 9-12 refer to the following article.

The Annual Red Apple Fair ------- to southern Newtown on October 25. This popular county
　　　　　　　　　　　　　　　　9.

fair ------- in Newtown for the last 10 years, and this year, organizers made a decision to move
　　　　10.

it to the town's largest park. The decision was the right one because a record number of -------
　　　　　　　　　　　　　　　　　　　　　　　　　　　　　　　　　　　　　　11.

showed up to sample delicious foods and watch performances by local musicians. -------.
　　　　　　　　　　　　　　　　　　　　　　　　　　　　　　　　　　　　　　12.

9. (A) are coming
(B) came
(C) come
(D) were coming

10. (A) has been held
(B) had held
(C) will be held
(D) would be held

11. (A) visitor
(B) visit
(C) visits
(D) visitors

12. (A) Organizers hope that everything goes well for this year's fair.
(B) Attendees at the fair also commented favorably on the new venue.
(C) The number of people at the fair was slightly less than last year's number.
(D) This year's fair lacked the live performances that previous fairs offered.

해결 TIP

9. 동사 자리: 동사의 수 일치
10. 동사 자리: 동사의 시제 일치
11. 명사 자리: a record number of + 복수 명사
12. 문장 삽입: 문맥에 맞는 문장 삽입

VOCA ···
fair *n.* 박람회, 축제 | **southern** *adj.* 남쪽의 | **county** *n.* 군, 주 | **organizer** *n.* 주최자, 조직자 | **a record number of** 기록적으로 많은 수의 |
show up 나타나다 | **sample** *v.* 맛보다, 시식하다 | **attendee** *n.* 참석자 | **comment** *n.* 논평 *v.* 논평하다 | **favorably** *adv.* 좋게, 호의적으로 |
venue *n.* 장소 | **slightly** *adv.* 약간 | **lack** *v.* ~이 없다, 부족하다 *n.* 부족 | **previous** *adj.* 이전의

Questions 13-16 refer to the following announcement.

Beauty Magazine welcomes letters from readers. Because space is ------- , not all submissions
                                                                      13.

can be printed. ------- . Letters with original ideas about the topic of beauty will be given priority.
                 14.

Letters must also meet certain requirements. For example, they cannot exceed 400 words.

We will edit letters which are ------- than the maximum. We ask you to include your name and
                              15.

contact information so that we can notify you if your letter is ------- for publication.
                                                                16.

---

13. (A) limiting
    (B) limit
    (C) limited
    (D) limits

14. (A) We let our readers choose which
       letters they want to see.
    (B) If you write us, we promise to print
       your letter in our magazine.
    (C) Letters about your personal
       experiences are the most likely to be
       published.
    (D) In fact, we only print a small portion
       of the letters we receive.

15. (A) older
    (B) wider
    (C) longer
    (D) better

16. (A) selected
    (B) opened
    (C) completed
    (D) continued

해결 TIP

13. 형용사 자리: 형용사 보어(과거분사형)
14. 문장 삽입: 문맥에 맞는 문장 삽입
15. 형용사 어휘: 주어를 확인
16. 동사 어휘: 수동태의 동사 어휘는 주어를 확인

VOCA ··

submission *n.* 제출(물) | **print** *v.* ~을 인쇄 출판하다 *n.* 인쇄물, 프린트 | **priority** *n.* 우선권 | **meet** *v.* 충족시키다 | **requirement** *n.* 요구, 조건 |
exceed *v.* 초과하다 | **edit** *v.* 편집하다 | **maximum** *n.* 최대(치) *adj.* 최대의 | **include** *v.* 포함하다 | **contact information** 연락처 | **so that**
~하기 위해서 | **notify** *v.* 통보하다 | **publication** *n.* 출판 | **limit** *v.* 제한하다 | **portion** *n.* 부분, 일부

실전 연습 02

Questions 17-20 refer to the following notice. 해설서 p.56

Thank you for staying with us at the MRT Hotel. ------- (17.). You will find a bottle of shampoo, a bar of soap, and a bottle of lotion in the cabinet. You may use ------- (18.) at no additional charge. Also, you will find information about our Green Hotel program. Customer ------- (19.) in the program enables our community to cut back on water and energy consumption. If you want to take part in the program, just place a memo in a ------- (20.) location on the table next to your bed.

---

17. (A) We are one of the city's fastest-growing travel agencies.
(B) Items such as soap and shampoo are available for sale in the lobby.
(C) Unfortunately, the shower in this room is not working.
(D) We hope that you enjoy your time here.

18. (A) their
(B) its
(C) it
(D) them

19. (A) participate
(B) participated
(C) participation
(D) participates

20. (A) noticeably
(B) noticeable
(C) notice
(D) notices

해결 TIP

17. 문장 삽입: 문맥에 맞는 문장 삽입
18. 대명사 자리: 격과 인칭 일치
19. 명사 자리: 복합 명사
20. 형용사 자리: 명사 수식 자리

VOCA ··

stay *v.* 머무르다 I **additional** *adj.* 추가의 I **charge** *n.* 요금 I **enable** *v.* ~를 할 수 있게 하다, ~를 가능하게 하다 I **cut back on** ~을 줄이다 I **consumption** *n.* 소비 I **take part in** ~에 참가하다 I **place** *v.* 놓다, 두다 I **travel agency** 여행사 I **such as** ~와 같은, 예를 들면

Questions 21-24 refer to the following e-mail.

To: Hong@dotmail.com
From: Lee1234@CandMagency.com
Date: April 1
Subject: Please tell us how we did.
Attachment: cmta.doc

Dear Customer,

Thank you for making a reservation with C&M Travel Agency. We'd like to hear about your recent

trip ------- California to Michigan on March 15. We would appreciate it if you could complete a
　　　 21.

short survey about your experience with our company. ------- should take only five minutes of
　　　　　　　　　　　　　　　　　　　　　　　　　　 22.

your time. Please complete the attached file and send it back to us. -------.
　　　　　　　　　　　　　　　　　　　　　　　　　　　　　　 23.

Your feedback will help ------- improve our service.
　　　　　　　　　　 24.

Thank you again for your business.

Ho Jun Lee, Chief Executive Officer
C&M Travel Agency

---

21. (A) from
(B) near
(C) at
(D) for

22. (A) Both
(B) Every
(C) They
(D) This

> **해결 TIP**
>
> **21. 전치사 어휘:** 방향을 나타내는 전치사
> **22. 대명사 자리:** 가리키는 앞명사 찾기
> **23. 문장 삽입:** 문맥에 맞는 문장 삽입
> **24. 대명사 자리:** 격 일치

23. (A) Your answers were extremely helpful to us.
(B) You must make a new reservation by next week.
(C) If we receive it by April 8, we will mail you a free gift.
(D) It should take an hour for you to complete it.

24. (A) our
(B) us
(C) ours
(D) their

VOCA ···

make a reservation 예약을 하다 | **appreciate** *v.* 고마워하다, 감사하다 | **complete** *v.* (서식 등을) 작성하다, 완성하다 *adj.* 완전한 | **survey** *n.* 설문 조사 | **experience** *v.* 경험하다, 겪다 *n.* 경험 | **attached** *adj.* 첨부된 | **feedback** *n.* 피드백, 조언 | **improve** *v.* 개선시키다 | **business** *n.* 사업, 거래 | **extremely** *adv.* 몹시, 매우

Questions 25-28 refer to the following notice.

The Owen Research Library is going to be renovated starting on April 2 and ending in late October. This renovation ------- storage space to accommodate our growing collections.
25.
The library will still remain open during the renovation work. Nevertheless, some sections will be temporarily ------- to on-site researchers. A list of these ------- sections will be on our Web site at
26.   **27.**
www.owenresearch.org. Researchers are urged to check the list or to contact the library prior to visiting. -------.
28.

---

25. (A) to increase
(B) increased
(C) increasing
(D) will increase

26. (A) unavailable
(B) unavailing
(C) unavailability
(D) unavailably

27. (A) inaccessibleness
(B) inaccessibility
(C) inaccessibly
(D) inaccessible

28. (A) Access to the library will be restricted to all users until October.
(B) It is impossible to predict when certain parts of the library will be closed.
(C) We apologize in advance for any inconvenience you may experience.
(D) Speak to a librarian to learn how to access the list.

해결 TIP

25. 동사 자리: 동사의 시제
26. 형용사 자리: 주격 보어 자리
27. 형용사 자리: 명사 수식 자리
28. 문장 삽입: 문맥에 맞는 문장 삽입

VOCA ···

renovation n. 보수, 수리, 개조 | **storage space** 저장 공간 | **accommodate** v. 수용하다 | **growing** adj. 증가하는, 커지는 | **remain** v. 남아 있다 | **nevertheless** adv. 그럼에도 불구하고 | **section** n. 부분, 부문 | **temporarily** adv. 일시적으로 | **on-site** adj. 현장의, 현지의 | **urge** v. 권고하다, 촉구하다 | **prior to** ~이전에 | **unavailing** adj. 소용 없는, 효과 없는 | **unavailably** adv. 효과 없이, 무익하게 | **restrict** v. 제한하다 | **apologize** v. 사과하다 | **in advance** ~이전에 | **access** n. 접근, 출입

Questions 29-32 refer to the following memo.

From: Hyo-ju Kim, Building Manager
To: All employees
Date: Thursday, March 2
Re: Construction work

As you know, renovations to our office building will start on Wednesday, March 15 and last until the end of the day on Monday, March 20. Accordingly, you may experience some -------.
29.

The south-side elevator will not function for the entire week. -------.
30.

I know that most of you ------- use this elevator. Unfortunately, you'll need to take the stairs.
31.

-------, the entrance on the southwest side of the building will be closed on Thursday. All other
32.

entrances to the building will remain open as usual during this time.

29. (A) inconvenience
(B) happiness
(C) addition
(D) contradiction

30. (A) Fortunately, a few people ever take this elevator.
(B) It needs to be repaired and inspected during that time.
(C) The elevator will be back in operation in three days.
(D) This elevator will not be affected by the renovations.

31. (A) regularize
(B) regular
(C) regularly
(D) regularity

32. (A) Nevertheless
(B) However
(C) Previously
(D) Moreover

해결 TIP

29. 명사 어휘: 동사 확인
30. 문장 삽입: 문맥에 맞는 문장 삽입
31. 부사 자리: 동사 수식 자리
32. 접속부사: 문맥에 맞는 접속부사 고르기

VOCA ···

renovation n. 개조, 수리 I **accordingly** adv. 그래서, 그런 이유로 I **experience** v. 경험하다 I **function** v. ∼역할을 하다, 기능을 하다, 작동을 하다, ∼로도 쓰이다 I **entire** adj. 전체의 I **unfortunately** adv. 불행하게도 I **stairs** n. 계단 I **entrance** n. 입구, 문 I **the southwest** n. 남서부(지방) adj. 남서부의 I **as usual** 평상시처럼 I **inspect** v. 조사하다, 검사하다 I **operation** n. (기계 등의) 조작, 운전; 운영 I **affect** v. 영향을 주다

실전 연습 03

Questions 33-36 refer to the following instructions.

해설서 p.58

The remodeling of Amarillo Automotive Repair Shop will be completed ------- October 3.
33.

After the remodeling, it will be open Monday through Friday from 6:00 A.M. to 5:00 P.M.

If you want to, you may leave your car at the shop. The store is ------- located next to a large,
34.

well-known shopping mall. -------. Fill in a card with your name and contact information, and
35.

write a brief description of the problem with your car. Then, seal your key in an envelope -------
36.

your request card and drop the envelope into the slot in front of the office door. We will look over

your car thoroughly. Then, we will call you in order to discuss the results and any suggested

repairs.

---

33. (A) by
(B) within
(C) at
(D) until

34. (A) convenience
(B) convenient
(C) conveniently
(D) conveniences

해결 TIP

33. 전치사 어휘: 완료(by) vs. 계속(until)
34. 부사 자리: 동사 수식 자리
35. 문장 삽입: 문맥에 맞는 문장 삽입
36. 전치사 어휘: ~와 함께

35. (A) We are located on the first floor of the shopping mall.
(B) A mechanic will look at your car the moment that you arrive.
(C) Simply explain the problem to the person on duty.
(D) Should you arrive when we are closed, please do the following.

36. (A) to
(B) above
(C) from
(D) along with

VOCA ···

complete *v.* 완성하다, 끝마치다 *adj.* 완전한 I **leave** *v.* 놓아두다, 남기고 가다 I **locate** *v.* 위치하다, 찾아내다 I **well-known** *adj.* 잘 알려진 I **fill in** 기입하다, 작성하다 I **contact information** 연락처 I **brief** *adj.* 짧은 I **description** *n.* 서술, 묘사 I **seal** *v.* 봉하다 I **envelope** *n.* 봉투 I **drop** *v.* 떨어지다, 떨어뜨리다 I **slot** *n.* (무엇을 집어넣도록 만든 가느다란) 구멍, 시간대 I **in front of** ~앞에 I **look over** 살펴보다 I **thoroughly** *adv.* 철저히 I **in order to** ~하기 위해 I **conveniently** *adv.* 편리하게

Questions 37-40 refer to the following notice.

We are offering a new service called RED Alerts. ------- you have registered, updates will be sent
37.

to your mobile phone if the air quality in your location is unsafe. -------.
38.

-------, our company is providing this service for free. ------- signing up for RED Alerts, you
39. 40.

should review the terms of service, which are on our Web site.

37. (A) Once
(B) Despite
(C) In order to
(D) Although

38. (A) It will also inform you when you can
expect better conditions.
(B) You can call to find out what is
happening in your area.
(C) Sign up during the next two weeks to
get this service for a special price.
(D) The alerts will be sent straight to your
e-mail when there is a problem.

39. (A) Moreover
(B) However
(C) In addition to
(D) Nevertheless

40. (A) Without
(B) Because
(C) Due to
(D) Prior to

해결 TIP

37. 접속사: 접속사와 전치사의 구분
38. 문장 삽입: 문맥에 맞는 문장 삽입
39. 접속부사: 문맥에 맞는 접속부사 고르기
40. 전치사 어휘: ~하기 전에

VOCA ··

alert n. 경보 adj. 경계하는 v. 경보를 발하다 I **register** v. 등록하다 I **update** n. 업데이트, 갱신, 최신, 새로운 정보 I **air quality** n. 대기·공기의 질 I
unsafe adj. 안전하지 못한 I **sign up** 등록하다, 가입하다, 신청하다 I **due to** ~때문에 I **review** v. 검토하다 I **terms** n. 조건, 조항 I **inform** v. 알
리다

Questions 41-44 refer to the following e-mail.

To: sue117@zonet.org
From: JSP@seework.net
Date: May 15

Dear Ms. Sue,

We recently reviewed your résumé. We were ------- with your experience. -------.
                                    41.   **42.**
We want to meet you, but we are very busy. As a result, we want to interview ------- by phone.
                                                                43.
Please confirm by e-mail ------- 2:00 P.M. on Friday, May 20, would be a suitable time for the call.
                                  44.

I look forward to your response.

Best regards,

Ji-Sung Park
Hiring Director

---

41. (A) impress
(B) impressive
(C) impressed
(D) impresses

42. (A) Please send your résumé as soon as you can.
(B) You also received an excellent education.
(C) You have barely done any work in the industry.
(D) In addition, you forgot to send your salary request.

43. (A) you
(B) your
(C) yours
(D) yourself

44. (A) whether
(B) at
(C) around
(D) next to

해결 TIP

41. 형용사 자리: 분사형 형용사
42. 문장 삽입: 문맥에 맞는 문장 삽입
43. 대명사 자리: 격 일치
44. 접속사: 명사절 접속사

VOCA ···

résumé *n.* 이력서 | **confirm** *v.* 확인하다, 확정하다 | **suitable** *adj.* 적당한, 적합한 | **response** *n.* 반응, 응답, 답변 | **impressive** *adj.* 인상적인 | **impressed** *adj.* 감명을 받은 | **barely** *adv.* 거의 ~ 않다 | **industry** *n.* 산업, 분야 | **whether** *conj.* ~인지 아닌지

Questions 45-48 refer to the following memo.

To: All employees
From: Hee-Ra Lee
Date: August 2
Subject: Technical Problems

This is to inform you that this is our last day using the old e-mail system. ------- 5:00 P.M. today,
                                                                                    45.

you won't be able to access the system at all. -------. Thus, it is essential that you save any
                                                      46.

important messages which you have stored in the e-mail program. Be aware that any unsaved

messages ------- permanently.
         47.

To learn more about the new e-mail program, watch the demonstration video, ------- describes
                                                                              48.

many helpful features and benefits.

If you still have questions or problems, contact helpdesk@JBT.com.

---

45. (A) As of
(B) Except for
(C) In addition to
(D) Aside from

46. (A) The system has been checked by
company technicians.
(B) You can continue sending and
receiving e-mails after that time.
(C) This includes any e-mails sent or
received in the past.
(D) A decision to change the program will
be made soon.

47. (A) to delete
(B) will be deleted
(C) have to delete
(D) were deleted

48. (A) which
(B) those
(C) so that
(D) what

해결 TIP

45 전치사 어휘· 시간이 전치사
46. 문장 삽입: 문맥에 맞는 문장 삽입
47. 동사 자리: 동사의 시제와 태
48. 접속사: 관계 대명사

VOCA ··

technical *adj.* 기술적인 I **access** *v.* 접근하다, 이용하다 *n.* 접근 I **essential** *adj.* 필수적인, 중요한 I **save** *v.* 저장하다 I **be aware that** ~라는 점
을 유념하다 I **unsaved** *adj.* 저장되지 않은 I **permanently** *adv.* 영구적으로 I **demonstration** *n.* 설명, 입증 I **describe** *v.* 묘사하다, 말하다, 서술
하다 I **feature** *n.* 특징 *v.* 특징을 이루다 I **benefit** *n.* 혜택, 이득

실전 연습 04

Questions 49-52 refer to the following memo.

해설서 p.60

To: All staff

The JUA Company is ------- to announce that Mr. Hong has been appointed Vice President.
49.
-------. Clearly, Mr. Hong's experience and commitment to this company are great. This is good
50.
timing for us because as of October 11, JUA is planning ------- some new products. We believe
51.
he will help our company increase its sales with these new products.

If you have any questions or concerns while we ------- this transition in leadership, please feel
52.
free to contact me.

Thank you,

Julia Park
Communication Director

---

49. (A) pleased
(B) pleasing
(C) pleasant
(D) pleasure

50. (A) Mr. Hong declined the promotion and chose to remain in his current position.
(B) Mr. Hong congratulated the company's newest Vice President.
(C) Mr. Hong is going to take over as the company's leader next month.
(D) Mr. Hong has been an employee at JUA for the last 18 years.

51. (A) to release
(B) releasing
(C) released
(D) release

52. (A) reconsider
(B) question
(C) undergo
(D) enjoy

해결 TIP

49. 형용사 자리: be pleased + to부정사
50. 문장 삽입: 문맥에 맞는 문장 삽입
51. to부정사: to부정사를 목적어로 취하는 동사
52. 동사 어휘: 뒤의 목적어 확인

VOCA ....

appoint *v.* 임명하다, 지명하다 | **vice president** 부사장 | **clearly** *adv.* 분명히, 알기 쉽게 | **commitment** *n.* 전념, 헌신 | **transition** *n.* (다른 조건으로의) 이행, 변경 | **feel free to V** 거리낌 없이 ~하다, 마음껏 ~하다 | **pleased** *adj.* 기쁜 | **take over** ~을 인계받다 | **release** *v.* 출시하다, 발표하다 | **reconsider** *v.* 재고하다 | **undergo** *v.* (변화 등을) 겪다

Questions 53-56 refer to the following e-mail.

To: Taewoo Kim <taewoo@melot.net>
From: Josephine Park <jpark@redbook.com>
Date: April 20
Attachment: Big Book of Basketball

Thank you for ------- articles for the third edition of our book. I enjoyed ------- them a lot.
                              53.   54.
However, I did find a few errors in the piece about the early history of basketball. I have marked

these and made notes for your review (see the attached file). Moreover, you have not signed the

contributor agreement yet. Please do so as soon as possible. You ------- the document from our
                                                                                                     55.
online author center. -------.
                                        56.

Sincerely,

Josephine Park, Editor
Red Books

---

53. (A) submitting
(B) to submit
(C) submit
(D) submission

54. (A) read
(B) reading
(C) reads
(D) to read

해결 TIP

53. 동명사: 전치사 뒤 동명사
54. 동명사: 동명사를 목적어로 취하는 동사
55. 동사 자리: 동사의 시제
56. 문장 삽입: 문맥에 맞는 문장 삽입

55. (A) had downloaded
(B) can download
(C) might download
(D) will have downloaded

56. (A) Please submit your manuscript as soon
as possible.
(B) Once you do that, we can begin to
process your payment.
(C) We will send you the necessary
document by mail.
(D) The signed document you sent was
just received.

VOCA ···

article n. 글, 기사 I **edition** n. (출간 횟수) 판 I **error** n. 오류, 실수 I **mark** v. 표시하다 I **make notes** ~를 기록하다, ~를 메모하다 I
contributor n. 기고자, 기부자, 기여자 I **author** n. 저자 I **manuscript** n. 원고 I **necessary** adj. 필수적인

Questions 57-60 refer to the following advertisement.

Reyes Construction has been in the home-improvement business for more than 30 years.

This company, ------- for its excellent service, renovates houses at very reasonable prices.
57.

Now, for a ------- time, we are providing customers with a 20 percent discount on all door
58.

replacements. But hurry—this ------- is not valid after March 20.
59.

If you are interested in improving your home, call Reyes Construction. -------.
60.

We're the best in the business.

57. (A) know
(B) known
(C) knew
(D) knowing

58. (A) limited
(B) limitation
(C) limit
(D) limits

59. (A) level
(B) project
(C) offer
(D) session

60. (A) Your payment has been processed.
(B) Please confirm your appointment by tomorrow.
(C) You can also visit our office at 43 Baker Street.
(D) You will be sent an invoice for the completed work.

해결 TIP

57. 분사구문: 명사 뒤에서 수식하는 분사
58. 형용사 자리: 명사 수식 자리
59. 명사 어휘: 앞에 있는 단어 확인
60. 문장 삽입: 문맥에 맞는 문장 삽입

VOCA ···

home improvement 주거 개선 | **renovate** v. 개조하다, 보수하다 | **reasonable** adj. (가격이) 알맞은, 합리적인 | **discount** n. 할인 v. 할인하다 | **replacement** n. 교체, 대체 | **valid** adj. 유효한 | **be interested in** ~에 관심이 있는, ~에 흥미가 있는 | **limited** adj. 제한된 | **level** n. 수준, 단계, 층 | **offer** n. 할인, 제안

Questions 61-64 refer to the following e-mail.

Dear Ms. Jackson,

We are happy to inform you that we have ------- your JL Mall membership application.
  61.
To get all the benefits from your membership, please ------- activate your account by visiting our
  62.
Web site at www.jlmall.org. Your user name is JLJackson1234, and your current password is

7777. You can change your password on our Web site. You can take advantage of our services

as soon as you register. -------. We know that you will find your JL membership ------- more
  63.   64.
rewarding than any other membership.

---

61. (A) revised
(B) begun
(C) accepted
(D) submitted

62. (A) in addition
(B) immediately
(C) nevertheless
(D) thus

63. (A) The service fee that you sent has been processed.
(B) Please read the terms of service to see how to use your membership.
(C) You have to wait three business days before using your membership.
(D) We are sorry to hear that you no longer want to be an JL Mall member.

64. (A) much
(B) very
(C) too
(D) so

해결 TIP

61. **동사 어휘:** 뒤에 목적어 확인
62. **부사 어휘:** 수식 받는 동사 확인
63. **문장 삽입:** 문맥에 맞는 문장 삽입
64. **비교급:** 비교급 강조 부사

VOCA ···

inform v. 알리다 I **application** n. 지원(서) I **activate** v. 작동시키다, 활성화시키다 I **account** n. 계좌, 계정 I **take advantage of** ~를 이용하다 I **register** v. 등록하다 I **rewarding** adj. 보람 있는 I **immediately** adv. 즉시 I **nevertheless** adv. 그럼에도 불구하고 I **fee** n. 요금 I **terms** n. (계약 등의) 조건

REVIEW TEST

해설서 p.62

Questions 1-4 refer to the following e-mail.

To : Kao74@savemail.net
From : Elliot.Kang@bluepubco.com
Date: March 8
Subject: Your Submission
Attachment: ekaoagree.doc

Dear Mr. Kao,

As you know, these days, many people are writing about cooking. After reviewing your submission, however, we believe that most of your content ------- superior. As a result, we
1.
want to use your submission. -------. If you accept our offer, your submission will appear in a
2.
cookbook ------- in October. We expect you ------- many specific tips in your edition.
3.   4.

I look forward to your response.

Best regards,

Elliot Kang
Blue Publishing Company

1.
(A) are
(B) be
(C) is
(D) being

2.
(A) Please find attached a contract with our proposed terms in it.
(B) You should be pleased to know that your submission is selling quite well.
(C) We do not feel that the quality of the paper is good enough to be published.
(D) Your article on your life as a chef is quite an interesting autobiography.

3.
(A) publish
(B) to be published
(C) is publishing
(D) have been published

4.
(A) to include
(B) including
(C) included
(D) inclusion

Questions 5-8 refer to the following letter.

10 August
Ms. Linda Kim
8676 Grandriver Street
Vancouver 2H4 8J7

Dear Ms. Kim,

-------. Please find below the estimate for the purchase and ------- of your water purifier.
  5.   6.
The total cost includes purchase price, labor, and tax, which comes to $1,300. The labor time

and costs are subject to adjustment.

If you want to -------, please contact ------- to arrange a time that is convenient for you.
              7.   8.

Thank you,

Jenny Kumamoto
JAY Water Purifier

---

5. (A) The proposal you made has been accepted.
     (B) Your water purifier will arrive at your home soon.
     (C) You still have not paid for the item you purchased.
     (D) Thank you for your interest in our product.

6. (A) installs
     (B) installed
     (C) installer
     (D) installation

7. (A) renew
     (B) proceed
     (C) work
     (D) visit

8. (A) my
     (B) me
     (C) mine
     (D) myself

Questions 9-12 refer to the following article.

Sang-Woo Park, the president of KB Industry, formally announced ------- the company is going
9.

to market a new high-definition television starting next week. According to the company's press

release, the television ------- good sound quality and a sharp image. Electronics industry analysts
10.

predict that this latest product should attract ------- more consumers and have positive sales
11.

performance. -------.
12.

9. (A) what
(B) which
(C) that
(D) as soon as

10. (A) feature
(B) featuring
(C) featured
(D) features

11. (A) much
(B) very
(C) high
(D) few

12. (A) This should benefit KB, which recorded
a loss last year.
(B) A company salesperson said the
television is already selling well.
(C) Few consumers appear to be interested
in the new product.
(D) Now that Mr. Kim has resigned, a
search for a new CEO will be held.

Questions 13-16 refer to the following e-mail.

To: yoon11@SMMed-Tech.com
From: james@BB.org
Date: April 6
Subject: Last Thursday

Dear Ms. yoon,

Thank you for ------- me last Thursday. I enjoyed our talk, and learning about SM Med-Tech's
        13.
many projects was very interesting. -------. I think that working with SM Med-Tech ------- great
                                    14.   15.
for BB Hospital. After holding a meeting, we have decided ------- forward with the collaboration.
                                                          16.

Please inform me of what the next steps are.

Best,

James Kim

---

13. (A) giving
(B) recommending
(C) making
(D) calling

14. (A) I'm looking forward to working at SM
        Med-Tech.
(B) We can conduct the second interview
    next week.
(C) I feel much better after having taken
    the medicine you gave me.
(D) It was a very educational experience
    for me.

15. (A) would be
(B) have been
(C) being
(D) to be

16. (A) to move
(B) moving
(C) moved
(D) being moved

PAR

RT 7

독해

OVERVIEW

지문을 읽고 그에 해당하는 질문에 알맞은 답을 고르는 문제이다. 지문은 문자 메시지와 온라인 채팅과 같은 문자 대화문부터 신문 기사나 웹사이트 페이지까지 그 종류가 다양하며, 그 형태도 1개의 지문으로 된 단일 지문, 2개의 지문으로 된 이중 지문, 3개의 지문으로 이루어진 삼중 지문 문제로 구분할 수 있다. 단일 지문 29문항, 이중 지문 10문항, 삼중 지문 15문항씩 총 54문항이 출제된다.

화자 의도 4%
문장 삽입 4%
동의어 6%
주제 15%
세부사항 30%
NOT / TRUE 18%
추론 25%

문제 유형

단일 지문(10개) ㅣ 이메일, 편지, 문자 메시지, 온라인 채팅, 광고, 기사, 양식, 회람, 공지, 웹페이지 등

이중 지문(2개) ㅣ 이메일-이메일, 기사-이메일, 웹페이지-이메일, 웹페이지(광고)-웹페이지(사용 후기)

삼중 지문(3개) ㅣ 다양한 세 지문들의 조합

출제 포인트

- 지문과 문제의 길이가 점점 길어지고 있다. 지문과 선택지를 일일이 대조할 필요가 있는 사실 확인 문제 유형의 비중을 늘려서 난이도를 조절하기도 한다.
- 유추 문제의 비중이 증가하고 있다. 지문에 나와 있는 정보를 토대로 알 수 있는 사실 확인 및 유추 문제가 많이 등장하고 있다.
- 동의어 문제가 매회 1~4문제의 출제 비율을 유지하고 있다.

PART 7 이렇게 대비하자!

- Part 7은 지문과 문항 수가 증가했고, 글의 흐름 파악이 더 중요해졌기 때문에 빠르고 정확한 독해력이 필요하다. 어휘력을 쌓고 문장의 구조를 파악하는 훈련을 통해 독해력을 뒷받침하는 기본기를 다져야 한다.
- 문자 메시지나 온라인 채팅은 난이도가 비교적 높지 않다. 그러나 구어체적 표현이 많이 나오고 문자 그대로의 사전적인 의미가 아닌 문맥상 그 안에 담겨 있는 숨은 뜻을 찾는 화자 의도 파악 문제가 꼭 출제되기 때문에 평소 구어체 표현을 숙지하고 대화의 흐름을 파악하는 연습을 한다.
- 질문의 키워드를 찾고 질문이 요구하는 핵심 정보를 본문에서 신속하게 찾아내는 연습이 필요하다.
- 본문에서 찾아낸 정답 정보는 선택지에서 다른 표현으로 제시되므로 같은 의미를 여러 가지 다른 표현들(paraphrased expressions)로 전달하는 연습이 필요하다.

PART 7 문제 풀이 접근법

1. 지문 순서대로 풀지 말자.

Part 7은 처음부터 또는 마지막부터 순서대로 풀지 않아도 된다. 15개의 지문 중에서 당연히 쉬운 것부터 먼저 풀고 어려운 문제는 시간이 남으면 푼다는 마음으로 풀어야 한다. 다음과 같은 순서로 문제를 풀어 보도록 한다.

첫 3개 지문 (147번~152번)

▼

광고, 온라인 채팅, 양식(청구서, 주문서, 초대장 등), 웹페이지

▼

이메일, 편지, 회람, 공지

▼

첫 번째 이중 지문, 첫 번째 삼중 지문,

▼

기사, 두 번째 이중 지문, 나머지 삼중 지문

2. 패러프레이징(Paraphrasing)된 정답을 찾는 것이 핵심이다.

같은 어휘는 절대 반복되지 않는다. 정답은 지문에 나온 표현을 다른 말로 바꿔 나온다.

> • **지문에서 나오는 표현** National Museum is located just minutes from Oxford Street Station in Richmont's shopping district. 국립 박물관은 Richmont의 쇼핑가에 있는 Oxford Street 역에서 단 몇 분 거리에 있다.
>
> • **문제** What is suggested about the Morlen Museum? 국립 박물관에 관하여 암시되는 것은?
>
> • **정답** It is conveniently located. 편리한 곳에 위치해 있다.

3. 지문 내용에 기반하여 정답을 찾는다.

정답은 반드시 지문 내용에 기반하여 사실인 것만 고른다. 절대 '그럴 것 같다, 그렇겠지'라고 상상하여 답을 고르면 안 된다. Part 7 문제 유형 중에는 추론해야 하는 문제들이 많이 나오기는 하지만 아무리 추론 문제이더라도 지문에 있는 근거 문장을 패러프레이징한 보기를 찾는 문제일 뿐이다. 추론 이상의 상상은 금물이다.

4. 문제를 먼저 읽고 키워드를 파악하자!

지문 유형 확인 ▶ **문제의 핵심어 확인** ▶ **지문 읽기** ▶ **문제 풀이**

• 주제나 목적, 대상을 묻는 문제는 대개 지문의 첫머리에 단서가 제시되므로 도입부 내용을 잘 확인하여 이 내용을 포괄할 수 있는 선택지를 고른다.

• 세부사항, 사실 확인 문제의 경우 핵심 단어 및 표현에 집중하여 질문에서 키워드를 파악하고 관련 내용이 언급된 부분을 지문에서 찾아 문제를 해결한다.

• 동의어 문제에서는 해당 단어의 대표적인 의미를 무작정 선택하는 것이 아니라 반드시 문맥상 어떤 의미로 쓰였는지 확인하여 정답을 찾는다.

주제·목적 문제

가장 핵심적인 내용을 파악해야 한다! 주제나 목적을 묻는 문제는 지문의 가장 핵심적인 내용을 파악해야 하며, 보통 지문의 앞부분에서 단서를 찾을 수 있다. 출제 비중이 매우 높은 문제 유형으로 매회 6~7문제 이상 출제된다.

🔍 질문 유형 확인하기

▶ 주제

What does the article **mainly discuss**? 기사는 주로 무엇에 대해 이야기하고 있는가?

What is the **main topic** of the notice? 공지의 주제는 무엇인가?

What is the memo **about**? 회람은 무엇에 관한 내용인가?

▶ 목적

What is the **purpose** of the article? 기사의 목적은 무엇인가?

Why was the e-mail **sent**? 이메일은 왜 발송되었는가?

Why did Mr. Hong **write** this letter? Mr. Hong은 편지를 왜 썼는가?

🙂 문제 풀이 전략

1 질문을 보고 글의 주제나 목적을 찾는 문제인지 확인한 후, 선택지보다 지문을 먼저 읽는다.

질문에 purpose, discuss, topic 등이 나오면 지문의 목적이나 주제를 묻는 문제이다.

2 주제나 목적은 글의 앞부분 또는 마지막 부분에서 단서를 찾는다.

영어 지문은 주로 글의 첫머리에 중심 내용이 나오는 두괄식 전개 구조이지만, 간혹, 글의 후반부에서 글쓴이의 의도를 정리하는 미괄식 전개 구조도 있으므로 유의한다.

3 지문의 내용을 다른 단어로 바꾸어 표현(paraphrasing)한 선택지에 유의하여 정답을 고른다.

지문에서 찾은 정답의 단서를 그대로 언급했거나 다른 표현으로 바꾸어 표현한 정답을 고른다.

Question 1 refers to the following memo.

To:	All employees
From:	Aileen Jang, Chief of Operations
Date:	April 9
Subject:	ID badges

We will install a new security system next Monday, April 16. After activating this system, LV employees always have to carry identification badges. There are digital identification codes in the plastic cards. As a result, they enable you to have access to all buildings on the LV campus. You can pick up badges in the Marketing Department office on Friday, April 11.

Keep in mind that employees won't be able to enter any LV facilities after April 16 without their new ID badges. If you have any questions or concerns, please contact your manager.

· 수신인
발신인
날짜
제목

· 회람의 목적
새로운 보안
설치 안내

· 주의 사항
· 문의 사항이 있을 경우
연락할 사람

1. What is the purpose of the memo?

(A) To inform employees of the temporary closing of a building
(B) To introduce a company policy
(C) To notify employees that a department's location has moved
(D) To address a recent security problem

1번은 다음 회람에 관한 문제입니다.

To:	All employees	수신인
From:	Aileen Jang, Chief of Operations	발신인
Date:	April 9	날짜
Subject:	ID badges	제목

수신인: 모든 직원들
발신인: Aileen Jang, 운영 실장
날짜: 4월 9일
제목: ID 명찰

❶ We will install a new security system next Monday, April 16. After activating this system, LV employees always have to carry identification badges. There are digital identification codes in the plastic cards. As a result, they enable you to have access to all buildings on the LV campus. You can pick up badges in the Marketing Department office on Friday, April 11.

회람의 목적
새로운 보안 시스템
설치 안내

우리는 다음 주 월요일 4월 16일에 새로운 보안 시스템을 설치할 것입니다. 이 시스템을 작동시킨 후에, LV 직원들은 신분 확인 명찰을 항상 소지해야 합니다. 이 플라스틱 카드 안에는 디지털 식별 코드가 있습니다. 그 결과, 그것은 여러분이 LV 캠퍼스 내에 있는 모든 건물에 접근할 수 있도록 해줍니다. 여러분은 4월 11일 금요일에 마케팅 부서에서 명찰을 가져갈 수 있습니다.

Keep in mind that employees won't be able to enter any LV facilities after April 16 without their new ID badges. If you have any questions or concerns, please contact your manager.

주의 사항
문의 사항이 있을 경우
연락할 사람

4월 16일 이후에는 직원들이 그들이 새 명찰 없이는 그 어떠한 LV 시설물에도 들어갈 수 없을 것이라는 사실을 명심하세요. 만약 어떤 질문이나 염려되는 것이 있다면, 여러분의 매니저에게 연락하시기 바랍니다.

1. What is the **purpose** of the memo?

  (A) To inform employees of the temporary closing of a building

  (B) To introduce a company policy

  (C) To notify employees that a department's location has moved

  (D) To address a recent security problem

이 회람의 목적은 무엇인가?

(A) 직원들에게 건물의 임시 폐쇄를 알리기 위해

(B) 회사 정책을 소개하기 위해

(C) 직원들에게 부서의 위치가 이동되었다라는 것을 통보하기 위해

(D) 최근의 보안 문제를 해결하기 위해

문제 풀이 전략 적용

① 질문을 보고 글의 주제나 목적을 찾는 문제인지 확인한 후, 선택지보다 지문을 먼저 읽는다.

purpose → 글의 목적을 묻는 문제이다.

② 주제나 목적은 글의 앞부분 또는 마지막 부분에서 단서를 찾는다.

지문의 전반부, We will install a new security system next Monday. → 새로운 보안 시스템 설치를 알리기 위한 글임을 알 수 있다.

③ 지문의 내용을 다른 단어로 바꾸어 표현(paraphrasing)한 선택지에 유의하여 정답을 고른다.

지문의 첫 문장에 메모의 목적이 제시되어 있다. 새 보안 시스템 설치로 인해 앞으로 직원들이 명찰을 지니고 다녀야 시설물 입장이 가능하다는 것을 알리는 것으로 회사 보안 시스템, 즉 회사 보안 정책이 변경된 것을 알리기 위한 글이다. 따라서 정답은 (B) To introduce a company policy이다.

VOCA ···

install *v.* 설치하다 | security *n.* 보안 | activate *v.* 작동시키다 | carry *v.* 지니고 다니다, 운반하다 | identification *n.* 신분 확인 | identification code 식별 코드 | enable *v.* 가능하게 하다 | access *v.* ~에 접근하다 | facility *n.* 시설 | without *prep.* ~없이 | temporary *adj.* 일시적인, 임시의

해설서 p.65

Questions 1-2 refer to the following text message.

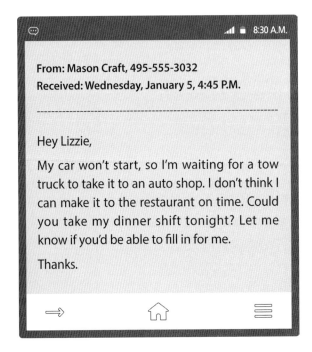

From: Mason Craft, 495-555-3032
Received: Wednesday, January 5, 4:45 P.M.

Hey Lizzie,

My car won't start, so I'm waiting for a tow truck to take it to an auto shop. I don't think I can make it to the restaurant on time. Could you take my dinner shift tonight? Let me know if you'd be able to fill in for me.

Thanks.

1. Why did Mason send the message?

(A) To inquire about car rental rates
(B) To arrange a substitute at his workplace
(C) To ask for a ride to an auto shop
(D) To postpone a meeting

2. What does Mason ask Lizzie to do?

(A) Bring tools from a garage
(B) Order a meal
(C) Call a restaurant
(D) Send a reply

VOCA ···

tow truck 견인차 ǀ auto (repair) shop 자동차 정비소 ǀ make it to ~에 이르다, 도착하다 ǀ on time 제시간에 ǀ fill in 대신 일을 봐주
다; 채우다, 기입하다 ǀ rate n. 요금; 비율 ǀ postpone v. 연기하다

Questions 3-4 refer to the following information.

Product of the Month: Jenny's Coconut Soap

Jenny's Coconut Soap is handmade by LA resident Jenny Kang. Ms. Kang sells the soap locally after contracting with BY Grocery. As long as you store the soap in a cool and dry location, you can use the organic coconut oil hand soap for over three months. Other organic soaps can be used for just one month. The soap is a popular item with many BY customers and is currently on sale for $10 for a pack of three bars. It has the following benefits.

- Make hands soft
- Features a delicate scent
- Made of purely organic materials
- Have no artificial chemicals
- Clean hands thoroughly

Also, you can receive 10 percent off your purchase of Jenny's Coconut Soap. Simply mention discount code GD88 to a cashier at BY Grocery in LA.

3. What is the purpose of the information?

(A) To announce the opening of a new store
(B) To describe a cleaning procedure
(C) To show how soap is made
(D) To market a local resident's merchandise

4. What is mentioned about the soap?

(A) It consists of natural ingredients.
(B) It is sold at several locations.
(C) It can be purchased in only single-bar packs.
(D) It will be sold only online.

VOCA ··

product *n.* 제품 I **soap** *n.* 비누 I **locally** *adv.* 지역에서, 현지에서 I **contract** *v.* 계약하다 *n.* 계약 I **grocery** *n.* 식료품점 I **store** *v.* 보관하다, 저장하다 I **organic** *adj.* 유기농의 I **benefit** *n.* 혜택, 장점, 이득 I **feature** *v.* 특징으로 삼다 *n.* 특징 I **delicate** *adj.* (색깔·향·냄새 등이) 은은한 I **scent** *n.* 향기 I **purely** *adv.* 순전히, 오직 I **artificial** *adj.* 인공적인 I **thoroughly** *adv.* 철저히 I **mention** *v.* 언급하다 I **opening** *n.* 개원식 I **consist of** ~로 구성되다

Questions 5-6 refer to the following e-mail.

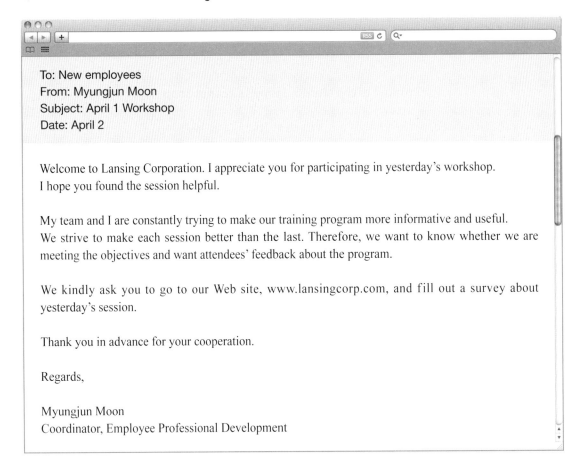

To: New employees
From: Myungjun Moon
Subject: April 1 Workshop
Date: April 2

Welcome to Lansing Corporation. I appreciate you for participating in yesterday's workshop.
I hope you found the session helpful.

My team and I are constantly trying to make our training program more informative and useful.
We strive to make each session better than the last. Therefore, we want to know whether we are
meeting the objectives and want attendees' feedback about the program.

We kindly ask you to go to our Web site, www.lansingcorp.com, and fill out a survey about
yesterday's session.

Thank you in advance for your cooperation.

Regards,

Myungjun Moon
Coordinator, Employee Professional Development

5. Why was the e-mail written?

(A) To congratulate some workers
(B) To request some input
(C) To announce an upcoming workshop
(D) To describe a program's benefits

6. What is indicated about Mr. Moon?

(A) He made changes to a company policy.
(B) He was recently promoted.
(C) He maintains the company Web site.
(D) He oversees training programs.

VOCA ···

participate v. 참가하다 | **helpful** adj. 도움이 되는 | **constantly** adv. 끊임없이 | **informative** adj. 유익한 | **useful** adj. 유용한, 도움이 되
는 | **strive** v. 노력하다, 애쓰다 | **meet** v. 충족시키다 | **objective** n. 목표, 목적 | **attendee** n. 참석자 | **kindly** adv. 친절하게, 정중히 | **fill
out** 기입하다 | **in advance** 미리 | **cooperation** n. 협조, 협력 | **coordinator** n. 조정자, 진행자, (의견 등을) 종합하는 사람

Questions 7-8 refer to the following notice.

Office Suite Available

A 1,000-foot office suite will be available to rent on Addison Road in Beltsville starting on May 1. The ideal tenant would be a small business looking for an open floor plan.

If that sounds like what you are looking for, you and your employees will be very satisfied. The space is located on the 16th floor and has windows on three sides that overlook downtown Beltsville. The view is simply amazing. The office is located in a modern building that features underground parking, three spacious elevators, and excellent security. For more information, please contact Britt Grouby at b.grouby@directrealtors. com.

---

7. What is the purpose of the notice?

(A) To ask for security fees
(B) To promote a new business
(C) To advertise an available position
(D) To announce a space for rent

8. What is NOT stated about the suite in the notice?

(A) It is currently unavailable.
(B) It features multiple elevators.
(C) It has windows on several sides.
(D) It is on the ground floor.

VOCA ···

available *adj.* 사물이 이용 가능한 | **rent** *v.* 임차하다 | **ideal** *adj.* 이상적인 | **tenant** *n.* 세입자, 임차인 | **open** *adj.* 탁 트인, 개방된 | **floor plan** 평면도 | **overlook** *v.* 내려다보다, 바라보다 | **simply** *adv.* 그야말로, 정말로 | **amazing** *adj.* 놀라운 | **modern** *adj.* 현대적인 | **feature** *v.* ~이 특징이다 | **underground parking** 지하 주차장 | **spacious** *adj.* 널찍한 | **security** *n.* 보안, 경비 | **ask for** ~에 대해 묻다 | **fee** *n.* 요금; 수수료 | **promote** *v.* 홍보하다 | **multiple** *adj.* 다수의, 많은 | **ground floor** 1층

UNIT 02

세부사항 문제

의문사와 질문의 키워드를 파악해야 한다! 세부 사항을 묻는 문제는 모든 질문이 의문사로 시작하며, 지문에서 질문의 키워드와 관련된 부분만 읽고 정답을 고를 수 있다. Part 7에서 가장 많이 출제되는 문제 유형으로 매회 20문제 이상 출제된다.

🔍 질문 유형 확인하기

▶ **인물·시간·장소**

Who most likely is Mr. Hong? Mr. Hong은 누구이겠는가?

When does the event start? 행사는 언제 시작하는가?

Where can more information be obtained? 더 자세한 정보는 어디에서 얻을 수 있는가?

▶ **요청·부탁**

What are the employees **asked** to do? 직원들은 무엇을 하도록 요청 받는가?

What does Mr. Leno **ask** Mr. Hong to do? Mr. Leno은 Mr. Hong에게 무엇을 하라고 요청하는가?

▶ **방법·이유**

How will the products be sent? 상품들은 어떻게 보내질 것인가?

Why did he miss the meeting? 그는 왜 회의에 빠졌는가?

 문제 풀이 전략

1 질문의 의문사를 확인한다.

세부사항을 묻는 질문은 Who, When, Where, What, How, Why(누가, 언제, 어디서, 무엇을, 어떻게, 왜) 등의 육하원칙으로 시작한다.

2 질문의 키워드를 파악한 후, 지문에서 언급된 부분을 찾는다.

질문의 키워드는 지문에서 언급된 내용을 다른 어휘로 바꾸어 표현(paraphrasing)하는 경우가 많으므로, 질문의 키워드가 그대로 언급되거나 비슷한 어휘나 표현이 나오면 선택지와 대조하면서 오답을 소거한다.

3 지문의 내용을 다른 어휘로 바꾸어 표현(paraphrasing)한 선택지에 유의하여 정답을 고른다.

지문에서 찾은 정답의 단서를 그대로 언급했거나 다른 어휘로 바꾸어 표현(paraphrasing)한 정답을 고른다.

Question 1 refers to the following invitation.

The BB Center Art Association
is going to host an exhibition.

Our Artists: Paintings and Drawings
by Chicago's Best Emerging Artists

Thursday, April 7, from 4:30 P.M. to 7:30 P.M.

Owen Performance Center
171 Grandriver Main Street
Chicago, IL 60007

Tickets to the event are $20 per person.

To make a reservation for your tickets,
please call or email by Friday, April 1.
TEL: 889-4000
E-mail: events@bbcenterarts.org

• 예술 협회 전시회

• 행사 세부 일정 안내
  (참가자, 전시 작품,
  시간, 장소, 비용)

• 티켓 예약 방법

1. What type of event is being held?

(A) A concert
(B) An art show
(C) A business convention
(D) An auction

1번은 다음 초대에 관한 문제입니다.

---

❶ The BB Center Art Association
is going to host an exhibition.
BB 센터 예술 협회는 전시회를 개최할 예정입니다.

Our Artists: Paintings and Drawings
by Chicago's Best Emerging Artists
우리의 예술가들: 시카고 최고 신인 예술가들의
회화와 소묘

Thursday, April 7, from 4:30 P.M. to 7:30 P.M.
4월 7일 목요일, 오후 4시 30분에서 오후 7시 30분까지

Owen Performance Center
171 Grandriver Main Street
Chicago, IL 60007
시카고, IL 60007의
Grandriver Main가 171번지에
있는 Owen 공연 센터에서 진행됩니다.

Tickets to the event are $20 per person.
행사 티켓은 인당 20달러입니다.

To make a reservation for your tickets,
please call or email by Friday, April 1.
TEL: 889-4000
E-mail: events@bbcenterarts.org
티켓을 예매하려면,
4월 1일 금요일까지 전화하거나 이메일을 보내세요.
전화: 889-4000
이메일: events@bbcenterarts.org

• 예술 협회 전시회

• 행사 세부 일정 안내
(참가자, 전시작품, 시간,
장소, 비용)

• 티켓 예약 방법

>> 세부사항을 묻는 문제

1. **What type of event** is being held?

(A) A concert
(B) An art show
(C) A business convention
(D) An auction

어떤 종류의 행사가 개최되는가?

(A) 콘서트
(B) 미술 전시회
(C) 비즈니스 컨벤션
(D) 경매

문제 풀이 전략 적용

① **질문의 의문사를 확인한다.**

어떤(What) 종류의 행사가 열리고 있는지를 묻는 세부 사항 문제이다. '어떤 종류의 행사(What type of event)'를 키워드로 잡아 지문에서 행사 관련 내용이 언급된 부분을 집중해서 읽는다.

② **질문의 키워드를 파악한 후, 지문에서 언급된 부분을 찾는다.**

지문의 첫 번째 줄 The BB Center Art Association is hosting an exhibition. → 예술 협회가 주최하는 전시회이므로 다른 종류를 언급한 (A), (C), (D)는 소거한다.

③ **지문의 내용을 다른 어휘로 바꾸어 표현(paraphrasing)한 선택지에 유의하여 정답을 고른다.**

지문의 첫 번째 줄 Art Association(예술 협회)란 단어가 보이고, 다음 줄에는 예술가들(Artists)에 의한 '회화와 소묘(paintings and drawings)'라고 나와 있다. 따라서 정답은 (B) An art show이다.
Paraphrasing! exhbition(전시회) → art show(미술 전시회)

VOCA ··

association *n.* 협회 | **host** *v.* 개최하다 | **exhibition** *n.* 전시회 | **emerging** *adj.* 떠오르는, 부상하는 | **per** *prep.* ∼당 | **person** *n.* 사람

해설서 p.66

Questions 1-2 refer to the following advertisement.

Superior Destination SM
Very good prices for each destination

Destination	Price
Seoul	$199
Daejeon	$299
Daegu	$299
Busan	$310
Jeju Island	$399

Make a reservation for your discounted trip. Our Web site is www.superiorsm.com. Also, browse our list of hotels so that you can find the best place to stay in the location you choose.

Terms & Conditions: Airfares are per person for economy flights. Transport to the airport via shuttle bus is included in deals, and you can have a buffet breakfast free of charge as long as you make a reservation for a hotel through our Web site.

---

1. What most likely is Superior Destination SM?

(A) An airline company
(B) A shuttle bus service
(C) A travel agency
(D) A hotel chain

2. What is included in deals?

(A) Travel guidebooks
(B) Hotel accommodations
(C) A tour guide
(D) A ride to the airport

VOCA ··

superior *adj.* 우수한 I **destination** *n.* 목적지, 도착지 I **browse** *v.* (정보를 찾아) 인터넷을 돌아다니다 I **airfare** *n.* 항공 요금 I **per** *prep.* ~당 I **transport** *n.* 운송, 수송, 이동 I **via** *prep.* ~을 통하여, ~을 경유하여 I **deal** *n.* 거래 I **free of charge** 무료로

Questions 3-5 refer to the following e-mail.

To	nwayans@cpomail.net
From	tbernell@swiftair.com
Date	June 29
Subject	Swift Frequent Flyers Club

Dear Ms. Wayans,

Thank you for joining the Swift Frequent Flyers Club. As a token of our appreciation, we have mailed you a special gift, compliments of Swift Air. You will be receiving a Gearup Travel Bag, a stylish and durable suitcase. The suitcase meets the carry-on luggage regulations set by all airlines. If you do not receive your Gearup Travel Bag within the next three weeks, please call Customer Service at 1-800-555-9844.

Also, make sure to log in to your Swift Frequent Flyer account and check out our weekly member specials. We are continually adding new packages for flights, hotels, and rental cars that our members can purchase at reduced rates. We hope you will enjoy all the benefits of your membership.

Sincerely,

Terrence Bernell
Swift Frequent Flyers Club

3. Why will Ms. Wayans receive a suitcase?

(A) She won a special contest.
(B) She lost one at an airport.
(C) She ordered one from a Web site.
(D) She joined an airline's club.

4. What is stated about the suitcase?

(A) It is available in different sizes.
(B) It may be exchanged for another color.
(C) It can be taken on board an airplane.
(D) It will be delivered to Ms. Wayans' office.

5. What is Ms. Wayans encouraged to do online?

(A) View discount offers
(B) Download an electronic ticket
(C) Confirm travel arrangements
(D) Create a customer account

VOCA ···

join v. 가입하다 I as a token of appreciation 감사의 표시로 I compliment n. 칭찬, 찬사 I durable adj. 내구성이 있는, 오래 가는 I suitcase n. 여행 가방 I meet v. 충족하다 I carry-on luggage (기내) 휴대용 가방 I make sure to 반드시 ~하다, ~을 확실히 하다 I log in to ~에 로그인하다 I account n. 계정 I continually adv. 계속해서, 끊임없이 I at a reduced rate 할인가로, 할인하여 I benefit n. 혜택, 이득 v. 득을 보다, 유용하다

Questions 6-8 refer to the following form.

Today's Date : 12/7
Maintenance Supervisor : Jasmine Kim
Maintenance Team Leader : Jenny Brown
Requested by : Greg Lee
Room Location : Owen Hall, Room 107

Requested for : 12/17
10:30 A.M. - 2:00 P.M. : lunch/guest speakers
9:30 A.M. : set up room; 2:30 P.M. : clean up room

If you need room setup, please specifically describe what is needed :
Conference setup is needed for 100 guests for luncheon and brief speeches. Please offer 10 rectangular tables with 10 seats each, all set to face the south wall in which the projection screen is located.

Please mention any additional equipment you need :
Podium, projector, and screen

6. Who most likely is organizing the event?

(A) Greg Lee
(B) Owen Hall
(C) Jasmine Kim
(D) Jenny Brown

7. By what time will the speeches end?

(A) 9:30 A.M.
(B) 10:30 A.M.
(C) 2:00 P.M.
(D) 2:30 P.M.

8. What was requested from the form?

(A) A special lunch menu
(B) A specific furniture arrangement
(C) Full names of guest speakers
(D) Replacement of damaged tables

VOCA ···

maintenance n. (정기적으로 점검, 보수하는) 유지 | supervisor n. 관리자 | setup n. 구조, 조직, 구성, 배열 | specifically adv. 구체적
으로 | describe v. 묘사하다 | luncheon n. 오찬 | speech n. 연설 | rectangular adj. 직사각형의 | face v. 마주하다, 향하다 | mention v.
(말, 글로) 간단히 말하다 | additional adj. 추가적인 | equipment n. 장비 | podium n. (연설자가 올라 설 수 있는) 단, 연단

Questions 9-11 refer to the following notice.

Staples Publishing Company
A great offer for all employees!

As an employee of Staples Publishing Company, you are entitled to huge discounts on all magazines published by our company. Please browse the included list of magazines. You can choose any number of subscriptions for the upcoming year. Just complete the address and billing fields in the attached form and check the box next to any magazine you would like to receive. After the form is complete, please deliver it to Jen Mackey in the subscriptions department.

We hope everyone can take advantage of this great opportunity.

	Regular Price for Yearly Subscription	Discounted Price for Yearly Subscription
Car News Monthly	$40/year	$15/year
Economics Worldwide	$80/year	$30/year
Busy Mom	$60/year	$22/year
Travel International Advice	$50/year	$20/year
Sports Worldly	$50/year	$20/year
Fast Bike	$40/year	$15/year

---

9. What is the purpose of the notice?

(A) To promote the acquisition of a new publisher
(B) To extend the date on a great offer
(C) To announce discounts on subscriptions to the public
(D) To inform employees of a special promotion

10. How can employees receive a discounted subscription?

(A) By visiting the company Web site
(B) By submitting a form to a fellow employee
(C) By calling the subscriptions department
(D) By ordering several magazines at one time

11. How much can an employee of Staples Publishing Company save on a yearly subscription to *Sports Worldly*?

(A) $15
(B) $20
(C) $30
(D) $50

사실확인 문제

선택지와 지문을 세부적으로 대조해야 한다! 주어진 4개의 선택지 중에서 지문의 내용과 일치하지 않거나 일치하는 것을 고르는 문제이다. 선택지와 질문의 키워드가 언급된 부분을 대조하면서 오답을 소거해야 한다. 매회 7~10문제가 출제된다.

🔍 질문 유형 확인하기

▶ 일치하는 정보 (TRUE)

What is **indicated** about the policy? 정책에 관하여 언급된 것은 무엇인가?

What is **stated** about the products? 제품들에 관하여 언급된 것은 무엇인가?

What is **mentioned** about the seminar? 세미나에 관하여 언급된 것은 무엇인가?

What is **true** about the system? 시스템에 관하여 사실인 것은 무엇인가?

▶ 일치하지 않는 정보 (NOT TRUE)

What is **NOT indicated** about the policy? 정책에 관하여 언급되지 않은 것은 무엇인가?

What is **NOT stated** about the products? 제품에 관하여 언급되지 않은 것은 무엇인가?

What is **NOT mentioned** about the seminar? 세미나에 관하여 언급되지 않은 것은 무엇인가?

What is **NOT true** about the system? 시스템에 관하여 사실이 아닌 것은 무엇인가?

문제 풀이 전략

① 질문과 선택지의 키워드를 파악한다.

질문에 나오는 이름, 숫자(날짜 또는 시간), 고유명사는 반드시 기억한다.

② 질문의 키워드가 언급된 부분을 지문에서 찾아 선택지와 대조하면서 오답을 소거한다.

선택지의 내용이 지문에 언급되지 않거나 잘못 언급되었는지, 지문의 내용과 일치하는지를 하나씩 대조하면서 오답을 소거한다.

③ 지문의 내용과 일치하거나 일치하지 않는 정답을 고른다.

정답은 지문에서 찾은 정답의 단서를 그대로 언급하기보다 다른 어휘로 표현(paraphrasing)된 경우가 많으므로 유의한다.

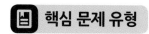

Questions 1-2 refer to the following advertisement.

Career Hope

• 회사명

Do you want an inexpensive way to attract new talented people for your company? Post your openings in *Career Hope*, an employment-related newspaper. It includes many things job seekers need in addition to job postings. It contains information about career fairs, professional advice about writing a résumé, and tips on how to do well in interviews.

• 회사가 하는 일

Career Hope is distributed to many locations around East Saint Louis, and it is completely free of charge to job seekers. Using *Career Hope* is a great idea for hiring companies. Each posting costs $30 and lasts for one month.

• 회사 위치와 요금 안내

Visit www.careerhopeprint.com/ad to make job postings. You can also view examples of effective job postings. Please upload the text you want to include in the posting, and then, pay the final fee.

• 웹사이트에서 할 수 있는 것

Please note that your text will not be edited by *Career Hope*. If you want to hire an editor to write your advertisement, please contact us at 785-884-2370. There will be an additional fee for this service.

• 유의 사항

---

1. What is indicated about *Career Hope*?

(A) It has several offices in East Saint Louis.
(B) It hosts a job fair every year.
(C) It charges $30 for each job posting.
(D) It is published once a month.

2. What is NOT mentioned as something that can be done on the *Career Hope* Web site?

(A) Making a payment
(B) Seeing sample postings
(C) Applying for a position
(D) Submitting a document

[1–2] 다음 광고에 관한 문제입니다.

Career Hope

Career Hope

• 회사명

Do you want an inexpensive way to attract new talented people for your company? Post your openings in *Career Hope*, an employment-related newspaper. It includes many things job seekers need in addition to job postings. It contains information about career fairs, professional advice about writing a résumé, and tips on how to do well in interviews.

• 회사가 하는 일

당신의 회사를 위한 새로운 재능 있는 사람을 끌어들일 저렴한 방법을 원하십니까? 고용 관련 신문 〈Career Hope〉에 구인 공고를 올리세요. 신문은 일자리 외에도 구직자가 필요로 하는 많은 것들을 포함하고 있습니다. 취업 박람회에 관한 정보와 이력서 쓰는 것에 대한 전문가들의 조언, 그리고 어떻게 하면 면접을 잘 볼 수 있는지에 대한 팁도 포함하고 있습니다.

Career Hope is distributed to many locations around East Saint Louis, and it is completely free of charge to job seekers. Using *Career Hope* is a great idea for hiring companies. ❶ Each posting costs $30 and lasts for one month.

• 회사 위치와 요금 안내

〈Career Hope〉는 East Saint Louis 주변의 많은 지역에 배포되고, 구직자들에게는 전액 무료입니다. 〈Career Hope〉를 이용하는 것은 고용 회사를 위해 아주 좋은 생각입니다. **각 공고는 30달러이며, 한달 동안 유지됩니다.**

❷ Visit www.careerhopeprint.com/ad to make job postings. You can also view examples of effective job postings. Please upload the text you want to include in the posting, and then, pay the final fee.

• 웹사이트에서 할 수 있는 것

구인 광고를 내기 위해 **careerhopeprint.com/ad**를 방문하세요. 당신은 또한 효과적인 구인 광고 예시들을 볼 수도 있습니다. 당신이 구인 광고에 포함시키고 싶은 문구를 업로드하고 나서 최종 요금을 지불하세요.

• 유의 사항

Please note that your text will not be edited by *Career Hope*. If you want to hire an editor to write your advertisement, please contact us at 785-884-2370. There will be an additional fee for this service.

당신의 글은 〈Career Hope〉에 의해서 편집되지 않을 것이라는 것을 알아두세요. 만약 당신의 광고글을 작성할 편집자를 고용하고 싶으면, 우리에게 785-884-2370으로 연락주세요. 이 서비스에 대한 추가 요금이 있을 것입니다.

VOCA ·······

inexpensive *adj.* 비싸지 않은 | employment-related *adj.* 고용과 관련된 | job seeker 구직자 | contain *v.* 포함하다 | career fair 취업 박람회 | résumé *n.* 이력서 | distribute *v.* 배포하다, 보급하다 | last *v.* 지속하다 | effective *adj.* 효과적인 | text *n.* 본문, 글, 문서 | edit *v.* 편집하다 | advertisement *n.* 광고 | additional *adj.* 추가적인

>> 일치하는 정보를 묻는 문제(TRUE)

1. What is indicated about *Career Hope*?

(A) It has several offices in East Saint Louis.
(B) It hosts a job fair every year.
(C) It charges $30 for each job posting.
(D) It is published once a month.

〈Career Hope〉에 관하여 언급된 것은 무엇인가?

(A) East Saint Louis에 몇 개의 사무실을 두고 있다.
(B) 매년 취업 박람회를 개최할 것이다.
(C) 각 구인 광고당 30달러를 부과한다.
(D) 한 달에 한 번 발행된다.

문제 풀이 전략 적용

1 질문과 선택지의 키워드를 파악한다.

〈Career Hope〉에 대해서 무엇이 언급(indicated)되는지를 묻는 문제이므로 〈Career Hope〉를 키워드로 삼아 지문에 언급된 부분을 찾는다.

2 질문의 키워드가 언급된 부분을 지문에서 찾아 선택지와 대조하면서 오답을 소거한다.

첫 번째 단락에 〈Career Hope〉가 취업 박람회에 관한 정보를 포함하고 있다는 이야기는 있었고, 두 번째 단락에 East Saint Louis 주변 지역에 〈Career Hope〉가 배포된다는 말은 있었다. 그러나 취업 박람회를 개최하거나 East Saint Louis에 몇 개의 사무실이 있다던가, 한 달에 한 번 발행된다는 말은 지문에서 언급된 적이 없었다.

3 지문의 내용과 일치하거나 일치하지 않는 정답을 고른다.

두 번째 단락에서 광고를 게시하는 건당 비용이 30달러라고 한 지문 내용을 언급했으므로 정답은 (C) It charges $30 for each job posting.이다.
Paraphrasing! Each posting costs $30 → It charges $30 for each ~ posting

>> 일치하지 않는 정보를 묻는 문제(NOT TRUE)

2. What is NOT mentioned as something that can be done on the *Career Hope* Web site?

(A) Making a payment
(B) Seeing sample postings
(C) Applying for a position
(D) Submitting a document

〈Career Hope〉 웹사이트에서 행해질 수 있는 것으로 언급되지 않은 것은 무엇인가?

(A) 요금을 지불하는 것
(B) 샘플 공고를 보는 것
(C) 일자리에 지원하는 것
(D) 서류를 제출하는 것

문제 풀이 전략 적용

1 질문과 선택지의 키워드를 파악한다.

질문에서 웹사이트를 키워드로 삼아 지문에서 〈Career Hope〉 웹사이트가 언급된 부분을 찾는다.

2 질문의 키워드가 언급된 부분을 지문에서 찾아 선택지와 대조하면서 오답을 소거한다.

지문 세 번째 단락에서 효과적인 구인 광고의 예시들이 있을 것이니, 당신이 구인 광고에 포함시키고 싶은 글을 게시한 후 최종 요금을 지불하라는 언급이 있으므로 (A), (B), 그리고 (D)는 언급되었으므로 하나씩 소거한다.

3 지문의 내용과 일치하거나 일치하지 않는 정답을 고른다.

Paraphrasing!
• view examples of ~ postings → Seeing sample postings
• upload ~ text → Submitting a document
• pay ~ fee → Making a payment
따라서, 보기에서 언급되지 않은 것은 일자리 지원에 관한 내용이므로 정답은 (C) Applying for a position이다.

Questions 1-2 refer to the following information.

BH

Design-A Awards are given annually to graphic design companies in order to recognize outstanding achievements. The Kensington Advertising League sponsors the awards, and only companies based in the Kensington area can receive the awards. There are five types of awards, and they are presented every October at the Kensington Regional Design Conference. All graphic design companies are encouraged to submit work and to visit the BH Web site for details.

---

1. What is mentioned about the Design-A Awards?

(A) They are awarded once every five years.

(B) They are only offered to firms in the local area.

(C) They are awarded to companies in various fields.

(D) They are held in different venues every year.

2. What can companies do on the Web site?

(A) Pay a fee

(B) Participate in a survey

(C) Reserve a booth

(D) Upload their work

VOCA ···

annually *adv.* 매년 I **recognize** *v.* 인지하다, 인정하다, 알아보다 I **outstanding** *adj.* 우수한, 뛰어난 I **achievement** *n.* 성취, 업적 I **sponsor** *v.* 후원하다 *n.* 후원업체 I **award** *n.* 상 *v.* 수여하다 I **present** *v.* 주다, 수여하다 I **work** *n.* 작품 I **venue** *n.* 장소 I **reserve** *v.* 예약하다

Questions 3-4 refer to the following brochure.

Real Tours
Italy's Finest Cities

For more than 10 years, Real Tours has offered customers the best tours. It has been featured in *World Interset Magazine* in addition to many other top travel publications. We have travel programs for many parts of Italy, especially Venice, Rome, Milan, and Florence.

A one-week visit to your chosen city is included in standard travel packages.

Every package includes:
• At least one tour guide
• Breakfast & lunch
• Ground transportation within the city
• Accommodations at a hotel for five nights
• Admission to three tourist attractions per day

For additional details, contact Marsha Kim at 02-847-9901.

---

3. What is indicated about Real Tours?

(A) It is currently under construction.
(B) It is offering discounts to first-time clients.
(C) It has been in business for more than a decade.
(D) It has recently opened a new branch.

4. What is NOT included in a standard travel package?

(A) Daytime meals
(B) Hotel stays
(C) Flight tickets
(D) Visits to famous places

VOCA ···

more than ~이상 I **feature** *v.* (신문 등에서) 특집 기사로 다루다 I **publication** *n.* 간행물 I **include** *v.* 포함하다 I **standard** *n.* 표준 *adj.*
표준의 I **ground** *n.* 땅, 지상 I **transportation** *n.* 운송, 수송 I **accommodations** *n.* 숙박(시설) I **admission** *n.* 입장 I **attraction** *n.* 끌림,
명소 I **construction** *n.* 공사 I **decade** *n.* 10년간 I **branch** *n.* 지점 I **daytime** *adj.* 낮의, 주간의

March 20 – *Lux Interior*, a popular home décor magazine, is marking its 20th year in publication. The magazine is celebrating the occasion by collaborating with renowned tableware designer Janson Co. to create a line of six commemorative plates. Each plate will depict a different type of kitchenware chosen by our readers from a selection of images that were included with a special article in last month's issue.

According to *Lux Interior*'s chief editor, Dianne Stein, Janson Co. was the obvious choice. "We wanted a company that we were familiar with and trusted, preferably one who has had its products showcased in our magazine," Ms. Stein said. "So we were all in favor of teaming up with Janson Co. for the project."

The collection can be purchased from Janson Co.'s online store beginning on the first of May. "Many of our readers have already asked to preorder the collectible plates," Ms. Stein noted, "but we have not yet decided on the prices."

5. What were readers of *Lux Interior* asked to do?

(A) Choose their favorite images
(B) Submit photos of their kitchen
(C) Preorder certain items online
(D) Try out some products

6. What does the article indicate about Janson Co.'s products?

(A) They are made of natural materials.
(B) They are sold worldwide.
(C) They have recently received an award.
(D) They have been featured in *Lux Interior*.

7. What has NOT been announced about the collection?

(A) Where it will be sold
(B) How much it will cost
(C) When it will be available
(D) How many designs will be produced

VOCA ··

mark *v.* 표시하다, 기념하다 | publication *n.* 출판, 발행, 출판물 | celebrate *v.* 축하하다, 기념하다 | occasion *n.* 행사, 때 | collaborate *v.* 협력하다, 공동으로 작업하다 | renowned *adj.* 유명한, 명성 있는 | tableware *n.* 식탁용 식기류 | commemorative plate 기념패 | depict *v.* 묘사하다 | obvious *adj.* 분명한, 명백한 | be familiar with ~와 친숙하다 | trusted *adj.* 신뢰할만한 | preferably *adv.* 가급적이면, 오히려 | showcase *v.* 전시하다, 소개하다 | in favor of ~에 찬성하여 | team up ~와 한 팀이 되다, 협력하다 | preorder *v.* 선주문하다 | note *v.* 언급하다, ~에 주목하다

Questions 8-10 refer to the following announcement.

An Invitation to the Speakmaster Course
From Evelyn Singh, Director, Woodbridge Location

Beginning February 21, there will be a series of weekly speaking classes here at our Woodbridge location. The course is designed for anyone who has to do public speaking, whether it be for work or school. It will enable you to not only improve your ability to speak in front of large groups, but it will also help you build confidence for your everyday life.

And what's more, every class session will be recorded. Upon completion of all classes, you will receive a DVD copy of all of your presentations to the group. You will also get a signed certificate verifying that you passed the course as well as an enlarged, framed photo of your class.

The registration fee for the 10 one-hour sessions is only $100. If you live far away from our Woodbridge location, we do offer this course at some of our other libraries at other times.

I take care of all registrations. If you would like to register, I can be reached by phone at 901-555-5571 or e-mail at e.singh@millerlibraries.gov.

Thank you,
Evelyn Singh

---

8. Where will the course be held?

(A) At a public school
(B) At a library
(C) At a community center
(D) At a store

9. What is NOT stated as being available to course participants?

(A) A recording of presentation
(B) An autograph from a famous speaker
(C) A group photo
(D) An official document

10. How can interested individuals enroll in the course?

(A) By emailing the instructor directly through a Web site
(B) By contacting the director of the Woodbridge location
(C) By sending in a completed registration form
(D) By attending an information session

VOCA ···

a series of 일련의 | **course** *n.* 강의, 과정 | **designed** *adj.* 설계된, 계획적인 | **public speaking** 공개연설 | **enable** *v.* ~를 할 수 있게 하다 | **improve** *v.* 개선되다, 나아지다 | **in front of** ~의 앞에서 | **build confidence** 자신감을 기르다 | **what's more** 게다가 | **record** *v.* 녹음하다, 녹화하다 | **on[upon] ~ing** ~하자마자 곧 | **enlarged** *adj.* 커진, 확장된 | **frame** *n.* 액자, 틀 | **registration fee** 등록비 | **at other times** 다른 때에는 | **reach** *v.* 전화로 연락하다; ~에 도달하다 | **directly** *adv.* 직접, 곧장

암시·추론 문제

지문의 전체 흐름을 이해해야 한다! 지문의 내용을 바탕으로 지문에 직접 언급되지 않은 사항을 추론하는 고난도 문제이다. 지문을 읽는 동안 지문의 전체 흐름을 이해하면서 오답을 소거해야 한다. 매회 0~6문제 가 출제된다.

🔍 질문 유형 확인하기

▶ **추론**

What is implied ~?

What is implied about the products? 그 제품들에 대해서 암시된 것은 무엇인가?

What is suggested ~?

What is suggested about Ms. Davis? Ms. Davis에 대해서 암시된 것은 무엇인가?

What can be inferred ~?

What can be inferred about the policy? 그 정책에 대해서 추론 가능한 것은 무엇인가?

What can be ~?

What can be learned from this announcement? 이 공지에서 무엇을 알 수 있는가?

[Who / What / When / Where] most likely ~?

Who most likely is Ms. Chan? Ms. Chan은 누구일 것 같은가?

Where would this memo most likely be found? 이 공지는 어디에서 볼 수 있을 것 같은가?

💁 문제 풀이 전략

1 질문을 읽고 추론 문제인지 확인한다.

질문에 imply, suggest, infer, most likely 등이 나오면 추론 문제이다.

2 질문의 implied, suggested, inferred 뒤에 나오는 키워드가 언급된 부분을 지문에서 찾아 선택지 와 하나씩 대조하면서 오답을 소거한다.

주의! 본인이 아는 지식이나 정보를 가지고 연상 및 추론을 하는 것이 아니라 반드시 지문의 단서에서 추론한 결론과 소거법을 통해 정답을 도출한다.

3 지문의 내용과 일치하는 정답을 고른다.

정답은 지문에서 찾은 정답의 단서를 그대로 언급하기보다 다른 어휘로 표현(paraphrasing)된 경우가 많으므로, 이 점을 반드시 유 의한다.

Question 1 refers to the following e-mail.

From:	Aileen Park
To:	Sue Kim
Date:	May 1
Subject:	New System

Dear Ms. Kim,

I would like to inform you that the company has decided to adopt the Tracker Time Reporting System (TTRS). The system is needed to record the staff hours. It is essential that all employees use the system. On April 20, I sent employees an e-mail explaining the system and described how to make an ID.

The system is going to be implemented on May 8, and all employees must have their IDs by May 5. Please click the TTRS icon on the company's homepage to make your ID. After creating your ID, it is possible to review your paycheck statements whenever you want to check them.

If you are faced with problems when you use the system, contact Mr. Kang, the help desk manager.

Thank you.

Aileen Park
Associate Director, Payroll Department

• 발신인
  수신인
  날짜
  제목

• 새로운 시스템
  도입 안내

• 전 직원들이 해야 할 일

• 문제가 있을 경우
  연락 방법

• 발신인 정보
  직책 및 부서

1. What is suggested about the new employee IDs?

(A) They require a fee to make.
(B) They are needed to access the Internet.
(C) They can be used to check salary statements.
(D) They are needed to enter a building.

1번은 다음 이메일에 관한 문제입니다.

From: Aileen Park
To: Sue Kim
Date: May 1
Subject: New System

발신: Aileen Park
수신: Sue Kim
날짜: 5월 1일
제목: 새로운 시스템

Dear Ms. Kim,

Ms. Kim에게,

I would like to inform you that the company has decided to adopt the Tracker Time Reporting System (TTRS). The system is needed to record the staff hours. It is essential that all employees use the system. On April 20, I sent employees an e-mail explaining the system and described how to make an ID.

저는 당신에게 우리 회사가 Tracker Time Reporting System (TTRS)을 채택하기로 결정했다는 것을 알려드립니다. 그 시스템은 직원 근무 시간을 기록하기 위해서 필요합니다. 모든 직원들이 그 시스템을 이용해야 합니다. 4월 20일에 저는 직원들에게 그 시스템을 설명하는 이메일을 보냈고, 그들의 ID를 만드는 방법을 설명하였습니다.

The system is going to be implemented on May 8, and all employees must have their IDs by May 5. Please click the TTRS icon on the company's homepage to make your ID. ❶ After creating your ID, it is possible to review your paycheck statements whenever you want to check them.

그 시스템은 5월 8일에 시행될 것이고 모든 직원들은 5월 5일까지 그들의 ID를 가지고 있어야 합니다. 당신의 ID를 만들기 위해서 회사 홈페이지에 있는 TTRS 아이콘을 클릭하세요. **당신의 ID를 만든 후, 당신의 급여 명세서를 확인하고 싶을 때마다 다시 보는 것이 가능합니다.**

If you are faced with problems when you use the system, contact Mr. Kang, the help desk manager.

만약 당신이 그 시스템을 사용하는 데에 문제가 있다면, 업무 지원 센터 매니저 Mr. Kang에게 연락해주세요.

Thank you.

감사합니다.

Aileen Park
Associate Director, Payroll Department

Aileen Park
경리부 차장

발신인
수신인
날짜
제목

새로운 시스템 도입 안내

전 직원들이 해야 할 일

문제가 있을 경우 연락 방법

발신인 정보 직책 및 부서

1. What is suggested about the new employee IDs?

(A) They require a fee to make.
(B) They are needed to access the Internet.
(C) They can be used to check salary statements.
(D) They are needed to enter a building.

신입 직원들 ID에 관해 암시된 것은 무엇인가?

(A) 요금을 내야 한다.
(B) 인터넷 접속을 위해 필요하다.
(C) 급여 명세서를 확인하는 데 사용될 수 있다.
(D) 건물에 입장하기 위해 필요하다.

문제 풀이 전략 적용

❶ 질문을 읽고 추론 문제인지 확인한다.
지문에 suggested(암시된)가 나왔으므로 추론 문제이다. new employee IDs(신입 직원 ID)에 관하여 암시된 (suggested) 것을 묻고 있으므로 employees' new ID를 키워드로 잡아 지문에서 관련 내용을 포착하고 ID 키워드 부분을 표시해둔다.

❷ 질문의 implied, suggested, inferred 뒤에 나오는 키워드가 언급된 부분을 지문에서 찾아 선택지와 하나씩 대조하면서 오답을 소거한다.
(A) 요금을 내야 한다는 말은 지문에서 언급된 적이 없으므로 소거한다.
(B) 지문에서 인터넷 접속에 대한 언급 자체가 없으므로 소거한다.
(C) 두 번째 단락에서 'ID를 만들면, 급여에 관한 정보를 확인할 수 있다'이라고 언급된 부분 확인한다.
(D) 건물 출입을 위해 필요하다는 말은 지문에 언급된 적이 없으므로 소거한다.

❸ 지문의 내용과 일치하는 정답을 고른다.
직원 신규 ID를 만들면 급여(paycheck)에 관한 정보를 확인 가능하다는 지문의 단서 문장을 바탕으로 직원 신규 ID가 직원들의 급여 정보를 확인하는 데 필요한 것임을 유추 가능하다. 따라서 정답은 (C) They can be used to check salary statements.이다.

VOCA ···

adopt *v.* 채택하다 ┃ **record** *v.* 기록하다 ┃ **essential** *adj.* 필수적인, 극히 중요한 ┃ **explain** *v.* 설명하다 ┃ **implement** *v.* 시행하다 ┃ **statement** *n.* 내역서, 명세서, 진술서 ┃ **face** *v.* 직면하다

Questions 1-3 refer to the following article.

Grand River (March 4) – There will be a big change in Grand River's biggest stationery store on March 29. Owner Aileen Keen's daughter, Sally, will take over the store's operations.

"The store has been managed by me for 20 years," Aileen said. "And I'm pleased to be turning it over to Sally. She had a part-time job at the store when she was a high school student. She helped me a lot while I was away on other business."

After she retires, Aileen is going to focus on her favorite activity, golf, which she learned from her grandfather when she was a child. She knows that the store will be in good hands.

---

1. What is the purpose of the article?

(A) To announce a retirement
(B) To sell a line of office supplies
(C) To report on a business closing
(D) To post a job opening

2. What is suggested about Sally?

(A) She met Aileen 20 years ago.
(B) She learned golf as a child.
(C) She has experience in running a store.
(D) She had worked at a high school.

3. What does Aileen plan to do?

(A) Register for a class
(B) Move to another city
(C) Go on a trip
(D) Engage in a recreational activity

VOCA ···

stationery *n.* 문구류, 문방구 I **instead of** *prep.* ~대신에 I **manage** *v.* 운영하다 I **turn over** ~을 넘기다, 맡기다 I **on business** 볼일이 있어, 업무로 I **retire** *v.* 은퇴하다 I **focus on** ~에 집중하다 I **be in good hands** 잘 관리되다 I **engage in** ~에 관여하다, ~에 참여하다 I **recreational activity** 여가 활동

Questions 4-7 refer to the following notice.

Springtime Fun

Check out the following schedule of spring events in Rennerdale. For more information about these events, visit www.rennerdale.org/events

Rennerdale Book Fair (2-9 April)
Readings and discussions featuring over 50 internationally acclaimed authors as well as book signings. At select participating bookstores and libraries throughout the city.

Rennerdale Theater Gala (8-25 April)
fifteen plays by emerging and renowned playwrights from all across the country. At the Cyan Arts Center.

Beats Festival (1-17 May)
The city's global music festival presents diverse music genres from around the world. At the Swan Lake Theater.

Visual Arts Exhibition (8-26 May)
Local amateur photographers and painters compete for the esteemed Ashura Prize. The winner to be announced on closing night. At the Ashura Art Museum.

Merriam Center - Grand Opening (14 May)
The concert venue's highly-anticipated opening night, featuring a special performance by world-famous singer Maybel Cheyenne. Book your tickets before they sell out.

---

4. What is suggested about all of the events?

(A) They will be held in the same city.
(B) They are free to the public.
(C) They will take place in the month of April.
(D) They feature local musicians and artists.

5. What is NOT listed among the events?

(A) Musical entertainment
(B) An art competition
(C) Theater performances
(D) A writing contest

6. What event will take place at multiple venues?

(A) The Rennerdale Book Fair
(B) The Rennerdale Theater Gala
(C) The Beats Festival
(D) The Visual Arts Exhibition

7. What is indicated about Ms. Cheyenne?

(A) She is from the Rennerdale area.
(B) She works as an event planner.
(C) She will perform in a new venue.
(D) She designed the Merriam Center.

VOCA ···

check out 확인하다 ┃ acclaimed *adj.* 찬사를 받는 ┃ select *adj.* 엄선된 ┃ throughout *prep.* 도처에, ~동안, ~내내 ┃ emerging *adj.* 최근에 생겨난, 신흥의, 떠오르는 ┃ renowned *adj.* 저명한 ┃ playwright *n.* 극작가, 각본가 ┃ diverse *adj.* 다양한 ┃ genre *n.* 장르 ┃ amateur *n.* 아마추어 (선수) ┃ compete *v.* 경쟁하다 ┃ esteemed *adj.* 존중/존경받는 ┃ closing night 폐막일 ┃ grand opening 개막식 ┃ venue *n.* 장소 ┃ highly-anticipated *adj.* 매우 기대되는 ┃ feature *v.* ~의 특징을 이루다, 출연하다 *n.* 특징, 기능 ┃ book *v.* 예약하다 ┃ sell out 다 팔리다, 매진되다

Questions 8-11 refer to the following e-mail.

To: e.dole@bermo.net
From: c.ferdinand@parzine.com.nz
Date: 3 February
Subject: Employment at Parzine
Attachment: Parzine_Elliot_C

Dear Mr. Dole,

Thank you for responding to our independent contractor job posting. We have reviewed your résumé and feel that you are well-suited for the job. Based on your writing portfolio and experience traveling the world, you would make a great addition to the team of freelance correspondents that contribute to our online travel magazine.

As this is a remote position, the work can be done from anywhere, and you will be paid per completed assignment. The job is ideal for people who have a flexible schedule and can take on different writing projects as they become available. Although assignments may not come steadily, you are guaranteed compensation for the time you spend working on them.

Attached is an employment contract for you to sign and return to us as soon as you can. Make sure to put "Parzine Writer – Elliot C" in your e-mail's subject line. If you have any questions in the meantime, do not hesitate to contact me. We have an assignment ready for you right now, but we cannot give it to you until we receive this document from you. We hope to be working with you very soon!

Sincerely,

Corinna Ferdinand, Chief Editor

8. Who most likely is Mr. Dole?

(A) An editor-in-chief
(B) A professional photographer
(C) An independent journalist
(D) A graphic designer

9. What is stated about Mr. Dole?

(A) He has previously worked with Parzine.
(B) He supervised a team of workers.
(C) He met Ms. Ferdinand at a convention.
(D) He has traveled internationally.

10. What is implied about the listed position?

(A) It involves attending weekly meetings.
(B) It involves an unpredictable work schedule.
(C) It requires high-level computer skills.
(D) It requires working in an office.

11. What does Ms. Ferdinand ask Mr. Dole to send her?

(A) A signed agreement
(B) A reimbursement form
(C) A project plan
(D) A work portfolio

VOCA ···

employment *n.* 고용, 취업 | respond *v.* 응답하다 | independent *adj.* 독립적인 | contractor *n.* 계약자, 도급업체 | job posting 구인광고 | review *v.* 검토하다, 복습하다 | well-suited *adj.* 적절한, 안성맞춤의 | based on 기반하여, 근거하여 | portfolio *n.* 포트폴리오 | freelance *adj.* 자유 계약의, 프리랜서로 일하는 | correspondent *n.* 편지글 쓰는 사람, 통신 기자, 투고자: 대응하는 것 | contribute *v.* 기여하다, 공헌하다 | per *prep.* ~당,~마다, 매, 일 | flexible *adj.* 유연한, 신축성 있는, 탄력적인 | steadily *adv.* 지속적으로, 점차, 끊임없이 | guarantee *v.* 보장하다, 장담하다 | in the meantime 그 동안에, 한편으로는 | hesitate *v.* 망설이다, 주저하다 | document *n.* 서류

FastPhone, Inc.
How to Set Up Online Bill Pay

Once you have activated your telephone service, please follow these simple steps to set up online bill pay:

1. Visit our Web site at www.fastphone.com, and create a user account.
2. Once you have created a user account, add your phone to the account by typing in the phone's serial number along with the PIN code located at the bottom of your user card.
3. Add your bank account information to the account. You may need to inform your bank that we will be charging your account depending on their rules.
4. To set up automatic bill pay, which will let you make recurring payments every month, select 'automatic bill pay' in the box located below the bank account information field.

It's as easy as that! You may then pay your monthly phone bill online. Or if you choose the automatic bill pay option, your bill payment will be automatically drafted from your bank account.

If you have any questions or concerns regarding our online bill pay service, please contact our technical support center at 800-555-0131 between 7:00 A.M. and 8:00 P.M. on weekdays.

12. What is indicated about Fastphone bill payments?

(A) They can be paid in person.
(B) They will soon increase.
(C) They are due each month.
(D) They can only be made online.

13. What is suggested about FastPhone, Inc.?

(A) It does not operate on the weekends.
(B) It has locations in different countries.
(C) It is going to release a new phone model.
(D) It has increased its activation fee.

VOCA ···

bill *n.* 청구서 | activate *v.* 활성화시키다, 작동시키다 | user account 사용자 계정 | serial number 일련번호 | along with ~와 함께 | bottom *n.* 맨 아래, 바닥 | bank account 은행 계좌 | charge *v.* 청구하다 | recurring *adj.* 되풀이하여 발생하는 | payment *n.* 지불 | field *n.* 필드 (특정 데이터 저장 지정 영역) | monthly *adj.* 매월의 | option *n.* 선택 | automatically *adv.* 자동적으로 | draft *v.* 뽑다 | concern *n.* 우려, 걱정 | technical support center 기술지원센터 | in person 몸소, 직접 | due *adj.* (돈을) 지불해야 하는 | activation *n.* 활성화

UNIT 05 문장 삽입 문제

지문의 흐름상 주어진 문장이 들어갈 적절한 위치를 고르는 문제로, 보통 2문제 정도 출제된다. 세부적인 정보보다 전체적인 문맥 파악이 중요한 문제 유형이다.

문맥상 흐름을 반드시 파악해야 풀 수 있으므로, 독해 실력과 지문의 흐름 판단력이 필요하다! 주어진 문장의 키워드가 될만한 지시어나 대명사, 접속부사 등을 근거로 지문에서 자연스럽게 문맥이 연결되는 위치를 고르는 게 관건이다. 마지막으로, 문장을 삽입한 후 지문의 문맥이 매끄러운 지 최종 체크할 것!

🔍 질문 유형 확인하기

▶ **문장 삽입**

In which of the positions marked [1], [2], [3], and [4] does the following sentence best belong?

"It is conveniently located across the street from the convention center."

[1], [2], [3], [4]로 표시된 곳 중에서 다음 문장이 들어가기에 가장 적절한 곳은 어디인가?

"그것은 컨벤션 센터 길 건너에 편리하게 위치되어 있습니다."

In which of the positions marked [1], [2], [3] and [4] does the following sentence best belong?

"Due to the handmade nature of this product, it is one of kind."

[1], [2], [3], [4]로 표시된 곳 중에서 다음 문장이 들어가기에 가장 적절한 곳은 어디인가?

"그 제품의 손으로 만들어지는 특성 때문에, 그 제품은 특별합니다."

문제 풀이 전략

1 **주어진 문장을 먼저 읽고, 접속사나 대명사 등의 단서를 파악한다.**

앞뒤 문장을 연결하는 접속사(and, so)나 접속부사(therefore, in addition), 그리고 앞에 나온 내용을 다시 언급하는 대명사 또는 반복적인 어구가 있는지 확인한다. 예를 들어 informal과 casual처럼 의미가 비슷한 단어가 주어진 문장과 지문에 나오면 유의해야 한다.

2 **지문에 표시된 위치의 앞뒤 문장을 읽고, 주어진 문장과 흐름상 연결되는지 확인한다.**

부연 설명, 비교와 대조, 원인과 이유, 조건, 예시 등 주어진 문장과 앞뒤 문장의 관계를 확인한다.

3 **정답 위치에 주어진 문장을 넣었을 때 문맥상 자연스러운지 확인한다.**

문장을 넣어서 지문을 읽었을 때, 문맥상 어색하지 않고 자연스러운지 마지막으로 확인한다.

Question 1 refers to the following e-mail.

To: Eric Hopkins <erichopkins@vincent.com> •→ 수신인

From: Wilma Mullins <wmullins@sche.org> 발신인

Subject: Special Rates 제목

Date: August 27 날짜

Dear Mr. Hopkins,

The Society of Chemical Engineers (SCHE) is going to be holding •→ 영국 런던에서 있을
its annual convention in London, England, this year from October 연례 회의 일정 안내
4-6. —[1]—. In case you have not yet made arrangements for
accommodations, we would like to inform you of a special deal that has •→ 특별 할인 안내
just been announced. Hillside Manor is offering SCHE members special
rates during the convention. —[2]—. For only 120 pounds a night, you
can get a double room, and for 205 pounds a night, you can reserve
a suite. Both offers represent savings of more than 40 percent off the
regular rates. —[3]—.

To take advantage of this special offer, use the special code •→ 할인 받는 방법
SCHECONVENTION when making your reservation at www.
hillsidemanor.com. —[4]—. But please hurry, as this offer is only valid
until September 15.

We look forward to seeing you at this year's conference. •→ 마무리 인사

Sincerely,

Wilma Mullins •→ 발신인 정보
SCHE Convention Organizer 직책

---

1. In which of the positions marked [1], [2], [3], and [4] does the following
sentence best belong?

"It is conveniently located across the street from the convention center."

(A) [1]
(B) [2]
(C) [3]
(D) [4]

1번은 다음 이메일에 관한 문제입니다.

To: Eric Hopkins <erichopkins@vincent.com>

From: Wilma Mullins <wmullins@sche.org>

Subject: Special Rates

Date: August 27

수신: Eric Hopkins 〈erichopkins@vincent.com〉

발신: Wilma Mullins 〈wmullins@sche.org〉

제목: 특별가

날짜: 8월 27일

• 수신인
 발신인
 제목
 날짜

Dear Mr. Hopkins,

Mr. Hopkins에게,

The Society of Chemical Engineers (SCHE) is going to be holding its annual convention in London, England, this year from October 4-6. In case you have not yet made arrangements for accommodations, we would like to inform you of a special deal that has just been announced. Hillside Manor is offering SCHE members special rates during the convention. ❶ It is conveniently located across the street from the convention center. For only 120 pounds a night, you can get a double room, and for 205 pounds a night, you can reserve a suite. Both offers represent savings of more than 40 percent off the regular rates.

• 영국 런던에서 있을
 연례 회의 일정 안내

• 특별 할인 안내

The Society of Chemical Engineers(SCHE)는 올해 10월 4일에서 6일까지 영국 런던에서 연례 회의를 열 것입니다. 당신이 숙박을 아직 마련하지 못한 경우에 대비해서, 우리는 방금 공지된 특별 요금을 당신께 알려드리고 싶습니다. Hillside Manor는 SCHE 회원들에게 회의 기간 동안에 특별 요금을 제공 중입니다. **그 것은 컨벤션 센터 길 건너에 편리하게 위치되어 있습니다.** 하룻밤에 오직 120파운드로 당신은 더블룸에서 지낼 수 있고, 205파운드로 당신은 스위트룸을 예약할 수 있습니다. 두 가지 모두 평상 시 가격보다 40퍼센트 이상을 절약할 수 있습니다.

To take advantage of this special offer, use the special code SCHECONVENTION when making your reservation at www.hillsidemanor.com. But please hurry, as this offer is only valid until September 15.

• 할인 받는 방법

이 특별 제안을 이용하려면, 당신이 www.hillsidemanor.com에서 예약을 할 때, 특별코드 SCHECONVENTION을 사용하세요. 하지만 이러한 혜택은 9월 15일까지만 유효하니 서두르세요.

We look forward to seeing you at this year's conference.

• 마무리 인사

우리는 당신을 올해 회의에서 뵙기를 고대합니다.

Sincerely,

진심으로,

Wilma Mullins

SCHE Convention Organizer

• 발신인 정보
 직책

Wilma Mullins

SCHE 회의 조직자

---

1. In which of the positions marked [1], [2], [3], and [4] does the following sentence best belong?

"It is conveniently located across the street from the convention center."

(A) [1]
(B) [2]
(C) [3]
(D) [4]

[1], [2], [3], 그리고 [4]로 표시되어 있는 자리 중 다음 문장이 들어갈 가장 적절한 곳은 어디인가?

"그것은 컨벤션 센터 길 건너에 편리하게 위치되어 있습니다."

(A) [1]
(B) [2]
(C) [3]
(D) [4]

문제 풀이 전략 적용

① **주어진 문장을 먼저 읽고, 접속사나 대명사 등의 단서를 파악한다.**

"It is conveniently located across the street from the convention center." (그것은 컨벤션 센터 길 건너에 편리하게 위치되어 있습니다.) → it이라는 대명사에서 단서를 찾는다.

② **지문에 표시된 위치의 앞뒤 문장을 읽고, 주어진 문장과 흐름상 연결되는지 확인한다.**

여기서 대명사 'It'은 Hillside Manor를 가리키고 있음을 파악한다.

③ **정답 위치에 주어진 문장을 넣었을 때 문맥상 자연스러운지 확인한다.**

바로 앞 문장에서 'Hillside Manor is offering SCHE members special rates during the convention' (Hillside Manor가 SCHE 회원들에게 회의 기간 동안에 특별가를 제공 중이다)라는 것을 알리고 이어서 'Hillside Manor는 컨벤션 센터 길 건너에 위치해 있다'라고 추가 정보인 위치를 소개하는 것이 문맥상 가장 자연스러우므로 정답은 (B) [2]이다.

VOCA ⋯⋯

hold *v.* 개최하다 | **convention** *n.* 협회, 회의, 대회 | **arrangement** *n.* 마련, 준비, 배열 | **accommodations** *n.* 숙소, 거처 | **announce** *v.* 발표하다 | **rate** *n.* 요금 | **represent** *v.* 대표하다 | **savings** *n.* 절약, 저축한 돈 | **regular rate** 정가 | **take advantage of** ~을 이용하다 | **valid** *adj.* 유효한 | **look forward to -ing** ~하기를 고대하다

Questions 1-2 refer to the following information.

Thank you for purchasing this product sold by Carlton Arts and Crafts. —[1]—. All Carlton products are guaranteed to have been made by hand by artisans. —[2]—. We guarantee the quality of all of our products, and we will provide you with a full refund should you be dissatisfied for any reason. —[3]—. Therefore, should you purchase another item of the same type, you will notice that each item is different in length, width, style, and appearance. —[4]—. If this item is made of cloth, do not machine-wash it. Instead, either hand-wash it or have it dry-cleaned.

1. What is stated about Carlton Arts and Crafts products?

(A) They are only sold in bulk.
(B) They come in the same size.
(C) They are hand-made.
(D) They come with a limited guarantee.

2. In which of the positions marked [1], [2], [3], and [4] does the following sentence best belong?

"Remember that this product is specially crafted, so it is one of a kind."

(A) [1]
(B) [2]
(C) [3]
(D) [4]

VOCA ···

guarantee *v.* 보장하다 I **by hand** 사람 손으로 I **artisan** *n.* 장인 I **dissatisfied** *adj.* 불만족스러워 하는 I **reason** *n.* 이유 I **therefore** *adv.* 그러므로 I **notice** *v.* 알아차리다, 주목하다 *n.* 알아챔, 주목 I **appearance** *n.* 외관, 모습, 외모 I **cloth** *n.* 천 I **machine-wash** *v.* (옷 등을) 세탁기로 빨다 I **instead** *adv.* 대신에 I **hand-wash** *v.* 손으로 씻다, 손빨래하다 I **dry-clean** *v.* 드라이클리닝을 하다 I **in bulk** 대량 으로 I **one of a kind** 독특한 것

Questions 3-6 refer to the following e-mail.

To	cbernard@homestylegrill.com
From	pcrew@westonsummerfestival.org
Date	May 25
Subject	Weston Summer Festival
Attachment	wsf.doc

Dear Mr. Bernard,

We have just received your application for a booth at the Weston Summer Festival. —[1]—. So, you may feel free to attend the festival to serve meals from your restaurant, Homestyle Grill.

You have been assigned to booth 42. It is located on the northern side of the festival grounds. Please see the attached map of the festival grounds so that you will know precisely where to go. —[2]—. If you have trouble finding it, you can simply ask one of the many volunteers who will be ready to assist people at the festival.

While the event starts at 9 in the morning, we request that vendors like you arrive no later than 7:30 A.M. —[3]—. This will enable everyone to set up their booths with a minimum amount of hassle. Vendors should park in the lot adjacent to Kenmore Street. Again, you can check the map for more details.

As a reminder, the festival will be held from Thursday, June 22, to Sunday, June 25. —[4]—. Please be aware that you need to submit an event fee of $250 so that you will have access to your booth.

Sincerely,

Peter Crew
Events Coordinator
Weston Summer Festival

3. What will Mr. Bernard most likely do at the festival?

(A) Operate rides
(B) Manage vendors
(C) Park cars
(D) Sell food

4. What did Mr. Crew send along with this e-mail?

(A) A receipt
(B) A map
(C) A registration form
(D) A schedule

5. When is Mr. Bernard first expected to arrive at the festival?

(A) On June 22 at 7:30 A.M.
(B) On June 22 at 9:00 A.M.
(C) On June 25 at 7:30 A.M.
(D) On June 25 at 9:00 A.M.

6. In which of the positions marked [1], [2], [3], and [4] does the following sentence best belong?

"We are pleased to let you know that there is still space available."

(A) [1]
(B) [2]
(C) [3]
(D) [4]

VOCA ··

application *n.* 지원(서) I booth *n.* 공간, 부스 I assign *v.* 할당하다 I locate *v.* 위치하다 I ground *n.* 지면, 땅, 부지 I attached *adj.* 첨부된 I precisely *adv.* 정확히 I volunteer *n.* 자원 봉사자 I vendor *n.* 행상인, 노점상 I no later than 늦어도 ~까지는 I enable *v.* 가능하게 하다 I set up ~을 세우다, 설치하다, 마련하다 I hassle *n.* 귀찮은 일 I adjacent *adj.* 인접한 I reminder *n.* 상기시키는 것 I aware *adj.* 인지하고 있는, 인식하고 있는 I access *n.* 접근 *v.* 접근하다 I coordinator *n.* 조정자, 책임자, 위원장

Questions 7-9 refer to the following memorandum.

To:	IT Department Staff
From:	Jennifer Archer
Date:	June 3
Subject:	Data Transition Project

Hello. For those of you I have not yet met, I am Jennifer Archer, the new director of IT. —[1]—.

Alongside Deidre Lee, the Chief Technology Officer, I will be focusing on managing the Data Transition Project. —[2]—. We will be devising a system to back up every employee's computer files to an off-site location. This will allow us to save both time and money. It will also help us to more easily secure sensitive information, as it will no longer be kept in multiple branch offices. —[3]—.

In the coming weeks, I will send out frequent progress reports. —[4]—. First, I will email each of you individual instructions regarding your role within two days. I will be available to take comments or suggestions related to the project in order to improve its efficiency. This will be a big change in how everyone accesses their files, so we will need to coordinate with other departments closely.

Thank you.

7. What is one purpose of the new project?

(A) To allow clients to access their files on mobile devices
(B) To improve communication between branch managers
(C) To decide the best way to attract more customers
(D) To lower expenses related to storing company data

8. According to the memorandum, what is Ms. Archer planning to do?

(A) Schedule a team meeting
(B) Send guidelines to employees
(C) Present some ideas to Mr. Lee
(D) Hire temporary workers

9. In which of the positions marked [1], [2], [3], and [4] does the following sentence best belong?

"It has been a pleasure to meet many of you during my first week here."

(A) [1]
(B) [2]
(C) [3]
(D) [4]

VOCA ·····

data transition 데이터 전환 | alongside *prep.* ~ 옆에, ~와 함께 | chief officer 실장, 최고 책임자 | focus on ~에 집중하다 | devise *v.* 고안하다 | off-site *adj.* (어느 장소에서) 떨어진, 부지 밖의 | allow *v.* 허락하다 | secure *v.* 얻어내다, 확보하다 | sensitive *adj.* 민감한, 예민한 | frequent *adj.* 잦은, 빈번한 | progress report 경과 보고서 | instruction *n.* 지침, 안내 | role *n.* 역할 | comment *n.* 논평 | efficiency *n.* 효율 | access *v.* 이용하다 | coordinate *v.* 조정하다, 협업하다

Questions 10-13 refer to the following Web page.

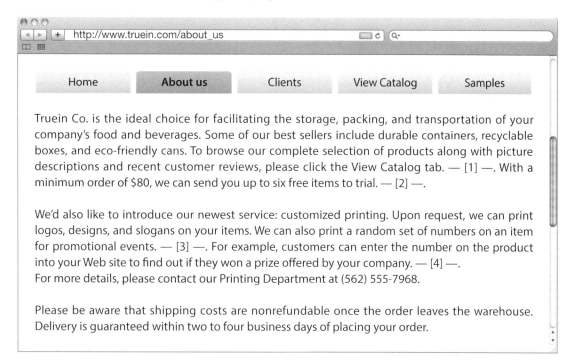

Truein Co. is the ideal choice for facilitating the storage, packing, and transportation of your company's food and beverages. Some of our best sellers include durable containers, recyclable boxes, and eco-friendly cans. To browse our complete selection of products along with picture descriptions and recent customer reviews, please click the View Catalog tab. — [1] —. With a minimum order of $80, we can send you up to six free items to trial. — [2] —.

We'd also like to introduce our newest service: customized printing. Upon request, we can print logos, designs, and slogans on your items. We can also print a random set of numbers on an item for promotional events. — [3] —. For example, customers can enter the number on the product into your Web site to find out if they won a prize offered by your company. — [4] —.
For more details, please contact our Printing Department at (562) 555-7968.

Please be aware that shipping costs are nonrefundable once the order leaves the warehouse. Delivery is guaranteed within two to four business days of placing your order.

10. For whom is the Web page most likely intended?

(A) Transportation services
(B) Local recycling centers
(C) Publishing firms
(D) Food preparation companies

11. What is NOT stated about Truein Co.?

(A) It gives a discount to first-time customers.
(B) It offers a limited number of sample items to customers.
(C) It writes messages on products at the customer's request.
(D) It posts the latest comments from customers.

12. What is indicated about orders placed through Truein Co.?

(A) They can be shipped at no cost with a minimum purchase of $80.
(B) They can be delivered within four working days.
(C) They can be paid for in installments.
(D) They can be exchanged within one month of the purchase date.

13. In which of the positions marked [1], [2], [3], and [4] does the following sentence best belong?

"Go to our Samples section for additional information."

(A) [1]
(B) [2]
(C) [3]
(D) [4]

VOCA ···

facilitate *v.* 용이하게하다 | storage *n.* 저장(고), 보관(소) | transportation *n.* 차편, 대중교통 | beverage *n.* 음료 | durable *adj.* 내구성이 있는 | container *n.* 용기 | recyclable *adj.* 재생 이용할 수 있는, 재활용 가능한 | eco-friendly *adj.* 친환경적인, 환경 친화적인 | browse *v.* 검색하다 | along with ~와 함께, ~와 마찬가지로 | trial *n.* 실험, 시험 | customized *adj.* 개개인의 요구에 맞춘, 맞춤형의 | slogan *n.* 슬로건, 구호, 표어 | random *adj.* 무작위의, 임의의 | nonrefundable *adj.* 환불되지 않는 | guarantee *v.* 보장하다

UNIT 06

동의어 문제

단어의 문맥적인 의미를 파악해야 한다! 동의어 문제는 주어진 단어의 사전적인 의미가 아니라 문맥상의 의미와 가장 가까운 단어를 고르는 문제이다. 매회 2문제 정도 출제된다.

동의어 문제는 단일지문과 복수지문에도 출제가 된다. 어휘 암기를 할 때, 한글 해석 뜻은 물론 동의어들을 함께 암기해두고 문맥에서 실제 어떻게 쓰이는지도 예문 들을 통해 파악하는 것이 필요하다!

🔍 질문 유형 확인하기

▶ **동의어**

단일지문의 경우

According to the notice, the word "as" in paragraph 2, line 4, **is closest in meaning to**
공지에 따르면, 두 번째 단락 네 번째 줄의 단어 "as"와 의미상 가장 가까운 것은

The word "cover" in paragraph 1, line 7, **is closest in meaning to**
첫 번째 단락, 일곱 번째 줄의 단어 "cover"와 의미상 가장 가까운 것은

이중·삼중 지문의 경우

In the e-mail, the word "assure" in paragraph 1, line 5, **is closest in meaning to**
이메일의 첫 번째 문단, 다섯 번째 줄의 단어 "assure"와 의미상 가장 가까운 것은

📝 문제 풀이 전략

1 질문을 읽고, 지문에서 해당 단어의 위치를 확인한다.

질문에서 언급한 단어가 들어 있는 문장을 지문에서 찾아 읽어본다.

2 해당 단어가 포함된 문장을 해석하고, 단어의 문맥적인 의미를 파악한다.

영어 단어는 특성상 한 단어에 여러 가지 의미가 있으므로 문장 속에서 어떤 의미로 쓰였는지 앞뒤 문맥을 잘 살펴야 한다.

3 정답을 찾는다.

빈칸에 해당 단어를 넣어서 읽었을 때, 문맥이 어색하지 않고 자연스럽게 연결되는지를 확인한다.

Question 1 refers to the following article.

(May 22) The city of Worcester has a cause to celebrate. It has managed to cut traffic jams in the downtown area by almost 25 percent compared to last year. According to transportation authorities, commutes were especially bad during the morning rush hour, but the conditions have improved significantly thanks to a smart initiative implemented last December to encourage citizens to commute by subway more often.

In order to attract more people to public transportation, subway fares were reduced, and the city decided to replace old subway trains with new ones and have them run more frequently. According to a survey of Worcester residents, these changes were important factors in their decision to use more public transportation. "The new schedules have made a huge impact," one resident said.

These measures appear to have had some positive effect in terms of financial viability of some subway operators. For example, the green subway line, which runs from Canal Street to Fergus Lane, rarely had any passengers, and operators once considered closing the line. However, this is no longer an issue since there are now enough passengers to maintain financial stability.

- 최근 시행된 교통 계획 안내

- 계획 시행 원인

- 추가 지하철 운행의 긍정적인 측면

1. The word "measures" in paragraph 3, line 1, is closest in meaning to

(A) distances
(B) actions
(C) standards
(D) successes

1번은 다음 기사에 관한 문제입니다.

(May 22) The city of Worcester has a cause to celebrate. It has managed to cut traffic jams in the downtown area by almost 25 percent compared to last year. According to transportation authorities, commutes were especially bad during the morning rush hour, but the conditions have improved significantly thanks to a smart initiative implemented last December to encourage citizens to commute by subway more often.

→● 최근 시행된 교통 계획 안내

(5월 22일) Worcester 시가 축하할 거리가 하나 생겼다. 이 도시는 지난해와 비교하여 시내 교통 체증을 25 퍼센트 가량 감소시켰다. 교통 관계자들에 따르면, 통근은 아침 출근 시간대에 특히 안 좋지만, 지난 12월 시민들이 더 자주 지하철로 통근을 하게끔 하기 위해 시행된 이 현명한 계획 덕분에 상황이 상당히 개선되었다.

In order to attract more people to public transportation, subway fares were reduced, and the city decided to replace old subway trains with new ones and have them run more frequently. According to a survey of Worcester residents, these changes were important factors in their decision to use more public transportation. "The new schedules have made a huge impact," one resident said.

→● 계획 시행 원인

더 많은 시민들이 대중교통을 이용하게끔 하기 위해, 지하철 요금이 인하되었고, 시는 낡은 지하철을 새 것으로 교체하고 더 자주 운행하기로 결정하였다. Worcester 시 거주자들을 대상으로 한 여론 조사에 따르면, 이러한 변화는 대중 교통의 사용을 늘리고자 하는 그들의 결정에 중요한 요인이었다. "이 새로운 운행 시간표들이 큰 영향을 끼쳤습니다." 라고 한 주민이 말했다.

❶ These measures appear to have had some positive effect in terms of financial viability of some subway operators. For example, the green subway line, which runs from Canal Street to Fergus Lane, rarely had any passengers, and operators once considered closing the line. However, this is no longer an issue since there are now enough passengers to maintain financial stability.

→● 추가 지하철 운행의 긍정적인 측면

이 조치들은 일부 지하철 운영자들에게 재정적 실현 가능성의 측면에서 어느 정도 긍정적인 영향을 끼친 것으로 보인다. 예를 들어, Canal가에서 Fergus가로 운행하는 녹색 지하철 노선은 승객들이 거의 없었기에, 지하철 운영자들은 한때 이 노선을 폐지하는 것을 고려했었다. 하지만, 이 계획은 재정 안정성을 유지하기 위한 승객들이 이제 충분하기에 더 이상 문제가 되지 않는다.

>> 동의어를 묻는 문제

1. The word "measures" in paragraph 3, line 1, is closest in meaning to

(A) distances
(B) actions
(C) standards
(D) successes

세 번째 단락, 첫 번째 줄의 단어 "measures"와 의미상 가장 가까운 것은

(A) 거리
(B) 조치
(C) 기준
(D) 성공

문제 풀이 전략 적용

1 **질문을 읽고, 지문에서 해당 단어의 위치를 확인한다.**

세 번째 단락, 첫 번째 줄에 있는 measures를 찾아서 이와 바꿔 쓸 수 있는 보기가 무엇인지 문맥을 통해 파악한다.

2 **해당 단어가 포함된 문장을 해석하고, 단어의 문맥적인 의미를 파악한다.**

These **measures** appear to have had some positive effect in terms of financial viability.
→ '이러한 **조치들**이 재정 실현 가능성에 어느 정도 긍정적인 영향을 끼친 것으로 보인다'라는 뜻이므로 이와 유사한 의미를 가진 보기를 찾는다.
• **measure** *n.* 대책, 수단, 조치

3 **정답을 찾는다.**

'조치'란 의미의 actions가 문장의 measures라는 어휘를 대신할 수 있다. 따라서 정답은 (B) actions이다.
• **action** *n.* 행동, 행위 = **measure** *n.* 수단, 조치 = **step** *n.* 단계, 조치 = **move** *n.* 움직임, 조치, 수단

VOCA ··

cause *n.* 원인 | **manage** *v.* 처리하다, 해내다 | **cut** *v.* 줄이다, 삭감하다 | **traffic jam** 교통 체증 | **compared to** ∼와 비교하여 | **transportation authority** 교통 관계자, 교통 공무원 | **rush hour** (출·퇴근) 혼잡 시간대 | **improve** *v.* 개선하다, 향상시키다, 나아지다 | **significantly** *adv.* 상당히, 중요하게 | **thanks to** ∼덕분에 | **initiative** *n.* 계획 | **implement** *v.* 시행하다, 수행하다 | **encourage** *v.* 격려하다, 용기를 북돋우다 | **impact** *n.* 영향 | **commute** *v.* 통근하다 | **resident** *n.* 거주민 | **schedule** *n.* 시간표; 일정 | **measure** *n.* 해결책, 조치 | **in terms of** ∼면에서, ∼에 관하여 | **financial** *adj.* 금융의, 재정의 | **viability** *n.* 실행 가능성 | **rarely** *adv.* 드물게, 좀처럼 ∼하지 않는 | **issue** *n.* 문제, 쟁점 | **maintain** *v.* 유지하다, 지키다 | **stability** *n.* 안정(성)

해설서 p.75

Questions 1-4 refer to the following information.

New York City
Cycling Center

Welcome to the New York City Cycling Center (NYCCC). We are an indoor recreation center intended to cater to the needs of cyclists of all levels.

Our services aim to help you enjoy the healthy sport of cycling while also achieving your fitness goals, whether they are just losing weight or winning bicycle races.

Our high-tech facilities offer the perfect environment for training. We have over a hundred lab-quality exercise bikes as well as a physiology lab that offers VO2 max and lactate threshold testing. There is also always a certified coach on duty to provide you with assistance.

General information is as follows:

Cycling Center Hours
Monday-Friday 6 A.M. to 10 P.M. Saturday-Sunday 7 A.M. to 9 P.M.

Office Hours
Monday-Friday 8 A.M. to 7 P.M.

Extension Numbers
Ext 110 for individual lessons   Ext 111 for physiological testing
Ext 112 for customer service   Ext 113 for pricing information

---

1. What is the purpose of the information?

(A) To provide general information about a fitness club
(B) To inform new employees of their responsibilities
(C) To detail the policies of a government organization
(D) To recruit volunteers for an upcoming event

2. What extension number should readers call to receive personal training?

(A) 110
(B) 111
(C) 112
(D) 113

3. The word "intended" in paragraph 1, line 2, is closest in meaning to

(A) firm
(B) directed
(C) meant
(D) indicated

4. What is NOT mentioned about the NYCCC?

(A) It was recently built.
(B) Its offices is closed on weekends.
(C) It provides high-quality equipment.
(D) Its facilities are open daily.

VOCA ··

cycling *n.* 자전거 타기, 사이클링 I intended *adj.* 의도하는, ~을 위해 만들어진 I cyclist *n.* 자전거 타는 사람, 사이클리스트 I aim *v.* 목표하다 I achieve *v.* 달성하다, 성취하다 I fitness *n.* 신체 단련 I lose weight 감량하다, 체중이 줄다 I bicycle race 자전거 경주 I high-tech *adj.* 최첨단의 I facility *n.* 시설 I training *n.* 훈련 I lab-quality *adj.* 실험실 수준의 I physiology *n.* 생리학 I lab *n.* 실험실 I VO2 max 최대 산소 섭취량 I lactate threshold 젖산 역치 I certified *adj.* 공인의, 증명된 I on duty 근무 중인 I provide *v.* 제공하다 I assistance *n.* 도움 I extension *n.* 구내전화, 내선 I inform A of B A에게 B를 알리다 I employee *n.* 직원 I responsibility *n.* 책임, 책무 I policy *n.* 방침, 정책 I government organization 정부 기관 I recruit *v.* 모집하다 I directed *adj.* 유도된, 지시 받은 I indicated *adj.* 표시된

254

Jenny Kang Joins NBN TV

NBN TV will broadcast a talk show about the economy hosted by Jenny Kang, who is known for her popular television program, *The Money Game*.

The program was created because, according to an online survey taken in May, viewers had felt that the lack of a talk show about the economy was the NBN's biggest weakness. Ms. Kang was NBN's first choice to host it. "We have long considered Ms. Kang one of the most competent financial reporters in the industry," said NBN producer Thomas Park, who has worked at the station for 20 years.

NBN's new show, which is currently untitled, will deal with a wide range of topics related to the economy. It will air at 7 P.M. on weekdays starting in late October.

5. What is the article mainly about?

(A) The retirement of a long-time producer
(B) The anniversary of a broadcasting station
(C) The process of creating TV programs
(D) The hiring of a new show host

6. According to the article, what happened in May?

(A) A studio was relocated.
(B) Ms. Kang was interviewed.
(C) A program was rescheduled.
(D) Feedback was given.

7. What is still undecided about the new TV program?

(A) Who will host the show
(B) What it will be called
(C) What time it will be aired
(D) When it will begin

8. The phrase "deal with" in paragraph 3, line 1, is closest in meaning to

(A) perform
(B) take over
(C) cover
(D) replace

VOCA ··
broadcast *v.* 방송하다 I **host** *v.* 주최하다, (TV·라디오 프로를) 진행하다 I **lack** *n.* 부족, 결여 *v.* 부족하다 I **weakness** *n.* 약함, 약점 I **consider** *v.* 고려하다, 생각하다 I **competent** *adj.* 능숙한, 유능한 I **station** *n.* 방송국 I **deal with** ~을 다루다 I **a wide range of** 다양한 I **air** *v.* 방송하다 I **long-time** *adj.* 오랜 I **relocate** *v.* 이전하다 I **take over** 인수하다

Questions 9-12 refer to the following letter.

Sammy Kim
2239 Tieman Road
Chicago, IL 60290
September 18

Dear Mr. Kim,

During our conversation on September 2, you informed me that you would like to rent one of our tour buses for the weekend of October 15 and 16. You also informed me that your party would consist of 75 individuals, and I told you a large-sized bus would be appropriate for that many people. However, you weren't sure that many people would be traveling. Nevertheless, I made a tentative reservation for you, and we agreed that you would get in touch with me within 10 days to confirm that a large-sized bus was appropriate. It has been over two weeks, and I still haven't received a confirmation from you.

So, I'm contacting you to find out if you are still planning to do business with us. Our tour buses are in high demand during the fall, and we would prefer to give another party the chance to reserve one of our large buses. Thus, if I do not receive any correspondence from you within the next five business days, I will cancel your reservation. Please contact me as soon as you can to inform me what you would like to do.

Sincerely,

Jon Voight

Jon Voight
General Manager
Skyway Bus and Tour

9. Why was this letter written?

(A) To invite another department to a meeting
(B) To seek a response from a potential customer
(C) To request some mechanical repairs to a bus
(D) To get a price quote from an industry competitor

10. What does the letter suggest about Mr. Voight?

(A) He will be away from the office for the next five days.
(B) He will speak with one of his superiors about an issue.
(C) He previously spoke with Mr. Kim about a matter.
(D) He has been on business trips with Mr. Kim before.

11. The word "tentative" in paragraph 1, line 4, is closest meaning to

(A) definite
(B) conditional
(C) cautious
(D) reluctant

12. What is Mr. Kim asked to do?

(A) Reply to Mr. Voight
(B) Reserve a smaller vehicle
(C) Get in touch with another branch
(D) Check the price on a receipt

VOCA ··

party *n.* (여행을 함께 하는) 단체 | consist of ~로 구성되다 | large-sized *adj.* 대형의 | appropriate *adj.* 적합한 | tentative *adj.* 잠정적인 | reservation *n.* 예약 | get in touch with ~와 연락하다 | do business with ~와 거래하다 | be in high demand 수요가 많다 | correspondence *n.* 서신, 편지 | potential *adj.* 잠재적인 | mechanical *adj.* 기계와 관련된 | repair *n.* 수리 | price quote 견적 | superior *n.* 상급자 | previously *adv.* 이전에 | on a business trip 출장 중인 | definite *adj.* 확실한 | conditional *adj.* 조건부의 | vehicle *n.* 차량 | receipt *n.* 영수증

Questions 13-16 refer to the following Web page.

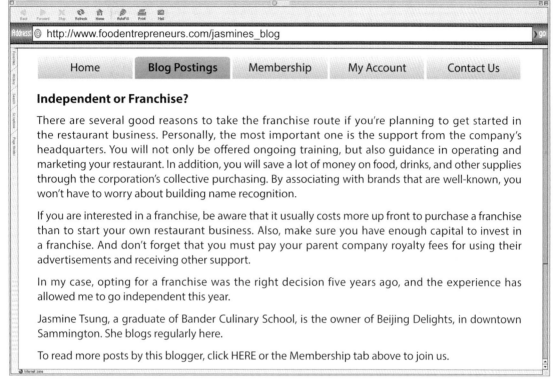

http://www.foodentrepreneurs.com/jasmines_blog

| Home | **Blog Postings** | Membership | My Account | Contact Us |

Independent or Franchise?

There are several good reasons to take the franchise route if you're planning to get started in the restaurant business. Personally, the most important one is the support from the company's headquarters. You will not only be offered ongoing training, but also guidance in operating and marketing your restaurant. In addition, you will save a lot of money on food, drinks, and other supplies through the corporation's collective purchasing. By associating with brands that are well-known, you won't have to worry about building name recognition.

If you are interested in a franchise, be aware that it usually costs more up front to purchase a franchise than to start your own restaurant business. Also, make sure you have enough capital to invest in a franchise. And don't forget that you must pay your parent company royalty fees for using their advertisements and receiving other support.

In my case, opting for a franchise was the right decision five years ago, and the experience has allowed me to go independent this year.

Jasmine Tsung, a graduate of Bander Culinary School, is the owner of Beijing Delights, in downtown Sammington. She blogs regularly here.

To read more posts by this blogger, click HERE or the Membership tab above to join us.

13. What is the purpose of the Web page?

(A) To share ideas about starting a business
(B) To provide instructions on setting up a blog
(C) To compare the services of two companies
(D) To post feedback from satisfied customers

14. What is NOT mentioned on the Web page as an advantage of running a franchise?

(A) Opportunities for training
(B) Advice on marketing
(C) Low supply costs
(D) Staffing assistance

15. The word "associating", in paragraph 1, line 5, is closest in meaning to

(A) socializing
(B) joining
(C) borrowing
(D) reserving

16. How can people read more of Ms. Tsung's work?

(A) By attending a class
(B) By sending an e-mail
(C) By joining a Web site
(D) By purchasing a book

VOCA ··

independent *adj.* 독자적인, 독립한 | **franchise** *n.* 제조자가 판매업자에게 주는 독점 판매권, 체인점; 체인점에 경영권을 주는 계약 | **route** *n.* 길, 경로, 노선 | **personally** *adv.* 개인적으로, 개인적인 의견을 말하자면 | **headquarters** *n.* 본사 | **ongoing** *adj.* 계속 진행 중인 | **guidance** *n.* 지도, 유도 | **in addition** 덧붙여, 게다가 | **collective** *adj.* 집단의, 단체의 | **purchasing** *n.* 구매(행위) | **well-known** *adj.* 유명한, 잘 알려진 | **name recognition** 인지도 | **capital** *n.* 자본, 자금 | **parent company** 모(母)회사, 본사 | **royalty fee** 로열티 | **In my case** 내 경우에는 | **opt for** ~를 선택하다 | **culinary school** 요리 학교 | **blogger** *n.* (인터넷) 블로거(블로그를 만드는 네티즌을 가르킴) | **above** *prep.* ~위에, (글에서) 위에서, 앞에서 | **socialize** *v.* 사람들과 사귀다, 교제하다 | **staffing** *n.* 직원, 직원 채용

문자 대화문과 화자 의도

문자 메시지는 2인 형태의 대화로 출제되고, 온라인 채팅은 3인 이상의 대화 형태로 출제된다. 문자 메시지나 온라인 채팅 지문에는 화자의 의도를 물어보는 새로운 문제 유형이 출제된다.

주로 2인 이상의 사람들이 메시지 또는 채팅 대화를 하는 유형으로, 회사 비즈니스 관련 대화 또는 일상적인 주제들을 다룬다. 구어체 표현이나 어떤 특정 문장이 문맥에 따라 다양한 의미를 가지므로, 대화의 흐름을 잘 파악하는 것이 중요하다!

🔍 지문 유형 확인하기

1. 자주 나오는 지문

2인이 주고 받는 문자 메시지에는 업무 관련 도움을 요청하는 대화 등이 출제된다.
3인 이상이 참여하는 온라인 채팅에는 프로젝트 진행 상황에 대한 보고나 서로 의견을 주고 받는 대화가 출제된다.

2. 대화의 목적, 이유, 요청 사항, 추가 요청 사항 등을 묻는다.

문자 메시지나 온라인 채팅을 하는 이유, 목적, 요청 사항은 대부분 지문의 앞부분에 나온다.
대화의 마무리 단계에서 추가 요청 사항이 나올 수 있다.

[주제·목적] What is the **main topic** of the text message chain? 문자 대화문의 주제는 무엇인가?

[요청 사항] What does Ms. Dole **ask** Ms. Kim to do? Ms. Dole이 Ms. Kim에게 무엇을 요청하는가?

3. 대화에 나오는 세부 정보를 묻는다.

질문에서 키워드를 파악하여 지문에서 키워드가 언급된 부분을 확인한다.

[사실확인] What is **true[NOT true]** about **Mr. Parker**? Mr. Parker에 대해 사실인 것은[아닌 것은] 무엇인가?

[세부사항] **Who** is **available** to **attend** the meeting? 회의에 참석할 수 있는 사람은 누구인가?

[세부사항] What is **indicated** about **Ms. Chen**? Ms. Chen에 관하여 알 수 있는 것은 무엇인가?

[암시·추론] What will most likely **happen** on **April 21**? 4월 21일에 무슨 일이 일어나겠는가?

[암시·추론] What is **suggested[implied]** about the **event**? 행사에 관하여 암시되는 것은 무엇인가?

4. 화자 의도를 묻는다.

질문에 주어진 표현이 문맥상 무엇을 의미하는지를 파악해야 한다. 지문에서 해당 표현을 찾아 앞뒤 문맥을 확인한다. 특히, 3인 이상이 대화하는 온라인 채팅의 경우에는 인물 간의 관계나 대화의 주제 또는 목적에 유의해야 한다.

Janet Lee

I wasn't able to finish writing the proposal for the finance meeting. What am I going to do?
재무 회의에 필요한 제안서 작성을 못 끝냈어요. 어떡하면 좋죠?

11:45 A.M.

Alex Whites

Actually, that meeting was postponed because of the annual board meeting.

11:46 A.M.   실은 그 회의가 연례 이사 회의 때문에 연기되었어요.

Janet Lee

Really? **That's good to hear**. Thanks for letting me know.
정말인가요? 그거 듣던 중 반가운 소리군요. 알려주셔서 감사해요.

11:52 A.M.

Q. At 11:52 A.M., what does Ms. Lee mean when she writes, "That's good to hear"?

오전 11시 52분에 Ms. Lee가 "그거 듣던 중 반가운 소리군요"라고 쓴 것은 무슨 의미인가?

Question 1 refers to the following text message chain.

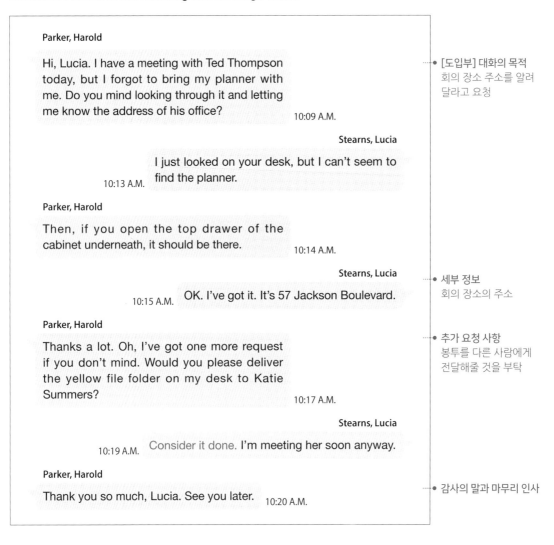

Parker, Harold

Hi, Lucia. I have a meeting with Ted Thompson today, but I forgot to bring my planner with me. Do you mind looking through it and letting me know the address of his office?

10:09 A.M.

[도입부] 대화의 목적
회의 장소 주소를 알려
달라고 요청

Stearns, Lucia

10:13 A.M.   I just looked on your desk, but I can't seem to find the planner.

Parker, Harold

Then, if you open the top drawer of the cabinet underneath, it should be there.

10:14 A.M.

Stearns, Lucia

10:15 A.M.   OK. I've got it. It's 57 Jackson Boulevard.

세부 정보
회의 장소의 주소

Parker, Harold

Thanks a lot. Oh, I've got one more request if you don't mind. Would you please deliver the yellow file folder on my desk to Katie Summers?

10:17 A.M.

추가 요청 사항
봉투를 다른 사람에게
전달해줄 것을 부탁

Stearns, Lucia

10:19 A.M.   Consider it done. I'm meeting her soon anyway.

Parker, Harold

Thank you so much, Lucia. See you later.   10:20 A.M.

감사의 말과 마무리 인사

문맥상 화자 의도를 묻는 문제

1. At 10:19 A.M., what does Ms. Stearns mean when she writes, "Consider it done"?

(A) She will give a document to Ms. Summers.
(B) She will organize Mr. Parker's desk.
(C) She will lock a cabinet.
(D) She will contact Mr. Thompson.

Question 2 refers to the following online chat discussion.

Walker, Chad [8:45 A.M.]

How are the preparations for this afternoon's negotiation session going? We have to land this contract so that those assembly lines will keep running smoothly.

Fontana, Maria [8:47 A.M.]

I'm in the large conference room. The chairs, laptop, and projector are being set up, so the room is almost ready.

Samuels, Kelly [8:49 A.M.]

I just spoke with the caterer. He said that the food for the luncheon will arrive no later than 11:30.

Walker, Chad [8:51 A.M.]

It sounds like you're both on top of things. Who's going to pick up the Reardon Mining executives from the airport?

Samuels, Kelly [8:51 A.M.]

I wasn't aware we were supposed to do that.

Fontana, Maria [8:52 A.M.]

Me, neither. What time are they arriving?

Walker, Chad [8:54 A.M.]

According to the schedule, five of them will be landing at the airport at 11:05. They're coming in on a flight from Dallas.

Samuels, Kelly [8:57 A.M.]

I could pick them up. But I need a vehicle big enough to carry everyone plus any luggage they've got.

Walker, Chad [8:59 A.M.]

Call Dave Harper at extension 386. He can set you up with a van. Maria, you should go with Kelly. It won't make a good impression if we only send one person.

Fontana, Maria [9:01 A.M.]

Sure, Chad. I'll head downstairs right now.

• 대화의 목적
  현재 진행 상황 문의

• [중반부] 준비 상황 보고
  - 회의실 준비 거의 완료
  - 오찬 음식 준비 거의 완료

• [후반부] 추가 요청 사항
  - 차량 요청
  - 두 명 모두 마중 나가기

문맥상 화자 의도를 묻는 문제

2. At 8:51 A.M., what does Mr. Walker mean when he writes, "It sounds like you're both on top of things"?

(A) A contract is on the top shelf.

(B) Some employees are doing their jobs well.

(C) Some projects have been completed.

(D) A negotiation is nearly finalized.

1번은 다음 문자 대화문에 관한 문제입니다.

Parker, Harold

Hi, Lucia. I have a meeting with Ted Thompson today, but I forgot to bring my planner with me. Do you mind looking through it and letting me know the address of his office?

안녕하세요, Lucia. 오늘 Ted Thompson과 미팅이 있는데, 깜빡 잊고 수첩을 가져오질 않았네요. 그것 좀 확인해서 그 분 주소를 제게 알려주실 수 있을까요?

오전 10:09

••• [도입부] 대화의 목적
회의 장소 주소를 알려 달라고 요청

Stearns, Lucia

I just looked on your desk, but I can't seem to find the planner.

방금 당신 책상을 봤는데, 수첩이 없는 것 같아요.

오전 10:13

Parker, Harold

Then, if you open the top drawer of the cabinet underneath, it should be there.

그럼 밑의 캐비닛 맨 윗서랍을 열면 거기 있을 거예요.

오전 10:14

Stearns, Lucia

OK, I've got it. It's 57 Jackson Boulevard.

네, 찾았어요. 주소는 Jackson 가 57번지예요.

오전 10:15

••• 세부 정보
회의 장소의 주소

Parker, Harold

Thanks a lot. Oh, I've got one more request if you don't mind. Would you please deliver the yellow file folder on my desk to Katie Summers?

정말 고마워요. 괜찮다면 하나 더 요청해도 될까요? 제 책상에 있는 노란색 서류철을 Katie Summers에게 전달해 줄 수 있을까요?

오전 10:17

••• 추가 요청 사항
봉투를 다른 사람에게 전달해줄 것을 부탁

Stearns, Lucia

❶ Consider it done. I'm meeting her soon anyway.

이미 처리된 걸로 봐 주세요. 제가 그녀를 곧 만날 예정이라서요.

오전 10:19

Parker, Harold

Thank you so much, Lucia. See you later.

정말 고마워요, Lucia. 이따 봐요.

오전 10:20

••• 감사의 말과 마무리 인사

1. At 10:19 A.M., what does Ms. Stearns mean when she writes, "Consider it done"?

(A) She will give a document to Ms. Summers.
(B) She will organize Mr. Parker's desk.
(C) She will lock a cabinet.
(D) She will contact Mr. Thompson.

오전 10시 19분에 Ms. Stearns이 "이미 처리된 걸로 봐 주세요."라고 쓴 것은 무슨 의미인가?

(A) Ms. Summers에게 서류를 줄 것이다.
(B) Mr. Parker의 책상을 정리할 것이다.
(C) 캐비닛을 잠귀둘 것이다.
(D) Mr. Thompson에게 연락할 것이다.

해설 '제 책상에 있는 노란색 서류철을 Katie Summers에게 전달해 줄 수 있을까요?'라고 Mr. Parker가 이야기했고, Ms. Stearns이 "Consider it done"이라고 말한 후, '그녀를 곧 만날 예정이라서요.'라고 한 것은 Mr. Parker의 요청을 들어 줄 수 있다는 뜻이므로 정답은 (A) She will give a document to Ms. Summers.이다.

VOCA ···

Do you mind~? (허락·동의를 구하는 표현) ~하는 걸 꺼리나요? | **look through** ~를 살펴보다, 검토하다 | **address** *n.* 주소 | **seem** *v.* ~인 것 처럼 보이다 | **planner** *n.* 계획표, 수첩, 기획자 | **drawer** *n.* 서랍 | **underneth** *adv.* ~의 밑에 | **I've got it.** 알았어요, 이해했어요, 받았어요. | **request** *n.* 요청 *v.* 요청하다 | **mind** *v.* 언짢아하다 | **deliver** *v.* 배달하다, 전달하다

2번은 다음 온라인 채팅 대화문에 관한 문제입니다.

Walker, Chad [오전 8:45]

How are the preparations for this afternoon's negotiation session going? We have to land this contract so that those assembly lines will keep running smoothly.

오늘 오후에 있을 협상 준비는 어떻게 되고 있나요? 그 조립 라인이 순조롭게 계속 가동될 수 있도록, 우리는 이 계약을 따내야 합니다.

Fontana, Maria [오전 8:47]

I'm in the large conference room. The chairs, laptop, and projector are being set up, so the room is almost ready.

저는 대회의실에 있어요. 의자, 노트북 컴퓨터, 그리고 프로젝터가 모두 설치되고 있고요. 회의실은 거의 준비가 다 되었습니다.

Samuels, Kelly [오전 8:49]

I just spoke with the caterer. He said that the food for the luncheon will arrive no later than 11:30.

저는 방금 식음료 공급자와 이야기했습니다. 그는 오찬 음식이 늦어도 11시 30분까지는 도착할 것이라고 말했어요.

Walker, Chad [오전 8:51]

❷ It sounds like you're both on top of things. Who's going to pick up the Reardon Mining executives from the airport?

두 분 모두 일을 잘 해내고 있는 것 같군요. 누가 공항에서 Reardon 광산의 중역들을 데려오실 건가요?

Samuels, Kelly [오전 8:51]

I wasn't aware we were supposed to do that.

저는 우리가 그걸 해야 하는지 몰랐네요.

Fontana, Maria [오전 8:52]

Me, neither. What time are they arriving?

저도 몰랐어요. 그들은 몇 시에 도착하나요?

Walker, Chad [오전 8:54]

According to the schedule, five of them will be landing at the airport at 11:05. They're coming in on a flight from Dallas.

제 일정에 따르면, 그분들 중 다섯 분이 11시 5분에 공항에 도착할 것입니다. 그들은 댈러스에서 비행기를 타고 오실겁니다.

Samuels, Kelly [오전 8:57]

I could pick them up. But I need a vehicle big enough to carry everyone plus any luggage they've got.

제가 그들을 모시러 갈 수 있을 것 같아요. 하지만 저는 짐과 함께 그분들이 탈 수 있을 만큼 충분한 크기의 큰 차량이 필요합니다.

Walker, Chad [오전 8:59]

Call Dave Harper at extension 386. He can set you up with a van. Maria, you should go with Kelly. It won't make a good impression if we only send one person.

Dave Harper에게 구내전화 386으로 전화하세요. 그는 당신에게 밴을 준비해 줄 수 있을거예요. Maria, 당신은 Kelly와 함께 가세요. 만약 우리가 한 명만 공항에 보낸다면, 좋은 인상을 주지 못할 거예요.

Fontana, Maria [오전 9:01]

Sure, Chad. I'll head downstairs right now.

물론이죠, Chad. 제가 지금 당장 아래층으로 갈게요.

• 대화의 목적
현재 진행 상황 문의

• [중반부] 준비 상황 보고
- 회의실 준비 거의 완료
- 오찬 음식 준비 거의 완료

• [후반부] 추가 요청 사항
- 차량 요청
- 두 명 모두 마중 나가기

2. At 8:51 A.M., what does Mr. Walker mean when he writes, "It sounds like you're both on top of things"?

(A) A contract is on the top shelf.

(B) Some employees are doing their jobs well.

(C) Some projects have been completed.

(D) A negotiation is nearly finalized.

오전 8시 51분에 Mr. Walker가 말한 "두 분 모두 일을 잘 해내고 있는 것 같군요."라고 쓴 것은 무슨 의미이겠는가?

(A) 계약서가 맨 윗 선반에 있다.

(B) 몇몇 직원들이 일을 잘하고 있다.

(C) 몇몇 프로젝트가 완료되었다.

(D) 협상이 거의 끝났다.

해설 Maria가 회의실 준비를 거의 다 해 놓았고, Kelly가 음식 준비 상황을 확인했다는 내용이 앞에 나온다. 따라서 둘 다 모두 일을 잘 하고 있다는 뜻이므로 정답은 (B) Some employees are doing their jobs well.이다.

VOCA ···

preparation *n.* 준비 | negotiation *n.* 협상 | land a contract 계약을 따내다 | assembly line 조립 라인 | run *v.* 운영하다, 작동하다 | caterer *n.* 식음료 공급자 | luncheon *n.* 오찬 | pick up 태우러 가다 | executive *n.* 경영진, 중역 | be supposed to ~하기로 되어있다 | land *v.* 착륙하다, 도착하다 | vehicle *n.* 차량 | carry *v.* 운반하다, 나르다 | luggage *n.* 짐 | extension *n.* 구내전화 | impression *n.* 인상 | head *v.* 가다, 향하다 | downstairs *adv.* 아래층으로

Questions 1-2 refer to the following text message chain.

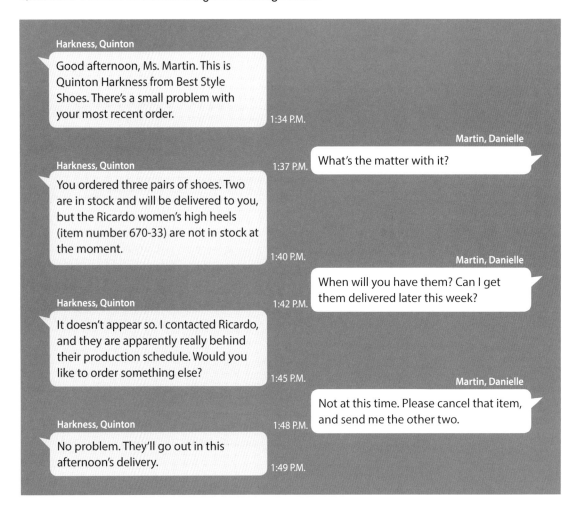

Harkness, Quinton

Good afternoon, Ms. Martin. This is Quinton Harkness from Best Style Shoes. There's a small problem with your most recent order.
1:34 P.M.

1:37 P.M. **Martin, Danielle**
What's the matter with it?

Harkness, Quinton

You ordered three pairs of shoes. Two are in stock and will be delivered to you, but the Ricardo women's high heels (item number 670-33) are not in stock at the moment.
1:40 P.M.

Martin, Danielle
When will you have them? Can I get them delivered later this week?
1:42 P.M.

Harkness, Quinton

It doesn't appear so. I contacted Ricardo, and they are apparently really behind their production schedule. Would you like to order something else?
1:45 P.M.

Martin, Danielle
Not at this time. Please cancel that item, and send me the other two.
1:48 P.M.

Harkness, Quinton

No problem. They'll go out in this afternoon's delivery.
1:49 P.M.

1. What is the problem with Ms. Martin's order?

(A) A price is incorrect.
(B) One of the items is not available.
(C) A quantity is wrong.
(D) Some of the items have been damaged.

2. At 1:48 P.M., what does Ms. Martin mean when she writes, "Not at this time"?

(A) She cannot visit Best Style Shoes today.
(B) She has not yet looked at other Ricardo shoes.
(C) She is not interested in buying a different product.
(D) She is too busy with her work.

VOCA ·····

recent *adj.* 최근의 I **order** *n.* 주문 *v.* 주문하다 I **matter** *n.* 문제 I **pair** *n.* 쌍, 짝, 켤레 I **stock** *n.* 재고, 재고품 I **deliver** *v.* 배달하다 I **appear** *v.* ~하게 보이다, ~인 것 같다 I **apparently** *adv.* 듣자 하니, 보아하니, 명백히 I **behind schedule** 예정보다 늦게 I **quantity** *n.* 양, 수량

Questions 3-4 refer to the following text message chain.

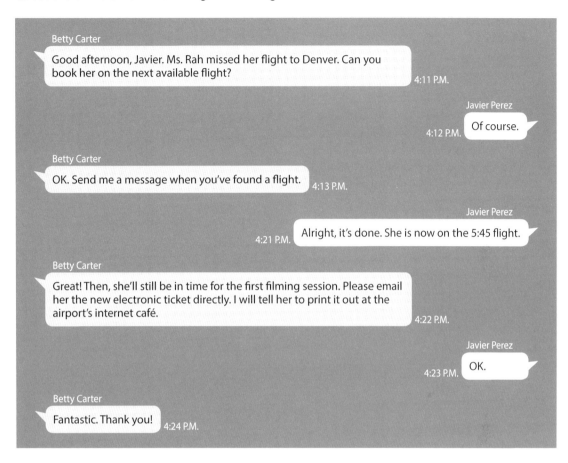

Betty Carter
Good afternoon, Javier. Ms. Rah missed her flight to Denver. Can you book her on the next available flight?
4:11 P.M.

Javier Perez
4:12 P.M. Of course.

Betty Carter
OK. Send me a message when you've found a flight.
4:13 P.M.

Javier Perez
4:21 P.M. Alright, it's done. She is now on the 5:45 flight.

Betty Carter
Great! Then, she'll still be in time for the first filming session. Please email her the new electronic ticket directly. I will tell her to print it out at the airport's internet café.
4:22 P.M.

Javier Perez
4:23 P.M. OK.

Betty Carter
Fantastic. Thank you!
4:24 P.M.

3. At 4:12 P.M., what does Mr. Perez mean when he writes, "Of course"?

(A) He will greet a client.
(B) He will reschedule a meeting.
(C) He will make a reservation.
(D) He will print out a ticket.

4. For what kind of business does Ms. Rah most likely work?

(A) A software company
(B) A production studio
(C) A restaurant
(D) An airline

VOCA ···

miss *v.* 놓치다 Ⅰ **available** *adj.* (사물이) 이용 가능한, (사람이) 시간이 있는 Ⅰ **filming** *n.* 촬영 Ⅰ **session** *n.* 기간 Ⅰ **directly** *adv.* 곧장, 똑
바로 Ⅰ **print out** 출력하다 Ⅰ **fantastic** *adj.* 기막히게 좋은, 환상적인 Ⅰ **client** *n.* 고객, 손님 Ⅰ **reschedule** *v.* (일정을) 다시 재조정하다 Ⅰ
production studio 제작사 Ⅰ **airline** *n.* 항공사

Questions 5-8 refer to the following online chat discussion.

Chapman, Carol [2:43 P.M.]
We're taking a break from the negotiations. I've got to return to the room in 15 minutes.

Lucas, Brian [2:45 P.M.]
How's everything going? Does it look like we'll get a good deal with Flint Manufacturing?

Chapman, Carol [2:46 P.M.]
We're not quite there. But I'm fairly optimistic at this moment, although there are still several things we need to discuss.

Atwell, Lucy [2:48 P.M.]
Have you asked them when they can begin production of our products? Winters, Inc. said they could start manufacturing them within a week, and for a fairly low price.

Chapman, Carol [2:50 P.M.]
If Flint is not willing to budge on the price, we may have to consider going with Winters.

Lucas, Brian [2:52 P.M.]
Do you still want those documents you asked for at lunch? I spoke with Judy, and she said everything is almost ready.

Chapman, Carol [2:55 P.M.]
Actually, I need those as soon as possible. Once they're done, please bring them here to the conference room. Just knock on the door and come in.

Atwell, Lucy [2:56 P.M.]
I can take them, Brian. I've got some other files to deliver, so give them to me when they're ready.

Lucas, Brian [2:57 P.M.]
Sure thing. I'll drop by your office soon.

Chapman, Carol [2:59 P.M.]
OK, I have to get back to the meeting. Thank you all for your help.

SEND

5. What is the conversation mainly about?

(A) A project deadline
(B) The status of a delivery
(C) A manufacturing issue
(D) The progress of some negotiations

6. What is suggested about Winters, Inc.?

(A) It is a competitor of Flint Manufacturing.
(B) It has already begun production.
(C) It will sign a contract with Ms. Chapman's company.
(D) It plans to acquire a business.

7. At 2:57 P.M., what does Mr. Lucas mean when he writes, "Sure thing"?

(A) He will negotiate with Winters, Inc.
(B) He will deliver some documents.
(C) He will print some files.
(D) He will make a lunch reservation.

8. What is Ms. Chapman most likely going to do next?

(A) Copy some papers
(B) Visit Ms. Atwell's office
(C) Enter a conference room
(D) Contact Winters, Inc.

VOCA ··

break *n.* 휴식(시간) l negotiation *n.* 협상 l fairly *adv.* 꽤 l optimistic *adj.* 낙관적인, 낙천적인 l manufacture *v.* 제조하다 l be willing to V 기꺼이 ~하는 l budge *v.* 약간 움직이다, 의견을 바꾸게 하다 l deliver *v.* 배달하다 l drop by 들르다 l negotiate *v.* 협상하다

Questions 9-12 refer to the following online chat discussion.

Bailey Ahn [8:43 A.M.] Good morning. I'm glad we're all able to get together online. I'd like to find out what progress has been made on the upcoming concert. Louis, you got a lot done last week, right?

Louis Perez [8:44 A.M.] Yes, the Arrow City Council finally issued us a permit to hold the concert at Shyrock Community Park.

Tran Van Thanh [8:45 A.M.] That's great news!

Kylie Bryce [8:46 A.M.] How wonderful! For a while, I was concerned that they wouldn't come around.

Louis Perez [8:47 A.M.] Same here. But when I mentioned that some of the performing artists were famous and that they could attract more tourists, they were convinced.

Baily Ahn [8:47 A.M.] Great. Does anyone else have updates?

Tran Van Thanh [8:48 A.M.] I just got off the phone with Midvale Burgers, and they've agreed to set up a hamburger stand at the concert. I've contacted other eateries as well, and I should have most of their replies by tomorrow afternoon.

Kylie Bryce [8:48 A.M.] I'm still looking for someone to replace the Helzon Trio. I'm meeting with Ellen Hattori and her band today, so hopefully I can sign a contract with them.

Baily Ahn [8:49 A.M.] Really? Wow! Her latest album was a big hit, so I'm sure many people would want to see her sing live.

---

9. What are the writers discussing?

(A) An outdoor event
(B) An online lecture
(C) A new menu
(D) A radio talk show

10. At 8:46 A.M., what does Ms. Bryce most likely mean when she writes, "I was concerned that they wouldn't come around"?

(A) She was not sure a council meeting would be held.
(B) She thought a restaurant would be closed.
(C) She was not sure a permit would be given.
(D) She thought a promotion would bring in more tourists.

11. What is Ms. Thanh expecting?

(A) Changes to a guest list
(B) Responses from restaurants
(C) A reply from an artist
(D) An update about an application

12. Who most likely is Ms. Hattori?

(A) An event organizer
(B) A journalist
(C) A singer
(D) A head chef

VOCA ···

progress *n.* 진전, 진척 | **upcoming** *adj.* 다가오는, 곧 있을 | **issue** *v.* 발급하다 | **permit** *n.* 허가증 | **come around** (생각, 의견을) 바꾸다 | **attract** *v.* 불러모으다 | **stand** *n.* 가판대, 좌판 | **eatery** *n.* 식당 | **replace** *v.* 대체하다, 교체하다 | **hopefully** *adv.* 바라건대 | **sign a contract** 계약하다 | **bring in** 유치하다

편지·이메일

수신인과 발신인, 제목부터 파악하자! 회사와 고객 또는 회사와 회사 사이의 비즈니스 상황에서 발생할 수 있는 다양한 주제가 출제된다. Part 7에서 가장 많이 출제되는 지문 유형으로 매회 3~5개 정도의 지문이 출제된다.

🔍 지문 유형 확인하기

1. 자주 나오는 지문

간행물 무료 구독 안내, 공연 일정 안내, 세미나 참석 확인, 상점 확장 이전 안내, 업체 정보, 배송 안내, 주문 오류, 인터넷 접속 문제, 숙박 서비스 불만, 업무 지원 요청 등이 출제된다.

2. 편지나 이메일의 주제 또는 목적을 묻는다.

제목(Subject:, Re:)이나 지문의 앞부분에 나온다.

What is the purpose of this e-mail? 이 이메일의 목적은 무엇인가?

Why was the letter sent? 편지는 왜 보내졌는가?
↳ I'm writing to inform[notify / confirm] you that ~ 당신에게 ~을 알려[통보/확인]드리기 위해 편지를 쓰고 있다
↳ I'm very pleased[sorry] to inform[notify] you that ~ 당신에게 ~을 알려드리게[통보드리게] 되어서 기쁘다[유감이다]

3. 수신인 또는 발신인의 신분, 직업, 지위 등을 묻는다.

수신인은 상단에 나오는 To: 부분을 확인하고, 발신인은 상단의 From: 부분이나 이메일 후반부에 나오는 이름이나 지위 등을 확인한다.

Who most likely is Mr. Brown? Mr. Brown은 누구일 것 같은가?
What is Ms. Chandler's position? Ms. Chandler의 직위는 무엇인가?
For whom is this letter written? 이 편지는 누구를 위해 쓰였는가?

4. 편지나 이메일에 동봉되거나 첨부된 것, 당부나 요청 사항 등을 묻는다.

주로 지문의 끝부분인 마지막 단락에 나온다.

What is **enclosed** with the e-mail? 이메일에 첨부된 것은 무엇인가?
↳ We have enclosed[included / attached] ~ 우리는 ~을 동봉했다[첨부했다]

What is Mr. Kim **asked[required]** to do? Mr. Kim은 무엇을 하도록 요청받는가?
↳ Please let me know ~ 저에게 ~을 알려주세요.
↳ Could you / Would you ~ ~해 주실 수 있나요?
↳ Keep[Bear] in mind that ~ ~을 명심하세요.

Questions 1-3 refer to the following letter.

Dear Ms. Park, ···• 수신인

We appreciate you writing a letter describing the exceptionally good service you received on February 3 from Ms. Angela Zhang. A copy of it has been placed in Ms. Zhang's personnel file.
···• 편지의 목적
직원의 서비스를 칭찬
하는 고객 편지에 대한
감사 표현

It is rare that a customer takes the time to formally acknowledge the good service that an employee has provided, so we would like to do something for you in return. Please accept the enclosed voucher, which entitles you to a 15 percent discount on any item you wish to buy from any of our locations in the future.
···• 세부 정보:
동봉·첨부
감사의 표시로 15%
할인을 받을 수 있는
상품권 제공

Sincerely,

Brian Bae
Brian Bae
Customer Service Manager
ENCLOSURE
···• 발신인
발신인
관련 정보

편지의 목적

1. What is the purpose of the letter?

(A) To express gratitude
(B) To introduce an upcoming sale
(C) To respond to a complaint
(D) To announce a new location

세부사항: 편지와 동봉된 것

2. What is enclosed with the letter?

(A) A catalog
(B) A prepaid mailing label
(C) A product sample
(D) A coupon

세부사항: 인물의 정체 또는 직업

3. Who is Mr. Bae?

(A) A company executive
(B) A factory supervisor
(C) A customer service manager
(D) A news reporter

[1-3] 다음 편지에 관한 문제입니다.

Dear Ms. Park,

Ms. Park에게,

① We appreciate you writing a letter describing the exceptionally good service you received on February 3 from Ms. Angela Zhang. **A copy of it has been placed in Ms. Zhang's personnel file.**

2월 3일 Ms. Angela Zhang으로부터 받으신 매우 훌륭한 서비스에 대해 자세히 적어 주신 서신에 감사 드립니다. 편지 사본은 Ms. Zhang의 파일에 보관될 것입니다.

③ It is rare that a customer takes the time to formally acknowledge the good service that an employee has provided, so we would like to do something for you in return. **②** Please accept the enclosed voucher, which entitles you to a 15 percent discount on any item you wish to buy from any of our locations in the future.

고객이 시간을 내서 직원이 제공한 훌륭한 서비스를 공식적으로 인정해 주시는 사례는 드뭅니다. 그래서 보답으로 고객님께 무언가 해드리고 싶습니다. 부디 동봉된 상품권을 받아주세요. 이 상품권은 앞으로 저희 매장 어디서든 고객님이 원하시는 어떤 상품이든 15% 할인을 받을 수 있도록 해드립니다.

Sincerely,

진심으로,

Brian Bae

Brian Bae
Customer Service Manager
ENCLOSURE

Brian Bae
고객 서비스 매니저
동봉물 재중

• 수신인

• 편지의 목적
직원의 서비스를 칭찬하는 고객 편지에 대한 감사 표현

• 세부 정보:
동봉·첨부
감사의 표시로 15% 할인을 받을 수 있는 상품권 제공

• 발신인
발신인
관련 정보

1. What is the purpose of the letter?

(A) To express gratitude
(B) To introduce an upcoming sale
(C) To respond to a complaint
(D) To announce a new location

편지의 목적은 무엇인가?

(A) 감사를 표현하기 위해
(B) 곧 있을 세일을 소개하기 위해
(C) 불만에 응대하기 위해
(D) 새 지점을 알리기 위해

해설 편지의 목적을 묻는 문제이다. 편지의 목적은 주로 글의 앞부분에 위치한다. 첫 번째 단락 첫 번째 줄 'We appreciate you writing a letter describing the exceptionally good service you received on February 3 from Ms. Angela Zhang.'에서 고객이 직원에게서 받은 매우 훌륭한 서비스에 감동해 편지를 보낸 것에 대한 감사를 표하고 있다. 따라서 정답은 (A) To express gratitude이다.

2. What is enclosed with the letter?

(A) A catalog
(B) A prepaid mailing label
(C) A product sample
(D) A coupon

편지와 함께 동봉된 것은 무엇인가?

(A) 카탈로그
(B) 선지불된 우편 라벨
(C) 제품 샘플
(D) 할인권

해설 세부 사항을 묻는 질문이므로 키워드 enclosed가 지문에 언급된 부분을 찾아본다. 두 번째 단락 세 번째 줄 'Please accept the enclosed voucher, which entitles you to a 15 percent discount on any item'에서 15% 할인을 제공하는 상품권을 동봉한다고 하였으므로 정답은 (D) A coupon이다.

3. Who is Mr. Bae?

(A) A company executive
(B) A factory supervisor
(C) A customer service manager
(D) A news reporter

Mr. Bae은 누구인가?

(A) 회사 간부
(B) 공장 관리자
(C) 고객 서비스 매니저
(D) 취재 기자

해설 세부 사항 질문이므로 키워드 Mr. Bae가 언급된 맨 마지막 부분에서 Customer Service Manager라는 직책을 확인할 수 있다. 따라서 정답은 (C) A customer service manager이다.

VOCA

appreciate v. 감사하다 | describe v. 설명하다 | exceptionally adv. 유난히, 특별히 | good service 좋은 서비스 | copy n. 한 부 | rare adj. 드문 | formally adv. 정식으로, 공식적으로 | acknowledge v. 인정하다 | in return 보답으로, 답례로 | accept v. 받아들이다, 수락하다 | enclosed adj. 동봉된 | voucher n. 상품권 | entitle v. 자격을 주다 | discount n. 할인 v. 할인하다 | item n. 상품 | location n. 지점, 위치 | in the future 미래에, 추후에 | gratitude n. 고마움, 감사 | upcoming adj. 다가오는, 곧 있을 | prepaid adj. 선불된

해설서 p.81

Questions 1-2 refer to the following e-mail.

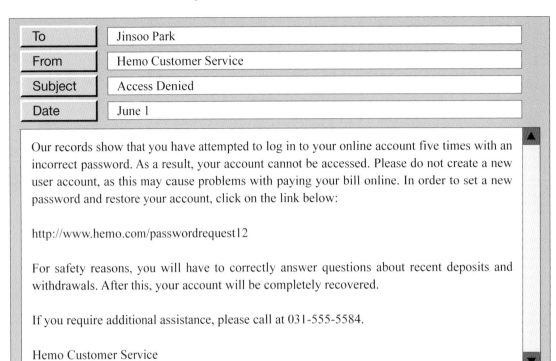

To	Jinsoo Park
From	Hemo Customer Service
Subject	Access Denied
Date	June 1

Our records show that you have attempted to log in to your online account five times with an incorrect password. As a result, your account cannot be accessed. Please do not create a new user account, as this may cause problems with paying your bill online. In order to set a new password and restore your account, click on the link below:

http://www.hemo.com/passwordrequest12

For safety reasons, you will have to correctly answer questions about recent deposits and withdrawals. After this, your account will be completely recovered.

If you require additional assistance, please call at 031-555-5584.

Hemo Customer Service

1. What is suggested about Mr. Park?

(A) He accessed a Web site from a mobile device.

(B) He forgot his password.

(C) He added his spouse as an account holder.

(D) He made more than one account.

2. What type of company is Hemo?

(A) A Web site developer

(B) An Internet service provider

(C) An online shopping mall

(D) A financial institution

VOCA ·······

record *n.* 기록 | attempt *v.* 시도하다 | account *n.* 계좌 | access *v.* 접근하다 *n.* 접근 | restore *v.* 복구하다 | deposit *n.* 예금, 예치 | withdrawal *n.* 인출 | completely *adv.* 완전히 | recover *v.* 복구하다, 회복하다 | assistance *n.* 도움, 지원 | spouse *n.* 배우자 | account holder 예금주 | institution *n.* 기관

Questions 3-4 refer to the following letter.

Alltria Bank
8291 Berry Drive
Sacramento, CA 92671
555-8993

December 8

Dear Ms. Huff,

Our records indicate that your checking account is overdrawn. On December 3, you wrote a check for $81.29 to the Federal Postal Service. However, your account balance at the time was $67.05. Unfortunately, your account does not have overdraft protection, so your account balance as of today is -$20.24. Please note that there is a $1/per day fee when your checking account is overdrawn. Please contact me as soon as possible to take care of this matter.

Sincerely,

Jeanie Chitalli

Jeanie Chitalli
Manager, Sacramento Branch
Alltria Bank
555-8993

---

3. What is the main purpose of the letter?

(A) To inform a customer of an issue with an account
(B) To convey gratitude for a recent performance
(C) To seek some information about account benefits
(D) To promote a closer branch to a loyal customer

4. What is indicated about Alltria Bank?

(A) Many customers overdraw their accounts.
(B) It provides overdraft protection without request.
(C) It is willing to compromise with its customers.
(D) It charges a fee for overdrawn accounts.

VOCA ··

record *n.* 기록 ∣ indicate *v.* 나타내다 ∣ checking account 당좌예금계좌 ∣ overdrawn *adj.* 초과 인출한 ∣ check *n.* 수표 ∣ Federal Postal Service 연방 우체국 ∣ postal service 체신부 ∣ account balance 계좌 잔고 ∣ overdraft *n.* 당좌 대월, 마이너스 통장 설정 ∣ fee *n.* 수수료 ∣ take care of ~을 처리하다 ∣ branch *n.* 지점 ∣ convey *v.* 전달하다, 전하다 ∣ gratitude *n.* 사의, 감사 ∣ performance *n.* 실적 ∣ seek *v.* 구하다, 찾다 ∣ benefit *n.* 혜택 ∣ promote *v.* 홍보하다 ∣ loyal customer 단골고객 ∣ request *n.* 요청 ∣ compromise *v.* 타협하다 ∣ charge *v.* 청구하다

Questions 5-7 refer to the following e-mail.

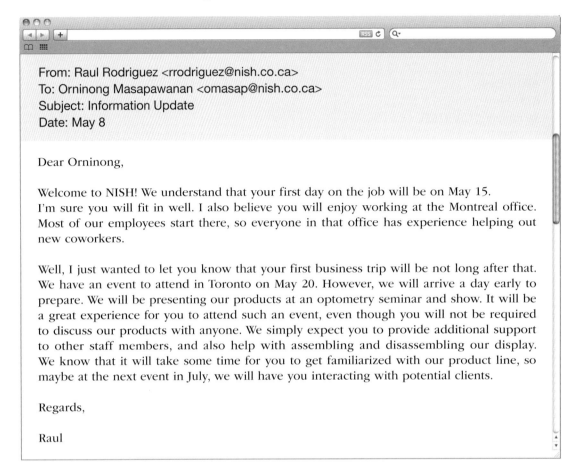

From: Raul Rodriguez <rrodriguez@nish.co.ca>
To: Orninong Masapawanan <omasap@nish.co.ca>
Subject: Information Update
Date: May 8

Dear Orninong,

Welcome to NISH! We understand that your first day on the job will be on May 15.
I'm sure you will fit in well. I also believe you will enjoy working at the Montreal office.
Most of our employees start there, so everyone in that office has experience helping out
new coworkers.

Well, I just wanted to let you know that your first business trip will be not long after that.
We have an event to attend in Toronto on May 20. However, we will arrive a day early to
prepare. We will be presenting our products at an optometry seminar and show. It will be
a great experience for you to attend such an event, even though you will not be required
to discuss our products with anyone. We simply expect you to provide additional support
to other staff members, and also help with assembling and disassembling our display.
We know that it will take some time for you to get familiarized with our product line, so
maybe at the next event in July, we will have you interacting with potential clients.

Regards,

Raul

5. What is a purpose of the e-mail?

(A) To greet a new colleague
(B) To confirm a reservation
(C) To suggest some topics for a speech
(D) To schedule a visit for an interview

6. When will Ms. Masapawanan probably arrive in Toronto?

(A) On May 14
(B) On May 15
(C) On May 19
(D) On May 21

7. What will Ms. Masapawanan NOT do in Toronto?

(A) Attend an optometry workshop
(B) Discuss products with clients
(C) Work on the display
(D) Assist coworkers

VOCA ···

business trip 출장 | **fit in** 어울리다, 맞다 | **attend** v. 참가하다, 참석하다 | **present** v. 소개하다, 제출하다 | **optometry** n. 검안, 시력
검사 | **require** v. 필요하다, 요구하다 | **additional** adj. 추가적인 | **staff member** 직원 | **assemble** v. 조립하다 | **disassemble** v. 분해하
다, 해체하다 | **display** n. 전시, 진열 | **familiarize** v. 익숙하게 하다 | **product line** 제품군 | **interact** v. 소통하다, 교류하다 | **potential**
adj. 가능성 있는, 잠재적인 | **schedule** n. 일정, 스케줄. v. 일정을 잡다 | **greet** v. 환영하다 | **assist** v. 돕다

Questions 8-11 refer to the following letter.

Nuvallis Furniture

Aubree Thompson
General Manager, Stanner's Home Décor
1400 Terrace Road
Brisbane 4000, Australia

3 July

Dear Ms. Thompson,

This letter is to inform you that Nuvallis will be relocating soon. Effective Tuesday, 17 July, we will be closing down our store in Brisbane. Starting Tuesday, 2 August, we will be operating from 250 Flannigan Drive in Gold Coast. Our new location has much more space, which will allow us to stock a wider selection of furniture.

Please be aware that we will not be open from 17 July to 1 August while we carry out the move. On the day of our grand reopening, we will hold a celebration where we will introduce some of our newest products and hold a raffle for prizes. We also invite you to participate in the Know Your Furniture competition.

We regret to inform you that there will be a modest price increase in our products and delivery services as we have invested considerably in building our new facility. However, since your company has been our loyal customer for over 10 years, you will be excluded from the above-mentioned price increases for one year. In addition, we will take 15 percent off any products you purchase in the month of August.

Also, as of August 2, our new telephone number will be 07-843-9526. We appreciate your business and look forward to serving you again in the future.

Sincerely,

Lydia Perkins

Lydia Perkins
Director of Operations, Nuvallis Furniture

---

8. What is suggested about Nuvallis Furniture?

(A) It currently has two locations.
(B) It will expand its inventory.
(C) It has purchased another company.
(D) It will hire additional delivery drivers.

9. The phrase "carry out" in paragraph 2, line 1, is closest in meaning to

(A) remove
(B) reconsider
(C) accomplish
(D) lift

10. What can a Nuvallis Furniture customer do on August 2?

(A) Tour a factory in Brisbane
(B) Enter a contest
(C) Get a special discount
(D) Participate in a product survey

11. What is NOT indicated about Stanner's Home Décor?

(A) It has been operating for at least 10 years.
(B) It is located in Brisbane.
(C) It will receive a price cut on purchases made at Nuvallis Furniture next month.
(D) It plans to increase its orders from Nuvallis Furniture.

VOCA ··

inform v. 알리다 | relocate v. 이전하다 | raffle n. 추첨식 판매법, 복권 판매 | invite v. (정식으로) 요청하다 | participate in 참가하다 |
modest adj. 별로 많지 않은 | invest v. 투자하다 | exclude v. 제외하다 | expand v. 확장하다 | inventory n. 재고품 목록 | remove v.
제거하다 | reconsider v. 재고하다 | accomplish v. 이루다, 성취하다 | lift v. 올리다, 들어올리다 | enter a contest 대회에 참가하다 |
survey n. 설문조사 | operate v. 영업하다; 작동되다, 가동되다 | price cut 가격 인하

광고

제목이나 도입부에서 광고 내용을 확인한다! 광고는 직원을 모집하는 구인 광고와 상품이나 서비스, 행사 등을 홍보하는 일반 상업 광고가 있다. 편지·이메일 유형 다음으로 가장 많이 출제되고 있으며, 매회 2~3개 정도의 지문이 출제된다.

🔍 지문 유형 확인하기

1. 자주 나오는 지문

구인 광고는 회사에 공석이 발생했을 때 직원을 모집하는 광고로, 담당 업무, 자격 요건, 지원 방법 등을 다룬다. 상품 및 서비스 광고는 업체의 제품이나 서비스 소개, 할인 이유, 할인 대상자, 할인율, 할인 기간 등을 다룬다. 중고 자동차 매매, 항공 카드 혜택, 스포츠용품 할인, 극장의 공연 광고 등이 출제된다.

2. 광고의 목적이나 모집하고 있는 직책 또는 광고 상품을 묻는다.

광고의 제목이나 앞부분에서 무엇을 광고하고 있는지 밝히고 있다.

What is the **main purpose** of the advertisement? 광고의 주요 목적은 무엇인가?

What position is being **advertised**? 어떤 직책이 광고되고 있는가?

What is being **advertised**? 무엇이 광고되고 있는가?
　↳ [관심] Are you interested in ~? ~에 관심이 있으신가요? / Are you looking for ~? ~을 찾고 계신가요?

3. 구인 광고는 지원 자격이나 지원 방법을 묻는다.

What is (NOT) a **requirement** for the position?
이 직책의 필수 조건은 무엇인가? / 이 직책의 필수 조건이 아닌 것은 무엇인가?
　↳ [자격 요건] experience in the field 그 분야에서의 경험, requirement for the position 직책의 필수 요건,
　　qualification 자격

How should the candidate **apply** for the position? 지원자는 이 직책에 어떻게 지원해야 하는가?
　↳ [지원 방법] visit our Web site 저희 웹사이트를 방문하세요, send your résumé via e-mail
　　이메일로 이력서를 보내주세요

4. 상품 광고는 상품의 특징, 할인 혜택, 구입 방법을 묻는다.

서비스나 행사 광고는 해당하는 대상, 할인 혜택, 장소, 날짜, 시간 등을 묻는다.

What is **indicated** about **product #949**? 제품번호 949에 대해 언급된 사실은 무엇인가?
　↳ [혜택] discount 할인, coupon 쿠폰, promotion 판촉 행사

What is **NOT** a **feature** of **product #949**? 제품번호 949의 특징이 아닌 것은 무엇인가?
　↳ [제품의 장점] innovative features 혁신적인 특징들, special products 특별한 제품들

Questions 1-3 refer to the following advertisement.

Job Opening: Mathematics Instructor

The Powell College of Technology is a leading private college offering degree and certification programs in the areas of technology, business, and health sciences. Instructors at the Powell College of Technology are responsible for the training and supervision of students as they prepare for their chosen career. Mathematics instructors are responsible for providing hands-on classroom instruction, preparing and utilizing approved lesson plans, and preparing student progress and grade reports.

Applicants must have prior teaching experience. A master's degree in mathematics and excellent speaking and written communication skills are required. Candidates must have at least five years of teaching experience. We offer competitive salaries and generous benefits.

Please send a copy of your résumé along with a cover letter and three letters of recommendation by August 23 to:

Ann Russo, Human Resources Director
Powell College of Technology
Columbia, South Carolina

- 구인 광고
- 회사 정보
  기술 대학의 수학
  강사 채용
- 업무 내용
  교실 수업, 수업 계획안
  을 준비, 학생의 학업
  진척도와 성적 보고
- 채용 조건
  교수 경력, 석사 학위
  의사소통 능력이 필수
- 지원 서류 및 지원 방법
  이력서, 자기소개서,
  추천서를 제출해야 함
- 회사 위치

세부사항: 채용 조건

1. What is NOT a requirement of the job?

(A) A degree
(B) Management skills
(C) Experience in teaching
(D) Outstanding speaking skills

세부사항: 지원 서류

2. What must the applicant submit by August 23?

(A) Information about salary
(B) Letters of recommendation
(C) Contact information of previous employers
(D) An online application form

세부사항: 지원 방법

3. How should the candidate apply for the job?

(A) By phone
(B) By e-mail
(C) By fax
(D) By mail

[1-3] 다음 광고에 관한 문제입니다.

Job Opening: Mathematics Instructor

채용 공고: 수학 강사

The Powell College of Technology is a leading private college offering degree and certification programs in the areas of technology, business, and health sciences. Instructors at the Powell College of Technology are responsible for the training and supervision of students as they prepare for their chosen career. Mathematics instructors are responsible for providing hands-on classroom instruction, preparing and utilizing approved lesson plans, and preparing student progress and grade reports.

Powell 기술대학은 기술과 비즈니스, 그리고 보건과학 분야에서 학위와 졸업장, 그리고 수료 프로그램을 제공하는 앞서가는 사립 대학입니다. Powell 기술대학의 강사들은 학생들이 선택한 진로를 준비할 때 학생들을 훈련시키고 감독하는 책임을 맡고 있습니다. 수학 강사는 실제 교실 수업을 제공하고 승인된 수업 계획안을 준비하고 활용하며 학생의 학업 진척도와 성적 보고를 준비할 책임이 있습니다.

❶ Applicants must have prior teaching experience. A master's degree in mathematics and excellent speaking and written communication skills are required. Candidates must have at least five years of teaching experience. We offer competitive salaries and generous benefits.

지원자들은 반드시 이전 교수 경력이 있어야 합니다. 수학 석사 학위, 그리고 탁월한 구술 및 문서상 의사소통 능력이 필요합니다. 지원자들은 적어도 5년 이상의 교수 경력이 있어야 합니다. 저희는 경쟁력 있는 급여와 풍부한 복지 혜택을 제공합니다.

❷ ❸ Please send a copy of your résumé along with a cover letter and three letters of recommendation by August 23 to:

자기소개서와 추천서 3부와 함께 귀하의 이력서 사본을 8월 23일까지 다음 주소로 보내주세요:

Ann Russo, Human Resources Director
Powell College of Technology
Columbia, South Carolina

Ann Russo, 인사부 부장
Powell 기술대학
컬럼비아, 사우스캐롤라이나

- 구인 광고

- 회사 정보
  기술 대학의 수학
  강사 채용
- 업무 내용
  교실 수업, 수업 계획안
  을 준비, 학생의 학업 진
  척도와 성적 보고

- 채용 조건
  교수 경력, 석사 학위
  의사소통 능력이 필수

- 지원 서류 및
  지원 방법
  이력서, 자기소개서,
  추천서를 제출해야 함

- 회사 위치

1. What is NOT a requirement of the job?

(A) A degree
(B) Management skills
(C) Experience in teaching
(D) Outstanding speaking skills

그 일자리에 대한 필수 조건이 아닌 것은 무엇인가?

(A) 학위
(B) 관리 능력
(C) 교수 경력
(D) 뛰어난 구술 능력

> **해설** 세부 사항 문제이므로 키워드 requirement가 언급된 부분을 지문에서 찾아 선택지와 대조하며 소거한다. 채용 조건은 두 번째 단락 첫 두 문장에 must와 required가 있는 부분에 언급되어 있다. 필수 요건 세 가지는 교수 경험, 수학과 석사 학위, 구술 및 문서상 의사소통 능력이다. 관리 능력은 언급되지 않았으므로 정답은 (B) Management skills이다.

2. What must the applicant submit by August 23?

(A) Information about salary
(B) Letters of recommendation
(C) Contact information of previous employers
(D) An online application form

지원자는 8월 23일까지 무엇을 제출해야 하는가?

(A) 연봉에 관한 정보
(B) 추천서
(C) 이전 고용주의 연락처
(D) 온라인 지원서

> **해설** 세부 사항 문제이므로 키워드 by August 23가 지문에 언급된 부분을 찾아본다. 세 번째 단락에서 언급된 3가지 제출해야 할 서류는 이력서, 자기소개서, 추천서이다. 따라서 정답은 (B) Letters of recommendation이다.

3. How should the candidate apply for the job?

(A) By phone
(B) By e-mail
(C) By fax
(D) By mail

지원자는 그 직책에 어떻게 지원해야 하는가?

(A) 전화로
(B) 이메일로
(C) 팩스로
(D) 우편으로

> **해설** 지원 방법을 묻는 세부 사항 문제이다. 세 번째 단락에서 지원 서류를 보내는 방법을 언급하며 우편 주소를 알려주고 있으므로 정답은 (D) By mail이다.

VOCA ···

leading *adj.* 선도하는, 일류의 ǀ certification *n.* 수료 ǀ responsible *adj.* 책임이 있는, 책임을 져야 할 ǀ supervision *n.* 감독, 관리 ǀ hands-on *adj.* 실제의, 직접 손으로 만지는 ǀ utilize *v.* 활용하다 ǀ approved *adj.* 공인된, 정평 있는 ǀ candidate *n.* 지원자 ǀ competitive *adj.* 경쟁의, 경합하는 ǀ generous *adj.* 많은, 풍부한, 인심 좋은 ǀ outstanding *adj.* 뛰어난 ǀ letter of recommendation 추천서

해설서 p.83

Questions 1-2 refer to the following advertisement.

Blackstone Chimney Services

We have offered our services with pride for more than 15 years. As you know, cold weather is coming and preparing your fireplace and chimney for use is important. So, for a limited time, Blackstone Chimney Services is offering you a special on cleanings so that it can keep your chimney functional and safe.

When you call for an appointment, you can use the promotional code AFE4410 to receive $20 off. We guarantee that certified technicians will come to your home within 24 hours in order to complete the work. As part of the promotion, we also inspect chimneys for home buyers or sellers, and provide certification that the chimney is safe.

In addition, we offer chimney rebuilding and repair services. Call Blackstone Chimney Services now at 773-9412.The promotional period ends on November 20.

---

1. What is indicated about the company?

(A) It is hiring new employees.
(B) It is an established business.
(C) It is celebrating an anniversary.
(D) It is improving its service.

2. What does promotional offer include?

(A) Fireplace repair
(B) Chimney inspections
(C) A free thermostat
(D) Chimney construction

VOCA ··

chimney n. 굴뚝 | **pride** n. 자부심 | **prepare** v. 준비하다 | **fireplace** n. 벽난로 | **functional** adj. 가동되는 | **appointment** n. 약속 | **guarantee** v. 보장하다 | **certified** adj. 증명된, 면허증을 가진 | **promotion** n. 홍보, 판촉 | **inspect** v. 점검하다 | **certification** n. 증명, 증명서 교부 | **promotional period** 행사 기간 | **established** adj. 인정받는, 확실히 자리를 잡은 | **thermostat** n. 온도 조절 장치

Questions 3-4 refer to the following advertisement.

KJA National

Ready for a Wonderful Holiday? KJA is here to help!

You can save up to $150 on companion fares from March 8 to July 27.
- Valid only for flights within the U.S.A.
- Applies to one companion fare only.
- Must book by February 11.

Visit www.kjanational.com in order to reserve your car and hotel as well. Moreover, join our loyalty club so that you can receive useful information, such as last-minute sales and all future discounts.

3. What is being discounted?

(A) Hotel packages
(B) Airplane tickets
(C) Car rentals
(D) The loyalty club annual fee

4. What is implied about KJA?

(A) It was recently established.
(B) It is based in the USA.
(C) It only offers discounts during the holidays.
(D) It just introduced its loyalty club.

VOCA ···

save v. 절약하다, 아끼다; 저장하다 | **up to** ～까지 | **companion** n. 동행자, 동반자 | **fare** n. 요금 | **valid** adj. 유효한 | **apply** v. 적용하다, 신청하다 | **book** v. 예약하다 | **last-minute** adj. 막바지의 | **establish** v. 설립하다 | **based in** ～에 기반을 둔 | **introduce** v. 도입하다

PART 7 ▪ UNIT 09. 광고   **283**

Tired of your commute?
Choose the Telegraph Connector!

The Telegraph Connector just introduced two new bus lines.
The Lee Line runs from Western Fairfax County into D.C. And the Gunston Line runs
north from the Pohick Peninsula to Union Station in D.C.
Use this advertisement for a complimentary one-way trip on the Connector!

Take a ride with us today!

The Telegraph Connector

t-connector.com

5. What is indicated about the Telegraph Connector?

(A) It recently expanded its routes.
(B) It has been around for a while.
(C) It is becoming increasingly popular.
(D) It offers discounts for groups.

6. What can customers receive with the advertisement?

(A) A discount on multiple fares
(B) A voucher for a toll
(C) A parking pass
(D) A free ride on the bus

VOCA ···

tired of ~에 진절머리가 난 | **commute** *n.* 통근 | **line** *n.* 노선 | **run** *v.* 운영하다 | **complimentary** *adj.* 무료의 | **one-way** *adj.* 편도의 | **trip** *n.* 여행, 이동 | **recently** *adj.* 최근에 | **expand** *v.* 확장하다 | **route** *n.* 경로, 노선 | **for a while** 한동안, 잠시 | **discount** *n.* 할인 | **multiple** *adj.* 많은, 다수의 | **fare** *n.* 요금 | **voucher** *n.* 할인권, 쿠폰 | **toll** *n.* 통행료 | **free ride** 무료승차

Questions 7-9 refer to the following advertisement.

Bagan Fitness and Recreation Center

Bagan Fitness and Recreation Center opened last month, bringing a spectacular new exercise facility to Belmont County. Located on top of a large hill, the 8,000 sq. ft. center offers a multitude of exercise options for everyone. From the olympic-size, ten-lane indoor swimming pool to its four indoor basketball courts, this place has it all!

In addition, Bagan Fitness and Recreation Center houses a daycare and play center. So, parents who visit for a workout can leave their young ones with our skillful and caring workers. And the kids will get plenty of exercise, too! The play center has a ball pool that kids just love. It also has a jungle gym, padded climbing walls, and an obstacle course.

For general information about Bagan Fitness and Recreation Center, feel free to visit our Web site at www.bagancenter.com. For information about pricing or to simply get directions, contact our front desk at 800-718-1000.

---

7. What is indicated about Bagan Fitness and Recreation Center?

(A) It will be opening soon.
(B) It offers swimming classes.
(C) It will host a sports competition.
(D) It is located in Belmont County.

8. What is available at Bagan Fitness and Recreation Center?

(A) Child care
(B) Basketball lessons
(C) Tennis courts
(D) Free parking

9. According to the advertisement, how can one get information about fees?

(A) By going to a Web site
(B) By emailing a director
(C) By calling a front desk
(D) By reading a pamphlet

VOCA

spectacular *adj.* 굉장한, 극적인 | exercise *n.* 운동 | facility *n.* 시설 | a multitude of 다수의 | option *n.* 선택권 | lane *n.* (수영장의) 레인 | basketball court 농구장 | in addition 게다가 | house *v.* 수용하다, 보관하다 | daycare center 탁아시설 | workout *n.* 운동 | skillful *adj.* 숙련된, 능숙한 | caring *adj.* 배려하는, 보살피는 | padded *adj.* 푹신한 | climbing wall 암벽등반용 인공 벽 | obstacle course 장애물 코스 | get directions 길 안내를 받다 | host *v.* 개최하다 | child care 보육, 탁아 | according to ~에 의하면 | fee *n.* 요금 | director *n.* 임원, 이사 | pamphlet *v.* 소책자

공지·회람

무엇을 전달하고 있는가? 언제, 어디서인가?를 확인한다! 공지는 기관이나 업체에서 이용자나 고객에게 필요한 주의 사항이나 변동 사항, 행사 안내 등 각종 정보를 알리는 글이고, 회람은 주로 회사 내부의 다양한 전달 사항을 알리는 글이다.

🔍 지문 유형 확인하기

1. 자주 나오는 지문

공지에서는 시설 보수 공사, 셔틀버스 운행 시간 변경, 열차 운임 인상, 재개점 행사, 교환 및 환불 정책 등이 출제된다. 사내 회람에서는 회사 정책, 인사 발령, 추가 근무, 보수 공사 등이 출제된다.

2. 공지나 회람의 목적 또는 주제를 묻는다.

What is the **purpose** of this announcement? 이 공지의 목적은 무엇인가?
Why was this memo **written**? 이 회람이 쓰여진 이유는 무엇인가?
What is being **announced**? 공지되고 있는 것은 무엇인가?

3. 공지나 회람을 전달받는 대상을 묻는다.

For whom is this memo most likely intended? 이 회람은 누구를 위한 것 같은가?
Where would the notice most likely be found? 공지를 주로 볼 수 있는 곳은 어디일 것 같은가?

4. 공지나 회람의 세부 정보를 묻는다.

What is **indicated** about the event? 행사에 대해 언급된 것은 무엇인가?
What will **take place** on October 1? 10월 1일에 어떤 일이 발생할 것인가?
What program is **offered every Friday**? 매주 금요일에는 어떤 프로그램이 제공되는가?
According to the notice, **what** is **NOT** being **offered**? 공지에 따르면, 제공되지 않는 것은 무엇인가?

Questions 1-2 refer to the following notice.

City Subway Service
Notice to All Passengers

The Subway Workers' Union has announced a 48-hour strike on the city's subway network that will begin at 8 P.M. tonight, July 18 and end at 8 P.M. on July 20. Normal service will resume on July 21. The strike will cause significant disruption, and we do not expect any subway trains to be operational during this period. We therefore offer the following advice for passengers: Passengers arriving at City Airport will be able to travel downtown. The City Express (not part of the subway network) will be fully operational, and we plan to double the number of trains operating on this line during the strike period.

For passengers downtown, a large number of extra services will be provided to help you move around the city. Extra bus and river services, including free travel across the river from Buxley Bridge to Fenstatton Embankment, will be provided.

For further information, go to www.citytransportation.org.

● 회사 이름
● 공지 대상
● 공지의 목적
지하철 파업으로
인한 불편 공지
● 세부 정보
파업 기간 동안 이용
가능한 교통 수단
● 세부 정보
추가 교통편에 대한
더 자세한 교통 정보는
웹사이트에서 제공

공지의 목적

1. What is the main purpose of the notice?

(A) To notify riders of alternate services
(B) To encourage travelers to take a bus to the airport
(C) To explain the reasons for a strike
(D) To publicize a new director of the City Express

세부사항: 웹사이트

2. What will happen on July 21?

(A) Buxley Bridge will be closed.
(B) The city subway system will run normally.
(C) Bus fares will be reduced.
(D) The number of trains will double.

[1-2] 다음 공지에 관한 문제입니다.

City Subway Service
Notice to All Passengers
도시 지하철 서비스
전 승객을 위한 공지

••••• 회사 이름
••••• 공지 대상

❶ The Subway Workers' Union has announced a 48-hour strike on the city's subway network that will begin at 8 P.M. tonight, July 18 and end at 8 P.M. on July 20. ❷ Normal service will resume on July 21. The strike will cause significant disruption, and we do not expect any subway trains to be operational during this period. ❶ We therefore offer the following advice for passengers: Passengers arriving at City Airport will be able to travel downtown. The City Express (not part of the subway network) will be fully operational, and we plan to double the number of trains operating on this line during the strike period.

••••• 공지의 목적
지하철 파업으로
인한 불편 공지

지하철 노조가 7월 18일 오늘 저녁 8시부터 시작해서 7월 20일 저녁 8시에 끝나는 도시 지하철 철도 노선의 48시간 파업을 선언했습니다. 지하철 정상 운행은 7월 21일에 재개될 것입니다. 이 파업은 엄청난 혼란을 일으킬 것이며 이 기간 동안 어떤 열차도 운행되지 않을 것이라 예상됩니다. 따라서 저희는 승객 여러분께 다음 사항을 권장합니다. City 공항에 도착하시는 승객분들은 시내로 이동하실 수 있습니다. (지하철 노선에 포함되지 않는) 도시 급행 열차는 전면 운행할 것이며 파업 기간 중에는 이 노선으로 운행하는 열차 수를 두 배로 늘릴 예정입니다.

❶ For passengers downtown, a large number of extra services will be provided to help you move around the city. Extra bus and river services, including free travel across the river from Buxley Bridge to Fenstatton Embankment, will be provided.

••••• 세부 정보
파업 기간 동안 이용
가능한 교통 수단

시내에서 이동하시는 승객을 위해서는 여러분들의 도시 주변 이동을 돕기 위해 많은 추가 서비스가 제공될 것입니다. Buxley 다리에서 Fenstatton 제방을 지나 강을 가로질러 이동하는 무료 운행 서비스를 비롯하여 추가 버스 및 선박 서비스가 제공될 것입니다.

For further information, go to www.citytransportation.org.

••••• 추가 정보
추가 교통편에 대한
더 자세한 교통 정보는
웹사이트에서 제공

좀 더 자세한 정보를 원하시면, www.citytransportation.org를 방문해 주세요.

1. What is the main purpose of the notice?

  (A) To notify riders of alternate services
  (B) To encourage travelers to take a bus to the airport
  (C) To explain the reasons for a strike
  (D) To publicize a new director of the City Express

공지의 주요 목적은 무엇인가?

  (A) 승객들에게 대체 서비스를 알리기 위해
  (B) 여행객들이 공항까지 버스를 탈 것을 장려하기 위해
  (C) 파업의 원인을 설명하기 위해
  (D) 도시 급행 열차의 새 책임자를 알리기 위해

> **해설** 글의 목적을 묻는 문제의 단서는 주로 지문 앞부분에서 찾을 수 있다. 첫 단락의 앞부분에서 지하철 노조의 파업이 있을 것을 알리며 중간쯤 'We therefore offer the following advice for passengers' 이하 부분에서 파업으로 인한 혼란을 피하기 위해 승객들에게 대책을 알리고 있다. 따라서 정답은 (A) To notify riders of alternate services이다.

2. What will happen on July 21?

  (A) Buxley Bridge will be closed.
  (B) The city subway system will run normally.
  (C) Bus fares will be reduced.
  (D) The number of trains will double.

7월 21일에 무슨 일이 일어날 것인가?

  (A) Buxley 다리가 폐쇄될 것이다.
  (B) 시 지하철 시스템이 정상적으로 운영될 것이다.
  (C) 버스 요금이 인하될 것이다.
  (D) 기차의 수가 두 배가 될 것이다.

> **해설** 세부 사항을 묻는 질문이다. 키워드는 July 21이다. 첫 번째 단락에서, 지하철 노조가 7월 18일부터 20일까지 파업을 선언했다고 하면서 정상 운행이 7월 21일에 재개될 것이라고 했으므로 정답은 (B) The city subway will run normally.이다.

VOCA ··

subway service 지하철 운행 서비스 I **workers' union** 노조 I **announce** v. 발표하다, 알리다 I **strike** n. 파업 I **network** n. (도로 · 신경 등의) 망, (인간 · 기업체의) 망, 관계 I **resume** v. 재개하다, 다시 시작하다 I **cause** v. 일으키다, 야기하다 I **significant** adj. 커다란, 엄청난 I **disruption** n. 혼란, 피해 I **expect** v. 예상하다 I **operational** adj. 운영상의 I **period** n. 기간 I **passenger** n. 승객 I **downtown** adv. 시내로, 도심지로 I **fully operational** 완전히 가동되는 I **plan to** ~할 계획이다 I **double** v. 두 배로 만들다 I **a large number of** 다수의, 많은 I **move around** 움직이다, 돌아다니다 I **including** prep. ~를 포함하여 I **notify** v. 알리다, 통지하다 I **publicize** v. 알리다, 홍보하다 I **fare** n. (교통) 요금 I **double** v. 두 배로 되다

해설서 p.85

Questions 1-2 refer to the following notice.

Notice to Moore City Contractors

Starting June 1, there will be some changes to the city's application process for building permits. Fees for building permit applications will remain the same. However, decisions on applications will now take 14 days instead of 7. Please keep this in mind when planning a construction project.

In addition, applications should now be submitted to the Development Services Office at our new building on Main Street. The Building Permit Office will be closed with the closing of the old Moore City Government Building.

Thank you for your cooperation.

Moore City Government

---

1. What is the purpose of the notice?

(A) To explain some changes to a government service
(B) To seek investment for a new building project
(C) To introduce a new schedule for employees
(D) To detail the closing of a private building

2. What is NOT stated about permit applications?

(A) Application fees will not be affected.
(B) It will take one week longer to receive a decision.
(C) They should be presented to a different office now.
(D) Many applications could be denied.

VOCA ··

application n. 신청 | **process** n. 절차 | **building permit** 건축 허가 | **fee** n. 수수료, 요금 | **decision** n. 결정 | **keep in mind** ~을 명심하다 | **submit** v. 제출하다 | **closing** n. 폐쇄 | **city government** 시 정부 | **cooperation** n. 협조 | **seek** v. 찾다, 구하다 | **investment** n. 투자 | **deny** v. 거부하다

Questions 3-4 refer to the following memo.

To: All employees
From: Marvin Greenwell, Director
Date: April 5
Subject: Road work

As most of you take the James Monroe Parkway to our facilities each day, it is important for you to know that the Maryland Department of Transportation will be doing some road work on the route and its exits. The project will get underway on April 12. At that time, one-mile sections of the road will be narrowed to one lane while the road gets resurfaced. Please plan ahead, as this is likely to cause considerable delays. Furthermore, on April 19, exit 4A, which is the exit to our facilities, will be closed. During this time, you will need to take exit 5A, and then, use Chantilly Boulevard to drive east three miles to our facilities. All work is expected to be completed by April 30. The Department of Transportation acknowledges that this project will cause traffic jams, but they ask you for patience while the work is being done.

3. What is being announced?

(A) A recent increase in traffic
(B) The opening of a new route
(C) Some repairs to a road
(D) A delay on a report

4. When will the employees have to take a detour?

(A) On April 5
(B) On April 12
(C) On April 19
(D) On April 30

VOCA ···

director *n.* 이사, 임원 I **road work** 도로 공사 I **facility** *n.* 시설, 기관 I **transportation** *n.* 운송, 수송 I **route** *n.* 노선 I **get underway** 진행시키다, 시작하다 I **section** *n.* 부분, 부문 I **narrow** *v.* 좁히다 I **lane** *n.* 차선 I **resurface** *v.* 표면 처리를 다시 하다 I **ahead** *adv.* 미리, 앞선 I **considerable** *adj.* 상당한 I **delay** *n.* 지연 I **furthermore** *adv.* 게다가 I **complete** *v.* 완료하다 I **acknowledge** *v.* 인정하다 I **traffic jam** 교통체증 I **patience** *n.* 인내심 I **repair** *n.* 수리, 수선 I **take a detour** 우회하다

NOTICE OF ROTARY CLUB MEETINGS
11 January

Business owners and leaders of other local organizations are invited to participate in the following meetings held by the Astoria Rotary Club.

Date: Tuesday, 2 February
Transportation Board, 7:00 P.M.

Date: Wednesday, 4 February
Tourism Board, 7:30 P.M.

Venue: Civic Center
The Main Hall, Third Floor
20213 Cleveden, Astoria

A full agenda will be posted on Monday, 14 January, in the main hall of the Civic Center and the lobbies of the Rotary Club headquarters. Local residents interested in addressing the board members at these meetings are required to submit a written request one week prior to the meeting.

Send requests to Max Mueller, Public Relations Officer.
Astoria Rotary Club
20213 Cleveden, Astoria
mmueller@astoriarotaryclub.au

---

5. What is the purpose of the notice?

(A) To announce new guidelines
(B) To inform members of an election
(C) To publicize upcoming events
(D) To promote commercial services

6. When is a discussion about attracting visitors to Astoria most likely to take place?

(A) On January 11
(B) On January 14
(C) On February 2
(D) On February 4

7. What should members of the public do if they want to speak during a board meeting?

(A) Write to Mr. Mueller
(B) Sign up online
(C) Arrive early to the meeting
(D) Register at the Civic Center

VOCA ··

organization *n.* 기관, 단체 l **invite** *v.* 초대하다, 초청하다, 권하다 l **participate in** ~에 참가하다 l **hold** *v.* 열다, 개최하다 l **transportation** *n.* 교통, 운송 l **tourism** *n.* 관광 l **agenda** *n.* 안건 l **post** *v.* 게시하다 l **headquarters** *n.* 본사 l **address** *v.* 발언하다, ~에게 말을 걸다 l **submit** *v.* 제출하다 l **written request** 서면 요청(문) l **prior to** ~에 앞서

Questions 8-10 refer to the following memo.

To: All staff
From: Thomas Marton, Director of Operations
Date: January 3
Subject: ID badges

We will be installing a new security system next Wednesday, January 11. Once the system becomes fully operational, Hertsworth staff members will be required to carry identification badges with them at all times. These badges, which are plastic cards embedded with digital codes, will allow employees to electronically access any building on the Hertsworth campus. The badges can be picked up in the Human Resources Department beginning on Thursday, January 5.

All department supervisors have been sent a schedule, and they will let their staff know when the badges will be available. Employees will not be able to enter any Hertsworth facility after January 11 without these new ID badges. If you have any questions or concerns, please direct them to your manager.

8. What is the purpose of the memo?

(A) To announce the renovation of a building
(B) To inform staff of a department's new office
(C) To report a security problem
(D) To introduce a company policy

9. What are employees being asked to do?

(A) Complete a form
(B) Obtain an identification card
(C) Use a different entrance
(D) Attend a workshop

10. Who are employees instructed to contact with their concerns?

(A) The facility maintenance personnel
(B) The director of operations
(C) Their department supervisors
(D) A security guard

VOCA ···

director of operations 운영 책임자 | **badge** n. 명찰 | **install** v. 설치하다 | **security system** 보안 시스템 | **fully** adv. 완전히, 충분히 | **operational** adj. 가동할 준비가 갖춰진 | **carry** v. 소지하다 | **at all times** 항상 | **embed** v. 단단히 끼워 넣다, 박혀있다 | **digital code** 디지털 암호 | **electronically** adv. 전자적으로, 컴퓨터로 | **direct** v. 지시하다, 안내하다, (편지 등을) ~에게 보내다 | **company policy** 사내 규정 | **obtain** v. 얻다, 구하다 | **entrance** n. 입구 | **personnel** n. 직원들 | **supervisor** n. 관리자, 감독관

기사

신문이나 잡지에 실리는 사회·경제 분야의 기사들은 다른 종류의 글에 비해 주제가 딱딱하고 어려운 어휘가 많이 등장하며, 길이도 긴 편이다. 보통 4~5문제가 출제된다.

🔍 지문 유형 확인하기

1. 자주 나오는 지문

▶ 기업의 업적 소개, 합병이나 구조 조정, 확장 이전, 신상품이나 새로운 서비스 홍보

▶ 축제 안내, 경연 대회나 국제 회의 개최 소식

▶ 음악과 매출의 관계, 시내버스 체제 개편에 따른 교통량 변화 등 연구나 설문조사 결과 등이 출제된다.

2. 기사의 주제 또는 목적을 묻는다.

What is the article **mainly about**? 기사는 주로 무엇에 관한 것인가?

What is the **purpose** of the article? 기사의 목적은 무엇인가?

3. 기사의 출처 및 예상 독자를 묻는다.

What kind of magazine is *Wall Street Zone*? 〈Wall Street Zone〉은 어떤 종류의 잡지인가?

Who is this article **intended for**? 이 기사는 누구를 위해 쓰였는가?

4. 기사의 세부 정보를 묻는다.

What is **(NOT) indicated** about this restaurant?
이 레스토랑에 대해 언급된 (언급되지 않은) 것은 무엇인가?

According to the article, **how** can people **find out more** about the product?
기사에 따르면, 사람들은 어떻게 제품에 대해 더 알 수 있는가?

Questions 1-4 refer to the following article.

Century Communications and Oram International to Merge

Greenville, October 10 - Century Communications and Oram International have announced that they will soon be merging. The two companies, which were previously headquartered in Martinsburg, West Virginia, and Winston-Salem, North Carolina, will be forming the largest internet service provider in the region.

The new company will be known as Century-Oram, and it is sure to do some great things. The two companies already have large customer bases. And after this merger, they will have little competition from their rivals. The new center of operations for Century-Oram will be in Roanoke, Virginia, at a newly constructed skyscraper named Century-Oram Tower.

Century-Oram will be looking to expand into Kentucky and southern Ohio by the end of next year. This move is likely to be a success as no other company has a strong presence in those markets.

• 기사 제목

• 기사의 주제
합병 안내

• 합병 이후 회사 이름과 회사 위치
두터운 고객층으로 인한 밝은 전망 및 회사 이전 위치 안내

• 시장 진출 계획
합병 이후 시장 진출 계획

기사의 주제

1. What is the purpose of this article?

(A) To announce a merger
(B) To explain a new service
(C) To report on sales figures
(D) To describe a market trend

세부사항: 기사의 출처

2. In what section of the newspaper would the article most likely appear?

(A) Entertainment
(B) Travel
(C) Business
(D) Sports

세부사항: 사업 분야

3. What kind of company will Century-Oram be?

(A) An internet service provider
(B) A computer retailer
(C) A phone manufacturer
(D) An advertising agency

세부사항: 본사 위치

4. Where will Century-Oram's headquarters be located?

(A) In Greenville
(B) In Winston-Salem
(C) In Roanoke
(D) In Martinsburg

[1-4] 다음 기사에 관한 문제입니다.

---

❶ Century Communications and Oram International to Merge
합병하려는 Century Communications와 Oram International

Greenville, October 10 – ❶ ❷ Century Communications and Oram International have announced that they will soon be merging. ❸ The two companies, which were previously headquartered in Martinsburg, West Virginia, and Winston-Salem, North Carolina, will be forming the largest internet service provider in the region.

Greenville, 10월 10일 – Century Communications와 Oram International이 곧 합병하게 될 것이라고 발표했다. 예전에 웨스트버지니아주의 마틴스버그와 노스캐롤라이나주의 윈스턴세일럼에 본사를 두었던 두 회사는 국내에서 가장 큰 인터넷 서비스 제공업체를 형성할 예정이다.

The new company will be known as Century-Oram, and it is sure to do some great things. The two companies already have large customer bases. And after this merger, they will have little competition from their rivals. ❹ The new center of operations for Century-Oram will be in Roanoke, Virginia, at a newly constructed skyscraper named Century-Oram Tower.

새로운 회사의 이름은 Century-Oram이고 반드시 대단한 일을 할 것이다. 두 회사는 이미 대규모의 고객층을 확보하고 있다. 그래서 이 합병 이후 경쟁사와의 경쟁은 거의 없을 것이다. **Century-Oram의 새로운 업무 중심지는 버지니아주의 로아노크에 있는** Century-Oram 타워라는 이름으로 새롭게 건설된 고층 건물에 자리잡을 예정이다.

Century-Oram will be looking to expand into Kentucky and southern Ohio by the end of next year. This move is likely to be a success as no other company has a strong presence in those markets.

Century-Oram은 연말까지 켄터키와 남부 오하이오로 확장할 계획이다. 이 움직임은 그쪽 시장들에서 강력한 입지를 가진 회사가 아무도 없기 때문에 성공할 것으로 보인다.

Right margin annotations:

• 기사 제목

• 기사의 주제
합병 안내

• 합병 이후 회사 이름과 회사 위치
두터운 고객층으로 인한 밝은 전망 및 회사 이전 위치 안내

• 시장 진출 계획
합병 이후 시장 진출 계획

1. What is the purpose of this article?

(A) To announce a merger
(B) To explain a new service
(B) To report on sales figures
(C) To describe a market trend

이 기사의 목적은 무엇인가?

(A) 합병을 알리기 위해
(B) 신규 서비스를 설명하기 위해
(C) 매출액을 보고하기 위해
(D) 시장 동향을 기술하기 위해

해설 기사의 목적을 묻는 문제이다. 기사의 주제와 목적은 기사의 제목과 앞부분에 제시되는 경우가 많다. 기사의 제목에서 두 회사가 합병한다는 것을 알리고 있고, 첫 단락의 첫 문장에서도 두 회사가 곧 합병할 예정임을 밝히고 있다. 따라서 정답은 (A) To announce a merger이다.

2. In what section of the newspaper would the article most likely appear?

(A) Entertainment
(B) Travel
(C) Business
(D) Sports

이 기사를 어디에서 찾을 수 있겠는가?

(A) 오락
(B) 여행
(C) 비즈니스
(D) 스포츠

해설 기사가 등장할 섹션을 묻는 추론 문제이다. 이 기사는 어느 한 부분에 정답 단서가 있는 것이 아니고 회사의 합병, 본사 위치, 사업 분야, 향후 전망 등을 다루고 있으므로 비즈니스 관련 기사라는 것을 파악할 수 있어야 한다. 따라서 정답은 (C) Business이다.

3. What kind of company will Century-Oram be?

(A) An internet service provider
(B) A computer retailer
(C) A phone manufacturer
(D) An advertising agency

Century-Oram은 어떤 회사인가?

(A) 인터넷 서비스 제공업체
(B) 컴퓨터 소매업체
(C) 휴대전화기 제조업체
(D) 광고 대행업체

해설 세부사항을 묻는 문제이다. 질문의 키워드 Century-Oram Web이 언급된 부분을 지문에서 찾아본다. 두 번째 단락에서 새로 합병될 회사의 이름이란 것을 알 수 있고 바로 앞에서 합병될 회사는 'the largest Internet service provider'가 될 것이라고 했으므로 정답은 (A) An Internet service provider이다.

4. Where will Century-Oram headquarters be located?

(A) In Greenville
(B) In Winston-Salem
(C) In Roanoke
(D) In Martinsburg

Century-Oram의 본사는 어디에 위치할 예정인가?

(A) Greenville에서
(B) Winston-Salem에서
(C) Roanoke에서
(D) Martinsburg에서

해설 세부사항을 묻는 문제이다. 두 번째 단락 마지막 부분에 headquarters가 center로 paraphrasing되었고 뒤에 신사옥의 위치가 언급되어 있다. 따라서 정답은 (C) In Roanoke이다.

VOCA ·

merge *v.* 합병하다 | previously *adv.* 이전에 | be headquartered ~에 본부를 두다 | competition *n.* 경쟁 | rival *n.* 경쟁자 | operation *n.* 운영, 가동 | skyscraper *n.* 고층 건물 | expand *v.* 확장하다 | strong *adj.* 튼튼한, 견고한 | market trend 시장 동향

Questions 1-2 refer to the following article.

Located on Maritime Way near Anglers' Wharf, Neptune's Bounty opened 10 years ago and swiftly established itself as the premier seafood restaurant in Portland. Neptune's Bounty offers a large selection of dishes prepared with fresh seafood, much of which is caught locally. Because of this insistence on the freshest of ingredients, the menu changes with the types of seafood in season. The restaurant was closed for two months for renovations, but it reopened last week. The interior now looks like the inside of an old wooden sailing ship. It also features tanks of live lobsters, fish, and other sea creatures. As a part of their grand reopening, Neptune's Bounty will offer all diners a free appetizer.

---

1. What is the purpose of the article?

(A) To advertise a business
(B) To promote cooking classes
(C) To compare different restaurants
(D) To describe tourist attractions

2. What is NOT indicated about Neptune's Bounty?

(A) It reopened last week.
(B) Its interior was redesigned.
(C) Its menu varies throughout the year.
(D) It has moved to a new location.

VOCA ··

maritime *adj.* 바다의 I **swiftly** *adv.* 신속히 I **establish** *v.* (입지를) 확고히 하다 I **premier** *adj.* 최고급의 I **seafood restaurant** 해산물 레스토랑 I **offer** *v.* 제공하다 I **a large selection of** 다양한 선택의 I **prepare** *v.* 준비하다 I **locally** *adv.* 지역적으로 I **insistence** *n.* 고집 I **ingredient** *n.* 재료 I **renovation** *n.* 수리 I **interior** *n.* 내부 I **wooden sailing ship** 목조 범선 I **lobster** *n.* 바닷가재 I **creature** *n.* 생물 I **free appetizer** 무료 전채 요리 I **advertise** *v.* 광고하다 I **compare** *v.* 비교하다 I **throughout the year** 일년 내내

Questions 3-4 refer to the following article.

After nearly 30 years as an executive for various companies in Vietnam, Thien Phouc Nguyen is widely regarded as one of the most successful businessmen in Southeast Asia. After retiring as President of Hanmon Enterprises, he visited many companies giving speeches on how to succeed in the region. Last year, he wrote and published the first of a planned series of five books on business. The first volume, *Market Barriers* (ASEAC Press, $19.95), is a study of many companies that have tried and failed to enter into the Southeast Asian market. This book is already being used in classrooms in America and Europe for MBA courses. The next book in the series is expected to be published later this year, but no firm date or title has been announced.

3. In what type of publication would the article mostly likely be found?

(A) A fashion magazine
(B) A travel brochure
(C) An instructional manual
(D) A business journal

4. What is indicated about *Market Barriers*?

(A) It is being read by graduate students.
(B) It features companies that have succeeded in Asia.
(C) It is being distributed only in North America.
(D) It is the fifth book in a series.

VOCA ··

nearly *adv.* 거의 ι **executive** *n.* 임원 ι **various** *adj.* 다양한 ι **widely** *adv.* 널리 ι **successful** *adj.* 성공적인 ι **retire** *v.* 은퇴하다 ι
president *n.* 사장, 회장 ι **give a speech** 연설하다 ι **succeed** *v.* 성공하다 ι **region** *n.* 지역 ι **publish** *v.* 출판하다 ι **barrier** *n.* 장벽 ι
MBA course 경영학 석사 코스 ι **firm** *adj.* 확정된 ι **title** *n.* 제목 ι **fashion magazine** 패션 잡지 ι **travel brochure** 여행 책자 ι
instructional manual 교육용 설명서 ι **business journal** 비즈니스 저널 ι **distribute** *v.* 배분하다, 배포하다

Questions 5-6 refer to the following article.

Economy Now

Latest News:

July 2, Los Angeles — Ji Young Lee, fashion designer and owner of the Life Apparel brand, announced that her company will be making big changes in the next six months. "Through market research, we discovered that the majority of our customers are in the upper one-third of the income bracket," said Ms. Lee. "This was a surprise for us because we always considered our brand to be accessible to everyone."

Because of this new information, several Life Apparel stores will be closing down, while others will be opened. Ms. Lee stated, "We need to move to where our customers are. Our research shows that most of our customers are well-to-do professionals living in urban areas. So, we will be closing down some of our stores located in suburban areas. We plan on opening stores in New York City, Washington, D.C., Los Angeles, Chicago, and Boston. Locations in Burke, Virginia; Lexington, Kentucky; Oakland, California; and Burnett, Washington; among others, will soon close their doors."

"We are excited to be making these big changes to the company. I'm sure it's going to make a big difference in our revenue. And I'm positive it will bring continued success to the Life Apparel brand," commented Ms. Lee.

---

5. What is suggested about the Life Apparel brand?

(A) It didn't start off as a clothing brand.
(B) It offers a huge selection of childrens' shoes.
(C) It is reviewing its inventory in some stores.
(D) It is most popular with city residents.

6. Where is a Life Apparel store currently located?

(A) In New York City
(B) In Burke
(C) In Washington, D.C.
(D) In Boston

VOCA ··

owner *n.* 주인, 소유자 I apparel *n.* 옷, 의류 I market research 시장 조사 I discover *v.* 발견하다 I majority of 다수의 I income *n.* 수입, 소득 I bracket *n.* 괄호, 등급, (가격·연령·소득 등의) 계층 I close down 문을 닫다 I well-to-do *adj.* 부유한, 잘사는 I professional *n.* 전문가 *adj.* 전문적인, 직업의 I urban *adj.* 도시의 I revenue *n.* 수익, 수입, 세익 I comment *n.* 논평, 언급 *v.* 논평하다, 견해를 밝히다

Airline to Expand Operations

CHATSWORTH ISLAND, Australia (22 November) — Rooback Air will start offering flights between Chatsworth Island and Melbourne on December 24. Round-trip service will be provided three times a day, and the flight time will be around 30 minutes.

Rooback Air CEO Jackson Ford explained that a rise in business trips between these two regions motivated the four-year-old airline's decision to increase its presence in Australia. "We're constantly responding to the wishes of the local community," he said.

Daily flights between Chatsworth Island and Melbourne used to be offered by Austravel Airways. However, last year, Austravel Airways was acquired by Beijing-based Shao Airways,

which discontinued its services in Chatsworth Island. Shao currently services Australia with only weekend flights between Beijing and Melbourne.

"Rooback Air's new travel services will allow same-day, round-trip flights across Australia for business meetings or leisure activities," Mr. Ford said.

Rooback Air has also partnered with Miter Tech Systems to design its Web site. Miter Tech Systems offers its services to over 40 regional airlines worldwide.

Rooback Air currently operates only in Australia, providing services to the cities of Sydney, Brisbane, Perth, and Adelaide.

---

7. What is the purpose of the press release?

(A) To provide details of a recent merger
(B) To introduce a new airline CEO
(C) To explain updates to a booking procedure
(D) To announce a new airline route

8. According to Mr. Ford, how will businesspeople in Chatsworth Island and Melbourne benefit from Rooback Air?

(A) They can buy tickets at lower prices.
(B) They will make more money from increased tourism.
(C) They can book flights faster than before.
(D) They will be able to travel more conveniently across the country.

9. What is implied about Miter Tech Systems?

(A) It is based in Beijing.
(B) It provides in-flight entertainment.
(C) It trains flight attendants.
(D) It develops Web sites.

10. What is suggested about Rooback Air?

(A) It acquired Austravel Airways.
(B) It provides flights within Australia only.
(C) It offers in flight internet service.
(D) It was founded last year in Chatsworth Island.

VOCA ···

round-trip *adj.* 왕복 여행의 I **rise** *n.* 증가, 상승 I **motivate** *v.* 동기를 부여하다 I **presence** *n.* 실재, 존재감 I **constantly** *adv.* 지속적으로 I **respond to** ~에 대응하다 I **local community** 지역 사회 I **acquire** *v.* 인수하다 I **discontinue** *v.* 중단하다 I **currently** *adv.* 현재는 I **regional** *adj.* 지방의, 지역의 I **merger** *n.* 합병 I **booking** *n.* 예약 I **in-flight** *adj.* 기내의 I **acquire** *v.* 얻다, 인수하다

양식

청구서, 영수증, 일정표 (invoice, receipt, schedule) 등 특정한 서식을 갖춘 양식 관련 문제는 Part 7 전반부에 거의 빠짐없이 출제되는 지문 유형이다. 보통 1~2문제가 출제되며, 지문이 길지 않으므로 여기서 시간을 절약할 수 있어야 한다는 사실을 명심하고, 문제를 보고 언급된 부분만 빠르게 찾아 답을 골라보도록 한다.

지문 유형 확인하기

1. 자주 나오는 지문

▶ 식당, 옷 가게, 철물점 등 상점의 영수증 및 청구서, 인테리어, 행사의 견적서, 참가 신청서, 행사 및 수업 일정 등이 출제된다.

2. 양식을 발행한 목적 또는 주체를 묻는다.

▶ 양식의 목적이나 양식을 발행한 주체에 대해 묻는다.

What kind of store most likely is Mintz Supplies? Mintz 공급업체의 업종은 무엇이겠는가?

For whom is the flyer most likely **intended**? 누구를 위한 광고이겠는가?

3. 양식의 세부 정보를 묻는다.

▶ 행사, 일정, 사람, 비용, 추후 계획, 기타 세부사항 등과 관련하여 묻는다. 또한, 양식과 관련하여 추론할 수 있는 사항들을 묻기도 한다.

What is **NOT included** in the invoice? 청구서에 포함되지 않은 것은 무엇인가?

What is **[indicated / stated]** on the receipt? 영수증에 언급되어 있는 것은 무엇인가?

How many products were **ordered**? 몇 개의 제품들이 주문되었나?

How can **customers receive** a **discount**? 고객들은 할인을 어떻게 받을 수 있나?

What is **suggested** about **Matador Books**? Matador 서적에 관해 암시되는 것은 무엇인가?

Questions 1-2 refer to the following invoice.

The Star Hotel
3815 Grandriver Ave.

Bill To: Sue Kim   **Date:** April 20
East Lansing, MI 48825   **Invoice number:** 314

Invoice for one-day conference to be held on May 28.

Item	Rate	Total
Standard Room Conference Space (300 guests)	$200.00/day	$200.00

Audiovisual equipment rental

2 wireless microphones	$40.00/unit	$80.00
1 projector	$100.00/unit	$100.00
1 projection screen	$70.00/unit	$70.00
Breakfast	$10.00/person	$3000.00
Lunch	$15.00/person	$4500.00

Subtotal	$7750.00
Tax	$620.00
Total	$8370.00

*Please send this amount by May 4 to reserve all services listed above.

- 업체명

- 청구서 정보
(수신인, 날짜,
청구서 번호)

- 세부 내역
(물품/가격)

- 요청 사항

사실확인: 행사 비용에 포함되지 않은 것

1. What is NOT included in the cost of the event?

(A) Overnight hotel stay
(B) Microphones
(C) Meals for participants
(D) Conference room rental

세부사항: 요청사항

2. What is Ms. Kim asked to do?

(A) Confirm a reservation
(B) Return audiovisual equipment
(C) Make a payment
(D) Select items from a menu

 **예제 풀이**

[1-2] 다음 청구서에 관한 문제입니다.

The Star Hotel
3815 Grandriver Ave.

The Star 호텔

3815 Grandriver가.

Bill To: Sue, Kim 청구인: Sue, Kim   **Date:** April 20 날짜: 4월 20일

East Lansing, MI 48825 East Lansing, MI 48825 **Invoice number:** 314 청구서 번호: 314

Invoice for one-day conference to be held on May 28.

5월 28일에 열릴 일일 컨퍼런스를 위한 청구서

Item 항목	**Rate** 가격	**Total** 합계
❶ Standard Room 일반 룸 ❶ Conference Space 회의 공간 **(300 guests)** (300명의 손님들을 위한)	$200.00 / day 200달러/하루에	$200.00 200달러

Audiovisual equipment rental 시청각 장비 대여

❶ 2 wireless microphones 2 무선 마이크	$40.00 / unit 40.00달러/개당	$80.00 80달러
1 projector 1 프로젝터	$100.00 / unit 100.00달러/개당	$100 100달러
1 projection screen 1 프로젝션 스크린	$70.00 / unit 70.00달러/개당	$70 70달러
❶ Breakfast 아침	$10.00 / person 10.00달러/한 사람당	$3000.00 3000달러
❶ Lunch 점심	$15.00 / person 15.00달러/한 사람당	$4500.00 4500달러

Subtotal 소계		$7750.00 7750달러
Tax 세금		$620.00 620달러
Total 합계		$8370.00 8370달러

❷ *Please send this amount by May 4 to reserve all services listed above.

*위에 언급된 모든 서비스를 예약하기 위해선 5월 4일까지 금액을 보내주세요.

• 업체명

• 청구서 정보
 (수신인, 날짜, 청구서 번호)

• 세부 내역
 (물품/가격)

• 요청 사항

1. What is NOT included in the cost of the event?

(A) **Overnight hotel stay**
(B) Microphones
(C) Meals for participants
(D) Conference room rental

행사 비용에서 포함되지 않은 것은 무엇인가?

(A) **하룻밤 동안의 호텔 숙박**
(B) 마이크
(C) 참가자들을 위한 식사
(D) 회의 룸 대여

> **해설** 행사 비용에 포함되지 않은 것을 물어보는 문제로 지문과 대조하여 오답을 소거를 한다.
> (B) Microphones → 청구서의 시청각 장비 대여 표에 wireless microphones(무선 마이크)가 언급되어 있으므로 소거한다.
> (C) Meals for participants → 청구서의 시청각 장비 대여 표에 Breakfast(아침) & Lunch(점심)이 언급되어 있으므로 소거한다.
> (D) Conference room rental → 청구서의 Standard Room(일반 룸), Conference Space(회의 공간)에서 회의실 대여가 가능함을 알 수 있으므로 소거한다.
> 따라서, 청구서 내역에는 언급된 적이 없는 (A) Overnight hotel stay가 정답이다.

2. What is Ms. Kim asked to do?

(A) Confirm a reservation
(B) Return audiovisual equipment
(C) **Make a payment**
(D) Select items from a menu

Ms. Kim이 하라고 요청 받은 것은 무엇인가?

(A) 예약을 확인한다
(B) 시청각 장비를 반환한다
(C) **돈을 지불한다**
(D) 메뉴에서 아이템을 고른다

> **해설** Ms. Kim이 요청 받는 것을 물었으므로 양식을 받는 사람이 부탁이나, 요청을 받은 것이 무엇인지 파악한다. 마지막 부분 'Please send this amount by May 4 to reserve all services listed above'와 같이 돈을 지불하라는 내용이 나오므로 이를 make a payment로 paraphrasing한 (C) Make a payment가 정답이다.

VOCA ··

invoice *n.* 청구서 | **standard** *adj.* 일반적인, 보통의 *n.* 기준, 규범 | **rate** *n.* 요금, 가격, 속도, 비율 | **audiovisual** *adj.* 시청각의 | **wireless** *adj.* 무선의 | **microphone** *n.* 마이크 | **amount** *n.* 양, 금액, 액수 | **reserve** *n.* 예약하다 | **overnight** *adv.* 하룻밤 동안, *adj.* 야간의, 일박(용)의 | **hotel stay** 호텔 숙박 | **rental** 임대(료), 대여 | **make a payment** 지불을 하다

Questions 1-2 refer to the following form.

Nonstop New Haven: The city's leading party hosts

We appreciate your business! Please make sure to fill out everything in the form below. One of our representatives will contact you with the appropriate package and pricing plan that will best meet your needs.

Full Name: _____	Telephone: _____
E-mail: _____	Event Date(s): _____

- **Party Locations:**
  - [ ] 183 Mulberry Lane
  - [ ] 2001 Tyconda Road
  - [ ] 72 Foxforth Avenue
  - [ ] 892 Grovington Drive

- **Event type:**

[ ] Award ceremony	[ ] Graduation party
[ ] Company dinner	[ ] other: _____

- **Expected number of guests:**
  - [ ] 40 or fewer [ ] 50-120 [ ] 121 or more

- **Local accommodations needed for some guests:** [ ] Yes [ ] No

- **List any special electronic equipment required:** _____

Nonstop New Haven

---

1. What will a Nonstop New Haven representative do?

    (A) Reduce prices for groups of 121 or more guests
    (B) Draft a proposal according to certain information
    (C) Guide guests to their seating area at an event
    (D) Send a list of nearby hotels

2. What is suggested about Nonstop New Haven?

    (A) It was started less than a year ago.
    (B) It requests clients bring their own electronic equipment.
    (C) It recently started providing private accommodations.
    (D) It owns four venues.

VOCA ···

leading *adj.* 가장 중요한, 선두적인 | **party host** 파티 주최자 | **appreciate** *v.* 감사하다, 감사히 여기다 | **business** *n.* 거래, 사업, 장사 | **fill out** 기입하다 | **appropriate** *adj.* 알맞은, 적절한 | **pricing plan** 요금 제도, 가격 계획표 | **meet** *v.* 충족하다 | **needs** *n.* (복수형) 요구 | **lane** *n.* (시골에 있는 좁은) 길 | **avenue** *n.* (도시의) 거리, －가 | **drive** *n.* (도로 명에 쓰이는) 번지 | **award ceremony** 시상식, 표창 수여식 | **company dinner** 회사 회식 | **graduation party** 졸업 파티

Questions 3-5 refer to the following invoice.

http://www.matadorbooks.com/invoice_63497

Matador Books

Order Number: 63497
Order Date: March 12
Estimated Shipping Date: March 16

Ship To:	Bill To:	
Ms. Nadia Stevens 74 Hanlon St. Apt 19 Tacoma, WA 98401	Ms. Rachel Fox Henley Dr. Newark, NJ 07101	
Title(s): *Management Policies*	**Author(s):** Charles Haywood	**Price** $28.95
Title(s): *Developing Managerial Skills*	**Author(s):** Jennie Wong	**Price** $37.62

Subtotal: $66.57

Tax: $4.35

Shipping and Handling: Free

Total Credit Card Charge: $70.92

Include a card (at no extra cost) if the order is a gift? *O* Yes __ No
Message on card: *Congratulations on the new job! We hope that these books will be useful in your new career. We already miss you.*

Sincerely,

The Staff at Fox & Marina Lawyers

3. What did Ms. Fox do on March 12?

(A) Exchanged a book
(B) Purchased a gift
(C) Tracked a shipment
(D) Picked up a package

4. What is suggested about Ms. Stevens?

(A) She has completed a book.
(B) She is Ms. Fox's supervisor.
(C) She was recently hired as a manager.
(D) She has registered for a university course.

5. What is indicated about Matador Books?

(A) It sells gift cards.
(B) It shipped an order at no additional cost.
(C) It processed an order a day after it was received.
(D) It publishes journals.

VOCA ··

estimated shipping date 예상 배송 기일 l **managerial skill** 경영 기술 l **subtotal** *n.* 소계, 잠정 집계 l **shipping and handling** 운송 및 취급, 배송 l **charge** *n.* 요금 l **useful** *adj.* 유용한 l **career** *n.* 직업, 직장생활 l **exchange** *v.* 교환하다 l **track** *v.* 추적하다 l **journal** *n.* (학회·전문 기관 등의) 정기 간행물, 잡지

Questions 6-9 refer to the following flyer.

Have you just moved to London?

Attend a London Welcomes You Orientation Hosted by the London Resident Committee
25 May, 10:30 A.M. – 2:30 P.M.
London Times Square
Big Ben Center
Open to Everyone

Schedule of Presentations

10:30 A.M.	How to Get Around: Available Public Transportation (Room 101)	
11:30 A.M.	Getting Housing in London (Room 103)	Waste Management Advice and Options (Room 104)
12:30 P.M.	Comprehending London's Local Banking System (Room 105)	Starting a Local Business in London (Room 104)
1:30 P.M.	What to do in London, Guide to Community Gatherings and Recreational Facilities (Room 101)	

Since two events may be held during the same time, attendees must choose which event best matches their interests. In addition, please be aware that due to high interests in the sessions on recreation and public transportation, you should plan on arriving early to secure a seat.

Although all presentations are in English, there are pamphlets available in Korean, Spanish, and French. Refreshments will be provided for purchase.

Following the last presentation, participants may join a one-hour guided tour throughout downtown London. This free tour will be provided by a long-time committee member and resident of London. For further details regarding these events, please visit www.welcometolondon.co.uk.

6. For whom is the flyer likely intended?

(A) Residents who are new to London
(B) London city councilors
(C) Tour guides working in London
(D) London Resident Committee members

7. Where will the most popular presentations occur?

(A) In Room 101
(B) In Room 103
(C) In Room 104
(D) In Room 105

8. What is indicated about the London Resident Committee?

(A) It provides materials in several languages.
(B) It will start to offer new services.
(C) It requires a membership fee.
(D) It holds monthly events.

9. According to the flyer, what can attendees do after the presentations?

(A) Enjoy free food and drinks
(B) Reserve seats for upcoming events
(C) Go on a tour of the city
(D) Sign up for a membership

VOCA ···

attend *v.* 참석하다 | host *v.* 개최하다, 주최하다 | resident *n.* 거주자, 주민 | committee *n.* 위원회 | open *adj.* 열려 있는 | get around 돌아다니다 | public transportation 대중교통 | housing *n.* 주택 | waste *n.* 폐기물, 쓰레기 | advice *n.* 조언, 충고 | comprehend *v.* 이 해하다 | local *adj.* 지역의, 현지의 | gathering *n.* 모임 | facility *n.* 시설 | choose *v.* 선택하다 | match *v.* 어울리다, 맞다 | interest *n.* 관심, 흥미 | in addition 게다가 | aware *adj.* 자각하고 있는 | due to ~ 때문에 | secure *v.* 얻어 내다, 확보하다 | refreshments *n.* 다과 | provide *v.* 제공하다 | following *adj.* 그 다음의 | participant *n.* 참석자 | join *v.* 함께하다, 가입하다 | detail *n.* 세부 사항 | regarding *prep.* ~에 관해 | committee *n.* 위원회 | upcoming *adj.* 다가오는

Questions 10-11 refer to the following schedule.

TGB Employees' Trip Itinerary for April 12

Name	Title	Departure City	Arrival City	Departure Time	Arrival Time
Andre Fisher	Reporter	Hong Kong, China	Manila, Philippines	8:40 A.M.	10:40 A.M.
Steven Lee	Cameraman	Hong Kong, China	Manila, Philippines	8:40 A.M.	10:40 A.M.
Natalie Bateman	Technical editor	Jakarta, Indonesia	Rome, Italy	8:50 A.M.	10:00 P.M.
Brian Mundy	Cameraman	Jakarta, Indonesia	Athens, Greece	9:05 A.M.	9:45 A.M.
Amy Bowman	News anchor	Jakarta, Indonesia	Rome, Italy	8:50 A.M.	10:00 P.M.

10. Where do the employees most likely work?

(A) At a manufacturing company
(B) At a broadcasting company
(C) At a trading company
(D) At a construction company

11. What is probably true about Mr. Fisher?

(A) His flight will be delayed.
(B) He will be flying with a coworker.
(C) He will be traveling to Europe.
(D) His seat will be upgraded.

VOCA ···

itinerary *n.* 여행 일정표 I **arrival** *n.* 도착 I **cameraman** *n.* 카메라맨, 촬영 기사 I **technical editor** 편집 기술자 I **news anchor** 뉴스 앵커 I **manufacturing company** 제조회사 I **broadcasting company** 방송국 I **trading company** 무역회사, 상사 I **construction company** 건설회사 I **coworker** *n.* 동료, 협력자

이중 지문

서로 관련된 두 개의 지문을 읽고 5문항을 풀어야 한다. 5문항 중에서 1~2개 문항은 두 지문을 연계시켜 추론하는 문제이다. 이중 지문은 1회당 2세트가 출제된다.

🔍 지문 유형 확인하기

1. 자주 나오는 지문

이중 지문은 아래와 같이 서로 같거나 다른 지문 유형 2개가 조합되어 나온다. 이외에도 다양한 지문들의 조합과 주제들이 가능하므로 다양한 이중 지문 문제를 접하고 풀어보는 연습이 필요하다.

✅ [이메일/편지] + [이메일/편지]
▶ 고객의 만족도를 묻는 이메일과 고객의 답장 이메일
▶ 고객의 불평 제기 이메일과 고객 불평에 대한 고객 서비스 센터의 답변 이메일
▶ 예약 및 일정 확인 등을 위해 이메일 교환

✅ [이메일/편지] + 일정표
▶ 컨퍼런스 세부 일정 변경 안내와 변경된 일정표
▶ 행사 관련 이메일/편지와 일정표 안내

✅ 광고 + [이메일/편지/초대장/기사]
▶ 행사, 공연, 채용 관련 광고와 행사, 공연, 채용 관련 문의 이메일
▶ 구인 광고와 이력서를 첨부한 이메일 답변

✅ 기사 + [이메일/편지]
▶ 협회 부회장 선출과 선출자 축하 이메일
▶ 지역 건설 계획 기사와 기사 관련 이메일
▶ 인물, 회사, 경제, 제품 등에 관한 기사와 문의 또는 오류 정정을 요청하는 이메일
▶ 식생활, 예술 등과 관련된 정보 기사와 기사에 대한 추가 정보를 요청하는 이메일

✅ 양식[청구서/초대장/일정표] + [이메일/편지]
▶ 사내 행사를 알리는 공지/회람과 사내 행사 등을 권고하는 이메일
▶ 구매 청구서와 오류 정정을 요청하는 이메일
▶ 초대장과 감사 의견을 표현하는 이메일
▶ 식당 호텔 서비스에 대한 의견을 요청하는 이메일과 고객 만족도를 나타내는 설문지
▶ 여행 일정 및 숙박 시설에 관한 표와 회의 참석을 위한 비행 및 숙박 예약 이메일
▶ 부재중 전화 메모와 메모와 관련된 내용을 담은 이메일

2. 각 지문의 주제나 목적 또는 대상을 묻는다.

What is the **purpose** of the memo? 회람의 목적은 무엇인가?

Why did Ms. Han **call** Mr. Brown? Ms. Han은 왜 Mr. Brown에게 전화했는가?

What is being **advertised**? 무엇이 광고되고 있는가?

3. 각 지문의 세부 정보를 묻는다.

Where was Ms. Kim on April 25? 4월 25일에 Ms. Kim은 어디에 있었는가?

How did the products change recently? 그 제품들은 최근에 어떻게 변했는가?

4. 두 지문의 내용을 비교하거나 연계해서 추론하는 문제가 나온다.

What is **NOT mentioned** in the memo? 회람에서 언급되지 않은 것은 무엇인가? 비교

What is most likely **true** about **Mr. Jang**? Mr. Jang에 대해 사실인 것은 무엇이겠는가? 비교

What is **implied** about the **company**? 회사에 대해 암시되는 것은 무엇인가? 연계 추론

 문제 풀이 전략

① 질문을 먼저 읽고 질문 유형을 파악하고 키워드를 찾는다.

질문의 순서와 내용의 순서가 다를 수도 있지만, 일반적으로 지문의 전개 순서와 질문의 순서가 동일하게 제시되는 경우가 많으므로 질문의 순서를 따라 본문에서 답을 찾아나간다. 두 지문 중 한 지문이 편지나 이메일인 경우에는 수신자와 발신자의 신분과 두 사람의 관계를 파악하는 문제가 자주 출제되므로 누가 누구에게 쓰는지 정확히 확인해야 한다.

② 문제를 먼저 보고 단일 지문에 관련된 문제인지, 이중 지문 연계형 문제인지 파악한다.

빠른 단서 포착을 위해 5개의 문제가 각각 두 지문 중 어느 지문과 관련되었는지를 파악해야 한다. 일반적으로 5개의 질문 중 상위 2~3개의 질문은 첫 번째 지문과 관련된 문제이므로 상위 3개 질문을 먼저 읽고 첫 번째 지문에서 답을 찾은 후에, 나머지 문제의 답을 두 번째 지문에서 찾는다.

③ 질문을 읽고 두 지문의 관계를 파악한 후, 문제부터 읽어 키워드를 확인하고 지문에서 그 키워드가 언급된 부분의 앞뒤를 살펴보며 답을 찾는다.

총 5문제 중 1~2 문제가 이중 지문 연계 문제로 중간에 출제된다. 그러므로 각 지문들 간의 공통된 주제를 미리 파악하면서 지문을 읽고 두 지문에 나타난 단서를 종합해 정답을 찾는다.

Questions 1-5 refer to the following e-mails.

To: Customer Service <customerservice@georgetownelectric.com>

From: Jeanie Syfu <j.syfu@speedmail.org>

Subject: Billing Issue

Date: September 15

To Whom It May Concern:

There seems to be a problem with my last electricity bill. Since the beginning of the new billing cycle, I have been paying a fixed rate of $50 a month for electricity. However, my bill for last month was for $73. I signed up for the fixed-rate service in order to save money on my electricity bills. However, this bill is $23 higher than what my contract states it should be. Please look into this matter right away, and let me know what happened.

Sincerely,

Jeanie Syfu

· 수신인
  발신인
  제목
  날짜

· 글의 목적
  예상보다 높은 금액의
  청구서를 받은 고객의
  항의 내용
· 세부 정보
  매월 고정 금액의 전기
  요금을 예상
· 이중 지문 연계
  고정 요금제를 신청했
  음에도 요금이 23달러
  더 부과되었음
· 맺음말

· 발신인

To: Jeanie Syfu <j.syfu@speedmail.org>

From: Customer Service <customerservice@georgetownelectric.com>

Subject: Re: Billing Issue

Date: September 16

Dear Ms. Syfu,

Thank you for contacting us regarding this matter. An investigation has revealed that a mistake was indeed made to your bill for last month. As you stated, you were overcharged by the amount indicated in your message. We have corrected this mistake, and the additional amount will appear as a credit on your bill for next month. Therefore, your bill for the month of September will be $27. We apologize for any inconvenience this problem may have caused. To compensate you further, we will take you 50 percent off of your power usage for the month of October.

· 수신인
  발신인
  제목
  날짜

· 글의 목적
  문제 해결을 알리고
  사과

· 이중 지문 연계
  더 부과된 금액은 계좌에
  입금됨

· 세부 정보
  다음 달 50% 할인 제공

To help us to ensure that our customers are receiving a high level of support, we kindly request that you complete a brief survey concerning the resolution of this issue. You can complete the survey form by visiting this link: www.georgetownelectric.com/customersurvey.

요청 사항
인터넷 설문조사

Thank you for your being a loyal customer of Georgetown Electric, and we look forward to your continued business in the future.

인사말

Regards,

John Bates
Customer Service Representative
Georgetown Electric Company

발신인
발신인 직책과 소속
회사

이메일의 목적

1. What is the purpose of the first e-mail?

(A) To call attention to a problem
(B) To set up an appointment
(C) To announce a new payment option
(D) To describe a company policy

사실확인

2. What is indicated about Ms. Syfu?

(A) She recommended Georgetown Electric to one of her friends.
(B) She would like to create a separate account.
(C) She expects to pay the same amount for electricity each month.
(D) She has canceled her contract with Georgetown Electric.

이중 지문 연계

3. How much money will be credited to Ms. Syfu's account in September?

(A) $23
(B) $27
(C) $50
(D) $73

세부사항

4. What does Mr. Bates encourage Ms. Syfu to do?

(A) Contact the accounting office
(B) Call his supervisor
(C) Renew a subscription
(D) Fill out a questionnaire

세부사항

5. What does Mr. Bates offer Ms. Syfu?

(A) A free month of service
(B) A discount
(C) A magazine
(D) A new phone

 **예제 풀이**

[1-5] 다음 이메일들에 관한 문제입니다.

To: Customer Service <customerservice@georgetownelectric.com>

From: Jeanie Syfu <j.syfu@speedmail.org>

Subject: ❶ Billing Issue

Date: September 15

수신: 고객 서비스 〈customerservice@georgetownelectric.com〉

발신: Jeanie Syfu 〈j.syfu@speedmail.org〉

제목: **청구서 발급 건**

날짜: 9월 15일

To Whom It May Concern:

담당자께,

There seems to be a problem with my last electricity bill. Since the beginning of the new billing cycle, I have been paying a fixed rate of $50 a month for electricity. However, my bill for last month was for $73. ❷ I signed up for the fixed rate service in order to save money on my electricity bills. ❸ However, this bill is $23 higher than what my contract states it should be. ❶ Please look into this matter right away, and let me know what happened.

제 최근 전기 요금 청구서에 문제가 있는 듯합니다. 새로운 청구서를 받기 시작한 후로 저는 한 달에 50달러의 정액 전기료를 지불해 왔습니다. 하지만 지난달 청구서는 73달러였습니다. **저는 전기요금을 절약하고자 정액 요금 서비스를 신청했습니다. 그런데 이 청구서는 제 계약이 명시한 금액보다 23달러 높게 나왔습니다.** 이를 검토하시고 문제가 무엇인지 알려주세요.

Sincerely,

감사합니다.

Jeanie Syfu

Jeanie Syfu

- 수신인
  발신인
  제목
  날짜

- 글의 목적
  예상보다 높은 금액의
  청구서를 받은 고객의
  항의 내용

- 세부 정보
  매월 고정 금액의 전기
  요금을 예상

- 이중 지문 연계
  고정 요금제를 신청했
  음에도 요금이 23달러
  더 부과되었음

- 맺음말

- 발신인

VOCA ··

electricity bill 전기 요금 청구서 I fixe rate 고정된 금액 I sign up for ~를 신청하다 I contract *n.* 계약서 I call attention to ~에 ~의 주의를 환기시키다

314

To: Jeanie Syfu ⟨j.syfu@speedmail.org⟩
From: Customer Service ⟨customerservice@georgetownelectric.com⟩
Subject: Re: Billing Issue
Date: September 16

수신: Jeanie Syfu ⟨j.syfu@speedmail.org⟩
발신: 고객 서비스 ⟨customerservice@georgetownelectric.com⟩
제목: 회신: 청구서 발급 건
날짜: 9월 16일

Dear Ms. Syfu,

친애하는 Ms. Syfu에게,

Thank you for contacting us regarding this matter. An investigation has revealed that a mistake was indeed made to your bill for last month. As you stated, you were overcharged by the amount indicated in your message. ❸ We have corrected this mistake, and the additional amount will appear as a credit on your bill for next month. Therefore, your bill for the month of September will be $27. We apologize for any inconvenience this problem may have caused. ❺ To compensate you further, we will take you 50 percent off of your power usage for the month of October.

이 문제에 대해 저희에게 연락을 주셔서 감사합니다. 지난 달 고객님의 청구서에 정말로 실수가 있었다는 사실이 조사에서 밝혀졌습니다. 그 결과, 고객님이 말씀하신 대로 고객님 메시지에 언급된 금액만큼 초과 청구되었습니다. 저희는 이 실수를 수정했으며 나머지 금액은 다음 달 귀하의 청구서에 공제액으로 표시될 것입니다. 따라서 9월 귀하의 청구서는 27달러가 될 것입니다. 이 문제로 인해 야기된 모든 불편에 대해 사과드립니다. **고객님께 더 보상해드리기 위해, 10월 전력 사용에 대해 50퍼센트 할인을 해드리겠습니다.**

To help us to ensure that our customers are receiving a high level of support, ❹ we kindly request that you complete a brief survey concerning the resolution of this issue. You can complete the survey form by visiting this link: www.georgetownelectric.com/customersurvey.

Thank you for your being a loyal customer of Georgetown Electric, and we look forward to your continued business in the future.

저희 고객들이 높은 수준의 서비스를 받는다는 사실을 확인하기 위해, 이 문제의 해결안에 대해 **간단한 설문조사 작성을 정중히 요청합니다.** 고객님께서 이 링크로 방문하셔서 설문지를 작성하실 수 있습니다: www.georgetownelectric.com/customersurvey. Georgetown 전기회사의 단골 고객이 되어주셔서 감사드리며, 앞으로도 지속적인 거래를 기대합니다.

Regards,

감사합니다.

John Bates
Customer Service Representative
Georgetown Electric Company

John Bates
고객 서비스 담당
Georgetown 전기회사

• 수신인
  발신인
  제목
  날짜

• 글의 목적
  문제 해결을 알리고
  사과

• 이중 지문 연계
  더 부과된 금액은 공제액
  표시됨

• 세부 정보
  다음 달 50% 할인 제공

• 요청 사항
  인터넷 설문조사

• 인사말

• 발신인
  발신인 직책과 소속
  회사

VOCA

contact *v.* 연락하다 | regarding *adv.* ~에 관하여 | matter *n.* 문제, 사항 | investigation *n.* 조사 | reveal *v.* 밝혀지다, 드러나다 | indeed *adv.* 정말, 확실히 | overcharge *v.* (금액을) 초과하여 청구하다 | amount *n.* 액수, 양, 총액 | indicated *adj.* 표시된, 나타난 | correct *v.* 수정하다, 바로 잡다 | appear *v.* 나타나다 | apologize *v.* 사과하다 | inconvenience *n.* 불편, 애로사항 | compensate *v.* 보상하다 | further *adv.* 더 | usage *n.* 사용량 | ensure *v.* 보장하다 | high level of 고도의 | kindly *adv.* 친절하게 | request *v.* 요청하다 | survey *n.* 설문조사 | concerning *prep.* ~에 관하여 | loyal customer 단골 고객 | look forward to ~하기를 고대한다 | continued *adj.* 계속되는, 지속된 | business *n.* 거래 | in the future 미래에도 | renew *v.* 갱신하다 | fill out 기입하다, 작성하다 | questionnaire *n.* 설문지

1. What is the purpose of the first e-mail?

첫 번째 이메일의 목적은 무엇인가?

(A) **To call attention to a problem**
(B) To set up an appointment
(C) To announce a new payment option
(D) To describe a company policy

(A) **문제점을 환기시키기 위해**
(B) 예약을 하기 위해
(C) 새로운 결제 방식을 안내하기 위해
(D) 회사방침을 설명하기 위해

해설 이메일 목적을 묻는 문제이다. 글의 목적은 제목이나 글의 앞부분 또는 간혹 맨 뒤에 제시된다. 이메일의 경우 제목(Subject:)을 확인해 본다. 제목은 '청구서 발급 건'이고 이메일에서 이에 대한 문제를 제기하며 끝부분에서 문제를 빨리 해결해 달라고 요청하고 있으므로 정답은 (A) To call attention to a problem이다.

2. What is indicated about Ms. Syfu?

Ms. Syfu에 대해 언급된 것은 무엇인가?

(A) She recommended Georgetown Electric to one of her friends.
(B) She would like to create a separate account.
(C) **She expects to pay the same amount for electricity each month.**
(D) She has canceled her contract with Georgetown Electric.

(A) 친구 중 한 명에게 Georgetown 전기회사를 추천했다.
(B) 별도의 계정을 만들기를 원한다.
(C) **매달 같은 금액의 전기요금을 지불할 것을 기대한다.**
(D) Georgetown 전기회사와의 계약을 취소했다.

해설 세부사항을 묻는 문제이다. Ms. Syfu가 키워드이므로 Ms. Syfu가 작성한 이메일에서 I로 언급된 부분과 선택지를 대조하며 소거한다. (A) 친구에게 Georgetown 전기회사를 추천했다는 언급이 없으므로 탈락이다. (B) 청구서 발급 전 문제를 해결해 줄 것을 요구했을 뿐이고 새로운 계정을 요청한 적은 없으므로 탈락이다. (D) 문제에 대한 시정을 요구했을 뿐이고 자신이 받는 서비스를 취소하겠다는 언급은 없으므로 탈락이다. (C) 그녀는 정액제 요금 서비스에 가입되어 있으므로 매달 동일한 금액의 전기요금을 지불할 것을 기대하는 것이 타당하다. 따라서 정답은 (C) She expects to pay the same amount for electricity each month.이다.

3. How much money will be credited to Ms. Syfu's account in September?

9월에 Ms. Syfu의 계정에는 얼마의 돈이 입금될 것인가?

(A) $23
(B) $27
(C) $50
(D) $73

(A) 23달러
(B) 27달러
(C) 50달러
(D) 73달러

해설 이중 지문 연계 유형 문제이다. 첫 번째 이메일에서는 23달러의 금액이 초과 청구되었다고 했고, 두 번째 이메일에서는 그 금액이 9월 청구서에 공제액으로 표시될 것이라고 했으므로 정답은 (A) $23이다.

4. What does Mr. Bates encourage Ms. Syfu to do?

(A) Contact the accounting office
(B) Call his supervisor
(C) Renew a subscription
(D) Fill out a questionnaire

Mr. Bates은 Ms. Syfu에게 무엇을 하도록 권유하는가?

(A) 회계 사무실에 연락한다
(B) 상사에게 연락한다
(C) 구독을 갱신한다
(D) 설문지를 작성한다

해설 세부사항을 묻는 문제이다. 키워드 encourage가 지문에서 kindly request로 표현되고 있다. 두 번째 이메일의 세 번째 단락 '이 문제의 해결안에 대해 간단한 설문 조사 작성을 정중히 요청합니다.'에서 Mr. Bates가 Ms. Syfu에게 간단한 설문조사에 응해 달라고 부탁하고 있으므로 정답은 (D) Fill out a questionnaire이다.

5. What does Mr. Bates offer Ms. Syfu?

(A) A free month of service
(B) A discount
(C) A magazine
(D) A new phone

Mr. Bates가 Ms. Syfu에게 제공한 것은 무엇인가?

(A) 한 달 무료 서비스
(B) 할인
(C) 잡지
(D) 새로운 전화기

해설 세부사항을 묻는 문제이다. 키워드 offer가 지문에서 유사한 단어인 give로 paraphrasing되었다. Mr. Bates가 Ms. Syfu에게 10월 전력 사용 요금을 50퍼센트 할인해주겠다고 하므로 정답은 (B) A discount이다.

해설서 p.91

Questions 1-5 refer to the following e-mails.

To	IT Department <itdepartment@vfb.com>
From	Nadia G. Pellins <ngpellins@vfb.com>
Date	July 20, 11:55 A.M.
Subject	Issues with the Online Account System

I work in the Mortgage Department, and I am sending you this e-mail because I have not been able to access our online account system all morning. I had no problems with it last Friday, but I keep getting an "access denied" message today every time I enter my password. Is anyone else in the company experiencing this problem, or is it just me that's having this problem? In any case, I need to enter account information into the system for five new loan applications before 6 P.M. today. Please help me to resolve this matter.

To: Nadia G. Pellins <ngpellins@vfb.com>
From: IT Department <itdepartment@vfb.com>
Date: July 20, 12:30 P.M.
Subject: Re: Issues with the Online Account System
Attachment: user_guide

Hello Nadia,

I apologize for the inconvenience. We started updating the online account system early Saturday morning and completed the work at 5:00 this morning. The update was purposely done during the weekend to ensure that the system would be accessible at the beginning of the work week today. Unfortunately, many employees have been receiving these "access denied" error messages this morning. We are in the process of fixing the problem, and the system should be fully operational in the next few hours, so you will have enough time to submit the loan applications for your clients.

Several employees have said they were able to access the system by resetting their password, so you may want to give this a try. You can find instructions for resetting your password in Section 2 of the system user guide, which has been attached to this e-mail. If you are still unable to access the system, please contact Kyoshiro Maruoka who will take care of any technical issues your department may have.

We appreciate your patience.

Simone Dilbert
IT Department Manager

1. Who most likely is Ms. Pellins?

(A) A recruitment consultant
(B) A system technician
(C) A loan applicant
(D) A bank clerk

2. In the first e-mail, the word "just" in line 4 is closest in meaning to

(A) only
(B) quite
(C) fairly
(D) also

3. According to Ms. Dilbert, when should Ms. Pellins be able to access the online account system again?

(A) By 5:00 Monday morning
(B) Before 6:00 Monday evening
(C) By Friday afternoon
(D) On the weekend

4. Why is Ms. Pellins referred to the system user guide?

(A) To find Mr. Maruoka's contact information
(B) To check the company's policy for accessing files
(C) To learn how to change her password
(D) To read instructions for submitting an application

5. What is true about Mr. Maruoka?

(A) He received an "access denied" error message.
(B) He is replacing Ms. Dilbert as the IT Department manager.
(C) He is an old client of Ms. Pellins.
(D) He will provide technical support for the Mortgage Department.

VOCA ··

issue *n.* 주제, 쟁점, 사안 | **online account system** 온라인 회계 시스템 | **mortgage** *n.* (담보) 대출(금), 융자(금) | **deny** *n.* 부인하다, 거부하다 | **every time** ~할 때마다 | **in any case** 어쨌든 | **apologize** *v.* 사과하다 | **inconvenience** *n.* 불편, 애로사항 | **purposely** *adv.* 고의로, 일부러 | **ensure** *v.* 확신하다 | **accessible** *adj.* 접근 가능한, 이용 가능한 | **unfortunately** *adv.* 불행하게도, 유감스럽게도 | **error message** 에러 메시지 | **process** *n.* 과정 | **fix the problem** 문제를 해결하다 | **fully operational** 완전히 가동 준비가 된 | **submit** *v.* 제출하다 | **loan application** 대출 신청 | **client** *n.* 고객 | **reset** *v.* (기기·조종 장치 등의 시간·숫자 등을) 다시 맞추다 | **attach** *adj.* 첨부하다 | **technical issue** 기술적 문제 | **appreciate** *v.* 고마워하다 | **patience** *n.* 참을성, 인내 | **refer** *v.* 언급하다, 조회하다

Questions 6-10 refer to the following Web page and online review.

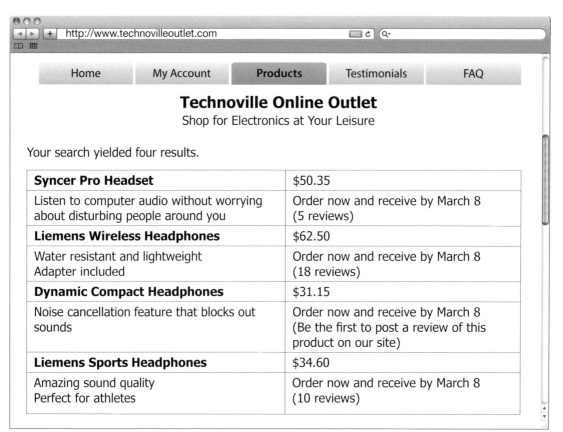

http://www.technovilleoutlet.com

| Home | My Account | Products | Testimonials | FAQ |

Technoville Online Outlet
Shop for Electronics at Your Leisure

Your search yielded four results.

Syncer Pro Headset	$50.35
Listen to computer audio without worrying about disturbing people around you	Order now and receive by March 8 (5 reviews)
Liemens Wireless Headphones	$62.50
Water resistant and lightweight Adapter included	Order now and receive by March 8 (18 reviews)
Dynamic Compact Headphones	$31.15
Noise cancellation feature that blocks out sounds	Order now and receive by March 8 (Be the first to post a review of this product on our site)
Liemens Sports Headphones	$34.60
Amazing sound quality Perfect for athletes	Order now and receive by March 8 (10 reviews)

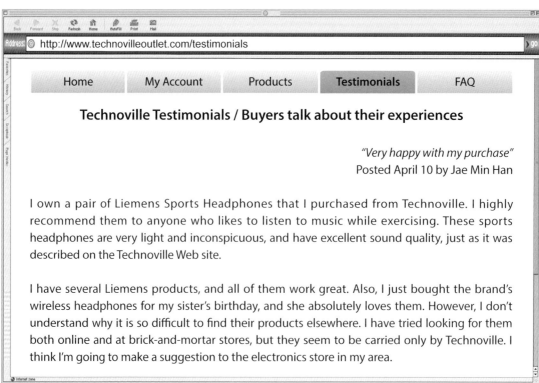

http://www.technovilleoutlet.com/testimonials

| Home | My Account | Products | Testimonials | FAQ |

Technoville Testimonials / Buyers talk about their experiences

"Very happy with my purchase"
Posted April 10 by Jae Min Han

I own a pair of Liemens Sports Headphones that I purchased from Technoville. I highly recommend them to anyone who likes to listen to music while exercising. These sports headphones are very light and inconspicuous, and have excellent sound quality, just as it was described on the Technoville Web site.

I have several Liemens products, and all of them work great. Also, I just bought the brand's wireless headphones for my sister's birthday, and she absolutely loves them. However, I don't understand why it is so difficult to find their products elsewhere. I have tried looking for them both online and at brick-and-mortar stores, but they seem to be carried only by Technoville. I think I'm going to make a suggestion to the electronics store in my area.

6. Why would shoppers most likely choose a Syncer Pro Headset?

(A) Because they often work close to other people
(B) Because they enjoy listening to music while working out
(C) Because they can save money on their purchase
(D) Because they don't want to be disturbed by noise outside

7. What item has NOT been evaluated on the Web site by customers?

(A) Syncer Pro Headset
(B) Liemens Wireless Headphones
(C) Dynamic Compact Headphones
(D) Liemens Sports Headphones

8. How much did the birthday present cost?

(A) $31.15
(B) $34.60
(C) $50.35
(D) $62.50

9. What is Mr. Han planning to do?

(A) Exchange an item
(B) Contact a local business
(C) Post another review
(D) Make a new purchase

10. In the online review, the word "carried" in paragraph 2, line 4, is closest in meaning to

(A) sold at a discount
(B) directed
(C) transported
(D) kept in stock

VOCA ···

yield v. (수익·결과·농작물 등을) 내다, 산출하다, 생산하다 | **wireless headphones** 무선 이어폰 | **testimonial** n. (어떤 것의 품질에 대한) 추천의 글 | **own** v. 소유하다 | **highly recommend** 매우 강력히, 적극 추천하다 | **inconspicuous** adj. 이목을 끌지 못하는, 눈에 잘 안 띄는 | **sound quality** 음질 | **describe** v. 말하다, 묘사하다 | **absolutely** adv. 전적으로, 틀림없이 | **elsewhere** adv. 다른 곳으로, 다른 곳에서도 | **sell** v. 팔다 | **direct** v. ~로 향하다, 지휘하다, (길을) 안내하다 | **transport** v. 수송하다, 실어 나르다 | **kept in stock** 상품을 구입해 두다, 재고가 있다

UNIT 14

삼중 지문

서로 관련된 세 개의 지문을 읽고 5문항을 풀어야 한다. 5문항 중에서 1~2개 문항은 두 지문을 연계시켜 추론하는 문제이다. 지문의 유형은 도표 등이 하나 이상 포함되어 있으며, 문제 풀이 방식은 이중 지문과 유사하다. 삼중 지문은 1회당 3세트가 출제된다.

삼중 지문은 이중 지문을 푸는 방법과 동일하게 접근하면 된다! 이중 지문보다 지문이 1개 늘었지만, 각 지문 길이가 비교적 짧은 편이므로 각 문제의 단서가 어느 지문에 해당하는 지만 잘 파악하면, 무리 없이 풀 수 있다. 최근, 인터넷, SNS의 발달 등으로 인해 삼중 지문에서도 문자 메시지, 웹사이트 지문들도 종종 등장하니 놀라지 말고, 각 지문에서의 단서를 찾아 문제를 해결하면 된다.

🔍 지문 유형 확인하기

1. 자주 나오는 지문

삼중 지문은 아래와 같이 서로 같거나 다른 지문 유형 3개가 조합되어 나온다. 이외에도 다양한 지문들의 조합과 주제들이 예상되므로 다양한 삼중 지문 문제를 접하고 풀어보는 연습이 필요하다.

☑ **이메일 + 웹사이트 + 쿠폰**

▶ 행사 또는 일정 안내 이메일 + 세부 사항 안내 사이트 + 할인 쿠폰

☑ **공지 + 양식 + [이메일/편지]**

▶ 행사 관련 공지 + 신청 양식 + 관련 이메일/편지

☑ **광고 + [청구서/온라인 구매 목록] + 이메일**

▶ 행사, 제품 및 서비스 광고 + [주문 양식 청구서/온라인 쇼핑 구매] + 확인 이메일

☑ **광고 + 이메일 + 이메일**

▶ 구인 광고 + 구직자 이메일 + 이력서 첨부 이메일

☑ **기사 + 일정표 + 이메일**

▶ 행사 및 시설 안내 기사 + 관련 일정표 + 관련 이메일

☑ **웹사이트 + 이메일 + 이메일**

▶ 광고 웹사이트 + 주문 문의 이메일 + 답변 이메일

☑ **웹사이트 + 고객 후기 + 이메일**

▶ 특정 정보 및 광고 웹 페이지 + 온라인 서평 후기 + 감사 또는 문의 이메일

2. 각 지문의 주제나 목적 또는 대상을 묻는다.

What is the **purpose** of the e-mail? 이메일의 목적은 무엇인가?

Why did Ms. Han **call** Mr. Brown? Ms. Han은 왜 Mr. Brown에게 전화했는가?

What is being **advertised**? 광고되고 있는 것은 무엇인가?

3. 각 지문의 세부 정보를 묻는다.

When did Ms. Kim take the class? Ms. Kim은 그 강의를 언제 수강했는가?

Which products were misdelivered? 어떤 물건들이 잘못 배송되었는가?

What are they **asked[required]** to do? 그들은 무엇을 하도록 요청[요구]되는가?

4. 두 지문의 내용을 비교하거나 연계해서 추론하는 문제가 나온다.

What is **NOT mentioned** in the letter? 편지에서 언급되지 않은 것은 무엇인가? 비교

What is most likely **true** about the class? 강의에 대해 사실인 것은 무엇이겠는가? 비교

What is **implied** about the **policy**? 정책에 대해 암시된 것은 무엇인가? 연계 추론

 문제 풀이 전략

1 지문이 하나 더 늘어났지만 문제 풀이 전략은 이중 지문과 동일하다.

삼중 지문 연계 지문은 등장하지 않으므로 문제 풀이는 기존의 이중 지문 문제 해결법과 동일함을 유의하자.

2 각 지문이 어떤 유형인지 파악하고 질문의 핵심 키워드를 확인한다.

질문을 보고 주제·목적 문제인지 세부사항 문제인지 확인하고 질문에서 단서 키워드를 잡는다.

3 단일 지문을 보고 푸는 문제와 두 개의 지문을 연계해서 풀어야 하는 문제를 구분한다.

예를 들어, 첫 번째 지문과 두 번째 지문의 연계 문제인지, 두 번째 지문과 세 번째 지문 연계 문제인지 확인한다.

4 세 개의 지문 중에는 일정표, 청구서, 목록, 영수증 등 다양한 서식 등이 포함된다.

지문이 세 개이므로 단일 지문이나 이중 지문에 비해 독해 시간이 다소 걸리지만, 세 개 지문 중에는 도표 등이 포함되어 있으므로 부담이 크게 늘어나지 않을 수도 있다.

Questions 1-5 refer to the following advertisement, online form, and e-mail.

The Chandler School of Fine Arts

Do you enjoy sketching, painting, or creating other types of artwork in your free time? Maybe you have an aptitude for art that you should develop more. Or perhaps you just want to learn about art. If so, consider taking classes at the Chandler School of Fine Arts.

We are currently accepting applications for the fall semester. Each courses lasts for three months and meets one to two times a week. To accommodate your busy schedule, classes are available in mornings, afternoons, and evenings from Monday through Saturday. The following are some of our most popular classes. For a complete listing, go to chandlerfa. com/fallschedule.

Class Name	Class Number	Instructor
Introduction to Oil Painting	53	Tim Haven
All About Sculpture	44	Lisa Watts
Advanced Watercolor Painting	87	Maria Gomez
How to Paint Like a Renaissance Artist	42	Enrico Eco

The semester begins on September 2. All classes cost $250, but there are additional fees for materials for some classes.

광고 주체
미술 학교

광고 대상
미술에 관심이 있거나
소질이 있는 사람

광고 목적:
가을 학기 미술 수강생
모집

수강 시간표
강의명, 강좌 번호,
강사명

개강일 및 수강료
9월 2일 개강, 전과목
동일 수강료 250달러

The Chandler School of Fine Arts
Online Registration Form

Name: Fred Thomas

Address: 45 W. Thompson Street, Chandler, AZ 85214

Telephone Number: 393-2396

E-mail Address: fred_t@privatemail.com

Date: August 27

Class(es):

Class Name	Class Number	Cost
A History of Painting	31	$250
Advanced Watercolor Painting	87	$315

How would you like to pay:

cash [✓]   check [ ]   credit card [ ]

Thank you for registering with the Chandler School of Fine Arts. You will receive a confirmation e-mail within 24 hours.

서식 종류
온라인 등록 신청서

수강 신청자 개인 정보

날짜

수강 신청 과목 및 비용
회화의 역사와 고급
수채화

지불 방법 선택
현금

24시간 이내 등록 확인
이메일 발송 예정

To: Fred Thomas <fred_t@privatemail.com>
From: Tina Powell <tpowell@chandlerfa.com>
Subject: Registration
Date: August 28

Dear Mr. Thomas,

Thank you for registering for classes at the Chandler School of Fine Arts. We are always pleased to welcome new students to our institute.

I would like to inform you of one change in your schedule. You registered for class number 31, A History of Painting. The instructor for that class has changed. Ms. Carmen Hooper will no longer teach it. Instead, Mr. Enrico Eco will be the instructor. He is a talented instructor, and I am positive you will enjoy learning from him.

Please note that you must pay for the classes in full by the end of the first week of classes.

Sincerely,

Tina Powell
The Chandler School of Fine Arts

- 수신인
  발신인
  제목
  날짜

- 이메일 발송 목적
  수강 신청을 확인해
  주기 위함

- 수강 변경 사항 안내
  31번 강의의 강사가
  변경됨

- 수강료 지급 기한 안내
  개강 첫 주가 끝나기
  전에 수강료를 지불해
  야 함

- 발신인 정보

동의어

1. In the advertisement, the word "aptitude" in paragraph 1, line 2, is closest in meaning to

   (A) desire
   (B) talent
   (C) interest
   (D) mood

사실확인

2. What is true about the classes at the Chandler School of Fine Arts?

   (A) They are held throughout the day.
   (B) They usually fill up fast.
   (C) They are taught by professional artists.
   (D) They are open only to skilled individuals.

이중 지문 연계

3. What is indicated about class number 87?

   (A) It is taught by a local artist.
   (B) Students must pay extra for supplies.
   (C) It is offered in the afternoon.
   (D) A limited number of people may take it.

세부사항: 지불 방법

4. How does Mr. Thomas intend to pay for his classes?

   (A) By check
   (B) With cash
   (C) With a credit card
   (D) By wire transfer

이중 지문 연계

5. What is indicated about Mr. Eco?

   (A) He will retire next semester.
   (B) He has been teaching for many decades.
   (C) He will teach more than one course.
   (D) He is popular among students.

[1-5] 다음 광고, 온라인 양식, 그리고 이메일에 관한 문제입니다.

The Chandler School of Fine Arts
Chandler 미술 학교

Do you enjoy sketching, painting, or creating other types of artwork in your free time? Maybe you have an ❶ aptitude for art that you should develop more. Or perhaps you just want to learn about art. If so, consider taking classes at the Chandler School of Fine Arts.

당신은 자유 시간에 스케치를 하거나 그림을 그리거나 다른 종류의 미술작품을 만드는 것을 즐깁니까? 아마도 당신은 더 개발할 필요가 있는 미술 **소질**을 지니고 있을 수도 있습니다. 또는 어쩌면 당신은 단지 미술에 대해 배우고 싶을 것입니다. 그러시다면, 당신은 Chandler 미술 학교의 수업을 듣는 것을 고려해 보세요.

We are currently accepting applications for the fall semester. Each courses lasts for three months and meets one to two times a week. To accommodate your busy schedule, classes are available in mornings, afternoons, and evenings from Monday through Saturday. The following are some of our most popular classes. For a complete listing, go to chandlerfa.com/fallschedule.

Chandler 미술 학교는 현재 가을 학기 지원서를 받고 있습니다. 각 수업은 3달 동안 진행되고, 일주일에 한 두 번 만납니다. 당신의 바쁜 일정을 수용하기 위해, 수업은 월요일부터 토요일까지 아침과 오후 저녁에 이용 가능합니다. 다음은 우리의 가장 인기 있는 몇몇 수업들입니다. 전체 목록을 보시려면, chandlerfa.com/fallschedule을 방문하세요.

Class Name 강의명	Class Number 강의 번호	Instructor 강사
Introduction to Oil Painting 유화 입문	53	Tim Haven
All About Sculpture 조각에 관한 모든 것	44	Lisa Watts
❸ Advanced Watercolor Painting 고급 수채화	87	Maria Gomez
❺ How to Paint Like a Renaissance Artist 르네상스 화가처럼 그림 그리는 법	42	❺ Enrico Eco

The semester begins on September 2. ❷ ❸ All classes cost $250, but there are additional fees for materials for some classes.

학기는 9월 2일에 시작합니다. **모든 수업은 비용이 250달러이지만 일부 수업은 추가 재료비가 있습니다.**

● 광고 주체
미술 학교

● 광고 대상
미술에 관심이 있거나 소질이 있는 사람

● 광고 목적:
가을 학기 미술 수강생 모집

● **수강 시간표**
강의명, 강좌 번호, 강사명

● 개강일 및 수강료
9월 2일 개강, 전과목 동일 수강료 250달러

VOCA

fine arts 미술 | artwork *n.* 미술품 | aptitude *n.* 소질, 적성 | perhaps *adv.* 어쩌면, 아마 | currently *adv.* 현재 | semester *n.* 학기 | last *v.* 지속하다 | the following *n.* 다음, 아래 | popular *adj.* 인기 있는 | listing *n.* 목록 | instructor *n.* 강사 | sculpture *n.* 조각품, 조각, 조소 | oil painting 유화 (그림, 화법) | accommodate *v.* 수용하다 | watercolor painting 수채화 | cost *v.* 비용이 들다 *n.* 비용 | material *n.* 재료, 자료

The Chandler School of Fine Arts
Online Registration Form

Chandler 미술 학교

온라인 등록 신청서

Name: Fred Thomas

Address: 45 W. Thompson Street, Chandler, AZ 85214

Telephone Number: 393-2396

E-mail Address: fred_t@privatemail.com

Date: August 27

이름: Fred Thomas

주소: W. Thompson가 45번지, 챈들러, 애리조나 85214

전화번호: 393-2396

이메일 주소: fred_t@privatemail.com

날짜: 8월 27일

Class(es):

강의(들):

Class Name 강의명	Class Number 강의 번호	Cost 비용
A History of Painting 회화의 역사	31	$250 250달러
Advanced Watercolor Painting 고급 수채화	87	❸ $315 315달러

How would you like to pay:

지불 방법:

❹ cash [✓]   check [　]   credit card [　]

현금　　　　수표　　　　　신용카드

Thank you for registering with the Chandler School of Fine Arts.
You will receive a confirmation e-mail within 24 hours.

Chandler 미술 학교에 등록해 주셔서 감사합니다. 당신은 24시간 이내에 확인 이메일을 받게 될 것입니다.

● 서식 종류
온라인 등록 신청서

● 수강 신청자 개인 정보

● 날짜

● 수강 신청 과목 및 비용
회화의 역사와 고급
수채화

● 지불 방법 선택
현금

● 24시간 이내 등록 확인
이메일 발송 예정

VOCA ···

registration *n.* 등록 | history *n.* 역사 | advanced *adj.* 고급의, 발전된 | watercolor painting 수채화 | cash *n.* 현금 | check *n.* 수표 |
register *v.* 등록하다 | confirmation *n.* 확인

To: Fred Thomas <fred_t@privatemail.com>
From: Tina Powell <tpowell@chandlerfa.com>
Subject: Registration
Date: August 28

수신: Fred Thomas 〈fred_t@privatemail.com〉
발신: Tina Powell 〈tpowell@chandlerfa.com〉
제목: 등록
날짜: 8월 28일

Dear Mr. Thomas,

Thomas 씨에게,

Thank you for registering for classes at the Chandler School of Fine Arts. We are always pleased to welcome new students to our institute.

Chandler 미술 학교 수업에 등록해 주셔서 감사합니다. 저희는 저희 학교에 신입생들을 맞이하게 되어 항상 기쁩니다.

I would like to inform you of one change in your schedule. You registered for class number 31, ❺ A History of Painting. The instructor for that class has changed. Ms. Carmen Hooper will no longer teach it. ❺ Instead, Mr. Enrico Eco will be the instructor. He is a talented instructor, and I am positive you will enjoy learning from him.

저는 귀하의 시간표에 한 가지 변경 사항이 있음을 알려드리고 싶습니다. 귀하는 강의 번호 31번 **회화의 역사**에 등록하셨습니다. **그 수업의 강사가 바뀌었습니다.** Ms. Carmen Hooper는 더 이상 그 과목을 가르치지 않을 것입니다. **대신 Mr. Enrico Eco가 강의할 것입니다.** 그는 재능 있는 강사라서 저는 귀하가 그에게서 배우는 것을 즐기시리라 확신합니다.

Please note that you must pay for the classes in full by the end of the first week of classes.

늦어도 수업이 있는 첫 번째 주의 말까지 수업료를 전액 지불하셔야 한다는 점을 유의하시기 바랍니다.

Sincerely,

감사합니다.

Tina Powell
The Chandler School of Fine Arts

Tina Powell
Chandler 미술 학교

• 수신인
발신인
제목
날짜

• 이메일 발송 목적
수강 신청을 확인해
주기 위함

• 수강 변경 사항 안내
31번 강의의 강사가
변경됨

• 수강료 지급 기한 안내
개강 첫 주가 끝나기
전에 수강료를 지불해
야 함

• 발신인 정보

VOCA ···

welcome v. 맞이하다, 환영하다 | **institute** n. 기관, 협회, 학원 | **talented** adj. 재능 있는 | **positive** adj. 확신하는, 긍정적인 | **in full** 완전히, 전부

1. In the advertisement, the word "aptitude" in paragraph 1, line 2 is closest in meaning to

(A) desire
(B) talent
(C) interest
(D) mood

광고 글에서, 첫 번째 문단 두 번째 줄의 "aptitude"와 의미상 가장 가까운 것은

(A) 갈망
(B) 재능
(C) 관심
(D) 분위기

> **해설** 동의어 찾기 문제이다. aptitude는 '소질, 적성'이라는 뜻으로 의미상 가장 가까운 단어는 talent(재능)이다. 따라서 정답은 (B) talent이다.

2. What is true about the classes at the Chandler School of Fine Arts?

(A) They are held throughout the day.
(B) They usually fill up fast.
(C) They are taught by professional artists.
(D) They are open only to skilled individuals.

Chandler 미술 학교의 수업들에 대해서 사실인 것은 무엇인가?

(A) 하루종일 열린다.
(B) 자리가 빨리 마감된다.
(C) 전문 예술가들이 수업을 가르친다.
(D) 수업들은 숙련된 개인들에게만 열린다.

> **해설** 첫 번째 광고 지문. 두 번째 단락을 보면 'classes are available in mornings, afternoons, and evening from Monday through Saturday'라고 하였으므로 수업이 월요일부터 토요일까지 하루 종일 진행된다는 사실을 알 수 있다. 정답은 (A) They are held throughout the day.이다.

3. What is indicated about class number 87?

(A) It is taught by a local artist.
(B) Students must pay extra for supplies.
(C) It is offered in the afternoon.
(D) A limited number of students may take it.

강의 번호 87번에 관하여 언급된 것은 무엇인가?

(A) 지역 미술가가 가르친다.
(B) 학생들은 제공품에 추가 비용을 지불해야 한다.
(C) 오후에 수업이 있다.
(D) 제한된 수의 학생들이 수강할 수 있다.

> **해설** 사실확인 유형의 문제이면서 두 개의 지문을 연계해서 봐야 답을 찾을 수 있는 문제이다. 키워드 class number 87이 지문에 나온 부분을 찾아본다. 온라인 등록 신청서에 강의 번호 87번은 수강료가 315달러이다. 첫 번째 지문인 광고 말미 'All classes cost $250, but there are additional fees for materials for some classes'에 모든 강좌의 수업료는 동일하게 250달러이지만 일부 과목에 재료비가 추가될 수 있다고 하였으므로 정답은 (B) Students must pay extra for supplies.이다.

4. How does Mr. Thomas intend to pay for his classes?

(A) By check
(B) With cash
(C) With a credit card
(D) By wire transfer

Mr. Thomas는 수업료를 어떻게 지불하고자 하는가?

(A) 수표로
(B) 현금으로
(C) 신용카드로
(D) 은행 이체로

> **해설** 세부사항을 묻는 문제이다. 온라인 등록 신청서 마지막 부분 'How would you like to pay'에서 원하는 지불 방식으로 'cash'에 체크를 했으므로 정답은 (B) With cash이다.

5. What is indicated about Mr. Eco?

(A) He will retire next semester.
(B) He has been teaching for many decades.
(C) He will teach more than one course.
(D) He is popular among students.

Mr. Eco에 관하여 알 수 있는 것은 무엇인가?

(A) 다음 학기에 은퇴할 것이다.
(B) 수십 년 간 가르쳐왔다.
(C) 한 과정 이상을 가르칠 것이다.
(D) 학생들 사이에서 인기가 많다.

> **해설** 신청서를 통해 Fred Thompson이 등록한 과정은 31번(회화의 역사)과 87번(Advanced Watercolor Painting)임을 알 수 있는데, 이 메일 두 번째 단락 'You registered for class number 31, A History of Painting. The instructor for that class has changed. Ms. Carmen Hooper will no longer teach it. Instead, Mr. Enrico Eco will be the instructor.'에서 '회화의 역사' 강사가 변경되었다고 하면서 새 강사로 Enrico Eco를 소개하고 있다. 광고를 보면 시간표에 강사 Enrico Eco가 가르치는 강의명이 'How to Paint Like a Renaissance Artist (르네상스 화가처럼 그림 그리는 법)'이므로 Enrico Eco이 두 과목을 강의할 거란 사실을 알 수 있다. 따라서 정답은 (C) He will teach more than one course.이다.

Questions 1-5 refer to the following article, e-mail, and announcement.

What a Job!

How would you like to eat the most delicious foods all day long and get paid? That's exactly the type of job Kevin Stevens has.

Kevin Stevens is a professional food taster. He works for Glencore Foods, an upscale catering service in Toronto. On average, his company makes food for 500 people a day, and Mr. Stevens gets to sample everything to make sure that the quality is high.

This job isn't as simple as it looks, though, as it requires a great deal of knowledge. Mr. Stevens studied nutrition as an undergraduate in Sydney, Australia, and then, he attended culinary school in Los Angeles, USA. Right after graduation, he worked as a chef in Milan, Italy, and Barcelona, Spain for a total of eight years. Upon returning to Canada two years ago, he started working at Glencore Foods and says about his job, "It's like a dream come true."

Cooking Life Magazine

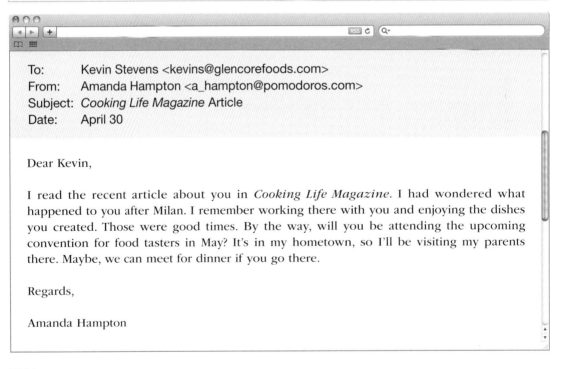

To: Kevin Stevens <kevins@glencorefoods.com>
From: Amanda Hampton <a_hampton@pomodoros.com>
Subject: *Cooking Life Magazine* Article
Date: April 30

Dear Kevin,

I read the recent article about you in *Cooking Life Magazine*. I had wondered what happened to you after Milan. I remember working there with you and enjoying the dishes you created. Those were good times. By the way, will you be attending the upcoming convention for food tasters in May? It's in my hometown, so I'll be visiting my parents there. Maybe, we can meet for dinner if you go there.

Regards,

Amanda Hampton

VOCA ··

taster *n.* 맛보는 사람, 맛 감별사 | upscale *adj.* 평균 이상의 | catering *n.* 음식 공급 | sample *v.* 맛보다, 시식하다 *n.* 샘플 | knowledge *n.* 지식 | nutrition *n.* 영양 | undergraduate *n.* 학부생, 대학생 | culinary *adj.* 요리의 | graduation *n.* 졸업 | chef *n.* 요리사 | wonder *v.* 궁금하다 | dish *n.* 요리 | by the way 그런데, 그건 그렇고 | upcoming *adj.* 다가오는 | convention *n.* 행사, 대회, 협회, 회의 | hometown *n.* 고향

Food Tasters Convention to Be Held Soon

The Food Tasters of North America (FTNA) is proud to announce that the fourth annual Food Tasters Convention is going to be held from May 15-17. The previous three conventions were held in Knoxville, Tennessee, but due to a scheduling conflict, the convention this year will take place in St. Louis, Missouri. Tickets cost $100 per person. Celebrity chef Walter Scott will be the keynote speaker. Noted individuals Kathy Kline and David Hurst will be in attendance, too.

1. What is suggested about Mr. Stevens?

(A) He earns a high salary at Glencore Foods.
(B) He enjoys his job.
(C) He prefers living in Europe.
(D) He has won several awards.

2. When did Mr. Stevens graduate from culinary school?

(A) 2 years ago
(B) 6 years ago
(C) 8 years ago
(D) 10 years ago

3. What was Ms. Hampton most likely doing when she met Mr. Stevens?

(A) She was studying at a university.
(B) She was employed as a food taster.
(C) She was working at a restaurant.
(D) She was learning to be a chef.

4. Where is Ms. Hampton's hometown?

(A) In Knoxville
(B) In Milan
(C) In St. Louis
(D) In Toronto

5. What is NOT mentioned about the Food Tasters Convention?

(A) How much it costs
(B) When it begins
(C) Who will be there
(D) What events will be held

VOCA ···

proud *adj.* 자랑스러운, 자랑스러워 하는 ǀ **previous** *adj.* 이전의 ǀ **conflict** *n.* 충돌, 갈등 ǀ **take place** 발생하다, 열리다 ǀ **keynote speaker** *n.* 기조 연설자 ǀ **celebrity** *n.* 유명 인사 ǀ **noted** *adj.* 유명한, 저명한 ǀ **individual** *n.* 개인 *adj.* 개개인의

Donoho Business Academy
45 Kensington Avenue, London, England

The Donoho Business Academy has been holding seminars on business matters for the past five decades. Our instructors are all either accomplished businesspeople or esteemed professors at local universities. They provide our students with the information they need to succeed in the business world. Our seminars are limited to 60 people, so it is crucial that you make your reservation now so to ensure you can get a seat. For more information or to make a booking, visit our Web site at www.donohoacademy.com or call us at 904-4557.

Here are this month's seminars:

Social Media and Your Business Saturday, 6 August 5:00 P.M. – 7:30 P.M. Tim Caldwell Kent University	**Breaking into the American Market** Saturday, 13 August 3:00 P.M. – 5:00 P.M. Amy Smythe The Baxter Group
Downsizing in Troubling Times Friday, 19 August 7:00 P.M. – 9:00 P.M. Joanna Pennyworth Chatham Consulting	**When to Take Your Company Public** Saturday, 27 August 11:00 A.M. – 1:30 P.M. Andrew Dalton Kincaid Financial

Registration Fees
Discounts are given for early registration:
Two weeks before the date of the seminar = 150 pounds
One week before the date of the seminar = 175 pounds
The day of the seminar = 200 pounds

Donoho Business Academy
Online Registration Form

Name: Claire York
E-mail: cyork@steadham.com
Telephone Number: 309-5683
Address: 32 Compass Street, Apartment 45B, London, England
Seminar Date: 19 August
Registration Submitted: 12 August

Thank you for registering for a seminar at the Donoho Business Academy. You will receive a confirmation e-mail within two hours of submitting this form.

To	cyork@steadham.com
From	customerrelations@donohoacademy.com
Date	17 August
Subject	Instructor Change

Dear Ms. York,

Thank you for submitting your payment for the upcoming seminar. I am obliged to inform you about a change to the seminar. The person originally scheduled to teach the seminar has fallen ill and will be unable to attend the event. However, Mr. Sean McManus, a professor at the London College of Finance, has agreed to teach the seminar in Ms. Pennyworth's place. Mr. McManus has taught courses here in the past, so you will still receive the quality education that you paid for.

Nevertheless, we understand if you wish to cancel your registration. While we normally only refund 50 percent of the price when students cancel, in this case, we will refund the full price of the fee. If we do not hear from you by the day of the seminar, we will assume that you would not like a refund.

Sincerely,

Simon Palmer
Donoho Business Academy

6. For whom is the advertisement intended?

(A) Educators
(B) University students
(C) Businesspeople
(D) Marketers

7. What is NOT mentioned about the seminars?

(A) They are broadcast on the Internet.
(B) The payment required for them varies.
(C) Some of them are taught by university professors.
(D) Seats in them can be booked online.

8. How much did Ms. York pay?

(A) 100 pounds
(B) 150 pounds
(C) 175 pounds
(D) 200 pounds

9. What is the purpose of the e-mail?

(A) To request payment for an event
(B) To advise a student that a refund has been processed
(C) To notify a participant about a change
(D) To mention that the time of a seminar has been altered

10. Which seminar is Mr. McManus going to teach?

(A) When to Take Your Company Public
(B) Breaking into the American Market
(C) Downsizing in Troubling Times
(D) Social Media and Your Business

VOCA ··

hold v. 개최하다 | decade n. 10년 | instructor n. 강사 | accomplished adj. 능숙한, 숙달된 | businesspeople n. 사업가 | esteemed adj. 존경 받는 | succeed v. 성공하다 | limit v. 제한하다 | crucial adj. 중요한 | ensure v. ~을 확실하게 하다 | break into 침입하다 | downsize v. 감축하다 | submit v. 제출하다 | upcoming adj. 다가오는 | originally adv. 원래 | fall ill 병이 나다 | pay for 지불하다 | nevertheless adv. 그럼에도 불구하고 | normally adv. 정상적으로 | refund v. 환불해주다 | in this case 이 경우에는 | assume v. 가정하다 | alter v. 바꾸다, 변경하다

REVIEW TEST

해설서 p.96

Questions 1-2 refer to the following job advertisement.

Love to snap pictures?
The Valley Monster team has a place for you!

Positions available:
Scheduling aide, yearbook picture assistant, portrait editor
Hiring full- and part-time employees.

Submit an application here: www.valleymonster.co.ca/hiring
An in-person interview is required. No experience necessary!

1. What kind of business most likely is Valley Monster?

(A) An appliance manufacturer
(B) A grocery store
(C) A sporting goods store
(D) A photography studio

2. What are job applicants asked to do?

(A) Email a schedule of available times
(B) Edit a sample document
(C) Submit a certificate
(D) Go to Valley Monster's Web site

Questions 3-4 refer to the following e-mail.

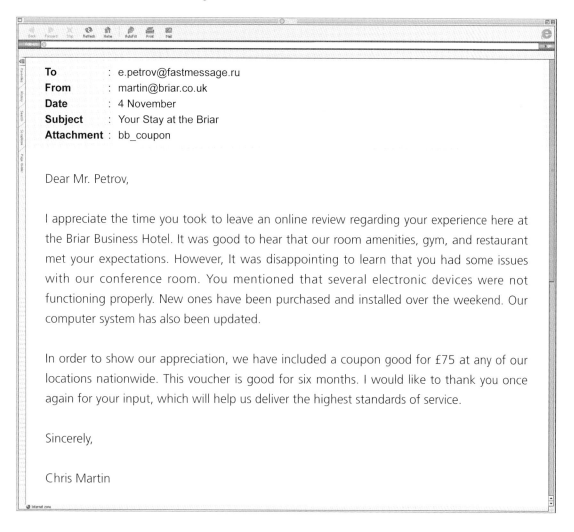

To   : e.petrov@fastmessage.ru
From   : martin@briar.co.uk
Date   : 4 November
Subject   : Your Stay at the Briar
Attachment : bb_coupon

Dear Mr. Petrov,

I appreciate the time you took to leave an online review regarding your experience here at the Briar Business Hotel. It was good to hear that our room amenities, gym, and restaurant met your expectations. However, It was disappointing to learn that you had some issues with our conference room. You mentioned that several electronic devices were not functioning properly. New ones have been purchased and installed over the weekend. Our computer system has also been updated.

In order to show our appreciation, we have included a coupon good for £75 at any of our locations nationwide. This voucher is good for six months. I would like to thank you once again for your input, which will help us deliver the highest standards of service.

Sincerely,

Chris Martin

---

3. Why did Mr. Martin write the e-mail?

(A) To reply to some customer comments
(B) To introduce a new service
(C) To make some travel arrangements
(D) To request a refund for a cancellation

4. What was recently improved at the Briar Business Hotel?

(A) A fitness center
(B) A restaurant menu
(C) A booking system
(D) A meeting room

Questions 5-6 refer to the following text message chain.

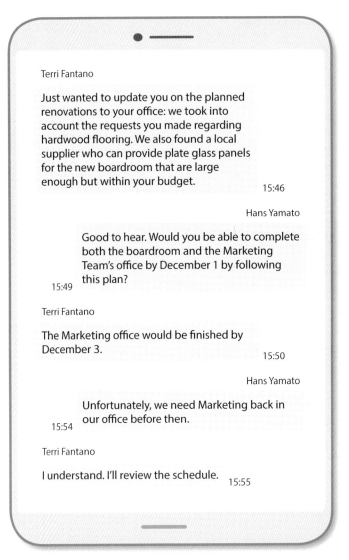

Terri Fantano

Just wanted to update you on the planned renovations to your office: we took into account the requests you made regarding hardwood flooring. We also found a local supplier who can provide plate glass panels for the new boardroom that are large enough but within your budget.

15:46

Hans Yamato

Good to hear. Would you be able to complete both the boardroom and the Marketing Team's office by December 1 by following this plan?

15:49

Terri Fantano

The Marketing office would be finished by December 3.

15:50

Hans Yamato

Unfortunately, we need Marketing back in our office before then.

15:54

Terri Fantano

I understand. I'll review the schedule.

15:55

5. What industry does Ms. Fantano most likely work in?

(A) Technology
(B) Marketing
(C) Construction
(D) Finance

6. At 15:55, what does Ms. Fantano most likely mean when she writes, "I understand"?

(A) She will lower a price.
(B) She will try to resolve an issue.
(C) She can use a different material.
(D) She can hire additional employees.

Questions 7-8 refer to the following instructions.

Residia.net—Online real estate

Account Access

To set your password, enter your e-mail address and user ID in the fields below. After that, click the tab, "Send temporary PIN." An e-mail will be sent to you automatically. Click on the link provided in the e-mail, and you will be redirected to a verification page. There, type in the personal identification number provided in the e-mail to access your account profile. Follow the steps provided in the "Set password" section to complete the process.

E-mail: daniel.kem@kemtech.com
Username: danielk96

Send Temporary PIN

---

7. Who most likely are the instructions for?

(A) Someone who is setting up a new computer
(B) Someone who has not created their log-in details
(C) Someone who is having software problems
(D) Someone who wishes to change their billing information

8. What is one thing the reader is instructed to do?

(A) Answer security questions
(B) Call customer support
(C) Fnter a specific number
(D) Print out a confirmation e-mail

Questions 9-11 refer to the following e-mail.

To	d.toth@worldemp.co.uk
From	a.munoz@worldemp.co.uk
Date	April 9
Subject	Newsletter Profile Information

Dear Mr. Toth,

It's our pleasure to welcome you to the accounting team here at World Emporium.

This e-mail is in regard to your employee profile, which will be published in our monthly newsletter. World Emporium's newsletter is sent to all our partners. Currently, we have a short biography, your role in the company, and your contact information. Now, we just need a photograph to appear next to your entry. Do you have a picture that you would like to use (it should be at least 1200 x 1600 pixels), or should we schedule for a member from the design team to stop by your office? Someone can come by either today or tomorrow.

Sincerely,

Alicia Munoz
Human Resources
World Emporium

9. What is implied about Mr. Toth?

(A) He is a new employee at World Emporium.
(B) He is making a company newsletter.
(C) He found an error in his staff profile.
(D) He recently received a pay raise.

10. What does Ms. Munoz ask Mr. Toth to provide?

(A) A résumé
(B) His contact details
(C) His job title
(D) An image

11. In the e-mail, the word "schedule" in paragraph 2, line 5, is closest in meaning to

(A) record
(B) check
(C) fit
(D) plan

Questions 12-14 refer to the following notice.

Announcement

Attention Boulder Fine Arts Theater Visitors

Our theater has been selected to be the host of the Colorado Independent Film Festival, which will run from October 1 to October 12. We would like to invite you back for this exciting event, which will feature short films, documentaries, and animated works by renowned filmmakers such as Mario Duke, Anna Scarius, Joanne Kim, and Rhody Scanlan. Of note is first-time director Edward Jimenez's thrilling debut film, which Stephen Vance, acclaimed critic of the *Atlanta Film Journal*, called "a breath of fresh air in cinema." Additional information about the featured directors and films can be found at www. bouldertheater.org, or you can download our mobile app to stay up-to-date on movie listings and special events.

12. What is indicated about the theater?

(A) It has received many awards.
(B) It holds a film festival every year.
(C) It will undergo construction starting in October.
(D) It is advertising a film festival online.

13. Who is Ms. Scanlan?

(A) A filmmaker
(B) A movie critic
(C) An actress
(D) A theater owner

14. Who was praised by Mr. Vance?

(A) Mr. Duke
(B) Ms. Scarius
(C) Ms. Kim
(D) Mr. Jimenez

Questions 15-18 refer to the following e-mail.

From: esmith@abcc.org
To: cnorton@kitchenjoy.co.nz
Subject: Registration and activities
Date: 20 April

Dear Ms. Norton,

This e-mail is to inform you that your registration and payment have been processed for the annual Allison Bay Culinary Conference (ABCC). —[1]—. We look forward to seeing you there again.

—[2]—. You left your choice of pre-conference activities blank on the form. I need that information to give to the entertainment coordinator, so he can finalize the itinerary for the attendees. —[3]—. Apart from the farmers' market and street food trips, this year, we are proud to offer participants a chance to visit a nearby organic farm. Additional information about these unique opportunities is available online. Please reply as soon as possible to let me know which tour you would like to join.

Also, note that these activities are covered by your fee. —[4]—. No extra payment will be required.

Sincerely,

Evan Smith
ABCC

15. Who most likely is Mr. Smith?

(A) An entertainment reporter
(B) A local farmer
(C) A conference organizer
(D) A street vendor

16. What is Ms. Norton asked to do?

(A) Submit a payment
(B) Change a reservation
(C) Download a form
(D) Select a tour option

17. What is indicated about Ms. Norton's fee for this year's event?

(A) It will stay the same.
(B) It is overdue.
(C) It will be reimbursed.
(D) It is affordable.

18. In which of the positions marked [1], [2], [3], and [4] does the following sentence best belong?

"I need one additional piece of information, however."

(A) [1]
(B) [2]
(C) [3]
(D) [4]

Questions 19-22 refer to the following online chat discussion.

Neil Ashton [10:52 A.M.]
Hi, Carley. Is Mill Avenue Designs done making the programs?

Carley Mendoza [10:54 A.M.]
I received an e-mail from Alyin this morning, and, unfortunately, they are behind schedule and can't deliver them on Tuesday. She says that they will be ready on Thursday morning.

Neil Ashton [10:55 A.M.]
Is that going to be enough time for our volunteers to include them in the participant packages?

Maja Anderson [10:56 A.M.]
Our sponsors are anxious to get their copies too. And I'd like to post a link to the digital version on our Web site by Friday.

Carley Mendoza [10:57A.M.]
Not to worry. As long as we get the materials by 1 P.M. on Thursday, we can still follow our planned timeline. Maja, I'll forward the file to our Web site developer once I get it.

Neil Ashton [10:59 A.M.]
Wonderful! Keep me up-to-date with any further details from Alyin. By the way, have you finalized who will give the keynote address?

Carley Mendoza [11:01 A.M.]
Yes. I am going to call Mr. Codrescu at Midland College in a moment to find out if he will need special equipment. Last Monday, I made sure that the main convention hall would be adequate for our 800 attendees.

Maja Anderson [11:02 A.M.]
That's great. Thank you, Carley. I'm sure this year's gathering will be a success.

SEND

---

19. What is the purpose of the discussion?

(A) To arrange a meeting with company sponsors
(B) To go over details of an event
(C) To check on an equipment order
(D) To confirm a convention venue

20. According to the discussion, when should the programs arrive?

(A) On Tuesday
(B) On Wednesday
(C) On Thursday
(D) On Friday

21. At 10:57 A.M., what does Ms. Mendoza most likely mean when she writes, "Not to worry"?

(A) She can keep to a schedule.
(B) She can update the programs.
(C) She can email some sponsors.
(D) She can find some volunteers.

22. What will Ms. Mendoza most likely do next?

(A) Revise a Web site
(B) Reserve a convention hall
(C) Contact an educational institution
(D) Call Mill Avenue Designs

C-sharp News

Glenn Wong, Staff Writer

Rastbury (June 4) - For nearly 90 years, C-sharp, Rastbury's popular jazz venue, has been serving the local community. Two years ago, it was put up for sale, but the building has remained on the market until recently. Last Tuesday, the venue was officially purchased for $1.2 million by Jim Gould, who was born just a few blocks away.

Yesterday afternoon, Mr. Gould invited members of the press into the historic building to talk about the purchase.

"I have always admired the aesthetics of this venue," he stated. "It should go without saying that I will keep the spirit of this place alive." Mr. Gould also owns Touchdown Pub, a popular diner in Rastbury. His comment was a reaction to rumors in the community that he was considering converting C-sharp into a second Touchdown Pub location. When the building went up for sale, Friends of C-sharp (FCS) was founded to address such concerns.

"The FCS would have liked to purchase the building to ensure that its musical tradition continues," explained FCS spokesperson Carolyn Brown, responding to Mr. Gould's statement. "We hope that Mr. Gould will be true to his word. We will work with him to ensure the continuing success of C-sharp."

Mr. Gould has stated that parts of the building will be renovated to ensure everyone's safety after a thorough inspection.

23. What is the article mainly about?

(A) A performance's recent reviews
(B) An executive's retirement
(C) A business' new ad campaign
(D) A building's future

24. What is suggested about Mr. Gould?

(A) He is well-liked in Rastbury.
(B) He will preserve a venue.
(C) He runs a major restaurant chain.
(D) He will allow the FCS to inspect C-sharp.

25. What is indicated about the FCS?

(A) It was formed two years ago.
(B) It is responsible for organizing concerts in Rastbury.
(C) It will buy several properties in Rastbury.
(D) It still does not agree with Mr. Gould's plans.

Questions 26-29 refer to the following advertisement.

The Arc Centre

Redesigned for mixed-use commercial and residential purposes, the Arc Centre caters to the needs of both business and residential tenants. —[1]—. Previously fully occupied by EMP Studios, executive suites and workspaces have been renovated into luxurious living quarters providing a breathtaking display of Hong Kong's Victoria Harbour. Fully equipped with advanced smart home technologies, every apartment has the latest in energy-saving and Internet-enabled comforts. —[2]—. However, the high-tech conveniences aren't only inside the residences.

Featured services include video conferencing rooms which can be reserved by residents or rented by companies with offices in the building. Part of the centre's commitment to green energy can be seen on the roof, where solar panels shade benches set among lush greenery. —[3]—. Tenants are also welcome to join the gym just down the street from the centre. Right next door to the Arc Centre is the Arc Mall, which has stores, restaurants, and a large game room—all popular with area families and workers. Within walking distance are two of the city's top schools.

The Arc Centre is the future of Hong Kong's urban landscape. —[4]—. Learn about becoming a resident by visiting our Web site at www.thearc.com.hk.

---

26. In the advertisement, the word "display" in paragraph 1, line 4, is closest in meaning to

(A) act
(B) arrangement
(C) exposition
(D) view

27. What does the Arc Centre offer its occupants?

(A) A fitness club
(B) Places to hold meetings
(C) A spacious parking garage
(D) A playground for children

28. What is mentioned about the Arc Centre?

(A) It is located near a shopping area.
(B) It is operated by EMP Studios.
(C) It provides access to public transportation.
(D) It has recently renovated its basement.

29. In which of the positions marked [1], [2], [3], and [4] does the following sentence best belong?

"This is a perfect area to escape the summer heat and socialize with the neighbors."

(A) [1]
(B) [2]
(C) [3]
(D) [4]

Questions 30-34 refer to the following memo and schedule.

To: Sharper Carrot Design staff
From: Anish Freeholm, General Affairs
Subject: December Itinerary
Sent: November 10
Attachment: Timetable

As you already know, the first two weeks in December are going to involve some challenges. Some departments will have to temporarily vacate their offices for set periods to enable workers to refloor, rewire, and paint the walls. Affected team members must place their office belongings into boxes before 4 P.M. the day before. (Refer to the attached timetable.) Floors will be vacated two rooms or offices at a time by on-site logistics staff. Please be aware that office suites scheduled for work on Monday will need to prepare before the weekend, on November 30.

Packing materials and boxes will be distributed. When you have finished, please write your name and department on them so that they can be put back in their correct locations afterward. Please be sure to arrange an area where you are able to keep working while your offices are unavailable. The executive conference room in office 712 will be open for anyone who needs a place to work. We encourage everyone to talk with their managers about the option of telecommuting for one or both days as well.

We thank you in advance for your cooperation. If you have questions or concerns regarding any part of the process, please reply directly to this e-mail.

Work Timetable - December 3 to December 13	
Mon., Dec 3 / Tue., Dec 4	Office 708 (Design studio) / Office 711 (Marketing & HR)
Thur., Dec 6 / Fri., Dec 7	Office 707 (Web design) / Office 709 (IT)
Tue., Dec 11 / Wed., Dec 12	Office 710 (Publishing & Sales) / Office 706 (Accounting)

30. Why was the memo sent to staff members?

(A) To address their concerns about a merger
(B) To announce upcoming promotions
(C) To ask for suggestions about a proposal
(D) To remind them of an upcoming remodeling project

31. What are employees instructed to do?

(A) Indicate which office items are theirs
(B) Work more hours in the office
(C) Revise their contact information
(D) Submit a form to their supervisors

32. What is stated about office 712?

(A) It will be provided as workspace for employees.
(B) A training session will be held there.
(C) It will be refurnished in a month.
(D) Video conferencing equipment will be set up there.

33. When should the Web Design Department be ready to vacate?

(A) On November 10
(B) On November 30
(C) On December 5
(D) On December 6

34. What is suggested about the Publishing Department?

(A) It has a project deadline approaching.
(B) It will reserve a conference room.
(C) It will appoint a new manager soon.
(D) It shares office space with another team.

To	helpdesk@intertop.co.kr
From	Mehran@weissnicht.de
Date	February 21
Subject	Registration

Hello,

I am currently unable to register my new Intertop tablet PC. I have read through the user's manual, and also checked for information on your company's Web site. Unfortunately, however, I was unable to locate the Intertop registration number required to complete the process. I then stopped by your retail outlet, where the staff told me to contact you via e-mail referencing the model number of the device. The model number is 05768936. Please advise where I can find the registration number.

Thank you,

Mehran Tebrizi

To	Mehran@weissnicht.de
From	helpdesk@intertop.co.kr
Date	February 22
Subject	Re: Registration

Dear Mr. Tebrizi,

Thanks for your inquiry dated 21 February. Using your e-mail address and the other information you gave, I determined that you bought an Intertop Topmaster 5000, service tag number 5982601. Your Intertop registration number is BK8W-A6SY-G85U.

For future services, I would recommend having the service tag number handy. This number can also be found on a sticker attached inside the cover of your owner's manual for your convenience. By providing this number, you allow us to direct your call to a service representative knowledgeable about your product and access the history of your prior service calls.

For further inquiries, I recommend contacting our service center by phone. Be ready to provide your name, service tag number, and details of the issue so that we can offer the quickest possible solution. Also, check out the FAQ section on our Web site for general information to ensure the best user experience.

Thanks again,

Leticia Han
Intertop Service Center Supervisor

35. What did Mr. Tebrizi do before writing his e-mail?

(A) He registered his device.
(B) He made a phone call.
(C) He visited a store.
(D) He returned his device.

36. How did Ms. Han confirm Mr. Tebrizi's purchase?

(A) By referring to a model number and an e-mail address
(B) By examining a registration number
(C) By speaking to the sales department
(D) By looking at an owner's manual

37. Where should Mr. Tebrizi look for his service tag number?

(A) On the back of a receipt
(B) On the bottom of his tablet PC
(C) Inside the cover of a guide
(D) In a section of a Web site

38. In the second e-mail, the word "direct" in paragraph 2, line 3, is closest in meaning to

(A) transfer
(B) correct
(C) manage
(D) instruct

39. How does Ms. Han suggest that Mr. Tebrizi contact a representative if he has a question?

(A) By phone
(B) By going to an Intertop branch office
(C) By e-mail
(D) By accessing an online account

Transition at Cambridge's Brown Mouse Restaurant Complete
By Louise Clairsen

CAMBRIDGE (January 5) - Andrea Desai, the current sous-chef at the Brown Mouse Restaurant working under head chef Nathan McLeod, has finalized the purchase of the eatery. Mr. McLeod will be moving to Keswick, where he plans to keep busy as a culinary instructor at a local university. "When Nathan told me he was leaving, I knew I had to seize the opportunity," said Ms. Desai.

Mr. McLeod stated, "Andrea has been with Brown Mouse for over a decade and was quite instrumental in helping me come up with most of our signature dishes." Since Ms. Desai took over this week, she has already changed up some of the restaurant's menu items, notably with a curry thyme dumpling that Daryl Davies of Cambridge Daily called, "stunningly delicious." The restaurant doesn't take reservations, but you can order ahead by calling 555-2344 or online at www.brownmouse.co.uk.

Brown Mouse Restaurant

The Month of January
A Taste of India Fixed Menu (£45 per person)

Appetizer
A) Toasted cumin and yogurt chicken kebabs
B) Curry thyme vegetable dumplings

Entrée
A) Tandoori lamb with potatoes
B) Spicy salmon linguini with cucumber-dill soup

Dessert
A) Rose chickpea cookies
B) Fried date sorbet

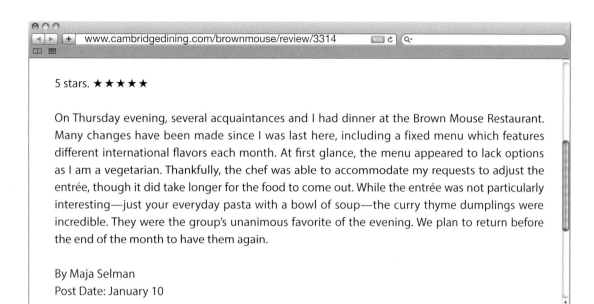

www.cambridgedining.com/brownmouse/review/3314

5 stars. ★ ★ ★ ★ ★

On Thursday evening, several acquaintances and I had dinner at the Brown Mouse Restaurant. Many changes have been made since I was last here, including a fixed menu which features different international flavors each month. At first glance, the menu appeared to lack options as I am a vegetarian. Thankfully, the chef was able to accommodate my requests to adjust the entrée, though it did take longer for the food to come out. While the entrée was not particularly interesting—just your everyday pasta with a bowl of soup—the curry thyme dumplings were incredible. They were the group's unanimous favorite of the evening. We plan to return before the end of the month to have them again.

By Maja Selman
Post Date: January 10

40. What is the purpose of the article?

(A) To announce the results of a cooking competition
(B) To publicize a change in a business' ownership
(C) To describe the difficulties of running a large restaurant
(D) To explain how to receive a discount voucher

41. Why is Mr. McLeod going to Keswick?

(A) To open a new restaurant
(B) To study online marketing
(C) To become a food critic
(D) To teach cooking

42. What detail from the article does Ms. Selman agree with?

(A) The restaurant's popularity has made it difficult to get a table.
(B) A menu item reviewed in a local publication is excellent.
(C) Some dishes are unusual for the Cambridge area.
(D) The staff members are very polite to the customers.

43. In the review, the word "take" in paragraph 1, line 5, is closest in meaning to

(A) withdraw
(B) permit
(C) require
(D) obtain

44. What dish did Ms. Selmen ask to have prepared differently?

(A) Chicken kebabs
(B) Spicy salmon
(C) Tandoori lamb
(D) Date sorbet

From:	Richard Halldorsson <rhalldorsson@icelandadv.com>
To:	Cynthia Rucker <cynthiar@sunmail.net>
Date:	June 10
Subject:	Options
Attachment:	cynthiarucker_schedule.rtf

Dear Ms. Rucker,

We appreciate your interest.

Our July packages only have a few spots remaining, as it's our most popular month. So please respond at your earliest convenience if you plan to register for one of them. They may be full by the end of the week!

Please note that not all the tours indicated in the attached document will be available to you, as you will have a travelling companion.

I hope to hear from you soon!

Sincerely,

Richard Halldorsson
Iceland Adventures Co.

Iceland Adventures Co.
July Programs Schedule

Tour Name	Date	Length	Prices (ISK)	Availability
Skogafoss Waterfall	July 10	9 A.M.–6 P.M.	41,000	3 spots remaining
Reynisfjara Beach	July 16	7 A.M.–4 P.M.	36,000	2 spots remaining
Diamond Beach	July 20	9 A.M.–6 P.M.	32,000	1 spot remaining
Reykjavik Shopping	July 27	10 A.M.–4 P.M.	8,000	2 spots remaining
Midnight Sun Hike	July 28	6 P.M.–4 A.M.	6,000	4 spots remaining

All tours leave from and arrive back at the Iceland Adventures headquarters. Be sure to come at least 20 minutes before your group is due to leave. The weather can be cold in some areas, so be sure to confirm beforehand whether you'll need to bring a heavy coat. Tours won't be called off due to inclement conditions, so you may wish to wear waterproof shoes. All meals are part of the package price, but you are encouraged to bring energy bars or other snacks.

To	Richard Halldorsson <rhalldorsson@icelandadv.com>
From	Cynthia Rucker <cynthiar@sunmail.net>
Date	June 11
Subject	Re: Options

Mr. Halldorsson,

Thank you for responding so quickly. The only day we can make time for a tour during our vacation in Iceland will be July 27. Please sign us up for that date. We will be staying in a rural part of the country for our first week and plan to do some hiking by ourselves.

Thanks!

Cynthia Rucker

45. What does the first e-mail indicate about Iceland Adventures Co.?

(A) It promoted Mr. Halldorsson in June.
(B) It offers trips exclusively in the summer.
(C) Its itinerary was recently updated.
(D) Its July packages are getting booked quickly.

46. According to Mr. Halldorsson, which tour is NOT an option for Ms. Rucker?

(A) Skogafoss Waterfall
(B) Diamond Beach
(C) Reykjavik Shopping
(D) Midnight Sun Hike

47. What does the schedule recommend that participants do?

(A) Bring an umbrella
(B) Arrive early to buy admission passes
(C) Check the weather forecast
(D) Pack some bottled water

48. What does the second e-mail suggest about Ms. Rucker?

(A) She frequently visits Iceland on vacation.
(B) She had technical difficulties with a Web site.
(C) She requires more trip details from Mr. Halldorsson.
(D) She will go on a hike without a guide.

49. What is the cost of the tour Ms. Rucker has selected?

(A) 36,000 ISK
(B) 32,000 ISK
(C) 8,000 ISK
(D) 6,000 ISK

Visiting the Washington History Museum (WHM)

One of South Bend's best-known attractions, the Washington History Museum, has been a prime destination for visitors since it opened in 1940. Visitors have the option of picking up an audio guide and looking around the museum at their own pace or getting a tour with one of our expert guides. For individual visitors, the cost of a guided tour is a flat fee of $5, but for groups larger than 10, we offer special pricing (see table below) and tours designed to fit your particular interests. Group reservations must be made at least 48 hours before your visit. To book a tour, email us at info@whm.org.

Group Pricing

Elementary and Middle School: $50 for up to 20 students; $100 for up to 50 students
High School and College: $75 for up to 20 students; $125 for up to 50 students
General: $85 for up to 20 guests; $140 for up to 50 guests

Washington History Museum (WHM) Exhibits

The First Midwestern City
Enjoy the largest collection of Cahokian artifacts in the world. Explore a full-sized reproduction of a block in the ancient city of Cahokia, getting a glimpse of the sophisticated urban life they had more than a millennium ago.

Prophets and Pioneers
This exhibit profiles important personalities of the 19th century. Watch filmed reenactments, and see firsthand records and personal effects of James Whitcomb Riley, Tecumseh, and others.

Dawn of a New Industry
This eye-opening examination of the origins of automobile manufacturing is on loan from the Searle Museum in Chicago from March 21 to April 30. The display, exhibiting some of the earliest automobiles and accounts of factory life, will take up the whole Tarkington Wing.

Growing Michiana
This gallery gives an in-depth background of our diverse culture. It examines the evolution of South Bend's population through the 20th and 21st centuries.

To: tours@whm.org
From: sueflowers@johnblainetech.edu
Subject: Reservation
Date: March 26

Group Name: John Blaine Tech
Group Size: 40

I'm the vice principal at John Blaine Tech, and I'd like to schedule a tour for a group of high school students. On previous visits, we've had the pleasure of being guided by Nairo Vidal. We'd really appreciate it if he could lead our tour once again. The group will be studying contemporary culture. If you have morning slots available in the first week of September, we'd like to schedule it for then.

Best,

Sue Flowers

50. What is implied about WHM?

(A) It has been in business for a long time.
(B) It has recently undergone renovations.
(C) It does not offer tours on the weekend.
(D) It provides complimentary history courses.

51. What is indicated about the Tarkington Wing?

(A) It will temporarily feature only one display.
(B) It is going to be expanded in the summer.
(C) It is exclusively open to researchers.
(D) It can be accessed for an extra fee.

52. How much will the John Blaine Tech group be charged for their tour?

(A) $75
(B) $100
(C) $125
(D) $140

53. Which exhibition would the John Blaine Tech group most likely be interested in touring?

(A) The First Midwestern City
(B) Prophets and Pioneers
(C) Dawn of a New Industry
(D) Growing Michiana

54. Who is Nairo Vidal?

(A) A John Blaine Tech staff member
(B) A university professor
(C) A WI IM employee
(D) A tour agency manager

MINI TEST

MINI TEST 01

해설서 p.109

1. Travelers whose trains are delayed more ------- two hours may be eligible for a discounted ticket.

(A) of
(B) as
(C) than
(D) from

2. Due to restricted seating, we require a ------- response so that we can reserve seats.

(A) busy
(B) quick
(C) sharp
(D) close

3. In order to promote a new range of first aid products, the Self Help Pharmacy ------- free samples tomorrow.

(A) providing
(B) was providing
(C) will be providing
(D) has been providing

4. Korrian Organization was forced to ------- its outdoor fundraising event due to inclement weather.

(A) donate
(B) postpone
(C) decorate
(D) prepare

5. Patients at Devana Hospital can access ------- medical records at any time of day.

(A) their
(B) they
(C) them
(D) theirs

6. Testing methods used in the laboratory must be ------- verified for precision and accuracy.

(A) regularity
(B) regular
(C) regularize
(D) regularly

7. Most of the glass producers are located in the southwest ------- of the town.

(A) amount
(B) distance
(C) area
(D) plan

8. The budget report will have to be ------- next Friday after the vice president approves it.

(A) submitting
(B) submits
(C) submitted
(D) submit

9. In ------- of the festival's twentieth anniversary, this year's event will run for three days straight.

(A) celebrate
(B) celebrates
(C) celebrated
(D) celebration

10. Consumer demand for more affordable fuel-efficient cars is expected to rise rapidly ------- the next five years.

(A) over
(B) toward
(C) behind
(D) against

Questions 11-14 refer to the following invitation.

May 11

Beth Rivers
4005 Floral Drive
Austin, Texas 78610

Dear Ms. Rivers,

Carl's Business Attire would like to show our appreciation for your loyal patronage by inviting you

to a -------. The grand reopening of our store at 945 Aspen Street ------- place on Friday, July 5,
    11.   **12.**

from 3:00 P.M. to 7:00 P.M.

It would be great if you could ------- us on this special occasion. -------.
                                 13.   **14.**

Thank you.

Sincerely,

Eric Wang

---

11. (A) society
    (B) conference
    (C) presentation
    (D) celebration

12. (A) took
    (B) taking
    (C) will take
    (D) would take

13. (A) join
    (B) find
    (C) hire
    (D) send

14. (A) Please contact Terrence Bodin if you have any questions.
    (B) Terrence Bodin should submit a full schedule by June 1.
    (C) Terrence Bodin can persuade him to start earlier.
    (D) Some new employees will be hired by June 1.

Questions 15-16 refer to the following text message.

From: Keith Hurst

1:50 P.M., March 20

My flight arrived a while ago. The driver isn't at the airport terminal. Could you find out where he's waiting to pick me up? It's been ten minutes now. I don't want to be late for the meeting. Thanks. See you in the office.

15. What is the purpose of the text message?

(A) To request driving directions
(B) To explain changes to a flight
(C) To check on transportation arrangements
(D) To postpone a business meeting

16. From where did Mr. Hurst send the message?

(A) His home
(B) An airport
(C) His office
(D) A taxi

Dalia's
3100 Smithson Way, Adelaide AD11
End-of-Season Clearance Sale
May 7 to May 22

Spring apparel – 50% to 70% off
Shoes – 25% off
Sportswear – 40% off
Jewelry and accessories – 25% off
Prices as marked

Present this flyer to receive an additional $15 off
any sunglasses purchase of $40 or more during this sale.
For each purchase of $75 or more during this clearance sale,
we will give a coupon for 10% off any item from the Summer Collection.
Coupons valid from May 28 to June 30.

Note: Dalia's will close on May 26 while our staff restock the inventory and
prepare our store for the Summer Collection.

17. What is the purpose of the flyer?

(A) To announce a store opening
(B) To introduce a new line of sportswear
(C) To provide information about new ownership
(D) To advertise a sale of seasonal merchandise

18. On what date could a customer be awarded a coupon?

(A) May 22
(B) May 26
(C) May 28
(D) June 30

Questions 19-21 refer to the following e-mail.

To	Thomas Donati <tdonati@dosmail.com>
From	Jewel Summers <jsummers@virgoeye.com>
Subject	Your Order
Date	October 15

We have received your recent e-mail. At Virgo Eyewear, customer satisfaction is our number one priority.

We regret that there was an issue with your last order. Our records indicate that one pair of item PF4938 (prescription sunglasses) and one pair of item PF8442 (prescription eyeglasses) should have been delivered to you. However, you said in your e-mail that two pairs of item number PF4938 were delivered instead and that you were charged for both of these as well as the item you didn't get.

We have shipped the eyeglasses to you by express mail this afternoon, so they should arrive at your home address tomorrow morning. As for the extra pair of sunglasses, you can either send them back to us or buy them at half price. Please inform us of your choice. If you wish to return the sunglasses, we will send a pre-paid mailing envelope to you. Once the package is received by us, the entire additional charge will be removed from your account. If you decide to keep the item, 50 percent of the additional charge will be removed from your account.

We sincerely apologize for any inconvenience this may have caused. We appreciate your business with Virgo Eyewear.

Best regards,

Jewel Summers
Customer Service Manager
Virgo Eyewear

19. Why did Ms. Summers send the e-mail?

(A) To confirm that she received a returned item
(B) To address an error reported by Mr. Donati
(C) To apologize for a delayed response to a complaint
(D) To encourage Mr. Donati to place an order

20. According to the e-mail, what will be sent to Mr. Donati upon request?

(A) An updated invoice
(B) An eyeglass prescription
(C) A product catalog
(D) A shipping envelope

21. What is indicated about item PF8442?

(A) It is Virgo Eyewear's best-selling item.
(B) It was included in a package with item PF4938.
(C) Mr. Donati will probably receive it on October 16.
(D) Mr. Donati purchased it online.

Questions 22-25 refer to the following letter.

Medical Developments Today
532 Stanfield Road, Toronto

July 17

Tony Huyen
4698 Rockwood Street
Toronto

Dear Mr. Huyen,

—[1]—. Thank you for being a subscriber to *Medical Developments Today*. We'd like to let you know that your current subscription expires on August 31. —[2]—. Just fill out and send back the renewal form that has been enclosed with this letter.

Medical Developments Today is the leading health magazine in the country and provides readers with the most recent news and developments in the medical world. —[3]—. As always, we are sure you'll continue to enjoy all of our content including the entertaining columns of Billy Grasp and the informative health tips from Professor Wanda Wilson. —[4]—.

Sincerely,

Sarah McQueen

Sarah McQueen
Circulation Manager
Enclosure

---

22. What is the main purpose of the letter?

(A) To offer health advice
(B) To issue a reminder
(C) To introduce a new product
(D) To promote a talk show

23. What is Mr. Huyen asked to do?

(A) Try out an item
(B) Comment on a column
(C) Return a form
(D) Enter a contest

24. What is suggested about Mr. Grasp?

(A) He develops medical tools.
(B) He travels around the world.
(C) He organizes seminars.
(D) He writes for a magazine.

25. In which of the positions marked [1], [2], [3], and [4] does the following sentence best belong?

"If you make your payment by the end of this month, you will receive Dr. Lin Chin's state-of-the-art thermostat at no charge."

(A) [1]
(B) [2]
(C) [3]
(D) [4]

Questions 26-30 refer to the following e-mails.

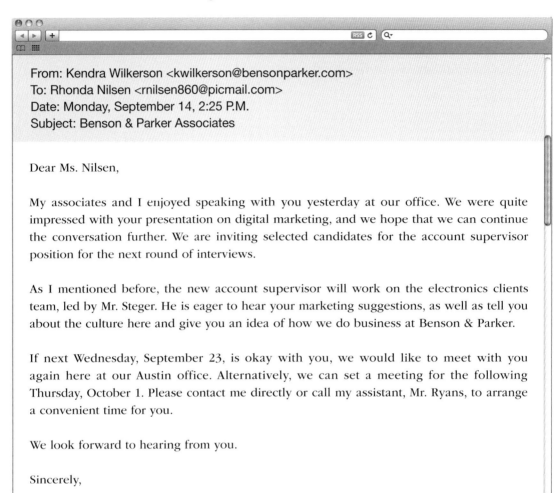

From: Kendra Wilkerson <kwilkerson@bensonparker.com>
To: Rhonda Nilsen <rnilsen860@picmail.com>
Date: Monday, September 14, 2:25 P.M.
Subject: Benson & Parker Associates

Dear Ms. Nilsen,

My associates and I enjoyed speaking with you yesterday at our office. We were quite impressed with your presentation on digital marketing, and we hope that we can continue the conversation further. We are inviting selected candidates for the account supervisor position for the next round of interviews.

As I mentioned before, the new account supervisor will work on the electronics clients team, led by Mr. Steger. He is eager to hear your marketing suggestions, as well as tell you about the culture here and give you an idea of how we do business at Benson & Parker.

If next Wednesday, September 23, is okay with you, we would like to meet with you again here at our Austin office. Alternatively, we can set a meeting for the following Thursday, October 1. Please contact me directly or call my assistant, Mr. Ryans, to arrange a convenient time for you.

We look forward to hearing from you.

Sincerely,

Kendra Wilkerson
Human Resources Manager

From	Rhonda Nilsen <rnilsen860@picmail.com>
To	Kendra Wilkerson <kwilkerson@bensonparker.com>
Date	Tuesday, September 15, 9:00 A.M.
Subject	Account Supervisor Position

Dear Ms. Wilkerson,

I am delighted to hear that you are considering me for the account supervisor position at your marketing firm. I would be more than happy to visit your office again to further share my ideas and tell you more about my experience here at Lyon Marketing Solutions.

Unfortunately, I am already scheduled to speak at a seminar in Orlando on the first date that you proposed; however, I will definitely be available on October 1. Also, to follow up on my interview this week, I have asked Mr. Praust, my manager at my current company, to send a reference letter on my behalf. If you wish to see more samples of my work, please let me know. I can either email them to you beforehand or bring them with me.

I am very much looking forward to my visit.

Sincerely,

Rhonda Nilsen

26. What is the purpose of the first e-mail?

(A) To recommend a product
(B) To schedule an interview
(C) To discuss a corporate account
(D) To provide a job description

27. What type of business is Benson & Parker?

(A) A Web design company
(B) An electronics company
(C) An accounting firm
(D) A marketing firm

28. According to the first e-mail, why does Mr. Steger want to meet Ms. Nilsen?

(A) To acquaint her with the company's style and expectations
(B) To assign her to an upcoming project
(C) To introduce her to some of his team members
(D) To give her a recommendation letter

29. When is Ms. Nilsen planning to be at a seminar?

(A) Monday
(B) Tuesday
(C) Wednesday
(D) Thursday

30. Who is NOT an employee of Benson & Parker?

(A) Ms. Wilkerson
(B) Mr. Ryans
(C) Mr. Steger
(D) Mr. Praust

MINI TEST 02

해설서 p.114

1. We request that passengers leave -------
for providing better service on our flights.

(A) suggest
(B) suggests
(C) suggestions
(D) suggesting

2. The latest vacuum cleaner from Saver
Technology operates more ------- than any
of its competitors.

(A) quietest
(B) quietly
(C) quietness
(D) quieter

3. Many ------- farmers trade their produce
at the St. Clair Market.

(A) local
(B) around
(C) close
(D) near

4. If you have any questions about Mr. Hiro's
talk, ------- will be available until 6 o'clock.

(A) him
(B) his
(C) he
(D) himself

5. While the building is being renovated,
members of the Accounting Department
will have to ------- their workspace with
employees from other departments.

(A) share
(B) allow
(C) cause
(D) invite

6. Following three quarters of continuous
growth, Sharman Distribution Depot is
looking to hire ------- sales representatives.

(A) additions
(B) additionally
(C) addition
(D) additional

7. Mr. Manashi will be representing the
company ------- negotiations with Napal
Tubular Accessories.

(A) because
(B) during
(C) once
(D) later

8. Mr. Arras is looking into other companies
even though a marketing firm has -------
assured him of a job.

(A) someday
(B) early
(C) soon
(D) already

9. Pertol Business Supply issues invoices
------- handles inquiries about online
payments.

(A) either
(B) for
(C) and
(D) after

10. Dr. William Thurston is an expert -------
work in developing new drugs has helped
reduce disease.

(A) that
(B) which
(C) them
(D) whose

Questions 11-14 refer to the following letter.

June 15

Sean Kirk
8843 Whitney Road
Cerritos, California 90703

Dear Mr. Kirk

As chairman of the Whitman Literary Association, I would like ------- you to speak at our annual
                                                                    11.
writer's conference on July 30 at the Plato Convention Center.

The ------- starts at 3 P.M. After the conference is over, dinner will be served at a nearby hotel.
    12.
If you decide to ------- our invitation, please inform me by June 30. -------.
                 13.   **14.**

Thank you.

Best regards,

Dean Chalmers

---

11. (A) inviting
    (B) to invite
    (C) invitation
    (D) invitingly

12. (A) event
    (B) change
    (C) display
    (D) interview

13. (A) win
    (B) receive
    (C) accept
    (D) create

14. (A) I look forward to your response.
    (B) Let me know your invoice number.
    (C) The convention schedule needs to be updated.
    (D) Please select an item from the dinner menu.

Questions 15-16 refer to the following ticket.

Passenger: Wendy Tyler
Ticket Number: 8940 23-55
Trip: To Bayou Valley, via Blue Line
Issued: August 5, 12:45 P.M.

Novaville   Depart: 1:20 P.M.
Platform 7   Seat: A12

Change trains at Stanley Station

Stanley City   Depart: 3:30 P.M.
Platform 12   Seat: D25

Bayou Valley   Arrive: 5:05 P.M.
Platform 9

Price: €21.00
Payment Method: Credit card

15. According to the ticket, when will Ms. Tyler leave Stanley City?

(A) At 12:45 P.M.
(B) At 1:20 P.M.
(C) At 3:30 P.M.
(D) At 5:05 P.M.

16. What is indicated about Ms. Tyler's trip to Bayou Valley?

(A) It includes transferring to a bus line.
(B) It was booked one week in advance.
(C) It requires her to take two trains.
(D) It was paid for by cash.

Questions 17-18 refer to the following online chat discussion.

Wilson, Edward [4:19 P.M.]
Are any of you going to the talk being given by Dr. Anthony Samuels this weekend?

Stuart, Amy [4:21 P.M.]
I had intended to go, but I changed my plans.

Wilson, Edward [4:23 P.M.]
What made you do that? Aren't you interested in hearing what he has to say?

Stuart, Amy [4:25 P.M.]
On the contrary, I'd love to attend his speech, but Mr. Jackson is sending me to meet Mr. Fritz in Berlin tomorrow, so I'm going to be out of the country.

Saville, Mary [4:27 P.M.]
That's too bad. I got my ticket for the talk, and I'm definitely looking forward to it. He's going to discuss some of the ideas from his latest book.

Wilson, Edward [4:28 P.M.]
The one on all the bestseller lists?

Saville, Mary [4:31 P.M.]
You got it. I read the book, but parts of it went over my head. I'm hoping that by attending the talk, I can gain some insights into it.

Stuart, Amy [4:33 P.M.]
You're so lucky you get to go. Would you mind taking notes and letting me see them?

Saville, Mary [4:36 P.M.]
Not at all. I always write down what speakers say at these kinds of events, so I'd be glad to share what I write with you.

Wilson, Edward [4:37 P.M.]
Okay, both of you have convinced me. I'm going to register for the event right now.

SEND

---

17. What is suggested about Mr. Jackson?

(A) He will attend the seminar.
(B) He is Ms. Stuart's boss.
(C) He works in Berlin.
(D) He knows Dr. Samuels.

18. At 4:31 P.M., what does Ms. Saville mean when she writes, "You got it"?

(A) Mr. Wilson should attend the event.
(B) She gave her ticket to Mr. Wilson.
(C) She is going to attend the event.
(D) Mr. Wilson is correct.

Questions 19-21 refer to the following e-mail.

To	Bruce Lennon <blennon@metcom.co.uk>
From	updates@sabs.org.uk
Date	30 October
Subject	Information

The Scottish Association of Biological Sciences (SABS) would like its members to be the first to be informed about our association sponsored Web lecture series. The SABS has teamed up with some of the nation's top industry leaders and scholars to offer online lectures on important topics in our field. The lectures are approximately two hours long and will take place every two months. At the end of each lecture, all attendees can engage in a 20-minute interactive Q&A session.

To take part in this wonderful opportunity to gain valuable insight into the industry and increase your overall knowledge of the field, visit our Web site at www.sabs.org.uk. There you will find the topics, dates, and times of this year's five lectures. Registration and payment instructions will also be available as well as the computer system requirements for participation.

We are also seeking lecturers. If you are qualified, contact our coordinator, Sandy Young, at syoung@sabs.org.uk.

19. Why did Mr. Lennon receive an e-mail?

(A) He is a member of the SABS.
(B) He has applied to study geography.
(C) He has organized a lecture series.
(D) He is scheduled to give a presentation.

20. What is indicated about the lectures?

(A) They are offered at no cost.
(B) They are held every month.
(C) They focus on a specific profession.
(D) They take place at the SABS headquarters.

21. What is NOT mentioned as something that can be found on the SABS Web site?

(A) Lecture topics
(B) Profiles of lecturers
(C) Dates of lectures
(D) Registration information

Questions 22-25 refer to the following article.

Fremont Township (January 8) – Clarkson County Commissioner Nadia Betlam announced this morning that the county will provide funding for road expansions along Highway 55 in two areas that are often heavily congested. The first phase of the project, which involves widening of the exit ramp to Pacific Boulevard, will begin on March 10. Ms. Betlam expects the construction to be completed in about a month, weather permitting. The second phase of the project will involve adding an extra lane to the three-kilometer stretch on the highway between Garrison Lane and Jacob Street. This work will begin in early April. Commissioners will finalize the schedule at their meeting next week. Ms. Betlam added that an experienced engineer will be hired to oversee the entire project.

22. Why is the roadwork necessary?

(A) The roads were damaged by heavy flooding.
(B) The roads have many uneven surfaces.
(C) The roads are too narrow for the amount of traffic.
(D) The roads are often too slippery in the winter.

23. What will probably be under construction in April?

(A) Highway 55
(B) Pacific Boulevard
(C) Garrison Lane
(D) Jacob Street

24. The word "stretch" in line 8 is closest in meaning to

(A) exaggeration
(B) section
(C) enlargement
(D) limit

25. According to the article, what will be completed next week?

(A) A roadwork schedule
(B) Extra lanes
(C) Three ramps
(D) A construction contract

Togo Commercial Movers
(480) 555-7310

Do you need to have your office or equipment moved? Whether your company has to relocate its office or just move some supplies to another location, Togo Commercial Movers is the answer to all your business moving needs.

Our services include:
- Short and long distance transportation
- Complete shipping preparation, which includes professional packing and safe delivery of items both domestically and internationally
- Free basic insurance coverage (Supplemental insurance is available from Helix LLC for an extra fee)

Headquartered in Mesa, Arizona, we have locations in major distribution regions throughout the country, including New York, Los Angeles, and Chicago. Togo is recognized by the Arizona Movers Association (AMA). To maintain this accreditation, all of our staff members are regularly trained and assessed to meet the high standards of the AMA.

We pair every Togo client with an experienced move coordinator so that every detail of the job is supervised from beginning to end.

PRICE ESTIMATE
Togo Commercial Movers
(480) 555-7310

DATE	February 10
COMPANY	RMC Financial

No.	Description	Amount
1	Transportation	$350.00
2	50 containers	$150.00
3	Packing (loading and unloading included)	$5,000.00
4	Insurance	$100.00

Subtotal: $5,600.00
Tax (10%): $560.00
Total: $6,160.00

The above costs are subject to change based on the actual labor and time necessary to complete the move.

To: Jack Walbert <j.walbert@togomovers.com>
From: Paul Han <p.han@rmcfinancial.com>
Date: February 12
Subject: Meeting follow-up

Dear Mr. Walbert,

I enjoyed our meeting last week. I have presented your estimate to the executive board, and they are satisfied with the costs. Please send us a contract, so we can proceed with the move.

During the meeting, Mr. Elman seemed very familiar with our industry. If it is possible, I would like him to be assigned to oversee our move. We hope to hear from you soon.

---

26. What does the advertisement indicate about Togo Commercial Movers?

(A) It is seeking new staff members.
(B) It has just moved its headquarters.
(C) It reassembles office equipment.
(D) It transports equipment internationally.

27. According to the advertisement, what service is available?

(A) Storage space rental
(B) Various training programs
(C) Expert packing
(D) Flexible scheduling

28. What is indicated about Togo Commercial Movers' employees?

(A) They have a background in financial management.
(B) They specialize in office renovation.
(C) They are certified by a professional organization.
(D) They all work in Mesa.

29. What is suggested about RMC Financial?

(A) It has multiple locations.
(B) It has purchased additional insurance.
(C) It is based in Chicago.
(D) It will merge with Helix LLC.

30. Who most likely is Mr. Elman?

(A) A moving specialist
(B) An AMA representative
(C) A RMC Financial executive
(D) An office assistant

MINI TEST 03

해설서 p.119

1. The food at the buffet is checked ------- to make sure it is restocked when needed.

(A) frequent
(B) frequently
(C) frequents
(D) frequency

2. Steamline Railways has recently raised its regular ------- to local destinations by 10 percent.

(A) fares
(B) values
(C) outputs
(D) assets

3. If Mr. Wirral takes the express train, he should make it on time ------- the executive meeting on Friday afternoon.

(A) for
(B) soon
(C) there
(D) while

4. The manager has asked that ------- computers be protected with secure passwords.

(A) we
(B) our
(C) ours
(D) ourselves

5. The accounting manager, Eunice Taft, will ------- how to use the new software at the workshop on Friday.

(A) write
(B) provide
(C) show
(D) prohibit

6. King Roofing takes pride in using only ------- materials in any work that they do.

(A) superiorities
(B) superiority
(C) superior
(D) superiors

7. Kilburn, Inc. welcomes your ------- concerning our products and services.

(A) suggest
(B) suggests
(C) suggested
(D) suggestions

8. Cottonbreeze is the most ------- addition to the Laurel Cosmetics line of perfumed soaps.

(A) late
(B) recent
(C) last
(D) former

9. We will watch a short video right before our keynote speaker is -------.

(A) introduction
(B) introduce
(C) introduced
(D) introduces

10. Museum patrons are advised to arrive early to gain entry, as ------- visitors are expected to attend the opening ceremony.

(A) any
(B) much
(C) every
(D) many

Questions 11-14 refer to the following notice.

Dear Readers,

Starborough Digest ------- announces the opening of starboroughdigest.com. -------.
                11.   12.

Subscribers will also enjoy interactive forums, quizzes, and surveys. ------- features will
                                                                    13.

encourage you to play a more direct role in the issues that concern you and your community.

The content will be offered to all subscribers at no additional cost. To access it, simply ------- on
                                                                                 14.

our new homepage. Nonsubscribers can also enroll by clicking the "I'd like to Sign Up" link.

Starborough Digest and starboroughdigest.com — we keep you connected and informed!

11. (A) often
    (B) particularly
    (C) enthusiastically
    (D) fully

12. (A) Our new Web site offers all the
        content of our print edition.
    (B) You can read instructions on our Web
        site.
    (C) You can access your account once
        our Web site is updated.
    (D) Our Web site also provides information
        regarding our competitors.

13. (A) Theirs
    (B) These
    (C) This
    (D) Their

14. (A) register
    (B) registers
    (C) registering
    (D) registered

CULVER ROAD PARKING LOT

Please take this ticket with you. Present the ticket when paying the parking lot attendant.

Date: 7 May   **Time in**: 11:25 A.M.

Only credit card or cash payments are accepted.

You can save up to $700 a year by getting a monthly pass!

For details, visit our Web site at culverlot.co.uk or call (034) 5555-1294.

15. How should customers pay for parking?

(A) By visiting the parking lot's Web site
(B) By using a prepaid card
(C) By making a payment to an attendant
(D) By depositing money into a meter

16. Why are customers encouraged to call the telephone number on the ticket?

(A) To get information about discounted parking fees
(B) To provide feedback about the quality of a service
(C) To reserve a parking spot for a week
(D) To inquire about a different payment option

Questions 17-18 refer to the following e-mail.

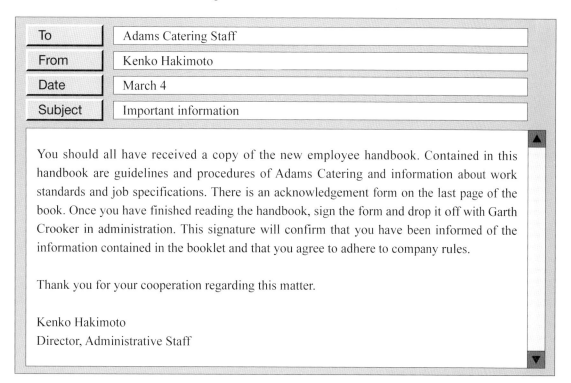

To	Adams Catering Staff
From	Kenko Hakimoto
Date	March 4
Subject	Important information

You should all have received a copy of the new employee handbook. Contained in this handbook are guidelines and procedures of Adams Catering and information about work standards and job specifications. There is an acknowledgement form on the last page of the book. Once you have finished reading the handbook, sign the form and drop it off with Garth Crooker in administration. This signature will confirm that you have been informed of the information contained in the booklet and that you agree to adhere to company rules.

Thank you for your cooperation regarding this matter.

Kenko Hakimoto
Director, Administrative Staff

17. What does Mr. Hakimoto discuss in the e-mail?

(A) A staffing change
(B) An orientation session
(C) A job opportunity
(D) A company manual

18. What does Mr. Hakimoto ask employees to do?

(A) Describe their job standards
(B) Submit a form
(C) Return some equipment
(D) Purchase a book

Questions 19-21 refer to the following article.

Central University News

December 22 — Eric Parker, one of Central University's longest-tenured professors, has been named the recipient of the Educator of the Year award at Central University. — [1]—.

Professor Parker teaches classes in the Biology Department, where he has been a mainstay for the past 27 years. His classes are always filled with students, and he is personally responsible for large numbers of Central University students deciding to become biology majors. — [2] —. Professor Parker teaches both undergraduate and graduate students, and he serves as the academic advisor for 32 students. He is also the faculty advisor for the university's Photography Club, which has helped increase that organization's popularity a great deal. — [3] —.

Professor Parker has earned the respect of students, faculty, and administrators alike, and he is well deserving of this award. — [4] —. A ceremony in his honor will be held at 3 P.M. on January 2 in the auditorium in Cedric Hall. The public is welcome to attend.

---

19. What is the purpose of the article?

(A) To honor a retiring employee
(B) To advertise a university class
(C) To announce the winner of an award
(D) To describe an upcoming internship

20. What is NOT true about Mr. Parker?

(A) His courses are popular among students.
(B) He has taught at his school for more than two decades.
(C) He used to work as a professional photographer.
(D) His club is well-known on campus.

21. In which of the positions marked [1], [2], [3], and [4] does the following sentence best belong?

"Many of them have gone on to work in related professions or to become educators themselves."

(A) [1]
(B) [2]
(C) [3]
(4) [4]

Questions 22-25 refer to the following letter.

Zing Electronics
September 10

Dear Customer,

There is exciting news at Zing Electronics! We invite you to come to Zing Electronics later this month and check out the improvements we've made to help make shopping more enjoyable for our customers.

As you may be aware, we are currently undergoing renovations to add 300 square feet to our store.

Our computer section will be double in size, which will enable us to offer a wider variety of accessories. We will also be expanding our music section to give you access to more audio equipment.

We will be celebrating our grand reopening on Friday, September 23. There will be demonstrations of new products. In addition, starting September 26, we will be open until 10:00 P.M. instead of 8:00 P.M.

Enclosed with this letter are Zing Electronics discount coupons, which are valid until September 30. We have also included a calendar showing our special sale days.

Sincerely,

Reginald Thompson
Zing Electronics Store Manager
Enclosure

---

22. What is the purpose of the letter?

(A) To announce a change in ownership
(B) To promote a new line of products
(C) To describe a store expansion
(D) To advertise a special sale

23. When will Zing Electronics host a special event?

(A) On September 10
(B) On September 23
(C) On September 26
(D) On September 30

24. What is NOT mentioned in this letter?

(A) Larger floor space
(B) Additional sales staff
(C) A greater selection of items
(D) Extended hours of operation

25. What is enclosed with the letter?

(A) Event information
(B) A survey form
(C) Product samples
(D) A membership card

Questions 26-30 refer to the following e-mail and list.

To: Abella Jude <ajude@cams.org.fr>
From: Lester Cross <lcross@cruiserrealestate.com>
Subject RE: Rental Property
Date: April 3
Attachment: List

Dear Ms. Jude,

We are responding to your e-mail from Tuesday, April 2, regarding rental homes in the Rosedale area. We work with both short-term and long-term apartment and house rentals, and we have experience with clients like you who plan to move to Canada for a limited period of time. I'm sure that we will find a place that's right for you.

You mentioned that you'll be working here for nine months, starting next month. The following are the rental preferences you have stated:

• A furnished one or two-bedroom unit
• A price range of $1,400 to $1,600 per month
• Within walking distance of a bus station (since you won't have a car)

Attached is a list of properties which best match your needs. And yes, I can certainly give you a tour of the properties on Thursday afternoon or Friday morning when you're in town this week, and I will be more than happy to come to your hotel to pick you up. Please email me to schedule a time. Finally, please convey our gratitude to your colleague, Ms. Kai Ling, as it is most appreciated when one of our customers recommends our services.

Sincerely,

Lester Cross
Cruiser Real Estate Rental Agent

Property Location	Rental Fee/Month	Availability	Details
45 Walnut Street	$1,550	May 2	2-bedroom house, furnished
1888 Shore Drive	$1,700	[Now]	2-bedroom apartment, furnished
760 Overland Lane	$1,600	June 2	1-bedroom apartment, furnished
24 Trask Street	$1,450	May 2	2-bedroom house, unfurnished

26. What is indicated about Ms. Jude?

(A) She is going on a vacation.
(B) She wants to purchase a new home.
(C) She will be moving to Rosedale temporarily.
(D) She has previously met Mr. Cross.

27. What information is Ms. Jude asked to provide?

(A) A move-in date
(B) A convenient meeting time
(C) A bank account number
(D) A certificate of employment

28. Who most likely is Ms. Ling?

(A) An owner of a rental home
(B) A Cruiser Real Estate client
(C) Mr. Cross's coworker
(D) Ms. Jude's neighbor

29. What is suggested about all the rental properties on the list?

(A) They are owned by Ms. Ling.
(B) They are close to public transportation.
(C) They have been newly built.
(D) They require a two-year lease.

30. Which property would probably best suit Ms. Jude's needs?

(A) 45 Walnut Street
(B) 1888 Shore Drive
(C) 760 Overland Lane
(D) 24 Trask Street

MINI TEST 04

해설서 p.124

1. Starways Supermarkets ------- opened six new local branches last year.

(A) success
(B) successes
(C) successful
(D) successfully

2. Benco Company's newest line of furniture is both ------- and attractive.

(A) durable
(B) durability
(C) durably
(D) durableness

3. With 22 specially modified electric vehicles, Das Bauer operates the most ------- transportation system in Germany.

(A) projected
(B) economical
(C) attentive
(D) internal

4. We will gladly repair or replace your GX3000 heater at no cost ------- two years of its purchase date.

(A) beneath
(B) off
(C) within
(D) on

5. Monthly timesheets for all employees must be ------- before the start of the next month.

(A) instructed
(B) informed
(C) decided
(D) completed

6. The security officers at Palace Apartments are trained to ensure the ------- of all tenants in the building.

(A) safety
(B) safest
(C) safe
(D) safely

7. Our client directory database has recently been updated and can be ------- online by staff members.

(A) access
(B) to access
(C) accessed
(D) accessing

8. Snacks and beverages will be available in the reception area ------- after the presentations.

(A) shortly
(B) recently
(C) extremely
(D) presently

9. Telco Motors introduced a hybrid vehicle, ------- consumers were quite receptive to it.

(A) or
(B) if
(C) than
(D) and

10. When overseas clients order goods from the Web site, remember to remind them of the ------- time of shipping.

(A) estimates
(B) estimated
(C) estimation
(D) estimating

Questions 11-14 refer to the following letter.

June 13

Dear Mr. Ristow,

Thank you for your purchase of our new GX555 personal tablet. We ------- to providing you with
11.

advanced, high-speed data technology. -------.
12.

If you are not 100 percent satisfied with your tablet, you will be issued a -------. Each of our items
13.

comes with a 60-day money-back guarantee. If you should have ------- questions regarding the
14.

operation of your new tablet, please contact us during our regular business hours, and we will be

glad to help you.

Sincerely,

Calvia Varga
Sales Manager

11. (A) are committed
(B) would be committing
(C) were committed
(D) will have committed

12. (A) The enclosed packet includes a
detailed product manual.
(B) As per your request, we have
upgraded your Internet service.
(C) Please indicate your preferred date
for us to perform the repair.
(D) Your payment is due on the first day
of every month.

13. (A) discount
(B) refund
(C) repair
(D) warranty

14. (A) further
(B) furthered
(C) furthering
(D) furthers

Questions 15-16 refer to the following information.

Thank you for purchasing a Maya Nanza scarf from our Fall Colors Collection. All of our materials are imported from the spectacular Tibetan Plateau in China. Our scarves are woven from 100 percent cashmere which goes through a hand dyeing process that does not harm the fabric or the environment. Color variations are a natural result of dyeing the cashmere. These variations give each scarf its own unique pattern. Dry-cleaning is strongly recommended in order to preserve the product's shape and to prevent wear and tear.

15. Where would this information most likely be found?

(A) In a magazine about weaving garments
(B) On a tag included with a woven product
(C) In a travel brochure to Tibet
(D) On a bottle of fabric dye liquid

16. What is stated about Maya Nanza products?

(A) They are made from various materials.
(B) They are sold only in China.
(C) They can be washed in water.
(D) They may have uneven coloration.

Harwood Bank

7044 Verde Street
Urbana, IL 61801

February 17

Marcela Reeves
825 Mesa Lane
Urbana, IL 61802
Re: Account #562302-344

Dear Ms. Reeves,

Thank you for sending us your new contact information. Accordingly, your account has been updated, and we will mail all subsequent bank statements and correspondence to your new home address.

Please note that your latest statement had already been sent to your previous address since your letter was received by us just today. However, you can check your account details (including current balance and recent transactions) by visiting our home page.

Thank you for your continued business.

Sincerely,

Anthony Hull
Customer Service Representative

17. What is the letter about?

(A) An incorrect transaction
(B) A change in payment policy
(C) A recently updated account
(D) A late payment

18. What does Mr. Hull suggest that Ms. Reeves do?

(A) Make a payment
(B) Contact customer service
(C) Complete a form
(D) Access a Web site

Questions 19-21 refer to the following advertisement.

Cross United
Job Openings

Nurses: Registered nurse positions (3 available). Applicants must be certified and have at least three years' experience in the medical field. Hours are 9 A.M. to 7 P.M., Monday to Thursday, and 9 A.M. to 4 P.M., Friday.

Office Assistant: A full-time position. The assistant's main duties are setting up patient appointments and processing bills. Additional daily duties include taking phone calls and sorting mail. Hours are 9 A.M. to 5 P.M., Monday to Friday. Applicants must possess at least one year of related work experience.

Interested applicants should visit www.crossunited.com and click on the Human Resource Department link to submit their cover letter, résumé, and copies of any other relevant documentation.

---

19. What most likely is Cross United?

(A) A community center
(B) An accounting firm
(C) A medical facility
(D) A pharmaceutical company

20. What is NOT required as a responsibility of the office assistant?

(A) Answering the telephone
(B) Handling payments
(C) Ordering office supplies
(D) Scheduling office visits

21. According to the advertisement, what is required for both types of positions listed?

(A) Three years of prior work experience
(B) Availability to work Monday through Friday
(C) Official certification
(D) Excellent leadership skills

Questions 22-25 refer to the following text message chain.

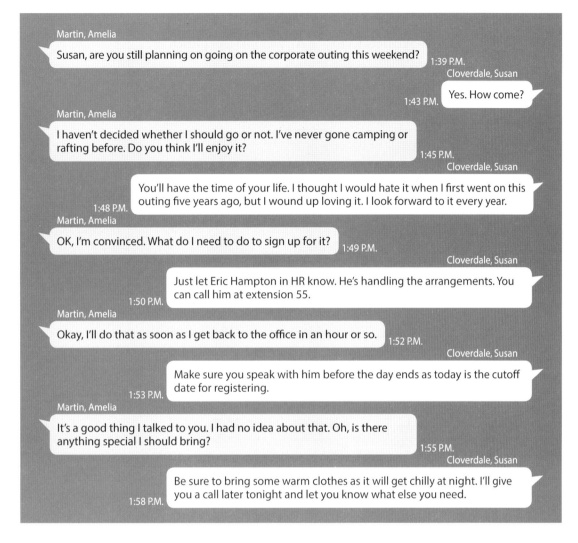

Martin, Amelia
Susan, are you still planning on going on the corporate outing this weekend? 1:39 P.M.

Cloverdale, Susan
1:43 P.M. Yes. How come?

Martin, Amelia
I haven't decided whether I should go or not. I've never gone camping or rafting before. Do you think I'll enjoy it? 1:45 P.M.

Cloverdale, Susan
1:48 P.M. You'll have the time of your life. I thought I would hate it when I first went on this outing five years ago, but I wound up loving it. I look forward to it every year.

Martin, Amelia
OK, I'm convinced. What do I need to do to sign up for it? 1:49 P.M.

Cloverdale, Susan
1:50 P.M. Just let Eric Hampton in HR know. He's handling the arrangements. You can call him at extension 55.

Martin, Amelia
Okay, I'll do that as soon as I get back to the office in an hour or so. 1:52 P.M.

Cloverdale, Susan
1:53 P.M. Make sure you speak with him before the day ends as today is the cutoff date for registering.

Martin, Amelia
It's a good thing I talked to you. I had no idea about that. Oh, is there anything special I should bring? 1:55 P.M.

Cloverdale, Susan
1:58 P.M. Be sure to bring some warm clothes as it will get chilly at night. I'll give you a call later tonight and let you know what else you need.

22. What is the text message chain mostly about?

(A) Plans for an upcoming conference
(B) A trip that Ms. Cloverdale just came back from
(C) An excursion the women will go on
(D) The items needed to go camping and rafting

23. What is suggested about Ms. Cloverdale?

(A) She has worked at the company for more than five years.
(B) She has gone on an outing with Ms. Martin before.
(C) She was recently hired at her company.
(D) She is uncomfortable spending time outdoors.

24. At 1:49 P.M., what does Ms. Martin mean when she writes, "OK, I'm convinced"?

(A) She has decided to go on the trip.
(B) She just purchased some new items.
(C) She needs to be convinced.
(D) She wants to hear a longer explanation.

25. What will Ms. Cloverdale do later in the day?

(A) Speak with Mr. Hampton
(B) Make arrangements for a trip
(C) Contact the HR Department
(D) Get in touch with Ms. Martin

HOLDING EVENTS AT TABERTON LIBRARY

The Roosevelt Room at the Taberton Library may be used for corporate events and private meetings. Please complete a request form to reserve the room.

Overview of Fees for Using the Roosevelt Room

	1-30 Participants	31-60 Participants	61-100 Participants
Library cardholders	$15	$30	$60
Nonmembers	$30	$60	$100
Company groups	$60	$90	$200

Taberton Library is open Monday to Saturday from 8:30 A.M. to 6:30 P.M. Events held after hours require a security guard to be on site. This arrangement can be made with the library for an extra fee. Alternatively, guests are also welcome to provide their own security guard.

TABERTON LIBRARY
The Roosevelt Room Reservation Request Form

Date and time: Tuesday, July 3, 6:45 P.M. – 8:45 P.M.
Individual/Group name: Welson Architecture
Contact person: Eric Hathers
Phone: 555-8839
E-mail: ehathers@welsonarchitecture.com
Expected number of participants: 78
Do you own a library card? No

I have read and consent to all policies regarding the use of the room. I understand that it is my responsibility to leave the room in its original state and to return all extra chairs and tables to the storage closet.

Signature: Eric Hathers
Date: June 18

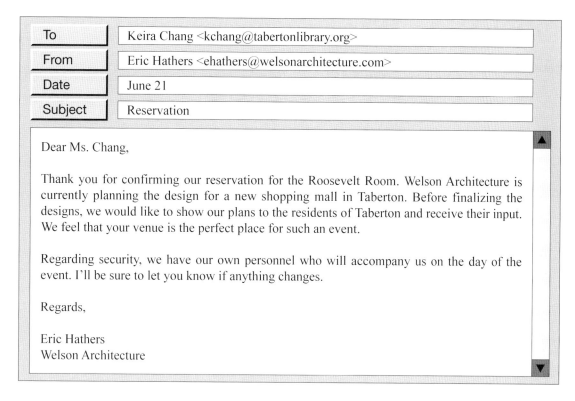

To	Keira Chang <kchang@tabertonlibrary.org>
From	Eric Hathers <ehathers@welsonarchitecture.com>
Date	June 21
Subject	Reservation

Dear Ms. Chang,

Thank you for confirming our reservation for the Roosevelt Room. Welson Architecture is currently planning the design for a new shopping mall in Taberton. Before finalizing the designs, we would like to show our plans to the residents of Taberton and receive their input. We feel that your venue is the perfect place for such an event.

Regarding security, we have our own personnel who will accompany us on the day of the event. I'll be sure to let you know if anything changes.

Regards,

Eric Hathers
Welson Architecture

26. What does the information indicate about Taberton Library?

(A) The library closes early on Saturdays.
(B) The library allows events to take place after its business hours.
(C) Some of the library's programs are free of charge.
(D) Taberton residents receive discounts on library room rentals.

27. How much will Welson Architecture be charged for the Roosevelt Room?

(A) $60
(B) $90
(C) $100
(D) $200

28. What is implied about the Roosevelt Room?

(A) It cannot be reserved on weekends.
(B) Extra furniture can be set up to accommodate large parties.
(C) It is available to companies only on Tuesdays.
(D) Library cardholders can book the room free of charge.

29. What is suggested about Welson Architecture?

(A) It is not required to pay an additional fee.
(B) It has used the Roosevelt Room before.
(C) It recently constructed a shopping mall.
(D) It regularly donates funds to the Taberton Library.

30. Why will Mr. Hathers hold a meeting?

(A) To plan a fundraiser for a project
(B) To announce the opening of a building
(C) To get feedback from people in the community
(D) To nominate individuals for awards

MINI TEST 05

해설서 p.129

1. Mr. Kaneko complimented ------- team for achieving their sales goals.

   (A) his
   (B) him
   (C) himself
   (D) he

2. Thanks to the hard work of Augen Corporation's sales staff, the company's goals for the fourth quarter have been -------.

   (A) meets
   (B) meeting
   (C) met
   (D) meet

3. The Rathburn Library offers an extensive ------- of business periodicals and journals both in print and online.

   (A) collects
   (B) collecting
   (C) collection
   (D) collected

4. During last week's press conference, Senator Janet White ------- answered a number of questions regarding pending issues.

   (A) calming
   (B) calms
   (C) calmly
   (D) calmer

5. The Borstein Financial Group has ------- costs by limiting overseas travel and implementing the use of video conferencing.

   (A) examined
   (B) reduced
   (C) stated
   (D) qualified

6. ------- all the items are finalized, we must consider the sales proposal only a draft.

   (A) Until
   (B) Yet
   (C) Despite
   (D) Still

7. Plantar Comfort Shoes belong to a new line of footwear that is ------- designed for people with problem feet.

   (A) specially
   (B) extremely
   (C) frankly
   (D) fairly

8. Sherm Travel Agency only hires employees with ------- skills, and a solid background in tourism.

   (A) organizational
   (B) organizes
   (C) organizations
   (D) organize

9. Sai Tao's paintings of the river were inspired ------- his childhood in Jiangsu Province.

   (A) by
   (B) to
   (C) at
   (D) on

10. Visitors who took the tour of the Lloyd Museum yesterday said that each exhibit represented an ------- example of history.

   (A) impressive
   (B) equipped
   (C) indecisive
   (D) acquired

Questions 11-14 refer to the following article.

Reyville, March 3 — Marvich's Toy Store has opened up a second location at 8373 Tinder Lane in the Bard Shopping Mall. Owner Jasper Marvich mentioned that he could not ------- the
11.
chance to further expand his business. "Once I found out that retail space was available in the mall, I immediately rented it out." Mr. Marvich also commented that while the Tinder Lane store is already -------, its official opening will be held on Friday, March 8, at 10:00 A.M. with a special
12.
ribbon-cutting ceremony and a raffle contest. -------. Marvich's sells the latest children toys,
13.
games, and various party supplies, ------- colorful confetti and birthday hats. Call 423-538-9843
14.
or go to www.marvichtoys.com for more information.

11. (A) sort out
(B) pass up
(C) go after
(D) look into

12. (A) operationally
(B) operational
(C) operation
(D) operated

13. (A) This event is open to the public.
(B) The opening was a success.
(C) The sale will last until next week.
(D) This space is much larger.

14. (A) includes
(B) inclusion
(C) inclusive
(D) including

Questions 15-16 refer to the following online chat discussion.

Thomas, Fred [11:01 A.M.]

I'm so disappointed. I was hoping to buy tickets for the speech being given by Edward Harvester, but I missed the deadline.

McMurtry, Robert [11:03 A.M.]

The deadline passed already? What a shame! I had intended to get a ticket as well.

Jones, Carla [11:05 A.M.]

Hold on a second. I just read on the Web site that tickets are still available. It appears that the registration date has been extended.

Thomas, Fred [11:07 A.M.]

That's great news. When is the new deadline?

Jones, Carla [11:09 A.M.]

According to the Web site, you have until 6 P.M. tomorrow to reserve tickets. However, you have to pay 10% more than the regular price.

McMurtry, Robert [11:11 A.M.]

I can live with that. Fred, do you want me to get a ticket for you?

Thomas, Fred [11:13 A.M.]

Yes, please. I'd like two. John Taylor in my office wants to go as well. Thanks for the news, Carla.

Jones, Carla [11:15 A.M.]

My pleasure. See both of you guys there.

SEND

15. What is the online chat discussion mostly about?

(A) The availability of tickets for an event
(B) The topic of an upcoming speech
(C) Where they will be sitting at a speech
(D) How many tickets they need to purchase

16. At 11:11 A.M., what does Mr. McMurtry mean when he writes, "I can live with that"?

(A) He is willing to go to the speech a bit late.
(B) He wants to attend the event with Ms. Jones.
(C) He does not mind paying a higher price.
(D) He is fine with Mr. Thomas buying the tickets.

Questions 17-18 refer to the following information.

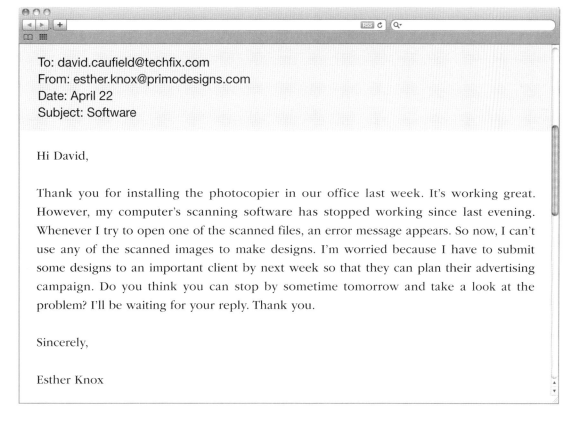

To: david.caufield@techfix.com
From: esther.knox@primodesigns.com
Date: April 22
Subject: Software

Hi David,

Thank you for installing the photocopier in our office last week. It's working great. However, my computer's scanning software has stopped working since last evening. Whenever I try to open one of the scanned files, an error message appears. So now, I can't use any of the scanned images to make designs. I'm worried because I have to submit some designs to an important client by next week so that they can plan their advertising campaign. Do you think you can stop by sometime tomorrow and take a look at the problem? I'll be waiting for your reply. Thank you.

Sincerely,

Esther Knox

17. What is the purpose of the e-mail?

(A) To request assistance
(B) To order a new photocopier
(C) To inquire about a company
(D) To submit a report

18. What is suggested about Ms. Knox?

(A) She has received a complaint from a client.
(B) She recently purchased a computer.
(C) She designs the interiors of office buildings.
(D) She is a graphic artist.

Questions 19-21 refer to the following e-mail.

From	Ji-Young Chang <jychang@tbacomputers.com>
To	Carl James <cjames@txtechconference.com>
Subject	Bonnie Thorpe
Date	30 January

Dear Carl,

I was supposed to depart for Texas this morning to be there in time to lead the workshop on Thursday. However, as you may be aware, there was a huge snowstorm yesterday here in Beijing, so all of the airports are shut down. I'm trying to book a new flight, but there hasn't been any word on the status of the airports. So I'm not sure if I will be able to make it to Texas by Thursday.

I've just talked to my colleague, Bonnie Thorpe, who has already arrived in Texas, and she said it would not be a problem for her to take my place. Bonnie is very proficient with the software I was planning to demonstrate at the workshop, and I know she'll do a good job. If you are okay with this arrangement, I will have Bonnie call you to get details on how to get reimbursed for any expenses related to the workshop and where to receive her conference pass. I will try my best to get there on Saturday before the conference ends. See you soon.

Sincerely,

Ji-Young

19. What is the purpose of the e-mail?

(A) To request a connecting flight
(B) To accept a job offer
(C) To explain a change in a plan
(D) To postpone the date of a conference

20. What has Ms. Thorpe agreed to do?

(A) Arrive in Texas later than originally planned
(B) Give a workshop at a conference
(C) Develop a software program with a colleague
(D) Recruit workers from her company's Beijing branch

21. What does Ms. Chang ask Mr. James to do?

(A) Reserve equipment to be used for a demonstration
(B) Update her on the local weather conditions
(C) Drop off a conference pass at an office
(D) Explain a reimbursement procedure to Ms. Thorpe

Recognizing Business Leaders
By Catherine Emerson, Writer for *the Herring Times*

KELLERTON (November 6) — The Technology & Innovation Committee (TIC) will honor leaders and innovators from various industries in the business world during the annual Business Awards Banquet on Saturday, December 10, at the Riveria Hotel. The event, originally started by TIC Chairman Ariel Won, presents prestigious awards such as the Most Popular Software Program and Top Innovator, given to the leader of this year's most innovative company.

According to a TIC representative, three individuals have been selected from a wide pool of qualified candidates for the Top Innovator award. The nominees this year for the award are: Lily Horvitz, founder of the digital marketing firm, Exceed Media; Spencer Donne, co-founder of Donne Pix, an image sharing Web site; and Josh Bruger, a nominee from our last banquet, whose famous Web site, Filmpop, provides detailed reviews of the latest movies. As usual, the TIC chairman will present the Top Innovator award.

Guests who are not members of TIC can also attend this gala by purchasing tickets for $60. Tickets are available to TIC members at the discounted price of $40. Tickets can be ordered by visiting www.tic.com or by calling 680-555-2391. "Anyone who keeps up with technology should consider becoming a member. It only costs $35 to join. Our members have access to many benefits," urges TIC representative Lucy Morgan. Everyone attending will be entered into the banquet's prize raffle, which includes a three-night trip to the famous Oceania Beach Resort.

22. What is suggested about TIC's Business Awards Banquet?

(A) It will be shown live on the Internet.
(B) It honors innovators from multiple industries.
(C) It can be attended by TIC members only.
(D) It will take place at a new location this year.

23. The word "last" in paragraph 2, line 9, is closest in meaning to

(A) following
(B) final
(C) previous
(D) current

24. Who will present the Top Innovator award?

(A) Ms. Won
(B) Ms. Horvitz
(C) Mr. Donne
(D) Mr. Bruger

25. What recommendation does Ms. Morgan make?

(A) To test a new product
(B) To vote for nominees
(C) To contact the Oceania Beach Resort
(D) To pay for a membership

Caress Beauty School
Presents

If you are considering working in the beauty industry, then Caress Beauty School (CBS), Portland's prestigious cosmetology institute, is the place for you. Venuscope is our yearly sampler course series that gives students the chance to explore different areas of cosmetology.

Select from one of the courses below. Each consists of six class sessions. You can find complete descriptions of each course by visiting our Web site at cbs.edu/venuscope.

Course 1: Hair Styling
Course Period: June 11-22
Class Days : Mondays, Tuesdays, and Fridays
Morning Classes: 8 A.M. – 11 A.M.
Evening Classes: 7 P.M. – 10 P.M.

Course 2: Make-up Techniques
Course Period : July 7-17
Class Days : Wednesday, Thursdays, and Saturdays
Afternoon Classes: 1 P.M. – 4 P.M.
Evening Classes: 7 P.M. – 10 P.M.

To sign up for the Venuscope program, you must pay a $15 registration fee and a $160 materials fee. For information about registering, contact Miriam Studebaker, the course coordinator, at mstudebaker@cbs.edu or at (301) 555-8294.

Can't enroll in the June and July program this year? Starting next year, CBS will offer the Venuscope program in February and March as well. In addition, CBS will provide an information session regarding the details about its ten-month licensing programs that begin on Monday, August 10. Please join us on July 21 to learn more.

To	Miriam Studebaker <mstudebaker@cbs.edu>
From	Vince Chow <vchow@tosmail.com>
Date	June 6
Subject	Inquiry

Dear Ms. Studebaker,

I am planning on registering for the Hair Styling sampler course. Please provide me with instructions on how to sign up.

I am fairly sure that I'll also be signing up for the ten-month program. I want to get more practice in addition to the in-class practice. Therefore, rather than buying the materials only for the Venuscope program, I would also like to purchase all of the supplies for the ten-month program. Please contact me to let me know if this would be possible. I hope to hear from you soon.

Sincerely,

Vince Chow

26. For whom is the information intended?

(A) Professional cosmetology instructors
(B) School program coordinators
(C) CBS personnel
(D) Future hair and make-up specialists

27. What is indicated about the Venuscope program?

(A) It is a requirement for the ten-month program.
(B) It will be offered more often in the future.
(C) It is available through the internet.
(D) It was advertised in a magazine.

28. When will the programs that lead to licensing be discussed?

(A) On June 6
(B) On June 11
(C) On July 21
(D) On August 10

29. In the e-mail, the word "fairly" in paragraph 2, line 1, is closest in meaning to

(A) frankly
(B) moderately
(C) equally
(D) reasonably

30. What is indicated about Mr. Chow?

(A) He will pay a reduced admission fee.
(B) He is willing to pay over $160 for materials.
(C) He wants to take classes in the morning.
(D) He has contacted the school before.

ACTUAL TEST

ACTUAL TEST

해설서 p.135

READING TEST

In the Reading test, you will read a variety of texts and answer several different types of reading comprehension questions. The entire Reading test will last 75 minutes. There are three parts, and directions are given for each part. You are encouraged to answer as many questions as possible within the time allowed.

You must mark your answers on the separate answer sheet. Do not write your answers in the test book.

PART 5

Directions: A word or phrase is missing in each of the sentences below. Four answer choices are given below each sentence. Select the best answer to complete the sentence. Then mark the letter (A), (B), (C), or (D) on your answer sheet.

101. Due to the city's new environmental laws, the amount of pollution has been significantly -------.

(A) reduced
(B) reduction
(C) reduce
(D) reduces

102. The revised WPM questionnaire measures work productivity more ------- than the one used last year.

(A) accuracy
(B) accurate
(C) accurately
(D) accuracies

103. Among ------- honored at the Carrigan International Film Festival were director Polly Grano and producer Ronald Foxsworth.

(A) them
(B) those
(C) whom
(D) whose

104. All of the brushes sold at Orion Cosmetics are made of natural materials and do not contain any ------- fibers.

(A) synthetic
(B) expected
(C) urgent
(D) capable

105. Kaymax Hardware's business hours will be ------- to 9:00 P.M. for the duration of its holiday sale.

(A) extending
(B) extendedly
(C) extended
(D) extends

106. The building manager of the Winen Tower was ------- notified of the water leak on the second floor.

(A) promptly
(B) steadily
(C) significantly
(D) timely

107. Boulder Architecture has created ------- to present to the City Council for the construction of the new shopping center.

(A) was designing
(B) designed
(C) designer
(D) designs

108. Experts predict that the price of commercial properties will decrease ------- 15 percent next year.

(A) before
(B) down
(C) by
(D) for

109. After accepting BMC Financial's job offer, Ms. Park decided to submit her ------- to her current company.

(A) resignation
(B) dedication
(C) qualification
(D) finalization

110. Recent studies conducted by Fit Care Max have shown that ------- exercising helps improve happiness and self-esteem.

(A) consist
(B) consistently
(C) consistent
(D) consistency

111. Applicants interested in working as an auditor at the Rennore Group should have received an accounting certificate ------- the arrangement of an interview.

(A) prior to
(B) previously
(C) apart from
(D) agreeable

112. Cervo Auto ------- that its new compact vehicle meets the safety requirements of the Transportation Department.

(A) adjusts
(B) restricts
(C) guarantees
(D) defines

113. Selected candidates will be placed in either Shanghai ------- Melbourne.

(A) and
(B) nor
(C) but
(D) or

114. By using electricity ------- by its solar panels, Fenick Mobile saves a lot of money on its utility bills.

(A) produces
(B) produce
(C) produced
(D) have produced

115. Out of all the restaurants located in the CT Shopping Center, Milword Bistro is the ------- to get to from our building.

(A) hardest
(B) more hardly
(C) hard
(D) most hardly

116. Dillman's Equipment specializes in ------- gear for athletes who participate in extreme sports.

(A) competing
(B) excessive
(C) definite
(D) protective

117. Grace Kim's independent film *Family Crossings* received such great reviews ------- three weeks of its release that the producers decided to show it in six other countries.

(A) above
(B) within
(C) while
(D) during

118. The data from Pateon Tech's customer survey is ------- used to help improve its software programs.

(A) simpleness
(B) simple
(C) simply
(D) simplicity

GO ON TO THE NEXT PAGE

119. Employees should make sure that the price of the item is correct before they request ------- for company card purchases.

(A) approval
(B) direction
(C) renewal
(D) explanation

120. According to *Travel Here*, Smith Island was ranked the world's most ------- destination last year.

(A) attracting
(B) attractively
(C) attraction
(D) attractive

121. Wayne Murdock runs a small repair shop that deals almost ------- with electronics.

(A) jointly
(B) exclusively
(C) kindly
(D) carefully

122. Presidential candidates Michael Roose and Vince Dalmer are in better standing with the voters than most of ------- rivals.

(A) theirs
(B) they
(C) their
(D) them

123. *Jump Nutrition* is one of Asia's most popular health magazines, with ------- in more than 30 countries.

(A) attendees
(B) viewers
(C) subscribers
(D) observers

124. We ask that you warmly greet conference participants as you meet them ------- the weekend.

(A) from
(B) throughout
(C) beyond
(D) with

125. Mayar, Inc. has made several attempts ------- the contract for developing the new apartment complex.

(A) is acquiring
(B) will acquire
(C) acquires
(D) to acquire

126. Professor Wilde is confident that her laboratory assistant will be able to conduct the experiment by -------.

(A) herself
(B) her own
(C) hers
(D) her

127. The primary ------- for moving to another office was lower rent.

(A) reasons
(B) reason
(C) reasonable
(D) reasoned

128. The product development team has ------- completed the prototype for the Skylight X250 smartphone and plans on presenting it to the board on Thursday.

(A) nearly
(B) constantly
(C) hardly
(D) regularly

129. Customers will be able to check the status of their order on the store Web site ------- the new system is installed.

(A) along with
(B) yet
(C) once
(D) in order for

130. For the purpose of -------, employees are required to create a password for their office computers.

(A) securer
(B) secure
(C) securely
(D) security

PART 6

Directions: Read the texts that follow. A word, phrase, or sentence is missing in some of the sentences. Four answer choices are given below each of these sentences. Select the best answer to complete the text. Then mark the letter (A), (B), (C), or (D) on your answer sheet.

Questions 131–134 refer to the following e-mail.

To: All Superplex Apparel Department Managers
From: Greta Silvers
Subject: Community Meeting

Next Friday, we plan on holding a community forum for ------- residents. There have
                                                          131.
been several complaints about the noise caused by the construction of our second store

on Leopold Street. So we want to address these issues, and hopefully, ------- a mutual
                                                                        132.
understanding with residents about the project. -------, we will see if they have any other
                                                133.
problems with the construction work. This will be a great opportunity to connect more

deeply with the community. As heads of your respective departments, we encourage each

and every one of you to participate in this forum next week. -------.
                                                            134.

Thank you.

Greta Silvers
Superplex Apparel

131. (A) concerning
     (B) concerned
     (C) concerns
     (D) concern

132. (A) finish
     (B) clear
     (C) develop
     (D) bring

133. (A) At the same time
     (B) Since
     (C) Although
     (D) On the other hand

134. (A) Attendance is mandatory for all
         supervisors.
     (B) The meeting has been moved to
         tomorrow.
     (C) I will describe the process in more detail.
     (D) We hope that you are able to join us.

GO ON TO THE NEXT PAGE

**We are currently accepting applications for a full-time position
at Catz Communications.**

Job title: Technical Support Representative

We are looking for a technical support representative who can handle various types of

technical issues. On a busy day, a representative can answer up to 50 ------- calls from
                                                                          135.
customers with specific questions about their internet service. In addition, the representative

must transfer calls to the appropriate department if needed.

One of the most important aspects of this position is the ability to identify and prioritize

problems that need ------- attention. This requires good analytical skills and the ability to
                     136.
make a sound ------- in a timely manner. -------. Therefore, it is crucial that the candidate
              137.   **138.**
can quickly adapt to any situation.

Go to www.catzcommunications.com to submit an application.

135. (A) moved
    (B) outgoing
    (C) incoming
    (D) disrupted

136. (A) postponed
    (B) indefinite
    (C) complex
    (D) immediate

137. (A) decisive
    (B) decision
    (C) to decide
    (D) decided

138. (A) At Catz Communications, we value
       every customer's feedback.
    (B) In this job, each day is different from
       the day before.
    (C) You can access directions to our store
       by visiting our Web site.
    (D) This position is perfect for full-time
       students as the hours are flexible.

From: support@flashcinema.com
To: s.durand@bmt.com
Subject: Flash Cinema Service
Date: June 10

Dear Ms. Durand,

Flash Cinema welcomes you to our video streaming service!

We are writing to confirm your ------- to Flash Cinema. You registered for the Premium
                                  139.
Viewers package, which is $10.00 per month and allows you to access unlimited television

shows and movies ------- on your computer or smart device. -------.
                   140.   **141.**

If you decide that you want to ------- your account, log in to our Web site at www.
                               142.
flashcinema.com/accounts. After you have done so, select the "Cancel Account" option.

We hope you enjoy our service.

The Flash Cinema Team

---

139. (A) utilization
(B) subscription
(C) completion
(D) confusion

140. (A) instantly
(B) instantaneous
(C) instant
(D) instance

141. (A) We regret to inform you that your
payment was not processed.
(B) As you have requested, we have
applied the extension.
(C) To sign up for an account, contact
customer service.
(D) You will be billed on the second of
each month.

142. (A) extend
(B) enhance
(C) open
(D) terminate

GO ON TO THE NEXT PAGE

Tyberion Adventure Co.
Outdoor equipment you can count on.

Thank you for purchasing a Tyberion Adventure hiking pole. It has been designed to serve

you ------- in the toughest situations. Although we have been manufacturing hiking sticks
　　143.

for over five decades, we know that there are always improvements to be made. To meet

our high ------- standards, we conduct rigorous tests on our hiking poles.
　　　144.

We have professional hikers use the equipment on the most rugged terrain. When

performing our quality control inspections, several hiking sticks are randomly selected and

------- the same kind of tests by other skilled hikers. -------.
　145.　　　　　　　　　　　　　　　　　　　146.

Check out our other outdoor gear and accessories on our Web site, tyberionadventure.com.

143. (A) expectedly
　　 (B) remotely
　　 (C) necessarily
　　 (D) faithfully

144. (A) reliability
　　 (B) academic
　　 (C) cost
　　 (D) health

145. (A) made by
　　 (B) tried out
　　 (C) put through
　　 (D) submitted to

146. (A) If even one pole fails, all production will
　　　 be halted.
　　 (B) These results show that we can cut
　　　 back costs in several areas.
　　 (C) An additional set of hiking poles are
　　　 recommended for long treks.
　　 (D) This process will allow workers to ship
　　　 items much faster.

PART 7

Directions: In this part you will read a selection of texts, such as magazine and newspaper articles, letters, and advertisements. Each text or set of texts is followed by several questions. Select the best answer for each question and mark the letter (A), (B), (C), or (D) on your answer sheet.

Questions 147-148 refer to the following advertisement.

Selling used refrigerator. Purchased brand-new five years ago, this Farno ZT50 refrigerator is in great condition. It has a beautiful stainless steel exterior. Perfect for any kitchen interior. Water filter was changed recently. No scratches, marks, or stains on the inside or the outside. Taking all reasonable offers. Owner moving abroad in three weeks, so must sell right away. Email Jimmy Manzer at jmanzer_25@mailweb.com.

147. What is suggested about the refrigerator?

(A) Its warranty expired five years ago.
(B) It uses very little electricity.
(C) Its water filter needs to be replaced.
(D) It has a stylish appearance.

148. Why is Mr. Manzer selling the refrigerator?

(A) He does not like its color.
(B) He is relocating overseas.
(C) He cannot afford its maintenance fees.
(D) He needs a larger model.

GO ON TO THE NEXT PAGE

Questions 149–150 refer to the following text message chain.

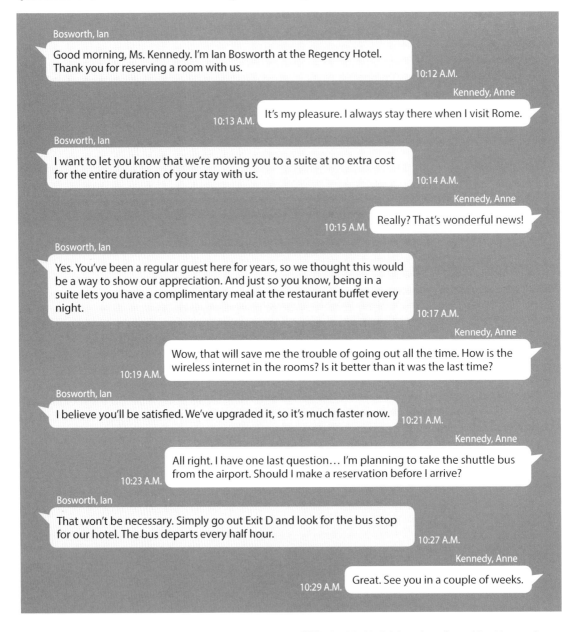

Bosworth, Ian
Good morning, Ms. Kennedy. I'm Ian Bosworth at the Regency Hotel. Thank you for reserving a room with us.
10:12 A.M.

Kennedy, Anne
10:13 A.M. It's my pleasure. I always stay there when I visit Rome.

Bosworth, Ian
I want to let you know that we're moving you to a suite at no extra cost for the entire duration of your stay with us.
10:14 A.M.

Kennedy, Anne
10:15 A.M. Really? That's wonderful news!

Bosworth, Ian
Yes. You've been a regular guest here for years, so we thought this would be a way to show our appreciation. And just so you know, being in a suite lets you have a complimentary meal at the restaurant buffet every night.
10:17 A.M.

Kennedy, Anne
Wow, that will save me the trouble of going out all the time. How is the wireless internet in the rooms? Is it better than it was the last time?
10:19 A.M.

Bosworth, Ian
I believe you'll be satisfied. We've upgraded it, so it's much faster now.
10:21 A.M.

Kennedy, Anne
All right. I have one last question… I'm planning to take the shuttle bus from the airport. Should I make a reservation before I arrive?
10:23 A.M.

Bosworth, Ian
That won't be necessary. Simply go out Exit D and look for the bus stop for our hotel. The bus departs every half hour.
10:27 A.M.

Kennedy, Anne
10:29 A.M. Great. See you in a couple of weeks.

149. Why does Mr. Bosworth contact Ms. Kennedy?

(A) To ask about a meal preference
(B) To inform her about an upgrade
(C) To move a reservation date
(D) To let her know about some repair work

150. At 10:19 A.M., what does Ms. Kennedy mean when she writes, "that will save me the trouble of going out all the time"?

(A) She will dine at a hotel restaurant often.
(B) She is worried about navigating through Rome.
(C) She is pleased that her room will have wireless Internet.
(D) She found a better public transportation option.

Questions 151-152 refer to the following memo.

From: Natalie Buckley
To: Lamar Foster
Re: Anniversary Dinner

As we discussed on Tuesday, I have compiled a list of venues. The one I think is best is the Grand Lao Hotel. They have several affordable and spacious dining rooms, and I heard that their executive chef is world famous! If not that, then I would suggest the Oceanic Inn. Many guests have written positive comments on their Web site, and they are conveniently located in the business district.

You had also asked me about transportation. Unfortunately, I don't know much about that, but I do know that Leslie Rivera arranged the buses for last year's corporate banquet. You can find her in the Human Resources Department (ext. 6735). She will likely have some useful information for you.

Please let me know if you have any further questions. I look forward to the event.

Natalie

151. Why did Ms. Buckley send the memo?

(A) To review the costs of a service
(B) To verify the reservation of a room
(C) To offer recommendations for an event
(D) To discuss comments by customers

152. Why should Mr. Foster contact Ms. Rivera?

(A) To request directions to a dinner party
(B) To submit an application for an open position
(C) To confirm the price of a venue
(D) To inquire about ideas for transportation

GO ON TO THE NEXT PAGE

Sales on the Rise

This time of year usually means that people are staying in and enjoying the comforts of their home. However, this year, many residents are making a surprising move by going out to enjoy the warmth of the local swimming center's indoor spa. With more customers out and about, local businesses have seen a nearly 40 percent increase in sales compared to last winter. Unsurprisingly, the popularity of the spa has also led to more residents using the swimming pool, which is regularly heated for the cold weather. Of course, the snowy winter has also been beneficial in more predictable ways: high sales of heavy coats and seasonal sports equipment, like snowboards.

153. What is the article mainly about?

(A) The cost of a spa service

(B) The details of an unexpected consumer trend

(C) The grand opening of a local swimming center

(D) The risks of snowy weather

154. According to the article, who has benefited from the weather change?

(A) Pool equipment manufacturers

(B) Restaurants

(C) Travel agencies

(D) Sporting goods stores

Questions 155-157 refer to the following e-mail.

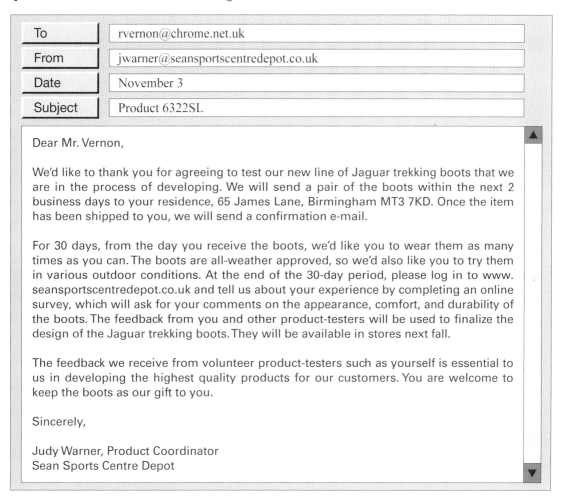

To: rvernon@chrome.net.uk

From: jwarner@seansportscentredepot.co.uk

Date: November 3

Subject: Product 6322SL

Dear Mr. Vernon,

We'd like to thank you for agreeing to test our new line of Jaguar trekking boots that we are in the process of developing. We will send a pair of the boots within the next 2 business days to your residence, 65 James Lane, Birmingham MT3 7KD. Once the item has been shipped to you, we will send a confirmation e-mail.

For 30 days, from the day you receive the boots, we'd like you to wear them as many times as you can. The boots are all-weather approved, so we'd also like you to try them in various outdoor conditions. At the end of the 30-day period, please log in to www.seansportscentredepot.co.uk and tell us about your experience by completing an online survey, which will ask for your comments on the appearance, comfort, and durability of the boots. The feedback from you and other product-testers will be used to finalize the design of the Jaguar trekking boots. They will be available in stores next fall.

The feedback we receive from volunteer product-testers such as yourself is essential to us in developing the highest quality products for our customers. You are welcome to keep the boots as our gift to you.

Sincerely,

Judy Warner, Product Coordinator
Sean Sports Centre Depot

---

155. Why was the e-mail sent?

(A) To confirm the receipt of a payment
(B) To inform a customer of a shipping delay
(C) To promote the launch of a new product
(D) To provide instructions to a volunteer

156. What is indicated about Sean Sports Centre Depot?

(A) Its head office is located in Birmingham.
(B) It has received complaints about its current products.
(C) Its Web site has been recently updated.
(D) It involves consumers in the product development process.

157. What is suggested about the Jaguar line?

(A) They are available in a wide range of colors.
(B) They are designed to be worn in many kinds of weather.
(C) They are being sold at a special price in November.
(D) They are endorsed by professional athletes.

GO ON TO THE NEXT PAGE ➡

Questions 158–160 refer to the following Web page.

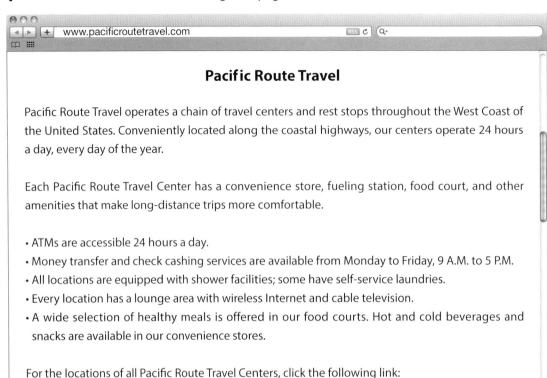

Pacific Route Travel

Pacific Route Travel operates a chain of travel centers and rest stops throughout the West Coast of the United States. Conveniently located along the coastal highways, our centers operate 24 hours a day, every day of the year.

Each Pacific Route Travel Center has a convenience store, fueling station, food court, and other amenities that make long-distance trips more comfortable.

• ATMs are accessible 24 hours a day.
• Money transfer and check cashing services are available from Monday to Friday, 9 A.M. to 5 P.M.
• All locations are equipped with shower facilities; some have self-service laundries.
• Every location has a lounge area with wireless Internet and cable television.
• A wide selection of healthy meals is offered in our food courts. Hot and cold beverages and
  snacks are available in our convenience stores.

For the locations of all Pacific Route Travel Centers, click the following link:
www.pacificroutetravel.com/locations.

158. What does the Web page describe?

(A) Travel packages
(B) Roadside facilities
(C) Low-priced hotels
(D) Moving services

159. What do only some locations offer?

(A) Laundry rooms
(B) Wireless Internet
(C) Food and drinks
(D) Shower areas

160. What information can most likely be found by clicking the link provided?

(A) Payment options
(B) Service fees
(C) Parking instructions
(D) Street addresses

Questions 161-164 refer to the following e-mail.

To	All Novad staff members
From	Niraj Sharma
Date	Wednesday, February 5
Subject	Opportunity

The Public Relations Department is seeking contributors to write articles on the latest trends and practices in the advertising industry. We will post the articles on the company's Web site so that current and prospective clients along with the general public can view them. We are looking for people who are able to write up to five articles of 400-500 words each per year.

This will give our employees an opportunity to share their experience and professional knowledge with a broader audience. The writer's name and job position at Novad will be displayed under the title of the article.

If you are interested in contributing, please come to the two-hour information session next Monday, February 10, at 10:45 A.M. in Room 410. The session will go over:

* The process of submitting articles
* How to write original and interesting articles
* Where to research relevant topics
* Company regulations regarding interviewing people both inside and outside of the company

If you are unable to be there, email me and let me know your date of availability. I'll arrange a separate time to meet you.

Niraj Sharma
Public Relations Manager
Novad LLC

161. What most likely is Novad?

(A) An advertisement agency
(B) A radio station
(C) A recruiting service
(D) A publishing firm

162. What does Mr. Sharma want contributors to do?

(A) Carry out a survey
(B) Market some products
(C) Send e-mails to all staff members
(D) Write articles for the company's Web site

163. What is indicated about the information session?

(A) It is mandatory for every employee.
(B) It will cover some company guidelines.
(C) It requires early registration.
(D) It will be led by the vice president.

164. Who is asked to send an e-mail to Mr. Sharma?

(A) Staff members who were recently hired
(B) Local reporters and journalists
(C) Employees who cannot attend the information session
(D) Potential clients of the company

GO ON TO THE NEXT PAGE

Dear Mr. Simmons,

It will be a privilege to host the awards ceremony for Baker Engineering on the night of November 19. I am sure that you and your guests will have a wonderful experience and that your event will be a complete success.

The Safeway Convention Center has held numerous events like this during the past decade, so our staff is fully aware of what to do for this kind of occasion. However, if you could let us know how many guests you are expecting, that would be helpful. — [1] —. If you do not know the exact number, a rough estimate will suffice.

Regarding the payment, it costs $2,500 to rent the Rose Ballroom for the entire evening. — [2] —. Since we will be catering the event, I have included a menu of the items we can prepare for you and your guests. Simply choose what you would like to eat and tell us the number of each dish you require. — [3] —. You can also select the buffet option. Many of our guests prefer this option.

Thank you again for choosing the Safeway Convention Center. — [4] —. Please feel free to contact me at 831-3595 anytime if there are any matters that you wish to discuss.

Clara Wellman
Events Coordinator
Safeway Convention Center

---

165. What is the main purpose of the letter?

(A) To inform a customer about the availability of a room
(B) To request payment for services provided
(C) To discuss preparations for an upcoming event
(D) To provide alternate choices for a venue

166. What does Ms. Wellman request that Mr. Simmons do?

(A) Arrange a time to plan guest accommodations
(B) Provide the exact time of a party
(C) Give her the names of the attendees
(D) Select some items from a menu

167. In which of the positions marked [1], [2], [3], and [4] does the following sentence best belong?

"We need to know how many chairs and tables will be required for the evening."

(A) [1]
(B) [2]
(C) [3]
(D) [4]

GOH at Glance

GOH, Inc. has been sponsoring the Make It Yours Engineering Competition for the last five years. Those between the ages of twelve and eighteen may register. This event has been drawing over 200 participants each year.

Aaron Grover, a Greensville resident and engineering professor at Greensville University, started Make It Yours eight years ago. Mr. Grover has 30 patents and has invented over 100 different products, most recently a robust water filter that is currently being used in many households across the globe. The International Inventors Hall of Fame aims to encourage young people from all over the world to consider a career in engineering.

GOH will also be directly involved in the competition. Xiao Tsu and Anna Shick from the Research and Development Department will be part of a panel of seven judges. Additionally, Gloria Berg from the Customer Service Department will be helping out with registration. If you are interested in participating in Make It Yours, please visit the Community Help page of the company Web site to view a list of volunteer opportunities. Who knows? You may be helping to select a future GOH employee.

168. Why most likely was the article written?

(A) To promote a new service
(B) To highlight an event
(C) To honor an employee
(D) To announce an award winner

169. What is suggested about GOH, Inc.?

(A) It nominates candidates for the International Inventors Hall of Fame.
(B) It makes water filters.
(C) It hires engineers.
(D) It provides internships for young people.

170. The word "drawing" in paragraph 1, line 3, is closest in meaning to

(A) illustrating
(B) gaining
(C) attracting
(D) provoking

171. According to the article, what can be found on the company's Web site?

(A) A list of Mr. Grover's inventions
(B) Details on how to apply to GOH, Inc.
(C) Information about available duties
(D) A customer survey

GO ON TO THE NEXT PAGE

Questions 172–175 refer to the following text message chain.

Blake, Gordon
Ms. Sikorski, this is Gordon Blake from Sigma Landscaping. I'd like to confirm that our work crew will be visiting your home this afternoon at 1.
10:14 A.M.

Sikorski, Tina
10:17 A.M.
That's correct, Mr. Blake. I'm looking forward to seeing the work your team can do.

Blake, Gordon
We'll do our best. We should have your front and back yard looking great in no time. And just to confirm… You want us to cut the grass and trim the hedges, right?
10:20 A.M.

Sikorski, Tina
10:21 A.M.
That's correct. But there's one more thing I'd like you to do.

Blake, Gordon
What's that?
10:22 A.M.

Sikorski, Tina
10:24 A.M.
There's an old tree stump in the backyard near the fountain that I'd really like to have removed. Could your team get rid of it for me?

Blake, Gordon
They'll have to take a look at it first before they can decide if they can do it or not. If they can't, they can go back later in the week and handle it. If it's a big job, though, there will be an extra fee.
10:27 A.M.

Sikorski, Tina
10:29 A.M.
That's understandable. Could you have the foreman give me the invoice today? I intend to pay with cash when the work is done.

Blake, Gordon
Of course. I'll be sure to let him know.
10:30 A.M.

Sikorski, Tina
10:31 A.M.
Thanks. I'll contact you again if I need anything else.

172. Why does Mr. Blake contact Ms. Sikorski?

(A) To describe fees for a service
(B) To request an extension
(C) To report on a project's results
(D) To confirm an appointment

173. What additional work does Ms. Sikorski request be done?

(A) The removal of a tree stump
(B) The installation of a fountain
(C) The planting of some flowers
(D) The trimming of some bushes

174. At 10:29 A.M., what does Ms. Sikorski mean when she writes, "That's understandable"?

(A) She does not understand what Mr. Blake wrote.
(B) The contract she signed earlier is acceptable.
(C) She is fine with being charged extra.
(D) The task must be completed before the evening.

175. According to the text message chain, what will Ms. Sikorski receive from the foreman?

(A) A bill
(B) A catalog
(C) A coupon
(D) A business card

GO ON TO THE NEXT PAGE

Questions 176–180 refer to the following e-mail and advertisement.

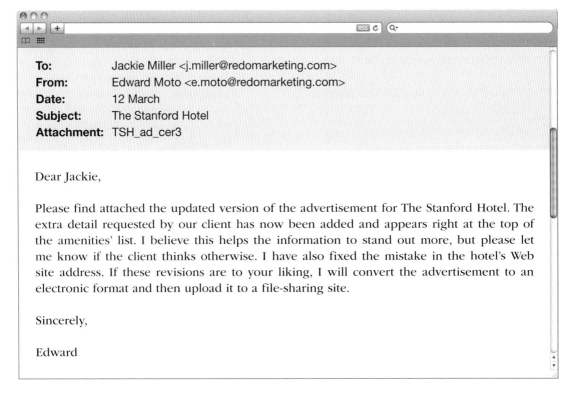

To: Jackie Miller <j.miller@redomarketing.com>
From: Edward Moto <e.moto@redomarketing.com>
Date: 12 March
Subject: The Stanford Hotel
Attachment: TSH_ad_cer3

Dear Jackie,

Please find attached the updated version of the advertisement for The Stanford Hotel. The extra detail requested by our client has now been added and appears right at the top of the amenities' list. I believe this helps the information to stand out more, but please let me know if the client thinks otherwise. I have also fixed the mistake in the hotel's Web site address. If these revisions are to your liking, I will convert the advertisement to an electronic format and then upload it to a file-sharing site.

Sincerely,

Edward

The Stanford Hotel
421 Bridge Street,
Margate, Kent CT9 5JP
United Kingdom

Do you need to break away from the busy city life? Then look no further. The Stanford Hotel rests on a beautiful shore and is surrounded by fresh coastal air. Come and enjoy a relaxing paradise, away from crowded streets and loud noises.

We offer the following amenities:
- Free shuttle service from the bus terminal and train station to the hotel
- Free continental breakfast in our amazing dining lounge
- Discounted rates for late spring, with rooms starting at just £60.00 per night

The Stanford Hotel, recognized by *Margate Gazette* for its affordability, is very close to the beach, but is still within walking distance to the local stores and cafés. So hurry on over and enjoy all that Margate has to offer! For more information, go to our Web site at www.thestanfordhotel.co.uk or call 01-271-324567.

176. Why did Mr. Moto send the e-mail?

(A) To check whether the file was sent to a client

(B) To ask Ms. Miller to approve some modifications

(C) To suggest Ms. Miller make further changes

(D) To apologize for mistakes in the file

177. Where most likely does Ms. Miller work?

(A) At a train station

(B) At a hotel

(C) At an advertising agency

(D) At a newspaper company

178. What did Mr. Moto add to a file?

(A) Information about transportation

(B) The directions to a hotel

(C) A phone number

(D) A price list

179. What is stated about The Stanford Hotel?

(A) It offers seasonal discounts.

(B) It recently launched its business.

(C) It is a historic landmark.

(D) It has a 24-hour restaurant.

180. What did the *Margate Gazette* indicate about The Stanford Hotel?

(A) The staff members are friendly.

(B) It has a private beach.

(C) It remodeled the lobby.

(D) The prices are reasonable.

GO ON TO THE NEXT PAGE

Open Seminar Series
Sponsored by Westfront University Hospital

Westfront University Hospital (WUH) is pleased to introduce its summer seminar series for pharmaceutical sales representatives. This series will provide a chance to listen to leading figures in our area who market new medicine to the public. For your convenience, the seminars will be held at Westfront University's School of Medicine. Seats are available on a first-come, first-served basis. Doors will open 30 minutes before the seminar begins.

Wednesday, 5 August, 6 P.M., Room 40

Speaker: Livia Togart, Regional Medicine Association
Increase Profits: Discover how to maximize profits in this slow economy.

Wednesday, 12 August, 6 P.M., Room 35

Speaker: Ryan Cleghorn, Medhearts Consultant Group
Customer Care: Learn effective ways to communicate better with your customers.

Saturday, 15 August, 3 P.M., Room 35

Speaker: Nakano Hitashi, Epstein Pharmaceutical Data, Inc.
Information Confidentiality: Get the latest details on how to keep data on new products secure.

Monday, 17 August, 7:30 P.M., Room 52

Speaker: Steve Ko, Westfront Accounting Solutions
Successful Financial Practices: Learn about new invoicing methods that ensure customers make their payments promptly.

Please email Daniel Duval at d.Duval@wuh_medinnovations.uk for more information.

To	Daniel Duval <d.Duval@wuh_medinnovations.uk>
From	Tristan Chai <tchai@dzprescription.com>
Date	16 August
Subject	Seminar Schedule

Dear Mr. Duval,

I am on your e-mail list, and I received your brochure regarding the summer seminar series. Since my pharmacy recently purchased software from Epstein Pharmaceutical Data, Inc., I was looking forward to their presentation. However, when I arrived at the School of Medicine yesterday afternoon, there was no one in Room 35. I went to the front desk, but the receptionist had no idea about the seminar. If the seminar has been moved to another time, please let me know exactly where and when it is scheduled to be held.

Sincerely,

Tristan Chai

181. In the brochure, the word "figures" in paragraph 1, line 3, is closest in meaning to

(A) numbers
(B) information
(C) people
(D) studies

182. What is mentioned about the seminars?

(A) They limit the number of participants to 50.
(B) They will be held at Westfront University Hospital.
(C) They are intended for those who promote medicine.
(D) They will have question and answer sessions.

183. What will be discussed at the seminar on August 17?

(A) How to make money during financial hardships
(B) How to ensure that bills are paid quickly
(C) How to analyze products' data
(D) How to connect successfully with clients

184. Whose lecture does Mr. Chai wish to attend?

(A) Mr. Cleghorn's
(B) Ms. Togart's
(C) Ms. Hitashi's
(D) Mr. Ko's

185. Why did Mr. Chai write the e-mail?

(A) To sign up for a seminar
(B) To request an update
(C) To join an e-mail list
(D) To apply for a position

GO ON TO THE NEXT PAGE

Questions 186–190 refer to the following letter, online form, and e-mail.

Jane Choi
20134 Elkins Road
Los Angeles, CA 90005

Dear Ms. Choi,

Enclosed are three author copies of your new novel, *Stardom Pathway*. It is now available for purchase on our Web site, www.galicapress.com, and it will be sold in select bookstores beginning April 29. So far, online sales of your novel have been brisk, and we expect sales to increase.

In addition to your complimentary copies, you can buy more copies of your novel at 65 percent off (use the online form on our Web site to order). This discount is also available for the other novels you have authored, *Spring Fever* and *Eternal Sun*.

As our valued author, you are also entitled to receive 15 percent off any other books published by Galica Press.

Thank you for choosing Galica Press.

Warm regards,

Sherry Henderson

Sherry Henderson
Marketing Manager
Galica Press
ENCLOSURES

Author Order Form

Author: Jane Choi
Date: April 10

Title	Copies	Price
Stardom Pathway	5	$37.50
Spring Fever	4	$20.00
Eternal Sun	2	$22.75

To purchase other books, please enter the author's name, the book title, and the desired number of copies in the corresponding boxes below:

Title: *Optical Flare*
Author: Gary Othstein
Number of Copies: 3
Total Price: $18.50

Note: Orders are shipped via standard mail and take three to five business days to arrive. If you choose the express option, we can deliver your order the very next day. Please contact customer support at customersupport@galicapress.com to arrange this service.

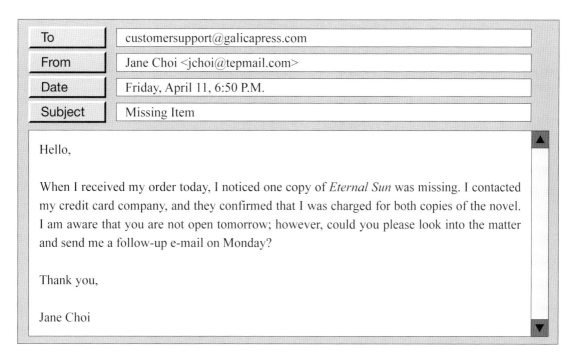

To	customersupport@galicapress.com
From	Jane Choi <jchoi@tepmail.com>
Date	Friday, April 11, 6:50 P.M.
Subject	Missing Item

Hello,

When I received my order today, I noticed one copy of *Eternal Sun* was missing. I contacted my credit card company, and they confirmed that I was charged for both copies of the novel. I am aware that you are not open tomorrow; however, could you please look into the matter and send me a follow-up e-mail on Monday?

Thank you,

Jane Choi

186. In the letter, the word "brisk" in paragraph 1, line 3, is closest in meaning to

(A) fresh
(B) strong
(C) attentive
(D) brief

187. How many free copies of *Stardom Pathway* have been sent to Ms. Choi?

(A) Two
(B) Three
(C) Four
(D) Eight

188. What is indicated about *Optical Flare*?

(A) It will be sold to Ms. Choi at a 15 percent discount.
(B) It was written collaboratively by Ms. Choi and Mr. Othstein.
(C) It received positive reviews from book critics.
(D) It will be available in select stores starting April 29.

189. What is most likely true about Ms. Choi?

(A) All of her books are bestsellers.
(B) She selected the express delivery option.
(C) One of her books is out of stock.
(D) She has switched to a new marketing agency.

190. What is suggested about customer support?

(A) It is managed by Ms. Henderson.
(B) It does not deal with shipping issues.
(C) It is located in Los Angeles.
(D) It does not operate on weekends.

GO ON TO THE NEXT PAGE

Questions 191-195 refer to the following Web page, article, and letter.

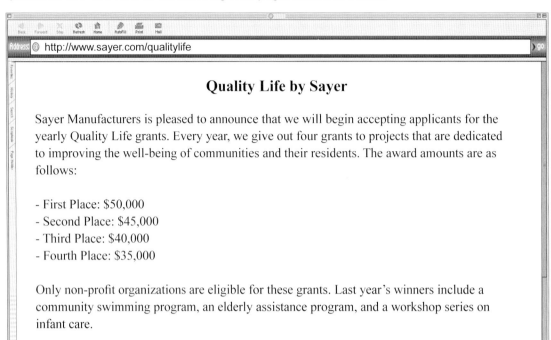

Philanthropy Corner

Quartz Gets Funding

by Thomas Dunn

Hillview, May 15 — The Quartz Foundation, based in Hillview, was awarded $40,000 through the Sayer Quality Life Grant Program to create a reading center. The center will provide an opportunity for children and teenagers residing in Hillview to increase their reading levels. Starting next month, the foundation will provide classes on 20th century literature. The foundation, which also operates the Hillview Public Library, is planning to donate a large number of fiction and nonfiction books to the center.

The Quartz Foundation was established 15 years ago in Hillview by a group of ten local residents who wanted to increase the community's awareness of education.

To the Editor:

I would like to call attention to an inaccuracy in Mr. Dunn's article in the May issue of *Philanthropy Corner*. Mr. Dunn wrote that Quartz was formed 15 years ago. Although Mr. Dunn's statement about Quartz's founders is correct, Quartz was, in fact, established 25 years ago.

As a former contributor, I am well aware that your magazine strives to publish insightful and trustworthy articles, and I understand that this error is a rare occurrence for your magazine.

Sincerely,

Jamie Boyd
President, Quartz Foundation

191. What is the purpose of the Web page?

(A) To publicize the opening of a medical center
(B) To seek participants for a sports competition
(C) To solicit applications for an award
(D) To announce the finalists for a grant

192. What prize did the Quartz Foundation receive?

(A) The first-place prize
(B) The second-place prize
(C) The third-place prize
(D) The fourth-place prize

193. According to the article, what will the grant enable the Quartz Foundation to do?

(A) Build a new library
(B) Conduct research on health
(C) Offer educational opportunities
(D) Improve working conditions of its employees

194. What does Ms. Boyd suggest about herself?

(A) She is a former employee of Mr. Dunn.
(B) She will be interviewed by a magazine writer.
(C) She helped establish the Quartz Foundation.
(D) She has written for *Philanthropy Corner* before.

195. According to Ms. Boyd, what is true about the Quartz Foundation in Mr. Dunn's article?

(A) It plans to apply for an additional grant.
(B) It was founded by local residents.
(C) It donates books to Hillview schools.
(D) It has cooking facilities.

GO ON TO THE NEXT PAGE

Castaway Band
For Immediate Release

Seattle, Washington, January 3 — The Castaway Band has announced its March tour dates. This tour includes a performance at the popular Orion Stadium, where the famous rock group made its debut 10 years ago.

Scheduled performances are listed below.

DATE	LOCATION	VENUE
March 2	Seattle	The Grand Stadium
March 5	Olympia	Orion Stadium
March 8	Spokane	Baron Theater
March 11	Kirkland	Foxwood Theater
March 14	Renton	Cumulus Arts Center

Tickets range from $80 (balcony level) to $120 (front-row) for all tour performances and can be purchased at participating venue box offices and X-One Music Stores. Members of the Castaway Band Fan Club can get $10 off tickets by ordering through the Members Only section at www.castawayboys.com. For more information about fan club benefits and annual dues, go to www.castawayband. com/membership_fanclub.

Contact: Sean Berstein, 206-555-7352, sberstein@castawayboys.com

Foxwood Theater
For Immediate Release

Canceled and Postponed Performances

Kirkland, Washington, February 22 — All of the performances scheduled for next month at the Foxwood Theater have been postponed or canceled due to emergency repairs being made to the building. With the exception of the Castaway Band concert, all ticket holders are asked to hold onto their tickets as they will be honored for the rescheduled date. For the most up-to-date information on performance dates, please visit Foxwood Theater's Web site, www.foxwoodtheater.org. Contact Stacy Kamshire at skamshire@foxwoodtheater.org to receive a refund for the canceled concert.

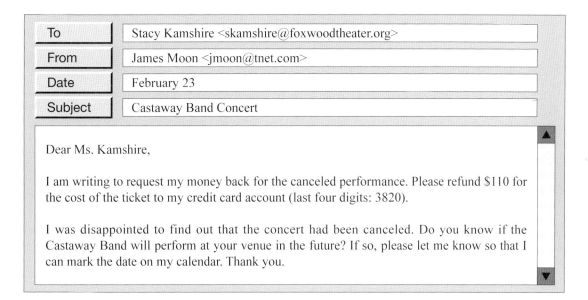

To	Stacy Kamshire <skamshire@foxwoodtheater.org>
From	James Moon <jmoon@tnet.com>
Date	February 23
Subject	Castaway Band Concert

Dear Ms. Kamshire,

I am writing to request my money back for the canceled performance. Please refund $110 for the cost of the ticket to my credit card account (last four digits: 3820).

I was disappointed to find out that the concert had been canceled. Do you know if the Castaway Band will perform at your venue in the future? If so, please let me know so that I can mark the date on my calendar. Thank you.

196. Where did the Castaway Band play their first concert?

(A) In Seattle
(B) In Olympia
(C) In Kirkland
(D) In Renton

197. What is suggested about the Castaway Band Fan Club?

(A) Its members have to pay a fee once a year.
(B) It meets annually in the month of March.
(C) Its members qualify for X-One Music Store discounts.
(D) It was founded ten years ago.

198. When will the Castaway Band be unable to play a scheduled performance?

(A) On March 2
(B) On March 5
(C) On March 11
(D) On March 14

199. According to the second press release, what will be posted on Foxwood Theater's Web site?

(A) New venue locations
(B) A revised list of dates
(C) Details about building repairs
(D) A refund request form

200. What is suggested about Mr. Moon?

(A) He is a member of the Castaway Band Fan Club.
(B) He is a colleague of Mr. Berstein.
(C) He wrote a review of an event.
(D) He used to work at the Foxwood Theater.

ANSWER SHEET

파고다 토익 기본 완성 RC - ACTUAL TEST

READING (Part V - VII)

NO.	ANSWER A B C D	NO.	ANSWER A B C D	NO.	ANSWER A B C D	NO.	ANSWER A B C D	NO.	ANSWER A B C D
101	Ⓐ Ⓑ Ⓒ Ⓓ	121	Ⓐ Ⓑ Ⓒ Ⓓ	141	Ⓐ Ⓑ Ⓒ Ⓓ	161	Ⓐ Ⓑ Ⓒ Ⓓ	181	Ⓐ Ⓑ Ⓒ Ⓓ
102	Ⓐ Ⓑ Ⓒ Ⓓ	122	Ⓐ Ⓑ Ⓒ Ⓓ	142	Ⓐ Ⓑ Ⓒ Ⓓ	162	Ⓐ Ⓑ Ⓒ Ⓓ	182	Ⓐ Ⓑ Ⓒ Ⓓ
103	Ⓐ Ⓑ Ⓒ Ⓓ	123	Ⓐ Ⓑ Ⓒ Ⓓ	143	Ⓐ Ⓑ Ⓒ Ⓓ	163	Ⓐ Ⓑ Ⓒ Ⓓ	183	Ⓐ Ⓑ Ⓒ Ⓓ
104	Ⓐ Ⓑ Ⓒ Ⓓ	124	Ⓐ Ⓑ Ⓒ Ⓓ	144	Ⓐ Ⓑ Ⓒ Ⓓ	164	Ⓐ Ⓑ Ⓒ Ⓓ	184	Ⓐ Ⓑ Ⓒ Ⓓ
105	Ⓐ Ⓑ Ⓒ Ⓓ	125	Ⓐ Ⓑ Ⓒ Ⓓ	145	Ⓐ Ⓑ Ⓒ Ⓓ	165	Ⓐ Ⓑ Ⓒ Ⓓ	185	Ⓐ Ⓑ Ⓒ Ⓓ
106	Ⓐ Ⓑ Ⓒ Ⓓ	126	Ⓐ Ⓑ Ⓒ Ⓓ	146	Ⓐ Ⓑ Ⓒ Ⓓ	166	Ⓐ Ⓑ Ⓒ Ⓓ	186	Ⓐ Ⓑ Ⓒ Ⓓ
107	Ⓐ Ⓑ Ⓒ Ⓓ	127	Ⓐ Ⓑ Ⓒ Ⓓ	147	Ⓐ Ⓑ Ⓒ Ⓓ	167	Ⓐ Ⓑ Ⓒ Ⓓ	187	Ⓐ Ⓑ Ⓒ Ⓓ
108	Ⓐ Ⓑ Ⓒ Ⓓ	128	Ⓐ Ⓑ Ⓒ Ⓓ	148	Ⓐ Ⓑ Ⓒ Ⓓ	168	Ⓐ Ⓑ Ⓒ Ⓓ	188	Ⓐ Ⓑ Ⓒ Ⓓ
109	Ⓐ Ⓑ Ⓒ Ⓓ	129	Ⓐ Ⓑ Ⓒ Ⓓ	149	Ⓐ Ⓑ Ⓒ Ⓓ	169	Ⓐ Ⓑ Ⓒ Ⓓ	189	Ⓐ Ⓑ Ⓒ Ⓓ
110	Ⓐ Ⓑ Ⓒ Ⓓ	130	Ⓐ Ⓑ Ⓒ Ⓓ	150	Ⓐ Ⓑ Ⓒ Ⓓ	170	Ⓐ Ⓑ Ⓒ Ⓓ	190	Ⓐ Ⓑ Ⓒ Ⓓ
111	Ⓐ Ⓑ Ⓒ Ⓓ	131	Ⓐ Ⓑ Ⓒ Ⓓ	151	Ⓐ Ⓑ Ⓒ Ⓓ	171	Ⓐ Ⓑ Ⓒ Ⓓ	191	Ⓐ Ⓑ Ⓒ Ⓓ
112	Ⓐ Ⓑ Ⓒ Ⓓ	132	Ⓐ Ⓑ Ⓒ Ⓓ	152	Ⓐ Ⓑ Ⓒ Ⓓ	172	Ⓐ Ⓑ Ⓒ Ⓓ	192	Ⓐ Ⓑ Ⓒ Ⓓ
113	Ⓐ Ⓑ Ⓒ Ⓓ	133	Ⓐ Ⓑ Ⓒ Ⓓ	153	Ⓐ Ⓑ Ⓒ Ⓓ	173	Ⓐ Ⓑ Ⓒ Ⓓ	193	Ⓐ Ⓑ Ⓒ Ⓓ
114	Ⓐ Ⓑ Ⓒ Ⓓ	134	Ⓐ Ⓑ Ⓒ Ⓓ	154	Ⓐ Ⓑ Ⓒ Ⓓ	174	Ⓐ Ⓑ Ⓒ Ⓓ	194	Ⓐ Ⓑ Ⓒ Ⓓ
115	Ⓐ Ⓑ Ⓒ Ⓓ	135	Ⓐ Ⓑ Ⓒ Ⓓ	155	Ⓐ Ⓑ Ⓒ Ⓓ	175	Ⓐ Ⓑ Ⓒ Ⓓ	195	Ⓐ Ⓑ Ⓒ Ⓓ
116	Ⓐ Ⓑ Ⓒ Ⓓ	136	Ⓐ Ⓑ Ⓒ Ⓓ	156	Ⓐ Ⓑ Ⓒ Ⓓ	176	Ⓐ Ⓑ Ⓒ Ⓓ	196	Ⓐ Ⓑ Ⓒ Ⓓ
117	Ⓐ Ⓑ Ⓒ Ⓓ	137	Ⓐ Ⓑ Ⓒ Ⓓ	157	Ⓐ Ⓑ Ⓒ Ⓓ	177	Ⓐ Ⓑ Ⓒ Ⓓ	197	Ⓐ Ⓑ Ⓒ Ⓓ
118	Ⓐ Ⓑ Ⓒ Ⓓ	138	Ⓐ Ⓑ Ⓒ Ⓓ	158	Ⓐ Ⓑ Ⓒ Ⓓ	178	Ⓐ Ⓑ Ⓒ Ⓓ	198	Ⓐ Ⓑ Ⓒ Ⓓ
119	Ⓐ Ⓑ Ⓒ Ⓓ	139	Ⓐ Ⓑ Ⓒ Ⓓ	159	Ⓐ Ⓑ Ⓒ Ⓓ	179	Ⓐ Ⓑ Ⓒ Ⓓ	199	Ⓐ Ⓑ Ⓒ Ⓓ
120	Ⓐ Ⓑ Ⓒ Ⓓ	140	Ⓐ Ⓑ Ⓒ Ⓓ	160	Ⓐ Ⓑ Ⓒ Ⓓ	180	Ⓐ Ⓑ Ⓒ Ⓓ	200	Ⓐ Ⓑ Ⓒ Ⓓ

ANSWER SHEET

MEMO

MEMO

해설서

3rd Edition

파고다교육그룹 언어교육연구소, 홍수림 | 저

빨더나오

토익 문법·독해·어휘 입문서

기본완성

RC

PAGODA Books

3rd Edition

해설서

비토익

토익 문법·독해·어휘 입문서

기본완성

RC

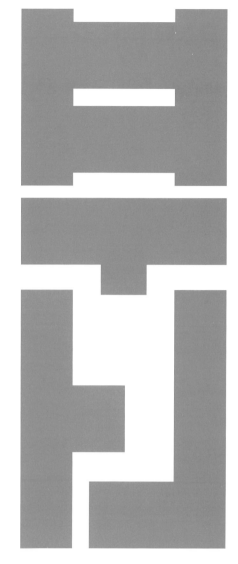
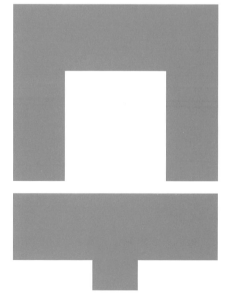

PART 5

UNIT 01. 문장의 구조와 동사 본서 p.24

+ check   1. (B)   2. (B)   3. (A)   4. (D)

1. 오늘 오후 모든 실험실 조교들은 안전 예방 교육에 반드시 참석해야 한다.

해설 빈칸은 주어 자리이다. 따라서 빈칸은 명사 자리인데, 해석상 실험실 '조교들이' 참석한다는 해석이 자연스러우므로 정답은 (B) assistants이다.

어휘 laboratory *n.* 실험실 | safety training session 안전 예방 교육

2. 모든 현장 공장 감독자들은 월요일까지 그들의 근무시간 기록표를 제출해야만 한다.

해설 품사 어형 문제로 조동사(must) 뒤에는 동사원형이 오므로 정답은 (B) submit이다.

어휘 on-site *adj.* 현장의 | supervisor *n.* 감독자, 관리자 | timesheet *n.* 근무시간 기록표

3. Bitec 게임사는 그 회사의 Hillstown 제조 시설을 개조하기 위한 계획을 세웠다.

해설 품사 어형 문제로 빈칸은 목적어 자리이므로 명사를 써야 한다. 보기 중 명사는 '계획'을 뜻하는 (A) plans와 '설계자, 계획표'란 의미의 (D) planner인데, 시설을 개조하기 위한 '계획'을 세웠다는 의미가 적절하므로 정답은 (A) plans이다.

어휘 renovate *v.* 개조하다, 보수하다 | manufacturing facility 제조 시설

4. Skymet 전자는 가장 합리적인 가격에 제품을 제공함으로써 고객들을 만족시켜 줄 것이다.

해설 어법상 적절한 어휘의 품사 형태를 묻는 문제이다. 동사 keep의 목적어인 its customers의 상태를 설명해 주는 목적격 보어 자리에는 형용사가 와야 한다는 사실을 알 수 있다. customers는 만족되는 대상이므로 정답은 수동형 분사 형용사인 (D) satisfied이다. 「keep + 누구 + satisfied」는 "누구를 만족시키다"는 뜻으로 자주 사용된다. (A)는 to부정사이므로 오답이고, (B)는 3인칭 단수형 동사이므로 빈칸에 들어갈 수 없다.

어휘 affordable *adj.* (가격이) 알맞은

Practice 본서 p.28

1. (D)	**2.** (A)	**3.** (C)	**4.** (B)	**5.** (D)
6. (C)	**7.** (A)	**8.** (C)	**9.** (A)	**10.** (B)
11. (B)	**12.** (D)	**13.** (B)	**14.** (A)	**15.** (B)
16. (A)	**17.** (D)	**18.** (A)	**19.** (B)	**20.** (C)

---

1. The Finance Department is very busy this month with their budget report.

2. The President of S&B Communications decided to offer internships to students.

3. The varying quality of products can make purchase decisions quite difficult.

4. You can renew subscriptions to *Beauty Updates Magazine* online or by telephone.

5. The government's new employment policy will enable businesses to create many jobs.

6. The President informed employees of the change in the payroll system.

7. The upgraded computer system is fully operational now and ready for use.

8. The Marketing Department encouraged employees to submit their feedback reports as soon as possible.

9. Moonfield Shopping Center reminded customers that their business hours will change from March 1.

10. Completion of this task is not expected until early April.

....

1. 재무팀은 그들의 예산 보고서로 이번 달에 매우 바쁘다.

해설 be동사 is는 2형식 동사이다. very는 부사일 뿐이므로 빈칸은 주격 보어 자리, 즉 주어의 상태를 설명하는 형용사 자리이다. 따라서 정답은 (D) busy이다. busier도 형용사이지만, 뒤에는 원급만 올 수 있으므로 비교급 busier는 답이 될 수 없다.

어휘 Finance Department 재무팀 | budget report 예산 보고서

2. Jaygen Holdings 사는 올해 노동력을 20% 증가시킬 것이다.

해설 빈칸은 동사 자리이다. 동사가 될 수 없는 -ing형태와 to부정사 형태, 그리고 수동태인 (B), (C), (D)를 탈락시키면 정답은 (A) will increase 이다.

어휘 workforce *n.* (특정 기업·조직 등의 모든) 노동자, 노동 인구

3. 월례 고객 설문 조사 때의 반응이 일관되게 긍정적이다.

해설 be동사 are는 2형식 동사이다. 형용사 주격 보어가 이미 positive로 나와 있는 상태이므로 빈칸은 문장의 필수요소가 아닌 수식어구 자리이며, 형용사 앞에 들어갈 수 있는 품사는 부사이다. 따라서 정답은 (C) consistently이다.

어휘 response n. 반응 | customer survey 고객 설문 조사 | positive adj. 긍정적인 | consistently adv. 일관적으로, 지속적으로, 끊임없이

4. S&B 커뮤니케이션의 사장은 학생들에게 인턴직을 제공하기로 결정했다.

해설 빈칸은 동사 자리이다. 동사가 될 수 없는 -ing 형태와 to부정사 형태인 (A)와 (D)는 탈락이고, (C)는 명사이므로 소거한다. 따라서 정답은 (B) decided이다.

어휘 offer v. 제공하다 | decide v. 결정하다

5. 제품들의 다양한 품질이 구매 결정을 꽤 어렵게 만든다.

해설 make는 5형식 동사이며 「make + 목적어 + 목적격 보어」 구문이다. purchase decisions가 목적어이고 빈칸은 목적격 보어 자리이다. 동사가 make일 때 목적격 보어 자리에 형용사나 명사가 들어갈 수 있으나, 목적어의 상태를 설명하고 있으므로 형용사 (D) difficult가 정답이다.

어휘 quality n. 품질 | purchase decision 구매 결정

6. 당신은 〈Beauty Updates Magazine〉의 구독을 온라인이나 전화로 갱신할 수 있다.

해설 빈칸은 renew의 목적어(명사) 자리이다. 명사는 (A)와 (C)이다. 해석상 '구독자'를 갱신하는 것이 아니라 '구독'을 갱신하는 것이므로 정답은 (C) subscriptions이다.

어휘 renew v. 갱신하다 | subscriber n. 구독자 | subscription n. 구독

7. 이번 주 토요일에, 그 백화점은 모든 쇼핑 고객들에게 15% 할인을 제공할 것이다.

해설 offer는 4형식 동사로 빈칸은 간접 목적어 자리이고, a 15 percent discount는 직접 목적어이다. 해석상 '쇼핑'이나 '가게'에게 할인해 주는 것이 아니라, '쇼핑하는 사람들'에게 할인을 제공하는 것이므로 정답은 (A) shoppers이다.

어휘 department store 백화점 | offer v. 제공하다 | shop v. 쇼핑하다 n. 가게, 상점 | shopper n. 쇼핑 고객

8. 마이애미로의 본사 이전이 4월에 있을 것이다.

해설 빈칸은 주어 자리이므로 명사가 와야 한다. 따라서 정답은 (C) relocation이다.

어휘 occur v. 발생하다, 일어나다 | relocate v. 이전하다

9. 정부의 새 고용 정책이 기업체들로 하여금 많은 일자리 창출을 가능하게 해 준다.

해설 enable은 5형식 동사이다. businesses가 목적어이고 빈칸은 목적격 보어 자리이다. enable은 목적격 보어 자리에 to부정사를 취하므로 정답은 (A) to create이다.

어휘 enable v. ~가 …를 할 수 있게 하다, 가능하게 하다 | create v. 창조하다, 만들다

10. Plaxco 회계법인은 작은 회사에서 500여명의 직원을 둔 대형 회사로 빠르게 성장했다.

해설 grow는 1형식 동사이다. 빈칸이 없어도 이미 완벽한 문장이므로, 문장을 완성하는데 영향을 주지 않는 부사가 와야 하므로 정답은 (B) quickly이다.

어휘 grow v. 성장하다

11. Johnsonville 공장의 직원들은 매달 말일에 월급을 받는다.

해설 빈칸은 주어 자리, 즉 명사 자리이다. 명사는 (A), (B), (C)인데 해석상 '직원들'이므로 정답은 (B) Workers이다.

어휘 salary n. 월급

12. 사장은 직원들에게 급여 체계의 변경을 알렸다.

해설 inform은 「inform A of B」의 형태로 쓰였으므로, 빈칸에는 명사가 들어가야 한다. 보기에서 정답이 될 수 있는 것은 (D) change이다.

어휘 inform v. 알리다 | payroll system 급여 시스템

13. 일부 고객들이 그 요리사의 새 디저트가 너무 달다고 불평했다.

해설 be동사 was는 2형식 동사이다. 따라서 빈칸은 주격 보어 자리로 주어의 상태를 보충 설명하는 형용사가 와야 한다. 따라서 정답은 (B) sweet이다.

어휘 complain v. 불평하다 | sweet adj. 달콤한

14. Frankston행 첫 번째 기차는 정확히 오늘 오전 10시에 출발할 것이다.

해설 depart는 1형식 동사이므로 이미 완벽한 문장이다. 따라서 빈칸은 뒤의 전치사구를 수식하는 자리이므로 부사 (A) precisely가 정답이다.

어휘 depart v. 출발하다 | precisely adv. 바로, 꼭, 정확히

15. 업그레이드된 컴퓨터 시스템은 이제 완전히 가동 가능하며, 사용할 준비가 되었다.

해설 be동사 is는 2형식 동사이다. fully는 수식어구이므로 빈칸은 주격 보어 자리로 주어의 상태를 보충 설명하는 형용사가 와야 한다. 따라서 정답은 (B) operational이다.

어휘 fully adv. 완전히, 충분히 | operational adj. 가동상의, 가동할 준비가 갖춰진

16. 마케팅 부서는 직원들이 가능한 한 빨리 그들의 피드백 보고서를 제출하도록 독려했다.

해설 encourage는 5형식 동사이다. employees는 목적어이고 빈칸은 목적격 보어 자리이다. encourage는 목적격 보어 자리에 to부정사를 취하므로 정답은 (A) to submit이다.

어휘 marketing department 마케팅 부서 | encourage v. 장려하다, 독려하다 | submit v. 제출하다

17. Mr. Song은 대표가 되기 전에, 그 회사의 여러 분야의 자리들에 있었다.

해설 문장에 동사가 보이지 않으며, 빈칸 뒤에 목적어로서 명사가 보이므로 빈칸은 동사 자리이다. (A)는 형용사, (B)는 명사, (C)는 동명사나 현재분사로 동사가 될 수 없다. 따라서 정답은 동사의 과거형인 (D) occupied이다.

어휘 prior to 전에, 이전에 I occupy v. 차지하다, 점령하다

18. Nahaju 그룹은 내년에 더 큰 사무 단지를 교외에 지을 것이다.

해설 빈칸은 동사 자리이다. 동사가 될 수 없는 -ing/to부정사 형태인 (B)와 (C)가 탈락하고 명사인 (D)도 탈락하므로 정답은 (A) will build이다.

어휘 office complex 사무실 단지 I suburb n. 교외 I build v. 짓다, 세우다

19. Moonfield 쇼핑 센터는 고객들에게 3월 1일부터 그들의 영업 시간이 변경될 것임을 상기시켰다.

해설 remind는 「remind A of B」, 「remind A that S + V」, 「remind A to 동사원형」 이렇게 3가지 형태로 쓰이는데, 빈칸 뒤에 주어와 동사가 왔으므로 「remind A that S + V」 형태가 되어야 한다. 따라서 정답은 (B) that이다.

어휘 remind v. 상기시키다 I business hours 영업 시간

20. 이 작업은 4월 초까지는 완료되지 않을 것으로 예상된다.

해설 빈칸은 주어 자리, 즉 명사 자리이다. 따라서 정답은 (C) Completion이다.

어휘 expect v. 기대하다, 예상하다 I completion n. 완성 I complete v. 완성하다, 완료하다 adj. 완전한

UNIT 02. 수 일치

본서 p.32

+ check   1. (B)   2. (A)   3. (A)   4. (D)

1. Arts Marketing 협회는 오늘 밤 Zenco 호텔에서 연례 학회를 개최한다.

해설 어법상 적절한 동사의 시제를 고르는 문제이다. 주어가(The Arts Marketing Association) 단수이므로 복수 동사 (A) hold와 (D) have held는 답에서 제외시킨다. 빈칸은 동사가 필요한 자리이므로 동사의 역할을 할 수 없는 현재분사 또는 동명사 형태의 (C) holding도 오답이다. 오늘 저녁에 열리게 되는 행사에 대해 언급하고 있으므로 미래형 또는 가까운 미래의 일을 나타내는 현재진행형이 빈칸에 어울린다. 따라서 정답은 (B) is holding이다.

어휘 association n. 협회 I annual adj. 연례의, 매년의 I hold v. 개최하다 I conference n. 회의, 학회

2. 관광객들 각각은 다음 행선지로 떠나기 전에 책자를 받는다.

해설 동사 자리 및 주어 동사 수 일치 문제로 each of the tourists 뒤에는 주어 each와 수 일치되는 단수 동사를 써야 한다. 따라서 정답은 (A) is이다.

어휘 tourist n. 관광객 I leave for ~로 향하다

3. 지난 몇 년간, 차량 소유와 관련된 비용은 많은 통근자들이 회사에 차를 가지고 다니지 못하게 했다.

해설 빈칸은 동사 자리인데, 주어가 the costs이므로 복수이다. (B)는 형

용사이므로 탈락이고, (D)는 명사이므로 탈락이다. (A)와 (C) 중에 복수 동사를 찾아야 하므로 정답은 (A) have prevented이다.

어휘 cost n. 비용 I own v. 소유하다 I prevent A from -ing A가 ~하는 것을 막다

4. 마케팅 부서의 Kelly Brady는 지난주 회의에서 신제품 홍보에 대한 그녀의 아이디어를 제시했다.

해설 빈칸은 동사 자리이다. 주어가 단수이므로 동사 자리에 단수 동사를 써야 한다. (B)와 (C)는 동사 자체가 될 수 없다. (A)는 복수 동사로 단수 동사 presents가 됐어야 했다. 따라서 정답은 (D) presented 이다. 과거 시제는 수 일치가 필요 없다는 점에 유의한다.

어휘 present v. ~을 제시하다

Practice

본서 p.36

1. (A)	**2.** (A)	**3.** (C)	**4.** (D)	**5.** (A)
6. (B)	**7.** (B)	**8.** (B)	**9.** (C)	**10.** (B)
11. (C)	**12.** (D)	**13.** (D)	**14.** (A)	**15.** (B)
16. (C)	**17.** (A)	**18.** (A)	**19.** (D)	**20.** (B)

기본 완성 훈련

① The new LX555 camera, designed for beginner photographers, is popular among young people.

② Our solid wood furniture comes with an extensive five-year warranty.

③ It is expected that productivity at the Thorndon Factory is going to increase this quarter.

④ Ms. Felix has made a considerable donation to the local community.

⑤ The customer service department is trained to deal with various complaints from customers.

6. Orders placed on the Cheap Buy Web site typically take four days to process.

7. Please read the manual carefully before installing your new word processing software.

⑧ Ms. Rares needs more information about the workshop before she can decide whether to attend.

⑨ Tom's Bistro offers customers friendly service as well as a variety of healthy foods.

10. Commuters can easily reach the central business district by taking the Yellow Rail Line.

4

1. 식당 매니저인 Mr. Lee는 정기적으로 새로운 메뉴를 개발한다.

해설 regularly는 부사일 뿐이고, 빈칸은 동사 자리이다. to부정사 형태인 (C)는 동사가 될 수 없다. 주어인 Mr. Lee는 단수 명사이므로 (A) develops가 정답이다.

어휘 develop v. 개발하다

2. 초보 사진작가들을 위해 고안된 새 LX555 카메라는 젊은이들 사이에서 인기가 있다.

해설 designed ~ photographers는 주어인 The new LX555 camera를 꾸며주는 수식어구이다. 따라서 빈칸은 동사 자리이다. -ing 형태인 (D)는 동사가 될 수 없다. (C)는 조동사 뒤에 쓸 수 있는 동사원형이다. 주어가 단수이므로 단수 동사 (A) is가 정답이다.

어휘 photographer n. 사진작가 | popular adj. 인기 있는

3. 영업 부장은 새로 온 인턴들의 교육을 면밀하게 감독한다.

해설 closely는 부사일 뿐이므로, 빈칸은 동사 자리이다. to부정사 형태인 (B)와 -ing 형태인 (D)는 동사가 될 수 없고, 주어가 단수 명사이므로 정답은 단수 동사 (C) monitors이다.

어휘 closely adv. 면밀히 | monitor v. 감시하다, 모니터 하다

4. 우리의 견고한 목재 가구에는 폭넓은 5년짜리 품질 보증서와 함께 나온다.

해설 빈칸은 동사 자리이다. -ing 형태인 (B)와 to부정사 형태인 (C)는 동사가 될 수 없고, 주어가 불가산 명사(furniture)이므로 단수 취급한다. 따라서 단수 동사 (D) comes가 정답이다.

어휘 solid adj. 견고한, 단단한 | extensive adj. 광범위한 | warranty n. 품질 보증서

5. 이번 분기에 Thorndon 공장의 생산성이 높아질 것으로 기대된다.

해설 빈칸은 주어 자리이므로 명사 자리이다. 명사는 (A), (C), (D)인데 동사 is가 나왔으므로 수 일치를 위해 단수 명사를 찾는다. 의미상 '농산물'이 아니라 '생산성'이 적절하므로 정답은 (A) productivity이다.

어휘 productivity n. 생산성 | quarter n. 분기

6. Ms. Felix는 지역 사회에 상당한 기부를 했다.

해설 빈칸은 동사 자리이다. ing 형태는 동사가 될 수 없고, 주어가 3인칭 단수이므로 정답은 단수 동사인 (B) has made이다.

어휘 considerable adj. 상당한 | donation n. 기부, 기증

7. 그 고객 서비스 부서는 고객들로부터 나오는 다양한 불만사항들을 처리하기 위한 교육을 받는다.

해설 주어는 서비스가 아니다. 해석상 고객 서비스가 교육받는 것이 아니고, 고객 서비스 부서가 교육받는 것이다. 따라서 복합 명사로 '고객 서비스 부서'를 찾아야 한다. (B)와 (D) 중에 답이 있다. 빈칸 뒤에 is가 나왔으므로 주어가 단수라는 것을 알 수 있다. 따라서 정답은 단수 명사 (B) department이다.

어휘 customer service department 고객 서비스 부서 | deal with ~을 다루다, (문제 등을) 처리하다 | complaint n. 불평, 불만

8. Comfy Dress 사는 소매업체들에게 적당한 가격의 최신 유행 의상을 10년 넘게 공급해왔다.

해설 빈칸은 동사 자리이다. to부정사와 -ing 형태는 동사가 될 수 없고, 주어가 고유명사 Comfy Dress, Inc.이므로 단수 취급한다. 따라서 단수 동사 (B) has supplied가 정답이다.

어휘 retailer n. 소매상[업체] | affordable adj. 가격이 합리적인 | trendy adj. 최신 유행의

9. Cheap Buy 웹사이트에 접수된 주문은 보통 처리되는 데 4일이 걸린다.

해설 typically는 부사일 뿐이고 빈칸은 동사 자리이다. to부정사와 -ing 형태는 동사가 될 수 없고, 주어가 Orders로 복수 명사이므로 복수 동사 (C) take가 정답이다.

어휘 typically adv. 일반적으로, 전형적으로 | process v. 처리하다 n. 과정, 공정

10. 새로운 워드 프로세싱 소프트웨어를 설치하기 전에 설명서를 주의 깊게 읽어 보세요.

해설 Please로 시작하는 문장은 명령문이다. 명령문은 수 일치와 상관없이 무조건 동사원형으로 시작하므로 정답은 (B) read이다.

어휘 carefully adv. 신중하게, 주의 깊게 | install v. 설치하다

11. 모든 건설 현장 노동자들은 10월 11일까지 보건 및 안전 교육을 이수해야만 한다.

해설 must는 조동사로 뒤에 무조건 동사원형을 취한다. 따라서 정답은 (C) complete이다.

어휘 construction n. 공사 | health and safety training 보건 및 안전 교육

12. 결함 있는 제품들 중 일부는 Newlands 창고로 수송될 것이다.

해설 Some은 전치사 다음에 오는 명사를 보고 수 일치를 시킨다. of라는 전치사 뒤에 products라는 복수 명사가 왔으므로 복수 동사가 와야 한다. to부정사 형태는 동사가 아니므로 (B)는 탈락이고, (C)는 조동사 다음에 쓰이는 동사원형이므로 탈락이다. (A)는 단수 동사이므로 수 일치가 안 맞아서 탈락이다. 따라서 정답은 복수 동사 (D) are이다.

어휘 defective adj. 결함 있는 | ship v. 실어 나르다, 수송하다 | warehouse n. 창고

13. 2,000명 이상의 사람들이 〈Jay' Fashion Magazine〉을 구독한다.

해설 빈칸은 동사 자리이므로 -ing형태인 (B)와 to부정사 (C)는 답에서 제외시킨다. 문장의 주어는 2,000 people로 복수이므로 정답은 복수동사 (D) subscribe이다.

어휘 subscribe v. 구독하다

14. 오늘 아침 호텔 로비에 많은 여행 가방들이 있었다.

해설 There로 시작하는 구문은 '~가 있다'라는 뜻으로 주어와 동사의 순서가 도치된다. 즉, 빈칸에는 동사가 와야 하고 many suitcases가 주어이다. 주어가 복수이므로 복수 동사인 (A)가 정답이다.

어휘 suitcase *n.* 여행 가방

15. 후보자들 중 한 명이 그의 이력서에 일부 부정확한 정보를 포함시켰다.

해설 「one of the + 복수 명사」는 '~중의 하나'라는 뜻으로, 주어가 one이므로 단수 동사가 나와야 한다. -ing와 to부정사 형태는 동사가 될 수 없고, (C)는 복수 동사이므로 탈락이다. 따라서 정답은 수 일치가 필요 없는 동사의 과거형 (B) included이다.

어휘 candidate *n.* 후보자 | inaccurate *adj.* 부정확한 | résumé *n.* 이력서

16. 만약 그 제품들에 대해 문의사항이 있다면, 저희 업무 지원 부서인 555-2349로 연락해주세요.

해설 빈칸은 동사 자리이다. -ing와 to부정사 형태는 동사가 될 수 없다. 대명사인 you는 복수 동사와 수 일치되므로 정답은 (C) have이다.

어휘 contact *v.* 연락하다

17. 올해 기술 학회 참가자들의 수가 감소할 것으로 예상된다.

해설 「the number of」는 '~의 수'라는 뜻으로 주어가 The number이므로 단수 취급한다. 빈칸은 동사 자리인데 (C)는 동사가 될 수 없다. 따라서 단수 동사 (A) is가 정답이다.

어휘 participant *n.* 참가자 | expect *v.* 기대하다

18. Ms. Rares는 참석 여부를 결정하기 전에 워크숍에 대한 더 많은 정보를 필요로 한다.

해설 빈칸은 동사 자리이다. -ing와 to부정사 형태는 동사가 될 수 없다. 주어가 여자이므로 대명사 she와 바꿔 쓸 수 있는데, she는 3인칭 단수이므로 단수 동사 (A) needs가 정답이다.

어휘 attend *v.* 참석하다

19. Tom's Bistro는 고객들에게 다양한 건강식품뿐만 아니라 친절한 서비스도 제공한다.

해설 빈칸은 동사 자리이다. 주어가 고유명사이므로 단수 취급한다. 따라서 단수 동사 (D) offers가 정답이다.

어휘 friendly *adj.* 친절한 | healthy *adj.* 건강에 좋은

20. 통근자들은 Yellow Rail Line을 타고 중심 업무 지구에 쉽게 도달할 수 있다.

해설 can이라는 조동사가 나왔으므로 동사원형이 와야 한다. 따라서 정답은 (B) reach이다.

어휘 easily *adv.* 쉽게 | central business district 중심 업무 지구 | reach *v.* 달성하다, 도달하다, 이르다

UNIT 03. 시제

+ check 1. (A) 2. (A) 3. (D) 4. (B)

1. Yohanas 호수가 마지막으로 완전히 언 것은 10년 전이었다.

해설 품사 어형 문제로 여기서 last가 동사(지속하다)가 아닌 부사(마지막으로)로 쓰였음을 파악할 수 있어야 한다. 따라서 빈칸은 동사 자리이고, 문장 맨 뒷부분에 과거를 나타내는 시간 부사구(a decade ago)가 쓰였으므로 정답은 과거 동사인 (A) froze이다.

어휘 last *adv.* 마지막으로 | completely *adv.* 완전히 | decade *n.* 10년

2. 우리 회사의 휴대폰 수출이 지난 3년간 늘어났다.

해설 빈칸은 동사 자리이다. 동사가 되지 않는 -ing 형태의 (B)는 탈락이다. 마지막 부분에 over the past three years가 나온 것이 현재완료 시제의 힌트이므로 정답은 (A) have increased이다.

어휘 export *n.* 수출

3. 직원들이 만족도 설문을 작성한 후에, 그들은 그 서식을 인사과 매니저에게 보낼 것이다.

해설 빈칸은 동사 자리이다. 문맥상 직원들이 만족 설문지를 완성한 후, 그 서식을 보낼 것이라는 뜻이므로 만족 설문지를 아직 완성하지 않은 상태이다. 따라서 빈칸은 문맥상 미래 시제가 맞지만, 시간접속사 after가 있다. 시간·조건 부사절에서는 미래를 현재시제로 바꿔야 하므로 정답은 (D) complete이다.

어휘 satisfaction survey 만족도 설문 조사 | form *n.* 서식, 양식

4. 승무원들은 귀하의 기내 수하물이 지정된 짐칸에 보관되도록 요청할 수 있습니다.

해설 요청 동사 ask가 있다. 요청, 제안 동사가 나오면 that절 뒤에 should가 생략되어 있다는 것을 알아차려야 한다. 따라서 빈칸 앞에는 should가 있으므로 동사원형을 찾아야 하므로 정답은 (B) be kept이다. (A)는 과거 동사나 과거분사이고, (C)는 3인칭 주어의 현재 시제 동사이다. (D)는 현재진행 시제이므로 답이 될 수 없다.

어휘 carry-on luggage 기내 수하물 | compartment *n.* 짐칸

Practice

1. (A)	**2.** (B)	**3.** (D)	**4.** (B)	**5.** (A)
6. (B)	**7.** (B)	**8.** (A)	**9.** (C)	**10.** (D)
11. (B)	**12.** (D)	**13.** (B)	**14.** (B)	**15.** (C)
16. (B)	**17.** (D)	**18.** (D)	**19.** (A)	**20.** (C)

기본 완성 훈련

1. Mr. Rockwell has been supervising the production schedule since he was appointed factory manager.

2. Dr. Cruz recommends that every patient visit his hospital for a routine checkup at least once a year.

3. Mr. Nakamoto , an expert in the field of science, was recently elected city mayor.

4. An increasing number of restaurants have offered customers discount coupons in the last few years.

5. Since Ms. Pham joined the company, sales have increased by almost 30 percent.

6. Until Ms. Kim relocates to the Beijing branch, she will be handling the Drefus account.

7. Kirks Department Store has been open for over 20 years.

8. Mr. Randall has been developing a new database over the past two months.

9. The IT Department will be accepting suggestions for the new security program until the end of this week.

10. Starting next Wednesday, the Vianox Shopping Center will be extending its business hours until 10 P.M.

---

1. Mr. Rockwell은 그가 공장 매니저로 임명된 이후로 생산 일정을 감독해 오고 있다.

해설 since 뒤에 주어가 나왔으니 빈칸에는 동사가 와야하므로 (A) was와 (C) is 중 하나가 답이 된다. 또한 since 앞에 쓰인 절은 항상 현재완료 시제를 쓰고 since 뒤에 주어와 동사를 갖춘 절을 쓸 때는 항상 과거 시제를 써야 하므로 정답은 (A) was이다.

어휘 **supervise** v. 관리/감독하다 | **appoint** v. 임명하다

2. Mr. Garcia는 지난 월요일에 마케팅 프로젝트를 완수했다.

해설 빈칸은 동사 자리이다. last Monday에서 last는 '지난'이라는 뜻으로 과거 시제와 함께 쓰이므로 정답은 (B) completed이다.

어휘 **complete** v. 완수/완료하다

3. Dr. Cruz 박사는 모든 환자가 정기 검진을 위해서 적어도 일년에 한 번은 그의 병원에 방문할 것을 권유한다.

해설 「recommend that S + (should) + 동사원형」이다. should가 생략되어 있으므로 정답은 동사원형인 (D) visit이다.

어휘 **recommend** v. 추천하다 | **patient** n. 환자

4. 과학 분야 전문가인 Mr. Nakamoto는 최근에 시장으로 선출되었다.

해설 빈칸은 동사 자리이다. recently는 과거 시제와 현재 완료 시제 둘 다에 쓰이므로 (A), (B), (D) 모두 가능하다. 주어인 Mr. Nakamoto는 3인칭 단수이므로 정답은 단수 동사인 (B) was이다.

어휘 **expert** n. 전문가 | **field** n. 분야 | **elect** v. 선출하다

5. 우리는 품질을 개선하고자 하는 당신의 노력에 항상 감사드립니다.

해설 빈칸은 동사 자리인데, always는 빈도부사로 현재 시제와 함께 쓰이므로 정답은 (A) appreciate이다.

어휘 **always** adv. 항상 | **effort** n. 노력

6. 지난 몇 년간 점점 많은 식당들이 고객들에게 할인 쿠폰을 제공해왔다.

해설 빈칸은 동사 자리이다. to부정사 형태는 동사가 될 수 없으므로 (D)는 탈락이다. 고객들에게 할인을 제공해 왔다는 능동의 의미이므로 수동태 동사 (C)도 탈락이다. in the last few years는 '지난 몇 년간'이라는 뜻으로 현재 완료 시제와 함께 쓰이는 표현이므로 정답은 (B) have offered이다.

어휘 **offer** v. 제공하다

7. 그 공장을 세우려는 시의 계획은 다음 주에 마무리될 것이다.

해설 빈칸은 동사 자리이다. next week은 '다음 주'라는 뜻으로 미래 시제와 함께 쓰이므로 정답은 (B) will be finalized이다.

어휘 **build** v. 짓다, 세우다

8. 고객들이 훌륭한 서비스와 맛있는 음식 때문에 대개 Sador's Diner로 돌아온다.

해설 빈칸은 동사 자리이다. 빈도부사 usually는 '보통'이라는 의미로 현재 시제와 함께 쓰이므로 정답은 (A)와 (C)가 가능하다. 주어가 복수이므로 수 일치를 위해 정답은 (A) return이다.

어휘 **usually** adv. 보통 | **return** v. 돌아오다, 반납하다

9. Ms. Pham이 회사에 입사한 이후로, 매출액이 거의 30퍼센트나 증가했다.

해설 「since + 과거 시제」가 나오면, '과거 이래로 현재까지 그래왔다'는 뜻이므로 현재 완료 시제가 정답이다. 따라서 정답은 (C) have increased이다.

어휘 **join** v. 합류하다, 가입하다

10. Ms. Kim이 베이징 지사로 이전할 때까지, 그녀는 Drefus 거래처를 다루게 될 것이다.

해설 빈칸은 동사 자리이며, 주어는 Ms. Kim으로 단수이므로 복수동사인 (B)는 탈락. 주절이 미래시제이므로 의미상 베이징 지사로 이전할 것이라는 미래시제가 적절해 보이지만, 종속절을 이끄는 시간 접속사 until은 미래를 나타낼 때 미래시제 대신 현재 시제를 취하므로 정답은 (D) relocates이다.

어휘 **handle** v. 다루다, 처리하다

11. Kirks 백화점은 20년 넘게 영업해오고 있다.

해설 「for + 기간」은 '~동안'이라는 뜻으로 현재 완료와 함께 쓰이므로, 정

답은 (A)와 (B)가 될 수 있다. 주어가 단수 명사이므로 단수 동사 (B) has been이 정답이다.

어휘　open v. 개업하다 adj. (상점·은행 등이) 영업을 하는

12. 지난 두 달 동안, Hu 교수 강의 참석자 수가 놀라울 정도로 늘었다.

해설　「during + 기간」은 현재 완료와 함께 쓰이고, 문맥상 '~동안'이라는 의미가 되어야 하므로 정답은 (D) During이다.

어휘　attendance n. 출석, 참석, 참석률, 참석자 수 l dramatically adv. 극적으로

13. Mr. Johnson은 미리 예약을 했다는 이유만으로 미술 축제에서 좌석을 얻을 수 있었다.

해설　빈칸은 동사 자리이다. 예약한 것이 좌석을 얻은 것보다 먼저 일어난 사건이므로 과거보다 더 이전인 과거완료 시제(대과거)를 써야 한다. 따라서 정답은 (B) had booked이다.

어휘　in advance 미리, 사전에 l book v. 예약하다

14. Mr. Randall은 지난 2개월 동안 새 데이터베이스를 개발해오고 있다.

해설　빈칸은 동사 자리이며, 'over the past two months'는 '지난 2개월 동안'이라는 의미로 현재완료 또는 현재완료진행 시제와 함께 쓰이는 시간부사구이므로 정답은 (B) has been developing이다.

어휘　database n. 데이터베이스 l past adj. 지난, 이전의

15. Ms. Reddy는 내년 4월에 새 공장이 문을 열면, 운영을 감독할 것이다.

해설　빈칸은 동사 자리이다. 뒷 문장의 when 시간 부사절에서 next April이면 미래 시제가 나와야 하는데, 시간, 조건 부사절에서는 미래 시제를 현재 시제로 바꾸므로 현재 시제(opens)가 쓰였다. 앞 문장의 주절은 시제를 바꾸지 않고 그대로 쓰기 때문에 해석상 미래 시제가 와야 하므로 정답은 (C) will oversee이다.

어휘　oversee v. 감독하다, 감시하다

16. IT 부서는 이번 주 말까지 새 보안 프로그램에 대한 제안을 수용할 것이다.

해설　빈칸은 동사 자리이므로 -ing와 to부정사 형태는 동사가 될 수 없다. until the end of this week(이번 주 말까지)라고 했으므로 미래 시제가 알맞다. 따라서 정답은 (B) will be accepting이다.

어휘　suggestion n. 제안 l accept v. 받아들이다, 수락하다

17. 다음 주 수요일부터 Vianox 쇼핑 센터는 영업 시간을 밤 10시까지 연장할 것이다.

해설　빈칸은 동사 자리이다. Starting next Wednesday가 미래 시제를 나타내고 있으므로 정답은 (D) will be extending이다.

어휘　business hours 영업 시간

18. Ms. Li와 Ms. Chau는 둘 다 Wantari 그룹에서 7년 이상 일해왔다.

해설　「for는 '~동안'」이라는 뜻으로 '기간'을 나타내며 현재 완료와 함께 쓰이므로 정답은 (D) have worked이다.

어휘　over adv. ~이상

19. 저녁 8시 이후에 사무실에 걸려온 전화들은 다음 날 아침에 답신될 것이다.

해설　주어 Phone calls가 복수 명사이므로 (C)와 (D)는 알맞지 않다. 또한 과거완료 시제는 문장에서 과거 시제의 사건이 언급되어야 정답이 될 수 있는데, 이 문장에는 과거 시제의 절이 포함되어 있지 않으므로 (B) 도 정답이 될 수 없다. 따라서 정답은 (A) will be returned이다.

어휘　phone call 걸려온 전화

20. Baprix 산업은 Detroit에 있는 제조 시설들을 곧 확장할 것이다.

해설　soon이 '곧'이라는 뜻으로 미래 시제와 함께 쓰이므로 정답은 (C) soon이다.

어휘　expand v. 확장시키다, 확장되다 l manufacturing n. 제조업 l facility n. 시설

UNIT 04. 능동태와 수동태

본서 p.48

✚ check　　1. (B)　　2. (B)　　3. (A)　　4. (D)

1. 최근 보고서는 현재의 경기 침체 동안에도 관광 산업이 놀랍게도 강세를 보이고 있음을 보여 준다.

해설　remain은 2형식 동사이다. 따라서 보어 형용사가 나와야 하는데, 이미 형용사 strong이 나와 있으므로 빈칸에는 없어도 문장이 완성되는 부사가 들어간다. 또한, 부사가 형용사 strong을 꾸미는 것도 가능하므로 정답은 (B) surprisingly이다.

어휘　economic recession 경기 침체

2. Birnham 극장에서의 연극 제작은 주로 지역 후원 업체들에 의해 자금을 조달 받는다.

해설　품사 어형 문제이다. 빈칸 앞뒤를 보면 「주어(Productions ~) + 동사(are -------) + 부사구(mainly by local sponsors)」의 구조를 갖추고 있다. (A)와 (D)는 명사나 동사인데, 문장에 동사 are가 이미 존재하므로 동사는 생각할 필요가 없고, 명사로 생각을 한다면, 2형식 동사 "are" 뒤에 명사를 넣으면 보어 자리에 명사가 들어오게 되어 주어와 동격이 되어야 한다. 주어와 fund는 동격이 아니므로 정답이 될 수 없다. (B)를 빈칸에 넣으면 현재 시제 수동태가 되고, (C)를 빈칸에 넣으면 현재진행형 능동태가 된다. fund는 3형식 동사이기 때문에 빈칸 뒤에 부사와 전치사구만 있고 목적어(명사)가 없으면 수동태가 되어야 한다. 따라서 정답은 (B) funded이다.

어휘　production n. (영화, 연극 등의) 제작 l mainly adv. 주로, 대부분 l sponsor n. 후원업체, 스폰서

3. 59.2 FM의 월례 경연 우승자들에게는 스튜디오에 와서 유명 라디오 진행자들을 만날 기회가 주어질 것이다.

해설　빈칸은 동사 자리이다. 그런데 give는 4형식 동사이다. 목적어(명사)가 두 개 나왔어야 했는데, 명사 the opportunity 한 개밖에 나오지 않았으므로 수동태가 되어야 됨을 알 수 있다. 수동태는 「be + p.p.」 형태를 띠어야 하므로 정답은 (A) will be given이다.

어휘　winner n. 우승자 l opportunity n. 기회 l radio host 라디오 진행자

4. 보안상의 이유로, 모든 직원들은 시설물에 들어올 때 신분증을 제시할 것이 요구된다.

해설 빈칸은 동사 자리이다. ask는 5형식 동사인데, 목적격 보어 자리에 to부정사가 나오는 5형식 동사로 문장 구조 단원에서 배웠다. 목적격보어 to부정사는 있지만 목적어(명사)가 빠져 있으므로 수동태를 찾아야 한다. (B)는 동사 자체가 될 수 없다. (A)는 현재 시제 능동태이다. (C)는 현재진행 능동태이다. (D)는 현재 시제 수동태이므로 정답은 (D) are asked이다.

어휘 security n. 안전, 보안 | personnel n. 직원들

Practice

본서 p.52

1. (A)	**2.** (A)	**3.** (C)	**4.** (A)	**5.** (A)
6. (D)	**7.** (D)	**8.** (A)	**9.** (B)	**10.** (B)
11. (B)	**12.** (A)	**13.** (B)	**14.** (A)	**15.** (B)
16. (C)	**17.** (A)	**18.** (A)	**19.** (B)	**20.** (A)

기본 완성 훈련

①. A large apartment complex will be built next to the Barhill train station.

②. The Employee of the Year has been nominated by the President of the company.

③. Changes to delivery schedules should be reported to the shipping manager directly.

④. This medication should be taken with a lot of water.

⑤. Hikers are encouraged to visit the park's information desk in order to get trail maps.

⑥. All desserts at the restaurant have been prepared by renowned chef Christy Kang.

⑦. Bromville Apartments' heating system is being inspected by the property management office this morning.

8. All team members can apply for a bonus once they have worked here for one year.

⑨. Applicants interested in the position are required to submit their résumés by November 30.

⑩. Any requests for a vacation must be submitted to the supervisor at least one week in advance.

---

1. 건설 작업자들은 그 프로젝트를 일정에 맞춰 완료했다.

해설 빈칸은 동사 자리이다. (C)의 -ing, (D)의 to부정사 형태는 동사가 될 수 없다. finish는 3형식 동사인데 빈칸 뒤에 목적어인 명사 '프로젝트'가 나왔으므로 능동태 (A) finished가 정답이다.

어휘 construction n. 건설, 공사 | crew n. 팀, 무리 | on schedule 예정대로

2. 대규모 아파트 단지가 Barhill 기차역 옆에 지어질 것이다.

해설 빈칸은 동사 자리이다. (B)는 명사이므로 탈락이다. build는 3형식 동사인데 빈칸 뒤에 전치사구, 즉 수식어구가 나와 있고 목적어가 될 수 있는 명사가 없으므로 수동태인 (A) will be built가 정답이다.

어휘 complex n. 단지, 복합 건물

3. 잡지에 있는 모든 이미지들이 SE 협회에 의해 아낌없이 제공되었다.

해설 have been provided는 현재 완료 시제의 수동태로 이미 완벽한 문장이다. 따라서 be p.p 사이에서 동사를 수식하는 부사 (C) generously가 정답이다.

어휘 magazine n. 잡지 | provide v. 제공하다 | generously adv. 관대하게, 아낌없이

4. 주간 영업 회의는 보통 아침에 진행된다.

해설 동사 is가 있으므로 (B)는 탈락이다. 단수 명사인 (C)는 앞에 관사가 있어야 하므로 정답이 될 수 없다. (A)를 넣으면 is conducted로 현재 시제 수동태가 되고, (D)를 넣으면 현재진행 능동태가 된다. conduct의 목적어(명사)가 빈칸 뒤에 없고, 전치사구(수식어구)만 있으므로 정답은 수동태인 (A) conducted이다.

어휘 usually adv. 일반적으로 | conduct v. (특정한 활동을) 하다

5. Furiko 사는 수년 동안 재정적인 문제에 직면해왔다.

해설 빈칸은 동사 자리이다. face는 3형식 동사로 목적어(명사)를 동반하는데, 빈칸 뒤에 목적어가 있으므로 능동태 (A), (C), (D)가 정답이 될 수 있다. for several years라는 기간은 현재완료 시제와 함께 쓰이므로 (A)와 (C)가 가능하지만 주어가 단수이므로 정답은 (A) has faced이다.

어휘 financial adj. 재정적인 | face v. (상황에) 직면하다

6. 올해의 (우수) 직원은 회사 대표에 의해서 지명되었다.

해설 빈칸은 동사 자리이다. nominate는 3형식 동사인데 빈칸 뒤에 목적어(명사)가 없으므로 수동태를 찾아야 한다. 따라서 정답은 (D) has been nominated이다.

어휘 nominate v. 지명하다, 임명하다

7. 배송 일정에 대한 변경 사항들은 배송 매니저에게 바로 보고되어야 한다.

해설 report는 '~을 보고하다'라는 의미의 3형식 동사로서 빈칸 뒤에 목적어 없이 전치사구가 연결되어 있으므로 수동태가 들어가야 할 자리이다. 보기 중 수동태는 (A)와 (D) 둘 뿐인데, 주어가 복수(Changes)이므로 단수형인 (A)는 답이 될 수 없다. 따라서 변경사항들이 매니저에게 즉시 보고되어야 한다는 의미를 완성하는 (D) should be

PART 5 UNIT 04

9

reported가 정답이다.

어휘 directly *adv.* 곧장, 바로

8. 당신의 모든 개인 정보가 안전하게 유지될 것이다.

해설 keep은 형용사를 목적격 보어로 취하는 5형식 동사이다. 그런데 문장이 수동태이므로 목적어는 빠지고, 목적격 보어만 남는다. 따라서 빈칸에는 목적격 보어 자리에 올 수 있는 형용사가 와야 한다. 따라서 정답은 (A) secure이다.

어휘 personal *adj.* 개인적인 | secure *adj.* 안전한, 안심하는 *v.* 얻어내다, 획득하다

9. 이 약은 많은 물과 함께 복용되어야 한다.

해설 조동사 뒤에는 동사원형이 와야 한다. (A)는 to가 붙어 있으므로 동사원형이 아니다. take는 3형식 동사인데 빈칸 뒤에 전치사구(수식어구)만 있고 목적어(명사)가 없으므로 수동태임을 알 수 있다. 따라서 정답은 (B) be taken이다.

어휘 medication *n.* 약, 약물 | take *v.* (약을) 복용하다 | a lot of 많은

10. 등산객들은 등반 코스 지도를 얻기 위해 공원 안내데스크 방문이 권장된다.

해설 encourage는 '목적어 + 목적격 보어'를 이끄는 5형식 동사이며, 목적격 보어로 to부정사를 취하는데, 문제에서 목적어가 주어 자리로 빠지는 수동태(are encouraged)로 쓰였으므로 to부정사가 바로 연결되어야 한다. 따라서 정답은 (B) to visit이다.

어휘 encourage *v.* 권장하다, 격려하다, 용기를 북돋우다 | trail *n.* 오솔길, 시골길, 산길

11. 모든 신입 직원들은 3월 말까지 오리엔테이션을 받아야 한다.

해설 should 뒤에는 동사원형이 와야 한다. (C)는 -ing 형태로 동사원형이 아니다. give는 '주다'라는 의미인데 여기서는 '받다'로 해석되므로 수동태임을 알 수 있고, give는 4형식 동사로 쓰이므로 수동태이지만 목적어가 뒤에 하나 남을 수 있음을 유의하자. 따라서 정답은 (B) be given이다.

어휘 orientation *n.* 오리엔테이션

12. 레스토랑에 있는 모든 후식들은 유명 요리사인 Christy Kang에 의해서 준비되었다.

해설 have been이라는 동사가 있으므로 빈칸에 동사 (B)는 올 수 없다. prepare는 3형식 동사로 빈칸 뒤에 목적어(명사)가 있어야 하는데, 전치사구(수식어구)만 있으므로 수동태를 찾으라는 의미이다. have been p.p.는 현재 완료 시제의 수동태이다. 따라서 정답은 (A) prepared이다.

어휘 renowned *adj.* 유명한, 명성 있는 | chef *n.* 요리사 | prepare *v.* 준비하다

13. Bromville 아파트의 난방 시설이 오늘 아침 관리 사무소에 의해 점검되고 있다.

해설 빈칸은 동사 자리이다. inspect는 3형식 동사로 빈칸 뒤에 목적어(명사)가 나와야 한다. 전치사구(수식어구)밖에 없으므로 현재 진행 수동태인 (B) is being inspected가 정답이다.

어휘 property management office 아파트 관리 사무소 | inspect *v.* 점검하다

14. 모든 팀원들은 이곳에서 1년간 일하게 되면 보너스를 신청할 수 있다.

해설 for one year는 현재 완료가 와야 한다는 힌트이므로 (A)와 (B)가 정답이 될 수 있다. work는 1형식 동사로 수동태는 쓸 수 없으므로, 정답은 (A) have worked이다.

어휘 apply for ~에 지원하다 | bonus *n.* 보너스, 상여금

15. Mr. Hassan는 Ms. Yang이 자리를 비운 동안 모든 호텔 예약을 처리할 것이다.

해설 조동사 will 뒤에 동사원형이 와야 하므로 (B)와 (C)가 정답이 될 수 있다. handle은 3형식 동사이고 빈칸 다음에 목적어 all hotel reservations가 왔으므로 능동태 (B) handle이 정답이다.

어휘 handle *v.* 다루다, 처리하다 | away *adv.* 자리에 없는, 결석한

16. 그 자리에 관심이 있는 지원자들은 11월 30일까지 이력서 제출이 요구된다.

해설 빈칸은 동사 자리이다. require는 5형식 동사이고 목적격 보어 자리에 to부정사를 취한다. 목적격 보어 자리에 to부정사는 있지만, 빈칸 뒤에 목적어(명사)는 없으므로 수동태 (C) are required가 정답이다.

어휘 applicant *n.* 지원자 | submit *v.* 제출하다 | résumé *n.* 이력서

17. 비행기 지연의 주된 원인은 엔진 결함과 관련이 있었다.

해설 전치사 by를 쓰지 않는 수동태 표현 「be related to」를 외우도록 하자. 정답은 (A) to이다.

어휘 cause *n.* 이유, 원인 | related *adj.* 관련된

18. 휴가를 받기 위한 신청서는 적어도 일주일 전에 상사에게 제출되어야 한다.

해설 be동사가 있으므로 동사 (C)는 답이 될 수 없다. be동사 뒤에 명사 (B)가 오면 주격 보어 자리에 명사가 온 것이므로 주어와 동격 관계여야 한다. '신청서≠제출'이므로 탈락이다. submit은 3형식 동사로 빈칸 뒤에 목적어(명사)가 있어야 하는데 없으므로 수동태인 (A) submitted가 정답이다.

어휘 request *n.* 요청, 신청서 *v.* 요구하다, 신청하다 | supervisor *n.* 상사 | in advance 미리

19. 그 실험실의 시험 결과는 실험이 성공했음을 보여준다.

해설 빈칸은 동사 자리이다. indicate의 목적어가 that절이므로 능동태인 (A)와 (B)가 가능한데, 주어가 복수이므로 복수 동사 (B) indicate가 정답이다.

어휘 laboratory *n.* 실험실 | experiment *n.* 실험 | indicate *v.* 나타내다

20. 학회 주최자들은 참석자들을 위해 교통편을 마련해 주었다.

해설 빈칸은 동사 자리이다. (D)의 -ing 형태는 동사가 될 수 없다. (B) arrangement는 명사이다. arrange는 3형식 동사이고 빈칸 뒤에 목적어(명사)가 있으므로 능동태 (A) have arranged가 정답이다.

어휘 arrange *v.* 마련하다, 주선하다 | transportation *n.* 교통수단

REVIEW TEST 01

본서 p.54

1. (A)	**2.** (D)	**3.** (B)	**4.** (A)	**5.** (A)
6. (C)	**7.** (B)	**8.** (B)	**9.** (A)	**10.** (B)
11. (B)	**12.** (B)	**13.** (C)	**14.** (A)	**15.** (B)
16. (A)	**17.** (A)	**18.** (A)	**19.** (A)	**20.** (B)
21. (B)	**22.** (A)	**23.** (C)	**24.** (B)	**25.** (D)
26. (A)	**27.** (A)	**28.** (C)	**29.** (A)	**30.** (D)

1. Mauri's Diners의 휴일 메뉴는 후추 치킨을 포함한다.

해설 빈칸은 문장의 본동사가 들어갈 자리이며, 주어는 The holiday menu로 단수이므로 이와 수 일치를 이루는 단수 동사 (A) includes 가 정답이다.

어휘 black pepper 후추

2. Ms. Kim은 직장에 보통 8시에 도착한다.

해설 arrives라는 현재 시제를 쓰고 있다. 현재 시제와 함께 쓰이는 부사는 usually이므로 정답은 (D) usually이다.

어휘 arrive v. 도착하다 | usually adv. 보통, 대개

3. 회계 관리자는 예산 보고서가 이달 말까지 완료될 것으로 기대한다.

해설 to부정사로 쓰인 to 다음에 '완료하다'라는 의미의 complete가 왔다. 빈칸 뒤에 목적어(명사)가 와야 하는데 없으므로 수동태인 (B) be completed가 정답이다.

어휘 complete v. 완료하다

4. Mr. Hong의 책 2판이 7월 1일에 출간되었다.

해설 빈칸은 동사 자리이다. (B)의 -ing 형태는 동사가 될 수 없고, (C)의 동사원형은 조동사가 없으므로 나올 수 없다. 주어가 단수이므로 정답은 (A) was이다.

어휘 edition n. (출간된 책의 형태로 본) 판, 호 | publish v. 출판하다

5. 최근에 있었던 시스템 업그레이드가 초기에는 감지되지 않았던 문제들을 발견했다.

해설 주격 관계대명사 that 뒤에 동사자리로 선행사와 수 일치를 시킨다. 선행사 problems는 복수이므로 정답은 (A) were이다.

어휘 discover v. 발견하다, 찾다, 알아내다 | initially adv. 처음에 | detect v. 감지하다, 발견하다

6. Geimon Tech Solutions의 모든 관리자들은 이달의 영업 워크숍에 참석해야 한다.

해설 should는 조동사이므로 빈칸에는 동사원형이 와야 한다. 따라서 정답은 (C) attend이다.

어휘 sales n. 영업 | attend v. 참석하다

7. 온라인으로 쇼핑하는 고객들의 수가 지난 10년 사이 급격하게 증가했다.

해설 주어가 the number로 단수이다. 단수 동사 (B)와 (C) 중에 over the past decade는 현재 완료 시제와 함께 쓰이는 표현이므로 정답은 (B) has이다.

어휘 the number of ~의 수 | rapidly adv. 빨리, 급속히, 순식간에

8. 컴퓨터의 기능 사양이 사용자 설명서에 상세히 적혀 있다.

해설 빈칸은 동사 자리이므로 동사 자리에 들어갈 수 없는 (C)는 오답이며, detail은 '~을 상세히 기록하다'라는 뜻의 3형식 동사로 빈칸 뒤에 목적어 없이 전명구가 바로 연결되어 있어 수동태가 들어갈 자리이므로 정답은 (B) are detailed이다.

어휘 technical adj. 기술적인 | specification n. 사양; 명세 | user manual 사용자 설명서 | detail v. 상세히 기록하다 n. 세부사항

9. 창문 수리의 총 비용은 원래의 견적을 초과할 것으로 예상된다.

해설 동사 is가 있으므로 (C)와 (D)는 답이 될 수 없다. expect는 5형식 동사로 목적격 보어 자리에 to부정사를 취한다. 목적격 보어는 있지만 목적어(명사)는 빠져 있는 형태이므로 수동태가 정답이다. be동사는 이미 나와 있으므로 (A) expected가 정답이다.

어휘 cost n. 비용 | repair n. 수리, 수선 | exceed v. 초과하다, 넘다 | estimate n. 견적서, 추정치

10. 경쟁력을 유지하기 위해서, HI 전자는 제품의 가격을 가끔 낮춘다.

해설 이 문장은 lowers라는 현재 시제 동사가 나온 문장이다. (A) previously, (C) recently는 보통 과거 시제와 함께 쓰이고, (D) soon 은 미래 시제와 함께 쓰이므로 답이 될 수 없다. occasionally는 현재 시제와 어울려 쓰이므로 정답은 (B) occasionally이다.

어휘 competitive adj. 경쟁력 있는 | lower v. 내리다, 낮추다 | occasionally adv. 가끔씩

11. Mr. Tam의 이력서를 검토했던 위원회 회원들은 그의 폭넓은 업무 경력에 매우 깊은 인상을 받았다.

해설 were이라는 be동사 뒤에는 형용사 보어가 나와야 하므로 정답은 형용사인 (B) impressed이다.

어휘 review v. 재검토하다 n. 검토 | résumé n. 이력서 | impressed adj. 감명[감동]을 받은, 인상 깊은

12. LM 비즈니스 상점은 아주 다양한 사무용품과 문구류를 공급하고 있다.

해설 빈칸은 동사 자리이다. 주어가 단수 명사이므로 (A)와 (C)는 정답이 될 수 없다. 또한 빈칸 뒤에 목적어가 있으므로 수동태인 (D)도 오답이다. 정답은 (B) supplies이다.

어휘 a wide range of 광범위한, 다양한 | supply v. 공급하다

13. 상품들이 당신의 부서로 배송되기 전에 주문 확인 번호를 체크해야 합니다.

해설 be동사 are가 있으므로 동사 (A)는 답이 될 수 없다. (D)를 빈칸에 넣으면 주격 보어 자리에 명사가 온 것이므로, 주어와 동격이 되어야 된다. items ≠ shipment이므로 답이 될 수 없다. ship은 3형식 동사로 목적어(명사)가 빈칸 뒤에 있어야 하는데 전치사구(수식어구)만 있으므로 수동태가 정답이다. be동사는 이미 나와 있으므로 p.p. 형태인 (C) shipped가 정답이다.

어휘 confirmation n. 확인 | ship v. 실어 나르다

14. 지난해, Tofuo 화학은 매일 약 14톤의 실리콘을 생산했다.

해설 빈칸은 동사 자리이다. (D) -ing나 (C) to부정사 형태는 동사가 될 수 없다. 주어가 고유명사여서 단수 취급해야 하므로 복수 동사인 (B)는 탈락이다. 따라서 정답은 (A) produced이다.

어휘 about adv. 약 | produce v. 생산하다

15. 온라인 쇼핑몰은 다른 제품들과의 가격 비교를 더 쉽게 해준다.

해설 빈칸은 동사 자리이다. (A) -ing와 (D) to부정사 형태는 동사가 될 수 없다. make는 5형식 동사로 it가 목적어(명사)이고 easier는 목적격 보어(형용사)이다. 목적어가 있으므로 정답은 능동인 (B) make이다.

어휘 compare v. 비교하다 | price n. 가격

16. Perstrom 사는 30여 년간 전자 제품을 제조해왔다.

해설 빈칸은 동사 자리이다. 「for + 기간」은 '~동안'이라는 뜻으로 현재 완료와 함께 쓰이는 표현이므로 (A)와 (D)가 답이 될 수 있다. manufacture의 목적어(명사)가 빈칸 뒤에 있으므로 정답은 능동태 (A) has manufactured이다.

어휘 manufacture v. 제조하다, 만들어 내다

17. 휴가 기간 동안 증가하는 수요를 맞추기 위해 임시 직원들이 고용될 것이다.

해설 빈칸은 동사 자리이다. 빈칸 뒤에 hire의 목적어(명사)가 없으므로 수동태 (A) will be hired가 정답이다.

어휘 temporary adj. 임시의, 일시적인 | meet v. 충족시키다 | demand n. 요구, 수요 | hire v. 고용하다

18. 최근 사업 확장 이후에, Chentora 사는 여러 명의 추가 직원들을 고용했다.

해설 빈칸에는 3형식 동사 hire의 목적어가 와야 하므로 명사 자리이다. several, additional은 명사를 꾸미는 형용사이다. 해석상 '고용'이 아니라 '직원'을 고용했다는 것이 적절하고, several 뒤에는 복수 명사가 와야 하므로 (A) employees가 정답이다.

어휘 hire v. 고용하다 | several adj. 몇몇의 | additional adj. 추가적인

19. 보안 요원들은 화재 경보가 울린 후 전 직원들이 그 구역을 비웠는지를 반드시 확인해야 한다.

해설 빈칸 앞에서 that절이 시작되었고, 주어 employees와 목적어 the premises 사이에 빈칸이 있으므로 빈칸은 동사 자리이다. 보기 중 유일한 동사인 (A) have vacated가 정답이다.

어휘 security guard 보안 요원, 경비원 | premises n. 부지, 지역, 구내 | fire alarm 화재경보기 | vacate v. 비우다

20. 그 재활용 정책은 그 회사가 운영비를 줄일 수 있도록 도와줄 것이다.

해설 help는 5형식 동사로 company는 목적어이고, 빈칸은 목적격 보어 자리이다. help는 목적격 보어 자리에 to부정사가 오는데 여기서 to는 생략 가능하다. 따라서 정답은 (B) reduce이다.

어휘 recycling policy 재활용 정책 | operating cost 운영비 | reduce v. 감소시키다

21. 기업들이 환경 보존의 중요성을 점점 더 인식하고 있다.

해설 become은 2형식 동사이다. 형용사 주격 보어가 이미 aware로 나와 있으므로 빈칸은 필요 없는 자리이다. 형용사 앞에 들어갈 수 있는 품사는 부사이므로 정답은 (B) increasingly이다.

어휘 aware adj. 알고 있는, 인지하고 있는 | conserve v. 보존하다 | increasingly adv. 점점 더, 갈수록 더

22. 마케팅 부서에서 15명 이상의 직원들이 성공적으로 영업 교육을 이수했다.

해설 from ~ department는 주어를 수식하고 있고, 주어는 '15명 이상의 직원들'로 복수이다. 빈칸은 동사 자리인데, -ing와 to부정사 형태는 동사가 될 수 없다. 따라서 복수 동사 (A) have가 정답이다.

어휘 successfully adv. 성공적으로, 잘 | complete v. 완료하다

23. 워크숍에 등록했던 직원들은 월간 사보를 받을 것이다.

해설 who ~ workshop은 주어인 Employees를 꾸미고 있는 수식어구이다. 빈칸 앞에 조동사 will이 나왔고, 빈칸 뒤에는 목적어(명사)가 있으므로 빈칸에는 동사원형이 와야된다. 따라서 정답은 (C) receive이다.

어휘 register v. 등록하다

24. Nari 사는 최근에 주요 은행들을 위해 고안된 새로운 보안 시스템을 개발했다.

해설 주어가 회사 이름으로 고유명사이므로 단수 취급한다. (A), (C), (D)는 모두 복수 동사이므로 탈락이다. 따라서 수 일치가 필요 없는 과거 시제 동사인 (B) developed가 정답이다.

어휘 recently adv. 최근에 | security system 보안 시스템 | develop v. 개발하다

25. 모든 공장 근로자들은 이 안전 규정을 따라야 하는 것이 필수이다.

해설 「It is essential that + S + (should) 동사원형」이므로 빈칸 앞에는 조동사 should가 생략되어 있다. 따라서 정답은 동사원형인 (D) follow이다.

어휘 essential adj. 필수적인 | safety regulation 안전 규정

26. 우리는 새 X5 차량에 대한 수요가 곧 증가할 것으로 예상한다.

해설 expect는 '예상하다, 기대하다'라는 뜻이다. 보통 앞으로의 일을 기대하므로 that절에는 미래 시제가 문맥상 맞다. 따라서 정답은 (A) will rise이다.

어휘 expect v. 예상하다 | demand n. 수요, 요구 (사항)

27. 내일 회의가 끝날 무렵에 충분한 시간이 있다면, Mr. Garson이 벤쿠버 미술 축제에 대해 잠깐 이야기할 것이다.

해설 '내일 회의에서'라는 말이 있기 때문에 미래 시제를 써야 하지만, if가 조건 부사절이므로 미래 시제 대신 현재 시제를 써야 한다. 따라서 정답은 (A)와 (C)가 될 수 있는데, there로 시작하는 문장은 주어와 동사가 도치된 것으로 주어가 불가산 명사 (enough time)이므로 단수 동사 (A) is가 정답이다.

어휘 enough adj. 충분한 | briefly adv. 짧게, 간단히

28. Ms. Ouellette이 새 지점의 관리자로 고용되었으며, 다음 달부터 전체의 사업 운영을 감독할 것이다.

해설 빈칸이 주어 she와 목적어 all business operations 사이에 있으므로 동사 자리인데, 문장 맨 끝에 starting next month가 있으므로 미래 시제인 (C) will oversee가 정답이다.

어휘 hire v. 고용하다 | location n. 장소, 위치 | business operation 사업 운영

29. 회사는 협력적인 업무 환경을 고취시킬 책임이 있다.

해설 to부정사로 쓰인 to 뒤에는 동사원형이 와야 하므로 (A)와 (B)가 답이 될 수 있다. promote의 목적어 a collaborative working environment가 있으므로 능동태인 (A) promote가 정답이다.

어휘 responsibility n. 책임(감) | collaborative adj. 협력적인 | working environment 근로 환경, 작업 환경

30. 직원 만족도 조사의 결과가 경영진에 의해 긍정적으로 여겨졌다.

해설 be동사 is가 있으므로 동사 (B)는 답이 될 수 없다. be동사 뒤에 명사 (C)가 오면 주격 보어 자리에 명사가 온 것이므로 주어와의 관계가 동격이어야 한다. '직원 만족도 조사 결과≠고려'이므로 탈락이다. consider는 5형식 동사로 목적어(명사)가 와야 하는데, 빈칸 뒤에 목적격 보어인 형용사 positive는 있지만 목적어(명사)는 없으므로 수동태가 정답이다. 이미 be동사는 나와 있으므로 (D) considered가 성답이다.

어휘 satisfaction n. 만족 | positive adj. 긍정적인 | management n. 경영진

UNIT 05. 명사

+ check　　1. (D)　　2. (B)　　3. (D)　　4. (D)

1. 데이터베이스에 접속하기 위해서는, 작성된 요청서와 Mr. Wood의 서면 허가가 필요하다.

해설 품사 어형 문제로 관사 a 뒤에는 명사가 와야 하고, 형용사 written의 수식을 받아야 하므로 빈칸은 명사 자리이다. 따라서 정답은 명사인 (D) authorization이다.

어휘 access v. 접속하다 | completed adj. 작성된, 완료된 | request form 요청서 | written adj. 서면으로 된

2. Modern 사무용 가구점은 선별된 물건들에 대해 최대 30퍼센트 할인을 제공하고 있다.

해설 빈칸은 동사 is offering의 목적어에 해당하는 명사 자리이며, 가구점이 최대 30퍼센트의 할인을 제공한다는 의미가 적절한데, '할인'을 뜻하는 명사 'discount'는 가산 명사로 빈칸 앞에는 관사가 없으므로 단수형은 쓸 수 없다. 따라서 복수형인 (B) discounts가 정답이다.

어휘 offer v. 제공하다 | up to ~까지

3. Goldland 체육관의 멤버십 가입 방법에 대한 동봉된 설명서를 읽어 주세요.

해설 품사 어형 문제로 정관사 뒤에 enclosed라는 형용사가 있으니 빈칸은 명사 자리이다. 보기 중 명사는 instructor와 instructions가 있는데, 문맥상, 동봉된 강사(instructor)가 아니라 동봉된 설명서(instructions)이므로 정답은 (D) instructions이다.

어휘 enclosed adj. 동봉된; 에워싸인 | sign up for ~에 가입하다, 신청하다

4. 건설업을 신장시키려는 노력에도 불구하고, 건설 허가증에 대한 요청 건수가 줄었다.

해설 빈칸 앞에 전치사가 있으므로 명사가 나와야 한다. 문맥상 '건축 허가증'에 대한 요청이 적절하다. 따라서 빈칸까지가 전치사의 목적어로 건축 '허가증'을 신청한다는 해석이 자연스럽다. 명사는 (A), (C), (D)이지만, 동명사 (C)는 동명사의 목적어가 없으므로 탈락이다. permit은 가산 명사인데 앞에 어떠한 한정사도 없으므로 정답은 복수 명사 (D) permits이다.

어휘 boost v. ~을 신장시키다 | request for ~에 대한 요청 | permit n. 허가증 v. ~을 허가하다

....

Practice

1. (B)	**2.** (B)	**3.** (D)	**4.** (B)	**5.** (B)
6. (B)	**7.** (A)	**8.** (B)	**9.** (D)	**10.** (B)
11. (C)	**12.** (D)	**13.** (A)	**14.** (C)	**15.** (D)
16. (C)	**17.** (C)	**18.** (A)	**19.** (D)	**20.** (C)

PART 5　UNIT 05

1. Gihans Architects received approval for the building project from the town council.

2. Mr. Morgan's ability to communicate with his clients is impressive.

3. MT Mart will provide refunds for all Reef Beauty Products purchased before August 12.

4. Due to the current drought conditions, agricultural water usage will increase.

5. Performances by popular musicians attracted large crowds at the festival.

6. The seminar will focus on how businesses can increase their sales through online services.

7. Mr. Park, an applicant for the customer service position, will be meeting with the interviewers tomorrow.

8. Vabimo Group's recent acquisition of Pexor Company helped expand its production capacities.

9. Please call our customer service line to arrange your furniture delivery this week.

10. Attendees at the annual travel conference must show their valid tickets at the main door.

....

1. Gihans 건축회사는 시의회로부터 건축 프로젝트에 대한 승인을 받았다.

해설 빈칸은 received의 목적어 자리이므로 명사가 와야 한다. 따라서 정답은 (B) approval이다.

어휘 approval *n.* 승인, 인정, 찬성 | town council 시의회

2. 고객들과 의사소통하는 Mr. Morgan의 능력은 인상적이다.

해설 소유격 뒤에는 명사가 들어가야 한다. 또한 빈칸은 주어 자리, 즉 명사 자리이기도 하다. 따라서 정답은 (B) ability이다.

어휘 communicate *v.* 의사소통하다 | impressive *adj.* 인상적인 | ability *n.* 능력

3. MT 마트는 8월 12일 이전에 구매된 모든 Reef 미용 제품에 대해서 환불해 줄 것이다.

해설 빈칸에는 provide의 목적어가 와야 하며 명사 자리이다. 정답은 (A)와 (D)가 될 수 있는데, refund는 가산 명사이므로 a refund 또는 refunds로 써야 한다. 따라서 정답은 (D) refunds이다.

어휘 purchase *v.* 구매하다 | refund *n.* 환불 *v.* 환불하다

4. 최신 차량 모델이 유럽 시장에서 성공할 것으로 예상된다.

해설 관사 a 뒤에는 명사가 나와야 하므로 정답은 (B) success이다.

어휘 latest *adj.* 최신의 | vehicle *n.* 차량, 탈것 | success *n.* 성공

5. 사무용품 구매는 Ms. Kang에 의해서 승인이 되어야 한다.

해설 사무용품이 승인이 되어야 하는 것이 아니고, 사무용품 구매(복합 명사)가 Ms. Kang에 의해 승인이 나야 한다는 것이다. 따라서 주어로 '구매'라는 명사가 나와야 한다. (A)와 (B) 중에 purchase는 가산 명사이므로 a purchase 또는 purchases가 답이 될 수 있다. 정답은 (B) purchases이다.

어휘 office supply 사무용품 | approve *v.* 승인하다

6. 현재의 가뭄 상태 때문에 농업용수의 사용이 증가할 것이다.

해설 가뭄 때문에 '물이 증가할 것이다'가 아니고, '물 사용(복합 명사)이 증가할 것이다'가 문맥상 적합하다. 따라서 빈칸은 주어로 '사용'이라는 명사가 나와야 하므로 정답은 (B) usage이다.

어휘 due to ~때문에 | drought *n.* 가뭄 | agricultural *adj.* 농업의

7. 그 축제에서 유명 음악가들에 의한 공연이 많은 관객을 사로잡았다.

해설 빈칸은 주어 자리이므로 명사가 와야 한다. 빈칸 앞에 관사가 없으므로 복수 명사인 (A) Performances가 정답이다.

어휘 attract *v.* 유혹하다, 마음을 끌다 | crowd *n.* 군중

8. 그 프로젝트를 제시간에 완료하기 위해서, 우리는 보조원을 고용할 필요가 있다.

해설 빈칸이 부정관사 an 다음에 있으므로 명사 자리이다. 또한 hire의 목적어 자리로도 볼 수 있다. 목적어 자리 역시 명사 자리이다. 명사 (A)와 (B) 중에 '도움을 고용하는 것'이 아니고, '보조해 주는 사람을 고용하는 것'이므로 정답은 (B) assistant이다.

어휘 on time 제시간에 | hire *v.* 고용하다 | assistance *n.* 도움, 원조, 지원 | assistant *n.* 보조자, 조수

9. 그 보안 프로그램에 대한 발표 일정이 변경되었다.

해설 빈칸은 정관사 뒤면서 주어 자리이므로 명사가 와야 한다. (A)와 (D) 중에 '발표자가 변경된 것'이 아니고 '발표 일정이 변경된 것'이므로 정답은 (D) presentation이다.

어휘 reschedule *v.* 일정을 변경하다

10. 그 세미나는 업체들이 온라인 서비스를 통해 그들의 매출액을 늘릴 수 있는 방법에 대해 중점을 둘 것이다.

해설 빈칸 뒤에 명사가 있다. 명사 앞에는 무조건 소유격이 와야 하므로 정답은 (B) their이다.

어휘 focus on ~에 초점을 맞추다 | sales *n.* 판매량

11. McJessop 컨설팅은 최근에 그들의 재무팀에 합류할 회계사들을 추가로 고용했다.

해설 빈칸은 employed의 목적어 자리로 명사가 와야 한다. 회계사를 고용할 것이므로 정답은 (C) accountants이다. 참고로 accountant는 가산 명사이므로 an accountant 또는 accountants로 써야 한다.

어휘 additional *adj.* 추가적인 I accounting *n.* 회계 I account *n.* 계좌 I accountant *n.* 회계원, 회계사

12. 고객 서비스 일자리의 지원자인 Mr. Park은 내일 면접관들과 만나게 될 것이다.

해설 빈칸은 관사 뒤이므로 명사가 와야 한다. 명사는 (B)와 (D)가 있는데, Mr. Park는 '지원서'가 아니고 '지원자'이므로 정답은 (D) applicant 이다.

어휘 interviewer *n.* 면접관 I application *n.* 지원(서) I applicant *n.* 지원자

13. 구독자들이 월말까지 회원권들을 갱신할 것이 권고된다.

해설 빈칸은 주어 자리로 명사가 와야 한다. 해석상 구독자들이 구독을 갱신하는 것이므로 정답은 (A) subscribers이다.

어휘 renew *v.* 갱신하다 I subscriber *n.* 구독자 I subscribe *v.* 구독하다 I subscription *n.* 구독

14. Vabimo 그룹의 최근 Pexor사 인수는 그 회사의 생산 능력을 확대하는 데 일조했다.

해설 recent는 명사를 꾸미는 형용사이고, Vabimo Group's라는 소유격 뒤에는 명사가 와야 하므로 정답은 (C) acquisition이다.

어휘 recent *adj.* 최근의 I expand *v.* 확대시키다, 확장되다 I capacity *n.* 능력, 역량 I acquisition *n.* 인수, 획득, 습득

15. 이번 주 고객님의 가구 배송 일정을 잡기 위해 저희 고객 상담 전화로 연락해 주세요.

해설 동사 arrange의 목적어가 필요하므로 'furniture ------'를 복합 명사로 만들어줘야 한다. 따라서 명사 (D) delivery가 정답이다.

어휘 line *n.* 전화(선) I arrange *v.* 마련하다, (일정 등을) 잡다 I delivery *n.* 배달

16. Klarksson 프로젝트의 완료가 회사의 매출액을 증가시킬 것으로 예상된다.

해설 빈칸은 주어 자리로 명사가 와야 하므로 정답은 (C) Completion 이다.

어휘 completely *adv.* 완전히 I completion *n.* 완료 I complete *a.* 완벽한 *v.* 완료하다

17. 연례 여행 학회의 참석자들은 중앙 출입구에서 그들의 티켓을 보여줘야만 한다.

해설 빈칸은 주어 자리로 명사가 와야 한다. 보기에서 명사는 (B)와 (C)이다. 문맥상 '참석자들'이 맞으므로 정답은 (C) Attendees이다.

어휘 attendance *n.* 출석, 참석(률), 참석자 수 I attendee *n.* 참석자

18. Terisan 커뮤니케이션에 의해 수집된 정보에 따르면, BX555 노트북 컴퓨터가 그래픽 디자이너들 사이에서 인기가 있다.

해설 According to는 전치사이므로 뒤에는 명사가 와야 한다. 따라서 정답은 (A) information이다.

어휘 collect *v.* 모으다, 수집하다 I popular *adj.* 인기 있는

19. Allwalk 신발 가게는 첫 구매자들에게 10% 할인 쿠폰을 제공한다.

해설 전치사 to 뒤에는 명사가 와야 한다. first-time은 형용사이다. 따라서 빈칸은 명사 자리이므로 (A)와 (D)가 될 수 있다. 그런데 구매자는 사람으로 가산 명사이므로 a buyer 또는 buyers로 써야 하기 때문에 정답은 (D) buyers이다.

어휘 first-time *adj.* 처음으로 해보는 I buyer *n.* 구매자

20. 천 권의 책과 비즈니스 저널의 디지털 모음집이 Hargort 도서관에 전시될 것이다.

해설 digital은 형용사이고 부정관사 a 뒤에는 명사가 와야 하므로 빈칸은 명사 자리이다. 부정관사 a가 있으므로 단수 명사 (C) collection이 정답이다.

어휘 display *v.* 진열하다, 전시하다 I digital *adj.* 디지털의 I collection *n.* 수집(품), 모음집

UNIT 06. 대명사

본서 p.66

+ check 1. (B) 2. (C) 3. (D) 4. (A)

1. Ms. Yamato는 그녀의 뛰어난 의사소통 능력 때문에 부서장으로 승진되었다.

해설 대명사의 격을 고르는 문제로 빈칸은 명사 communication skills. 앞에 소유격이 올 자리이다. 따라서 정답은 (B) her이다.

어휘 promote *v.* 승진시키다 I department head 부서장 I communication skill 의사소통 능력

2. 스튜디오 제작 인턴들은 종종 그들 스스로 야근하고 있음을 알게 된다.

해설 동사 find가 5형식「find + 목적어 + 목적격 보어」으로 쓰인 형태로, 목적격 대명사가 필요한 자리이다. 의미상 인턴들 스스로가 야근하고 있음을 알게 된다는 문맥이므로 주어와 목적어가 일치해야 한다. 따라서 재귀대명사 (C) themselves가 정답이다.

어휘 work overtime 늦게까지 일하다, 야근하다

3. 현 주차 허가증을 가지고 있는 사람들만이 그들의 차량을 회사로 가져올 수 있다.

해설 수식어 문제로 holding부터 permits까지가 주어인 빈칸을 수식하는 형태이다. whose는 소유격 관계대명사로 선행사가 필요한데 선행사가 없으므로 탈락이다. they, each라는 대명사는 수식을 받을 수 없는 명사이다. those는 지시대명사 that의 복수형으로 대명사이다. 일반적으로 대명사는 수식을 받을 수 없는데, "those = people" 이라는 것도 알고 있어야 한다. those는 '사람들'이라는 명사로서, 주어 역할과 수식을 받을 수 있는 역할 모두가 가능하므로 정답은 (D) those이다.

어휘 parking permit 주차 허가증 I vehicle *n.* 차량

4. 부서장들은 그들의 직원들 서로가 얘기할 것을 촉구한다.

해설 문맥상 '직원들이 서로 상호 간에 연락하다'라는 의미가 되어야 하므로 정답은 (A) one another이다. (B)는 '다른 나머지 하나', (C)는 '또 다른', (D)는 '다른'이라는 의미이므로 오답이다. (A) one another은 '서로서로'라는 뜻이다.

어휘 urge v. 촉구하다, 권고하다 | staff n. (전체) 직원 | communicate v. 의사소통하다

Practice

본서 p.70

1. (C)	**2.** (B)	**3.** (C)	**4.** (D)	**5.** (C)
6. (D)	**7.** (A)	**8.** (D)	**9.** (D)	**10.** (B)
11. (C)	**12.** (B)	**13.** (D)	**14.** (B)	**15.** (C)
16. (A)	**17.** (B)	**18.** (A)	**19.** (A)	**20.** (D)

기본 완성 훈련

1. Mr. Park wants all staff to communicate directly with him about the new marketing project.

2. All employees who have unused vacation days should use them by October 30.

3. The company policy requires that our computers be protected with a secure password.

4. After the proposal had been reviewed by three managers, it was finally accepted.

5. Mr. Jang has proven himself to be a hardworking and useful member of the R&D Department.

6. If anyone has completed their quarterly reports, please inform the team leader.

7. The brand's sales have been much better than those of last year.

8. Ms. Hong managed to move the heavy desk by herself.

9. Many students at Korire University work as interns before starting their first professional job.

10. At Giny's Store, we take pleasure in providing each of our customers with excellent service.

1. Mr. Park은 새로운 마케팅 프로젝트에 관해서 모든 직원들이 그와 직접 이야기하기를 원한다.

해설 전치사 다음은 전치사의 목적어 자리이고 대명사의 목적격이 와야 하므로 정답은 (C) him이다.

어휘 directly adv. 곧장, 즉시, 직접적으로

2. Dr. Kim이 사무실에 없는 동안에는 그녀의 업무 비서에게 전화해 주세요.

해설 명사 앞에 빈칸이 있다. 명사 앞에는 소유격이 들어가므로 정답은 (B) her이다.

어휘 administrative assistant 업무 비서

3. 휴가를 아직 사용하지 못한 모든 직원들은 10월 30일까지 그것들을 써야 한다.

해설 빈칸은 use의 목적어 자리이므로 대명사의 목적격이 들어가야 한다. 따라서 정답은 (C) them이다. 목적어 자리에 themselves가 들어가려면 주어와 목적어가 같아야 하므로 정답이 아니다.

어휘 vacation day 휴가

4. 회사 방침은 우리의 컴퓨터들이 안전한 비밀번호로 보호될 것을 요구한다.

해설 빈칸이 명사 computers 앞에 있으므로 정답은 소유격 (D) our이다.

어휘 secure adj. 안전한

5. Anopar 산업은 3월에 주요 경쟁사인 Pukom 사를 인수할 것이다.

해설 빈칸 뒤에는 명사가 나와 있다. 명사 앞에는 소유격이 와야 하므로 정답은 (C) its이다.

어휘 acquire v. 인수하다 | main adj. 주된 | competitor n. 경쟁자

6. 새 XV20 노트북 컴퓨터 일부가 운송 중에 파손되었다.

해설 (A) Anything이 주어로 들어가면 단수 취급을 하므로 동사 were와 맞지 않다. (B) Every는 형용사로 쓰이므로 주어 자리에 들어갈 수 없다. (C) Each는 형용사와 대명사 모두 가능하므로 주어 자리에 올 수는 있지만 단수 취급이므로 동사 were와 맞지 않다. (D) Some은 형용사와 대명사 모두 가능하므로 주어 자리에 올 수 있으며, Some은 동사 were와도 수 일치되므로 정답은 (D) Some이다.

어휘 damaged adj. 파손된 | transit n. 운송, 수송

7. 제안서는 세 명의 매니저에 의해 검토된 후에 최종 수락되었다.

해설 빈칸은 be동사 was 앞이므로 주어 자리이다. 따라서 주격 대명사 (A) it가 정답이다. 재귀 대명사는 주어 자리에 올 수 없다.

어휘 proposal n. 제안(서) | accept v. 받아주다, 수락하다

8. 우리 직원들이 사용하는 컴퓨터들 중 대다수는 그들의 것이 아니라 회사가 제공한 것이다.

해설 빈칸은 be동사 뒤 보어 자리이며, '직원들이 사용하는 컴퓨터 대다수가 그 직원들의 컴퓨터가 아니다'라는 의미로 '소유격 + 명사 (their [=the employees'] + computers)' 형태인 소유대명사가 들어가야 적절하므로 정답은 (D) theirs이다.

어휘 not A but B A가 아니라 B인 | provide v. 제공하다

9. Mr. Jang은 스스로를 R&D 부서에서 근면하고 유능한 멤버임을 입증해 보였다.

해설 빈칸은 목적어 자리로 Mr. Jang이 스스로를 근면하고 유능한 사람으로 입증해 보였다는 의미인데, 이처럼 주어와 목적어가 같은 대상일 때는 재귀대명사를 써야 하므로 정답은 (D) himself이다.

어휘 prove v. 입증시키다, 증명시키다 I hardworking adj. 근면한, 부지런한 I useful adj. 유능한, 훌륭한

10. 그 복사기 부품이 없어서 그 비서가 복사기를 수리할 수 없었다.

해설 '부품'이라는 명사 앞에 빈칸이 있으므로 소유격이 정답이다. 보기 모두 소유격이지만, 빈칸이 지칭하는 명사는 사물, 즉 복사기이므로 정답은 (B) its이다.

어휘 copy machine 복사기 I part n. 부품 I available adj. 구할 수 있는, 이용할 수 있는, (시간적) 여유가 있는

11. 누구든 분기별 보고서를 완료했다면, 팀장에게 알려 주세요.

해설 빈칸은 주어 자리이다. 재귀대명사인 (A)와 (D)는 주어 자리에 올 수 없고, (B) other는 형용사로 주어 자리에 올 수 없다. 따라서 정답은 (C) anyone이다.

어휘 complete v. 끝마치다, 완료하다 adj. 완전한 I quarterly report 분기별 보고서

12. 비록 Carlam 미용 제품과 GoodNature 화장품이 올해에 수익을 내지 못했지만, 내년에는 둘 다 수익을 낼 것으로 기대한다.

해설 (A) another는 대명사와 형용사로 쓰이지만, 단수 취급하므로 단수 동사 expects가 와야 한다. (C) other는 형용사로만 쓰이므로 빈칸의 주어 자리에 올 수 없다. (D) the other는 대명사와 형용사로 쓰이지만 '나머지 하나'라는 의미로 단수 취급하므로 동사 expect와 수일치가 맞지 않다. (B) both는 대명사와 형용사로 모두 이 문장에서는 주어 자리에 대명사 both로 쓰인 것이고, Carlam 뷰티 제품과 GoodNature 화장품 둘 다를 가리키므로 정답은 (B) both이다.

어휘 unprofitable adj. 수익성이 없는 I revenue n. 수익

13. 그 브랜드의 매출액이 작년의 그것(매출액)보다 훨씬 더 좋았다.

해설 빈칸은 sales를 받는 자리이다. 앞에 언급한 명사를 다시 받을 때, that이나 those를 쓰는데 복수 명사를 받았으므로 정답은 (D) those이다.

어휘 sales n. 판매량 I much better (비교급) 훨씬 나은

14. 비록 많은 사람들이 Ms. Wilson의 의견에 반대했지만, Mr. Taylor는 그것에 동의했다.

해설 (A) the other는 형용사와 대명사의 역할 모두 가능하므로 주어 자리엔 올 수 있지만, '나머지'라는 의미로 문맥상 맞지 않다. (D) other는 형용사로 주어 자리에 올 수 없다. (C) himself도 재귀대명사로 주어 자리에 올 수 없다. (B) many는 형용사로도 쓰이지만, '많은 사람들'이라는 의미의 명사로도 사용 가능하므로 주어 자리에 올 수 있다. 정답은 (B) many이다.

어휘 disagree v. 동의하지 않다 I opinion n. 의견 I agree v. 동의하다

15. Ms. Hong은 그녀 혼자서 용케도 그 무거운 책상을 옮겼다.

해설 by herself는 '그녀 스스로, 홀로'라는 의미로 정답은 (C) herself이다.

어휘 manage 간신히 해내다, 용케 해내다 I heavy adj. 무거운

16. La Rouge Pictures는 전 유럽에서 선두적인 영화 배급업체들 중 하나이다.

해설 (B) other는 형용사로 전치사 뒤의 명사 자리에 올 수 없다. (C) every도 형용사로 전치사 뒤의 명사 자리에 쓸 수 없다. (D) the other는 형용사와 대명사 모두로 쓰이지만 '나머지'라는 의미로 문맥상 맞지 않다. (A) all은 형용사와 대명사 모두 가능하므로, 전치사 다음의 명사 자리에 올 수 있고 문맥도 맞으므로 정답은 (A) all이다.

어휘 leading adj. 선두적인 I distributor n. 배급업체

17. Korire 대학교의 많은 학생들은 그들의 첫 전문 직업을 갖기 전에 인턴사원으로 일한다.

해설 빈칸 뒤에 명사 job이 왔다. 명사 앞에는 소유격을 쓰므로 정답은 (B) their이다.

어휘 professional adj. 전문적인 n. 전문가

18. 제 홍콩 사무실 방문이 취소되었다는 것을 Ms. Lin에게 알려 주세요.

해설 that절 내의 has been canceled가 동사이므로 visit은 동사가 아니라 명사로 쓰인 것이다. 명사 앞에는 소유격을 쓰므로 정답은 (A) my이다.

어휘 inform v. 알리다 I visit n. 방문 v. 방문하다 I cancel v. 취소하다

19. Giny's 상점에서는 저희 고객들 각각에게 훌륭한 서비스를 제공한다는 것에서 즐거움을 느낍니다.

해설 빈칸에는 providing의 목적어가 와야 한다. (B) the other는 형용사와 대명사 모두로 쓰이지만 '나머지'라는 의미이므로 문맥상 어색하다. (C) other와 (D) every는 형용사로만 쓰이므로 간접 목적어 자리(명사 자리)에 올 수 없다. (A) each는 형용사와 대명사 둘 다 쓰이므로 목적어 자리에 올 수 있다. 정답은 (A) each이다.

어휘 take pleasure in ~을 즐기다

20. 많은 사람들이 안 좋은 날씨에도 불구하고 음악 축제에 참석했다.

해설 (A) Others와 (B) The others는 명사 역할을 하므로 명사 people 앞에 쓰일 수 없다. (C) Every는 형용사 역할을 하며 단수 취급하므로 단수 명사와 함께 쓰이는데, people은 복수 명사이므로 답이 될 수 없다. Many는 형용사와 대명사 역할이 모두 가능하며, 명사 people을 수식하는 형용사 자리이므로 정답은 (D) Many이다.

어휘 despite prep. ~에도 불구하고 I attend v. 참석하다

UNIT 07. 형용사

check   1. (A)   2. (C)   3. (C)   4. (B)

1. Linear Stage의 혁신적인 연극 공연들은 현대의 사회적인 쟁점들을 강조한다.

해설 품사 어형 문제로 's는 소유격을 의미하고, 소유격 뒤에는 명사가 나오는데 이미 명사(theatrical performances)가 나와 있다. 즉, 소유격과 명사 사이에는 형용사가 들어갈 수 있다는 점을 눈치챌 수 있어야 한다. 보기 중 형용사는 innovative(혁신적인)와 innovated(혁신된)인데, '혁신된' 연극이라는 뜻보다는 '혁신적인' 연극이라는 것이 문맥상 더 알맞으므로 정답은 (A) innovative이다.

어휘 theatrical *adj.* 연극의, 공연의 | performance *n.* 공연 | highlight *v.* ~을 강조하다 | contemporary *adj.* 현대의; 동시대의 | issue *n.* 쟁점, 문제 | innovative *adj.* 혁신적인

2. 고객을 확보할 가능성을 높이기 위해 당신은 영업 발표를 설득력 있게 만들어야 한다.

해설 make는 5형식 동사로 목적어(your sales presentation) 뒤의 빈칸은 목적격 보어 자리이다. 목적격 보어자리에는 목적어와 동격일 땐 명사, 상태를 설명할 땐 형용사가 온다. 문맥상 빈칸에는 목적어를 설명하는 형용사가 필요한 자리이므로 정답은 (C) persuasive이다.

어휘 possibility *n.* 가능성 | acquire *v.* 얻다, 획득하다

3. 영업 사원들은 반드시 전문성 있게 갖춰 입어야 하며 까다로운 고객들과 논쟁하게 되는 상황을 피해야 한다.

해설 동사 become의 보어인 형용사가 필요한데, 보기 중 형용사는 '논란의 여지가 있는'을 뜻하는 (A) arguable과 '논쟁을 좋아하는, 시비를 거는'이란 의미의 (C) argumentative가 있다. 문맥상 까다로운 고객들과 논쟁하게 되는 것을 피해야 한다는 의미가 적절하므로 (C) argumentative가 정답이다.

어휘 professionally *adv.* 전문적으로 | demanding *adj.* 요구가 많은, 까다로운

4. 준비된 새 회계 소프트웨어 프로그램으로, 대부분의 부기 오류들을 막을 수 있다.

해설 품사 어형 문제로 빈칸 앞의 are는 2형식 동사로 빈칸은 주격 보어자리 즉, 상태를 설명하는 형용사 자리이다. 따라서 명사인 (D) prevention은 탈락시킨다. (A) preventing을 넣어 보면 현재 진행형이 되면서, '~을 예방 중이다'라는 뜻이 되는데, '~을'에 해당하는 목적어가 빈칸 뒤에 나와 있지 않으므로 답이 될 수 없다. 남은 preventable과 preventive 중에서 preventable은 '예방할 수 있는'이란 뜻이고, preventive는 '예방을 위한'이란 뜻인데, 문맥상 '예방할 수 있는'이 맞으므로 정답은 (B) preventable이다.

어휘 in place ~할 준비가 되어 있는 | bookkeeping *n.* 부기, 장부 기입 | error *n.* 실수, 오류

Practice

본서 p.78

1. (A)   **2.** (D)   **3.** (C)   **4.** (C)   **5.** (C)
6. (A)   **7.** (A)   **8.** (A)   **9.** (C)   **10.** (A)
11. (A)   **12.** (A)   **13.** (A)   **14.** (B)   **15.** (A)
16. (B)   **17.** (C)   **18.** (A)   **19.** (A)   **20.** (B)

기본 완성 훈련

1. Mr. Jones plans to conduct training with several members of the sales team.

2. After months of negotiations, the two companies appeared agreeable to the terms of the merger.

3. Carefully reviewing comments from each customer will help improve our services.

4. Once the factory is fully operational, it will need a workforce of 500.

5. The controversial policy change was resolved in a timely manner.

6. According to the survey results, most customers found Lebtro's new leather jackets very attractive.

7. Bahilo Advisory Group provides a wide variety of financial services.

8. Despite being dropped on the floor a few times, the mobile phone is still functional.

9. The warm weather is likely to last throughout the month.

10. It is crucial that all client information is kept confidential.

---

1. Elbart Bay는 그곳의 저렴한 숙박 시설로 인해 젊은 여행객들 사이에서 인기 있는 휴양지이다.

해설 소유격 its와 명사 accommodation 사이에 빈칸이 있으므로 형용사인 (A) affordable이 정답이다.

어휘 holiday destination 휴양지 | accommodation *n.* 숙박(시설) | affordable *adj.* (가격이) 합리적인, 비싸지 않은

2. 오늘날 많은 사람들은 너무 바빠서 그들의 식습관에 관심을 기울일 수 없다.

해설 are는 be동사로 2형식 동사이다. 빈칸에는 주격 보어가 와야 하며, 상태를 설명하는 형용사 자리이다. 따라서 정답은 (D) busy이다. 「too ~ to ~는 '너무 ~해서 ~할 수 없다'라는 뜻이다.

어휘 pay attention to ~에 유의하다 | diet *n.* 식습관 | busy *adj.* 바쁜

18

3. 이것은 실험적인 교수법이기 때문에 Dr. Wu는 학생들의 피드백을 받기를 원한다.

해설 부정관사 an과 명사 teaching method 사이에 빈칸이 있으므로 형용사 (C) experimental이 정답이다.

어휘 feedback *n.* 피드백 | experimental *adj.* 실험적인

4. Mr. Jones는 영업팀의 여러 팀원들과 교육을 할 계획이다.

해설 another, each, every는 단수 가산 명사와 함께 쓰이므로 members가 올 수 없다. several은 복수 가산 명사와 함께 쓰이므로 정답은 (C) several이다.

어휘 conduct *v.* 실시하다 | training *n.* 교육, 훈련

5. 수개월간의 협상 후에, 두 회사는 합병 조건에 동의한 것처럼 보였다.

해설 appear은 2형식 동사이다. 따라서 빈칸은 주격 보어 자리로서 형용사가 들어가야 하므로 정답은 (C) agreeable이다.

어휘 negotiation *n.* 협상 | appear *v.* ~인 것처럼 보이다 | terms *n.* (계약) 조건 | merger *n.* 합병 | agreeable *adj.* 동의하는, 받아들일 수 있는

6. 각 고객들의 코멘트를 신중하게 검토하는 것은 우리 서비스를 개선하는 데 도움을 줄 것이다.

해설 a few는 셀 수 있는 복수 명사와 써야 하므로 customers가 와야 한다. all과 most는 셀 수 있을 땐 복수로 쓰고, 셀 수 없을 땐 단수로 쓰는데 이 경우 고객은 셀 수 있으므로 customers가 와야 한다. each는 단수 취급하므로 customer와 쓸 수 있다. 따라서 정답은 (A) each 이다.

어휘 carefully *adv.* 신중히, 조심스럽게 | improve *v.* 개선하다, 향상시키다

7. 일단 공장이 완전히 가동이게 되면, 500명의 노동력이 필요할 것이다.

해설 부사 fully는 필요 없는 수식어구이고, 빈칸은 is라는 2형식 동사 다음의 주격 보어 자리이므로 상태 설명 형용사가 와야 한다. 따라서 정답은 (A) operational이다.

어휘 once *conj.* 일단 ~하면, ~하자마자 | fully *adv.* 완전히, 충분히 | workforce *n.* 노동력, 노동 인구

8. 관광 산업에 대한 그의 깊이 있는 이해 덕분에, Mr. Pareto는 Gofirst Travels에 의해 고용되었다.

해설 소유격 대명사 his와 명사 understanding 사이에 빈칸이 있으므로 형용사 (A) deep이 정답이다.

어휘 hire *v.* 고용하다 | tourism industry 관광 산업

9. 논란을 일으켰던 정책 변경은 시기적절하게 해결되었다.

해설 관사 a와 명사 manner 사이에 빈칸이 있으므로 정답은 형용사인 (C) timely이다.

어휘 controversial *adj.* 논란이 많은 | resolve *v.* 해결하다 | in a timely manner 적시에, 빠른 시일 내에

10. 설문 조사 결과에 따르면, 대부분의 고객들은 Lebtro의 새 가죽 재킷이 아주 매력적이라고 생각했다.

해설 find는 5형식 동사로 빈칸은 목적격 보어 자리이다. 가방의 상태가 매력적이라는 의미가 되는 것이 자연스러우므로 목적격 보어 자리에는 형용사가 와야 한다. 정답은 (A) attractive이다.

어휘 attractive *adj.* 매력적인 | attraction *n.* 끌림, 명소

11. CariBags가 만든 그 여행 가방들은 튼튼하면서도 스타일이 좋다.

해설 2형식 동사 are 다음에는 주격 보어 자리이므로 상태 설명 형용사가 와야 한다. 「both A and B」는 'A, B 둘 다 모두'라는 뜻으로 A, B 대등하게 형용사 두 개를 연결했으므로 정답은 (A) durable이다.

어휘 suitcase *n.* 여행 가방, 커다란 수하물 가방 | trendy *adj.* 최신 유행의 | durable *adj.* 내구성이 있는, 오래가는, 튼튼한

12. Bahilo Advisory 그룹은 매우 다양한 금융 서비스를 제공한다.

해설 부정관사 a와 명사 variety 사이에 빈칸이 있으므로 빈칸은 형용사 자리이다. 따라서 정답은 (A)와 (D)가 될 수 있는데, 최상급은 보통 정관사 the와 함께 쓰이므로 정답은 (A) wide이다.

어휘 a wide variety of 매우 다양한

13. Frankston 노선 열차들 중 일부는 대대적인 수리가 필요하다.

해설 전치사 of와 명사 repairs 사이에 빈칸이 있으므로 형용사 (A) extensive가 정답이다. extended는 '연장된'이라는 의미로 맞지 않다.

어휘 in need of ~을 필요로 하는 | repair *n.* 수리 *v.* 수리하다 | extensive *adj.* 아주 넓은, 대규모의, 광범위한

14. 바닥에 여러 번 떨어뜨렸음에도 불구하고, 그 휴대폰은 여전히 작동된다.

해설 빈칸은 be동사 is 뒤 주격 보어 자리로, still은 문장 성분에 영향을 주지 않는 부사이므로 걷어내면 주어를 서술하는 형용사나 주어와 동격을 이루는 명사가 들어갈 수 있는데, 휴대폰이 작동된다는 의미가 적절하므로 정답은 (B) functional이다.

어휘 drop *v.* 떨어뜨리다 | function *n.* 기능; 특징 | functional *adj.* 작동되는; 기능상의

15. Hurley's 까페의 고객들은 새 아이스티가 충분히 달다고 말했다.

해설 '새로 나온 아이스티가 충분히 달다'는 의미로 빈칸은 that절의 보어 자리이므로 형용사 (A) sweet가 정답이다. 빈칸 뒤에 enough는 '충분한'이라는 뜻의 형용사뿐만 아니라 '충분히'라는 뜻의 부사이기도 하므로 어떤 품사로 쓰였는지는 의미상 확인을 해야 답으로 형용사를 수식할 부사를 고를 지 아니면 부사를 수식할 형용사를 고를 지 결정을 할 수 있다. enough는 부사로 쓰일 때 형용사나 부사 뒤에서 수식한다.

어휘 enough *adj.* 충분한

16. 직원 회의에 있던 모든 사람들이 안전이 가장 중요한 우선 사항들 중 하나라는 점에 동의했다.

해설 정관사 the와 priority라는 명사 사이에 빈칸이 있으므로 빈칸은 형용사 자리이다. 따라서 정답은 (B) important이다.

어휘 safety *n.* 안전 | priority *n.* 우선 사항, 우선(권) | important *adj.* 중요한

17. 그 광고 캠페인은 회사 매출액을 증가시키는 데 있어서 성공적이었다.

해설 2형식 동사인 be동사 다음에 빈칸이 있으므로 주격 보어 자리이고 상태 설명 형용사가 와야 한다. (B)와 (C)가 형용사이지만, successive는 '연속적인'이라는 뜻이므로 이 문장과 문맥상 어울리지 않는다. successful은 '성공적인'이라는 의미로 적합하다. 따라서 정답은 (C) successful이다.

어휘 successful *adj.* 성공적인 | successive *adj.* 연속적인, 연이은

18. 모든 고객 정보를 기밀로 유지하는 것은 매우 중요하다.

해설 keep은 5형식 동사이므로 빈칸은 keep의 목적격 보어 자리이다. 목적격 보어 자리에는 상태 설명 형용사가 쓰이므로 정답은 (A) confidential이다.

어휘 crucial *adj.* 중요한 | confidential *adj.* 기밀의

19. Perco 산업은 환경운동을 조직하는 데 20년 넘게 활동해왔다.

해설 빈칸은 be동사의 현재완료시제 형태 뒤 주격 보어 자리이며, Perco 산업이 '활동해왔다'는 의미로, 주어를 서술해주는 형용사가 들어가야 적절하므로 정답은 (A) active이다.

어휘 organize *v.* 조직하다 | environmental activity 환경운동

20. 많은 도로 사고들은 주의 깊은 계획과 운전자 교육을 통해 예방이 가능하다.

해설 2형식 동사 are 다음의 주격 보어 자리이므로 상태 설명 형용사가 쓰여야 한다. 따라서 정답은 (B) preventable이다.

어휘 road accident 도로 사고 | careful *adj.* 주의 깊은, 세심한

UNIT 08. 부사

본서 p.82

➕ **check** 1. (B)   2. (C)   3. (A)   4. (D)

1. 분석가들은 Halcyon 전자가 올해 상당히 더 많은 수익을 얻을 것으로 예상한다.

해설 품사 어형 문제로 빈칸에는 to부정사인 to gain의 목적어가 필요하다. 즉, 명사가 필요하다는 것인데, 이미 명사 revenue가 뒤에 나와 있다. 명사 앞에 형용사 more가 위치해 있으므로 정답은 형용사 수식 부사인 (B) substantially이다. 부사가 형용사를 꾸미고, 형용사가 명사를 꾸미는 형태이다.

어휘 revenue *n.* 수익 | substantially *adv.* 상당히, 많이

2. Canterra 상담 서비스는 특별히 중간 규모의 소매 업체들의 요구에 부응하기 위하여 고안되었다.

해설 품사 어형 문제로 이 문장은 빈칸 앞에 「be p.p.」라는 수동태를 갖추고 있다. 수동태는 완벽한 문장이므로 빈칸은 문장 구조상 필요 없는 부사가 들어가는 것이 옳다. 다시 말해, design은 3형식 동사이지만 수동태는 목적어가 주어 자리로 가면서 목적어가 빠져 있는 구조이므로 빈칸에는 목적어(명사)가 필요 없다. 정답은 부사 (C) specifically이다.

어휘 consulting service 상담 서비스 | design *v.* 고안하다 | meet requirements 요구에 부응하다 | medium-sized *adj.* 중간 규모의 | retail *n.* 소매

3. Kamal 전자는 고객들과 적극적으로 소통함으로써 매출을 높이기를 바라고 있다.

해설 품사 어형 문제로 전치사 뒤에는 명사나 동명사가 올 수 있는데, 전치사 by 뒤에 동명사 interacting이 왔다. 따라서 문장을 완성하는 데 있어서 빈칸은 필요 없는 자리이고, 동명사를 수식할 수 있어야 한다. 동명사를 수식하는 품사는 부사이므로 정답은 (A) actively이다.

어휘 increase *v.* 증가시키다 | sales *n.* 매출액, 판매량 | interact with ~와 소통하다, 교류하다

4. 곧 게시될 공지에 따르면, 본관 입구는 보수 공사를 위해 다음 주 동안 폐쇄될 것이다.

해설 which 이하의 관계절의 구조가 「will be posted + -------」와 같이 수동태를 취하고 있다. 수동태는 완벽한 문장이므로 빈칸에는 문장 구조를 완성하는 데 있어서 필요 없는 부사가 들어가는 것이 옳다. 따라서 빈칸은 동사 be posted를 수식하는 부사 (D) shortly이다.

어휘 post *v.* ~을 게시하다 | shortly *adv.* 곧

Practice

본서 p.86

1. (D)   **2.** (D)   **3.** (C)   **4.** (D)   **5.** (B)

6. (A)   **7.** (D)   **8.** (C)   **9.** (C)   **10.** (C)

11. (C)   **12.** (C)   **13.** (D)   **14.** (D)   **15.** (A)

16. (D)   **17.** (B)   **18.** (B)   **19.** (A)   **20.** (D)

기본 완성 훈련

1. The Goodread Bookstore on Riverside Street (frequently) hosts big discount events.

2. By hiring additional employees, productivity increased (substantially) at Woodtown Manufacturing.

3. One of the most (widely) respected jazz events is held in Seoul.

4. The new surgical laser is designed to (significantly) shorten patients' recovery times.

5. Customers' responses to the new product packaging have been (consistently) positive.

6. Fragile items should be packaged (separately).

7. (Over) 1,000 customers recently subscribed to *Rover Auto Magazine*.

8. Regend University is well-known for its (remarkably) diverse student body.

9. Providing more public transportation options has proven effective in reducing air pollution in the city.

10. (Lately), Mr. Ko has been working overtime in order to meet the project deadline.

....

1. Riverside 거리에 있는 Goodread 서점은 대규모 할인 행사를 자주 연다.

해설 이미 3형식의 완벽한 문장이므로 빈칸에는 없어도 되는 부사가 들어 가야 된다. 동사 앞에서 동사를 수식하는 부사 (D) frequently가 정답 이다.

어휘 host v. (행사 등을) 주최하다. 열다 | frequently adv. 빈번히, 자주

2. 거의 200명의 직원들은 우리의 기본 과정을 성공적으로 마쳤다.

해설 have와 과거분사 사이에는 부사가 들어가므로 정답은 (D) successfully이다.

어휘 complete adj. 완전한 v. 완료하다, 끝마치다 | successfully adv. 성공적으로

3. Ms. Chen은 Broaden의 보안 시스템 제작에 깊이 연관되어 있다.

해설 '깊이 연관되어 있다'는 의미로 수동태인 been involved 사이에 들어 갈 수 있는 품사는 부사이므로 정답은 (C) deeply이다.

어휘 involved in ~에 관련된 | creation n. 제작 | security n. 보안, 안보

4. 추가 종업원들을 고용함으로써, Woodtown 제조사의 생산성이 상당 히 증가했다.

해설 1형식 동사인 increased로 문장이 끝났다. 따라서 빈칸은 부사 자리 로 정답은 (D) substantially이다.

어휘 hire v. 고용하다 | additional adj. 추가적인 | productivity n. 생 산성

5. 가장 널리 인정 받는 재즈 행사 중 하나가 서울에서 개최된다.

해설 형용사 respected 앞에 빈칸이 있으므로 부사 자리이다. 따라서 정답 은 (B) widely이다.

어휘 widely adv. 광범위하게, 폭넓게 | respected adj. 존경받는, 높이 평가되는

6. 모든 생산 작업장 직원들은 기계를 작동하기 전에 작업장 안전에 관한 교육을 받아야 한다.

해설 문장이 끝났다고 생각해서 부사를 고르게 되면 '안전하게 작업장에 관 한 교육을 받아야 한다'라고 해석되어 의미가 맞지 않다. 이런 경우는 앞의 workplace와 함께 복합명사가 되는 명사 safety를 골라야 한 다. '작업장 안전에 관한 교육을 받아야 한다'가 의미상 맞으므로 정답 은 명사 (A) safety이다.

어휘 production floor 생산 작업장 | workplace safety 작업장 안전 | operate 작동하다, 가동하다, 운영하다 | machinery 기계류

7. 새로운 수술용 레이저는 환자들의 회복 기간을 상당히 줄여 주기 위해 고안되었다.

해설 이미 3형식으로 완벽한 문장이 있으므로 빈칸은 필요 없는 자리이고, 동사 앞에 왔으므로 부사 (D) significantly가 정답이다.

어휘 surgical adj. 외과의, 수술의 | shorten v. 줄이다 | recovery time 회복 기간 | significantly adv. 상당히

8. Froissart 사는 Metz 중공업을 약 천만 달러에 매입했다.

해설 빈칸은 수 형용사 10을 수식하는 부사 자리이므로 정답은 (C) approximately이다.

어휘 purchase v. 구매하다 | heavy industry 중공업

9. 신제품 포장재에 대한 고객들의 반응이 일관되게 긍정적이었다.

해설 형용사 positive 앞에 빈칸이 있으므로 부사 (C) consistently가 정답 이다.

어휘 response n. 반응 | packaging n. 포장(재) | positive adj. 긍 정적인 | consistently adv. 일관되게, 지속적으로

10. 경영진은 재디자인된 회사 로고에 완전히 만족스러워 하지는 않았다.

해설 빈칸은 수동태 동사구문의 과거분사인 satisfied를 수식하는 부사자리 이다. 따라서 (C) completely가 정답이다.

어휘 management n. 경영진 | satisfied adj. 만족하는, 만족스러워 하 는 | redesigned adj. 재디자인된 | completely adv. 완전히

11. 깨지기 쉬운 물건들은 따로따로 포장되어야 한다.

해설 빈칸에 들어갈 단어가 빠지더라도 이미 완벽한 문장이므로 빈칸은 동사 be packaged를 수식하는 부사 자리이다. 따라서 정답은 (C) separately이다.

어휘 fragile adj. 깨지기 쉬운 | package v. 포장하다 | separately adv. 각각, 따로따로

12. 접수 담당직 지원자들은 반드시 메시지와 기타 정보를 정확히 전달할 수 있어야 한다.

해설 '메시지를 정확히 전달하다'는 의미로 빈칸은 농사 relay를 수식 하는 자리이며, 동사를 수식하는 품사는 부사이므로 정답은 (C) accurately이다.

어휘 receptionist n. 접수 담당자 | relay v. (정보 등을) 전달하다

13. EPPN 광고사에 의해 디자인된 광고는 제품을 소비자들에게 더 매력 적으로 해줄 것이다.

해설 빈칸 뒤에 부사를 고르면 make를 수식하게 되어 의미상 맞지 않고, make는 형용사를 목적격 보어로 취하는 5형식 동사로 시험에 출제된 다는 점을 명심하고 make가 나오면 목적어 뒤에 형용사 보어를 고른 다. 정답은 형용사 (C) attractive이다.

어휘 marketing campaign 광고 | attractive adj. 매력적인 | consumer n. 소비자

14. 직원들은 시기적절하게 프로젝트를 완료하기 위해 협력해서 일할 것으로 기대된다.

해설   work는 '일하다'라는 의미로 쓰일 때 목적어나 보어를 취하지 않는 1형식 동사이므로 빈칸에는 동사 work를 수식하는 부사가 들어가야 한다. 따라서 정답은 (D) collaboratively이다.

어휘   complete v. 완료하다 | in a timely manner 시기적절하게

15. Kamal 전자는 고객들과 적극적으로 소통함으로써 매출을 높이기를 바라고 있다.

해설   '고객들과 적극적으로 소통함으로써'라는 의미로 전치사(by)와 동명사(interacting) 사이에 위치하여 동명사를 수식하는 품사는 부사이므로 정답은 (A) actively이다.

어휘   increase v. 증가시키다 | sales n. 매출액, 판매량 | interact with ~와 소통[교류]하다

16. 1,000명이 넘는 고객들이 최근에 〈Rover Auto Magazine〉을 구독했다.

해설   빈칸은 수 형용사 1,000을 수식하는 부사 자리이며, 보기 중 over는 부사로 쓰일 때 '(특정 숫자) 이상'을 뜻하여 1,000명이 넘게 구독했다는 의미를 완성하므로 정답은 (D) Over이다.

어휘   recently adv. 최근에 | subscribe to ~을 구독하다

17. Regend 대학교는 놀라울 정도로 다양한 학생 집단으로 유명하다.

해설   빈칸 뒤에 diverse student body라는 「형용사 + 명사」의 구조가 있으므로 빈칸에는 형용사를 수식하는 부사가 들어가야 한다. 따라서 정답은 (B) remarkably이다.

어휘   diverse adj. 다양한 | student body 한 대학의 학생 전체

18. 참석자들은 회의가 끝날 때 방에서 조용히 나가도록 요구 받는다.

해설   빈칸 앞의 exit the room으로 '동사 + 목적어'의 3형식 구조가 완성되었으므로 빈칸에는 부사가 들어가야 한다. 따라서 (B) quietly가 정답이다.

어휘   attendee n. 참석자 | exit v. 나가다

19. 더 많은 대중 교통 옵션들을 제공하는 것이 시내의 대기 오염을 줄이는 데 있어서 효과적인 것으로 드러났다.

해설   '효과적인 것으로 드러났다'라는 의미로 해석상으로는 부사가 들어갈 자리로 보이지만, prove는 '~임이 드러나다'라는 뜻으로 쓰일 때 주격 보어를 취하는 2형식 동사이므로 정답은 형용사인 (A) effective이다.

어휘   proven adj. 입증된, 증명된 | effective adj. 효과적인

20. 최근 들어 Mr. Ko는 프로젝트 마감일을 맞추기 위해 야근하고 있다.

해설   완벽한 문장이고 문장 맨 앞에 빈칸이 있으므로 부사가 들어가야 하는 자리임을 알 수 있다. (A) Late는 형용사와 부사로 모두 쓰이지만 '늦게 일했다'는 의미는 문맥상 적합하지 않다. (B)와 (C)는 최상급, 비교급인데, 품사는 late와 마찬가지로 형용사와 부사로 쓰이지만 역시 문맥상 '가장 늦게, 더 늦게'는 어울리지 않는다. '최근에'라는 의미가 문맥상 가장 잘 어울리므로 정답은 (D) Lately이다.

어휘   meet v. 충족시키다, 만나다 | work overtime 야근하다 | project deadline 프로젝트 마감일

UNIT 09. 전치사

본서 p.92

+ check   1. (C)   2. (C)   3. (C)   4. (A)

1. 모든 대여 도서들을 다음 주 월요일 이전에 반드시 도서관에 반납해 주세요.

해설   전치사 선택 문제이다. within은 기간 전치사로 뒤에 기간이 나와야 하는데, next Monday라는 시점이 나왔으므로 탈락이다. 보기 중 시점을 나타내는 전치사는 before로, 빌린 책들을 다음 주 월요일 전에 반납하라는 의미가 적절하다. 즉, before가 문맥상으로도 적절하므로 정답은 (C) before이다.

어휘   return v. 반납하다; 돌려주다 | borrowed adj. 빌린; 차용한

2. 이번 주 토요일이 시의 금융가에 위치한 우리 은행 최신 지점의 공식 개점일이다.

해설   전치사 선택 문제이다. 보기의 의미를 살펴보면 (A) ~로(방향) (B) ~아래에(위치) (C) ~안에(지역/공간), ~ 후에(시간의 경과) (D) ~까지(시점)로, 문맥상 구역 안에 위치되어 있는 것이 맞으므로 정답은 (C) in이다.

어휘   official adj. 공식적인; 공적인 | opening n. 개막식, 개관식 | latest adj. 최근의, 최신의 | branch n. 지사, 지점 | financial district 금융가

3. 당신의 연회 파티 전에, 저희 음식 공급자 중 한 명이 손님 수와 메뉴 선택을 확인하기 위해 당신에게 전화할 것이다.

해설   연결어 문제로 빈칸 뒤에는 명사구가 위치해 있는데, 접속사 (A)와 (B)는 문장인 「주어 + 동사」를 이끌기 때문에 탈락이다. Prior to는 '~전에'라는 뜻의 전치사로서 전치사는 뒤에 명사(구)를 이끈다. 문맥상으로도 손님 수와 메뉴를 확인하기 위해 연회 '전에' 연락을 줄 것이라는 의미가 적절하므로 정답은 (C) Prior to이다.

어휘   reception n. 연회; 접수처 | caterer n. 음식 공급자, 연회업자 | confirm v. 확인해주다

4. 영세 소매업자들은 서로 협력함으로써 이득을 볼 수 있기 때문에 지역 사업 단체를 결성한다.

해설   보기를 보면 동사 어휘 문제로 benefit이 전치사 from을 동반하여 '~로부터 혜택을 얻다'라는 의미로 쓰인다는 것을 알고 있으면 쉽게 풀 수 있는 문제이다. 해석을 해봐도 소매업자들이 서로 협력하여 이득을 볼 수 있기 때문에 단체를 결성한다는 문맥이므로 정답은 (A) benefit이다.

어휘   retailer n. 소매업자[체], 소매상 | cooperate v. 협력하다 | one another 서로 | form v. 형성하다 | association n. 단체, 연맹

....

Practice

본서 p.96

1. (B)	**2.** (A)	**3.** (D)	**4.** (C)	**5.** (A)
6. (A)	**7.** (A)	**8.** (A)	**9.** (C)	**10.** (A)
11. (B)	**12.** (C)	**13.** (D)	**14.** (A)	**15.** (B)
16. (D)	**17.** (C)	**18.** (A)	**19.** (D)	**20.** (D)

1. Elkor Spa Resort is conveniently located (within walking distance) (of major tourist attractions).

2. Patrons can get help (from librarians) (through the library's online help desk).

3. Please read the instructions (in the manual) (prior to assembling the couch).

4. The conference room is located (near the entrance) (of the building).

5. The estimate (for your office renovation) will be provided (within two working days).

6. H&PCH Architects will not make changes (to the floor plan) (without the client's prior approval).

7. Before he came (to Busan), Mr. Kang had worked (as a bank manager).

8. The tour may differ (from the description) (in the brochure) (depending upon the weather conditions).

9. Please note that e-mails received (after 10 P.M.) will be checked the following morning.

10. (During the past three months), the number (of students) (at Pullmans Academy) has increased dramatically.

1. Spicy Leaf 레스토랑은 개인 행사를 위해 7월 10일 월요일에 문을 닫을 예정이다.

해설 전치사 for는 '~때문에'라는 뜻으로 문맥상 적합하므로 정답은 (B) for 이다.

어휘 private *adj.* 사적인

2. Panjala 경영 대학원의 지원이 연중 내내 받아들여진다.

해설 throughout the year는 '연중 내내'라는 의미로 정답은 (A) throughout이다.

어휘 application *n.* 지원(서) | accept *v.* 받아들이다

3. Starzie 화학은 추가 자금으로 새로운 실험 장비를 구매했다.

해설 '추가 자금으로 새 실험 장비를 구매했다'는 의미로 '~로'라는 뜻의 수단의 전치사인 (D) with가 정답이다.

어휘 lab equipment 실험 장비 | extra *adj.* 추가의 | funds *n.* 자금, 기금

4. 통근자들은 대중 교통을 이용함으로써 에너지를 보존하는 걸 도울 수 있다.

해설 「by -ing」는 '~함으로써'라는 의미이므로 정답은 (C) by이다.

어휘 conserve *v.* 보존하다 | public transportation 대중 교통

5. 춥고 눈이 많이 내리기 때문에 스키 시즌이 3월 말까지 계속될 것이다.

해설 해석상 until과 by가 가장 잘 어울리지만, until은 계속적 의미일 때 쓰고 by는 완료의 의미일 때 쓰인다. 이 문장에서는 last가 '지속하다'라는 계속적 의미로 쓰였으므로 정답은 (A) until이다.

어휘 heavily *adv.* 심하게 | last *v.* 지속하다, 계속하다

6. Elkor Spa 리조트는 주요 관광 명소에서 걸어 다닐 수 있는 거리 내에 편리하게 위치해 있다.

해설 빈칸 뒤에 명사가 있으므로 부사 (C)와 접속부사 (B)는 탈락이다. 전치사 (A)와 (D) 중에 문맥상 '걸어 다닐 수 있는 거리 내에'가 맞으므로 정답은 (A) within이다.

어휘 conveniently *adv.* 편리하게 | walking distance 도보 거리

7. 손님들은 도서관의 온라인 지원 창구를 통해 사서로부터 도움을 받을 수 있다.

해설 in case of '~라는 경우에,' among '~사이에,' such as '~와 같은' 모두 문맥상 적합하지 않으므로 답이 될 수 없고, through '~을 통해서'가 문맥상 잘 어울리므로 정답은 (A) through이다.

어휘 patron *n.* 손님 | librarian *n.* 사서

8. 긴 의자를 조립하기 전에 설명서에 있는 안내 사항들을 읽어주세요.

해설 '긴 의자를 조립하기 전에 안내 사항들을 읽어 달라'는 의미가 적절하므로 '~전에'라는 뜻의 전치사 (A) prior to가 정답이다.

어휘 instruction *n.* 안내사항, 설명 | manual *n.* 설명서 | assemble *v.* 조립하다 | couch *n.* 긴 의자

9. 그 회의실은 빌딩 입구 근처에 위치해 있다.

해설 해석상 next와 near가 가장 자연스럽지만, next는 전치사 to와 함께 쓰일 때 명사를 동반할 수 있으므로 next는 탈락이다. 참고로 next는 형용사 또는 부사로 쓰인다. 따라서 전치사인 (C) near가 정답이다.

어휘 located *adj.* 위치한 | entrance *n.* (출)입구

10. Mr. Jang은 8년이 넘는 기간 동안 Sognet 공업에서 일해왔다.

해설 문맥상 for가 '~ 동안'이란 의미로 가장 적합하다. for는 현재 완료(has p.p.)와 함께 쓰이므로 정답은 (A) for이다.

어휘 more than ~이상

11. 귀하의 사무실 개조를 위한 견적서가 영업일 2일 이내에 제공될 것이다.

해설 빈칸 다음에 '영업일 2일'이라는 시점이 아닌 기간이 나왔다. 시점 전치사 (C)와 (D)는 탈락이고, (A)는 접속사이라서 부적절하다. '영업일 2일 내로 제공될 것이다'가 적합하므로 정답은 (B) within이다.

어휘 estimate *n.* 견적서

12. 모든 세입자들은 임대 계약에 포함되어 있는 규칙들을 따라야 한다.

해설 문맥상 '임대 계약에 포함되어 있는 규칙들'이므로 정답은 (C) in이다.

어휘 tenant *n.* 세입자 | lease agreement 임대 계약

13. H&PCH 건축 사무소는 고객의 사전 승인 없이 평면도에 수정을 가하지 않을 것이다.

해설 보기에 모두 전치사가 나왔다. 해석상 without '~없이'라는 의미가 문맥상 가장 적합하므로 정답은 (D) without이다.

어휘 floor plan (건물의) 평면도 | prior *adj.* 사전의, 이전의 | approval *n.* 승인

14. 그가 부산에 오기 전에, Mr. Kang은 은행 관리자로 일했었다.

해설 보기에 모두 전치사가 나왔다. as '~로서'가 문맥상 가장 적합하므로 정답은 (D) as이다.

어휘 manager *n.* 운영자, 관리자

15. 관광은 날씨 상황에 따라 안내 책자에 기술된 것과 다를 수 있습니다.

해설 「depending on/upon」은 '~에 따라'라는 의미이므로 정답은 (B) upon이다.

어휘 differ from ~와 다르다 | description *n.* 기술, 서술

16. 밤 10시 이후에 수신된 이메일은 다음 날 아침에 확인된다는 점에 유의하세요.

해설 such as는 '~와 같은'이란 의미로 문맥상 적합하지 않다. during 다음에는 기간이 와야 하는데, 10 P.M.은 기간이 아닌 시점이다. between은 두 개의 대상이 있어야 하므로 탈락이다. after 뒤에는 시점인 10 P.M.도 올 수 있고 문맥상 적합하므로 정답은 (D) after이다.

어휘 note *v.* 주의하다, 언급하다

17. 직원 휴게실 청소를 담당하는 직원들은 그 구역을 하루에 세 번 점검해야 한다.

해설 「be responsible for」는 '~할 책임이 있다'는 의미의 관용 표현이므로 (C) for가 정답이다.

어휘 staff lounge 직원 휴게실

18. 새 보안 업데이트를 설치하기 전에 중요한 모든 파일들을 저장해주세요.

해설 '보안 업데이트를 설치하기 전에 파일들을 저장하라'는 의미가 적절하므로 '~전에'라는 뜻의 전치사 (A) before가 정답이다.

어휘 save *v.* 저장하다 | install *v.* 설치하다 | security update 보안 업데이트

19. 지난 3개월 동안 Pullmans 아카데미가 보유한 학생 수는 급격히 늘어났다.

해설 보기에 모두 전치사가 나왔다. 문맥상 during '~동안에'라는 의미가 가장 적합하며, during 다음에 the past three months라는 기간이 나오는 것이 적합하므로 정답은 (D) During이다.

어휘 the number of ~의 수 | dramatically *adv.* 극적으로

20. 고장 난 급수 파이프 때문에, Blues 식당은 추후 공지가 있을 때까지 문을 닫을 것이다.

해설 「until further notice」는 '추후 공지가 있을 때까지'라는 의미의 관용 표현이므로 (D) until이 정답이다.

어휘 due to ~때문에 | broken *adj.* 고장 난 | close *v.* 폐쇄하다

REVIEW TEST 02

본서 p.98

1. (A)	2. (B)	3. (D)	4. (C)	5. (D)
6. (B)	7. (C)	8. (D)	9. (D)	10. (A)
11. (C)	12. (B)	13. (B)	14. (D)	15. (A)
16. (C)	17. (B)	18. (B)	19. (B)	20. (B)
21. (A)	22. (A)	23. (B)	24. (D)	25. (A)
26. (C)	27. (B)	28. (D)	29. (A)	30. (B)

1. Jorcom 광고사는 조직 관리 기술을 보유한 판매 사원들을 고용하고자 한다.

해설 전치사와 명사 사이에 빈칸이 있으므로 형용사인 (A) organizational이 정답이다.

어휘 hire *v.* 고용하다 | organizational *adj.* 조직(상)의

2. 대부분의 경우에, 그 소프트웨어로 당신의 컴퓨터에 있는 모든 파일들을 복구할 수 있다.

해설 every는 단수 취급하므로 복수 명사 files와 함께 쓰일 수 없다. as는 접속사나 전치사로 쓰인다. 접속사 as로 쓰인 경우에는 두 개의 문장이 연결되어야 하는데 문장은 한 개밖에 없다. 전치사 as로 쓰인 경우에는 as files가 전치사구가 되어 문장의 목적어가 사라져 버리므로 탈락이다. next는 형용사나 부사로 쓰이는데 문맥상 적합하지 않으므로 탈락이다. all은 복수 가산 명사와 단수 불가산 명사와 함께 쓰인다. 이 문장에서는 복수 가산 명사인 files와 함께 쓰였고, 문맥도 자연스러우므로 정답은 (B) all이다.

어휘 recover *v.* 회복되다, 되찾다

3. Dreambird 가구는 모든 고객들에게 모든 구매에 대해서 환불 보장을 제공한다.

해설 문맥상 빈칸에는 '구매자'가 아닌 '구매'가 들어가야 하므로 (B), (C)는 탈락이다. (A)와 (D)가 될 수 있는데, '구매'는 가산 명사이다. all은 복수 가산 명사와 단수 불가산 명사와 같이 쓰이므로 복수 가산 명사인 (D) purchases가 정답이다.

어휘 money-back guarantee 환불 보장

4. 도쿄 지사에서의 판매량은 베이징 지사의 판매량보다 눈에 띄게 더 높다.

해설 2형식 동사 be가 쓰였고, 주격 보어 자리에 상태 설명 형용사 higher가 이미 있으므로 빈칸은 부사 (C) noticeably이다.

어휘 sales *n.* 판매량 | noticeably *adv.* 현저히

5. Mr. Oh는 직원 회의를 위한 안건을 내일 보낼 것이다.

해설 보기에 모두 전치사가 나왔다. 해석상 '~을 위해서, ~을 위한'이라는 의미의 for가 가장 적합하므로 정답은 (D) for이다.

어휘 agenda *n.* 안건 | staff meeting 직원, 회의

6. El Grande 레스토랑은 모든 요리에 우수한 재료들만을 사용한다.

해설 명사 ingredients 앞에 빈칸이 있으므로 형용사 (B) superior가 정답이다.

어휘 ingredient *n.* 재료 | superior *adj.* 우수한

7. 환경 친화적 기능들이 그 제품을 가치 있게 만들어 준다.

해설 make는 5형식 동사로 빈칸은 목적격 보어 자리이다. 목적어의 상태를 설명하는 형용사가 와야 하므로 정답은 (C) valuable이다.

어휘 environmentally-friendly *adj.* 환경 친화적인 | feature *n.* 기능, 특징

8. 빈번한 우편물 수신자 명단 업데이트는 그 시장을 겨냥하는 데 성공적으로 기여했다.

해설 have와 과거분사 사이에는 부사가 들어가야 하므로 정답은 (D) successfully이다.

어휘 frequent *adj.* 자주, 빈번한 | contribute *v.* 기여하다, 공헌하다 | target *v.* 겨냥하다, 목표로 삼다 *n.* 목표, 대상, 표적

9. Jassom 사는 새로운 제품에 관한 당신의 제안을 환영한다.

해설 소유격 다음에 빈칸이 있으며, welcome의 목적어 자리이기도 하므로 명사가 와야 한다. 따라서 정답은 (D) suggestions이다.

어휘 welcome *v.* 환영하다 | concerning *prep.* ~에 관한 | suggestion *n.* 제안

10. 다양한 부서의 공동 작업의 결과로, 그 회의는 원활하게 진행되었다.

해설 정관사 the와 명사 departments 사이에 빈칸이 있으므로 형용사 (A)와 (C)가 답이 될 수 있으나, 해석상 '다양한'이 자연스러우므로 정답은 (A) various이다.

어휘 collaboration *n.* 공동 작업, 협력 | smoothly *adv.* 순조롭게 | various *adj.* 다양한 | variable *adj.* 변화를 줄 수 있는

11. 에어컨은 구매일로부터 6개월 이내에 무상으로 반품할 수 있다.

해설 빈칸 뒤에 6 months라는 '시점'이 아닌 '기간'이 나왔다. 시점을 써야 하는 (A), (B), (D)는 모두 탈락이다. within 다음에는 기간이 와야 하고, 문맥상 적합하므로 정답은 (C) within이다.

어휘 air conditioner 에어컨 | purchase *n.* 구매 | free of charge 무료로

12. 그 회사의 새로운 웹사이트는 제품 정보를 고객들에게 더 쉽게 접근할 수 있도록 만들 것이다.

해설 make의 목적어인 product information이 나와 있고, 목적격 보어 자리에 상태 설명 형용사 accessible이 나와 있다. 따라서 빈칸은 필요 없는 자리이며 형용사 앞이므로 부사 (B) readily가 정답이다.

어휘 accessible *adj.* 접근 가능한 | readily *adv.* 손쉽게, 순조롭게

13. 임대차 계약서에 따르면, 세입자들이 집세를 밀리면 벌금을 내야 한다.

해설 임대차 계약서에 적혀 있는 내용에 따라, 세입자가 집세를 밀릴 경우 벌금을 내야 한다는 의미이므로 '(특정인이 진술한 내용이나 계약 조항 등에) 따르면'이라는 의미의 (B) According to가 정답이다.

어휘 lease agreement 임대차 계약(서) | tenant *n.* 세입자, 임차인 | fine *n.* 벌금 | rent *n.* 집세 | except for ~을 제외하고 | according to ~에 따르면 | such as ~와 같이 | instead of ~ 대신에

14. 증가하는 생산성의 결과로, 그 회사는 직원들에게 인센티브를 제공하고 있다.

해설 빈칸은 형용사 increasing 뒤에 있으므로 명사 (A)와 (D)가 가능하다. 문맥상 '증가하는 생산자'가 아니고, '증가하는 생산성'이므로 정답은 (D) productivity이다.

어휘 productivity *n.* 생산성 | offer *v.* 제공하다

15. 그 문제들이 제품 결함에 관한 것이든, 파손된 물건에 관한 것이든, 혹은 분실된 상품에 관한 것이든 모두가 Ms. Cherry에게 전달된다.

해설 빈칸 앞은 접속사 Whether가 이끄는 부사절(~이든 아니든)이므로 빈칸은 주절의 주어 자리이며 동사가 복수(are)이므로 단수 동사를 취하는 (B), (C), (D)는 모두 답에서 제외시킬 수 있다. all은 가산 복수와 불가산 명사를 모두 받을 수 있으므로 정답은 (A) all이다.

어휘 whether *conj.* ~이든 아니든 | defect *n.* 결함 | damaged *adj.* 파손된 | missing *adj.* 분실된, 잃어버린 | merchandise *n.* 상품 | forward *v.* 전달하다

16. 탑승객들은 승무원들로부터 세관 신고 양식을 받을 수 있다.

해설 보기에 모두 전치사가 나와 있다. 문맥상 '~로부터 얻다, 구하다'가 적합하므로 정답은 (C) from이다.

어휘 passenger *n.* 승객 | obtain *v.* 얻다, 구하다 | customs *n.* 세관

17. 지난달 회의의 회의록에 따르면, 모든 멤버들이 참석했다.

해설 빈칸은 전치사 뒤이므로 명사 자리이다. 해석상 '종업원'이 아니고 '참석'이 맞으므로 정답은 (B) attendance이다

어휘 minutes *n.* 회의록 | attendant *n.* 종업원 | attendance *n.* 참석, 참석자 수, 출석(률)

18. 분석가들은 연료비가 내년에 증가할 것이라고 믿고 있다.

해설 빈칸은 that절 내의 주어 자리로 명사가 와야 한다. '연료가 증가하는 것'이 아니고 '연료비가 증가하는 것'이므로 정답은 (B) prices이다. 참고로 price는 가산 명사이므로 a price 또는 prices로 써야 한다.

어휘 analyst *n.* 분석가 | believe *v.* 믿다 | fuel *n.* 연료 | rise *v.* 증가하다, 오르다 *n.* 증가

19. 공장 노동자들은 청력 보호 장치를 착용해야 한다.

해설 '보호 장치'로 복합 명사이다. 따라서 정답은 (B) protection이다.

어휘 wear *v.* 입다. 쓰다. 착용하다 | hearing *n.* 청력. 청각 | device *n.* 장치 | protection *n.* 보호

20. Mr. Lee는 마케팅 부서 자리의 최종 후보자들을 직접 인터뷰할 예정이다.

해설 빈칸 앞은 3형식의 완벽한 문장이므로 빈칸은 필요 없는 자리이다. 빈칸은 주어 자리가 아니므로 주어 자리에 올 수 있는 주격 대명사 (A) she는 올 수 없다. 빈칸 뒤에 명사가 없으므로 명사 앞에 오는 소유격 (B) her도 올 수 없다. (B) her를 목적격이라고 봐도 빈칸은 목적어 자리가 아니므로 답이 될 수 없다. 소유대명사인 (C) hers 역시 올 수 없다. 필요 없는 자리에 재귀대명사를 넣으면 강조 역할이 되므로 정답은 (D) herself이다.

어휘 candidate *n.* 후보자

21. 세미나에 참석하기를 원하는 사람들은 Mr. Chang에게 연락해야 한다.

해설 빈칸은 주어 자리이다. (C) Other는 형용사로 쓰이므로 주어 자리에 올 수 없다. 재귀대명사인 (D) Themselves도 주어 자리에 올 수 없다. (A) Those는 people과 같은 의미로 복수이고 (B) Anyone은 단수이다. who 다음에 want라는 복수 동사가 온 것을 보면 빈칸에는 복수 명사가 와야 함을 알 수 있다. 따라서 정답은 (A) Those이다.

어휘 attend *v.* 참석하다 | contact *v.* 연락하다

22. Ms. Smythe는 다른 한 명의 디자이너가 휴가 중이었기 때문에 디자인 작업을 마무리하기 위해 야근을 해야 했다.

해설 두 명 중 한 명을 먼저 언급하고 나머지 한 명을 뒤에 언급할 때는 the other를 쓰므로 정답은 (A) the other이다. (B)와 (C)는 명사이므로 뒤에 designer라는 명사가 올 수 없다. (D) other는 형용사로 명사 designer 앞에 올 수 있지만, 가산 명사일 땐 복수 명사와, 불가산 명사일 땐 단수 명사와 함께 쓰인다. 이 문장에서 (D)가 정답이 되려면, designer는 가산 명사이므로 designers가 와야 한다.

어휘 work overtime 야근하다

23. 많은 동료들은 회사를 그만둔 후에도 꾸준히 서로 연락한다.

해설 전치사 with 다음에는 명사가 와야 한다. (C) other는 형용사이므로 올 수 없다. (B) another는 형용사와 명사 모두로 쓰이지만, 문맥상 동료들이 또 다른 사람과 연락하는 것이 아니고 동료들끼리 서로 연락하는 것이므로 답이 될 수 없다. (D) each도 '각각'이라는 의미로 맞지 않다. (A) one another는 '서로'라는 뜻의 대명사이므로 전치사 뒤에 쓸 수 있고, 문맥도 맞으므로 정답은 (A) one another이다.

어휘 colleague *n.* 동료 | stay in touch 연락을 유지하다

24. 많은 학생들이 Kumar 교수의 역사 강의에 참석할 것으로 기대된다.

해설 Another와 Every는 단수 가산 명사와 쓰이는데, students는 복수 명사이므로 (A), (C)는 탈락이다. much는 셀 수 없는 명사와 쓰이는데, students는 셀 수 있는 명사이므로 탈락이다. Many는 복수 가산 명사와 쓰이므로 students와 쓸 수 있다. 따라서 정답은 (D) Many이다.

어휘 expect *v.* 기대하다. 예상하다 | attend *v.* 참석하다 | lecture *n.* 강의

25. 몇몇 직원들은 도로 공사의 소음이 그들의 근무에 방해가 된다고 생각했다.

해설 5형식 동사 found를 사용한 문장이며 빈칸은 목적격 보어 자리이므로 형용사 (A) disruptive가 정답이다.

어휘 disruptive *adj.* 지장을 주는

26. 고객 서비스 직원들은 모든 불만과 문의 사항들에 지체 없이 대응해야 한다.

해설 조동사와 동사원형 사이는 동사 수식 부사 자리이므로 정답은 (C) promptly이다.

어휘 associate *n.* (사업직장) 동료 | respond *v.* 대응하다, 반응하다 | complaint *n.* 불만, 항의 | inquiry *n.* 문의

27. 기업들은 직장에서 평등의 중요성을 점점 더 인식하고 있다.

해설 2형식 be동사 are 다음에 주격 보어 형용사인 aware가 왔다. 2형식의 완벽한 문장이 나왔으므로 빈칸은 필요 없는 자리이다. 부사가 정답이며, 더욱이 형용사 앞이므로 (B) increasingly가 정답이다.

어휘 aware *adj.* 인식하고 있는, 알고 있는 | increasingly *adv.* 점점 더. 갈수록 더

28. 모든 사무실 컴퓨터들은 현재 업데이트된 소프트웨어로 바르게 작동하고 있다.

해설 work가 1형식 동사이므로 빈칸은 부사 자리이다. 따라서 정답은 (D) correctly이다.

어휘 work *v.* 작동하다

29. 워크샵에 관한 추가적인 세부 사항들은 내일 확인될 것이다.

해설 보기에 모두 전치사가 나왔다. 해석상 concerning '~에 관하여'라는 의미가 가장 적합하므로 정답은 (A) concerning이다.

어휘 additional *adj.* 추가적인 | detail *n.* 세부 사항

30. Garrison 법률 센터는 20년이 넘는 기간 동안 지역 사회에 서비스를 제공해왔다.

해설 빈칸 앞의 for가 이미 전치사이므로 between, from, during과 같은 전치사를 또 넣을 수 없다. over는 전치사로도 쓸 수 있지만, 숫자 앞에서는 '~이상'이라는 의미의 부사로도 쓰이므로 정답은 (B) over 이다.

어휘 serve *v.* (서비스를) 제공하다 | local community 지역 사회

UNIT 10. 접속사

+check　　1. (C)　　2. (A)　　3. (B)　　4. (A)

1. 그 회사의 CEO가 계약 조건을 만족스럽게 제시하지 않으면, 이사진은 Skycross 항공과의 합병을 승인하지 않을 것이다.

해설　빈칸 앞에도 문장이고, 빈칸 뒤에도 문장이다. 문장과 문장을 연결할 수 있는 접속사가 빈칸에 들어가야 한다. 보기에 나온 것들은 모두 접속사이기 때문에 해석을 해봐야 하는데, 만족스러운 조건을 제시하지 '않으면' 승인하지 않을 것이라는 문맥이므로 정답은 (C) unless이다.

어휘　merger *n.* 합병 | contract terms 계약 조건

2. 쇼핑객들은 물건을 새로 구매할 때 쿠폰을 받을 것이다.

해설　빈칸을 기준으로 앞에도 문장이고, 빈칸 뒤에도 문장이다. 따라서 빈칸은 절과 절을 이어줄 수 있는 접속사가 필요한 자리이다. 보기 중 접속사는 when뿐이므로 정답은 (A) when이다.

어휘　coupon *n.* 쿠폰, 할인권 | make a purchase 구매하다

3. 직원들 일부가 학회 참석차 자리를 비우기 때문에 이번 주 부서 회의는 연기될 것이다.

해설　빈칸을 기준으로 앞에도 문장이고, 빈칸 뒤에도 문장이다. 따라서 빈칸은 두 개의 문장을 이어줄 수 있는 (부사절) 접속사가 필요한 자리이다. 보기를 살펴보면, (A) 명사절 접속사(~인지 아닌지) (B) 부사절 접속사(~ 때문에) (C) 접속부사(그러므로) (D) 접속부사(게다가)이므로 해석할 필요 없이 정답은 (B) because이다.

어휘　postpone *v.* 연기하다 | be away 떠나다

4. Mr. Watts는 대리들이 6월의 연수회와 7월의 워크숍 둘 다 참가해야 한다고 제안한다.

해설　상관접속사 문제이다. 「both A and B: A, B 둘 다」의 구조를 취하므로 정답은 (A) both이다.

어휘　suggest *v.* 제안하다 | assistant manager 대리 | participate in ~에 참가하다

Practice

본서 p.106

1. (C)	**2.** (D)	**3.** (B)	**4.** (A)	**5.** (D)
6. (A)	**7.** (D)	**8.** (D)	**9.** (A)	**10.** (A)
11. (B)	**12.** (D)	**13.** (A)	**14.** (B)	**15.** (B)
16. (C)	**17.** (A)	**18.** (A)	**19.** (C)	**20.** (C)

기본 완성 훈련

1. In addition to free delivery, the company offers discounts on large orders.

2. Prior to joining our company, Ms. Patel worked for a competing firm.

3. The internet helps companies connect with customers as well as make new business contacts.

4. Employees may join the workshop as long as they sign up in advance.

5. The new store is so popular that it had to hire additional staff.

6. The heating system will be upgraded due to its poor energy efficiency.

7. We will not disclose our customers' information without their consent.

8. Staff will not be eligible for a bonus unless they meet or exceed their sales quotas.

9. Since RZAI, Inc. has done so well in Los Angeles, it will open a branch in Seoul.

10. The client database system was updated so that employees could find information more quickly.

---

1. Halmont는 인기 있는 관광지이며, 외국인 투자를 환영합니다.

해설　문장이 두 개 나와 있으므로 빈칸은 두 개의 문장을 연결할 수 있는 접속사 자리이다. (A)와 (B)는 전치사이고, (C)와 (D)가 접속사인데, 문맥상 '그리고'라는 의미가 적합하므로 (C) and이다.

어휘　popular *adj.* 인기 있는 | tourist destination 관광지

2. 무료 배달 서비스 이외에도, 그 회사는 대량 주문에 대한 할인도 제공한다.

해설　빈칸 뒤에 명사가 있으므로 빈칸에는 전치사가 와야 한다. (B)와 (D) 중 문맥상 (D) In addition to가 정답이다.

어휘　offer *v.* 제공하다, 제안하다 | discount *n.* 할인

3. Ms. Patel은 우리 회사에 합류하기 전에 경쟁사에서 근무했다.

해설　구조상 네 개의 보기가 모두 빈칸에 들어갈 수 있지만 문맥상 '이전에, 앞서'라는 의미의 (B) Prior to가 정답이다.

어휘　competing firm 경쟁사

4. 구내식당은 개조 작업을 진행하는 동안 폐쇄될 것입니다.

해설　빈칸 뒤에 「주어 + 동사」의 구조가 있으므로 접속사인 (A) while이 정답이다. 나머지는 모두 전치사이기 때문에 정답이 될 수 없다.

어휘　undergo *v.* 겪다 | renovation *n.* 개수, 정비

5. 직원들은 6시까지만 근무하도록 규정되어 있었음에도 불구하고 많은 이들이 자주 초과 근무를 했다.

해설　(A)와 (C)는 전치사이기 때문에 「주어 + 동사」 앞에 사용할 수 없다. (B) So as to는 뒤에 동사원형이 와야 한다. 빈칸 뒤의 구조상 접속사인 (D) Even though가 정답이다.

어휘　employee *n.* 직원 | require *v.* 요구하다

6. 인터넷은 기업들이 새로운 비즈니스 인맥을 형성하는 것뿐만 아니라 고객들과 소통하는 것에도 도움을 준다.

해설　「A as well as B」는 'B뿐만 아니라 A도 역시'라는 의미로 A와 B가 대등하게 와야 한다. 문장에서 A와 B가 전치사구로 대등하게 왔으므로 정답은 (A) as well as이다.

어휘　business contact 사업상 도움이 될 인맥

7. 재활용 정책은 지출을 감소시킬 수 있기 때문에 승인될 것이다.

해설　빈칸은 두 개의 문장을 연결할 수 있는 접속사 자리이다. (A)는 전치사이고 (B)는 접속부사이다. 접속사인 (C)와 (D)가 가능한데, 문맥상 '~때문에'라는 의미가 적합하므로 정답은 (D) because이다.

어휘　recycling *n.* 재활용 | decrease *v.* 감소하다, 감소시키다 | expense *n.* 지출

8. 직원들은 사전에 등록하기만 하면 워크숍에 참가할 수 있다.

해설　빈칸은 두 개의 문장을 연결할 수 있는 접속사 자리이다. (A)는 전치사이고 (B) so as to 다음에는 동사원형이 와야 한다. 접속사인 (C)와 (D)가 가능한데, 문맥상 '~하기만 하면'이라는 (D) as long as가 정답이다.

어휘　sign up ~에 등록하다 | in advance 미리

9. 새 상점은 인기가 너무 좋아서 추가 직원을 고용해야 했다.

해설　「so 형용사/부사 that 주어 + 동사」는 '너무 ~해서 ~하다'라는 의미로 정답은 (A) so이다.

어휘　additional *adj.* 추가적인

10. 그 난방 시스템은 낮은 에너지 효율성 때문에 업그레이드될 것이다.

해설　빈칸 다음에 명사가 왔으므로 빈칸에는 전치사가 들어갈 수 있다. (A)와 (C)는 전치사, (B)는 접속부사, (D)는 접속사이다. 문맥상 '~ 이래로'가 아니고 '~때문에'가 적합하므로 정답은 (A) due to이다. since가 전치사로 쓰일 때는 '~때문에'라는 뜻이 아니라 '~이래로'라는 뜻으로 쓰인다는 점에 유의한다.

어휘　heating system 난방 시스템 | poor *adj.* (질적으로) 좋지 못한, 형편없는 | efficiency *n.* 효율, 능률

11. 텔레비전 광고 두 편을 제작하기 위해 예산이 수정되었다.

해설　빈칸 다음에 동사원형이 왔다. (A)는 접속사이므로 뒤에 주어와 동사가 와야 하고, (C)는 전치사이므로 뒤에 명사가 와야 하고, (D)는 접속부사이다. 「in order to + 동사원형」은 '~하기 위해서'라는 의미로 정답은 (B) in order to이다.

어휘　advertisement *n.* 광고

12. 우리는 고객들의 동의 없이는 고객들의 정보를 공개하지 않을 것이다.

해설　빈칸 다음에 명사가 나왔으므로 빈칸에는 전치사가 올 수 있다. (A), (B), (C)는 모두 접속사이므로 유일한 전치사인 (D) without가 정답이다.

어휘　disclose *v.* 공개하다 | consent *n.* 동의 *v.* 동의하다

13. 대회 우승자들은 상점 상품권이나 현금 중 하나를 받는 것을 선택할 수 있다.

해설　빈칸 뒤에 「A (a store gift certificate) or B (cash)」 구조가 연결되어 있으므로 상관접속사 「either A or B」 'A, B 둘 중 하나'를 떠올릴 수 있어야 한다. 따라서 정답은 (A) either이다.

어휘　contest *n.* 대회 | gift certificate 상품권 | cash *n.* 현금

14. 직원들이 판매 할당량을 충족 및 초과 달성하지 못한다면, 보너스의 자격이 주어지지 않을 것이다.

해설　빈칸은 두 개의 문장을 연결할 수 있는 접속사 자리이다. (A)와 (C)는 접속부사이고, (D)는 전치사이다. 유일한 접속사인 (B) unless가 정답이다.

어휘　be eligible for ~에 자격이 있는 | exceed *v.* 초과하다 | quota *n.* 할당량

15. RZAI 사는 로스앤젤레스에서 너무 잘 해왔기 때문에 서울에 지점을 열 것이다.

해설　빈칸은 두 개의 문장을 연결할 수 있는 접속사 자리로 (A)와 (B)가 가능하다. 문맥상 '~때문에'가 적합하므로 정답은 (B) Since이다.

어휘　branch *n.* 분점, 지사

16. 소설의 성공 이후에, Kylie Chung은 이제 영화 각본도 집필했다.

해설　빈칸 다음에 명사가 나왔으므로 빈칸에는 전치사가 들어갈 수 있다. (A)와 (B)는 접속사이고, (D)는 부사이다. following은 바로 뒤에 명사가 오는 경우 전치사로 쓰이므로 정답은 (C) Following이다.

어휘　success *n.* 성공 | script *n.* 대본

17. 수리에 청구된 금액이 정확하지 않아서 새 송장을 첨부해드렸습니다.

해설　빈칸은 두 개의 문장을 연결할 수 있는 접속사 자리이다. (B)를 제외하고는 모두 접속사이다. 문맥상 '그리고'라는 의미로 연결하는 것이 가장 자연스러우므로 정답은 (A) and이다.

어휘　charge *v.* 청구하다 | repair *v.* 수리하다 *n.* 수리 | attach *v.* 첨부하다 | invoice *n.* 송장, 청구서

18. 이 여행 가방 브랜드는 가벼우면서 내구성도 좋은 것으로 알려져 있다.

해설　상관접속사 중 and와 짝을 이루는 것은 both이므로 (A) both가 정답이다.

어휘　luggage *n.* 짐가방 | lightweight *adj.* 가벼운 | durable *adj.* 내구성이 있는, 튼튼한

19. 직원들이 정보를 더 빨리 찾을 수 있도록 고객 데이터베이스 시스템이 업데이트되었다.

해설　빈칸 앞뒤로 주어, 동사를 갖춘 절이 연결되어 있어, 빈칸에는 두 절을 이어줄 수 있는 부사절 접속사가 들어가야 할 자리이므로 전치사 (A),

(D)는 정답에서 제외시킨다. 직원들이 정보를 더 빨리 찾을 수 있도록 하기 위해 시스템이 업데이트되었다는 의미가 적절하므로 목적을 나타내는 접속사 (C) so that이 정답이다.

어휘 client *n.* 고객 | because of ~때문에 | whereas *conj.* ~와는 대조적으로 | so that ~하도록 | in spite of ~에도 불구하고

20. 모든 직원들은 작년에 참석했다고 하더라도, 다음 주 안전 교육 세션에 참석해야 한다.

해설 빈칸 앞뒤로 주어, 동사를 갖춘 절이 연결되어 있어, 빈칸에는 두 절을 이어줄 수 있는 부사절 접속사가 들어가야 할 자리이므로 전치사 (A), (B), (D)를 해석 없이 소거시킬 수 있다. 따라서 정답은 (C) even if이다.

어휘 participate in ~에 참여하다 | between *prep.* ~사이에 | despite *prep.* ~에도 불구하고 | even if 설령 ~라 해도 | during *prep.* ~동안에

UNIT 11. 명사절 접속사

본서 p.110

+check   1. (B)   2. (B)   3. (C)   4. (B)

1. 저의 대만 여행이 후일로 연기되었다는 것을 Ms. Chang에게 알려주세요.

해설 inform은 사람 간접 목적어 뒤에 that절을 직접 목적어로 갖는 4형식 동사이므로 정답은 (B) that이다. to와 of는 전치사이므로 뒤에 절이 올 수 없고, because가 이끄는 절은 부사절이기 때문에 목적어가 될 수 없다.

어휘 postpone *v.* 연기하다, 미루다 | to a later date 후일로

2. 우리는 가장 정확한 정보를 제공하기 위해 무엇을 해야 하는지 결정해야만 한다.

해설 빈칸은 동사 determine의 목적어 자리이다. 즉, 명사가 필요한데, 뒤에 주어가 빠진 불완전한 절이 와 있다. 불완전한 절을 명사로 만들어서 determine의 목적어(명사) 역할을 하도록 해야 하는데, 불완전한 문장을 명사로 이끄는 명사절 접속사는 what이므로 정답은 (B) what이다.

어휘 accomplish *v.* 성취하다 | provide *v.* 제공하다 | accurate *adj.* 정확한, 정밀한

3. 최고 재무 책임자는 회사가 사무용품을 Faremex 사에서 주문할지 아니면, Callico 사에서 주문할지를 결정할 것이다.

해설 will decide의 목적어가 필요하므로 명사절 접속사가 와야 한다. 부사절 접속사인 although와 전치사 to를 지우고 의미상 '주문할지 말지'를 결정해야 하는 것이므로 정답은 (C) whether이다.

어휘 Chief Financial Officer 최고 재무 책임자(=CFO)

---

4. Mr. Yoon이 모든 출품작들의 평가를 끝내는 대로, 그는 누구의 작품을 선정할지 결정할 것이다.

해설 빈칸 앞에는 동사 determine이, 빈칸 뒤에는 '명사(work) + 수동태 (will be chosen)' 구조가 이어지고 있으므로 work를 수식하여 뒤에 오는 절을 이끌면서 determine의 목적어 기능을 할 수 있는 의문사가 와야 된다. 따라서 '누구의 작품이 선정될 것인지를 결정해야 한다'는 의미를 완성하는 의문 형용사 (B) whose가 정답이다.

어휘 evaluate *v.* 평가하다 | entry *n.* 출품작 | determine *v.* 결정하다 | work *n.* 작품

Practice

본서 p.114

1. (A)	**2.** (D)	**3.** (A)	**4.** (B)	**5.** (A)
6. (B)	**7.** (D)	**8.** (A)	**9.** (A)	**10.** (B)
11. (A)	**12.** (A)	**13.** (A)	**14.** (A)	**15.** (A)
16. (A)	**17.** (B)	**18.** (B)	**19.** (D)	**20.** (D)

기본 완성 훈련

①The warranty guarantees that the machine will be replaced if it has defects.

②The recent survey result indicates that most travelers book their flights online.

③The President will decide whether to merge with the company.

④Regardless of whether a candidate is hired, we keep all applications on file for one year.

⑤City officials insist that the new fuel tax will reduce traffic congestion.

⑥Please be aware that the HR Department will be interviewing new employees in conference room A today.

⑦The technician will determine exactly what caused the building's power failure.

⑧Please ensure that all labels are put on the boxes properly before sending them to the warehouse.

9. Despite the increased volume, 96 percent of the packages were delivered on time.

10. Tamiloy Jewelry customers can get 10 percent off their purchases as long as they spend $300 or more.

1. 품질 보증서는 기계에 결함이 있을 경우 교체해 줄 것임을 보증한다.

해설 빈칸에는 guarantee의 목적어 역할을 할 수 있고 뒤에 있는 절을 이끌 수 있는 명사절 접속사가 필요하다. 명사절을 이끄는 접속사 (A) that과 (C) what 중에서 빈칸 뒤에 완전한 절이 나와 있으므로 정답은 (A) that이다.

어휘 warranty *n.* 품질 보증서 ㅣ guarantee *v.* 보증하다 ㅣ defect *n.* 결함

2. 최근 설문조사 결과는 대부분의 여행객들이 온라인으로 그들의 비행편을 예약한다는 것을 나타내고 있다.

해설 빈칸에는 indicates의 목적어 역할을 할 수 있고 뒤에 있는 절을 이끌 수 있는 명사절 접속사가 필요하다. 명사절 접속사 (A) which, (B) what, (D) that 중에서 빈칸 뒤에 완전한 절이 나와 있으므로 정답은 (D) that이다.

어휘 indicate *v.* 나타내다, 가리키다 ㅣ book *v.* 예약하다 ㅣ flight *n.* 비행편

3. 사장은 그 회사와 합병할지 안할 지를 결정할 것이다.

해설 (C)와 (D)는 접속사로 두 개의 문장을 연결한다. 빈칸 뒤에는 주어와 동사도 없고, decide의 목적어도 없으므로 탈락이다. whether는 명사절 자리에서 to부정사와 함께 명사구를 이끌 수 있다. 따라서 whether to ~가 명사 역할로 decide의 목적어 역할을 하므로 정답은 (A) whether이다.

어휘 merge *v.* 합병하다

4. 지원자가 고용되었는지에 관계없이, 우리는 1년 간 모든 지원서를 파일로 보관해둔다.

해설 빈칸은 전치사 Regardless of (~와는 관계없이)의 목적어 자리이면서 동시에 빈칸 뒤에 연결된 완전한 절(a candidate is hired)을 이끌어야 하므로 명사절 접속사가 필요하다. 따라서 정답은 (B) whether이다.

어휘 candidate *n.* 지원자, 후보자 ㅣ hire *v.* 고용하다 ㅣ keep ~ on file ~을 파일로 보관하다

5. 지난 분기에 유가가 오를 것이라는 사실은 아무도 몰랐다.

해설 (B), (C), (D)는 문맥상 적합하지 않다. 이 문장에서 that은 동격의 that 역할을 한다. 즉, that은 명사의 내용을 반복하는 동격절을 이끌 수 있다. 「The fact = that절」이므로 정답은 (A) that이다.

어휘 oil *n.* 기름, 석유 ㅣ price *n.* 가격 ㅣ quarter *n.* 분기

6. 사용 설명서에는 그 믹서기를 찬 음료와 뜨거운 음료 모두를 만드는 데 사용할 수 있다고 적혀 있다.

해설 빈칸에 (A), (C), (D)가 오면 state의 목적어는 없으므로 정답이 될 수 없다. that은 명사절 접속사로 that절 전체가 state의 목적어(명사)가 될 수 있으므로 정답은 (B) that이다.

어휘 instruction *n.* 지시 ㅣ manual *n.* 설명서 ㅣ state *v.* 진술하다, 명시하다 ㅣ blender *n.* 믹서기

7. 그 연구는 우리의 신제품이 젊은 구매자들에게 매력적일지 밝혀줄 것이다.

해설 빈칸에 (B)가 오면 determine의 목적어가 없어지므로 답이 될 수 없다. (C) either는 상관접속사로 「either A or B」로 쓰이는데, A와 B가 대등한 형태로 와야 하므로 탈락이다. (A)와 (D)는 명사절 접속사로, 빈칸 다음에 나오는 주어와 동사를 포함하여 명사절이 되므로 determine의 목적어 역할이 가능하다. what 다음에는 불완전한 문장이 오고, whether 다음에는 완전한 문장이 와야 하므로 정답은 (D) whether이다.

어휘 determine *v.* 밝히다 ㅣ appeal *v.* 관심을 끌다

8. 이사회는 회사 보험 정책에 몇 가지 변경이 있어야 한다고 제안했다.

해설 (B)와 (D)가 앞 명사 board를 수식하는 형태로 고르면 의미도 이상해질 뿐 아니라 board가 주어가 되어 be made와 수일치도 안 맞게 된다. 이 문장은 빈칸 뒤에 명사절 접속사 that이 생략이 된 형태이고 빈칸은 주절의 동사 자리가 된다. 빈칸 뒤에 that이 생략된 명사절이 목적어로 있으므로 빈칸에는 능동태 동사가 와야 하므로 정답은 (A) proposed이다.

어휘 board *n.* 이사회 ㅣ insurance *n.* 보험

9. 시 공무원들은 새로운 유류세가 주차 교통혼잡을 감소시킬 것이라고 주장한다.

해설 보기에 모두 명사절을 이끄는 접속사가 나왔다. 빈칸에는 insist의 목적어 역할을 할 수 있는 명사절 접속사가 와야 한다. (B) what은 다음에 불완전한 문장이 와야 하므로 탈락이다. 나머지 보기 중에서 문맥상 '~라는 것'이라는 의미의 명사절을 이끄는 접속사 (A) that가 정답이다.

어휘 official *n.* 공무원, 임원 ㅣ insist *v.* 주장하다

10. 회사는 그래픽 디자이너가 너무 바쁘기 때문에 주간 회보를 중단할 것이다.

해설 빈칸 앞에 완벽한 문장이 나왔으므로 명사절 접속사 whether는 올 수 없다. therefore와 in addition은 접속부사로 두 개의 문장을 연결할 수 없다. 따라서 정답은 부사절 접속사인 (B) because이다.

어휘 end *v.* 종료하다 ㅣ newsletter *n.* 회보

11. 그 여론조사는 21-35세의 소비자들이 우리 경쟁사의 제품을 선호한다는 것을 보여준다.

해설 보기에 모두 명사절을 이끄는 접속사가 나왔다. 명사절은 명사의 기능을 하기 때문에 show의 목적어 역할을 할 수 있다. 하지만 what 다음에는 불완전한 문장이 와야 하므로 탈락이다. 나머지 보기 중에 문맥상 '~라는 것'이라고 해석되는 (A) that가 정답이다.

어휘 poll *n.* 여론조사 ㅣ show *v.* 나타내다, 보여주다

12. 오늘 A 회의실에서 인사부가 실시하는 신입직원 면접이 있다는 것을 유념하세요.

해설 that절을 이끄는 관용적인 형용사 표현도 존재한다. 「be aware that + 완전한 문장」의 형태로 정답은 (A) that이다.

어휘 aware *adj.* 알고 있는, 인지하고 있는

13. 기록에 따르면 당신은 연례 안과 정기검진을 받을 시기가 되었다.

해설 빈칸은 that절 내의 주어 자리이다. 주어 자리에는 목적격 대명사 them와 소유격 대명사 its, 그리고 재귀대명사 itself는 올 수 없으므로 정답은 (A) it이다.

어휘 record n. 기록 | indicate v. 나타내다, 보여주다 | exam n. 조사, 검사

14. 뛰어난 판매 실적을 고려해 보면 Mr. Wang이 급여 인상을 받았다는 것은 별로 놀랍지 않다.

해설 It은 가주어이고 that이 진주어이다. 「It ~ that ~」 구문으로 정답 (A) that이다.

어휘 given prep. ~을 고려할 때 | hardly adv. 거의 ~아니다 | surprising adj. 놀라운

15. Mr. Kim은 나흘간 해외로 출장을 갈 것이라고 말했다.

해설 빈칸에 부사절 접속사 (D) while과 등위접속사 (C) and가 오면 said의 목적어가 없으므로 정답이 될 수 없다. (A) that과 (B) what 중에서 빈칸 뒤에 완전한 절이 나와 있으므로 정답은 (A) that이다.

어휘 business trip 출장

16. 그 기술자는 정확히 무엇이 건물의 정전을 일으켰는지 알아낼 것이다.

해설 본동사 determine 뒤에 주어가 빠진 채 '동사 + 목적어' 형태의 불완전한 절이 연결되어 있으며, '무엇이 정전을 일으켰는지를 알아낼 것이다'라는 의미가 자연스러우므로 의문 대명사로 쓰인 (A) what이 정답이다.

어휘 technician n. 기술자, 기사 | determine v. 알아내다, 밝히다 | exactly adv. 정확히 | cause v. 일으키다, 발생시키다 | power failure 정전

17. 박스를 창고에 보내기 전에, 상표가 박스에 제대로 붙어 있는지 확실히 해두세요.

해설 ensure의 목적어 역할을 하는 명사가 필요하다. 또한 빈칸 다음에 주어와 동사가 왔으므로 빈칸에는 명사절을 이끄는 접속사가 필요하다. 명사절 접속사 (B), (C), (D) 중에서 문맥상 '~라는 것'이라는 의미가 가장 자연스러우므로 정답은 (B) that이다.

어휘 ensure v. 반드시 ~하게 하다, 보장하다 | label n. 상표 v. 라벨을 붙이다 | properly adv. 적절하게 | warehouse n. 창고

18. Milleott 사가 새 공장을 지을 것인지의 여부는 시장의 장기 동향에 달려 있다.

해설 접속사 (A)와 (C)를 빈칸에 넣으면 depend의 주어가 없으므로 정답이 될 수 없다. 전치사 (D)를 넣으면 빈칸 다음에 주어와 동사가 나올 수 없다. 따라서 명사절 접속사 whether를 넣으면 whether절이 명사로 depends에 주어가 되므로 정답은 (B) Whether이다.

어휘 depend on ~에 의존하다, ~에 달려 있다 | long-term adj. 장기적인

19. 증가된 양에도 불구하고, 96퍼센트의 소포가 예정대로 배달되었다.

해설 빈칸 다음에 명사가 나와 있으므로 빈칸은 전치사 자리이다. 따라서 정답은 (D) Despite이다.

어휘 volume n. 양, 음량 | package n. 소포, 상자 | deliver v. 배달하다 | on time 예정대로

20. 300달러 또는 그 이상을 구매한다면, Tamiloy 보석상 고객들은 구매한 것의 10%를 할인 받을 수 있다.

해설 두 개의 문장을 연결하는 부사절 접속사를 찾아야 한다. 「as long as」는 '만약 ~라면, 하기만 하면'의 부사절 접속사로 정답은 (D) as long as이다.

어휘 purchase v. 구매하다 n. 구매 | spend v. (돈을) 쓰다, (시간을) 보내다

UNIT 12. 형용사절 접속사

본서 p.118

+check   1. (B)   2. (C)   3. (D)   4. (C)

1. Statusville의 첫 번째 초등학교로서의 역할을 한 Kellogg 가에 있는 Shireton Manor가 완전히 리모델링 될 것이다.

해설 콤마와 콤마 사이는 수식어구가 들어가야 한다. 따라서 they나 what(=the thing which)은 답이 될 수 없다. what은 명사절 접속사이기도 하고, 선행사를 포함한 관계대명사이기도 하다. 둘이 서로 같은 말이다. 이때 'what = the thing which'로, 선행사 the thing을 포함하고 있기 때문에 앞에 선행사 Shireton Manor와 겹쳐서 답이 될 수 없다. 빈칸 뒤에 주어가 없으므로 주격 관계대명사이고 선행사는 사물(Shireton Manor)이므로 정답은 (B) which이다.

어휘 serve v. 도움이 되다, 기여하다 | remodel v. 개조하다

2. 요청하셨던 회원 가입 신청서를 첨부 파일에서 확인하시고 신청서를 꼼꼼히 작성해 주십시오.

해설 빈칸 앞은 명령문 구조로서 완벽한 문장이다. 빈칸 뒤부터는 수식어구인데, 빈칸 뒤에 request의 목적어가 빠져 있으니 목적격 관계대명사 수식어구를 찾아야 한다. 선행사가 사물(application)이므로 정답은 (C) that이다.

어휘 attached adj. 첨부된 | membership application 회원 신청서 | fill out 작성하다 | completely adv. 완전히

3. 미술관이 선정한 작품의 화가들은 모두 4월 2일까지 연락 받을 것이다.

해설 빈칸부터 gallery까지 주어 All artists를 수식하는 수식어구이다. 빈칸 뒤에 수동태로 완벽한 문장이 왔다. 즉, 완벽한 문장을 이끌며 선행사를 수식할 수 있는 소유격 관계대명사가 정답이다. 따라서 정답은 (D) whose이다.

어휘 artist n. 화가, 예술가 | contact v. 연락하다

4. 지원서 5번 박스에, 면접을 위해 당신이 가장 시간이 되는 특정 날짜 표시를 해 주세요.

해설 빈칸 앞, 뒤로 완전한 문장이 연결되어 있으므로 불완전한 문장을 이 끄는 (A) what은 먼저 답에서 제외시킨다. 완전한 문장을 이끌면서 앞에 오는 시간 명사(date)를 꾸며 주는 관계부사 (C) when이 정답 이다. (D) where는 관계부사로 쓰일 때 앞에 장소 명사를 취한다.

어휘 application *n.* 지원서 I indicate *v.* 표시하다 I particular *adj.* 특정한 I available *adj.* 시간이 있는

....

Practice

본서 p.122

1. (C)	**2.** (A)	**3.** (B)	**4.** (C)	**5.** (B)
6. (A)	**7.** (A)	**8.** (B)	**9.** (A)	**10.** (A)
11. (C)	**12.** (A)	**13.** (B)	**14.** (B)	**15.** (B)
16. (C)	**17.** (A)	**18.** (D)	**19.** (B)	**20.** (B)

기본 완성 훈련

1. Many of the applicants (who applied for the job) were well-qualified.

2. Starshine Corp., (whose advertisements appear frequently on TV), is launching a new product.

3. The document (which describes the new marketing strategies) will be on your desk by tomorrow.

4. Subscribers (who do not receive their magazines by August 15) should contact the customer service center.

5. Red Cedar Plant, (which manufactures recycled paper products), has relocated to Midville.

6. Some replacement parts (that were shipped to LNK Warehouses) never arrived.

7. The list of employees (who are promoted) will be announced tomorrow.

8. JAK Frequent Traveler members (whose enrollment ends this month) should pay their fees by the 26th.

9. Fuel prices, (which have increased steadily for months), are forecast to go down in September.

10. Any items left in the building (which are not claimed within a week) will be discarded.

....

1. 그 자리에 지원한 많은 지원자들은 매우 자격이 있었다.

해설 빈칸은 주어 Many of the applicants와 동사 applied 사이에 있으 므로 수식어구가 들어가야 한다. 빈칸 뒤에 주어가 없으므로 주격 관 계대명사가 오면 정답이 될 수 있다. when은 관계부사로 완벽한 문장 이 나와야 한다. what 앞에는 선행사가 올 수 없으므로 이 역시 탈락 이다. 따라서 정답은 (C) who이다.

어휘 applicant *n.* 지원자 I well-qualified *adj.* 매우 자격이 있는

2. 우리가 검토한 제안서는 이사회에서 발표될 것이다.

해설 주어는 The proposal이고 동사는 will be이므로 그 사이에 낀 부분 은 수식어구이다. 빈칸 뒤에 reviewed의 목적어가 빠져 있으므로 목 적격 관계대명사가 와야 하며 선행사는 사물(proposal)이므로 정답은 (A) which이다.

어휘 proposal *n.* 제안서 I review *v.* 검토하다 *n.* 검토 I present *v.* 발표하다

3. TV에 자주 광고를 내는 Starshine 사는 신제품을 출시할 것이다.

해설 빈칸 뒤에는 1형식의 완벽한 문장이 왔으므로 소유격 관계대명사를 찾 아야 한다. 따라서 정답은 (B) whose이다.

어휘 advertisement *n.* 광고 I appear *v.* 나타나다

4. 새 마케팅 전략을 설명해 주는 서류는 내일 책상에 놓겠습니다.

해설 관계대명사 which 다음에 올 수 있는 동사 자리이다. 주격 관계대명 사 뒤의 동사는 반드시 선행사(document)와 수 일치를 해야 하므로 정답은 (C) describes이다.

어휘 marketing strategy 마케팅 전략

5. Crowde 개발은 Falcon Central Complex에 대한 디자인이 거의 완료되었다는 것을 발표했다.

해설 빈칸에는 announce의 목적어 역할을 할 수 있고 뒤에 있는 절 을 이끌 수 있는 명사절 접속사가 필요하다. 부사절 접속사인 (C) because, (D) while는 답이 될 수 없고 빈칸 뒤에 완전한 절이 나와 있으므로 정답은 (B) that이다.

어휘 announce *v.* 알리다, 발표하다 I almost *adv.* 거의 I complete *v.* 완료하다

6. 8월 15일까지 잡지를 받지 못한 구독자들은 고객 서비스 센터로 연락 해야 한다.

해설 who 앞에 사람 선행사가 필요하다. 사람 명사로는 (A)와 (B)가 가 능한데, who 다음에 나온 동사가 복수 동사이므로 선행사 역시 복수 명사가 와야 한다. 정답은 (A) Subscribers이다.

어휘 receive *v.* 받다 I contact *v.* 연락하다 I subscriber *n.* 구독자

7. Dr. Kim은 연례 건강 검진 전 12시간동안 식사를 하지 말라고 요청했 다.

해설 이 문장에서 that은 선행사가 없으므로 관계대명사가 아니고 명사절 을 이끄는 접속사이다. 빈칸은 that절 내의 주어이므로 주격 대명사가 들어가야 한다. 따라서 정답은 (A) we이다.

어휘 request *v.* 요청하다 I health check-up 건강 검진

8. 재생 종이 제품을 제조하는 Red Cedar 공장은 Midville로 이전했다.

해설 빈칸 다음에 주어가 없기 때문에 접속사 (A)와 관계부사 (C)는 답이 될 수 없다. 왜냐하면 접속사와 관계부사 모두 완벽한 문장이 따라와야 하기 때문이다. 따라서 빈칸에는 주격 관계대명사가 와야 하며, 선행사가 사물인 Red Cedar Plant이므로 정답은 (B)와 (D)가 될 수 있지만, that은 콤마와 함께 쓸 수 없으므로 정답은 (B) which이다.

어휘 manufacture v. 제조하다

9. 영업팀이 고용한 인턴들 중의 한 명이 일을 매우 잘하고 있다.

해설 이 문장은 접속사가 없는데 동사가 두 개인 점을 고려하여, interns 뒤에 목적격 관계대명사 whom이 생략되었다는 것은 파악해야 한다. 따라서 이 문장의 주어는 one이고 빈칸이 동사 자리이다. 주어가 단수이므로 단수동사 (A) is가 정답이다.

어휘 hire v. 고용하다 I perform v. 수행하다 I exceptionally adv. 특별히

10. 새 소프트웨어를 사용할 사람들을 위한 교육은 오전 9시로 일정이 잡혔다.

해설 이 문장의 주어는 A training session이고 동사는 is scheduled 이므로 그 사이에는 수식어구가 와야 한다. 빈칸 다음에 주어가 없기 때문에 주격 관계대명사가 와야 하며, 선행사가 사람들(those = people)이므로 정답은 (A) who이다.

어휘 training session 교육 훈련 I schedule v. 일정을 잡다

11. LNK 사의 창고로 배송된 교체 부품 일부가 아예 도착하지 않았다.

해설 that이 주격 관계대명사로 쓰였기 때문에 빈칸에는 동사가 들어가야 한다. 빈칸 다음에 목적어도 없으므로 수동태를 찾아야 하며, 정답은 (B)와 (C)가 될 수 있다. 하지만 선행사가 복수이므로 정답은 (C) were shipped이다.

어휘 replacement parts 교체 부품

12. 승진된 직원들의 명단이 내일 발표될 것이다.

해설 빈칸 뒤에 주어가 없으므로 빈칸에는 주격 관계대명사가 와야 한다. 선행사는 list와 employees가 될 수 있지만, 빈칸 다음의 동사 are를 통해 선행사가 복수인 employees임을 알 수 있다. 따라서 정답은 (A) who이다.

어휘 promote v. 승진시키다. 홍보하다 I announce v. 발표하다

13. 그 연구조사는 생물학 분야에서 상을 받았던 세 명의 연구원들에 의해 수행되었다.

해설 빈칸 다음에 주어가 없으므로 접속사 because는 올 수 없다. what 앞에는 선행사가 올 수 없으므로 이 역시 정답이 될 수 없다. 따라서 빈칸에는 주격 관계대명사가 와야 하며, 선행사는 사람(three researchers)이므로 정답은 (B) who이다.

어휘 study n. 연구 조사 I conduct v. 수행하다 I field n. 분야 I biology n. 생물학

14. 5,000명의 관중들을 수용할 수 있는 확장된 **PG** 스포츠 종합 단지는 10월에 문을 열 예정이다.

해설 콤마와 콤마 사이에는 수식어구가 온다. 빈칸 다음에 주어가 없으므로 주격 관계대명사가 와야 하며, 선행사가 사물(PG Sports Complex)이므로 정답은 (B)와 (C)가 될 수 있다. that 앞에는 콤마를 사용할 수 없으므로 정답은 (B) which이다.

어휘 expand v. 확장하다 I accommodate v. 수용하다 I spectator n. 관중

15. 현재 서울에서 AC 테크놀로지 공장을 관리하는 Mr. Kang이 다음 달에 운영 부사장으로 승진할 것이다.

해설 문장의 주어는 Mr. Kang, 본동사는 will be promoted이므로 빈칸은 주어와 본동사 사이에 들어갈 주어가 빠진 불완전한 절을 이어줄 수 있는 관계대명사가 필요한 자리이다. 이때 선행사는 Mr. Kang으로 사람이며, 빈칸 앞에 콤마가 있는 계속적 용법으로 쓰인 문장이므로 정답은 (B) who이다.

어휘 currently adv. 현재 I plant n. 공장 I promote v. 승진시키다

16. Ms. Lang은 Mr. Yoon이 왜 그의 예산 보고서를 늦게 제출했는지 알고 싶어한다.

해설 빈칸에는 뒤에 연결된 완전한 절을 이끌어 동사 know의 목적어 역할을 해야 하는 자리이므로 명사절 접속사가 들어갈 자리이다. 따라서 앞뒤로 완전한 절이 필요한 부사절 접속사 (B)나 불완전한 절을 이끄는 관계대명사 (D)를 답에서 제외시키면, 의문부사 (A)와 (C)가 남는데, Mr. Yoon이 왜 보고서를 늦게 제출했는지를 알고 싶어한다는 의미가 적절하므로 이유를 나타내는 (C) why가 정답이다.

어휘 submit v. 제출하다 I budget report 예산 보고서 I late adv. 늦게

17. 최근에 회사는 직원들에게 은퇴 계획에 대하여 묻는 설문 조사를 실시했다.

해설 명사절 접속사 whether와 if, 부사절 접속사 since 다음에는 모두 완벽한 문장이 와야 한다. 빈칸 뒤에는 주어가 있지 않으므로 (A)의 that을 명사절 접속사가 아닌 주격 관계대명사 that으로 보고 선행사 survey를 수식한다고 보면 정답은 (A) that이다.

어휘 recently adv. 최근에 I carry out 실시하다 I survey n. 설문 조사 I retirement n. 은퇴 I plan n. 계획

18. 이번 달에 회원 기간이 끝나는 JAK 상용 여행자 회원들은 26까지 회비를 내야 한다.

해설 이 문장의 주어는 members이고 동사는 should pay이다. 따라서 빈칸에는 앞 명사 members를 수식하는 형용사절 접속사 즉, 관계 대명사가 들어가야 하며, 빈칸 다음은 1형식의 완벽한 문장이므로 소유격 관계대명사가 들어가야 한다. 따라서 정답은 (D) whose이다.

어휘 enrollment n. 등록 I end v. 끝나다

19. 유가가 몇 달 동안 꾸준히 증가해왔지만 9월에는 내려갈 전망이다.

해설 빈칸은 문장의 주어이면서 동시에 관계대명사 which의 선행사 자리이다. 따라서 명사가 와야 하고, which 다음의 복수 동사 have를 통해 빈칸에는 복수 명사가 나와야 함을 알 수 있다. 따라서 정답은 (B) prices이다.

어휘 steadily adv. 꾸준하게 I forecast v. 예측하다

20. 건물 내에 남겨두고 1주일 이내에 찾아가지 않는 물품은 폐기될 예정입니다.

해설 which는 주격 관계대명사이고 선행사가 building이 아니라 items이다. 복수 동사가 와야 하므로 정답은 (B)와 (D)가 될 수 있다. claim의 목적어가 없기 때문에 수동태를 찾아야 하므로 정답은 (B) are이다.

어휘 claim v. 주장하다, 요구하다 | discard v. 버리다, 폐기하다

REVIEW TEST 03
본서 p.124

1. (C)	2. (B)	3. (B)	4. (B)	5. (D)
6. (D)	7. (C)	8. (A)	9. (C)	10. (D)
11. (A)	12. (A)	13. (B)	14. (B)	15. (A)
16. (C)	17. (C)	18. (B)	19. (C)	20. (C)
21. (A)	22. (D)	23. (D)	24. (A)	25. (B)
26. (D)	27. (A)	28. (A)	29. (C)	30. (B)

1. 그 프로젝트를 위한 아이디어가 채택된 직원은 누구든지 상금을 받을 것이다.

해설 빈칸 다음은 완전한 수동태 문장이므로 빈칸에는 소유격 관계대명사가 필요하다. 선행사가 사람(employee)이므로 정답은 (C) whose이다.

어휘 adopt v. 채택하다 | award n. 상

2. 매출 신장을 위한 다양한 노력에도 불구하고, 회사의 이윤은 증가하지 않았다.

해설 빈칸 뒤에 명사가 왔다. 따라서 빈칸은 전치사 자리이므로 부사인 (A)는 소거한다. 전치사는 (B)가 문맥상 '~에도 불구하고'가 적합하므로 정답은 (B) Despite이다.

어휘 boost v. 신장시키다 | revenue n. 이윤, 수입

3. Ms. Wilson은 곧 은퇴하는데, 우수 직원상을 수여 받을 것이다.

해설 빈칸에 주격 대명사 (A)를 넣으면 문장이 되어 버리므로 답이 될 수 없다. 콤마와 콤마 사이에는 문장이 아닌 수식어구가 들어가야 한다. 빈칸 다음에 주어가 없으므로 빈칸에는 주격 관계대명사가 와야 하고, 선행사가 사람(Ms. Wilson)이므로 정답은 (B) who이다.

어휘 retire v. 은퇴하다 | present v. 수여하다

4. Jackie 식당의 스테이크 요리는 밥이나 스위트 감자 중 하나의 사이드 메뉴와 함께 제공된다.

해설 either 뒤에 rice와 sweet potatoes가 연결되어 있는 구조이므로 상관접속사 either A or B (A, B 둘 중 하나)를 떠올릴 수 있어야 한다. 따라서 정답은 (B) or이다.

어휘 dish n. 요리 | come with ~이 딸려 있다

5. 주로 젊은 근로자들에게 많이 의존하는 매장들은 적합한 지원자를 찾는 데 애를 먹고 있다.

해설 관계대명사 that 다음에는 동사가 꼭 필요하므로 빈칸에는 동사가 와야 한다. 선행사는 복수(stores)이므로 정답은 복수 동사 (D) rely이다.

어휘 heavily adv. 심하게, 아주 많이, 무겁게 | rely v. 의지하다

6. 그 조립 기계는 오늘 필요한 부품이 도착하기만 하면 내일 수리될 것이다.

해설 빈칸 앞뒤로 주어, 동사를 갖춘 절이 연결되어 있으므로 두 절을 이어줄 수 있는 부사절 접속사가 필요한 자리이며, 필요한 부품이 도착하기만 하면 수리될 거라는 의미가 적절하므로 '~하는 한, ~하기만 하면'이라는 뜻의 (D) as long as가 정답이다.

어휘 assembly n. 조립 | fix v. 수리하다 | part n. 부품

7. 세무 사무소의 결론은 그 회사가 예산 책정을 개선할 필요가 있다는 것이었다.

해설 (A)와 (D)는 빈칸 앞에 선행사가 없으므로 답이 될 수 없다. (B) what 다음에는 불완전한 문장이 와야 하는데 완전한 문장이 왔으므로 답이 될 수 없다. (C)는 빈칸 앞에 선행사가 없으므로 관계대명사가 아닌 명사절로 봐야 한다. 명사절을 이끄는 접속사 that 다음에 완전한 문장이 올 수 있고, that절이 명사로 이 문장에서 주격 보어 역할을 하므로 정답은 (C) that이다.

어휘 conclusion n. 결론 | tax consulting firm 세무 사무소 | budgeting n. 예산 편성

8. 그 임대차 계약서는 세입자와 임대주가 사인하기만 하면 공인될 것이다.

해설 빈칸 앞뒤로 주어, 동사를 갖춘 절이 연결되어 있으므로 두 절을 이어줄 수 있는 부사절 접속사가 필요한 자리이며, 계약서에 사인하는 대로 공인될 거라는 의미가 적절하므로 '~하기만 하면; ~하자마자'라는 뜻의 (A) once가 정답이다.

어휘 lease agreement 임대차 계약(서) | official adj. 공인된, 공식적인 | tenant n. 세입자 | landlord n. 임대주

9. Go Aid는 아시아 전역의 생활 환경을 개선하는 것을 목표로 하는 단체이다.

해설 what 앞에는 선행사가 올 수 없으므로 답이 될 수 없다. 빈칸 다음에 2형식의 완전한 문장이 왔으므로 빈칸에는 소유격 관계대명사가 와야 한다. 선행사가 사물(an organization)이므로 정답은 (C) whose이다.

어휘 living condition 생활 환경

10. FG 광고는 저렴한 요금을 제공하는 반면 DTO 광고는 평판이 더 좋다.

해설 빈칸에는 두 개의 문장을 연결하는 접속사가 와야 한다. 등위 접속사 (B)는 문두에 올 수 없고, 접속부사 (C)는 부사이므로 문장을 연결할 수 없다. (A)와 (D) 중에서 문맥상 '반면에'가 적합하므로 정답은 (D) While이다.

어휘 advertising n. 광고, 광고업 | reasonable adj. 가격이 저렴한

11. 제 10회 조경 콘퍼런스에서 Ms. Petal은 그녀가 지난달에 디자인한 정원 설계도를 발표할 것이다.

해설 이 문장에는 동사가 두 개인데 접속사가 없다. 따라서 선행사 plan 뒤에 앞에는 목적격 관계대명사 which가 생략되었음을 파악하면 빈칸은 designed의 주어자리라는 것을 알 수 있으므로 정답은 (A) she이다.

어휘 present v. 발표하다 | gardening plan 정원 설계도

12. 구매 부서는 Adalet사에서 새 복사기를 구매할지를 결정할 것이다.

해설 빈칸에는 guarantee의 목적어 역할을 할 수 있고 뒤에 있는 절을 이끌 수 있는 명사절 접속사가 필요하다. 명사절 접속사가 아닌 (B) neither와 (D) even if는 답이 될 수 없고 뒤에 주어, 동사가 있는 완전한 절이 아니라 to부정사가 나와 있으므로 정답은 (A) whether이다.

어휘 purchase v. 구매하다 | photocopier n. 복사기

13. 국제 무역을 규제하는 법이 개정되었다.

해설 which라는 관계대명사 다음에는 동사가 와야 한다. 그러나 international trade는 복합 명사이므로 빈칸은 동사 자리이다. 빈칸 다음에 international trade가 있으므로 능동태를 찾아야 하고, 선행사가 단수(the law)이므로 단수 동사를 찾아야 한다. 따라서 정답은 (B) regulates이다.

어휘 regulate v. 규제하다, 조절하다 | international trade 국제무역

14. 우리는 그 부품들이 즉시 교체되어야 한다고 요청했지만, 수리 예약을 잡는 데는 며칠이 걸렸다.

해설 빈칸에는 두 개의 문장을 연결하는 접속사가 필요하다. (A)와 (C)는 접속부사로 문장을 연결할 수 없고, (D)는 등위접속사로 문두에 올 수 없다. 따라서 정답은 양보접속사 (B) Although이다.

어휘 request v. 요청하다 n. 요청 | immediate adj. 즉각적인 | replacement n. 교체

15. 우리는 아시아 시장에서의 판매를 증대시켜 줄 프로젝트를 시작했다.

해설 unless는 조건 접속사로 두 개의 문장을 연결해 주지만, 빈칸 다음에 주어가 없으므로 탈락이다. that이 빈칸에 오면 주격 관계대명사로 선행사 project를 수식하게 되므로 정답은 (A) that이다.

어휘 sales n. 판매(량)

16. Ms. Kang과 Ms. Lee 둘 다 기획위원회에 임명되지 않았다.

해설 빈칸 뒤에 'A (Ms. Kang) nor B (Ms. Lee)' 구조가 연결되어 있으므로 상관접속사 「neither A nor B: A, B 둘 다 아닌」를 떠올릴 수 있어야 한다. 따라서 정답은 (C) neither이다.

어휘 appoint v. 임명하다 | planning committee 기획위원회

17. 만약 미납 지불이 없다면, 고객은 24시간 기술 지원을 받을 수 있다.

해설 두 개의 문장을 연결하는 접속사가 필요하다. (A)는 전치사이고 (B)는 접속부사이다. 부사절 접속사 (C)와 (D) 중에 문맥상 적합한 (C) unless가 정답이다.

어휘 outstanding adj. 미지불된, 미해결된, 뛰어난, 두드러진 | payment n. 지불

18. 그녀의 비행기가 지연되었기 때문에, Ms. Kang은 주주총회에 참석할 수 없었다.

해설 빈칸에는 두 개의 문장을 연결할 수 있는 접속사가 필요하다. (A)와 (D)는 전치사이고 (C)는 관계부사이다. 문맥상 '~때문에'라는 의미의 접속사가 들어가는 것이 적합하므로 정답은 (B) as이다.

어휘 delay v. 미루다, 연기하다 | shareholder n. 주주

19. B&C 상점은 많은 고객 불만사항을 받은 직후 반품 정책을 변경했다.

해설 빈칸 다음에 전치사 after가 있다. (A)와 (B)는 접속사로 다음에 주어와 동사가 와야 하므로 정답이 될 수 없다. (D)는 전치사로 뒤에 명사가 와야 하므로 탈락이다. '~직후에'라는 의미의 shortly after는 문맥상 잘 어울리므로 정답은 (C) Shortly이다.

어휘 return policy 반품정책 | shortly adv. 곧

20. 에너지를 절약하기 위해 건물에서 나가기 전에 컴퓨터를 꺼 주세요.

해설 빈칸 다음에 -ing 형태의 동명사가 있다. (B)와 (D)는 접속사이므로 뒤에 주어와 동사가 와야 하고, (A)는 접속부사이다. (C)는 접속사와 전치사의 역할 모두 가능하지만, 빈칸 다음에 동명사가 왔으므로 정답은 전치사로 쓰인 (C) before이다.

어휘 turn off 끄다 | leave v. 떠나다

21. 우리는 공장의 전체 조립 라인 문제를 점검할 수 있는 새 장치를 가지고 있다.

해설 (D) near는 전치사로 다음에 동사가 올 수 없다. 빈칸 다음에 주어가 없으므로 that이 빈칸에 오면 주격 관계대명사로 선행사 device를 꾸미게 되므로 정답은 주격 관계대명사 (A) that이다.

어휘 check v. 점검하다 | entire adj. 전체의 | assembly n. 조립

22. 그 회사는 생산 지연에도 불구하고 새 RVM-593 전화기를 일정대로 출시했다.

해설 빈칸 뒤에 명사가 나오므로 전치사인 (D) In spite of가 정답이다.

어휘 release v. 발표하다, 출시하다 | on schedule 예정대로, 일정대로

23. 투어를 오전 정각 10시에 시작할 수 있도록 모든 가이드 여러분은 오전 9시까지 출근하시기 바랍니다.

해설 두 개의 문장을 연결하는 부사절 접속사를 찾아야 한다. (A)는 명사절 접속사로 정답이 될 수 없다. (B), (C), (D) 중에 문맥상 적절한 것은 (D) so that이다.

어휘 promptly adv. 정확히, 제시간에

24. 모든 서비스 계약서는 관리자와 판매 사원 모두에 의해 서명되어야 한다.

해설 「both A and B」는 'A B 둘 다 모두' 구문의 형태로 정답은 (A) both이다.

어휘 sign v. 서명하다 | sales representative 판매 사원

25. 세미나에 참석하기를 원하는 사람들은 Ms. Lee에게 10월 24일까지 연락해야 한다.

해설 빈칸은 who의 선행사 자리이므로 사람이 와야 한다. 또한 빈칸은 주어 자리이므로 소유격 대명사인 (D) Their는 답이 될 수 없다. (C) They는 대명사이기 때문에 관계대명사의 수식을 받을 수 없다. (A)와 (B)가 가능한데 who 다음의 동사가 wants라는 단수 동사이므로 정답은 (B) Anyone이다.

어휘 attend v. 참석하다 | contact v. 연락하다

26. 그 보고서는 회의 전에 Carol이 수정해야 하는 수치들을 포함하고 있다.

해설 that은 목적격 관계대명사로 선행사 figures를 수식한다. 빈칸에는 동사가 와야 하는데, (C)는 동사가 아니라서 탈락이고 (A)는 주어가 단수이므로 단수 동사인 corrects가 와야 하므로 탈락. 빈칸 다음에 목적어가 없는 이유는 that이 목적격 관계대명사이기 때문이다. 그러므로 목적어가 없는 것이 아니라 앞에 있는 것이므로 수동태 (B) has been corrected는 답이 될 수 없다. 따라서 정답은 (D) will correct 이다.

어휘 figure n. 수치 | correct v. 수정하다

27. Mr. Kim은 내일 마감인 보고서를 작성하고 있다.

해설 빈칸 앞에 선행사 the report가 있고 빈칸 뒤에는 동사 is가 있으므로 빈칸에는 주격 관계대명사 (A) that이 정답이다. since는 전치사 혹은 접속사인데, 이것들은 뒤에 동사가 올 수 없으므로 정답이 될 수 없다.

어휘 due adj. 기한이 된

28. 파트타임 직원들은 어젯밤 수정된 일정표를 확인해야 합니다.

해설 빈칸 앞에 선행사 the schedule이 있고 빈칸 뒤에 동사 was revised가 있으므로 빈칸에 들어가야 하는 정답은 주격 관계대명사 (A) which이다.

어휘 part-time adj. 파트타임인 | revise v. 수정하다

29. Ms. Shim에게 당신이 프로젝트 매니저를 맡아줄 수 있는지 금요일까지 알려 주세요.

해설 빈칸 뒤의 절이 빈칸 앞 동사 know의 목적어가 되도록 명사절 접속사를 선택해야 한다. 보기 중 명사절 접속사는 whether밖에 없으므로 (C) whether가 정답이다.

어휘 available adj. 시간이 있는 | lead v. 이끌다

30. 새 주민센터에 관한 기사는 편집장에 의해 검토되는 대로 발행될 것이다.

해설 빈칸 앞뒤로 주어, 동사를 갖춘 절이 연결되어 있으므로 두 절을 이어줄 수 있는 부사절 접속사가 필요한 자리이며, 편집장이 그 기사를 검토하는 대로 발행될 거라는 의미가 적절하므로 '~하자마자'라는 뜻의 (B) as soon as가 정답이다.

어휘 community center 주민센터 | review v. 검토하다 | chief editor 편집장

UNIT 13. to부정사
본서 p.128

check   1. (A)   2. (C)   3. (A)   4. (A)

1. Dytex 사는 모든 매니저들이 분기별 워크숍에 참석하는 것을 필수 요건으로 두고 있다.

해설 문맥상 의미상의 주어는 all managers이다. 따라서 의미상의 주어를 쓸 때는 전치사 for가 앞에 위치하므로 정답은 (A) for이다. '매니저들이 워크숍에 참석하는 것이 필수 요건이다.'에서 '참석하는 것'은 문법상의 주어이고, '매니저들'은 의미상의 주어이다.

어휘 requirement n. 필수 요건 | attend v. 참석하다 | quarterly adj. 분기의

2. 기념일 축하를 위한 가장 인기 있는 방법 중 하나는 야유회를 가는 것이다.

해설 이 문장의 주어는 one이고 동사는 is이다. 따라서 그 사이에 있는 부분은 모두 수식어구이다. way라는 명사는 항상 to부정사의 수식을 받는 명사이므로 정답은 (C) to celebrate이다.

어휘 anniversary n. 기념일 | picnic n. 야유회, 소풍

3. 우리는 가까운 시일 내에 당신으로부터 소식 듣기를 바랍니다.

해설 빈칸 앞에 동사 hear가 있기 때문에 동사 (B) hear와 (D) heard는 답이 될 수 없고, 빈칸 앞의 hope의 목적어가 와야 할 자리인데 hope는 목적어로 to부정사를 취하는 동사이다. 따라서 정답은 (A) to hear이다.

어휘 hope v. 바라다 | in the near future 가까운 시일 내에

4. Emerson은 자사의 모든 직원들이 정직과 공정성을 가지고 거래에 임할 것을 기대한다.

해설 expect라는 동사는 5형식 동사로 목적격 보어 자리에 to부정사를 취한다. 빈칸은 목적격 보어 자리이므로 정답은 (A) to conduct이다.

어휘 expect A to B A가 B할 것을 기대하다 | dealing n. 거래 (행위) | honesty n. 정직성, 솔직함 | fairness n. 공정성

Practice
본서 p.132

1. (A)   **2.** (D)   **3.** (A)   **4.** (B)   **5.** (B)

6. (A)   **7.** (C)   **8.** (D)   **9.** (C)   **10.** (C)

11. (A)   **12.** (D)   **13.** (A)   **14.** (A)   **15.** (A)

16. (A)   **17.** (A)   **18.** (D)   **19.** (A)   **20.** (B)

1. Because the weather is unusually cold, Matton Hotels are currently offering discount coupons to attract customers.

2. Due to the low sales figures, we made a decision to discontinue the Bluestone Bicycle line.

3. The Human Resources Department asked employees to submit ideas to improve workplace performance.

4. The President of JBK Company has decided to offer university students internships this summer.

5. The employees are happy to discuss ways to improve customer services.

6. The company is committed to increasing its domestic sales.

7. Requirements for the editor position include a journalism degree.

8. The restaurant is planning a special menu to celebrate its fifth anniversary.

9. To get to the Roseblossom Café, use the elevator on the south side of the lobby.

10. The city council organized the town hall meeting to be held on May 20.

---

1. 날씨가 이례적으로 춥기 때문에 Matton 호텔들은 고객들을 끌어들이기 위해 현재 할인 쿠폰을 제공하고 있다.

해설　주절에는 이미 3형식의 완전한 문장이 왔으므로, 빈칸은 필요 없는 수식어구이다. 문장 맨 마지막에 오는 수식어구는 보통 부사이다. to부정사는 '~하기 위해서'라는 의미로 부사 기능을 하므로 정답은 (A) to attract이다.

어휘　weather n. 날씨 | unusually adv. 이례적으로 | attract v. 끌어들이다

2. 낮은 매출액 때문에 우리는 Bluestone 자전거 제품군을 단종 시키기로 결정했다.

해설　주절은 3형식 문장으로 완전하므로 빈칸은 필요 없는 수식어구이다. decision이라는 명사는 to부정사의 수식을 받는 어휘이므로 정답은 (D) to discontinue이다.

어휘　low adj. 낮은 | sales figures 매출액

3. 인사부는 직원들에게 업무 성과를 향상시키기 위한 아이디어를 제출하라고 요청했다.

해설　ask는 5형식 동사로 목적격 보어 자리에 to부정사가 들어간다. 목적어는 employees이고 빈칸이 목적격 보어 자리이므로 정답은 (A) to submit이다.

어휘　human resources department 인사부 | submit v. 제출하다

4. JBK 회사의 사장은 올 여름 대학생들에게 인턴직을 제공하기로 결정했다.

해설　빈칸은 동사 자리이다. (A)는 명사이고, to부정사와 -ing 형태는 동사가 될 수 없으니 정답은 (B) has decided이다.

어휘　internship n. 인턴직, 인턴사원 근무 (기간)

5. 직원들은 고객 서비스를 향상시키기 위한 방법에 관해 토론하게 되어 기쁘다.

해설　이미 2형식의 완전한 문장이므로 빈칸부터는 수식어구가 와야 하며, 문맥상 그 수식어구는 happy라는 형용사를 꾸며야 한다. 보기 중에 형용사를 꾸미는 부사 기능을 할 수 있는 것은 to부정사 밖에 없으므로 정답은 (B) to discuss이다.

어휘　way n. 방법, 방식 | discuss v. 토론하다

6. 그 회사는 국내 판매를 증진시키는 것에 전념한다.

해설　「be committed to」에서 to는 to부정사가 아닌 전치사 to이다. 따라서 to 다음에는 동사원형이 아니라, 명사나 동명사가 나와야 한다. 이 문장에서는 빈칸 뒤에 명사가 나오므로 빈칸에는 동명사가 와야 한다. 빈칸 뒤에 나오는 명사는 동명사의 목적어라 할 수 있다. 따라서 정답은 (A) increasing이다.

어휘　commit v. 헌신하다, 전념하다 | domestic adj. 국내의

7. 편집자 자리를 위한 요건들에는 저널리즘 학위를 포함한다.

해설　빈칸은 주어 자리이므로 명사가 와야 한다. 보기에서 명사 역할을 할 수 있는 것은 (A), (B), (C)이지만 동명사 Requiring과 to부정사 To require는 동사의 성질을 가지기 때문에 목적어가 따라와야 하므로 정답은 (C) Requirements이다.

어휘　requirement n. 요건, 요구 | editor n. 편집자 | position n. 자리, 직책 | journalism n. 저널리즘, 언론계 | degree n. 학위

8. Okoms Global 은행은 외국어를 배우는 것에 강한 흥미가 있는 직원들을 고용하길 원한다.

해설　빈칸은 전치사 다음에 있다. 전치사 다음에는 명사나 동명사가 올 수 있고, to부정사는 올 수 없다. 따라서 (A)는 탈락이고, 동사인 (B)와 (C)도 탈락이다. 따라서 정답은 (D) learning이다.

어휘　interest n. 관심, 흥미 | learn v. 배우다

9. 무더위는 월말까지 계속될 것으로 보인다.

해설　「be likely + to부정사」이므로 정답은 (C) to last이다.

어휘　heat wave 무더위, 장기간의 혹서 | likely adj. ~할 것 같은 | through prep. ~동안, 쭉 내내

10. 이 자리에 지원하기 위해, 회사 웹사이트를 방문하세요.

해설 「------ + 전명구, 명령문」구조이므로 빈칸은 부사구를 이끌어야 하므로 부사적으로 쓰일 수 있는 to부정사 (C) To apply 가 정답이다.

어휘 apply for ~에 지원하다

11. 경매에서 팔릴 모든 물건들은 사전에 조사되어야 한다.

해설 주어 All items와 동사 must be inspected 사이에 수식어구가 필요한 자리이다. 주어와 동사 사이에 오는 수식어구는 보통 주어(명사)를 수식하므로 형용사 기능을 하는 것이 와야 한다. (B)와 (C)는 동사이므로 탈락이고, to부정사는 형용사 기능을 하므로 가능하다. 이 문장에서 sell의 목적어가 없으므로 to부정사를 수동태 형태로 써야 하기 때문에 정답은 (A) to be sold이다.

어휘 sell v. 팔다 | beforehand adv. 미리, 사전에

12. 소유주들은 더 많은 고객을 끌어들이기 위해 식당을 개조하려고 계획하고 있다.

해설 빈칸에는 동사 plan의 목적어가 필요한데, 동명사를 목적어로 취하지 않기 때문에 (A)는 정답이 될 수 없고, 과거분사 (B)는 빈칸 뒤에 목적어 the restaurant가 있기 때문에 사용할 수 없다. plan은 to 부정사를 목적어로 사용하는데, 빈칸 뒤에 목적어가 있기 때문에 능동태인 (D) to remodel이 정답이다.

어휘 attract v. 끌어들이다 | remodel v. 개조하다

13. 구독을 갱신하기 위해서는 온라인 설문조사를 먼저 작성해야 한다.

해설 「in order to + 동사원형」이므로 정답은 (A) renew이다.

어휘 subscription n. 구독 | renew v. 갱신하다

14. 인사부는 IT 분야에서 경력이 있는 직원들을 더 고용하고자 한다.

해설 hope은 to부정사만을 목적어로 취하는 동사이므로 정답은 (A) to hire이다.

어휘 hope v. 희망하다 | hire v. 고용하다

15. 그 레스토랑은 5주년을 기념하기 위해 특별 메뉴를 계획하고 있다.

해설 이미 3형식의 완전한 문장이므로 빈칸부터는 수식어구가 나와야 한다. (A)의 to부정사는 수식어구 기능을 한다. (D)의 전치사구 역시 수식어구 기능을 하지만 빈칸 뒤에 명사, 즉 to부정사의 목적어가 있으므로 정답은 (A) to celebrate이다. 여기서 to부정사는 '~하기 위해서'라는 의미의 부사 역할로 쓰였다.

어휘 celebrate v. 기념하다, 축하하다 | anniversary n. 기념일

16. Roseblossom 카페에 도착하기 위해서, 로비의 남쪽 끝에 있는 엘리베이터를 이용하세요.

해설 콤마 앞은 수식어구이고, 빈칸부터 문장이 시작되는데 동사가 없다. 따라서 빈칸에는 동사가 와야 하며, 동사부터 시작하는 문장은 명령문이다. 명령문은 동사원형으로 시작하므로 정답은 (A) use이다.

어휘 get to ~에 도착하다

17. 우리가 고객들로부터의 피드백을 주의 깊게 분석하는 것은 필수적이다.

해설 「It(가주어) ~ for 진주어 ~ to부정사」 구문으로 정답은 (A) for이다.

어휘 essential adj. 필수적인 | analyze v. 분석하다

18. Drytech 사의 회장인 Mr. Park은 3월에 은퇴할 의사를 발표했다.

해설 소유격 뒤의 빈칸이므로 명사가 들어가야 한다. 정답은 (D) intention 이다.

어휘 announce v. 발표하다 | retire v. 은퇴하다 | intention n. 의사, 의도

19. 노동자들은 새 안전 기준에 더 익숙해질 필요가 있다.

해설 2형식 동사 become 뒤에는 보어 역할을 하는 형용사가 따라와야 한다. more는 부사이므로 빈칸에는 형용사가 와야 하므로 정답은 (A) familiar이다.

어휘 familiar adj. 익숙한 | safety standard 안전 기준

20. 시의회는 5월 20일에 개최되는 시청 회의를 준비했다.

해설 to hold일 경우 hold의 목적어가 나와야 하는데, 빈칸 뒤에 목적어가 없으므로 수동태를 써야 한다. be동사는 이미 있으므로 p.p. 형태인 (B) held가 정답이다.

어휘 organize v. 준비하다, 조직하다

UNIT 14. 동명사

본서 p.136

+ check 1. (C) 2. (D) 3. (C) 4. (B)

1. 출장 요리 서비스를 예약하기 전에 당신의 행사 담당자에게 특별한 식사 요청 사항들을 알려 주세요.

해설 품사 어형 문제이다. 전치사 before 뒤에는 명사나 동명사가 올 수 있다. 그런데 복합 명사를 제외하고는 명사 두 개를 열거해서 쓸 수 없기 때문에 빈칸에 명사를 쓰면, 빈칸 뒤에도 명사가 있으므로 답이 될 수 없다. 즉, 빈칸에 동명사를 넣어서 a catering service를 동명사의 목적어(명사)로 봐야 한다. 따라서 정답은 (C) booking이다.

어휘 catering service 출장 요리 서비스, 음식 제공 서비스

2. 경비 부서는 Westland 호텔의 손님들과 직원들을 위한 안전 규칙과 지침을 마련하는 것을 책임진다.

해설 전치사 뒤에 명사(safety regulations)가 와 있으므로 빈칸에는 형용사도 가능하고, 전치사 뒤에 동명사를 넣어서 safety regulations를 동명사의 목적어로 볼 수도 있다. 그런데 문맥상 안전 규칙을 수립하는 것에 책임이 있다는 뜻이므로 정답은 동명사인 (D) establishing이다.

어휘 be responsible for ~을 책임지다 | safety regulation 안전 규칙 | guideline n. 지침

3. 당신이 바라던 책을 찾기 위해, 도서관에 새로 업데이트된 전자 데이터베이스 활용을 적극 권장합니다.

해설 recommend 뒤에는 목적어(명사)가 필요하다. 즉, 명사인 (A)와 명사 역할을 할 수 있는 (B), (C)가 가능한데, 명사 (A)를 넣으면 빈칸 뒤에 정관사를 낀 명사가 있어서 답이 될 수 없다. 복합명사를 제외하고는, 명사 두 개를 열거해서 쓸 수 없기 때문이다. to부정사와 동명사는 동사의 성질 때문에 목적어 the library's newly updated electronic database를 취할 수 있는데, (B)와 (C) 중에서 recommend는 동명사만을 목적어로 취하는 특별한 동사이므로 정답은 (C) utilizing이다. 동명사를 목적어로 취하는 동사를 따로 암기해 두자.

어휘 desired *adj.* 바랐던, 희망했던 | recommend *v.* 권장하다

4. PS 컨설팅은 사람들이 직장에서 더 효과적으로 일할 수 있게 해주는 기술을 제공하는 데 전념하고 있다.

해설 be committed to에서 to는 전치사이다. 따라서 동명사 (B)나 명사 (C)를 취해야 한다. 그런데 빈칸 뒤에 명사가 또 있다는 것은 동명사의 목적어가 연결되어 있다는 의미이므로 정답은 (B) providing이다.

어휘 be committed to -ing ~하는 데 전념하다

Practice

본서 p.140

1. (B)	**2.** (A)	**3.** (D)	**4.** (B)	**5.** (A)
6. (C)	**7.** (A)	**8.** (B)	**9.** (A)	**10.** (A)
11. (C)	**12.** (D)	**13.** (C)	**14.** (C)	**15.** (A)
16. (B)	**17.** (C)	**18.** (C)	**19.** (C)	**20.** (D)

기본 완성 훈련

1. (Hiring additional engineers) for the project will be our first priority.

2. Lulpite Corporation discontinued (producing home appliances).

3. All the information about (interviewing applicants) is kept in the HR office.

4. The theater owner prevented the audience from (recording the performance).

5. By (updating the assembly line process), production numbers can be increased.

6. Bostex, Inc., a global consumer appliance supplier, works to meet the demand for steam irons.

7. After carefully (reviewing the seating chart), let me know what changes should be made.

8. A good way of (attracting customers) is to give them a money-back guarantee.

9. Customers will receive free movie tickets, for (participating in the survey).

10. The person in charge of (dealing with urgent requests) is Mr. Morales.

----

1. 공사 현장에 오는 방문자들은 안전모와 보안경을 써야 한다.

해설 빈칸은 주어 자리이므로 명사나 동명사가 들어가야 한다. 동명사는 동사의 성질 때문에 동명사의 목적어가 나와야 하는데 빈칸 뒤에는 아무것도 없으므로 '방문자들'을 뜻하는 (B) Visitors가 정답이다.

어휘 protective *adj.* 보호하는, 보호용의

2. 프로젝트를 맡을 추가적인 엔지니어들을 고용하는 것은 우리의 최우선 사항이 될 것이다.

해설 동사 will be가 있으므로 동사 (B)와 (C)는 탈락이다. (D)는 과거 동사일 경우에는 탈락이고, 과거분사 형용사가 되는 경우에도 빈칸에 형용사가 들어가면 결국 주어는 engineers로 복수이다. 그러면 보어가 단수 명사 our first priority이므로 탈락이다. 동명사가 주어가 되는 것이 적절하므로 (A) Hiring이 정답이다. 여기서 additional engineers는 동명사의 목적어이다.

어휘 additional *adj.* 추가적인 | priority *n.* 우선 사항

3. 이 공고는 운전자들에게 주차 건물에서 너무 큰 차량들에 대한 규제를 알리기 위해 의도된 것이다.

해설 inform은 「inform + 사람 of 사물: ~에게 …을 알리다」의 구조를 취하는 동사이므로 빈칸은 명사 자리이며, 빈칸 뒤에 전명구가 연결되어 있으므로 목적어를 동반하는 동명사도 들어갈 수 없다. 따라서 정답은 (D) restrictions이다.

어휘 notice *n.* 공고(문) | intend *v.* 의도하다 | oversized *adj.* 너무 큰, 특대의 | vehicle *n.* 차량 | parking garage 주차장 (건물)

4. Lulpite 사는 가정용 기기를 생산하는 것을 중단했다.

해설 discontinue는 목적이 자리에 동명사만을 취하며, home appliances는 동명사의 목적어이다. 빈칸에 일반 명사인 (C)를 넣으면 그 뒤에 명사를 동반하지 않아야 하므로 정답은 (B) producing이다.

어휘 discontinue *v.* 중단하다 | home appliance 가정용 (전자) 기기 | produce *v.* 생산하다

5. 지원자들을 인터뷰하는 것에 대한 모든 정보는 인사부 사무실에 보관되어 있다.

해설 전치사 뒤에 동명사 -ing가 나왔으므로 빈칸은 동명사의 목적어로 명사 자리이다. (A)와 (B) 중에 '지원서를 인터뷰하는 것'이 아니고 '지원자들을 인터뷰하는 것'이므로 정답은 (A) applicants이다.

어휘 applicant *n.* 지원자 | application *n.* 지원서

6. Kitchen-Pro 스토브의 쟁반들은 수월한 청소를 위해 뺄 수 있다.

해설 빈칸은 형용사 easy의 수식을 받는 명사 자리이며, 수월한 청소를 위해 쟁반을 뺄 수 있다는 의미가 적절하므로 '청소'를 뜻하는 -ing형 명사인 (C) cleaning이 정답이다. (B) cleaners도 명사이지만 의미상 맞지 않다.

어휘 tray n. 쟁반 | remove v. 제거하다, 빼다 | cleaner n. 청소부; 청소기 | cleaning n. 청소

7. 극장 소유주는 관객이 공연을 녹화하지 못하도록 했다.

해설 「prevent A from -ing 'A가 ~하지 못하게 하다'」이므로 정답은 (A) recording이다.

어휘 prevent v. 막다, 예방하다, 방지하다 | audience n. 청중, 관객 | record v. 기록하다, 녹음[녹화]하다

8. 조립 라인 공정을 업데이트 함으로써, 생산량이 늘어날 수 있다.

해설 전치사 By 뒤에는 명사나 동명사가 와야 하는데, 빈칸 뒤에 목적어가 나와 있으므로 동명사 (B) updating이 정답이다.

어휘 assembly n. 조립 | process n. 공정, 과정

9. 세계적인 가전제품 공급자인 Bostex 사는 증기 다리미에 대한 수요를 충족시키기 위해서 노력한다.

해설 부정관사 a 뒤에는 단수 명사가 와야 한다. global은 형용사이므로 빈칸은 명사 자리이다. 명사는 (A)와 (B)인데, 동명사는 동사의 성질 때문에 동명사의 목적어를 수반하여야 한다. 빈칸 뒤에는 목적어가 없으므로 정답은 (A) supplier이다.

어휘 global adj. 세계적인 | meet v. 충족시키다, 만나다 | demand v. 요구하다 n. 수요, 요구 | supplier n. 공급자, 공급 회사

10. 신중하게 좌석 배치도를 검토한 후에, 어떤 변화가 이뤄져야 하는지를 나에게 알려 주세요.

해설 전치사 After 다음에 동명사 -ing가 왔고, 동명사의 목적어(the seating chart)도 나왔다. 따라서 빈칸은 필요 없는 자리이다. 필요 없는 자리이면서 동명사 앞의 빈칸이므로 동명사를 수식할 수 있는 부사가 정답이다. 따라서 정답은 (A) carefully이다.

어휘 carefully adv. 신중하게, 주의하여 | review v. 재검토하다 n. 재검토 | seating chart 좌석 배치도

11. 승진을 수락한 후, Mr. Jang은 조수 한명을 찾기 시작했다.

해설 전치사 After 다음에는 명사나 동명사가 와야 한다. 그런데 빈칸 뒤에 명사가 나왔고 이는 동명사의 목적어로 볼 수 있기 때문에 정답은 동명사 (C) accepting이다.

어휘 promotion n. 승진

12. 다음 주 수요일은 KJ 은행의 개업 3주년을 기념한다.

해설 's는 '~의'라는 의미의 소유격이므로 빈칸에는 명사가 나와야 한다. 명사는 (B)와 (D)이다. (B) openness는 '솔직함, 마음이 열려 있음'이라는 뜻으로 문맥상 적합하지 않다. 따라서 '개업'이라는 뜻의 (D) opening이 정답이다.

어휘 mark v. 기념하다, 표시하다, 나타내다 | anniversary n. 기념일

13. 웹사이트에서 영화 티켓을 구매하는 데 단지 몇 분만 걸린다.

해설 빈칸은 동사 자리이다. 주어가 명사구(Purchasing a movie ticket)로 단수 취급하므로 정답은 (C) takes이다.

어휘 purchase v. 구매하다

14. 고객들을 끌어들이는 좋은 방법 중 하나는 그들에게 환불을 보장해 주는 것이다.

해설 전치사 of 뒤에는 명사나 동명사가 와야 한다. 또한 빈칸 뒤에 명사가 또 있다는 것은 동명사의 목적어가 나왔다는 의미이므로 정답은 동명사 (C) attracting이다.

어휘 way n. 방법 | money-back guarantee 환불 보장

15. 오늘 오후 늦게 도착할 주문 번호 9734 제품의 수령을 꼭 확인해 주세요.

해설 빈칸은 confirm의 목적어 자리, 즉 명사 자리이다. 명사는 (A)와 (D)인데, 동명사는 동사의 성질 때문에 동명사의 목적어가 또 나와야 한다. 그런데 빈칸 뒤에는 명사가 없으므로 정답은 (A) receipt이다.

어휘 make sure 반드시 ~하도록 하다, ~을 확실히 하다 | confirm v. 확정하다, 확인하다 | order n. 주문, 주문품 | receipt n. 수령, 영수증

16. 학생들은 교과서의 보충 자료로서 권장 도서 목록이 부과된다.

해설 빈칸은 관사 뒤 명사 자리이며, 권장 도서 목록이 보충물로 부과된다는 의미가 적절하므로 '보충(물)'이라는 뜻의 (B) supplement가 정답이다.

어휘 assign v. 부과하다; 배정하다 | reading list 도서 목록 | textbook n. 교과서 | supplement n. 보충(물) v. 보충하다 | supplementary adj. 보충의

17. BRT 스포츠 시계는 기능 손상 없이 물에서 착용 가능하다.

해설 전치사 without 뒤에 동명사 losing이 연결되어 있으므로 그 뒤에는 동명사의 목적어 역할을 하는 명사가 와야 한다. 따라서 정답은 (C) functionality이다.

어휘 lose v. 잃다 | functional adj. 기능 위주의, 실용적인 | functionality n. (상품의) 기능

18. 고객들이 설문 조사에 참가해서 무료 영화 티켓을 받을 것이다.

해설 전치사 for 다음에는 명사나 동명사가 나와야 한다. 보기에 나온 명사는 (C) 뿐이다. 또한 participate는 1형식 동사로 동명사의 목적어가 나올 필요가 없다. 따라서 정답은 동명사 (C) participating이다.

어휘 receive v. 받다 | survey n. 설문 조사

19. 축제 참가자들은 세계의 진품 요리들을 먹어볼 수 있습니다.

해설 빈칸은 주어 자리로 명사가 와야 한다. (A), (C), (D)가 명사인데, 동명사 (A)는 동명사의 목적어가 나와야 하므로 답이 될 수 없다. (C)와 (D) 중에 문맥상, '축제의 참석이 먹어볼 수 있는 것'이 아니고 '축제의 참석자들이 먹어볼 수 있는 것'이므로 정답은 (C) Attendees이다.

어휘 attendee n. 참석자 | attendance n. 참석, 참석자 수, 출석(률)

20. 긴급 요청의 처리 담당자는 Mr. Morales이다.

해설 전치사 of 다음에는 명사나 동명사가 와야 하는데 dealing이라는 동명사가 나왔다. 따라서 동명사의 목적어인 명사가 나와야 하는데, urgent가 형용사이므로 빈칸에는 명사가 들어가야 한다. 명사는 (A), (B), (D)인데, 동명사 (B)는 동명사의 목적어로 빈칸 뒤에 명사가 나와야 하므로 탈락이고, request는 가산 명사이므로 a request 또는 requests로 써야 하므로 정답은 (D) requests이다.

어휘 in charge of ~을 맡아서, ~을 담당하는 | urgent *adj.* 긴급한, 시급한 | request *v.* 요청하다 *n.* 요청

UNIT 15. 분사
본서 p.144

+ check   1. (A)   2. (B)   3. (B)   4. (C)

1. 비행기가 정시에 이륙하기 위해 승객들은 오전 9시까지 배정된 좌석에 있어야 한다.

해설 품사 어형 문제로 빈칸이 소유격과 명사(seats) 사이에 위치해 있다. 소유격과 명사 사이에는 형용사가 들어갈 수 있으므로 정답 후보를 assigned와 assigning으로 좁힐 수 있는데, 과거분사 assigned는 수동의 의미(배정된), 현재분사 assigning은 능동의 의미(배정하는)로, 배정된 좌석이 문맥상 적절하므로 정답은 (A) assigned이다.

어휘 passenger *n.* 승객 | take off 이륙하다 | on time 정시에

2. Tungston 제조사는 직원들에게 직장 안전에 중점을 둔 다양한 교육 프로그램들을 제공하고자 한다.

해설 빈칸 앞에 이미 완벽한 문장이 와 있으므로 빈칸은 문장에서 필요 없는 수식어구 자리이다. (A), (C), (D)는 모두 동사인데, 문장에 동사 intend가 이미 있으므로 더 이상 동사는 필요 없다. 따라서 정답은 빈칸 앞의 명사 training programs를 수식할 수 있는 분사 형용사 (B) focusing이다.

어휘 intend *v.* ~할 의도이다 | safety *n.* 안전 | focus on ~에 초점을 맞추다

3. Tory 자동차가 5년 만에 전기 자동차 산업에서 선두가 되었나는 것은 상당히 놀랍다.

해설 「it ~ that」 가주어 진주어 구문이다. 빈칸은 주격 보어로서 형용사가 필요한 자리이므로 (B)와 (C)가 답이 될 수 있다. It은 가주어이며, 진주어는 that 이하의 "Tory 자동차가 단 5년 만에 전기 자동차 산업에서 리더가 된 것"이다. 주격 보어와 진주어의 관계를 살펴봤을 때, 5년 만에 리더가 된 것이 놀라움을 받는 것이 아니라 놀라움을 주는 것이므로 정답은 현재분사 능동인 (B) amazing이다.

어휘 leader *n.* 선두, 선도자 | industry *n.* 산업, ~업 | just *adv.* 바로, 막 | amaze *v.* 놀라게 하다 | amazing *adj.* 놀라운

4. Mr. Doan은 연례 성과 평가 일정을 잡기 일주일 전에 직원들에게 통지할 것이다.

해설 빈칸이 접속사(when)와 명사구(annual performance reviews) 사이에 위치해 있으며 주어가 없는 상태에서 빈칸에 알맞은 동사 형태를 고르라는 문제이므로, when절의 주어가 주절의 주어와 동일하여 생략되고 동사가 분사 형태로 바뀐 분사구문이 와야 하는 문장으로 판단할 수 있다. 빈칸 뒤에 목적어가 연결되어 있다는 점에서 빈칸은 현재분사 능동이 필요한 자리이다. 따라서 정답은 (C) scheduling이다.

어휘 annual *adj.* 연례의 | performance review 성과 평가

Practice
본서 p.148

1. (A)	**2.** (A)	**3.** (B)	**4.** (A)	**5.** (D)
6. (D)	**7.** (A)	**8.** (B)	**9.** (A)	**10.** (C)
11. (A)	**12.** (B)	**13.** (A)	**14.** (B)	**15.** (C)
16. (B)	**17.** (D)	**18.** (B)	**19.** (A)	**20.** (D)

기본 완성 훈련

1. WBC Health manufactures disposable medical equipment for use in hospitals and clinics.

2. New workers must attend the assigned training sessions taking place this week.

3. The redesigned logo for *Beauty Tips Magazine* has won several awards.

4. The recently released report shows that fourth quarter sales increased.

5. Customers purchasing items in bulk may be eligible for volume discounts.

6. Extensive repairs are needed before the bridge over Sunflower Creek can reopen.

7. Newly hired employees are required to attend a very demanding three-week training course.

8. Despite the convenience of online shopping malls, consumers are still hesitant to buy clothes they cannot try on first.

9. All boxes left behind the loading dock will be discarded this weekend

10. Our company will hold interviews for experienced programmers next month.

1. WBC 보건은 병·의원용 일회용 의료 장비를 제조한다.

해설 복합 명사 medical equipment 앞에 빈칸이 있으므로 형용사가 와야 한다. (A)는 일반 형용사이고, (B)와 (C)는 분사 형용사이다. 보기에 일반 형용사가 있으면 분사 형용사보다 유력한 답이 된다. 따라서 정답은 (A) disposable이다.

어휘 manufacture *v.* 제조하다 | medical *adj.* 의학의, 내과의 | disposable *adj.* 일회용의

2. 신입 직원들은 이번 주에 있을 지정된 교육에 참석해야 한다.

해설 관사 the와 명사 training sessions 사이에 빈칸이 있으므로 형용사가 정답이다. 분사 형용사 (A)와 (D) 중에 '지정하는 교육'이 아니고 '지정된 교육'이므로 정답은 (A) assigned이다.

어휘 attend *v.* 참석하다 | training session 교육

3. 〈Jenny's Adventures〉는 다가오는 연휴 기간의 가장 기대되는 영화들 중 하나이다.

해설 명사 movies 앞에 빈칸이 있으므로 형용사가 들어가야 한다. 분사 형용사 (B)와 (C) 중에 '기대하는 영화'가 아니고 '기대되는 영화'이므로 정답은 (B) anticipated이다.

어휘 anticipate *v.* 기대하다, 예상하다

4. 증가하는 인구 때문에 주택 건설 업체에 대한 수요가 높다.

해설 정관사 the와 명사 population 사이에 빈칸이 있으므로 형용사가 와야 한다. 분사 형용사 (A)와 (C) 중에 grow는 1형식 자동사이므로 현재분사인 (A) growing이 정답이다.

어휘 population *n.* 인구 | home builder 주택 건설업체 | be in high demand 수요가 많다

5. 새로 디자인된 〈Beauty Tips Magazine〉의 로고는 몇 회의 상을 받았다.

해설 관사와 명사 사이에 빈칸이 있으므로 형용사가 와야 한다. 형용사는 (C)와 (D)가 가능한데, '다시 디자인하는 로고'가 아니고 '다시 디자인된 로고'이므로 정답은 (D) redesigned이다.

어휘 redesign *v.* 다시 디자인하다

6. 그 자리에 지원하는 데 관심 있는 지원자들은 인사부에 연락해야 한다.

해설 interest는 '~의 관심을 끌다'는 의미의 감정동사로, 감정동사가 사람을 수식/서술할 때는 과거분사를, 사물을 수식하거나 서술할 때는 현재분사를 쓰는 데 수식을 받는 명사가 사람(Candidates)이므로 정답은 과거분사 형태의 형용사 (D) interested이다.

어휘 candidate *n.* 지원자, 후보자 | apply for ~에 지원하다 | position *n.* 자리, 직책

7. 최근 발표된 보고서는 4분기 판매량이 증가했음을 보여준다.

해설 빈칸 뒤의 명사 report를 수식할 형용사가 필요하다. 형용사는 (A)와 (B)가 가능한데, '발표하는' 보고서가 아니고 '발표된' 보고서이므로 정답은 (A) released이다.

어휘 release *v.* 발표하다

8. 상품을 대량으로 구매하는 고객들은 대량 구매 할인 자격을 얻을 수 있다.

해설 문장에 동사 may be가 이미 있기 때문에 빈칸에 동사인 (A)와 (D)는 들어갈 수 없고, 분사인 (B)와 (C)가 가능한데, '구매되는' 고객이 아니

고 '구매하는' 고객이므로 정답은 (B)이다. 또한 분사가 앞의 명사를 뒤에서 수식할 때 목적어를 동반하면 현재분사이고 목적어를 동반하지 않으면 과거분사이다. 이 문장에서는 목적어 items가 있으므로 정답은 (B) purchasing이다.

어휘 in bulk 대량으로 | discount *n.* 할인

9. Sunflower Creek을 가로지르는 다리를 재개통하기 전에 광범위한 수리가 요구된다.

해설 명사 repairs 앞에 빈칸이 있으므로 형용사가 정답이다. 일반 형용사 (A)와 분사 형용사 (D)가 될 수 있는데, 일반 형용사가 보기에 나오면 분사 형용사보다 유력한 답이 되므로 정답은 (A) Extensive이다.

어휘 repair *v.* 수리하다 | *n.* 수리, 수선

10. 새로 고용된 직원들은 매우 힘든 3주 훈련 코스에 참석하도록 요구된다.

해설 부사 very와 명사 three-week training course 사이에 빈칸이 있으므로 형용사를 찾아야 한다. 형용사는 (B)와 (C)가 될 수 있지만, demanding이라는 형용사가 '힘든'이라는 의미로 문맥상 적합하다. 따라서 정답은 (C) demanding이다.

어휘 newly *adv.* 새롭게 | hire *v.* 고용하다 | demanding *adj.* 부담이 큰, 힘든, 요구가 많은

11. J&J 기술에 의해서 만들어진 그 웹사이트는 4월에 업계의 상을 받았다.

해설 이미 3형식의 완벽한 문장으로 빈칸에는 수식어구가 들어가야 한다. (D)는 명사로 수식할 수 없고, (C) 부사는 수식은 가능하나 문맥상 적합하지 않다. (A)와 (B)는 형용사로 명사 the Web site를 수식한다. '만든 웹사이트'가 아니라 '만들어진 웹사이트'이므로 정답은 (A)이다. 또한 앞의 명사를 꾸미고 있는데 빈칸 뒤에 목적어가 따라 나오지 않았으므로 정답은 과거분사인 (A) created이다.

어휘 create *v.* 만들다, 창조하다

12. 준비위원들은 회사 야유회가 흥미진진하고 재미있기를 바란다.

해설 be동사 뒤 빈칸에 상태를 설명하는 보어로 형용사가 들어가야 한다. (B)와 (D) 중 선택해야 하는데, 야유회가 '흥분시키는' 것이므로 능동의 의미가 있는 현재분사 (B) exciting이 정답이다.

어휘 organizer *n.* 주최자, 준비자 | enjoyable *adj.* 즐거운

13. 고위 경영진은 사용자 설명서가 혼란스러워 다시 쓸 필요가 있을지 몰라 우려한다.

해설 2형식 동사 is 뒤에 빈칸이 있으므로 주격 보어 자리, 즉 상태 설명 형용사가 와야 한다. 형용사는 (A)와 (D)인데, 주격 보어이므로 주어와의 관계를 확인한다. 그 설명서가 '혼란을 받고 느낀 것'이 아니고, '혼란을 주고 일으키는 것'이므로 정답은 (A) confusing이다.

어휘 confusing *adj.* (무엇이) 혼란스러운 | confused *adj.* 혼란스러워 하는

14. 그 호텔의 업데이트된 웹사이트는 고객들이 온라인으로 예약할 수 있도록 해줄 것이다.

해설 소유격 's와 명사 Web site 사이에 빈칸이 있으므로, 빈칸에는 형용

사가 들어가야 한다. 형용사는 (A)와 (B)가 가능한데, '업데이트하는' 웹사이트가 아니라 '업데이트된' 웹사이트이므로 정답은 (B) updated 이다.

어휘 book *v.* 예약하다

15. Camera Servicing Group으로도 알려져 있는 CSG는 매달 전문 가들을 위한 수업을 주최한다.

해설 문장에 이미 동사 hosts가 있고 쉼표 사이의 삽입 구문이므로 빈칸에 는 동사가 들어가선 안 된다. 분사인 (A)와 (C) 중 선택해야 하는데, 빈칸 뒤에 목적어가 없으므로 과거분사 (C) known이 정답이다.

어휘 host *v.* 주최하다 ǀ professional *n.* 전문가

16. 제품이 광고에 나온 대로 작동하지 않았기 때문에 많은 고객들이 실망 했다.

해설 2형식 동사 were 다음에 빈칸이 있으므로 주격 보어 자리, 즉 상태 설 명 형용사가 와야 한다. 보기 중 형용사는 (A)와 (B)인데, 주격 보어이 므로 주어와의 관계를 본다. '고객들이 실망을 주고 일으킨 것'이 아니 고, '고객들이 실망을 받고 느낀 것'이므로 정답은 (B) disappointed 이다.

어휘 disappointing *adj.* 실망스러운 ǀ disappointed *adj.* 실망한, 낙담한

17. 온라인 쇼핑몰의 편리함에도 불구하고, 소비자들은 여전히 먼저 입어 볼 수 없는 옷을 사는 것에 주저한다.

해설 be동사 are 뒤에 빈칸이 있으므로 주격 보어 자리, 즉 상태 설명 형용 사가 와야 한다. 보기 중 형용사는 분사 형용사인 (A)와 일반 형용사 (D)가 있다. 정답은 (D) hesitant이다.

어휘 consumer *n.* 소비자 ǀ convenience *n.* 편리함, 편의성 ǀ still *adv.* 여전히 ǀ hesitant *adj.* 주저하는, 망설이는, 머뭇거리는

18. 직원들에게 가장 최근의 프로젝트 진행 상황을 알게 하기 위해서, 우 리는 회사 웹사이트를 매일 업데이트한다.

해설 keep은 5형식 동사로 목적어와 목적격 보어를 이끈다. 이 문장에서 목적어는 employees이고 빈칸은 목적격 보어 자리이다. keep은 목 적격 보어 자리에 상태 설명 형용사가 들어가므로 정답은 (B)와 (C)가 가능하다. 목적어와의 관계를 봤을 때, 직원들이 '알려주는 쪽'이 아니 고 '알림을 받는 쪽'이므로 정답은 (B) informed이다.

어휘 inform *v.* 알리다 ǀ daily *adv.* 하루, 매일

19. 하역장 뒤에 남겨진 모든 상자들은 이번 주말에 폐기될 예정이다.

해설 문장에 이미 will be discarded라는 동사가 있기 때문에 동사인 (B) 와 (D)는 정답이 될 수 없고, 분사인 (A)와 (C) 중 선택해야 한다. 상 자가 '남겨지는' 것이며, 빈칸 뒤에 목적어도 없으므로 과거분사인 (A) left가 정답이다.

어휘 loading dock 하역장 ǀ discard *v.* 버리다

20. 우리 회사는 다음 달 경력직 프로그래머들의 면접을 주최한다.

해설 전치사 for와 명사 programmers 사이에 빈칸이 있으므로 형용사가 와야 한다. 따라서 정답은 (D) experienced이다.

어휘 experienced *adj.* 경험 있는, 경력 있는, 능숙한

UNIT 16. 비교

본서 p.152

check   1. (A)   2. (A)   3. (D)   4. (C)

1. 귀하의 일정을 변경하셔야 한다면, 저희에게 가능한 한 일찍 연락해 주세요.

해설 as ~ as 사이에는 형용사나 부사가 들어갈 수 있는데, 앞에 어떤 품 사를 수식하는지에 따라 결정된다. as ~ as에 들어갈 품사가 앞의 동사(contact)를 수식하므로 빈칸은 동사 수식 부사가 필요하다. 따 라서 정답은 (A) early이다.

어휘 reschedule *v.* 일정을 변경하다

2. Liv 식당의 성공은 주로 다른 식당들이 하는 것보다 고객들에게 더 빨리 음식을 제공한다는 사실에 기인한다.

해설 that절이 주어, 동사, 목적어를 갖춘 완벽한 문장이므로 빈칸은 문 장 구조에 영향을 미치지 않는 부사 자리이며, 빈칸 뒤에 than이 있 으므로 비교급이 필요함을 알 수 있다. 따라서 정답은 비교급 부사인 (A) more quickly이다.

어휘 attribute A to B A를 B의 결과로 여기다 ǀ serve *v.* 음식을 제공 하다

3. Office Network의 점원들 중 Mr. Bryson이 매장에 전시된 제품 에 대해 가장 많이 알고 있다.

해설 is는 2형식 동사이므로 빈칸에는 주격 보어로서 상태를 설명하는 형 용사가 와야 한다. 형용사는 (A), (C), (D)인데, 형용사가 들어갈 빈칸 앞에 the가 나왔다는 것은 최상급이 필요함을 말해 주는 결정적 힌 트가 된다. 또한 문장 맨 앞의 'Of the sales clerks(점원들 중에서)' 와 같이 범위를 한정하는 것은 최상급 문장이라는 의미이므로 정답 은 (D) most knowledgeable이다.

어휘 display *v.* 전시하다 ǀ knowledgeable *adj.* 아는 것이 많은

4. 새로운 소프트웨어가 설치되고 나면, XM120 스마트폰은 더 이상 구식 비디오 응용 프로그램을 지원하지 않을 것이다.

해설 '더 이상 ~ 아닌'을 뜻하는 관용 표현 no longer를 알아둬야 한다. 빈칸 뒤 longer를 보고 no를 바로 선택할 수 있는 문제이다. 따라서 정답은 (C) no이다.

어휘 install *v.* 설치하다 ǀ support *v.* 지원하다 ǀ application *n.* 응 용 프로그램, 애플리케이션

Practice

본서 p.156

1. (A)	**2.** (D)	**3.** (C)	**4.** (A)	**5.** (D)
6. (A)	**7.** (A)	**8.** (D)	**9.** (D)	**10.** (C)
11. (C)	**12.** (B)	**13.** (A)	**14.** (C)	**15.** (D)
16. (C)	**17.** (D)	**18.** (D)	**19.** (B)	**20.** (D)

기본 완성 훈련

1. (Geartech's flagship product) is more expensive than (that of Noble Connect's).

2. The industry association is looking for (a conference venue) that is even larger than (MC Convention Center).

3. Islet Travel is famous for offering the cheapest (flights available from Chicago to New York).

4. Martin Co. plans to have the most extensive (network of bus routes in the country) by next year.

5. JH Company's new (computer monitor) is much slimmer than (its model from the year before).

6. Marrich, Inc. believes (its product) is superior to (those made by its competitors).

7. (Print advertising) is usually more expensive than (online advertising) due to additional overhead costs.

8. (No one) at the Anderson Corporation has worked more energetically for the launch of the new smartphone than (Justine Kim).

9. (Of all the applicants), (Mr. Hong) seems to be the most qualified.

10. Falanx Corp. has been more narrowly focused on manufacturing computer components (in recent years).

....

1. Geartech의 주력 상품은 Noble Connect의 그것 보다 더 비싸다.

해설 more expensive라는 비교급 표현이 있으므로 '~보다'라는 뜻이 적합하다. 따라서 정답은 (A) than이다.

어휘 flagship product 주력(대표) 상품 | expensive adj. 비싼

2. 산업 협회는 MC 컨벤션 센터보다 훨씬 더 큰 컨벤션 센터를 찾고 있다.

해설 비교급 앞에 빈칸이므로 비교급 강조 표현을 써야 한다. 비교급은 much, still, a lot, far, even으로 강조할 수 있으므로 정답은 (D) even이다.

어휘 association n. 협회 | venue n. (모임을 위한) 장소

3. 우발적인 손상을 피하기 위해 가능한 한 가장 튼튼한 포장 재료를 사용하는 것이 중요하다.

해설 정관사 the와 명사 packing materials 사이에 빈칸이 있으므로 빈칸에는 형용사가 와야 한다. 보기 중 유일한 형용사인 (C) strongest가 정답이다.

어휘 material n. 재료 | accidental adj. 우발적인 | strong adj. 강한

4. Clover Suites는 그 나라의 많은 리조트들 중에서 가장 아름답다.

해설 2형식 동사 is 다음에 빈칸이 왔으므로 주격 보어 자리, 즉 상태 설명 형용사가 적합한 자리이다. 형용사는 (A)와 (D)인데, the 뒤에는 비교급이 아닌 최상급을 써야 하고, among이라는 전치사는 '~사이에서 가장'이라는 최상급의 의미를 찾으라는 힌트이다. 따라서 정답은 (A) most beautiful이다.

어휘 among prep. ~사이에 | beautiful adj. 아름다운

5. DRM 전자는 어제 시장에서 가장 작은 태블릿 PC를 출시했다.

해설 정관사 the와 명사 tablet pc 사이에 빈칸이 있으므로 형용사가 들어가야 한다. 그런데 the가 있고 '시장에서'라는 범위 한정이 들어갔다는 것은 최상급을 찾으라는 의미이다. 최상급은 (C)와 (D)인데, small은 음절이 짧아서 the smallest로 쓰인다. 따라서 정답은 (D) smallest 이다.

어휘 release v. 출시하다

6. Mr. Lee는 작년에 산 것만큼 내구성 강한 여행 가방을 원한다.

해설 as와 as 사이에 빈칸이 있으므로 무조건 원급이 필요한데, 형용사인 (A)와 부사인 (C)가 있다. a suitcase 뒤에 「주격 관계대명사 + be동사(which is)」가 생략되어 있다는 것을 간파하고 be동사 뒷자리에 올 수 있는 형용사인 (A) durable을 정답으로 선택해야 한다.

어휘 suitcase n. 여행 가방 | durable adj. 내구성이 있는

7. Cedar 택시의 공항 픽업 서비스는 다른 어떠한 경쟁업체보다 더 편리하다.

해설 비교구문 more ~ than은 문장 성분에 영향을 주지 않으므로 걷어내면, 빈칸은 be동사 뒤 보어 자리이며, 서비스가 편리하다는 의미이므로 형용사 (A) convenient가 정답이다.

어휘 pick-up service 공항으로 여행자를 마중 나가는 서비스 | competitor n. 경쟁업체

8. Islet 여행사는 시카고에서 뉴욕으로 가는 가장 싼 항공편을 제공하는 것으로 유명하다.

해설 정관사 the와 명사 flights 사이에 빈칸이 있으므로 빈칸에는 형용사가 와야 한다. 형용사는 (D)뿐이고, 빈칸 앞에 the가 있으므로 최상급으로 쓰였음을 알 수 있다. 따라서 정답은 (D) cheapest이다.

어휘 flight n. 비행, 항공편 | available adj. 이용 가능한 | cheap adj. (값이) 싼

9. 그 도시 계획자들은 건물의 도면을 보자 더 쉽게 설득 당했다.

해설 이미 수동태의 완벽한 문장이므로 빈칸은 필요 없는 자리이다. 따라서 정답은 (D) easily이다.

어휘 convince v. 납득시키다 | plan n. 도면

10. Martin 사는 내년까지 국내에서 가장 광범위한 버스 노선 네트워크를 보유할 계획이다.

해설 정관사 the와 명사 network 사이에 빈칸이 있으므로 빈칸은 형용사 자리이다. 형용사는 (B)와 (C)이다. 빈칸 앞에 the가 있으므로 비교급이 아닌 최상급이 정답이다. 따라서 정답은 (C) most extensive이다.

어휘 route *n.* 길, 노선 | extensive *adj.* 광범위한

11. 직원들은 새 소프트웨어로 이전보다 더 정확히 고객들의 피드백을 분석할 수 있다.

해설 이미 3형식의 완전한 문장이 나와 있으므로 빈칸은 필요 없는 자리이다. 따라서 정답은 부사인 (C) more accurately이다.

어휘 analyze *v.* 분석하다 | accurately *adv.* 정확히

12. JH 사의 새로운 컴퓨터 모니터는 전년도 모델보다 훨씬 더 얇다.

해설 2형식 동사 are가 나왔으므로 빈칸은 주격 보어 자리로 상태 설명 형용사가 와야 된다. much는 비교급을 강조하는 것이고, than은 '~보다'라는 뜻이므로 빈칸에는 형용사의 비교급이 들어가는 것이 적절하다. 따라서 정답은 (B) slimmer이다.

어휘 slim *adj.* 얇은, 날씬한

13. Marrich 사는 자사의 제품이 경쟁업체들이 만든 것보다 더 우수하다고 믿는다.

해설 비교의 뜻이지만 than이 아닌 to를 사용하는 관용 표현 be superior to '~보다 뛰어난'을 기억해 두자. 따라서 정답은 (A) to이다.

어휘 superior *adj.* 우수한

14. 인쇄 광고는 보통 추가 간접비 때문에 온라인 광고보다 더 비싸다.

해설 2형식 동사 is가 있으므로, 빈칸은 주격 보어 자리로 상태 설명 형용사가 온다. 형용사는 (A)와 (C)인데, 뒤에 than이 있으므로 비교급을 찾으라는 말이다. 따라서 정답은 (C) more expensive이다.

어휘 print *n.* (인쇄된) 활자 *v.* 인쇄하다 | advertising *n.* 광고, 광고업 | overhead cost 간접비 | expensive *adj.* 비싼

15. 새 스마트폰의 출시를 위해 Anderson 사의 그 누구도 Justine Kim보다 더 열정적으로 일하지 않았다.

해설 빈칸 뒤에 than이 보이므로 비교급을 써야 하며, work는 1형식 동사이므로 비교급 부사가 와야 한다. 따라서 정답은 (D) more energetically이다.

어휘 launch *n.* 출시 *v.* 출시하다

16. 모든 지원자들 중에서 Mr Hong이 가장 자격이 있는 것처럼 보인다.

해설 to be는 to부정사이지만, 동사의 성질 때문에 상태 설명이 필요하다. 따라서 빈칸에 형용사가 들어가야 하므로 정답은 (C) qualified이다.

어휘 seem *v.* ~인 것 같다 | qualified *adj.* 자격이 있는

17. 항공편이 5시간 이상 지연되어서 고객 회의도 연기되었다.

해설 「more than '~이상」,이라는 뜻으로 정답은 (D) than이다.

어휘 postpone *v.* 연기하다 | flight *n.* 항공편, 비행

18. 요즘에는 대부분의 고객 불만 사항들이 이전보다 더 쉽게 해결된다.

해설 완전한 수동태 문장이고 필요 없는 부사 easily가 왔다. than이 있기 때문에 부사를 비교급으로 써야 하므로 정답은 (D) more이다.

어휘 nowadays *adv.* 요즘에는 | resolve *v.* 해결하다

19. Lapan 전자에 관한 Mr. Kim의 최신 기사는 투자자들에게 고무적이다.

해설 소유격 's 뒤에 명사 article이 왔으므로 그 사이에는 형용사가 와야 한다. 따라서 정답은 (B) most recent이다.

어휘 encouraging *adj.* 고무적인 | recent *adj.* 최근의 | most recent 최신

20. Falanx 사는 지난 몇 년간 컴퓨터 부품을 제조하는 것에 더 제한적으로 집중했다.

해설 be focused는 수동태이므로 빈칸에는 부사가 와야 한다. 따라서 정답은 (D) narrowly이다.

어휘 focus *v.* 집중하다 | narrowly *adv.* 제한적으로, 좁게

REVIEW TEST 04

1. (C)	2. (C)	3. (D)	4. (B)	5. (B)
6. (D)	7. (A)	8. (D)	9. (A)	10. (B)
11. (B)	12. (C)	13. (B)	14. (A)	15. (B)
16. (C)	17. (B)	18. (A)	19. (B)	20. (B)
21. (A)	22. (B)	23. (C)	24. (C)	25. (C)
26. (D)	27. (C)	28. (B)	29. (C)	30. (B)

1. 최종 검토자가 내일 아침 이사회에 제안서를 제출해야 한다.

해설 정관사 The 뒤에는 명사가 와야 한다. final은 형용사이므로 빈칸이 명사 자리이다. 명사 (A), (B), (C) 중에 B 동명사는 동명사의 목적어도 필요하고 관사와도 함께 쓰일 수 없으므로 탈락이다. 명사 (A)와 (C) 중에 문맥상 '검토가 제출하는 것'이 아니고 '검토하는 사람이 제출하는 것'이므로 정답은 (C) reviewer이다.

어휘 final *adj.* 마지막의 | proposal *n.* 제안서 | reviewer *n.* 검토자, 논평가

2. 새 공장 설비는 레버를 사용하여 원하는 높이로 설정할 수 있다.

해설 정관사 the 뒤에는 명사가 와야 하는데, 명사 height가 있으므로 그 사이의 빈칸에는 형용사가 와야 된다. 형용사 (C)와 (D) 중에 height를 자연스럽게 꾸며 주는 형용사를 골라야 하는데, '바라는 높이'가 아니고 '바랐던 높이'이므로 정답은 (C) desired이다.

어휘 set *adj.* 설정하다 | height *n.* 높이 | lever *n.* 레버, 지렛대 | desired *adj.* 바랐던, 희망했던

3. 식물원을 둘러보고자 하시는 고객들께서는 온라인이나 정문에서 티켓을 구매하실 수 있습니다.

해설 wishing은 to부정사를 동반하는 형용사이므로 정답은 (D) to explore이다.

어휘 botanical garden 식물원 | explore *v.* 답사하다, 탐구하다

PART 5 REVIEW TEST 04

4. 새로운 소프트웨어는 사람들이 복잡한 프로젝트를 쉽게 준비할 수 있게 해 준다.

해설 전치사 with 다음에는 명사나 동명사가 와야 한다. 동명사는 뒤에 목적어가 나와야 하는데, 빈칸 뒤에 명사가 없으므로 정답은 (B) ease이다.

어휘 organize v. 조직하다, 준비하다 | complex adj. 복잡한 | ease n. 쉬움, 용이함

5. 신제품을 개발하기 전에, Xpando 사는 광범위한 조사를 했다.

해설 전치사 Before 다음에는 명사나 동명사가 와야 한다. to부정사는 전치사 뒤에 올 수 없으므로 (D)는 탈락이다. 빈칸 뒤에 명사가 또 있다는 것은 동명사의 목적어라는 의미이므로 정답은 동명사 (B) developing이다.

어휘 extensive adj. 광범위한, 폭넓은 | develop v. 개발하다, 발달시키다

6. Rousse 식당의 인상적인 새 메뉴가 월 수익을 20퍼센트 증가시켰다.

해설 명사 앞의 형용사 자리이므로 (D) impressive가 정답이다. 분사 (C) impressed도 형용사 역할을 할 수는 있지만 '감동받은, 깊은 인상을 받은'이라는 뜻으로 의미상 답이 될 수 없다.

어휘 increase v. 증가시키다, 늘리다 | monthly adj. 매월의 | revenue n. 수익, 수입

7. 그 회사의 주 공장은 다음 달에 생산량을 증가시키는 것을 계획하고 있다.

해설 plan은 to부정사만을 목적어로 취하므로 정답은 (A) to increase이다.

어휘 plant n. 공장

8. 회의실을 예약하기 위한 요청서는 접수 담당자에게 제출되어야 한다.

해설 빈칸은 주어 자리로 명사가 온다. 명사는 (A), (B), (D)이다. 동명사는 뒤에 목적어(명사)가 나와야 하는데, 빈칸 뒤에 명사가 없으므로 (B)는 탈락이다. 또한 request는 가산 명사이므로 a request 또는 requests를 써야 하므로 정답은 (D) Requests이다.

어휘 reserve v. 예약하다 | submit v. 제출하다 | receptionist n. 접수 담당자 | request n. 요청, 신청서 v. 요청하다

9. 제안된 합병에 대한 보고서가 내일 발표될 것이다.

해설 정관사 the와 명사 merger 사이에 빈칸이 있으므로 빈칸에는 형용사가 온다. 형용사는 (A)와 (B)가 가능한데, '제안하는 합병'이 아니고 '제안된 합병'이므로 정답은 (A) proposed이다.

어휘 merger n. 합병 | release v. 발표하다 | propose v. 제안하다 | proposal n. 제안서

10. LPS 중공업은 신제품이 소매 시장에서 성공을 거두기를 바란다.

해설 부정관사 a 다음에는 명사가 와야 하므로 빈칸은 명사 자리이다. 명사는 (B)와 (D)인데, 동명사는 부정관사와 함께 쓸 수 없으므로 정답은 (B) success이다.

어휘 retail n. 소매 v. 소매하다 | marketplace n. 시장 | succeed v. 성공하다 | success n. 성공 | successfully adv. 성공적으로

11. 모든 현재 직원들은 새로 만들어진 행정 보조 자리에 지원할 자격이 있다.

해설 administrative assistant position이라는 명사 앞에 형용사 자리이므로 분사형 형용사 (B) created가 정답이다.

어휘 current adj. 현재의 | be eligible to부정사 ~할 자격이 있다 | administrative adj. 행정의, 관리의 | position n. 자리

12. 근로자들의 기술을 향상시키기 위해 교육에 합당한 양의 비용을 들이는 것은 불가피하다.

해설 부정관사 a와 명사 amount 사이에 빈칸이 있으므로 형용사가 와야 한다. 형용사는 (C)와 (D)가 가능한데, 문맥상 정답은 (C) reasonable 이다.

어휘 boost v. 늘리다 | workforce n. 노동 인구, 노동력 | devote v. 바치다 | amount n. 총액, 양 | unavoidable adj. 불가피한 | reasonable adj. 합리적인, 합당한

13. 매장 관리자의 검토를 위해서 수정된 분기 보고서를 내일 제출해 주세요.

해설 quarterly report이라는 명사 앞에 형용사 자리로 형용사 역할을 할 수 있는 분사 중에서 '수정된' 보고서로 수동의 의미가 있으므로 과거분사 (B) revised가 정답이다.

어휘 submit v. 제출하다 | quarterly adj. 분기의 | review n. 검토, 평가

14. 철강의 공급 과잉이 공급 가격을 매우 매력적으로 만들어 주었다.

해설 make는 5형식 동사로 목적어로 supplier prices가 왔다. 빈칸은 목적격 보어 자리로 상태 설명 형용사가 와야 한다. 형용사인 (A)와 (C) 중에서 목적어와의 관계를 봤을 때, '공급 가격들이 매료된 것'은 문맥상 적합하지 않으므로 정답은 (A) attractive이다.

어휘 oversupply n. 공급 과잉 | steel n. 철강 | supplier price 공급 가격 | attractive adj. 매력적인

15. 적절한 안전 예방 조치는 작업장의 모든 사고를 예방 가능하게 해 줄 것이다.

해설 동사 make는 5형식 동사이며 빈칸은 목적격 보어 자리이므로 형용사 (B) preventable이 정답이다.

어휘 proper adj. 적절한, 제대로 | safety precaution 안전 예방 조치 | preventable adj. 막을 수 있는, 예방할 수 있는

16. 모든 승객들은 탑승 요원에게 그들의 탑승권과 여권을 보여줄 것을 요구 받는다.

해설 ask는 5형식 동사로 목적격 보어 자리에 to부정사를 취한다. ask를 수동태로 썼으므로 목적어는 빠지고 바로 목적격 보어 to부정사가 왔다. 따라서 정답은 (C) present이다.

어휘 boarding agent 탑승 요원 | present v. 제시하다

17. B.N. 사는 경험 있고 동기 부여된 직원들을 찾고 있다.

해설 명사인 employees 앞에서 형용사 두 개가 and로 대등하게 연결된 형태이므로 정답은 (B) experienced이다.

어휘 seek v. 찾다 | motivated adj. 동기 부여된, 자극 받은 | experienced adj. 경험 있는, 능숙한

18. Mulberry로의 모든 건물들은 두 대의 차량을 주차할 수 있는 진입로를 갖추고 있다.

해설 전치사(of)와 명사구(two vehicles) 사이는 전치사의 목적어로서 명사의 기능과 명사구를 목적어로 취하는 동사의 기능을 동시에 할 수 있는 동명사 자리이므로 (A) parking이 정답이다.

어휘 property n. 건물; 부동산 | driveway n. 진입로 | capable of ~을 할 수 있는

19. 그 회사의 부사장은 우리 발표에 완전히 만족했다.

해설 was 뒤에 형용사 보어 자리이다. 동사 (A)와 (B)는 탈락이고 분사형 중에서 '사람이 만족하다'라는 의미로 수동의 의미가 있으므로 정답은 (D) satisfied이다.

어휘 completely adv. 완전히

20. Genhardt 자동차는 현재 공급 추적 소프트웨어의 교체를 고려하고 있다.

해설 consider는 목적어 자리에 동명사만을 취하므로 정답은 (B)와 (C)가 될 수 있다. 그런데 change의 목적어 their supply tracking software가 있으므로 능동 형태인 (B) changing이 정답이다.

어휘 currently adv. 현재 | supply tracking software 공급 추적 소프트웨어

21. 위원회의 추천 사항 중 하나가 즉시 시행될 것이다.

해설 정관사 the 뒤에는 명사가 와야 하는데, 동명사는 관사와 함께 쓸 수 없으므로 (B)는 정답이 될 수 없다. 「one of the + 복수 명사」 형태로 (A)와 (C)가 가능한데, 위원회에 의해서 만들어진 '추천자'가 아니고, '추천 사항'이므로 정답은 (A) recommendations이다.

어휘 implement v. 시행하다 | recommendation n. 추천, 추천서

22. 초기의 예산 견적은 금요일까지 회계부서에 제출되어야 한다.

해설 빈칸은 주어 자리로 명사가 들어가야 한다. 동명사 (C)는 뒤에 동명사의 목적어가 나와야 하는데 빈칸 뒤에 명사가 없으므로 탈락이다. 또한 빈칸 앞에 부정관사 an이 있으므로 단수 명사인 (B) estimate가 정답이다.

어휘 initial adj. 초기의, 처음의 | budget n. 예산 | estimate n. 견적서 | estimation n. 짐작, 평가, 평가치

23. 학회에서 전문성 개발 방법을 가르치는 것에 관심이 있는 사람들은 10월 10일까지 등록해야 한다.

해설 전치사 뒤에는 명사나 동명사가 와야 하고, to부정사는 올 수 없으므로 (A)는 탈락이다. 따라서 정답은 (C) teaching이다.

어휘 professional development 전문성 개발

24. 다음 관광 장소를 안내하기 전에, 모든 참가자 분들이 버스에 자리해 있는지 꼭 확인해야 한다.

해설 전치사 뒤 목적어 자리로, 뒤에 이미 명사 목적어가 있으므로 동명사

(D) announcing이 정답이다. 대개 명사구를 목적어로 취하지 않는 과거분사 (A) announced는 오답이며, 빈칸 뒤에 명사가 바로 오지 않고, 정관사 the가 있다는 점에서 명사나 형용사도 불가하다.

어휘 make sure 반드시 ~하다 | participant n. 참가자

25. Goldway 은행의 휴대폰 어플리케이션에서 사용자들이 겪고 있는 가끔 발생하는 문제들이 새 버전으로 해결될 것이다.

해설 문장의 주어는 issues, 본동사는 will be resolved로, 빈칸은 명사 issues를 수식하는 형용사 자리이며, '가끔(씩 일어나는) 문제들'이란 의미가 적절하므로 형용사 (C) occasional이 정답이다. occasion이 동사로 쓰일 때는 '~을 야기하다'라는 뜻의 타동사이므로 (A) occasioned는 '야기된'을 뜻하여 문맥상 어색하다.

어휘 issue n. 문제, 사안 | experience v. 겪다, 경험하다 | application n. 어플리케이션, 응용장치 | resolve v. 해결하다

26. Mr. Jones은 내일 회의에서 초대 받은 청중들에게 연설할 것이다.

해설 명사 audience 앞에 빈칸이 있으므로 형용사가 들어가야 한다. 형용사는 (C)와 (D)인데, '초대하는 청중들'이 아니고 '초대된 청중들'이므로 정답은 (D) invited이다.

어휘 give a speech 연설하다 | audience n. 청중

27. 행사의 가장 중요한 후원 업체들은 Indulsion 사와 M&K 사이다.

해설 정관사 The 뒤에 명사가 있으므로 빈칸은 형용사 자리이다. 따라서 정답은 (C) most prominent이다.

어휘 sponsor n. 후원업체, 후원자 | prominent adj. 중요한, 유명한, 현저한, 눈에 잘 띄는

28. 소비자들은 차세대 Mango 노트북 컴퓨터가 시판될 날을 간절히 기다린다.

해설 이미 완전한 3형식 문장이므로 빈칸에는 부사가 와야 한다. 따라서 정답은 (B) eagerly이다.

어휘 await v. 기다리다 | eagerly adv. 간절히, 열망하여 | go on sale 시판되다

29. 수익 감소는 추가로 영업 사원을 고용하는 것을 어느 때보다 더 어렵게 만들었다.

해설 make는 5형식 동사로 가목적어는 it이고 진목적어는 to부정사 이하다. 빈칸은 목적격 보어 자리로 상태 설명 형용사가 들어가야 한다. 형용사는 (A)와 (C)가 가능하지만 than이 있으므로 정답은 (C) harder이다.

어휘 decline n. 감소 | sales associate 영업 사원 | hard adj. 어려운

30. 사과 샐러드는 어제 그녀가 만든 키위 샐러드보다 더 달콤하다.

해설 2형식 동사 is 다음의 빈칸에는 주격 보어, 즉 상태 설명 형용사가 온다. 형용사는 (A), (B), (D)인데 뒤에 than이 있으므로 정답은 (B) sweeter이다.

어휘 sweet adj. 달콤한

VOCA

UNIT 01. 동사

본서 p.165

....

Practice

1. (C) **2.** (C) **3.** (A) **4.** (B) **5.** (B)
6. (D) **7.** (A) **8.** (C) **9.** (D) **10.** (C)

....

1. 고객들을 끌어들이기 위해서, Blue Stone 호텔들은 현재 할인을 제공하고 있다.

해설　빈칸에 들어갈 동사 어휘는 customers를 목적어로 취할 수 있어야 한다. 토익에서 '고객'을 목적어로 잘 취하는 동사 중의 하나가 attract이다. '고객들을 끌어들이다'는 문맥상 자연스러우므로 정답은 (C) attract이다.

어휘　discount *n.* 할인 | await *v.* ~을 기다리다 | contact *v.* 연락하다, 접촉하다 | reimburse *v.* 배상하다

2. 새 컬러 인쇄기는 토너 카트리지 하나로 문서를 10,000페이지까지 생산해낸다.

해설　컬러 프린터기가 최대 10,000페이지의 문서를 생산해낸다는 의미가 자연스러우므로 '생산하다'라는 의미의 (C) produces가 정답이다.

어휘　up to 최대 ~까지 | toner cartridge (잉크) 토너 카트리지 | categorize *v.* 분류하다 | limit *v.* 제한시키다 | spend *v.* (시간을) 보내다, (돈을) 쓰다

3. 모든 고객들은 10달러 이상의 구매에 대해 할인 쿠폰을 제공받았다.

해설　수동태 문장으로, 수동태는 목적어가 주어로 빠지게 되므로 동사 뒤에 목적어가 없어야 된다. 그런데 수동태임에도 불구하고 빈칸 뒤에 명사(목적어)가 있다는 것은 원래 목적어가 두 개였다는 뜻이다. 따라서 4형식 동사를 찾아야 하므로 정답은 (A) offered이다.

어휘　purchase *n.* 구매 | advertise *v.* 광고하다

4. 우리는 직원들이 사무실 안에 있는 동안 신분 배지를 항상 착용하도록 요구한다.

해설　빈칸 뒤에 목적어(employees)와 to부정사(to wear)가 연결되어 있으므로 목적격 보어로 to부정사를 취하여 5형식 동사로 쓰일 수 있는 (B) ask가 정답이다.

어휘　at all times 항상

5. 모든 직원들은 반드시 회사 정책들을 따라야 한다.

해설　빈칸에 들어갈 동사는 전치사 with와 함께 다니는 동사이어야 한다. give와 assign은 「give/assign + 목적어 + to 명사」로 전치사 to와 함께 쓰이므로 탈락이다. 「comply with」는 '~를 준수하다, 지키다, 순응하다'라는 뜻으로 전치사 with를 동반하므로 정답은 (B) comply이다.

어휘　comply *v.* 준수하다, 따르다 | assign *v.* 할당하다

6. Hidden 스튜디오와 Cliff 제작사는 그 영화를 협력하여 작업하기 위한 합의에 이르렀다.

해설　「reach an agreement」는 '합의에 도달하다'라는 뜻으로 관용적 표현처럼 쓰이므로 목적어인 agreement만 보고도 (D) reached를 선택할 수 있어야 한다.

어휘　collaboratively *adv.* 협력하여

7. 당신은 지역 사업 연합회 가입을 통해 혜택을 얻을 수 있다.

해설　빈칸에 들어갈 동사는 전치사 from과 함께 다니는 동사이어야 하므로 정답은 (A) benefit이다. 「benefit from」은 '~로 부터 혜택을 얻다'라는 뜻이다. serve는 보통 serve as로 쓰여 '~의 역할을 하다'라는 뜻이다.

어휘　association *n.* 협회 | assist *v.* 돕다 | serve *v.* 제공하다

8. Hill 사에 의해 생산된 바닥재는 다양한 모양, 크기와 색상들로 나온다.

해설　문장의 형식을 물어보는 문제이다. 빈칸 동사 뒤에 목적어도, 보어도 아무것도 없다. 단지, 전치사와 명사로 이루어진 수식어구만 존재한다. 따라서 1형식 동사를 찾으라는 문제이므로 정답은 (C) comes이다.

어휘　flooring *n.* 바닥재 | a variety of 여러 가지의 | come in (물품, 상품이) 들어오다, 나오다

9. 병가 신청서는 부장에게 이메일로 제출되어야 한다.

해설　빈칸에 들어갈 동사의 어휘는 중간에 있는 수식어구와 상관없이, 주어와 어울리는 동사를 찾는 것이 포인트이다. 신청서가 이메일로 제출되어야 하므로 정답은 (D) submitted이다.

어휘　sick leave 병가 | select *v.* 선택하다, 고르다 | solve *v.* 해결하다

10. 모든 직원들은 자신들의 책상을 청소할 것을 요구받는다.

해설　선택지에 나온 단어를 빈칸에 넣으면 수동태가 된다. (D) worked는 1형식 동사이므로 수동태가 될 수 없으므로 탈락이다. 수동태 뒤에 to부정사가 나왔다는 것은 5형식 동사 중 목적격 보어로 to부정사를 취하는 동사를 찾으라는 신호다. 5형식 동사의 목적어는 주어로 빠지고, 목적격 보어 자리에 있던 to부정사가 빈칸 뒤에 남은 것이다. require는 「require + 목적어 + to부정사」 형태로 쓰인다. 따라서 정답은 (C) required이다.

어휘　create *v.* 만들다, 창조하다 | require *v.* 요구하다

UNIT 02. 명사

본서 p.169

····································

Practice

1. (C)	**2.** (B)	**3.** (C)	**4.** (A)	**5.** (B)
6. (C)	**7.** (A)	**8.** (A)	**9.** (B)	**10.** (A)

····································

1. 그 새로운 레스토랑은 매우 다양한 건강 요리를 제공한다.

해설　덩어리 표현을 알아 두자. 「a variety of」는 '여러 가지의, 다양한'이란 뜻이다. 따라서 정답은 (C) variety이다.

어휘　**wide** *adj.* 넓은 | **dish** *n.* 요리 | **sense** *n.* 감각 | **situation** *n.* 상황 | **variety** *n.* 여러 가지, 각양각색 | **condition** *n.* 상태, 조건

2. 청구서에 기재되어 있는 인건비는 예상 견적이다.

해설　수식어에 상관없이 뼈대만 보고 어휘를 찾자. 빈칸에 올 명사는 are라는 2형식 동사 뒤에 오는 주격 보어가 된다. 명사 보어는 주어와 동격 관계이다. 즉, 주어와 같은 개념이 빈칸에 들어가야 한다. 주어가 '비용'이므로 비용=개발, 비용=시도, 비용=요구 모두 말이 되지 않으므로 탈락이다. 비용=견적이 제일 자연스러우므로 정답은 (B) estimate이다.

어휘　**labor cost** 인건비 | **indicate** *v.* 나타내다, 보여주다, 명시하다 | **estimate** *n.* 견적(서), 추정치, 추산 | **attempt** *n.* 시도 | **requirement** *n.* 요구 조건

3. Platinum 상 수상자가 다음달 〈Technological Spotlight Magazine〉에 실릴 것이다.

해설　Platinum 상의 수상자가 잡지에 실릴 거라는 의미가 자연스러우므로 '수령인'을 뜻하는 (C) recipient가 정답이다.

어휘　**feature** *v.* 특징으로 삼다

4. Hanscro 슈퍼마켓은 건강에 관심이 많은 쇼핑객들을 끌기 위해 아주 많은 종류의 유기농 제품들을 판매한다.

해설　덩어리 표현을 알아두자. 「a range of」는 '다양한'이라는 의미이며 명사 range 앞에 강조를 위해 아주 다양하다는 뜻으로 형용사 full이나 wide, broad와 같은 형용사가 붙을 수 있다. 따라서 정답은 (A) range이다.

어휘　**organic product** 유기농 제품 | **attract** *v.* 끌어들이다 | **health-conscious** *adj.* 건강을 의식하는 | **range** *n.* 다양성; 범위 | **degree** *n.* 정도 | **focus** *n.* 초점; 주목 | **growth** *n.* 성장

5. QVPE 사는 이번 분기에 Kavabean 사를 매입하려는 의도를 발표했다.

해설　빈칸 뒤에 to부정사가 나왔다는 것은 빈칸에 들어갈 명사가 to부정사의 수식을 받는다는 말이다. 매입하겠다는 '이상, 창조, 설명'을 발표하는 것은 모두 어색하다. 매입하겠다는 '의사'를 발표하는 것이 가장 자연스럽다. 따라서 정답은 (B) intention이다.

어휘　**ideal** *n.* 이상(형) *adj.* 이상적인 | **creation** *n.* 창조, 창작 | **explanation** *n.* 설명 | **intention** *n.* 의사, 의도, 목적

6. 저희와 지속적으로 거래해 주신 것에 감사드리며 우리는 당신께 회원 카드를 제공해 드리고 싶습니다.

해설　전치사 of와 함께 어울려 쓰는 명사 어휘를 찾으면 된다. (A) response는 전치사 to와 어울려 쓰므로 탈락이다. 「in response to」는 '~에 반응하여'라는 뜻이다. 「in appreciation of」는 '~을(에) 감사하여'라는 뜻으로 쓰이므로 전치사 in과 of가 힌트가 되어 정답은 (C) appreciation이다.

어휘　**response** *n.* 반응 | **mention** *n.* 언급, 진술 *v.* 언급하다 | **appreciation** *n.* 감사, 감상, 감탄 | **comment** *n.* 의견, 논평

7. 고객 만족을 향상시키기 위해, 우리는 제품 품질을 향상시키는 것에 전념한다.

해설　복합 명사로 덩어리 표현을 알아두자. 'customer satisfaction'은 '고객 만족'이라는 복합 명사다. 따라서 정답은 (A) satisfaction이다.

어휘　**be committed to** ~에 헌신하다, 전념하다 | **consideration** *n.* 고려, 사려 | **hospitality** *n.* 환대, 접대

8. 우리는 운영비를 절약할 가장 효과적인 방법에 대해 토의했다.

해설　빈칸 뒤에 to부정사가 나왔다는 것은 빈칸에 들어갈 명사가 to부정사의 수식을 받는다는 의미이다. way는 to부정사의 수식을 자주 받는 명사이다. '절약할 가장 효과적인 (B) 명세 사항, (C) 자격, (D) 숙박 시설'은 모두 어색하므로 탈락이다. 따라서 정답은 (A) ways이다.

어휘　**discuss** *v.* 토론하다 | **effective** *adj.* 효과적인 | **save** *v.* 절약하다 | **operating cost** 운영비 | **way** *n.* 방법 | **specification** *n.* 설명서, 사양 | **qualification** *n.* 자격, 자질 | **accommodation** *n.* 숙박 (시설)

9. 이달의 (우수) 직원 추천서는 오늘 오후 4시까지 제출되어야 한다.

해설　수식어구 빼고 뼈대만 보면 빈칸은 주어 자리이므로 주어와 동사와의 관계만 보고 답을 찾아 보자. '성과(실적), 사건, 권한'이 제출될 수 없다. 그러나 추천서는 제출될 수 있으므로 정답은 (B) Nominations이다.

어휘　**performance** *n.* 실적, 성과, 공연 | **nomination** *n.* 지명, 추천(서), 임명 | **incident** *n.* 사건 | **authority** *n.* 권한, 권위자

10. 판매 직원이 솔선해서 잠재 고객들과 접촉해야 한다.

해설　initiative는 생김새는 형용사 같지만 실제 품사는 명사이다. 생김새와 실제 품사가 다르면 다른 명사들보다 정답이 될 확률이 높다. 「take the initiative」는 '솔선해서 하다'라는 뜻이므로 정답은 (A) initiative이다.

어휘　**representative** *n.* 대표, 대리인, 직원 | **initiative** *n.* 개시, 솔선수범, 주도(권) | **outcome** *n.* 결과 | **advice** *n.* 충고 | **prediction** *n.* 예측, 예견

UNIT 03. 형용사

본서 p.173

....

Practice

1. (B)	2. (C)	3. (C)	4. (A)	5. (A)
6. (B)	7. (C)	8. (A)	9. (B)	10. (D)

....

1. 경험 있는 기술자들은 대부분의 컴퓨터 문제를 확인하는 데 고작 10분 밖에 안 걸린다.

해설 어휘 문제라고 모두 다 읽을 필요는 없다. 빈칸에 들어갈 형용사는 명사 technicians를 꾸며 주므로 빈칸의 어휘는 technicians와 문맥상 잘 어울리면 정답이 될 수 있다. '상대적인 기술자, 결정적인 기술자, 유리한 기술자'는 모두 말이 되지 않는다. 문맥상 '경험 있는 기술자' 또는 '노련한 기술자'가 자연스러우므로 정답은 (B) Experienced 이다.

어휘 technician n. 기술자 | identify v. 확인하다, 찾다 | relative adj. 상대적인 | conclusive adj. 결정적인 | advantageous adj. 이로운, 유리한 | experienced adj. 경험 있는, 노련한

2. 당신의 새로운 소프트웨어가 당신의 운영 체제와 호환이 가능한지를 확인해야 한다.

해설 빈칸 뒤에 with가 있으므로 빈칸의 어휘는 전치사 with를 동반할 수 있는 형용사이어야 한다. 전치사 with를 동반할 수 있는 것은 compatible이므로 정답은 (C) compatible이다. 「be compatible with」는 '~와 호환할 수 있다'라는 뜻이다.

어휘 operating system (컴퓨터) 운영 체제 | reflective adj. 반사하는, 반영하는 | reportable adj. 보고할 수 있는 | compatible adj. 호환 되는 | irregular adj. 불규칙한

3. Golden 유기농 농장은 친환경적 관행을 중요하게 여긴다.

해설 environmentally friendly는 '환경 친화적인'이라는 뜻으로 관용적 표현처럼 쓰이므로 부사 environmentally만 보고도 (C) friendly를 선택할 수 있어야 하며, friendly가 '~친화적인'이라는 뜻의 '-ly'형 형용사인 점에 주의한다.

어휘 practice n. 관행, 관례 | general adj. 일반적인 | exposed adj. 노출된 | considerate adj. 사려 깊은

4. 참가자들은 컨벤션에 입장하기 위해 사진이 있는 유효한 신분증을 보여줘야 한다.

해설 photo ID를 수식하기에 알맞은 형용사를 고르는 문제로 '유효한 신분증을 보여줘야 한다'는 의미가 자연스러우므로 '유효한'이라는 뜻의 (A) valid가 정답이다.

어휘 participant n. 참가자 | ID n. 신분증(=identification) | convention n. 컨벤션, 대회

5. 애플리케이션에 대한 기술적인 지원을 받으려면 Mr. Hong에게 연락해주세요.

해설 빈칸에 들어갈 형용사는 명사 assistance를 꾸미므로 빈칸의 어휘는 assistance와 함께 말이 되면 바로 정답이 될 수 있다. '흥미 있는 지원, 의존적인 지원, 역사적인 지원'은 모두 문맥상 말이 되지 않는다. '기술적인 지원'이 가장 자연스러우므로 정답은 (A) technical이다.

어휘 assistance n. 도움, 원조, 지원 | application n. 응용장치, 애플리케이션 | technical adj. 기술적인 | interested adj. 관심[흥미] 있어 하는 | dependent adj. 의존적인 | historical adj. 역사적인

6. 직원들은 제때에 그들의 일을 해야 한다.

해설 timely는 부사처럼 보이지만 형용사이다. 명사에 -ly를 붙이면 형용사가 된다. 이럴 땐 생김새와 실제 품사가 다른 것이 답이 될 확률이 높아진다. 「in a timely manner는 '시기 적절하게'이므로, 정답은 (B) timely이다.

어휘 timely adj. 시기 적절한, 때맞춘 | in a timely manner 시기적절하게, 적시에, 제때에 | favorite adj. 가장 좋아하는 | recent adj. 최근의

7. 그 계약서의 조건에 대해서 알아 두시오.

해설 빈칸 뒤에 전치사 of가 힌트이다. 전치사 of와 함께 다니는 형용사 어휘를 찾으면 된다. (A)와 (B)는 딱히 어울려 쓰이는 전치사가 존재하지 않는다. (D) 「be known for는 '~로 알려져 있다'라는 뜻으로 전치사 for를 동반한다. (C) 「be aware of는 '~을 알아차리다, ~을 알다'라는 뜻으로 전치사 of를 동반하므로 정답은 (C) aware이다.

어휘 contract n. 계약(서) v. 계약하다 | terms and conditions (계약)조건 | noted adj. 유명한, 잘 알려져 있는 | proposed adj. 제안된 | aware adj. ~을 알고 있는 | known adj. 알려진

8. 그 회사는 화학 분야에서 열심히 일하기를 열망하는 모든 지원자들을 환영한다.

해설 빈칸에 들어갈 형용사 어휘는 다 읽을 필요 없이 빈칸 뒤에 나온 to부정사가 힌트이다. 즉, to부정사와 함께 다니는 형용사를 찾으라는 말인데, eager가 to부정사와 함께 다니는 형용사 어휘이므로 정답은 (A) eager이다. 기억이 나지 않는다면 Grammar 파트 to부정사 부분을 꼭 다시 살펴보자!

어휘 welcome v. 환영하다 adj. 환영하는 | applicant n. 지원자 | chemistry n. 화학 | field n. 분야 | eager adj. 열렬한, 간절히 바라는 | capable adj. ~ 할 수 있는 | probable adj. 있을 것 같은 | possible adj. 가능한

9. 갑작스러운 정전으로 인해, 몇몇 직원들이 중요한 파일들을 저장할 수 없었다.

해설 복합명사로 쓰인 power outage (정전)를 수식하기에 알맞은 형용사를 고르는 문제이다. 정전이 갑자기 일어나서 파일을 저장하지 못했다는 의미이므로 '갑작스러운'이라는 뜻의 (B) sudden이 정답이다.

어휘 power outage 정전 | be unable to ~할 수 없다 | save v. 저장하다 | convenient adj. 편리한 | sudden adj. 갑작스러운 | inadequate adj. 불충분한 | upcoming adj. 다가오는

10. Mr. Nguyen의 짧은 부재 기간 동안 그의 동료 중 하나가 직장에서 그의 직무를 대신할 것이다.

해설 답을 찾기 위해 이 문장을 다 읽을 필요는 없다. 어차피 빈칸에 들어갈 어휘는 뒤에 있는 명사 absence를 꾸미는 형용사이어야 하므로 absence와 의미상 잘 어울리면 정답이다. '강한 부재, 생산적인 부재, 중요한 부재'는 모두 말이 되지 않는다. '짧은 부재'는 잠깐 자리를 비웠다는 뜻이므로 말이 된다. 따라서 정답은 (D) brief이다.

어휘 absence n. 부재, 결근 | colleague n. 동료 | cover v. 대신하다, 씌우다, 덮다 | duty n. 의무, 직무, 임무 | workplace n. 직장, 업무 현장 | productive adj. 생산적인

UNIT 04. 부사

본서 p.177

Practice

1. (C)	**2.** (C)	**3.** (A)	**4.** (B)	**5.** (C)
6. (D)	**7.** (D)	**8.** (C)	**9.** (C)	**10.** (D)

1. 수하물 청구 서식을 고객 서비스 센터에 제출하기 전에 꼼꼼하게 작성해 주세요.

해설 동사 fill out (작성하다)을 수식하기에 알맞은 부사를 고르는 문제로 '꼼꼼하게 작성해 달라'는 의미가 자연스러우므로 '꼼꼼하게, 완벽하게'라는 뜻의 (C) completely가 정답이다.

어휘 baggage claim form 수화물 청구 서식 | submit v. 제출하다 | comparatively adv. 비교적 | sometimes adv. 때때로 | massively adv. 엄청나게

2. 당신은 그 기사를 대략 3페이지 정도 써야 한다.

해설 '3페이지'라는 숫자가 나왔다. 숫자 앞에 올 수 있는 부사를 찾아야 한다. '거의, 대략'이라는 뜻의 about이 적절하다. 따라서 정답은 (C) about이다.

어휘 article n. 기사 | more adv. 더 | rather adv. 오히려, 차라리 | about adv. 대략, 거의 | quite adv. 꽤, 상당히

3. 낮은 월급 때문에, 그 회사의 직원들은 반복적으로 급여 인상을 요청했다.

해설 빈칸에 들어갈 부사는 requested를 꾸미므로 request와 가장 잘 어울리는 부사를 찾아야 한다. '믿을 수 없을 정도로 요청한다, 간략한 요청한다, 정확히 요청한다'는 모두 문맥상 말이 되지 않는다. '반복적으로 요청한다'가 가장 자연스러우므로 정답은 (A) repeatedly이다.

어휘 low adj. 낮은 | request v. 요청하다 | pay raise 급여 인상 | repeatedly adv. 반복적으로 | incredibly adv. 믿을 수 없을 정도로, 엄청나게 | shortly adv. 곧, 이내 | exactly adv. 정확히

4. 최근 연구에 따르면, 대졸자들 사이의 실업률이 올해 상당히 더 높다.

해설 비교급 형용사 higher (더 높은)를 수식하기에 알맞은 부사를 고르는 문제로 '상당히 더 높다'는 의미가 자연스러우므로 '상당히'라는 뜻의 (B) considerably가 정답이다.

어휘 according to ~에 따라 | unemployment rate 실업률 | college graduates 대졸자 | deeply adv. 깊게 | densely adv. 밀집하여 | nearly adv. 거의

5. 새 GX890 프린터는 산업 디자이너들에 의해 강력히 추천된다.

해설 '강력히 추천하다'라는 뜻으로 highly[strongly] recommend는 항상 함께 사용되므로 덩어리째 암기하는 게 좋다. 정답은 (C) highly이다.

어휘 loosely adv. 느슨하게 | readily adv. 손쉽게, 순조롭게 | highly adv. 매우 | gradually adv. 점차적으로

6. 비록 오늘은 늦었지만, Ms. Kim은 보통 8시 정각에 직장에 도착한다.

해설 이 문제는 부사 어휘 문제처럼 보이지만 사실은 시제 문제이다. arrives라는 현재 시제가 나왔으므로 현재 시제와 주로 어울리는 빈도 부사를 찾아야 한다. 따라서 정답은 (D) usually이다. 기억이 나지 않는다면 Grammar 파트에서의 시제 부분을 꼭 다시 살펴보자!

어휘 late adj. 늦은 adv. 늦게 | greatly adv. 대단히, 크게 | evenly adv. 고르게 | weakly adv. 힘없이, 약하게 | usually adv. 보통, 대개

7. 직원들을 위한 집중 훈련 프로그램들 중 다수가 아주 성공적이었다.

해설 빈칸에 들어갈 부사는 형용사 successful을 꾸미므로 successful과 가장 잘 어울리는 부사를 찾아야 한다. '예의 바르게 성공적인, 마음대로 성공적인, 실험적으로 성공적인'은 모두 말이 되지 않는다. '아주 성공적인'이 가장 자연스러우므로 정답은 (D) extremely이다.

어휘 intensive adj. 집중적인, 철두철미한 | successful adj. 성공적인 | courteously adv. 예의 바르게 | optionally adv. 마음대로 | experimentally adv. 실험적으로 | extremely adv. 아주, 극도로

8. Ober 의류는 더 많은 고객들을 유치하기 위해 적정 가격의 비즈니스 정장을 판매한다.

해설 reasonably priced는 '적정하게 가격이 매겨진, 적정 가격의'라는 뜻으로 관용적 표현처럼 쓰이므로 빈칸 뒤의 priced만 보고도 (C) reasonably를 선택할 수 있어야 한다.

어휘 business attire 비즈니스 정장 | attract v. 불러모으다, 끌어들이다 | specifically adv. 분명하게, 명확하게 | totally adv. 완전히, 전적으로 | slightly adv. 약간, 조금

9. 그 버스는 Maxerit 호텔에서 도심까지 대략 40분이 걸린다.

해설 숫자 앞에 빈칸인 경우 '대략'이라는 뜻의 부사가 답이다. 따라서 정답은 (C) approximately이다.

어휘 city center n. 도심부 | neatly adv. 깔끔하게, 말쑥하게 | finally adv. 마침내, 결국에 | approximately adv. 거의, 대략, ~가까이 | closely adv. 밀접하게

10. 우리가 현재 귀사를 위해 실시하고 있는 설문 조사는 다음 주 화요일까지 집계될 것이다.

해설 부사 어휘 문제처럼 보이지만 이 문제는 사실 시제 문제이다. are conducting이라는 현재진행형 시제가 나왔으므로 현재진행형과 어울리는 부사를 찾아야 한다. 따라서 정답은 (D) currently이다. 기억이 나지 않는다면 Grammar 파트에서의 시제 부분을 꼭 다시 살펴보자!

어휘 conduct v. 실시하다, 수행하다 | compile v. (자료 등을) 엮다, 편찬하다 | commonly adv. 흔히, 보통 | previously adv. 이전에 | ordinarily adv. 정상적으로, 보통, 대개 | currently adv. 현재

REVIEW TEST
본서 p.178

1. (B)	**2.** (A)	**3.** (A)	**4.** (B)	**5.** (D)
6. (A)	**7.** (B)	**8.** (D)	**9.** (B)	**10.** (B)
11. (C)	**12.** (C)	**13.** (C)	**14.** (C)	**15.** (C)
16. (B)	**17.** (C)	**18.** (C)	**19.** (B)	**20.** (C)
21. (C)	**22.** (C)	**23.** (B)	**24.** (C)	**25.** (C)
26. (D)	**27.** (B)	**28.** (A)	**29.** (A)	**30.** (B)

1. 물리치료 병동은 병원 입구에서 먼 곳에 위치해 있다.

해설 빈칸은 명사 hospital의 한정을 받는 명사 자리로 '병원 입구에서 멀리 떨어져 있다'는 의미가 자연스러우므로 '입구'라는 뜻의 (B) entrance가 정답이다.

어휘 physical therapy 물리 요법 | locate v. 위치시키다 | far from ~에서 먼 | distance n. 거리 | format n. 구성, 방식 | dimension n. 크기, 규모

2. PT 음료회사의 마케팅 이사는 그 직위에 Ms. Kanakuro를 추천했다.

해설 빈칸은 Ms. Kanakuro를 목적어로 취하는 동사 자리로 '그 자리에 Ms. Kankuro를 적극 추천했다'는 의미가 자연스러우므로 '추천하다'라는 뜻의 (A) recommended가 정답이다.

어휘 beverage n. 음료 | director n. 이사 | position n. 직위, 일자리 | conclude v. 결론을 내리다 | deserve v. ~할 만하다 | record v. 녹음하다

3. 면접에 참석할 때는 회사에 관한 기본적인 지식을 갖고 있는 것이 도움이 된다.

해설 빈칸은 명사 knowledge를 수식하는 형용사 자리로 '회사에 관한 기본 지식을 갖는 것이 도움이 된다'는 의미가 자연스러우므로 '기본적인'이라는 뜻의 (A) basic이 정답이다.

어휘 attend v. 참석하다 | helpful adj. 도움이 되는 | anxious adj. 염려하는 | hard adj. 어려운, 힘든 | reckless adj. 무모한

4. 소포를 뜯어보기 전에 배송 라벨에 적힌 정보를 읽는 것이 중요하다.

해설 빈칸 앞 shipping과 복합명사를 이루기에 적절한 명사 자리로 '배송 라벨에 적힌 정보'라는 의미가 자연스러우므로 '라벨'을 뜻하는 (B) label이 정답이다.

어휘 crucial adj. 중대한, 결정적인 | include v. 포함하다 | shipping n. 운송, 발송 | signal n. 신호 | type n. 종류, 유형

5. Ms. Johnson은 전국 미술 경연대회에서 그녀의 그림으로 대상을 수상했다.

해설 빈칸은 문장의 동사 자리로 'Ms. Johnson이 그녀의 그림으로 대상을 수상했다'는 의미가 자연스러우므로 '수여하다'라는 뜻의 (D) awarded가 정답이다. 참고로 award는 두 개의 목적어를 취하여 '~에게 ...을 주다'라는 기본 의미를 갖는 4형식 동사이므로 문제에서처럼 수동태 문장에서도 명사구를 목적어로 취할 수 있음에 유의하고, 오히려 이것이 문제를 푸는 단서가 될 수 있음을 알아두자.

어휘 national adj. 전국의 | contest n. 경연대회 | win v. 이기다, 승리하다 | obtain v. 얻다, 획득하다

6. Stern 식당의 수석 요리사는 지역 농장에서 신선한 유기농 농산물을 주문한다.

해설 빈칸은 organic과 함께 명사 produce를 수식하는 형용사 자리로 '신선한 유기농 농산물을 주문한다'는 의미가 자연스러우므로 '신선한'이라는 뜻의 (A) fresh가 정답이다.

어휘 bistro n. 작은 선술집 | executive chef 수석 요리사 | order v. 주문하다 | organic adj. 유기농의, 화학 비료를 쓰지 않는 | produce n. 농작물 | local adj. 지역의 | gentle adj. 온화한 | durable adj. 오래가는, 내구성이 있는 | effective adj. 효과적인

7. Riverton's 교통부는 도시의 버스와 지하철 서비스를 감독한다.

해설 빈칸은 문장의 동사 자리로 '교통부가 시의 버스와 지하철 서비스를 감독한다'는 의미가 자연스러우므로 '감독하다'라는 뜻의 (B) oversees가 정답이다.

어휘 transportation department 교통부 | predict v. 예상하다 | view v. 보다; 여기다 | commute v. 통근하다

8. Ms. Nguyen의 스타트업 회사를 위한 아이디어는 뉴질랜드에서 휴가를 보내는 동안 형성되었다.

해설 빈칸은 문장의 주어 자리로 '스타트업 회사를 위한 아이디어가 휴가 기간 동안 형성되었다'는 의미가 자연스러우므로 '아이디어'라는 뜻의 (D) idea가 정답이다. 참고로 명사 idea는 전치사 for나 of를 동반한다는 점에서 빈칸 뒤의 전치사 for가 문제를 푸는 단서가 된다는 점을 알아두자.

어휘 startup company 스타트업 기업, 신생기업 | form v. 형성시키다, 만들어 내다 | vacation n. 휴가 | content n. 내용물; 목차 | fact n. 사실 | value n. 가치

9. Heilen 식료품점의 특별 할인은 9월 15일까지만 가능하다.

해설 빈칸은 앞의 형용사 available을 수식하는 부사 자리로 '특별 할인이 9월 15일까지만 이용 가능하다'는 의미가 자연스러우므로 '오직 ~만'이라는 뜻의 (B) only가 정답이다.

어휘 special discount 특별 할인 | available *adj.* 이용 가능한 | hardly *adv.* 거의 ~하지 않는 | only *adv.* 오로지, 단지 | barely *adv.* 겨우, 간신히 | carefully *adv.* 주의 깊게

10. 〈Essential Knife Techniques〉은 장차 요리사가 되려는 모든 사람들의 영상 수집품에 훌륭한 추가 자료가 될 것이다.

해설 빈칸은 명사 addition을 수식하는 형용사 자리로 '〈Essential Knife Techniques〉이란 컨텐츠가 훌륭한 추가 자료가 될 것이다'라는 의미가 자연스러우므로 '훌륭한'이라는 뜻의 (B) great가 정답이다.

어휘 addition *n.* 추가된 것, 추가물 | library *n.* 수집품; 도서관 | aspiring *adj.* 장차 ~가 되려는 | like *prep.* ~와 같은 | high *adj.* (위치상) 높은 | constant *adj.* 끊임없는, 지속적인

11. Mr. Ido의 부재 시에, 부매니저가 가게를 운영할 것이다.

해설 빈칸은 Mr. Ido의 한정을 받는 명사 자리로 'Mr. Ido의 부재 시에, 부매니저가 가게를 운영할 것이다'라는 의미가 자연스러우므로 '부재'라는 뜻의 (C) absence가 정답이다. 참고로 「in 사람's absence는 '~의 부재 시에'」라는 관용표현이므로 기억해두자.

어휘 essential *adj.* 필수의, 가장 중요한 | assistant manager 부매니저 | run *v.* 운영하다 | situation *n.* 상황 | example *n.* 예, 본보기 | duty *n.* 임무, 직무

12. Dyno 사가 예상 수익을 초과 달성하였으므로 직원들은 연말에 보너스를 받을 것이다.

해설 빈칸은 주절의 목적어 자리로 'Dyno 사가 예상 수익을 초과 달성했다'는 의미가 자연스러우므로 '수익'이라는 뜻의 (C) earnings가 정답이다.

어휘 surpass *v.* 능가하다, 뛰어넘다 | projected *adj.* 예상된, 추정된 | employee *n.* 직원 | combination *n.* 조합 | trip *n.* 여행

13. 예산안에 있는 자료를 확인하시고 언급할 내용이 있으실 경우 Mr. Patel에게 전화 주십시오.

해설 빈칸은 if절의 목적어 자리로 '예산안을 확인하고 언급할 내용이 있다면 Mr. Patel에게 전화하라'는 의미가 자연스러우므로 '언급할 내용, 논평'이라는 뜻의 (C) comments가 정답이다.

어휘 confirm *v.* 확인하다 | budget proposal 예산안 | operation *n.* 운영 | policy *n.* 규정 | price *n.* 가격

14. Lamar 무선인터넷은 오늘 아침 Heather Hill 지역의 나쁜 수신 상태에 대해 진심으로 사과 드립니다.

해설 빈칸은 '수신 상태'라는 뜻으로 쓰인 명사 reception을 수식하는 명사 자리로 '나쁜 수신 상태에 대해 사과한다'는 의미가 자연스러우므로 '나쁜, 좋지 못한'이라는 뜻의 (C) poor가 정답이다.

어휘 wireless internet 무선인터넷 | sincerely *adv.* 진심으로 | apologize *v.* 사과하다 | district *n.* 지구, 지역 | pale *adj.* 창백한 | mild *adj.* 순한 | less *adj.* 덜한

15. 모든 연구실 기술자들은 위험한 화학 물질을 다룰 때면 공식 안전 절차들을 준수해야 한다.

해설 빈칸 앞 safety와 복합명사를 이루기에 적절한 명사 자리로 '안전 절차들을 준수해야 한다'라는 의미가 자연스러우므로 '절차, 규정'을 뜻하는 (C) procedures가 정답이다.

어휘 technician *n.* 기술자 | adhere to ~을 고수하다 | official *adj.* 공식적인 | safety *n.* 안전 | handle *v.* 다루다 | chemical *n.* 화학 물질 | matter *n.* 문제, 사안 | installation *n.* 설치

16. 곧 있을 행사에 대해 일찍 공지를 받으시려면 귀하의 연락처를 제공해 주시기 바랍니다.

해설 빈칸은 명사 events를 수식하는 형용사 자리로 '곧 있을 행사에 관한 공지를 일찍 받으려면, 연락처를 제공하라'는 의미가 자연스러우므로 '곧 있을, 다가오는'이라는 뜻의 (B) upcoming이 정답이다.

어휘 notification *n.* 알림, 통지 | contact information 연락처 | latest *adj.* 최신의 | prepared *adj.* 준비된 | advanced *adj.* 진보된; 고급의

17. Lascaux 플라자의 정원은 유명 야외 예술가인 Jean Dernier에 의해 계획되었다.

해설 빈칸은 문장의 동사 자리로 'Lascaux 플라자 정원이 유명 예술가에 의해 기획되었다'는 의미가 자연스러우므로 '계획하다'라는 뜻의 (C) planned가 정답이다.

어휘 popular *adj.* 인기가 많은 | outdoor *adj.* 옥외의, 야외의 | artist *n.* 예술가 | concern *v.* 우려하다 | assume *v.* 가정하다 | affect *v.* 영향을 끼치다

18. 지난 몇 개월 동안은 이례적으로 더웠지만, 최근에 눈이 많이 와서 지역 스키장들이 혜택을 보았다.

해설 빈칸 뒤 문장 전체를 꾸며주는 부사 자리로 '최근에 눈이 많이 와서 스키장들이 혜택을 보았다'는 의미가 자연스러우므로 '최근에'라는 뜻의 (C) recently가 정답이다. 해석상 혼동될 수 있는 (A) soon은 미래시제와 어울리며, (C) recently는 현재완료나 과거시제와 어울리므로 수식 받는 문장이 현재완료시제(has snowed)로 쓰였다는 점도 문제 해결의 단서가 될 수 있다는 점을 참고로 알아두자.

어휘 unusually *adv.* 몹시, 평소와 달리 | heavily *adv.* 심하게, 많이 | benefit *v.* 득을 보다

19. 어떤 모델을 제작할지에 대한 제조사의 결정은 연구 결과에 달려 있다.

해설 빈칸은 be 동사 뒤 보어 자리로 '어느 모델을 제작할지에 대한 제조사의 결정이 연구 결과에 달려 있다'는 의미가 자연스러우므로 '~에 달려 있는, ~에 좌우되는'이라는 뜻의 (B) dependent가 정답이다. 참고로 형용사 dependent는 전치사 on이나 upon을 동반한다는 점에서 빈칸 뒤 on이 문제 해결의 단서가 될 수 있으니 참고해두자.

어휘 manufacturer *n.* 제조사 | decision *n.* 결정 | result *n.* 결과 | responsive *adj.* ~에 반응하는(to) | reliable *adj.* 믿을 수 있는 | subsequent *adj.* 그 다음의, 차후의

20. 모든 도서관 직원은 업무를 마칠 때 책꽂이를 철저히 정리해야만 한다.

해설 빈칸 앞 library와 복합명사를 이루기에 적절한 명사 자리로 '도서관 직원들이 철저히 정리해야 한다'라는 의미가 자연스러우므로 '직원들, 인원'을 뜻하는 (B) personnel이 정답이다.

어휘 thoroughly *adv.* 철저히, 완전히 | organize *v.* 정리하다, 조직하다 | bookshelf *n.* 책꽂이 | research *n.* 연구 (조사) | personnel *n.* 직원들

21. 작년 11월에 디자인된 Fleet Footwear의 새 운동화가 마침내 다음 주에 생산을 시작할 것이다.

해설 빈칸은 동사 begin을 수식하는 부사 자리로 '작년 11월에 디자인된 운동화가 마침내 생산을 시작할 것이다'라는 의미가 자연스러우므로 '마침내, 결국'이라는 뜻의 (C) finally가 정답이다.

어휘 design *v.* 디자인하다, 설계하다 | training shoes 운동화 | production *n.* 생산 | extremely *adv.* 극도로, 극히 | precisely *adv.* 정확히 | lately *adv.* 최근에

22. 부사장을 위한 은퇴식이 11월 24일 토요일 Webster 센터의 Morely 강당에서 개최될 것이다.

해설 문장의 주어는 retirement reception으로 은퇴식이 개최될 것이라는 의미가 자연스러우므로 '(행사를) 개최하다'라는 의미를 갖는 (D) held 가 정답이다. 해석상 opened도 가능해 보이지만, opened는 문이나 뚜껑 등 닫혀 있는 것을 또는 점포 등을 '열었다'라는 의미이므로 retirement reception을 주어로 받기에 어색하다.

어휘 retirement reception 은퇴 연회 | vice president 부사장 | auditorium *n.* 강당

23. Dr. Nasseri는 인상적인 자격증 때문에 부서의 매니저로 임명되었다.

해설 빈칸은 문장의 동사 자리로 '인상적인 자격증 때문에 부서장으로 임명되었다'라는 의미가 자연스러우므로 '임명하다'라는 뜻의 (B) appointed가 정답이다. 참고로 appoint는 목적어와 목적보어를 취하는 5형식 동사로 수동태 문장에서도 명사 보어가 연결될 수 있다는 점에 유의한다.

어휘 department *n.* 부서 | impressive *adj.* 인상적인 | credentials *n.* 자격증

24. Starker 식당은 모든 연령대의 손님들의 관심을 끌 만한 다양한 메뉴를 제공한다.

해설 빈칸은 문장의 목적어 자리로 'Starker 식당이 다양한 메뉴를 제공한다'는 의미가 자연스러우므로 '다수, 다량'이라는 뜻의 (C) array가 정답이다. 참고로 「an array of는 '다양한'」라는 의미의 관용표현이므로 덩어리째 암기해두자.

어휘 appeal to ~의 관심을 끌다 | diner *n.* 식사하는 사람 | ingredient *n.* 재료 | object *n.* 물건 | entity *n.* 독립체 | an array of 다양한

25. Gatlin 건설자재는 한 달에 한 번씩 모든 창고의 재고를 조사한다.

해설 빈칸은 부사구에 들어갈 부사 자리로 '한 달에 한 번'이라는 의미를 완성하는 (B) Once가 정답이다.

어휘 inspect *v.* 조사하다 | stock *n.* 재고, 재고품 | warehouse *n.* 창고 | instantly *adv.* 즉각, 즉시 | once *adv.* 한 번 | already *adv.* 이미, 벌써

26. Wraith 1200 태블릿 PC는 향상된 비산 방지 화면을 특징으로 하고 있다.

해설 빈칸은 문장의 동사 자리로, '향상된 비산 방지 화면을 특징으로 한다'는 의미가 자연스러우므로 '~을 특징으로 삼다'라는 뜻의 (D) features가 정답이다.

어휘 improved *adj.* 향상된, 개선된 | shatter-resistant *adj.* 비산 방지의(유리가 깨졌을 때 유리조각이 흩어지는 것을 방지하는 기술) | sample *v.* 시도해보다 | endure *v.* 견디다 | adjust *v.* 조정하다

27. 여전히 명시되지 않은 기계적 문제로 인해 항공편은 취소되었다.

해설 빈칸은 '명시되지 않은'이라는 뜻의 형용사 unspecified를 수식하는 부사 자리로 '여전히 명시되지 않은 기계 결함 때문에 항공편이 취소되었다'는 의미가 자연스러우므로 '여전히, 아직도'라는 뜻의 (B) still 이 정답이다.

어휘 due to ~때문에 | mechanical *adj.* 기계적인 | unspecified *adj.* 명시되지 않은, 불특정한 | flight *n.* 항공편 | cancel *v.* 취소하다 | early *adv.* 일찍 | well *adv.* 잘 | much *adv.* 많이

28. Ms. Phan은 화학 공학을 전공했음에도 불구하고 현재 영업 마케팅 부에서 근무한다.

해설 빈칸은 동사 works를 수식하는 부사 자리로 'Ms. Phan이 화학 공학을 전공했지만, 지금은 영업 마케팅 부서에서 근무한다'는 의미가 자연스러우므로 '지금'이라는 뜻의 (A) now가 정답이다.

어휘 chemical engineering 화학 공학 | therefore *adv.* 그러므로, 그러니 | fairly *adv.* 상당히, 꽤 | quite *adv.* 상당히, 꽤

29. 업그레이드된 기계장치는 공장이 더 짧은 시간 동안 더 많은 상품을 생산하게 해주었다.

해설 빈칸은 '기계장치'를 뜻하는 명사 machinery를 수식하는 형용사 자리로 '업그레이드된 기계장치가 생산 시간을 줄여주었다'는 의미가 자연스러우므로 '업그레이드된'이라는 뜻의 (A) Upgraded가 정답이다.

어휘 enable *v.* ~을 가능케 하다 | unit *n.* (상품의) 한 개 | anticipated *adj.* 예상된 | imposed *adj.* 부과된

30. Smith 병원 환자들을 돕겠다는 Dr. Berringer의 열정은 20년이 지난 후에도 여전히 높다.

해설 빈칸은 Dr. Berringer의 한정을 받는 명사 자리로 'Dr. Berringer의 열정이 20년이 지난 후에도 여전히 높다'는 의미가 자연스러우므로 '열정, 열의'를 뜻하는 (B) enthusiasm이 정답이다.

어휘 patient *n.* 환자 | remain *v.* 여전히 ~이다 | likeness *n.* 유사성, 닮음 | addition *n.* 추가된 것, 부가물 | collection *n.* 수집품, 소장품

PART 6

UNIT 02. 실전 연습 01

1. (B)	2. (A)	3. (B)	4. (B)
5. (A)	6. (A)	7. (A)	8. (D)
9. (B)	10. (A)	11. (D)	12. (B)
13. (C)	14. (D)	15. (C)	16. (A)

[1-4] 다음 설명서에 관한 문제입니다.

유지 보수 설명서

1 최대의 효과를 내려면 이 설명들을 따라주십시오. 마른 천으로 테이블을 **2** 닦아 주십시오. 남아 있는 어떠한 얼룩이든 젖은 천으로 지울 수 있습니다. 표면이 깨끗해졌을 때, 왁스를 발라 주는 것이 좋습니다. 이것은 테이블을 **3** 반짝거리게 만들어 줄 것입니다. 이 과정을 서너 번 **4** 반복해 주시기 바랍니다.

1. (A) 귀하께서는 이 방법을 절대 한 번 이상 사용할 필요가 없을 것입니다.
(B) 최대의 효과를 내려면 이 설명들을 따라 주십시오.
(C) 이 방법은 얼룩을 제거하는 데 효과적이지 않습니다.
(D) 당신이 사용하는 천은 반드시 축축해야 합니다.

해설 지문의 첫 문장을 삽입하는 문제로, (A)와 (C)는 this method가 어떤 방법인지에 대한 설명이 전혀 없이 this method가 나왔으므로 첫 문장으로 올 수 없다. (D)는 빈칸 다음 문장에 마른 천으로 닦으라고 나오는 것과는 반대되는 내용이며, 첫 문장으로도 어울리지 않으므로 탈락이다. 제목 자체가 유지 보수 설명서이고 뒤에 설명들이 따라 나오고 있으므로 Follow these instructions ~.(설명들을 따라 주십시오.)가 오는 것이 가장 자연스럽다. 따라서 정답은 (B) Follow these instructions for maximum performance이다.

2. Please가 나오면 명령문이라는 힌트이다. 명령문은 주어 없이 동사원형으로 시작하므로 정답은 (A) wipe이다.

3. 해설 make는 5형식 동사로 the table이 목적어이고, 빈칸은 목적격 보어 자리이다. make는 목적격 보어 자리에 형용사나 명사를 쓴다. 목적격 보어와 목적어와의 관계가 동격이 아닌 상태를 설명하므로 형용사가 빈칸에 들어가야 한다. 따라서 정답은 (B) shiny이다.

4. 해설 맨 마지막에 'three to four times'가 나와 있으므로 문맥상 서너 번 '반복하다'라는 동사가 필요하다. 따라서 정답은 (B) repeat이다.

[5-8] 다음 이메일에 관한 문제입니다.

수신: Sue77@mymail.net
발신: JayJang@pinkinc.com
날짜: 4월 8일

Ms. Song에게,

저희는 마케팅 부서의 공석과 관련해 귀하의 이력서를 최근에 검토했습니다. 비록 귀하께서는 업무 경험을 **5** 가지고 있지 않지만, 귀하의 탄탄한 학업 성적과 자기소개서는 매우 인상적 **6** 입니다. 이러한 이유로, 저희 매니저인 David Kim과 저는 귀하와 전화로 이야기를 나눠보고자 합니다. **7** 이것이 저희 모두에게 가장 편할 것 같습니다. 통화하기 편한 시간이 언제인지 **8** 확인해 주시기 바랍니다.

귀하의 답변을 기다리겠습니다.

감사합니다.

Jay Jang
채용 담당 이사, Pink 사

5. 해설 do라는 조동사가 나와 있으므로 빈칸에는 동사원형이 나와야 한다. 따라서 정답은 (A) have이다.

6. 해설 빈칸은 동사 자리이다. 동사가 아닌 (C)와 (D)는 탈락이다. 주어가 두 개 언급되어 복수이므로 정답은 (A) are이다.

7. **(A) 이것이 저희 모두에게 가장 편할 것 같습니다.**
(B) 지난주에 전화로 당신과 이야기할 수 있어서 매우 좋았습니다.
(C) 그런 방식으로 우리는 당신과 대면 면접을 할 수 있습니다.
(D) Mr. Kim이 조만간 당신과 점심 식사를 하기를 기대하고 있습니다.

해설 (B)에는 was라는 과거 시세가 나왔는데, 지문에서는 과거에 이미 전화 인터뷰를 한 것이 아닌, 앞으로 하고 싶다고 말하고 있으므로 (B)는 탈락이다. (C)에서 in person은 직접 대면해서 면접을 본다는 의미인데, 앞 문장에서 전화로 이야기하고 싶다고 하였으므로 탈락이다. (D)는 전화로 인터뷰를 하고 싶은 것이지 점심을 먹는 내용은 없었으므로 탈락이다. 빈칸 앞의 문장이 '탄탄한 학업 성적과 자기소개서가 매우 인상적이어서 당신과 전화로 이야기하고 싶다'는 내용이므로 '이러한 방식(=전화 인터뷰)이 모두에게 가장 편리할 것'이라는 내용이 이어지는 것이 가장 자연스럽다. 따라서 정답은 (A) We think this will be most convenient for all of us.이다.

8. 해설 Please가 나오면 명령문이라는 힌트이다. 명령문은 주어 없이 동사원형으로 시작하므로 정답은 (D) confirm이다.

PART 6 UNIT 02

연례 Red Apple 박람회가 10월 25일 남부 Newtown에서 **9** 하게 되었다. 이 인기 있는 지역 박람회는 Newtown 공원에서 지난 10년 동안 **10** 열려왔지만, 올해는 박람회 주최측이 박람회를 시내에서 가장 큰 공원으로 옮기로 결정했다. 그 결정은 옳은 결정이었다. 왜냐하면 기록적인 수치의 많은 **11** 방문자들이 맛있는 음식을 맛보고 그 지역 음악가들의 공연을 보기 위해서 왔기 때문이다. **12** 박람회의 참가자들은 또한 새로운 장소에 대해서도 호의적으로 이야기했다.

9. 해설 빈칸은 동사 자리이다. 주어가 단수이다. 그런데, (A), (C), 그리고 (D)는 모두 복수 동사이므로 주어와 동사의 수 일치가 맞지 않아 탈락이다. (B)는 과거 시제로 수 일치를 필요로 하지 않는다. 따라서 정답은 (B) came이다.

10. 해설 빈칸은 동사 자리이다. 'for the last 10 years'라는 문구가 나오면 현재 완료 시제의 힌트이다. 따라서 정답은 (A) has been held 이다.

11. 해설 빈칸은 주어 자리로 명사 자리이다. (A)와 (D)가 명사인데, 기록적으로 많은 수치의 방문자들이 왔다는 의미가 되어야 하므로 복수 명사를 써야 한다. 따라서 정답은 (D) visitors이다. a number of = many(많은) 이라는 뜻으로 뒤에 복수 명사가 나옴에 유의하자.

12. (A) 조직 위원들은 올해의 박람회와 관련한 모든 일이 잘되길 희망한다.
(B) **박람회 참가자들은 또한 새로운 장소에 대해서도 호의적으로 이야기했다.**
(C) 박람회에 참여한 인원이 작년 수치보다 약간 더 적었다.
(D) 올해 박람회에는 이전 박람회들이 선보였던 라이브 공연이 없었다.

해설 빈칸 바로 앞 문장에서 박람회 장소를 넓은 장소로 옮긴 것은 옳은 결정이었다고 하면서, 그렇게 판단하는 이유는 많은 방문자들이 왔기 때문이라고 언급했다. 따라서 빈칸에는 박람회 장소를 넓은 장소로 옮긴 것이 옳은 판단이 될 수 있는 근거를 찾아야 하므로 정답은 (B) Attendees at the fair also commented favorably on the new venue.이다. (A), (C), (D)는 글의 내용과 맞지 않는다.

〈Beauty Magazine〉은 독자님들이 보내주시는 편지를 환영합니다. 지면 공간이 **13** 제한되어 있기 때문에, 제출된 글들이 모두 게재될 수 없습니다. **14** 사실, 저희는 저희가 받은 글의 아주 일부분만을 게재합니다. 아름다움이라는 주제에 대한 독창적인 아이디어를 담은 편지들에게 우선권이 주어질 것입니다. 또한, 편지는 특정 요구 조건을 만족시켜야 합니다. 예를 들어, 편지는 400자를 초과해서는 안 됩니다. 저희는 최대 400자보다 **15** 더 긴 글들은 편집할 예정입니다. 귀하의 글이 게재되기로 **16** 선정되었는지를 알려 드릴 수 있도록 귀하의 성함과 연락처를 포함시켜 주실 것을 요청드립니다.

13. 해설 is라는 동사가 있으므로 빈칸에 또 동사가 나올 수 없다. 따라서 (B)와 (D)는 탈락이다. 문맥상 지면 공간이 제한되어 있다는 뜻이고 타동사인 limit의 목적어도 보이지 않으므로 수동태가 적절하다. be동사는 이미 제시되어 있으므로 빈칸에는 과거분사만 들어가면 된다. 따라서 정답은 (C) limited이다.

14. (A) 저희는 독자들에게 그들이 보고 싶은 편지를 고를 수 있게 합니다.
(B) 만일 저희에게 편지를 주신다면, 저희 잡지에 여러분의 편지를 게재해 드릴 것을 약속 드립니다.
(C) 여러분의 개인 경험에 관한 편지들이 게재될 가능성이 가장 높습니다.
(D) **사실, 저희는 저희가 받은 글의 아주 일부분만을 게재합니다.**

해설 빈칸 앞의 문장에서 '제출된 글이 모두 (잡지에) 게재될 수 없다'고 했고, 빈칸 뒤의 문장에서는 '아름다움이라는 주제에 대한 독창적인 아이디어를 담은 글들에게 우선권이 주어진다'고 하고 있으므로 빈칸 앞뒤 문맥상 그 사이에 들어가기에 가장 자연스러운 내용은 '받은 글의 일부분을 게재한다'이다. 따라서 정답은 (D) In fact, we only print a small portion of the letters we receive.이다.

15. 해설 글자 수가 400자를 초과해서는 안 된다고 하고 있으므로, 최대 글자 수보다 긴 글을 다듬을 것이라는 내용이 적절하다. 따라서 정답은 (C) longer이다.

16. 해설 글을 제출한 사람의 이름과 연락처를 포함시키라는 것은 글이 잡지에 실리기로 선정되었는지 여부를 통보하기 위한 것이므로 정답은 (A) selected이다.

UNIT 03. 실전 연습 02 본서 p.190

17. (D)	**18.** (D)	**19.** (C)	**20.** (B)
21. (A)	**22.** (D)	**23.** (C)	**24.** (B)
25. (D)	**26.** (A)	**27.** (D)	**28.** (C)
29. (A)	**30.** (B)	**31.** (C)	**32.** (D)

MRT 호텔에 머물러 주셔서 감사합니다. **17** 저희는 고객님께서 이곳에서 즐거운 시간을 보내시기를 희망합니다. 캐비닛 안에 샴푸 한 통, 비누 하나, 로션 한 통이 있을 것입니다. 고객님은 **18** 그것들을 추가 비용 없이 사용하셔도 됩니다. 또한, 귀하께서는 저희 Green 호텔 프로그램에 관한 정보를 보게 될 것입니다. 고객님의 프로그램 **19** 참여는 저희 지역 공동체가 물과 에너지 소비를 줄이는 것을 가능하게 해 줍니다. 만약 그 프로그램에 참여하길 원하시면, 고객님의 침대 옆 테이블 위 **20** 눈에 띄는 장소에 메모를 놓아두시기만 하면 됩니다.

17. (A) 저희는 이 도시에서 가장 빠르게 성장하는 여행사 중의 하나입니다.

(B) 비누와 샴푸 같은 물품들은 로비에서 판매 중입니다.

(C) 안타깝게도, 이 방의 샤워기가 작동하지 않습니다.

(D) 저희는 고객님께서 이곳에서 즐거운 시간을 보내시기를 희망합니다.

해설 이 글은 호텔에 대한 글이므로 여행사(travel agency)에 대해 언급한 (A)는 문맥상 맞지 않다. (B) 빈칸 뒤의 문장에서 캐비닛 안에 비누와 샴푸가 있을 것이라고 했으므로 문맥상 맞지 않다. (C)는 지문 다음 문장에서 캐비닛 안에 있는 샴푸, 비누 등을 추가 비용 없이 사용할 수 있다고 말하면서 샤워기가 고장 났다고 하는 것은 앞뒤가 맞지 않다. 지문의 첫 문장은 주로 인사치레이다. 'MRT 호텔을 이용해 주어서 감사하고, 이곳에서 즐거운 시간을 보내길 바란다'라는 내용이 가장 자연스럽다. 따라서 정답은 (D) We hope that you enjoy your time here.이다.

---

18. 해설 빈칸은 use의 목적어 자리이므로 대명사의 목적격을 찾아야 한다. 샴푸, 비누, 로션 세 가지를 언급하고 있으므로 (C)와 (D) 중 복수형 대명사 (D) them이 정답이다.

---

19. 해설 빈칸은 주어에 해당하는 명사 customer를 수식하는 분사 자리이거나 customer와 복합명사를 이루는 명사 자리인데, customer는 '고객'을 뜻하는 가산 명사이므로 문제에서처럼 단수로 쓸 때는 관사나 소유격 등의 한정사 없이는 쓸 수 없다. 따라서, customer 단독으로는 주어로 쓸 수 없으며, 불가산 명사나 participation과 함께 '고객 참여'라는 의미의 복합명사 형태가 적절하므로 정답은 (C) participation이다.

---

20. 해설 빈칸이 부정관사 a와 명사 location 사이에 있으므로 형용사가 와야 하는 자리이다. 따라서 정답은 (B) noticeable이다.

[21-24] 다음 이메일에 관한 문제입니다.

수신: Hong@dotmail.com

발신: Lee1234@CandMagency.com

날짜: 4월 1일

제목: 저희가 어땠는지 말씀해 주세요.

첨부 파일: cmta.doc

고객님에게,

C&M 여행사로 예약해 주신 것에 대해 감사드립니다. 저희는 고객님의 최근 3월 15일자 캘리포니아 **21** 에서 미시간으로의 여행이 어땠는지 듣고 싶습니다. 고객님께서 저희 회사와 함께한 고객님의 경험에 대해 간단한 설문 조사를 완성해 주시면 감사하겠습니다. **22** 이것은 대략 고객님의 시간 중 5분밖에 안 걸릴 것입니다. 첨부된 파일을 완성해서 그것을 저희에게 보내 주시기 바랍니다. **23** 저희가 4월 8일까지 그것을 받는다면 고객님께 무료 선물을 보내드리겠습니다. 고객님의 피드백은 **24** 저희가 저희 서비스를 개선하는 데 도움이 될 것입니다.

다시 한번 저희 회사와 거래해 주셔서 감사합니다.

이호준, 최고경영자

C&M 여행사

---

21. 해설 「from A to B」는 'A에서(부터) B로'라는 뜻이다. 따라서 정답은 (A) from이다.

---

22. 해설 (A) Both는 2개를 가리키는데, 빈칸 주변에는 2개가 언급된 것이 없다. (B) Every는 형용사로만 쓰이므로 주어(명사) 자리인 빈칸에 들어갈 수 없다. (C) They는 복수를 의미하는데, 빈칸 주변에 복수 명사가 나온 것이 없다. (D) This는 단수로, 단수 명사 'a short survey'를 가리키므로 정답은 (D) This이다.

---

23. (A) 고객님의 답변이 저희에게 아주 큰 도움이 되었습니다.

(B) 반드시 다음 주까지 새로운 예약을 하셔야 합니다.

(C) 저희가 4월 8일까지 그것을 받는다면, 고객님께 무료 선물을 보내드리겠습니다.

(D) 그것을 작성하시는 데 한 시간이 걸릴 것입니다.

해설 빈칸 앞에는 설문 조사가 5분밖에 걸리지 않으니 설문 조사를 부탁한다는 내용이 나왔다. (A)는 과거 시제를 써서 이미 '당신의 대답들이 도움이 되었다'라고 말하므로 탈락이다. (B)는 설문 조사를 부탁하는 문장 다음에 나오기에는 문맥상 맞지 않다. (D)는 빈칸 앞의 문장에서 대략 5분이 걸린다고 했는데, 다시 1시간이 걸린다는 것은 앞뒤가 맞지 않는 말이다. (C) 설문 조사를 부탁하면서 '4월 8일까지 그것(설문 조사 응답)을 보내 주면 무료 선물을 보내 준다.'라고 말하면서 설문에 응해 줄 것을 부탁하는 것이 적절하다. 따라서 (C) If we receive it by April 8, we will mail you a free gift.가 정답이다.

---

24. 해설 빈칸은 help의 목적어 자리이다. (A)는 소유격으로 명사 앞에 써야 한다. (C)는 '우리의 것'을 돕는 것이 아니므로 탈락이다. (D)는 여행사 입장에서 '우리'를 돕는 것이므로 '그들'이 나오는 것은 맞지 않으며 소유격이 아닌 목적격 자리이다. 따라서 목적어 자리이므로 목적격인 (B) us가 정답이다.

[25-28] 다음 공지에 관한 문제입니다.

Owen 연구 도서관은 4월 2일부터 10월 말까지 보수가 이루어질 예정입니다. 이 수리는 점점 불어나는 저희의 소장 도서들을 수용할 보관 공간을 **25** 늘려갈 것입니다. 도서관은 보수 작업을 하는 동안에도 여전히 문을 열 예정입니다. 그럼에도 불구하고, 도서관의 일부 섹션들은 일시적으로 현장의 연구원들에게 **26** 이용 불가할 것입니다. 이 **27** 접근 불가능한 섹션들의 목록은 저희 웹사이트 www.owenresearch.org에 게시될 것입니다. 연구원들은 방문 전에 그 목록을 확인하거나 도서관에 연락해 보시길 권고드립니다. **28** 귀하가 겪게 될 불편에 대해 미리 사과의 말씀 드립니다.

---

25. 해설 빈칸은 동사 자리이다. 따라서 (A)와 (C)는 탈락이다. (B)와 (D) 중에서 문맥상 도서관 보수 공사를 통해 보관 공간을 넓힐 예정이므로 정답은 미래 시제 (D) will increase이다.

---

26. 해설 빈칸은 be동사 뒤의 보어 자리이므로 상태를 설명하는 형용사가 필요하다. 따라서 정답은 (A) unavailable이다.

27. 해설 빈칸이 명사 sections 앞에 있으므로 빈칸에는 형용사가 와야 한다. 따라서 정답은 (D) inaccessible이다.

28. (A) 10월까지 모든 이용자들에게 도서관 접근이 제한될 것입니다.
(B) 도서관의 특정 파트가 언제 폐쇄될 것인지를 예측하는 것은 불가능합니다.
(C) 귀하가 겪게 될 불편에 대해 미리 사과의 말씀 드립니다.
(D) 그 목록에 접근하는 법을 배우려면 사서에게 말씀하십시오.

해설 (A) 앞에서 일부만 접근이 제한된다고 하였으므로 문맥상 맞지 않다. (B)는 마지막 문장에 넣기에 문맥상 맞지 않다. (D) '그 목록에 접근하는 법을 배우려면 사서에게 말씀하세요.'는 목록 확인을 위한 웹사이트 주소를 앞에서 이미 알려 주었으므로 문맥상 맞지 않다. 맨 마지막에 들어갈 문장으로는 '이러한 불편을 끼쳐서 사과드린다'라는 내용이 가장 적절하다. 따라서 정답은 (C) We apologize in advance for any inconvenience you may experience.이다.

[29-32] 다음 회람에 관한 문제입니다.

발신: Hyo-Ju Kim, 건물 매니저
수신: 모든 직원들
날짜: 목요일, 3월 2일
회신: 건설 공사

아시다시피, 우리 사무실 건물의 수리가 3월 15일 수요일부터 시작해서, 3월 20일 월요일 저녁까지 계속될 것입니다. 따라서 여러분은 몇 가지 **29** 불편을 겪게 될 수도 있습니다. 남쪽에 있는 엘리베이터는 일주일 내내 작동하지 않을 것입니다. **30** 그 기간 동안 그것은 수리되고 점검될 필요가 있습니다. 저는 여러분들 대부분이 이 엘리베이터를 **31** 정기적으로 사용한다는 것을 알고 있습니다. 안타깝게도, 여러분은 계단을 이용해야 합니다. **32** 게다가, 그 건물의 남서쪽에 있는 출입구도 목요일에 폐쇄될 것입니다. 그 건물의 다른 모든 출입구들은 이 기간 동안 평상시대로 개방될 것입니다.

29. 해설 수리가 시작되면 고객들이 불편을 겪게 될 수 있으므로 정답은 (A) inconvenience이다.

30. (A) 다행히, 사람들이 거의 엘리베이터를 타지 않습니다.
(B) 그 기간 동안 그것은(= 엘리베이터) 수리되고 점검될 필요가 있습니다.
(C) 3일 후면 엘리베이터가 다시 정상 가동할 것입니다.
(D) 이 엘리베이터는 건물 수리에 의해 영향을 받지 않을 것입니다.

해설 빈칸 바로 앞의 문장이 엘리베이터가 작동을 안 할 것이라는 내용이고, 빈칸 뒤의 문장은 여러분이 정기적으로 이용하나 계단을 대신 이용하라는 내용이므로 (A) '다행히, 사람들이 거의 엘리베이터를 타지 않는다.'는 문맥상 맞지 않다. 빈칸 앞의 문장이 '엘리베이터가 일주일 내내 작동하지 않을 것이'므로 3일 후면 작동할 것이라는 (C)는 문맥상 맞지 않다. (D)는 엘리베이터가 일주일 내내 작동하지 않는 것은 건물 수리의 영향을 받는 것이므로 지문의 내용과 맞지 않아 답

이 될 수 없다. 그것은(= 엘리베이터) 일주일 내내 작동이 안 되고, (B) '그 기간 동안 엘리베이터는 수리되고 점검되는 것'이므로 정답은 (B) It needs to be repaired and inspected during that time.이다.

31. 해설 이미 3형식의 완전한 문장이므로 빈칸은 수식어가 올 자리이다. 동사 앞에 온 빈칸이므로 부사가 와야 한다. 따라서 정답은 (C) regularly이다.

32. 해설 빈칸 앞의 문장을 보면, 계단을 이용하라고 나오는데 이것은 빌딩 수리로 인한 불편함이다. 그런데, 빈칸 뒤 문장에도 출입구가 닫힐 거라는 불편함이 또 언급 되어 있다. 따라서 '게다가'라는 뜻의 접속부사가 문맥상 적절하다. 정답은 (D) Moreover이다.

UNIT 04. 실전 연습 03
본서 p.194

33. (A)	**34.** (C)	**35.** (D)	**36.** (D)
37. (A)	**38.** (A)	**39.** (A)	**40.** (D)
41. (C)	**42.** (B)	**43.** (A)	**44.** (A)
45. (A)	**46.** (C)	**47.** (B)	**48.** (A)

[33-36] 다음 지시문에 관한 문제입니다.

Amarillo 자동차 수리점의 리모델링이 10월 3일 **33** 까지 완료될 것입니다. 리모델링이 후, 그 가게는 월요일부터 금요일까지 오전 6시부터 오후 5시까지 문을 열 것입니다. 만약 여러분이 원한다면, 자신의 차를 가게에 두고 가도 좋습니다. 그 가게는 잘 알려진 큰 쇼핑몰 옆에 **34** 편리하게 위치해 있습니다. **35** 만약 저희가 문을 닫았을 때 오셨다면, 다음의 사항들을 이행하십시오. 귀하의 성함과 연락처를 카드에 작성하고 귀하의 차에 대한 문제점을 짧게 기술하십시오. 그러고 나서, 신청 카드와 **36** 함께 (차) 열쇠를 봉투 안에 넣어 봉하고, 그 봉투를 사무실 문 앞에 있는 투입구에 밀어 넣으십시오. 저희가 여러분의 차를 꼼꼼하게 살펴볼 것입니다. 그러고 나서, 저희는 여러분에게 검사 결과와 어떤 수리가 필요한지 말씀드리기 위해 전화를 드릴 것입니다.

33. 해설 (B) within 뒤에는 기간이 와야 하므로 탈락이다. (C) 날짜 앞에는 전치사 on이 들어가야 하므로 (C)도 탈락이다. 빈칸 뒤에 시점이 나왔는데, (A)와 (D)는 시점 전치사이다. 그런데 by는 완료적인 의미일 때 쓰이고, until은 계속적인 의미로 쓰인다. will be completed를 보면 완료적인 의미임을 알 수 있다. 따라서 정답은 (A) by이다.

34. 해설 be동사와 과거분사(located) 사이는 무조건 부사가 올 자리이다. 따라서 정답은 (C) conveniently이다.

35. (A) 저희는 쇼핑몰 1층에 위치해 있습니다.

(B) 수리공은 여러분이 도착하자마자 여러분의 차를 살펴볼 것입니다.

(C) 근무 중인 사람에게 문제를 간단히 설명해 주십시오.

(D) 만약 저희가 문을 닫았을 때 오셨다면, 다음의 사항들을 이행하십시오.

해설 (A)는 빈칸 앞에서 이미 쇼핑몰 옆에 위치해 있다고 말해 주고 있으므로 탈락이다. 빈칸 뒤의 문장에서 차의 문제가 무엇인지 메모해 놓고 가라고 했으므로 수리공이 손님이 도착하자마자 차를 살펴볼 것이라는 (B)와, 근무 중인 사람에게 문제를 간단히 설명하라는 (C)도 지문의 내용과 맞지 않다. (D)에서 the following(다음의 사항들)이란 빈칸 뒤에 나오는 사항들을 가리킨다. (사항들: 자신의 이름과 연락처를 카드에 작성하고, 자신의 차에 대한 문제를 짧게 기술하고, 신청 카드와 함께 (차) 열쇠를 봉투 안에 넣어 봉하고, 그 봉투를 사무실 문 앞에 있는 투입구에 밀어 넣기) 따라서 정답은 (D) Should you arrive when we are closed, please do the following.이다.

36. 해설 문맥상 신청 카드와 함께 차 열쇠를 봉투 안에 넣고 함께 봉하라는 뜻이므로 정답은 (D) along with이다.

[37-40] 다음 공지에 관한 문제입니다.

저희는 RED Alerts라고 불리는 새로운 서비스를 제공하고 있습니다. **37** 일단 등록을 하시면, 귀하가 계신 곳의 대기 상태가 위험한 경우, 업데이트 사항이 귀하의 휴대 전화로 전송될 것입니다. **38** 이 것은 또한 언제 상황이 나아질 것으로 예상되는지 알려드릴 것입니다. **39** 게다가, 저희 회사는 이 서비스를 무료로 제공하고 있습니다. RED Alerts에 등록하기 **40** 전에, 귀하께서는 저희 웹사이트에 있는 서비스 약관을 검토해주십시오.

37. 해설 빈칸 뒤에 문장이 두 개 있다는 것은 빈칸에 접속사가 필요하다는 뜻이다. (B)는 전치사이고, (C) In order to는 그 뒤에 동사원형이 와야 하므로 탈락이다. 두 개의 문장을 연결할 수 있는 접속사는 (A)와 (D)인데 의미상 (A)가 자연스러우므로 정답은 (A) Once이다.

38. **(A) 이것은 또한 언제 상황이 나아질 것으로 예상되는지도 알려드릴 것입니다.**

(B) 귀하는 귀하의 지역에서 무슨 일이 벌어지고 있는지 알아보기 위해 전화를 걸 수 있습니다.

(C) 이 서비스를 특가로 구매하기 위해 다음 2주 동안에 가입하세요.

(D) 문제가 있을 때 경보가 곧바로 귀하의 이메일로 전송될 것입니다.

해설 바로 앞 문장에서 대기 질이 좋지 않을 경우 휴대 전화로 통보한다고 했으므로 언제 상황이 개선될 것으로 보이는지도 알려 주겠다고 하는 게 문맥상 자연스럽다. 정답은 (A) It will also inform you when you can expect better conditions.이다.

39. 해설 (C)는 전치사로 빈칸 뒤에 명사가 나와야 한다. (A), (B), (D)는 접속부사로 문장 맨 앞에 들어갈 수 있다. 그런데 문맥상 빈칸 앞에서 서비스가 어떤 서비스인지 설명했고, 빈칸 뒤에는 그 서비스가 무료라고 하면서 서비스에 대한 추가 정보를 제공하고 있으므로 문맥상 '게다가' 라는 뜻의 접속부사가 필요하다. 따라서 (A) Moreover가 정답이다.

40. 해설 빈칸 뒤에 동명사가 왔으므로 빈칸에는 전치사가 들어가야 한다. (B)는 접속사로 주어와 동사가 나와야 한다. (A), (C), (D)는 모두 전치사인데 문맥상 '등록하기 전에 서비스 약관을 검토해 달라'는 뜻이 되어야 한다. 따라서 정답은 (D) Prior to이다.

[41-44] 다음 이메일에 관한 문제입니다.

수신: sue117@zonet.org

발신: JSP@seework.net

날짜: 5월 15일

Mr. Sue에게

저희는 최근에 귀하의 이력서를 검토했습니다. 저희는 귀하의 경력에 **41** 감명을 받았습니다. **42** 귀하는 또한 훌륭한 교육도 받았습니다. 저희는 귀하를 만나보고 싶지만, 저희가 매우 바쁩니다. 따라서 저희는 **43** 귀하를 전화상으로 인터뷰하고 싶습니다. 5월 20일 금요일 오후 2시가 전화 통화하기에 편한 시간 **44** 인지 아닌지를 이메일로 확인해 주십시오.

귀하의 답변을 기다립니다.

감사합니다.

Ji-Sung Park

고용 담당 이사

41. 해설 '우리가 인상적이다'라는 뜻이 아니고 '우리가 감명을 받았다'라는 뜻이므로 수동태가 되어야 한다. 따라서 정답은 (C) impressed 이다.

42. (A) 귀하의 이력서를 가급적 빨리 보내 주세요.

(B) 당신은 또한 훌륭한 교육도 받았습니다.

(C) 귀하는 그 분야에서 일해 본 적이 거의 없습니다.

(D) 게다가 귀하는 월급 신청서 보내는 것을 잊으셨습니다.

해설 (A)는 빈칸 앞에서 당신의 이력서를 최근에 검토했다고 했으므로 말이 되지 않는다. (C)는 당신의 경력에 대해 인상 깊었다는 앞 문장과 문맥상 맞지 않는다. (D)는 이력서를 검토했다는 말이 나오고 있는 상황에서 말이 되지 않는다. 당신의 경력이 인상 깊었는데 '(B) 또한 훌륭한 교육까지도 받아서' 당신과 면접 일정을 잡고 싶다는 내용이 적절하다. 따라서 정답은 (B) You also received an excellent education.이다.

43. 해설 빈칸은 interview의 목적어 자리이다. (B) 소유격은 뒤에 명사를 동반해야 한다. (C)는 당신을 인터뷰하고 싶은 것이지 당신의 것을 인터뷰하고 싶은 것이 아니다. (D)는 목적어 자리에 -self를 쓰려면 주어와 목적어가 같아야 한다. 주어 we와 yourself는 함께 쓸 수 없으므로 탈락이다. 따라서 빈칸은 목적어 자리이므로 목적격인 (A) you가 정답이다.

44. 해설 (B), (C), (D)는 모두 전치사인데, 하나의 문장에 confirm이라는 동사와 would be라는 동사 2개가 있어 어법에 맞지 않다. whether라는 명사절 접속사를 넣으면 동사가 들어간 whether절 전체가 명사로서 confirm의 목적어가 될 수 있다. 따라서 정답은 (A) whether이다.

PART 6 UNIT 04

59

수신: 모든 직원들
발신: Hee-Ra Lee
날짜: 8월 2일
제목: 기술적인 문제들

이것은 여러분에게 오늘이 기존 이메일 시스템을 사용하는 우리의 마지막 날임을 알려 드리기 위한 것입니다. 오늘 오후 5시 **45** 부로, 당신은 이 시스템에 일체 접근할 수 없을 것입니다. **46** 이는 과거에 주고 받은 어떤 이메일이든 모두 포함합니다. 따라서, 당신이 이메일 프로그램에 보관해 놓았던 중요한 메시지들을 저장해 두는 것이 필수적입니다. 저장되지 않은 메시지들은 모두 영구적으로 **47** 지워질 것이라는 사실을 알아두십시오.

새로운 이메일 프로그램에 대해서 더 자세히 알고자 한다면, 도움이 되는 많은 특징과 장점을 묘사해 **48** 둔 교육용 비디오를 보십시오.

그래도 궁금한 사항이나 문제가 있다면, helpdesk@JBT.com으로 연락해 주십시오.

45. 해설 모두 전치사이다. 따라서 문맥상 알맞은 것을 골라야 한다. 문맥상 '오늘 오후 5시부로[부터]'가 적절하므로 정답은 (A) As of이다.

46. (A) 그 시스템은 회사 기술자들에 의해 점검되었습니다.
(B) 당신은 그 시간 이후에도 계속해서 이메일을 보내고 받을 수 있습니다.
(C) 이는 과거에 주고 받은 어떤 이메일이든 모두 포함합니다.
(D) 프로그램을 바꾸는 결정이 곧 내려질 것이다.

해설 (A)는 현재 완료 시제로 문제가 다 해결되었다는 뜻인데, 빈칸 앞에는 '문제가 있으니, 앞으로 이메일 프로그램에 접근이 안될 것이다'라고 하며 미래 시제로 말하고 있으므로 시제가 적절하지 않다. (B)는 빈칸 앞의 오후 5시부터 이메일 프로그램에 접근이 안 될 것이라는 내용에 어긋난다. 프로그램을 바꾸는 결정이 곧 내려질 것이라는 (D)는 문맥상 어울리지 않는다. 이메일 시스템에 문제가 있으니 오후 5시부터 접근이 안 될 것이고, 이는 과거에 발신 또는 수신되었던 모든 이메일들을 포함한다고 했으므로 정답은 (C) This includes any e-mails sent or received in the past.이다.

47. 해설 빈칸은 that절 속의 동사 자리이다. 동사 delete의 목적어가 없으므로 수동태를 골라야 한다. 수동태 (B)와 (D) 중에 문맥상 과거 시제가 아닌 미래 시제가 와야 하므로 정답은 (B) will be deleted이다.

48. 해설 (C)는 접속사이므로 주어와 동사를 동반해야 한다. (D)는 선행사를 포함한 관계대명사로 the thing which로 바꿔서 쓸 수 있는데, 앞에 the demonstration video라는 선행사가 있으므로 답이 될 수 없다. 빈칸 뒤에 주어가 없으므로 주격 관계대명사가 들어가야 한다. 선행사 the demonstration video가 사물이므로 which나 that이 가능하나 that은 빈칸 앞의 콤마와 함께 쓸 수 없으므로 정답은 (A) which이다.

UNIT 05. 실전 연습 04
본서 p.198

49. (A)	50. (D)	51. (A)	52. (C)
53. (A)	54. (B)	55. (B)	56. (B)
57. (B)	58. (A)	59. (C)	60. (C)
61. (C)	62. (B)	63. (B)	64. (A)

[49-52] 다음 회람에 관한 문제입니다.

수신: 전 직원

JUA 사는 Mr. Hong이 부사장에 임명되었음을 알리게 되어 **49** 기쁩니다. **50** Mr. Hong는 지난 18년 동안 JUA 사에서 직원으로 일해왔습니다. 명백히, Mr. Hong의 경험과 이 회사에 대한 헌신은 대단한 것입니다. JUA 사는 10월 11일부로 몇몇 신제품을 **51** 출시할 계획이기 때문에 우리로서는 지금이 좋은 시기입니다. 우리는 그가 신제품들로 우리 회사의 판매량을 증가시키는 데 도움이 될 것이라고 믿습니다.

우리가 이 지도부 변경 과정을 **52** 겪는 동안, 어떠한 질문이나 염려가 있으면, 언제든지 저에게 연락을 주십시오.

감사합니다.

Julia Park
홍보 부장

49. 해설 「be pleased + to부정사」는 '~하게 되어 기쁘다'라는 뜻이다. 따라서 정답은 (A) pleased이다.

50. (A) Mr. Hong는 승진을 사양하고 현재의 자리에 계속 있기를 선택했습니다.
(B) Mr. Hong는 회사의 신임 부사장을 축하했습니다.
(C) Mr. Hong는 다음 달에 리더를 맡게 될 것입니다.
(D) 그가 지난 18년 동안 JUA 사에서 직원으로 일해왔습니다.

해설 (A)는 빈칸 앞에서 부사장으로 임명되었다고 했고, 마지막 문장에 나온 '지도부 변경'이라는 내용과도 어긋나므로 탈락이다. (B)는 빈칸 앞에 Mr. Hong가 부사장으로 임명되었다는 내용이 있으므로 답이 될 수 없다. (C)는 빈칸 앞 문장에서 현재 완료 시제로 '이미 임명이 되었다'고 했으므로 '리더를 맡게 될 것'이라는 미래 시제는 맞지 않다. Mr. Hong가 부사장으로 이미 임명되었고, (D) '그가 지난 18년 동안 JUA 사를 위해 일해온 사람'이라고 소개하는 것이 가장 자연스럽다. 따라서 정답은 (D) Mr. Hong has been an employee at JUA for the last 18 years.이다.

51. 해설 plan은 to부정사를 목적어로 취하는 동사이므로 정답은 (A) to release이다.

52. 해설 문맥상 지도부 변경 과정을 겪는 동안 질문이 있으면 연락을 달라는 것이므로 정답은 (C) undergo이다.

[53-56] 다음 이메일에 관한 문제입니다.

수신: Taewoo Kim 〈taewoo@melot.net〉
발신: Josephine Park 〈jpark@redbooks.com〉
날짜: 4월 20일
첨부: Big Book of Basketball

저희 책의 제 3판에 사용할 기사들을 **53** 제출해 주셔서 감사합니다. 저는 그 기사들을 정말 재미있게 **54** 읽었습니다. 그러나 저는 기사에서 농구의 초기 역사에 관한 몇 가지 오류를 발견했습니다. 제가 이것들을 표시해 놓았고 검토하시라고 메모를 달아 놓았습니다. (첨부된 파일을 보십시오.) 게다가, 귀하는 기고자 동의서에 아직 사인하지 않았습니다. 가능하면 빨리 해 주시기 바랍니다. 저희 온라인 저자 센터에서 그 서류를 **55** 다운로드 받으실 수 있습니다. **56** 일단 귀하께서 그렇게 해 주시면, 저희가 귀하의 입금 처리를 시작할 수 있습니다.

감사합니다.

Josephine Park, 편집자
Red Books

---

53. 해설 전치사 뒤에 명사나 동명사가 모두 가능하지만 빈칸 뒤에 명사가 또 있다면 동명사의 목적어로 나온 것이다. 따라서 정답은 (A) submitting이다.

· ·

54. 해설 enjoy는 동명사를 목적어로 취하므로 정답은 (B) reading 이다.

· ·

55. 해설 문맥상 '서류를 다운로드 했었다, 할지도 모른다, 할 것이다'가 아니라, '서류를 다운로드 할 수 있다'가 가장 적절하다. 따라서 정답은 (B) can download이다.

· ·

56. (A) 귀하의 원고를 가능하면 빨리 제출하십시오
    (B) 일단 귀하께서 그것을 해주시면 저희는 입금 처리를 시작할 수 있습니다.
    (C) 저희가 필요한 서류를 귀하께 우편으로 보내드리겠습니다.
    (D) 귀하께서 보낸 사인된 서류를 막 받았습니다.

해설 (A)는 이메일 전반부에서 원고(기사)를 제출해 줘서 감사하다고 하면서 원고가 재미있었다고 했으므로 말이 되지 않는다. (C)는 문맥상 적절하지 않다. 서류에 아직 사인을 하지 않았다고 했으므로 (D) '당신이 보냈던 사인된 서류를 막 받았다'고 과거 시제를 사용하는 것 역시 문맥상 어울리지 않는다. (B)에서 '그렇게 해 주시면'은 '서류를 온라인 저자 센터에서 다운로드 받아서 사인하는 것'을 의미한다. 따라서 정답은 (B) Once you do that, we can begin to process your payment.이다.

[57-60] 다음 광고에 관한 문제입니다.

Reyes 건설은 주택 개조 사업을 30여 년 이상 해왔습니다. 탁월한 서비스로 **57** 알려진 이 회사는 매우 합리적인 가격에 집을 개조해 드립니다.

현재 저희는, **58** 제한된 기간 동안만 고객들에게 모든 문 교체에 20% 할인을 제공하고 있습니다. 하지만 서두르십시오. 이 **59** 할인은 3월 20일 이후에는 유효하지 않습니다.

만약 당신의 집을 개조하는 것에 관심이 있으시면, Reyes 건설로 전화 주십시오. **60** 또한, Baker 거리 43번지에 있는 저희 사무실을 방문해도 좋습니다.

저희는 업계 최고입니다.

---

57. 해설 주어는 This company이고 동사는 renovates이다. 따라서 빈칸은 수식어구 자리이고, company를 꾸며 주는 형용사가 필요한 자리이다. 문맥상 '아는 회사'가 아니고 '알려진 회사'이어야 하므로 과거분사가 맞다. 또한 앞의 명사를 꾸미고 있는데, 빈칸 뒤에 목적어가 나와 있지 않으므로 정답은 (B) known이다.

· ·

58. 해설 부정관사와 명사 사이에 있는 빈칸은 형용사 자리이다. 형용사는 과거분사 형용사로 (A)밖에 없으므로 정답은 (A) limited이다.

· ·

59. 해설 앞에서 일정 기간 동안만 20% 할인을 제공해 준다고 하였으므로 빈칸에는 '제안, 할인'을 뜻하는 명사가 필요하다. 따라서 정답은 (C) offer이다.

· ·

60. (A) 당신의 대금 지불이 처리되었습니다
    (B) 내일까지 약속을 확인해주세요.
    (C) 또한, Baker 거리 43번지에 있는 저희 사무실을 방문해도 좋습니다.
    (D) 당신은 완료된 작업에 대한 청구서를 받게 될 것입니다.

해설 이 글은 주택 개조 회사의 광고문이므로 대금 지불이 처리되었다는 (A)는 내용과 맞지 않다. (B)는 앞서 약속 일정에 대해 논의된 사항이 없으므로 답이 될 수 없다. 고객을 찾고 있는 광고문인데 (D)에서는 완료된 작업에 대한 청구서에 대해 언급하고 있으므로 답이 될 수 없다. 빈칸 앞에서 집을 개조하는 것에 관심이 있는 경우 연락을 취할 방법을 소개하고 있으므로, 빈칸에서 그 방법 아니면 다른 방법도 소개하는 것이 가장 자연스럽다. 따라서 정답은 (C) You can also visit our office at 43 Baker Street.이다.

Ms. Jackson에게,

저희는 고객님의 JL 쇼핑몰 멤버십 신청을 저희가 **61** 받아들였다는 사실을 알리게 되어 기쁩니다. 고객님의 멤버십으로 모든 혜택을 얻으려면, 저희 웹사이트 www.jlmall.org에 방문하셔서 고객님의 계정을 **62** 즉시 활성화시키십시오. 고객님의 사용자 이름은 JLJackson1234이고 현재 비밀번호는 7777입니다. 비밀번호는 저희 웹사이트에서 변경하실 수 있습니다. 저희 멤버십에 등록하시자마자 저희 서비스 이용이 가능하십니다. **63** 멤버십 이용 방법을 알아보시려면, 서비스 약관을 읽어 보세요. 저희는 고객님께서 JL 멤버십이 다른 어떤 멤버십보다 **64** 훨씬 더 가치가 있다는 것을 아시게 될 것입니다.

61. 해설 문맥상 당신의 신청이 받아들여졌음을 알려 준다는 내용이므로 정답은 (C) accepted이다.

62. 해설 문맥상 '혜택을 받으려면 즉시 계정을 활성화시켜라'라는 뜻이므로 정답은 (B) immediately이다.

63. (A) 고객님께서 보내신 서비스 요금이 처리되었습니다.
(B) 멤버십 이용 방법을 알아보시려면 서비스 약관을 읽어 보세요.
(C) 멤버십을 사용하려면 영업일 기준으로 3일을 기다리셔야 합니다.
(D) 고객님께서 더 이상 JL 쇼핑 회원이 되는 것을 원치 않으니 안타깝습니다.

해설 (A)에서 '고객님이 보낸 서비스 요금'이라고 과거 시제를 썼는데, 서비스 요금을 보냈다는 언급은 이메일에 없으므로 탈락이다. (C)는 이미 앞 문장에서 고객이 계정을 등록하자마자 즉시 서비스를 이용할 수 있다고 언급했으므로 오답이다. 첫 문장에서 회원 신청을 한 것에 대해 그것이 받아들여졌다는 이야기가 나오므로 (D)는 문맥상 맞지 않는다. 빈칸 앞에서 '서비스를 이용할 수 있다'는 내용이 나왔으므로, (B) '멤버십을 이용하는 방법을 알아보려면 서비스 약관을 읽어보라'는 내용이 가장 자연스럽다. 따라서 정답은 (B) Please read the terms of service to see how to use your membership.이다.

64. 해설 완벽한 비교급 문장이므로 빈칸은 수식어구가 들어갈 자리이다. 비교급 앞에서 비교급을 강조하는 표현을 찾아야 한다. 따라서 정답은 (A) much이다.

---

1. (C)	2. (A)	3. (B)	4. (A)
5. (D)	6. (D)	7. (B)	8. (B)
9. (C)	10. (D)	11. (A)	12. (A)
13. (D)	14. (D)	15. (A)	16. (A)

[1-4] 다음 이메일에 관한 문제입니다.

수신: Kao74@savemail.net
발신: Elliot.Kang@bluepubco.com
날짜: 3월 8일
제목: 투고 원고
첨부파일: ekaoagree.doc

Mr. Kao에게,

당신도 아시다시피, 요즘 많은 사람들이 요리에 관한 글을 쓰고 있습니다. 그러나 당신이 투고한 원고를 검토한 후, 우리는 당신의 대부분의 자료가 뛰어 **1** 나다는 것을 알게 되었습니다. 그 결과, 우리는 당신이 투고한 글을 사용하고 싶습니다. **2** 우리의 제안 조건들이 적혀 있는 계약서가 첨부되어 있으니 확인해 주시기 바랍니다. 만약 당신이 우리 제안을 수락한다면, 투고하신 글은 10월에 출간될 요리 책에 게재될 것입니다. 우리는 출간될 판에 당신이 구체적인 팁을 많이 **4** 포함시켜 주기를 기대합니다.

귀하의 답변을 기다리겠습니다.

감사합니다,

Elliot Kang
Blue 출판사

어휘 **these days** 요즘에 ǀ **review** *v.* 검토하다 ǀ **submission** *n.* 제출(물) ǀ **specific** *adj.* 구체적인 ǀ **response** *n.* 반응. 응답. 답변 ǀ **autobiography** *n.* 자서전

---

1. 해설 빈칸은 that절 속의 동사 자리이다. (D) ing형태는 동사가 될 수 없다. (B) 조동사가 있어야 동사원형이 나올 수 있으므로 오답이다. most는 전치사 of 뒤에 있는 명사와 수를 일치시킨다. content가 '내용'을 뜻하는 셀 수 없는 명사로 쓰였으므로, 단수 취급한다. 따라서 빈칸은 단수동사 (C) is가 정답이다.

2. **(A) 저희의 제안 조건들이 적혀 있는 계약서가 첨부되어 있으니 확인해 주시기 바랍니다.**
(B) 당신의 투고 원고가 꽤 잘 팔리고 있다는 것을 아시면 기쁠 것입니다.
(C) 저희는 그 원고의 질이 출간할 만큼 훌륭하지 않다고 생각합니다.
(D) 요리사로서 당신의 인생에 대한 당신의 글은 상당히 흥미로운 자서전입니다.

해설 (B)는 현재 책이 출간되기 전 상황이므로 문맥상 맞지 않다. (C)는 빈칸 앞의 문장이 '당신이 투고한 글이 출판되었으면 좋겠다'이므로 앞뒤가 맞지 않는 말이다. (D)는 책을 아직 출간하지도 않았는데 '당

신의 글은 흥미로운 자서전이다'라고 말할 수 없다. 빈칸 앞의 문장이 '당신이 제출한 글이 출판되었으면 좋겠다'이고, 빈칸 뒤의 문장은 '만약 당신이 우리의 제안을 받아들인다면'이다. 따라서 빈칸에는 '우리의 계약서를 살펴보시고 우리의 제안을 생각해 보라'고 하는 것이 가장 자연스럽다. 따라서 정답은 (A) Please find attached a contract with our proposed terms in it.이다.

3. **해설** 빈칸 이하가 없어도 완벽한 문장이므로 빈칸은 a cookbook을 꾸며 주는 수식어구가 들어갈 자리이다. (A), (C), (D) 모두 동사이므로 탈락이다. 수식어 역할은 to부정사 밖에 없다. 또한, to publish의 목적어가 없으므로 to부정사를 수동태로 써야 한다. 따라서, 정답은 (B) to be published이다.

4. **해설** expect는 5형식 동사이다. you가 목적어이고 빈칸은 목적격 보어 자리이다. expect는 목적격 보어에 to부정사가 올 수 있으므로 정답은 (A) to include이다.

[5-8] 다음 편지에 관한 문제입니다.

8월 10일
Ms. Linda Kim
Grandriver 가 8676번지
밴쿠버 2H4 8J7

Ms. Kim에게,

⑤ 저희 제품에 관심을 가져 주셔서 감사합니다. 귀하의 정수기 구매와 ⑥ 설치에 대한 견적서를 아래에서 확인하십시오. 총 금액은 구매 비용, 노동력, 그리고 세금을 포함하며, 총 1,300달러가 됩니다. 노동 시간과 비용은 조정될 수 있습니다.

만약 귀하께서 ⑦ 계속 진행하길 원하신다면, 귀하에게 편하신 시간을 정할 수 있도록 ⑧ 저에게 연락을 주십시오.

감사드리며,

Jenny Kumamoto
JAY 정수기

어휘 estimate *n.* 견적서 | water purifier 정수기 | labor *n.* 노동 | be subject to ~의 대상이다, ~하기 쉽다 | adjustment *n.* 수정, 조정 | arrange *v.* 정하다, 마련하다, 준비하다 | convenient *adj.* 편리한 | renew *v.* 재개하다, 갱신하다 | proceed *v.* 진행하다

5. (A) 당신이 만든 제안서가 받아들여졌습니다.
(B) 당신의 정수기가 곧 집에 도착할 것입니다.
(C) 당신이 구매한 물품에 대해 아직 비용을 지불하지 않았습니다.
(D) 저희 제품에 관심을 가져 주셔서 감사합니다.

해설 (A)의 '당신이 만든 제안서가 받아들여졌다'의 '제안서'라는 단어는 이 글의 내용과 어울리지 않는다. (B)는 빈칸 뒤에 견적서라는 말이 나오는 것으로 보아 아직 사지 않은 것을 알 수 있으므로, 정수기가 곧 도착한다는 것은 말이 되지 않는다. (C)도 아직 사지 않았으므로 '구매한 물품'은 말이 되지 않는다. 글의 첫 문장이므로 (D) '우리 제품에 관심 가져 줘서 고맙다'고 말하면서, 구매 제품과 설치 비용에 대한 견적

서를 안내하는 것이 자연스럽다. 따라서 정답은 (D) Thank you for your interest in our product.이다.

6. **해설** 'the purchase'와 빈칸은 전치사 for의 목적어 자리이다. 따라서 명사 자리이다. 명사는 (C)와 (D)이지만 문맥상 '설치하는 사람'이 아니라 '설치'가 맞으므로 정답은 (D) installation이다.

7. **해설** 문맥상 '견적서를 보고 거래를 계속 진행하고 싶으면'이라는 의미이므로 정답은 (B) proceed이다.

8. **해설** 빈칸은 contact의 목적어 자리이다. (A)는 소유격 뒤에는 명사가 있어야 하므로 오답이다. (C) '나의 것'에 연락한다는 것은 말이 되지 않는다. (D) 목적어 자리에 -self가 들어가려면 주어와 목적어가 같아야 한다. 명령문의 주어는 생략되긴 하지만 사실 you이므로, you와 myself는 호응이 안 된다. 따라서 빈칸은 목적어 자리이기 때문에 목적격 (B) me가 정답이다.

[9-12] 다음 기사에 관한 문제입니다.

KB 산업의 Sang-Woo Park 사장은 회사가 다음 주부터 새로운 고화질 텔레비전을 시장에 내놓을 ⑨ 것이라고 공식 발표했다. 회사의 보도 자료에 따르면, 그 텔레비전은 좋은 음질과 선명한 화질을 ⑩ 특징으로 하고 있다. 전자 제품 산업 분석가들은 이 최신 제품이 ⑪ 훨씬 더 많은 소비자들을 끌어들여 긍정적인 판매 실적도 낼 것이라고 예측한다. ⑫ 이는 작년에 손실을 기록한 바 있는 KB에게 유익할 것이다.

어휘 formally *adv.* 공식적으로, 정식으로 | market *n.* 시장 *v.* (상품을) 내놓다, 광고하다 | high-definition *adj.* 고화질의 | according to ~에 따르면 | press release 보도 자료 | sound quality 음질 | sharp *adj.* 날카로운, 선명한 | industry *n.* 산업, 업계 | analysis *n.* 분석 | latest *adj.* 최신의 | attract *v.* 끌어 모으다, (어떤 반응을) 불러 일으키다 | positive *adj.* 긍정적인

9. **해설** 본동사 announced의 목적어로서 주어, 동사, 목적어를 모두 갖춘 완전한 절이 연결되어 있으므로 완전한 절을 이끌어 주거나 목적어, 보어 자리에 올 수 있는 명사절 접속사가 필요하다. 따라서 정답은 (C) that이다.

10. **해설** 빈칸은 동사 자리이다. 따라서 (B)는 탈락이다. 주어가 단수이므로 (A)도 탈락이다. (C)와 (D) 중에 문맥상 이번에 출시할 이 제품은 현재 이런 '특징을 가지고 있다'는 뜻이므로 과거 시제가 아닌 현재 시제가 적절하다. 따라서 정답은 (D) features이다.

11. **해설** 비교급 앞에서 비교급을 강조하는 부사는 much, even, still, far, a lot 등인데 보기 중에는 much밖에 없으므로 정답은 (A) much 이다.

12. **(A) 이는 작년에 손실을 기록한 바 있는 KB에게 유익할 것이다.**
(B) 한 회사의 영업 사원에 따르면 그 텔레비전은 이미 잘 팔리고 있다고 한다.
(C) 그 신제품에 관심을 보이는 소비자들이 거의 없는 것으로 보인다.
(D) Mr. Kim이 사임했기 때문에 신임 CEO에 대한 탐색이 벌어질 것이다.

해설 (B)는 제품을 내놓을 예정이지 이미 팔고 있지는 않으므로 답이 될 수 없다. (C)도 아직 제품을 내놓지 않았으므로 소비자들의 관심이 어떤지 알 수가 없다. (D)는 새로운 CEO를 뽑는다는 내용이 아니므로 문맥상 어울리지 않는다. 빈칸 앞에 '더 많은 고객들을 끌어들일 것이고 긍정적인 판매 실적도 낼 것'이라는 내용이 나오므로 빈칸에는 '이것(This)이 KB에게 이로울 것이다'라는 내용이 오는 것이 가장 자연스럽다. 따라서 정답은 (A) This should benefit KB, which recorded a loss last year.이다.

[13-16] 다음 이메일에 관한 문제입니다.

수신: yoon11@SMMedTech.com
발신: james@BB.org
날짜: 4월 6일
제목: 지난주 목요일

Ms. yoon에게,

지난주 목요일에 저에게 **13** 전화 주셔서 고맙습니다. 당신과 이야기를 한 것도 좋았고, SM 의료기기에서 이루어지고 있는 다양한 프로젝트에 대해서 알게 된 것도 유익했습니다. **14** 그것은 저에게 매우 교육적인 경험이었습니다. 저는 SM 의료기기와 일하는 것이 BB 병원에 매우 좋 **15** 을 것이라고 생각합니다. 회의를 연 후, 저희는 협력하며 **16** 나아가기로 결정했습니다. 다음 단계는 무엇인지 저에게 알려 주십시오.

감사합니다.

James Kim

어휘 collaboration *n.* 공통 작업, 협조, 협력 | inform *v.* 알리다, 통지하다 | step *n.* 단계 | look forward to -ing ~를 고대하다 | conduct *v.* 하다, 시행하다

13. 해설 문맥상 전화를 해 주어서 고맙고, 당신과 이야기하는 것이 좋았다는 말이므로 정답은 (D) calling이다.

14. (A) 저는 SM 의료기기에서 일하게 되길 고대하고 있습니다.
(B) 저희는 다음 주에 두 번째 인터뷰를 실시할 것입니다.
(C) 저는 당신이 준 약을 먹은 뒤로 훨씬 나아졌습니다.
(D) 그것은 저에게 매우 교육적인 경험이었습니다.

해설 (A) 빈칸 뒤의 문장을 보면, 내가 SM 의료기기에 입사해서 일하는 것이 아니고 SM 의료기기와 함께 협력해서 일하는 것이라는 것을 알 수 있으므로 답이 될 수 없다. (B) 역시 입사 인터뷰가 아니라 협력에 대한 논의를 한 것이므로 상관없는 문장이다. (C) 혼동을 유발하기 위해 '병원'이라는 단어를 통해 연상할 수 있는 '약'이라는 단어를 사용한 오답이다. (D) 여기서 It이 가리키는 것은 '당신과 이야기한 것과 다

양한 프로젝트에 대해서 알게 된 것'이다. 따라서 정답은 (D) It was a very educational experience for me.이다.

15. 해설 빈칸은 that절 속의 동사 자리이다. 동사는 (A)와 (B)인데, (B)는 주어와의 수 일치에 어긋나 문맥상 '함께 일하는 것이 앞으로 이로울 것이라고 생각한다'이므로 현재의 추측을 나타내는 조동사가 적절하다. 따라서 정답은 (A) would be이다.

16. 해설 decide는 목적어로 to부정사만을 취하는 동사이므로 정답은 (A) to move이다.

PART 7

UNIT 01. 주제·목적 문제

Practice

본서 p.214

1. (B)	**2.** (D)	**3.** (D)	**4.** (A)	**5.** (B)
6. (D)	**7.** (D)	**8.** (D)		

[1-2] 다음 문자 메시지에 관한 문제입니다.

보낸 사람: Mason Craft, 495-555-3032
받은 날짜: 1월 5일 수요일, 오후 4:45

안녕하세요, Lizzie.

제 차가 시동이 걸리지 않아서, 정비소에 가져가려고 견인차를 기다리는 중이에요. 제가 시간 맞춰서 식당에 갈 수 없을 것 같아요. **1** 오늘 밤 제 저녁 교대 근무를 해줄 수 있나요? **2** 저 대신해 줄 수 있으면 알려주세요.

고마워요.

1. Mason은 메시지를 왜 보냈는가?
　(A) 차량 대여료를 문의하기 위해
　(B) 그의 직장에 대리인을 마련하기 위해
　(C) 자동차 정비소에 차량을 요청하기 위해
　(D) 회의를 연기하기 위해

해설　지문 후반부, 오늘 밤 내 저녁 교대 근무를 해줄 수 있냐는 부탁을 하고 있으므로 (B) To arrange a substitute at his workplace가 정답이다.

2. Mason은 Lizzie에게 무엇을 해달라고 요청하는가?
　(A) 차고에서 공구를 가져온다
　(B) 음식을 주문한다
　(C) 식당에 전화한다
　(D) 답장을 보낸다

해설　지문 후반부, 대신해 줄 수 있으면 알려 달라고 요청하고 있으므로 (D) Send a reply가 정답이다.

[3-4] 다음 정보에 관한 문제입니다.

이 달의 상품: Jenny의 코코넛 비누

3 Jenny의 코코넛 비누는 로스엔젤레스 거주자인 Jenny Kang의 손으로 만들어집니다. **4** Ms. Kang은 비누를 BY 식료품점과 계약 후 지역 내에서 팝니다. 그 비누를 시원하고 건조한 곳에 보관해 둔다면, 그 유기농 코코넛 오일 손 비누를 3개월 이상 사용할 수 있습니다. 다른 유기농 비누들은 겨우 1달간만 사용할 수 있습니다. Jenny의 코코넛 비누가 BY 고객들에게 인기 상품이며, **4** 현재 3개씩을 한 팩으로 해서 10달러에 판매 중입니다. 이는 다음과 같은 혜택을 지닙니다.

- 손을 부드럽게 만듭니다.
- 은은한 향이 특징입니다.
- **4** 순전히 유기농 재료로 이루어져 있습니다.
- **4** 인공적인 화학 물질을 포함하지 않습니다.
- 손을 철저하게 씻을 수 있습니다.

또한, 귀하는 Jenny의 코코넛 비누 구매 가격에서 10퍼센트 할인을 받으실 수 있습니다. 단지 할인 코드 GD88을 LA에 있는 BY 식료품점의 계산원에게 언급해주기만 하면 됩니다.

3. 정보의 목적은 무엇인가?
　(A) 새로운 가게의 개점을 알리기 위해서
　(B) 씻는 절차를 묘사하기 위해서
　(C) 비누가 어떻게 만들어지는지 보여 주기 위해서
　(D) 지역 거주자의 상품을 홍보하기 위해서

해설　글의 목적은 주로 앞부분에서 언급된다. 제목 자체가 '이번 달 제품'으로, 상품을 광고하는 것이고, 첫 번째 단락의 앞부분에서 로스엔젤레스 거주자인 Ms. Kang이 지역에서 수제비누를 판다고 하면서 제품의 장점과 구매 방법을 안내하며 홍보하고 있다. Jenny's Coconut Soap이 a local resident's merchandise로 paraphrasing되었다. 따라서 정답은 (D) To market a local resident's merchandise이다.

4. 비누에 대해서 언급된 것은 무엇인가?
　(A) 천연 재료로 이루어져 있다.
　(B) 여러 장소에서 판매가 된다.
　(C) 비누 1개가 한 팩인 것만 구입할 수 있다.
　(D) 온라인에서만 판매가 될 것이다.

해설　선택지를 하나씩 소거하며 정답을 찾는다. BY 식료품점에서만 판매한다고 나와 있으므로 (B)는 탈락이다. 비누 3개가 한 팩으로 팔고 있으므로 (C)도 탈락이다. 온라인에서만 판다는 이야기는 나와 있지 않고, 식료품점에 가서 산다고 했으므로 (D)도 탈락이다. organic(유기농)이라는 말이 계속 나오고 인공적인 화학 물질을 포함하고 있지 않다고 하였으므로 정답은 (A) It consists of natural ingredients이다.

[5-6] 다음 이메일에 관한 문제입니다.

수신: 신입 직원들
발신: Myungjun Moon
제목: 4월 1일 워크숍
날짜: 4월 2일

Lansing 사에 오신 걸 환영합니다. 어제 워크숍에 참석해 주신 것을 감사드립니다. 저는 그 모임이 여러분에게 도움이 되었길 바랍니다.

6 저희 팀과 저는 저희의 훈련 프로그램을 유익하고 도움이 되도록 만들기 위해서 끊임 없이 노력하고 있습니다. 저희는 매번 모임을 이전보다 더 낫게 만들기 위해 노력합니다. 그러므로, 저희는 저희가 그 목표를 달성하고 있는지를 알고 싶고, 그 프로그램에 관한 참석자들의 피드백을 원합니다.

5 저희는 여러분이 저희의 웹사이트 www.lansingcorp.com에 가서, 어제 모임에 관한 설문조사를 작성해 주시길 정중히 요청드립니다.

여러분의 협조에 미리 감사 드립니다.

감사합니다.

6 Myungjun Moon
위원장, 직원 전문 개발

---

5. 이메일이 왜 쓰여졌는가?

(A) 몇몇 직원들을 축하하기 위해

(B) 의견을 요청하기 위해

(C) 직원들에게 곧 있을 워크숍을 알리기 위해

(D) 프로그램의 혜택에 대해서 알리기 위해

해설 이 글은 마지막 부분에 글의 목적이 나왔다. 이메일 마지막 단락에서 '저희는 여러분이 저희의 웹사이트 www. lansingcorp.com에 가서, 어제 모임에 관한 설문조사를 작성해 주시길 정중히 요청드립니다'라고 하였으므로 정답은 (B) To request some input이다.

---

6. Mr. Moon에 대해서 언급된 것은 무엇인가?

(A) 사내 정책을 변경했다.

(B) 최근에 승진했다.

(C) 회사 웹사이트를 관리한다.

(D) 훈련 프로그램을 감독한다.

해설 선택지를 하나씩 소거하며 정답을 찾는다. 두 번째 단락 첫 번째 줄에서 '저희 팀과 저는 훈련 프로그램을 유익하게 만들려고 노력한다'는 말이 있었고, 맨 마지막 부분에 coordinator라는 직책이 나왔으므로 조직하고 조정하는 즉, 총괄하는 사람이다. 따라서 정답은 (D) He oversees training programs.이다.

[7-8] 다음 공지에 관한 문제입니다.

사무실 임대 가능

7 Beltsville의 Addison 가에 있는 1,000피트 사무실이 5월 1일부터 임대 가능합니다. 개방된 평면을 찾고 있는 소규모 사업체에게 적합합니다. 이것이 귀하가 찾고 있는 것이라면, 귀하와 직원들은 매우 만족할 것입니다. **8** 사무실은 16층에 위치해 있으며, 삼면에 Beltsville 도심을 내려다보는 창이 있습니다. 전망이 정말 근사합니다. 이 사무실은 지하 주차장, 세 대의 널찍한 엘리베이터, 탁월한 보안을 특징으로 하는 현대적인 건물에 위치해 있습니다. 더 많은 정보를 원하시면, Britt Grouby에게 b.grouby@directrealtors.com으로 연락 주십시오.

---

7. 이 공지의 목적은 무엇인가?

(A) 경비료에 대해 문의하기 위해

(B) 신규 업체를 홍보하기 위해

(C) 충원 중인 직책을 광고하기 위해

(D) 임대 공간을 알리기 위해

해설 공지의 처음 부분에서 'Beltsville의 Addison 가에 있는 1,000피트 사무실이 5월 1일부터 임대 가능합니다'이라는 내용이 나오므로, 임대 가능한 사무실을 알리기 위해 공지했음을 알 수 있다. 따라서 정답은 (D) To announce a space fo rent이다.

---

8. 공지에서 이 사무실에 대해 언급되지 않은 것은 무엇인가?

(A) 현재 이용할 수 없다.

(B) 여러 대의 엘리베이터가 특징이다.

(C) 여러 면에 창문이 있다.

(D) 1층에 있다.

해설 공지의 중간 부분에서 "사무실은 16층에 위치해 있으며, 삼면에 Beltsville 도심을 내려다보는 창이 있습니다."이라는 내용이 나오므로, 정답은 (D) It is on the ground floor.이다.

UNIT 02. 세부사항 문제

Practice

본서 p.222

1. (C)	**2.** (D)	**3.** (D)	**4.** (C)	**5.** (A)
6. (A)	**7.** (C)	**8.** (B)	**9.** (D)	**10.** (B)
11. (C)				

[1-2] 다음 광고에 관한 문제입니다.

Superior Destination SM
목적지마다 매우 좋은 가격

목적지	가격
서울	199달러
대전	299달러
대구	299달러
부산	310달러
제주도	399달러

1 귀하의 할인된 여행을 예약하세요. 저희 웹사이트는 www. superiorsm.com입니다. 또한, 귀하가 선택한 지역에서 숙박할 최고의 장소를 찾으려면 저희 호텔 리스트를 검색해 보세요.

조건: 항공 요금은 일반석에 대한 1인당 비용입니다.

2 저희 웹사이트를 통해서 호텔을 예약한다면 거래에는 셔틀버스를 이용하여 공항으로 가는 것을 포함하며, **아침식사로 무료 뷔페를 이용할 수 있습니다.**

---

1. Superior Destination SM은 무엇이겠는가?

(A) 항공사

(B) 셔틀버스 서비스

(C) 여행사

(D) 호텔 체인점

해설 광고 중간 부분에서 핵심 키워드 주변을 살펴보면 항공 요금이 나와서 항공사라고 착각하기 쉽지만, 여행사가 자신들의 웹사이트를 통해서 할인된 여행 지역을 제시하고, 자사의 웹사이트를 통해서 호텔도 예약하라고 하고 있으므로 항공사가 아닌 여행사임을 알 수 있다. 따라서, 정답은 (C) A travel agency이다.

2. 거래에 포함된 것은 무엇인가?

(A) 여행 안내책자

(B) 호텔 숙박

(C) 여행 가이드

(D) 공항까지 태워다 주는 것

해설 키워드가 나오는 마지막 부분 'Transport to the airport via shuttle bus is included in deals'에서 셔틀버스를 이용하여 공항으로 가는 것이 거래에 포함되어 있음을 밝히고 있으므로 정답은 (D) A ride to the airport이다. Transport to the airport가 A ride to the airport로 paraphrasing되었다.

[3-5] 다음 이메일에 관한 문제입니다.

수신: nwayans@cpomail.net

발신: tbernell@swiftair.com

날짜: 6월 29일

제목: Swift Frequent Flyers 클럽

Ms. Wayans에게,

3 Swift Frequent Flyers 클럽에 가입해 주셔서 감사합니다. 감사의 표시로, 고객님께 Swift 항공사가 드리는 특별한 선물을 발송했습니다. 고객께서는 요즘 유행하는 튼튼한 Gearup 여행 가방을 받으실 겁니다. **4** 이 여행 가방은 모든 항공사가 정해 놓은 기내용 수하물 규정을 충족합니다. 앞으로 3주 이내에 고객님의 Gearup 여행 가방을 받지 못하신다면, 고객 서비스 1-800-555-9844로 전화해 주십시오.

5 또한, 반드시 고객님의 Swift Frequent Flyer 계정으로 로그인하셔서 저희 주간 회원 할인가를 확인해 주세요. 저희는 회원들이 할인된 요금으로 구매하실 수 있는 비행기, 호텔, 렌터카를 위한 새로운 패키지 상품을 계속 추가하고 있습니다. 고객님께서 모든 회원 혜택을 누리시길 바랍니다.

진심으로,

Terrence Bernell

Swift Frequent Flyers 클럽

---

3. Ms. Wayans는 왜 여행 가방을 받을 것인가?

(A) 특별한 경연에서 우승했다.

(B) 공항에서 여행 가방을 잃어버렸다.

(C) 웹사이트에서 여행 가방을 주문했다.

(D) 항공사 클럽에 가입했다.

해설 이메일 도입부에서 'Frequent Flyers 클럽에 가입해 주셔서 감사합니다. 감사의 표시로 고객님께 Swift 항공사가 드리는 특별한 선물을 발송했습니다.'라고 말한 후, 선물이 여행 가방이라고 알려주고 있으므로 정답은 (D) She joined an airline's club.이다.

---

4. 여행 가방에 관하여 언급된 것은 무엇인가?

(A) 다양한 크기로 이용 가능하다.

(B) 다른 색으로 교환될 수 있다.

(C) 비행기 탑승 시에 가져갈 수 있다.

(D) Ms. Wayans의 사무실로 배달될 것이다.

해설 여행 가방을 키워드로 잡고 지문을 살펴본다. '이 여행 가방은 모든 항공사가 정해 놓은 기내용 수하물 규정을 충족합니다.'라고 설명했으므로 (C) It can be taken on board an airplane.가 정답이다.

---

5. Ms. Wayans는 온라인으로 무엇을 하라고 권장 받는가?

(A) 할인 혜택들을 본다

(B) 전자 티켓을 다운로드한다

(C) 여행 일정을 확인한다

(D) 고객 계정을 만든다

해설 '또한, 반드시 고객님의 Swift Frequent Flyer 계정으로 로그인하셔서 저희 주간 회원 할인가를 확인해 주세요. 저희는 저희 회원들이 할인된 요금으로 구매하실 수 있는 비행기, 호텔, 렌터카를 위한 새로운 패키지 상품을 계속 추가하고 있습니다.'라고 할인가로 제공되는 패키지 상품을 이용할 것을 권장하고 있으므로 (A) View discount offers가 정답이다.

[6-8] 다음 양식에 관한 문제입니다.

오늘 날짜: 12월 7일

유지보수 관리자: Jasmine Kim

유지보수팀 리더: Jenny Brown

6 **요청자:** Greg Lee

방 위치: Owen홀 107호

요청 사항: 12월 17일

7 오전 10시 30분~오후 2시: 점심/초청 연사들

오전 9시 30분: 방을 쓸 수 있게 준비, 오후 2시 30분: 방 청소

만약 방 세팅이 필요하다면, 구체적으로 무엇이 필요한지 알려주세요:

8 오찬과 짧은 연설을 위해서 100명의 손님을 수용할 회의실 준비가 필요합니다. 각 10개의 좌석이 있는 10개의 직사각형 테이블을 마련해 주시고, 전부 프로젝션 스크린이 있는 남쪽 벽을 향하도록 배치해주세요.

필요한 어떤 추가 장비가 있으면 적어주세요:

연단, 영사기, 그리고 스크린

---

6. 행사를 준비하고 있는 사람은 누구이겠는가?

(A) Greg Lee

(B) Owen Hall

(C) Jasmine Kim

(D) Jenny Brown

해설 핵심 키워드 Who(사람)는 맨 위에 언급되어 있는데 Jenny Brown, Jasmine Kim, Greg Lee 중에서 행사를 위해 여러가지 사항을 요청한 사람은 Requested by에 언급되어 있다. 따라서 정답은 (A) Greg Lee이다.

---

7. 몇 시쯤 연설이 끝날 것인가?

(A) 오전 9시 30분

(B) 오전 10시 30분

(C) 오후 2시

(D) 오후 2시 30분

해설 시간 관련 단어가 Requested for 부분에 보인다. 연설과 점심은 오후 2시까지이며 guest speakers를 통해 speeches가 있을 것임을 유추할 수 있다. 따라서 연설이 끝나는 시간은 오후 2시이므로 정답은 (C) 2:00P.M.이다.

---

8. 양식에서 요청된 것은 무엇인가?
(A) 특별한 점심 메뉴
(B) 구체적인 가구 배치
(C) 초청 연사의 성과 이름
(D) 손상된 테이블의 교체

해설 '만약 방 세팅이 필요하다면, 구체적으로 무엇이 필요한지 알려주세요.' 부분에 요청 사항을 자세히 썼으므로 답은 그 안에 있다. 10개의 직사각형 테이블을 마련하고, 프로젝션 스크린이 있는 남쪽 벽을 향하도록 배치해달라고 했으므로 정답은 (B) A specific furniture arrangement이다.

[9-11] 다음 공지에 관한 문제입니다.

Staples 출판사
전 직원들을 위한 멋진 제안!

9 Staples 출판사의 직원으로서, 여러분은 우리 회사에서 발행되는 모든 잡지에 대한 큰 할인을 받으실 수 있습니다. 여기 포함된 잡지 목록을 훑어 보십시오. 내년에 몇 권이든 구독을 선택하실 수 있습니다. 첨부된 서식에 주소와 청구서 필드를 기입하시고, 받아보고 싶으신 잡지의 옆 상자에 체크 표시를 해 주십시오. **10** 서식을 기입하신 뒤, 구독부의 Jen Mackey에게 가져다 주십시오.

여러분 모두가 이 멋진 기회를 이용하실 수 있기를 희망합니다.

	연간 구독 정상가	연간 구독 할인가
〈Car News Monthly〉	40달러/년	15달러/년
〈Economics Worldwide〉	80달러/년	30달러/년
〈Busy Mom〉	60달러/년	22달러/년
〈Travel International Advice〉	50달러/년	20달러/년
11 〈Sports Worldly〉	50달러/년	20달러/년
〈Fast Bike〉	40달러/년	15달러/년

9. 이 공지의 목적은 무엇인가?
(A) 새로운 출판사의 인수를 홍보하기 위해
(B) 멋진 제안의 기한을 연장하기 위해
(C) 대중들에게 구독 할인을 발표하기 위해
(D) 직원들에게 특별 판촉을 알리기 위해

해설 공지의 첫 번째 단락에서 직원들에게 회사에서 발행되는 모든 잡지에 할인을 해 준다고 했으므로 정답은 (D) To inform employees of a special promotion이다.

---

10. 직원들은 어떻게 할인된 구독을 받을 수 있는가?
(A) 회사 웹사이트를 방문함으로써
(B) 동료 직원에게 서식을 제출함으로써
(C) 구독부에 전화함으로써
(D) 한번에 여러 개의 잡지를 주문함으로써

해설 공지의 마지막 부분에서 서식을 완성한 후, 사내 특정 직원에게 전달하라고 했으므로 정답은 (B) By submitting a form to a fellow employee이다.

---

11. Staples 출판사 직원은 〈Sports Worldly〉의 연간 구독에서 얼마나 절약할 수 있는가?
(A) 15달러
(B) 20달러
(C) 30달러
(D) 50달러

해설 잡지들의 정상가와 할인가 대조표에 〈Sports Worldly〉를 보면 연간 정상가는 50달러, 할인가는 20달러이므로 직원들은 30달러를 할인 받을 수 있음을 알 수 있다. 정답은 (C) $30이다.

UNIT 03. 사실확인 문제

Practice

1. (B)	2. (D)	3. (C)	4. (C)	5. (A)
6. (D)	7. (B)	8. (B)	9. (B)	10. (B)

[1-2] 다음 정보에 관한 문제입니다.

BH

1 매년 Design-A Awards는 그래픽 디자인 회사에게 뛰어난 업적을 인정해주기 위해 주어집니다. 켄징턴 광고업자 연맹이 그 상을 후원하고, 켄징턴 지역에 있는 회사들만이 그 상을 받을 수 있습니다. 5가지 종류의 상들이 있고, 켄징턴 지역 디자인 컨퍼런스에서 매년 10월에 시상됩니다. **2** 모든 그래픽 디자인 회사들은 작품을 제출할 것이 촉구되며, 자세한 사항을 알아보려면 BH 웹사이트를 방문하세요.

---

1. Design-A Awards에 관하여 언급된 것은 무엇인가?
(A) 5년마다 한 번 주어진다.
(B) 지역 회사들에게만 주어진다.
(C) 다양한 분야의 회사들에게 수여된다.
(D) 매년 다른 장소에서 열린다.

해설 켄징턴 지역에 있는 회사들만이 상을 받을 수 있다는 내용이 있으므로 (B) They are only offered to firms in the local area.가 정답이다. 첫 문장에서 매년 그래픽 디자인 회사에게 주는 상이라고 소개하고 있으므로 (A)와 (C)는 정답이 될 수 없다. 또한 매년 켄징턴 지역 디자인 컨퍼런스에서 시상이 된다고 언급했으므로 (D)도 오답이다.

2. 회사들은 웹사이트에서 무엇을 할 수 있는가?

(A) 요금을 낸다.

(B) 설문조사에 참여한다.

(C) 부스를 예약한다.

(D) 그들의 작품을 업로드한다.

해설 질문의 키워드 Web site를 찾아내면 정답을 알아낼 수 있다. 마지막 문장에 Web site에 들어가면 작품을 제출할 수 있다는 내용이 있으므로 submit를 upload로 paraphrasing한 (D) Upload their work가 정답이다.

[3-4] 다음 안내책자에 관한 문제입니다.

Real Tours
이탈리아의 매력적인 도시들

3 10년 넘게, Real Tours는 고객들에게 최고의 여행을 제공해왔습니다. 저희는 많은 최고의 여행 간행물 이외에도 〈World Interest〉 잡지에도 소개되어왔습니다. 저희 여행사는 이탈리아의 여러 지역에 관한 여행 프로그램이 있으며, 베니스, 로마, 밀란, 그리고 플로렌스에 관해서는 더욱 특별한 프로그램을 가지고 있습니다.

선택된 도시로의 1주일 간의 방문이 기본 여행 패키지에 포함됩니다.

4 모든 패키지에는 다음이 포함됩니다:

• 적어도 1명의 여행 가이드
• 아침식사와 점심식사
• 도시 내의 육상 교통
• 호텔에서의 5박
• 하루 세 곳의 관광 명소 입장

더 자세한 사항을 원하시면, Marsha Kim에게 02-847-9901로 연락하세요.

3. Real Tours에 대해서 언급된 것은 무엇인가?

(A) 현재 공사 중이다.

(B) 처음 방문한 고객들에게 할인을 제공한다.

(C) 10년 이상 운영된 업체이다.

(D) 최근에 새로운 지점을 열었다.

해설 고유명사 Real Tours가 키워드이다. 첫 줄에 언급된 '10년 넘게, Real Tours는 고객들에게 최고의 여행을 제공해왔습니다'가 'It has been in business for more than a decade'로 paraphrasing되었다. 따라서 정답은 (C) It has been in business for more than a decade.이다.

4. 기본 여행 패키지에 포함되지 않는 것은 무엇인가?

(A) 점심 식사

(B) 호텔 숙박

(C) 비행기 티켓

(D) 유명한 장소 방문

해설 소거법으로 선택지와 지문을 대조해서 정답을 찾는다. (A) Daytime meals는 Breakfast & lunch에 해당한다. (B) Hotel stays는 Accommodations at a hotel for five nights에 해당한다. (D) Visits to famous places는 Admission to three tourist attractions per day에 해당한다. Flight tickets는 언급되지 않았다. 따라서, 정답은 (C) Flight tickets이다.

[5-7] 다음 기사에 관한 문제입니다.

3월 20일 – 유명 홈 인테리어 잡지인 〈Lux Interior〉가 발간 20주년을 기념한다. 잡지사는 여섯 개의 기념패를 제작하기 위해 유명 식기 디자인 업체인 Janson 사와 함께 작업함으로써 이 특별한 날을 기릴 것이다. **5** 각 기념패는 지난 호 특집 기사에 실린 여러 사진들 가운데 우리 독자들이 뽑은 다양한 종류의 주방용품들을 묘사할 것이다.

〈Lux Interior〉의 편집장인 Dianne Stein에 따르면, Janson 사는 확실한 선택이었다고 한다. Ms. Stein은 **6** "저희는 저희를 잘 알고, 믿음이 가는 회사를 원했고, 되도록이면 저희 잡지에 제품 소개를 했던 곳이기를 바랍니다."라고 하면서, "그래서 저희는 모두 그 프로젝트를 위해 Janson 사와 함께 일하는 것에 찬성했습니다."라고 말했다.

이 컬렉션들은 5월 1일부터 Janson 사의 온라인 상점에서 구매가 가능하다. "벌써 많은 독자 분들이 소장용 접시의 선주문을 요청하셨습니다."라고 하면서, **7** "하지만 우리가 아직 가격을 결정하지 못했습니다."라고 Ms. Stein이 말했다.

5. 〈Lux Interior〉 독자들은 무엇을 하라고 요구 받았는가?

(A) 가장 마음에 드는 이미지를 고른다

(B) 그들의 주방 사진들을 제출한다

(C) 온라인에서 특정 품목들을 선주문한다

(D) 몇 제품을 시험 사용한다

해설 '각 기념패는 지난 호 특집 기사에 실린 여러 사진들 가운데 우리 독자들이 뽑은 다양한 종류의 주방용품들을 묘사할 것이다.'에서 지난 달 독자들에게 잡지에 실린 이미지 중 하나를 선택하라는 요청을 했음을 유추할 수 있으므로 정답은 (A) Choose their favorite images이다.

6. 기사가 Janson 사 제품에 관하여 언급한 것은 무엇인가?

(A) 천연재료로 만들어졌다.

(B) 전세계적으로 팔린다.

(C) 최근 수상 경력이 있다.

(D) 〈Lux Interior〉에 실린 적이 있다.

해설 Janson 사를 선택한 이유로 '저희는 저희에게 친숙하고, 믿음이 가는 회사를 원했고, 되도록이면 저희 잡지에 제품 소개를 했던 곳이기를 바랍니다.'라는 문장이 나왔으므로 (D) They have been featured in Lux Interior.가 정답이다.

7. 컬렉션에 관하여 알려지지 않은 것은 무엇인가?

(A) 어디서 판매될지

(B) 비용이 얼마나 들지

(C) 언제 이용 가능한지

(D) 얼마나 많은 디자인이 만들어질지

해설 '하지만 저희가 아직 가격을 결정하지 못했습니다.'라고 했으므로 정답은 (B) How much it will cost이다.

Speakmaster 강좌로의 초대
🔟 Evelyn Singh, Woodbridge 지점 담당 이사로부터

2월 21일부터 이곳 Woodbridge 지점에서 매주 연설 교실이 열릴 것입니다. 이 강좌는 회사나 학교에서 사람들 앞에서 말을 해야 하는 사람들을 위해 고안되었습니다. 이 강좌는 여러분이 많은 사람들 앞에서 말하는 능력을 향상시킬 뿐만 아니라, 일상생활에서 자신감을 쌓는 데에도 도움을 줄 것입니다.

9️⃣ 게다가 매 수업 세션이 녹화될 것입니다. 모든 수업이 완료되면, 여러분이 사람들 앞에서 발표한 모든 모습을 담은 DVD 사본을 받게 될 것입니다. 또한 이 과정을 통과했음을 인증하는 서명된 증명서와 확대하여 액자에 넣은 수업 사진을 받게 될 것입니다.

1시간짜리 10회 세션의 등록비는 100달러밖에 되지 않습니다. 저희 Woodbridge 지점으로부터 먼 곳에 거주하신다면, 저희가 다른 시간대에 다른 도서관에서 이 강좌를 제공하기도 합니다.

제가 모든 등록을 처리하고 있습니다. **8️⃣ 🔟** 등록을 원하시면, 저에게 901-555-5571로 전화 주시거나 e.singh@millerlibraries.gov로 이메일 주십시오.

감사합니다.
Evelyn Singh

---

8. 강좌는 어디에서 열릴 것인가?
(A) 공립학교에서
(B) 도서관에서
(C) 지역 문화 센터에서
(D) 매장에서

해설 공지의 마지막 단락에서 등록을 원하면, 자신의 번호 901-555-5571로 전화 주시거나 e.singh@millerlibraries.gov로 이메일 달라고 되어 있어 마지막 이메일 주소의 도메인을 보고 도서관이 강좌를 주최한 것임을 알 수 있다. 정답은 (B) At a library이다.

---

9. 수강생들이 이용할 수 있는 것으로 언급되지 않은 것은 무엇인가?
(A) 발표 녹화본
(B) 유명 연사의 사인
(C) 단체 사진
(D) 공식 서류

해설 공지의 두 번째 단락에서 매 수업 세션이 녹화될 것이며 모든 수업이 완료되면, 수강생들이 사람들 앞에서 발표한 모든 모습을 담은 DVD 사본을 받게 될 것이라고 했다. 또한 이 과정을 통과했음을 인증하는 서명된 증명서 및 확대하여 액자에 넣은 수업 사진을 받게 될 것이라고 했다. 따라서 (A), (C), (D)는 소거시킨다. 유명 연사의 사인에 대한 언급은 없으므로 정답은 (B) An autograph from a famous speaker이다.

---

10. 관심 있는 사람이 이 강좌에 어떻게 등록할 수 있는가?
(A) 웹사이트를 통해 강사에게 직접 이메일을 보냄으로써
(B) Woodbridge 지점 담당 이사에게 연락함으로써
(C) 작성된 등록 신청서를 보냄으로써
(D) 설명회에 참석함으로써

해설 공지의 제목 부분 "From Evelyn Singh, Director, Woodbridge Location"에서 공지를 적은 사람은 Woodbridge 지점 담당 이사임을 알 수 있다. 또한 마지막 단락 '등록을 원할 때 자신의 번호 901-555-5571로 전화를 하거나 e.singh@millerlibraries.gov로 이메일 하라'고 했으므로 정답은 (B) By contracting the director of the Woodbridge location이다.

UNIT 04. 암시·추론 문제

Practice
본서 p.238

1. (A) **2.** (C) **3.** (D) **4.** (A) **5.** (D)
6. (A) **7.** (C) **8.** (C) **9.** (D) **10.** (B)
11. (A) **12.** (C) **13.** (A)

[1-3] 다음 기사에 관한 문제입니다.

Grand River (3월 4일) – Grand River 최대 규모의 문구점에 3월 29일 큰 변화가 있을 예정이다. **1️⃣** 소유주 Aileen Keen의 딸 Sally가 매장 경영을 맡을 예정이다.

"그 가게는 20년 동안 제가 운영해왔습니다."라고 Aileen이 말했다. **1️⃣** "그리고 저는 이 가게를 Sally에게 넘겨 주게 되어 기쁩니다. **2️⃣** 그녀는 고등학생일 때 그 문구점에서 아르바이트로 일을 했었습니다. 그녀는 제가 다른 볼일이 있어 밖에 나가 있는 동안에 저를 많이 도왔습니다."

은퇴 후 Aileen은 그녀가 어렸을 때, 그녀의 할아버지로부터 배웠던 **3️⃣** 가장 좋아하는 활동인 골프에 몰두할 것이다. 그녀는 가게가 잘 관리될 거라는 것을 알고 있다.

---

1. 기사의 목적은 무엇인가?
(A) 은퇴를 발표하기 위해
(B) 사무용품을 팔기 위해
(C) 가게 폐업을 보도하기 위해
(D) 채용 공고를 내기 위해

해설 글의 목적은 보통 글의 앞부분 아니면 맨 마지막 부분에 나온다. 첫 단락에서 큰 변화가 있을 것이고, Aileen Kim 대신에 그녀의 딸 Sally가 가게를 운영할 것임을 알리고 있다. 두 번째 단락 '그리고 저는 이 가게를 Sally에게 넘겨 주게 되어 기쁩니다.'를 통해서도 Aileen이 은퇴한다는 것을 알 수 있다. 따라서 정답은 (A) To announce a retirement이다.

---

2. Sally에 대해서 암시된 것은 무엇인가?
(A) Aileen을 20년 전에 만났다.
(B) 어렸을 때 골프를 배웠다.
(C) 가게를 운영한 경험이 있다.
(D) 고등학교에서 일을 했었다.

해설 선택지를 하나씩 소거하면서 정답을 찾아본다. (A) 20년 전에 만났다는 이야기는 없고, '20년 동안 가게를 운영했다'라는 이야기는 있다. (B) 골프를 배운 사람은 Sally가 아니고 Aileen이다. (D) 고등학생 때 일을 했었다는 것이지 고등학교에서 일을 했었던 것은 아니다. (C) 그녀는 고등학생 때, 엄마를 도와 가게에서 일을 했기 때문에 가게를 운영한 경험이 있다고 볼 수 있다. 따라서 정답은 (C) She has experience in running a store.이다.

---

3. Aileen은 무엇을 할 계획인가?
(A) 수업에 등록한다.
(B) 또 다른 도시로 이사한다.
(C) 여행을 간다.
(D) 여가 활동을 한다.

해설 의문사와 키워드(Ms. Aileen plan to do)가 있으므로 세부 사항 문제이다. Ms. Aileen plan이 지문에서는 Ms. Aileen is going to으로 paraphrasing된 마지막 단락을 보면 은퇴 후에 골프를 즐기겠다고 하였으므로 정답은 (D) Engage in a recreational activity이다.

[4-7] 다음 공지에 관한 문제입니다.

Springtime Fun

4 Rennerdale에서 열리는 아래의 봄 행사 일정을 확인하세요. 이 행사들을 위한 더 많은 정보를 위해, www.rennerdale.org/events 를 방문하세요.

Rennerdale 도서전 (4월 2~9일)
국제적으로 호평을 받는 50여 명의 작가들이 출연하는 낭독회와 토론회 및 책 사인회. **6** 시 전역에 있는 엄선된 참가 서점들과 도서관들에서.

Rennerdale 극장 갈라 (4월 8~25일)
전국의 모든 곳에서 신예와 유명작가들이 쓴 **5** 15개의 연극. Cyan 아트 센터에서.

Beats 축제 (5월 1~17일)
5 시의 지구촌 음악 축제가 전 세계의 다양한 음악 장르를 선보인다. Swan 호수 극장에서.

시각 예술 전시회 (5월 8~26일)
5 지역 아마추어 사진작가들과 화가들이 인정 받는 Ashura 상을 위해 경쟁한다. 우승자는 폐막일 밤에 발표될 예정, Ashura 미술관에서.

7 **Merriam 센터 – 개장 (5월 14일)**
세계적으로 유명한 가수 Maybel Cheyenne의 특별 공연을 포함한 콘서트 장의 몹시 기대되는 개막일 밤. 매진되기 전에 표를 예매하세요.

4. 모든 행사들에 관하여 알 수 있는 것은 무엇인가?
(A) 같은 도시에서 열릴 것이다.
(B) 일반인은 무료이다.
(C) 4월에 열릴 것이다.
(D) 지역 음악가들과 화가들이 출연한다.

해설 첫 문장에서 'Rennerdale에서 열리는 아래의 봄 행사 일정을 확인하세요.'이라고 했으므로 (A) They will be held in the same city.가 정답이다.

---

5. 행사들 중에 목록에 없는 것은 무엇인가?
(A) 음악회
(B) 미술 경연
(C) 연극 공연
(D) 백일장

해설 (A)는 The city's global music festival, (B)는 Local amateur photographers and painters compete for the esteemed Ashura Prize', (C)는 Fifteen plays 에서 각각 언급되어 있다. 따라서 정답은 (D) A writing contest이다.

---

6. 여러 장소에서 열릴 행사는 무엇인가?
(A) Rennerdale 도서전
(B) Rennerdale 극장 갈라
(C) Beats 축제
(D) 시각 예술 전시회

해설 Rennerdale 도서전을 소개할 때, '시 전역에 있는 엄선된 참가 서점들과 도서관들에서.'라고 장소를 알려주고 있으므로 (A) The Rennerdale Book Fair가 정답이다.

---

7. Ms. Cheyenne에 관하여 언급된 것은 무엇인가?
(A) Rennerdale 지역 출신이다.
(B) 행사 기획자로 일한다.
(C) 새로운 장소에서 공연할 것이다.
(D) Merriam 센터를 설계했다.

해설 Merriam 센터의 개관식이 5월 14일이라고 했는데, 이 날 유명한 가수인 Maybel Cheyenne이 특별 공연을 한다고 했으므로 (C) She will perform in a new venue.가 정답이다.

[8-11] 다음 이메일에 관한 문제입니다.

수신: e.dole@bermo.net
발신: c.ferdinand@parzine.com.nz
날짜: 2월 3일
제목: Parzine에서의 고용
첨부: Parzine_Elliot_C

Mr. Dole에게,

8 독립 외주용역 구인 공고에 지원해 주셔서 감사합니다. 우리는 당신의 이력서를 검토했고, 당신이 그 일에 잘 맞을 거라고 생각합니다. **8** **9** 당신의 저술물 포트폴리오와 전 세계를 여행한 경험을 기반으로, 당신은 우리의 온라인 여행 잡지에 기고하는 프리랜서 기자 팀에 큰 보탬이 될 것입니다.

이것은 원격직이기 때문에, 어느 곳에서든 그 일을 할 수 있으며, 과제를 완료할 때마다 급여가 지급될 것입니다. **10** 그 일은 유연한 스케줄을 가진 사람들에게 이상적이며 그들이 시간이 날 때 다양한 글쓰기 프로젝트를 맡을 수 있습니다. **10** 비록 과제들이 꾸준히 들어

오지 않을 수도 있지만, 작업에 들어간 시간에 대한 보상은 보장 받습니다.

11 첨부된 것은 가능한 한 빠른 시일 내에 당신이 서명해서 우리에게 돌려주셔야 하는 고용 계약서입니다. 반드시 당신의 이메일 제목란에 "Parzine 작가 – Elliot C"를 기재해 주세요. 그 동안 질문이 있으면, 주저하지 말고 제게 연락해 주세요. 우리는 지금 당신을 위해 준비된 과제가 있습니다만, 당신에게서 이 서류를 받을 때까지 그것을 드릴 수 없습니다. 조만간 당신과 함께 일하기를 바랍니다.

진심으로,

Corinna Ferdinand, 편집장

---

8. Mr. Dole는 누구이겠는가?
(A) 편집장
(B) 전문 사진작가
(C) 독립 기자
(D) 그래픽 디자이너

해설 첫 문장에서 '독립 외주용역 구인 공고에 지원해 주셔서 감사합니다'라고 했으므로 지원자임을 알 수 있고, 그 뒤 네 번째 줄에 'freelance correspondents' 기자라고 언급돼 있으므로 (C) An independent journalist 가 정답이다.

---

9. Mr. Dole에 관하여 언급된 것은 무엇인가?
(A) 이전에 Parzine과 일한 적이 있다.
(B) 작업자 팀을 감독했다.
(C) 컨벤션에서 Ms. Ferdinand를 만났다.
(D) 전세계를 여행했다.

해설 지문 첫 단락 후반부에서 '당신의 저술물 포트폴리오와 전 세계를 여행한 경험을 기반으로.'라는 구문이 있으므로 (D) He has traveled internationally.가 정답이다.

---

10. 수록된 직책에 관하여 암시된 것은 무엇인가?
(A) 주간 회의 참석을 포함한다.
(B) 예측할 수 없는 업무 일정을 포함한다.
(C) 고급 컴퓨터 기술이 필수이다.
(D) 내근이 필수이다.

해설 두 번째 문단에서 '그 일은 유연한 스케줄을 가진 사람들에게 이상적이며'과 '비록 과제들이 꾸준히 들어오지 않을 수도 있지만,'이라는 구문이 있으므로 (B) It involves an unpredictable work schedule. 가 정답이다.

---

11. Ms. Ferdinand는 Mr. Dole에게 무엇을 보내달라고 요청하는가?
(A) 서명된 계약서
(B) 상환 양식
(C) 프로젝트 계획
(D) 저술물 포트폴리오

해설 마지막 문단, '첨부된 것은 가능한 한 빠른 시일 내에 당신이 서명해서 우리에게 돌려주셔야 하는 고용 계약서입니다.'라고 했으므로, 정

답은 contract를 agreement로 paraphrasing된 (A) A signed agreement가 정답이다.

[12-13] 다음 정보 카드에 관한 문제입니다.

FastPhone 사
온라인 청구서 결제를 신청하는 방법

고객님의 전화 서비스를 활성화하신 뒤, 온라인 청구서 결제를 신청하기 위해 다음의 간단한 절차를 따라 주십시오.

1. 저희 웹사이트 www.fastphone.com을 방문하셔서 사용자 계정을 만들어 주십시오.
2. 사용자 계정을 만드신 뒤, 전화기의 시리얼 번호와 함께 사용자 카드 맨 아래에 있는 PIN 코드를 입력하여 계정에 전화기를 추가해 주십시오.
3. 계정에 고객님의 은행 계좌 정보를 추가해 주십시오. 은행의 규정에 따라, 저희가 계좌에서 청구할 것임을 은행에 알려주셔야 할 수도 있습니다.
4. 매달 반복 지불을 하게 해 주는 '자동 청구서 결제'를 신청하려면, 은행 계좌 정보 필드 하단에 위치한 상자에서 '자동 청구서 결제'를 선택해 주십시오.

12 이렇게 아주 간단합니다! 이렇게 하시면 온라인으로 매달 전화 청구서를 지불하실 수 있을 것입니다. 또는 자동 청구서 결제 옵션을 선택하시면, 청구서 지불이 자동으로 고객님의 은행 계좌에서 인출될 것입니다.

13 저희의 온라인 청구서 결제 서비스에 질문이나 우려 사항이 있으시면, 주중 오전 7시부터 오후 8시 사이에 저희 기술지원센터 800-555-0131로 연락 주십시오.

---

12. Fastphone 청구서 결제에 대해 언급된 것은 무엇인가?
(A) 직접 지불될 수 있다.
(B) 곧 인상될 것이다.
(C) 매달 지불해야 한다.
(D) 온라인으로만 결제할 수 있다.

해설 정보 카드 중간 부분에서 매달 온라인으로 매달 전화 청구서를 지불하실 수 있다고 했으므로 정답은 (C) They are due each month.이다.

---

13. FastPhone 사에 관하여 암시된 것은 무엇인가?
(A) 주말에는 운영하지 않는다.
(B) 여러 나라에 지점이 있다.
(C) 새 전화 모델을 출시할 것이다.
(D) 개통료가 인상되었다.

해설 지문 맨 하단, '저희의 온라인 청구서 결제 서비스에 질문이나 우려 사항이 있으시면, 주중 오전 7시부터 오후 8시 사이에 저희 기술지원센터 800-555-0131로 연락 주십시오.'에서 질문이 있으면 주중에 연락을 달라고 했으므로, 주말에는 운영하지 않음을 유추할 수 있다. 정답은 (A) It does not operate on the weekends.이다.

UNIT 05. 문장 삽입 문제

Practice

1. (C)	**2.** (C)	**3.** (D)	**4.** (B)	**5.** (A)
6. (A)	**7.** (D)	**8.** (B)	**9.** (A)	**10.** (D)
11. (A)	**12.** (B)	**13.** (B)		

[1-2] 다음 정보에 관한 문제입니다.

Carlton 미술 공예품이 판매하는 이 제품을 구매하신 것에 대해 감사드립니다. 모든 Carlton 제품들은 장인들에 의해 수작업으로 만들어짐을 보장합니다. 저희는 이것과 모든 저희의 모든 제품들의 품질도 보장해드리고, 만약 귀하가 어떤 이유로든 만족하지 않는다면, 우리는 귀하에게 100퍼센트 환불도 제공해 드릴 것입니다. **2** 이 제품은 특별히 공들여 제작되어서, 세상에 단 하나뿐이라는 점을 기억해주세요. 그래서 만약 귀하가 같은 유형의 또 다른 물건을 구매한다면, 귀하는 두 개의 물건이 길이, 넓이, 스타일, 그리고 외관이 다르다라는 것을 알 수 있을 것입니다. **1** 만약 이 물건이 천으로 만들어진 것이라면, 그것을 세탁기로 빨지 마세요. 대신에 그것을 손으로 세탁하거나, 드라이클리닝을 하시기 바랍니다.

1. Carlton 미술 공예 제품에 대해서 언급된 것은 무엇인가?
(A) 대량으로만 판매한다.
(B) 동일한 크기로 되어 있다.
(C) 수제 제작된다.
(D) 제한된 보증이 딸려 있다.

해설 선택지를 지문과 대조해 정답을 찾는다. 제품은 손으로 만들어진다고 하였으므로 (A)의 대량 판매는 답이 될 수 없다. 손으로 만들어져서 상품마다 길이와 스타일이 다 다르다고 하였으므로 같은 크기로 출시되는 것도 아니다. 따라서 (B)도 탈락이다. 어떤 이유로든 마음에 들지 않으면 100퍼센트 환불을 해주겠다고 하였으므로 (D)도 탈락이다. 지문 초반에 수작업으로 제작된다고 했으므로 정답은 (C) They are hand-made.이다

---

2. [1], [2], [3], [4]로 표시된 곳 중에서 다음 문장이 들어가기에 가장 적절한 곳은 어디인기?

"이 제품은 특별히 공들여 제작되어서, 세상에 단 하나뿐이라는 점을 기억해주세요."

(A) [1]
(B) [2]
(C) [3]
(D) [4]

해설 앞뒤 관계를 잘 살피는 것이 이 문제의 포인트이다. 수작업으로 특별 제작되어서 단 하나밖에 없는 상품이라고 하였으므로 뒤에 나올 문장은 그러한 특성을 뒷받침할 수 있어야 한다. [3] 뒤의 문장을 보면, '두 상품이 길이, 넓이, 스타일, 그리고 외관이 다를 수 있다'고 하며 손으로 만든 독특한 특성을 뒷받침을 하고 있다. 연결어 therefore도 단서이다. '수작업으로 제작되어서 독특하다. 그래서 상품마다 외관이 다를 수 있다'이므로 정답은 (C) [3]이다.

[3-6] 다음 이메일에 관한 문제입니다.

수신: cbernard@homestylegrill.com
발신: pcrew@westonsummerfestival.org
날짜: 5월 25일
제목: Weston 여름 축제
첨부파일: wsf.doc

Mr. Bernard에게,

저희는 Weston 여름 축제에서 부스를 신청한 귀하의 지원서를 방금 받았습니다. **6** 저희는 귀하에게 여전히 이용 가능한 공간이 있다는 것을 알려드리게 되어 기쁩니다. 그래서 **3** 귀하는 귀하의 레스토랑인 Homestyle Grill에서 식사 제공을 하기 위해 축제에 참가해도 좋습니다.

귀하에게는 42번 부스가 할당되었습니다. 그것은 축제장의 북쪽에 위치해 있습니다. **4** 귀하가 정확하게 어디로 가야 할지 알려면 첨부된 축제장의 지도를 확인하세요. 만약 귀하가 그것을 찾는 데에 어려움이 있다면, 축제에서 사람들을 도울 준비가 되어 있는 많은 자원 봉사자들 중 한 명에게 그냥 물어보면 됩니다.

축제는 오전 9시에 열리지만, 저희는 귀하와 같은 **5** 모든 판매상들이 늦어도 오전 7시 30분까지는 도착할 것을 요청드립니다. 이것은 모든 이들의 혼란을 최소화하고 그들의 부스를 함께 세우도록 해줄 것입니다. 판매상인들은 Kenmore 가에 인접한 곳에 주차를 해야 합니다. 다시 한번, 귀하는 그 위치를 보려면 지도를 보시면 됩니다.

다시 한번 상기시키자면, **5** 축제는 6월 22일 목요일에서 6월 25일 일요일까지 열릴 것입니다. 그리고 귀하의 부스(공간)를 이용하기 위해서는, 행사 요금 250달러를 내야 함을 양지하시기 바랍니다.

감사합니다.

Peter Crew
행사 위원장
Weston 여름 축제

---

3. Mr. Bernard가 축제에서 무엇을 하겠는가?
(A) 차를 운전한다.
(B) 판매상을 관리한다.
(C) 차를 주차한다.
(D) 음식을 판매한다.

해설 질문의 키워드를 지문에서 찾아본다. 첫 번째 단락에서 '귀하는 귀하의 레스토랑 Homestyle Grill에서 식사를 제공하기 위해서 축제에 참가해도 좋습니다.'라고 하고 있으므로 정답은 (D) Sell food이다.

---

4. Mr. Crew가 이메일과 함께 보낸 것은 무엇인가?
(A) 영수증
(B) 지도
(C) 등록 신청서
(D) 일정

해설 send along with가 키워드이다. 두 번째 단락에서 attached로 표현되었다. '첨부된 지도를 보라.'고 하였으므로 정답은 (B) A map이다.

5. Mr. Bernard는 언제 처음 축제에 도착할 것으로 기대되는가?

    (A) 6월 22일 오전 7시 30분에

    (B) 6월 22일 오전 9시에

    (C) 6월 25일 오전 7시 30분에

    (D) 6월 25일 오전 9시에

해설 세 번째 단락에서 '축제는 오전 9시에 열리지만, 저희는 귀하와 같은 모든 판매상인들이 늦어도 오전 7시 30분까지는 도착할 것을 요청드립니다.'라고 하고 있고, 네 번째 단락에서 '축제는 6월 22일 목요일부터 6월 25일 일요일까지 진행된다'고 하였으므로 정답은 (A) On June 22 at 7:30 AM이다.

---

6. [1], [2], [3], [4]로 표시된 곳 중에서 다음 문장이 들어가기에 가장 적절한 곳은 어디인가?

    "저희는 귀하에게 여전히 이용 가능한 공간이 있다는 것을 알려드리게 되어 기쁩니다."

    (A) [1]

    (B) [2]

    (C) [3]

    (D) [4]

해설 '공간'이라는 뜻의 space가 나왔다. space와 비슷한 단어는 booth이다. [1] 앞의 문장에 'booth를 신청하다'라는 문장이 나와 있다. so라는 접속사도 힌트다. '여전히 이용 가능한 booth, 즉 space가 있다. 그래서 귀하는 식사를 제공하기 위해 축제에 참가해도 좋다'라는 뜻이므로 정답은 (A) [1]이다.

[7-9] 다음 회람에 관한 문제입니다.

수신: IT 부서 직원

발신: Jennifer Archer

날짜: 6월 3일

제목: 데이터 전환 프로젝트

안녕하세요. 아직 만나지 못한 분들께 인사 드리자면, 저는 IT 부서의 새 이사 Jennifer Archer입니다. **9** 제가 이곳에서 보낸 첫 주 동안 여러분을 많이 만날 수 있어 기뻤습니다.

저는 최고 기술 책임자이신 Deidre Lee님과 함께 데이터 전환 프로젝트 관리에 집중할 것입니다. **7** 저희는 모든 직원의 컴퓨터 파일을 외부 장소에 백업하는 시스템을 고안할 예정입니다. 이는 우리 회사가 시간과 돈을 모두 절약하게 해줄 겁니다. 또한, 민감한 정보가 다수의 지점 사무실에 보관되지 않게 함으로써 이 정보를 더 쉽게 보호할 수 있도록 도와줄 것입니다.

앞으로 몇 주간, 저는 경과 보고서를 자주 보내드릴 겁니다. **8** 먼저, 여러분 각자에게 여러분의 역할과 관련한 개별 지침을 이틀 안에 이메일로 보낼 것입니다. 프로젝트의 효율성을 향상시키기 위해 프로젝트 관련 코멘트나 제안을 받겠습니다. 모두가 파일을 이용하는 방법에 있어 큰 변화가 될 테니, 다른 부서들과 긴밀하게 협업해야 할 것입니다.

감사합니다.

---

7. 새 프로젝트의 한 가지 목적은 무엇인가?

    (A) 고객들이 모바일 장치에서 파일을 이용하기 위해

    (B) 지점 매니저들 사이의 소통을 개선하기 위해

    (C) 더 많은 고객을 끌어들이기 위한 최고의 방법을 결정하기 위해

    (D) 회사 자료 보관과 관련된 비용을 줄이기 위해

해설 두 번째 단락에서 모든 직원의 컴퓨터 파일을 외부 장소에 백업하는 시스템을 고안할 예정이라고 하면서, 이것이 회사가 시간과 돈 모두를 절약하게 해줄 거라고 했으므로 (D) To lower expenses related to storing company data가 정답이다.

---

8. 회람에 따르면, Ms. Archer는 무엇을 하려고 계획 중인가?

    (A) 팀 회의 일정을 잡는다

    (B) 직원들에게 지침을 보낸다

    (C) Mr. Lee에게 아이디어를 제시한다

    (D) 임시 직원을 고용한다

해설 세 번째 단락에서 각자에게 역할과 관련한 개별 지침을 이틀 안에 이메일로 보낼 거라고 했으므로 (B) Send guidelines to employees가 정답이다.

---

9. [1], [2], [3], [4]로 표시된 곳 중에서 다음 문장이 들어가기에 가장 적절한 곳은 어디인가?

    "제가 이곳에서 보낸 첫 주 동안 여러분을 많이 만날 수 있어 기뻤습니다."

    (A) [1]

    (B) [2]

    (C) [3]

    (D) [4]

해설 첫 번째 단락에서 아직 만나지 못한 사람들에게 인사를 드린다면서, 본인을 IT 부서에 새로 온 이사, Jennifer Archer라고 소개하며 회람을 시작하고 있어, 주어진 문장이 이 다음에 이어지기에 자연스러우므로 (A) [1]이 정답이다.

[10-13] 다음 웹페이지에 관한 문제입니다.

http://www.truein.com/about_us

홈	회사 소개	고객들	카탈로그 보기	샘플

10 Truein 사는 귀하의 음식과 음료의 보관, 포장, 그리고 운송을 용이하게 하는 데 이상적인 선택입니다. 저희의 베스트셀러 중에는 내구성이 좋은 용기, 재활용이 가능한 상자, 그리고 친환경적인 캔들이 포함되어 있습니다. **11** 사진 설명 및 최근의 고객 후기들과 함께 제품 전체를 둘러보시려면, '카탈로그 보기' 탭을 클릭해 주시기 바랍니다. **11** 최소 80달러의 주문으로, 저희는 무료 테스트 제품을 최대 6개까지 배송해 드립니다. **13** "추가 정보를 얻으려면, 저희 Samples 섹션으로 이동해주시기 바랍니다."

또한 저희의 가장 최신 서비스를 소개해 드리고자 합니다: 그것은 맞춤 제작형 인쇄입니다. **11** 요청을 받으면 저희가 로고, 디자인, 그리고 슬로건을 귀하의 물품에 인쇄해 드립니다. 또한 저희는 판촉 행사용으로 제품에 무작위로 정해진 번호들을 찍어드릴 수 있습니다. 예를 들어, 고객들은 웹사이트에 제품 번호를 입력하여 그들이 귀사가 제공하는 상에 당첨되었는지 확인해 보실 수 있습니다. 더 자세한 정보를 얻으려면, 저희 인쇄 부서로 (562) 555-7968로 연락 주시기 바랍니다.

일단 주문이 창고를 출발하면 배송비는 환불되지 않는다는 점을 유의해 주시기 바랍니다. **12** 배송은 주문 후 영업일 기준으로 2~4일 이내로 해드릴 것을 보장합니다.

10. 이 웹페이지는 누구를 대상으로 하겠는가?
(A) 운송 서비스
(B) 지역 재활용 센터
(C) 출판사
(D) 음식 준비 업체

해설 첫 번째 단락에서 Truein 사라는 회사가 음식과 음료와 관련된 서비스를 제공하는 데 이상적인 선택이라고 하면서, 자사를 소개하고 있으므로, 대상 업체는 음식 준비 업체이다. 정답은 (D) Food preparation companies이다.

11. Truein 사에 관하여 언급되지 않은 것은 무엇인가?
(A) 신규 고객들에게 할인해 준다.
(B) 고객들에게 한정된 샘플 상품들을 제공한다.
(C) 고객의 요청에 따라 제품에 메시지를 적는다.
(D) 고객들의 최근 의견들을 게시한다.

해설 보기와 지문에 언급된 내용을 각각 대조 시켜 본다. (B)는 'we can send you up to six free items to trial(저희는 무료 테스트 제품을 최대 6개까지 배송해 드립니다)', (C)는 'Upon request, we can print logos, designs, and slogans on your items (요청을 받으면 저희가 로고, 디자인, 그리고 슬로건을 귀하의 물품에 인쇄해 드립니다)', (D)는 'To browse our complete selection of products along with picture descriptions and recent customer reviews (사진 설명 및 최근의 고객 후기들과 함께 제품 전체를 둘러보시려면)'에 해당하지만 (A)는 지문에 언급된 바 없다. 따라서 (A) It gives a discount to first-time customers.가 정답이다.

12. Truein 사를 통해서 한 주문에 관하여 언급된 것은 무엇인가?
(A) 최소 80달러를 구매하면 무료로 배송된다.
(B) 영업일로 4일 이내에 배송될 수 있다.
(C) 할부로 지불 가능하다.
(D) 구매일로 한달 이내에 교환 가능하다.

해설 세 번째 단락을 보면 배송은 주문 후 영업일 2~4일 이내로 해준다고 했으므로 (B) They can be delivered within four working days.가 정답이다. working days가 business days로 paraphrasing되었다.

13. [1], [2], [3], [4]로 표시된 곳 중에서 다음 문장이 들어가기에 가장 적절한 곳은 어디인가?

"추가 정보를 얻으려면, 저희 Samples 섹션으로 이동해주시기 바랍니다."

(A) [1]
(B) [2]
(C) [3]
(D) [4]

해설 [2] 앞에서 최소 80달러를 주문하면, 무료 테스트 제품을 최대 6개까지 배송해 준다고 했으므로, 주어진 문장은 [2] 뒤에 위치하는 것이 적절하다. 따라서 정답은 (B) [2]가 정답이다.

UNIT 06. 동의어 문제

Practice
본서 p.254

1. (A)	**2.** (A)	**3.** (C)	**4.** (A)	**5.** (D)
6. (D)	**7.** (B)	**8.** (C)	**9.** (B)	**10.** (C)
11. (B)	**12.** (A)	**13.** (A)	**14.** (D)	**15.** (B)
16. (C)				

[1-4] 다음 정보에 관한 문제입니다.

뉴욕시
사이클링 센터

뉴욕시 사이클링 센터에 오신 것을 환영합니다. **1** 저희는 모든 단계의 사이클리스트들의 구미를 맞추기 **3** 위해 고안된 실내 레크리에이션 센터입니다.

고객님이 건강에 좋은 사이클링을 즐기시는 동시에, 단순히 체중 감량이든 자전거 경주에서 승리하는 것이든 신체단련 목표를 달성하는 것을 도와드리는 것이 저희 서비스의 목표입니다.

4 저희의 최첨단 시설은 훈련을 위한 완벽한 환경을 제공합니다. 저희는 100대 이상의 실험실 수준의 연습용 자전거와 최대 산소 섭취량 및 젖산 역치 검사를 제공하는 생리학 실험실을 갖추고 있습니다. 또한 고객님을 도와드릴 공인 코치가 항상 근무하고 있습니다.

일반 정보는 다음과 같습니다.

4 사이클링 센터 영업시간
월–금 오전 6시부터 오후 10시까지
토–일 오전 7시부터 오후 9시까지

사무실 운영시간
4 월~금 오전 8시부터 오후 7시까지

구내 전화
2 내선 110번: 개인 레슨   내선 111번: 생리학 검사
내선 112번: 고객 서비스   내선 113번: 가격 정보

1. 이 정보의 목적은 무엇인가?

(A) 피트니스 클럽에 대한 일반적인 정보를 제공하기 위해

(B) 신규 직원들에게 책무를 알리기 위해

(C) 정부 기관의 정책을 상세히 알리기 위해

(D) 곧 있을 행사를 위한 자원 봉사자들을 모집하기 위해

해설   정보 지문 서두에서 '저희는 모든 단계의 사이클리스트들의 구미를 맞추기 위해 고안된 실내 레크리에이션 센터입니다.'라고 언급했으므로 해당 업체를 소개하기 위한 글임을 알 수 있다. 정답은 (A) To provide general information about a fitness club입니다.

2. 개인 트레이닝을 받으려면 독자들은 내선번호 몇 번으로 전화를 해야 하는가?

(A) 110

(B) 111

(C) 112

(D) 113

해설   내선 번호가 "Ext 110 for individual lessons"라고 나와 있으므로 정답은 (A) 110이다.

3. 첫 번째 단락, 두 번째 줄의 "intended"와 의미상 가장 가까운 것은

(A) 확고한

(B) 유도된

(C) 의도된

(D) 나타낸

해설   문맥상 "모든 사이클리스트들을 위해 (의도되어) 만들어진" 뜻으로 정답은 (C) meant이다.

4. NYCCC에 대해 언급되지 않은 것은 무엇인가?

(A) 최근에 지어졌다.

(B) 사무실을 주말에 운영하지 않는다.

(C) 고품질의 기구들을 제공한다.

(D) 이 시설은 매일 문을 연다.

해설   사무실은 월요일에서 금요일까지 운영된다고 언급되어 있으므로 (B) 는 소거한다. '저희의 최첨단 시설은 훈련을 위한 완벽한 환경을 제공합니다'라고 언급되어 있으므로 (C)도 소거한다. 사이클링 센터 영업 시간에 월요일부터 일요일까지 일주일 내내 운영된다고 언급되어 있으므로 (D)도 소거한다. 센터의 설립 시기는 언급되어 있지 않으므로, 정답은 (A) It was recently built이다.

[5-8] 다음 기사에 관한 문제입니다.

5 Jenny Kang이 NBN TV에 합류하다

NBN TV는 인기 텔레비전 프로그램인 〈The Money Game〉으로 유명한 Jenny Kang이 진행하는 경제 토크쇼를 방영할 것이다.

6 지난 5월에 있었던 온라인 설문조사에 따르면, 이 프로그램은 시청자들이 경제 관련 토크쇼의 부족이 NBN의 가장 큰 약점이라고 생각하기 때문에 만들어졌다. Ms. Kang은 진행자로 NBN의 첫 번째 선택이었다. NBN 방송국에서 20년 동안 근무한 프로듀서 Thomas Park는 "우리는 오랫동안 Ms. Kang을 업계에서 가장 유능한 금융 전문 진행자 중 한 명으로 생각해왔습니다."라고 말했다.

7 현재 타이틀이 정해지지 않은 NBN의 새로운 쇼는 경제에 대한 전반적인 것들을 **8** 다룰 것입니다. 그것은 10월 말부터 평일 오후 7시에 방송될 것입니다.

5. 기사가 주로 이야기하는 것은 무엇인가?

(A) 오래 근무한 프로듀서의 은퇴

(B) 방송국의 기념일

(C) TV 프로그램의 제작 과정

(D) 새로운 쇼 호스트의 고용

해설   첫 번째 단락에서 새 경제 토크쇼를 방영한다고 하면서 진행자로 Jenny Kang을 언급했고, 두 번째 단락에서는 Jenny Kang이 발탁된 이유에 대해 설명하고 있으므로 정답은 (D) The hiring of a new show host이다.

6. 기사에 따르면, 5월에 무슨 일이 일어났는가?

(A) 스튜디오가 새로운 곳으로 이전되었다.

(B) Ms. Kang이 인터뷰를 했다.

(C) 프로그램 일정이 변경되었다.

(D) 피드백이 주어졌다.

해설   키워드 May를 지문에서 찾아보면 두 번째 단락에서 '지난 5월에 있었던 온라인 설문조사에 따르면'이라고 하면서 시청자들의 의견을 언급하고 있으므로 정답은 (D) Feedback was given.이다.

7. 새로운 TV 프로그램에 대해서 아직 결정되지 않은 것은 무엇인가?

(A) 누가 그 쇼를 진행할 것인지

(B) 그 쇼가 무엇이라고 불릴지

(C) 몇 시에 방송이 될 것인지

(D) 언제 시작할 것인지

해설   키워드 undecided가 지문에서는 currently untitled로 paraphrasing되어 있다. 마지막 단락에 '현재 타이틀이 정해지지 않은 NBN의 새로운 쇼는 경제에 대한 다양한 주제들을 다룰 것입니다'라고 하였으므로 그 쇼의 명칭이 정해지지 않은 것을 알 수 있다. 10월 말을 시작으로 평일 오후 7시에 방송한다고 하였으므로 (C)와 (D)는 이미 결정되었다. 제목과 첫 번째 문단에서도 알 수 있듯이 Jenny Kang이 그 쇼를 진행할 것이므로 (A)도 이미 결정되었다. 따라서 정답은 (B) What it will be called이다.

8. 세 번째 단락 첫 번째 줄의 구 "deal with"와 의미상 가장 가까운 것은

(A) 실행하다

(B) 인수하다

(C) 다루다

(D) 교체하다

해설   '현재 타이틀이 정해지지 않은 NBN의 새로운 쇼는 경제에 대한 다양한 주제들을 다룰 것입니다'라고 해석되므로 deal with는 '다루다'라는 뜻이다. 따라서 비슷한 의미를 갖는 (C) cover가 정답이다.

[9-12] 다음 편지에 관한 문제입니다.

Sammy Kim
2239 Tieman 가로
시카고, IL 60290
9월 18일

Mr. Kim에게,

10 9월 2일 우리가 대화할 때, 10월 15일~16일 주말에 저희 관광버스들 중 한 대를 임대하고 싶다고 알려 주셨습니다. **고객님의 일행이 75명일 것이라고 알려 주셨고, 저는 그렇게 많은 사람들에게는 대형 버스가 적절할 것이라고 말씀드렸습니다. 그러나 고객님은 그렇게 많은 사람들이 여행할 것인지 확신하지 못하셨습니다. 그럼에도 불구하고 저는 **11** 잠정 예약을 해드렸고, 대형 버스가 적절할지 고객님께서 열흘 내에 연락 주셔서 확인해 주시기로 했었습니다. 2주가 지났으나, 아직 고객님의 확인을 받지 못했습니다.

그래서 **9** 아직 저희와 거래할 계획이신지 알아보기 위해 연락드립니다. 저희 관광버스는 가을에 수요가 높으며, 다른 단체에 저희 대형 버스 중 한 대를 예약할 기회를 드리고 싶습니다. **12** 그러므로, 앞으로 영업일 기준으로 5일 이내에 고객님의 회신이 없다면, 고객님의 예약을 취소하겠습니다. **9** 어떻게 하고 싶으신지 가능한 빨리 저에게 연락 주십시오.

진심으로,

Jon Voight
Jon Voight
총지배인
Skyway Bus and Tour

9. 이 편지는 왜 쓰여졌는가?
(A) 회의에 다른 부서를 초대하기 위해
(B) 잠재적인 고객의 회신을 요청하기 위해
(C) 버스의 수리를 요청하기 위해
(D) 업계 경쟁사의 견적을 받기 위해

해설 편지의 두 번째 단락에서 '아직 저희와 거래할 계획이신지 알아보기 위해 연락드립니다'라는 내용과 어떻게 하고 싶으신지 가능한 빨리 저에게 연락 주십시오.'를 통해 잠재적인 고객의 연락을 요청하기 위해 이메일을 보냈음을 알 수 있다. 따라서 정답은 (B) To seek a response from a potential customer이다.

10. 이 편지는 Mr. Voight에 대해 암시되는 것은 무엇인가?
(A) 앞으로 5일간 사무실을 비울 것이다.
(B) 이 문제에 대해 상급자와 이야기할 것이다.
(C) Mr. Kim와 이전에 이 사안에 대해 이야기를 했다.
(D) Mr. Kim와 이전에 출장을 갔다.

해설 편지의 첫 번째 단락에서 '9월 2일 우리가 대화할 때, 10월 15일~16일 주말에 저희 관광버스들 중 한 대를 임대하고 싶다고 알려 주셨습니다'라는 내용이 나오므로, 전에 관광버스 임차 문제로 이야기를 나눴음을 알 수 있다. 따라서 정답은 (C) He previously spoke with Mr. Kim about a matter.이다.

11. 첫 번째 단락, 네 번째 줄의 단어 "tentative"와 의미상 가장 가까운 것은
(A) 확실한
(B) 조건부의
(C) 조심스러운
(D) 꺼리는

해설 문맥상 고객이 단체 인원수를 확인하지 못했지만 일단 관광버스를 예약해 두었다는 의미로, "tentative"가 '잠정적인'의 의미로 쓰였으므로 이와 바꿔쓸 수 있는 형용사는 '조건부의'라는 의미의 (B) conditional 이다.

12. Mr. Kim은 무엇을 하도록 요청 받는가?
(A) Mr. Voight에게 회신한다
(B) 더 작은 차량을 예약한다
(C) 다른 지점에 연락한다
(D) 영수증의 가격을 확인한다

해설 편지의 두 번째 단락에서 '그러므로, 앞으로 영업일 기준으로 5일 이내에 고객님의 회신이 없다면, 고객님의 예약을 취소하겠습니다. 어떻게 하고 싶으신지 가능한 빨리 저에게 연락 주십시오.'라는 내용이 나오므로, Mr. Kim에게 회신해 달라고 요청하고 있음을 알 수 있다. 따라서 정답은 (A) Reply to Mr. Voight이다.

[13-16] 다음 웹페이지에 관한 문제입니다.

http://www.foodentrepreneurs.com/jasmines_blog

홈	**블로그 게시물**	멤버십	내 계정	연락하기

개인 창업이냐, 프랜차이즈냐?

13 만약 레스토랑 사업을 시작하실 계획이라면, 프랜차이즈의 길을 선택할만한 몇 가지 타당한 이유가 있습니다. 개인적으로, 가장 중요한 것은 본사로부터의 지원입니다. 당신은 **14** 계속되는 교육을 제공받을 뿐만 아니라 당신이 레스토랑을 운영하고 마케팅 하는 것에 있어서도 지도를 받을 것입니다. 게다가, 당신은 음식과 음료, 그리고 다른 보급품들에 있어서도 회사의 공동구매를 통해 많은 돈을 절약할 수 있습니다. 잘 알려진 브랜드와 **15** 제휴를 맺음으로써, 당신은 인지도를 쌓는 것에 대해 신경을 쓰지 않아도 됩니다.

프랜차이즈 창업에 관심이 있으시다면, 개인 레스토랑 사업을 시작하는 것보다 프랜차이즈 영업권을 구매하는 것이 보통 초기 비용이 더 든다는 점을 알아두세요. 그리고, 프랜차이즈에 투자할 자본이 충분해야 합니다. 또한 모회사에 그들의 광고 이용과 그 밖의 다른 지원을 받는 것에 대해 로열티를 지급해야 한다는 점도 잊지 마세요.

저 같은 경우에는, 5년 전 프랜차이즈 창업을 선택한 것이 옳은 결정이었고, 그 경험이 제가 올해 개인 사업을 하는 것을 가능하게 해줬어요.

16 Bander 요리 학교 졸업생인 Jasmine Tsung은 Sammington 시내에 있는 Beijing Delights의 주인이며 여기에 정기적으로 글을 올린다.

16 이 블로거가 작성한 게시물을 더 읽으시려면, '여기'를 클릭하시거나 가입을 위해 상단의 멤버십 탭을 클릭하세요.

13. 웹 페이지의 목적은 무엇인가?

(A) 사업을 시작하는 것에 대한 아이디어를 공유하기 위해

(B) 블로그를 시작하는 것에 대한 설명서를 제공하기 위해

(C) 두 회사의 서비스를 비교하기 위해

(D) 만족한 고객들의 피드백을 게시하기 위해

해설 지문의 주제나 목적은 대개 전반부에 등장한다. 웹페이지의 탭에서 글의 성격이 "블로그 게시물"임을 알 수 있고, 첫 문장에서 '레스토랑 사업을 시작할 때 프랜차이즈를 선택해야 할 이유가 몇 가지 있다'고 했으므로 정답은 (A) To share ideas about starting a business이다.

---

14. 웹 페이지에서 프랜차이즈 운영의 장점으로 언급되지 않은 것은 무엇인가?

(A) 교육을 받을 기회

(B) 마케팅에 관한 조언

(C) 낮은 공급 비용

(D) 직원 보조 지원

해설 질문의 'advantage of running a franchise'를 키워드로 삼아 지문에 등장한 단서와 보기를 대조한다. (A) be offered ongoing training, (B) guidance in operating and marketing your restaurant, (C) you will save a lot of money on food, drinks, and other supplies through the corporation's collective purchasing와 매칭시킬 수 있으나 직원 파견 지원에 관한 내용은 없었으므로 정답은 (D) Staffing assistance이다.

---

15. 첫 번째 단락, 다섯 번째 줄의 단어 "associating"와 의미상 가장 가까운 것은

(A) 어울리다

(B) 함께 하다

(C) 빌리다

(D) 예약하다

해설 '잘 알려진 브랜드와 제휴를 맺음으로써, 당신은 인지도를 쌓는 것에 대해 신경을 쓰지 않아도 됩니다.' 문장에서의 associate는 '제휴하다'는 뜻으로 쓰였으므로 문맥상 이를 대신할 수 있는 보기는 '함께 하다'는 뜻의 (B) joining이다.

---

16. 사람들은 어떻게 Ms. Tsung의 글을 더 읽을 수 있는가?

(A) 수업에 참석함으로써

(B) 이메일을 보냄으로써

(C) 웹사이트에 가입함으로써

(D) 책을 구입함으로써

해설 질문의 키워드는 Ms. Tsung으로서 이 이름은 지문 하단에 언급되어 있고, 맨 마지막 문장에서 이 블로거가 작성한 게시물을 더 읽으려면, '여기'를 클릭하거나 가입을 위해 상단의 멤버십 탭을 클릭하라고 했으므로 click Membership tab을 paraphrasing한 (C) By joining Web site가 정답이다.

UNIT 07. 문자 대화문과 화자 의도

Practice

본서 p.266

1. (B)	2. (C)	3. (C)	4. (B)	5. (D)
6. (A)	7. (B)	8. (C)	9. (A)	10. (C)
11. (B)	12. (C)			

[1-2] 다음 문자 대화문에 관한 문제입니다.

Harkness, Quinton

안녕하세요, Ms. Martin, 저는 Best Style Shoes의 Quinton Harkness예요. 당신이 가장 최근 주문하신 건에 약간의 문제가 있어서요. 오후 1:34

Martin, Danielle

오후 1:37 무슨 문제인가요?

Harkness, Quinton

귀하께서 세 켤레의 신발을 주문하셨는데, 두 켤레는 재고가 있어서 귀하에게 배달이 될 것이지만, **❶** Ricardo 여성용 하이힐 (물품 번호 670-33)은 현재 재고가 없어요. 오후 1:40

Martin, Danielle

언제 입고되나요? 제가 이번 주 늦게 그것들을 배송받을 수 있을까요? 오후 1:42

Harkness, Quinton

그럴 것 같지가 않아요. 제가 Ricardo에 연락해 봤는데, **❶** 그들이 생산 일정이 많이 미뤄진 게 틀림 없어요. 그 밖에 다른 것을 주문하고 싶으신가요? 오후 1:45

Martin, Danielle

❷ 지금은 없습니다. 그 물건은 취소해 주시고, 저에게 나머지 두 켤레만 보내주세요. 오후 1:48

Harkness, Quinton

알겠습니다. 두 켤레는 오늘 오후에 배달될 거예요. 오후 1:49

---

1. Ms. Martin의 주문에 무슨 문제가 있는가?

(A) 가격이 정확하지 않다.

(B) 물품 하나가 구매가 불가능하다.

(C) 수량이 잘못 되었다.

(D) 상품의 일부가 손상되었다.

해설 키워드 problem을 지문에서 찾아본다. 그녀의 최근 주문에 문제가 있다고 하면서, 생산 일정이 많이 미뤄졌기 때문에 Ricardo 여성용 하이힐은 구입할 수 없다고 하므로 정답은 (B) One of the items is not available이다.

---

2. 오후 1시 48분에 Ms. Martin이 "지금은 없어요"라고 쓴 것은 무슨 의미인가?

(A) 그녀는 Best Style Shoes에 방문할 수 없다.

(B) 그녀는 Ricardo의 다른 신발들을 아직 살펴보지 않았다.

(C) 그녀는 다른 물건을 구매하는 것에는 관심이 없다.

(D) 그녀는 일로 매우 바쁘다.

해설 지문에서 해당 표현을 찾아 앞뒤 문맥을 확인해본다. '그 밖에 다른 것을 주문하고 싶으신가요?'라고 물었을 때, "Not at this time"라고 대답을 한 후, '그 물건은 취소해 주시고, 나머지 두 컬레만 보내주세요'라고 한 것은 다른 물건을 주문하고 싶지 않다는 뜻이므로 정답은 (C) She is not interested in buying a different product.이다.

[3-4] 다음 문자 대화문에 관한 문제입니다.

Betty Carter

안녕하세요, Javier. Ms. Rah가 덴버로 가는 비행기를 놓쳤다고 해요. ❸ 이용 가능한 다음 비행기를 예약해줄 수 있으신가요?   오후 4:11

Javier Perez

❸ 물론이죠.   오후 4:12

Betty Carter

알겠어요. 비행편 찾으시면 메시지를 보내주세요.   오후 4:13

Javier Perez

좋아요, 다 됐어요. 5시 45분 비행기로 예약했어요.   오후 4:21

Betty Carter

잘 됐네요! ❹ 그러면 여전히 첫 촬영에 시간 맞춰 도착할 수 있겠어요. 그 분에게 직접 이메일로 전자 항공권을 보내주세요. 제가 그녀에게 그걸 공항 인터넷 카페에서 프린트 하라고 일러둘게요.   오후 4:22

Javier Perez

알겠어요.   오후 4:23

Betty Carter

잘됐어요. 고마워요.   오후 4:24

---

3. 4시 12분에, Mr. Perez가 "물론이죠."라고 쓴 것은 무슨 의미인가?

(A) 고객을 환영할 것이다.

(B) 회의 일정을 다시 잡을 것이다.

(C) 예약을 할 것이다.

(D) 티켓을 출력할 것이다.

해설 바로 앞 문장에서 Can you book her on the next available flight?이라는 부탁이 있었으므로 Of course.라는 대답은 요청한

업무를 수락한다는 의미이다. 따라서 정답은 (C) He will make a reservation.이다.

---

4. Ms. Rah는 어떤 종류의 업체에서 일하겠는가?

(A) 소프트웨어 회사

(B) 제작 스튜디오

(C) 레스토랑

(D) 항공사

해설 filming session이라는 키워드를 통해 직업을 유추할 수 있다. 촬영을 수반하는 업무를 맡은 사람이므로 (B) A production studio에서 근무한다고 유추하는 것이 적절하다.

[5-8] 다음 온라인 채팅 대화문에 관한 문제입니다.

Chapman, Carol [오후 2시 43분]

우리는 ❺ 협상하다가 지금 잠시 쉬는 시간이에요. ❽ 저는 15분 후에 회의실로 다시 돌아가야 해요.

Lucas, Brian [오후 2시 45분]

❺ 다 잘 되어가고 있나요? 우리가 Flint 제조사와 좋은 조건에 계약을 할 수 있을 것 같나요?

Chapman, Carol [오후 2시 46분]

아직 거기까지는 얘기를 못 했어요. 여전히 논의해야 할 것들이 몇 가지 있기는 하지만, 제가 보기에는 현재 꽤 낙관적이에요.

Atwell, Lucy [오후 2시 48분]

❻ 그들이 제품 생산을 언제 시작할 수 있는지 얘기해 보셨나요? Winters 사는 1주일 내로 꽤 저렴한 가격에 제조를 시작할 수 있다고 하던대요.

Chapman, Carol [오후 2시 50분]

❻ Flint가 가격을 조정하려고 하지 않으면, Winters 사와 거래하는 걸 고려해야 할 수도 있어요.

Lucas, Brian [오후 2시 52분]

당신이 점심에 요청했던 그 서류들을 여전히 원하나요? 제가 Judy와 이야기해 봤는데, 그녀가 거의 다 준비되었다고 했어요.

Chapman, Carol [오후 2시 55분]

사실, 가능하면 빨리 그 서류들이 필요해요. 그것들이 다 되면, 여기 회의실로 가져다 주세요. 그냥 문을 노크하시고 들어오시면 됩니다.

Atwell, Lucy [오후 2시 56분]

❼ 제가 가져갈게요, Brian. 전달할 다른 파일들도 있으니 준비가 되면 저에게 그것들을 주세요.

Lucas, Brian [오후 2시 57분]

❼ 물론이죠. 제가 당신의 사무실에 곧 들르도록 할게요.

Chapman, Carol [오후 2시 59분]

네, ❽ 저는 이제 회의실로 돌아가야 해요. 모두들 도와줘서 고마워요.

---

5. 대화는 주로 무엇에 대한 것인가?

(A) 프로젝트 마감기한

(B) 배송 상황

(C) 제조상의 문제점

(D) 일부 협상의 진척

해설 글의 주제를 묻는 문제이므로 지문의 앞부분에서 단서를 찾아본다. Chapman이 협상 도중 휴식을 취하고 있다고 말하자 Lucas가 어떻게 진행되고 있는지 경과를 묻고 있으므로 정답은 (D) The progress of some negotiations이다.

6. Winters 사에 대해서 암시된 것은 무엇인가?
   (A) Flint 제조사의 경쟁사이다.
   (B) 제품 생산을 이미 시작했다.
   (C) Chapman의 회사와 계약에 서명할 것이다.
   (D) 업체를 인수할 계획이다.

해설 키워드인 Winters 사가 언급된 부분과 선택지를 대조해가며 소거한다. (B) 1주일 내로 제조를 시작할 수 있다고 약속했으므로 아직 시작한 것은 아니다. (C) Chapma의 회사와 계약할 회사는 Flint 제조사다. (D)는 언급이 없었다. '우리는 Flint 제조사와 계약을 해야 하는데, 그들이 제품을 얼마나 빠르게 만들 수 있는지' 물으면서, 'Winters 사는 꽤 저렴한 가격에 1주일 내 제조에 들어갈 수 있다'고 하면서 두 회사의 조건을 서로 비교하고 있다. Flint가 가격을 조정하려고 하지 않으면 winters 사와 거래해야 한다고 하기 때문에 winters 사는 Flint 사의 경쟁사임을 알 수 있다. 따라서 정답은 (A) It is a competitor of Flint Manufacturing.이다.

7. 오후 2시 57분에 Mr. Lucas가 "물론이죠."라고 쓴 것은 무슨 의미인가?
   (A) Winters 사와 협상할 것이다
   (B) 몇몇 서류들을 전달할 것이다
   (C) 파일 몇 개를 인쇄할 것이다
   (D) 점심 예약을 할 것이다

해설 화자의 의도를 물어보는 문제는 앞뒤 관계를 잘 살펴야 한다. 특히, 온라인 채팅은 3명 이상 대화를 하므로 앞뒤 관계를 더욱 더 잘 살피는 것이 중요하다. Lucas가 Chapman에게 회의실로 가져다 주려고 서류를 준비 중인데, Atwell이 어차피 자신도 전달할 파일들이 있으니 Lucas에게 서류가 준비되면 자신에게 가져다 달라고 한다. 따라서 Lucas가 Chapman에게 직접 가져다 주는 것이 아니고 Atwell에게 주겠다는 의미이다. 따라서 정답은 (B) He will deliver some documents. 이다.

8. Ms. Chapman은 다음에 무엇을 하겠는가?
   (A) 몇몇 서류들을 복사한다.
   (B) Ms. Atwell의 사무실을 방문한다.
   (C) 회의실로 들어간다.
   (D) Winters 사와 접촉한다.

해설 마지막 줄에서 그가 회의실로 돌아갈 것임을 알 수 있다. 따라서 정답은 (C) Enter a conference room.이다.

[9-12] 다음 온라인 채팅 대화문에 관한 문제입니다.

Bailey Ahn [오전 8:43]
안녕하세요. 온라인상에서 함께 만날 수 있게 되어 기쁩니다. **9** 곧 있을 콘서트에 어떤 진전이 있어왔는지 알고 싶네요. Louis, 지난 주에 많은 일을 했죠, 그렇죠?

Louis Perez [오전 8:44]
9 10 네, Arrow 시 의회가 마침내 우리에게 Shyrock 커뮤니티 공원에서 콘서트를 열 수 있는 허가증을 내주었습니다.

Tran Van Thanh [오전 8:45]
아주 좋은 소식이네요!

Kylie Bryce [오전 8:46]
대단하네요! 한동안, **10** 그들이 생각을 바꾸지 않을까봐 걱정했거든요.

Louis Perez [오전 8:47]
10 저도 그랬어요. 하지만, 공연 예술가들 중 몇몇은 인기가 많고, 그들이 더 많은 관광객을 불러모을 수 있다고 얘기했을 때, 그들이 납득하더라고요.

Baily Ahn [오전 8:47]
좋아요. 그 밖의 다른 소식이 있나요?

Tran Van Thanh [오전 8:48]
제가 방금 Midvale Burgers와 전화 통화를 했는데, 그들이 콘서트를 할 때 햄버거 가판을 설치하겠다고 했어요. **11** 제가 다른 식당들과도 연락을 했고, 내일 오후쯤에는 대부분의 답변들을 받게 될 겁니다.

Kylie Bryce [오전 8:48]
저는 아직 Helzon Trio를 대체할 사람을 찾고 있는 중입니다. **12** 오늘 Ellen Hattori와 그녀의 밴드와 미팅을 할 거여서, 바라건대, 그들과 계약할 수 있으면 좋겠어요.

Baily Ahn [오전 8:49]
정말이요? 와! **12** 그녀의 최신 앨범이 큰 히트를 쳐서 분명 많은 사람들이 그녀의 노래를 라이브로 보고 싶어할 거예요.

9. 글쓴이들이 논의하고 있는 것은 무엇인가?
   (A) 야외 행사
   (B) 온라인 강의
   (C) 신 메뉴
   (D) 라디오 토크쇼

해설 Bailey Ahn이 처음에 곧 있을 콘서트가 어떻게 되어 가고 있는지 알고 싶다고 했고, Louis Perez이 이어서 시의회가 마침내 공원에서 콘서트 할 수 있도록 허가해주었다고 했으므로 정답은 (A) An outdoor event이다.

10. 오전 8시 46분에, Ms. Bryce가 "그들이 생각을 바꾸지 않을까봐 걱정했거든요"라고 쓴 것은 무슨 의미이겠는가?
    (A) 의회가 열릴 거라고 확신하지 못했다.
    (B) 식당이 문을 닫을 거라고 생각했다.
    (C) 허가증이 발급될 거라고 확신하지 못했다.
    (D) 홍보가 더 많은 관광객들을 불러들일 것이라고 생각했다.

해설　Louis Perez가 시의회가 공원에서의 콘서트를 허가해주었다고 하자, Kyile Bryce가 '그들의 생각이 바뀌지 않을까봐 걱정했다(I was concerned that they wouldn't come around.)고 한 것이고, Louis Perez는 자기도 마찬가지였다고 하며, 그들을 설득했다는 내용이 이어지고 있으므로 Kylie Bryce는 허가가 날 거라는 확신이 없었음을 나타낸 것으로 볼 수 있다. 따라서 (C) She was not sure a permit would be given.이 정답이다.

---

11. Ms. Thanh이 기대하고 있는 것은 무엇인가?
　　(A) 손님 명단의 변경
　　(B) 식당의 반응
　　(C) 예술가의 답변
　　(D) 애플리케이션의 업데이트

해설　Ms. Thanh가 다른 식당에도 연락했다고 하면서, 내일 오후에 대부분의 답변을 들을 수 있을 것이라고 했으므로 정답은 (B) Responses from restaurants이다.

---

12. Ms. Hattori는 누구이겠는가?
　　(A) 행사 기획자
　　(B) 기자
　　(C) 가수
　　(D) 수석 요리사

해설　Ms. Hattori가 질문의 키워드로서 Kylie Bryce가 Ellen Hattori를 먼저 언급했는데, 그녀와 그녀의 밴드가 계약하기를 바란다고 했고, Baily Ahn은 그녀의 최신 앨범이 큰 히트를 쳐서, 많은 사람들이 보러 올 것이라고 했으므로 Ellen Hattori는 가수임을 알 수 있다. 따라서 정답은 (C) A singer이다.

UNIT 08. 편지·이메일

Practice
본서 p.274

1. (B) **2.** (D) **3.** (A) **4.** (D) **5.** (A)
6. (C) **7.** (B) **8.** (B) **9.** (C) **10.** (B)
11. (D)

[1-2] 다음 이메일에 관한 문제입니다.

수신: Jinsoo Park
발신: Hemo 고객 서비스
제목: 접근 거부
날짜: 6월 1일

1 귀하께서는 온라인에서 귀하의 계좌에 틀린 비밀번호로 5번 로그인을 시도한 기록이 있습니다. 그 결과, 귀하께서는 현재 계좌에 접근할 수 없습니다. 새로운 사용자 계좌를 만들지 마세요. **2** 귀하

가 온라인으로 돈을 지불할 때 문제를 일으킬 수도 있습니다. 귀하의 비밀번호를 확인하고 계좌를 복구하려면 아래에 있는 링크를 이용하세요.

http://www.hemo.com/passwordrequest12

안전상의 이유로, 귀하께서는 **2** 최근 예금과 인출에 관한 질문에 정확하게 응답하셔야 합니다. 이후 귀하의 계정은 완전히 복구될 것입니다.

만약 추가적인 도움을 원하시면, 031-555-5584번으로 전화를 주십시오.

Hemo 고객 서비스

---

1. Mr. Park에 대해 암시되는 것은 무엇인가?
　　(A) 모바일 장치로 웹사이트에 접근했다.
　　(B) 그의 비밀번호를 잊어버렸다.
　　(C) 그의 배우자를 예금주로 추가했다.
　　(D) 한 개 이상의 계좌를 만들었다.

해설　글의 주제나 목적은 지문의 앞부분이나 맨 마지막 부분에 나온다. 이 이메일에서는 앞부분에 나와 있다. '올바르지 않은 비밀번호로 인해서, 계좌에 접근할 수 없다'라는 말이 나와 있으므로 정답은 (B) He forgot his password.이다.

---

2. Hemo는 어떤 종류의 회사인가?
　　(A) 웹사이트 개발업체
　　(B) 인터넷 서비스 제공업체
　　(C) 온라인 쇼핑몰
　　(D) 금융 기관

해설　키워드 Hemo는 지문에서 이메일을 보낸 발신 회사이다. 계좌, 비밀번호, 인출, 예금 등 인터넷 뱅킹과 관련된 단어들이 나오고 있으므로 정답은 (D) A financial institution이다.

[3-4] 다음 편지에 관한 문제입니다.

Alltria 은행
8291 Berry가
새크라멘토, 캘리포니아 92671
555-8993

12월 8일

Ms. Huff에게,

3 저희 기록에 의하면 고객님의 당좌예금계좌가 초과 인출되었습니다. 고객님은 12월 3일에 연방 체신청에 81달러 29센트의 수표를 쓰셨습니다. 그러나 당시 고객님의 잔고는 67달러 5센트였습니다. 유감스럽게도 고객님의 계좌는 당좌 대월 보호가 되어있지 않으므로, 오늘 현재 고객님의 잔고는 -20달러 24센트입니다. **4** 당좌 예금계좌에서 초과 인출이 되면 매일 1달러의 수수료가 있음을 유의해주십시오. 이 문제를 처리하기 위해 가능한 빨리 저에게 연락 주십시오.

진심으로,

Jeanie Chitalli

Jeanie Chitalli

Sacramento 지점 매니저

Alltria 은행

555-8993

---

3. 이 편지의 주요한 목적은 무엇인가?

(A) 고객에게 계좌의 문제를 알리기 위해

(B) 최근 실적에 대한 감사를 표하기 위해

(C) 계좌 혜택에 대한 정보를 찾기 위해

(D) 단골고객에게 더 가까운 지점을 홍보하기 위해

해설 편지의 처음 부분에서 계좌에서 초과인출된 문제를 알리기 위해 고객에게 연락했음을 알 수 있다. 따라서 정답은 (A) To inform a customer of an issue with an account임을 알 수 있다.

....

4. Alltria 은행에 관하여 언급된 것은 무엇인가?

(A) 많은 고객들이 계좌에서 초과 인출한다.

(B) 요청하지 않아도 당좌 대월 보호를 제공한다.

(C) 고객과 기꺼이 타협할 의향이 있다.

(D) 초과 인출된 계좌에 대해 수수료를 청구한다.

해설 편지의 중간 부분에서 이 은행은 초과 인출된 당좌예금계좌에 대해 매일 1달러의 수수료를 청구함을 알 수 있다. 따라서 정답은 (D) It charges a fee for overdrawn accounts.이다.

[5-7] 다음 이메일에 관한 문제입니다.

발신: Raul Rodriguez 〈rrodriguez@nish.co.ca〉

수신: Orninong Masapawanan 〈omasap@nish.co.ca〉

제목: 정보 업데이트

일자: 5월 8일

Orninong에게,

5 NISH에 오신 것을 환영합니다! 당신이 5월 15일부터 일하게 될 것이라고 알고 있습니다. 당신이 잘 적응할 것이라고 확신합니다. 또한 당신이 몬트리올 사무소에서 즐겁게 일할 것이라고 믿습니다. 우리 직원들 대부분이 그곳에서 근무를 시작하므로, 그 사무실의 모든 사람들이 새로운 동료를 도운 경험이 있습니다.

음, 당신의 첫 번째 출장이 곧 있을 것임을 알려드리고 싶었습니다. **6** 5월 20일 토론토에서 참가해야 할 행사가 있습니다. 하지만, 저희는 준비를 위해 하루 일찍 도착할 것입니다. 우리는 검안 세미나 및 쇼에서 우리 제품들을 소개할 것입니다. 당신이 우리 제품에 대해 누구와 이야기할 필요는 없지만, 이러한 행사에 참석하는 것은 큰 경험이 될 것입니다. 그저 다른 직원들을 지원해주고, 전시 조립 및 해체를 도와주면 됩니다. **7** 우리 제품군에 익숙해지려면 시간이 걸릴 것임을 알고 있으므로, 아마 다음 7월 행사 때 당신이 잠재 고객들과 이야기를 하도록 할 것 같습니다.

Raul 드림

---

5. 이 이메일의 목적은 무엇인가?

(A) 새로 온 동료를 맞이하기 위해

(B) 예약을 확인하기 위해

(C) 연설을 위한 주제 몇 개를 제안하기 위해

(D) 인터뷰를 위한 방문 일정을 정하기 위해

해설 이메일의 첫 단락에서 오신 걸 환영한다는 인사로 시작하고 있으며, 차후 출장 일정 안내와 이메일의 세 번째 단락에서 Most of our employees라며 발신인과 수신인을 우리라고 표현하며 업무적인 이야기를 나누고 있으므로 둘의 관계는 동료임을 알 수 있다. 따라서 정답은 (A) To greet a new colleague이다.

....

6. Ms. Masapawanan는 언제 토론토에 도착할 것 같은가?

(A) 5월 14일

(B) 5월 15일

(C) 5월 19일

(D) 5월 21일

해설 이메일의 두 번째 단락에서 '5월 20일 토론토에서 참가해야 할 행사가 있습니다. 하지만, 저희는 준비를 위해 하루 일찍 도착할 것입니다.'라는 내용이 나오므로, 행사 전날인 5월 19일에 도착할 것임을 알 수 있다. 따라서 정답은 (C) On May 19이다.

....

7. Ms. Masapawanan이 토론토에서 하지 않을 것은 무엇인가?

(A) 검안 워크숍에 참석한다

(B) 고객들과 제품에 대해 이야기한다

(C) 전시 작업을 한다

(D) 동료들을 도와준다

해설 이메일의 세 번째 단락에서 '우리 제품군에 익숙해지려면 시간이 걸릴 것임을 알고 있으므로, 아마 다음 7월 행사 때 당신이 잠재 고객들과 이야기를 하도록 할 것 같습니다.'라는 내용이 나오므로, Ms. Masapawanan이 이번 토론토 행사에서는 고객들과 제품에 대해 이야기하지 않을 것임을 알 수 있다. 따라서 정답은 (B) Discuss products with clients이다.

[8-11] 다음 편지에 관한 문제입니다.

Nuvallis 가구

Aubree Thompson

총책임자, Stanner's 실내장식용품

Terrace가 1400번지

11 브리즈번 4000, 호주

7월 3일

Ms. Thompson에게,

이 서신은 Nuvallis가 곧 이전한다는 것을 알려드리기 위한 것입니다. 7월 17일 화요일부로, 브리즈번에 있는 저희 가게는 문을 닫습니다. **10** 8월 2일 화요일부터 저희는 골드코스트, Flannigan가 250번지에서 영업을 할 것입니다. **8** 저희의 새 지점은 훨씬 더 넓은 공간을 가지고 있는데, 이것은 저희가 더 다양한 종류의 가구를 들여놓을 수 있도록 해줄 것입니다.

9 저희가 이전을 하는, 7월 17일부터 8월 1일까지는 문을 열지 않으니 유념해 주세요. **10** 재개점일 당일 날, 저희는 최신 제품들 중 일부를 소개하고 경품이 걸린 추첨 행사를 열 것입니다. '당신의 가구를 알아라' 대회에도 참가해 주실 것을 요청 드립니다.

저희가 새 시설을 짓는 데 상당한 투자가 있었기 때문에 저희 제품과 배달 서비스에 약간의 가격 인상이 있을 것임을 알려 드리게 되어 송구스럽습니다. 하지만, **11** 귀사는 10년이 넘게 저희의 단골 고객이셨기 때문에, 일년 동안 상기의 가격 인상에서 제외될 것입니다. 게다가, 8월에는 귀사가 구매하는 모든 제품들에 대해 15퍼센트를 할인해 드리겠습니다.

또한, 8월 2일자로, 저희의 새 전화 번호는 07-843-95260이 됩니다. 귀사의 거래에 감사 드리며 후에 또 서비스를 제공할 수 있기를 고대하겠습니다.

진심을 담아,

Lydia Perkins

Lydia Perkins
운영 책임자, Nuvallis 가구

---

8. Nuvallis 가구에 대해 암시된 것은 무엇인가?
(A) 현재 지점이 두 개 있다.
(B) 품목을 확대할 것이다.
(C) 다른 회사를 인수했다.
(D) 배달 기사들을 추가로 고용할 것이다.

해설 '저희의 새 지점은 훨씬 더 넓은 공간을 가지고 있는데, 이것은 저희가 더 다양한 종류의 가구를 들여놓을 수 있도록 해줄 것입니다.'라고 했으므로 정답은 (B) It will expand its inventory.이다.

9. 두 번째 단락, 첫 번째 줄의 단어 "carry out"과 의미상 가장 가까운 것은
(A) 제거하다
(B) 재고하다
(C) 수행하다
(D) 들어 올리다

해설 'carry out'이 언급된 문장을 확인한다. while we carry out the move는 '이전 작업을 수행하는 동안'이라는 의미이므로 carry out과 의미상 가장 가까운 것은 (C) accomplish이다.

10. Nuvallis 가구 고객은 8월 2일에 무엇을 할 수 있는가?
(A) 브리즈번에 있는 공장을 견학할 수 있다
(B) 대회에 참가할 수 있다
(C) 특별 할인을 받을 수 있다
(D) 제품 조사에 참여할 수 있다

해설 Starting Tuesday, 2 August, we will be operating(8월 2일 화요일부터 영업할 것입니다)이라고 했으므로 8월 2일은 매장을 이전하여 재개업하는 날이다. 그러므로 재개점일 당일이 8월 2일을 가리키는 것인데, 이 구문 이후에 나오는 내용에 '당신의 가구를 알아라' 대회에도 참가해 주실 것을 요청 드립니다.'라 했으므로 정답은 (B) Enter a contest이다.

---

11. Stanner's 실내 장식용품에 대해 언급되지 않은 것은 무엇인가?
(A) 최소 10년 동안 영업을 해 왔다.
(B) 브리즈번에 위치해 있다.
(C) 다음 달에 Nuvallis 가구에서 구매 시 할인을 받을 것이다.
(D) Nuvallis 가구에서의 주문을 늘릴 예정이다.

해설 '귀사는 10년이 넘게 저희의 단골 고객이셨기 때문에'를 통해 (A)를 소거한다. 편지 윗부분의 브리즈번 주소를 보고 (B)를 소거한다. 편지를 보낸 날짜가 7월 3일인데 8월에는 귀사가 구매하는 모든 제품들에 대해 15퍼센트를 할인해 드리겠습니다.라고 했으므로 (C)도 소거한다. 지문에 언급되지 않은 (D) It plans to increase its orders from Nuvallis Furniture.가 정답이다.

UNIT 09. 광고

Practice
본서 p.282

1. (B)	**2.** (B)	**3.** (B)	**4.** (B)	**5.** (A)
6. (D)	**7.** (D)	**8.** (A)	**9.** (C)	

[1-2] 다음 광고에 관한 문제입니다.

Blackstone 굴뚝 서비스

1 저희는 15년 이상 자부심을 가지고 서비스를 제공해왔습니다. 아시다시피, 추운 날씨가 오고 있고 여러분의 벽난로와 굴뚝을 사용할 수 있도록 준비하는 것은 중요합니다. 따라서 여러분의 굴뚝이 정상적으로 작동하고 안전할 수 있도록 하기 위해서 Blackstone 굴뚝 서비스는 여러분에게 한시적으로 청소 특별가를 제공 중입니다.

여러분이 예약 전화를 주실 때, 여러분은 20퍼센트 할인을 받을 수 있는 쿠폰 번호 AFE4410을 이용할 수 있습니다. 저희는 검증된 기술자들이 작업을 완료하기 위해 여러분의 집에 24시간 이내에 방문할 것을 보장해 드립니다. **2** 판촉 행사의 일환으로, 저희는 또한 집을 사는 사람이나 파는 사람들을 위해 여러분의 굴뚝을 점검해 주고, 굴뚝이 안전하다는 증서를 제공합니다.

게다가, 저희는 굴뚝 개축과 수리에 대한 서비스를 제공합니다. Blackstone 굴뚝 서비스로 지금 773-9412번으로 전화 주세요. 판촉 홍보 할인 기간은 11월 20일에 끝납니다.

---

1. 회사에 관하여 언급된 것은 무엇인가?
(A) 새로운 직원들을 고용하고 있다.
(B) 확고히 자리잡은 사업체이다.
(C) 기념일을 축하하고 있다.
(D) 서비스를 개선시키고 있다.

해설 회사를 'we'로 언급한 부분을 지문에서 찾아보며 선택지를 소거해야 한다. 맨 첫 줄에 '저희는 15년 이상 자부심을 가지고 서비스를 제공해왔습니다'라고 말하고 있으므로 자리잡은 안정된 사업체라는 것을 알 수 있다. 따라서 정답은 (B) It is an established business.이다.

2. 홍보용으로 제공되는 것에 포함되는 것은 무엇인가?

(A) 벽난로 수리

(B) 굴뚝 점검

(C) 무료 온도조절장치

(D) 굴뚝 공사

해설　키워드 promotional이 지문에 언급된 부분을 찾아본다. 두 번째 단락 끝에서 '판촉 행사의 일환으로, 저희는 또한 집을 사는 사람이나 파는 사람들을 위해 여러분의 굴뚝을 점검해 주고, 굴뚝이 안전하다는 증서를 제공합니다'라고 하였으므로 정답은 (B) Chimney inspections이다. (A)와 (D)는 이 회사가 제공하는 다른 서비스이고, (C)는 언급되지 않았다.

[3-4] 다음 광고에 관한 문제입니다.

③ KJA National

멋진 휴가를 갈 준비가 되셨습니까? KJA National가 도와드리겠습니다!

③ 여러분은 3월 8일에서 7월 27일까지 동행자 요금을 최대 150달러까지 절약할 수 있습니다.

- 미국 내 ③ 비행편에만 유효합니다.
- 한 명의 동행자 요금에만 적용됩니다.
- ④ 2월 11일까지 예약해야만 합니다.

여러분의 차와 호텔도 예약하려면 www.kjanational.com을 방문하세요. 게다가, 막바지 할인 및 추후 모든 할인행사와 같은 유용한 정보를 받을 수 있도록 로열티 클럽에 가입하세요.

3. 무엇이 할인되고 있는가?

(A) 호텔 패키지

(B) 비행기 티켓

(C) 자동차 렌트

(D) 로열티 클럽의 연회비

해설　지문에서 키워드 discount가 언급된 부분을 확인해본다. '동행자 요금을 최대 150달러까지 절약할 수 있고 이는 미국 내 비행편에만 적용된다'고 했으므로 정답은 (B) Airplane tickets이다.

4. KJA에 관하여 알 수 있는 것은 무엇인가?

(A) 최근에 설립되었다.

(B) 미국 내에 사업 기반을 두고 있다.

(C) 휴가 기간에만 할인을 제공한다.

(D) 로열티 클럽을 막 도입했다.

해설　최근에 설립되었다는 말은 언급되지 않았으므로 (A)는 소거한다. 3월 8일부터 7월 27일까지 할인된다고 했지, 휴가 기간에만 할인을 제공한다는 것이 아니므로 (C)도 소거한다. 로열티 클럽에 대해 도입된 시기를 밝히지 않았으므로 (D)도 소거한다. 'Valid only for flights within USA'를 통해 미국 내에서만 항공 서비스를 제공한다는 것을 알 수 있으므로 정답은 (B) It is based in the USA.이다.

[5-6] 다음 광고에 관한 문제입니다.

출퇴근에 지치셨나요?
Telegraph Connector를 선택하세요!

⑤ Telegraph Connector는 최근에 두 개의 새로운 버스 노선을 도입했습니다. Lee 노선은 Western Fairfax County에서 D.C.까지 운행합니다. Gunston 노선은 Pohick Peninsula부터 D.C.의 Union Station까지 북쪽으로 운행합니다. ⑥ 이 광고를 이용하여 Connector에 무료로 편도 승차해 보십시오!

오늘 저희와 함께 타보세요!
The Telegraph Connector
t-connector.com

5. Telegraph Connector에 관하여 언급된 것은 무엇인가?

(A) 최근에 노선을 확장했다.

(B) 한동안 운행되어 왔다.

(C) 점점 인기가 많아지고 있다.

(D) 단체에 할인을 제공한다.

해설　광고의 도입 부분에서 최근 두 개의 버스 노선을 도입했다고 했으므로 정답은 (A) It recently expanded its routes.이다.

6. 고객들은 이 광고로 무엇을 받을 수 있는가?

(A) 다수의 요금 할인

(B) 통행료 할인권

(C) 주차권

(D) 버스 무료승차

해설　광고의 마지막 부분에서 무료로 버스에 편도 승차하기 위해 이 광고를 이용해 보라고 했으므로 정답은 (D) A free ride on the bus이다.

[7-9] 다음 광고에 관한 문제입니다.

Bagan 피트니스 레크리에이션 센터

⑦ Bagan 피트니스 레크리에이션 센터는 지난달에 개장했으며, Belmont County에 굉장한 새로운 운동 시설을 가져왔습니다. 큰 언덕 꼭대기에 위치한 이 8천 제곱피트의 센터는 모든 사람들을 위한 다양한 운동 선택권을 제공합니다. 올림픽 규모의 10레인 실내 수영장부터 4개의 실내 농구장까지, 이곳은 모든 운동시설을 갖추고 있습니다!

⑧ 또한 Bagan 피트니스 레크리에이션 센터에는 보육·놀이센터가 있습니다. 그러므로 운동하러 방문한 부모님들은 어린 자녀들을 능숙하고 잘 보살피는 직원들에게 맡기실 수 있습니다. 그리고 아이들도 많은 운동을 할 것입니다! 놀이센터에는 아이들이 정말 좋아하는 볼풀이 있습니다. 또한 정글짐, 푹신한 암벽등반 인공벽, 장애물 코스가 있습니다.

Bagan 피트니스 레크리에이션 센터에 대한 전반적인 정보를 보시려면, 저희 웹사이트 www.bagancenter.com을 방문해 주십시오. ⑨ 가격 정책이나 길 안내를 받으시려면, 저희 안내 데스크에 800-718-1000으로 연락 하십시오.

7. Bagan 피트니스 레크리에이션 센터에 관하여 언급된 것은 무엇인가?

    (A) 곧 문을 열 것이다.

    (B) 수영 강습을 제공한다.

    (C) 운동 경기를 주최할 것이다.

    (D) Belmont County에 위치해 있다.

해설 광고의 앞 부분에서 피트니스 레크리에이션 센터는 지난 달에 개장했으며, Belmont County에 굉장한 새로운 운동 시설을 가져왔다는 것을 알 수 있으므로 정답은 (D) It is located in Belmont County. 이다.

---

8. Bagan 피트니스 레크리에이션 센터에서 무엇을 이용할 수 있는가?

    (A) 보육

    (B) 농구 강습

    (C) 테니스 코트

    (D) 무료 주차

해설 광고의 중간 부분에서 Bagan 피트니스 레크리에이션 센터는 보육/놀이센터가 있다고 했으므로 정답은 (A) Child care임을 알 수 있다.

---

9. 이 광고에 의하면, 요금에 관한 정보를 어떻게 받을 수 있는가?

    (A) 웹사이트에 방문함으로써

    (B) 임원에게 이메일을 보냄으로써

    (C) 안내 데스크에 전화함으로써

    (D) 소책자를 읽음으로써

해설 광고의 마지막 부분에서 가격 정책이나 길 안내를 받으려면, 안내 데스크에 800-718-1000으로 전화 달라고 했으므로 정답은 (C) By calling a front desk임을 알 수 있다.

UNIT 10. 공지·회람

Practice

본서 p.290

1. (A)   **2.** (D)   **3.** (C)   **4.** (C)   **5.** (C)

6. (D)   **7.** (A)   **8.** (D)   **9.** (B)   **10.** (C)

[1-2] 다음 공고에 관한 문제입니다.

Moore 외주업체 분들께 공지합니다.

1 6월 1일부터 시의 건축 허가 신청 절차가 최소 변경될 것입니다. **2** 건축 허가 신청 수수료는 변동이 없을 것입니다. 그러나, 신청에 대한 결정에 기존의 7일이 아닌 14일이 소요될 것입니다. 건설 프로젝트를 계획하실 때 이점을 유념하십시오.

2 뿐만 아니라, 신청서를 이제 Main 가에 있는 저희 새 건물의 Development Services Office에 제출하셔야 합니다. Building Permit Office는 예전의 Moore 시 정부 청사가 폐쇄되면서 문을 닫을 것입니다.

협조해 주셔서 감사합니다.

Moore 시 정부

---

1. 이 공지의 목적은 무엇인가?

    (A) 정부 서비스의 변경을 설명하기 위해

    (B) 새 건설 프로젝트를 위한 투자하기 위해

    (C) 직원들을 위한 새 일정을 소개하기 위해

    (D) 민간 건물의 폐쇄를 상세히 알리기 위해

해설 공지의 첫 번째 단락에서 6월 1일부터 시의 건축 허가 신청 절차가 변경될 것이라고 했으므로 공지의 목적은 (A) To explain some changes to a government service임을 알 수 있다.

---

2. 허가증 신청에 관하여 언급되지 않은 것은 무엇인가?

    (A) 신청 수수료는 영향을 받지 않을 것이다.

    (B) 결정이 되는데 1주일이 더 걸릴 것이다.

    (C) 이제 다른 사무실에 제출되어야 한다.

    (D) 많은 신청이 기각될 수 있다.

해설 공지의 두 번째, 세 번째 단락에서 각각 건축 허가 신청 수수료는 변동이 없을 것이며 신청에 대한 결정은 기존의 7일이 아닌 14일이 소요될 것이라 했다. 또한 신청서를 Main 가에 있는 새 건물의 Development Services Office에 제출해야 한다고 했으며 그 이유는 Building Permit Office는 예전의 Moore 시 정부 청사가 폐쇄되면서 문을 닫을 것이기 때문이라 했다. 따라서 정답은 (D) Many applications could be denied.임을 알 수 있다.

[3-4] 다음 회람에 관한 문제입니다.

수신: 전 직원

발신: Marvin Greenwell 이사

일자: 4월 5일

제목: 도로 작업

3 여러분이 대부분 매일 James Monroe 가를 거쳐서 출근하기 때문에, Maryland 교통부가 이 노선 및 출구에 도로공사를 할 예정이라는 것을 알고 계시는 게 중요합니다. 이 프로젝트는 4월 12일에 시작될 것입니다. 그때 도로 표면 작업을 다시 하는 동안 도로의 1마일 구간이 한 차선으로 좁혀질 것입니다. 이로 인해 상당한 지연이 야기될 가능성이 높으므로 미리 준비해 주십시오. **4** 게다가 4월 19일에는 우리 회사쪽 출구인 4A 출구가 폐쇄될 것입니다. 이 기간 동안 여러분은 5A 출구로 나온 다음 Chantilly 가를 이용하여 동쪽으로 3마일 운전하여 회사로 와야 할 것입니다. 모든 작업은 4월 30일에 완료될 예정입니다. 교통부는 이 프로젝트가 교통 혼잡을 야기할 것임을 인정하지만, 작업이 진행되는 동안 인내심을 가져줄 것을 요청하고 있습니다.

3. 무엇이 발표되고 있는가?
(A) 최근의 교통량 증가
(B) 새로운 노선의 개장
(C) 도로의 일부 보수
(D) 보고서의 지연

해설 회람의 처음 부분에서 '여러분이 대부분 매일 James Monroe 가를 거쳐서 출근하기 때문에, Maryland 교통부가 이 노선 및 출구에 도로 공사를 할 예정이라는 것을 알고 계시는 게 중요합니다.'라는 내용이 나오므로, 도로 공사에 대해 직원들에게 알려주고 있음을 알 수 있다. 따라서 정답은 (C) Some repairs to a road이다.

....

4. 직원들은 언제 우회해야 하는가?
(A) 4월 5일
(B) 4월 12일
(C) 4월 19일
(D) 4월 30일

해설 메모의 중간 부분에서 '게다가 4월 19일에는 우리 회사쪽 출구인 4A 출구가 폐쇄될 것입니다. 이 기간 동안 여러분은 5A 출구로 나온 다음 Chantilly 가를 이용하여 동쪽으로 3마일 운전하여 회사로 와야 할 것입니다.'라는 내용이 나오므로, 4월 19일에 우회하여 출근해야 함을 알 수 있다. 따라서 정답은 (C) On April 19이다.

....

[5-7] 다음 공지에 관한 문제입니다.

5 로터리 클럽 모임 공지
1월 11일

5 사업체 소유주 및 기타 지역 기관장 분들은 Astoria 로터리 클럽에서 열리는 다음의 모임들에 참가하시도록 초대됩니다.

날짜: 2월 2일 화요일
교통 위원회, 저녁 7시
날짜: **6** 2월 4일 수요일
관광 위원회, 저녁 7시 30분
장소: 시민회관 본관 3층
20213 Cleveden, Astoria

전체 안건들은 1월 14일 월요일, 시민회관 본관과 로터리 클럽 본사의 로비에 게재될 것입니다. **7** 이 모임에서 위원회 구성원들의 발언에 대해 관심이 있으신 지역 주민들께서는 모임 일주일 전에 서면 요청서를 제출해 주실 것을 요청 드립니다.

7 요청서는
홍보관 Max Mueller
Astoria 로터리 클럽
20213 Cleveden, Astoria
mmueller@astoriarotaryclub.au
앞으로 보내 주십시오.

────────────────────────────

5. 이 공지의 목적은 무엇인가?
(A) 새로운 지침을 알리기 위해
(B) 구성원들에게 선거에 대해 알려주기 위해
(C) 다가오는 행사를 알리기 위해
(D) 상업용 서비스를 홍보하기 위해

해설 공지의 목적을 묻는 문제로 제목을 확인하면, 모임 공지(NOTICE OF ROTARY CLUB MEETINGS)임을 알 수 있고, 첫 번째 단락에서 로터리 클럽 모임에 참석할 것을 권하고 있으므로 정답은 (C) To publicize upcoming events이다.

....

6. Astoria에 관광객을 유치하는 것에 관한 논의는 언제 열리겠는가?
(A) 1월 11일에
(B) 1월 14일에
(C) 2월 2일에
(D) 2월 4일에

해설 관광객 유치에 대한 논의 날짜를 묻고 있다. attracting visitors를 키워드로 삼아 행사 날짜를 언급하는 부분에서 단서를 잡으면, 관광위원회 모임은 2월 4일(Date: Wednesday, 4 February / Tourism Board, 7:30 P.M.)이라고 나와 있으므로 정답은 (D) On February 4이다.

....

7. 일반 대중들이 위원회 모임에서 발언하고 싶으면 무엇을 해야 하는가?
(A) Mr. Mueller에게 글을 쓴다.
(B) 온라인으로 등록한다.
(C) 모임에 일찍 도착한다.
(D) 시민회관에 등록한다.

해설 발언 희망자들이 해야 할 일을 묻고 있다. 이사회 모임 발언 희망자들에 대한 안내사항을 확인하면, 위원회 구성원들의 발언에 관심이 있는 주민들은 서면 요청을 해달라고 하면서, 요청서를 Max Mueller에게 제출해달라고 했으므로 정답은 (A) Write to Mr. Mueller이다.

[8-10] 다음 회람에 관한 문제입니다.

수신: 전 직원
발신: Thomas Marton, 운영 책임자
날짜: 1월 3일
제목: 신분 확인 배지

저희는 다음 주 수요일인 1월 11일에 새 보안 시스템을 설치할 예정입니다. **8** 시스템이 완전히 가동되기 시작하면, Hertsworth 직원들은 늘 신분증 배지를 소지할 것이 요구됩니다. 플라스틱 카드에 디지털 코드가 박힌 이 배지들은 직원들이 Hertsworth 캠퍼스에 있는 모든 건물에 전자 출입이 가능하도록 해줄 것입니다. **9** 이 배지들은 1월 5일, 목요일부터 인사부에서 수령할 수 있습니다.

전 부서장들은 일정표를 받았고, 그들이 배지가 언제 수령 가능한지 직원들에게 알려줄 것입니다. 직원들은 1월 11일 이후 새 신분 확인 배지 없이는 Hertsworth의 전 시설에 출입이 불가합니다. **10** 기타 문의사항이나 용건이 있으신 분은 여러분의 매니저와 상의하기 바랍니다.

────────────────────────────

8. 회람의 목적은 무엇인가?
(A) 건물의 보수를 알리기 위해
(B) 직원들에게 부서의 새 사무실을 알리기 위해
(C) 보안 문제를 보고하기 위해
(D) 회사 정책을 소개하기 위해

해설 '시스템이 완전히 가동되기 시작하면, Hertsworth 직원들은 늘 신분증 배지를 소지할 것이 요구됩니다.'를 통해 새 정책을 알려주고 있으므로 정답은 (D) To introduce a company policy이다.

9. 직원들은 무엇을 하도록 요구 받는가?
(A)서류를 작성한다
(B)신분증을 받는다
(C)다른 출입문을 이용한다
(D)워크숍에 참석한다

해설 '이 배지들은 1월 5일, 목요일부터 인사부에서 수령할 수 있습니다.'라고 했으므로 (B) Obtain an identification card가 정답이다.

10. 용건이 있는 직원들은 누구에게 연락하라고 지시 받는가?
(A)시설 유지보수 직원
(B)운영 책임자
(C)부서 관리자
(D)보안 요원

해설 '기타 문의사항이나 용건이 있으신 분은 여러분의 매니저와 상의하기 바랍니다.'라고 했으므로 (C) Their department supervisors가 정답이다.

UNIT 11. 기사

Practice
본서 p.298

1. (A)	**2.** (D)	**3.** (D)	**4.** (A)	**5.** (D)
6. (B)	**7.** (D)	**8.** (D)	**9.** (D)	**10.** (B)

[1-2] 다음 기사에 관한 문제입니다.

1 Anglers' Wharf 부근의 Maritime Way에 위치한 Neptune's Bounty가 10년 전에 문을 열어 포틀랜드의 최고급 해산물 레스토랑으로 빠르게 자리 잡았습니다. Neptune's Bounty는 신선한 해산물로 준비된 다양한 요리를 선보이고 있으며, 그것들 중 많은 것들이 이 지역에서 잡아 올린 것입니다. **2** 가장 신선한 재료만을 고집하고 있기 때문에, 메뉴는 계절에 맞는 해산물 종류에 따라 바뀌고 있습니다. 레스토랑은 지난 두 달 동안 수리를 위해 휴업했으나, 지난주에 다시 문을 열었습니다. 현재 내부는 오래된 목조 범선 내부처럼 보입니다. 또한 살아 있는 가재와 물고기, 다른 해산물이 들어 있는 수족관을 선보입니다. 그들의 재오픈 기념으로, Neptune's Bounty는 모든 손님들에게 무료로 전채 요리를 제공할 것입니다.

1. 이 기사의 목적은 무엇인가?
(A) 사업체를 광고하기 위해
(B) 요리 수업을 홍보하기 위해
(C) 다른 레스토랑들을 비교하기 위해
(D) 관광 명소를 설명하기 위해

해설 기사의 도입부에서 포틀랜드에서 자리 잡은 지 10년이 된 레스토랑을 소개하고 있다. 따라서 이 기사의 목적으로 가장 적절한 답은 (A) To advertise a business이다.

2. Neptune's Bounty에 관해 언급되지 않은 것은 무엇인가?
(A) 지난주에 다시 문을 열었다.
(B) 내부를 새롭게 꾸몄다.
(C) 메뉴가 일년 내내 바뀐다.
(D) 새로운 장소로 옮겼다.

해설 기사의 내용과 선택지의 내용을 비교 또는 대조하여 기사의 내용과 일치하지 않는 정보를 찾는 문제이다. 먼저 문장 'but it reopened last week'를 통해 (A)는 지문의 내용과 일치하는 정보임을 알 수 있다. 문장은 두 달간의 수리 후에 현재 내부가 오래된 목조 범선 내부와 같다라고 했으므로 (B)는 지문의 내용과 일치할 수 있다. 마지막으로 문장에서 (C) 역시 사실임을 확인할 수 있다. 그런데 레스토랑을 이전했다는 정보는 기사 어디에서도 찾을 수 없으므로 정답은 (D) It has moved to a new location.이다.

[3-4] 다음 기사에 관한 문제입니다.

여러 베트남 회사의 임원을 지낸 지 30년이 지나서, Thien Phouc Nguyen은 동남아시아에서 가장 성공한 기업인 중 한 명으로 널리 인정받고 있다. Hanmon Enterprises의 사장으로 퇴직한 후에, 그는 이 지역에서 어떻게 성공할 수 있는지에 대해 연설하면서 여러 회사를 방문했다. **3** 지난해 그는 사업에 관해 5권으로 계획한 시리즈 중 첫 번째 책을 집필하여 출판했다. 제 1권인 〈Market Barriers〉 (ASEAC 출판, 19.95달러)는 동남아시아 시장에 진입하려 했으나 실패한 여러 기업들에 대한 연구이다. **4** 이 책은 이미 미국과 유럽의 MBA 과정 교실에서 사용되고 있다. 시리즈의 다음 책은 올해 말에 출판될 예정이나, 확정된 출판 날짜와 제목은 알려진 바 없다.

3. 어떤 종류의 출판물에서 이와 같은 기사를 찾아볼 수 있겠는가?
(A) 패션 잡지
(B) 여행 안내책자
(C) 교육용 설명서
(D) 비즈니스 저널

해설 주어진 기사가 어떤 종류의 출판물에서 볼 수 있을 것 같은지를 묻는 질문이다. 이와 같은 문제는 명확하게 답이 주어지기보다는 기사의 내용을 바탕으로 적절한 답을 유추해야 한다. 기사는 30년 동안 여러 베트남 회사의 임원을 지낸 Thien Phouc Nguyen에 관한 글이고, 기사의 중반부에서 기사는 Nguyen이 집필한 저서를 소개하고 있다. 이와 같은 기사는 비즈니스 분야의 출판물에서 볼 수 있을 것이다. 따라서 문제의 정답은 (D) A business journal이다.

4. 〈Market Barriers〉에 관해 언급된 것은 무엇인가?

(A) **대학원생들에게 읽혀지고 있다.**

(B) 아시아에서 성공한 기업들을 다루고 있다.

(C) 북미 지역에만 배포되고 있다.

(D) 시리즈 중에서 다섯 번째 책이다.

해설 Nguyen의 저서 〈Market Barriers(비즈니스 장벽)〉에 관한 세부 정보를 묻고 있다. 지문에서 이 책이 이미 미국과 유럽의 MBA 과정 교실에서 사용되고 있다는 언급을 통해 미국과 유럽에서 MBA 과정을 밟고 있는 대학원생들의 교재로 사용되고 있다는 사실을 알 수 있다. 따라서 정답은 (A) It is being read by graduate students.이다.

[5-6] 다음 기사에 관한 문제입니다.

〈Economy Now〉

최신 뉴스:

7월 2일, Los Angeles – 패션 디자이너이자 Life 의류 브랜드 소유주인 Ji Young Lee는 향후 6개월간 이 회사에 큰 변화가 있을 것이라고 발표했다. "우리는 시장조사를 통해 우리 고객의 대부분이 소득계층 상위 1/3에 속하는 것을 발견했습니다."라고 Ms. Lee는 말했다. "이것은 놀라운 결과였습니다. 우리 브랜드가 모든 사람들에게 이용 가능하다고 항상 생각했기 때문입니다."

이러한 새로운 정보로 인해, Life 의류 점포 몇 군데가 문을 닫을 것이며, 다른 곳에서 문을 열 것이다. "우리는 우리 고객들이 있는 곳으로 이전해야 합니다. **5** 조사 결과 대부분의 우리 고객들이 도시 지역의 부유한 전문가들임을 알게 되었습니다. 따라서 우리는 교외 지역에 위치한 점포 몇 곳을 폐점할 것입니다. **6** 우리는 뉴욕, 워싱턴, 로스앤젤레스, 시카고, 보스턴에 점포를 열 계획입니다. 버지니아주의 버크시, 켄터키주의 렉싱턴시, 캘리포니아주의 오클랜드시, 워싱턴주의 버넷시 등에 위치한 점포는 곧 폐점할 것입니다."라고 Ms. Lee는 설명했다.

"우리는 이러한 큰 변화를 추진하게 되어 기쁩니다. 이는 우리 수입에 큰 차이를 가져올 것이라 확신합니다. 그리고 Life 의류 브랜드가 지속적으로 성공하게 해 줄 것이라 확신합니다"라고 Ms. Lee는 논평했다.

---

5. Life 의류 브랜드에 대해서 암시된 것은 무엇인가?

(A) 의류 브랜드로 출발하지 않았다.

(B) 다양한 아동화를 제공한다.

(C) 일부 점포의 재고를 검토하고 있다.

(D) **도시 거주자들에게 가장 인기가 있다.**

해설 기사의 중간 부분에서 조사 결과 대부분의 우리 고객이 도시 지역의 부유한 전문가들임을 알게 되었다고 했으므로 정답은 (D) It is most popular with city residents.임을 알 수 있다.

---

6. Life 의류 점포는 현재 어디에 위치해 있는가?

(A) 뉴욕에

(B) **버크에**

(C) 워싱턴에

(D) 보스턴에

해설 기사의 중간 부분에서 뉴욕, 워싱턴, 로스앤젤레스, 시카고, 보스턴에 점포를 열 계획이고 버지니아주의 버크시, 켄터키주의 렉싱턴시, 캘리

포니아주의 오클랜드시, 워싱턴주의 버넷시 등에 위치한 점포는 곧 폐점할 것이라고 했으므로 정답은 (B) In Burke 임을 알 수 있다.

[7-10] 다음 보도자료에 관한 문제입니다.

7 항공사의 운영 확장

채츠워스섬과, 호주(11월 22일) – **7** 12월 24일에 Rooback 항공사는 채츠워스섬과 멜버른을 오가는 비행편을 제공하기 시작할 것이다. 왕복 서비스는 하루에 세 번 제공되며, 비행 시간은 30분 정도이다.

두 지역 사이의 출장의 증가는 호주에서 인지도를 높이려는 4년 된 항공사가 이와 같은 결정을 하게 한 계기가 되었다고 Rooback 항공사의 최고 경영자인 Mr. Jackson Ford가 설명했다. "우리는 지속적으로 지역사회의 바람에 응답하고 있습니다."

Austravel 항공사는 채츠워스섬과 멜버른을 오가는 매일 항공편을 제공했었다. 하지만, 작년 Austravel 항공사는 베이징에 본사를 둔 Shao 항공에 의해 인수되었고, 채츠워스섬에서의 서비스를 중단했다. Shao는 현재 호주에서 베이징과 멜버른 사이의 주말 항공편만을 제공한다.

8 "Rooback의 새로운 여행 서비스는 호주 일대의 업무 회의나 여가 활동을 위한 당일 왕복 여행을 가능하게 할 것입니다."라고 Mr. Ford는 말했다.

9 Rooback 항공사는 그들의 웹사이트를 개발하기 위해 Miter Tech System과 제휴를 맺었다. Miter Tech Systems는 전세계 40개 이상의 지역 항공사들에게 그들의 서비스를 제공한다.

10 Rooback 항공사는 현재 시드니, 브리즈번, 퍼스 그리고 애들레이드에 서비스를 제공하면서, 오직 호주에서만 운행하고 있다.

---

7. 이 언론 보도의 목적은 무엇인가?

(A) 최근 합병의 세부 사항을 제공하기 위해

(B) 새로운 항공사의 최고 경영자를 소개하기 위해

(C) 업데이트된 예약 절차를 설명하기 위해

(D) **새로운 비행 항로를 알리기 위해**

해설 보도의 목적을 묻고 있다. 제목과 첫 번째 문장을 확인하면 항공사에서 확장된 노선 운항 서비스를 제공한다고 했으므로 정답은 (D) To announce a new airline route이다.

---

8. Mr. Ford에 따르면, 채츠워스섬 멜버른의 기업인들은 Rooback 항공사로부터 어떻게 혜택을 받을 것인가?

(A) 더 저렴한 가격으로 티켓을 구매할 수 있다.

(B) 관광의 증가로 더 많은 돈을 벌 것이다.

(C) 항공편 예약을 더 빨리 할 수 있을 것이다.

(D) **국내 전역을 더 편리하게 여행할 수 있을 것이다.**

해설 기업인들이 받는 혜택을 묻고 있다. 'Rooback의 새로운 여행 서비스는 호주 일대의 업무 회의나 여가 활동을 위한 당일 왕복여행을 가능하게 할 것입니다.'에서 당일 왕복 여행이 가능해질 거라고 했으므로 정답은 (D) They will be able to travel more conveniently across the country.이다.

9. Miter Tech Systems에 관하여 알 수 있는 것은 무엇인가?

(A) 베이징에 본사가 있다.

(B) 기내 오락을 제공한다.

(C) 비행 승무원들을 훈련시킨다.

(D) 웹사이트를 개발한다.

해설 Miter Tech Systems에 관하여 암시되는 것을 묻고 있다. Miter Tech Systems를 키워드로 삼아 단서를 잡으면, 항공사가 웹사이트 개발을 위해 Miter Tech Systems와 제휴 한다고 한 부분에서 (partnered with Miter Tech Systems to design its Web site) 이 회사는 웹사이트와 관련된 서비스를 제공하는 곳임을 알 수 있다. 따라서 정답은 (D) It develops Web sites.이다.

---

10. Rooback 항공사에 관하여 알 수 있는 것은 무엇인가?

(A) Austravel 항공을 인수했다.

(B) 호주 내에서만 운항한다.

(C) 기내 인터넷 서비스를 제공한다.

(D) 작년에 채츠워스섬에 설립되었다.

해설 Rooback 항공사에 관하여 암시되는 것을 묻고 있다. Rooback Air를 키워드로 삼아 단서를 잡으면, Rooback Air currently operates only in Australia의 내용을 토대로 이 항공사가 현재는 호주에서만 운항함을 알 수 있다. 따라서 정답은 (B) It provides flights within Australia only.이다.

UNIT 12. 양식

Practice

본서 p.306

1. (B)	**2.** (D)	**3.** (B)	**4.** (C)	**5.** (B)
6. (A)	**7.** (A)	**8.** (A)	**9.** (C)	**10.** (B)
11. (B)				

[1-2] 다음의 양식에 관한 문제입니다.

Nonstop New Haven: 우리 도시의 선두적인 파티 주최자

저희 회사를 찾아주셔서 감사합니다! 아래의 양식을 모두 작성해 주시기 바랍니다. **1** 저희 회사 직원이 귀하의 필요에 가장 적절한 패키지와 비용 계획을 가지고 귀하에게 연락드릴 것입니다.

성명: _____	전화번호: _____
이메일: _____	행사 날짜: _____

- **2** 파티 장소:
  [ ] 183 Mulberry 가
  [ ] 2001 Tyconda 가
  [ ] 72 Foxforth 가
  [ ] 892 Grovington 가

- 행사 종류

[ ] 시상식	[ ] 졸업 파티
[ ] 회사 회식	[ ] 기타: _____

- 예상 손님 인원:
  [ ] 40명 이하 [ ] 50-120명 [ ] 121명 이상

- 손님을 위한 인근 숙소 필요 여부:
  [ ] 네 [ ] 아니오

- 특정 전자 장비를 대여하고 싶으시면 말씀해 주십시오:
  _____

Nonstop New Haven

---

1. Nonstop New Haven 직원은 무엇을 할 것인가?

(A) 121명 이상의 손님이 있을 경우 비용을 깎아준다

(B) 특정 정보에 따라 제안서를 작성한다

(C) 행사에서 손님들을 자리로 안내한다

(D) 인근 호텔 목록을 보낸다

해설 양식을 작성하면 직원이 전화해서 적절한 패키지 상품을 소개하고 고객의 필요에 가장 잘 맞는 요금을 알려주겠다고 했으므로 appropriate package and pricing plan that will best meet your needs를 proposal로 paraphrasing한 (B) Draft a proposal according to certain information이 정답이다.

---

2. Nonstop New Haven에 대해 암시된 것은 무엇인가?

(A) 1년이 채 되지 않은 회사이다

(B) 고객들이 자신의 전자 장비를 가져오도록 요청한다

(C) 최근 전용 숙소를 제공하기 시작했다

(D) 네 개의 행사장을 가지고 있다

해설 고객이 작성할 양식의 Party Locations(파티 장소) 부분을 보면 네 곳 중 선택하도록 되어 있다. 따라서 네 개의 지점이 있다고 말하는 (D) It owns four venues.이다.

[3-5] 다음 청구서에 관한 문제입니다.

http://www.matadorbooks.com/invoice_63497

Matador 서적

주문 번호: 63497

3 주문 날짜: 3월 12일

예상 배송일: 3월 16일

배송지:	요금 청구지:	
4 Ms. Nadia Stevens	**3** Ms. Rachel Fox	
74 Hanlon St. Apt 19	Henley Dr.	
터코마, 워싱턴 98401	뉴어크, 뉴저지 07101	
제목:	저자:	가격:
4 <Management Policies>	Charles Haywood	28.95달러
제목:	저자:	가격:
4 <Developing Managerial Skills>	Jennie Wong	37.62 달러

소계: 66.57달러

세금: 4.35달러

5 배송 및 취급수수료: 무료

신용카드 전체 부과 금액: 70.92달러

선물용 주문이라면 카드를 포함하나요? (추가 요금 없음)

✓ 네 ___ 아니오

카드 메시지:

4 새로운 일을 하게 되신 것을 축하 드립니다! 우리는 이 책들이 당신의 새로운 경력에 도움이 되기를 희망합니다. 벌써 당신이 그립습니다.

진심으로,

Fox & Marina 법무법인 직원 일동

---

3. Ms. Fox는 3월 12일에 무엇을 했는가?

(A) 책을 한 권 교환했다.

(B) 선물을 구입했다.

(C) 배송품을 추적했다.

(D) 소포를 가져왔다.

해설 지문에서 Ms. Fox와 3월 12일 관련 정보에 주목한다. 주문일이 3월 12일(Order date: March 12)이며, 청구지 주소에서 이름이 Ms. Rachel Fox로 되어 있으므로 3월 12일에 Ms. Fox가 선물을 구매했음을 알 수 있다. 따라서 정답은 (B) Purchased a gift이다.

---

4. Ms. Stevens에 대해서 암시된 것은 무엇인가?

(A) 책을 완성했다.

(B) Ms. Fox의 상사이다.

(C) 최근에 관리자로 채용되었다.

(D) 최근에 대학 과정을 등록했다.

해설 'Ms. Stevens'를 키워드로 삼아 해당 내용을 찾는다. 배송지에서 수령인인 Nadia Stevens를 확인하고, 카드 메시지와 선물로 보내지는 책 제목(Management Policies, Developing Managerial Skills)을 확인하면, 최근 관리직을 새로 얻은 것에 대한 축하의 뜻으로 Ms. Stevens가 책을 선물 받았음을 알 수 있다. 따라서 정답은 (C) She was recently hired as a manager.이다.

---

5. Matador 서적에 관하여 언급된 것은 무엇인가?

(A) 상품권을 판매한다.

(B) 추가 요금 없이 주문품을 배송했다.

(C) 주문이 접수된 다음날 처리를 했다.

(D) 학술지를 발행한다.

해설 청구서에서 Matador 서적과 관련된 정보를 찾으면, 배송료와 취급수수료가 무료(Shipping and Handling: Free)임을 알 수 있다. 따라서 정답은 (B) It shipped an order at no additional cost.이다.

[6-9] 다음 전단에 관한 문제입니다.

6 이제 막 런던으로 이사 오셨나요?

런던 거주민 위원회가 주최하는

6 '런던은 당신을 환영합니다' 오리엔테이션에 참가하세요.

5월 25일, 오전 10:30 – 오후 2:30

London Times 광장

Big Ben 센터

누구나 참석 가능합니다

6 발표 일정		
오전 10:30	**7** 다니는 방법: 이용 가능한 대중교통 (101호)	
오전 11:30	**6** 런던에서 집 구하기 (103호)	쓰레기 관리 조언과 옵션 (104호)
오후 12:30	런던의 현지 은행 시스템 이해하기 (105호)	**6** 런던에서 현지 사업 시작하기 (104호)
오후 1:30	**7** 런던에서 할 것, 주민 모임과 오락 시설 안내 (101호)	

두 행사가 같은 시간에 진행될 수도 있으니, 참석자들은 가장 관심이 있는 행사를 선택해야 합니다. **7** 게다가, 오락과 대중교통 세션에 대한 관심들이 높기 때문에 빨리 오셔서 자리를 확보하셔야 한다는 점을 유념하시기 바랍니다.

8 모든 발표는 영어로 진행되지만, 한국어, 스페인어, 프랑스어 팸플릿들이 준비되어 있습니다. 다과는 구매하실 수 있습니다.

9 마지막 발표 후에, 참가자들은 한 시간 동안 가이드가 안내 하는 런던 시내 관광에 참여하실 수 있습니다. 이 무료 관광은 장기간 활동한 위원회 회원과 런던 거주민에 의해 제공됩니다.

이 행사와 관련하여 더 많은 정보를 원하면, www.welcometolondon.co.uk을 방문해 주시기 바랍니다.

---

6. 전단은 누구를 위한 것이겠는가?

(A) 런던에 새로 온 거주민들

(B) 런던 시 의원들

(C) 런던에서 일하고 있는 관광 가이드들

(D) 런던 거주민 협의회 회원들

해설 전단의 제목 및 일정표의 프레젠테이션 주제를 확인하면, 런던으로 이사 온 시민을 위한 오리엔테이션이며, 프레젠테이션 주제들이 런던의 대중교통, 주택, 쓰레기 관리, 오락시설에 관한 내용이므로 정답은 (A) Residents who are new to London 이다.

---

7. 가장 인기 있는 발표는 어디서 진행될 것인가?

(A) 101호에서

(B) 103호에서

(C) 104호에서

(D) 105호에서

해설 가장 인기 있는 발표에 대해 언급된 내용을 찾는다. 오락과 대중교통 세션에 대한 관심이 높으므로 자리 확보를 위해서는 일찍 와야 한다고 했는데 대중교통 관련 세션(How to Get Around: Available Public Transportation: Room 101)과 오락 관련 세션(What to do in London, Guide to Community Gatherings and Recreational Facilities: Room 101) 모두 101호에서 진행함을 알 수 있으므로 정답은 (A) In Room 101이다.

8. 런던 거주민 위원회에 관하여 언급된 것은 무엇인가?

(A) 여러 언어로 자료를 제공한다.

(B) 새로운 서비스를 제공하기 시작할 것이다.

(C) 회비를 요구한다.

(D) 월간 행사를 주최한다.

해설 런던 거주민 위원회의 활동과 제공 서비스 등에 대한 정보에 주목한다. 여러 언어로 된 팸플릿을 제공한다고 했으므로 정답은 (A) It provides materials in several languages.이다.

---

9. 전단에 의하면, 참석자들이 발표 후에 할 수 있는 것은 무엇인가?

(A) 무료 음식과 음료를 즐긴다

(B) 다가오는 행사의 좌석을 예약한다

(C) 시내 관광을 한다

(D) 회원으로 등록한다

해설 발표 이후의 활동에 대해 언급된 것을 찾는다. 발표 이후에 참가자들은 가이드가 딸린 런던 시내 투어에 참가한다고 했으므로 정답은 (C) Go on a tour of the city이다.

[10-11] 다음 일정에 관한 문제입니다.

4월 12일 TGB 직원 출장 일정표

이름	⑩ 직책	출발 도시	도착 도시	출발 시각	도착 시각
⑪ Andre Fisher	기자	홍콩, 중국	마닐라, 필리핀	오전 8시 40분	오전 10시 40분
⑪ Steven Lee	카메라맨	홍콩, 중국	마닐라, 필리핀	오전 8시 40분	오전 10시 40분
Natalie Bateman	편집 기술자	자카르타, 인도네시아	로마, 이탈리아	오전 8시 50분	오후 10시
Brian Mundy	카메라맨	자카르타, 인도네시아	아테네, 그리스	오전 9시 5분	오전 9시 45분
Amy Bowman	뉴스 앵커	자카르타, 인도네시아	로마, 이탈리아	오전 8시 50분	오후 10시

10. 직원들은 어디서 일할 것 같은가?

(A) 제조회사에서

(B) 방송국에서

(C) 무역회사에서

(D) 건설회사에서

해설 여행 일정표의 직책 타이틀에 "Reporter, Cameraman, Technical editor, News anchor"라고 나와 있으므로 직원들은 방송국에서 일함을 알 수 있다. 정답은 (B) At a broadcasting company이다.

---

11. Mr. Fisher에 대해 무엇이 사실이겠는가?

(A) 그의 항공편은 지연될 것이다.

(B) 동료와 함께 비행기를 탈 것이다.

(C) 유럽으로 여행을 갈 것이다.

(D) 그의 좌석은 업그레이드될 것이다.

해설 여행 일정표에 Mr. Fisher와 같은 여행 일정(홍콩/마닐라/오전 8:40/오전 10:40)을 가진 사람이 Steven Lee이므로 정답은 (B) He will be flying with a coworker.이다.

UNIT 13. 이중 지문

Practice

1. (D) **2.** (A) **3.** (B) **4.** (C) **5.** (D)

6. (A) **7.** (C) **8.** (D) **9.** (B) **10.** (D)

[1-5] 다음 두 이메일에 관한 문제입니다.

수신: IT부 ⟨itdepartment@vfb.com⟩

발신: Nadia G. Pellins ⟨ngpellins@vfb.com⟩

날짜: 7월 20일, 오전 11시 55분

제목: 온라인 계좌 시스템과 관련된 문제들

---

1 **5** 저는 대출부에서 일하며, 제가 오늘 오전 내내 저희 온라인 계좌 시스템에 접속할 수가 없어서 이렇게 이메일을 보냅니다. 지난 주 금요일에는 문제가 없었지만, 오늘 제가 비밀번호를 입력할 때마다 "접속 거부" 메시지가 뜹니다. 회사 내에서 이러한 문제를 겪는 사람이 또 있나요, 아니면 이 문제를 가진 사람은 저 **2** 뿐인가요? **3** 어쨌든 제가 오늘 오후 6시 전에 다섯 개의 새 대출 신청에 대한 계좌 정보를 시스템에 입력해야 합니다. 제가 이 문제를 해결할 수 있도록 도와주세요.

수신: Nadia G. Pellins ⟨ngpellins@vfb.com⟩

발신: IT부 ⟨itdepartment@vfb.com⟩

날짜: 7월 20일, 오후 12시 30분

제목: 회신: 온라인 계좌 시스템과 관련된 문제들

첨부: 사용 설명서

안녕하세요 Nadia,

불편함을 드려 사과 드립니다. 저희가 토요일 아침 일찍 온라인 계좌 시스템을 업데이트하기 시작했고 오늘 아침 5시에 그 일을 완료했습니다. 오늘 주간 근무가 시작할 때 시스템 접속을 확실히 하기 위해 주말 동안 업데이트가 의도적으로 이루어졌습니다. 안타깝게도, 오늘 아침에 많은 직원들이 이 "접근 거부" 오류 메시지를 받았습니다. 우리는 그 문제를 해결하는 중에 있으며, **3** 시스템은 앞으로 수 시간 안에 완전히 작동하게 될 것이니, 당신의 고객들을 위해 대출 신청서 제출을 위한 충분한 시간을 가질 것입니다.

몇몇 직원들은 그들의 비밀번호를 재설정함으로써 시스템에 접속할 수 있었다고 말했으니, 당신이 이를 시도해봐도 좋을 것 같습니다. **4** 당신의 비밀번호를 재설정하기 위한 설명을 이 이메일에 첨부된 시스템 사용 설명서 2절에서 찾을 수 있습니다. **5** 만약 그렇게 했는데도 시스템에 접속할 수 없다면, 당신의 부서가 겪을 수도 있는 기술적 문제들을 처리할 Kyoshiro Maruoka에게 연락해 주세요.

당신의 인내에 감사 드립니다.

Simone Dilbert
IT 매니저

---

1. Ms. Pellins는 누구이겠는가?
(A) 채용 컨설턴트
(B) 시스템 기술자
(C) 대출 신청자
(D) 은행원

해설 '저는 대출부에서 일하며, 제가 오늘 오전 내내 저희 온라인 계좌 시스템에 접속할 수가 없어서 이렇게 이메일을 보냅니다.'를 통해 Ms. Pellins의 직업을 유추할 수 있으므로 (D) A bank clerk가 정답이다.

....

2. 첫 번째 이메일, 네 번째 줄의 단어 "just"와 의미상 가장 가까운 것은
(A) ~뿐인
(B) 꽤
(C) 상당히
(D) 또한

해설 '회사 내에서 이러한 문제를 겪는 사람이 또 있나요, 아니면 이 문제를 가진 사람은 저뿐인가요?'라는 의미이므로 just와 의미상 가장 가까운 것은 (A) only 이다.

....

3. Ms. Dilbert의 따르면, Ms. Pellins는 언제 온라인 계좌 시스템에 다시 접속할 수 있겠는가?
(A) 월요일 오전 5시쯤
(B) 월요일 저녁 6시 이전
(C) 금요일 오후쯤
(D) 주말에

해설 첫 이메일에서 '제가 오늘 오후 6시 전에 다섯 개의 새 대출 신청에 대한 계좌 정보를 시스템에 입력해야 합니다.'라고 했는데, 답장에서 '시스템은 앞으로 수 시간 안에 완전히 작동하게 될 것이니, 당신의 고객들을 위해 대출 신청서 제출을 위한 충분한 시간을 가질 것입니다.'라고 설명하고 있으므로 정답은 (B) Before 6:00 Monday evening 이다.

....

4. Ms. Pellins는 왜 시스템 사용 설명서를 조회하겠는가?
(A) Mr. Maruoka의 연락처를 찾기 위해
(B) 파일에 접속하기 위한 회사 정책을 확인하기 위해
(C) 그녀의 비밀번호 변경 방법을 알기 위해
(D) 신청서 제출에 대한 지시문을 읽기 위해

해설 두 번째 이메일에서 '당신의 비밀번호를 재설정하기 위한 설명을 시스템 사용 설명서 2절에서 찾을 수 있습니다.'라고 했으므로 (C) To learn how to change her password가 정답이다.

....

5. Mr. Maruoka에 관하여 사실인 것은 무엇인가?
(A) "접속 거부" 오류 메시지를 받았다.
(B) IT부서 매니저로서 Mr. Dillbert를 대신할 것이다.
(C) 그는 Ms. Pellins의 오랜 고객이다.
(D) 그는 주택 담보 대출 부서를 위한 기술 지원을 제공할 것이다.

해설 두 번째 이메일 마지막 문장이 '만약 그렇게 했는데도 시스템에 접속할 수 없다면, 당신의 부서가 겪을 수도 있는 기술적 문제들을 처리할 Kyoshiro Maruoka에게 연락해 주세요.'인데, 첫 번째 이메일에서 Ms. Pellins가 I work in the Mortgage Department(저는 대출부에서 일하며)라고 소속을 밝혔으므로 (D) He will provide technical support for the Mortgage Department.가 정답이다.

[6-10] 다음 웹페이지와 온라인 리뷰에 관한 문제입니다.

http://www.technovilleoutlet.com

홈	내 계정	**제품**	추천의 글	자주 묻는 질문들

Technoville 온라인 아웃렛
시간 날 때 전자제품을 보러 오세요.

당신의 검색으로 네 개의 결과를 가져왔습니다.

Syncer 프로 헤드셋	50.35달러
6 당신 주변에 있는 사람들을 방해할 걱정 없이 컴퓨터 오디오를 들으세요.	지금 주문하시면, 3월 8일까지 받습니다. (리뷰 5개)
Liemens 무선 헤드폰	**8** 62.50달러
방수가 되고, 가벼운 어댑터 포함	지금 주문하시면 3월 8일까지 받습니다. (리뷰 18개)
Dynamic 콤팩트 헤드폰	31.15달러
소리를 차단하는 잡음 제거 기능	지금 주문하시면 3월 8일까지 받습니다. **7** (우리 사이트에 이 제품 리뷰를 제일 먼저 올리세요.)
Liemens 스포츠 헤드폰	34.60달러
놀라운 음질 운동선수용으로 안성맞춤	지금 주문하시면 3월 8일까지 받습니다 (리뷰 10개)

---

http://www.technovilleoutlet.com/testimonials

홈	내 계정	제품	**추천의 글**	자주 묻는 질문들

Technoville 추천의 글 / 구매자들이 그들의 경험에 관해 얘기한다.

"구매에 아주 만족합니다"
Jae Min Han, 4월 10일 게시

저는 Technoville에서 구매한 Liemens 스포츠 헤드폰 하나를 가지고 있습니다. 운동하면서 음악을 듣는 것을 좋아하는 분들이라면 누

구에게든 그 제품을 적극 추천합니다. 이 스포츠 헤드폰은 Technoville 웹사이트에 기술되어 있는 것과 똑같이 아주 가볍고 눈에 잘 띄지 않으며, 음질이 아주 훌륭합니다.

저는 Liemens 제품을 몇 개 가지고 있고, 그들 모두 아주 잘 작동합니다. **8** 그리고, 제 여동생의 생일을 맞아 그 브랜드의 무선 헤드폰을 구입했는데, 그녀가 너무나도 좋아합니다. 하지만, 그 회사의 제품들을 왜 다른 곳에서는 찾기가 힘든지 이해가 되지 않습니다. 제가 온라인과 오프라인 상점에서 모두 그 회사 제품들을 찾으려고 해봤지만 **10** 오직 Technoville에서만 취급하는 것 같습니다. **9** 저는 제가 사는 지역에 있는 전자제품 판매점에 제안을 할 계획입니다.

6. 쇼핑객들은 왜 Syncer 프로 헤드셋을 선택하겠는가?
(A) **종종 다른 사람들과 가까이서 일하기 때문에**
(B) 운동하면서 음악을 즐겨 듣기 때문에
(C) 물건을 구매할 때 돈을 아낄 수 있기 때문에
(D) 밖에서 나는 소음에 방해 받고 싶어하지 않기 때문에

해설 '제품 설명에 당신 주변에 있는 사람들을 방해할 걱정 없이 컴퓨터 오디오를 들으세요' 라고 나와있으므로 (A) Because they often work close to other people가 정답이다.

7. 웹사이트에서 고객들이 평가하지 않은 제품은 무엇인가?
(A) Syncer 프로 헤드셋
(B) Liemens 무선 헤드폰
(C) **Dynamic 콤팩트 헤드폰**
(D) Liemens 스포츠 헤드폰

해설 Dynamic Compact Headphones를 설명하는 부분에서 '우리 사이트에 이 제품 리뷰를 제일 먼저 올리세요.'라고 권하고 있으므로 (C) Dynamic Compact Headphones가 정답이다.

8. 생일 선물은 얼마의 비용이 들었나?
(A) 31.15달러
(B) 34.60달러
(C) 50.35달러
(D) **62.50달러**

해설 리뷰 평가에서 Liemens라는 브랜드의 제품을 논하고 있는데 '제 여동생의 생일을 맞아 그 브랜드의 무선 헤드폰을 구입했는데' 라고 했으므로 웹페이지 표의 내용에 따라 (D) $62.50가 정답이다.

9. Mr. Han은 무엇을 할 계획인가?
(A) 물품을 교환한다.
(B) **지역 업체 한 곳에 연락한다**
(C) 다른 리뷰를 올린다
(D) 새로 구매한다

해설 '저는 제가 사는 지역에 있는 전자제품 판매점에 제안을 할 계획입니다.'라고 했으므로 (B) Contact a local business가 정답이다.

10. 온라인 리뷰에서, 두 번째 단락, 네 번째 줄의 단어, "carried"와 의미상 가장 가까운 것은
(A) 할인되어 판매된
(B) 지시 받은
(C) 운반된
(D) **재고가 있는**

해설 '그것들은 오직 Technoville에서만 취급하는 것 같습니다.'라는 의미이므로 carried와 의미상 가장 가까운 것은 (D) kept in stock이다.

UNIT 14. 삼중 지문

Practice
본서 p.332

1. (B)	**2.** (D)	**3.** (C)	**4.** (C)	**5.** (D)
6. (C)	**7.** (A)	**8.** (C)	**9.** (C)	**10.** (C)

[1-5] 다음 기사, 이메일, 그리고 공지에 관한 문제입니다.

아! 이런 직장도 있을까!

당신은 하루 종일 가장 맛있는 음식을 먹고 그것에 대한 봉급을 받는다면 어떻겠습니까? 그것은 바로 Kevin Stevens가 가지고 있는 업무의 유형입니다.

Kevin Stevens는 전문적인 음식 맛 감별사입니다. 그는 Toronto에 있는 최고의 식음료 제공업체인 Glencore Foods에서 일합니다. 평균적으로 그의 회사는 하루에 500인분의 음식을 만들고, Mr. Stevens은 품질이 높은 수준을 유지하도록 하기 위해, 모든 것을 맛봅니다.

이 직업은 많은 지식을 요구하기 때문에, 보이는 것처럼 간단하지 않습니다. Mr. Stevens은 호주 시드니에서 학부생으로 영양을 공부했고, 그리고 나서 그는 미국 로스앤젤레스에 있는 요리 학교를 다녔습니다. **2** 졸업 직후, 그는 즉시 이탈리아 밀라노와 스페인 바르셀로나에서 **2** 총 8년간 요리사로 일했습니다. 그는 2년 전 캐나다로 돌아오자마자 Glencore 식품에서 일을 하기 시작했고, **1** 자신의 직업에 대해 '꿈이 현실이 된 거 같아요'라고 말합니다.

〈Cooking Life〉 잡지

수신: Kevin Stevens 〈kevins@glencorefoods.com〉
발신: Amanda Hampton 〈a_hampton@pomodoros.com〉
제목: Cooking Life 잡지 기사
날짜: 4월 30일

Kevin에게,

저는 〈Cooking Life〉에 실린 당신에 대한 최근 기사를 읽었어요. 저는 밀라노 이후에 당신이 잘 지내고 있는지 궁금했어요. **3** 저는 당

신과 거기서 일했던 것과 당신이 만들었던 음식을 즐겼던 것을 기억하고 있어요. 좋은 시간이었어요. 그건 그렇고, **4** 당신은 5월에 열리는 곧 있을 음식 맛 감별사들을 위한 대회에 참석할 예정인가요? 그곳은 저의 고향이어서 저는 그곳에 제 부모님을 찾아뵐 예정입니다. 만약 당신이 그곳에 있다면 만날 수도 있을 거 같아요.

진심으로,

Amanda Hampton

곧 열리는 음식 맛 감별사 대회

북미 음식 맛 감별사(FTNA)는 제 4회 연례 **5** 음식 맛 감별사 대회가 5월 15일부터 17일까지 열릴 것이라는 점을 알리게 되어 자랑스럽습니다. 이전 세 번의 대회는 테네시 녹스빌에서 열렸었지만, 일정이 겹치는 바람에, **4** 올해의 행사는 미주리 세인트루이스에서 열릴 것입니다. **5** 표는 1인당 100달러입니다. 유명 요리사인 Walter Scott이 기조 연설자가 될 것입니다. 저명한 Kathy Kline과 David Hurst도 참석할 예정입니다.

---

1. Mr. Stevens에 대해서 암시된 것은 무엇인가?
(A) Glencore Foods에서 높은 급여를 받는다.
(B) 그의 일을 즐긴다.
(C) 유럽에서 사는 것을 선호한다.
(D) 여러 상을 받았다.

해설 Mr. Stevens가 키워드이므로 첫 번째 지문에서 그에 대한 언급이 있는 부분과 선택지를 대조하며 정답을 찾아본다. (A) Glencore Foods에서 일한다고 했을뿐 높은 급여를 받는다는 언급은 없었다. (C) 호주와 유럽에서 공부하거나 일했지만 유럽을 선호한다는 내용은 없었다. (D) 그가 하는 일이 중요한 일이고 전문적인 일이긴 하지만 상을 받았는지 알 수 없다. 자신의 직장에 대해 '꿈이 현실이 된 것 같다'라고 말하고 있으므로 정답은 (B) He enjoys his job.이다.

---

2. Mr. Stevens은 언제 요리 학교를 졸업했는가?
(A) 2년 전
(B) 6년 전
(C) 8년 전
(D) 10년 전

해설 요리 학교 졸업 시점을 묻고 있다. 기사의 세 번째 단락에서, 그는 요리 학교를 다녔고 졸업하자마자 8년간 요리사로 일했다고 했다. 그리고 2년 전에 Glencore Foods에 새로 직장을 얻었다는 말이 나오므로 졸업한 시기는 지금으로부터 10년 전이다. 따라서 정답은 (D) 10 years ago이다.

---

3. Ms. Hampton은 Mr. Stevens와 알고 지낼 때, 무엇을 했는가?
(A) 대학에서 공부하고 있었다.
(B) 맛 감별사로 일하고 있었다.
(C) 레스토랑에서 일을 하고 있었다.
(D) 요리사가 되기 위해 배우고 있었다.

해설 이메일과 관련된 문제이다. Ms. Hampton이 보낸 이메일에서, '당신(Mr. Stevens)과 일했던 기억이 있고, 당신(Mr. Stevens)이 만들었던 음식을 즐겼다'는 이야기가 나오므로, Mr. Stevens이 요리사로 일했던 레스토랑에서 함께 일을 했던 것이다. 따라서 정답은 (C) She was working at a restaurant.이다.

---

4. Ms. Hampton의 고향은 어디인가?
(A) 녹스빌에서
(B) 밀라노에서
(C) 세인트루이스에서
(D) 토론토에서

해설 두 번째 지문과 세 번째 지문을 연계해서 읽어야 답할 수 있는 문제이다. 이메일에서는 대회가 Ms. Hampton의 고향에서 열릴 것이라고 하고 있고, 공지에서는 올해의 대회가 St. Louis, Missouri에서 열린다고 하였으므로 정답은 (C) In St. Louis이다.

---

5. '음식 맛 감별사 대회'에 대해서 언급되지 않은 것은 무엇인가?
(A) 참석하는 데 드는 비용이 얼마인지
(B) 언제 시작 하는지
(C) 누가 올 것인지
(D) 어떤 행사들이 열릴 것인지

해설 Food Tasters Convention에 관한 내용은 세 번째 지문에 소개되었으므로 공지의 내용을 선택지와 대조하며 오답을 소거한다. (A)는 표 값이 1인당 100달러라고 언급되어 있으므로 탈락이다. (B)는 행사가 5월 15일에서 17일까지 열릴 것이라고 언급되어 있으므로 탈락이다. (C)는 지문 끝부분 Noted individuals가 있는 부분에서 참석할 사람들이 언급되었으므로 역시 탈락이다. 이 대회에서 어떤 행사가 열릴 것인지 구체적으로 언급된 곳이 없으므로 정답은 (D) What events will be held이다.

[6-10] 다음 광고, 양식과 이메일에 관한 문제입니다.

Donoho 경영 아카데미
45 Kensington 가, 런던, 영국

Donoho 경영 아카데미는 지난 50년 동안 사업상의 문제에 관한 세미나를 개최해 오고 있습니다. **7** 저희의 강사들은 모두 뛰어난 기업인들이거나 국내 대학들에서 존경 받는 교수들입니다. **6** 강사들은 사업세계에서 성공하기 위하여 수강생들이 알아야 하는 정보들을 그들에게 제공합니다. 저희 세미나는 인원이 60명으로 제한되어 있어서, 좌석을 보장받기 위해서는 지금 예약을 하는 것이 중요합니다. **7** 추가 정보가 필요하거나, 예약을 하시려면, 저희 웹사이트 www.donohoacademy.com를 방문하시거나 904-4557로 전화해 주시기 바랍니다.

이번 달에 개최되는 세미나는 다음과 같습니다.

소셜 미디어와 당신의 사업	미국 시장으로의 진입
8월 6일 토요일	8월 13일 일요일
오후 5:00 – 오후 7:30	오후 3:00 – 오후 5:00
Tim Caldwell	Amy Smythe
Kent 대학교	Baxter 그룹

🔟 불황기에 감축하기	회사 상장 시기
8월 19일 금요일	8월 27일 토요일
오후 7:00 – 오후 9:00	오전 11:00 – 오후 1:30
Joanna Pennyworth	Andrew Dalton
Chatham 컨설팅	Kincaid 금융

7 등록 비용

조기 등록시, 할인이 제공됩니다.

수업 당일로부터 2주 전 = 150 파운드

8 수업 당일로부터 1주 전 = 175 파운드

수업 당일 = 200 파운드

Donoho 경영 아카데미
온라인 등록 양식

이름: Claire York

이메일: cyork@steadham.com

전화 번호: 309-5683

주소: 32 Compass 가, Apartment 45B, 런던, 영국

8 수업 날짜: 8월 19일

등록 양식 제출일: 8월 12일

Donoho 경영 아카데미의 수업에 등록해 주셔서 감사합니다. 귀하께서는 이 양식을 제출하시고 2시간 내에 확인 이메일을 받으실 것입니다

수신: cyork@steadham.com

발신: customerrelations@donohoacademy.com

날짜: 8월 17일

제목: 강사 교체

Ms. York에게,

귀하께서 참여할 예정인 곧 다가오는 세미나에 대한 수업료를 지불해 주셔서 감사합니다. **9** 저는 귀하께 그 세미나의 변경 사항에 대하여 알려 드리려고 합니다. 원래 그 세미나에서 강의하기로 한 사람이 아파서 그 세미나에 참석할 수 없을 것입니다. 하지만, **10** 런던 금융 대학 교수인 Mr. Sean McManus가 Ms. Pennyworth 대신 그 과정을 가르치기로 약속했습니다. Mr. McManus는 과거에 여기서 강의를 한 적이 있으므로, 귀하께서는 귀하가 수업료를 지불한 양질의 교육을 받으실 겁니다.

그럼에도 불구하고, 우리는 귀하께서 등록을 취소하고 싶으시다면 이해합니다. 보통 저희는 수강생들이 수강 취소를 하실 때 수강료의 50퍼센트만 환불해 드리는 반면에, 이번 경우에는, 수강료 전액을 환불해드릴 것입니다. 만약 저희가 세미나 당일까지 귀하로부터 어떤 요청도 듣지 못한다면, 저희는 귀하께서 수업에 참여하실 의향이 있어서, 환불을 요청하지 않는 것으로 간주할 것입니다.

감사합니다.

Simon Palmer

Donoho 경영 아카데미

---

6. 누구를 위한 광고인가?

(A) 교육자들

(B) 대학생들

(C) 사업가들

(D) 마케팅 담당자들

해설 안내문 두 번째 줄에서 강사들은 사업 세계에서 성공하기 위하여 수강생들이 알아야 하는 정보들을 그들에게 제공한다고 하였으므로, 광고의 대상은 (C) Businesspeople 임을 알 수 있다.

---

7. 세미나들에 관하여 언급되지 않은 것은 무엇인가?

(A) 인터넷으로 방송된다.

(B) 세미나 참석 금액은 각기 다르다.

(C) 몇몇 세미나는 대학 교수들이 강의한다.

(D) 세미나 좌석들을 온라인으로 예약할 수 있다.

해설 안내문의 마지막 부분에 더 빨리 등록할 시에, 더 적게 지불한다고 언급하였고 수업일 1, 2주전의 가격이 다름을 확인할 수 있다. 따라서 (B)는 소거한다. 또한 수업은 몇몇 성공한 기업가들과, 대학교수들에 의하여 지도된다고 언급되어 있다. 또한, 정보나 예약을 하려면 웹사이트나 전화를 이용하라고 명시되어 있다 정답은 (A) They are broadcast on the Internet.이다.

---

8. Ms. York가 지불한 금액은 얼마인가?

(A) 100 파운드

(B) 150 파운드

(C) 175 파운드

(D) 200 파운드

해설 이중 지문 연계형 두 지문을 내용적으로 연계하여 해결하는 문제이다. 등록 양식에서 수업날짜는 8월 19일이고, 양식 제출 날짜가 8월 12일임을 확인할 수 있다. 안내문에서 수업 일주일 전에 등록할 시에 175파운드임을 알 수 있다. Ms. York가 일주일 전에 등록하였음을 확인할 수 있으므로 (C) 175 pounds가 정답이다.

---

9. 이메일의 목적은 무엇인가?

(A) 세미나 수업료 지불을 요청하기 위해

(B) 환불이 처리되었음을 참가자들에게 알리기 위해

(C) 변경 사항을 알리기 위해

(D) 세미나 시간이 변경되었음을 언급하기 위해

해설 이메일의 첫 번째 단락 두 번째 줄에서 수업의 변화에 대하여 알려준다고 하였으므로 (C) To notify a participant about a change가 정답이다.

---

10. Mr. McManus가 강의할 세미나는?

(A) 회사 상장 시기

(B) 미국 시장으로의 진입

(C) 불황기에 감축하기

(D) 소셜 미디어와 당신의 사업

해설 이중 지문 연계형 두 지문을 내용적으로 연계하여 해결하는 문제이다. 이메일의 첫 번째 단락 세 번째 줄에서 Sean McManus가 Pennyworth 대신 강의를 한다고 명시되어 있고 광고에서 원

래 Pennyworth가 강의하려고 한 과목은 (C) Downsizing in Troubling Times임을 확인할 수 있다.

REVIEW TEST
본서 p.336

1. (D)	2. (D)	3. (A)	4.(D)	5. (C)
6. (B)	7. (B)	8. (C)	9. (A)	10. (D)
11. (D)	12. (D)	13. (A)	14. (D)	15. (C)
16. (D)	17. (A)	18. (B)	19. (B)	20. (C)
21. (A)	22. (C)	23. (D)	24. (B)	25. (A)
26. (D)	27. (B)	28. (D)	29. (C)	30. (D)
31. (A)	32. (C)	33. (A)	34. (D)	35. (C)
36. (A)	37. (C)	38. (D)	39. (A)	40. (B)
41. (D)	42. (B)	43. (C)	44. (B)	45. (C)
46. (B)	47. (C)	48. (D)	49. (C)	50. (A)
51. (A)	52. (C)	53. (D)	54. (C)	

[1-2] 다음 구인 광고에 관한 문제입니다.

1 사진 찍기를 좋아하세요?
2 Valley Monster 팀에 당신을 위한 자리가 있습니다.

지원 가능 직책:
일정 편성 비서, **1** 졸업 앨범 사진 보조, 인물 사진 편집
정규직 혹은 파트타임 직원 채용

2 지원서는 이 곳으로 제출하세요: www.valleymonster.co.ca/hiring
대면 면접 필수. 경력 무관!

어휘 snap v. 사진 찍다 | aide n. 조수 | yearbook n. 졸업 앨범 | assistant n. 조수 | portrait n. 인물 사진 | application n. 지원서 | in-person adj. 직접의

---

1. Valley Monter은 어떠한 유형의 업체이겠는가?
(A) 가전제품 제조업체
(B) 식료품 가게
(C) 스포츠 용품점
(D) 사진 스튜디오

해설 지문의 첫 문구가 '사진 찍기를 좋아하세요?'이며, 졸업 앨범 사진 보조, 인물 사진 편집 등의 내용을 토대로 Valley Monster가 사진관임을 알 수 있으므로 정답은 (D) A photography studio이다.

---

2. 입사 지원자에게 무엇을 하도록 요구하는가?
(A) 근무 가능 시간표를 이메일로 보낸다
(B) 견본 문서를 편집한다
(C) 자격증을 제출한다
(D) Valley Monster 웹사이트에 접속한다

해설 광고 하단부에 지원서를 www.valleymonster.co.ca/hiring으로 보내라고 했으므로 정답은 (D) Go to Valley Monster's Web site이다.

[3-4] 다음 이메일에 관한 문제입니다.

수신: e.petrov@fastmessage.ru
발신: martin@briar.co.uk
날짜: 11월 4일
제목: 귀하의 Briar 체류
첨부: bb_쿠폰

Mr. Petrov님,

3 이곳 Briar 비즈니스 호텔에서 고객님께서 경험하신 것에 대해 시간을 내어 온라인 리뷰를 남겨주셔서 감사 드립니다. 저희의 객실 편의시설과 피트니스 센터, 레스토랑이 고객님의 기대를 만족시켰다니 기쁩니다. **4** 그러나, 저희 컨퍼런스룸 때문에 문제를 겪으셨다는 것을 알게 되어 안타깝습니다. 몇 대의 전자 장비가 제대로 기능하지 않았다고 언급하셨습니다. 주말 동안 새로운 장비를 구매하여 설치했습니다. 저희의 컴퓨터 시스템 역시 업데이트되었습니다.

감사를 표하기 위해 전국에 있는 저희 지점 어느 곳에서나 이용 가능한 75 파운드 쿠폰을 동봉했습니다. 이 쿠폰은 6개월 동안 이용 가능합니다. 저희가 최고급 수준의 서비스를 제공할 수 있도록 도움을 주신 고객님의 조언에 다시 한번 감사 드리고 싶습니다.

진심으로,

Chris Martin

어휘 appreciate v. 감사하다 | review v. 검토, 리뷰 | amenity n. 편의 시설 | expectation n. 예상, 기대 | disappointing adj. 실망스러운 | issue n. 문제 | mention v. 언급하다 | electronic device 전자기기 | function v. 기능하다 | properly adv. 제대로 | purchase v. 구매하다 | install v. 설치하다 | include v. 포함하다 | nationwide adv. 전국적으로 | input n. (시간/지식 등의) 조언, 투입 | standard n. 기준

---

3. Mr. Martin은 왜 이메일을 썼는가?
(A) 고객의 코멘트에 답변하기 위해
(B) 새로운 서비스를 소개하기 위해
(C) 여행 준비를 주선하기 위해
(D) 취소에 대한 환불을 요청하기 위해

해설 첫 번째 단락에서 고객인 Mr. Petrov에게 Briar 호텔에서 경험했던 것들에 대한 온라인 리뷰를 남겨줘서 고맙다는 인사로 시작하여, 좋았던 점과 안 좋았던 점을 차례로 지적하며, 지문이 전개되고 있으므로 정답은 (A) To reply to some customer comments이다. an online review regarding your experience here가 some customer comments로 paraphrasing되었다.

---

4. 최근에 무엇이 Briar 비즈니스 호텔에서 개선되었는가?
(A) 피트니스 센터
(B) 레스토랑 메뉴
(C) 예약 시스템
(D) 회의실

해설 첫 번째 단락에서 고객이 컨퍼런스실 때문에 문제를 겪은 사실을 알게 되어 안타깝다며, 제대로 작동하지 않은 전자 장비를 새 것으로 구매하여 설치했다고 했으므로 정답은 (D) A meeting room이다. a conference room이 a meeting room으로 paraphrasing되었다.

[5-6] 다음 문자 메시지에 관한 문제입니다.

Terri Fantano

⑤ 귀하의 사무실 수리 계획을 업데이트해드리려고 합니다. 견목 바닥재에 관한 귀하의 요청을 고려했습니다. 또한 새 중역 회의실에 들어갈, 귀하의 예산에 맞으면서도 충분히 큰 판유리를 제공해줄 수 있는 지역 공급회사를 찾았습니다. (15:46)

Hans Yamato

좋은 소식이네요. ⑥ 이 계획에 따라 중역 회의실과 마케팅 팀의 사무실 둘 다 12월 1일까지 끝내실 수 있으신가요? (15:49)

Terri Fantano

⑥ 마케팅 사무실은 12월 3일에 완성될 겁니다. (15:50)

Hans Yamato

⑥ 안타깝게도 마케팅 팀이 그 전에 우리 사무실에 다시 돌아와야 해요. (15:54)

Terri Fantano

⑥ 알겠습니다. 일정을 검토해보겠습니다. (15:55)

어휘 renovation n. 개조, 수리 | take into account ~을 고려하다 | request n. 요청 | hardwood n. 견목 | flooring n. 바닥재 | local adj. 지역의 | supplier n. 공급 업체 | plate glass 판유리 | panel n. 판 | boardroom n. 중역 회의실 | budget n. 예산 | complete v. 끝내다, 완성하다 | unfortunately adv. 안타깝게도 | review v. 검토하다

5. Ms. Fantano는 어떤 업계에서 일하겠는가?

(A) 기술
(B) 마케팅
(C) 건설
(D) 금융

해설 15:46분, Ms. Fantano의 메시지에서 사무실 수리 계획을 업데이트하려고 한다면서, 견목 바닥재에 관한 요청을 고려했고, 예산에 맞는 선에서 충분히 큰 판유리를 제공해 줄 수 있는 공급 업체를 찾았다는 내용을 토대로 Ms. Fantano가 건설업에 종사하는 사람임을 알 수 있으므로 정답은 (C) Construction이다.

6. 15시 55분에 Ms. Fantano가 '알겠습니다'라고 쓴 것은 무슨 의미이겠는가?

(A) 가격을 낮출 것이다.
(B) 문제를 해결해보려 할 것이다.
(C) 다른 자재를 사용할 수 있다.
(D) 추가 직원을 고용할 수 있다.

해설 15:49분 ~ 15:54분 대화에서, Mr. Yamato가 중역 회의실과 마케팅 팀의 사무실 두 개 모두를 12월 1일까지 끝낼 수 있냐고 물었고, Ms. Fantano가 마케팅 팀 사무실은 12월 3일에 완성될 거라고 하자, Mr. Yamato가 마케팅 팀이 그 전에 돌아와야 한다고 한 말에 대해 Ms. Fantano가 '알겠다(I understand)'고 하면서 일정을 다시 확인하겠다고 한 것이므로 정답은 (B) She will try to resolve an issue.이다.

[7-8] 다음 설명서에 관한 문제입니다.

Residia.net—온라인 부동산

계정 접근

⑦ 패스워드를 설정하시려면, 귀하의 이메일 주소와 이용자 ID를 아래 있는 칸들에 입력하십시오. 그 뒤 "임시 PIN번호 전송" 탭을 클릭하십시오. 이메일이 귀하에게 자동으로 보내질 것입니다. 그 이메일에 있는 링크를 클릭하시면 인증 페이지로 넘어갑니다. 거기서 ⑧ 귀하의 계정 프로필에 접속하시려면, 이메일로 제공된 개인 신분 확인 번호를 입력하십시오. "패스워드 설정 전송" 부분에서 제공하는 단계를 따라 절차를 마무리하십시오.

이메일: daniel.kem@kemtech.com
사용자명: danielk96

임시 PIN 번호 전송

어휘 enter v. 입력하다 | field n. (데이터 저장 지정 영역) 필드 | temporary adj. 임시적인 | automatically adv. 자동으로 | provide v. 제공하다 | redirect v. 다시 보내다, 전송하다 | verification n. 조회, 확인 | personal identification 개인 식별 | account profile 계정 프로필 | complete v. 끝내다, 완성하다 | process n. 절차

7. 이 설명서는 누구를 위한 것이겠는가?

(A) 새 컴퓨터를 설치하는 사람
(B) 로그인 정보를 아직 만들지 않은 사람
(C) 소프트웨어 문제를 겪고 있는 사람
(D) 비용 청구 정보를 변경하고 싶어 하는 사람

해설 첫 번째 줄에서 패스워드를 설정하려면, 이메일 주소와 이용자 ID를 입력하라고 했으므로 설명서의 대상은 아직 로그인 정보를 만들지 않은 사람이다. 따라서 정답은 (B) Someone who has not created their log-in details이다.

8. 읽는 사람이 하라고 지시 받은 것은 무엇인가?

(A) 보안 질문에 답변한다
(B) 고객 지원센터에 전화한다
(C) 특정 번호를 입력한다
(D) 확인 이메일을 출력한다

해설 세 번째 줄에서 계정 프로필에 접속하려면, 이메일로 제공된 개인 신분 확인 번호를 입력하라고 했으므로 정답은 (C) Enter a specific number이다. type in the personal identification number가 Enter a specific number로 paraphrasing되었다.

PART 7 REVIEW TEST

[9-11] 다음 이메일에 관한 문제입니다.

수신: d.toth@worldemp.co.uk
발신: a.munoz@worldemp.co.uk
날짜: 4월 9일
제목: 소식지 프로필 정보

Mr. Toth님,

9 귀하를 이곳 World Emporium의 회계팀으로 모시게 되어 기쁩니다.

이 이메일은 저희 회사의 월간 소식지에 발행될 당신의 직원 프로필에 관한 것입니다. World Emporium의 소식지는 우리 회사의 모든 파트너들에게 보내집니다. 현재 저희는 짧은 약력과 회사에서의 귀하의 직무, 그리고 당신의 연락처를 갖고 있습니다. **10** 이제 당신의 기재사항 옆에 보여질 사진만 있으면 됩니다. 사용하고 싶은 사진이 있으신가요(적어도 1200x1600 픽셀이 되어야 합니다), 아니면 **11** 디자인팀 사람과 일정을 잡아서 귀하의 사무실에 들르도록 할까요? 누군가가 오늘이나 내일 들을 수 있습니다.

진심으로,

Alicia Munoz
인사팀
World Emporium

어휘 newsletter *n.* 소식지, 회보 | accounting team 회계팀 | emporium *n.* 큰 상점 | publish *v.* 발행하다, 출판하다 | currently *adv.* 현재 | biography *n.* 전기 | role *n.* 역할 | contact information 연락처 | appear *v.* 나타나다, 보이다 | entry *n.* 기재사항, 항목

9. Mr. Toth에 관하여 알 수 있는 것은 무엇인가?
   (A) World Emporium의 신입 직원이다.
   (B) 회사 소식지를 제작하고 있다.
   (C) 자신의 직원 프로필에서 오류를 발견했다.
   (D) 최근 급여 인상을 받았다.

해설 첫 번째 단락에서 Mr. Toth에게 World Emporium의 회계팀으로 모시게 되어 기쁘다는 말을 토대로 Mr. Toth가 이 회사의 신입 직원임을 알 수 있으므로 정답은 (A) He is a new employee at World Emporium.이다.

10. Ms. Munoz는 Mr. Toth에게 무엇을 제공해달라고 요청하는가?
    (A) 이력서
    (B) 자세한 연락처
    (C) 직위
    (D) 사진

해설 두 번째 단락에서 Mr. Toth가 기재한 내용들 옆에 보여질 사진만 있으면 된다고 했으므로 정답은 (D) An image이다. a photograph가 an image로 paraphrasing되었다.

11. 이메일의 두 번째 단락, 열 번째 줄의 구 "일정을 잡다"와 의미상 가장 가까운 것은
    (A) 기록하다
    (B) 확인하다
    (C) 들어맞다
    (D) 계획하다

해설 해당 문장에서 schedule은 '일정을 잡다'라는 의미로 쓰였으므로 보기 중 이를 대신할 수 있는 것은 '계획하다'를 뜻하는 (D) plan이다.

[12-14] 다음 공지에 관한 문제입니다.

공지

Boulder 예술 극장 관람객 여러분께 알립니다.

저희 극장이 10월 1일부터 12일까지 진행되는 Colorado 독립영화 축제의 주최 극장으로 선정되었습니다. **13** Mario Duke와 Anna Scarius, Joanne Kim, Rhody Scanlan 같은 저명한 영화감독들에 의한 단편 영화와 다큐멘터리, 애니메이션 작품들을 선보일 이 흥미진진한 행사에 여러분을 초대하오니 다시 방문해주시기 바랍니다. **14** 매우 흥미로운 작품은 'Atlanta 영화 저널'의 간판 비평가 Stephen Vance가 '영화 속 신선한 공기의 숨결'이라고 묘사한 신인 연출가 Edward Jimenez의 신나는 데뷔작입니다. **12** 참가 연출자들과 영화들에 관한 추가 정보는 www.bouldertheater.org에서 보실 수 있으며 저희의 모바일 앱을 다운로드 하시면 상영작과 특별 행사에 관한 최신 정보를 받아 보실 수 있습니다.

어휘 fine art *n.* (순수) 예술 | host *n.* 개최지 | run *v.* (일정 기간 동안) 계속되다 | feature *v.* (출연자, 전시물 등으로) 포함하다 | animated *adj.* 만화영화로 된 | renowned *adj.* 저명한 | filmmakers *n.* 영화감독 | of note 중요한, 아주 흥미로운 | first-time *adj.* 처음으로 해보는 | director *n.* 감독, 연출자 | thrilling *adj.* 아주 신나는 | acclaimed *adj.* 호평을 받는 | critic *n.* 비평가 | call *v.* ~을 라고 묘사하다 | up-to-date *adj.* (정보가) 최신의 | hold *v.* 개최하다, 주최하다 | undergo *v.* (어떤 일을) 겪다

12. 극장에 관하여 알 수 있는 것은 무엇인가?
    (A) 많은 상을 받았다.
    (B) 매년 영화 축제를 개최한다.
    (C) 10월부터 공사를 한다.
    (D) 온라인으로 영화 축제를 광고하고 있다.

해설 참가 연출자들과 영화들에 관한 추가 정보는 www.bouldertheater.org에서 볼 수 있으며 모바일 앱을 다운로드 하면 상영작과 특별 행사에 관한 최신 정보를 받아 볼 수 있다고 했으므로 정답은 (D) It is advertising a film festival online.이다.

13. Ms. Scanlan은 누구인가?
    (A) 영화 감독
    (B) 영화 평론가
    (C) 여배우
    (D) 극장 소유주

해설　Mario Duke와 Anna Scarius, Joanne Kim, Rhody Scanlan 과 같은 저명한 영화 감독들에 의한 단편 영화와 다큐멘터리, 애니 메이션 작품들을 선보일 행사에 초대한다고 했으므로 정답은 (A) A filmmaker이다.

14. 누가 Mr. Vance로부터 칭찬 받았는가?
　(A) Mr. Duke
　(B) Ms. Scarius
　(C) Ms. Kim
　(D) Mr. Jimenez

해설　〈Atlanta 영화 저널〉의 간판 비평가 Stephen Vance가 '영화 속 신 선한 공기의 숨결'이라고 묘사한 신인 연출가 Edward Jimenez의 신나는 데뷔작이라고 말한 내용을 토대로 정답은 (D) Mr. Jimenez 이다. called "a breath of fresh air in cinema."가 praised로 paraphrasing되었다.

[15-18] 다음 이메일에 관한 문제입니다.

발신: esmith@abcc.org
수신: cnorton@kitchenjoy.co.nz
제목: 등록과 활동
날짜: 4월 20일

Ms. Norton께,

연례 Allison Bay 요리 학회(ABCC)의 등록과 대금 지불이 처리되 었음을 알려드립니다. 다시 뵙는 날을 기대합니다.

18 그런데 추가 정보 한 가지가 필요합니다. **15** 양식에서 식전 활 동 선택란을 공란으로 남겨주셨더군요. 엔터테인먼트 진행자에게 알 려주어서 참가자들에게 나눠줄 일정표를 마무리 짓게 하기 위해 이 정보가 필요합니다. 올해에는 농산물 직거래 장터와 노점 음식 투어 외에도 참가자들에게 근처 유기농장을 방문할 기회를 제공하게 되 었음을 기쁘게 여깁니다. 이러한 독특한 기회들에 관한 추가 정보는 온라인으로 이용하실 수 있습니다. **16** 되도록 빠른 시일 내에 답장 을 주셔서 어느 투어에 참여하고 싶으신지 알려주시기 바랍니다.

17 또한 이 활동은 지불하신 참가비에 포함되어 있음을 유의하시 기 바랍니다. 어떠한 추가 요금 지불도 요구하지 않습니다.

진심을 담아,

Evan Smith
ABCC

어휘　process v. 처리하다 ǀ culinary adj. 요리의 ǀ conference n. 학회, 회의 ǀ blank adj. (글자가 없는) 빈 ǀ coordinator n. 진행자 ǀ itinerary n. 일정표 ǀ apart from prep. ~ 외에도 ǀ farmers' market (농산물) 생산자 직거래 장터 ǀ organic adj. 유기농의 ǀ note v. 주목하다, 주의 하다 ǀ cover v. 포함시키다

15. Mr. Smith는 누구이겠는가?
　(A) 연예 기자
　(B) 지역 농부
　(C) 학회 행사 담당자
　(D) 노점상인

해설　첫 번째 단락에서 Allison Bay 요리 학회 등록과 납부가 처리되었다 고 알려주었으며, 두 번째 단락에서 Ms. Norton에게 식전 활동 선택 란을 공란으로 남겨두었다면서, 참가자들에게 나눠줄 일정표를 마무리 짓 게 하기 위해 이 정보가 필요하다고 하여 등록 정보를 추가 요청한 것 으로 미루어 정답은 (C) A conference organizer이다.

---

16. Ms. Norton은 무엇을 하도록 요구 받는가?
　(A) 대금을 지불한다
　(B) 예약을 변경한다
　(C) 양식을 내려 받는다
　(D) 관광 옵션을 선택한다

해설　두 번째 단락 끝에서 되도록 빠른 시일 내에 답장을 보내어 어느 투어 에 참여하고 싶은지 알려달라고 했으므로 정답은 (D) Select a tour option이다. let me know which tour you would like to join이 Select a tour option으로 paraphrasing되었다.

---

17. 올해 행사를 위한 Ms. Norton의 참가비에 관하여 알 수 있는 것은?
　(A) 동일하게 유지될 것이다.
　(B) 지불기한이 지났다.
　(C) 환급될 것이다.
　(D) 저렴하다.

해설　세 번째 단락에서 해당 활동들이 지불한 참가비에 포함되어 있으니 추가 요금 납부가 필요 없다고 했으므로 정답은 (A) It will stay the same.이다.

---

18. [1], [2], [3], [4]로 표시된 곳 중에서 다음 문장이 들어가기에 가장 적절 한 곳은 어디인가?

　"그런데 추가 정보 한 가지가 필요합니다."

　(A) [1]
　(B) [2]
　(C) [3]
　(D) [4]

해설　두 번째 단락, 첫 번째 문장에서 Ms. Norton에게 식전 활동 선택란을 공란으로 남겨두었다고 하여, 주어진 문장이 이 앞에 위치하는 것이 문맥상 자연스러우므로 정답은 (B) [2]이다.

[19-22] 다음 온라인 대화 토론에 관한 문제입니다.

Neil Ashton [오전 10:52]
안녕, Carley. **19 20** Mill Avenue 디자인이 프로그램 제작 다 끝냈나요?

Carley Mendoza [오전 10:54]
오늘 오전에 Alyin으로부터 이메일을 받았는데요. **19 20** 안타깝지만 일정보다 늦어지고 있어서 화요일에 가져다 줄 수 없다고 하네요. 목요일 오전에 준비될 거라고 했어요.

Neil Ashton [오전 10:55]
그 시간이면 우리 자원봉사자들이 그것들을 참가자 패키지에 넣을 충분한 시간이 되나요?

Maja Anderson [오전 10:56]
후원자들도 한 부씩 받고 싶어 하세요. 그리고 저는 디지털 버전으로 연결되는 링크를 금요일까지 우리 웹사이트에 게시하고 싶고요.

Carley Mendoza [오전 10:57]
21 걱정하실 것 없어요. **21** 자료를 목요일 오후 1시까지 받기만 하면 우리가 계획한 일정대로 할 수 있어요. Maja, 제가 파일을 받는 대로 웹사이트 개발업자에게 전달할게요.

Neil Ashton [오전 10:59]
좋아요! Alyin으로부터 추가적으로 들어오는 세부사항이 있으면 바로 알려주세요. 그런데 기조연설은 누가 할 건지 결정했나요?

Carley Mendoza [오전 11:01]
네. **22** Midland 대학교의 Mr. Codrescu에게 곧 전화해서 혹시 특별한 장비가 필요한지 알아볼 거예요. 지난 주 월요일에는 대회의장이 우리의 800명의 참가자들에게 적절하다는 걸 확인했어요.

Maja Anderson [오전 11:02]
그거 잘 됐네요. 고마워요, Carley. 올해 모임은 반드시 성공적일 거예요.

어휘　**behind schedule** 일정보다 늦은 | **be anxious to-V** ~ 하기를 열망하다, 간절히 바라다 | **post** *v.* 게시하다 | **timeline** *n.* 일정 | **forward** *v.* 전달하다 | **up-to-date** *adj.* 최신 정보를 알고 있는 | **further** *adj.* 더 이상의 | **keynote address** 기조연설 | **in a moment** 곧, 바로 | **adequate** *adj.* 적절한 | **gathering** *n.* 모임 | **arrange** *v.* 마련하다 | **go over** *v.* 검토하다 | **convention** *n.* 집회 | **venue** *n.* 장소 | **keep to** 따르다, 지키다

---

19. 토론의 목적은 무엇인가?
(A) 회사 후원자들과의 회의를 마련하기 위해
(B) 행사 세부사항을 검토하기 위해
(C) 장비 주문에 관하여 확인하기 위해
(D) 집회 장소를 확인하기 위해

해설　Mr. Ashton이 오전 10시 52분에 Mill Avenue 디자인이 프로그램 제작을 다 끝냈는지 물어본 내용과 10시 59분에 기조 연설자는 누구로 결정했는지에 대한 질문, 그리고 11시 1분에 Ms. Mendoza가 지난주 월요일에 대회의장의 수용 여부를 확인했다는 내용 등을 토대로 대화 참가자들이 행사에 관한 세부 사항들을 논의하는 중임을 알 수 있으므로 정답은 (B) To go over details of an event이다.

20. 논의에 따르면, 프로그램은 언제 도착할 것인가?
(A) 화요일
(B) 수요일
(C) 목요일
(D) 금요일

해설　오전 10시 52분 ~ 10시 54분 대화에서, Mr. Ashton이 Ms. Mendoza에게 프로그램 제작이 다 끝났는지에 대한 질문에, Ms. Mendoza가 일정보다 늦어지고 있어서 목요일 오전에 준비될 거라고 하면서, 자료를 오후 1시까지 받기만 하면 계획한 일정대로 할 수 있다고 했으므로 정답은 (C) On Thursday이다.

---

21. 오전 10시 57분에 Ms. Mendoza가 "걱정하실 것 없어요."라고 쓴 것은 무슨 의미이겠는가?
(A) 일정을 지킬 수 있다.
(B) 프로그램을 갱신할 수 있다.
(C) 후원자들에게 이메일을 보낼 수 있다.
(D) 자원봉사자들을 찾을 수 있다.

해설　오전 10시 52분 ~ 10시 54분 대화에서, Ms. Mendoza가 프로그램 제작 일정이 늦어지고 있어서 목요일 오전에 준비될 거라고 하자, Mr. Ashton과 Ms. Anderson의 우려 섞인 목소리에 Ms. Mendoza가 'Not to worry (걱정하실 것 없어요)'라면서 자료를 목요일 오후 1시까지만 받으면 계획한 일정대로 할 수 있다고 말한 것이므로 정답은 (A) She can keep to a schedule.이다.

---

22. Ms. Mendoza는 다음에 무엇을 하겠는가?
(A) 웹사이트를 수정한다.
(B) 회의장을 예약한다.
(C) 교육기관에 연락한다.
(D) Mill Avenue Designs에 전화한다.

해설　오전 11시 1분 메시지에서, Ms. Mendoza가 Midland 대학교의 Mr. Codrescu에게 곧 전화하겠다고 했으므로 정답은 (C) Contact an educational institution이다. College가 educational institution으로 paraphrasing되었다.

[23-25] 다음 기사에 관한 문제입니다.

C-sharp 뉴스
Glenn Wong, 전속 작가

Rastbury (6월 4일) – Rastbury의 유명 재즈 행사장인 C-sharp는 거의 90년 동안 지역 사회에 기여해 왔다. **25** 이곳은 2년 전 팔려고 내놓았으나 최근까지 시장에 남아 있었다. **23** 지난 화요일 이 행사장은 이곳에서 몇 블록 떨어지지 않은 곳에서 태어났던 Jim Gould에게 120만 달러에 공식적으로 팔렸다.

어제 오후 Mr. Gould는 매입에 대해 이야기하기 위해 이 역사적인 건물로 언론 사람들을 초청했다.

23 24 "저는 항상 이 행사장의 미학적 특징을 동경했죠," 그가 말했다. "제가 이 건물의 정신을 유지할 것이라는 사실은 말할 필요도 없습니다." Mr. Gould는 Rastbury의 유명한 식당인 Touchdown Pub 또한 소유하고 있다. 그의 발언은 그가 C-sharp를 제 2의 Touchdown Pub으로 개조할 것이라는 지역 사회의 루머에 대한 반응이었다. **25** 이 건물을 팔려고 내놓았을 때, 이러한 우려를 다루기 위해 프렌즈 오브 C-sharp (FCS)가 설립되었다.

"FCS는 이 건물의 음악적 전통을 확실히 지속할 수 있도록 이 건물을 매입하고 싶었습니다." FCS의 대변인 Carolyn Brown이 Mr. Gould의 말에 답했다. "Mr. Gould가 하신 말을 지키셨으면 하고 바랍니다. C-sharp의 계속되는 성공을 위해 그분과 함께 일하겠습니다."

23 Mr. Gould는 철저한 검사 뒤 모두의 안전을 위해 건물의 일부를 보수하겠다고 밝혔다.

어휘 nearly *adv.* 거의 | popular *adj.* 인기가 많은 | venue *n.* 장소, 행사장 | serve *v.* 도움이 되다, 기여하다 | local *adj.* 지역의 | recently *adv.* 최근 | officially *adv.* 공식적으로 | purchase *v.* 구매하다 | press *n.* 언론 | historic *adj.* 역사적으로 중요한 | admire *v.* 칭찬하다, 존경하다 | aesthetic *n.* 미학적 특징 | It goes without saying that ~는 말할 필요도 없다 | spirit *n.* 정신, 영혼 | alive *adj.* 살아 있는, 생기 넘치는 | own *v.* 소유하다 | diner *n.* 식사하는 사람, 손님 | reaction *n.* 반응 | rumor *n.* 루머, 소문 | consider *v.* 고려하다 | convert *v.* 전환하다, 개조하다 | founded *adj.* 설립된 | address *v.* 다루다 | concern *n.* 우려, 걱정 | ensure *v.* 반드시 ~하게 하다 | spokesperson *n.* 대변인 | respond to ~에 응하다, 대응하다 | statement *n.* 성명, 진술 | continuing *adj.* 계속되는 | success *n.* 성공 | renovate *v.* 보수하다, 개조하다 | safety *n.* 안전 | thorough *adj.* 빈틈없는, 철저한 | inspection *n.* 검사

23. 기사는 무엇에 관한 것인가?
(A) 어떤 공연의 최근 리뷰
(B) 한 임원의 은퇴
(C) 한 사업체의 새 광고
(D) 한 건물의 미래

해설 첫 번째 단락에서 어떤 행사장이 이곳 출신인 Jim Gould에게 공식적으로 팔렸다는 내용을 시작으로, 세 번째 단락의 Jim Gould의 인터뷰에서 그가 이 행사장의 미학적 특징을 동경했다고 하면서, 이 건물의 정신을 계속 유지하겠다고 한 것과, 마지막 단락에서 Mr. Gould가 철저한 검사 뒤에 안전을 위해 건물 일부를 보수하겠다고 한 내용 등을 토대로 향후 건물에 관한 계획을 다룬 기사임을 알 수 있으므로 정답은 (D) A building's future이다.

24. Mr. Gould에 관하여 알 수 있는 것은 무엇인가?
(A) Rastbury에서 인기가 많다.
(B) 어떤 장소를 보존할 것이다.
(C) 큰 레스토랑 체인을 운영한다.
(D) FCS가 C-sharp를 검사하게 할 것이다.

해설 세 번째 단락의 Jim Gould의 인터뷰에서 그가 이 행사장의 미학적 특징을 동경했다고 하면서, 이 건물의 정신을 계속 유지하겠다고 말했으므로 정답은 (B) He will preserve a venue.이다.

25. FCS에 관하여 알 수 있는 것은 무엇인가?
(A) 2년 전 만들어졌다.
(B) Rastbury에서 콘서트를 조직하는 일을 맡고 있다.
(C) Rastbury에서 몇 개의 부동산을 매입할 것이다.
(D) 여전히 Mr. Gould의 계획에 동의하지 않는다.

해설 첫 번째 단락에서 2년 전에 해당 건물을 팔려고 내놓았으나 최근까지 시장에 남아 있었다고 말한 내용과 세 번째 단락에서 이 건물을 팔려고 내놓았을 때, 이러한 우려들을 해결하기 위해 FCS가 설립되었다고 한 내용을 토대로 FCS가 2년 전에 설립되었음을 알 수 있으므로 정답은 (A) It was formed two years ago.이다. found가 form으로 paraphrasing되었다.

[26-29] 다음 광고에 관한 문제입니다.

Arc 센터

상업과 주거의 다목적을 위해 다시 새롭게 디자인된 Arc 센터는 기업과 개인 임차인 모두의 필요를 충족시킵니다. **26** 전에는 EMP 스튜디오가 전부 사용하던 이 건물의 특실과 작업 공간은, 홍콩의 빅토리아 항구의 숨이 멎을 듯 아름다운 경관을 보여주는 호화로운 주거공간으로 개조되었습니다. 최신 스마트 홈 기술이 완벽히 탑재된 각 아파트는 에너지 절약과 인터넷 사용의 편리함에 있어 최신 기술을 보유하고 있습니다. 그러나 이 최첨단 편의 시설은 주거공간에만 한정된 것이 아닙니다.

27 특별 서비스로는 거주자들이 예약할 수 있거나, 건물에 사무실을 둔 회사들이 대여할 수 있는 화상 회의실을 포함합니다. 친환경 에너지에 대한 센터의 헌신 일부는 옥상에서 볼 수 있는데, 이곳에는 무성한 화초들 사이에 태양 전지판이 설치된 그늘막 벤치가 놓여 있습니다. **29** 여름의 열기에서 탈출해 이웃들과 교류하기에 완벽한 장소입니다. 또한 센터 바로 아래쪽 거리에 있는 피트니스 센터에서는 신규 가입하는 세입자들을 환영합니다. **28** Arc 센터 바로 옆에는 Arc 몰이 있으며, 이곳에는 매장과 레스토랑, 대형 오락실이 있어 가족과 직원들에게 모두 인기 만점입니다. 걸어갈 수 있는 거리에는 이 도시에서 가장 좋은 학교 두 곳이 있습니다.

Arc 센터는 홍콩 도시 경관의 미래입니다. 저희 웹사이트 www.thearc.com.hk를 방문하셔서 거주자가 되는 것에 대해 알아보십시오.

어휘 redesign *v.* 다시 디자인하다 | mixed-use *adj.* 다목적 이용의 | commercial *adj.* 상업의 | residential *adj.* 주거의 | purpose *n.* 목적 | cater to ~를 충족시키다 | tenant *n.* 세입자 | previously *adv.* 이전에, 미리 | occupy *v.* 사용하다, 거주하다 | executive suite 임원실 | renovate *v.* 개조하다 | luxurious *adj.* 호화로운 | living quarter 거처 | breathtaking *adj.* 숨이 막히는 | scene *n.* 경치 | equipped *adj.* 장비가 갖춰진 | advanced *adj.* 진보한, 최첨단의 | latest *adj.* 최신의 | energy-saving *adj.* 에너지 절약의 | comfort *n.* 안락, 편안 | convenience *n.* 편의, 편리 | residence *n.* 주택, 거주지 | feature *v.* 특별히 포함하

다, 특징으로 삼다 I reserve *v.* 예약하다, 예매하다 I rent *v.* 대여하다 I resident *n.* 주민 I commitment *n.* (돈, 시간, 인력의) 투입 I green energy 친환경 에너지 I roof *n.* 옥상 I solar panel 태양 전지판 I shade *n.* 햇빛 가리개 I lush *adj.* 무성한, 우거진 I greenery *n.* 화초, 녹색 나뭇잎 I popular *adj.* 인기가 많은 I distance *n.* 거리 I urban landscape 도시 경관

---

26. 광고에서 첫 번째 단락, 네 번째 줄의 단어 "경관"과 의미상 가장 가까운 것은

(A) 행동

(B) 배치

(C) 설명

(D) 경관

해설 해당 문장에서 display는 '경관'이라는 의미로 쓰였으므로 보기 중 이와 같은 의미를 갖는 (D) view가 정답이다.

- -

27. Arc 센터는 입주자들에게 무엇을 제공하는가?

(A) 피트니스 클럽

(B) 회의를 할 장소

(C) 널찍한 주차장

(D) 아이들을 위한 놀이터

해설 두 번째 단락에서 특별 서비스로 거주자들이 예약할 수 있거나 건물에 사무실을 둔 회사들이 대여할 수 있는 화상 회의실이 포함되어 있다고 했으므로 정답은 (B) Places to hold meetings이다. residents가 occupants로 paraphrasing되었다.

- -

28. Arc 센터에 관하여 언급된 것은 무엇인가?

(A) 쇼핑 구역 근처에 자리하고 있다.

(B) EMP 스튜디오가 운영한다.

(C) 대중 교통 이용을 제공한다.

(D) 최근 지하층을 개조했다.

해설 두 번째 단락에서 Arc 센터 바로 옆에 Arc 몰이 있고, 이곳에 매장과 레스토랑, 대형 오락실이 있어 가족과 직원들에게 인기가 많다고 했으므로 정답은 (A) It is located near a shopping area.이다.

- -

29. [1], [2], [3], [4]로 표시된 곳 중에서 다음 문장이 들어가기에 가장 적절한 곳은 어디인가?

"여름의 열기에서 탈출해 이웃들과 교류하기에 완벽한 장소입니다."

(A) [1]

(B) [2]

(C) [3]

(D) [4]

해설 두 번째 단락에서 친환경 에너지에 대한 센터의 헌신 일부를 옥상에서 볼 수 있다고 하면서, 이곳의 무성한 화초들 사이에 태양 전지판이 설치된 그늘막 벤치가 놓여 있다고 하여 주어진 문장이 이어지기에 자연스러우므로 정답은 (C) [3]이다.

[30-34] 다음 회람과 일정표에 관한 문제입니다.

수신: Sharper Carrot 디자인 직원들

발신: Anish Freeholm, 총무부

제목: 12월 일정

날짜: 11월 10일

첨부 파일: 일정표

이미 아시다시피 12월의 첫 2주에는 약간의 어려움이 있을 것입니다. **30** 인부들이 바닥재를 다시 깔고, 전기 배선 공사를 다시 하고, 벽에 페인트칠을 할 수 있게 해주기 위해 일부 부서들이 일정 기간 동안 사무실을 일시적으로 비워야 합니다. **31 33** 해당 팀원들은 사무실 내 소지품을 전날 오후 4시 전에 상자에 넣어야 합니다. (첨부한 일정표를 참조하세요.) 현장 물류 직원들이 각 층에서 한 번에 두 개씩 방이나 사무실을 비울 겁니다. 월요일에 작업이 예정되어 있는 사무실들은 주말 전 11월 30일에 준비하셔야 한다는 점 유의하시기 바랍니다.

31 포장재와 상자는 지급될 것입니다. 나중에 맞는 자리에 되돌려 놓기 위해 일을 마친 후에는 이름과 부서를 써놓으시기 바랍니다. 사무실을 이용할 수 없는 기간 동안은 반드시 근무를 계속할 수 있는 공간을 마련하시기 바랍니다. **32** 712호 사무실에 있는 중역 회의실은 근무 장소가 필요한 모든 분들에게 개방합니다. 하루 혹은 이틀 모두 재택근무를 하는 옵션에 관하여 매니저와 상의하는 것도 직원 여러분 모두에게 권장합니다.

협조에 미리 감사 드립니다. 절차의 어느 부분이든 궁금하거나 우려되는 점이 있으시다면 이 이메일에 바로 답장 부탁드립니다.

어휘 general affairs 총무 I itinerary *n.* 일정 I attachment *n.* 첨부파일 I timetable *n.* 시간표 I involve *v.* 수반하다 I challenge *n.* 어려움 I vacate *v.* 비우다 I set *adj.* 정해진 I refloor *v.* 바닥재를 다시 깔다 I rewire *v.* 전기 배선 공사를 다시 하다 I affect *v.* 영향을 주다 I place *v.* 두다, 놓다 I belongings *n.* 소지품 I on-site *adj.* 현장의 I logistics *n.* 물류 I aware *adj.* 알고 있는 I office suite *n.* 사무실 I packing materials 포장재 I distribute *v.* 배포하다 I be sure to-V 반드시 ~해라 I arrange *v.* 준비하다, 마련하다 I unavailable *adj.* 이용할 수 없는 I executive *adj.* 중역의, 간부의 I conference room 회의실 I telecommute *v.* 재택 근무하다 I in advance *adv.* 미리, 사전에 I cooperation *n.* 협조 I process *n.* 과정, 절차

작업 일정표 – 12월 3일 – 12월 13일	
12/3 월 / 12/4 화	708호 (디자인 스튜디오) / 711호 (마케팅 & 인사)
33 12/6 목 / 12/7 금	**33** 707호 (웹디자인) / 709호 (IT)
12/11 화 / 12/12 수	**34** 710호 (출판 & 영업) / 706호 (회계)

30. 직원들에게 왜 사내 공지사항을 보냈는가?

(A) 합병에 관한 우려를 다루기 위해

(B) 다가오는 승진을 발표하기 위해

(C) 기획안에 관한 제안을 요청하기 위해

(D) 다가오는 개조 공사를 상기시켜주기 위해

해설 첫 번째 지문 도입부에서 12월 첫 2주에는 약간의 어려움이 있을 것이라며, 건물 리모델링 공사를 위해 일부 부서들이 일정 기간 사무실을 비워야 한다고 말했으므로 정답은 (D) To remind them of an upcoming remodeling project이다.

---

31. 직원들은 무엇을 하라고 지시받는가?

(A) 어느 사무용품이 자신들의 것인지 표시한다.

(B) 사무실에서 더 많은 시간을 근무한다.

(C) 연락처를 수정한다.

(D) 상사에게 양식을 제출한다.

해설 첫 번째 지문, 첫 번째와 두 번째 단락에서 해당 팀원들이 사무실 내 소지품을 상자에 넣어야 한다고 하면서, 포장재와 상자가 지급될 것이고, 일과 후에 이름과 부서를 적으라고 했으므로 정답은 (A) Indicate which office items are theirs이다.

---

32. 712호 사무실에 관하여 무엇이라고 말하는가?

(A) 직원들을 위한 업무 공간으로 제공될 것이다.

(B) 교육 모임이 열릴 것이다.

(C) 한 달 후에 비품이 다시 지급될 것이다.

(D) 화상회의 장비가 설치될 것이다.

해설 712호 사무실이 언급된 첫 번째 지문, 두 번째 단락에서 712호 사무실에 있는 중역 회의실은 근무 장소가 필요한 모든 사람들에게 개방된다고 했으므로 정답은 (A) It will be provided as workspace for employees.이다. open for anyone who needs a place to work 가 provided as workspace for employees로 paraphrasing되었다.

---

33. 웹디자인 부서는 언제 나갈 준비를 해야 하는가?

(A) 11월 10일

(B) 11월 30일

(C) 12월 5일

(D) 12월 6일

해설 Web Design 부서가 언급된 두 번째 지문, 일정표를 보면 웹디자인 부서의 공사가 12월 6일로 잡혀 있는 것을 알 수 있는데, 첫 번째 지문 첫 번째 단락에서 공사를 하는 부서의 팀원들이 공사 전날 오후 4시 전에 사무실 내 소지품을 상자에 넣어야 한다고 했으므로 웹디자인 부서가 나갈 준비를 해야 하는 날짜는 12월 5일이다. 따라서 정답은 (C) On December 5이다.

---

34. 출판부에 관하여 알 수 있는 것은 무엇인가?

(A) 프로젝트 마감기한이 얼마 남지 않았다.

(B) 회의실을 예약할 것이다.

(C) 곧 새 매니저를 임명할 것이다.

(D) 사무실을 다른 팀과 함께 쓴다.

해설 Publishing 부서가 언급된 두 번째 지문, 일정표를 보면 12월 11~12일에 출판부가 영업부와 710호 사무실을 같이 쓰게 될 것임을 알 수 있으므로 정답은 (D) It shares office space with another team.이다.

[35-39] 다음 이메일들에 관한 문제입니다.

수신: helpdesk@intertop.co.kr

발신: Mehran@weissnicht.de

날짜: 2월 21일

제목: 등록

안녕하세요,

현재 저의 새 Intertop 태블릿 PC를 등록할 수 없습니다. 사용자 매뉴얼을 꼼꼼히 읽어봤고 정보를 찾으려고 회사 웹사이트도 확인해봤어요. 그러나 안타깝게도 절차를 마무리 짓는 데 요구되는 Intertop 등록 번호를 찾을 수가 없더군요. **35** 그리고 나서 소매점에 들러봤더니 직원이 당신에게 이메일로 기기의 모델 번호를 알려주면서 연락하라고 하더군요. **36** 모델 번호는 05768936입니다. 등록 번호를 어디서 찾을 수 있는지 알려주시기 바랍니다.

고맙습니다.

Mehran Tebrizi

어휘 **read through** 꼼꼼히 읽다 I **locate** v. 정확한 위치를 찾다 I **process** n. 과정, 절차 I **stop by** ~에 들르다 I **retail outlet** 소매점 I **reference** v. 참조문으로 인용하다

수신: Mehran@weissnicht.de

발신: helpdesk@intertop.co.kr

날짜: 2월 22일

제목: 회신: 등록

Mr. Tebrizi께,

2월 21일의 문의 고맙습니다. **36** 고객님께서 주신 이메일 주소와 기타 정보를 이용하여 Intertop Topmaster 5000(서비스 태그 번호 5982601)을 구매하셨다는 것을 알아냈습니다. **고객님의 Intertop 등록 번호는 BK8W-A6SY-G85U입니다.**

37 향후의 서비스를 위해 서비스 태그 번호를 이용하기 쉬운 곳에 보관하실 것을 권장합니다. 이 번호는 고객님의 편의를 위해 사용자 매뉴얼 표지 안쪽에 붙어있는 스티커에서도 확인하실 수 있습니다. 이 번호를 제시하시면 **38** 저희가 고객님의 전화를 제품에 관해 많이 알고 있는 고객 상담원에게 돌려주고 **고객님의 이전 상담 전화의 기록도 이용할 수 있게 됩니다.**

39 추가 문의사항이 있으시다면 저희 서비스 센터에 전화로 연락하실 것을 권장합니다. 가능한 가장 빠른 해결책을 제공해드리기 위해 성함과 서비스 태그 번호, 문제점의 세부사항을 알려주실 수 있게 준비하시기 바랍니다. 또한 사용자에게 최고의 경험을 보장하기 위해 일반적인 정보는 저희 웹사이트의 '자주 물어보는 질문' 코너를 확인하시기 바랍니다.

다시 한번 감사 드립니다.

Leticia Han
Intertop 서비스 센터 책임자

어휘 **determine** *v.* 알아내다 I **handy** *adj.* 이용하기 편한 곳에 있는 I **service representative** 고객 상담원 I **knowledgeable** *adj.* 박식한 I **access** *n.* 이용 권한 I **FAQ(frequently asked questions)** 자주 묻는 질문

---

35. Mr. Tebrizi은 이메일을 쓰기 전에 무엇을 했는가?
(A) 기기를 등록했다.
(B) 전화를 했다.
(C) 매장을 방문했다.
(D) 기기를 반품했다.

해설 Mr. Tebrizi가 쓴 첫 번째 지문, 이메일에서 자신이 소매점에 들렀더니 직원이 이메일로 기기의 모델 번호를 알려주라고 했다고 말했으므로 정답은 (C) He visited a store.이다.

---

36. Ms. Han은 어떻게 Mr. Tebrizi의 구매 품목을 확인했는가?
(A) 모델 번호와 이메일 주소를 참조함으로써
(B) 등록 번호를 조사함으로써
(C) 영업부에 물어 봄으로써
(D) 사용자 매뉴얼을 봄으로써

해설 Mr. Tebrizi가 쓴 첫 번째 지문, 이메일에서 상점 직원이 알려준 대로 기기의 모델 번호를 언급했으며, Ms. Han이 회신한 두 번째 지문, 이메일에서 Mr. Tebrizi가 제공한 이메일 주소와 기타 정보를 이용하여 Intertop Topmaster 5000을 구매했다는 사실을 알아냈다고 했는데, 바로 이 모델 번호가 기타 다른 정보(the other information)에 해당하므로 정답은 (A) By referring to a model number and an e-mail address이다.

---

37. Mr. Tebrizi는 어디에서 서비스 태그 번호를 찾아야 하는가?
(A) 영수증 뒷면에서
(B) 태블릿 PC의 바닥에서
(C) 안내서 표지 안쪽에서
(D) 웹사이트의 한 코너에서

해설 service tag number가 언급된 두 번째 지문, 두 번째 단락에서 향후 서비스를 위해 서비스 태그 번호를 이용하기 쉬운 곳에 보관할 것을 권장한다며, 이 번호는 사용자 매뉴얼 표지 안쪽에 붙어있는 스티커에서도 확인할 수 있다고 했으므로 정답은 (C) Inside the cover of a guide이다. be found가 look for로, owner's manual이 guide로 paraphrasing되었다.

---

38. 두 번째 이메일에서, 두 번째 단락 세 번째 줄의 단어 direct와 의미상 가장 가까운 것은
(A) (전화를 다른 사람 번호로) 돌려주다
(B) 바로잡다
(C) 관리하다
(D) 지시하다

해설 해당 문장에서 direct는 '전화를 다른 번호로 돌려주다'라는 의미로 쓰였으므로 보기 중 transfer 로 paraphrasing되었다. 정답은 (A) transfer이다.

---

39. Ms. Han는 Mr. Tebrizi가 질문이 있을 경우 어떻게 직원에게 연락하라고 제안하는가?
(A) 전화로
(B) Intertop 지사에 가서
(C) 이메일로
(D) 온라인 계정에 접속해서

해설 두 번째 지문, 세 번째 단락에서 추가 문의사항이 있다면 서비스 센터에 전화로 연락하실 것을 권장한다고 했으므로 정답은 (A) By phone이다. For further inquiries가 if he has a question으로 paraphrasing되었다.

[40-44] 다음 기사와 광고, 이용후기에 관한 문제입니다.

Cambridge Brown Mouse 식당의 변동 완료
Louise Clairsen 작성

케임브리지 (1월 5일) – **40** 주방장 Nathan McLeod 아래에서 근무하고 있는 Brown Mouse 식당의 현 부주방장 Andrea Desai가 식당의 매입을 완료했다. **41** Mr. McLeod는 Keswick로 이동해서 지역 대학교의 요리 강사로써 계속 바쁘게 지낼 계획이다. Ms. Desai는 "Nathan이 떠나겠다고 말했을 때 저는 기회를 잡아야 한다는 걸 알았죠."라고 말했다. Mr. McLeod는 "Andrea는 Brown Mouse와 10년 이상 함께 했고 제가 대부분의 대표 요리를 개발하는 데 아주 중요한 도움을 주었습니다."라고 말했다. **42** Ms. Desai는 이번 주에 식당을 인수한 후 메뉴 품목 중 일부를 이미 바꾸었으며 눈에 띄는 것은 〈Cambridge Daily〉의 Daryl Davies가 '놀라울 정도로 맛있다'고 평가한 카레 백리향 덤플링이다. 이 식당은 예약은 받지 않지만 555-2344에서 전화상으로 또는www.brownmouse.co.uk에서 온라인으로 미리 주문을 할 수 있다.

어휘 **transition** *n.* 변화 I **sous-chef** *n.* 부주방장 I **eatery** *n.* 식당 I **culinary** *adj.* 요리의 I **seize** *v.* 붙잡다 I **instrumental** *adj.* 중요한 I **come up with** ~을 생산하다 I **signature dish** 요리사의 가장 유명한 요리 I **take over** 인수하다 I **notably** *adv.* 특히, 눈에 띄게 I **thyme** *n.* 백리향 I **stunningly** *adv.* 놀랍도록

Brown Mouse 식당

1월
인도 정식의 맛(1인당 45파운드)

애피타이저
A) 구운 쿠민과 요거트 치킨 케밥
B) 카레 백리향 채소 덤플링

🔲 **주요리**
A) 양고기 탄도리와 감자
B) 🔲 매운 연어 링귀니와 오이 딜 수프

디저트
A) 장미 병아리콩 쿠키
B) 데이트 튀김 셔벗

어휘 fixed menu 정식 | entrée n. 주요리 | cucumber n. 오이 | chickpea n. 병아리콩

---

www.cambridgedining.com/brownmouse/review/3314

별점 5. ★★★★★

목요일 저녁에 몇 명의 지인들과 함께 Brown Mouse 식당에서 식사를 했습니다. 지난 번에 온 이후 매달 다른 국제적인 맛을 특징으로 하는 정식을 비롯해서 많은 변화가 있었더군요. 🔲 저는 채식주의자이기 때문에 처음에 봤을 때, 선택 메뉴가 부족해 보였습니다. 🔲 비록 음식이 나오는 데 더 오래 걸리기는 했지만, 고맙게도 요리사께서 제 요구를 받아들여서 주요리를 조정해주셨습니다. 주요리는 특별히 흥미로울 게 없었지만 – 그냥 일상적으로 먹는 파스타와 수프 한 그릇 – 🔲 카레 백리향 덤플링은 믿을 수 없을 정도였습니다. 저희가 그냥 저녁에 만장일치로 가장 좋아한 것이었어요. 이 달이 가기 전에 그것들을 먹으러 다시 갈 계획입니다.

Maja Selman
게시 날짜: 1월 10일

어휘 acquaintance n. 아는 사람, 지인 | feature v. ~을 특징으로 하다 | flavor n. 맛, 풍미 | glance n. 흘낏 봄 | accommodate v. 수용하다 | adjust v. 조정하다 | incredible adj. 믿을 수 없는

---

40. 기사의 목적은 무엇인가?
(A) 요리 대회의 결과를 발표하기 위해
(B) 사업체 소유권의 변경을 알리기 위해
(C) 대형 식당 운영의 어려움을 설명하기 위해
(D) 할인 쿠폰 받는 방법을 설명하기 위해

해설 첫 번째 지문 기사의 도입부에서 주방장 Nathan McLeod 아래에서 근무하고 있는 Brown Mouse 식당의 현 부주방장 Andrea Desai가 식당의 매입을 완료했다고 했다고 했으므로 정답은 (B) To publicize a change in a business' ownership이다.

---

41. Mr. McLeod는 왜 Keswick에 가는가?
(A) 새 식당을 열기 위해
(B) 인터넷 마케팅을 공부하기 위해
(C) 음식 비평가가 되기 위해
(D) 요리를 가르치기 위해

해설 Mr. McLeod와 Keswick이 언급된 첫 번째 지문 기사에서 Mr. McLeod가 Keswick로 이동해서 지역 대학교의 요리 강사로서 계속 바쁘게 지낼 계획이라고 했으므로 정답은 (D) To teach cooking이다. keep busy as a culinary instructor가 teach cooking으로 paraphrasing되었다.

---

42. Ms. Selman은 기사의 어떤 세부사항에 동의하는가?
(A) 식당의 인기 때문에 자리를 얻는 것이 어려웠다.
(B) 지역 간행물에서 평가한 메뉴 품목이 훌륭했다.
(C) 일부 요리가 Cambridge 지역에서는 특이한 것이었다.
(D) 직원들이 고객들에게 매우 공손했다.

해설 첫 번째 지문 기사에서 Ms. Desai가 이번 주에 식당을 인수한 후에 메뉴 품목 중 일부를 이미 바꾸었다고 했고, 눈에 띄는 것은 〈Cambridge Daily〉의 Daryl Davies가 '놀라울 정도로 맛있다'고 평가한 카레 백리향 덤플링이라고 했는데, Ms. Selman이 쓴 세 번째 지문 이용후기에서 카레 백리향 덤플링의 맛이 믿을 수 없을 정도였다고 했으므로 정답은 (B) A menu item reviewed in a local publication is excellent.이다.

---

43. 이용 후기 첫 문단, 다섯 번째 줄의 단어 take에 의미상 가장 가까운 것은
(A) 물러나다
(B) 허용하다
(C) 필요로 하다
(D) 입수하다

해설 해당 질문에서 take는 '시간이 걸리다'라는 의미로 쓰였으므로 보기 중 이와 바꿔 쓸 수 있는 것은 '요구하다, 필요로 하다'라는 뜻의 (C) require이다.

---

44. Ms. Selmen은 어떤 요리를 다르게 준비해달라고 요구했는가?
(A) 치킨 케밥
(B) 매운 연어
(C) 양고기 탄도리
(D) 데이트 셔벗

해설 Ms. Selman이 쓴 세 번째 지문 이용후기에서 자신이 채식주의자여서 선택 메뉴가 두 가지로 제한되어 고르느라 힘들었다고 하면서, 음식이 나오는 데 더 오래 걸리기는 했지만, 요리사가 주요리를 파스타와 수프로 조정해주었다고 했는데, 두 번째 지문 식당 광고에서 주요리의 두 옵션 중 정답은 수프가 포함된 (B) Spicy salmon이다.

[45-49] 다음 두 이메일과 일정표에 관한 문제입니다.

발신: Richard Halldorsson ⟨rhalldorsson@icelandadv.com⟩
수신: Cynthia Rucker ⟨cynthiar@sunmail.net⟩
날짜: 6월 10일
제목: 옵션
첨부: cynthiarucker_일정.rtf

Ms. Rucker님,

귀하의 관심에 감사 드립니다.

45 7월이 가장 인기가 많은 달이기에, 저희의 7월 패키지에는 소수의 자리만 남아 있습니다. 그러니 그 중 하나에 등록하시려면 편하신 시간에 가능한 빨리 연락 주십시오. **45** 이번 주 말에는 전부 마감될지도 모릅니다!

46 귀하는 동반자가 있으시니, 첨부된 서류에 있는 모든 투어가 이용 가능하지는 않다는 점을 염두에 두시기 바랍니다.

곧 답변을 듣게 되길 바랍니다!

진심으로,

Richard Halldorsson
Iceland Adventures 사

어휘 appreciate v. 감사하다 | spot n. 자리 | remain v. 남다 | popular adj. 인기가 많은 | respond v. 답장하다 | register v. 등록하다 | note v. ~에 주목하다, 주의하다 | indicated adj. 표시된, 나타난 | attached adj. 첨부된 | document n. 서류, 문서 | companion n. 동행, 동반자

Iceland Adventures 사
7월 프로그램 일정

투어명	날짜	소요 시간	가격 (ISK)	이용 가능
Skogafoss 폭포	7월 10일	오전 9시 – 오후 6시	41,000	잔여석 3
Reynisfjara 해변	7월 16일	오전 7시 – 오후 4시	36,000	잔여석 2
46 Diamond 해변	7월 20일	오전 9시 – 오후 6시	32,000	**46** 잔여석 1
Reykjavik 쇼핑	**49** 7월 27일	오전 10시 – 오후 4시	**49** 8,000	잔여석 2
Midnight Sun 하이킹	7월 28일	오후 6시 – 오전 4시	6,000	잔여석 4

모든 투어는 Iceland Adventures 본사에서 출발하고 돌아옵니다. 여러분의 그룹이 출발하기 적어도 20분 전에 와주시기 바랍니다. **47** 일부 지역의 날씨가 쌀쌀할 수 있으므로 두꺼운 코트를 챙겨야 하는지 사전에 확인하시기 바랍니다. 궂은 날씨로 인해 투어가 취소되지는 않을 것이므로 방수가 되는 신발을 신으시는 게 좋습니다. 모든 식사는 패키지 가격에 포함되어 있지만, 에너지 바나 다른 간식을 가져오시는 것을 권장 드립니다.

어휘 availability n. 이용 가능성 | waterfall n. 폭포 | headquarters n. 본사 | confirm v. 확인하다 | beforehand adv. 사전에 | call off 취소하다, 중지하다 | inclement adj. 좋지 못한, 궂은 | waterproof adj. 방수의 | encourage v. 장려하다

수신: Richard Halldorsson ⟨rhalldorsson@icelandadv.com⟩
발신: Cynthia Rucker ⟨cynthiar@sunmail.net⟩
날짜: 6월 11일
제목: 답장: 옵션

Mr. Halldorsson님,

이렇게 빨리 답장 주셔서 감사합니다. **49** 아이슬란드에서의 휴가기간 중 저희가 투어를 할 시간이 되는 유일한 날은 7월 27일이에요. 그 날짜에 저희를 등록해 주세요. **48** 첫째 주는 그 나라의 시골 지역에서 머물면서 저희끼리 하이킹을 하려고 합니다.

감사합니다!

Cynthia Rucker

어휘 vacation n. 휴가 | sign up 신청하다 | rural adj. 시골의, 지방의

---

45. 첫 번째 이메일은 Iceland Adventures 사에 대해 무엇을 알려주는가?

(A) Mr. Halldorsson을 6월에 승진시켰다.
(B) 여름에만 여행을 제공한다.
(C) 여행 일정이 최근 업데이트되었다.
(D) 7월 패키지가 빠르게 예약되고 있다.

해설 Mr. Halldorsson이 Ms. Rucker에게 보낸 첫 번째 지문, 첫 번째 단락에서 7월이 가장 인기가 많은 달이라서, 7월 패키지에는 소수의 자리만 남아 있다고 하면서, 이번 주 말에는 전부 마감될지도 모른다고 했으므로 정답은 (D) Its July packages are getting booked quickly.이다.

---

46. Mr. Halldorsson에 따르면, 어떤 투어가 Ms. Rucker에게 선택지가 될 수 없는가?

(A) Skogafoss 폭포
(B) Diamond 해변
(C) Reykjavik 쇼핑
(D) Midnight Sun 하이킹

해설 Mr. Halldorsson이 Ms. Rucker에게 보낸 첫 번째 지문, 두 번째 단락에서 Ms. Rucker가 동반자가 있어서 첨부된 서류에 있는 투어를 다 이용할 수는 없다고 했는데, 두 번째 지문, 일정표를 보면 Diamond 해변의 잔여석은 1개이므로 정답은 (B) Diamond Beach 이다.

---

47. 일정은 참가자들이 무엇을 하라고 권하고 있는가?

(A) 우산을 가져온다

(B) 입장권 구입을 위해 일찍 도착한다

(C) 일기예보를 확인한다

(D) 물을 챙겨온다

해설 두 번째 지문의 설명 부분에서 날씨가 갑자기 바뀔 수 있으니 두꺼운 코트를 챙겨야 하는지 사전에 확인하기 바란다고 했으므로 정답은 (C) Check the weather forecast이다.

---

48. Ms. Rucker에 관하여 두 번째 이메일에서 알 수 있는 것은 무엇인가?

(A) 휴가로 아이슬란드에 자주 방문한다.

(B) 웹사이트에서 기술적 문제를 겪었다.

(C) Mr. Halldorsson에게 더 자세한 여행 정보를 요청한다.

(D) 가이드 없이 하이킹을 할 것이다.

해설 Ms. Rucker가 Mr. Halldorsson에게 보낸 세 번째 지문에서 첫째 주는 그 나라의 시골 지역에 머물면서 자신들끼리 하이킹을 하려 한다고 했으므로 정답은 (D) She will go on a hike without a guide. 이다. do some hiking by ourselves가 go on a hike without a guide로 paraphrasing되었다.

---

49. Ms. Rucker가 선택한 투어 요금은 얼마인가?

(A) 36,000 ISK

(B) 32,000 ISK

(C) 8,000 ISK

(D) 6,000 ISK

해설 Ms. Rucker가 Mr. Halldorsson에게 보낸 세 번째 지문에서 아이슬란드에서의 휴가 중 투어를 할 시간이 되는 유일한 날은 7월 27일이라고 했는데, 두 번째 지문, 일정표에서 7월 27일 일정을 확인하면 Reykjavik 쇼핑 – 8,000 ISK이므로 정답은 (C) 8,000 ISK이다.

[50-54] 다음 정보와 브로셔, 이메일에 관한 문제입니다.

워싱턴 역사박물관 (WHM) 방문

50 사우스벤드에서 가장 잘 알려진 명소 중 하나인 워싱턴 역사박물관은 1940년에 문을 연 이래 방문객들의 주된 목적지가 되어 왔습니다. 방문객들은 오디오 가이드를 씌냅해서 스스로의 페이스로 박물관을 둘러보거나 저희 박물관의 전문 가이드와 함께 투어를 할 수 있습니다. 개인 방문객의 경우 가이드 투어는 고정 비용 5달러이지만 열 명 이상의 단체에게는 특별 할인(아래의 표를 보십시오)과 단체의 특정한 관심사에 맞춘 투어를 제공합니다. 단체 예매는 적어도 방문 48시간 전에 하셔야 합니다. 투어를 예약하시려면 info@whm.org로 이메일 주십시오.

단체 비용

초등학생과 중학생: 20명까지 50달러; 50명까지 100달러

52 **고등학생과 대학생:** 20명까지 75달러; 50명까지 125달러

일반: 20명까지 85달러; 50명까지 140달러

어휘 **attraction** *n.* 명소 | **prime** *adj.* 주된, 주요한 | **destination** *n.* 목적지 | **visitor** *n.* 방문객 | **pace** *n.* 속도 | **expert** *adj.* 전문가의, 전문적인 | **individual** *adj.* 개인의 | **cost** *n.* 비용 | **particular** *adj.* 특정한 | **interest** *n.* 흥미 | **reservation** *n.* 예약

워싱턴 역사박물관(WHM) 전시

최초의 중서부 도시

세계에서 가장 큰 Cahokian 유물 컬렉션을 즐기십시오. 실제 사이즈로 제작한 고대 Cahokia 도시의 한 블록을 탐험하며 천 년도 전에 이들이 누렸던 세련된 도시의 삶을 엿보십시오.

예언자와 선구자

이 전시는 19세기의 중요 인물들을 다룹니다. 영화로 제작된 재연을 관람하시고, James Whitcomb Rile, Tecumseh와 다른 이들이 직접 작성한 자료와 이들의 일상용품도 살펴보십시오.

새로운 산업의 시작

51 자동차 제조업 시초의 이 놀라운 관찰은 시카고에 있는 Searle 박물관에서 3월 21일부터 4월 30일까지 대여할 것입니다. 최초의 자동차 몇 대와 공장에서의 삶에 관한 이야기를 보여주는 이 전시는 Tarkington 부속건물 전체를 차지할 것입니다.

성장하는 Michiana

53 이 갤러리는 우리의 다양한 문화 배경을 깊이 다룹니다. 20세기와 21세기 South Bend의 인구 발전을 살펴봅니다.

어휘 **exhibit** *n.* 전시 | **artifact** *n.* 유물, 공예품 | **explore** *v.* 탐험하다 | **reproduction** *n.* 복사, 복제 | **block** *n.* (도로로 나뉘는) 구역, 블록 | **ancient** *adj.* 고대의 | **glimpse** *n.* 언뜻 봄 | **sophisticated** *adj.* 세련된, 정교한 | **urban** *adj.* 도시의 | **prophet** *n.* 예언자 | **pioneer** *n.* 개척자, 선구자 | **profile** *v.* 개요를 알려주다, 작성하다 | **personality** *n.* 인물 | **reenactment** *n.* 재연 | **firsthand** *adv.* 직접, 바로 | **record** *n.* 기록 | **dawn** *n.* 새벽, 여명 | **industry** *n.* 산업 | **eye-opening** *adj.* 놀랄 만한, 경이로운 | **examination** *n.* 조사, 검사 | **automobile** *n.* 자동차 | **manufacturing** *n.* 제조 | **on loan** 차용하여 | **display** *n.* 전시 | **account** *n.* 이야기, 설명 | **in-depth** *adj.* 상세한, 면밀한 | **diverse** *adj.* 다양한 | **culture** *n.* 문화 | **evolution** *n.* 진화, 발전 | **population** *n.* 인구

수신: tours@whm.org
발신: sueflowers@johnblainetech.edu
제목: 예약
날짜: 3월 26일

단체명: John Blaine 기술고
52 단체 수: 40

52 저는 John Blaine 기술고의 교감이고 고등학생 단체를 위해 투어 일정을 잡고 싶습니다. **54** 저번 방문 때 Nairo Vidal가 저희 가이드를 해주셔서 좋았습니다. 다시 한번 저희 투어를 진행해주실 수 있다면 감사하겠습니다. **53** 저희 단체는 동시대 문화를 공부하고 있을 것입니다. 9월 첫 번째 주에 아침 시간 자리가 있으시다면 그때로 일정을 잡고 싶습니다.

인사를 드리며,
Sue Flowers

어휘 **vice principal** 교감 l **previous** *adj.* 이전의 l **appreciate** *v.* 감사하다 l **contemporary** *adj.* 동시대의

---

50. WHM에 관해 무엇을 알 수 있는가?
(A) 오랜 시간 동안 영업해왔다.
(B) 최근 보수공사를 했다.
(C) 주말에는 투어를 제공하지 않는다.
(D) 무료 역사 강의를 제공한다.

해설 첫 번째 지문 안내문의 첫 번째 단락에서 South Bend에서 가장 잘 알려진 명소 중 하나인 워싱턴 역사박물관이 1940년에 문을 연 이래 방문객들의 주된 목적지가 되어 왔다고 했으므로 정답은 (A) It has been in business for a long time.이다.

---

51. Tarkington 부속건물에 관하여 알 수 있는 것은 무엇인가?
(A) 당분간 하나의 전시만 할 것이다.
(B) 여름에 확장될 것이다.
(C) 연구원들에게만 독점적으로 공개되었다.
(D) 추가 비용을 내면 이용할 수 있다.

해설 Tarkington Wing이 언급된 두 번째 지문 브로셔의 'Dawn of a New Industry'에서 자동차와 공장의 삶에 관한 이야기를 보여주는 전시가 3월 21일 ~ 4월 30일까지 Tarkington 부속건물 전체를 차지할 거라고 했으므로 정답은 (A) It will temporarily feature only one display.이다.

---

52. John Blaine Tech 단체는 투어에 요금을 얼마나 지불해야 하는가?
(A) 75 달러
(B) 100 달러
(C) 125 달러
(D) 140 달러

해설 John Blaine 기술고가 보낸 세 번째 지문 이메일에서 단체 수가 40명임을 알 수 있고, 도입부에서 자신을 John Blaine 기술고의 교감으로 소개하며, 고등학생 단체를 위해 투어 일정을 잡고 싶다고 했는데, 첫 번째 지문 안내문의 'Group Pricing'에서 고등학생과 대학생 단체가 20명까지 75달러; 50명까지 125달러라고 했으므로 John Blain 기

술고 단체가 지불해야 할 요금은 (C) $125이다.

---

53. John Blaine 기술고가 투어에서 가장 관심 있어 할 전시는 무엇이겠는가?
(A) 중서부 최초의 도시
(B) 예언자와 선구자
(C) 새 산업의 시작
(D) 성장하는 Michiana

해설 John Blaine 기술고가 보낸 세 번째 지문 이메일에서 방문할 학생들이 동시대 문화를 공부하고 있을 거라고 했는데, 두 번째 지문 브로셔의 'Growing Michiana'를 보면 이 갤러리에서 다양한 문화 배경을 다루며, 20세기와 21세기 사우스벤드의 인구 발전을 살펴본다고 했으므로 John Blaine 단체가 가장 관심 있어 할 전시는 (D) Growing Michiana이다.

---

54. Nairo Vidal은 누구인가?
(A) John Blaine 기술고 직원
(B) 대학 교수
(C) WHM 직원
(D) 여행사 매니저

해설 John Blaine Tech가 보낸 세 번째 지문 이메일에서 지난 방문 때 Nairo Vidal가 가이드를 해주어서 좋았다며, 다시 한번 Nairo Vidal가 단체 투어를 이끌어주면 고맙겠다고 했으므로 정답은 (C) A WHM employee이다.

MINI TEST

MINI TEST 01

본서 p.358

1. (C)	**2.** (B)	**3.** (C)	**4.** (B)	**5.** (A)
6. (D)	**7.** (C)	**8.** (C)	**9.** (D)	**10.** (A)
11. (D)	**12.** (C)	**13.** (A)	**14.** (A)	**15.** (C)
16. (B)	**17.** (D)	**18.** (A)	**19.** (B)	**20.** (D)
21. (C)	**22.** (B)	**23.** (C)	**24.** (D)	**25.** (B)
26. (B)	**27.** (D)	**28.** (A)	**29.** (C)	**30.** (D)

1. 열차가 두 시간 넘게 지연된 승객들은 할인된 표를 받을 자격이 있다.

해설 more than은 '~이상'이라는 뜻으로 숫자 앞에 많이 쓰이므로 꼭 알아두도록 하자. 따라서 정답은 (C) than이다.

어휘 delay *v.* 연기하다, 지연시키다 I eligible *adj.* ~할 자격이 있는 I discounted *adj.* 할인된

2. 한정된 좌석 때문에, 우리는 자리 예약을 할 수 있도록 빠른 응답을 받아야 한다.

해설 보기를 확인해보니 형용사 어휘 문제이다. 빈칸에 들어갈 형용사는 어차피 명사 response를 꾸미므로 response와 가장 어울리는 어휘를 찾으면 된다. 따라서 바쁜 반응(응답), 날카로운 반응(응답), 가까운 반응(응답)은 모두 이상하다. '빠른 반응(응답)'이 가장 자연스러우므로 정답은 (B) quick이다.

어휘 restricted *adj.* 제한된, 한정된 I seating *n.* 좌석, 자리 I reserve *v.* 예약하다 I busy *adj.* 바쁜 I quick *adj.* 빠른, 신속한 I sharp *adj.* 날카로운, 급격한 I close *adj.* 가까운, 친밀한

3. 응급 처치 물품의 신제품 판촉을 위해, Self Help 약국은 내일 무료 견본을 제공할 것이다.

해설 빈칸은 동사 자리이다. 동사가 될 수 없는 (A)는 탈락이다. 나머지는 시제를 잘 살펴보아야 한다. 문장 마지막에 tomorrow가 있으므로 정답은 미래진행 시제인 (C) will be providing가 정답이다.

어휘 promote *v.* 홍보하다, 판촉하다 I first aid 응급 처치 I pharmacy *n.* 약국 I free *adj.* 무료의 I provide *v.* 제공하다

4. Korrian 기관은 악천후 때문에 야외 기금 마련 행사를 연기할 수밖에 없었다.

해설 보기를 확인해보니 동사 어휘 문제이다. 문맥상 날씨가 안 좋아서 야외 행사를 연기해야 했다는 의미가 적합하므로 (B) postpone이 정답이다.

어휘 organization *n.* 기관, 조직 I be forced to 어쩔 수 없이 ~하다 I outdoor *adj.* 야외의 I fundraising *n.* 기금 모금 I due to ~때문에 I inclement *adj.* (날씨 등이) 궂은

5. Devana 병원의 환자들은 하루 중 어느 때라도 그들의 의료 기록을 볼 수 있다.

해설 보기를 확인해보니 대명사의 격을 물어보는 문제이다. 빈칸 뒤에 medical records라는 명사가 나와있다. 명사 앞에는 무조건 소유격이므로 정답은 (A) their이다.

어휘 access *v.* 접속하다; 접근하다, 이용하다 I medical record 의료 기록

6. 실험실에서 사용되는 실험 방법은 정밀함과 정확성을 위해 정기적으로 검증 받아야만 한다.

해설 be p.p. 사이에는 무조건 부사가 정답이다. 덧붙여, be p.p.는 수동태로서 완벽한 문장이다. 따라서 빈칸은 필요 없는 수식어 자리라 할 수 있다. 따라서 정답은 부사인 (D) regularly이다.

어휘 method *n.* 방법(론) I laboratory *n.* 실험실 I verify *v.* 입증하다 I precision *n.* 정확함, 정밀함 I accuracy *n.* 정확함

7. 유리 제조업체들 중 대부분이 그 도시의 남서 지역에 위치해 있다.

해설 보기를 확인해보니 명사 어휘 문제이다. 문맥상 제조업체들 대부분이 남서 '지역'에 위치해 있다는 의미가 적절하므로 정답은 (C) area이다.

어휘 be located in ~에 위치해 있다

8. 예산 보고서는 부사장이 그것을 승인한 후 다음 주 금요일에 제출되어야 할 것이다.

해설 to 뒤에 be라는 동사가 있으므로 빈칸에 동사를 또 넣을 순 없다. 따라서 (B)와 (D)는 답이 될 수 없다. (A)를 넣으면, 빈칸 뒤에 submit의 목적어가 있어야 하는데, 빈칸 뒤에는 목적어(명사)가 없다. next Friday는 부사이다. 따라서 정답은 수동태의 형태인 (C) submitted가 정답이다.

어휘 budget report 예산 보고서 I vice president 부사장 I approve *v.* 승인하다

9. 그 축제의 20번째 기념일을 축하하여, 올해의 행사는 3일 연속 계속될 것이다.

해설 전치사 in 뒤에는 명사가 와야 한다. 따라서 정답은 (D) celebration 이다.

어휘 festival *n.* 축제 I anniversary *n.* 기념일 I run *v.* (얼마의 기간 동안) 계속되다 I straight *adv.* 내리, 잇달아 I in celebration of ~을 축하하여

10. 더 저렴하고 연비가 좋은 차량들에 대한 소비자 수요가 향후 5년에 걸쳐 급속히 증가할 것으로 예상된다.

해설 문맥상 향후 5년에 걸쳐서 (동안) 소비자 수요가 급속히 증가할 것으로 예상된다는 뜻이므로 정답은 (A) over이다. (A) ~동안에(기간), ~을 넘어 (B) ~쪽으로, ~을 향하여(방향) (C) ~뒤에(위치) (D) ~에 반대하여, ~에 맞서서

어휘 demand *n.* 수요; 요구 (사항) I affordable *adj.* (가격이) 알맞은 I fuel-efficient *adj.* 연료 효율이 좋은 I rapidly *adv.* 빠르게, 급속히

5월 11일
Beth Rivers
4005 Floral 로
오스틴, 텍사스 78610

Ms. Rivers에게,

Carl's Business Attire는 고객님을 **11** 축하연에 초대함으로써 지속적인 후원에 감사의 뜻을 전하고자 합니다. 945 Aspen 가에 있는 저희 가게의 멋진 재개업식은 7월 5일 금요일 오후 3시부터 7시까지 **12** 개최될 예정입니다.

이 특별 행사에 **13** 함께 해주시면 감사하겠습니다. **14** 궁금한 내용이 있으신 경우, Terrence Bodin에게 연락 주시기 바랍니다.

감사합니다.

진심으로,

Eric Wang

어휘 show one's appreciation for ~에 대해 감사를 표하다 | occasion n. 행사 | take place (행사 등이) 개최되다

---

11. **해설** 해당 문장에서는 단골 고객을 어디에 초대하여 감사의 뜻을 표하고자 한다고 했고, 바로 뒤에서 The grand reopening of our store (가게의 재개업식)로 시작하는 문장이 연결되어 있으므로 '축하연'에 초대함으로써 감사의 뜻을 표한다는 문맥이 적절하므로 정답은 (D) celebration이다. (A) society(사회), (B) conference(학회), (C) presentation(발표)는 모두 문맥상 어색하다.

12. **해설** 빈칸은 동사 자리이다. 따라서 (B)번은 탈락이다. 나머지 보기를 확인해보니, 시제 문제임을 알 수 있다. 이 글을 쓴 날이 5월 11일인데, grand reopening을 하는 날짜는 7월 5일이다. 즉, 미래시제가 정답이다. 따라서 정답은 (C) will take이다.

13. **해설** 지문 초반에서 초대 의사를 밝히면서, 행사 장소와 시점을 언급했으므로 이 특별 행사에 함께 해주면 감사하겠다는 의미가 적절하므로 정답은 (A) join이다.

14. **(A) 궁금한 내용이 있으신 경우, Terrence Bodin에게 연락 주시기 바랍니다.**
    (B) Terrence Bodin은 6월 1일까지 전체 일정을 제출해야 합니다.
    (C) Terrence Bodin은 그가 더 일찍 시작하도록 설득할 수 있습니다.
    (D) 몇몇 신입 직원들이 6월 1일까지 채용될 것입니다.

    해설 고객들을 초대하는 초대장이므로 마지막 문장에서 궁금한 내용이 있는 경우 담당자에게 연락 달라는 내용이 적절하므로 정답은 (A) Please contact Terrence Bodin if you have any questions이다.

발신: Keith Hurst
3월 20일 오후 1시 50분

15 16 제 비행기가 조금 전에 도착했어요. 운전기사가 공항 터미널에 없네요. 저를 픽업하러 그가 어디서 기다리고 있는지 알려주시겠어요? 지금 10분이 지났어요. 회의에 늦고 싶지 않아서요. 감사합니다. 사무실에서 뵐게요.

어휘 a while ago 조금 전에 | airport terminal 공항 터미널 | pick up ~을 (차에) 태우러 가다

---

15. 문자 메시지의 목적은 무엇인가?
    (A) 운전해서 가는 길을 요청하기 위해
    (B) 비행편 변경을 설명하기 위해
    (C) 교통편 준비를 확인하기 위해
    (D) 비즈니스 회의를 연기하기 위해

    해설 글의 목적을 물어보는 문제이다. 목적을 묻는 문제는 지문 앞부분이나 맨 마지막에 단서가 나온다. 보통 두괄식이 많다. 문자 메시지 첫머리를 확인해보니, 운전기사가 공항에 없으므로 어디에서 기다리고 있는지 확인해 알려달라고 하는 것으로 보아 확인을 요청하는 글이므로 정답은 (C) To check on transportation arrangements이다.

16. Mr. Hurst는 메시지를 어디에서 보냈는가?
    (A) 그의 집
    (B) 공항
    (C) 그의 사무실
    (D) 택시

    해설 장소와 관련된 언급에 주목해보면, 공항에 좀 전에 도착해 있는데 운전기사가 아직 안 왔다는 내용이므로 Mr. Hurst가 공항에 도착해서 이 메시지를 보낸 것임을 알 수 있다. 따라서 정답은 (B) An airport이다.

Dalia's
3100 Smithson 길, 애들레이드 AD11
17 계절 마감 창고 정리 세일
18 5월 7일부터 22일까지

표시된 가격에서
봄 의류 – 50퍼센트에서 70퍼센트까지 할인
신발 – 25퍼센트 할인
운동복 – 40퍼센트 할인
보석과 엑세서리류 – 25퍼센트 할인

이번 세일 기간 동안 40달러 이상의 선글라스 구매에 대한 15달러를 추가로 할인 받으시려면 이 전단을 제시해 주세요. **18** 이 재고 정리 세일 기간에 75달러 이상의 구매에 한해서 여름 컬렉션의 전 제품에 대한 10퍼센트 할인 쿠폰을 지급해 드립니다. 쿠폰은 5월 28일부터 6월 30일까지 유효합니다.

주목: Dalia's는 직원들이 재고를 다시 채우고, 매장의 여름 컬렉션을 준비하는 5월 26일에는 영업하지 않습니다

어휘 clearance sale 재고 정리 세일 | apparel *n.* 의복, 의류 | purchase *n.* 구매 | valid *adj.* 유효한 | restock *v.* 재고를 다시 채우다

17. 전단의 목적은 무엇인가?

(A) 상점 개점을 알리기 위해

(B) 새로운 운동복 라인을 소개하기 위해

(C) 새로운 소유권에 대한 정보를 제공하기 위해

(D) 계절 상품의 할인을 광고하기 위해

해설 전단의 목적을 물어보는 문제이다. End-of-Season Clearance Sale (계절 마감 창고 정리)라는 단어와 70% off 라는 단어 등을 보아하니, 할인판매를 광고하는 것이다. 따라서 정답은 (D) To advertise a sale of seasonal merchandise이다.

18. 고객은 며칠에 쿠폰을 받을 수 있는가?

(A) 5월 22일

(B) 5월 26일

(C) 5월 28일

(D) 6월 30일

해설 이 재고 정리 세일 기간에 75달러 이상을 구매하면 모든 제품을 10% 할인 받을 수 있는 쿠폰을 제공한다고 했고 할인 행사 기간은 상단 제목에서 기간을 확인해보면 5월 7일부터 22일까지이므로 정답은 (A) May 22이다.

[19-21] 다음 이메일에 관한 문제입니다.

수신: Thomas Donati ⟨tdonati@dosmail.com⟩

발신: Jewel Summers ⟨jsummers@virgoeye.com⟩

회신: 귀하의 주문

날짜: **21** 10월 15일

저희는 귀하께서 최근에 보내주신 이메일을 받았습니다. Virgo Eyewear에서는 고객 만족이 저희의 최우선 사항입니다.

저희는 귀하의 이전 주문에 문제가 있었다니 유감입니다. 저희 기록에는 PF4938 제품 한 개(처방된 선글라스)와 PF8442 제품 한 개(처방된 안경)가 귀하께 배달되었어야 하는 것으로 나타납니다. **19** 그러나 귀하는 이메일에서 상품 번호 PF4938 두 개가 대신 배달되었고, 귀하께서 받지 못하신 상품뿐만 아니라, 이 둘 모두에 대해서도 청구가 되었다고 했습니다.

21 저희는 오늘 오후에 그 안경을 속달 우편으로 배송했으므로 내일 아침에 귀하의 자택에 도착할 것입니다. 추가된 선글라스에 대해서는, 귀하께서 그것을 저희에게 반송해주시거나 반값에 구매하실 수 있습니다. **20** 귀하가 선택하신 것을 저희에게 알려주세요. 만약 선글라스를 반품하기를 바라신다면, 저희가 선불된 우편 봉투를 당신께 보내겠습니다. 소포를 받는 대로, 총 추가 요금은 귀하의 계좌에서 삭제될 것입니다. 만약 귀하가 그 물건을 갖기로 결정하신다면, 50퍼센트의 추가 요금이 빠져나갈 것입니다.

저희는 이 일이 초래했을 불편함에 대해 진심으로 사과드립니다. Virgo Eyewear와의 거래에 감사드립니다.

안부를 전하며,

Jewel Summers

고객 서비스 관리자

Virgo Eyewear

어휘 number one priority 최우선 순위 | regret *v.* 유감스럽게 생각하다 | issue *n.* 문제 | indicate *v.* 나타내다, 보여주다 | a pair of 한 쌍[벌]의 | prescription *n.* 처방 | instead *adv.* 대신에 | charge *v.* 청구하다 | ship *v.* 배송하다 | express mail 속달 우편 | as for ~에 대해 말하자면 | extra *adj.* 추가의 | inform *v.* 알리다 | return *v.* 반품하다 | pre-paid *adj.* 선불의 | mailing envelope 우편봉투 | package *n.* 소포, 꾸러미 | additional *adj.* 추가의 | remove *v.* 제거하다 | account *n.* 계좌; 이용 계정 | inconvenience *n.* 불편 | cause *v.* 야기하다, 초래하다 | customer service 고객 서비스

19. Ms. Summers는 왜 이메일을 보냈는가?

(A) 그녀가 반품된 물건을 받았음을 확인하기 위해

(B) Mr. Donati가 알린 오류를 처리하기 위해

(C) 불만 사항에 대한 뒤늦은 답변에 사과하기 위해

(D) Mr. Donati가 주문을 하도록 권하기 위해

해설 이메일을 보낸 이유, 즉 글의 목적을 물어보는 문제이다. 주문한 물건과 다른 물건이 오고 청구도 잘못되었음을 알리고 있는 Mr. Donati의 이메일에 대한 처리 사항을 알려주고 있으므로 정답은 (B) To address an error reported by Mr. Donati이다.

20. 이메일에 따르면, 요청하면 무엇이 Mr. Donati에게 보내질 것인가?

(A) 업데이트된 청구서

(B) 안경 처방전

(C) 제품 카탈로그

(D) 배송용 봉투

해설 잘못 배달된 선글라스를 반품하거나 반값에 구매할 수 있다고 안내하며, 반품을 원할 시 선불용 우편봉투를 발송해줄 것이라고 하므로 정답은 (D) A shipping envelope이다. mailing envelope가 shipping envelope으로 paraphrasing되었다.

21. PF8442 제품에 관하여 언급된 것은 무엇인가?

(A) Virgo Eyewear의 가장 잘 팔리는 상품이다.

(B) PF4938 상품과 함께 소포에 포함되어 있었다.

(C) Mr. Donati는 아마도 그것을 10월 16일에 받을 것이다.

(D) Mr. Donati는 그것을 온라인으로 구매했다.

해설 PF8442 제품에 관한 내용에 주목해보면, 선글라스(PF4938)와 안경(PF8442)를 한 개씩 주문했지만 선글라스만 두 개가 배달되고 안경이 누락되어 오늘 오후에 배송하였고, 안경이 내일 아침에 도착할 것이라고 안내하므로 편지를 쓴 날짜를 확인해야 한다. 편지를 쓴 날짜가 10월 15일이므로, 안경(PF8442)을 받을 날짜는 그 다음 날인 10월 16임을 알 수 있다. 따라서 정답은 (C) Mr. Donati will probably receive it on October 16이다.

[22-25] 다음 편지에 관한 문제입니다.

Medical Developments Today
532 Stanfield 가, 토론토

7월 17일

Tony Huyen
4698 Rockwood 가
토론토

23 Mr. Huyen에게,

〈Medical Developments Today〉를 구독해 주셔서 감사합니다. **22** 귀하의 현재 정기 구독이 8월 31일에 만료됨을 알려드리고자 합니다. **25** 이달 말까지 결제하시면, Dr. Lin Chin의 최첨단 온도 조절기를 무료로 받게 됩니다. **23** 이 우편에 동봉된 갱신 양식을 작성하셔서 다시 보내주십시오.

〈Medical Developments Today〉는 국내의 선두적인 건강 잡지이며 독자들에게 의료계의 최신 뉴스 및 동향을 제공합니다. 항상 그랬듯이, **24** Billy Grasp의 재미있는 칼럼과 Wanda Wilson 교수의 유익한 건강 팁을 포함한 모든 내용들을 계속해서 즐기실 것이라고 확신합니다.

진심으로,

Sarah McQueen

Sarah McQueen
유통 관리자
동봉물 재중

어휘 subscriber *n.* 구독자, 기부자 | fill out 작성하다 | renewal form 갱신 양식 | enclose *v.* 동봉하다 | leading *adj.* 선두의 | informative *adj.* 유익한 | issue *v.* 발행하다 | reminder *n.* (약속이나 해야 할 일 등) 상기시켜 주는 편지 | try out 테스트해보다 | comment on ~에 대해 논평하다 | write for ~에 기고하다 | thermostat *n.* 온도 조절 장치

22. 편지의 주된 목적은 무엇인가?
(A) 건강 조언을 제공하기 위해
(B) 상기시켜 주기 위해
(C) 신제품을 소개하기 위해
(D) 토크쇼를 홍보하기 위해

해설 편지의 목적을 물어보는 문제이므로, 편지의 서두를 확인해보면, 현재 정기 구독이 8월 31일에 만료됨을 알려드리고자 한다고 했으므로 정기 구독이 8월 31일자로 만료됨을 상기시켜주고 있다. 따라서 정답은 (B) To issue a reminder이다.

23. Mr. Huyen은 무엇을 하도록 요청 받는가?
(A) 제품을 테스트해본다
(B) 칼럼에 대해 논평한다
(C) 양식을 반환한다
(D) 경연 대회에 참가한다

해설 Mr. Huyen은 편지의 수신인으로, 첫 단락 후반부를 보면, 동봉된 갱신 양식을 작성하셔서 다시 보내달라고 요청하고 있으므로 정답은 (C) Return a form이다.

24. Mr. Grasp에 관하여 알 수 있는 것은 무엇인가?
(A) 의료 도구를 개발한다.
(B) 세계 일주 여행을 한다.
(C) 세미나를 기획한다.
(D) 잡지에 기고한다.

해설 Mr. Grasp가 언급되는 둘째 단락 후반부에서 Billy Grasp의 재미있는 칼럼을 포함한 모든 내용들을 즐길 것이라고 했으므로 Mr. Grasp가 잡지에 기고한다는 것을 알 수 있으므로 정답은 (D) He writes for a magazine이다.

25. [1], [2], [3], [4]로 표기된 곳 중에서 다음 문장이 들어가기에 가장 적절한 곳은 어디인가?

"이달 말까지 결제하시면, Lin Chin 박사의 최첨단 온도 조절기를 완전히 무료로 받게 됩니다."

(A) [1]
(B) [2]
(C) [3]
(D) [4]

해설 해당 문장은 이달 말까지 결제하면 Lin Chin 박사의 최첨단 온도 조절기를 무료로 받을 수 있다는 내용이므로 정기 구독이 만료된다는 내용의 문장 뒤에 오는 것이 가장 적절하다. 즉 [2]에 나오는 것이 가장 적절하므로 정답은 (B) [2]이다.

[26-30] 다음 이메일들에 관한 문제입니다.

발신: Kendra Wilkerson 〈kwilkerson@bensonparker.com〉
수신: Rhonda Nilsen 〈rnilsen860@picmail.com〉
날짜: 9월 14일, 월요일, 오후 2시 25분
제목: Benson & Parker Associates

Ms. Nilsen에게,

어제 저희 사무실에서 제 동료들과 저는 당신과 나눈 대화가 매우 즐거웠습니다. **26** 저희는 디지털 마케팅에 대한 당신의 프레젠테이션에 대단히 깊은 인상을 받았으며, 추후에 좀 더 대화를 나누기를 희망합니다. 저희는 다음 회차의 회계 관리직 면접을 위해 선별된 후보자들을 초대하고 있습니다.

전에 말씀 드린 바와 같이, 새 회계 관리자는 Mr. Steger가 이끄는 전자제품 고객팀에서 근무할 것입니다. **28** 그는 당신에게 이곳의 문화에 대해 얘기해 주고, 우리가 Benson & Parker에서 어떻게 비즈니스를 하는지에 대한 아이디어를 줄 뿐만 아니라, 당신의 마케팅 제안들에 대해서도 매우 듣고 싶어합니다.

만약 **29** 다음 주 수요일인 9월 23일이 괜찮으시다면, **26** 이 곳 오스틴 사무실에서 당신을 다시 뵙기를 바랍니다. 이 시간이 안 되시면, 저희가 **29** 10월 1일인 다음 주 목요일로 일정을 다시 잡을 수 있습니다. 당신이 편한 시간에 일정을 잡기 위해 제게 직접 연락을 주시거나 제 비서 Mr. Ryans에게 전화주셔도 됩니다.

귀하로부터 소식을 듣기를 고대합니다.

진심으로,

Kendra Wilkerson
인사 부장

어휘 **associate** *n.* 동료 ǀ **quite** *adv.* 꽤, 상당히 ǀ **impressed**
adj. 깊은 인상을 받은, 감명을 받은 ǀ **further** *adv.* 더 나아가,
더 ǀ **selected** *adj.* 선발된, 엄선된 ǀ **candidate** *n.* 후보자 ǀ
eager *adj.* 간절히 바라는, 열렬한 ǀ **suggestion** *n.* 제안 ǀ
alternatively *adv.* 그 대신, 그렇지 않으면 ǀ **following** *adj.*
그 다음의

발신: Rhonda Nilsen 〈rnilsen860@picmail.com〉
수신: Kendra Wilkerson 〈kwilkerson@bensonparker.com〉
날짜: 9월 15일, 화요일, 오전 9시
제목: 회계 관리직

Ms. Wilkerson에게,

27 저를 당신의 마케팅 회사의 회계 관리직에 고려하고 있다는 소식
을 듣게 되어 매우 기쁩니다. 저는 기꺼이 당신의 사무실을 다시 방
문하여 제 아이디어를 공유하고, 이곳 Lyon Marketing Solutions
에서의 제 경험에 대해 더 말씀 드리고 싶습니다.

29 안타깝게도, 저는 당신이 제안하신 첫 번째 날짜에는 이미 올랜
도에서 열리는 세미나의 연설 일정이 잡혀 있습니다. 하지만 저는
10월 1일에는 확실히 시간이 될 것입니다. 또한, 이번 주 제 면접에
대한 추가 조치로, **30** 현 회사의 제 관리자인 Mr. Praust에게 저를
위해 추천서를 보내달라고 요청했습니다. 제 작업 견본들을 더 보길
원하시면, 제게 알려주십시오. 제가 미리 이메일로 보내드리거나 직
접 가지고 가겠습니다.

방문하기를 고대하겠습니다.

진심으로,

Rhonda Nilsen

어휘 **consider** *v.* 고려하다 ǀ **propose** *v.* 제안하다 ǀ **follow up
on** ~에 대한 후속[추가] 조치를 하다 ǀ **on one's behalf** ~을
대신해서 ǀ **beforehand** *adv.* 사전에, 미리

---

26. 첫 번째 이메일의 목적은 무엇인가?

(A) 제품을 추천하기 위해

(B) 면접 일정을 잡기 위해

(C) 회사 계좌에 관해 논의하기 위해

(D) 직무 기술서를 제공하기 위해

해설 첫 번째 이메일의 목적을 물어보는 문제이다. 보통 처음 부분이나 마
지막 부분에 목적이 나오므로 먼저 첫 부분을 확인해보면, 프레젠테이
션에 감명 받았고 대화를 더 나누고 싶다고 하면서, 현재 회계 관리직
을 위한 선별된 후보자들을 초대 중이라 하며 이메일 마지막 부분에서
도, 다시 한번 만나보고 싶다고 하면서 약속 날짜를 잡으려고 하므로
면접 일정을 잡기 위한 이메일임을 알 수 있다. 따라서 정답은 (B) To
schedule an interview이다.

---

27. Benson & Parker 사의 업종은 무엇인가?

(A) 웹디자인 회사

(B) 전자 회사

(C) 회계 법인

(D) 마케팅 회사

해설 두 번째 이메일 지문의 발신인(Rhonda Nilsen)과 수신인(Kendra
Wilkerson)을 확인해 보면, 발신인이 말하는 수신인의 회사 업종을
확인할 수 있다. 저를 당신의 마케팅 회사의 회계 관리직에 고려하고
있다는 소식을 듣게 되어 매우 기쁘다고 말하고 있다. 따라서 정답은
(D) A marketing firm이다.

---

28. 첫 번째 이메일에 따르면, Mr. Steger는 Ms. Nilsen을 왜 만나고 싶
어 하는가?

(A) 그녀에게 회사의 방식과 기대에 대해 알려주기 위해

(B) 그녀를 곧 있을 프로젝트에 배정하기 위해

(C) 그의 팀원들에게 그녀를 소개하기 위해

(D) 그녀에게 추천서를 써주기 위해

해설 두 번째 단락에서 새 회계 관리자는 Mr. Steger가 이끄는 팀에서
일하게 될 거라는 내용 확인할 수 있다. 이어서 만나서 이곳 문화와
Benson & Parker 사에서 비즈니스를 하는 방법에 대해 알려주고
한다고 하므로 정답은 (A) To acquaint her with the company's
style and expectations이다. the culture here and an idea of
how we do business는 company's style and expectations로
paraphrasing되었다.

---

29. Ms. Nilsen은 세미나에 언제 참석할 계획인가?

(A) 월요일

(B) 화요일

(C) 수요일

(D) 목요일

해설 이중 지문 연계 문제이다. 먼저 두 번째 이메일에서 Ms. Nilsen의 일
정을 확인하며 두 번째 단락에서 첫 번째 제안한 날짜는 세미나 일정
이 있어서 안 된다고 하였는데, 첫 번째 이메일에서 Ms. Wilkerson
이 처음에 제안한 날짜는 Wednesday, September 23(9월 23일 수
요일)이므로 정답은 (C) Wednesday이다.

---

30. Benson & Parker 사의 직원이 아닌 사람은 누구인가?

(A) Ms. Wilkerson

(B) Mr. Ryans

(C) Mr. Steger

(D) Mr. Praust

해설 보기의 이름과 지문을 잘 대조해 봐야 한다.

• Ms. Wilkerson이 쓴 첫 번째 이메일, From: Kendra Wilkerson
〈kwilkerson@bensonparker.com〉 / 이메일 하단의 발신자와 직
급을 확인할 수 있다. Kendra Wilkerson, Human Resources
Manager → (A) Ms. Wilkerson은 Benson & Parker 사의 인사부
장이다.

- 첫 번째 이메일, Please contact me(= Mr. Wilkerson) directly or call my assistant, Mr. Ryans ➡ (B) Mr. Ryans은 Mr. Wilkerson의 비서이다.
- 첫 번째 이메일, As I(= Mr. Wilkerson) mentioned before, the new account supervisor will work on the electronics clients team, led by Mr. Steger. ➡ (C) Mr. Steger는 Benson & Parker 사 전자제품 고객팀장이다.

따라서 정답은 Ms. Nilsen이 쓴 두 번째 이메일의 I have asked Mr. Praust, my(= Ms. Nilsen's) manager at my current company, to send a reference letter on my behalf에서 보면 Mr. Praust는 Benson & Parker 사가 아닌 현재 Ms. Nilsen이 다니고 있는 회사의 관리자이므로 정답은 (D) Mr. Praust이다.

MINI TEST 02

1. (C)	2. (B)	3. (A)	4. (C)	5. (A)
6. (D)	7. (B)	8. (D)	9. (C)	10. (D)
11. (B)	12. (A)	13. (C)	14. (A)	15. (C)
16. (C)	17. (B)	18. (D)	19. (A)	20. (C)
21. (B)	22. (C)	23. (A)	24. (B)	25. (A)
26. (D)	27. (C)	28. (C)	29. (B)	30. (A)

1. 저희 항공편에서 더 나은 서비스를 제공하기 위해 저희는 승객들께 제안들을 남겨 주실 것을 요청 드립니다.

해설 빈칸은 leave의 목적어 자리로 명사 자리이다. 따라서 명사 (C)와 동명사 (D)가 가능하다. 동명사는 동사 성질 때문에 suggesting의 목적어(명사)가 뒤따라 나와야 하는데 빈칸 뒤에는 전치사구만 있고 목적어(명사)는 없다. 따라서 정답은 (C) suggestions이다.

어휘 passenger *n.* 승객 | provide *v.* 제공하다 | flight *n.* 비행기, 항공편 | suggestion *n.* 제안

2. Saver 전자의 최신식 진공청소기는 경쟁업체들의 그 어떤 제품들보다도 조용히 작동한다.

해설 진공청소기가 무언가를 작동시키는 것이 아니라, 진공청소기가 작동한다는 의미이어야 하므로, 이미 1형식으로 완벽한 문장이다. 즉, 빈칸은 필요 없는 자리로 문장 맨 끝에 있다. 따라서 부사인 (B) quietly가 정답이다.

어휘 latest *adj.* 최신의 | operate *v.* 작동하다 | competitor *n.* 경쟁자, 경쟁 상대 | quietly *adv.* 조용히

3. 많은 지역 농부들이 St. Clair 시장에서 자신의 농작물을 거래한다.

해설 빈칸은 명사 앞에 위치하므로 형용사가 정답이다. (B)는 '약', '~쯤'이라는 뜻으로 부사이므로 탈락이다. 나머지 형용사 어휘 중에, 문맥상 '많은 지역 농부들'이라는 의미가 적절하므로 정답은 (A) local이다.

어휘 trade *v.* 거래하다, 교역하다 | produce *n.* 농작물, 생산물 | local *adj.* 현지의, 지역의

4. Mr. Hiro의 강연에 관한 질문이 있다면, 그는 6시까지 시간이 될 것이다.

해설 If라는 접속사가 앞의 문장과 뒤의 문장을 연결하고 있다. 따라서 빈칸은 뒤의 문장의 주어 자리이다. 따라서 주격 (C) he가 정답이다.

어휘 talk *n.* 강연, 연설 | available *adj.* (사람이) 시간이 있는; (사물이) 이용 가능한

5. 건물이 개조되고 있는 동안, 회계 부서 직원들은 다른 부서 직원들과 업무 공간을 공유해야 한다.

해설 보기를 확인해보니, 동사 어휘 문제이다. 건물이 개조되는 동안, 회계 부서 직원들이 다른 부서 직원들과 업무 공간을 공유할 것이란 문맥이 적절하므로 정답은 (A) share이다. 「share A with B (A를 B와 공유하다)」의 패턴을 기억해 두자.

어휘 renovate *v.* 개조하다 | workspace *n.* 작업/업무 공간

6. 세 분기에 걸친 지속적인 성장에 따라, Sharman Distribution Depot는 더 많은 영업 담당자들을 고용하려고 생각하고 있다.

해설 빈칸 뒤에 영업 담당자라는 명사가 나오고 있으므로, 빈칸은 형용사 자리이다. 따라서 정답은 (D) additional이다.

어휘 quarter *n.* 분기 | continuous *adj.* 지속적인 | sales representative 판매원, 영업 담당자 | additional *adj.* 추가적인

7. Mr. Manashi는 Napal Tubular Accessories와의 협상 동안 회사를 대표하게 될 것이다.

해설 빈칸 뒤에는 명사가 존재하므로 부사절 접속사 (A)와 (C)는 답이 될 수 없다. 접속사는 주어와 동사를 동반한 문장이 와야 한다. (D)는 부사로 '더 늦게'라는 뜻을 가지고 있는데, 부사 뒤에 명사를 쓸 수 없다. (B)는 전치사로서, 명사를 동반할 수 있다. 따라서 정답은 (B) during이다.

어휘 represent *v.* 대표하다 | negotiation *n.* 협상, 교섭

8. Mr. Arras는 한 마케팅 회사가 이미 그에게 일자리를 보장했지만 다른 회사들을 알아보고 있다.

해설 보기를 확인해보니, 부사 어휘 문제이다. 앞의 절은 다른 회사들을 알아보고 있다는 내용이고 뒤의 절은 어떤 회사가 그에게 일자리를 장담했다는 내용이므로, 한 회사가 이미 일자리를 장담했지만 Mr. Arras는 다른 회사들을 알아보고 있다는 문맥이 적절하므로 정답은 (D) already이다.

어휘 look into ~을 조사하다; ~을 주의 깊게 살피다 | assure *v.* 장담하다, 확언하다

9. Pertol Business Supply는 청구서를 발부하고 온라인 납부에 관한 문의를 처리한다.

해설 빈칸 앞뒤로 동사와 목적어가 나란히 연결되어 있으므로 동일한 문장 성분을 이어주는 등위접속사가 필요한 자리이다. 청구서를 발부하고 (and), 문의를 처리한다는 의미이므로 정답은 (C) and이다.

어휘 issue *v.* 발행하다 | invoice *n.* 청구서 | handle *v.* 처리하다

10. Dr. William Thurston는 새로운 약을 개발하여 질병을 줄이는 데 일조한 전문가이다.

해설 이미 빈칸 앞에는 2형식 문장으로 완벽한 문장이 왔다. 따라서 빈칸부터는 수식어구가 와야 한다. 보기를 확인해보니, 관계대명사가 나와 있다. 관계대명사는 선행사를 수식하는 수식어구 역할이다. 그런데 빈칸 뒤의 문장이 5형식으로 완벽한 문장으로 나왔으므로 빈칸은 소유격 관계대명사가 정답이다. 선행사는 an expert이다. 따라서 정답은 (D) whose이다.

어휘 expert *n.* 전문가 | reduce *v.* 감소시키다, 줄이다

[11-14] 다음 편지에 관한 문제입니다.

6월 15일

Sean Kirk
8843 Whitney 로
세리토스, 캘리포니아 90703

Mr. Kirk에게,

Whitman 문학 협회장으로서, 7월 30일, Plato 컨벤션 센터에서 있을 연례 작가 컨퍼런스에서 당신이 연설하도록 **11** 초대하고 싶습니다.

12 행사는 오후 3시에 시작합니다. 컨퍼런스가 끝난 후에는, 근처에 있는 호텔에서 저녁 식사가 제공될 것입니다. 저희 초대를 **13** 수락하기로 결정하신다면, 제게 6월 30일까지 알려주세요. **14** 당신의 답변을 기다리겠습니다.

감사합니다.

안부를 전하며,

Dean Chalmers

어휘 chairman *n.* 의장, 회장 | literary *adj.* 문학의, 문학적인 | association *n.* 협회 | annual *adj.* 연례의 | nearby *adj.* 근처의, 가까운 곳의 | invitation *n.* 초대(장)

11. 해설 「would like to V」라는 표현을 알아두자. '~하고 싶다'라는 뜻이다. 따라서 정답은 (B) to invite이다.

12. 해설 앞 문장에서 7월 30일, Plato 컨벤션 센터에서 연례 작가 컨퍼런스가 있다고 했으므로 컨퍼런스를 받을 수 있는 명사는 '행사'이다. 이 행사(= 컨퍼런스)가 오후 3시에 시작된다는 의미로 연결되는 것이 적절하므로 정답은 (A) event이다. (B) change(변화), (C) display(진열), (D) interview(면접)은 모두 문맥상 어색하다.

13. 해설 지문의 도입부에서 컨퍼런스에서의 연설을 위해 Mr. Kirk를 초대하고 싶다고 했으므로 초대를 수락하기로 결정한다면 자신에게 얘기해 달라고 연결되어야 적절하므로 정답은 (C) accept이다.

14. (A) 당신의 답변을 기다리겠습니다.
(B) 귀하의 청구서 번호를 알려주십시오.
(C) 컨벤션 일정이 업데이트되어야 합니다.
(D) 저녁 식사 메뉴에서 하나를 선택해주십시오.

해설 초대 수락 여부에 대한 응답을 6월 30일까지 달라고 했으므로 응답을 기다리겠다는 내용이 나와야 가장 적합하다. 따라서 정답은 (A) I look forward to your response이다.

[15-16] 다음 표에 관한 문제입니다.

승객: Wendy Tyler
표 번호: 8940 23-55
여행지: **16** Bayou Valley, Blue Line 경유
발행일: 8월 5일, 오후 12시 45분

| **16** Novaville | 출발 시각: 오후 1시 20분 |
| 7번 승강장 | 좌석 번호: A12 |

---

16 Stanley 역에서 기차를 갈아타세요.

| **15** Stanley 시 | 출발 시각: 오후 3시 30분 |
| 12번 승강장 | 좌석 번호: D25 |

| Bayou Valley | 도착 시각: 오후 5시 5분 |
| 9번 승강장 | |

가격: 21.00유로
지불 수단: 신용카드

어휘 passenger *n.* 승객 | issue *v.* 발행하다 | platform *n.* (기차역의) 플랫폼, 승강장 | payment method 지불 수단[방법] | credit card 신용카드

15. 표에 따르면, Ms. Tyler는 언제 Stanley 시를 떠날 것인가?
(A) 오후 12시 45분에
(B) 오후 1시 20분에
(C) 오후 3시 30분에
(D) 오후 5시 5분에

해설 Stanley City를 키워드로 삼아 해당 내용 포착하자. Stanley City, Depart: 3:30 P.M. Stanley 시에서 출발 시각이 오후 3시 30분임을 확인할 수 있다. 따라서 정답은 (C) At 3:30 P.M.이다. depart = leave임을 알아두도록 한다.

16. Ms. Tyler의 Bayou Valley 여행에 관하여 언급된 것은 무엇인가?
(A) 버스 노선으로의 환승을 포함한다.
(B) 일주일 전에 예약되었다.
(C) 두 개의 기차를 탈 것을 요구한다.
(D) 현금으로 지불되었다.

해설 trip to Bayou Valley를 키워드로 삼아 Bayou Valley까지의 여행 경로를 확인해보자. Novaville을 출발하여 Bayou Valley에 도착할 때까지 Stanley 역에서 기차를 갈아타라고 했으며, 좌석번호도 바뀌어 있는 점으로 보아 총 두 개의 기차를 타는 것으로 파악할 수 있다. 따라서 정답은 (C) It requires her to take two trains이다.

Wilson, Edward [오후 4:19]

이번 주말에 Dr. Anthony Samuels가 하는 강연에 가시는 분 있나요?

Stuart, Amy [오후 4:21]

저는 가려고 했는데, 계획을 바꿨어요.

Wilson, Edward [오후 4:23]

무엇이 당신의 계획을 바뀌게 만들었나요? 박사님 이야기를 듣는 것에 관심이 없는 건가요?

Stuart, Amy [오후 4:25]

그와 반대로, 저는 그의 강연에 참석하고 싶지만, **17** Mr. Jackson이 내일 베를린에서 Mr. Fritz를 만나라고 저를 보내기 때문에, 출국을 하게 됐어요.

Saville, Mary [오후 4:27]

정말 유감이네요. 제가 강연티켓을 구해서 엄청 고대하고 있거든요. **18** Samuels 박사는 자신의 최근 저서에 나오는 몇 가지 견해들에 대해서 논의할 거예요.

Wilson, Edward [오후 4:28]

18 베스트셀러 목록에 있는 그 책이요?

Saville, Mary [오후 4:31]

18 바로 그거예요. 그 책을 읽었는데, 책의 일부분이 이해하기 너무 어려웠어요. 저는 강연에 참여해 그 책에 대한 식견을 가질 수 있기를 희망해요.

Stuart, Amy [오후 4:33]

그곳에 간다니 참 좋겠네요. 메모를 해서 저한테 좀 보여주시면 안 될까요?

Saville, Mary [오후 4:36]

문제 없어요. 저는 늘 이런 종류의 행사에서 강사가 말하는 것들을 필기하니까, 제가 필기한 것을 기꺼이 공유할게요.

Wilson, Edward [오후 4:37]

좋아요, 두 분 다 저에게 확신을 주셨네요. 지금 당장 강연 신청을 해야겠어요.

어휘 intend *v.* 의도하다 | interested in ~에 흥미가 있는 | on the contrary 그와 반대로 | attend *v.* 참석하다 | out of ~ 밖에 | definitely *adv.* 분명히 | latest *adj.* 가장 최근의 | insight *n.* 통찰력, 식견 | take notes 메모하다 | convince *v.* 설득하다 | register *v.* 등록하다

---

17. Mr. Jackson에 대하여 암시된 것은 무엇인가?

(A) 세미나에 참석할 것이다.

(B) Ms. Stuart의 상사이다.

(C) 베를린에서 일한다.

(D) Dr. Samuels를 알고 있다.

해설 오후 4시 25분에 Mr. Jackson이 Ms. Stuart에게 내일 베를린에서 Mr. Fritz를 만나라고 보냈다고 했으므로, Mr. Jackson이 Ms. Stuart의 상사임을 추론할 수 있다. 따라서 정답은 (B) He is Ms. Stuart's boss이다.

18. Ms. Saville가 오후 4시 31분에 "바로 그거예요"라고 쓴 것은 무슨 의미인가?

(A) Mr. Wilson이 행사에 참여해야만 한다.

(B) 그녀가 자신의 티켓을 Mr. Wilson에게 주었다.

(C) 그녀는 행사에 참석할 것이다.

(D) Mr. Wilson의 말이 맞았다.

해설 화자가 말하고자 하는 의도를 파악하는 문제이다. 오후 4시 27분 채팅의 세 번째 문장에서 Ms. Saville가 Dr. Samuels가 최근 책의 몇 가지 견해에 대하여 논의한다고 했고, 오후 4시 28분에 Mr. Wilson의 그 책이 베스트셀러 목록 1위에 있는 책이냐고 물어보았고, 오후 4시 31분에 You got it이라고 말했으므로 Mr. Wilson의 말이 맞았음을 짐작할 수 있다. 따라서 정답은 (D) Mr. Wilson is correct이다.

[19-21] 다음 이메일에 관한 문제입니다.

수신: Bruce Lennon 〈blennon@metcom.co.uk〉

발신: updates@sabs.org.uk

날짜: 10월 30일

제목: 정보

19 스코틀랜드 생물과학협회(SABS)는 회원님들이 협회가 주최하는 웹 강연 시리즈에 관하여 가장 먼저 알기를 바랍니다. **20** SABS는 몇몇 국내 정상의 업계 선두 업체들 및 학자들과 우리 분야의 주요 화제들에 대한 온라인 강의를 제공하고자 팀을 이루었습니다. 강의는 대략 두 시간이 걸리며 두 달마다 열릴 예정입니다. 각 강의의 끝에서, 모든 참석자들은 20분짜리 대화형 질의응답 시간에 참여할 수 있습니다.

21 업계에 대한 소중한 통찰력을 얻고 그 분야에 대한 전반적인 지식을 늘릴 수 있는 이 멋진 기회에 참여하시려면 저희 웹사이트 www.sabs.org.uk를 방문하세요. 거기서 여러분은 올해 있을 다섯 강의의 주제와 날짜, 시간대를 찾으실 수 있을 겁니다. 참여를 위한 컴퓨터 시스템 요건뿐만 아니라 등록과 지불 안내 역시 이용하실 수 있습니다.

우리는 또한 강연자를 찾고 있습니다. 자격을 갖추고 계시다면, 저희 진행자 Sandy Young에게 syoung@sabs.org.uk로 연락해 주세요.

어휘 biological *adj.* 생물학의 | sponsor *v.* 주관[주최]하다; 후원하다 | team up 팀을 이루다; 협력하다 | approximately *adv.* 대략 | take place 열리다, 발생하다 | attendee *n.* 참석자 | engage in ~에 관여하다[참여하다] | interactive *adj.* 대화형의; 상호적인 | take part in ~에 참여하다, 참가하다 | gain *v.* 얻다 | valuable *adj.* 소중한, 가치 있는 | insight *n.* 통찰력; 이해 | overall *adj.* 전반적인 | instruction *n.* 지시, 설명 | requirement *n.* 요구 조건 | seek *v.* 구하다, 찾다 | qualified *adj.* 자격이 있는

---

19. Mr. Lennon은 왜 이메일을 받았는가?

(A) SABS의 회원이다.

(B) 지리학을 공부하기 위해 지원했다.

(C) 강의 시리즈를 조직했다.

(D) 발표하기로 일정이 잡혀 있다.

해설 왜 이메일을 받게 되었는지를 물어보고 있다. 글의 첫머리에서 이메일을 보낸 이유를 확인할 수 있다. SABS 협회가 주최하는 강연에 대한

소식을 그 회원들에게 가장 먼저 알리고 싶다고 하므로 수신자인 Mr. Lennon은 SABS의 회원임을 알 수 있다. 따라서 정답은 (A) He is a member of the SABS이다.

20. 강의에 관하여 언급된 것은 무엇인가?

(A) 무료로 제공된다.

(B) 매달 열린다.

(C) 특정 분야에 중점을 둔다.

(D) SABS 본사에서 열린다.

해설 lectures를 키워드로 삼아 보기와 해당 내용 대조해보자. SABS는 몇몇 국내 정상의 업계 선두주자 및 학자들과 팀을 이루어 우리 분야(= Biological Science)에서 중요한 주제들에 대한 온라인 강의를 제공할 거라고 하고 있다. 따라서 정답은 (C) They focus on a specific profession이다. field는 profession으로 paraphrasing되었다.

21. SABS 웹사이트에서 발견될 수 있는 것으로 언급되지 않은 것은 무엇인가?

(A) 강의 주제

(B) 강사의 프로필

(C) 강의 날짜

(D) 등록 정보

해설 보기와 지문 내용 대조해 봐야 한다.

• To take part in this wonderful opportunity ~, visit our Web site at www.sabs.org.uk. There you will find the topics, dates, and times of this year's five lectures. ➔ (A) Lecture topics, (C) Dates of lectures

• Registration and payment instructions will also be available ➔ (D) Registration information

하지만 강사 프로필은 웹사이트에서 찾을 수 없다. 따라서 정답은 (B) Profiles of lecturers이다.

[22-25] 다음 기사에 관한 문제입니다.

Fremont 군구 (1월 8일) – **22** Clarkson 카운티 위원 Nadia Betlam은 카운티에서 종종 교통 체증이 매우 심한 55번 고속도로를 따라 있는 두 지역에 도로 확장을 위한 자금을 제공할 것이라고 오늘 아침 말표했다. 프로젝트의 첫 번째 단계는 Pacific 대로로 향하는 출구 경사로의 확장과 관련이 있으며, 3월 10일에 시작될 것이다. Ms. Betlam은 날씨만 좋다면 공사가 약 한 달 안에 완료될 것으로 예상한다. **23** 프로젝트의 두 번째 단계는 Garrison 로와 Jacob 가 사이의 고속도로에 3킬로미터 **24** 구간에 차선을 추가하는 것을 포함한다. 이 작업은 4월 초에 시작될 것이다. **25** 위원들은 다음 주 그들의 회의에서 그 일정을 최종 확정 지을 것이다. Ms. Betlam은 전체 프로젝트를 감독하기 위해 경험 많은 엔지니어가 고용될 것이라고 덧붙였다.

어휘 commissioner *n.* (위원회) 위원 | funding *n.* 자금 조달 | congested *adj.* 혼잡한, 붐비는 | phase *n.* 단계; 국면 | involve *v.* ~와 관련이 있다; 포함하다 | widening *n.* 확장 | exit ramp 출구 경사로 | permit *v.* 허용하다 | lane *n.* 차선 | finalize *v.* 마무리 짓다, 완결하다 | oversee *v.* 감독하다, 관리하다 | entire *adj.* 전체의; 완전한

22. 도로 공사는 왜 필요한가?

(A) 도로가 심한 홍수로 파손되었다.

(B) 도로의 표면이 많이 고르지 못하다.

(C) 도로가 교통량을 수용하기에 너무 좁다.

(D) 도로가 겨울에 종종 너무 미끄럽다.

해설 왜 도로 공사가 필요한지에 관한 단서를 찾으면, Clarkson 카운티에서 교통 정체가 심한 55번 고속도로를 따라 있는 두 지역에 도로 공사를 위한 자금이 지원될 예정이라고 나와있으므로 정답은 (C) The roads are too narrow for the amount of traffic이다.

23. 4월에는 무엇이 공사 중이겠는가?

(A) 55번 고속도로

(B) Pacific 대로

(C) Garrison 로

(D) Jacob 가

해설 in April을 키워드로 삼아 해당 내용 포착해보자. 프로젝트의 두 번째 단계는 55번 고속도로에 3킬로미터 구간의 차선을 추가하는 것이며, 이 작업은 4월 초에 시작될 예정이라고 하였으므로 정답은 (A) Highway 55이다.

24. 8번째 줄의 단어 "stretch"와 의미상 가장 가까운 것은

(A) 과장

(B) 구역

(C) 확장

(D) 제한

해설 프로젝트의 두 번째 단계는 Garrison 로와 Jacob 가 사이의 고속도로 상의 3킬로미터 '구간'에 차선을 추가할 것이라는 내용이다. 문맥상 stretch가 section으로 paraphrasing되었다. 따라서 (B) section가 정답이다.

25. 기사에 따르면, 다음 주에 무엇이 완료될 것인가?

(A) 도로 공사 일정

(B) 추가 차선

(C) 세 개의 경사로

(D) 공사 계약

해설 next week를 키워드로 삼아 해당 내용을 포착해보자. 위원들이 다음 주 회의에서 일정을 확정 지을 예정이라고 하였으므로 정답은 (A) A roadwork schedule이다.

[26-30] 다음 광고, 견적서, 그리고 이메일에 관한 문제입니다.

Togo 기업 이사 업체

(480) 555-7310

귀하의 사무실이나 장비를 옮겨야 하나요? **26** 귀하의 회사가 사무실을 이전해야 하든, 단순히 자재들을 다른 장소로 옮기기만 하면 되든, 귀하의 모든 이사 요구에 대한 답은 Togo 기업 이사 업체입니다.

저희 서비스는 다음을 포함하고 있습니다.

● 단거리와 장거리 운송

- ㉗ 전문 포장 및 ㉖ 국내외 모두 안전한 물품 배송을 포함한 완벽한 배송 준비
- ㉙ 무료 기본 보험 보장 (추가 비용으로 Helix LLC의 추가 보험을 이용할 수 있습니다.)

저희는 아리조나 주의 메사에 본사를 두고 있으며, 뉴욕, 로스앤젤레스, 시카고를 포함하여 국내 전역의 주요 유통 지역에 지점들을 가지고 있습니다. ㉘ Togo는 아리조나 이삿짐센터 협회(AMA)의 공인을 받았습니다. 인가 상태를 유지하고자, AMA의 높은 기준을 맞추기 위해 저희 모든 직원들은 정기적으로 교육과 평가를 받습니다.

저희는 처음부터 끝까지 업무가 낱낱이 감독될 수 있도록 ㉚ 모든 Togo 고객 분들께 경험 많은 이사 코디네이터를 정해 드립니다.

어휘   whether A or B A이든 B이든 | relocate v. 이전하다 | supplies n. 자재, 물자 | needs n. 요구 | packing n. 포장 | domestically adv. 국내에서 | insurance coverage 보험 (보상 범위) | supplemental adj. 추가의, 보충의 | distribution n. 유통 | including prep. ~을 포함하여 | accreditation n. 인가 | assess v. 평가하다 | meet v. 충족시키다 | pair v. 짝을 짓다 | experienced adj. 경험이 많은 | supervise v. 감독하다

가격 견적서
Togo 기업 이사 업체
(480) 555-7310

날짜: 2월 10일
회사: ㉙ RMC 금융

번호	세목	금액
1	운송	350달러
2	컨테이너 50개	150달러
3	포장 (하역 포함)	5,000달러
4	㉙ 보험	100달러

소계: 5,600달러
세금(10%): 560달러
총계: 6,160달러

상기 비용은 이사를 완료하는 데 필요한 실제 노동력과 시간을 바탕으로 변경될 수 있습니다.

어휘   packing n. 포장 | loading and unloading 하역 | subtotal n. 소계

수신: Jack Walbert 〈j.walbert@togomovers.com〉
발신: Paul Han 〈p.han@rmcfinancial.com〉
날짜: 2월 12일
제목: 회의 후속 조치

Mr. Walbert에게,

지난주 회의는 즐거웠습니다. 당신이 보내준 견적서를 이사회에 제출했고, 그분들이 비용에 만족해 했습니다. 이사 업무가 진행될 수 있도록 우리에게 계약서를 보내주세요.

회의 기간 동안, ㉚ Mr. Elman은 저희 업계를 매우 잘 알고 있는 것 같습니다. 가능하다면, 저는 우리의 이사를 감독하는데 그가 배정되기를 바랍니다. 곧 당신으로부터 소식을 듣길 바랍니다.

어휘   estimate n. 견적서 | executive board 이사회 | proceed with ~을 (계속) 진행하다 | familiar with ~에 정통한[잘 아는] | assign v. 배정하다, 맡기다 | oversee v. 감독하다

---

26. Togo 기업 이사 업체에 관하여 광고가 나타내는 것은 무엇인가?
(A) 새 직원들을 구하고 있다.
(B) 얼마 전에 본사를 옮겼다.
(C) 사무용 장비를 재조립한다.
(D) 장비를 해외로 운송한다.

해설   광고문에서 회사명(Togo Commercial Movers) 및 사무실이나 장비 이전이 필요하냐고 말한 초반 문장을 통해 이 업체가 이삿짐센터임을 알 수 있고, 그들이 제공하는 서비스 항목들 중 물건을 국내외로 모두 안전하게 배달한다고 했으므로 (D) It transports equipment internationally가 정답이다. delivery ~ items가 transits equipment로 paraphrasing되었다.

---

27. 광고에 따르면, 어떤 서비스가 이용 가능한가?
(A) 저장 공간 임대
(B) 다양한 교육 프로그램
(C) 전문 포장
(D) 유연한 일정 관리

해설   광고문에서 Togo 기업 이사 업체가 제공하는 서비스 항목들 중 전문 포장(professional packing)이 포함되어 있다고 했으므로 (C) Expert packing이 정답이다. professional이 expert로 paraphrasing되었다.

---

28. Togo 기업 이사 업체의 직원들에 관하여 알 수 있는 것은 무엇인가?
(A) 재무 관리에 이력이 있다.
(B) 사무실 수리를 전문으로 한다.
(C) 전문 기관에 의해 공인되었다.
(D) 모두 메사에서 일한다.

해설   광고문의 세 번째 단락에서 자신들이 이삿짐센터 협회의 공인을 받았고, 이 인가 상태를 유지하기 위해 그 협회의 높은 기준을 맞추고자 직원들이 정기적으로 교육 및 평가를 받는다고 했으므로 (C) They are certified by a professional organization가 정답이다. recognized, accreditation이 certified로, Arizona Movers Association(AMA)가 professional organization으로 paraphrasing되었다.

29. RMC 금융에 관하여 알 수 있는 것은 무엇인가?

(A) 여러 지점을 가지고 있다.

(B) 추가 보험을 구매했다.

(C) 시카고에 본사를 두고 있다.

(D) Helix LLC와 합병할 것이다.

해설 RMC 금융이 언급된 두 번째 지문의 거래 내역을 보면 보험료로 100 달러가 기재되어 있는데(Insurance: $100,00), 광고문의 서비스 항목들 중 기본 보험은 무료로 제공하지만, 추가 요금을 내면 Helix LLC의 보험을 추가로 들 수 있다고 했으므로 RMC Financial이 추가 보험을 들 것임을 알 수 있다. 따라서 (B) It has purchased additional insurance가 정답이다. supplemental이 additional로 paraphrasing되었다.

---

30. Mr. Elman은 누구이겠는가?

(A) 이사 전문가

(B) AMA 대표

(C) RMC 금융 간부

(D) 사무 보조원

해설 Mr. Elman이 언급된 세 번째 지문에서 Mr. Elman이 자신들의 업계를 매우 잘 알고 있는 것 같으니 가능하면 이사 감독자로 그가 배정되기를 바란다고 했는데, 첫 번째 지문 맨 마지막 문장을 보면 이사 감독을 위해 모든 고객들에게 경험 많은 이사 코디네이터를 붙여 준다고 했으므로 Mr. Elman은 이사 전문 코디네이터임을 알 수 있다. 따라서 (A) A moving specialist가 정답이다. experienced move coordinator가 moving specialist로 paraphrasing되었다.

MINI TEST 03

1. (B)	**2.** (A)	**3.** (A)	**4.** (B)	**5.** (C)
6. (C)	**7.** (D)	**8.** (B)	**9.** (C)	**10.** (D)
11. (C)	**12.** (A)	**13.** (B)	**14.** (A)	**15.** (C)
16. (A)	**17.** (D)	**18.** (B)	**19.** (C)	**20.** (C)
21. (B)	**22.** (B)	**23.** (B)	**24.** (B)	**25.** (A)
26. (C)	**27.** (B)	**28.** (B)	**29.** (B)	**30.** (A)

1. 그 뷔페의 음식은 그것들이 필요할 때에 다시 채워지는 것을 확실히 하기 위해서 자주 점검된다.

해설 동사가 is p.p. 형태로 수동태 형태이다. 이미 수동태로서 완벽한 문장이다. 왜냐하면 check는 3형식 동사인데, 수동태는 목적어를 쓰지 않으므로 3형식의 목적어 (명사)는 쓸 필요가 없어졌으므로 is p.p.로 문장이 끝이 날 수 있다. 따라서 빈칸은 더 이상 필요 없는 수식어구 자리이다. 따라서 부사인 (B) frequently가 정답이다.

어휘 **make sure** 확실히 하다 I **restock** v. 다시 채우다, 보충하다 I **frequent** v. 자주 다니다 adj. 잦은

2. Steamline 철도는 최근 지역 행선지까지의 기본 운임을 10퍼센트 인상했다.

해설 문맥상 기본 운임비를 인상했다는 의미기 적절하므로 정답은 (A) fares이다.

어휘 **raise** v. 올리다, 인상하다 I **destination** n. 행선지, 목적지 I **fare** n. (교통) 요금, 운임 I **value** n. 가치 I **output** n. 생산량, 산출량 I **asset** n. 자산, 재산

3. Mr. Wirral이 급행열차를 탄다면, 금요일 오후에 열릴 간부 회의에 정시에 도착할 것이다.

해설 (B)와 (C)는 부사로서, 뒤에 명사 the executive meeting를 동반할 수 없다. (D)는 접속사로서, 빈칸 뒤에 주어와 동사 문장이 나왔어야 했다. (A)는 전치사로 뒤에 명사를 동반할 수 있으므로 정답은 (A) for 이다.

어휘 **express train** 급행열차 I **make it** ~에 도착하다 I **on time** 정각에, 시간을 어기지 않고 I **executive meeting** 간부 회의

4. 관리자는 우리의 컴퓨터를 안전한 비밀번호로 보호할 것을 요청했다.

해설 보기를 확인해보니, 대명사 격을 물어보는 문제이다. 빈칸 뒤에 명사가 있으므로 명사 앞은 소유격이 올 자리이다. 따라서 정답은 (B) our 이다.

어휘 **protect** v. 보호하다 I **secure** adj. 안전한

5. 회계 부장 Eunice Taft는 금요일에 있을 워크숍에서 새로운 소프트웨어의 사용 방법을 보여줄 것이다.

해설 문맥상 새로운 소프트웨어를 어떻게 사용하는지 보여줄 것이라는 문맥이 적합하므로 정답은 (C) show이다.

어휘 **accounting** n. 회계

6. King Roofing은 그들이 하는 어떠한 작업이든 우수한 자재들만을 사용하는 것을 자랑스럽게 생각한다.

해설 materials가 명사인데, 명사 앞에 빈칸이 있다. 명사 앞에는 형용사가 들어가야 한다. 따라서 정답은 (C) superior이다.

어휘 **roofing** n. 지붕 재료, 지붕 공사 I **take pride in** ~을 자랑하다 I **material** n. 재료, 자재

7. Kilburn 사는 저희 제품과 서비스에 관한 귀하의 의견을 환영합니다.

해설 your은 소유격이다. 소유격 뒤에는 항상 명사가 있어야 한다. 따라서 정답은 (D) suggestions이다.

어휘 **welcome** v. 환영하다 I **concerning** prep. ~에 관한

8. Cottonbreeze는 Laurel 화장품의 향수 비누 라인에 가장 최근에 추가된 것이다.

해설 보기를 확인해보니, 형용사 어휘 문제이다. Cottonbreeze란 상품이 향수 비누 제품에 가장 최근에 추가되었다는 의미가 적절하므로 정답은 (B) recent이다. late는 예정된 시간을 지나 늦었다는 의미이며, last는 '가장 최근의'라는 의미로 쓰이지만 이미 최상급의 의미가 내포되어 있어 앞에 최상급 표현(the most)과 함께 쓸 수 없으므로 답이 될 수 없다.

어휘 addition *n.* 부가물, 추가된 것 | perfumed soap 향수 비누

9. 기조 연설자가 소개되기 직전에 우리는 짧은 영상을 시청할 것이다.

해설 before가 앞의 문장과 뒤의 문장을 연결하는 형태이다. 뒤의 문장에서 is라는 동사가 있으므로 동사인 (B)와 (D)는 탈락이다. 명사 (A)를 is라는 2형식 동사 뒤 주격보어 자리에 넣으면, 주격보어 자리에 명사가 오게 되므로 주어와 동격이 되어야 한다. 그러나 Our keynote speaker = introduction은 맞지 않는다. (C)는 넣게 되면 수동태가 되며, 수동태이므로 목적어(명사)가 나오지 않아도 문장이 성립된다. 따라서 정답은 (C) introduced이다.

어휘 right before ~하기 직전에 | keynote speaker 기조 연설자

10. 많은 방문객들이 개회식에 참석할 것으로 예상되므로, 박물관 고객들은 입장을 위해 일찍 도착할 것을 권고받는다.

해설 보기를 확인해보니 한정사 문제이다. much는 불가산명사와 써야 하는데 visitors는 복수 가산명사이다. every는 항상 단수 취급하므로 visitor가 됐어야 맞다. any는 가산명사와 불가산명사를 모두 수식할 수 있지만 의미상 many가 더 적합하다. many는 복수가산명사와 함께 쓰인다. visitors가 복수이고, 복수를 썼다는 것은 가산명사라는 것을 알 수 있다. 문맥상 많은 방문자들이 참석할 것으로 기대가 된다는 뜻이므로 정답은 (D) many이다.

어휘 patron *n.* 고객; 후원자 | gain entry 입장하다 | opening ceremony 개회식

[11-14] 다음 공지에 관한 문제입니다.

독자님들께,

〈Starborough Digest〉는 starboroughdigest.com의 오픈을 ⑪ 의욕적으로 알려드립니다. ⑫ 저희의 새 웹사이트는 인쇄판과 동일한 내용을 제공할 것입니다. 또한, 독자님께서는 대화형 포럼, 퀴즈, 그리고 설문도 즐기실 것입니다. ⑬ 이 특징들은 여러분과 여러분의 지역 사회에 관련된 사안들에서 더 직접적인 역할을 하도록 부추길 것입니다.

이 콘텐츠는 모든 독자들에게 추가 비용 없이 제공될 것입니다. 그것을 이용하시려면, 저희의 새 홈페이지에서 ⑭ 등록만 하시면 됩니다. 비구독자들 역시 "등록하고 싶어요" 링크를 클릭하여 등록하실 수 있습니다.

〈Starborough Digest〉와 starboroughdigest.com은 여러분을 계속 세상과 연결시켜 드리고 정보를 제공합니다!

어휘 announce *v.* 알리다, 발표하다 | subscriber *n.* 구독자 | interactive *adj.* 대화형의 | forum *n.* 포럼, (토론의) 장 | feature *n.* (신문·텔레비전 등의) 특집, 섹션; 특징 | encourage *v.* 장려하다, 권장하다 | play a role 역할을 하다 | issue *n.* 사안, 문제 | concern *v.* ~에 영향을 미치다, ~에 흥미를 갖다 | at no additional cost 추가 비용 없이 | access *v.* 접속하다, 이용하다 | simply *adv.* 그냥, 그저 | enroll *v.* 등록하다 | content *n.* 내용(물) | print edition 인쇄판

11. 해설 보기를 확인해보니, 부사 어휘 문제이다. 동사 announces를 수식하기에 알맞은 부사를 고르는 문제인데, 〈Starborough Digest〉란 잡지사가 웹사이트의 오픈을 '의욕적으로' 알린다는 의미가 적절하므로 정답은 (C) enthusiastically이다.

12. (A) 저희의 새 웹사이트는 인쇄판의 모든 내용을 제공할 것입니다.
(B) 저희의 웹사이트에서 사용법을 읽어보실 수 있습니다.
(C) 일단 저희 웹사이트가 업데이트되면 여러분의 계정에 접속할 수 있습니다.
(D) 저희 웹사이트도 저희 경쟁사들에 관한 정보를 제공합니다.

해설 starboroughdigest.com의 오픈을 시작하고, 빈칸 다음 문장은 세부사항에 대한 내용이므로 빈칸에는 오픈하는 업체가 웹사이트에서 제공하는 세부내용이 들어가는 것이 적절하므로 정답은 (A) Our new Web site offers all the content of our print edition이다.

13. 해설 빈칸 뒤에 명사가 존재하므로 (A) "Theirs"는 소유대명사로 이 자체가 명사이므로 뒤에 명사를 또 동반할 수 없다. (C)는 단수를 의미하므로 복수 명사 앞에 올 수 없으므로 소거한다. (D)는 소유격으로 빈칸 뒤에 명사를 동반할 수는 있으나, '그들의 특징들이'라는 뜻이 되는데, '그들'이라는 대명사를 쓰려면, 앞에 '그들'을 받을 수 있는 명사가 먼저 있어야한다. '그들'을 받는 명사가 앞에 나온 '구독자'라고 봐도 문맥상 이상하고, 'forums, quizzes, and surveys'의 특징이라고 봐도 문맥상 이상하다. (B)는 복수이므로 복수 명사 features를 받기에 적절하다. these features은 앞에 나온 'forums, quizzes, and surveys'를 의미한다. 따라서 정답은 (B) These이다.

14. 해설 부사구 To access it을 제외하면 주절이 주어가 없이 부사(simply)로 시작하므로 명령문이라는 것을 알 수 있다. 따라서 '등록하다'는 의미로 동사원형인 (A) register를 정답으로 선택한다.

[15-16] 다음 안내문에 관한 문제입니다.

CULVER 가 주차장

이 표를 소지해주시기 바랍니다. ⑮ 주차장 요원에게 요금을 지불하실 때, 이 표를 제시해 주세요.

날짜: 5월 7일   **출입 시각:** 오전 11시 25분

신용카드 또는 현금 지불만 가능합니다.
⑯ 월 정기권을 구매하시면, 1년에 700달러까지 절약하실 수 있습니다! 자세한 사항은, 저희 웹사이트 culverlot.co.uk를 방문하시거나 (034) 5555-1294로 전화 주세요.

어휘 parking lot 주차장 | attendant *n.* 종업원, 안내원 | credit card 신용카드 | cash *n.* 현금 | payment *n.* 지불 | accept *v.* 수용하다, 받아들이다 | save *v.* 절약하다 | monthly pass 월 정기권 | detail *n.* 세부 사항

15. 고객들은 주차 요금을 어떻게 지불해야 하는가?

(A) 주차장 웹사이트를 방문함으로써

(B) 선불 카드를 사용함으로써

(C) 안내원에게 지불함으로써

(D) 미터기에 돈을 예금함으로써

해설 주차 요금 지불에 관한 언급을 주목해보자. 지불할 때 주차요원에게 이 표를 보여주라고 안내하였다. 따라서 정답은 (C) By making a payment to an attendant이다.

---

16. 고객들은 왜 표에 나와 있는 전화번호로 전화하도록 권장되는가?

(A) 할인된 주차 요금에 관한 정보를 구하기 위해

(B) 서비스 품질에 관한 의견을 제공하기 위해

(C) 주차장 자리를 일주일 동안 예약하기 위해

(D) 다른 지불 수단에 관해 문의하기 위해

해설 전화번호가 언급된 부분을 주목해보면, 바로 위에서 월 정기권을 구매하면 1년에 700달러를 절약할 수 있다고 하며 월 정기권의 할인 혜택에 대해 알리고, 그에 대한 세부 정보를 얻으려면 웹사이트 방문과 전화 문의를 하라고 안내하고 있으므로 정답은 (A) To get information about discounted parking fees이다.

[17-18] 다음 이메일에 관한 문제입니다.

수신: Adams 출장요리업체 직원들

발신: Kenko Hakimoto

날짜: 3월 4일

제목: 중요한 정보

17 여러분은 모두 새로운 직원 안내서를 한 부씩 받아 보셨을 것입니다. 이 책자에 실린 내용들은 Adams 출장요리업체의 지침과 절차들이자, 작업 표준과 직무 내용에 관한 정보입니다. 마지막 장에 답신 양식이 있습니다. 이 안내서를 다 읽으시면 **18** 그 양식에 서명을 하셔서 관리부의 Garth Crooker에게 맡겨 주십시오. 이 서명은 여러분이 그 책자에 수록된 정보를 숙지하고 회사 규율을 준수하는 데 동의했음을 확인해 줄 것입니다.

이 사안에 관한 여러분의 협조에 감사 드립니다.

Kenko Hakimoto

행정실장

어휘 contain v. ~이 들어 있다. ~를 포함하다 ǀ guideline n. 지침 ǀ procedure n. 절차 ǀ work standard 작업 표준 ǀ job specification 직무 내용 ǀ acknowledgement n. 답신; 인정 ǀ drop something off ~을 맡기다, (들러서) 주다 ǀ administration n. 관리, 행정 ǀ signature n. 서명 ǀ confirm v. 확인해주다 ǀ adhere to ~을 지키다[준수하다]

---

17. Mr. Hakimoto는 이메일에서 무엇에 관해 이야기하는가?

(A) 직원 교체

(B) 오리엔테이션

(C) 채용 기회

(D) 회사 안내서

해설 이메일에서 무엇을 이야기하고 있느냐를 물어보고 있다. new employee handbook을 언급하며 안내서의 내용을 설명한 후 직원들에게 안내서의 내용을 숙지하라는 지시를 내리고 있으므로, 이 메일의 주제는 안내서에 관한 것이므로 정답은 (D) A company manual이다. employee handbook이 A company manual로 paraphrasing되었다.

---

18. Mr. Hakimoto는 직원들에게 무엇을 하라고 요청하는가?

(A) 그들의 작업 표준을 설명한다

(B) 양식을 제출한다

(C) 일부 장비를 반납한다

(D) 책을 구입한다

해설 이메일 중반에서 책 속에 있는 양식에 서명을 해서 관리부에 제출하라는 말이 있으므로 정답은 (B) Submit a form이다. drop ~ off이 submit으로 paraphrasing되었다.

[19-21] 다음 기사에 관한 문제입니다.

Central 대학뉴스

12월 22일 – Central 대학에서 가장 오래 재직한 교수님들 중 한 분인 **19** Eric Parker가 Central 대학의 올해의 교육자상 수상자로 지명되었다.

20 Parker 교수는 지난 27년 동안 그가 중심 인물로 있었던 생물학과에서 학생들을 가르친다. **20** 그의 수업은 항상 학생들로 가득 차 있으며, 그는 생물학 전공자가 되려고 결정하는 Central 대학 학생들 대다수에 개인적으로 책임이 있다. **21** 그들 중 많은 사람들이 그쪽 직종에서 일하거나 그들도 교육자가 되었다. Parker 교수는 학부생과 대학원생을 모두 가르치고, 32명의 학생들의 지도 교수이다. **20** 그는 또한 대학 사진 동아리의 고문 교수이고 이것은 그 조직(동아리)의 인기를 상승시키는 데 크게 도움이 되었다.

Parker 교수는 학생들, 교수단 그리고 교직원들에게 똑같이 존경을 받고 있어, 이 상을 받을 충분한 자격이 있다. 그의 시상식은 1월 2일 오후 3시에 Cedric Hall 강당에서 열릴 예정이다. 일반인도 참석할 수 있다.

어휘 tenured adj. 종신직의, 종신 제직권을 가진 ǀ be named ~로 지명되다 ǀ recipient n. 받는 사람, 수령인 ǀ award n. 상 ǀ biology n. 생물학 ǀ mainstay n. 중심, 대들보, 기둥 ǀ personally adv. 개인적으로 ǀ be responsible for ~에 책임이 있다 ǀ major n. 전공 ǀ undergraduate adj. 학부생의 ǀ graduate student 대학원생 ǀ serve as ~의 역할을 하다 ǀ academic advisor 지도 교수 ǀ faculty n. 교수단 ǀ photography n. 사진 찍기, 사진[촬영]술 ǀ organization n. 조직 ǀ popularity n. 인기도 ǀ respect n. 존경 ǀ administrator n. 행정 직원 ǀ deserving of ~을 받을 만한 ǀ ceremony n. 의식, 식 ǀ in one's honor ~에게 경의를 표하여, ~을 기념하여 ǀ auditorium n. 강당 ǀ public n. 대중 ǀ attend v. 참석하다

19. 기사의 목적은 무엇인가?
(A) 은퇴 직원을 기리기 위해
(B) 대학 수업을 광고하기 위해
(C) 수상자를 발표하기 위해
(D) 곧 있을 인턴직을 설명하기 위해

해설 글의 첫 단락에 보면 Eric Parker가 올해의 교육자 상에 지명되었다는 내용이 나오며, 그 뒤에는 그가 왜 이 상을 받기에 적합한지에 대한 내용이 나오기 때문에 (C) To announce the winner of an award가 정답이다.

20. Mr. Parker에 대한 설명으로 맞지 않는 것은 무엇인가?
(A) 그의 수업 과목이 학생들 사이에서 인기다.
(B) 그는 20년 넘게 그의 학교에서 가르쳤다.
(C) 그는 전문 사진작가로 일했었다.
(D) 그의 동아리는 캠퍼스에서 유명하다.

해설 그가 사진 동아리의 고문 교수라는 이야기는 나오지만 그가 전문 사진작가로 일했다는 내용은 나오지 않으므로 (C) He used to work as a professional photographer가 정답이다.

21. [1], [2], [3], [4]로 표시된 곳 중 다음 문장이 들어가기에 가장 적절한 곳은 어디인가?

"그들 중 많은 사람이 그쪽 직종에서 일하거나 그들도 교육자가 되었다"

(A) [1]
(B) [2]
(C) [3]
(D) [4]

해설 Many of them ~에서 them에 해당하는 내용이 앞에 나와야 하고, the profession(그 직종)이라고 했기 때문에 어떤 직종을 말하는 것인지 그에 대한 내용이 앞에 나와야 하므로 [2]번에 들어가는 것이 자연스럽다. them은 학생들이고, the profession은 biology를 가리키는 것이다. '학생들이 생물학을 전공하는 데 영향을 끼쳤을 뿐만 아니라 생물학을 전공하게 된 학생들 중 다수는 그쪽 분야의 직업을 갖게 되었다'라고 내용이 전개되는 것이 자연스럽다. 따라서 정답은 (B) [2]이다.

[22-25] 다음 편지에 관한 문제입니다.

Zing 전자
9월 10일

고객님께,

Zing 전자에 신나는 소식이 있습니다! **22** 이달 달 말에 Zing 전자에 나오셔서 고객 분들의 쇼핑이 더 즐겁도록 도와 드리기 위해 저희가 실시한 개선 사항들을 확인해 보실 것을 권유 드립니다.

알고 계시겠지만, **24** 저희는 현재 가게에 300평방 피트를 추가하기 위한 보수공사를 진행 중입니다.

저희 컴퓨터 매장은 규모가 두 배가 될 것입니다. **24** 이는 더욱 다양한 부대용품들을 제공할 수 있도록 해줄 것입니다. 저희는 또한 고객님께서 더 많은 오디오 장비를 구하실 수 있도록 음악 매장을 확장할 것입니다.

23 저희는 9월 23일 금요일에 재개장을 기념할 것이며, **신제품의 시연**이 있을 예정입니다. 게다가, **24** 9월 26일부터는 오후 8시 대신 오후 10시까지 영업을 합니다.

이 편지에 **25** 동봉된 것은 Zing 전자의 할인 쿠폰이며, 9월 30일까지 유효합니다. 또한 저희는 특별 할인 판매일을 보여주는 달력도 함께 포함시켰습니다.

진심으로,

Reginald Thompson
Zing 전자 매장 관리자
동봉물 재중

어휘 check out ~을 확인하다 | improvement *n.* 개선 | enjoyable *adj.* 즐거운 | undergo *v.* (특히 변화·안 좋은 일 등을) 겪다 | renovation *n.* 개조, 보수 | add *v.* 추가하다 | square feet 평방 피트 | accessory *n.* 부속품, 액세서리 | celebrate *v.* 축하하다 | demonstration *n.* 시연 | in addition 게다가, 더욱이 | instead of ~ 대신에 | enclose *v.* 동봉하다 | discount coupon 할인권 | valid *adj.* 유효한 | calendar *n.* 달력, 일정표

22. 편지의 목적은 무엇인가?
(A) 소유권 변경을 알리기 위해
(B) 새로운 제품 라인을 홍보하기 위해
(C) 가게 확장을 알리기 위해
(D) 특별 할인을 광고하기 위해

해설 편지의 목적을 물어보는 문제이다. 보통 초반 부분에 목적이 나오므로, 편지의 첫머리를 확인해보면, 매장에서 고객 편의를 위해 개선한 점들을 확인하러 이달 말 가게에 들러줄 것을 요청하고 있다. 현재 가게 확장을 위해 보수공사가 진행 중이라고 하고 있으므로 정답은 (C) To describe a store expansion이다. renovations to add 300 square feet이 expansion으로 paraphrasing되었다.

23. Zing 전자는 언제 특별 행사를 열 것인가?
(A) 9월 10일에
(B) 9월 23일에
(C) 9월 26일에
(D) 9월 30일에

해설 Zing 전자의 행사와 관련된 정보에 주목해보면, 재개장 기념식이 9월 23일에 있을 거라고 하고 있으므로 정답은 (B) On September 23이다. be celebrating our grand reopening이 host a special event로 paraphrasing되었다.

24. 편지에 언급된 것이 아닌 것은 무엇인가?
(A) 더 큰 바닥 면적
(B) 추가된 판매사원들
(C) 더 많은 제품들
(D) 연장된 영업 시간

해설 편지에 언급되지 않은 사실을 확인하는 문제이다. 지문과 보기를 잘 대조해 봐야 한다.

• we are currently undergoing renovations to add 300 square feet to our store → (A) Larger floor space

• Our computer section will be double in size, which will enable us to offer a wider variety of accessories. → (C) A greater selection of items

• In addition, starting September 26, we will be open until 10:00 P.M. instead of 8:00 P.M. → (D) Extended hours of operation

따라서 추가된 판매사원들에 대한 내용은 언급된 바 없으므로 정답은 (B) Additional sales staff이다.

---

25. 편지와 동봉된 것은 무엇인가?

(A) 행사 정보

(B) 설문지 양식

(C) 제품 견본

(D) 회원카드

해설 마지막 단락에서 동봉된 것은 할인 쿠폰과 달력이라고 밝히고 있다. 특히 달력은 할인 행사가 표시된 것이므로 정답은 (A) Event information이다.

[26-30] 다음 이메일과 목록에 관한 문제입니다.

수신: Abella Jude ⟨ajude@cams.org.fr⟩
발신: Lester Cross ⟨lcross@cruiserrealestate.com⟩
회신: 임대 부동산
날짜: 4월 3일
첨부: 목록

Ms. Jude에게,

Rosedale 지역의 주택 임대에 관하여 4월 2일 화요일에 보내신, 당신의 이메일에 답변 드립니다. **26** 저희는 단기 및 장기 아파트와 주택 임대 모두를 취급하며, 당신과 같이 한정된 기간 동안 캐나다로 이전할 계획인 고객들과의 경험이 있습니다. 저는 분명 저희가 당신에게 맞는 곳을 찾아 드릴 거라고 확신합니다.

당신은 다음 달부터 이곳에서 9개월 간 근무를 할 것이라고 얘기했습니다. 아래는 당신이 언급한 임대 선호 사항들입니다:

• 가구가 있는 방 하나 또는 두 개짜리
• 월 1,400달러에서 1,000달러의 가격대
• **29** 버스정류장에서 걸어갈 수 있는 거리 이내 (당신이 차가 없으므로)

당신의 요구에 가장 잘 맞는 건물들의 목록이 첨부되어 있습니다. 그리고, 네, **27** 저는 당신이 시내에 있는 이번 주 목요일 오후 또는 금요일 오전에 건물들을 물론 보여드릴 수 있고, 당신을 데리러 기꺼이 호텔로 가겠습니다. **27** 일정을 잡기 위해 제게 이메일을 보내주세요. 마지막으로, **28** 우리의 고객 중 한 분이 저희의 서비스를 추천해주시는 건 정말 감사한 일이므로, 당신의 동료인 Ms. Kai Ling에게 감사 인사를 전해 주세요.

진심으로,

Lester Cross
Cruiser 부동산 중개인

어휘 regarding *prep.* ~에 관한 | rental *adj.* 임대의 | limited *adj.* 제한된, 한정된 | following *adj.* 다음의 | preference *n.* 선호 | furnished *adj.* 가구가 갖추어진 | range *n.* 범위 | per *prep.* ~당, ~마다 | within walking distance 걸어서 갈 수 있는 거리 이내에 있는 | attach *v.* 첨부하다 | property *n.* 건물, 부동산 | match *v.* 일치하다, 어울리다 | schedule *v.* 일정을 잡다 | convey *v.* 전달하다 | gratitude *n.* 감사 | colleague *n.* 동료 | appreciate *v.* 감사하다

건물 위치	임대료/월	이용 가능일	세부사항
30 45 Walnut 가	1,550달러	5월 2일	방 2개짜리 주택, 가구 완비
1888 Shore 가	1,700달러	[현재]	방 2개짜리 아파트, 가구 완비
760 Overland 가	1,600달러	6월 2일	방 1개짜리 아파트, 가구 완비
24 Trask 가	1,450달러	5월 2일	방 2개짜리 주택, 가구 없음

어휘 location *n.* 위치 | availability *n.* 이용 가능성 | unfurnished *adj.* 가구가 갖춰지지 않은

---

26. Ms. Jude에 관하여 언급된 것은 무엇인가?

(A) 휴가를 갈 것이다.

(B) 새 집을 구매하기를 원한다.

(C) Rosedale로 잠시 이전할 것이다.

(D) Mr. Cross를 이전에 만났었다.

해설 Ms. Jude에 대한 내용에 주목해보면, 이메일 첫 단락에서 Rosedale 지역의 임대 주택에 관한 Ms. Jude의 이메일에 답변을 드린다고 하고 있다. Ms. Jude 처럼 캐나다에 임시로 거주하는 사람들에 대한 경험이 있다고 하였으므로 Ms. Jude가 한정된 기간 동안 캐나다로 이사할 계획임을 알 수 있다. 따라서 Ms. Jude가 Rosedale 지역의 임대 주택으로 잠시 이사할 거라는 사실 확인할 수 있으므로 정답은 (C) She will be moving to Rosedale temporarily이다. for a limited period of time이 temporarily로 paraphrasing되었다.

---

27. Ms. Jude는 어떤 정보를 제공하도록 요청 받는가?

(A) 입주 날짜

(B) 편한 약속 시간

(C) 은행 계좌번호

(D) 재직 증명서

해설 이메일 지문의 후반부에서 요청 사항을 확인할 수 있다. 원하는 부동산을 둘러볼 수 있도록 목요일 오후와 금요일 오전 중 시간을 정하여 이메일을 달라고 요청하고 있으므로 정답은 (B) A convenient meeting time이다.

28. Ms. Ling은 누구이겠는가?

(A) 어느 임대 주택의 주인

(B) Cruiser 부동산 고객

(C) Mr. Cross의 동료

(D) Ms. Jude의 이웃

해설 Ms. Ling를 단서로 언급된 부분을 확인해보자. 이메일 끝부분에서 Ms. Ling는 Cruiser 부동산의 서비스에 만족하여 동료인 Ms. Jude 에게 업체를 추천했으므로 Cruiser 부동산의 고객임을 알 수 있다. 따라서 정답은 (B) A Cruiser Real Estate client이다.

---

29. 목록에 있는 모든 임대 건물들에 관하여 알 수 있는 것은 무엇인가?

(A) Ms. Ling이 소유하고 있다.

(B) 대중교통과 가깝다.

(C) 새로 지어졌다.

(D) 2년 임대를 요구한다.

해설 rental properties on the list를 키워드로 삼아 해당 내용을 살펴보 자. 이메일 지문에서 Ms. Jude의 요구에 가장 잘 맞는 건물들의 목록 이 첨부되어 있다고 하고 있으므로, Ms. Jude의 선호 사항 3가지가 언급된 부분을 확인해 본다. 이 중 세 번째 항목(버스 정류장에서 걸어 서 갈 수 있는 거리)이 (B)에 부합하므로 정답은 (B) They are close to public transportation이다. within walking distance of a bus station이 close to public transportation으로 paraphrasing되었 다.

---

30. Ms. Jude의 요구 사항에 적합한 건물은 어느 곳일 것 같은가?

(A) 45 Walnut 가

(B) 1888 Shore 가

(C) 760 Overland 가

(D) 24 Trask 가

해설 이메일에서 Ms. Jude가 구하는 건물에 대한 정보를 확인해보면, 다음 달에 건물에 입주할 예정이고, 이메일의 날짜가 4월 3일(Date: April 3)이므로 입주할 시기는 5월로 판단 가능하다. 가구가 완비된 1~2개 의 침실/월 1,400~1,600달러의 가격대를 원한다. 두 번째 목록 지문 에서 Ms. Jude의 요구 사항에 부합되는 건물을 확인할 수 있다. 45 Walnut Street/$1,550/May 2/2-bedroom house, furnished. 따라서 (A) 45 Walnut Street가 정답이다.

MINI TEST 04

본서 p.382

1. (D)	**2.** (A)	**3.** (B)	**4.** (C)	**5.** (D)
6. (A)	**7.** (C)	**8.** (A)	**9.** (D)	**10.** (B)
11. (A)	**12.** (A)	**13.** (B)	**14.** (A)	**15.** (B)
16. (D)	**17.** (C)	**18.** (D)	**19.** (C)	**20.** (C)
21. (B)	**22.** (C)	**23.** (A)	**24.** (A)	**25.** (D)
26. (B)	**27.** (D)	**28.** (B)	**29.** (A)	**30.** (C)

1. Starways 슈퍼마켓은 작년에 여섯 개의 신규 지점을 성공적으로 열 었다.

해설 이미 3형식으로 완벽한 문장이다. 따라서 빈칸은 필요 없는 자리인 데, 동사 앞이므로 부사가 들어가야 하는 자리이다. 따라서 정답은 (D) successfully이다.

어휘 **branch** *n.* 지사, 분점 I **success** *n.* 성공 I **successful** *adj.* 성 공적인 I **successfully** *adv.* 성공적으로

2. Benco 사의 최신 가구 제품은 내구성도 있고 매력적이다.

해설 「Both A and B」라는 형태이고 A, B에는 서로 대등한 성분이 와야 한다. B자리에 attractive라는 형용사가 왔으므로 A자리에도 형용사 가 와야 한다. 따라서 정답은 (A) durable이다.

어휘 **newest** *adj.* 최신의 I **line** *n.* (상품의) 종류 I **furniture** *n.* 가구 I **attractive** *adj.* 매력적인

3. 스물 두 대의 특별히 개조된 전기차량을 가지고, Das Bauer는 독일 에서 가장 경제적인 운송 시스템을 운영한다.

해설 보기를 확인해보니, 형용사 어휘 문제이다. 문맥상 '가장 ~한 운송수 단'에 어울리는 어휘는 economical(경제적인)이다. 따라서 정답은 (B) economical이다.

어휘 **specially** *adv.* 특별하게 I **modified** *adj.* 개조된, 수정된 I **vehicle** *n.* 탈것, 차량 I **operate** *v.* 운영하다 I **transportation** *n.* 운송 I **projected** *adj.* 예상된 I **attentive** *adj.* 주의를 기울이는 I **internal** *adj.* 내부의

4. 우리는 구입일로부터 2년 이내에는 당신의 GX3000 난방기를 기꺼이 무상으로 수리나 교환을 해줄 것이다.

해설 보기를 확인해보니, 전치사 문제이다. 빈칸 뒤를 보니, two years라는 기간을 나타내는 명사가 나와 있다. 기간 전치사는 within밖에 없다. 따라서 정답은 (C) within이다.

어휘 **gladly** *adv.* 기꺼이 I **repair** *v.* 수리하다 I **replace** *v.* 교체하다, 대 신하다 I **at no cost** 무료로 I **purchase date** 구매일

5. 전 직원들의 월례 근무시간 기록표는 다음 달이 시작하기 전에 작성되 어야 한다.

해설 보기를 확인해보니, 동사 어휘 문제이다. 주어가 근무시간 기록표 인데, 기록표가 작성되어야 한다는 의미가 적절하므로 정답은 (D) completed이다.

어휘 **timesheet** *n.* 출퇴근 기록 용지

6. Palace 아파트의 경비원들은 건물의 모든 세입자들의 안전을 보장하기 위해 교육을 받는다.

해설 정관사 the 뒤에 빈칸이 있다. 즉, 빈칸은 명사 자리이다. 따라서 정답은 (A) safety이다.

어휘 security officer 경비원 | train v. 훈련하다, 교육하다 | ensure v. 보장하다 | tenant n. 세입자

7. 우리의 고객 주소록 데이터베이스는 최근에 갱신되었으며, 직원들은 온라인 접근이 가능하다.

해설 can be라는 동사가 있으므로 동사인 (A)는 탈락이다. (A)를 명사로 볼 수도 있으나, 명사가 be동사 뒤에 들어가면 주격보어 자리에 명사가 왔으므로 주어와 동격이 되어야 하는데, database와 access는 동격이 될 수 없다. to부정사 (B)가 주격보어 자리에 오면 역시나, to부정사의 명사적 역할로 쓰이게 되는 것이다. 그럼 명사 역할이 주격보어 자리에 들어간 것이므로 주어와 동격이 되어야 하는데 database = to access는 될 수 없다. (C)를 넣으면 수동태가 되고, (D)를 넣으면 능동태가 되는데, access의 목적어(명사)가 빈칸 뒤에 없다. online은 단지 부사일 뿐이다. 따라서 수동태 (C) accessed가 정답이다.

어휘 directory n. 주소록, 안내 책자 | database n. 데이터베이스 | update v. 갱신하다, 업데이트하다

8. 발표 직후에 간식과 음료가 로비에 준비될 것이다.

해설 shortly after라는 표현을 알아두자. 발표 '직후'라는 뜻이다. 따라서 정답은 (A) shortly이다. recently는 보통 과거시제나 현재 완료와 함께 쓰인다. presently는 현재시제와 함께 사용된다.

어휘 snack n. 간식 | beverage n. 음료 | available adj. 이용 가능한; 구할 수 있는 | reception area 안내실, 로비 | presentation n. 발표

9. Telco 자동차가 하이브리드 차량을 소개했고, 소비자들은 그것에 꽤 수용적이었다.

해설 앞의 문장과 뒤의 문장을 연결할 접속사가 필요하다. (C)는 '~보다' 라는 뜻으로 비교급에서 쓰이므로 탈락이다. (A)와 (D)는 등위접속사이고, (B)는 부사절 접속사인데, 문맥상, Telco 자동차는 하이브리드 자동차를 소개했고 소비자들이 이에 상당히 수용적이었다는 의미가 자연스러우므로 순접의 관계로 이어주는 등위접속사가 적절하다. 따라서 정답은 (D) and이다.

어휘 introduce v. 소개하다, 도입하다 | hybrid n. 혼성, 혼합 | consumer n. 소비자 | receptive to ~을 선뜻 받아들이는

10. 해외 고객들이 웹사이트에서 물품을 주문하면, 추정되는 배송 시간을 그들에게 다시 한번 알려 주어야 한다는 것을 기억하시오.

해설 관사와 명사 사이에 빈칸이 있으므로 형용사가 들어가야 한다. 형용사는 (B) 과거분사 형용사(수동)와 (D) 현재분사 형용사(능동)가 있다. 추정하는 배송 시간이 아니라, 추정되는 배송 시간이 적절하므로 정답은 (B) estimated이다.

어휘 overseas adj. 해외의 | goods n. 물품, 상품 | remind v. 다시 한 번 일깨우다, 상기시키다 | shipping n. 배송 | estimate v. 추정하다, 추산하다

[11-14] 다음 편지에 관한 문제입니다.

6월 13일

Mr. Ristow에게,

GX555의 신제품 개인용 태블릿 구매를 감사드립니다. 저희는 최첨단 고속 데이터 기술을 제공해 드리는 데 **11** 전념하고 있습니다. **12** 동봉된 꾸러미에는 자세한 제품 안내서가 포함되어 있습니다.

만일 귀하께서 태블릿에 100% 만족하지 못하신다면, 귀하께서는 **13** 환불을 받으실 것입니다. 저희의 각 제품에는 60일 환불 보증이 포함되어 있습니다. 귀하께서 새로운 태블릿 작동에 관한 문의 사항이 **14** 더 있으시다면, 정규 영업 시간 내에 저희에게 연락을 주시면 기꺼이 도와드리겠습니다.

진심으로,

Calvia Varga
판매 관리인

어휘 come with ~가 딸려오다, 포함되다 | money-back adj. 환불 가능한 | guarantee n. 보증 | be committed to -ing ~에 전념/헌신하다 | packet n. 꾸러미 | detailed adj. 상세한, 세부적인

11. 해설 「be committed to -ing」라는 표현을 숙지하고 있자. '~에 헌신하다, ~에 전념하다'라는 뜻이다. commit의 목적어가 없이 전치사 to가 왔으므로 수동태가 정답이다. 수동태는 (A)와 (C)이다. 문맥상, 우리가 당신에게 ~을 제공하는 것에 헌신하고 있다는 뜻이므로 일반적인 사실을 말하는 현재시제가 적절하다. 따라서 정답은 (A) are committed이다.

12. (A) 동봉된 꾸러미에는 자세한 제품 안내서가 포함되어 있습니다.
(B) 귀하의 요청에 따라, 저희는 귀하의 인터넷 서비스를 업그레이드 했습니다.
(C) 저희가 복구를 할 수 있도록 선호하는 날짜를 표시해주세요.
(D) 귀하의 납부 마감일은 매월 첫째 날입니다.

해설 편지 서두에 태블릿 구매에 감사 드린다는 내용이 나오고 있다. 빈칸 뒤의 문장에서, 마음에 들지 않을 경우, 환불을 받을 수 있고, 60일 환불 보증도 있다는 내용이 나오므로, 빈칸에는 동봉된 패킷에 제품 상세 안내서가 있다는 문장이 적합하다. 따라서 정답은 (A) The enclosed packet includes a detailed product manual이다.

13. 해설 태블릿이 100퍼센트 만족스럽지 않다면 귀하에게 환불을 해주겠다는 의미가 적합하며, 빈칸 뒤에서 각 제품에 60일 환불 보증 (money-back guarantee) 조건이 포함되어 있다고 했으므로 정답은 (B) refund이다.

14. 해설 questions라는 명사 앞에 빈칸이 있으므로 형용사가 들어가야 한다. further가 동사로 사용되어 과거분사형, 현재분사형으로 쓰일 수 있지만 여기서는 동사적 의미가 아니라 '추가의, 더 이상의'라는 의미의 형용사가 필요하므로 정답은 (A) further이다.

Maya Nanza 스카프의 가을 컬러 컬렉션을 구매해 주셔서 감사합니다. 저희 재료는 모두 장관을 이루는 중국의 티베트 고원에서 수입됩니다. 🔟 저희 스카프는 직물이나 환경에 해를 끼치지 않는 수제 염색 과정을 거치는 100퍼센트 캐시미어로 짜서 만듭니다. 🔟 색의 차이는 캐시미어를 염색하는 데서 온 자연스러운 결과입니다. 이 차이는 각 스카프에 그것만의 독특한 패턴을 줍니다. 제품의 모양을 보존하고, 마모되는 것을 막기 위해 드라이클리닝이 강력히 권장됩니다.

어휘   import v. 수입하다 | spectacular adj. 장관을 이루는, 극적인 | weave v. (실이나 천 등을) 짜다, 엮어서 만들다 (weave-wove-woven) | cashmere n. 캐시미어(고급 옷에 쓰이는 모직) | go through ~을 거치다. 겪다 | hand dyeing 손으로 염색하는 | harm v. 해를 끼치다 | fabric n. 직물 | variation n. 변화, 차이 | natural adj. 자연스러운, 당연한 | unique adj. 독특한 | preserve v. 보존하다, 지키다 | prevent v. 예방하다, 막다 | wear and tear (일상적 사용에 의한) 마모, 손상

15. 이 안내문은 어디에서 발견되겠는가?

(A) 옷 짜기를 다룬 잡지에서

(B) 손으로 짠 제품에 포함된 태그에서

(C) 티베트 여행 안내서에서

(D) 직물 염료 병에서

해설   안내문 첫 단락을 확인해보면, 티베트 고원에서 수입된 직물에 수제 염색을 거친 100퍼센트 캐시미어로 짠 제품이며, 제품 유의사항을 뒤에서 설명하는 것으로 보아 제품 성분 정보가 포함된 옷이라는 것을 알 수 있다. 따라서 정답은 (B) On a tag included with a woven product이다.

16. Maya Nanza 제품에 관하여 언급된 것은 무엇인가?

(A) 다양한 직물로 제작된다.

(B) 중국에서만 판매된다.

(C) 물세탁이 가능하다.

(D) 고르지 않은 천연색일 것이다.

해설   Maya Nanza 제품에 관한 언급에 주목해 보자. 천연 염색으로 인하여 색이 고르지 않을 수 있다고 하므로 정답은 (D) They may have uneven coloration이다. Color variations가 uneven coloration으로 paraphrasing되었다.

Harwood 은행

7044 Verde 가

어배너, 일리노이 61801

2월 17일

Marcela Reeves

825 Mesa 로

어배너, 일리노이 61802

회신: 계좌 번호 562302-344

Ms. Reeves께,

저희에게 고객님의 새 연락처를 보내주셔서 감사합니다. 그에 따라, 🔟 고객님의 계좌가 업데이트되었고, 이후의 모든 입출금 내역서 및 서신을 고객님의 새로운 집 주소로 우편 발송하겠습니다.

고객님의 편지를 오늘에서야 받았기 때문에 고객님의 최근 내역서는 이미 이전 주소로 발송되었음을 참고해 주시기 바랍니다. 하지만 🔟 고객님께서는 저희 홈페이지를 방문하셔서 계좌 정보(현재의 잔액과 최근 거래들을 포함)를 확인하실 수 있습니다.

고객님의 지속적인 거래에 감사 드립니다.

진심으로,

Anthony Hull
고객 서비스 담당자

어휘   Re prep. ~와 관련하여(= regarding) n. 회신 | accordingly adv. 그에 따라 | subsequent adj. 그 이후의, 그 다음의 | bank statement 입출금 내역서 | correspondence n. 서신 | note v. 주목하다, 주의하다 | including prep. ~을 포함하여 | balance n. 잔액, 잔고 | transaction n. 거래

17. 무엇에 관한 편지인가?

(A) 부정확한 거래

(B) 지불 정책 변경

(C) 최근 갱신된 계좌

(D) 체납

해설   편지 첫머리를 확인해보자. 새 연락처를 보내주어 연락처 정보가 갱신되었으며 차후 모든 입출금 내역서와 서신은 새로운 집 주소로 발송될 예정이라고 하였으므로 정답은 (C) A change in payment policy 이다.

18. Mr. Hull은 Ms. Reeves에게 무엇을 하라고 제안하는가?

(A) 비용을 납부한다

(B) 고객 서비스에 연락한다

(C) 서식을 작성한다

(D) 웹사이트에 접속한다

해설   제안 및 요청 사항을 나타내는 표현에 주목해보자. 제안 및 요청 사항은 주로 후반부에 언급된다. 최근 입출금 내역이 이전 주소로 발송이 되었기 때문에 계좌 내역 조회는 홈페이지를 통해 확인해 볼 것을 안내하고 있으므로 정답은 (D) Access a Web site이다. visiting our home page가 Access a Web site으로 paraphrasing되었다.

Cross United
구인

간호사: 공인 간호사 자리 (세 자리 지원 가능). 지원자는 반드시 자격증이 있어야 하며 🔟 의료 분야에서 최소 3년의 경력이 있어야 합

니다. **21** 근무 시간은 월요일에서 목요일은 오전 9시에서 오후 7시까지이며, 금요일은 오전 9시에서 오후 4시까지입니다.

사무 보조: 정규직. **20** 보조원의 주요 업무는 환자 예약을 잡고 청구서를 처리하는 일입니다. 일일 추가 업무는 전화를 받고 우편물을 분류하는 일이 포함됩니다. **21** 근무 시간은 월요일에서 금요일, 오전 9시부터 오후 5시까지입니다. 지원자는 최소 1년의 관련 업무 경력을 보유해야 합니다.

관심 있는 지원자분들은 www.crossunited.com을 방문하셔서 인사부 링크를 클릭하여 자기소개서, 이력서, 기타 관련 증빙 서류 사본을 제출하십시오.

어휘 registered *adj.* 공인된; 등록된 I certified *adj.* 자격증을 소지한, 공인의 I field *n.* 분야 I full-time position 정규직, 상근직 I duty *n.* 직무 I process *v.* 처리하다 I sort *v.* 분류하다 I possess *v.* 소유하다 I cover letter 자기소개서 I résumé *n.* 이력서 I relevant *adj.* 관련된 I documentation *n.* 증빙 서류

---

19. Cross United는 무엇이겠는가?
(A) 시민 문화 회관
(B) 회계 회사
(C) 의료 시설
(D) 제약 회사

해설 Cross United의 모집 광고이므로 광고 대상을 확인해보자. Nurses: Registered nurse positions에서 간호직 모집이라는 것을 확인할 수 있다. 사무 보조원 모집 내용에서 직무 중에 환자의 예약을 잡는 업무가 있다. 즉, Cross United를 의료 시설로 볼 수 있다. 따라서 정답은 (C) A medical facility이다.

---

20. 사무 보조원의 직무로 요구되는 것이 아닌 것은 무엇인가?
(A) 전화 받는 것
(B) 지불 처리하는 것
(C) 사무용품 주문하는 것
(D) 사무실 방문 일정을 예약하는 것

해설 office assistant를 키워드로 보기와 지문을 대조해봐야 한다.
• Additional daily duties include taking phone calls ➡ (A) Answering the telephone
• The assistant's main duties are setting up patient appointments and processing bills ➡ (B) Handling payments, (D) Scheduling office visits
사무용품을 주문하는 업무는 언급되지 않았으므로 정답은 (C) Ordering office supplies이다.

---

21. 광고에 따르면, 열거된 두 유형의 직책에 모두 요구되는 것은 무엇인가?
(A) 3년간의 이전 근무 경력
(B) 월요일부터 금요일까지 근무 가능해야 함
(C) 공식 자격증
(D) 뛰어난 리더십 자질

해설 간호사와 사무 보조원의 자격 요건 중 같은 항목을 확인해보자. 간호사의 근무 시간은 월요일부터 금요일까지이다. 사무 보조원의 근무 시간은 월요일부터 금요일까지이다. 두 직책의 공통 근무 조건은 주 5일제라는 것을 알 수 있다. 따라서 정답은 (B) Availability to work Monday through Friday이다.

[22-25] 다음 문자 대화문에 관한 문제입니다.

Martin, Amelia [오후 1:39]
Susan, 아직 **22** **23** 이번 주말에 회사 야유회를 가는 것에 대하여 계획 중인가요?

Cloverdale, Susan [오후 1:43]
네, 무슨 일이세요?

Martin, Amelia [오후 1:45]
저는 아직 야유회에 가야 할지 말아야 할지 결정 못했어요. **23** 저는 캠핑이나 래프팅을 전혀 해본 적이 없거든요. 제가 즐길 수 있을 거라고 생각하세요?

Cloverdale, Susan [오후 1:48]
아주 멋진 시간을 보낼 거예요. **23** 저도 5년 전에 처음 야유회를 갔을 때 아주 싫어할 거라고 생각했었는데, 막상 가보니 마음에 들었어요. 저는 매년 야유회를 고대하고 있어요.

Martin, Amelia [오후 1:49]
24 네, 확신이 드네요. 야유회를 신청하려면 뭘 해야 하나요?

Cloverdale, Susan [오후 1:50]
인사부의 Eric Hampton에게 알려주시기만 하면 돼요. 그분이 준비하고 있거든요. 내선번호 55번으로 연락하면 돼요.

Martin, Amelia [오후 1:52]
알겠어요. 한 시간 정도 후에 사무실에 돌아가자마자 바로 해야겠네요.

Cloverdale, Susan [오후 1:53]
오늘이 등록 마감일이니까, 오늘 업무 종료 전에 그와 이야기하도록 하세요.

Martin, Amelia [오후 1:55]
당신과 얘기해보길 잘했네요. 그건 전혀 생각하지 못했어요. 아 참, 제가 특별히 가져가야 할 게 있나요?

Cloverdale, Susan [오후 1:58]
밤이면 쌀쌀해지니까 꼭 따뜻한 옷 몇 벌 가져가세요. **25** 이따 오늘 밤 전화해서 다른 필요한 것들을 알려드릴게요.

어휘 corporate *adj.* 회사의, 기업의 I outing *n.* 소풍 I how come 왜 I rafting *n.* (래프팅) 뗏목 타기 I wind up 결국 ~하게 되다 I sign up 신청하다 I HR 인사팀 I handle *v.* 다루다 I arrangement *n.* 준비 I extension *n.* 내선번호 I cutoff *n.* (신청의) 마감일 I chilly *adj.* 쌀쌀한

---

22. 주로 무엇에 대한 문자 대화문인가?
(A) 다가오는 회의에 관한 계획
(B) Ms. Cloverdale가 막 다녀온 여행
(C) 여자들이 가려고 하는 단체 여행
(D) 캠핑과 래프팅을 가는 데 필요한 물품들

해설 오후 1시 39분에 회사 야유회를 갈 것인지 묻고 오후 1시 45분에 아직 회사 야유회를 가야 할지 말아야 할지 결정 못했다고 했으므로 회사 야유회, 즉 단체 여행에 관한 문자 메시지임을 알 수 있다. 따라서 정답은 (C) An excursion the women will go on이다.

23. Ms. Cloverdale에 대하여 암시된 것은 무엇인가?
    (A) 5년 이상 회사에서 일을 해왔다.
    (B) 전에 Ms. Martin와 야유회를 갔었다.
    (C) 최근에 그녀의 회사에 고용됐다.
    (D) 야외에서 시간을 보내는 것을 불편해한다.

해설 오후 1시 48분에 Ms. Cloverdale가 5년 전 처음 이 야유회를 갔다고 했는데, 'this outing'은 앞에서 언급한 회사 야유회(corporate outing)를 말하는 것이므로, Ms. Cloverdale는 이 회사에서 적어도 5년 이상 근무했음을 짐작할 수 있다. 따라서 정답은 (A) She has worked at the company for more than five years.이다.

24. Ms. Martin이 오후 1시 49분에 "네, 확신이 드네요"라고 쓴 것은 무슨 의미인가?
    (A) 여행을 가기로 결정했다.
    (B) 이제 막 몇 가지 새로운 물품을 구매했다.
    (C) 납득할 필요가 있다.
    (D) 보다 긴 설명을 듣기를 원한다.

해설 화자가 말하고자 하는 의도를 파악하는 문제이다. 오후 1시 49분에 보낸 메시지의 두 번째 문장에서 야유회 등록을 어떻게 해야 하는지를 묻고 있으므로, 회사 야유회를 가기로 결정했음을 알 수 있다. 따라서 정답은 (A) She has decided to go on the trip이다.

25. Ms. Cloverdale는 그 날 이후에 무엇을 하겠는가?
    (A) Mr. Hampton과 이야기한다
    (B) 여행을 위한 준비를 한다
    (C) 인사부로 연락을 한다
    (D) Ms. Martin에게 연락을 한다

해설 오후 1시 58분에 보낸 메시지의 두 번째 문장에서 오늘 밤에 Ms. Martin에게 전화해서 다른 필요한 것들을 알려준다고 했으므로 정답은 (D) Get in touch with Ms. Martin이다.

[26-30] 다음 안내문, 서식, 그리고 이메일에 관한 문제입니다.

TABERTON 도서관에서의 행사 개최

Taberton 도서관의 Roosevelt 룸은 기업 행사 및 사적인 모임을 위해 이용하실 수 있습니다. 룸 예약을 위해 신청서를 작성해주세요.

Roosevelt룸 이용 요금 안내

	참가자 1-30명	참가자 31-60명	참가자 61-100명
도서관 카드 소지자	15달러	30달러	60달러
비회원	30달러	60달러	100달러
27 회사 단체	60달러	90달러	200달러

Taberton 도서관은 월요일에서 토요일, 오전 8시 30분부터 오후 6시 30분까지 문을 엽니다. **26** 운영 시간 이후에 열리는 행사는 현장 보안 요원이 필요합니다. 이에 대해서는 추가 비용으로 도서관에서 마련해 드릴 수 있습니다. **29** 그렇지 않으면, 방문하시는 분들이 자체 보안 요원을 두시는 것도 환영합니다.

어휘 corporate *adj.* 기업의, 회사의 | private *adj.* 사적인, 개인 소유의 | complete *v.* 작성하다 | request form 신청서 | reserve *v.* 예약하다 | after hours 근무[영업] 시간 후에 | security guard 보안 요원, 경비원 | on site 현장에 | alternatively *adv.* 그렇지 않으면, 그 대신에

TABERTON 도서관
Roosevelt 룸 예약 신청서

날짜와 시간: 7월 3일, 화요일, 오후 6:45 - 오후 8:45분
개인/단체명: **27** Welson 건축
담당자: Eric Hathers
전화번호: 555-8839
이메일: ehathers@welsonarchitecture.com
예상 참가자 수: **27** 78
도서관 카드가 있습니까? 아니오

저는 방 이용에 관한 모든 방침들을 읽었고, 이에 동의합니다. 방을 원래의 상태로 해 놓고, **28** 모든 여분의 의자와 테이블을 창고에 반납하는 것이 저의 책임이라는 것을 알고 있습니다.

서명: Eric Hathers
날짜: 6월 18일

어휘 contact person 담당자 | consent to ~에 동의하다 | policy *n.* 방침, 정책 | understand *v.* 이해하다, 알다 | original state 원래의 상태 | return *v.* 반납하다, 돌려보내다 | storage closet 창고, 저장소

수신: Keira Chang 〈kchang@tabertonlibrary.org〉
발신: Eric Hathers 〈ehathers@welsonarchitecture.com〉
날짜: 6월 21일
제목: 예약

Ms. Chang에게,

저희 Roosevelt 룸 예약을 확인해주셔서 감사합니다. Welson 건축은 현재 Taberton 지역에 새로운 쇼핑몰을 위한 디자인을 계획하고 있습니다. 그 디자인을 확정하기 전에, **30** 우리의 계획을 Taberton 주민들께 보여드리고 그들의 조언을 듣고 싶습니다. 우리는 귀하의 모임 장소가 그러한 행사를 위해 더할 나위 없이 좋다고 생각합니다.

29 보안에 관하여, 우리는 행사 당일에 우리와 동행할 자체 인력이 있습니다. 어떠한 변경 사항이라도 있다면 귀하께 꼭 알려드리겠습니다.

안부를 전하며,

Eric Hathers
Welson 건축

어휘 confirm *v.* 확인해주다 | finalize *v.* 마무리 짓다, 완결하다 | resident *n.* 주민 | input *n.* 조언 | regarding *prep.* ~에 관하여 | personnel *n.* 인원, 직원들 | accompany *v.* 동행하다

26. Taberton 도서관에 관하여 안내문은 무엇을 나타내는가?
(A) 토요일에 일찍 문을 닫는다.
(B) 행사가 업무 시간 이후에 열릴 수 있도록 해준다.
(C) 도서관 프로그램들 중 일부는 무료이다.
(D) Taberton 주민들은 도서관 룸 대여 시 할인 받는다.

해설 Taberton 도서관에서의 행사 관련 안내를 다룬 첫 번째 지문에서 표 하단을 보면 도서관 운영 시간은 오전 8시 30분부터 오후 6시 30분까지인데, 그 시간 이후에 열리는 행사들은 안전 요원이 함께 있어야 한다는 내용을 토대로 안전 요원만 배치한다면 운영 시간 후에도 행사 개최가 가능함을 알 수 있으므로 (B) The library allows events to take place after its business hours가 정답이다. held after hours가 take place after ~ business hours로 paraphrasing되었다.

27. Welson 건축은 Roosevelt 룸 이용에 얼마를 청구 받을 것인가?
(A) 60달러
(B) 90달러
(C) 100달러
(D) 200달러

해설 신청서 양식인 두 번째 지문에서 '개인/단체명(Individual/Group name)'란에는 회사 이름(Welson Architecture)이, '예상 참가자 수(Expected number of participants)'에는 78명이 적혀 있으므로 첫 번째 지문의 Roosevelt Room 이용료 항목에서 이 두 가지를 모두 충족시키는 비용은 200달러이므로(61~100 Participants + Company groups = $200달러) (D) $200가 정답이다.

28. Roosevelt 룸에 관하여 암시되는 것은 무엇인가?
(A) 주말에는 예약될 수 없다.
(B) 많은 인원을 수용하기 위해 여분의 가구가 비치될 수 있다.
(C) 화요일은 회사들만 이용할 수 있다.
(D) 도서관 카드 소지자들은 룸을 무료로 예약할 수 있다.

해설 신청서 양식인 두 번째 지문 하단의 서약 내용에서 모든 추가 의자와 테이블들을 창고에 다시 가져다 놓겠다고 했으므로 여분의 가구가 이용 가능하다는 점을 짐작할 수 있다. 따라서 (B) Extra furniture can be set up to accommodate large parties가 정답이다. chairs and tables가 furniture로 paraphrasing되었다.

29. Welson 건축에 관하여 알 수 있는 것은 무엇인가?
(A) 추가 비용을 낼 필요가 없다.
(B) 전에 Roosevelt 룸을 이용한 적이 있다.
(C) 최근에 쇼핑몰을 세웠다.
(D) Taberton 도서관에 기금을 기부한다.

해설 첫 번째 지문의 표 하단을 보면 운영 시간 (8:30 A.M. to 6:30 P.M.) 이후의 행사들은 보안 인력이 있어야 하는데, 도서관에서 제공하게 되면 추가 비용이 들지만, 직접 데려와도 좋다고 했고 두 번째 지문에서 Welson 건축이 원하는 이용 시간은 운영 시간 이후이며, Welson 건축의 담당자, Eric Hathers가 보낸 세 번째 지문, 두 번째 단락을 보면 행사 당일 날 우리와 동행할 보안 인력이 있다고 했으므로 Welson 건축은 추가 비용을 낼 필요가 없음을 알 수 있다. 따라서 (A) It is not required to pay an additional fee가 정답이다.

30. 왜 Mr. Hathers는 회의를 열 것인가?
(A) 프로젝트를 위한 모금행사를 계획하기 위해
(B) 건물 개관을 발표하기 위해
(C) 그 지역 사회의 주민들에게서 피드백을 받기 위해
(D) 수상 후보자들을 지명하기 위해

해설 Mr. Hathers가 쓴 세 번째 지문, 첫 번째 단락을 보면 Taberton 주민들에게 자신들의 계획을 보여주고 그들의 의견을 받고 싶다고 했으므로 (C) To get feedback from people in the community가 정답이다. receive ~ input이 get feedback으로, the residents of Taberton이 people in the community로 paraphrasing되었다.

MINI TEST 05

본서 p.390

1. (A)	**2.** (C)	**3.** (C)	**4.** (C)	**5.** (B)
6. (A)	**7.** (A)	**8.** (A)	**9.** (A)	**10.** (A)
11. (B)	**12.** (B)	**13.** (A)	**14.** (D)	**15.** (A)
16. (C)	**17.** (A)	**18.** (D)	**19.** (C)	**20.** (B)
21. (D)	**22.** (B)	**23.** (C)	**24.** (A)	**25.** (D)
26. (D)	**27.** (B)	**28.** (C)	**29.** (D)	**30.** (B)

1. Mr. Kaneko는 매출액 목표를 달성한 것에 대해 그의 팀을 칭찬했다.

해설 보기를 확인해보니, 대명사의 격을 물어보는 문제이다. 빈칸 뒤에 명사가 있다. 명사 앞에는 무조건 소유격이 성립이다. 따라서 정답은 (A) his이다.

어휘 compliment *v.* 칭찬하다 | achieve *v.* 달성하다 | sales goal 매출 목표

2. Augen 사의 영업 직원들의 노고 덕분에, 회사의 4분기 목표가 달성되었다.

해설 have been이라는 동사가 있으므로 동사인 (A)와 (D)는 답이 될 수가 없다. (B)를 빈칸에 넣으면 현재 완료 진행형 시제의 능동태가 되고, (C)를 빈칸에 넣으면 현재완료 시제의 수동태가 되는데, 3형식 동사 meet(만족시키다)의 목적어(명사)가 빈칸 뒤에 없으므로 수동태가 정답이다. 따라서 정답은 (C) met이다.

어휘 sales staff 영업 직원 | goal *n.* 목표 | quarter *n.* 분기

3. Rathburn 도서관은 다양한 비즈니스 정기간행물들과 학술지 소장품들을 인쇄판과 온라인으로 제공한다.

해설 부정관사 an이 있으므로 그 뒤에는 명사가 존재해야 한다. extensive는 형용사이므로 빈칸에 명사를 넣어야 한다. 명사는 동명사 (B)와 명사 (C)가 있다. 동명사는 동사에서 명사가 된 것이므로, collect처럼 3형식 성질을 가지고 있다. 따라서 목적어가 있어야 하는데 빈칸 뒤에 collecting의 목적어(명사)가 없으므로 동명사는 답이 될 수 없다. 따라서 정답은 (C) collection이다.

어휘 offer v. 제공하다 | extensive adj. 아주 많은, 대규모의 | periodical n. 정기간행물 | journal n. 저널, 학술지

4. 지난주 기자회견 동안, Janet White 상원의원은 현안에 관한 많은 질문들에 침착하게 답했다.

해설 콤마 앞에는 전치사구 수식어구가 있고, 콤마 뒤에는 이미 3형식으로 완벽한 문장이다. 따라서 빈칸은 문장 필수 성분이 필요 없는 자리이다. 게다가 동사 앞에 빈칸이 있으니 부사가 올 자리이다. 따라서 정답은 (C) calmly이다.

어휘 press conference 기자회견 | senator n. 상원의원 | a number of 많은, 다수의 | regarding prep. ~에 관하여 | pending issue 현안, 미결 사항

5. Borstein 금융 그룹은 해외 여행을 제한하고 화상 회의의 이용을 시행함으로써 비용을 줄였다.

해설 문맥상 해외 여행을 제한하고 화상 회의를 시행하여 비용을 줄였다는 의미가 적절하므로 정답은 (B) reduced이다.

어휘 limit v. 제한하다 | overseas adj. 해외의 | implement v. 시행하다, 실행하다 | video conferencing 화상 회의 | examine v. 조사하다 | reduce v. 줄이다 | state v. 진술하다 | qualify v. 자격을 얻다

6. 모든 물품들이 확정될 때까지, 우리는 영업 제안서를 초안으로만 고려해야 한다.

해설 콤마 앞에도 문장이 있고, 뒤에도 문장이 있다. 즉, 문장 두개를 연결할 접속사가 필요하다. (B)는 등위접속사로 문두에 오지 않는다. (C)는 접속사가 아니라 전치사이다. (D)는 부사이다. 따라서 정답은 접속사 (A) Until이다.

어휘 finalize v. 완결하다, 마무리 짓다 | consider v. 고려하다 | sales proposal 영업 제안서 | draft n. 원고, 초안 v. 초안을 작성하다

7. Plantar Comfort Shoes는 발에 문제가 있는 사람들을 위해 특별히 고안된 새로운 신발 라인에 속해 있다.

해설 보기를 확인해보니, 부사 어휘 문제이다. 빈칸에 들어갈 부사는 designed를 꾸미므로 designed라는 말과 어울려야 한다. 문맥상 발에 문제가 있는 사람들을 위해 '특별히' 만들어졌다는 의미가 적절하므로 정답은 (A) specially이다.

어휘 belong to ~에 속해 있다 | footwear n. 신발류 | design v. 고안하다

8. Sherm 여행사는 조직적인 기량을 지니면서, 관광업의 탄탄한 배경을 겸비한 직원만을 채용한다.

해설 with라는 전치사 뒤에는 명사가 있어야 하는데, 이미 명사 skills가 있다. 따라서 빈칸은 형용사 자리이다. 따라서 정답은 (A) organizational이다.

어휘 hire v. 고용하다 | employee n. 직원 | skill n. 기량 | solid adj. 확실한, 탄탄한 | background n. 배경 | tourism n. 관광업

9. Sai Tao의 강 그림들은 Jiangsu 지역에서의 그의 어린 시절에서 영감을 받았다.

해설 were inspired라는 것은 수동태의 형태이다. 보통의 수동태는 전치사 by를 취하므로 정답은 (A) by이다. 전치사 by를 취하지 않는 수동태들은 꼭 따로 외워두도록 하자.

어휘 painting n. 그림 | inspire v. 영감을 주다 | province n. 주(州)[도(道)], 지방

10. 어제 Lloyd 박물관 관광을 했던 방문객들은 각각의 전시품이 역사의 인상적인 사례들을 보여주었다고 말했다.

해설 보기를 확인해보니, 형용사 어휘 문제이다. 빈칸 뒤에 등장하는 명사구 example of history를 수식하여, 전시실이 역사의 인상적인 사례를 보여주었다는 내용이 적절하므로 정답은 (A) impressive이다.

어휘 exhibit n. 전시품 | represent v. 대표하다, 나타내다

[11-14] 다음 기사에 관한 문제입니다.

Reyville, 3월 3일 – Marvich's 장난감 가게가 8373 Tinder 가의 Bard 쇼핑몰에 두 번째 매장을 열었다. 주인인 Jasper Marvich는 그의 사업을 더 확장시킬 수 있는 기회를 **11** 놓칠 수 없었다고 말했다. "그 쇼핑몰에서 소매점 자리가 났다는 사실을 알자마자 즉시 그곳을 임대했습니다." Mr. Marvich는 또한 Tinder 가의 상점이 이미 **12** 운영될 준비가 되어 있긴 하지만, 3월 8일 금요일 오전 10시에 특별 개점식 및 복권 추첨 행사와 함께 공식적으로 문을 열 거라고도 말했다. **13** 이 행사는 대중에게 개방된다. Marvich's 장난감 매장은 최신 어린이용 장난감과 게임, 그리고 형형색색의 색종이 조각과 생일 모자를 **14** 포함한 다양한 파티용품을 판매한다. 추가 정보를 얻으려면 423–538–9843으로 전화하거나 www.marvichtoys.com에 방문하면 된다.

어휘 retail space 소매점 | rent out ~을 임대하다 | ribbon-cutting ceremony 개관식, 개점식 | raffle contest 복권 추첨 행사 | latest adj. 최신의 | party supplies 파티용품 | colorful adj. 다채로운, 형형색색의 | confetti n. (행사 때 뿌리는) 색종이 조각 | be open to the public 대중에게 개방되다

11. 해설 앞에서 Marvich's 장난감 가게가 두 번째 매장을 열었다고 했으며, 빈칸 뒷문장에서 가게 주인이 쇼핑몰에 자리가 났을 때, 바로 그곳을 임대했다고 했으므로 사업 확장의 기회를 놓칠 수 없었다고 해야 적절하므로 정답은 (B) pass up이다.

12. 해설 already는 부사이므로 신경 쓰지 말고, be동사 뒷자리에 빈칸이 있으므로 주격보어 자리에 올 수 있는 상태설명 형용사가 필요하다. 형용사는 (B)와 과거분사 형용사 (D)가 있다. 보통 형용사가 보기에 두 개일 땐, 분사보다는 일반 형용사가 정답이다. 정확히 더 따져보면, operational은 '운영상의' 또는 '사용할 준비가 된'의 의미를 가지고 있고, operated는 타동사 operate의 과거분사로 '가동되는, 운용되는'의 의미를 가지는데, 이 상점이 이미 사용할 준비가 되긴 했지만, 특정 시점에 공식 오픈할 거란 의미가 적절하므로 (B) operational이 정답이다.

13. (A) 이 행사는 대중에게 개방된다.
(B) 개점은 성공적이었다.
(C) 세일은 다음 주까지 계속될 것이다.
(D) 이 공간은 훨씬 더 크다.

해설 Tinder 가의 Bard 쇼핑몰에 두 번째 매장을 열었다. 3월 8일 금요일 오전 10시에 특별 개점식 및 복권 추첨 행사와 함께 공식적으로 문을 열 거라고도 말했다. 최신 어린이용 장난감과 게임, 그리고 형형색색의 색종이 조각과 생일 모자를 포함한 다양한 파티용품을 판매한다는 내용이 맞으므로, 그 사이에는 행사의 개방 대상자를 언급해야 한다. 따라서 정답은 (A) This event is open to the public이다.

14. 해설 문장의 본동사는 sells이므로 동사 (A)는 탈락이다. 이미 빈칸 앞에는 3형식으로 완벽한 문장(뼈대)이 왔으므로 명사인 (B)는 뼈대역할을 하므로 답이 될 수 없다. 빈칸부터는 뼈대가 아닌, 수식어구가 와야 한다. (C)의 형용사를 빈칸에 넣으면 그 형용사가 뒤에 명사를 꾸민다. 그럼 결국에 꾸밈 받은 명사(뼈대)가 3형식 문장 뒤에 존재하게 된다. 따라서 답이 될 수 없다. 완벽한 3형식 문장 뒤에는 명사 같은 뼈대가 아닌, 수식어구가 와야 하기 때문이다. including은 전치사로 뒤에 명사를 동반하며, 전치사구는 수식어구 역할이므로 정답이 될 수 있다. 따라서 정답은 (D) including이다.

[15-16] 다음 온라인 채팅 대화문에 관한 문제입니다.

Thomas, Fred [오전 11:01]
너무 실망스럽습니다. Edward Harvester의 연설 입장권을 구매하고 싶었는데, 마감 기한을 놓쳤어요.

McMurtry, Robert [오전 11:03]
벌써 마감 기한이 지났나요? 정말 안타깝네요! 저도 입장권을 구할 생각이었는데 말이죠.

Jones, Carla [오전 11:05]
잠깐만요. ⑮ 제가 방금 웹사이트에서 아직 입장권 구매가 가능하다고 읽었어요. 등록 일자가 연장되었다고 나와 있었던 것 같아요.

Thomas, Fred [오전 11:07]
정말 좋은 소식이네요. 새로운 마감 기한은 언제인가요?

Jones, Carla [오전 11:09]
웹사이트에 따르면, 두 분은 내일 오후 6시까지 입장권을 예매해야 해요. ⑯ 하지만 정상 가격보다 10% 더 지불해야 해요.

McMurtry, Robert [오전 11:11]
⑯ 그건 감수할 수 있어요. Fred, 제가 당신 입장권도 예매해 드릴까요?

Thomas, Fred [오전 11:13]
네, 부탁 드려요. 전 두 장을 원해요. 제 사무실의 John Taylor도 가고 싶어 하거든요. Carla, 좋은 소식 고마워요.

Jones, Carla [오전 11:15]
도움이 되어 저도 기뻐요. 두 분 다 강연에서 봬요.

어휘 disappointed *adj.* 실망한 | miss *v.* 놓치다 | deadline *n.* 마감일 | shame *n.* 애석한 일 | as well 마찬가지로 | hold on 기다리다 | appear *v.* 나타나다, ~인 것 같다 | extend *v.* 연기하다, 미루다 | according to *prep.* ~에 따르면 | regular price 정가

15. 주로 무엇에 대한 온라인 채팅 대화인가?
(A) 어떤 행사 입장권의 구입 가능성
(B) 곧 있을 연설의 주제
(C) 연설회에서 그들이 앉을 자리
(D) 구매해야 할 입장권의 수

해설 온라인 채팅 대화의 전체 내용이 Edward Harvester가 하는 강연 입장권의 마감 기한이 지났지만 웹사이트에 마감 기한 연장이 발표되었고, 그래서 채팅 대화 참여자들이 입장권 구입에 대해 얘기를 나누고 있다. 따라서 정답은 (A) The availability of tickets for an event 이다.

16. Mr. McMurtry가 오전 11시 11분에 "그건 감수할 수 있어요"이라고 쓴 것은 무슨 의미인가?
(A) 강연에 약간 늦게 가고 싶어 한다.
(B) Ms. Jones와 같이 행사에 참여하고 싶어 한다.
(C) 더 높은 가격을 지불하는 것에 신경 쓰지 않는다.
(D) Mr. Thomas가 입장권들을 사는 것이 그에게 괜찮다.

해설 화자가 말하는 의도를 파악하는 문제이다. 오전 11시 09분에 Jones가 보낸 메시지에 따르면, 마감 기한이 연장된 입장권이 정상 가격보다 10% 높게 팔리고 있다고 했고, 오전 11시 11분에 보낸 McMurtry의 메시지에서 Fred에게 입장권을 대신 사주길 원하냐고 물었으므로 정답은 (C) He does not mind paying a higher price.이다.

[17-18] 다음 이메일에 관한 문제입니다.

수신: david.caufield@techfix.com
발신: esther.knox@primodesigns.com
날짜: 4월 22일
제목: 소프트웨어

안녕하세요 David,

지난주 저희 사무실에 복사기를 설치해 주셔서 감사합니다. 그것은 아주 잘 작동하고 있습니다. 하지만 ⑰ 제 컴퓨터의 스캐닝 소프트

웨어가 어제 저녁부터 작동이 멈추었습니다. 제가 스캔한 파일 중 하나를 열려고 할 때마다, 오류 메시지가 나타납니다. 그래서 현재, **18** 저는 디자인을 만들기 위해 스캔한 이미지들을 전혀 사용할 수 없습니다. 저는 중요한 고객들에게 그들이 광고 캠페인을 계획할 수 있도록 다음 주까지 일부 디자인을 제출해야 하기 때문에, 걱정이 됩니다. **17** 내일 중으로 들러 주셔서 이 문제를 확인해 주실 수 있나요? 당신의 답변을 기다리고 있겠습니다. 감사합니다.

진심으로,

Esther Knox

어휘   install v. 설치하다 | photocopier n. 복사기 | whenever conj. ~할 때마다 | error message 오류 메시지, 오류창 | submit v. 제출하다 | stop by 들르다 | take a look 살펴 보다, 점검하다

---

17. 이메일의 목적은 무엇인가?

(A) 지원 요청을 하기 위해
(B) 새 복사기를 주문하기 위해
(C) 회사에 관해 문의하기 위해
(D) 보고서를 제출하기 위해

해설   이메일의 목적을 물어보는 문제이다. 이메일을 쓰게 된 목적을 초반부에서 확인해보면, 컴퓨터의 스캐닝 프로그램이 작동하지 않는다고 문제점을 언급하면서 직접 방문해 문제를 확인해 주기를 요청하고 있으므로 정답은 (A) To request assistance이다. take a look at the problem이 assistance로 paraphrasing되었다.

---

18. Ms. Knox에 관하여 알 수 있는 것은 무엇인가?

(A) 고객에게서 불평을 받았다.
(B) 최근에 컴퓨터를 구매했다.
(C) 사무실 건물의 실내 디자인을 한다.
(D) 그래픽 아티스트이다.

해설   이메일의 하단, Esther Knox에서 Ms. Knox는 이메일의 발신인으로 확인된다. 고객에게 제출해야 할 디자인 작업을 위해 스캔한 이미지 파일을 사용해야 한다고 언급하고 있다. 즉, 그래픽 관련 작업을 하는 사람임을 알 수 있으므로 정답은 (D) She is a graphic artist이다.

[19-21] 다음 이메일에 관한 문제입니다.

발신: Ji-Young Chang 〈jychang@tbacomputers.com〉
수신: Carl James 〈cjames@txtechconference.com〉
제목: Bonnie Thorpe
날짜: 1월 30일

Carl에게,

20 저는 목요일 워크숍을 주관하기 위해 오늘 아침에 미리 텍사스로 출발하기로 되어 있었습니다. 하지만 아시다시피, 어제 이곳 베이징에 큰 눈보라가 휘몰아쳐서 공항 전체가 폐쇄되었습니다. 저는 새 항공편을 예약하려고 노력 중이나 공항 상황에 대한 어떠한 소식도 없습니다. 그래서 제가 목요일까지 텍사스에 도착할 수 있을지 확실치 않습니다.

벌써 텍사스에 도착한 **19 20** 제 동료, Bonnie Thorpe와 제가 방금 얘기해 봤는데, 그녀는 자신이 저를 대신하는 것은 문제 없을 거라고 말했습니다. Bonnie는 제가 워크숍에서 보여드리려고 했던 소프트웨어에 매우 능숙하기에, 저는 그녀가 잘할 것이라는 것을 알고 있습니다. 이 조정안이 괜찮으시다면, **21** Bonnie에게 워크숍과 관련된 비용을 보상 받는 방법과 컨퍼런스 출입증을 수령하는 곳에 대한 정보를 얻기 위해 당신에게 전화하라고 말해 두겠습니다. 저는 컨퍼런스가 끝나기 전인 토요일에 그곳에 도착하기 위해 최선을 다하겠습니다. 곧 뵙겠습니다.

진심으로,

Ji-Young

어휘   be supposed to ~하기로 되어 있다 | depart for ~를 향해 떠나다 | in time 시간에 맞춰, 늦지 않게 | lead v. 이끌다, 주관하다 | shut down 문을 닫다, 폐쇄하다 | book v. 예약하다 | status n. 상태 | take one's place ~를 대신하다 | proficient adj. 능숙한 | demonstrate v. 보여주다, 설명하다 | arrangement n. 계획, 준비 | reimburse v. 변제하다, 보상하다 | pass n. 출입증

---

19. 이메일의 목적은 무엇인가?

(A) 연결 비행편을 요청하기 위해
(B) 일자리 제의를 수용하기 위해
(C) 계획의 변경을 설명하기 위해
(D) 컨퍼런스 날짜를 연기하기 위해

해설   이메일의 목적은 보통 처음 부분에 있다. Ji-Young은 목요일 워크숍을 위해 오늘 오전에 출발하기로 되어 있었지만 그렇지 못했고, 제시간에 도착할 수 있을지 확실치 않다. 그래서 동료인 Bonnie Thorpe에게 이야기해서 그녀가 자신을 대신해도 괜찮다는 답변을 받았다. 따라서 계획 변경을 설명하기 위한 것이므로 정답은 (C) To explain a change in a plan이다.

---

20. Ms. Thorpe는 무엇을 하는 데 동의했는가?

(A) 텍사스에 원래 계획했던 것보다 늦게 도착하는 데
(B) 컨퍼런스에서 워크숍을 하는 데
(C) 동료와 소프트웨어 프로그램을 개발하는 데
(D) 그녀 회사의 베이징 지사로부터 직원들을 채용하는 데

해설   Ms. Thorpe를 키워드로 삼아 해당 내용을 포착해보자. Bonnie Thorpe가 Ji-Young의 일을 대신해 줄 수 있다고 하고 있다. Ji-Young이 하기로 예정되어 있던 일을 확인해보면, 목요일 워크숍을 주관하는 일이라는 것을 알 수 있다. 따라서 정답은 (B) Give a workshop at a conference이다.

---

21. Ms. Chang은 Mr. James에게 무엇을 해달라고 요청하는가?

(A) 시연을 위해 사용될 장비를 예약한다
(B) 지역 날씨 상황을 업데이트한다
(C) 사무실에 컨퍼런스 출입증을 놓고간다
(D) Ms. Thorpe에게 환급 절차를 설명한다

해설　Ms. Chang(= Ji-Young Chang), Mr. James(= Carl James)
가 각각 이메일 발신인과 수신인임을 확인하고, 지문 하단에서 요청
과 관련된 표현을 찾아보자. Ji-Young은 Thorpe에게 환급 절차와
관련해 James에게 전화해 보라고 말하면서 환급과 관련된 정보를
Thorpe에게 알려줄 것을 요청하고 있으므로 정답은 (D) Explain a
reimbursement procedure to Ms. Thorpe이다.

[22-25] 다음 기사에 관한 문제입니다.

기업주들의 공로를 인정하기
〈Herring Times〉의 작가 Catherine Emerson의 글

켈러턴 (11월 6일) – **22** 과학기술과 혁신 위원회(TIC)는 12월 10
일, 토요일, Riveria 호텔에서 열릴 연례 비즈니스 시상식 연회 동
안 재계의 다양한 산업계 지도자들과 혁신가들에게 상을 줄 것이다.
24 원래 TIC 회장 Ariel Won에 의해 시작된 이 행사는 올해의 가
장 혁신적인 회사 지도자에게 주어지는 Most Popular Software
Program과 Top Innovator와 같은 명망 높은 상을 수여한다.

TIC 대표에 따르면, Top Innovator 상의 수상 자격을 갖춘 많은 후
보자들 중에서 세 사람이 선발되었다. 올해의 수상 후보자들은 디지
털 마케팅 회사 Exceed Media의 설립자 Lily Horvitz, 이미지 공유
웹사이트 Donne Pix의 공동 설립자 Spencer Donne, 그리고 **23**
지난 시상식의 후보자였던, 최신 영화에 대한 상세한 평을 제공하는
유명 웹사이트 Filmpop의 소유주인 Josh Bruger이다. **24** 늘 그렇
듯이, TIC 회장이 Top Innovator 상을 수여할 것이다.

TIC의 회원이 아닌 내빈들도 60달러에 표를 구매하여 이 경축 행사
에 참석할 수 있다. TIC 회원은 40달러의 할인가로 표를 구할 수 있
다. 표는 www.tic.org를 방문하거나 680-555-2391에 전화로 주
문할 수 있다. "기술 정보를 계속 알고자 하는 사람이라면 누구나 회
원 가입을 고려해야 합니다. **25** 가입을 위해 35달러의 비용만 지불
하시면 됩니다. 저희 회원들은 많은 혜택을 누리고 있습니다."라며
TIC 대표 Lucy Morgan은 강하게 권한다. 참석하는 사람들은 모두
유명한 Oceania Beach 리조트의 3박 여행을 포함한 연회의 경품
추첨에 참가하게 된다.

어휘　recognize *v.* (공로를) 인정하다 | honor *v.* 영예를 주
다, 예우하다 | awards banquet 시상식 연회 | present
v. 주다, 수여하다 | prestigious *adj.* 명망 높은, 일류의 |
representative *n.* 대표, 대리인 | pool *n.* 이용 가능 인력 |
qualified *adj.* 자격이 있는 | candidate *n.* 지원자, 후보
자 | nominee *n.* 후보자 | founder *n.* 설립자 | detailed
adj. 자세한, 세부적인 | as usual 늘 그렇듯이 | gala *n.* 경축
행사 | keep up with (최신 정보를) 알게 되다, 알다 | have
access to ~을 이용하다, ~에 접근하다 | urge *v.* 강력히 권
하다 | prize raffle 경품 추첨

22. TIC의 비즈니스 시상식 연회에 관하여 알 수 있는 것은 무엇인가?
　(A) 인터넷에서 생중계될 것이다.
　(B) 다양한 산업의 혁신가들에게 상을 준다.
　(C) TIC 회원들만 참석할 수 있다.
　(D) 올해 새로운 장소에서 열릴 것이다.

해설　TIC의 비즈니스 시상식 연회에 관련된 언급을 찾아보자. 기사 초반에
언급되었듯이 재계의 다양한 산업계 지도자들과 혁신가들에게 수상의

영예를 안겨줄 예정이므로 정답은 (B) It honors innovators from
multiple industries이다.

23. 두 번째 단락, 아홉 번째 줄의 단어, "last"와 의미상 가장 가까운 것은
　(A) 다음의
　(B) 최종의
　(C) 이전의
　(D) 현재의

해설　last의 동의어를 물어보는 문제이다. 지난 시상식 연회의 후보자가
Josh Bruger라는 의미이므로 문맥상 적절한 어휘는 '이전의'라는 뜻
의 previous이다. 따라서 정답은 (C) previous이다.

24. 누가 Top Innovator 상을 수여할 것인가?
　(A) Ms. Won
　(B) Ms. Horvitz
　(C) Mr. Donne
　(D) Mr. Bruger

해설　상을 수여하는 것과 관련된 정보에 주목해보자. Top Innovator 상은
TIC 회장인 Ariel Won이 처음 만들었으며 매년 상도 회장이 수여한
다고 했으므로 이번에도 Ariel Won 회장이 수여할 예정이라는 것을
알 수 있다. 따라서 정답은 (A) Ms. Won이다.

25. Ms. Morgan은 무엇을 권고하는가?
　(A) 신제품을 시험한다
　(B) 후보자들에게 투표한다
　(C) Oceania Beach 리조트에 연락한다
　(D) 회원권을 산다

해설　권고 및 제안과 관련된 표현에 주목해보자. Lucy Morgan이 권하
고 있는 부분을 보면 기술 정보를 계속 알고자 하는 사람이라면 누
구나 회원 가입을 고려해야 한다고 말하며 35달러만 내면 된다
고 하면서, 회원 가입을 제안하고 있다. 따라서 정답은 (D) To pay
for a membership이다. becoming a member가 pay for a
membership으로 paraphrasing되었다.

[26-30] 다음 안내문과 이메일에 관한 문제입니다.

Caress 미용 학교가
선사합니다.

26 미용업계에서 일하는 것을 고려하고 있다면, 포틀랜드의 일
류 미용 학교인 Caress 미용 학교(CBS)가 당신을 위한 곳입니다.
Venuscope는 학생들에게 다양한 미용 분야를 탐구할 기회를 제공
하는 저희의 연례 시범 강좌입니다.

아래의 강좌들 중에서 하나를 선택하세요. 각 과정은 여섯 개의 수업
시간으로 구성되어 있습니다. 저희 웹사이트 cbs.edu/venuscope
를 방문하시면 각 강좌의 자세한 설명들을 볼 수 있습니다.

강좌 1: 헤어 스타일링
강좌 기간: 6월 11일–22일
수업 요일: 월요일, 화요일, 금요일

오전 수업: 오전 8시 – 오전 11시
저녁 수업: 오후 7시 – 오후 10시

강좌 2: 메이크업 기술
강좌 기간: 7월 7일–17일
수업 요일: 수요일, 목요일, 토요일
오후 수업: 오후 1시 – 오후 4시
저녁 수업: 오후 7시 – 오후 10시

30 Venuscope 프로그램을 등록하시려면, 15달러의 등록비와 160달러의 재료비를 지불하셔야 합니다. 등록에 관한 정보를 원하시면, 강좌 기획자 Miriam Studebaker에게 mstudebaker@cbs.edu 또는 (301) 555–8294로 연락하시기 바랍니다.

27 올해 6월과 7월 프로그램은 등록할 수 없으시다구요? 내년부터, CBS는 2월과 3월에도 Venuscope 프로그램을 제공할 것입니다. 게다가, **28** CBS는 8월 10일, 월요일에 시작되는 10개월 과정의 자격 프로그램에 대한 상세 내용에 관해 설명회를 제공할 것입니다. 더 많은 정보를 위해 7월 21일에 저희와 함께 하세요.

어휘 prestigious *adj.* 명망 높은, 일류의 | cosmetology *n.* 미용술, 미용업 | sampler course 시범 강좌 | explore *v.* 탐험하다 | consist of ~로 구성되다 | description *n.* 설명, 기술 | sign up for ~에 등록하다, 가입하다 | registration fee 등록비 | enroll in ~에 등록하다 | information session 설명회 | regarding *prep.* ~에 관하여 | licensing program 자격 프로그램

수신: Miriam Studebaker ⟨mstudebaker@cbs.edu⟩
발신: Vince Chow ⟨vchow@tosmail.com⟩
날짜: 6월 6일
제목: 문의

Ms. Studebaker께,

저는 헤어 스타일링 시범 강좌 등록을 계획하고 있습니다. 제게 등록 방법에 대한 안내문을 보내주세요.

저는 10개월 프로그램도 등록할 것이라고 **29** 꽤 확신합니다. 수업 중에 하는 실습 외에도 더 많은 실습을 하고 싶습니다. 그래서 **30** Venuscope 프로그램을 위한 재료만을 사기보다는, 10개월 프로그램을 위한 기자재들도 모두 구매하고 싶습니다. 이것이 가능할지 제게 연락해서 알려주세요. 곧 연락 받기를 바랍니다.

진심으로,

Vince Chow

어휘 inquiry *n.* 문의, 질문 | plan on ~을 계획하다 | practice *n.* 실습, 연습 | rather than ~보다는

---

26. 안내문은 누구를 대상으로 한 것인가?
(A) 전문 미용 강사들
(B) 학교 프로그램 기획자들
(C) CBS 직원들
(D) 미래의 헤어 및 메이크업 전문가들

해설 안내문 첫머리를 확인해보자. 안내문 제목을 확인해보면, Caress Beauty School Presents이므로 미용 학교 소개와 제공 강좌를 확인할 수 있는 글이다. Course 1: Hair Styling / Course 2: Make-up Techniques 미용업계에서 일할 것을 고려하며 다양한 미용 분야를 탐험할 기회를 찾는 사람들을 위한 안내문이므로 정답은 (D) Future hair and makeup specialists이다.

---

27. Venuscope 프로그램에 관하여 언급된 것은 무엇인가?
(A) 10개월 프로그램을 위한 요건이다.
(B) 앞으로는 더 자주 제공될 것이다.
(C) 인터넷을 통해 이용할 수 있다.
(D) 잡지에 광고되었다.

해설 Venuscope 프로그램에 관한 언급을 찾아보자. CBS가 내년부터 6월과 7월뿐만 아니라 2월과 3월에도 Venuscope 프로그램을 제공할 예정이므로 더 자주 프로그램이 제공될 것이다. 따라서 정답은 (B) It will be offered more often in the future이다.

---

28. 자격증으로 이어지는 프로그램들은 언제 논의될 것인가?
(A) 6월 6일에
(B) 6월 11일에
(C) 7월 21일에
(D) 8월 10일에

해설 자격증 연관 프로그램에 관한 언급을 찾아보면, 8월 10일에 시작하는 10개월 과정 자격 연관 프로그램의 상세 내용에 관해 설명회를 가질 예정이며, 이에 관해 더 알고자 한다면 7월 21일에 참가할 것을 제안하고 있으므로 정답은 (C) On July 21이다. 8월 10일은 10개월 과정이 시작하는 날이니 주의하자.

---

29. 이메일에서 두 번째 단락, 첫 번째 줄의 단어 "fairly"와 의미상 가장 가까운 것은
(A) 솔직하게
(B) 적정하게
(C) 동등하게
(D) 상당히

해설 fairly의 동의어를 물어보는 문제이다. 10개월 프로그램도 등록할 것이라고 '꽤' 확신한다는 내용이므로 문맥상 적절한 어휘는 reasonably이다. 따라서 정답은 (D) reasonably이다.

---

30. Mr. Chow에 관하여 언급된 것은 무엇인가?
(A) 할인된 입학금을 지불할 것이다.
(B) 재료비로 160달러 이상을 지불할 용의가 있다.
(C) 오전 수업을 듣기를 원한다.
(D) 전에 그 학교에 연락한 적이 있다.

해설 Mr. Chow는 이메일 발신인이다. 이메일 지문을 보면, 10개월 프로그램을 위한 기자재도 구입하길 원하고 있다. 안내문 지문에서, 기자재 비용에 관한 정보를 찾을 수 있는데, Mr. Chow가 기본 재료비 160달러에 추가로 10개월 프로그램을 위한 기자재를 구입할 생각임을 알 수 있다. 따라서 정답은 (B) He is willing to pay over $160 for materials이다.

ACTUAL TEST

101. (A)	102. (C)	103. (B)	104. (A)	105. (C)
106. (A)	107. (D)	108. (C)	109. (A)	110. (B)
111. (A)	112. (C)	113. (D)	114. (A)	115. (A)
116. (D)	117. (B)	118. (C)	119. (A)	120. (D)
121. (B)	122. (C)	123. (C)	124. (A)	125. (D)
126. (A)	127. (B)	128. (A)	129. (C)	130. (D)
131. (B)	132. (C)	133. (A)	134. (D)	135. (C)
136. (D)	137. (B)	138. (B)	139. (B)	140. (A)
141. (D)	142. (D)	143. (D)	144. (A)	145. (C)
146. (A)	147. (B)	148. (B)	149. (C)	150. (A)
151. (C)	152. (D)	153. (B)	154. (C)	155. (D)
156. (B)	157. (B)	158. (B)	159. (B)	160. (D)
161. (A)	162. (D)	163. (B)	164. (C)	165. (C)
166. (D)	167. (A)	168. (B)	169. (D)	170. (C)
171. (C)	172. (D)	173. (A)	174. (C)	175. (A)
176. (B)	177. (C)	178. (A)	179. (D)	180. (D)
181. (B)	182. (C)	183. (B)	184. (C)	185. (B)
186. (B)	187. (B)	188. (A)	189. (B)	190. (D)
191. (C)	192. (D)	193. (C)	194. (D)	195. (B)
196. (B)	197. (A)	198. (C)	199. (B)	200. (A)

101. 시의 새 환경법 때문에 오염량이 상당이 줄어들었다.

해설　be동사 뒤에는 보어가 들어갈 자리로 항상 형용사가 정답으로 출제된다. 보기 중 형용사가 없을 때는 형용사의 역할을 하는 분사를 선택한다. 여기서는 현재완료 수동태를 만들어 주는 과거분사가 필요하므로 (A) reduced가 정답이다. 명사도 보어로 사용될 수 있지만 부사 significantly의 수식을 받는 자리이므로 (B) reduction은 정답이 될 수 없다.

어휘　environmental law 환경법 | pollution n. 오염, 공해 | significantly adv. 상당히, 크게

102. 개정된 WPM 설문지는 지난해 사용했던 것보다 업무 생산성을 더 정확하게 측정한다.

해설　이미 빈칸 앞은 3형식 문장으로 완벽하다. 따라서 빈칸은 필요 없는 자리이다. 더군다나, 3형식 문장이 끝난 후 맨 마지막에 빈칸이 왔으므로 부사가 들어가야 한다. 따라서 정답은 (C) accurately이다.

어휘　questionnaire n. 설문지 | measure v. 측정하다 | work productivity 업무 생산성

103. Carrigan 국제영화제에서 상을 받은 사람들 중에는 감독 Polly Grano와 제작자 Ronald Foxsworth가 있다.

해설　빈칸 뒤에 관계대명사 who로 시작하는 구문이나 분사구문, 형용사구, 전치사구 등이 있을 때는 이것들의 수식을 받아 '~하는 사람들'이라는

의미가 되도록 those를 정답으로 선택한다. 여기서는 빈칸 뒤의 분사구인 honored at the Carrigan International Film Festival을 보고 (B) those를 정답으로 선택해야 한다. 보기 중 those가 없을 때는 anyone이 정답으로 출제된다. 관계대명사로 시작하는 절에는 반드시 동사가 있어야 하므로 (C)나 (D)는 정답이 될 수 없다.

어휘　honor v. 명예를 주다 | director n. (영화·연극의) 감독 | producer n. (영화·연극의) 제작자

104. Orion 화장품이 판매하는 모든 브러시는 천연 소재로 만들어지며 합성 섬유는 전혀 들어있지 않다.

해설　빈칸 앞의 are made of ~부터 빈칸 뒤의 fibers까지만 보고 정답을 선택한다. '천연 소재로 만들어지며 합성 섬유는 전혀 함유하지 않는다'가 자연스러우므로 (A) synthetic이 정답이다. natural과 synthetic이 서로 대조되고 있다.

어휘　natural material 천연 소재 | contain v. ~이 함유되어 있다 | synthetic fiber 합성 섬유 | expected adj. 예상되는 | urgent adj. 긴급한, 시급한 | capable adj. 유능한

105. Kaymax 철물점의 영업 시간은 연휴 세일 기간 동안 오후 9시까지 연장될 것이다.

해설　보기 중 be동사 뒤에 들어갈 수 있는 것은 분사인 (A)와 (C) 두 가지이다. 동사의 형태를 능동태로 할 것인지 수동태로 만들 것인지 선택하는 문제이며, 빈칸 뒤에 목적어가 없을 때는 수동태가 정답이므로 (C) extended를 선택한다.

어휘　hardware n. 철물 | business hours 영업 시간 | duration n. (지속되는) 기간 | extend v. 연장하다 | extendedly adv. 오래; 광범위하게; 널리

106. Winen 타워의 건물 관리자는 2층의 누수 현상에 대해 즉각 통보 받았다.

해설　빈칸 뒤의 notified of the water leak만 보면 정답을 알 수 있다. 건물의 누수 현상은 상식적으로 즉각 통보해야 할 일이므로 (A) promptly가 정답이다. (D) timely는 대부분 형용사로 사용하므로 동사를 수식하는 자리인 빈칸에 들어갈 수 없다.

어휘　notify v. (공식적으로) 알리다 | water leak n. 누수 | promptly adv. 지체 없이 | steadily adv. 꾸준히 | significantly adv. 상당히 | timely adj. 시기적절한, 때맞춘

107. Boulder 건축사무소는 새 쇼핑센터의 건설을 위해 시의회에 제출할 디자인을 설계했다.

해설　타동사인 has created의 목적어가 필요하므로 빈칸에는 명사인 (C) 혹은 (D)가 들어가야 한다. 단수 명사인 (C)를 사용하려면 앞에 관사가 있어야 하므로 복수명사 (D) designs를 선택한다.

어휘　present v. 보여 주다 | city council 시의회

108. 전문가들은 내년에 상업용지의 가격이 15퍼센트까지 떨어질 것이라고 예상한다.

해설　증가, 감소의 양이나 정도를 나타낼 때는 전치사 by를 사용한다. 빈칸 앞뒤의 will decrease와 15 percent를 보고 15퍼센트까지 떨어질 것이라는 의미가 되도록 (C) by를 선택한다.

어휘　expert *n.* 전문가 | predict *v.* 예측하다 | commercial property 상업용지

109. Ms. Park는 BMC 금융의 채용 제안을 수락한 후 현재 근무 중인 회사에 사직서를 제출하기로 결심했다.

해설　명사 어휘 문제이다. 다른 회사의 일자리 제안을 수락했으므로 지금 다니는 회사에는 사직서를 제출하는 게 상식적이므로 (A) resignation가 정답이다.

어휘　accept *v.* 받아들이다 | job offer 일자리 제의 | current *adj.* 현재의, 지금의 | resignation *n.* 사직서 | dedication *n.* 전념, 헌신 | qualification *n.* 자격, 자격증 | finalization *n.* 마무리; 최종 승인

110. Fit Care Max가 실시한 최근의 연구는 지속적으로 운동하는 것이 행복과 자존감을 향상시키는 데 도움을 준다는 것을 보여주었다.

해설　to부정사나 동명사, 분사와 같은 준동사는 부사가 수식하므로 (B) consistently가 정답이다. exercise는 자동사라서 동명사 exercising도 뒤에 목적어가 없음에 유의한다.

어휘　conduct *v.* (특정한 활동을) 하다 | exercise *v.* 운동하다 | improve *v.* 개선하다, 향상시키다 | self-esteem *n.* 자존감 | consist of ~로 이루어져 있다 | consistent *adj.* 한결같은, 일관된 | consistently *adv.* 일관되게, 지속적으로

111. Rennore 그룹에서 회계 감사관으로 근무하는 데 관심 있는 지원자는 면접 일정을 잡기에 앞서 회계사 자격증을 받았어야 한다.

해설　빈칸 앞의 should have ~ 부터 빈칸 뒤 the arrangement of an interview를 보고 정답을 고른다. '면접 일정을 잡기에 앞서 회계사 자격증이 있어야 한다'가 자연스러운 문장이므로 (A) prior to가 정답이다.

어휘　applicant *n.* 지원자 | auditor *n.* 회계 감사관 | accounting certificate 회계사 자격증 | arrangement *n.* 계획, 예정 | prior to ~에 앞서 | previously *adv.* 이전에 | apart from ~외에는 | agreeable *adj.* 기분 좋은; 쾌활한

112. Cervo 자동차는 자신들의 새 소형차가 교통부의 안전성 요건을 충족한다는 것을 보장한다.

해설　보기에 있는 네 개의 동사 중 that절을 목적어로 취할 수 있는 것은 guarantee밖에 없으므로 (C) guarantees를 정답으로 선택한다.

어휘　compact vehicle 소형차 | safety requirement 안전성 요건 | transportation department 교통부 | adjust *v.* 조정하다 | restrict *v.* (크기·양·범위 등을) 제한하다 | guarantee *v.* 보장하다, 약속하다 | define *v.* 정의하다, 규정하다

113. 선발된 지원자는 상하이나 멜버른에 배치될 것이다.

해설　상관접속사 문제는 짝을 지어서 외워 두면 해결된다. 빈칸 앞에 있는 either의 짝은 or이다. 따라서 정답은 (D) or이다.

어휘　selected *adj.* 선발된 | candidate *n.* 후보자 | place *v.* 배치하다

114. Fenick Mobile은 태양 전지판에 의해 생산되는 전기를 사용함으로써 공과금에서 많은 돈을 절약한다.

해설　by로 시작하는 전치사구이므로 동사를 사용할 수는 없다. 보기 중 유

일하게 동사가 아닌 과거분사로 사용할 수 있는 (C) produced를 정답으로 선택한다.

어휘　electricity *n.* 전기, 전력 | solar panel *n.* 태양 전지판 | save *v.* 절약하다 | utility bill 공과금

115. CT 쇼핑센터에 있는 모든 식당 중 Milword Bistro가 우리 건물에서 가기에 가장 어렵다.

해설　빈칸 앞에 be동사가 있으므로 빈칸에는 보어가 될 형용사가 필요하다. 형용사인 (A)와 (C) 중 빈칸 앞에 있는 정관사 the나 문장에 들어있는 of all 같은 최상급 정답의 단서를 보고 (A) hardest를 선택한다.

어휘　located *adj.* ~에 위치한 | bistro *n.* 작은 식당 | get to ~에 도착하다, 닿다

116. Dillman's Equipment는 극한 스포츠 경기에 참가하는 운동선수들을 위한 보호 장비를 전문으로 한다.

해설　빈칸 뒤 gear와 함께 사용하는 형용사는 protective밖에 없다. protective[safety] gear[equipment/clothing](보호[안전] 장비[의복]) 같은 단어는 토익시험에 자주 등장하므로 반드시 알고 있어야 한다. 따라서 정답은 (D) protective이다.

어휘　specialize in ~을 전문으로 하다 | athlete *n.* 운동선수 | extreme sports 극한 스포츠 | competing *adj.* 대립되는, 경쟁하는 | excessive *adj.* 지나친, 과도한 | definite *adj.* 확실한, 확고한 | protective *adj.* 보호하는

117. Grace Kim의 독립 영화 〈Family Crossings〉가 개봉된 지 3주 이내에 매우 훌륭한 평가를 받았기 때문에 제작자들은 영화를 추가로 6개국에서 개봉하기로 결정했다.

해설　three weeks라는 기간 표현 앞에 쓸 수 있는 전치사는 within이므로 정답은 (B) within이다. during은 숫자로 표시하는 기간 표현(예, four years, five business days 등) 앞에는 사용하지 않고, 기간의 명칭(예, vacation, holiday sale 등) 앞에 사용한다.

어휘　independent film 독립 영화 | review *n.* 평가 | release *n.* 개봉 | producer *n.* 제작자[사]

118. Pateon 전자의 고객 설문조사 데이터는 단순히 소프트웨어 프로그램의 향상을 돕는 데만 사용한다.

해설　「be + ------- + p.p.」, 「be + ------- + V-ing」, 「have + ------- + p.p.」와 같이 완성된 동사의 형태 중간에 빈칸이 들어있는 경우 항상 부사가 정답이므로 (C) simply를 선택해야 한다. 토익시험에 가장 많이 출제되는 형태는 「be + ------- + p.p.」이다.

어휘　customer survey 고객 설문 조사

119. 직원들은 법인카드를 이용한 구매의 승인을 요청하기 전에 상품의 가격이 정확한지 확인해야 한다.

해설　빈칸에는 동사 request의 목적어에 해당하는 명사가 와야 할 자리이다. 보기를 보아하니 명사 어휘 문제이다. 문장 전체의 내용을 가장 자연스럽게 만들어주는 것은 (A) approval이다.

어휘　make sure 확실하게 하다 | correct *adj.* 맞는, 정확한 | request *v.* 요청하다, 신청하다 | company card *n.* 법인카드 | approval *n.* 승인 | direction *n.* 지시, 명령 | renewal *n.* 갱신 | explanation *n.* 설명

120. 〈Travel Here〉지에 따르면 Smith 섬이 작년에 세계에서 가장 매력적인 관광지로 평가되었다.

해설 관사와 명사 사이에 빈칸이 있을 때는 항상 형용사가 들어가서 명사를 수식해야 한다. 분사도 형용사의 역할을 할 수 있지만 형용사와 분사가 보기에 함께 있을 때는 매우 특수한 경우를 제외하고 형용사가 정답이다. 그러므로 정답은 (D) attractive이다.

어휘 **rank** v. (등급·등위·순위를) 매기다, 평가하다 | **destination** n. 여행지, 목적지 | **attractive** adj. 매력적인 | **attraction** n. 명소

121. Wayne Murdock은 거의 오로지 전자제품만을 취급하는 작은 수리점을 운영한다.

해설 빈칸 바로 앞뒤에 있는 동사 deal with, 부사 almost와 어울리게 사용할 수 있는 부사는 '거의 오로지' 전자제품만을 취급한다라는 의미가 되는 (B) exclusively밖에 없다.

어휘 **run** v. (사업체 등을) 운영하다, 관리하다 | **repair shop** 수리점 | **deal with** ~을 처리하다, 취급하다 | **electronics** n. 전자 제품 | **jointly** adv. 공동으로 | **exclusively** adv. 오로지, 오직; 독점적으로 | **kindly** adv. 친절하게 | **carefully** adv. 주의하여, 조심스럽게

122. 대선후보 Michael Roose와 Vince Dalmer는 유권자들 사이에서 대부분의 경쟁자들보다 좋은 평판을 얻고 있다.

해설 대명사의 격을 판단하는 문제에서 명사 앞에 빈칸이 있으므로 소유격 대명사인 (C) their가 정답이다.

어휘 **presidential candidate** 대선후보 | **standing** n. 지위, 평판 | **voter** n. 투표자, 유권자 | **rival** n. 경쟁자, 경쟁 상대

123. 〈Jump Nutrition〉은 아시아의 가장 인기 있는 건강잡지 중 하나로서 30개 이상의 나라에 구독자가 있다.

해설 빈칸 뒤의 in more than 30 countries를 보면 의미상 네 개의 보기가 모두 들어갈 수 있는데, 빈칸 앞에 있는 magazines를 보고 (C) subscribers가 정답임을 판단할 수 있다.

어휘 **attendee** n. 참석자 | **viewer** n. 시청자 | **subscriber** n. 구독자 | **observer** n. 보는 사람, 목격자

124. 주말 내내 학회 참가자들을 마주칠 때 따뜻하게 환영해주시기 바랍니다.

해설 the weekend라는 기간명사와 함께 사용했을 때 의미가 통하는 것은 (B) throughout뿐이다. throughout the weekend는 '주말 동안, 주말 내내'라는 뜻이다.

어휘 **warmly** adv. 따뜻하게 | **greet** v. 맞다, 환영하다 | **conference** n. 회의, 학회 | **participant** n. 참가자 | **throughout** prep. ~동안 죽, 내내 | **beyond** prep. ~저편에

125. Mayar 사는 새 아파트 단지 개발의 계약을 얻어내려고 여러 번 시도했다.

해설 빈칸 앞에 문장의 동사 has made가 이미 있으므로 더 이상 동사를 사용하면 안 된다. 보기 중 동사가 아닌 것은 준동사인 (D) to acquire뿐이다.

어휘 **make an attempt** 시도하다, 꾀하다 | **contract** n. 계약(서) | **apartment complex** 아파트 단지 | **acquire** v. 습득하다, 얻다

126. Wilde 교수는 자신의 연구실 조수가 실험을 혼자 진행할 수 있을 것이라고 확신한다.

해설 빈칸 앞에 전치사 by가 있으므로 빈칸에는 목적어가 필요하다. 목적어에는 목적격 (D), 소유대명사 (C), 재귀대명사 (A)가 모두 들어갈 수 있는데, 문장 속 행위의 주체인 her laboratory assistant가 보기에 있는 대명사(she)와 동일 대상이라서 재귀대명사가 정답이다. 그러므로 (A) herself가 정답이 된다. 더 빠르고 정확한 문제풀이를 위해 by 뒤에 빈칸이 있는 문제가 출제될 때는 항상 재귀대명사가 정답이라는 사실을 기억하는 게 좋다.

어휘 **confident** adj. 자신감 있는 | **laboratory assistant** 연구실 조수 | **conduct** v. 실시하다 | **experiment** n. 실험 | **by oneself** 혼자; 다른 사람 없이

127. 다른 사무실로 옮긴 주된 이유는 낮은 임대료였다.

해설 빈칸 앞에 관사와 형용사가 있으므로 빈칸에는 명사가 들어가야 한다. 그러므로 (A)나 (B)가 정답인데, 동사가 단수형인 was이므로 단수명사인 (B) reason을 선택해야 한다.

어휘 **primary** adj. 주된, 주요한 | **lower** v. 낮추다 | **rent** n. 임차료 | **reasonable** adj. 합리적인

128. 제품 개발팀은 Skylight X250 스마트폰의 시제품을 거의 완료했으며 목요일에 그것을 이사회에 발표할 예정이다.

해설 네 개의 보기 (A) 거의 끝마쳤다, (B) 끊임없이 끝마쳤다, (C) 거의 끝마치지 못했다, (D) 정기적으로 끝마쳤다 중 자연스러운 것은 (A) nearly이다. 빈칸 뒤에 숫자, all, every, entire, finished, completed 등이 있는 문제에서는 거의 예외 없이 nearly나 almost가 정답으로 출제된다는 사실을 기억하면 매년 서너 번 정도 쉽고 빠르게 문제를 해결할 수 있다.

어휘 **product development team** 제품 개발팀 | **complete** v. 완료하다, 끝마치다 | **prototype** n. 시제품 | **plan on** ~할 예정/계획이다 | **present** v. 공개하다, 발표하다 | **board** n. 이사회 | **nearly** adv. 거의 | **constantly** adv. 끊임없이 | **hardly** adv. 거의 ~아니다 | **regularly** adv. 정기적으로, 규칙적으로

129. 고객들은 일단 새 시스템이 설치되면 매장 웹사이트에서 주문 상황을 확인할 수 있을 것이다.

해설 (A)는 전치사이고, (B)는 부사, (C)는 접속사이다. (D)는 바로 뒤에 「명사＋to부정사」가 붙어서 「in order for＋N＋to-V」의 구조가 되어야 하는데, 이 때는 for＋N이 in order to-V의 의미상 주어가 된다. 빈칸 뒤에 절이 있기 때문에 빈칸에 들어갈 수 있는 것은 접속사인 (C) once이다.

어휘 **customer** n. 손님, 고객 | **status** n. 상황 | **order** n. 주문 | **install** v. 설치하다 | **along with** ~와 함께 | **once** conj. ~하자마자; 일단 ~하면

130. 직원들은 보안을 위해 자신들의 사무실 컴퓨터의 암호를 만들도록 요구 받는다.

해설 전치사 of 뒤에 빈칸이 있으므로 목적어가 필요하다. 명사인 (A)와 (D)가 들어갈 수 있는데, '안전을 위해'가 의미상 더 적절하고, 사람을 나타내는 securer 앞에는 관사 a나 the가 필요하므로 (D) security가 정답이다.

어휘 **for the purpose of** ~의 목적으로, ~을 위해 | **be required to** ~하라는 요구를 받다 | **password** *n.* 암호 | **secure** *adj.* 안전한 | **securer** *n.* 안전하게 하는 사람; 보증하는 사람 | **security** *n.* 보안

[131-134] 다음 이메일에 관한 문제입니다.

수신: 모든 Superplex 의류 부서장들
발신: Greta Silvers
제목: 주민 회의

다음 주 금요일 우리는 **131** 관심 있는 주민들을 위한 지역 사회 토론회를 개최할 예정입니다. Leopold 가에 우리의 두 번째 매장을 짓는 공사로 인해 유발되는 소음에 대해 여러 건의 항의가 있었습니다. 그래서 우리는 이 사안을 다루고, 바라건대 프로젝트에 관하여 주민들과 상호 이해를 **132** 증진시킬 것입니다. **133** 동시에 우리는 공사 작업과 관련하여 혹시 다른 문제도 있는지 알아볼 것입니다. 이것은 지역 사회와 더 깊게 가까워질 수 있는 좋은 기회가 될 것입니다. 우리는 각 부서의 장으로서 여러분 중 한 사람도 빠짐없이 다음 주 이 토론에 참여할 것을 권장합니다. **134** 여러분이 참여할 수 있기 바랍니다.

감사합니다.

Greta Silvers
Superplex 의류

어휘 **apparel** *n.* 의류 | **department manager** 부서장 | **subject** *n.* 주제 | **community** *n.* 주민, 지역 사회 | **plan on** ~할 예정이다 | **hold** *v.* 열다, 개최하다 | **forum** *n.* 토론회 | **complaint** *n.* 불평, 항의 | **noise** *n.* 소음 | **cause** *v.* 야기하다 | **address** *v.* 대처하다 | **issue** *n.* 주제, 쟁점, 사안 | **hopefully** *adv.* 바라건대 | **develop mutual understanding** 상호 간의 이해를 증진하다 | **opportunity** *n.* 기회 | **connect with** ~와 마음이 통하다, 잘 지내다, 가까워지다 | **respective** *adj.* 각자의, 각각의 | **head of the department** 부서장 | **encourage** *v.* 권장하다, 장려하다 | **each and every** 어느 ~이나, 한 사람[하나]도 빠짐없이 | **participate** *v.* 참가하다, 참여하다

---

131. 해설 빈칸 앞에 전치사 for가 있고 빈칸 뒤에 명사 residents가 있으므로 빈칸에는 형용사가 들어가서 명사를 수식해야 하므로 (B) concerned가 정답이다. (A)는 '~에 관한[관련된]'이라는 뜻의 전치사인데, 전치사 두 개를 연달아 쓸 수는 없으므로 정답이 될 수 없다.

132. 해설 '상호 간 이해를 증진시킨다'는 의미를 만들 때 동사 develop를 사용해서 develop mutual understanding라고 표현한다. 토익 시험에 자주 등장하는 develop relationship(관계를 발전시키다) 같은 표현도 함께 외워두는 게 좋다. 따라서 정답은 (C) develop이다.

133. 해설 앞 문장에서는 상호 간 이해를 증진시키는 것, 뒷문장에서는 또 다른 문제가 있는지 알아보는 것을 언급하면서 토론회의 여러 가지 목적을 나열하고 있으므로 '동시에'라는 의미의 (A) At the same time이 알맞다. 빈칸은 접속부사가 들어가야 할 자리이므로 접속사인 (B)나 (C)는 정답이 될 수 없다.

134. (A) 모든 관리자에게 출석은 의무입니다.
(B) 회의는 내일로 옮겨졌습니다.
(C) 제가 그 과정을 더 자세하게 묘사하겠습니다.
(D) 여러분이 참여할 수 있길 바랍니다.

해설 빈칸 앞 문장에서 모든 사람의 참가를 장려한다고 했으므로 모든 감독자의 참석이 의무라고 말하고 있는 (A)는 문맥상 맞지 않다. (B) 회의가 내일로 옮겨졌습니다, (C) 절차를 더 자세히 설명하겠습니다 등은 지문과 전혀 상관없는 내용이다. 이메일을 마무리 짓기에 가장 좋은 문장은 (D) We hope that you are able to join us.이다.

[135-138] 다음 광고에 관한 문제입니다.

Catz 커뮤니케이션이 현재 정규직 지원서를 받고 있습니다.

직책: 기술 지원 직원

다양한 유형의 기술적인 문제를 처리할 수 있는 기술지원 직원을 찾고 있습니다. 바쁜 날에는 직원 한 명이 인터넷 서비스에 대한 특정한 질문이 있는 고객으로부터 **135** 걸려오는 전화를 최대 50통까지 받을 수 있습니다. 게다가, 직원은 필요한 경우 적절한 부서로 전화를 연결시켜줘야 합니다.

이 직책의 가장 중요한 측면 중 하나는 **136** 즉각적인 주목이 필요한 문제를 규명하고 우선순위로 처리하는 능력입니다. 이것은 분석력과 시기적절하게 타당한 **137** 결정을 내리는 능력을 요합니다. **138** 이 직책에서는 매일매일이 전날과 다릅니다. 그러므로 지원자가 어떤 상황이든 빠르게 적응할 수 있는지가 중요합니다.

지원서를 제출하려면 www.catzcommunications.com으로 가세요.

어휘 **currently** *adv.* 현재, 지금 | **accept** *v.* 받아들이다 | **application** *n.* 지원[신청](서) | **full-time position** 정규직 | **job title** 직위, 직책 | **technical support** 기술 지원 | **representative** *n.* 대리인 | **look for** ~을 바라다[기대하다] | **handle** *v.* 다루다 | **technical issue** 기술적 문제 | **up to** ~까지 | **incoming call** 걸려오는 전화 | **specific** *adj.* 구체적인, 명확한, 분명한 | **in addition** 덧붙여, 게다가 | **transfer** *v.* 넘겨주다 | **appropriate** *adj.* 적절한 | **aspect** *n.* 측면 | **identify** *v.* 찾다, 발견하다 | **prioritize** *v.* 우선적으로 처리하다 | **attention** *n.* 주의, 주목 | **require** *v.* 필요로 하다 | **analytical skill** 분석력 | **sound** *adj.* 견실한, 믿을 만한, 타당한 | **make a decision** 결정을 하다 | **in a timely manner** 시기적절하게 | **therefore** *adv.* 그러므로 | **crucial** *adj.* 중대한, 결정적인 | **candidate** *n.* 후보자 | **adapt to** ~에 적응하다 | **situation** *n.* 상황, 처지, 환경

---

135. 해설 빈칸 앞의 answer up to 50와 빈칸 뒤의 calls from customers를 봤을 때 고객으로부터 걸려오는 전화를 최대 50통까지 받는다가 자연스러우므로 (C) incoming이 정답이다.

136. 해설 우선순위로 처리한다는 뜻의 동사 prioritize는 '즉각적인 주목이 필요한 문제(problems that need immediate attention)'가 목적어이므로 정답으로 (D) immediate를 선택해야 한다.

137. 해설　빈칸 앞에 관사 a와 형용사 sound가 있으므로 빈칸에는 명사인 (B) decision이 들어가야 한다.

138. (A) Catz 커뮤니케이션은 모든 고객의 의견을 소중히 여깁니다.
(B) 이 직책에서는 매일매일이 전날과 다릅니다.
(C) 저희 웹사이트를 방문하시면 저희 매장에 오시는 길을 알 수 있습니다.
(D) 이 자리는 시간이 유동적이라서 정규 학생들에게 안성맞춤입니다.

해설　빈칸 뒷문장인 '그러므로 지원자가 어떤 상황이든 빠르게 적응할 수 있는지가 중요합니다'를 보면 빈칸에는 (B) In this job, each day is different from the day before.가 들어가야 문맥이 자연스럽다.

[139-142] 다음 이메일에 관한 문제입니다.

발신: support@flashcinema.com
수신: s.durand@bmt.com
제목: Flash Cinema 서비스
날짜: 6월 10일

Ms. Durand에게,

Flash Cinema가 저희 동영상 스트리밍 서비스에 오신 고객님을 환영합니다!

Flash Cinema **139** 가입을 확인시켜드리고자 메일 드립니다. 고객님은 Premium Viewers 패키지에 등록하셨으며 매월 10달러에 컴퓨터나 스마트 기기에서 **140** 즉시 텔레비전 쇼와 영화를 무제한으로 이용하시게 해드립니다. **141** 요금은 매월 2일에 청구될 것입니다.

계정을 **142** 종료하기로 결정하셨다면, 저희 웹사이트 www.flashcinema.com/accounts에 로그인하시면 됩니다. 로그인하신 후 "계정 취소" 옵션을 선택하세요.

즐거운 서비스가 되시기 바랍니다.

Flash Cinema 팀

어휘　subject *n.* 주제 | subscription *n.* (서비스) 사용 | access *v.* 이용하다 | unlimited *adj.* 무제한의 | instantly *adv.* 즉각, 즉시 | device *n.* 장치[기기] | bill *v.* 청구서, 계산서를 보내다 | terminate *v.* 종료하다

139. 해설　보기 네 개의 명사 중 바로 뒤에 to를 붙여서 '~에 서비스 이용 가입[구독]'이라는 뜻으로 사용하는 것은 subscription밖에 없으므로 (B) subscription가 정답이다. 동사형 subscribe도 subscribe to의 형태로 사용한다는 것을 알고 있어야 한다.

140. 해설　빈칸 앞에 '동사＋목적어(access unlimited television shows and movies)'의 3형식 문장 형태가 완성되어 있으므로 빈칸에는 부사가 들어갈 자리이다. 따라서 (A) instantly가 정답이다.

141. (A) 귀하의 요금이 처리되지 않았음을 알려드리게 되어 유감입니다.
(B) 귀하가 요청하신 대로 저희가 연장을 시켜드렸습니다.
(C) 계정을 신청하시려면 고객서비스로 연락주십시오.
(D) 요금은 매월 2일에 청구될 것입니다.

해설　이용자가 가입한 서비스 명칭과 월 요금, 이용 방법 등을 설명하는 내용 뒤에 이어지는 문장이므로 지불금액이 처리되지 않았음을 알리는 문장 (A)나 서비스 연장을 알려주는 문장 (B), 가입방법을 알려주는 (C)는 알맞지 않다. 가장 자연스럽게 이어질 수 있는 문장은 (D) You will be billed on the second of each month.이다.

142. 해설　뒷문장에서 '계정 취소' 옵션을 선택하라고(select the "Cancel Account" option) 말하고 있으므로 빈칸에 알맞은 동사는 서비스의 종료를 나타내는 terminate이다. 따라서 정답은 (D) terminate이다.

[143-146] 다음 정보에 관한 문제입니다.

Tyberion Adventure 사
믿을 수 있는 야외 장비

Tyberion Adventure 등산용 지팡이를 구매해 주셔서 고맙습니다. 저희 제품은 가장 힘든 환경에서도 **143** 충실하게 도움을 드릴 수 있도록 설계되었습니다. 저희는 50년이 넘는 기간 동안 등산용 지팡이를 생산해왔음에도 불구하고 개선의 여지는 항상 있다는 것을 알고 있습니다. 저희는 저희 자신의 높은 **144** 신뢰도 기준을 충족시키기 위해 등산용 지팡이에 대한 엄격한 테스트를 실시합니다.

저희는 전문 등산가들이 가장 기복이 심한 지형에서 장비를 사용하도록 합니다. 품질관리 검사를 수행할 때는 몇몇 등산용 지팡이를 무작위로 선택해서 다른 숙련된 등산가들에 의한 같은 유형의 테스트를 **145** 거치게 합니다. **146** 하나의 지팡이라도 테스트에서 떨어지면 모든 생산이 중단됩니다.

저희 웹사이트 tyberionadventure.com에서 다른 야외 장비와 액세서리도 확인해보세요.

어휘　outdoor equipment[gear] 야외 장비 | count on ~을 믿다 | hiking pole[stick] 등산용 지팡이 | serve *v.* 도움이 되다, 기여하다 | faithfully *adv.* 충실히 | tough *adj.* 힘든, 어려운 | manufacture *v.* 제조하다, 생산하다 | improvement *n.* 향상 | reliability *n.* 신뢰도 | meet standards 기준에 부합되다 | conduct *v.* 실시하다 | rigorous *adj.* 철저한, 엄격한 | rugged *adj.* 기복이 심한 | terrain *n.* 지형, 지역 | perform *v.* 수행하다 | quality control *n.* 품질 관리 | inspection *n.* 조사, 검사 | randomly *adv.* 무작위로 | put through ~을 겪다 | skilled *adj.* 숙련된, 노련한 | fail *v.* (시험에) 떨어지다 | production *n.* 생산 | halt *v.* 중단시키다 | check out ~을 확인하다

143. 해설　가장 험한 환경에서도(in the toughest situations) 일상적인 상황과 마찬가지로 제 역할을 한다는 의미의 문장이 되어야 하므로 '충실하게'라는 뜻의 부사 (D) faithfully가 정답이다.

144. 해설 제조업체가 엄격한(rigorous) 테스트를 하는 이유는 제품의 신뢰성을 위한 것이라고 하는 게 자연스러우므로 (A) reliability가 정답이다.

145. 해설 무작위로 선택한 제품이 테스트를 통과하게 한다는 의미가 되도록 (C) put through를 선택하면 자연스러운 문장이 된다.

146. (A) 하나의 지팡이라도 테스트에서 떨어지면 모든 생산이 중단됩니다.
(B) 이 결과들은 우리가 여러 가지 영역에서 비용을 줄일 수 있다는 것을 보여줍니다.
(C) 긴 트레킹에는 등산용 지팡이를 한 세트를 더 추천드립니다.
(D) 이 과정은 근로자들이 물건들을 훨씬 더 빨리 배송할 수 있게 할 것입니다.

해설 바로 앞에서 제품의 신뢰도를 테스트하는 방식을 설명하고 있으므로 이것과 연관된 내용인 (A) If even one pole fails, all production will be halted.를 넣어야 문맥의 흐름이 자연스러워진다.

[147-148] 다음 광고에 관한 문제입니다.

중고 냉장고 판매. Farno ZT50 냉장고 5년 전 신형으로 구입. 최상의 상태. **147** 아름다운 스테인리스 스틸로 된 외관. 어떠한 부엌 인테리어에도 안성맞춤. 급수 필터 최근 교체함. 내/외부에 긁힌 자국, 흔적, 얼룩 없음. 모든 합리적인 제안 받음. **148** 주인이 3주 후에 해외로 이사하는 관계로 즉시 판매해야 함. Jimmy Manzer에게 jmanzer_25@mailweb.com로 이메일 바람.

어휘 purchase v. 구매하다 | reasonable adj. 타당한

147. 냉장고에 관해서 알 수 있는 것은 무엇인가?
(A) 5년 전에 품질 보증기간이 만료되었다.
(B) 전기를 아주 적게 소모한다.
(C) 급수 필터를 교체해야 한다.
(D) 멋스러운 외관을 자랑한다.

해설 냉장고에 대해 암시된 것을 찾는 문제이다. 아름다운 스테인리스 스틸로 된 외관, 어떠한 부엌 인테리어에도 안성맞춤이라고 했으므로 beautiful을 stylish로, exterior를 appearance로 paraphrasing한 (D) It has a stylish appearance.가 정답이다.

148. Mr. Manzer가 냉장고를 파는 이유는 무엇인가?
(A) 색상이 마음에 안 든다.
(B) 해외로 이사한다.
(C) 유지비를 감당할 수 없다.
(D) 더 큰 모델이 필요하다.

해설 왜 냉장고를 파는지를 묻고 있다. Owner moving abroad in three weeks, so must sell right away(주인이 3주 후에 해외로 이사하는 관계로 즉시 판매해야 함)를 통해 moving abroad를 relocating overseas로 paraphrasing한 (B) He is relocating overseas.가 정답임을 알 수 있다.

[149-150] 다음 문자 대화문에 관한 문제입니다.

Bosworth, Ian
좋은 아침이에요, Ms. Kennedy. 저는 Regency 호텔의 Ian Bosworth입니다. 저희 객실을 예약해 주셔서 감사합니다.
오전 10:12

Kennedy, Anne
오전 10:13 천만에요. 제가 로마에 방문할 때 저는 항상 거기서 머물러요.

Bosworth, Ian
149 저는 고객님께서 저희 호텔에 머무르는 전체 기간 동안 무료로 고객님을 스위트룸으로 옮겨드리고자 한다는 것을 알려드리려고 연락 드립니다.
오전 10:14

Kennedy, Anne
오전 10:15 정말이요? 좋은 소식이네요!

Bosworth, Ian
네, 고객님은 수년간 저희 단골 고객이시기에 저희는 이것이 저희의 감사를 보여드리는 한 방편이 될 것이라 생각했습니다. 참고로 말씀 드리자면, **150** 스위트룸에 머무르시면, 고객님은 매일 저녁 레스토랑 뷔페에서 무료로 식사하실 수 있습니다.
오전 10:17

Kennedy, Anne
와, **150** 항상 나가서 먹는 수고는 덜겠네요. 객실에서 와이파이 연결 상태는 어떤가요? 지난번보다 나은가요?
오전 10:19

Bosworth, Ian
고객님께서 만족하실 거라고 믿습니다. 저희 호텔은 그것을 업그레이드시켰고, 이제 훨씬 더 빠릅니다.
오전 10:21

Kennedy, Anne
좋아요. 아, 마지막 질문이 있습니다... 저는 공항에서 셔틀버스를 탈 계획이에요. 제가 도착하기 전에 예약을 해야 하나요?
오전 10:23

Bosworth, Ian
그러실 필요 없습니다. 그냥 D 출구로 나오셔서 저희 호텔의 버스 정류장을 찾으세요. 그 버스는 매 30분마다 출발합니다.
오전 10:27

Kennedy, Anne
오전 10:29 잘됐네요. 몇 주 뒤에 봬요.

어휘 pleasure n. 기쁨, 즐거움 | suite n. 스위트룸(호텔의 큰 고급 객실) | entire adj. 전체의 | duration n. 기간 | complimentary adj. 무료의 | satisfied adj. 만족한 | make a reservation 예약을 하다 | necessary adj. 필수적인 | depart v. 출발하다

149. Mr. Bosworth가 Ms. Kennedy에게 연락하는 이유는 무엇인가?

(A) 좋아하는 식사를 물어보기 위해

(B) 업그레이드에 관하여 알려주기 위해

(C) 예약 날짜를 옮기기 위해

(D) 수리 작업에 관하여 알려주기 위해

해설 대화의 서두에서 별도의 비용 추가 없이 체류 전 기간 동안 Ms. Kennedy의 방을 스위트룸으로 업그레이드시켜 주기로 했다는 것을 알리기 위해 그녀에게 연락했다고 문자 메시지를 보내는 이유를 밝히고 있다. 따라서 (B) To inform her about an upgrade가 정답이다.

---

150. 오전 10시 19분에, 그녀가 "항상 나가서 먹는 수고를 덜겠네요"라고 쓸 때, Ms. Kennedy가 의도한 것은 무엇인가?

(A) 호텔 식당에서 종종 식사할 것이다.

(B) 로마의 이곳저곳을 찾아다니는 것이 걱정된다.

(C) 그녀의 방에 무선 인터넷이 있어서 기쁘다.

(D) 더 나은 대중교통 옵션을 찾았다.

해설 스위트룸에 머무르면, 매일 저녁 레스토랑 뷔페에서 무료로 식사할 수 있다는 말 뒤에 Ms. Kennedy가 'that will save me the trouble of going out all the time'이라고 말했으므로 호텔 밖으로 나가서 먹지 않아도 된다는 의미이다. 와이파이에 대한 내용은 그 뒤에 나오며 (B), (D)와 관련된 내용은 언급되지 않았다. 따라서 (A) She will dine at a hotel restaurant often.이 정답이다.

[151-152] 다음 회람에 관한 문제입니다.

발신: Natalie Buckley

수신: Lamar Foster

회신: 기념일 저녁 식사

저희가 화요일에 상의했던 대로, ⬛151 제가 장소 리스트를 모아봤어요. 제가 가장 좋다고 생각하는 곳은 Grand Lao 호텔이에요. 괜찮은 가격대에 넓은 방이 여러 개 있고, 총괄 요리사가 세계적으로 유명하다네요! 그곳이 아니라면 다음으로는, Oceanic Inn을 제안할게요. 많은 손님들이 그곳의 웹사이트에 긍정적인 후기를 남겼고, 상업 지역에 있기 때문에 가기가 편리하겠네요.

저에게 교통편에 대해서도 물어봤죠. 불행히도, 그거에 대해서는 제가 아는 게 별로 없어요. 근데 ⬛152 Leslie Rivera가 작년 회사 만찬 때 버스를 마련했던 걸로 알고 있어요. 인사부(내선번호 6735)에서 그녀를 찾을 수 있을 거예요. ⬛152 그녀가 아마 낭신을 위한 유용한 정보들을 가지고 있을 거예요.

또 다른 질문이 있으면 저에게 알려주세요. 행사 기대하고 있겠습니다.

Natalie

어휘 compile v. 엮다. | venue n. 장소 | affordable adj. (가격이) 알맞은 | spacious adj. 널찍한 | conveniently adv. 편리하게, 알맞게 | transportation n. 교통

---

151. Ms. Buckley가 메모를 보낸 이유는 무엇인가?

(A) 서비스 비용을 검토하기 위해

(B) 방 예약을 확인하기 위해

(C) 행사를 위한 추천을 하기 위해

(D) 고객의 후기에 대해 상의하기 위해

해설 지문의 주제나 목적을 묻는 문제는 대부분 지문 초반의 몇 줄만 읽으면 정답이 나온다. 첫 번째 단락에서 장소에 대한 리스트를 정리해보았고, Grand Lao 호텔을 추천하고, 차선으로 Oceanic Inn을 추천하고 있다. 따라서 행사 장소를 제안하기 위해 쓴 이메일이라는 것을 알 수 있으므로 (C) To offer recommendations for an event가 정답이다.

---

152. Mr. Foster가 Ms. Rivera에게 연락해야 하는 이유는 무엇인가?

(A) 저녁 식사 파티로 가는 길을 물어보기 위해

(B) 공석으로 있는 자리에 지원서를 제출하기 위해

(C) 장소의 가격을 확인하기 위해

(D) 교통수단에 대한 정보를 알아보기 위해

해설 두 번째 단락에서 Leslie Rivera가 작년 만찬 때 버스를 마련했기 때문에 필요한 정보가 있을 것이라고 했으므로 Ms. Rivera에게 연락을 해봐야 하는 이유는 교통편에 대해 물어보기 위해서이다. 따라서 정답은 (D) To inquire about ideas for transportation이다.

[153-154] 다음 기사에 관한 문제입니다.

상승하는 매출

연중 이때쯤이면 보통 사람들은 자신의 집에 머물며 안락함을 즐기곤 합니다. 하지만 ⬛153 올해는, 많은 주민들이 지역 수영 센터의 실내 스파에서 따뜻함을 즐기기 위해 밖으로 나가는 이례적인 움직임을 보이고 있습니다. 밖으로 나온 손님이 많아지면서, 전년 겨울 대비 지역 업체들의 판매액이 40퍼센트 가까이 증가했습니다. 아니나 다를까, 스파의 인기로 인해 더 많은 주민들이 보통 추운 날씨를 대비해서 정기적으로 데워지는 수영장을 찾고 있습니다. ⬛154 물론 눈이 많이 오는 겨울은 더 예측 가능한 방식으로 도움이 되기도 하는데, 두꺼운 코트나 스노보드 같은 계절 스포츠 장비의 높은 판매량이 그것입니다.

어휘 comfort n. 안락, 편안 | out and about 어디를 돌아다니는 | unsurprisingly adv. 아니나 다를까 | popularity n. 인기 | predictable adj. 예측할 수 있는

---

153. 이 기사는 주로 무엇에 관한 것인가?

(A) 스파 이용료

(B) 예상치 못한 소비자 동향의 세부 사항

(C) 지역 수영 센터 개장

(D) 눈 오는 날씨의 위험

해설 지문의 주제를 묻는 문제이므로 첫 몇 줄을 잘 읽어봐야 한다. 예년 같으면 사람들이 실내에 머물러 있을 텐데, 올해는 실내 스파를 즐기러 밖에 나가는 사람들이 많다고 말하면서 이것을 '이례적 움직임'이라고 표현하고 있다. 이어지는 내용은 이러한 예상치 못했던 소비자 동향에 대한 설명이다. 따라서 (B) The details of an unexpected consumer trend가 정답이다.

---

154. 기사에 따르면, 날씨의 변화로 가장 혜택을 받을 사람은 누구인가?

(A) 수영장 장비 제조업체

(B) 식당

(C) 여행사

(D) 스포츠용품 판매점

해설 문제에 benefited from the weather change라는 키워드가 있으므로 지문을 훑어봐서 이 키워드가 언급되는 부분을 찾는다. 그리고 키워드가 paraphrasing되어 있는 the snowy winter has also been beneficial이 들어간 지문의 마지막 문장에서 정답을 찾아낸다. 계절 스포츠용품(seasonal sports equipment)의 판매가 늘어난다고 (high sales) 했으므로 스포츠용품 판매점이 혜택을 본다. 따라서 정답은 (D) Sporting goods stores이다.

[155-157] 다음 이메일에 관한 문제입니다.

수신: rvernon@chrome.net.uk
발신: jwarner@seansportscentredepot.co.uk
날짜: 11월 3일
제목: 제품 6322SL

Mr. Vernon에게,

155 저희가 개발 중인 Jaguar 트레킹 부츠의 새로운 제품군 시험에 동의해 주셔서 감사합니다. 영업일 2일 이내에 그 부츠 한 켤레를 귀하의 거주지인 65 James 가, 버밍엄 MT3 7KD로 보내드리겠습니다. 물건이 귀하께 배송되는 대로, 확인 이메일을 보내겠습니다.

귀하께서 부츠를 받은 날로부터 30일 동안, 최대한 많이 착용해 주시기 바랍니다. **157** 그 부츠는 어떤 날씨에도 사용 가능하므로 다양한 야외 환경에서 신어 보셨으면 합니다. 30일의 기간이 끝날 때, www.seansportscentredeopt.co.uk로 로그인한 후, 부츠의 외양, 편안함, 그리고 내구성에 관한 귀하의 의견을 요구하는 온라인 설문조사를 작성하여 귀하의 경험에 대해 말씀해 주십시오. 귀하와 상품을 시험한 다른 분들의 피드백은 Jaguar 트레킹 부츠의 디자인을 마무리하는 데 사용될 것입니다. 그 부츠는 내년 가을에 상점에서 구입할 수 있을 것입니다.

156 여러분과 같은 상품 시험 지원자들에게서 받은 피드백은 저희 고객들을 위한 최고급 품질의 제품을 개발하는 데 매우 중요합니다. 그 부츠는 저희가 드리는 선물이니 간직하세요.

진심으로,

Judy Warner, 제품 관리자
Sean Sports Center Depot

어휘 be in the process of ~하는 중이다 | business day
n. 영업일 | residence n. 주택, 거주 | ship v. 배송하다 |
confirmation n. 확인 | all-weather approved 모
든 날씨에 사용이 가능한 | various adj. 다양한 | outdoor
adj. 야외의 | condition n. 환경, 상태, 상황 | complete v.
작성하다 | survey n. 설문조사 | comment n. 의견, 평 |
appearance n. 외양, 외관 | comfort n. 안락, 편안 |
durability n. 내구성 | finalize v. 마무리 짓다, 완결하다 |
volunteer n. 지원자, 자원봉사자 | essential adj. 필수적인,
매우 중요한

---

155. 이메일은 왜 보내졌는가?
(A) 지불 수령을 확인하기 위해
(B) 고객에게 배송 지연을 알리기 위해
(C) 신제품의 출시를 홍보하기 위해
(D) 자원자에게 안내문을 제공하기 위해

해설 이메일의 목적은 이메일의 첫머리에서 확인해보자. 첫 문장인 '저희가 개발 중인 Jaguar 트레킹 부츠의 새로운 제품군 시험에 동의해 주셔서 감사합니다.'에서 이메일의 수신인이 신제품을 테스트할 예정이며, 30일간 신제품 테스트 시 요구 사항을 안내하고 있다. 따라서 제품 테스트의 방법과 요구 사항을 안내하기 위한 이메일이라는 것을 알 수 있다. 따라서 정답은 (D) To provide instructions to a volunteer 이다.

---

156. Sean Sports Centre Depot에 관하여 언급된 것은 무엇인가?
(A) 본사가 버밍엄에 있다.
(B) 그들의 현 제품들에 관하여 불평을 받았다.
(C) 웹사이트가 최근에 업데이트되었다.
(D) 제품 개발 과정에 소비자들을 참여시킨다.

해설 Sean Sports Centre Depot에 관련된 정보에 주목해보자. 이메일 마지막 단락에서 최고의 제품을 개발하기 위해 테스터들의 피드백은 중요하다고 하고 있으므로 고객들의 피드백이 제품 개발 과정에 반영된다는 것을 알 수 있으므로 정답은 (D) It involves consumers in the product development process.이다.

---

157. Jaguar 제품군에 관하여 알 수 있는 것은 무엇인가?
(A) 다양한 색상으로 나와 있다.
(B) 다채로운 날씨에 신을 수 있도록 디자인되었다.
(C) 11월에 특별가로 판매될 것이다.
(D) 프로 운동선수들이 홍보한다.

해설 Jaguar 제품군 관련 정보에 주목해보자. The boots are all-weather approved. Jaguar 신제품인 부츠는 어떤 날씨에도 괜찮다라고 말하고 있다. 따라서 정답은 (B) They are designed to be worn in many kinds of weather.이다. all-weather approved 가 designed to be worn in many kinds of weather로 paraphrasing되었다.

[158-160] 다음 웹페이지에 관한 문제입니다.

www.pacificroutetravel.com

Pacific Route 여행

158 Pacific Route 여행은 미국의 서해안 도처에 있는 여행 센터와 휴게소 체인점을 운영합니다. 해안 고속도로를 따라 편리하게 위치해 있는 저희 센터는 일년 내내 하루 24시간 운영합니다.

각 Pacific Route 여행 센터는 편의점, 주유소, 푸드코트와 장거리 여행을 더욱 편안하게 해주는 기타 편의시설들을 포함하고 있습니다.

- 현금자동입출금기는 하루 24시간 동안 이용 가능합니다.
- 송금과 수표 현금화 서비스는 월요일에서 금요일, 오전 9시부터 오후 5시까지 이용 가능합니다.
- 모든 지점에는 샤워 시설을 갖추고 있습니다; **159** 일부 지점에는 셀프서비스 세탁실이 있습니다.
- 모든 지점은 무선 인터넷과 케이블 텔레비전이 있는 휴게실이 있습니다.
- 푸드코트에서는 아주 다양한 건강식이 제공됩니다. 냉온 음료와 간식거리들은 저희 편의점에서 이용 가능합니다.

160 모든 Pacific Route 여행 센터의 위치를 알기 위해, 아래의 링크를 클릭해주세요: www.pacificroutetravel.com/locations.

어휘 **rest stop** 휴게소 | **throughout** *prep.* ~전역에, ~도처에 | **West Coast** 서부 해안 | **conveniently located** 편리한 곳에 위치한 | **convenience store** 편의점 | **fueling station** 주유소 | **food court** 푸드코트 (쇼핑센터 내 여러 종류의 식당들이 모여 있는 구역) | **amenity** *n.* 생활 편의 시설 | **ATM (Automated Teller Machine)** *n.* 현금입출금기 | **accessible** *adj.* 접근 가능한, 이용 가능한 | **money transfer** 현금 이체 | **check cashing service** 수표를 현금으로 바꾸는 서비스 | **be equipped with** ~을 갖추다 | **self-service laundry** 셀프서비스 빨래방 | **lounge** *n.* 휴게실 | **wireless Internet** 무선 인터넷 | **snack** *n.* 간식

---

158. 웹페이지는 무엇을 설명하는가?

(A) 여행 패키지

(B) 도로변 시설

(C) 가격이 저렴한 호텔

(D) 이사 서비스

해설 글의 첫머리를 확인해보자, 해안 고속도로를 따라있는 Pacific Route 여행사가 24시간 연중무휴로 운영하는 여행 센터와 휴게소에 대해 설명하고 있다. 따라서 정답은 (B) Roadside facilities이다. travel centers and rest stops, located along the coastal highways 가 Roadside facilities로 paraphrasing되었다

---

159. 일부 지점에서만 제공하는 것은 무엇인가?

(A) 세탁실

(B) 무선 인터넷

(C) 음식과 음료

(D) 샤워실

해설 일부 지점이 언급된 내용에 주목하자, 샤워실은 모든 지점마다 있고, 일부에만 있는 것은 셀프서비스 빨래방이다. 따라서 정답은 (A) Laundry rooms이다.

---

160. 제공된 링크를 클릭함으로써 어떤 정보를 찾을 수 있겠는가?

(A) 결제 방식

(B) 수수료

(C) 주차 안내문

(D) 거리 주소

해설 link를 키워드로 삼아 해당 내용을 포착해보자, 글의 맨 하단 For the locations of all Pacific Route Travel Centers, click the following link에서 Pacific Route 여행 센터의 위치를 알려면 링크를 클릭하라는 안내를 확인할 수 있다. 따라서 정답은 (D) Street addresses이다. locations가 street addresses로 paraphrasing되었다.

[161-164] 다음 이메일에 관한 문제입니다.

수신: 모든 Novad 직원들
발신: Niraj Sharma
날짜: 2월 5일, 수요일
제목: 기회

161 홍보 부서는 광고업계의 최신 동향과 관행에 대한 기사를 쓸 기고자를 찾고 있습니다. 현재 그리고 잠재 고객들과 더불어 일반 대중들이 볼 수 있도록, 저희는 회사의 웹사이트에 그 기사들을 게시할 것입니다. 162 저희는 1년에 각 400~500자의 기사를 최대 5개까지 쓸 수 있는 사람들을 찾고 있습니다.

이것은 저희 직원들에게 그들의 경험과 전문적인 지식을 더 많은 청중들과 공유할 수 있는 기회를 줄 것입니다. 작가의 이름과 Novad에서의 직책은 기사의 제목 아래에 보여질 것입니다.

기고에 관심이 있으시면, 다음 주 월요일인 2월 10일, 오전 10시 45분에 410호실로 2시간짜리 설명회에 와 주세요. 163 설명회가 다룰 내용은 다음과 같습니다.

* 기사 제출 절차
* 독창적이고 흥미로운 기사를 쓰는 방법
* 관련 있는 주제들을 조사할 수 있는 장소
* 163 회사 안팎에서 사람들을 인터뷰하는 것에 관한 회사 규정

164 만약 여러분이 그곳에 올 수 없다면, 제게 이메일을 보내 여러분이 가능한 날짜를 알려주십시오. 제가 여러분을 만나기 위해 따로 시간을 마련하도록 하겠습니다.

Niraj Sharma
홍보 담당자
Novad LLC

어휘 **Public Relations Department** 홍보 부서 | **seek** *v.* 찾다, 구하다 | **contributor** *n.* 기고자 | **latest** *adj.* 최신의 | **trend** *n.* 경향, 유행 | **practice** *n.* 관행 | **advertising industry** 광고업계 | **post** *v.* 게시하다, 게재하다 | **prospective client** 잠재 고객 | **up to** ~까지 | **per** *prep.* ~마다, ~당 | **share** *v.* 공유하다, 나누다 | **professional** *adj.* 전문적인 | **broad** *adj.* 폭넓은 | **audience** *n.* 청중 | **job position** 직책 | **contribute** *v.* 기여하다, 기고하다 | **information session** 설명회 | **go over** 다루다, 검토하다 | **process** *n.* 절차, 과정 | **submit** *v.* 제출하다 | **original** *adj.* 독창적인 | **interesting** *adj.* 흥미로운 | **research** *v.* 연구하다 | **relevant** *adj.* 관련 있는 | **regulation** *n.* 규정 | **regarding** *prep.* ~에 관하여 | **interview** *v.* 인터뷰하다, 면접을 보다 | **availability** *n.* 이용 가능성 | **arrange** *v.* 준비하다 | **separate** *adj.* 각각의, 별도의

---

161. Novad는 무엇이겠는가?

(A) 광고 대행사

(B) 라디오 방송국

(C) 취업 서비스

(D) 출판사

해설 Novad가 언급된 부분에 주목해보자. All Novad staff members가 수신인이며, Novad의 직원들이다. 광고업계의 최신 동향과 관행에 대한 글을 써줄 기고자를 내부에서 찾고 있는 글이다. 홍보업계의 최신 경향과 관행에 대한 기사를 고객과 일반 대중들이 볼 수 있도록 올릴 것이라는 내용이 언급되므로 이 업체는 광고 대행사임을 알 수 있다. 따라서 정답은 (A) An advertisement agency이다.

162. Mr. Sharma는 기고자들이 무엇을 하기를 바라는가?

(A) 설문조사를 수행한다

(B) 제품을 홍보한다

(C) 모든 직원들에게 이메일을 발송한다

(D) 회사의 웹사이트에 기사를 작성한다

해설 Mr. Sharma는 편지의 발신인이며, contributors를 키워드로 삼아 해당 내용을 포착해보자. 광고업계에 관한 기사를 쓸 지원자를 찾고 있으며, 회사 웹사이트에 지원자가 쓴 기사를 올릴 예정이라고 하고 있다. 1년에 최대 5번의 기사를 써줄 기고자를 찾고 있으므로 정답은 (D) Write articles for the company's Web site이다.

163. 설명회에 관하여 언급된 것은 무엇인가?

(A) 모든 직원들에게 의무적이다.

(B) 몇 가지 회사 지침들을 다룰 것이다.

(C) 사전 등록이 필요하다.

(D) 회사의 부사장이 이끌 것이다.

해설 information session을 키워드로 삼아 단서를 포착해보자. 기고에 관심 있는 사람들은 설명회에 참석하라고 하면서, 다룰 내용들을 열거하고 있다. 그 중에 회사 안팎에서 사람들을 인터뷰하는 것에 관한 회사의 규정을 언급하고 있다. 따라서 정답은 (B) It will cover some company guidelines이다. company regulations가 company guidelines로 paraphrasing되었다

164. 누가 Mr. Sharma에게 이메일을 보내라고 요구 받는가?

(A) 최근에 고용된 직원들

(B) 지역 리포터와 기자들

(C) 설명회에 참석할 수 없는 직원들

(D) 기업의 잠재 고객들

해설 Mr. Sharma는 편지의 발신인이고, 수신인은 회사의 직원들이다. send an e-mail을 키워드로 삼아 단서를 포착해보자. 설명회에 참석할 수 없는 사람들은 이메일을 보내달라고 하고 있다. 앞에서 기사를 기고하고 싶은 사람은 설명회에 참석해달라고 안내하므로 이메일을 보내야 하는 사람은 설명회에 참석할 수 없는 직원들이다. 따라서 정답은 (C) Employees who cannot attend the information session이다.

[165-167] 다음 편지에 관한 문제입니다.

Mr. Simmons에게,

11월 19일 밤에 Baker Engineering을 위한 시상식을 주최하게 된 것은 영광입니다. 저는 귀하와 귀하의 손님들이 멋진 경험을 할 것이며 당신의 이벤트가 매우 성공적일 것임을 확신합니다.

Safeway 컨벤션 센터는 이와 같은 다양한 이벤트들을 지난 10년 동안 진행해 와서 **165** 저희 직원들은 이러한 행사를 어떻게 진행해야 하는지에 대해 충분히 숙지하고 있습니다. 하지만 귀하께서 저희에게 몇 명의 손님들이 오실 것으로 예상하는지 알려 주신다면 매우 도움이 될 것입니다. **167** 우리는 그날 저녁에 몇 개의 의자와 테이블이 필요한지 알아야 합니다. 정확한 인원수를 모르신다면, 대략적인 예상 인원수로도 충분합니다.

지불과 관련해서는, 저녁 내내 Rose Ballroom을 대여하는 것으로 2,500달러입니다. 저희가 이 행사에서 음식을 준비할 것이기 때문에, 귀하와 귀하의 손님들을 위해 저희가 준비할 수 있는 메뉴 항목들을 포함시켰습니다. **166** 무엇을 드시고 싶은지 고르시고, 각 음식이 몇 인분씩 필요한지 알려 주십시오. 귀하께서는 또한 뷔페 옵션을 선택하실 수도 있습니다. 저희 고객들 중 많은 분들이 이 옵션을 선호합니다.

Safeway 컨벤션 센터를 선택해 주셔서 다시 한번 감사드립니다. 상의하고 싶으신 문제가 있으면 언제든 831-3595로 저에게 연락 주십시오.

Clara Wellman
행사 진행자
Safeway 컨벤션 센터

어휘 privilege *n.* 특권 | host *v.* (행사를) 주최하다 | awards ceremony 시상식 | guest *n.* 손님 | experience *n.* 경험 | complete *adj.* 완전한 | numerous *adj.* 많은 | expect *v.* 기대하다 | helpful *adj.* 도움이 되는 | exact *adj.* 정확한 | rough *adj.* 대략적인 | estimate *n.* 추산, 추정치 | suffice *v.* 충분하다 | payment *n.* 지불 | cater *v.* (행사에) 음식을 공급하다 | prepare *v.* 준비하다 | simply *adv.* 그냥, 그저 | dish *n.* 요리 | require *v.* 요구하다 | matter *n.* 문제

165. 이 편지의 주 목적은 무엇인가?

(A) 방이 이용 가능하다는 것을 고객에게 알려주기 위해

(B) 제공된 서비스에 대한 지불을 요청하기 위해

(C) 다가올 행사에 대한 준비를 상의하기 위해

(D) 장소에 대한 다른 선택 사항을 제공하기 위해

해설 Safeway 컨벤션 센터가 행사 진행을 맡게 되어 진행될 행사에 대한 세부 사항을 점검하고 있는 글이므로 (C) To discuss preparations for an upcoming event가 정답이다.

166. Ms. Wellman가 Mr. Simmons에게 하도록 요청한 것은 무엇인가?

(A) 손님들 숙박 계획을 위한 시간을 정한다

(B) 파티의 정확한 시간을 알려준다

(C) 참석자들의 이름을 그녀에게 준다

(D) 메뉴에서 몇 개를 선택한다

해설 세 번째 단락을 보면, Safeway 컨벤션 센터가 음식 서비스를 제공하기 때문에, 원하는 음식을 선택해 알려달라는 말이 나온다. 따라서 (D) Select some items from a menu가 정답이다.

167. [1], [2], [3], [4]라고 표시된 곳 중 다음 문장이 들어가기에 가장 적절한 곳은 어디인가?

"우리는 그날 저녁에 몇 개의 의자와 테이블이 필요한지 알아야 합니다"

(A) [1]
(B) [2]
(C) [3]
(D) [4]

해설 의자와 테이블이 얼마나 필요한지 '숫자'와 관련된 내용이므로, 바로 앞에 몇 명의 손님이 올 것인지 알려 달라고 말한 다음인 [1]에 오는 것이 가장 자연스럽다. [1]에서 인원수를 알고자 하는 구체적인 이유가 언급되고, 다음 문장에서 정확한 숫자를 모른다면 예측 인원수도 괜찮다고 말하는 것이 문맥상 자연스럽다. 따라서 (A) [1]이 정답이다.

[168-171] 다음 사보에 관한 문제입니다.

GOH 대략 살펴보기

168 GOH 사는 지난 5년간 Make It Yours 공학 경연대회를 후원해 왔습니다. 12살에서 18살 사이의 연령대가 등록 가능합니다. 이 행사는 매년 200명 이상의 참가자를 **170** 불러 모았습니다.

Greensville 주민이자 Greensville 대학의 공학 교수인 Aaron Grover는 8년 전 Make It Yours를 시작했습니다. Mr. Grover는 30개의 특허가 있으며, 현재 전 세계의 많은 가정에서 사용되고 있는 가장 최근에 발명한 강력한 정수기 필터 등 100개 이상의 다양한 제품들을 발명했습니다. 국제 발명가 명예의 전당은 세계 각국의 젊은이들이 공학 분야의 직업을 고려하도록 장려하는 것을 목표로 하고 있습니다.

GOH도 경연대회에 직접 참여할 것입니다. 연구개발 부서의 Xiao Tsu와 Anna Shick가 일곱 명의 심사위원단에 있을 것입니다. 더불어, 고객 서비스 부서의 Gloria Berg가 등록하는 것을 도울 것입니다. 만약 당신이 Make It Yours에 참여하는 것에 관심이 있으시다면, **171** 자원봉사 기회의 목록을 확인하기 위해 회사 웹사이트의 지역사회 돕기 페이지를 방문해 주십시오. ☞기 알겠습니까? **169** 당신이 미래의 GOH의 직원을 선발하는 데 도움을 주게 될지도 모릅니다.

어휘 glance *n.* 흘끗 봄 ǀ sponsor *v.* 후원하다 ǀ engineering *n.* 공학 ǀ competition *n.* 경연, 경쟁 ǀ register *v.* 등록하다 ǀ draw *v.* 끌어들이다 ǀ participant *n.* 참여자 ǀ resident *n.* 주민 ǀ patent *n.* 특허 ǀ invent *v.* 발명하다 ǀ robust *adj.* 강력한, 튼튼한 ǀ water filter 정수기 필터 ǀ household *n.* 가정 ǀ across the globe 전 세계에서 ǀ inventor *n.* 발명가 ǀ Hall of Fame 명예의 전당 ǀ aim to ~하는 것을 목표로 하다 ǀ encourage *v.* 장려하다, 권장하다 ǀ panel *n.* 패널(특정한 문제에 대해 조언·견해를 제공하는 전문가 집단) ǀ judge *n.* 심사위원 ǀ help out 돕다 ǀ volunteer *n.* 자원봉사, 자원봉사자

168. 이 기사가 쓰여진 이유는 무엇이었겠는가?

(A) 새로운 서비스를 홍보하기 위해
(B) 행사를 조명하기 위해
(C) 직원에게 영예를 주기 위해
(D) 수상자를 발표하기 위해

해설 기사의 첫머리에 주목해보자. GOH 사가 후원하는 Make It Yours 경연대회라는 행사를 언급하는 것으로 시작하여 이에 대한 세부 정보를 제공하고 있으므로 정답은 (B) To highlight an event이다.

169. GOH 사에 관하여 알 수 있는 것은 무엇인가?

(A) 국제 발명가 명예의 전당을 위한 후보자들을 지명한다.
(B) 정수기 필터를 만든다.
(C) 엔지니어들을 고용한다.
(D) 젊은이들을 위한 인턴직을 제공한다.

해설 GOH에 대해 언급된 내용에 주목해보자. GOH가 후원해 온 Make It Yours 공학 경연대회 소개를 하고 있다. 국제 발명가 명예의 전당의 취지는 전 세계 젊은이들이 공학 관련 직업을 고려하도록 장려하는 것이라고 이야기하고 있다. Make It Yours에 참여하는 것이 GOH의 다음 직원을 뽑는 일로 이어질 수도 있다는 내용은 GOH에서 엔지니어를 뽑는다는 사실로 유추할 수 있다. 따라서 정답은 (C) It hires engineers.이다.

170. 첫 번째 단락, 세 번째 줄의 "drawing"과 의미상 가장 가까운 것은

(A) 보여주는
(B) 얻는
(C) 끌어 오는
(D) 유발하는

해설 drawing의 동의어를 물어보는 문제이다. This event has been drawing over 200 participants each year란 이 행사는 200명 이상의 참가자를 '끌어 왔다'는 뜻이므로 문맥상 가장 적절한 어휘는 (C) attracting이다.

171. 기사에 따르면, 회사의 웹사이트에서 무엇을 발견할 수 있는가?

(A) Mr. Grover의 발명품 목록
(B) GOH 사 지원 방법에 대한 상세 정보
(C) 할 수 있는 직무에 관한 정보
(D) 고객 설문조사

해설 Web site를 키워드로 삼아 해당 내용을 포착해보자. 회사 웹사이트에서 자원봉사 기회가 적힌 목록을 확인할 수 있다고 말하고 있다. 따라서 정답은 (C) Information about available duties이다. volunteer opportunities가 available duties로 paraphrasing되었다.

Blake, Gordon [오전 10:14]

Mr. Sikorski, 저는 Sigma 조경의 Gordon Blake입니다. **172** 저희 작업반이 오늘 오후 1시에 고객님 댁에 방문한다는 것을 확인하고자 합니다.

Sikorski, Tina [오전 10:17]

맞아요, Mr. Blake. 당신의 작업반이 작업하는 것을 보기를 기대하고 있습니다.

Blake, Gordon [오전 10:20]

저희는 최선을 다할 것입니다. 저희는 곧 고객님의 앞뜰과 뒤뜰을 보기 좋게 만들어야 합니다. 그리고 확인 차 여쭤보는데… 고객님께서는 저희가 잔디를 깎고 생울타리를 다듬는 것을 원하시는 거지요, 그렇지요?

Sikorski, Tina [오전 10:21]

맞아요. 그런데, 당신이 해주실 일이 한 가지 더 있어요.

Blake, Gordon [오전 10:22]

그것이 무엇인가요?

Sikorski, Tina [오전 10:24]

173 분수 근처에 있는 뒤뜰에 제가 정말 제거하고 싶은 오래된 나무 그루터기가 있습니다. 저를 위해 귀하의 작업반이 그루터기를 제거해 주실 수 있나요?

Blake, Gordon [오전 10:27]

작업반이 제거할 수 있을지 없을지 결정하기 전에 먼저 그루터기를 봐야 할 것 같습니다. 만약 불가능하다면, 주중에 다시 가서 처리할 수 있습니다. **174** 만약에 손이 많이 가는 큰 작업이면, 추가 요금이 발생할 것입니다.

Sikorski, Tina [오전 10:29]

174 그건 이해할 수 있어요. **175** 오늘 작업 감독관이 제게 청구서를 주시도록 해줄 수 있나요? 작업이 완료되면 현금으로 지불하려고 해요.

Blake, Gordon [오전 10:30]

175 물론입니다. 제가 감독관한테 그렇게 말해 놓겠습니다.

Sikorski, Tina [오전 10:31]

감사합니다. 작업이 끝날 때, 만약 필요한 것이 있으면 말씀드릴게요.

어휘 confirm v. 확인하다 | crew n. 동료 | look forward to ~을 고대하다 | do one's best 최선을 다하다 | yard n. 뜰 | in no time 곧 | trim v. 정돈하다 | hedge n. 울타리 | stump n. 그루터기 | remove v. 제거하다 | get rid of ~을 제거하다 | take a look 보다 | though adv. 하지만 | extra fee n. 추가 비용 | understandable adj. 이해할 수 있는 | foreman n. 공장장, 감독 | invoice n. 청구서

172. 왜 Mr. Blake이 Ms. Sikorski에게 연락하는가?

(A) 서비스 요금을 기술한다

(B) 연장을 요청한다

(C) 프로젝트 결과에 대해 보고한다

(D) 약속을 확인한다

해설 오전 10시 14분에 Mr. Blake이 Sigma 조경의 작업반이 오늘 오후 1시에 Ms. Sikorski의 집에 방문하는 것을 확인한다고 말하였으므로 (D) To confirm an appointment가 정답이다.

173. Ms. Sikorski가 추가로 요청한 일은 무엇인가?

(A) 나무 그루터기 제거

(B) 분수대 설치

(C) 꽃 심기

(D) 몇몇 덤불을 다듬기

해설 오전 10시 24분에 Ms. Sikorski가 뒤뜰에 정말 제거하고 싶은 오래된 나무 그루터기가 있다고 이야기하였으므로 (A) The removal of a tree stump가 정답이다.

174. 오전 10시 29분에, Ms. Sikorski가 "그건 이해할 수 있어요"라고 쓴 것은 무슨 의미인가?

(A) Mr. Blake이 쓴 글을 이해하지 못한다.

(B) Ms. Sikorski이 먼저 서명한 계약은 수용할 만하다.

(C) 추가 요금을 내도 괜찮다.

(D) 그 일은 저녁 전에 완료되어야 한다.

해설 화자가 말하고자 하는 의도를 파악하는 문제이다. 오전 10시 27분에 Mr. Blake이 나무 그루터기를 제거하는 작업을 할 때 손이 많이 가는 큰 작업이면 추가 요금이 발생할 것이라고 하였고, 이에 10시 29분에 Ms. Sikorski는 그건 이해할 수 있다고 하였으므로 Mr. Blake의 말에 대해 수긍한 것임을 알 수 있다. 따라서 정답은 (C) She is fine with being charged extra.이다.

175. 문자 대화문에 따르면, Ms. Sikorski는 작업반장에게 무엇을 받을 것인가?

(A) 청구서

(B) 카탈로그

(C) 쿠폰

(D) 명함

해설 오전 10시 29분에 Ms. Sikorski가 Mr. Blake에게 작업 감독관이 청구서를 주도록 해 줄 수 있냐고 물어보았고 오전 10시 30분에 Mr. Blake이 작업 감독관한테 이야기해 놓겠다고 하였으므로 (A) A bill이 정답이다.

수신: Jackie Miller ⟨j.miller@redomarketing.com⟩

발신: Edward Moto ⟨e.moto@redomarketing.com⟩

날짜: 3월 12일

제목: The Stanford 호텔

첨부문서: TSH_ad_cer3

Jackie님께,

The Stanford 호텔의 업데이트된 광고 버전을 첨부하오니 확인 바랍니다. 저희 고객들이 요청한 추가적인 세부 사항이 현재 추가되었고, 편의시설 목록의 오른쪽 상단에 나타납니다. 저는 이렇게 하면 정보가 더 잘 눈에 띌 것이라고 생각하는데, 고객 분이 달리 생각하신다면 제게 알려주시기 바랍니다. 또한 호텔 웹사이트 주소에 있던 오류도 수정했습니다. 만약 이러한 수정사항들이 마음에 드신다면, 광고를 전자문서 형태로 변환한 후 파일공유 사이트에 업로드 할 예정입니다.

진심으로,

Edward

어휘 attach v. 첨부하다 | amenity n. 생활 편의 시설 | stand out 쉽게 눈에 띄다 | otherwise adv. 달리, 다르게 | fix v. 수리하다, 바로잡다 | revision n. 수정 사항 | liking n. 좋아함, 애호, 취향 | upload v. 게시하다, 업로드하다

The Stanford 호텔

421 Bridge가,

Margate, Kent CT9 5JP

영국

분주한 도시 생활로부터 벗어날 필요가 있으신가요? 그렇다면 멀리 찾으실 필요가 없습니다. The Stanford 호텔은 아름다운 해안가 위에 세워져 있으며 상쾌한 해안 공기로 둘러 쌓여 있습니다. 혼잡한 도로와 시끄러운 소음으로부터 벗어나, 편안한 낙원으로 와서 즐기세요.

저희는 다음의 편의 사항들을 제공합니다.

– 버스정류장과 기차역에서부터 호텔까지의 무료 셔틀 서비스

– 멋진 식사 라운지에서의 무료 유럽식 조식

– 늦봄 할인 가격 적용, 1박에 60파운드부터 시작하는 객실

⟨Margate Gazette⟩에서 저렴한 가격으로 이름을 알린 The Stanford 호텔은 해변과 매우 가깝지만, 지역 상점과 카페는 걸어서 갈 수 있는 거리에 있습니다. 그러니, 빨리 오셔서 Margate에서 즐거운 시간들을 보내세요. 더 많은 정보를 원하시면, 저희 웹사이트 www.thestanfordhotel.co.uk를 방문하시거나 01-271-324567로 전화 주십시오.

어휘 coastal air 해안 공기 | rate n. 요금 | recognize v. 알아보다, 인정하다 | affordability n. 감당할 수 있는 적당한 가격 | within walking distance 걸어갈 수 있는 거리에

---

176. Mr. Moto는 왜 이메일을 보냈는가?

(A) 파일이 고객에게 보내졌는지 확인하기 위해

(B) Ms. Miller가 변경 사항들을 승인하도록 요청하기 위해

(C) Ms. Miller가 더 변경할 것을 제안하기 위해

(D) 파일의 오류들에 대해 사과하기 위해

해설 이메일 첫 번째 문장에서 첨부한 파일을 확인해달라고 요청했고, 마지막 문장에서 수정 사항들이 마음에 든다면, 광고를 사이트에 업로드 하겠다고 했으므로 수정사항에 대한 승인을 받기 위해 이메일을 보냈음을 알 수 있다. 따라서 정답은 (B) To ask Ms. Miller to approve some modifications이다.

177. Ms. Miller는 어디에서 일하겠는가?

(A) 기차역에서

(B) 호텔에서

(C) 광고 대행사에서

(D) 신문사에서

해설 Ms. Miller가 Mr. Moto에게 보낸 이메일 첫 번째 문장에서 The Stanford 호텔 광고의 업데이트 버전을 첨부했으니 확인해달라고 하면서, 마지막 문장에서 수정한 내용이 마음에 든다면 광고문을 전자 양식으로 변경하여 파일공유 사이트에 업로드 할 거라고 했으므로 Ms. Miller는 광고 관련 업무에 종사할 것으로 유추할 수 있다. 따라서 정답은 (C) At an advertising agency이다.

178. Mr. Moto는 파일에 무엇을 추가하였는가?

(A) 교통 정보

(B) 호텔 위치

(C) 전화 번호

(D) 가격 정보

해설 질문의 add와 file을 키워드로 삼아 단서를 포착해보자. 이메일 지문에서 고객이 요청한 추가 정보가 편의시설 목록의 맨 위에 추가되었다고 했는데, 광고 지문에서 편의시설(amenities) 목록에서 가장 먼저 나오는 내용이 숙소까지 오는 셔틀 서비스, 즉 교통수단과 관련된 정보이므로 정답은 (A) Information about transportation이다.

179. The Stanford 호텔에 관하여 언급된 것은 무엇인가?

(A) 계절 할인을 제공한다.

(B) 최근에 사업을 시작했다.

(C) 역사적 명소이다.

(D) 24시간 운영하는 식당이 있다.

해설 광고 지문에서 늦봄에 숙박료를 할인해준다는 내용이 언급되어 있으므로 정답은 (A) It offers seasonal discounts.이다. Discounted rates for late spring이 seasonal discounts로 paraphrasing되었다.

180. ⟨Margate Gazette⟩가 The Stanford 호텔에 관하여 언급한 것은 무엇인가?

(A) 직원들이 친절하다.

(B) 사유지 해변을 소유하고 있다.

(C) 로비를 재단장하였다.

(D) 가격이 합리적이다.

해설 질문의 〈Margate Gazette〉를 키워드로 삼아 단서를 포착해보자. 광고 지문, 세 번째 단락에서 The Stanford 호텔의 적당한 가격 (affordability)이 〈Margate Gazette〉에 의해 인정 받았다는 내용을 토대로 정답은 (D) The prices are reasonable.이다. affordability 가 The prices are reasonable로 paraphrasing되었다.

[181-185] 다음 안내 책자와 이메일에 관한 문제입니다.

공개 세미나 시리즈
Westfront 대학병원 후원

182 Westfront 대학병원 (WUH)은 제약 회사 영업 직원들을 위한 여름 세미나를 소개하게 되어 기쁩니다. 이 시리즈는 저희 업계에서 일반 대중에게 새로운 약을 마케팅하는 **181** 선두주자들의 말을 들을 수 있는 기회를 제공할 것입니다. 여러분의 편의를 위하여, 세미나들은 Westfront 의과 대학에서 열릴 것입니다. 좌석은 선착순으로 이용할 수 있습니다. 세미나가 열리기 30분 전에 문이 열릴 것입니다.

8월 5일, 수요일, 오후 6시, 40호실
발표자: Livia Togart, 지역 의료 협회
수익 늘리기: 오늘날의 저성장 경제 속에서 수익을 최대화하는 방법 찾기

8월 12일, 수요일, 오후 6시, 35호실
발표자: Ryan Cleghorn, Medhearts 자문 위원단
고객 서비스: 고객들과 더 뛰어난 의사소통을 하는 효과적인 방법 익히기

8월 15일, 토요일, 오후 3시, 35호실
발표자: Nakano Hitashi, Epstein 제약 데이터(주)
정보 기밀: 신제품의 정보를 안전하게 지킬 수 있는 최신 방법 알아보기

183 8월 17일, 월요일, 오후 7시 30분, 52호실
발표자: Steve Ko, Westfront 회계 솔루션
성공적인 금융 연습: 고객들이 신속하게 지불하도록 하는 새로운 청구서 작성 방법 익히기

더 많은 정보를 얻으려면, Daniel Duval에게 d.duval@wuh_medinnovations.uk로 이메일 보내주세요.

어휘 sponsor v. 후원하다 | pharmaceutical adj. 제약의 | sales representative 영업 직원 | leading adj. 선두적인 | figure n. 인물 | market v. 상품을 내놓다, 광고하다 | public n. 대중 | School of Medicine 의과 대학 | first-come, first-served basis 선착순 | maximize v. 최대화하다 | profit n. 수익 | confidentiality n. 기밀, 비밀 | latest adj. 최신의 | secure adj. 안전한 | accounting n. 회계 | successful adj. 성공적인 | financial adj. 재정적인, 금융의 | practice n. 관행, 연습 | invoicing n. 청구서 작성 | ensure v. 확실히 하다, 보장하다 | make a payment 지불하다 | promptly adv. 신속하게

수신: Daniel Duvalle 〈d.duval@wuh_medinnovations.uk〉
발신: Tristan Chai 〈tchai@dzprescription.com〉
날짜: 8월 16일
제목: 세미나 일정

Mr. Duval께,

저는 당신의 이메일 명단에 있고, 여름 세미나 시리즈에 관한 당신의 안내 책자를 받았습니다. **184** 저의 제약 회사가 최근에 Epstein 제약 데이터(주)로부터 소프트웨어를 구매했기 때문에, 저는 그들의 발표를 매우 기대하고 있었습니다. 하지만 제가 어제 오후에 의과 대학에 도착했을 때, 35호실에는 아무도 없었습니다. 저는 안내 데스크로 갔지만, 접수 담당자는 세미나에 관해 아는 것이 전혀 없었습니다. **185** 만약 세미나가 다른 시간대로 옮겨진 것이라면, 정확히 어디에서 언제 있을 예정인지 제게 알려주세요.

진심으로,

Tristan Chai

어휘 regarding prep. ~에 관한 | pharmacy n. 약국 | look forward to ~을 기대하다 | receptionist n. 접수 담당자 | exactly adv. 정확히

---

181. 안내 책자에서, 첫 번째 단락, 세 번째 줄의 "figures"와 의미상 가장 가까운 것은
(A) 수
(B) 정보
(C) 사람
(D) 연구

해설 figures의 동의어를 찾는 문제이다. leading figures in our area who market new medicine to the public은 '새로운 약을 내놓고 마케팅 및 홍보를 하는 선두적인 인물들'이라는 의미이므로 정답은 (C) people이다.

---

182. 세미나에 관하여 언급된 것은 무엇인가?
(A) 참여자의 수를 50명으로 제한한다.
(B) Westfront 대학병원에서 개최될 것이다.
(C) 약을 홍보하는 사람들을 대상으로 한 것이다.
(D) 질의응답 시간을 가질 것이다.

해설 안내 책자 지문에서, 세미나에 대한 정보를 주목해보자. 첫 문장에서 제약 회사의 영업 직원들을 위한 세미나를 소개하게 되어 기쁘다고 하고 있다. 따라서 정답은 (C) They are intended for those who promote medicine.이다. pharmaceutical sales representatives 가 those who promote medicine으로 paraphrasing되었다.

---

183. 8월 17일의 세미나에서 논의될 것은 무엇인가?
(A) 재정적으로 어려울 때 돈을 버는 방법
(B) 청구서가 신속히 납부되도록 확실히 하는 방법
(C) 제품 정보를 분석하는 방법
(D) 고객들과 성공적으로 연락하는 방법

해설 8월 17일 세미나 주제에 주목하자. 8월 17일 세미나의 주제는 고객들이 지불을 신속하게 하도록 하는 청구서 작성 방법이다. 따라서 정답

은 (B) How to ensure that bills are paid quickly이다. ensure customers make their payments promptly가 ensure that bills are paid quickly로 paraphrasing되었다.

184. Mr. Chai는 누구의 강의를 참석하길 희망하는가?

    (A) Mr. Cleghorn의

    (B) Ms. Togart의

    (C) Mr. Hitashi의

    (D) Mr. Ko의

해설 Mr. Chai가 희망하는 강의 및 발표자에 관한 정보에 주목하자. 이메일에서 Mr. Chai는 Epstein 제약 데이터(주) 주최의 발표를 기대하고 있다고 말했다. Epstein 제약 데이터(주) 주최의 발표자를 확인하기 위해 첫 번째 안내책자 지문을 보자. 발표자의 소속 회사가 Epstein 제약 데이터(주)이므로 세미나의 발표자는 Nakano Hitashi임을 알 수 있다. 따라서 정답은 (C) Ms. Hitashi's이다.

185. Mr. Chai는 왜 이메일을 썼는가?

    (A) 세미나 등록을 위해

    (B) 최신 정보를 요청하기 위해

    (C) 이메일 명단에 가입하기 위해

    (D) 직책에 지원하기 위해

해설 발신자의 요청 사항에 주목해보자. Estein 제약 데이터(주)의 세미나 일정이 변경되었다면 세미나 변경 장소와 시간을 알려달라고 요청하고 있으므로 정답은 (B) To request an update이다.

[186-190] 다음 편지, 온라인 서식, 그리고 이메일에 관한 문제입니다.

Jane Choi

20134 Elkins 로

로스앤젤레스, 캘리포니아 90005

Ms. Choi에게,

187 귀하의 신작 소설, 〈Stardom Pathway〉의 저자 증정본 세 부가 동봉되어 있습니다. 이제 저희 웹사이트, www.galicapress.com에서 구매가 가능하며, 4월 29일부터 엄선된 서점에서 판매될 것입니다. 지금까지, 귀하의 소설 온라인 판매가 **186** 활발해서, 매출액이 증가할 것으로 예상됩니다.

무료 부수 외에도, 그 이상의 귀하의 소설책을 65퍼센트 할인된 가격에 (주문을 위해 저희 웹사이트 상의 온라인 서식을 이용하세요) 구매하실 수 있습니다. 이 할인은 귀하께서 저술하신 다른 소설들인 〈Spring Fever〉와 〈Eternal Sun〉에도 이용 가능합니다.

188 저희의 소중한 저자로서, 귀하께서는 Galica 출판사가 발행한 기타 모든 도서들에 대해 15퍼센트 할인도 받으실 수 있습니다.

Galica 출판사를 선택해주셔서 감사 드립니다.

안부 전하며,

Sherry Henderson

Sherry Henderson

마케팅 매니저

Galica 출판사

동봉물 재중

어휘 enclosed *adj.* 동봉된 | author *n.* 작가, 저자 *v.* 저술하다 | copy *n.* (책, 신문 등의) 한 부 | select *adj.* 엄선된 | brisk *adj.* 활발한, 빠른 | in addition to ~이외에 | complimentary *adj.* 무료의 | valued *adj.* 소중한 | be entitled to ~할 자격이 있다

저자 주문서

저자: Jane Choi

날짜: 4월 10일

제목	부수	가격
〈Stardom Pathway〉	5	37.50달러
〈Spring Fever〉	4	20.00달러
〈Eternal Sun〉	2	22.75달러

다른 책들을 구매하시려면, 아래의 해당 박스 안에 저자의 이름과, 도서명, 그리고 희망 부수를 입력해주세요:

제목: **188** Optical Flare

저자: Gary Othstein

부수: 3

총액: 18.50달러

주(註): 주문은 일반우편으로 배송되며 도착하는 데 영업일로 3~5일이 걸립니다. **189** 속달 옵션을 선택하시면, 귀하의 주문품을 익일에 배송해드릴 수 있습니다. 이 서비스를 이용하시려면 고객지원부 customersupport@galicapress.com로 연락해주세요.

어휘 enter *v.* 입력하다 | book title 도서명 | desired *adj.* 바랐던, 희망했던 | corresponding *adj.* ~에 해당하는, 상응하는 | via *prep.* ~을 통하여 | standard mail 일반우편 | business day 영업일 | arrange *v.* 처리하다; 마련하다

수신: customersupport@galicapress.com

발신: Jane Choi (jchoi@tepmail.com)

날짜: **189** 4월 11일 **190** 금요일, 오후 6시 50분

제목: 누락된 물건

안녕하세요.

189 제가 오늘 주문품을 받았을 때, 〈Eternal Sun〉 한 부가 빠져 있는 걸 알게 되었습니다. 제가 신용카드사에 연락을 취했는데, 그들이 두 소설 모두 청구가 되었다는 걸 확인해 주었습니다. **190** 저는 귀사가 내일 문을 열지 않는다는 사실을 알고 있습니다만, 이 일을 알아보시고 월요일에 제게 후속 조치 이메일 보내주시겠습니까?

감사드리며,

Jane Choi

어휘 notice *v.* 알아차리다 | missing *adj.* 빠져 있는, 분실된 | confirm *v.* 확인해주다 | charge *v.* 청구하다 | look into ~을 조사하다 | matter *n.* 일, 사안 | follow-up *n.* 후속 조치

186. 편지에서, 첫 번째 단락의 세 번째 줄에 나온 "brisk"와 의미상 가장 가까운 것은

(A) 신선한

(B) 강한

(C) 주의를 기울이는

(D) 짧은

해설　brisk가 쓰인 문장을 확인하면 지금까지 소설의 온라인 판매가 활발해서, 매출액이 증가할 것으로 예상된다는 내용이므로 이 문장에서 brisk는 '빠른, 활발한'의 의미로 쓰였다. '강한, 강세인'을 뜻하는 (B) strong가 정답이다.

187. Ms. Choi에게 〈Stardom Pathway〉는 무료로 몇 부가 보내졌는가?

(A) 2부

(B) 3부

(C) 4부

(D) 8부

해설　첫 번째 지문, 첫 번째 단락에서 Ms. Choi의 신작 소설, 〈Stardom Pathway〉 저자 증정본 세 부를 동봉했다고 했고, 두 번째 단락에서 무료 증정본 이외는 65퍼센트 할인가로 구매할 수 있다고 했으므로 동봉된 세 부가 무료로 제공되었음을 알 수 있다. 따라서 (B) Three가 정답이다. complimentary가 질문에서 free로 paraphrasing되었다.

188. 〈Optical Flare〉에 관하여 알 수 있는 것은 무엇인가?

(A) Ms. Choi에게 15퍼센트 할인되어 판매될 것이다.

(B) Ms. Choi와 Mr. Othstein가 공동 집필했다.

(C) 책 비평가들로부터 호평을 받았다.

(D) 4월 29일부터 엄선된 서점에서 이용 가능하다.

해설　〈Optical Flare〉가 언급된 두 번째 지문을 먼저 보면 해당 책 제목의 저자는 Gary Othstein으로 되어 있어, Ms. Choi의 저작물이 아님을 알 수 있는데, 첫 번째 지문을 보면 Galica Press에서 출판된 기타 다른 도서들은 15퍼센트를 할인해주겠다고 했으므로 Ms. Choi는 〈Optical Flare〉를 15퍼센트 할인된 가격에 구매할 수 있다. 따라서 (A) It will be sold to Ms. Choi at a 15 percent discount.가 정답이다.

189. Ms. Choi에 관하여 사실인 것은 무엇이겠는가?

(A) 그녀의 책 모두가 베스트셀러이다.

(B) 속달 배송 옵션을 선택했다.

(C) 그녀의 책들 중 하나가 품절되었다.

(D) 새 마케팅 대행업체로 바꿨다.

해설　Ms. Choi가 쓴 세 번째 지문을 먼저 확인하면 주문한 물건을 오늘 받았다고 했는데(When I received my order today), 지문 맨 앞의 날짜 정보에서 오늘이 4월 11일이라는 것을 알 수 있고(Date: Friday, April 11, 6:50 P.M.), 두 번째 지문을 보면 주문서 작성일은 4월 10일(Date: April 10)이고, Note에서는 속달 옵션을 선택하면 바로 그 다음 날 배송된다고 했으므로 Ms. Choi는 속달 우편을 선택했음을 알 수 있다. 따라서 (B) She selected the express delivery option.이 정답이다. choose가 select로 paraphrasing되었다.

190. 고객 지원부에 관하여 알 수 있는 것은 무엇인가?

(A) Ms. Henderson가 관리한다.

(B) 배송 문제들을 처리하지 않는다.

(C) 로스앤젤레스에 위치해 있다.

(D) 주말에는 운영되지 않는다.

해설　Ms. Choi가 customer support에 보낸 세 번째 지문을 보면, 내일은 문을 열지 않으니 그 문제에 대해 월요일에 연락을 주겠다고 했는데 오늘이 금요일이므로 문을 열지 않는 요일은 토요일임을 알 수 있다. 따라서 (D) It does not operate on weekends.가 정답이다. not open이 not operate로 paraphrasing되었다.

[191-195] 다음 웹 페이지, 기사, 그리고 편지에 관한 문제입니다.

Sayer와 함께 하는 더 좋은 삶

191 Sayer 제조사는 연례 Quality Life 보조금을 받을 지원자들을 받기 시작할 것임을 알리게 되어 기쁩니다. 매년, 우리는 지역 사회와 그 주민들의 복지를 향상시키는 데 전념하는 프로젝트들에 네 개의 보조금을 제공합니다. 상금은 다음과 같습니다:

– 1등: 50,000달러

– 2등: 45,000달러

– **192** 3등: 40,000달러

– 4등: 35,000달러

비영리 기관들만이 이 보조금을 받을 수 있는 자격이 됩니다. 지난해의 수상자들은 지역 수영 프로그램, 어르신들의 지원 프로그램 및 영유아 보육에 대한 워크숍 강좌들을 포함합니다.

이 링크에서 보조금 신청서를 다운로드해주세요.

어휘　grant *n.* 보조금 | give out 나눠주다 | be dedicated to ~에 전념하다 | well-being *n.* 행복, 안녕 | resident *n.* 거주자, 주민 | award amount 상금 | non-profit organization 비영리 기관 | winner *n.* 수상자 | elderly *adj.* 나이든 분의, 어르신의 | infant care 영유아 보육

〈Philanthropy Corner〉

Quartz가 재정 지원을 받다
Thomas Dunn 글

Hillview, 5월 15일 – **192** Hillview에 본사를 둔 Quartz 재단은 독서 센터를 만들기 위해 Sayer Quality Life 보조금 프로그램을 통해 4만 달러를 수여 받았다. **193** 이 센터는 Hillview에 거주하는 아이들과 10대들의 독서 수준을 높이기 위한 기회를 제공할 것이다. 다음 달부터, 재단은 20세기 문학에 대한 강좌들을 제공할 것이다. Hillview 공공 도서관도 운영하고 있는 그 재단은 센터에 상당량의 소설과 비소설 도서들을 기부할 계획이다.

Quartz 재단은 교육에 대한 지역 사회의 인식을 높이고자 했던 **195** 10명의 지역 주민들에 의해 15년 전에 Hillview에 설립되었다.

어휘　funding *n.* 재정 지원 | award *v.* 수여하다 | reside in ~에 거주하다 | donate *v.* 기부하다 | awareness *n.* 인식, 관심

편집자 분께,

〈Philanthropy Corner〉의 5월호에 실린 Mr. Dunn의 기사에 오류가 있어 알려드리고자 합니다. Mr. Dunn은 Quartz가 15년 전에 구성되었다고 기술했습니다. **195** Quartz의 설립자들에 관한 Mr. Dunn의 진술이 맞기는 하나, Quartz는 사실 25년 전 설립되었습니다.

194 전(前) 기고가로서, 귀사의 잡지가 통찰력 있고, 신뢰할 수 있는 기사들을 출간하려고 애쓴다는 점은 잘 알고 있으며, 귀사의 잡지에는 이러한 오류가 드문 일이라는 걸 이해하고 있습니다.

진심으로,

Jamie Boyd
Quartz 재단, 대표

어휘 **call attention to** ~에 주의를 기울이다 | **inaccuracy** *n.* 오류, 부정확 | **statement** *n.* 진술(서) | **former** *adj.* 이전의 | **contributor** *n.* 기고가 | **strive** *v.* 고군분투하다 | **insightful** *adj.* 통찰력 있는 | **trustworthy** *adj.* 신뢰할 수 있는 | **rare** *adj.* 드문, 희귀한 | **occurrence** *n.* 발생, 출현

---

191. 웹 페이지의 목적은 무엇인가?

(A) 의료원의 개원을 알리기 위해
(B) 스포츠 대회 참가자들을 찾기 위해
(C) 상금을 위한 신청을 요청하기 위해
(D) 보조금의 최종 후보자들을 발표하기 위해

해설 첫 번째 지문, 맨 처음 문장에서 Sayer 제조사가 보조금 신청자들을 받기 시작할 것임을 발표하고 있으며 등수에 따른 상금의 액수도 제시하고 있으므로 보조금 신청자들을 모집하기 위한 것임을 알 수 있다. 따라서 (C) To solicit applications for an award가 정답이다.

---

192. Quartz 재단은 어떤 상을 받았는가?

(A) 1등 상
(B) 2등 상
(C) 3등 상
(D) 4등 상

해설 Quartz 재단이 언급된 두 번째 지문을 보면 이 회사가 4만 달러를 수상했다고 보도했는데 보조금 신청 모집을 알리는 첫 번째 지분에서 4만 달러의 수상금은 3등에 해당하므로(Third Place: $40,000) (C) The third-place prize가 정답이다.

---

193. 기사에 따르면, 보조금은 Quartz 재단으로 하여금 무엇을 할 수 있게 해줄 것인가?

(A) 새 도서관을 건립한다
(B) 건강에 대한 연구를 수행한다
(C) 교육 기회를 제공한다
(D) 직원들의 근무 조건을 개선한다

해설 Quartz 재단이 언급된 두 번째 지문을 보면 이 회사가 독서 센터를 만들기 위해 4만 달러의 보조금을 타게 되었다고 하면서, 그 지역 아이들의 독서 수준을 높이는 기회를 제공할 것이라고 하므로 (C) Offer educational opportunities가 정답이다.

---

194. Ms. Boyd이 자기 자신에 대해 내비치는 것은 무엇인가?

(A) Mr. Dunn의 전 직원이다.
(B) 잡지 기자의 인터뷰를 받을 것이다.
(C) Quartz 재단의 설립을 도왔다.
(D) 이전에 〈Philanthropy Corner〉에 글을 썼다.

해설 Ms. Boyd이 〈Philanthropy Corner〉의 편집자에게 보낸 세 번째 지문을 보면 두 번째 단락에서 자신이 이 잡지의 전 기고자(As a former contributor)였다는 것을 내비치고 있으므로 (D) She has written for Philanthropy Corner before.이 정답이다.

---

195. Ms. Boyd에 따르면, Mr. Dunn의 기사에서 Quartz 재단에 관하여 사실인 것은 무엇인가?

(A) 추가 보조금을 신청할 계획이다.
(B) 지역 주민들에 의해 설립되었다.
(C) Hillview 학교들에 도서를 기부할 것이다.
(D) 취사 시설이 있다.

해설 Ms. Boyd가 쓴 세 번째 지문을 보면 첫 번째 단락에서 Mr. Dunn의 기사의 오류를 지적하겠다고 얘기하면서, Quartz의 설립자들에 관한 진술은 옳다고 했으므로 Mr. Dunn가 쓴 두 번째 지문에서 설립자에 관한 내용을 찾으면 두 번째 단락에서 그는 Quartz 재단이 10명의 지역 주민들이 모여 설립되었다고 진술했다. 따라서 (B) It was founded by local residents.가 정답이다. established가 founded로 paraphrasing되었다.

[196-200] 다음 보도 자료들과 이메일에 관한 문제입니다.

Castaway 밴드
언론 보도

워싱턴, 시애틀, 1월 3일 – Castaway 밴드가 3월 공연 일정들을 발표했습니다. 이 투어는 유명한 Orion 경기장에서의 공연을 포함하는데, **196** 그 유명 락그룹이 그곳에서 10년 전 데뷔 무대를 가졌습니다.

예정된 공연들은 아래에 열거되어 있습니다.

날짜	지역	장소
3월 2일	시애틀	Grand 경기장
3월 5일	**196** 올림피아	Orion 경기장
3월 8일	스포캔	Baron 극장
198 3월 11일	커클랜드	Foxwood 극장
3월 14일	렌턴	Cumulus 아트센터

200 티켓은 모든 투어 공연들에 대해 80달러(발코니석)에서 120달러(앞좌석)까지 다양하며 참가 장소들의 매표소와 X-One 음악 상점에서 구매할 수 있습니다. **200** Castaway 밴드 팬클럽 회원들은 www.castawayboys.com의 회원 전용 섹션에서 주문하여 티켓에서 10달러를 할인 받을 수 있습니다. **197** 팬클럽 혜택과 연회비에 관한 더 많은 정보를 보시려면, www.castawayband.com/membership_fanclub를 방문하면 됩니다.

연락처: Sean Berstein, 206-555-7352, sberstein@castawayboys.com

어휘 **debut** *n.* 데뷔, 첫 출연 | **venue** *n.* (모임) 장소 | **range** *v.* 다양하다 | **box office** 매표소 | **annual due** 연회비

Foxwood 극장
언론 보도

취소 및 연기된 공연들

워싱턴, 커클랜드, 2월 22일 – **198** Foxwood 극장에서 다음 달에 예정된 공연들 모두가 건물의 긴급 수리 작업으로 연기되거나 취소되었습니다. Castaway 밴드 공연을 제외하고, 모든 티켓 소지자들은 변경된 날짜로 이행될 것이므로 그들의 티켓을 계속 가지고 있어야 합니다. **199** 공연 날짜에 대한 최신 정보를 보시려면, Foxwood 극장 웹사이트, www.foxwoodtheater.org를 방문해 주세요. 취소된 공연의 환불을 받으려면 Stacy Kamshire에 skamshire@foxwoodtheater.org로 연락하세요.

어휘 emergency *n.* 긴급, 비상 | repair *n.* 수리 작업 | with the exception of ~을 제외하다 | hold onto ~을 그대로 소지하다 | honor *v.* 이행하다, 받아들이다 | up-to-date *adj.* 최신의 | refund *n.* 환불

수신: Stacey Kamshire ⟨skamshire@foxwoodtheater.org⟩
발신: **200** James Moon ⟨jmoon@tnet.com⟩
날짜: 2월 23일
제목: Castaway 밴드 공연

Ms. Kamshire에게,

취소된 공연을 위한 환불을 요청하고자 이메일을 드립니다. **200** 제 신용카드 계좌에서 티켓 비용으로 빠져나간 110달러를 환불해주세요 (마지막 네 자리: 3820).

저는 그 공연이 취소되었다는 걸 알고 실망했습니다. Castaway 밴드가 향후에 당신이 있는 곳에서 공연을 하게 될지 알고 계시나요? 만약 그러시다면, 제 달력에 날짜를 표시해 둘 수 있도록 제게 알려주세요. 감사합니다.

어휘 money back 환불 | digit *n.* 숫자

---

196. Castaway 밴드는 첫 공연을 어디에서 가졌나?
(A) 시애틀에서
(B) 올림피아에서
(C) 커클랜드에서
(D) 랜톤에서

해설 첫 번째 지문에서 Castaway 밴드가 3월 투어 일정을 발표했다고 하면서, 이 밴드가 10년 전 데뷔 무대를 가진 Orion 경기장의 공연 일정도 포함하고 있다고 했는데, 아래의 일정표를 확인하면 Orion 경기장이 있는 지역은 올림피아이므로 (B) In Olympia가 정답이다.

---

197. Castaway 밴드 팬클럽에 관하여 알 수 있는 것은 무엇인가?
(A) 그곳 회원들은 일년에 한 번 회비를 내야 한다.
(B) 매년 3월에 만난다.
(C) 그곳 회원들은 X–One 음악 상점 할인을 받을 수 있다.
(D) 10년 전에 만들어졌다.

해설 첫 번째 지문 하단부를 보면 Castaway Band 팬클럽은 티켓 주문 시 10퍼센트 할인을 받을 수 있다고 하면서, 팬클럽의 혜택과 연회비에 관한 정보를 특정 웹사이트 페이지에서 확인하라고 안내하고 있으므로 (A) Its members have to pay a fee once a year.가 정답이다. annual dues가 pay a fee once a year로 paraphrasing되었다.

---

198. Castaway 밴드는 언제 예정된 공연을 할 수 없을 것인가?
(A) 3월 2일에
(B) 3월 5일에
(C) 3월 11일에
(D) 3월 14일에

해설 커클랜드의 Foxwood 극장에서 발표한 두 번째 지문을 보면 Foxwood 극장에서 열리기로 예정된 모든 공연들이 연기되거나 취소되었다고 하면서, Castaway 밴드 공연을 제외한 나머지 공연들은 모두 연기만 되었다는 걸 나타내고 있으므로 이 극장에서의 Castaway 밴드 공연은 취소되었음을 짐작할 수 있다. 따라서 첫 번째 지문의 Castaway 밴드 공연 일정표에서 Foxwood 극장의 공연 날짜를 확인하면 3월 11일이므로 (C) On March 11가 정답이다.

---

199. 두 번째 보도 자료에 따르면, Foxwood 극장의 웹사이트에 무엇이 게시될 것인가?
(A) 새로운 개최 장소
(B) 수정된 날짜 목록
(C) 건물 수리에 관한 정보
(D) 환불 신청서

해설 두 번째 지문에서 Foxwood Theater's Web site를 키워드로 삼아 단서를 찾으면, 지문 하단에 공연 일정을 위한 최신 정보를 위해 해당 사이트를 방문하라고 했으므로 그곳에 변경된 날짜가 업데이트될 것임을 알 수 있다. 따라서 (B) A revised list of dates가 정답이다. the most up-to-date information on ~ dates가 revised list of dates로 paraphrasing되었다.

---

200. Mr. Moon에 관하여 알 수 있는 것은 무엇인가?
(A) Castaway 밴드 팬클럽의 회원이다.
(B) Mr. Berstein의 동료이다.
(C) 행사 리뷰를 썼다.
(D) 과거에 Foxwood 극장에서 일한 적이 있다.

해설 첫 번째 지문의 공연 티켓 가격 정보와(모든 공연은 80달러에서 120달러임)와, 팬 클럽 회원들은 티켓 가격에서 10달러를 할인 받을 수 있다는 정보를 토대로 세 번째 지문에서 Mr. Moon이 110달러를 환불해 달라고 한 이유가 Mr. Moon이 그 밴드의 팬 클럽이기 때문임을 유추해 낼 수 있어야 한다. 따라서 (A) He is a member of the Castaway Band Fan Club.이 정답이다.